Talmud Bavli Indexed Reference Guide

HaMafteach
המפתח ®

THE R' MORDECHAI (MARCUS) RETTER Z"L EDITION

Talmud Bavli Indexed Reference Guide

HaMafteach®

A-Z

An Indexed Reference Guide to the
Talmud Bavli (Babylonian Talmud) and its Mishnayos,
designed to enable the student of the Talmud
to locate significant subject matter, laws, anecdotes,
maxims, parables, sayings, Biblical exegesis, Biblical and
Talmudic personalities, and commentaries of the Sages;
also included is a phonetic-transliteration of
Hebrew and Aramaic words and phrases,
and a new integrated glossary

Daniel Retter

Copyright Registration:
Title of Work: HaMafteach® (English Version)
TX 7-481-168 (2012)

Copyright Registration Numbers (previous versions):
TXu001575424 (2007);
TXu001661086 (2008);
TXu001615037 (2008);
TXu001615041 (2008).

Copyright © 2011, 2012 by Daniel Retter
Riverdale, New York U.S.A.

ISBN # 978 965 301 326 1

First Edition:
First Printing – November, 2011
Second Printing – January, 2012

Second Edition:
August, 2012

Sole Distributor:
Koren Publishers Ltd.
POB 4044, Jerusalem 91040, Israel
POB 8531, New Milford, CT 06776, USA

Graphic Design:
Ben Gasner Studio
Jerusalem, Israel

Printed in USA

DEDICATION

The R' Mordechai (Marcus) Retter z"l Edition of the HaMafteach®

27 Kislev 5680 - 28 Elul 5767
December 8, 1920 - September 11, 2007

My father, R' Mordechai (Marcus) Retter *z"l*, was a man of letters and foremost, a *talmid chacham*. As a young boy growing up in Vienna, he was raised in a house of Ruzhiner Chasidim, imbued with the philosophy of *Torah im Derech Eretz*. He possessed an encyclopedic knowledge of Tanach, and he spoke and wrote perfect Hebrew, German, English, Yiddish, and Latin. He could effortlessly translate every word of the *selichos*, *yotzros*, the Book of Job, and of course Rashi's *dikduk*. He recalled in "photographic" detail his life in Vienna and London, both before and during the war, especially relating to *chasidishe* Rebbes, Rabbis, political personalities and events, of both a personal and historical nature.

After escaping to London via Dr. Solomon Schonfeld's *Kindertransport*, my father began working during the war as a diplomatic aide to Lord Wedgeworth of the British Parliament. He never tired of telling us about his interaction with members of Parliament and the British Foreign Office. He was appointed by Lord Wedgeworth to examine mail written in German, which was sent to and from Britain, in order to ascertain whether it contained secret codes to be used against the British. His usefulness to the British war effort was such, that he was only one of very few refugees who was not interned for the duration of the war on the Isle of Man, as an enemy alien. He told us of his trips in 1945 immediately after the war to Bergen Belsen, Warsaw, and the DP camps, where, as the representative of the Chief Rabbi's Religious Emergency Council, he brought to the wretched survivors kosher food, *taleisim*, and *tefillin*. He would jokingly refer to his emergency mobile synagogue as "the original Mitzvah Tank."

My father *z'l* developed a close relationship with Rabbi Dr. Solomon Schonfeld, and he became his trusted and untiring assistant. He was elected Secretary of the Union of Hebrew Orthodox Congregations of London. He coined the well known name "Kedassia," which represents even today, the accepted symbol for kosher food supervised by the Union of Hebrew Orthodox Congregations of London. He explained to me that he chose the name "Kedassia," to assure for all time that the "Kedassia" supervision would always be "LeMehadrin" kosher, as the word "Kedassia" was an acronym for "Kedas Kah" which means "according to the law of the Torah."

My father *z"l* possessed the personality, bearing, and dignity of a world-class diplomat and statesman. Unfortunately, the war robbed him of his youth and his ability to pursue a diplomatic or legal career, which he had greatly desired. But Hashem, in His ultimate wisdom, led him on the path to a far higher purpose. He joined with, and worked alongside, his father-in-law, my grandfather, R' Yechiel HaKohen Rosenblatt *z"l*. Together they built our family's business, which currently, and for many decades, supports needy individuals, *hachnasas kallah,* and *bikur cholim*, as well as large and small institutions of Torah throughout the world.

My father *z"l* was the family's role model for honesty, selflessness, and a deep and abiding faith in God, despite his many personal challenges. He never took a vacation in his life. It was not so much that he was a workaholic; he simply never made time for a vacation because he considered it to be non-productive time, and instead stayed at his father-in-law's side continuously. I remember my father *z"l* once suffered from an ulcer, and the doctor ordered him to take a walk in Riverside Park. As we walked together on a Sunday afternoon, he remarked to me, "Danny, you mean all these people here in the park also suffer from ulcers?" His constant admonition to us that "the worst thing a person can do is 'kill' time" remains etched in my memory.

During his reflective moments, my father *z"l* told me he considered himself to be the "Yosef," whom God had sent to enrich others and not himself. In London, he worked tirelessly for the Jewish community, including on behalf of refugees like himself, who had escaped from all over Europe. He was the youngest serving member on the Board of Deputies of British Jews, which was the central organ of Jewry in London.

In 1949, my father *z"l* and mother *a"h* moved their young family to America. My father *z"l* devoted himself to my grandfather and to the family business, nurturing its growth and success with Hashem's help. He was a model of rectitude in all of his dealings with vendors, suppliers, and everyone else who wanted to do business with my grandfather. Nor would he ever accept any commissions from newly graduated yeshiva bochurim and Kolel Yungerleit, who had placed their real estate licenses with him as their broker,

to further their real estate careers. Late at night and at all times during the day, he greeted representatives from every conceivable *mosad* who visited him and my grandfather for support, with a warm smile and kind words. He never let them leave without a check, together with warm words or good advice.

His numerous accomplishments and appointments included being the official United Nations representative of the "Religious Jewish Weekly" a.k.a. "Der Yid," the yearly chairman of the Yeshiva M'kor Chaim (Rav Paler's Yeshiva) dinner, the Pressburg and Slonim Yeshiva dinners, the Talmud Torah Beis Yechiel of Nitra dinner, and the Alexander Yeshiva Tifereth Shmiel dinner. He was also the annual guest speaker at the Satmar Bikur Cholim Ladies Luncheon, which drew over one thousand ladies in attendance. He was also the *Maggid Shiur* of the weekly Chumash class, teaching the commentary of the Orach Chaim Hakodosh, at Rabbi Vorhand's Shul on the Upper West Side, where he and Rabbi Vorhand founded the Daf Yomi *shiur* over 35 years ago, before Daf Yomi took root in many other communities. He often taught the Daf as well, to the delight of the other *lomdim*.

Since my father *z"l* was buried in Eretz Yisrael on erev Rosh Hashanah, there was no *shiva* period to enable the community to demonstrate their love and respect for him. Instead, as the family prepared for a private *sheloshim* ceremony, we were inundated with calls from complete strangers begging us to allow the public to attend and mourn my father *z"l*'s passing. I will never forget how the leading Rebbes, Rabbis, and *Roshei Yeshiva*, together with hundreds and hundreds of friends and neighbors from all over New York and even Eretz Yisrael, assembled for the *sheloshim*, and listened to the haunting chant of the *Kel Malei Rachamim* by Chazan Yitzchak Meir Helfgot, who volunteered for the *zechus* to honor "Reb Mordechai *z"l*," whom he had never met.

What was my father's legacy? For one, he left us with the conviction that extremism on the left or right was anathema, and that we must follow the Rambam's *shvil hazahav* (golden mean). He constantly warned us against shaming him by any act that could bring disgrace upon our family. He abhorred vanity, and despised anyone who was boastful or arrogant, no matter that person's station in life.

How can a son honor his beloved
father after his passing? Some pay
for buildings, while others dedicate
institutions in order to perpetuate their
father's memory. I have chosen to dedicate
this HaMafteach® to his memory, because
this is exactly the sort of *sefer* he would
have loved. The Talmud is a collection of
different texts, their etymology in *Lashon
HaKodesh* and Aramaic, with traces of
Greek and Latin. The HaMafteach®'s
translation and transliteration of these
languages into English would have
certainly brought my father great joy. If,
indeed, this HaMafteach®, identified with
R' Mordechai Retter *z"l*, will be found in
every *beis midrash*, and public and private
library, I will have been fortunate enough
to have succeeded in honoring my father
beyond his own lifetime. There is no
greater *kibud av* I would wish to have.

Daniel Retter

AUTHOR'S NOTE

Dear Student of the Talmud,
It can only be due to Hashem's blessings, that the HaMafteach® has been so warmly and widely received by the Torah world, its primary intended beneficiary. I have received many messages of encouragement, together with constructive comments, and so I rejoice with the knowledge that the HaMafteach® has found a warm place in the Batei Medroshot, in the homes, and in the "hearts," of those who have a genuine love of the Talmud.

This second edition incorporates all of the constructive comments, that the editorial board of the HaMafteach® has reviewed, and found worthy of including in this second edition. We have added a few new Entries, and we have cross referenced a few existing Entries, to enable you to locate the particular Talmudic source for which you may be searching.

I ask you to welcome to the HaMafteach® "family," Koren Publishers of Jerusalem Ltd., and its President Meir Miller, who are now publishing and distributing the HaMafteach®. I extend my gratitude to Feldheim Publishers, my first distributor, with my special thanks to R' Yitzhak Feldheim, whose integrity and faithfulness, is a shining example to be followed by all those in the business world. Once again, I thank Ben Gasner who continues to beautify the HaMafteach®, with his graphics designs skill. I thank my son in law Alain (Avrohom Dovid) Schiff, for his discreet but critical contribution to the success of the HaMafteach®.

We at the HaMafteach® welcome your messages and suggestions at comments@HaMafteach.org. We endeavor to respond to each and every one of your comments.

Sincerely,
Daniel Retter
August 19, 2012
2 Rosh Chodesh Elul 5772

(Translated from original Hebrew)

Blessing from Rabbi Chaim Kanievsky

BS"D

15 Av, 5767

Upon entering the private office of Rabbi Chaim Kanievsky, *shlita*, we showed him *HaMafteach on the Talmud* by R' Daniel Retter. He received it warmly and said, "This is a good thing! A book like this, an index of the Talmud, does not need my approbation!" and then wished it blessings and success.

Rabbi Kanievsky approved this text in the presence of Dr. Moshe Rothschild, Rabbi Shmuel Sluzch, and Daniel Retter.

בס"ד

ברכת מרן הגר"ח קנייבסקי שליט"א

כאשר נכנסנו אל הקודש פנימה, אל מרן הגר"ח קנייבסקי שליט"א,
והראינו לו את המפתח של ר' דניאל רטר על הש"ס,
הוא קיבלנו במאור פנים, ואמר:

דבר טוב הוא!
ספר כזה, שהוא מפתח לש"ס, אינו צריך את הסכמתי!
וברך בברכה ובהצלחה.

בט"ו באב תשס"ז
היה נוסח זה לעיני מרן שליט"א
בנוכחות ד"ר משה רוטשילד, הרב שמואל סלושץ, ודניאל רֶטֶר

(Translated from original Hebrew)

Blessing from Rabbi Aharon Leib Steinman

BS"D

15 Av, 5767

Upon our meeting with Rabbi Aharon Leib Steinman, *shlita*, and his seeing Daniel Retter's HaMafteach, he was very happy with the idea, and blessed it with success.

Rabbi Steinman approved of this text in the presence of Rabbi Yaakov Shulevitz and Daniel Retter.

בס"ד

ברכת מרן הגראי"ל שטיינמן שליט"א

בהכנסנו אל מרן הגראי"ל שטיינמן שליט"א,
ובראותו את המפתח של ר' דניאל רטר על הש"ס,
הוא שמח על הרעיון,
וברך אותו בהצלחה.

בט"ו באב תשס"ז
היה נוסח זה לעיני מרן שליט"א
בנוכחות הרב יעקב שולביץ ודניאל רֶטר

(Translated from original Hebrew)

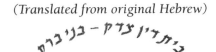

Beth Din Zedek of Bnei Brak

Under the Auspices of Maran HaGaon S.Y. Nissim Karelitz *shlita*

BS"D

A unique Torah creation has been brought before us, written and edited by R' Elchanan Kohn, *shlita*, author of the *sefarim Mafteach Sugyot v'Inyanei HaShas*. He has done this on behalf of the distinguished patron of the sages, R' Daniel Retter of Riverdale, New York.

This work contains indices for direct searches of the Talmud: a list of entries for the entire Talmud in alphabetical order, a list of entries for each individual tractate in alphabetical order, and a list of additional sources that deal with topics on every page of the Talmud, arranged in order of their appearance in the Talmud.

R' Daniel Retter conceived the idea for such an index, entrusted the project to R' Elchanan Kohn, *shlita*, and served as an advisor and editor.

R' Elchanan Kohn has granted to R' Daniel Retter and anyone acting on his behalf full rights to this work.

Since R' Daniel Retter has invested so much time, effort, and money in this work, it is proper that no one infringe upon his exclusive right to publish a

work of this nature. It has been divinely ordained that R' Daniel Retter receive the privilege to grace K'lal Yisrael with this important work, which allows for quick, direct, and simple access to every matter that appears in the Babylonian Talmud.

For the honor of the Torah, we have affixed our signatures to this document, this 22nd day of Iyar 5767, here in the city of Bnei Brak.

Nissim Karelitz
Sariel Rosenberg
Yoel Friedman

B"H, Being that this project strengthens one's general familiarity with the Talmud, it is very close to my heart, and I commend its author.

He who awaits the redemption,
Shmuel HaLevi Wosner

(Translated from original Hebrew)

Tzvi Elimelech Halberstam
Av Beis Din of Sanz
Kiryat Sanz, Netanya

With the help of God,
Tuesday of Parashas Re'eh, 23 Menahem Av 5767

Let us come and appreciate the efforts of our dear and honored friend, Rabbi Daniel Retter of New York, may he enjoy long life, whose heart has sought to enlighten the eyes with three catalogued indices and source books for finding entries throughout the Talmud. He has invested much time, effort, and toil to arrange these matters in proper order, and has hired the steadfast hands of Rabbi Elchanan Kohn, *shlita*, to assist him. Praise God, it has turned out beautifully, and will definitely be of use and assistance to those who immerse themselves in the Torah of Hashem.

He should be commended for his efforts, and thank God, Daniel's personality combines love of the living Torah with a love of kindness, and he cleaves to Hashem's attributes just as our sages, of blessed memory, stated (*Vayikra Rabbah*, 4:1, and *Devarim Rabbah*, 5:4): "There are two matters kept in God's right hand: righteousness and Torah. Righteousness, as it says, 'Righteousness fills your right hand,' and Torah, as it says, 'From His right hand, a fiery law unto them.'"

Fortunate is his lot for benefiting the masses. Only a worthy individual could accomplish such a thing. I hereby bless him that he continue to produce other meritorious works that will magnify and glorify the Torah. May *Hashem Yisbarach* constantly assist him, that wherever he may turn he be successful and see a sign of great blessing and fortune from Above, and may only goodness, health, divine enlightenment, and kindness pursue him throughout his life.

Tzvi Elimelech Halberstam

(Translated from original Hebrew)

שמואל קמנצקי
Rabbi S. Kamenetsky

2018 Upland Way
Philadelphia, Pa 19131

Home: 215-473-2798
Study: 215-473-1212

BS"D, 26 Tishrei 5767

To the Honorable Rabbi Daniel Retter, *shlita*;

I was impressed by the index of the Talmud that lists every topic and its related subjects, making it so easy for one to find what his heart desires. He certainly deserves credit for doing a great service for the masses. This index is also of use to English speakers, who can now use the index to easily find what they seek in their own language.

I am certain that this book will be received joyously, and with much appreciation for all that R' Daniel has invested of his own resources and understanding. May he be blessed to be counted among those who work for the public good, may the merit of their Torah study be attributed to him, and may he be blessed from Above with blessings for all good.

Shmuel Kamenetsky

(Translated from original Hebrew)

Shlomo Moshe Amar
Rishon Lezion Chief Rabbi Of Israel
President of the Great Rabbinical Court

שלמה משה עמאר
הראשון לציון הרב הראשי לישראל
נשיא בית הדין הרבני הגדול

BS"D, 10 Kislev, 5771

Approbation

I have seen excerpts from the sefer Mafteach al HaShas that was written and edited by R' Elchanan Kohn, *shlita*, author of the *sefarim "Mafteach Sugyot v'Inyanei HaShas."*

I understand that this has been a formidable project, in that he has included within it an alphabetical subject index, something that is very good and useful for seekers of Torah.

May R' Daniel Retter, who has invested his time and resources in publishing this important work, be blessed from heaven.

May he blessed that Hashem grant him success in this endeavor, that he merit to disseminate his Torah with grace and favor, and that his work be accepted by the rabbis and their students.

He who anticipates Hashem's merciful salvation,

Shlomo Moshe Amar
Rishon Lezion Chief Rabbi of Israel

(Translated from original Hebrew)

ISRAEL MEIR LAU
CHIEF RABBI
TEL-AVIV-JAFFA, ISRAEL

ישראל מאיר לאו
הרב הראשי
תל-אביב-יפו, ישראל

B"SD, 18 Av, 5767
August 2, 2007

My friend, Rabbi Daniel Retter, *shlita*, of New York, a lover of Torah and those who study it, visited me bearing the fruits of his study, *Sefer Mafteach Al HaShas*, within which are thousands of entries by order of tractate. Every issue, topic, and expression mentioned in the Talmud, whether in *halacha* or *aggadah*, can now be easily found courtesy of this index.

My friend R' Daniel Retter, *shlita*, conceived of this idea, and charged an outstanding Torah scholar to organize this index. He personally supervises and participates in every stage of the project, whether in Hebrew or English, and he even intends to publish it in other languages.

I firmly believe that his entire goal and intention are to benefit the masses and to magnify and glorify the Torah. There is great utility in such a work for those who immerse themselves in the Sea of the Talmud, as it "shows them a path through the seas, and a channel in the mighty waters."

The utility of such a work is double for English speakers, a book like this does not yet exist in their language.

I bless R' Daniel that Hashem grant this work success and that it be received with favor in the study halls and every house of Torah. May the merit of the Torah protect him and his family, that they be blessed with all good things.

With love of the Torah,

Rabbi Israel Meir Lau

(Translated from original Hebrew)

Grand Rabbi
Moishe L. Rabinovich
of Munkach

1417 – 49th Street
Brooklyn, N. Y. 11219

משה יהודא ליב ראבינאוויטש

אבדק"ק מונקאטש

ברוקלין, ניו יורק

BS"D
9 Elul, 5767

To the Honorable Rabbi Daniel Retter,

Shalom. I have seen his important work, a magnificent index of every issue in the Talmud, Torah, and Oral Law, through which every scholar and seeker of Hashem's word can find whatever he seeks, and from what I have seen, it is a wondrous treasure. With Hashem's help, may it be of great use to all students of the Torah. Fortunate is his lot that he merited to author, publish, and promote it for the benefit of the masses. May his strength remain steadfast for the Torah.

With abundant blessings,

Moishe L. Rabinovich

בס"ד

הרב דוב בערל וויין

שדרות בן מימון 15, ירושלים 92262

5 Elul 5767

Daniel Retter has done a great service to the Torah world and the Jewish people generally with the publication of this magnificent volume. It will be of immense aid to anyone interested in expanding one's Torah knowledge and of the infinite genius of the Talmud and its immortal scholars. I am unworthy of giving approbations but this is a work that stands by itself in its importance and necessity. May Daniel Retter be blessed in seeing this project through to its completion.

With Torah blessings,

Rabbi Berel Wein
Rav, Beit Knesset Hanassi, Jerusalem
Senior Lecturer, Yeshiva Ohr Sameach, Jerusalem
Director, Destiny Foundation

דוד קאהן

ביהמ"ד גבול יעבץ
ברוקלין, נוא יארק

בס"ד

My good friend, the well known lawyer and ASKAN Daniel Retter Esq., came to me with three different compilations of indices to enable Talmudic scholars and laymen to find any topic in the Talmud. He has named them „Index Daniel Retter al hashas".

I believe that he merited to bring his magnificent idea to concretization because of his fervent attachment to learning Torah as well as his commitment to the needs of the community.

More Power to him! May he always be deemed worthy to be an instrument to enhance Torah study and fulfilling the needs of the TSIBBUR.

דוד קאהן
אני החותם מוקירו לעד

(Translated from original Hebrew)

Tel: 548-4765

YOUNG ISRAEL OF RIVERDALE

4502 HENRY HUDSON PARKWAY EAST
RIVERDALE, NEW YORK 10471

Mordechai Willig, Rabbi

4 Tevet, 5768

Our master, the Hazon Ish, writes that in our time, we call searching "exertion." Placing searching on the same level as the "exertion" [necessary for proper study] is the ruin of the entire ideal of exerting oneself for the Torah. R' Isaac Hutner wrote similarly in his introduction to *Otzar Mefarshei Hatalmud* (Bava Metzia, Volume II). But what can one do when he wants to toil and exert himself in the study of Torah, but cannot remember the source in the Talmud necessary for further investigation?

Therefore, let us appreciate that my friend, R' Daniel Retter, has devised a new and wonderful idea: an index of the entire Talmud.

It seems to me that by creating this index and assisting his own study, R' Daniel has benefited others. R' Daniel has been delivering a daily *shiur* in *daf yomi* to our congregation for many years now, and studying at such a pace does not allow sufficient time for investigating any issue connected to the *daf* being studied that particular day. Now that the index has appeared, every *talmid chacham* and lecturer can immediately find the topic he is searching for.

R' Daniel deserves much credit for benefitting the masses.

Mordechai Willig

CONTENTS

PREFACE

A Few Beginning Words

The basic book of traditional Jewish thought, practice and values is the Talmud. Its two versions – The Jerusalem Talmud and the Babylonian Talmud – are the repository of the Oral Law of Sinai and the wisdom of Jewish Torah scholarship over millennia. It may very well be the most intensely studied book in human history. It has been the main component of the Jewish studies curriculum in yeshiva and synagogue study halls for centuries on end. Scholarship in Jewish life has always meant Talmudic scholarship.

The final redaction of the Talmud took place in the sixth century CE and commentaries, explanations, debates, novellae, and discussions regarding its contents have continued until this very day. There is no other book that equals its influence and inspiration over an entire people and faith. It is unique in every way and withstands any comparison to any other work.

The Talmud can be maddeningly difficult to deal with. Written in Aramaic dialect, it really contains no clear rules of organization, punctuation, or style. It assumes that you know it all before you even begin to study it. It is a book

of Godly personalities and deep insight into the human condition and the world that we inhabit. It is a book of love, of compassion, of striving spirituality but also of withering candor. It is inspiring and revealing, and it has nurtured generation upon generation of Jews through harrowing times and difficulties. But it does not give up its secrets and insights easily. It is not light or cursory reading material. And even the scholar, if not possessed of especially gifted powers of memory, will find it difficult to locate subjects and sayings which one knows to be in the Talmud – but where?

Enter therefore the HaMafteach® –The Talmud Bavli Indexed Reference Guide by Daniel Retter, the fabulous work that you now hold in your hands. It is this latest contribution to Talmudic scholarship that opens the maze of the Talmud to uncomplicated navigation. All of the wisdom of the Talmud is now available for easy perusal and location. This will be a boon to all those interested in studying the Talmud, and assimilating its wisdom. From veteran scholars to neophytes just beginning their way in the study of Talmud this book will light and lighten their path toward understanding

its eternal words and wisdom. Like all
great tools in life, after using this book
even once, one will wonder how he ever
get along without it until now. Efficiently
organized with great scholarship and
presented with unusual clarity, this book
belongs in the library of every individual
Jewish home, school, yeshiva and study
hall. I am convinced that it will become
a staple in future methods of Talmudic
study and instruction.

Rabbi Berel Wein

FOREWORD

From the Editors of the Talmudic Encyclopedia

רבי דניאל היה נותן בהם סימנים

The work of the Tannaim did not come to an end with the passing of Rabbi Yehuda Hanasi, the redactor of the Mishnah; rather, it changed. The Amoraim in their day treated the words of the Tannaim like a living book, and frequently quoted the Tannaim to back up their own assertions. The book of the *Mishnah* stood as a collective memory, and they derived further laws and sayings from its intricacies. Sometimes an Amora had to amend the version as taught by a Tanna. "R' Yosef said to the reciter of Tannaic statements: 'do not include the word *humility,*'" i.e., remove the word *humility* from the version you have memorized (Sotah 49b). Here you have a generation of giants of the spirit, who still needed someone to memorize the statements of the previous generations. Such mastery has not passed from the world, and for many years there were a few known Sages of Israel who could pass the pin test: they could tell which word in each folio was perforated by a pin when poked through the entire volume.

However, God planted limited numbers of such sages in each generation, such that there is not even one per city or two for each tribe. Many are those who stand before the books of the Talmud who cannot succeed in finding what they seek within. Even if they do remember which tractate it is in, they do not know exactly where, nor do they know the exact quote. They no longer have at their side that wondrous reciter who could come up with the exact quote whenever asked. It is not uncommon that someone is entirely unaware that the particular subject he is dealing with at the moment is discussed somewhere in the Talmud.

Over the course of the generations, books have been composed for the purpose of assisting students to find what they are searching for. Some anthologies had entries in order of their appearance in the weekly Torah reading, with the assumption that the average Jew was familiar with that order. Even Maimonides, for example, was of the point of view that "the wisdom of our sages has gone lost, and the understanding of our intellects is hidden… only a handful of people understand these issues." (Maimonides, introduction to Yad HaChazaka). By "these issues," he meant the Babylonian Talmud, and as a solution, he divided his work into "individual laws of every issue." He did not wish to

establish the practical *halacha*; rather, he wanted to hand his students a sort of index of the Talmudic world, without which one could not find his bearings in the Sea of the Talmud, whose laws are interspersed and woven throughout the individual tractates.

It is nevertheless still necesary for the student with a general familiarity of the Talmud to find each issue–whether familiarity by the weekly Torah reading, or by dividing the entire Torah into fourteen sections, each with its own subsections. Yet, the Torah once again became the lot of the few. Although we lack familiarity with these issues, at least the childhood studies of the alphabet have not gone lost. Based on this, writers over the subsequent generations composed more and more reference guides and encyclopedias arranged in alphabetical order. Rabbi Yitzchak Lampronti did such in his work *Pahad Yitzchak*, as did Rabbi Yosef Engel in *Beit HaOtzar* and Rabbi Chizkiyah Medini in *Sdei Chemed*. The trend has continued with the editing of the *Talmudic Encyclopedia*, which is a work still in progress.

As the corpus of Talmudic discussion continued to grow, it included all of the treasures of the Oral Law from the times of the Tannaim and the Rishonim, and contemporary authorities, the decisors and yeshiva heads of today. Once again, one who concentrates on the basic Oral Law of the Babylonian Talmud will become lost in the infinite sea. In the end he is searching for how the Amoraim could be so sure of certain issues that they could "claim to be witnesses." The student cannot distinguish between certain knowledge of a deed and certain knowledge of an intent, and neither is there anyone who can clarify if the Amoraim meant testimony in the legal sense. He now wants to finds the only two instances in the Talmud where the Amoraim used this expression as a concept and not as a literal statement.

If he were to use the concordance reference of the Talmud to find a particular word, he would be inundated by tens and hundreds of references, most of which will be totally irrelevant to the matter at hand. The same would be true if he were to use a computer search, which can find each far-flung word, but which lacks the necessary intelligence to distinguish which results are relevant. See how much we praise

the Tanna Rabbi Yehuda, who used an acronym to remember the names of the ten plagues brought on Egypt. The order of the plagues has been preserved among the masses in the merit of those who devised mnemonics, and this mnemonic serves every one in Israel. Did not our sages teach us (Eruvin 54b) that the Torah is only acquired through mnemonics? Elsewhere (Shabbat 104b) the Gemara expounded the order of the letters of the alphabet; for example, *samech* and *ayin*, if read literally as whole words, mean "support the eye." "Make mnemonics in the Torah, and acquire it." Because of these mnemonics, the Torah has been preserved in our possession, just as the sages further stated (Eruvin 53a), the Judeans who were exacting in their language and who would make mnemonics for themselves maintained their Torah knowledge.

We also appreciate Daniel Retter, who also has formulated mnemonics, and has eased our familiarization with the Talmud.

Rabbi Dr. Avraham Steinberg
President, Yad HaRav Herzog Institute
Administrative Director of the Talmudic
Encyclopedia

Rabbi Uri Dassberg, *z"l*
Vice President, Yad HaRav Herzog Institute
Editorial Board of the Talmudic
Encyclopedia

INTRODUCTION

B'siyata d'Shemaya

Dear Student of the Talmud, You hold in your hands the HaMafteach®, the first user-friendly, comprehensive, indexed reference guide to the entire Babylonian Talmud.

Many have asked why this has never been published before. I too have often wondered, why is there no index in the back of every Hebrew and English edition of the Talmud? This question has gnawed at me for years.

I think the answer may lie in the history of the Talmud.

It is at the very core of our belief as God-fearing Jews that Moses received the Written Torah, as well as the Oral Torah, on Mt. Sinai directly from God, in the year 2448 after Creation, 1313 BCE. The Written Torah was subsequently transmitted by Moses to the Jewish Nation, and thereafter from generation to generation, to the present time. The original text and form of the Written Torah did not evolve over generations; rather, we possess the Written Torah today, exactly as it was on the day it was given to Moses, uninterrupted and unchanged, for the past 3,323 years.

Not so the Oral Torah! The Oral Torah was transmitted by Moses to the Jewish Nation orally, and thereafter handed down from generation to generation for the next 1,500 years. In the year 3925 (164 CE), Rabbi Yehudah HaNasi, also called *Rabeinu HaKadosh* or *Rebbi*, redacted all of the previous forty generations' cumulative knowledge of the Oral Torah in **written** form, which was called the Mishnah.

The exigent circumstances which brought about this monumental change in the transmission of the Oral Law is described below by the Rambam:

"Our Holy Teacher (*Rabeinu Hakadosh*) wrote the Mishnah. From the time of Moshe until Our Holy Teacher, (*Rabeinu Hakadosh*), no one had written a work from which the Oral Law was publicly taught. Rather, in each generation, the head of the court or the prophet of the time wrote down for his private use notes on the traditions he had heard from his teachers, but he taught in public from memory. So too, each individual wrote down, according to his ability, parts of the explanation of the Torah and of its laws that he had heard, as well as the new matters that developed in each generation, which

had not been received by tradition, but had been deduced by applying the Thirteen Principles for Interpreting the Torah, and had been agreed upon by the Great Rabbinical Court. Such had always been done, until the time of Our Holy Teacher (*Rabeinu Hakadosh*). He gathered together all the traditions, all the enactments, and all the explanations and interpretations that had been heard from Moshe Our Teacher or had been deduced by the courts of all the generations in all matters of the Torah; and he wrote the Book of the Mishnah from all of them. And he taught it in public, and it became known to all Israel; everyone wrote it down and taught it everywhere, so that the Oral Law would not be forgotten by Israel. And why did Our Holy Teacher do so, and did not leave the matter as it had been? Because he saw that the students were becoming fewer and fewer, calamities were continually happening, wicked government was extending its domain and increasing in power, and the Israelites were wandering and reaching remote places. He thus wrote a work to serve as a handbook for all, so that

it could be rapidly studied and would not be forgotten; throughout his life, he and his court continued giving public instruction in the Mishnah." (Rambam, Introduction to the *Yad HaChazakah*)

The written Mishnah did not end with Rebbi's passing in the year 3949 (189 CE). For the next 286 years, the Tannaim and the Amoraim analyzed, criticized, dissected, and expanded the Mishnah-Gemara, until the "Oral Law" was "closed" by Ravina and Rav Ashi in the year 4235 (475 CE). Even so, for the next sixty-five years, additional editing and rulings were made by the Rabbanan Savurai, such as Rav Yosef of the Academy of Pumbedisa, Mar Zutra, and Rav Achai, as well as others of their generation. The Talmud was finally closed in the middle of the sixth century, in approximately the year 4300 (540 CE).

This history of the Talmud reveals that it was a "work in progress" until after the Rabbanan Savurai, and hardly ready for an index. Also, there is no record that the newly written Mishnah by Rebbi, followed by the written Talmud, was ever uniformly paginated, even though it was classified and divided by Rebbi into six parts, namely *Zeraim*, *Moed*, *Nashim*,

Nezikin, *Kodashim*, and *Taharos*. Therefore, without uniform pagination, and with an expanding text, an index was not yet possible.

Also, it must not be forgotten that before the onset of the printing press, the Talmud was written by hand, and the "luxury" of an index was probably not the highest priority.

In 5205 (1445 CE), Johannes Gutenberg invented the movable type printing press in Germany. Approximately twenty-five years later, in 5230 (1470 CE), almost 1,000 years after the Talmud was "closed," the first Hebrew book was published. There is a scholarly dispute if that book was the *Aruch*, a Talmudic lexicon, or Rashi's commentary on the Torah. Approximately thirteen years later, in 5243 (1483 CE), Joshua Solomon Soncino and his nephew Gershom Soncino, from the Italian town of Soncino, published tractate Berachos, the first-ever printed edition of the Talmud. This was followed by tractate Beitzah and a few other popular tractates. The Soncino edition of the Talmud inaugurated the page format (*tzuras hadaf*) of the Talmud, which featured the Talmud's text in square letters in the middle of the page, with Rashi on the inside margin and Tosafos on the outside margin, printed in scripted text. However, Soncino never published a complete set of the Talmud, nor do we have any record that any editions of the Talmud, during this period, included the *daf* and *amud* pagination with which we are familiar.

Between 1520 and 1548, Daniel Bomberg, a non-Jew from Antwerp, Belgium, printed several editions of the complete Talmud, in Venice, utilizing the same format (*tzuras hadaf*) as the Soncino Talmud. However, it was Bomberg who introduced the *daf* and *amud* pagination of the complete Talmud, which we use today.[1]

Finally, the Talmud was now ready for an index! It was already "closed" for more than 1,000 years, relatively easy and economical to reproduce en masse via the printing press, and most important, finally possessed a standard *daf* and *amud* pagination that was accepted throughout

---

[1] It was not until 1886, when the Widow and Brothers Romm published the Vilna Shas, which truly and universally standardized the Talmud's pagination. This was accomplished by uniformly printing each word on each line with identical margins, spacing, and text layout. This was unlike the previous editions, which although following the daf and amud pagination, were not uniformly formatted word for word within the Talmud's page itself.

the world by Talmudic scholars and laymen alike.

It is therefore not surprising that a few years after Bomberg began printing the complete Talmud, in approximately 1535-1540, Rabbi Joshua Boaz of Italy, compiled his *Mesoras HaShas*, which cross-referenced the Talmudic sources of the subject being studied, to other tractates. This apparently served the needs of Talmud scholars for the next five hundred years, who were able to locate identical or similar Talmudic subjects throughout the Shas.

However, the *Mesoras HaShas* was not designed to locate a particular source in the Talmud without knowledge of the initial location beforehand. It was not an "index" as that word is commonly understood.

Perhaps the reason for the continued absence of an index for five centuries, was that the study of the Talmud was generally restricted to a select group of *bnei Torah*. This select group, while discrete, was limited to yeshiva students from age six through high school, yeshiva graduates, Kolel students, *Roshei Yeshiva*, Rabbis, and devoted laymen, who would set aside time throughout their busy work week to "learn for the sake of learning." As

extensive as this group appears to be, in reality it was a select and limited group, as it only included a miniscule component of the strictly observant Jewish population.

Furthermore, there was no real need or demand by members of this group for an index to Shas. This was because many members of this limited group learned the Talmud "day and night" and already knew Shas "by heart," whether literally or virtually. When it became necessary to locate a particular subject in the Talmud, these scholars or students could always rely on their teachers, study partners, or older *bnei Torah*, to help them find a Talmudic source if they had difficulty finding it themselves. But this was a frustrating exercise.

There may be another reason for the absence of an index to the Talmud. The Talmud is written in the Aramaic and Hebrew languages. Any Hebrew or English language index would have to capture the "essence" of the subject matter being sought, rather than applying a word to a search engine, as with computer programs. This "essence" would include idiomatic expressions referring to the subject matter, obscure and unfamiliar Aramaic words, complex and esoteric topics found in the

Talmud or its commentaries, and even those words or expressions not found literally in the Talmud itself.

An example of this "essence" would be *pidyon haben* (redemption of the firstborn son). If one were to look for a source in the Talmud for the custom of having a *seudas mitzvah* (ceremonial feast) for a *pidyon haben*, one could find this source only in the Talmudic anecdote about Rav and Shmuel relating to this *mitzvah*. However, this singular Talmudic source, in *Bava Kama 80a*, refers to this *seudas mitzvah* as "*yeshua haben*," which Rashi ad loc. interprets as the *mitzvah* of the *seudah* (meal) of *pidyon haben*. Rashi explains that "*yeshua*" is the equivalent of the Aramaic word "*purkan*" which means "to save or redeem." The HaMafteach® locates this source under the Entry "*pidyon haben*," although the word *pidyon haben* is not found anywhere in Bava Kama 80a. The HaMafteach® thus captures the "essence" of the search for *pidyon haben* though not through the literal text of *yeshua haben*, which would have defeated the purpose of finding a source for the *seudas mitzvah* of a *pidyon haben*.

A computer database, however, would find this *seudas mitzvah* reference only if it was asked to search for "*yeshua haben*," which is unusual terminology for "*pidyon haben*," and with which most people are not familiar. This highlights the major conceptual difference between the HaMafteach® and a computer-based search engine.

In addition, an English index would present an even greater challenge. This is because of the index's need to transliterate, rather than to just translate, the original Aramaic and Hebrew texts into English. Also, an English index would have to utilize transliterated expressions familiar to Talmudic scholars, as well as English translations understood by ordinary laymen. It would serve no purpose to solely employ literal English translations for Talmudic concepts and subjects, because often there are no adequate English translations.

An example would be the word "*get*," which is easily translated as "divorce." However, the words "*terumah*" or "*maaser*" cannot be translated as "tithes," since *maaser* is more properly described as a "tithe," but "*terumah*" is sui generis.

With the popularity of the Daf Yomi movement, which started in 1923 through the initiative of Rabbi Meir

Shapiro *z"l* (may his memory be for a blessing), this limited group of Shas devotees expanded considerably. This expansion grew substantially with the advent of the complete Soncino English Talmud in 1952. The Talmud's popularity increased even more significantly with the English translation and elucidation of the Talmud by ArtScroll, as well as Hebrew translations and elucidations by Chavruta, Mesivta, and other Talmudic supplements, in both Hebrew and English. In addition, the *baal teshuvah* and *kiruv* movements introduced the Talmud to many hundreds of thousands of Jewish youth and men who had never before opened, let alone studied, the Talmud.

Also, the 7.5-year Daf Yomi cycle has added many new participants as each new tractate begins. In Eretz Yisrael, a trend has recently developed where *yeshivos* learn one complete *daf* for the entire day. Of course, there are still hundreds of thousands of Talmudic students and laymen who simply learn Talmud as part of a yeshiva curriculum, or as their daily fare of Talmud.

This expanded group of Daf Yomi participants, as well as many Talmud students, needed an index to the Talmud to assist in their studies. But an index which was geared to all backgrounds and would capture the "essence" of a Talmudic subject did not exist, until the advent of the HaMafteach®.

As I developed the concept of the HaMafteach®, I recognized that it would require the endorsement of both its concept and contents by the universally recognized *Gedolim* (Sages) of Eretz Yisrael and America. It was during the infancy of this project that I showed a sample of the HaMafteach® to these *Gedolim*, both in Eretz Yisrael and the United States. I was extremely heartened by their immediate reactions. One of these well-known *Gedolim*, with whom I spent almost an hour (to the astonishment of those waiting outside his room) at his summer residence, asked me: "Doniel, when will you start and finish the Talmud Yerushalmi?" This was of course "music to my ears."

It is fitting, therefore, that some of the *haskamos* and *berachos* (approbations and blessings) which you will find at the beginning of the HaMafteach® are dated more than five years ago. Usually, the author of a *sefer* seeks a *haskama* and/or *beracha* only after his work is completed.

However, the HaMafteach® dictated that both its concept as well as its contents receive in advance the wholehearted endorsement of the *Gedolim,* both in Eretz Yisrael and in the United States. I therefore felt it appropriate to first consult with these *Gedolim* before embarking on the HaMafteach® in both Hebrew and English.

I thank Hashem that the HaMafteach® was warmly embraced by these *Gedolim.* Moreover, I was encouraged by them to complete the HaMafteach® as quickly as possible, so that it would be available to the Torah community, as well as the Jewish community at large, as soon as possible.

I therefore pray that *b'ezras Hashem,* the HaMafteach® will find favor in "the eyes of man and God" (Proverbs 3:4).

Highlights of the HaMafteach®
The HaMafteach® contains approximately 6,600 major subject Entries, 27,000 minor Sub-Entries, 42,000 Talmudic reference sources (*mar'eh mekomos*), and 2,800 transliterated or dual-referenced Glossary entries.

Who will use the HaMafteach®?

1. Students of the Talmud who wish to immediately locate a particular subject, phrase, Biblical or Talmudic personality, exegesis, parable, or anecdote;

2. A rabbi, or teacher of the Talmud, who wishes to discuss a topic not being studied in class, which requires Talmudic sources;

3. A *chaburah* (Talmud study group) leader who wishes to prepare a *shiur* relating to a particular topic, and requires all of the basic Talmudic sources;

4. A speaker who wishes to draw on Talmudic sources for the particular occasion;

5. An author who wishes to write about the Talmud or on related topics, and requires authoritative information relating to lesser-known, unusual, or unique subjects and topics found in the Talmud.

The HaMafteach® will be a companion to every edition of the Talmud, whether at home, in the yeshiva, or in a public library.

On a personal note, I am aware that the HaMafteach® may contain errors, of both omission and commission. These errors are my fault alone. I ask of you a personal favor. If you find an error, whether a missing Entry or an incorrect or incomplete source, or if you have a comment or suggestion to improve the HaMafteach®, please email us at comments@hamafteach.org. If our editors determine that we have erred,

then *b'ezras Hashem*, the next edition of the HaMafteach® will reflect your correction(s).

Please remember, the HaMafteach® is not a computer program. I have intentionally not included every single Abbaye or Rava found in Shas, which a computer program can and will print out. We have striven to include only those entries which a serious user will require in order to locate a basic subject or topic in the Talmud, and which will enable him to develop his studies from that source. Our Talmudic board has patiently reviewed every single Entry, and we have consciously classified and categorized the Entries in a user-friendly manner, so that you will be

able to find the Entry or source as quickly and easily as possible. Your comments or suggestions will help improve the next edition, so that Hashem's Torah will be glorified.

Daniel Retter
Riverdale, New York
28 Elul 5771
September 28, 2011

לע"נ הרה"ח ר' מרדכי
בן ר' קלונמוס אריה ז"ל
Commemorating the fourth *yahrzeit* of my father, R' Mordechai ben R' Klonymous Aryeh *z'l*

ACKNOWLEDGEMENTS

The HaMafteach® is the fruit of the labor of several extraordinary individuals. I acknowledge first and foremost Rav Elchanan Kohn of Bnei Brak. I was fortunate to have been introduced to Rav Elchanan (as he is popularly known), in the year 2006. I described to him my dream of authoring a *Mafteach* to Shas. R' Elchanan not only encouraged me to personally undertake this project, he also graciously agreed to be its chief scholar. From our first meeting in Jerusalem, and many subsequent meetings in Bnei Brak over the past five years, I have been in almost daily contact with him by e-mail, phone, and in person, as we developed the outline and guidelines of this project. It was our goal that the HaMafteach® would be comprehensive, accurate, and most important, efficient and user-friendly, so as to be welcome in the homes of those who love the Torah and the Talmud. I also wish to thank R' Elchanan's wife, Rebbetzin Nechamah Kohn, whose efforts and assistance in the translation of this work were invaluable.

At the earliest stage of this project, I sought the acceptance, blessings, and endorsement for the HaMafteach® from *Gedolim* and Rabbis in Eretz Yisrael and America. I first approached Rav Dovid Cohen, the renowned *posek* (decisor) for many benevolent and charitable organizations throughout the United States, as well as the personal rabbi and advisor to many thousands of individuals throughout the world. As I showed him the earliest drafts of the HaMafteach®, we discussed the awesome breadth of this undertaking, yet he encouraged me to continue the work. R' Dovid presented me with the first in a series of *haskamos* and *michtevei berachah* (approbations and endorsements) for the HaMafteach®, which convinced me that the HaMafteach® would have its rightful place in every Jewish library which contained a Shas. I shall always be grateful to R' Dovid Cohen, who was the first to offer his blessings for the idea as well as for the success of the HaMafteach®.

Afterwards, I met with Rabbi Berel Wein in Jerusalem, who was my *Mara d'Asra* in Miami Beach, Florida, where I lived before returning to New York. From our first meeting, until a few weeks before the publication of the HaMafteach®, Rabbi Wein has provided me with sound judgment, experienced counsel, and practical advice, which enabled the

HaMafteach® to see the "light of day." Rabbi Wein took precious time away from his family during his visits to the United States to give me guidance and counsel, and I so appreciate his selflessness in that regard.

I wish to acknowledge the support and encouragement of Rabbi Dr. Abraham Steinberg of Jerusalem, the editor of The Talmudic Encyclopedia. Dr. Steinberg immediately grasped the enormous value of the HaMafteach®, and graciously offered to write the preface to the Hebrew edition.

I also wish to publicly thank Rabbi Yaakov Shulevitz, who played a most valuable role "behind the scenes," to enable the HaMafteach® to come to fruition. His friendship with, and entrée to, the *Gedolei Eretz Yisrael*, is unsurpassed by anyone I know.

One of the greatest challenges to publishing the HaMafteach® was the decision of which Entries to include and which not to include, in order to meet the intellectual needs of our readers from diverse backgrounds. After we selected the Entries based on our own Talmudic experience and expectations, I reached out to my own *Mara d'Asra*, Rabbi Mordechai

Willig, the rabbi of my shul, The Young Israel of Riverdale, for his assistance. Rabbi Willig endorsed the HaMafteach® in glowing terms, and also worked tirelessly to secure a significant number of diverse Entries for the HaMafteach® from his own students, colleagues, laymen and lovers of the Talmud, from all walks of life. I wish to publicly thank Rabbi Mordechai Willig for his efforts on behalf of the HaMafteach®, and for continuously encouraging me over the past six years to complete this work.

I wish to publically acknowledge and thank my beloved children, Alain and Lea Schiff, Dr. Avi and Tamar Retter, and Avi and Yael Kamelhar, who reviewed the final manuscript, and have all made noteworthy suggestions and changes which have been incorporated into the final draft. I would like to thank my son Aaron for his continuing help from the birth of this project. He served beyond the call of duty one owes to one's father. I thank his wife, Alizza, for selflessly encouraging his efforts and time on behalf of the HaMafteach®. All of my children have supported all of my efforts and undertakings related to Torah and *chesed* projects. All of my children's devotion to

Torah and *yiras Shamayim,* are well-known in their communities. I am so proud of them and their families. The life they live is a template of *Torah im derech eretz* and a daily *Kiddush Hashem.*

Ben Gasner created this beautifully designed book and he deserves a special prize for this masterpiece, in consonance with the verse, "This is my God and I shall beautify Him." Both the stunning cover, as well as the clear and attractive page layout, were his craftsmanship. In his hand, the HaMafteach® became so much more than an index. It became a repository of our Talmud's brilliance, which is now so much more accessible to the Jewish community. I want to thank Mrs. Mindel Kassorla of Ben's graphic design studio in Jerusalem. Her thoughtful and often pointed questions, as well as her critical observations throughout the final editing process, were indispensible to assure that the HaMafteach® would serve its purpose. I respect and admire her perseverance and patience, which are deeply appreciated. I also wish to acknowledge the hard work of Nili Boim of Ben's office, who worked together with Mindel and Ben on this project. Her diligence and knowledge contributed to

the completion of the HaMafteach®. I wish to thank Rabbi Meir Erlanger and Deena Nataf of Feldheim Publishers for their assistance in the final proofreading and editing of this sefer. I wish to acknowledge the efforts of Rabbi Avi Grossman, who contributed to some of the translations of the HaMafteach®. I am in great debt to Rabbi Yoel Domb, whose editing of the HaMafteach® was conducted with exacting and brilliant insight and analysis.

I want to thank the members of my daily Daf Yomi *shiur* at the Young Israel of Riverdale, with whom I have the *zechus* to say the *shiur* for the past twenty-two years. Together, we have almost finished three cycles of Shas. Much of my inspiration for this project came through my *chaverim* at the *shiur,* because I realized how often all of us, which includes rabbis, teachers, doctors, lawyers, and businessmen, were frustrated by our inability to "put one's finger" on a Gemara just learned "a few *mesechtas,*" or even *perakim* ago. These faithful members of "the *daf*" include Herbert Ausubel, Howard Berenstein, Dr. Judah Burns, Harvey Feldschreiber, Rabbi Elchonon Finkelstein, Rabbi Michael Gervis, Rabbi Siggy Handelman, Yissocher Heinemann, Nachman Horowitz, Avi

Kamelhar (my dear son-in-law), Dr. John Mann, Rabbi Moshe Neiss, Steven Rapp, Harvey Rosenfeld, Kenny Scharf, and Chaim Sharp. I am also indebted to my "daily *daf*" *chavrusa* and president of our shul, Dr. Aryeh Rosenbaum, with whom I prepare the following day's *daf* each morning after the Daf Yomi *shiur*.

When I approached R' Yaakov and R' Yitzchak Feldheim to offer them the opportunity to publish and distribute the HaMafteach®, supported by their legendary and venerable publishing house, they immediately agreed. I thank them for their wonderful cooperation.

I would like to take this opportunity to acknowledge my law colleague, Barry Werbin, Esq., who heads the intellectual property department of the law firm where I am counsel, Herrick, Feinstein LLP in Manhattan. I cannot thank Barry enough for his guidance in advising me concerning the complex domestic and international copyright laws involved, in order to properly register and protect this work. The copyright protection indicated on the front cover was implemented through Barry's sage and experienced counsel. His advice and guidance in this complex field of law was provided

to me as a "mitzvah" (*pro bono*), so that the HaMafteach® would be available to all those who both love and respect the Talmud, a group in which Barry counts himself.

And now to both the easiest yet most difficult part of this acknowledgement. How can I thank a life partner?! My wife, Margie, is an accomplished attorney who has raised our four children, founded and organized the not-for-profit Din Legal Centers to protect and represent abused spouses before *beis din*, and advises our family 24/7 throughout year. At the same time, there is no more gracious hostess in the world. Yet, despite all of this work, Margie has been my *ezer kenegdo* for all of my life. As I tell her constantly, "I have never regretted acting on your advice; I have only regretted not taking it often enough."

I asked Margie whether I should undertake this project. Her answer was "Yes! And I will help you with it," which was the single most important encouragement I needed. As I explained to her the nature of this project, she encouraged me to spend whatever time would be needed, even to devote much of my day and night to the HaMafteach®. It

was she who insisted that I speak to the *Gedolim* before I started the HaMafteach®. Margie's contribution to this effort also involved her staying alone many nights when I was in Eretz Yisrael, or waiting home alone during the late hours of the night, as I worked on the HaMafteach® at our local *beis midrash*. Can you imagine the time we spent debating the appropriate translation of "*Nashim da'atan kalos*?!" (See Kiddushin 80a; Shabbos 33a). Perhaps her greatest contribution was her constant encouragement, despite many doubting moments when I felt the project would never get off the ground. Margie would never let me abandon this project!

I wish to take this opportunity to express to her in this public forum my gratitude for her emotional dedication to me, as well as my greatest respect for her *binah yeseirah*.

I am the product of my parents and grandparents. I thank my father, R' Mordechai Retter *z"l*, and my mother, Mrs. Betty Retter *a"h*, who brought me into this world. It was they who nourished my soul with the love of learning Torah, as well as the love of Hashem's world. I wish to memorialize my grandfather, R' Yechiel HaKohen Rosenblatt *z"l*, and my grandmother, Riva (Rachla) Rosenblatt *a"h*, who totally and unequivocally trusted and believed in Hashem's dominion over this world. I have inherited this belief from them as well.

I want to finally thank my beloved father in law, R' Leib (Leo) Rapaport *z"l*, who deserved to see this day. He looked after me and loved me as a son.

I am wholly indebted to Hashem for giving me the strength, the sense, and the years, to start and complete this holy project.

Daniel Retter

GUIDELINES

For the use of the HaMafteach® Talmud Bavli Indexed Reference Guide

To maximize the usefulness of the HaMafteach®, we have attempted to ease the method by which one can locate any particular subject in the Talmud. The HaMafteach® is especially designed to serve the needs of the public from all backgrounds.

Purpose of the HaMafteach®

1. To refer the user – through an easy and convenient search – to significant subject matter, laws, anecdotes, maxims, parables, sayings, Biblical exegesis, Biblical and Talmudic personalities, and commentaries of the Sages in *Shas Bavli* (the Babylonian Talmud).

2. To aid those who wish to prepare an extended *shiur, chaburah, drasha*, etc.

General Rules

1. The Entries have been selected very carefully and with great thought in order to allow a quick and easy search to locate significant subjects in the Talmud.

2. The HaMafteach® is not based on a computer search program, whose database contains extraneous and unnecessary information. Nor was it designed to find Talmudic sources based exclusively on the exact wording found in the Talmud like a computer program. Instead, the HaMafteach® may be compared to a Talmudic scholar, who is fluent in Talmudic "language," and is ready to aid the user in a logical and intuitive manner to find a desired subject, by anticipating how the user would normally search for a particular subject matter.

> For example, the words "we are witnesses" (*anan sahadi*) appears in several places throughout the Talmud. However, in the HaMafteach®, this phrase is cited in relation to two *sugyos* (contexts) only, because it is only in these two locations that "we are witnesses" is meant as a significant legal *concept*. In the other locations, the words "we are witnesses" are used as a non-contextual *expression* only, with no characteristic link to the *sugya*, and thus the expression is otherwise not cited in the HaMafteach®.

3. We have included multiple Sub-Entries in various Categories to anticipate all of the

reasonable ways one would search for a subject, whether by concept, Keyword, phrase, name, or subject.

Definitions of Terminology in These Guidelines

1. **Entry**: Bold font, which refers the reader to a Talmudic source.

   Examples:

   a. **Acha DeRav Yirmiyah** *(Entry)* ....Shabbos 56b
   b. **Aaron** *(Entry)*
      Aaron, Annointing ....Krisos 5b
      Aaron, Golden Calf ....Sanhedrin 7a

2. **Sub-Entry**: Various Entries under the main Entry.

   Examples:

   a. **Absorption** *(Entry)*
      Absorption in food giving taste to another food *(Sub-Entry)* ....Chullin 111b-112a
      Absorption in meat, impossible when blood flows *(Sub-Entry)* ....Chullin 8b
   b. **Acknowledge** *(Entry)*
      Acknowledged barley, claimed wheat *(Sub-Entry)* ....Bava Metzia 5a, 100b;
      ....Bava Kama 35b-36a; Shevuos 38b, 40a-40b
      Acknowledged debt, answered elusively *(Sub-Entry)* ....Bava Basra 175a;
      ....Sanhedrin 29a-29b

      Acknowledging in part *(Sub-Entry I)*
         Acknowledging in part, "here it is" *(Sub-Entry II)* ....Bava Metzia 4a-5a
         Acknowledging in part, against witnesses *(Sub-Entry II)* ....Bava Basra 128b-129a
      Acknowledgement by litigant *(Sub-Entry I)*
         Acknowledgement by litigant *(Sub-Entry II)* ....Kiddushin 65b; Gittin 40b, 64a;
         ....Bava Metzia 3b
         Acknowledgement by litigant, *kiddushin* *(Sub-Entry II)* ....Kiddushin 65a-65b

3. **Category**: If an Entry contains multiple components with more than three Sub-Entries, it may then be divided into Categories.

   Example:

   Abbaye
     Behavior — *(Category)*
       Abbaye inspected his property ....Chullin 105a
       Abbaye, juggling ....Succah 53a
       Abbaye, priestly gifts ....Chullin 133a
     Learning — *(Category)*
       Abbaye, advice about guarantee of marriage contract ....Bava Basra 174b
       Abbaye, arrogant man ....Chullin 51a
       Abbaye, invalid bill for troublesome people ....Bava Basra 168b

4. **Sources**: The page (folio) where the subject matter of the Entry may be found in the

Talmud (ex. a below). The letter "a" following the source page indicates the front page of the folio. The letter "b" following the source page indicates the back page. Multiple Sources in the same tractate are separated by a comma (ex. b). Multiple Sources in different tractates are separated by semicolons (ex. c). When there is a cross-reference, the other Entry is bolded (ex. d).

Examples:

a. Abba Kohen Bardela, acts of acquisition .... *(Source)* Bava Metzia 10a-10b
b. Accessory and primary, blessing .... *(Source)* Berachos 35b-36a, 41a, 44a
c. Abraham, angels .... *(Source)* Yoma 37a; Bava Metzia 86b-87a; Kiddushin 32b
d. Abba bar Abba .... *(Source) see* **Avuha DeShmuel**, page 37

How to Find a Subject or Phrase

Keywords: Start by looking for an Entry using a Keyword(s) which comprise(s) the subject or phrase being sought. We have made every effort to list of all the possible ways to search for a particular subject.

Example:

If one is searching for the saying, *"Everywhere you find G-d's strength, you find His humility"* (Megillah 31a), he may find this by searching for a Keyword, as follows:

Everywhere, G-d's humility .... Megillah 31a
God's strength, humility .... Megillah 31a
Greatness of G-d, humility .... Megillah 31a
Humility, God's .... Megillah 31a
Strength, Divine, humility .... Megillah 31a

Transliteration, Translation, Phonetic Key

A well-known Talmudic expression, phrase, or dictum may be found by searching for the Aramaic or Hebrew transliteration of the Keywords which make up the phrase, as found verbatim in the Talmud's text. Please note that when using the transliteration key, the citation is to the page in the HaMafteach® (not the Talmud), which will direct one to the source in the Talmud.

Examples:

a. **Anavah** .... *see* **Humility**, page 288
b. **Gedulas Hashem** .... *see* **Greatness of G-d, humility**, page 258
c. **Hakadosh Baruch Hu** .... *see* **G-d**, page 245

Sometimes, Talmudic concepts are listed under both their conventional English translation and their transliteration. For example, *Brairah* is listed under its transliteration as well as its translation, "Retroactive classification."

Personalities in the Talmud

If one wishes to find a personality mentioned in the Talmud, he will generally be able to

do so if that person is associated with a historic episode or a well-known halacha. It is impractical to list all of the instances in the Talmud where, for example, Abbaye (about 2,500 instances) or Rava (about 4,000 instances) are mentioned! A computer database would include all of these instances, but this would defeat the purpose of the HaMafteach®.

Linking Words

Many phrases and maxims in the Talmud begin with a common preposition or a "linking" word or words, such as "All…", "No man…", "There are…", and "Just as…".

Generally, these prepositions or links have been omitted as Entries if they do not characterize the saying.

For example, the linking word *keshem*, meaning "*Just as*," is found about three hundred times in the Talmud, but is included in the HaMafteach® as an Entry in only three places, where it characterizes the saying. One instance is "*Keshem shenichnas lebris…*" ("Just as [the baby] will enter into the covenant…"; Yevamos 65b). Here, the word *keshem* characterizes the saying because it is the blessing.

However, where the word *keshem* is found as part of a well-known Talmudic saying, we have not referenced the phrase under that word. Instead, the subject is listed by multiple-Entry (Key)words to reflect the substance of the Talmudic saying.

Example:

"'Just as' *(keshem)* one may not interrupt [his learning] for *tefilah*, one may also not interrupt [his learning] for *Kriyas Shema*."

This is listed as follows:

Prayer, interrupting learning ....Shabbos 11a
Shema, interrupting one's learning ....Shabbos 11a
Interrupting learning for *Shema* and prayer ....Shabbos 11a

Omissions of Significant Words in Entries

We have also omitted as Entries words which do not characterize the saying, even if their meaning is important. For example, "Israel" appears as an Entry only sixteen times, while it appears about three thousand times in the Talmud! On the other hand, the Category "Non-Jews" is found in more than one hundred Entries. The reason is that the word "Israel" is not conceptually significant unless it comes to differentiate an ordinary Jew from a Kohen, Levi or non-Jew. "Non-Jew," on the other hand, is considered significant with respect to every halacha or *aggadah* linked to non-Jews.

Examples:

a. Where the word "Israel" is featured as an Entry word:
    Israel, nation more cherished than angels ....Chullin 91b-92a
In this saying, the word Israel is the essence of the saying.

b. Where the word "Israel" is not the Entry word, but instead the Entry word reflects the essence of the saying:

"Hashem does not inflict punishment [i.e., sickness] upon Israel unless He first creates its remedy." This is listed as follows:

Remedy before illness ....Megillah 13b

Excerpts of Key Phrases

Generally, the Entry word cites the Talmud's Key text word(s) verbatim, unless, if out of its proper context, a different meaning would result.

For example, the well-known rule of "A man does not think up a *gezeirah shavah* by his own reasoning" (Niddah 19b) is not listed in its original form, because the Key phrase – "*Gezeirah shavah* by one's own reasoning" – is inaccurate; to the contrary, a man does not think up a *gezeirah shavah* by his own reasoning. Instead, the rule is listed as "*Gezeirah shavah*, from one's teacher."

Excerpts of Well-Known Phrases

An excessively lengthy saying is listed in abridged form. We have generally replaced the missing words with a comma.

For example: "*Gezeirah Shavah*, from one's teacher."

Subject with Several Opinions

When a subject has diverse opinions with identical opening words, we have listed only one of these opinions. The reason is that the Source will lead to both or multiple opinions.

For example, we have listed the Entry, "Kindling on Shabbos, to differentiate it from other works" (Shabbos 70a) without listing the conflicting opinion: "Kindling on Shabbos, to exempt from stoning penalty." Both opinions will be found in Shabbos 70a.

Multiple Phrases

A subject that may be cited in the Talmud with multiple phrases using the same opening word (for example, "*Gezeirah shavah*") is listed in the HaMafteach® only by the most significant citation, (i.e., "*Gezeirah shavah*, from one's teacher.") Generally, all the Sub-Entries having similar opening words are arranged in close proximity under the same Entry. Thus, one who is looking for "*Gezeirah shavah*, by one's own reasoning" will find this concept in "*Gezeirah shavah*, from one's teacher."

Cross-Referencing Words by Substance and Meaning

When searching for the Source of a subject, occasionally only one critical component of the subject matter is known. The HaMafteach® has therefore cross-referenced both the general subject and its critical components.

Example:

There is a well-known saying, "Four things need encouragement" [which the Talmud teaches us are Learning, Livelihood, Prayer, and Torah].

This saying may be found by its Keywords...

Encouragement, four things ....Berachos 32b
Four things need encouragement ....Berachos 32b
Need encouragement ....Berachos 32b

...or by any of its components (the substantive content):

Learning, encouragement ....Berachos 32b
Livelihood, encouragement ....Berachos 32b
Prayer, encouragement ....Berachos 32b
Torah, encouragement ....Berachos 32b

Guidelines for a Quicker and More Efficient Search

1. When a subject can be listed in several possible word forms, the noun will be used, i.e., "mistake" and not "mistaken."

2. In order to easily find a phrase, the HaMafteach® omits generic words.

For example, in the phrase, "Everyone whose fear of G-d precedes his wisdom," the words "everyone" and "whose" are omitted, as well as words such as, *and*, *by one*, *that*, *the*, etc.

Order of Listing of the Talmudic Sources

1. The Entries and Sources found in the HaMafteach® encompass all of Talmud Bavli, including the Mishnaic tractates that have no Gemara (i.e., Kilayim and Uktzin). A source concerning a subject that is only briefly mentioned in a Mishnah, but is discussed at length in the corresponding Gemara, will be listed in the HaMafteach® according to its place in the Gemara.

For example, "*Shema*, midnight" appears in the first Mishnah of Berachos (2a), but in the HaMafteach®, the source is the location where the Gemara thoroughly discusses this subject (Berachos 4a-4b, 9a).

2. When a subject is found in numerous places in the Talmud, the Sources are generally listed in descending conceptual order, beginning with the main source (for instance, "king"; see example, below), then the Source(s) of less importance ("prince"), then the Source where the subject is mentioned only incidentally or with an additional new insight ("minister"). Finally, the least "important" source where the subject is mentioned without any additional insight ("citizen") will be listed according to the Talmudic order of tractates. However, all sources that are found within the same tractates are always grouped together. Where there are other Sources, we have given priority to the order of the Talmud, i.e., Berachos before Shabbos.

Example:

Sabbatical year, work done before ....Sheviis 1:1-8, 2:1-6 (*king*); Yevamos 83a (*prince*);
....Rosh Hashanah 9b 10b (*minister*); Succah 34a 44a (*citizen*); Taanis 3a (*citizen*);
........................Moed Katan 3b-4a (*citizen*); Bava Basra 26b-27a (*citizen*); Zevachim 110b (*citizen*).

In this example, the "king" is listed first, then the "prince" and the "minister" (conceptual order). Finally, the "citizen" is listed, all Sources for which are listed according to the order of the Talmud.

Entry Titles

We have listed many diverse sayings that begin with the same word. Examples are "No" and "*Ein*." Also, the Talmud begins some of its well-known sayings with a number (1,2, 3,4,5,6,7,8,9,10,20,30,40,50,60,70,80, 90, 100, 1,000, 6,000). Each of these numbers is found as an Entry except for the number 90, since it is part of the famous Mishnah dealing with the developmental age of man.

Alphabetical Order and Category Division

The Entries and the Categories are organized in alphabetical order. The Sub-Entries are also organized alphabetcally under each Entry. When a Sub-Entry is further divided into multiple Sub-Entries (*Sub-Entry II*, as explained above), it is removed from the alphabetical order and placed after the other single Sub-Entries. When an Entry is divided into categories, all Sub-Entries which do not belong to the main Categories are grouped in the last Category under "Misc."

Spelling of Biblical names in the HaMafteach®

The English spelling of proper names of Biblical personalities are as listed below. Many well known Biblical names pronounced in English are not spelled phonetically, (e.g. Achashveirush= Ahasuerus). Therefore, we have followed the traditional spelling for Biblical names (e.g Sorah = Sarah).

Aaron	Ahimelech	Bezalel	Eglon
Abel	Ahitophel	Bigthan	Elazar
Abigail	Amasa	Bilhah	Eldad
Abihu	Amlaek	Boaz	Eli
Abijah	Amaziah	Cain	Eliab
Abimelech	Amos	Caleb	Eliezer
Abiram	Amram	Canaan	Elijah
Abishag	Amraphel	Chileab	Elimelech
Abner	Asa	Cyrus	Elisha
Abraham	Asher	Dan	Elkanah
Absalom	Azariah	Daniel	Enosh
Achan	Balaam	Darius	Ephraim
Adam	Baladan	Dathan	Ephron
Adonijah	Balak	David	Er
Ahab	Barak	Deborah	Esau
Ahasuerus	Baruch	Delilah	Esther
Ahaz	Bathsheba	Dinah	Eve
Ahaziah	Benajah	Doeg	Ezekiel
Ahijah	Benjamin	Edom	Ezra

Gabriel	Jethro	Miriam	Rebecca
Gad	Jezebel	Moab	Reuben
Gedaliah	Joab	Mordechai	Ruth
Gehazi	Job	Moses	Samson
Gideon	Jochebed	Naamah	Samuel
Gog	Joel	Naaman	Sarah
Goliath	Jonah	Naboth	Sarai
Haggai	Jonathan	Nabal	Saul
Haman	Joseph	Nadab	Sennacherib
Haran	Joshua	Nahshon	Seth
Hezekiah	Josiah	Nahum	Sheba
Hiel	Jotham	Naomi	Shechem
Hiram	Judah	Nebuchadnezzar	Shem
Hosea	Keturah	Nebuzaradan	Shemaiah
Iddo	Korah	Nehemiah	Shimei
Isaac	Kozbi	Nimrod	Sihon
Isaiah	Laban	Noah	Sisera
Ishmael	Lappidoth	Obadiah	Solomon
Ishvi	Leah	Obed	Tamar
Israel	Levi	Og	Tobijah
Issacher	Maacah	Omri	Uriah
Jacob	Malachi	On	Uzzah
Jael	Manasseh	Orpah	Uzziah
Japheth	Manoah	Othniel	Vashti
Jehoahaz	Memucan	Paltiel	Zebulun
Jehoiachin/ Jechoniah	Menahem	Peninnah	Zechariah
Jehoiakim	Mephiboshet	Pharaoh	Zedekiah
Jehonathan	Merab	Pharaoh Neco	Zelophehad
Jehoram	Merari	Phinehas	Zephaniah
Jehoshaphat	Merodach	Potiphar	Zichri
Jehu	Methusael	Puah	Zimri
Jephthah	Micah	Queen of Sheba	Zipporah
Jeroboam	Michael	Rachel	
Jesse	Michal	Rahab	

Note:

For your convenience, we have published two independent editions of the English HaMafteach®, as well as two independent editions of the Hebrew HaMafteach®, as follows:

The first English edition is organized by subject matter (A-Z).
The second English edition is organized by individual Tractates.
The first Hebrew edition is organized by subject matter (Alef-Tav).
The second Hebrew edition is organized by individual Mesechtas.

HaMafteach®

Aaron

Aaron, anointing ....Krisos 5b
Aaron, golden calf ....Sanhedrin 7a
Aaron, happy with Moses' success ....Shabbos 139a
Aaron, humility ....Chullin 89a
Aaron kept silent at his sons' death ....Zevachim 115b
Aaron, leprosy ....Shabbos 97a
Aaron loved peace ....Sanhedrin 6b

Abandon

Abandon all trade, Torah ....Kiddushin 82b
Abandoned child ....Kesubos 15b; Kiddushin 73a-73b
Abandoned eternal life ....Shabbos 10a, 33a; Taanis 21a; Beitzah 15b
Abandoning broken item which caused damage ....Bava Kama 29a-30a
Abandoning slave, freedom ....Gittin 39a; Yevamos 48a; Nazir 62b; Kiddushin 72b

Abba

Abba Aricha, fire sparks ....Chullin 137b
Abba bar Abba ....*see* **Avuha DeShmuel**, page 37
Abba bar Marta, debt ....Shabbos 121b; Yevamos 120a
Abba bar Marta, wax ....Yevamos 120a
Abba bar Minyumi, cancelled debts of *sheviis* ....Gittin 37b
Abba bar Zavda, sterile (unable to procreate) ....Yevamos 64b
Abba Chilkiyah ....Taanis 23a-23b
Abba Kohen Bardela, acts of acquisition ....Bava Metzia 10a-10b
Abba Yose, the last of pious men ....Sotah 49b
Abba, Rav Yirmiyah's father, repentance ....Shabbos 56b

Abba Saul

Abba Saul, Absalom's eye ....Niddah 24b
Abba Saul, height ....Niddah 24b
Abba Saul, measuring ....Beitzah 29a
Abba Saul, Og's femur ....Niddah 24b

Abba Umna

Abba Umna, bloodletting ....Taanis 21b-22a
Abba Umna, heavenly greeting ....Taanis 21b

Abba Ploni, slave ....Berachos 16b

Abbaye
Behavior —

Abbaye inspected his property .... Chullin 105a
Abbaye, juggling .... Succah 53a
Abbaye, priestly gifts .... Chullin 133a
Abbaye, protection in outdoor bathroom .... Berachos 62a
Abbaye refrained from making *eruv* .... Eruvin 68a

Learning —

Abbaye, advice about guarantee of marriage contract .... Bava Basra 174b
Abbaye, arrogant man .... Chullin 51a
Abbaye, invalid bill for troublesome people .... Bava Basra 168b
Abbaye, judges' scribes .... Bava Basra 136a; Sanhedrin 29b
Abbaye, learning entire Shas .... Berachos 20a
Abbaye, Rav Yosef's lecture .... Berachos 28b
Abbaye relied on who reviewed his learning .... Yevamos 64b

Ruling —

Abbaye, disciples .... Bava Basra 22a
Abbaye, feast for completion of Tractate .... Shabbos 118b-119a
Abbaye, irrigation of field .... Gittin 60b
Abbaye, mistake in ruling .... Kesubos 60b

Misc. —

Abbaye, "greater the man, greater his evil urge" .... Succah 52a
Abbaye, dreams interpretation .... Berachos 56a-56b
Abbaye, his donkey returned to him .... Gittin 45a
Abbaye, launderer's fee .... Shabbos 19a
Abbaye, making use of signature and forgery .... Bava Basra 167a
Abbaye, Nachmani .... Gittin 34b; Meilah 20b; Shabbos 33a
Abbaye, orphan .... Kiddushin 31b
Abbaye, ransom of *tefillin* .... Gittin 45b
Abbaye, received heavenly greeting .... Taanis 21b-22a
Abbaye, *seder maarachah* .... Yoma 14b, 33a-34a
Abbaye stared at Sage .... Yevamos 106a
Abbaye, unusual occurrences at his death .... Moed Katan 25b
Abbaye, urge for forbidden relations .... Succah 52a
Abbaye, wine for his widow's support .... Kesubos 65a
Abbaye, woman whose two husbands died .... Yevamos 64b
Abbaye's widow, episode .... Kesubos 65a

Abbaye and Rabbah

Abbaye and Rabbah, Eli's offspring .... Yevamos 105a; Rosh Hashanah 18a
Abbaye and Rabbah, long life .... Yevamos 105a; Rosh Hashanah 18a

Abbaye and Rava

Abbaye and Rava, place of Divine Presence .... Berachos 48a
Abbaye and Rava, ruling .... Kiddushin 52a; Bava Metzia 22b; Bava Kama 73a; Sanhedrin 27a

Abbaye's mother

Abbaye's mother, baby .... Yoma 78b; Kesubos 50a
Abbaye's mother, health .... Shabbos 66b, 133b, 134a; Eruvin 29b; Yoma 78b; Moed Katan 12a;
                                    Kesubos 10b, 39b, 50a; Gittin 67b, 70a; Avodah Zarah 28b
Abbaye's mother, medicine .... Shabbos 66b, 133b-134a; Eruvin 29b; Gittin 67b, 70a
Abbaye's mother, nurse .... Kiddushin 31b

Abbaye's mother, preventing disturbances .... Eruvin 65a
Abbaye's mother, suspicion .... Yevamos 25a; Moed Katan 18b
Abel and Cain .... Sanhedrin 37b; Yevamos 62a
Abiathar
Abiathar my son says thus .... Gittin 6b
Abiathar, *Urim Vetumim* .... Yoma 73b
Abigail
Abigail, beauty .... Megillah 15a
Abigail, prophecy .... Megillah 14a-14b
Abigail went towards David .... Pesachim 3b; Megillah 14a-14b
Abijah son of Jeroboam .... Moed Katan 28b
Abimelech, episode with Sarah .... Bava Kama 92a; Sanhedrin 58b; Makos 9a-9b
Abishag
Abishag, beauty .... Sanhedrin 39b
Abishag, David and Adonijah .... Sanhedrin 22a
Abishai
Abishai and Ishvi, David .... Sanhedrin 95a
Abishai, worth like *Sanhedrin's* majority .... Berachos 62b
Abizreihu, commandments of non-Jews .... Sanhedrin 74b
Abner
Abner, death .... Sanhedrin 49a
Abner, funeral and reason of punishment .... Sanhedrin 20a
Abominable, prohibition to make oneself, bodily needs .... Makos 16b
Abortion
Abortion, damage caused by man .... Bava Kama 43a, 49a-49b
Abortion, damage caused by ox .... Bava Kama 42a, 48b-49a
Abortion, damage caused by an ox goring occasionally .... Bava Kama 41b-42b
Abortion, non-Jew .... Sanhedrin 57b
About to
About to be collected, like collected .... Sotah 25a-25b; Yevamos 38b; Kesubos 81a; Gittin 37a; Bava Metzia 62a; Shevuos 48b
About to be cut, impurity .... Chullin 72b-73a
About to be picked, like land .... Shevuos 43a; Kesubos 50b-51a; Gittin 39a; Sanhedrin 15a; Bava Metzia 100b
About to be redeemed like redeemed .... Bava Kama 76b-77b
About to be shorn, like shorn .... Gittin 39a
About to be sprinkled, impurity .... Menachos 101b-102b
About to be shaved, like shaved .... Gittin 39a
About to be torn out, like torn out .... Gittin 39a
About to throw like throwing .... Bava Kama 76b; Menachos 79b, 101b-102b; Pesachim 13b; Temurah 22b; Krisos 24b; Meilah 5a-6a
Abraham .... *see also* **Patriarchs**, page 475
Aggadah —
Abraham, "happy is the man" .... Avodah Zarah 18b-19a
Abraham, blessings .... Yevamos 63a
Abraham, commandments given through his merit .... Sotah 17a; Chullin 88b-89a
Abraham, first convert .... Succah 49b; Chagigah 3a
Abraham takes out of from *Gehinnom* .... Eruvin 19a

Episodes —

Abraham, "from a string to a shoelace" .... Chullin 89a; Sotah 17a
Abraham and Haran, birth .... Sanhedrin 69b
Abraham and Sarah, Rabbi Benaah .... Bava Basra 58a
Abraham and Isaac, upright ones .... Avodah Zarah 25a
Abraham, angels .... Yoma 37a; Bava Metzia 86b-87a; Kiddushin 32b
Abraham, captive and eulogy .... Bava Basra 91a-91b
Abraham, circumcision .... Nedarim 32a-32b
Abraham, daughter .... Bava Basra 16b, 141a
Abraham, did not wonder .... Bava Basra 15b
Abraham, Eliezer in Cave of Machpelah .... Bava Basra 58a
Abraham, enslavement of his offspring .... Nedarim 32a
Abraham, inn in Be'er Sheva .... Sotah 10a-10b
Abraham, modesty with Sarah .... Bava Basra 16a
Abraham, old age .... Bava Metzia 87a; Sanhedrin 107b
Abraham, promise and acquisition of *Eretz Yisrael* .... Bava Basra 100a
Abraham, Shem's priesthood .... Nedarim 32b
Abraham, spirit's defense .... Sanhedrin 44b
Abraham, Temple destruction .... Menachos 53b
Abraham, trials, tests .... Avos 5:3
Abraham, visiting the sick .... Sotah 14a
Abraham, war .... Sanhedrin 96a, 108b; Nedarim 32a
Abraham, when did he discover G-d .... Nedarim 32a
Abraham's healing stone .... Bava Basra 16b
Abraham's servants, woman screamed .... Succah 31a

Names —

Abraham, Avram .... Berachos 13a
Abraham, Eytan Haezrachi .... Bava Basra 15a
Abraham, his mother's name .... Bava Basra 91a
Abraham, Nadiv .... Succah 49b; Chagigah 3a
Abraham, numerical value .... Nedarim 32b
Abraham, seven shepherds .... Succah 52b

Piety —

Abraham, called G-d "Master" .... Berachos 7b
Abraham, humility .... Chullin 88b; Sotah 17a
Abraham, integrity .... Nedarim 32a
Abraham, *maseches Avodah Zarah* .... Avodah Zarah 14b
Abraham observed the commandments .... Yoma 28b

Misc. —

Abraham, astrology and medicine .... Bava Basra 16b
Abraham, difficulties in raising his children .... Sanhedrin 19b
Abraham, learning laws from him .... Yoma 28b
Abraham minted coin .... Bava Kama 97b

Absalom

Absalom, events .... Sotah 10b-11a
Absalom, mentioned close to Gog .... Berachos 10a
Absalom, *nezirus* .... Temurah 14b; Nazir 4b
Absalom, no son after him .... Sotah 11a
Absalom, revolt .... Temurah 14b; Nazir 4b-5a

Absalom, shaving of *nazir* .... Nazir 4b-5a
Absalom, struck on his hair .... Sotah 10a
Absalom, World to Come .... Sanhedrin 103b

Absence
Absence, collecting .... Bava Kama 112b
Absence, judgment of ox .... Bava Kama 45a
Absence, refuting witnesses .... Kesubos 19b-20a
Absence, testimony .... Bava Kama 112a-112b
Absence, verdict .... Sanhedrin 79b

Absorbed
Absorbed, expelled in the same way .... Pesachim 30b
Absorbed forbidden substance, kidney .... Chullin 97a
Absorbed in his work, jobs causing improper thoughts .... Bava Metzia 91a
Absorbed in metal, partly heated .... Pesachim 74a
Absorbed in utensils, sacrifice .... Zevachim 94b-97a
Absorbed in wheat and grapes .... Avodah Zarah 65b
Absorbed like putting down .... Shabbos 102a
Absorbed meager food, removing finger-like quantity .... Chullin 97a
Absorbed, roasted food .... Pesachim 76a; Chullin 96b-97a, 97b, 112a
Absorbed, sacrifice .... Zevachim 93a, 95b, 96b, 97a-97b

Absorption
Absorption in food giving taste to another food .... Chullin 111b-112a
Absorption in meat, impossible when blood flows .... Chullin 8b

Abundance, prayer .... Taanis 22b

Abyss, depth and *aggadah* .... Succah 53b

Accept
Accept my opinion, judge .... Avos 4:8
Accepted prayer, tears .... Bava Metzia 59a
Accepting commandments, convert .... Bechoros 30b
Accepting converts .... Yevamos 47a-47b, 109b; Bechoros 30b
Accepting converts, punishment .... Yevamos 109b
Accepting derogatory speech .... Niddah 61a
Accepting disqualified judge .... Sanhedrin 23a-23b, 24a-24b, 25b; Bava Basra 128a
Accepting idol as divinity .... Sanhedrin 61a-61b
Accepting yoke of Torah .... Avos 3:5

Accessories
Accessories for *beis din*, fear .... Sanhedrin 7b
Accessories for Pesach lamb, Shabbos .... Pesachim 65b-66a, 68a-69a; Eruvin 103a
Accessories of idolatrous cult .... Temurah 28b; Avodah Zarah 51b-52a; Chullin 8b
Accessories to accessories of man's work .... Keilim 16:7
Accessories to prepare food, work on Yom Tov .... Beitzah 28a-28b; Megillah 7b; Shabbos 137b

Accessories for commandment
Accessories for commandment, override .... Yevamos 6a
Accessories for commandment, punishment .... Succah 38a
Accessories for commandment, Shabbos .... Pesachim 65b-66a, 69b; Shabbos 130a, 131a-132a, 133a;
.... Yevamos 14a; Menachos 72a, 96a
Accessories for commandment, sprinkling .... Pesachim 69a

Accessory
Accessory and primary, blessing .... Berachos 35b-36a, 41a, 44a

Accessory, more severe than primary .... Zevachim 48b-49a, 63a; Menachos 91b; Bechoros 14b
Accessory to fruit, considered as fruit .... Orlah 1:7-8
Accessory to fruit, tithe .... Maasros 4:5-6
Accidentally
Accidentally, confusing between works .... Krisos 19b-20a
Accidentally, forbidden fats or forbidden relations .... Krisos 19b; Sanhedrin 62b
Accidentally killing bird, Shabbos .... Shabbos 75a
Accidentally, leprous marks .... Shabbos 133a
Accidentally, personal use .... Pesachim 33a
Accidentally, slaughtering of sacrifices .... Chullin 13a, 31b; Zevachim 46b-47a; Menachos 110a
Accidentally, transgression .... Pesachim 25b-26b; Shabbos 29b
Accompany
Accompany me and I shall go .... Bava Kama 92b
Accompanying dead .... *see* **Funeral**, page 241
Accompanying fellow on his journey .... Berachos 31a; Sotah 46b
Accompanying on a *parsah*, crouched donkey .... Bava Metzia 33a
Accompanying those who commit transgression .... Sanhedrin 9a; Makos 5b
Accompanying those who perform commandment .... Sanhedrin 9a; Makos 5b
Accounts of government .... Shabbos 11a
Accuser
Accuser cannot become defender .... Rosh Hashanah 26a
Accuser, transgression .... Avos 4:11
Accusers on High .... Sanhedrin 44b
Accustomed
Accustomed their tongue, episode .... Yevamos 63a
Accustomed to say, happy .... Berachos 17a
Ach and rak, to exclude .... Sanhedrin 49a
Ach, bonfire .... Shabbos 20a
Acha DeRav Yirmiyah, repentance .... Shabbos 56b
Achan .... Sanhedrin 43b-44b
Acharayius .... *see* **Security**, page 597; *see also* **Warranty**, page 732
Acharecha leploni .... *see* **Double bequest**, page 175
Achei Yosef .... *see* **Brothers of Joseph**, page 78
Acher
Acher entered Pardes .... Chagigah 14b
Acher, episode .... Chagigah 15a-15b; Chullin 142a
Acheirim, Rabbi Meir .... Horayos 13b-14a
Achilah .... *see* **Eat**, page 185
Achinu atah .... *see* **Brother, "you are our brother,"** page 78
Achiyah Hashiloni .... *see* **Ahijah Hashiloni** page 16
Achizas eynayim .... *see* **Camel, illusion**, page 85
Achorei Keilim .... *see* **Container, outer side**, page 125
Achos ishto .... *see* **Sister of wife**, page 630
Achrazta ledardeki .... *see* **Announcement, not effective for children**, page 26
Achsadrah .... *see* **Vestibule**, page 722
Achsah, Caleb's daughter .... Temurah 16a
Achsanai .... *see* **Guest**, page 261
Achsania .... *see* **Host**, page 285
Achsarah, maos lo menuyos .... *see* **Overcharging, sale without knowing quantity**, page 466

Achshur darei..*see* **Generation, new one better than previous one**, page 248
Achuzah..*see* **Patrimony**, page 476
Achzari...*see* **Cruel**, page 134

Acknowledged
Acknowledged barley, claimed wheat.........................Bava Metzia 5a, 100b; Bava Kama 35b-36a;
....Shevuos 38b, 40a-40b
Acknowledged debt, answered elusively...........................Bava Basra 175a; Sanhedrin 29a-29b
Acknowledged without shame...Zevachim 101a
Acknowledging, exempting from penalty............................Bava Kama 14b-15a, 64b, 74b-75b
Acknowledging having seduced, flaw...Kesubos 41a
Acknowledging promissory note, *migo*...............................Kesubos 19a; Bava Basra 154a-155a, 170a;
....Shabbos 78b-79a; Bava Metzia 7a, 72b

Acknowledging in part
Acknowledging in part, "here it is"..Bava Metzia 4a-5a
Acknowledging in part, against witnesses...Bava Basra 128b-129a
Acknowledging in part, bill partly paid..Kesubos 87a-87b; Shevuos 45a
Acknowledging in part, oath...Kiddushin 11b
Acknowledging in part, quantity..............................Kiddushin 11b; Shevuos 39b; Bava Metzia 55a
Acknowledging in part, slave...Bava Metzia 100a-100b

Acknowledgement by litigant
Acknowledgement by litigant....................................Kiddushin 65b; Gittin 40b, 64a; Bava Metzia 3b
Acknowledgement by litigant, *kiddushin*...Kiddushin 65a-65b
Acknowledgement by litigant, in front of two...Bava Basra 40a
Acknowledgement by litigant, was refuted...Gittin 40b

Acknowledgement, verbal
Acknowledgement, verbal, act of acquisition....................Kesubos 101b-102b; Bava Basra 149a
Acknowledgement, verbal, why does it compel..............................Gittin 14a; Bava Basra 144a
Acknowledgement, verbal, writing bill...Sanhedrin 29b

Acquire
Acquire a friend..Avos 1:6, 1:16
Acquire! like a donkey...Bava Basra 142b-143a
Acquire! text of act of acquisition...Bava Metzia 9b
Acquire! to make someone else acquire..Nedarim 48b
Acquiring one's world in one instant...Avodah Zarah 10b, 17a, 18a

Act
Act adds up to act, Divine Judgment..Sotah 8b-9a
Act, annulling handle, impurity...Succah 13b-14a
Act, continuing, first thought...Zevachim 41b-42a; Menachos 16a-16b
Act for impurity of food..Eruvin 28b
Act forbidden on Shabbos, not to use its result................Chullin 15a; Bava Kama 71a; Kesubos 34a;
....Terumos 2:3; Gittin 53b
Act, idolatrous sacrifice...Sanhedrin 63a
Act, lashes..............Shevuos 3b-4a, 21a; Makos 4b, 13b, 15b-16a, 20b; Pesachim 63b, 84a; Chullin 83a, 91a;
....Temurah 3b, 4b
Act, moving lips.......................Krisos 3b-4a; Bava Metzia 90b-91a; Sanhedrin 65a-65b; Makos 13b-14a
Act of child...Chullin 12b-13a; Taharos 8:6
Act of child, impurity...Keilim 17:15; Chullin 12b-13a
Act of teacher, ruling..............Bava Basra 83a, 130b; Shabbos 21a, 126b; Pesachim 51a-51b; Niddah 65b
Act, conspiring witnesses' testimony...Bava Kama 5a

A

Act, replacing sacrifice .... Temurah 3a
Act, requirement to bring sin offering .... Krisos 3b-4a; Sanhedrin 65a-65b
Act, second, levirate marriage .... Yevamos 50a-52a, 53a-53b, 96a-96b
Act to purify utensil ....Kiddushin 59a-59b; Shabbos 52b, 58b; Succah 13b-14a; Menachos 69b; Keilim 25:9
Acts, "your acts will draw you near" .... Eduyos 5:7
Acts at this time .... Rosh Hashanah 16b
Acts like Zimri .... Sotah 22b
Acts, numerous .... Avos 3:9, 3:17
Acts of righteous, greatness .... Kesubos 5a
Acts of righteous, like sand .... Bava Basra 7b

Act of acquisition
  Acquisition —
Act of acquisition, consecrated items Treasury ....Kiddushin 28b-29a; Maaser Sheni 4:6; Gittin 52a
Act of acquisition, custodians .... Bava Metzia 98b-99a; Kiddushin 47b; Bava Kama 79a
Act of acquisition for settlement .... Sanhedrin 6a
Act of acquisition, gift by sick person .... Kesubos 55b-56a; Bava Basra 152a-153a, 156a-157a;
.... Gittin 14b-15a
Act of acquisition of animal, riding and bridle .... Bava Metzia 8a-9b
Act of acquisition of ship .... Bava Basra 75b-76b; Kesubos 85a
Act of acquisition of stolen item ...... see **Despairing**, page 161; see also **Change of owner**, page 96
Act of acquisition, order to acquire .... Bava Basra 52b-53a
Act of acquisition, sale without knowing quantity .... Bava Metzia 46b
Act of acquisition, stolen item .... Kesubos 31b
Act of acquisition together with land .... see **Kinyan Agav**, page 341
Acts of acquisition, rent .... Bava Kama 79a-79b
  Cases —
Act of acquisition by forbidden act .... Bava Kama 70b
Act of acquisition by mistake .... Gittin 14a
Act of acquisition by money, from the Torah....Bava Metzia 47b-48b; Eruvin 81b; Kiddushin 28b;
.... Bechoros 13a-13b; Chullin 83a
Act of acquisition, divided domain .... Bava Basra 54b-56a
Act of acquisition, of part of fruit .... Bava Basra 86b-87a, 105a, 106b-107a
Act of acquisition, paid in part .... Bava Metzia 77b-78a
Act of acquisition, promissory note .... Bava Basra 76a, 173a
  Eruv —
Act of acquisition for family members, eruv techumin .... Eruvin 82b
Act of acquisition from baker, eruv .... Eruvin 81a-81b
Act of acquisition of eruv chatzeiros .... Nedarim 88b; Eruvin 73b, 79b-80a; Gittin 64b
  For whom —
Act of acquisition, married woman .... Kiddushin 23b-24a; Nedarim 88a-88b; Sanhedrin 71a
Act of acquisition, non-Jew .... Bechoros 13a-13b; Avodah Zarah 71a-72a
Act of acquisition of non-Jew in Eretz Yisrael, tithes .... Gittin 47a-47b; Menachos 31a;
.... Bava Metzia 101a; Bechoros 11b
Acts of acquisition, for Canaanite slave .... Kiddushin 23b; Pesachim 88b; Nedarim 88b
Acts of acquisition of Canaanite slave .... Kiddushin 22b-23a, 8a
Acts of acquisition of Hebrew maidservant .... Kiddushin 9b, 11b-12a
Acts of acquisition of Hebrew slave .... Kiddushin 16a, 14b
  How —
Act of acquisition by acknowledgement ...see **Acknowledgement, verbal, act of acquisition**, page 7

Act of acquisition by barter .... *see* **Barter**, page 43

Act of acquisition by bridle, ten together .... Kiddushin 27b

Act of acquisition by *chazakah* .... *see* **Chazakah**, page 99

Act of acquisition by cloth .... Bava Metzia 7a

Act of acquisition by courtyard .... *see* **Courtyard**, page 130

Act of acquisition by handing over, animal .... Kiddushin 25b; Bava Kama 11b; Bava Basra 86b

Act of acquisition by legal document .... *see* **Legal document**, page 361

Act of acquisition by money .... *see* **Money**, page 421

Act of acquisition by pulling .... *see* **Pulling to purchase**, page 510

Act of acquisition by utensil .... *see* **Utensil of buyer, act of acquisition**, page 718

Act of acquisition by utensils placed on animal .... Bava Metzia 9b

Act of acquisition by walking .... Bava Basra 100a

Marriage —

Act of acquisition by speech, dowry .... Kesubos 102b; Kiddushin 9b; Moed Katan 18b

Act of acquisition of wife .... *see* **Kiddushin**, page 337

Acts of acquisition of divorce certificate .... Gittin 21a, 78a-78b

Acts of acquisition of divorce certificate, courtyard .... Gittin 21a, 77a-78a, 79a-79b;
.... Bava Metzia 11b-12a

Acts of acquisition of widow awaiting levirate marriage .... Kiddushin 13b-14a; Yevamos 54a

Misc. —

Act of acquisition by money, wheat in buyer's attic .... Bava Metzia 49b

Act of acquisition, closed alley .... Bava Basra 84b-85b

Act of acquisition, destined to be written in bill .... Bava Basra 40a

Act of acquisition of debt, three men .... Gittin 13a-14a; Kiddushin 48a; Bava Basra 144a, 148a

Act of acquisition of ship by renting place .... Bava Basra 76b

Act of acquisition, prohibition of prostitute's fee .. Pesachim 90a; Temurah 29b-30a; Bechoros 56b

Act of acquisition by cloth

Act of acquisition by cloth, *eruv* .... Eruvin 49a-49b

Act of acquisition by cloth, returning .... Nedarim 48b

Act of acquisition by cloth, whose utensils .... Bava Metzia 47a-47b

Act of acquisition, Rabbinical

Act of acquisition, Rabbinical, conventional .... Bava Metzia 74a-74b

Act of acquisition, Rabbinical, four cubits .... Bava Metzia 10a-10b

Act of acquisition, Rabbinical, without act .... Bechoros 18a-18b; Bava Metzia 12b; Gittin 30a

Acts of acquisition, Rabbinical, Rabbinical theft .... Gittin 60b-61a

Acts of acquisition, Rabbinical, three men .... Gittin 13a-14a

Ad

Ad beli dai .... *see* **Unlimited blessings, tithe**, page 715

Ad bichlal .... *see* **Ad, includes**, page 9

Ad hayom hazeh, explanation .... Yoma 54a

Ad, includes .... Chullin 46a, 54b-55a; Arachin 18a-18b; Berachos 26b-27a; Eruvin 82b; Pesachim 117b;
.... Rosh Hashanah 30b; Succah 41b; Nazir 6b; Menachos 68b; Niddah 58b

Ad shelo notzarti, prayer .... Berachos 17a

Ada Deila, height .... Niddah 24b

Adam

Sin —

Adam, feared night .... Avodah Zarah 8a

Adam, garments .... Sotah 14a

Adam, mortification for repentance .... Eruvin 18b

A

Adam, punishment .... Pesachim 118a
Adam, sin .... Sanhedrin 38b
Adam, ungratefulness .... Avodah Zarah 5a-5b
Misc. —
Adam and Rabbi Benaah .... Bava Basra 58a
Adam, book .... Bava Metzia 85b-86a
Adam, creation .... Sanhedrin 38a-38b
Adam, decided about world population .... Berachos 31a
Adam, future .... Sanhedrin 38b; Avodah Zarah 5a
Adam, *Gan Eden* .... Bava Basra 75a; Sanhedrin 59b
Adam, height .... Chagigah 12a; Sanhedrin 38b
Adam, his beauty .... Bava Metzia 84a; Bava Basra 58a
Adam, his first day .... Sanhedrin 38b
Adam, meaning according to initials .... Sotah 5a
Adam, men who encompassed History .... Bava Basra 121b
Adam, pleased with Eve .... Yevamos 63a
Adam, sacrifice .... Chullin 60a; Shabbos 28b; Avodah Zarah 8a
Adam, seven shepherds .... Succah 52b
Adam, sleep to create Eve .... Sanhedrin 39a
Adam .... *see* **Man**, page 386
Adam karov le'atzmo .... *see* **Man considered like his own relative**, page 388
Adar
Adar, bar mitzvah .... Arachin 31b
Adar, first and second .... Nedarim 63a-63b
Adar, full or missing .... Rosh Hashanah 19b-20a; Bechoros 58a; Sanhedrin 11a; Arachin 9b
Adar, joy and *mazal* .... Taanis 29a-29b
Adar sheni .... Bava Metzia 102a-102b; Bava Basra 105a
Adar sheni .... *see also* **Leap year**, page 357
Adar, communal needs .... Shekalim 1:1-2; Megillah 13b; Moed Katan 6a
Adar I, Purim .... Megillah 6b-7a; Rosh Hashanah 19b
Adar, tree .... Beitzah 15b
Adarchan, episode .... Avodah Zarah 10b
Adding
Adding apartment to courtyard, claim .... Bava Basra 60a
Adding blessing for oneself .... Taanis 13b
Adding equivalent to subtracting .... Sanhedrin 29a
Adding judges .... Sanhedrin 42a
Adding mortar, impurity .... Eduyos 7:8
Adding personal prayer in *Shemoneh Esrei* .... Berachos 29b
Adding to building, Temple .... Chullin 83b
Adding to fire, damage .... Bava Kama 10a-10b
Adding to permitted quantity, Shabbos .... Menachos 64a-64b
Adding to permitted quantity, Yom Tov .... Beitzah 17a, 22b; Pesachim 37a
Adding to sum of dowry .... Kesubos 66a-66b; Bava Metzia 104b
Adding to Temple Courtyard .... Sanhedrin 16b; Shevuos 14b-15a, 16a
Adding to weaving, amount for Shabbos violation .... Krisos 17a, 19b; Shabbos 104b, 105a
Adding warmth, keeping food warm .... Shabbos 39b
Adding warmth, which substance .... Shabbos 47b-48a, 49a, 51b; Bava Basra 19a

Adding a month
Adding a month, at daytime .... Sanhedrin 11b
Adding a month, cold weather .... Sanhedrin 18b
Adding a month, episode .... Sanhedrin 26a
Adding a month, Hezekiah .... Sanhedrin 12a-12b
Adding a month, impurity .... Sanhedrin 12a-12b
Adding a month, king .... Sanhedrin 18b
Adding a month, protest against Sage .... Berachos 63a-63b
Adding a month, season .... Rosh Hashanah 21a; Sanhedrin 12b-13b
Adding a month, when .... Rosh Hashanah 7a; Sanhedrin 11b-12a, 12b, 87a; Eduyos 7:7
Adding a month, where .... Sanhedrin 11b; Berachos 63a
Adding a month, who .... Sanhedrin 10b
Adding to commandments
Adding to commandments, general .... Rosh Hashanah 28b; Eruvin 95b-96a
Adding to commandments, *lulav* .... Sanhedrin 88b; Succah 31a-31b
Adding to commandments, priestly blessing .... Rosh Hashanah 28b
Adding to commandments, sprinkling blood .... Zevachim 80a
Adding to commandments, succah .... Succah 48a
Adding to commandments, *tefillin* .... Sanhedrin 88b-89a; Eruvin 95b-96a
Adding to commandments, *tzitzis* .... Sanhedrin 88b-89a; Menachos 40b-41a
Addition
Addition to coin .... Bechoros 5b, 50a; Bava Basra 90a-90b; Menachos 77a
Addition to impurity, *terumah* .... Pesachim 14a-14b
Addition to Jerusalem area .... Shevuos 15a-15b
Addition to measures and coins .... Bava Basra 90a-90b; Menachos 77a
Addition to Sabbatical year .... Sheviis 1:1-8, 2:1-6; Yevamos 83a; Rosh Hashanah 9b, 10b;
.... Succah 34a, 44a; Taanis 3a; Moed Katan 3b-4a; Bava Basra 26b-27a; Zevachim 110b
Addition to Shabbos and Yom Tov .... Rosh Hashanah 9a; Yoma 81b
Addition to Shabbos, Tiberias .... Shabbos 118b
Addition to Temple Courtyard .... Shevuos 14a-15a, 16a; Sotah 45a; Sanhedrin 2a, 14b, 16b
Addition to Yom Kippur .... Yoma 81a-81b
Addition to Yom Kippur, woman .... Succah 28a-28b
Addition to *kesubah*
Addition to *kesubah*, custom .... Kesubos 12a-12b
Addition to *kesubah*, for whom .... Kesubos 90a
Addition to *kesubah*, permission to add .... Kesubos 54b
Additional impurity, *terumah* .... Pesachim 14a-14b
Additional limb
Additional limb, blemishes of *Kohen* .... Bechoros 45a
Additional limb, impurity of corpse .... Bechoros 45a; Niddah 49b
Additional limb is like missing one, *treifah* .... Chullin 58b
Ade'ata denafshei ke'avid .... *see* **Non-Jew, acting in self-interest**, page 448
Adhesion, lung .... Chullin 46b
Adirim, adages .... Menachos 53a-53b
Adjacent parts of land, to whom? .... Bava Basra 12b
Adjured
Adjured from Mount Sinai .... Shevuos 21b, 22b, 23b, 25a-25b, 27a-27b; Yoma 73b;
.... Nedarim 8a; Nazir 4a; Makos 22a
Adjuring, oath for testimony .... Shevuos 32a

Administrator

Administrator, bequest .... Bava Basra 131b-132a, 144a, 150b; Gittin 14a

Administrator, his wife's oath .... Kesubos 86b

Administrator in one's house, distance .... Berachos 63a

Administrator, legal document on his name .... Bava Basra 52a-52b

Administrator, without reason .... Gittin 14a; Bava Basra 131b, 144a

Administrators of Temple .... Shekalim 5:2

Admon

Admon, *halacha* .... Kesubos 109a

Admon, Jerusalem's judges .... Kesubos 104b-105a

Admonition, when to keep silent .... Yevamos 65b

Adonijah

Adonijah, Avishag forbidden to him .... Sanhedrin 22a

Adonijah son of Hagit .... Sanhedrin 21b

Adrachta, bill .... Kesubos 104b; Bava Kama 112b; Bava Metzia 17b; Bava Basra 169a

Adult

Adult supervising, divorce certificate .... Gittin 23a

Adult supervising, ritual slaughter .... Succah 42b

Adult girl

Adult girl, annulment of vow .... Nedarim 89a-89b

Adult girl before us, *chazakah* .... Kiddushin 79a

Adult girl, signs .... Niddah 47a-47b

Adult girl to *Kohen Gadol* .... Yevamos 58b-59a, 61b

Adult girl to minor boy, Jerusalem .... Sanhedrin 104a

Adult girl, washing and adorning .... Taanis 13b

Adulterer

Adulterer .... *see also* **Man guilty of forbidden relations**, page 387

Adulterer, took away bride from canopy .... Yevamos 110a; Bava Metzia 104a

Adulterer warned about snake .... Nedarim 91b

Adulterer who fled and saved .... Nedarim 91b

Adulterers, what must witnesses testify .... Makos 7a; Bava Metzia 91a

Adulteress .... *see* **Woman guilty of forbidden relations**, page 758

Adultery, signs of misconduct .... Yevamos 24b-25a

Adulthood

Adulthood, signs .... Niddah 47a-47b

Adulthood, six months .... Niddah 65a; Kesubos 39a; Kiddushin 79a

Advance cancellation of legal document .... Bava Basra 49a; Kesubos 19b

Advancing marriage, episode .... Kesubos 62b

Advantage outweighed by loss .... Avos 5:12

Advice

Advice from one's wife .... Bava Metzia 59a

Advice given for one's own interests .... Sanhedrin 76b

Advice, good, levirate marriage .... Yevamos 44a

Advice, Rabbi Yehoshua .... Sotah 49b

Advocate

Advocate, by commandment .... Avos 4:11

Advocate, one among a thousand .... Shabbos 32a

Affar .... *see* **Dust**, page 183; *see also* **Earth**, page 185

Affected by
Affected by testimony, disqualified .... Bava Basra 43a-44b, 46b-47a; Kiddushin 43b
Affected by trial, judge .... Bava Basra 43a
Affixing *mezuzah* .... Menachos 32b-33b
Afflictions
Afflictions on communal fast days .... Taanis 12b, 13a
Afflictions on *Tisha B'Av* .... Taanis 29b, 30a-30b
Afflictions on Yom Kippur .... Yoma 74a, 74b, 76a-77b
Afik, significance .... Eruvin 65a
Afikoman
Afikoman .... Pesachim 119b
Afikoman, after Pesach lamb .... Pesachim 86a, 119b
Afikoman, eating after .... Pesachim 119b-120a
After
After a week etc., until when .... Gittin 77a
After oath, until when .... Gittin 77a
After Rebbi etc. .... Sanhedrin 32b
After your conversion, *kiddushin* .... Kiddushin 62a; Yevamos 92b, 93b; Kesubos 58b; Bava Metzia 16b
After thirty days
After thirty days, act of acquisition .... Kesubos 82a, 86b
After thirty days, divorce certificate .... Kesubos 86b
After thirty days, *kiddushin* .... Kiddushin 19b, 59a-60a
Afternoon prayer .... *see* **Mincha**, page 411
Against your will you live .... Avos 4:22
Agar natar .... *see* **Interest, salary for money kept**, page 314
Agav
Agav .... *see* **Kinyan Agav**, page 341
Agav churfei lo iyen .... *see* **Sharp-minded, too sharp to see details**, page 610
Agav onsei gamar umakneh .... *see* **Forced to sell**, page 234
Age
Temple and sacrifices —
Age of burnt offering and guilt offering .... Menachos 48b; Temurah 19b
Age of *Kohanim*, Temple .... Chullin 24b
Age of *Leviim*, Temple .... Chullin 24a
Age of sacrifices
Age of sacrifices .... Parah 1:1-3; Rosh Hashanah 10a
Age of sacrifices, hours .... Zevachim 25b
Age of sacrifices, young sheep .... Chullin 23a-23b; Menachos 91b; Parah 1:3
Misc. —
Age, evaluation for endowment .... Arachin 18a
Age for marriage .... Kiddushin 29b-30a
Age for vows .... Niddah 45b
Age, forty, drinking better than eating .... Shabbos 152a
Age of *bar mitzvah* and *bas mitzvah* .... Niddah 45b
Age of man, development .... Avos 5:21
Age of son, trustworthiness .... Kiddushin 63b-64a
Age, sixty years old, Rav Yosef .... Moed Katan 28a
Age to beget children .... Sanhedrin 68b-69b
Age, twenty, land sale .... Bava Basra 155a-156a

A

Agent
Commandments —
Agent, "choose the best ones" .... Bava Metzia 22a
Agent, better to do by oneself .... Kiddushin 41a
Agent for *eruv techumin* .... Eruvin 31b; Meilah 21a
Agent for first fruit who died .... Bava Basra 81b-82a; Gittin 47b
Agent, quantity for *terumah* .... Terumos 4, 3-5; Kesubos 99b-100a; Kiddushin 41a-41b; Bechoros 61a
Agent to separate tithes .... Terumos 3:4; Kiddushin 59a
Agent who made a mistake, tithe of animal .... Bechoros 61a

Marriage —
Agent for divorce certificate, elgibility .... Gittin 23a-23b, 62b; Kiddushin 41b
Agent for *kiddushin* who died .... Nazir 11b-12a; Gittin 64a
Agent for *kiddushin*, who gave first .... Kiddushin 78b-79a
Agent who cannot himself give divorce certificate .... Gittin 29b-30a

Monetary matters —
Agent appointed before witnesses .... Bava Kama 104a-104b
Agent, bought without telling for whom .... Bava Metzia 74a
Agent, cases in which he keeps a benefit .... Kesubos 98b
Agent, changed instruction in purchase .... Bava Kama 102a-102b; Meilah 21a-21b; Kesubos 99a-99b
Agent for gift, beneficiary died .... Gittin 14b-15a
Agent for oneself, trickery .... Kiddushin 58b-59a
Agent, fraud .... Kesubos 99b-100a
Agent, warranty .... Bava Basra 169b
Agent who caused damage .... Kiddushin 42b; Eruvin 75b; Kesubos 85a, 99b; Bava Metzia 108a; Bechoros 61a
Agent who changed instruction in sale .... Kesubos 98b-99b
Agent who slaughtered and sold stolen animal .... Bava Kama 78b-79a

Principles —
Agent, "I carried out your mission" .... Yoma 71a
Agent appointment, effective for what .... Kiddushin 41a-42a
Agent appoints agent .... Kiddushin 41a
Agent, can he become witness? .... Kiddushin 43a-43b; Gittin 5b
Agent carries out his mission .... Eruvin 31b-32a; Nazir 12a; Gittin 64a-64b; Chullin 12a
Agent, for mission that does not apply to him .... Gittin 23b
Agent for transgression .... Kiddushin 42b-43a; Bava Kama 51a, 79a; Bava Metzia 10b
Agent, mission that sending man is not competent to do .... Nazir 12a-12b; Kiddushin 23b
Agent, non-Jew .... Kiddushin 41b; Gittin 23b; Bava Metzia 71b-72a
Agent who changed his mission .... Meilah 20b-21a

Vow —
Agent asking permission, wording of vow .... Nedarim 54a-54b; Chullin 104a; Meilah 20b
Agent for man forbidden by vow to benefit, prohibition .... Nedarim 36b
Agent for sick person, act of acquisition .... Gittin 14b, 62b, 63a-63b
Agent for wife's vow .... Nedarim 8b
Agent, no agent for sin .... Kiddushin 42b-43a; Bava Kama 51a, 79a
Agent of *beis din*, collateral .... Bava Metzia 113a-113b
Agent of *beis din*, man refusing to come to convocation .... Bava Kama 112b-113a; Moed Katan 16a
Agent, second, for divorce .... Gittin 66a-67a, 71b-72a
Agent sent for divorce .... Gittin 29a-30a, 62b-63a; Bava Metzia 76a-76b

Agent to annul vows..Nedarim 72b; Nazir 12b; Bava Metzia 96a
Agents, G-d's, *Kohanim*..........................Nedarim 35b-36a; Kiddushin 23b; Yoma 19a-19b
Agents, G-d's, report on the spot...Bava Basra 25a
Agents to perform commandment, protection............Pesachim 8b; Chullin 142a; Yoma 11a;
....Kiddushin 39b

Misc. —
Agent appointment, source.....................Kiddushin 41a-42a; Berachos 34b; Chagigah 10b;
....Nedarim 72b; Nazir 12b; Bava Metzia 96a
Agent for payment, responsibility...Kesubos 85a
Agent, murder..Kiddushin 43a
Agent, personal use........Meilah 20b-21a; Chagigah 10b; Kesubos 98b; Nedarim 54a; Kiddushin 42b, 50a
Agent to obtain fellow's forgiveness...Makos 10b

Aggadah
Aggadah and *halacha*, episode..Bava Kama 60b
Aggadah, draws people like water..........................Chagigah 14a; Shabbos 87a
Aggadah, people prefer...Sotah 40a
Aggadah, Rabbi Avuhu appeased Sage..Sotah 40a
Agil, significance...Shabbos 64a
Agirah, significance..Sanhedrin 7a
Agmon, significance...Kiddushin 62b
Agras daughter of Machalas..Pesachim 112b
Agreement
Agreement between Israel and Rome...Avodah Zarah 8b
Agreement to sell husband's property.........Kesubos 95a; Bava Basra 49b-50a; Gittin 55b
Agriculture...see **Field**, page 221
Agrippas, King
Agrippas, King, bride..Kesubos 17a
Agrippas, King, flattery...Sotah 41b
Agrippas, King, population of Israel..Pesachim 64b
Agudah...see **Bundle**, page 79
Agudos agudos..............................see **Groups, not to separate into groups**, page 260
Agunah ("Anchored" woman – unable to remarry)
Death and signs —
Agunah, deceased man's distinctive signs.........Yevamos 120a-120b; Bava Metzia 27b; Bechoros 46b
Agunah, deceased man's garments...Bava Metzia 27b
Agunah, deceased man's name...Yevamos 115b-116a
Agunah, hearing dying man's voice...Yevamos 122a
Agunah, husband drowned..Yevamos 121a-121b
Agunah, indications of death..Yevamos 120b
Agunah, war...Yevamos 114a-115b

Trustworthiness —
Agunah, contradiction between witnesses.........Kesubos 22b; Yevamos 88b; Bava Basra 31b
Agunah, disqualified witnesses' testimony.........................Yevamos 25a-25b, 122a
Agunah, minor and non-Jew..Yevamos 121b-122a
Agunah, mutually biased, women's testimony...............Yevamos 117a-118a, 119b-120a
Agunah, presumption declaration..Yevamos 114b-115a
Agunah, quarrel...Yevamos 116a-116b
Agunah, trustworthiness about herself...Yevamos 116b
Agunah, trustworthiness of non-Jewish court..................................Gittin 28b-29a

Agunah, witness from witness .... Yevamos 87b, 122a; Shabbos 145a-145b; Bechoros 46b
Agunah, witnesses examination .... Yevamos 122a-122b
Agunah, woman inquires before marrying .... Yevamos 25a, 93b-94a, 115a, 116b

Misc. —
Agunah, concern about rumor .... Yevamos 91b-92a
Agunah, husband came back .... Yevamos 88b-89a, 90b-91b, 89a
Agunah, *kesubah* .... Yevamos 116b-117a
Agunah, levirate marriage .... Yevamos 11a
Agunah, widow awaiting levirate marriage .... Yevamos 92a-92b, 93b-94a, 114b, 118b;
Shevuos 32b; Eduyos 1:12

Ahab
Ahab and Elijah .... Chullin 5a; Sanhedrin 113a
Ahab and Jehoshaphat .... Chullin 4b-5a
Ahab, drawings on chariot .... Sanhedrin 39b
Ahab, false prophets .... Sanhedrin 89a
Ahab, his merits .... Sanhedrin 102b
Ahab, his Torah knowledge .... Sanhedrin 103b
Ahab, prophecies announcing his death .... Sanhedrin 39b
Ahab, wickedness .... Sanhedrin 102b
Ahab, World to Come .... Sanhedrin 104b
Ahab's right hand, punishment .... Sanhedrin 90a-90b

Ahasuerus
Ahasuerus, anger about number of slain .... Megillah 16b
Ahasuerus, his wickedness and his reign .... Megillah 11a
Ahasuerus, mistake about seventy years .... Megillah 11b-12a
Ahasuerus ruled over whole world .... Megillah 11a-11b
Ahasuerus, years of reign .... Megillah 11b

Ahavah bemilchemes Torah .... *see* **Love through Torah war**, page 379

Ahavas Olam, Shema .... Berachos 12a

Ahaz
Ahaz, early sunset .... Sanhedrin 96a
Ahaz, king .... Sanhedrin 103a, 103b
Ahaz, premature death .... Pesachim 87b
Ahaz, World to Come .... Sanhedrin 104a

Ahaziah .... Sanhedrin 102b

Ahiman, Shaishai and Talmai .... Yoma 10a; Sotah 34b

Ahimelech, David .... Menachos 95b-96a

Ahitophel
Ahitophel, "my teacher and my friend" .... Sanhedrin 106b
Ahitophel, David's curse .... Succah 53b; Makos 11a
Ahitophel, David's wars .... Berachos 3b; Sanhedrin 16a-16b
Ahitophel, evil in his heart .... Chagigah 15b
Ahitophel, thought he would reign .... Sanhedrin 101b
Ahitophel, wills .... Bava Basra 147a
Ahitophel, wisdom .... Sanhedrin 106b
Ahitophel, World to Come .... Sanhedrin 104b-105a
Ahitophel, years of life .... Sanhedrin 69b, 106b

Ahijah Hashiloni
Ahijah Hashiloni, men who encompassed History .... Bava Basra 121b

Ahijah Hashiloni, Jeroboam .... Sanhedrin 102a

Ahuv lemaalah venechmad lematah .... *see* **Loved Above**, page 379

Ai

Ai, war .... Bava Basra 121b

Ai, Yair's death .... Bava Basra 121b

Air

Air in *Eretz Yisrael* .... Bava Basra 158b

Air out of *Eretz Yisrael*, impurity .... Shabbos 15b; Nazir 54b-55a; Gittin 8b

Air, polluted, in pit .... Bava Kama 50b, 53a, 54a

Air space

Air space and disqualified *s'chach* .... Succah 17a-18a

Air space in clay, reptile and purification .... Pesachim 20a-20b; Shabbos 138b; Keilim 8:1-8

Air space in clay utensils .... Keilim 2:1; Zevachim 3a; Chullin 20a, 24b-25a

Air space in courtyard, act of acquisition .... Bava Metzia 102a

Air space in utensil, act of acquisition .... Avodah Zarah 71b

Air space of Altar .... Zevachim 62b, 104a; Pesachim 34a, 77a

Air space of Altar, sanctification .... Zevachim 87b

Air space in s'chach

Air space in *s'chach*, dimension .... Succah 17b, 18a

Air space in *s'chach*, *lavud* .... Succah 18a

Air space in *s'chach*, underneath .... Succah 19a

Akavia

Akavia ben Mehalalel, praises .... Berachos 19a; Pesachim 64b

Akavia, difference of opinion .... Eduyos 5:6; Berachos 19a; Pesachim 64b

Akavia said "Look at three things" .... Avos 3:1

Akeidas Yitschak .... *see* **Binding of Isaac**, page 57

Akeidas Yitschak .... Sanhedrin 89b

Akimas sefasayim .... *see* **Speech**, page 649

Akirah .... *see* **Raising item**, page 535

Akiva nechamtanu .... *see* **"Rabbi Akiva, you have consoled us,"** page 518

Al daas beis din .... *see* **Will of *beis din***, page 747

Al daas rabim .... *see* **Vow according to several persons**, page 726

Al de'atfes atfuch .... *see* **Drowning, man who drowned others will be drowned**, page 182

Al hachadashim anu boshim .... *see* **Surprising things, do not add**, page 665

Al hachalukin anu mitztaarin .... *see* **Dispute, do not add**, page 167

Al Hamichyah .... Berachos 37a-37b, 44a

Al Hamichyah .... *see* **Blessing, final, on seven species**, page 64

Al Hanissim

Al Hanissim, Bircas HaMazon .... Shabbos 24a

Al Hanissim, Mussaf .... Shabbos 24a-24b

Al kol tzarah shelo tavo .... *see* **Tragedy which we hope will not happen**, page 699

Al korcha atah chai .... *see* **Against your will you live**, page 13

Al meduchah zo yashav .... *see* **"On this mortar he sat,"** page 460

Al menas .... *see* **Condition**, page 120

Al Netilas Lulav .... *see* **Blessing, *al netilas lulav***, page 63

Al regel achas .... *see* **Leg, "on one leg,"** page 361

Al shloshah devarim haolam omeid .... *see* **Three things, world stands on**, page 688

Al taamin be'atzmecha .... *see* **Believe, do not believe in yourself**, page 51

Al taamod al hamekach .... *see* **Haggle, do not haggle if you do not have money**, page 263

Al taan kesil .... *see* **Answer a fool according to his foolishness**, page 29

Al taas atzmecha keorchei hadayanim .... *see* **Lawyer, avoid being**, page 356

Al taasem atarah .... *see* **Do not make them a crown**, page 172

Al tachzik tovah le'atzmecha .... *see* **Consider, do not consider you did something great**, page 125

Al tadun ad shetagiya limkomo ...... *see* **Judge, do not judge before being in other's place**, page 328

Al tarbeh sichah im ha'ishah .... *see* **Conversation with woman**, page 127

Al tehi tzadik harbeh .... *see* **Righteous, do not be too righteous**, page 568

Al teratzeh beshaas kaaso .... *see* **Appeasing, do not appease man during anger**, page 30

Al tetzer tzaras machar .... *see* **Worry, do not worry about tomorrow's troubles**, page 764

Al tevakesh gedulah .... *see* **Look for, do not look for wealth**, page 377

Al timna tov mibe'alav .... *see* **Do not withhold good from its recipient**, page 172

Al tishtadel liroso bekalkalaso .... *see* **Try, do not try to see your friend's disgrace**, page 705

Al tistakel bakankan .... *see* **Look at what is inside pitcher**, page 377

Al tisvada larashus .... *see* **Authorities, do not get close to**, page 36

Al tisyaesh mehapuranus .... *see* **Lose hope, do not lose hope of retribution**, page 378

Al titosh Toras imecha .... *see* **Forsake, do not forsake your mother's Torah**, page 236

Al toche'ach letz .... *see* **Reprove, do not reprove scoffer**, page 560

Al yedei rofeh ploni .... *see* **Physician, "by this physician,"** page 486

Al yeshaneh beno me'echav ...... *see* **Preference, no preferential treatment to one child**, page 500

Al yiftach peh laSatan .... *see* **Opening mouth to *Satan***, page 461

Al yimana mibeis hamidrash .... *see* **Diligence in house of study**, page 164

Al yipater ela mitoch halacha .... *see* **Leaving friend, law**, page 359

Al yotzi atzmo mehaklal .... *see* **Society, not to stay out of**, page 641

Alcoholic beverage

Alcoholic beverage, blessing .... Bava Basra 96b

Alcoholic beverage darkens girls' skin .... Shabbos 80b

Alcoholic beverage for *havdala,* popular drink .... Pesachim 107a

Alcoholic beverage for *kiddush,* popular drink .... Pesachim 107a

Alcoholic beverage made from hop, episode .... Bava Metzia 42b-43a

Alcoholic beverage, new, health .... Eruvin 55b-56a; Pesachim 42a

Alcoholic beverage of non-Jew .... Avodah Zarah 31b

Alcoholic beverage, old, harmful .... Bava Basra 91b

Alcoholic beverage, Rebbi .... Pesachim 107a

Alcoholic beverage, smelling during prayer .... Eruvin 65a

Alcoholic beverage to cure teeth .... Bava Kama 35a

Alcoholic beverage, wealth .... Pesachim 113a

Aleph, ayin .... Megillah 24b; Berachos 32a

Alexander Mokdon (Macedonia)

Alexander Mokdon, Africa .... Tamid 32a-32b

Alexander Mokdon, deceased man's eye .... Tamid 32b

Alexander Mokdon, questions .... Tamid 31b-32a

Alexander, Shimon Hatzaddik .... Yoma 69a

Alexandria

Alexandria, craftsmen in Temple .... Yoma 38a

Alexandria, destruction .... Succah 51b

Alexandria, illegitimate children .... Bava Metzia 104a

Alexandria, Rabbi Yehoshua's answers .... Niddah 69b

Alexandria, surgery on animals .... Sanhedrin 33a, 93a; Bechoros 28b

Alexandria, synagogue .... Succah 51b

Alexandrians
Alexandrians, goat to Azazel .... Yoma 66b
Alexandrians, questions .... Niddah 69b
Alexandrians, raw meat .... Menachos 100a
Algavish stones .... Berachos 54b
Aliah, best of one's property .... Bava Kama 16b; Nedarim 56a; Menachos 108b
Alimony .... *see* **Supporting,** page 664
Aliyah laaretz .... *see* **Emigration to** *Eretz Yisrael,* page 195
Aliyah laregel .... *see* **Pilgrimage,** page 488
Aliyah laTorah .... *see* **Called up to Torah,** page 85
Aliyas Chananiah .... *see* **Attic of Chananiah, Book of Ezekiel,** page 36
Aliyas Ezra .... *see* **Emigration of Ezra,** page 195
All
"All" comes to add laws, deduction .... Niddah 33a
"All these troubles for an uncertainty" .... Chagigah 4b
All of you are duty-bound to honor Me .... Bava Metzia 32a; Yevamos 5b
Allusion to non-Jew on Shabbos .... Shabbos 150a
Almanah, significance .... Kesubos 10b
Almonds
Almonds, bitter, tithes .... Chullin 25b; Eruvin 28b; Maasros 1:4
Almonds, blessing .... Eruvin 28b
Alone
Alone at night, Sage .... Berachos 43b; Pesachim 112b; Chullin 91a-91b
Alone he will stay, punishment for leper .... Arachin 16b
Alos hashachar .... *see* **Dawn, announcing in Temple,** page 147
Also
Also to conquer queen in my house, Rabbi Yose .... Pesachim 100a
Also to you! .... Megillah 27b
Altar
Altar, base .... Zevachim 53b-54b, 62a; Middos 3:1
Altar, bowls for libations .... Succah 48a-48b
Altar, cavities .... Succah 49a-49b; Zevachim 61b; Middos 3:2-3
Altar, damaged .... Zevachim 59a, 60a-60b
Altar damaged, size .... Chullin 18a; Succah 48b-49a
Altar, dimensions .... Menachos 59b, 97a-98a; Eruvin 4a; Succah 45a; Zevachim 54a, 61b-62a;
.... Middos 3:1-3, 3:6
Altar, how to encircle .... Zevachim 64a-64b; Succah 48b
Altar, idolatrous, annulling .... Avodah Zarah 53b-54a
Altar in Heaven .... Chagigah 12b; Menachos 110a
Altar in second Temple .... Zevachim 61b-62a; Middos 3:1
Altar in Tabernacle, Shiloh and Nov .... Zevachim 59b-60a, 61b
Altar, iron .... Middos 3:4
Altar of numerous stones .... Avodah Zarah 53b
Altar, painting and washing .... Middos 3:4
Altar, place .... Yoma 33b; Zevachim 53b-54a, 58a-59a, 63b
Altar, private altar .... Zevachim 108b
Altar sheds tears, divorce .... Sanhedrin 22a; Gittin 90b
Altar, *sikrah* thread .... Zevachim 53a; Menachos 97b; Bechoros 17b; Middos 3:1
Altar, stones .... Middos 3:4

A

Altar, golden
    Altar, golden, base .... Zevachim 50a
    Altar, golden, not to take down invalid sacrifices .... Zevachim 27b
    Altar, golden, sprinklings of Yom Kippur .... Yoma 58b-59a
Alu lo yerdu .... *see* **Taking down offering from Altar, non-*Kohen*** page 670;
    .... *see also* **Sacrifices (Placed on Altar)**, page 580
Aluf, monarchy .... Sanhedrin 99b
Alufenu mesubalim, *aggadah* .... Berachos 17a-17b
Aluv vesheino aluv .... *see* **Humble man, moves back before others**, page 287
Aluvah kallah .... *see* **Bride, pitiful, golden calf**, page 77
Alyah .... *see* **Tail**, page 670
Am haaretz .... *see* **Ignoramus**, page 297
Amad lafush ulekasef .... *see* **Standing to rest or to load one's burden**, page 654
Amah ivriyah .... *see* **Maidservant, Hebrew**, page 384
Amah traiksin .... *see* **Temple, *amah traiksin***, page 679
Amah, *shiur* .... *see* **Cubit**, page 135
Amalek
    Amalek and king, order .... Sanhedrin 20b
    Amalek, erasing .... Bava Basra 21a-21b; Sanhedrin 20b; Megillah 7a
    Amalek, Saul .... Yoma 22b
Amalgam of nations, do not have compassion .... Beitzah 32b
Amanah .... *see* **Honesty**, page 282
Amanah bemechirah .... *see* **Cost price sale**, page 129
Amasa
    Amasa and Joab .... Sanhedrin 49a
    Amasa, David's nephew .... Shabbos 55b
Amasla .... *see* **Justification**, page 330
Amaziah
    Amaziah, idolatry .... Sanhedrin 103a
    Amaziah, Josiah's uncle .... Megillah 10b
Ambidextrous, writing .... Shabbos 103a
Amcha, wicked not included .... Makos 8b; Yevamos 22b; Bava Kama 94b; Bava Metzia 48b, 62a;
    .... Bava Basra 4a; Sanhedrin 85a
Ameimar, kept distance from a bribe .... Kesubos 105b
Amen
    Amen, after *bone Yerushalayim* .... Berachos 45b
    Amen, *El Melech Ne'eman* .... Shabbos 119b; Sanhedrin 111a
    Amen, how .... Berachos 45a, 47a
    Amen, like taking oath .... Shevuos 29b, 36a
    Amen, raising flag .... Succah 51b
    Amen, reward .... Shabbos 119b; Nazir 66b; Berachos 53b; Sanhedrin 110b
    Amen, significance .... Shabbos 119b; Sanhedrin 111a; Shevuos 36a
    Amen, when .... Berachos 45b, 53b
    Amen, *yehei shemei rabba* .... *see* ***Yehei shemei rabba***, page 768
Ami Shapir Naah, mortgage (*apotiki*) .... Gittin 41a; Niddah 19a
Amgosha
    Amgosha digs in graves .... Bava Basra 58a
    Amgosha, explanation .... Shabbos 75a
Amidah is prayer, source .... Berachos 6b, 26b

Amirah legoy .... *see* **Asking a non-Jew**, page 34
Amiraso lagavoha .... *see* **Speech, act of acquisition for consecrated items Treasury**, page 649
Ammon
  Ammon .... Sanhedrin 103a, 103b
  Ammon, World to Come .... Sanhedrin 104a
Ammon and Moab
  Ammon and Moab, conquest by Sihon .... Gittin 38a; Sanhedrin 94b; Chullin 60b
  Ammon and Moab, destruction .... Sanhedrin 96b
  Ammon and Moab, tithes .... Yadayim 4:3; Chagigah 3b; Yevamos 16a
Ammon hamelech .... *see* **King Ammon**, page 341
Ammon, Naamah the Ammonite .... Bava Kama 38b
Ammonite
  Ammonite girl to *Kohen* .... Yevamos 77a-77b
  Ammonite man and not Ammonite woman .... Yevamos 69a, 76b-77a, 88b;
  .... Kesubos 7b; Kiddushin 67b, 75a; Chullin 62b
  Ammonite who married Egyptian woman .... Kiddushin 67b
  Ammonites, disqualified to marry into Jewish people ... Yevamos 76b-77a; Nazir 23b; Horayos 10b
  Ammonites, Sennacherib .... Berachos 28a; Yadayim 4:4
Amniotic liquid in field, damage by animal .... Bava Kama 58a-58b
Amnon and Tamar .... Sanhedrin 21a
Amod venaaseh melachtenu .... *see* **Stand and we shall do our work**, page 654
Amora
  Amora, episodes about forgiveness .... Sotah 40a
  Amora to Rabbi Shila, Rav .... Yoma 20b
  Amoraim of Pumbedita, who were they .... Sanhedrin 17b
  Amoraim, order of sitting in Heaven .... Bava Metzia 85b
Amos
  Amos, derogatory speech to Jeroboam .... Pesachim 87b
  Amos, princes of mankind .... Succah 52b
  Amos, wealth .... Nedarim 38a
Amounts
  Amounts, cannot be different for everyone .... Bava Basra 29a; Shabbos 35b; Megillah 18b; Gittin 14a;
  .... Chullin 9a, 32a
  Amounts for Torah, according to Zechariah's scroll .... Eruvin 21a
Amrafel, Nimrod .... Eruvin 53a
Amrah li em .... *see* **Mother said to me**, page 425
Amram
  Amram, marriage to Jochebed .... Bava Basra 119b-120a; Sanhedrin 58b; Sotah 12a
  Amram, men who encompassed History .... Bava Basra 121b
Amru davar echad .... *see* **Tannaim,** several said same thing, page 672
Amud anan .... *see* **Pillar of cloud**, page 488
Amulet
  Amulet, against evil eye .... Berachos 55b; Bava Basra 118a-118b
  Amulet, carrying on Shabbos .... Shabbos 53b, 60a, 61a-62a
  Amulet, cure .... 66b; Shabbos 61a-61b
  Amulet, episode about demons' laughter .... Pesachim 111b
  Amulet, holiness .... Shabbos 61b-62a
  Amulet, verses .... Shabbos 61b, 115b
  Amulets against demons .... Pesachim 111b

Ana Hashem, Yom Kippur confession .... Yoma 36b-37a
Anah
  Anah, mules .... Pesachim 54a
  Anah, Tzivon .... Bava Basra 115b; Pesachim 54a
Analogy
  Analogy, all laws included .... Krisos 22b; Nedarim 7a
  Analogy, all sacrifices .... Zevachim 97b-98a; Menachos 82b-83a
  Analogy and similar words, preference .... Zevachim 48a; Gittin 41b
  Analogy, explicitly .... Zevachim 49b
  Analogy, for leniency and stringency ...... Yevamos 8a; Shabbos 83b; Kiddushin 68a; Avodah Zarah 46b
  Analogy from analogy, sacrifice ...... Zevachim 41a, 49b-50a, 55a, 57a; Yoma 57a; Menachos 28a, 78a, 82b
  Analogy, refuting .... Menachos 82b; Bava Kama 63b, 106b
Analyzing words of bill .... Bava Metzia 104a-104b
Anan, Rav Huna's resentment .... Kesubos 69a-69b
Ananei kavod .... *see* **Clouds of Glory,** page 112
Ananim, clouds .... Taanis 6b
Anavah .... *see* **Humility,** page 288
Androgynous .... *see* **Androgyny,** page 22
Androgyny
  Androgyny, blemish .... Yevamos 83b-84a
  Androgyny, circumcision on Shabbos .... Shabbos 136b-137a
  Androgyny, doubt .... Yevamos 82b-84a
  Androgyny, firstborn animal .... Bechoros 41b
  Androgyny, his wife's *terumah* .... Yevamos 81a
  Androgyny, impurity after giving birth to .... Niddah 28a, 40a; Bava Basra 127a
  Androgyny, intimate relations .... Yevamos 82b, 84a
  Androgyny, laws .... Bikurim 4:1-5; Shabbos 136b-137a; Niddah 28b; Bechoros 42a; Arachin 4a-4b
  Androgyny, seminal and blood discharges .... Niddah 28a-28b; Zavim 2:1
Aneinu, prayer on fast day .... Taanis 11b, 13b-14a
Angel
  Angels —
    Angel, Matatron .... Sanhedrin 38b
    Angel, *Ofan* .... Chagigah 12b-14a
    Angel, world minister .... Yevamos 16b
    Angels *Chayos* .... Chagigah 12b-13a
  Episodes —
    Angel of Rome, city of refuge .... Makos 12a
    Angel of the sea, episode .... Bava Basra 74b
    Angel, Rabbi Yehudah .... Shabbos 25b
    Angel, rebuke about *tzitzis* .... Menachos 41a
    Angel, struggle with Jacob .... Chullin 91a-92a
    Angels and men, death .... Kesubos 104a
    Angels, creation of man .... Sanhedrin 38b
    Angels roast meat, Adam .... Sanhedrin 59b
    Angels, ship containing flour .... Taanis 24b
    Angels, visiting Abraham ...... Yoma 37a; Kiddushin 32b; Bava Metzia 86b-87a
  Misc. —
    Angel, Aramaic language .... Sotah 33a; Shabbos 12b
    Angel interceding among a thousand .... Shabbos 32a

Angel makes fetus forget his learning .... Niddah 30b
Angel of rain, water of festival .... Taanis 25b
Angel, prohibition to draw an angel .... Avodah Zarah 42b-43b; Rosh Hashanah 24a-24b
Angels, *aggadah* .... Chagigah 13a-14a
Angels, G-d took advice from angels .... Sanhedrin 38b
Angels, like Tarshish .... Chullin 91b
Angels protecting man .... Taanis 11a; Chagigah 16a
Angels, Sages .... Nedarim 20b
Angels, Shabbos .... Shabbos 119b
Angels welcoming deceased .... Kesubos 104a

Angel of Death
    Angel of Death, city of Luz .... Sotah 46b
    Angel of Death, evil urge .... Bava Basra 16a
    Angel of Death, eyes .... Avodah Zarah 20b
    Angel of Death, here or there .... Bava Metzia 36b
    Angel of Death, how does he kill .... Avodah Zarah 20b
    Angel of Death, Miriam Magdela Nashia .... Chagigah 4b-5a
    Angel of Death, Patriarchs .... Bava Basra 17a
    Angel of Death, Rabbi Yehoshua ben Levi .... Kesubos 77b
    Angel of Death, Rav Chisda .... Makos 10a
    Angel of Death, righteous men .... Moed Katan 28a
    Angel of Death, synagogue .... Bava Kama 60b
    Angel of Death, women .... Berachos 51a

Anger
  Behavior —
    Anger, distance .... Avos 2:10, 5:11; Berachos 29b; Taanis 4a
    Anger, do not appease during anger .... Avos 4:18
    Anger, four traits .... Avos 5:11
    Anger, man is known by his anger .... Eruvin 65b
    Anger of teacher, keeping silent .... Berachos 63b
    Anger, virtue of man avoiding anger .... Pesachim 113b

  Episodes —
  Anger, Eliab and David .... Pesachim 66b
  Anger, exhibited, episodes .... Shabbos 105b; Kiddushin 32a
  Anger, I do not have, Moses .... Nedarim 32a
  Anger, son and disciple .... Bava Basra 116a, 141a
  Anger, wicked .... Sanhedrin 113b
  Anger, written in Torah .... Zevachim 102a
  Angry, murder on way to *Eretz Yisrael* .... Nedarim 22a-22b

  Misc. —
  Anger against friend, communal sacrifice .... Zevachim 41b
  Anger destroys house .... Sotah 3b
  Anger, *Eretz Yisrael* .... Nedarim 22a
  Anger, G-d's .... Berachos 7a, 54b; Avodah Zarah 4a-4b; Pesachim 87b; Sanhedrin 105b
  Anger, ill effects .... Nedarim 22a
  Anger, liver and bile .... Berachos 61b
  Anger of Sage, Torah burns in him .... Taanis 4a
  Anger, sends his wife to her mother .... Pesachim 87b
  Anger, wisdom disappears .... Pesachim 66b

Angry man

Angry man, compared to idolater..Shabbos 105b
Angry man, his life is no life..Pesachim 113b

Animal

Aggadah —

Animal, fed copiously..Kiddushin 82b
Animal, to show inferiority to man..Chullin 5b
Animals, giant, D'bei Ilai...Chullin 59b
Animals, giant, feast for righteous..Bava Basra 74b-75a
Animals, giant, stories..Bava Basra 73b; Zevachim 113b
Animals of righteous men, protected from forbidden foods.........Chullin 5b, 6a, 7a;
....Yevamos 99b; Kesubos 28b; Gittin 7a
Animals, parable for tribes..Sotah 11b

Damages —

Animal, borrowed or rented who died....................................Bava Metzia 97a-98b
Animal, breaching wall in front of animal............................Bava Kama 55b-56a
Animal, damage...*see also* **Ox**, page 467
Animal damaging field, by amniotic liquid...........................Bava Kama 58a-58b
Animal in fellow's field...Bava Kama 81b
Animal, large, theft..Sanhedrin 25b
Animal, small, theft...........Bava Kama 79b-80a; Bava Metzia 5b; Sanhedrin 25b; Temurah 15b
Animal, taken out in sun...Sanhedrin 76b-77a
Animal, thieves took it out..Bava Kama 56a-56b
Animal turning its head, damages..Bava Kama 21a-21b
Animal under sun, liability..Bava Kama 56a
Animal which lost its value with custodian.............................Bava Metzia 96b
Animals causing damage, slaughtering.....................................Bava Kama 23b
Animals considered natural damagers from the first time..........Bava Kama 16a-16b
Animals, dangerous, killing them...Sanhedrin 15b
Animals, harmful, keeping them...Bava Kama 80a-80b

Monetary matters —

Animal, act of acquisition, pulling and riding........................Bava Metzia 8b-9b
Animal bound, act of acquisition...Bava Metzia 9b
Animal, head of flock, act of acquisition.................................Bava Kama 52a
Animal, lost...Bava Metzia 27a, 28b, 30b-31a, 32a
Animal, seizing freely grazing.................................Bava Basra 36a; Kesubos 84b
Animal, ways to purchase................Kiddushin 25b-26a; Bava Kama 11b; Bava Basra 86b
Animals in deals, caring..Bava Metzia 69a
Animals, included in sale..Bava Basra 77b
Animals, one yoke for all...Kiddushin 27b

Prohibitions —

Animal, bestiality...Sanhedrin 54b-55a
Animal cheek, *treifah*..Chullin 55b
Animal coupled to man, stoning...Sanhedrin 54a, 55a-55b
Animal coupled to non-Jew......................................Avodah Zarah 15b, 22a-23a
Animal, difficulty in delivery..Chullin 68a-68b
Animal, forbidden profit..Kiddushin 57a
Animal from second tithe..Succah 40b-41a
Animal, giving it man's food...Taanis 20b

Animal, *kosher* ....*see* **Treifah**, page 702
Animal, Sabbatical year produce ....Sheviis 8:1
Animal, seclusion with ....Kiddushin 81b, 82a
Animal sold to non-Jew ....Avodah Zarah 14b-15a, 16a-16b, 20b; Bechoros 2a-3a
Animal used for idolatry, permitted ....Temurah 29a
Animal with non-cloven hooves, well-known ....Chullin 75b
Animals and beasts, *kashrus* ....Chullin 42a, 80a
Animals, idolatry ....Temurah 29a
Animals, impure, prohibition of business ....Sheviis 7:3-4; Pesachim 23a
Animals, mixed mating ....*see* **Sinning animals**, page 629
Animals, mixture ....Zevachim 72a-72b
Animals preferred to their wives, idolaters ....Avodah Zarah 22b; Gittin 38a
Animals, working with two species ....Kilayim 8:2-4; Bava Metzia 8b

Sacrifice —
Animal ....*see also* **Sacrifice**, page 578
Animal, close to Jerusalem ....Shekalim 7:4-5; Kiddushin 55a-55b
Animal, dirty, sacrifice ....Bechoros 41a; Temurah 28b
Animal, impure, sacrifice ....Zevachim 34a
Animal, redeemed ....*see* **Redeemed sacrifices**, page 551
Animal reserved in case of loss, sacrifice ....Temurah 24a
Animal without blemish, rare ....Menachos 101a
Animals, sacrificial, deductions ....Nazir 35a-35b

Scientific facts —
Animal, evil urge ....Berachos 61a
Animal has no *mazal* ....Bava Kama 2b; Shabbos 53b
Animal, produce of its land ....Pesachim 52b
Animal, small, abundant care ....Bava Metzia 69a
Animal, small, gestation and dropping young ....Rosh Hashanah 8a
Animal, small, wealth ....Chullin 84a-84b
Animal used to some person, value ....Bava Metzia 93b
Animals, dangers ....Beitzah 25b
Animals, gestation and bringing forth ....Bechoros 7b-8a; Bava Basra 16a
Animals in sea, similar to land animals ....Chullin 127a

Shabbos —
Animal, born on Shabbos ....Shabbos 128b
Animal carrying chain on Shabbos ....Shabbos 51b-52a
Animal carrying out, camels ....Shabbos 54a-54b
Animal carrying out, Shabbos ....Shabbos 52b-54b, 58a
Animal, dead, *muktzeh* ....Beitzah 2a, 6b, 27b; Shabbos 45b, 156b; Chullin 14a
Animal, driving donkey on Shabbos ....Shabbos 153b-154b; Avodah Zarah 15a
Animal, fallen in water, Shabbos ....Shabbos 117b, 124a, 128b; Beitzah 37a
Animal, feeding it from plant connected to ground ....Shabbos 122a; Eruvin 79a
Animal, feeding it on Shabbos ....Shabbos 106b, 155a-156a; Beitzah 23b
Animal, food eaten by another ....Shabbos 140b-141a
Animal, partition ....Eruvin 15a-15b
Animal, preparing food for it on Shabbos ....Shabbos 155a-155b, 156b
Animal, prohibition to work animal on Shabbos ....Avodah Zarah 15a
Animal, pushing it in courtyard on Shabbos ....Shabbos 128b
Animal, slaughtered, Shabbos ....Chullin 14a-15a; Kesubos 34a; Bava Kama 71a

Animal, *techumin* ....Beitzah 37a-37b, 40a; Eruvin 97b
Animals, care on Shabbos ....Shabbos 53a-53b
Animals grazing, *muktzeh* ....Beitzah 40a-40b; Shabbos 45b, 157a
Animals, *muktzeh* ....Shabbos 19b
Misc. —
Animal, feeding animal before eating ....Berachos 40a; Gittin 62a
Animal for wall of succah ....Succah 23a-23b
Animal, included in best category ....Chullin 70b-71a, 84a; Nedarim 81a; Bava Kama 17b
Animal, signs ....Chullin 59a
Animals, same laws as ox ....Bava Kama 54b
Animal and its young
Animal and its young, blemished sacrifice ....Bechoros 15a
Animal and its young, by which law ....Chullin 78a-78b
Animal and its young, father ....Chullin 78b-79a; Bechoros 45b
Animal and its young, improper slaughtering ....Chullin 80a-80b
Animal and its young, in Temple Courtyard ....Chullin 80a-80b
Animal and its young, informing buyer ....Chullin 83a, 83b
Animal and its young, *Kohen* ....Bechoros 45b
Animal and its young, order ....Chullin 82a
Animal and its young, precedence ....Chullin 82a
Animal and its young, sacrifice ....Chullin 78a, 80a-81b
Animal and its young, slaughtering by two ....Chullin 82a-82b
Animal and its young, Yom Tov ....Shabbos 117b, 124a; Beitzah 37a
Animal found in mother's womb
Animal found in mother's womb, impurity ....Chullin 72a-72b, 73a, 74b-75a
Animal found in mother's womb, laws ....Chullin 74a-74b, 92b; Bechoros 12a-12b
Animal found in mother's womb, sacrifice ....Chullin 75a
Animal found in mother's womb, slaughtering ....Chullin 75b; Menachos 30b
Animal found in mother's womb, source ....Chullin 69a
Animal found in mother's womb, *treifah* ....Chullin 75a-75b
Ankle ....Yevamos 103a
Annotation, *"delo ke'asmachta"* ....Bava Basra 44b
Announcement
Announcement ....*see also* **Auction**, page 36
Announcement before death penalty ....Sanhedrin 43a, 89a
Announcement by *beis din*, sale ....Kesubos 100b; Arachin 21b-22b
Announcement, disqualified witnesses ....Sanhedrin 26b
Announcement for lost item ....Bava Metzia 28a-28b
Announcement for priesthood, pregnant woman ....Yevamos 36a, 119b
Announcement, not effective for children ....Eruvin 64a
Announcement, orphans' property ....Kesubos 100b; Arachin 21b-22b
Announcement, *treifah* animal in town ....Chullin 94b-95a
Announcer in Temple ....Yoma 20b
Announcing annulment of vows ....Nedarim 23a-23b
Annul
Annul your will before His will ....Avos 2:4
Annulled and did not annul ....Makos 16a-16b; Chullin 141a
Annulled personal opinion ....Shabbos 92a-92b, 144b; Eruvin 28a, 29b
Annulling husband's approbation to vow ....Nedarim 69a; Kesubos 79a

Annulling one's position, Hillel and Shamai...Eduyos 1:4
Annulling verdict of *beis din*..Sanhedrin 31a
Annulling vow
  When —
  Annulling vow, before it applies...Nedarim 89b-90a
  Annulling vow, before marriage.................................Nedarim 70b, 72b, 73b-74a; Kesubos 57b
  Annulling vow, before vow....................................Nedarim 72b-73a, 75a-76b; Nazir 12b
  Annulling vow, for future...Nazir 21b-22a
  Annulling vow on Shabbos...Shabbos 46b, 157a; Nedarim 77a-77b
  Annulling vow, time of wedding arrived.......................................Nedarim 70b, 73b-74a
  Annulling vow, until when..................................Nedarim 76b, 87b; Shabbos 157a
  Annulling vows..*see also* **Permitting vows**, page 482

  Misc. —
  Annulling vow by agent..................................Nedarim 72b; Nazir 12b; Bava Metzia 96a
  Annulling vow by mistake...Nedarim 86b-87a
  Annulling vow, father and fiancé..............Nedarim 66b-67a, 68a-68a, 70a-70b, 71a-71b, 72a, 78b
  Annulling vow for one species..Nedarim 87a-87b
  Annulling vow, half annulling by father......................Nedarim 68a-69a, 71b; Nazir 19a, 21b
  Annulling vow, half vow...Nedarim 82b-83b
  Annulling vow, impossibility...Nedarim 89a-89b
  Annulling vow instead of permitting vow....................................Nedarim 77b-78a
  Annulling vow of two wives together...Nedarim 73a
  Annulling vow, so as not to displease her husband.................................Yevamos 90b
  Annulling vow, so-and-so and fruit..Nedarim 82a-82b
  Annulling wife's consecrating vow................Kesubos 59a-59b, 66a, 70a; Nedarim 85a-86b;
                                                                                   Yevamos 93a; Kiddushin 63a

  Annulling vow of *nazir*
    Annulling vow of *nazir*, sacrifices...Nazir 28a-28b
    Annulling vow of *nazir*, source..Nedarim 4b
    Annulling vow of *nazir*, when husband said "You also"..................Nazir 22b-23a
Annulment
  Divorce certificate —
  Annulment of agent, in front of one man..Gittin 33b
  Annulment of appraisal announcement; divorce...Arachin 21b
  Annulment of divorce certificate...................Gittin 32a-34a; Yevamos 90b; Kiddushin 59a
  Annulment of divorce certificate, lashes.............................Kiddushin 12b; Yevamos 52a
  Misc. —
  Annulment in greater quantity...*see* **Mixture**, page 417
  Annulment in greater quantity, impurity of corpse...................................Niddah 27b
  Annulment in sixty times the same volume.....................Avodah Zarah 69a; Chullin 97a-99b
  Annulment of *chametz*..Pesachim 6b-7a
  Annulment of *chametz*, from the Torah..Pesachim 4b, 10a
  Annulment of Heavenly decree.............................Rosh Hashanah 17b-18a; Yevamos 105a
  Annulment of mission..Kiddushin 59b
  Annulment of *orlah* in two hundred times its volume.....................................Pesachim 48a
  Annulment of sale, fraud in price.....................Bava Metzia 49b-50b; Kiddushin 42b; Bava Basra 95a
  Annulment of straw, domains...Eruvin 78b-79a
  Annulment of straw, impurity........................Succah 4a; Eruvin 78b-79a; Oholos 15:6-7
  Annulment of utensil use, *muktzeh*...........................Shabbos 43a, 47b, 128b, 154b

Annulment of idolatrous
Annulment of idolatrous Altar .... Avodah Zarah 53b-54a
Annulment of idolatrous impurity .... Avodah Zarah 52a-52b
Annulment of idolatrous item, by Jew .... Avodah Zarah 42a, 52b-53a
Annulment of idolatrous item, by whom .... Avodah Zarah 43a, 64b
Annulment of idolatrous item, cases .... Avodah Zarah 42a-42b, 43a, 44b, 53a-53b
Annulment of idolatrous item, Nimrod's tower .... Avodah Zarah 53b
Annulment of idolatrous item, pruning idolatrous tree .... Avodah Zarah 42a, 49b
Annulment of idolatrous item, removing new addition .... Avodah Zarah 47b
Annulment of idolatrous sacrifice .... Avodah Zarah 50a-50b

Annulment of ownership
Annulment of ownership, annulled his house .... Eruvin 26a-26b, 69b
Annulment of ownership, carried out afterwards .... Eruvin 68b-69a
Annulment of ownership, closing his house .... Eruvin 79b
Annulment of ownership, Cuthean .... Chullin 6a
Annulment of ownership, dead .... Eruvin 70a-71a
Annulment of ownership, *eruv* .... Eruvin 67a, 69b-70a
Annulment of ownership, for everyone .... Eruvin 26b, 70a
Annulment of ownership, for which items .... Eruvin 66a-67a, 75b
Annulment of ownership, laws concerning man annulling .... Eruvin 26b, 69b
Annulment of ownership, non-Jew .... Eruvin 63b-64a
Annulment of ownership, resident non-Jew .... Avodah Zarah 64b
Annulment of ownership, second time .... Eruvin 68b, 69b, 79b
Annulment of ownership, when .... Eruvin 71a

Anochi
Anochi, heard from G-d .... Makos 24a
Anochi, initials .... Shabbos 105a

Anointing
Anointing baby .... Yoma 78b
Anointing hands, *Bircas HaMazon* .... Berachos 53b
Anointing impure person with *terumah* .... Niddah 32a
Anointing, mourner .... Taanis 13b
Anointing on Yom Kippur .... Yoma 77b
Anointing oneself like drinking .... Yoma 76b; Niddah 32a; Shabbos 86a
Anointing, second tithe .... Yevamos 74a
Anointing stomach on Shabbos .... Shabbos 147b; Sanhedrin 101a
Anointing with anointing oil, prohibition .... Krisos 5a, 6b-7a
Anointing with oil of Sabbatical year .... Sheviis 8:2
Anointing with rose oil, Shabbos .... Shabbos 111b, 128a; Bava Metzia 113b

Anointment
Anointment of Aaron .... Krisos 5b
Anointment of kings .... Horayos 11b; Krisos 5b
Anointment of *Kohen Gadol* .... Horayos 11b; Krisos 5b; Yoma 5a
Anointment of measuring utensils in Temple .... Menachos 8b, 57b, 88a-88b, 90a
Anointment with oil, meal offering .... Menachos 74b-75a, 106a

Anshei Alexandria .... *see* **Alexandrians**, page 19

Anshei
Anshei maaseh, Rabbi Chanina ben Dosa .... Sotah 49b
Anshei Mishmar, shaving and laundering .... Taanis 17a; Moed Katan 14a

Anshei Maamad
Anshei Maamad, fasts .... Taanis 27b
Anshei Maamad, prayer .... Taanis 27b-28b; Yoma 37b
Anshei Maamad, prohibitions .... Taanis 17a
Anshei Maamad, Torah reading .... Taanis 27b-28a
Anshei Maamad, why .... Taanis 27a

Answer
"Answer me, G-d, answer me," Elijah .... Berachos 6b, 9b
Answer a fool according to his foolishness .... Shabbos 30b
Answer, I gave one and you give the other .... Bava Kama 17b
Answer stolen .... Meilah 7b
Answer, to prophet .... Sanhedrin 105a
Answer, unsatisfactory, not adopted as law .... Yevamos 91b; Bava Basra 135a
Answer, unsatisfactory, on verse .... Kiddushin 68a; Pesachim 59b; Niddah 33a
Answering before hearing .... Bava Basra 98b
Answering elusively, acknowledging debt .... Bava Basra 175a; Sanhedrin 29a-29b
Answering in feminine gender, modesty .... Shabbos 140b
Answering first things first, wise man .... Avos 5:7
Answering on same level .... Beitzah 20b
Answering softly calms anger .... Berachos 17a
Answers correctly, wise man .... Avos 5:7
Answers, insufficient to permit danger .... Avodah Zarah 30a

Ant
Ant, "Your justice is eternal" .... Chullin 63a
Ant, living, combining with dead ones .... Makos 16b
Ant, missing limb, lashes .... Nazir 51b-52a
Ant, theft .... Eruvin 100b
Ants, destroying with earth .... Moed Katan 6b-7a
Ants, episode about experiment .... Chullin 57b
Ants, sheaves of poor .... Peah 4:11; Chullin 134a

Ant-hills
Ant-hills, containing sheaves of poor .... Peah 4, 10-11; Chullin 134a
Ant-hills, destroying .... Moed Katan 6b-7a
Ant-hills, tithes .... Maasros 5:7

Antoninus
Antoninus and Rebbi .... Avodah Zarah 10a-10b
Antoninus, radish and horseradish .... Avodah Zarah 11a; Berachos 57b

Anusah .... *see* **Rape victim**, page 536

Apartment
Apartment, additional to courtyard, claim .... Bava Basra 60a
Apartment, empty, damage .... Bava Kama 21a
Apartment in building, sale .... Bava Basra 61b

Apikoros .... *see* **Heretic**, page 277

Apotiki .... *see* **Mortgage**, page 423

Apotropa .... *see* **Administrator**, page 12

Apotropus .... *see* **Custodian**, page 136

Appeal
Appeal .... Sanhedrin 33b
Appeal about divorce certificate .... Gittin 6b, 3a, 9a, 46b; Yevamos 65a

Appeal against judge attesting legal document .... Kesubos 21b-22a
Appeal against ruling of *beis din* .... Sanhedrin 31a
Appeal, two witnesses .... Kesubos 26a-26b; Gittin 9a; Kiddushin 73b; Bava Basra 32a

Appearance
Appearance, amulet on Shabbos .... Shabbos 61b
Appearance arising suspicion, in secret .... Shabbos 64b-65a, 146b; Beitzah 9a; Avodah Zarah 12a
Appearance, blemishes of *Kohen* .... Bechoros 43a
Appearance, circumcision of overweight baby .... Shabbos 137a
Appearance, idolatry .... Avodah Zarah 12a-12b
Appearance, ladder on Yom Tov .... Beitzah 9a
Appearance, muzzling animal threshing *terumah* .... Bava Metzia 90a
Appearance of coin, asceticism .... Avodah Zarah 50a; Pesachim 104a
Appearance, *s'chach* .... Succah 10b

Appearing
Appearing false, legal document .... Kesubos 21b, 85a-85b; Gittin 26b
Appearing to be arrogant .... Pesachim 55a

Appeasing
Appeasing, do not appease man during anger .... Avos 4:18
Appeasing, not when man is angry .... Berachos 7a

Apple
Apple, parable for Israel .... Shabbos 88a
Apples, Jacob's scent .... Taanis 29b

Application of deceased's will .... Gittin 14b-15a, 40a; Kesubos 70a
Applying double prohibition .... *see* **Double prohibition**, page 176
Applying hands on sacrifice .... *see* **Semichah**, page 600
Appraisers .... Bava Basra 107a-107b; Avodah Zarah 72a
Appraises for himself, custodian .... Kesubos 98a
Apprentice, advised his master to divorce .... Gittin 58a
Approval, Divine, of decrees .... Makos 23b

Approving vow
Approving vow, cases .... Nedarim 79a
Approving vow internally .... Nedarim 79a
Approving vow, kept silent to upset his wife .... Nedarim 78b-79a
Approving vow, permitting .... Nedarim 69a
Apron for woman, decree .... Bava Kama 82a
Apt to be mixed even if was not mixed .... Kiddushin 25a; Menachos 103b; Niddah 66b
Arabs
Arabs .... *see also* **Ishmaelites**, page 318
Arabs, G-d's regret .... Succah 52b
Arabs, inferior nation .... Kesubos 66b
Arachin .... *see* **Donation valuation**, page 174
Aram, decrees .... Gittin 17a
Aramaic
Aramaic language .... Bava Kama 83a; Sanhedrin 38b
Aramaic language, angels .... Sotah 33a; Shabbos 12b
Aramaic language, communal prayer .... Sotah 33a; Shabbos 12b
Aramaic language, requests in prayer .... Sotah 33a; Shabbos 12b
Aramaic man, put dead under bed .... Berachos 8b; Pesachim 112b
Aravah .... *see* **Willow**, page 748

A

Arayos..*see* **Forbidden relations**, page 233

Arbaah devarim...*see* **Four indemnities**, page 238

Arboriculturist, rights...Bava Metzia 109a-109b

Arch, *Sefer Hayashar*..Avodah Zarah 25a

Arch on arch, tent of corpse...Parah 3:6

Area of graves.........................Nazir 64b-65b; Bava Basra 101b-102b; Oholos 16:3-5

Arel...*see* **Uncircumcised**, page 714

Argument

   Argument, changing in *beis din*.......................................Bava Basra 31a

   Argument for people repenting......................................Avodah Zarah 4b-5a

   Argument for Satan..Berachos 19a, 60a; Kesubos 8b

   Argument on behalf of purchaser......................Bava Basra 23a, 41a; Gittin 58b

   Arguments on behalf of heir.......................................Bava Basra 23a, 52a

Ari D'bei Ilai..Chullin 59b

Arifah...*see* **Decapitating**, page 152

Arioch, Shmuel..Shabbos 53a

Ariri..*see* **Childless person**, page 104

Aristobolus, siege......................Sotah 49b; Bava Kama 82b; Menachos 64b

Ark

   Ark..*see also* **Poles of Ark**, page 493

   Ark and tablets, dimensions...Bava Basra 14a

   Ark, bore its bearers..Sotah 35a

   Ark, borne by *Kohanim* and *Leviim*..................................Sotah 33b

   Ark, David's feast...Pesachim 36b

   Ark, David's mistake..Sotah 35a

   Ark, episode of Uzza...Sotah 35a-35b

   Ark, going out to war..Sotah 42b-43a

   Ark in Temple, general...........Yoma 3b, 72b; Bava Basra 14a-14b, 98b-99a; Menachos 98a-98b

   Ark in Temple, miracle of its position.......Bava Basra 98b-99a; Yoma 21a; Megillah 10b

   Ark of Covenant, impurity...Megillah 26b

   Ark of Noah...Sanhedrin 108b

   Ark, Oved Edom...Berachos 63b-64a

   Ark, place of concealment..Yoma 54a

   Ark, put away..............................Horayos 12a; Yoma 52b, 53b-54a; Krisos 5b

   Ark, second Temple..Yoma 21b

   Ark, song in desert...Avodah Zarah 24b

   Ark, song of cows...Avodah Zarah 24b

Arkan, Greek...Bava Basra 164b

Arkaos..*see* **Idolaters' courts**, page 294

Armed robber............................Bava Kama 57a-57b; Bava Metzia 22a, 95a

Army

   Army, non-Jewish...Chullin 123a

   Army peacefully passing through country, fast.........................Taanis 22a

   Army, Sennacherib's.........................Shabbos 113b; Sanhedrin 95b-96a

Arnon river, miracle for Israel.................................Berachos 54a-54b

Arod...*see* **Wild donkey**, page 747

Aron hakodesh...*see* **Holy Ark**, page 282

Aron Mikdash..*see* **Ark in Temple**, page 31

Arona, place of Temple...Zevachim 116b

Aronos .... *see* **Coffin**, page 112
Around
   Around, four corners .... Eruvin 57a
   Around G-d, eighteen thousand rows of righteous .... Succah 45b; Sanhedrin 97b
Arriving early at synagogue .... Berachos 8a
Arrogance
   Arrogance, avoiding acts appearing like arrogance .... Berachos 17b; Pesachim 55a
   Arrogance because of wealth, forgetting G-d .... Berachos 32a
   Arrogance, Elam nation .... Sanhedrin 24a; Kiddushin 49b
   Arrogance, poverty in Torah .... Sanhedrin 24a; Kiddushin 49b
   Arrogance .... *see also* **Pride**, page 503
   Arrogance, severity and punishment .... Sotah 4b-5b
Arrogant man
   Arrogant man, Abbaye asked him .... Chullin 51a
   Arrogant man, *Gehinnom* .... Bava Basra 10b, 78b; Avodah Zarah 18b
   Arrogant man is not accepted by society .... Sotah 47b
   Arrogant man, shame and punishment .... Bava Basra 98a
Arrow
   Arrow in eyes of Satan .... Kiddushin 30a, 81a-81b; Succah 38a; Menachos 62a
   Arrow in eyes of Satan, episode .... Kiddushin 81a-81b
   Arrows, male, *s'chach* .... Succah 12b, 15a
   Arrows of G-d cease but Israel survives .... Sotah 9a
Arusah .... *see* **Betrothed girl**, page 55
Arvis **prayer**
   Arvis prayer, optional .... Berachos 27b; Shabbos 9b; Yoma 87b
   Arvis prayer, importance .... Berachos 6b
   Arvis prayer, time .... Berachos 27a
   Arvis prayer, time of *Shema* .... Berachos 2b-3a
As if by accident, Shabbos .... Shabbos 121b
Asa hamelech .... *see* **King Asa**, page 341
Asa, king .... Sotah 10a
Asarah B'Teives .... Rosh Hashanah 18b
Asarah rishonim ...... *see* **Ten men who first arrived in synagogue**, page 680
Asei .... *see* **Positive commandment**, page 495
Asei lecha Rav .... *see* **Make yourself a Rav**, page 386
Asei retzono kiretzoncha .... *see* **Do His will like your will**, page 172
Asei shabatecha chol .... *see* **Make your Shabbos a weekday**, page 386
Aseres Hadibros .... *see* **Ten Commandments**, page 680
Aseres yemei teshuvah .... *see* **Ten days of Repentance**, page 680
Ash
  Prohibitions —
   Ash of consecrated items Treasury .... Temurah 34a
   Ash of deceased man, forbidden benefit .... Temurah 34a; Pesachim 27b
   Ash of stove-top, *muktzeh* .... Beitzah 8a-8b
   Ash on wound, tattooing .... Makos 21a
  Misc. —
   Ash, curing wound .... Bava Kama 35a
   Ash for grooms .... Bava Basra 60b
   Ash from Altar, place .... Meilah 12a

Ash from Altar, personal use .... Meilah 9a-9b

Ash from Altar, benefit .... Meilah 11b-12a

Ash from Altar, taking down from Altar .... Yoma 23b-24a; Tamid 5:5

Ashes of deceased person .... Niddah 27b-28a, 57b; Oholos 2:2

Ash of Isaac, place of Altar .... Zevachim 62a

Ash pile on Altar .... Tamid 28b

Ash of Red Heifer

Ash of Red Heifer, Abraham .... Sotah 17a; Chullin 88b

Ash of Red Heifer, how .... Sotah 16b; Temurah 12b; Parah 6:1

Ash of Red Heifer, impurity .... Parah 9:7-9

Ash of Red Heifer, mixed .... Parah 9:7; Bechoros 23a

Ash of Red Heifer, secular use .... Menachos 51b-52a

Ash of Red Heifer, sanctification .... Parah 6:2, 5:4; Temurah 12b; Yevamos 72b; Sotah 16b;
Shabbos 137a; Yoma 43a; Arachin 3a; Kiddushin 58b; Bechoros 29a

Asham talui .... *see* **Guilt offering for doubtful culpability**, page 262

Asham .... *see* **Guilt offering**, page 262

Asheirah

Asheirah, general .... Avodah Zarah 45b, 48a; Eruvin 79b

Asheirah, impurity of idolatry .... Avodah Zarah 48b

Asheirah, pillar and beam .... Eruvin 80b

Asheirah, pruned .... Avodah Zarah 42a, 49b

Asheirah, sitting and walking .... Avodah Zarah 48b

Asheirah, stumbling-block .... Sanhedrin 55a

Asher

Asher kideshanu, Rabbinical .... Shabbos 23a; Succah 46a

Asher Yatzar badin, blessing .... Berachos 58b

Asher Yatzar, blessing .... Berachos 60b

Asher kideshanu .... *see* **Who sanctified us**, page 742

Asher Yatzar badin .... *see* **Blessing, Who formed with justice**, page 64

Asher Yatzar .... *see* **Blessing, *Asher yatzar***, page 63

Ashkavta D'Rebbi .... Kesubos 103b

Ashmadai and Solomon .... Gittin 68a-68b

Ashmoros halaylah .... *see* **Parts of the night**, page 472

Ashrei

Ashrei, Psalm cherished by David .... Berachos 10a

Ashrei three times .... Berachos 4b

Ashrei, without the letter *nun* .... Berachos 4b

Ashuris, origin .... Sanhedrin 21b-22a; Zevachim 62a

Ashvuyei gumos .... *see* **Leveling holes**, page 366

Asimon, explanation .... Bava Metzia 47b

Asked

Asked in improper way .... Taanis 4a

Asking a child, cut letter .... Menachos 29a-29b, 34a

Asking a Rav, law .... Avos 1:16

Asking before festival, laws .... Pesachim 6a-6b; Megillah 32a

Asking demons on Shabbos .... Sanhedrin 101a

Asking for Divine justice against someone .... Berachos 55a; Bava Kama 93a; Rosh Hashanah 16b

Asking for forgiveness .... *see* **Appeasing**, page 30

Asks correctly, wise .... Avos 5:7

Asks His angels, G-d's behavior...Sanhedrin 38b
Asking a non-Jew
   Asking a non-Jew, by allusion..Shabbos 150a
   Asking a non-Jew, circumcision on Shabbos..Eruvin 67b-68a
   Asking a non-Jew, for a sick person..Shabbos 129a; Beitzah 22a
   Asking a non-Jew, for after Shabbos...Shabbos 150a
   Asking a non-Jew, prohibitions..Bava Metzia 90a-90b
   Asking a non-Jew, to buy property in *Eretz Yisrael*.................Bava Kama 80b; Gittin 8b
Askupah..*see* **Doorsill**, page 175
Asmachta deRabbanan...*see* **Source**, page 648
Asmachta....................*see* **Commitment by presumption**, page 117; *see also* **Presumption**, page 502
Aspaklaria meira..Succah 45b
Aspaklaria..*see* **Vision**, page 724
Aspargus...*see* **Wine and alcohol**, page 751
Ass, Balaam..Sanhedrin 105b
Assembly for Heaven's sake..Avos 4:11
Assistant
   Assistant schoolteacher...Bava Basra 21a
   Assistant to *Kohen Gadol*.................Yoma 12b-13a, 39a; Megillah 9b; Nazir 47b; Sotah 42a; Horayos 12b
Associate
   Associate, do not associate with the wicked..Avos 1:7
   Associating G-d's Name in one's pain...Berachos 63a
   Associating G-d's Name to something else, punishment..............Succah 45b; Sanhedrin 63a
Assufi...*see* **Abandoned child**, page 1
Assur, said where excising of soul is concerned...Yoma 74a
Assyrian script
   Assyrian script, origin..Sanhedrin 21b-22a; Zevachim 62a
   Assyrian script, source...Sanhedrin 21b-22a; Zevachim 62a
Astrologers
   Astrologers, prohibition to consult..Pesachim 113b
   Astrologers, Sage or schoolteacher...Yevamos 21b
Astrology
   Astrology, Abraham..Bava Basra 16b
   Astrology, he knows paths of Heaven...Berachos 58b
Astronomy
   Astronomy..Pesachim 94a; Eruvin 56a
   Astronomy, commandment to calculate...Shabbos 75a
   Astronomy, stars..................................Berachos 58b-59a; Pesachim 94a; Eruvin 56a
Asu she'eino zocheh kezocheh.......*see* **Theft, Rabbinical, before act of acquisition**, page 686
Asukim beoto inyan................................*see* **Retracting from purchase, until when**, page 563
Asusa bebeis hamidrash.......................*see* **Good health, house of study**, page 254
Asuyim lehashil.......................................*see* **Lent, items usually lent**, page 363
At Bash
   At Bash, inversed letters...Succah 52b
   At Bash, reversed alphabet...Shabbos 104a
At that time, punishment..Sanhedrin 102a
Ata chonantanu
   Ata chonantanu, forgot..Berachos 29a
   Ata chonantanu, havdala...Berachos 33a-33b; Pesachim 105b

Ata chonantanu, where .... Niddah 8a-8b; Berachos 29a, 33a

Atem eidai .... *see* **Witnesses, designated, acknowledgment**, page 754

Athens, Rabbi Yehoshua .... Bechoros 8b-9a

Atirah, prayer .... Succah 14a; Yevamos 64a

Atoned owner

Atoned owner, guilt offering .... Pesachim 73a; Shevuos 12a; Temurah 20b

Atoned owner, sin offering .... Meilah 7a-7b; Bechoros 33a; Temurah 24a

Atonement

Sacrifices —

Atonement, "my sacrifice will not expiate" .... Krisos 7a

Atonement by burnt offering .... Yoma 36a-36b; Zevachim 5b, 6a-7a

Atonement by eating sacrifice .... Pesachim 59b

Atonement by goat to Azazel .... Shevuos 12b

Atonement by guilt offering .... Krisos 22b

Atonement by guilt offering for doubtful culpability .... Yoma 85b; Krisos 25a, 26b

Atonement by increase in value of consecrated items .... Menachos 80a, 81a; Temurah 25b;
.... Krisos 27a

Atonement by sin offering, positive commandment .... Zevachim 7a-7b

Atonement by Yom Kippur goats .... Shevuos 12b, 7b-9a, 10b

Atonement of dead, communal sin offerings .... Temurah 15a-15b; Horayos 6a

Atonement of *Kohanim*, Yom Kippur .... Yoma 50b, 51b, 61a; Shevuos 13b-14a; Menachos 92a

Atonement of Yom Kippur in Temple .... Yoma 44a

Atonement, superficial, missing *mitzvah* in sacrificial service .... Zevachim 6a; Yoma 5a;
.... Menachos 93b

Atonement, superficial, sacrifice for positive commandment .... Zevachim 7b

When —

Atonement by suffering .... Berachos 5a-5b

Atonement, groom's sins .... Yevamos 63b

Atonement, sick person .... Nedarim 41a

Atonement, thing coming from transgression .... Temurah 20b

Atonement when attaining high position .... Sanhedrin 14a

Atonement, when we shall count on G-d .... Shabbos 89b

Misc. —

Atonement for dead .... Sanhedrin 47a-47b

Atonement for having reduced size of moon .... Chullin 60b

Attacking ship .... Bava Kama 97a

Attention when walking, damage .... Bava Kama 27b

Attestation

Attestation, mutual, trustworthiness .... Kesubos 24a; Avodah Zarah 61b

Attestation of divorce certificate .... Gittin 9a

Attestation of legal document

Attestation of legal document, acknowledging .... Kesubos 19a; Bava Basra 154a-155a, 170a;
.... Shabbos 78b-79a; Bava Metzia 7a, 72b

Attestation of legal document, cases .... Kesubos 20a-21a

Attestation of legal document, contents .... Bava Basra 52b

Attestation of legal document, empty line .... Bava Basra 163a-163b

Attestation of legal document, judges .... Kesubos 21a-22a

Attestation of legal document, minor .... Kesubos 28a

Attestation of legal document, Rabbinical .... Kesubos 21b, 28a; Gittin 15b

Attestation of legal document, reading .... Kesubos 109a
Attestation of legal document, relative .... Bava Basra 57a
Attestation of legal document, who may .... Bava Metzia 20b
Attic of Chananiah, Book of Ezekiel .... Shabbos 13b; Chagigah 13a; Menachos 45a
Attitude
Attitude of piety, fraud .... Bava Metzia 52b
Attitude of Sodom, refusing even when not losing .... Bava Kama 20a-21a; Eruvin 49a;
.... Kesubos 103a; Bava Basra 12b, 59a, 168a
Attributes
Attributes, G-d's, oath .... Shevuos 35b
Attribute of piety, fraud .... Bava Metzia 52b
Attribute of Sodom, refusing even when not losing .... Bava Kama 20a-21a; Eruvin 49a;
.... Kesubos 103a; Bava Basra 12b, 59a, 168a
Attribute of justice
Attribute of justice, mourning .... Moed Katan 27b
Attribute of justice, what differences are there .... Sanhedrin 111b
Attributes of justice and compassion .... Rosh Hashanah 17b
Attributing
Attributing bad occurrence to bad person .... Bava Basra 109b
Attributing to one's own merit .... Berachos 10b
Attributing to other cause .... see **Doubt**, page 176
Atuna .... see **Athens, Rabbi Yehoshua**, page 35
Auction
Auction, sale by widow .... Kesubos 98a
Auction to redeem consecrated item .... Arachin 21b-22a, 27a-27b
Audacity, oath .... Shevuos 42b; Kesubos 18a; Gittin 51b
Authorities
Authorities, do not get close to .... Avos 1:10
Authority .... see also **Leadership**, page 356
Authority buries those who attain it .... Yoma 86b
Authority, distance and damages .... Avos 1:10, 2:3
Authority given by *Reish Galusa* .... Sanhedrin 5a
Authority, keeping away from .... Avodah Zarah 17a; Sanhedrin 14a, 92a
Authority of Sages, episode concerning collapse .... Berachos 60a; Kesubos 62a
Authority of Sages to annul commandment .... Yevamos 89b-90b
Authority of *beis din*
Authority of *beis din*, decrees to strengthen .... Yevamos 67b, 90b; Kesubos 99b, 100a-100b;
.... Gittin 33a-34a
Authority of *beis din*, Divine endorsement .... Yerushalmi Nedarim 23b
Authority of *beis din*, heirs .... Kiddushin 42a-42b
Authority of *beis din*, mistake .... Kesubos 100a-100b
Authorization .... see *Semichah*, page 600
Av, month of mourning .... Yevamos 43a-43b; Taanis 26b, 29b
Avak
Avak lashon hara .... Bava Basra 164b-165a; Arachin 15b-16a
Avak ribbis is not returned .... Bava Metzia 61b-62b, 67a; Temurah 6a-6b
Avak sheviis, punishment .... Kiddushin 20a-20b; Succah 40b; Arachin 30b
Avar z'mano .... see **Past its time**, page 475
Avdan, episode .... Yevamos 105b

Aveidah .... *see* **Lost item**, page 378
Aveilus .... *see* **Mourning**, page 427
Aveirah .... *see* **Transgression**, page 700
Avel ein lo peh .... *see* **Mourner cannot speak**, page 427
Avenger
   Avenger, exile .... Makos 10b, 12a; Sanhedrin 49a
   Avenger, intentional murderer .... Sanhedrin 49a
   Avenger, murderer came out of City of Refuge .... Makos 12a
   Avenger, murderer on the way to City of Refuge .... Makos 10b
Average
   Average land, closing door before borrowers .... Bava Kama 8a
   Average land, collecting ...... Gittin 49b, 50a; Bava Kama 7b-8a; Kesubos 110a
   Average men, we are .... Berachos 61b
   Average people, resurrection .... Rosh Hashanah 16b-17a
Avid dina lenafshei .... *see* **Self help**, page 599
Avim, clouds .... Taanis 6b
Avim
   Avim, Philistine chiefs .... Chullin 60b
   Avim, reason for their name .... Chullin 60b
Avimi son of Rabbi Avuhu, *melaveh d'malkah* meal .... Shabbos 119b
Avimi
   Avimi, forgot his learning .... Menachos 7a
   Avimi hit Rav Chisda .... Menachos 7a; Arachin 22a
   Avimi, Pumbedisa's sharp ones .... Sanhedrin 17b
   Avimi tested Eifa .... Shevuos 28b-29a
Avinu
   Avinu, G-d .... Berachos 35b
   Avinu Malkeinu, Rabbi Akiva .... Taanis 25b
Avnet .... *see* **Belt**, page 52
Avodah zarah .... *see* **Idolatry**, page 295
Avodah .... *see* **Service**, page 603; *see also* **Work**, page 760
Avoid disturbances in house of study .... Eruvin 60a; Avodah Zarah 74b
Avon, willful sin .... Yoma 36b; Krisos 25b
Avos
   Avos Beis Din, pairs of Sages .... Chagigah 16a-16b
   Avos Melachos, list .... Shabbos 73a
   Avos Melachos, number .... Shabbos 49b
   Avos Hatumah, levels .... Keilim 1:1-4; Bava Kama 2a-2b
Avos nezikin .... *see* **Primary categories of damage**, page 504
Avos .... *see* **Patriarchs**, page 475
Avreich, kingship .... Bava Basra 4a
Avtalyon, pairs .... Chagigah 16a
Avuha bar Ihi, food for servant .... Kesubos 61a
Avuha DeShmuel
   Avuha DeShmuel, Abba bar Abba .... Berachos 18b
   Avuha deShmuel, deposit .... Berachos 18b
   Avuha deShmuel, Divine Presence in synagogue .... Megillah 29a
   Avuha DeShmuel, his daughters .... Shabbos 65a-65b
   Avuha DeShmuel, his granddaughters' captivity .... Kesubos 23a

Awe and fear, learning.. Berachos 22a; Moed Katan 15a

Awesome, "from those who sanctify You".. Zevachim 115b

Ax

    Ax, learning Torah not for Heaven's sake... Nedarim 62a; Avos 4:5

    Ax, purity of Pesach lamb.. Pesachim 70a-70b; Shekalim 8:3

Ayah... *see* **Buzzard, long distance vision**, page 83

Ayalah... *see* **Deer**, page 157

Ayalah (an expert on blemishes of first born animals).. Bechoros 29a

Ayef, need to wash oneself.. Yoma 77a

Ayil venafik azuzei.. *see* **Sale on credit, buyer refuses to pay**, page 585

Ayin hara.. *see* **Evil eye**, page 204

Ayin yafah.. *see* **Generosity**, page 248

Aylonis, significance.. Kesubos 11a

Az kanamer.. *see* **Strong as a leopard**, page 659

Az panim.. *see* **Impudent**, page 300

Azazel... *see* **Goat to Azazel**, page 253

Azharah mikal vachomer.............................. *see* **Deduction, prohibition from "all the more so,"** page 156

Azharah... *see* **Warning in Torah**, page 731

B

Ba bemachteres .... *see* **Surreptitiously coming, page 665**
Ba ladun bidvar chadash .... *see* **Deduction, exceptional law, page 156**
Ba laolam .... *see* **Existing already, page 209**
Ba letaher, mesayin .... *see* **Comes to purify himself, page 115**
Ba min haklal .... *see* **Deduction, law being exception to rule, page 156**
Ba zeh velimed al zeh .... *see* **Deduction, worker and employee, page 155**
Baal chov .... *see* **Borrower, page 73;** *see also* **Lender, page 363**
Baal hanes lo makir niso .... *see* **Miracle, one who experiences it is not aware, page 413**
Baal keishto .... *see* **Husband like his wife, page 289**
Baal mum .... *see* **Blemished animal, page 62**
Baalei amanah .... *see* **Trustworthy men, page 705**
Baalei chaim .... *see* **Animal, page 24**
Baalei teshuvah .... *see* **Repenting people, page 559**
Babos, one *maseches* .... Bava Kama 102a

Baby
   Baby born, overriding Shabbos .... Shabbos 129b
   Baby, danger if does not drink milk .... Yevamos 114a
   Baby, dead, put under bed .... Berachos 8b; Pesachim 112b
   Baby, distance from his excrement .... Succah 42b
   Baby, eating wheat .... Berachos 40a
   Baby found, doubt about lineage .... Kesubos 15b
   Baby having animal form, can he live? .... Niddah 23a-23b
   Baby, healing on Shabbos .... Shabbos 66b, 123a-123b, 147b

Babylon
  Aggadah —
   Babylon, abundance .... Taanis 10a, 29b
   Babylon, advantage of dwelling in .... Kesubos 111a
   Babylon, *aggadah* .... Sanhedrin 24a; Zevachim 113b
   Babylon, curse .... Berachos 57b-58a; Sanhedrin 109a
   Babylon, illnesses .... Kesubos 77b
   Babylon, joy on festivals .... Shabbos 145b
   Babylon, mixed with Mishnah .... Sanhedrin 24a
  Laws —
   Babylon, blessings .... Berachos 57b

B

Babylon, communal fast days .... Taanis 11b, 12b
Babylon, divorce certificates .... Gittin 6a-6b
Babylon immigrants, lineage .... Kiddushin 69b-70a, 71b
Babylon, lineage .... Kiddushin 69b, 71a-72a; Kesubos 111a
Misc. —
Babylon, Bursif .... Shabbos 36a-36b; Succah 34a
Babylon, exorbitant taxes .... Shabbos 149b-150a
Babylon, frontiers .... Gittin 6a-6b; Kiddushin 71b, 72a
Babylon, precision in speech .... Gittin 65b
Babylon and _Eretz Yisrael_
Babylon and _Eretz Yisrael_, clothes .... Shabbos 145b
Babylon and _Eretz Yisrael_, hate .... Yoma 66b; Menachos 100a
Babylon and _Eretz Yisrael_, pleasant .... Sanhedrin 24a
Babylon and _Eretz Yisrael_, Sages .... Taanis 23b; Megillah 28b; Chullin 122a
Babylon and _Eretz Yisrael_, tough temperament .... Taanis 23b; Chullin 122a
Babylonians
Babylonians, raw meat .... Menachos 100a
Babylonians, foolish, bread .... Nedarim 49b; Beitzah 16a
Babylonians, foolish, obscure explanations ..... Pesachim 34b; Yoma 57a; Zevachim 60b; Menachos 52a
Babylonians, foolish, went to _Eretz Yisrael_ .... Kesubos 75a
Bachelor
Bachelor, forbidden jobs .... Kiddushin 82a
Bachelor in city, G-d proclaims .... Pesachim 113a-113b
Bachurei Yisrael .... see **Young men of Israel**, page 774
Backs toward G-d's _Heichal_ .... Yoma 76b-77a; Kiddushin 72b; Succah 53b
Bad
Bad .... see also **Harmful**, page 270
Bad affair, episode .... Bava Kama 99b
Bad is not good, sun .... Shabbos 129a
Bad news, faith .... Berachos 60a
Bad news, tearing garment .... Moed Katan 26a
Bad occurrence, ascribed to bad person .... Bava Basra 109b
Bad on good, separating _terumah_ .... Yevamos 89a-89b; Terumos 3:1; Kiddushin 46b, 46b;
                                                        Bava Metzia 56a; Bava Basra 84b, 143a; Temurah 5a
Bad payment, reimbursing little by little .... Bava Metzia 77b
Bad reputation, not to remarry her after divorce .... Gittin 45b-46b; Yevamos 25a; Kesubos 74b
Bad thing, not to answer .... Megillah 15a; Avodah Zarah 10b
Bad wife .... see **Wife, bad**, page 745
Bad women, stories .... Yevamos 63b; Sanhedrin 22b
Bad smell
Bad smell, distance .... Berachos 25a
Bad smell, distance from city .... Bava Basra 25a
Bad smell, sneezing .... Berachos 24b
Bad spirit
Bad spirit, food .... Niddah 17a
Bad spirit, under bed .... Pesachim 112a
Bad spirit, washing hands .... Shabbos 108b-109a; Pesachim 111b-112a
Bad spirit, water .... Pesachim 111a

Bad
Bad, item to hang others upon .... Bava Metzia 24a
Bad, linen .... Yoma 71b

Baderech sherotzeh leilech .... see **Way on which one wants to go**, page 737

Bag
Bag and purse, lending .... Bava Metzia 27b
Bag for *tefillin*, holiness .... Berachos 23b-24a

Bagrus .... see **Adulthood**, page 12

Baha, Amora .... Temurah 29a

Bahul al mamono .... see **Hurry, worried for one's money**, page 289

Baker
Baker, man without field must depend on him .... Menachos 103b-104a
Baker's utensils, impurity .... Keilim 15:2-5; Eduyos 7:7

Baking, crust .... Shabbos 19b-20a, 37b

Baki .... see **Knowledgeable**, page 344

Bakol
Bakol, Abraham's daughter .... Bava Basra 16b, 141a
Bakol mikol kol, Avos blessing .... Bava Basra 16b

Balaam
Balaam, advice to Pharaoh .... Sanhedrin 106a
Balaam, bad blessing .... Taanis 20a; Sanhedrin 105b-106a
Balaam, blessings and prophecies .... Sanhedrin 105b-106a
Balaam, daughters of Moab .... Sanhedrin 106a
Balaam, death .... Sanhedrin 106a-106b
Balaam, enemy's kisses .... Sanhedrin 105b
Balaam, *Gehinnom* .... Gittin 57a
Balaam, general .... Sanhedrin 105a-105b
Balaam, his age .... Sanhedrin 106b
Balaam, one-eyed .... Niddah 31a
Balaam, preventing G-d's anger .... Berachos 7a; Avodah Zarah 4a-4b; Sanhedrin 105b
Balaam, privacy of tents entrances .... Bava Basra 60a
Balaam, three traits .... Avos 5:19

Bal talin .... see **Paying on time**, page 470

Bal tashchis .... see **Waste**, page 734

Bal te'acher .... see **Delay**, page 157

Bal teshaktzu .... see **Repulsive acts**, page 561

Bal tigra .... see **Subtracting from commandments**, page 660

Bal tosif .... see **Adding to commandments**, page 11

Bal yachel .... see **Vow, not to transgress one's word**, page 726

Baladan son of Baladan .... Sanhedrin 96a

Balak, Ruth .... Nazir 23b

Bald on this side and that side .... Bava Kama 60b

Ball, unintentional murderer .... Sanhedrin 77b-78a

Bamah .... see **Private altar**, page 504

Bameh, to explain or to refute .... Eruvin 82a; Sanhedrin 24b-25a

Banei chayei umezonei .... see **Life, children and livelihood, fate**, page 369

Banim kesimanim .... see **Sons like signs**, page 644

Bank of river, *chazakah* .... Bava Metzia 108a

Bankrupt .... Kesubos 108b-109a

Banners of the Tribes in desert, public domain .... Shabbos 5a, 98a
Bar Avin, eulogy .... Moed Katan 25b
Bar bei Rav Dechad Yoma .... Chagigah 5b
Bar bei Rav dechad yoma .... *see* **Student for one day,** page 660
Bar Galil, lecture on Heavenly Chariot .... Shabbos 80b
Bar Hadia, dreams .... Berachos 56a-56b
Bar Kappara
    Bar Kappara, episode about oath .... Yevamos 32b
    Bar Kappara, Rebbi .... Nedarim 50b-51a
    Bar Kappara, Rebbi's rebuke .... Moed Katan 16a
    Bar Kappara, scoffing disciple .... Berachos 39a
Bar Kipok, his foot .... Moed Katan 25b
Bar Kochba .... Sanhedrin 93b
Bar metzra .... *see* **Neighbor,** page 441
Bar Mitzvah
    Bar Mitzvah, Adar .... Arachin 31b
    Bar Mitzvah, age .... Niddah 45b; Avos 5:21
    Bar Mitzvah, Pesach Sheni .... Pesachim 93a
Bar Nafcha, Rabbi Yochanan .... Bava Metzia 85b
Bar Nassan ruled after Rav Ashi .... Moed Katan 28a
Bar Orian
    Bar Orian and illustrious lineage .... Menachos 53a
    Bar Orian, standing before .... Shabbos 31b
Bar Shatia, fool at times .... Kesubos 20a; Yevamos 31a-31b
Bar Shishach, non-Jewish festival .... Avodah Zara 65a
Bar Yochni, episode .... Bechoros 57b
Bara, in the past .... Berachos 52b
Barak, excommunication of Meroz .... Shevuos 36a; Moed Katan 16a
Barbarians .... Yevamos 63b
Barber, non-Jew and for non-Jew .... Avodah Zara 29a
Barchi Nafshi
    Barchi Nafshi, David .... Berachos 10a
    Barchi Nafshi, wicked .... Berachos 10a
Barchu es Hashem Hamevorach .... Berachos 50a
Barefoot, patched shoes .... Yoma 77a
Bareheaded, prohibition for man .... Kiddushin 31a
Bari Veshema .... *see* **Certainty and doubt,** page 91
Bari, judges' oath .... Bava Metzia 2b
Barkai, dawn .... Yoma 28a-28b; Menachos 100a
Barley
    Barley, cure .... Nedarim 41b
    Barley given to Rabbi Elazar .... Kesubos 77a
    Barley, meal offering .... Menachos 60b
    Barley, *omer* .... Menachos 68b, 84a
    Barley, quantity .... Keilim 17:8
    Barley to animal, pure language .... Pesachim 3b
Barn, dimensions .... Bava Basra 98b
Barrel
    Barrel and beam, damage .... Bava Kama 31b-32a

Barrel and jug, purchase..Bava Kama 27a-27b
Barrel, breaking on Shabbos.......................................Beitzah 33b; Shabbos 146a
Barrel, impurity of corpse...Oholos 9:16
Barrel, liability of who moves..Bava Metzia 82b-83a
Barrel of workers, episode...Bava Metzia 83a
Barrel on Shabbos, works..Shabbos 74b
Barrel, opening on Shabbos...Shabbos 146a-146b
Barrel, plugging on Shabbos..Shabbos 141a
Barrel which opened, mixture..Zevachim 74b
Bars in tabernacle...Shabbos 98b
Barter
Barter, cases of purchase..Kiddushin 28a-28b
Barter, donkey for cow..Bava Metzia 47a
Barter, fruit..Bava Metzia 46b-47b
Barter, money.................Bava Metzia 45b-46b, 47a; Kiddushin 28a
Barter, purchase of field..Kiddushin 13a
Barter, utensil...Bava Metzia 46b-47b
Baruch...*see* **Blessed**, page 722
Blessings —
Baruch Dayan Haemes...Berachos 60a
Baruch Hamakom Shearago...................................Shabbos 13b
Baruch Hamavdil, issue of Shabbos.................Shabbos 150b
Baruch Hashem, Jethro...Sanhedrin 94a
Baruch Hashem yom yom, Hillel............................Beitzah 16a
Baruch Rofe Cholim..Berachos 60a
Baruch Shehechezarta Avedasi................Avodah Zarah 52b
Baruch Shelo Nassa Panim.......................................Shabbos 13b
Misc. —
Baruch ata ba'ir...Bava Metzia 107a
Baruch, beginning and end of blessings.........Berachos 11a, 46a; Pesachim 104b-105a; Kesubos 7b
Baruch Hu Uvaruch Shemo..Yoma 37a
Baruch Shem in *Shema*..Pesachim 56a
Baruch Shem, in Temple..........................Berachos 63a; Taanis 16b
Baruch Hu Uvaruch Shemo........*see* **Blessed be He and blessed be His name**, page 62
Barzilai the Gileadite...Avodah Zarah 38b
Bas kol..*see* **Divine voice**, page 169
Bas
Bas mitzvah, age...Niddah 45b
Bas Nadiv, Abraham............................Succah 49b; Chagigah 3a
Bas ploni leploni..Moed Katan 18b
Bas, quantity...Menachos 77a
Bas Yaanah, writing...Chullin 64b-65a
Bas ploni leploni.........*see* **Daughter of so-and-so to so-and-so**, page 145
Bas talmid chacham.................*see* **Daughter of scholar**, page 145
Base of utensils, impurity..Keilim 25:6
Baseless hatred
Baseless hatred, Jerusalem...Yoma 9b
Baseless hatred, punishment..Shabbos 32b
Bashful one to *Gan Eden*...Avos 5:20

Bashfulness, Jews' characteristic .... Nedarim 20a
Basilica, idolatrous .... Avodah Zarah 16b
Basin
 Basin in Temple .... Zevachim 21b-22a, 58b-59a; Yoma 37a
 Basin in Temple, place .... Middos 3:6; Zevachim 59a
 Basin, *mikveh* .... Gittin 15b-16a; Avodah Zarah 72a
Basis (base or support)
 Basis, cases .... Shabbos 44b-45a, 142b
 Basis, dusk .... Shabbos 44b-45a
 Basis to fire, lamp .... Shabbos 46b-47a
 Basis to forbidden and permitted item, *muktzeh* .... Shabbos 47a, 117a, 120b, 125b, 141b; Beitzah 21b
Basket
 Basket, brought in private domain .... Eruvin 33b; Shabbos 5a, 101a
 Basket full of books .... Megillah 28b
 Basket in sky, episode .... Bava Basra 74a
 Basket in street, private domain .... Shabbos 8a
 Basket of peddler, Rabbi Yochanan ben Nuri .... Gittin 67a
 Basket of spices, Rabbi Elazar ben Azariah .... Gittin 67a
 Basket, partly carrying out on Shabbos .... Shabbos 91b-92a
Bassar aniya azla aniyusa .... *see* **Poverty pursues pauper**, page 496
Bassar basra .... *see* **Last use**, page 354
Bassar Bechalav .... *see* **Meat with milk**, page 399
Bassar, meaning according to initials .... Sotah 5a
Bassheva .... *see* **Bathsheba**, page 45
Basyah
 Basyah, conversion .... Sotah 12a-12b
 Basyah, Moses and Caleb .... Megillah 13a
 Basyah, sent her hand .... Sotah 12b
Bas .... *see* **Daughter**, page 144; *see also* **Girl**, page 251
Bat, eyeless .... Sanhedrin 98b
Batei irei chomah .... *see* **House in walled city**, page 287
Batei nirin, Shabbos work .... Shabbos 105a
Bath, virgin became pregnant in bath .... Chagigah 14b-15a
Bathhouse
 Bathhouse and oil press, sale .... Bava Basra 67b-68a, 78b
 Bathhouse, danger .... Pesachim 112b
 Bathhouse, episode concerning collapse .... Berachos 60a; Kesubos 62a
 Bathhouse, health .... Shabbos 41a
 Bathhouse heated with straw of Sabbatical year .... Sheviis 8:11
 Bathhouse, idolatrous .... Avodah Zarah 44b, 51b
 Bathhouse, modesty .... Shabbos 41a
 Bathhouse, prayer and learning ...... Avodah Zarah 44b Berachos 24b, 26a Shabbos 10a-10b, 40b, 150a;
                  Kiddushin 33a Zevachim 102b
 Bathhouse, prayer and thanksgiving .... Berachos 60a
 Bathhouse, quickly growing plants .... Avodah Zarah 38b
Bathing
 Bathing in teacher's presence .... Pesachim 51a
 Bathing, is it recommended .... Shabbos 50b
 Bathing with relatives .... Pesachim 51a

B

Bati, Shvor Malka .... Avodah Zarah 76b

Bathsheba

Bathsheba, David's mistakes .... Shabbos 56a

Bathsheba, David's trial .... Sanhedrin 107a-107b

Bathsheba, her father's age at her birth .... Sanhedrin 69b

Bathsheba, rebuke to Solomon .... Sanhedrin 70b

Bathsheba, Urijah's divorce certificate .... Shabbos 56a; Kesubos 9a-9b

Bava ben Butha, candles .... Nedarim 66b

Bava Kama and **Bava Metzia,** *mesechtos nezikin* .... Bava Kama 102a; Avodah Zarah 7a

Bavel .... *see* **Babylon**, page 39

Bavliim .... *see* **Babylonians**, page 40

Bazichim of Temple .... Pesachim 64b

Be

Be among Aaron's disciples .... Avos 1:12

Be diligent to learn .... Avos 2:14; Sanhedrin 38b

Be in your own eyes like a wicked .... Niddah 30b

Be innocent .... *see* **Appearance**, page 30

Be strong as a leopard .... Avos 5:20

Be tail to lions .... Avos 4:15

Be careful

Be careful in *Shema* .... Avos 2:13

Be careful lest they learn to lie .... Avos 1:8

Be careful, lenient commandment .... Avos 2:1

Be careful of a Sage who forgot .... Berachos 8b

Be careful of Nachmani and his Torah .... Pesachim 112b

Be careful of Rabbi Akiva .... Kiddushin 81a

Be careful of your friend's honor .... Berachos 28b

Be careful, scribe .... Sotah 20a

Beam

Beam and barrel, damage .... Bava Kama 31b-32a

Beam in forest or in city, same price .... Bava Kama 11a

Beam on pit, partition .... Eruvin 86a-86b

Beam stolen, decree .... Gittin 55a; Succah 31a

Beams, *muktzeh* .... Beitzah 2b, 31a-31b; Shabbos 157a

Beams of figs, how to obtain them .... Tamid 29b-30a

Beams of my house never saw my garments .... Shabbos 118b

Beams of Rabbi Chanina ben Dosa .... Taanis 25a

Beams, tent of dead .... Oholos 12:5, 12:6-7; Succah 22a

Beam for closed alley

Beam for closed alley, at an angle .... Eruvin 8b

Beam for closed alley, closed alley opened to land .... Shabbos 6a-6b; Eruvin 12b

Beam for closed alley, from idolatrous tree .... Eruvin 80b

Beam for closed alley, higher than twenty .... Eruvin 2a-3b; Succah 2a

Beam for closed alley, how .... Eruvin 13b-14a

Beam for closed alley, out of closed alley .... Eruvin 8b-9a

Beam for closed alley, repairing closed alley .... Eruvin 2b, 11b-12b; Shabbos 117a-117b

Beam for closed alley, why is it effective? .... Eruvin 3a, 5a, 8b, 12b

Beams for closed alley, combining .... Succah 18a, 22a-22b; Eruvin 14a

B

Bean
Bean, size of blood stain ....Niddah 58b-59a
Bean, size of leprous marks ....Negaim 6:1-4
Beans, wording of vow ....Nedarim 53b

Bear
Bear, Persians ....Kiddushin 72a; Megillah 11a; Avodah Zarah 2b
Bears and children, Elisha ....Sotah 46b-47a

Beard
Beard, "your beard is long" ....Berachos 11a
Beard, beauty of man's face ....Shabbos 152a
Beard, cantor ....Chullin 24b
Beard, leprous mark ....Negaim 10:9
Beard of grave diggers ....Bava Basra 58a
Beard, shaving ....Makos 20b, 21a
Beard, with which item is it forbidden to shave ...... Makos 20b-21a; Nazir 40b, 58b; Kiddushin 35b
Beard, Joseph's brothers did not recognize him ....Yevamos 88a; Kesubos 27b; Bava Metzia 39b

Bearing grudge and revenging ....Yoma 23a

Beast
Beast and animals, names ....Kilayim 8:5-6
Beast in milk ....Chullin 116a
Beast, included in "animals" category ....Chullin 59a, 70b-71a, 84a; Nedarim 81a; Nazir 35b;
                                                                             Bava Kama 17b, 54b; Zevachim 115b
Beast, its signs ....Chullin 59a-59b
Beast, prohibition to offer as sacrifice ....Zevachim 34a
Beast, wild, for which sin ....Avos 5:9
Beasts, work ....Avodah Zarah 16b

Beating grain
Beating grain, peeling on Shabbos ....Beitzah 13b
Beating grain, plants ....Shabbos 75a
Beating grain, secondary category of work ....Shabbos 73b
Beating grain, unusual manner ....Kesubos 60a; Yevamos 114a

Beautiful
"Beautiful man in Israel," why mention "Israel" ....Arachin 13b-14a
Beautiful, esrog ....Succah 31a-31b
Beautiful, lulav ....Succah 29b, 31a
Beautiful women in Tanach ....Megillah 15a; Bava Basra 58a; Sanhedrin 39b

Beautiful captive
Beautiful captive, David's warriors ....Kiddushin 76b; Sanhedrin 21a
Beautiful captive, general ....Yevamos 47b-48b; Kiddushin 21b-22a
Beautiful captives, David ....Sanhedrin 21a

Beautify
Beautify yourself before Him by commandments ....Shabbos 133b; Succah 11b; Nazir 2b
Beautifying commandment ....see **Hiddur**, page 278

Beauty
Beauty, disturbance for learning ....Nedarim 50b
Beauty of Japheth, Greek language ....Megillah 9b
Beauty of non-Jew, prohibition to praise ....Avodah Zarah 20a; Arachin 14a
Beauty of Rabbi Eliezer's sons ....Nedarim 20b
Beauty of righteous men ....Bava Metzia 84a; Berachos 5b; Bava Basra 58a

Beauty of woman, how..Shabbos 80b; Kesubos 59b
Beauty spot, women's blemishes..Kesubos 75a
Beauty will wither in grave, Rabbi Yochanan.......................................Berachos 5b
Because
Because I am a male I lost?..........................Kesubos 108b; Bava Basra 139b, 140b
Because of change, majority..Bechoros 42b
Because of commandment carried out with item................................Berachos 39b
Because of first dispensation, impurity...Pesachim 95b-96a
Because of first dispensation, prohibition......Yevamos 7b-8a; Zevachim 32b; Menachos 9b, 43a, 45a;
....Arachin 3b
Because of the snake..Shabbos 55b
Because of, thought in sacrifice..Pesachim 62a, 62b
Because, preparing food on Yom Tov...............Pesachim 46b-48a, 62a; Beitzah 21a
Because, Sage's expression...Pesachim 114b
Bechor..*see* **Firstborn**, page 226
Bed
Bed and coins, *muktzeh*...Shabbos 44b-45a
Bed, Aramean placed deceased man under bed............Berachos 8b; Pesachim 112b
Bed, dismantled, impurity...Succah 16a; Keilim 18:9
Bed, episode about dirtying...Shabbos 46a-46b
Bed, food underneath...Pesachim 112a
Bed, impurity of couch...Keilim 18:3-5
Bed, impurity of part of bed..Succah 16a; Keilim 18:5
Bed, north and south..Berachos 5b
Bed of married woman, prohibition to sit on it..............................Shabbos 140b
Bed of Rav, Rav Kahana hid underneath..Berachos 62a
Bed of Sage...Bava Basra 58a
Bed on which Torah scroll is put............................Menachos 32b; Moed Katan 25a
Bed, sleeping with one's daughter.........................Kiddushin 81b; Berachos 24a
Bed, support for succah...Succah 21b
Bed turned upside down, mourner..........................Moed Katan 15a, 26b-27a
Bed under *s'chach*...Succah 10b-11a, 20b-21b
Bed, vow, what is included..Nedarim 56a-56b
Bed with canopy, tent in succah..Succah 10b-11a, 19b
Bed with others, *Shema*..Berachos 24a
Bededami....................................*see* ***Agunah***, presumption declaration, page 15
Bedek habayis.................................*see* **Temple Treasury, sacrifice**, page 679
Bedek habayis, sacrifice..................Temurah 6b, 13a; Yoma 63b; Zevachim 113b
Bedikas chametz.............................*see* **Searching for *chametz***, page 594
Beehive
Beehive, hunting on Shabbos..Beitzah 36a-36b
Beehive, impurity of food...Bava Basra 80a-80b
Beehive in tent of corpse..Oholos 9:1-14
Beehive, large, *muktzeh*..Shabbos 35a
Beehive like land.............Bava Basra 65b-66a, 80b; Sheviis 10:7; Shabbos 95a; Uktzin 3:10
Beehive on Shabbos, works..Shabbos 74b
Beehive, private domain...Shabbos 8a
Beehive upside down, *lavud*..Shabbos 8a
Beer...*see* **Alcoholic beverage**, page 18

Bees

Bees and mustard, chasing away .... Bava Basra 18a-18b, 25b
Bees, castration to obtain honey .... Bava Basra 80a
Bees, leaving swarm .... Bava Basra 80a
Bees, saving one's bees with fellow's money .... Bava Kama 81b, 114b

Beet

Beet, blessing .... Berachos 39a
Beet, health .... Eruvin 28b-29a; Berachos 39a
Beets water, healing face .... Shabbos 133b-134a

Befanai nichtav .... *see* **Before me it was written**, page 48

Before

Before a blind (person) .... *see* **Stumbling-block**, page 660
Before commandment, blessing .... Pesachim 7b; Succah 39a
Before commandment, *tefillin* .... Menachos 35b
Before drinker, put wine .... Sotah 10a
Before G-d, how much more so .... Shabbos 74b
Before morning prayer, prohibitions .... Berachos 5b
Before morning prayer, saying *shalom* .... Berachos 14a
Before prayers, eating .... Berachos 28b; Shabbos 9b-10a
Before prayers, forbidden acts .... Shabbos 9b-10a; Berachos 28b; Succah 38a
Before Sabbatical year .... Sheviis 1:1-8, 2:1-6; Yevamos 83a; Rosh Hashanah 9b, 10b; Succah 34a, 44a;
.... Taanis 3a; Moed Katan 3b-4a; Bava Basra 26b-27a; Zevachim 110b
Before Temple destruction, bad omens .... Yoma 39b
Before, there is no "before" or "after" in the Torah .... Pesachim 6b
Before Whom you are toiling .... Avos 2:14
Before world, Creation .... Pesachim 54a; Nedarim 39b

Before him

Before him, testimony .... Bava Kama 112a-112b
Before him, testimony in *beis din* .... Sanhedrin 79b

Before me it was written

Before me it was written, general .... Gittin 2a-3a, 5b-6a, 9a, 15a-17a, 86a; Bava Metzia 55b
Before me it was written, married without .... Gittin 5a-5b, 86a; Bava Metzia 55b
Before me it was written, who and when .... Gittin 4a-6b, 16b, 24a
Before praying man, not to pass .... Berachos 27a

Before time

Before time, animal and its young .... Chullin 80b-81b
Before time, Azazel .... Yoma 63b-64a
Before time, eight and thirty days .... Parah 1:4
Before time, *nazir* and *zav* .... Chagigah 9b
Before time, on same day .... Menachos 5a; Yoma 62b; Zevachim 12a
Before time, outside sacrifices .... Yoma 62b-63a; Zevachim 114a-115b
Before time, secular use .... Meilah 12a
Before time, tithe .... Bechoros 21a-21b, 56a, 57b; Temurah 19b

Begging at doors, how much will charity collector give .... Bava Basra 9a

Beginning

"Beginning of wisdom is fear of G-d" .... Berachos 17a
Beginning and end of Mishnah, two reasons .... Sanhedrin 62b; Bava Metzia 41a
Beginning and end of sentence, contradiction .... Pesachim 59b-60b
Beginning, because of end .... Nedarim 72a

Beginning commandment, completing it..Sotah 13b

Beginning in pain, suffering..Kiddushin 40b

Beginning of *Adar*, joy..Taanis 29a

Beginning of *Av*, reducing joy..Taanis 29b

Beginning of intimate relations makes *kiddushin*............................Kiddushin 10a-10b

Beginning of judgment, Torah.............................Sanhedrin 7a; Kiddushin 40b

Beginning of Mishnah, added because of end...........Zevachim 91b; Shabbos 30a; Eruvin 16a;

............Yevamos 98a, 102a; Kesubos 90a; Nedarim 28b, 72a; Nazir 21b-22a; Bava Kama 49b, 94b;

............Bava Metzia 62b; Sanhedrin 57a; Chullin 68a, 1'09b; Bechoros 46b

Beginning of Mishnah, explained first...........................Nedarim 2b-3a; Nazir 2a-2b

Beginning with negligence..................Bava Kama 21b, 56a, 58a-58b; Bava Metzia 36b, 42a, 93a

Beginning with negligence, damaging field by amniotic liquid.............Bava Kama 58a-58b

Behavior

Behavior, according to religion of Moses and *Yehudis*....................Kesubos 72a-72b

Behavior, pleasant...Kesubos 17a

Beheima, included in chayah category.............Chullin 70b-71a, 84a; Nedarim 81a; Bava Kama 17b

Behind

Behind a lion, better than behind a woman..Berachos 61a

Behind a synagogue...Berachos 6b

Behind a woman, better than behind a non-Jew.....................................Berachos 61a

Behind doors of *Heichal*, gold...Middos 4:1

Behind G-d you shall walk...Sotah 14a

Behind Heavenly curtain, decrees...Berachos 18b

Behonos metzora..*see* **Toes, leper**, page 695

Bein

Bein Haarbayim, explanation...Zevachim 11b

Bein Hazemanim, Nissan and *Tishrei*..Berachos 35b

Bein hashmashos..*see* **Dusk**, page 183

Bein hazemanim..................................*see* **Interval**, *Nissan* and *Tishrei*, page 316

Bein Ulam lamizbeach...............................*see* **Between** *Ulam* **and Altar**, page 56

Beino lebeina..................................*see* **Between husband and wife, vows**, page 56

Beinonis...*see* **Average land**, page 37

Beis

Temple —

Beis Avtinas and *Hanitzutz*...Tamid 25b; Middos 1:1

Beis Chonyo..............................Megillah 10a; Avodah Zarah 52b; Menachos 109a, 109b

Beis Chonyo, disqualified items...Avodah Zarah 52b

Beis Hadeshen, three..Zevachim 104b

Beis Haeven, staying in for Red Heifer..Yoma 2a

Beis Hamitbachayim, Temple..Middos 3:5

Beis Hamokad in Temple, sleep..Tamid 26b

Beis Hamokad, room in Temple.....................Yoma 15b-16a, 17a-17b; Middos 1:5-9

Beis Haparvah, immersion..Yoma 34b-35a

Beis Hapras, checking...............................Bechoros 29a; Oholos 18:4-5; Chagigah 25b

Beis Pagi, out of Temple Courtyard..............................Menachos 78b; Pesachim 63b

Beis She'an, its fruit..Eruvin 19a

Beis She'an, tithe...Chullin 6b-7a

Beis Yaazek...Rosh Hashanah 23b

B

Misc. —

Beis geim yissach Hashem, house of idolaters .... Berachos 58b

Beis hashlachin, explanation .... Bava Basra 68a-68b

Beis Hatzevitah, explanation .... Chagigah 22b

Beis Hatzevitah, utensils .... Keilim 25:7-9

Beis kur, does not correspond to its name .... Bava Metzia 104a; Bava Basra 7a

Beis achizah .... *see* **Handle**, page 268

Beis Avtinas

Beis Avtinas, incense .... Shekalim 5:1-2; Yoma 38a

Beis Avtinas refused to teach their skill .... Yoma 38a

Beis chomah .... *see* **House in walled city**, page 287

Beis din .... *see also* **Sacrifice for mistake**..., page 581, **Sanhedrin**, page 588; **Ruling**, page 574, **Judge**, page 327

How —

Beis din, commandment to appoint .... Sanhedrin 16b; Makos 7a

Beis din, even number of judges .... Sanhedrin 17a

Beis din, even number of judges in *Sanhedrin* .... Sanhedrin 3b

Beis din for each tribe .... Sanhedrin 16b

Beis din, odd number of judges .... Sanhedrin 3b

Beis din, out of *Eretz Yisrael* .... Makos 7a

Beis din sitting, parties must leave the rooms .... Sanhedrin 30a

Monetary matters —

Beis din, fraud .... Kiddushin 42b; Kesubos 99b, 100a-100b

Beis din, free decision, doubt in monetary matters .... Bava Basra 35a; Kesubos 85b, 94a-94b

Beis din, free decision, two bills .... Kesubos 94a; Bava Basra 34b-35a

Beis din important, commitment to pay a fine .... Nedarim 27b

Beis din, orphans .... Bava Kama 36b-37a; Kiddushin 42a-42b; Yevamos 67b; Kesubos 100a; Gittin 34a

Beis din permission, damage .... Bava Kama 6a, 30a-30b, 62b, 81b; Bava Metzia 118b

Beis din who sold, warranty .... Kesubos 97a, 100a

Ruling —

Beis din, condition, redeeming communal sacrifice .... Shevuos 11a-12a; Kesubos 106b; Menachos 79b

Beis din, disciples forbidden to ask questions .... Bava Kama 96b

Beis din does not annul another *beis din*'s decree .... Avodah Zarah 36a; Megillah 2a;

.... Moed Katan 3b; Gittin 36b; Eduyos 1:5

Beis din, made a mistake .... Bava Basra 138b, 164a; Yevamos 106a; Kesubos 21a; Sanhedrin 30a

Beis din, permitting .... Avodah Zarah 37a; Eduyos 8:4

Time —

Beis din, Monday and Thursday .... Bava Kama 82a

Beis din, night .... Sanhedrin 34b; Yevamos 104a, 2"2 113b-114a; Niddah 50a

Beis din, on *chol haMoed* .... Moed Katan 14b

Beis din, on Shabbos eve .... Sanhedrin 35a

Beis din, prohibition in Shabbos .... Beitzah 36b

Beis din, time for sessions .... Shabbos 10a

Women —

Beis din, *chalitzah* .... Yevamos 101a-102a, 104a, 105b-106a

Beis din, warning .... Sotah 24a, 27a

Beis din, women not used to .... Gittin 41a

Misc. —

Beis din changing decision, causes disrespect .... Bava Basra 32a; Kesuvos 26b

Beis din, communal needs .... Shekalim 1:1-2

Beis din, consecrated money in collection box..Pesachim 90b; Eruvin 32a
Beis din, decrees..Yevamos 46b, 47b; Kiddushin 62b
Beis din, Divine Presence..Berachos 6a
Beis din of Shem..Avodah Zarah 36b
Beis din retracted, sacrifice..Horayos 3b-4a
Beis din, Sadducee, burned a woman..Sanhedrin 52b

Beis Garmu
Beis Garmu refused to teach their skill..Yoma 38a
Beis Garmu, showbread..Shekalim 5:1-2; Yoma 38a

Beis habaal vehashelachin..*see* **Field, irrigated or dependant only on rain**, page 221
Beis habliyah..*see* **Throat**, page 690
Beis hakiseh..*see* **Toilets**, page 695
Beis haknesses..*see* **Synagogue**, page 667
Beis hakosos..*see* **Reticulum**, page 563
Beis hamidrash..*see* **House of study**, page 287
Beis HaMikdash..*see* **Temple**, page 678
Beis hamitbachayim..*see* **Room for preparation of sacrifices, Temple**, page 571
Beis hapras..*see* **Field, doubtful impurity**, page 221
Beis hasetarim..*see* **Covered parts of body**, page 131
Beis Hillel..*see* **House of Hillel**, *halacha*, page 286
Beis kevaros..*see* **Cemetery**, page 90
Beis kibul..*see* **Clay utensil, container**, page 110
Beis shaar..*see* **Gatehouse**, page 245
Beis Shamai..*see* **House of Shamai**, page 286
Beis She'an..*see* **Beis She'an**, page 49
Beis sohar..*see* **Prison, Rabbi Eliezer**, page 504
Beis vaad lachachamim..*see* **Meeting place for Sages**, page 402

Beitar
Beitar, destruction..Gittin 57a-58a
Beitar, *Tisha B'Av*..Taanis 29a

Bekius..*see* **Knowledge**, page 344
Belaos..*see* **Worn out garments**, page 764

Believe
Believe, do not believe in yourself..Berachos 29a
Believing derogatory speech..Niddah 61a

Believers sons of believers..Shabbos 97a

Bell
Bell, carrying out on Shabbos..Shabbos 58a
Bell, impurity..Shabbos 58a-58b
Bells of horse, Jerusalem..Pesachim 50a
Bells on *Kohen Gadol*'s robe..Zevachim 88b

Belongings, possibility to consecrate..Bava Kama 69-69b; Arachin 20b-21a

Belongs to so-and-so, trustworthiness..Bava Basra 52a

Beloved
Beloved is Israel, agent..Yoma 52a
Beloved, Israel and man..Avos 3:14

Belshazzar
Belshazzar, Daniel..Sanhedrin 22a
Belshazzar, years of reign..Megillah 11b

B

B

Belt
Belt for prayer ....Shabbos 10a
Belt of Sage, king ....Zevachim 19a
Belt, priestly vestments ....Yoma 6a, 12b; Zevachim 18b-19a
Belt, wet, sickness ....Bava Metzia 113b
Bemakom chilul Hashem ....*see* **Desecration of G-d's Name, honor to teacher**, page 160
Bemakom she'ein ish ....*see* **Place where there is no man**, page 490
Ben Arza, Temple officers ....Shekalim 5:1-2

Ben Azzai
Ben Azzai, diligent ....Sotah 49b
Ben Azzai, "discussed in front of Sages" ....Sanhedrin 17b
Ben Azzai, entered Pardes ....Chagigah 14b
Ben Azzai, garlic peel ....Bechoros 58a
Ben Azzai, "I am like Ben Azzai" ....Kiddushin 20a
Ben Azzai, marriage ....Kesubos 63a; Yevamos 63b; Sotah 4b
Ben Azzai, Rabbi Akiva ....Bava Basra 158b
Ben Azzai, Rabbi Akiva's daughter ....Kesubos 63a
Ben Azzai, Rabbi Yishmael's disciple ....Chullin 71a
Ben Azzai, serving Rabbi Akiva ....Nedarim 74b
Ben Azzai, toilets ....Berachos 62a

Ben Bag Bag
Ben Bag Bag, "break his teeth" ....Bava Kama 27b
Ben Bag Bag, Turn it over, turn it over, all can be found in it (Torah) ....Avos 5:26
Ben bakar, age ....Parah 1:2; Rosh Hashanah 10a
Ben chorin haosek baTorah ....*see* **Free man, only by studying Torah**, page 239
Ben Dama, snake ....Avodah Zarah 27b
Ben Drusai ....Shabbos 20a, 36b; Avodah Zarah 38a; Menachos 57a
Ben Elassa, haircut ....Nedarim 51a; Sanhedrin 22b
Ben Hae Hae, according to the effort is the reward ....Avos 5:26

Ben Ish Chai
Ben Ish Chai ....Berachos 18a-19a
Ben Ish Chai, Benaiah ....Berachos 18a-19a
Ben Kamtzar refused to teach his skill ....Yoma 38a-38b
Ben Katin, openings of Temple basin ....Yoma 37a; Yoma 25b; Zevachim 21b

Ben Koziba
Ben Koziba ....Sanhedrin 93b
Ben Koziba, years of reign ....Sanhedrin 97b
Ben Nanas ....Bava Metzia 2b
Ben pekuah ....*see* **Animal found in mother's womb**, page 26
Ben Peturah, one jug of water ....Bava Metziah 62a
Ben Satda, sorcery ....Shabbos 104b

Ben Sira
Ben Sira, beautiful woman ....Yevamos 63b; Sanhedrin 100b
Ben Sira, commentaries and reading ....Sanhedrin 100b
Ben Sira, guest invites guest ....Bava Basra 98b
Ben sorer umoreh ....*see* **Rebellious son**, page 550
Ben tisha larishon ....*see* **Nine months old from first marriage**, page 445

Ben Torah
Ben Torah and illustrious lineage ....Menachos 53a

Ben Torah, standing before .... Shabbos 31b
Ben Tzitzis Hakesess .... Gittin 56a
Ben yomo, utensil .... Avodah Zarah 67b, 75b-76a
Ben Zoma
    Ben Zoma, "discussed in front of Sages" .... Sanhedrin 17b
    Ben Zoma, entered Pardes .... Chagigah 14b
    Ben Zoma, lecturer .... Sotah 49b
Benaiah ben Yehoyada
    Benaiah ben Yehoyada .... Berachos 18a-19a
    Benaiah ben Yehoyada, immersion .... Berachos 18b
Bench, partial damage .... Bava Kama 10b
Beneficial for one, detrimental for another organ .... Pesachim 42b
Benefit
    Benefit —
        Benefit, no benefit from slander .... Arachin 15b
        Benefit of partners, dividing .... Kesubos 93a-93b
        Benefit of storekeeper .... Bava Metzia 51b
        Benefit of storekeeper, Rabbi Yehudah .... Bava Metzia 40a-40b
    Consecrated items —
        Benefit from non-holy animal slaughtered in Temple Courtyard .... Kiddushin 57b-58a;
        .... Pesachim 22a
        Benefit from priestly garments .... Yoma 68b-69a; Tamid 27a
        Benefits from consecrated item Treasury, permitted .... Shekalim 7:5-7
    Corpse —
        Benefit, ash of corpse .... Temurah 34a
        Benefit from corpse .... Avodah Zarah 29b
        Benefit from corpse's hair .... Arachin 7b
        Benefit from grave .... Sanhedrin 47b
        Benefit from shrouds .... Yevamos 66b
    Idolatry —
        Benefit from idolatrous knife, slaughtering .... Chullin 8a-8b
        Benefit from wine of idolaters .... Avodah Zarah 29b
    Impurity —
        Benefit from impure *terumah* .... Yevamos 73b, 74a; Pesachim 32a; Shabbos 25a-25b
        Benefit from impure *tevel* .... Shabbos 26a
        Benefit, impurity of forbidden to benefit substance .... Bechoros 9b-10b
    Prohibitions —
        Benefit and destruction simultaneous, Sabbatical year .... Succah 40a; Bava Kama 101b-102a
        Benefit, ashes of buried forbidden food .... Temurah 34a
        Benefit from *chametz* .... Pesachim 21b, 23a, 28a-28b, 30a, 32a-32b
        Benefit from firstborn donkey .... Kiddushin 57b; Bechoros 9b-10b, 12b
        Benefit from stoned ox .... Kiddushin 56b; Bava Kama 41a-41b; Pesachim 22b
        Benefit, meat with milk .... Kiddushin 57b; Menachos 101b; Chullin 114b-116a
    Property —
        Benefits from daughter's property .... Kesubos 46b-47a
        Benefits from sale of *kesubah* .... Bava Kama 89a
        Benefits of earnings, of wife .... Bava Kama 89a; Kesuvos 83b
        Benefits of one's divorcee .... Gittin 17b, 18a
        Benefits of wife, husband's gift .... Bava Basra 51a-51b

B

Benefits of wife, parallel to which right . . . Kesubos 47b
Benefits or capital, dried tree . . . Bava Metzia 79a, 109b-110a; Kesubos 95b

Misc. —
Benefit from forbidden item, in unusual way . . . Pesachim 24b-25a
Benefit from sale, who . . . Nedarim 31a-31b
Benefit, mixed species in vineyard . . . *see* **Vineyard**, page 723
Benefit, permission . . . Pesachim 22a-23a
Benefit of society, decrees . . . Gittin 32a-53a
Benefit to righteous and to world . . . Sanhedrin 72a
Benefit to wicked and to world . . . Sanhedrin 72a

Benefitting
Benefitting from this world, by little finger . . . Kesubos 104a
Benefitting from ignoramus, like clay utensil . . . Sanhedrin 52b
Benefitting from meal with a Sage . . . Berachos 64a
Benefitting from one's work, value . . . Berachos 8a
Benefitting man in his absence . . . Kiddushin 23a
Benefitting of radiance of Divine Presence . . . Berachos 17a
Benefitting Sage from one's belongings . . . Kesubos 111b; Berachos 34b; Sanhedrin 92a, 99a
Benefitting without blessing . . . Berachos 35a-35b, 48b
Benefits without the other losing, consecrated item . . . Bava Metzia 99b; Bava Kama 20b-21a

Benei Brak . . . *see* **B'nai Braq**, page 69
Benevolent, Israel . . . Yevamos 79a
Benin dichrin . . . *see* **Inheritance of mother's** *kesubah*, page 309

Benjamin
Benjamin, concubine in Gibeah . . . Bava Basra 116a, 121a
Benjamin, his sons . . . Sotah 36b
Benjamin, pain about Temple . . . Yoma 12a
Benjamin written in full, *shoham* stones . . . Sotah 36b

Benos . . . *see* **Daughters**, page 144

Bequeathing
Bequeathing because of death . . . Gittin 66a; Bava Basra 151b
Bequeathing his property to so-and-so . . . Bava Basra 128b-131a, 133a
Bequeathing oath to sons . . . Shevuos 47a, 48a-48b
Bequeathing one's property during life, cries out . . . Bava Metzia 75b

Bequest
Bequest . . . *see also* **Sick person**, page 623
Bequest after bequest . . . *see* **Double bequest**, page 175
Bequest by sick, undetermined coin . . . Gittin 13a-13b
Bequest of Geniva, wine . . . Gittin 65b-66a
Bequest of healthy man, for after his death . . . Bava Basra 135b; Bava Metzia 19a-19b
Bequest, she lost her *kesubah* . . . Bava Basra 132a-133a, 150a; Peah 3:7

Beraisa
Beraisa, dispute and *halacha* . . . Eruvin 9b; Niddah 46b
Beraisa, erroneous . . . Gittin 73a
Beraisos Rabbi Chiya and Rabbi Oshiah . . . Chullin 141a-141b
Beraisos, who is the author? . . . Yevamos 43a, 82b

Berachah
Berachah acharonah . . . Berachos 12a, 37a-37b, 38b-39a, 44a; Niddah 51b-52a
Berachah me'ein sheva . . . Shabbos 24b

Berachah acharonah .... *see* **Final blessing**, page 222

Berachah, berachos .... *see* **Blessing**, page 62

Bereshis, utterance .... Rosh Hashanah 32a

Beriah .... *see* **Creature**, page 133

Beris bein habesarim .... *see* **Covenant between parts**, page 131

Berov am hadras melech .... *see* **Multitude, king's glory**, page 431

Berries of myrtle .... Succah 11b, 33a-33b

Besamim .... *see* **Fragrant spices**, page238; *see also* **Perfume**, page 481

Besar Shema vetaama .... *see* **Mixture, name and taste**, page 418

Beshalom, said to deceased .... Moed Katan 29a

Besieged city, disqualified *kohanos* .... Kesubos 27a; Avodah Zarah 71a

Best

Best, "this also is for the best," faith .... Berachos 60b-61a

Best, how .... Gittin 48b-49b

Best in the flock .... Yoma 34b, 70b; Megillah 28a

Best of butchers, partner of Amalek .... Kiddushin 82a

Best of physicians to *Gehinnom* .... Kiddushin 82a

Best, this also is for the best, episode .... Taanis 21a; Sanhedrin 108b-109a

Best, who and from where .... Gittin 48b-49b; Bava Kama 5a

Best, whose .... Bava Kama 6b-8a; Kesubos 110a

Best land

Best land, how to evaluate .... Gittin 48b-49b

Best land, who and source .... Gittin 48b-49b; Bava Kama 5a

Best land, whose .... Bava Kama 6b-7a Kesubos 110a, 8a, 59a; Gittin 48b-49b

Best of best land, repayment of debt .... Bava Metzia 66b

Besulah, different meanings .... Niddah 8b

Besulah .... *see* **Virgin**, page 724

Besulim .... *see* **Virginity**, page 724

Beteilah daato .... *see* **Annulled personal opinion**, page 26

Bethuseans, sanctifying new moon .... Rosh Hashanah 22b

Betrothal

Betrothal during festival .... Moed Katan 18b

Betrothal during mourning period .... Yevamos 43a-43b

Betrothed girl

Rights —

Betrothed girl, burial .... Kesubos 53a

Betrothed girl, inheritance .... Kesubos 47a-47b

Betrothed girl, *kesubah* .... Kesubos 89b, 47a-47b, 54b; Bava Metzia 17b

Betrothed girl, supporting .... Kesubos 53b

Misc. —

Betrothed girl, annulment of vow .... Nedarim 67a-68a, 70a-70b, 74b; Yevamos 29b; Kesubos 39a, 46b; Kiddushin 4a

Betrothed girl, learning Torah .... Pesachim 49b; Berachos 57a; Sanhedrin 59a

Betrothed girl, levirate marriage .... Yevamos 13b

Betrothed girl, mourning .... Kesubos 53a

Betrothed girl, pregnant, doubt .... Kiddushin 75a; Yevamos 69b-70a; Kesubos 13b-14a

Betrothed girl, *sotah* .... Yevamos 58a-58b; Kiddushin 27b; Sotah 18a-18b, 23b-26a

Betrothed girl, stoning .... Sanhedrin 66b; Kesubos 44b-45b, 49a

Betrothed girl, *terumah* .... Kesubos 57b-58b; Kiddushin 5a, 10b-11a

Betrothed girl, time of wedding..Kesubos 57a-57b; Nedarim 73b
Betrothed girl to one's brother, marriage by mistake..Yevamos 95b
Betrothed proselyte girl, stoning...Kesubos 44a-44b

Better
Better be a fool during whole life...Eduyos 5:6
Better close neighbor...Bava Metzia 108b; Kesubos 85b
Better jump into furnace than humiliate fellow...Berachos 43b; Kesubos 67b
Better marry anyone than stay alone...Kesubos 75a; Yevamos 118b; Kiddushin 7a, 41a; Bava Kama 111a
Better fingernail of first Sages...Yoma 9b
Better not to have been created..Eruvin 13b; Berachos 17a
Better not to make vow...Menachos 81a; Nedarim 9a; Chullin 2a
Better one hot pepper than basket full of sweet peppers...Megillah 7a; Chagigah 10a; Yoma 85b
Better they sin involuntarily...Shabbos 148b; Beitzah 30a; Bava Basra 60b

Between
Between *Chumashim*, space..Bava Basra 13b
Between courtyards, carrying out..Eruvin 98b-99b
Between courtyards, domain...Eruvin 77a, 83b-85b, 91b
Between Divine names, importance...Berachos 33a
Between Divine names, vengeance...Sanhedrin 92a
Between husband and wife, vows..Nedarim 79b, 81b
Between husband and wife, what is considered..Nedarim 81a-81b
Between poles, *karmelis*..Shabbos 7a
Between servant of G-d, reviewing hundred and one times.....................................Chagigah 9b
Between teeth, combining...Chullin 103b
Between *Ulam* and Altar, leaving that place..Yoma 44a-44b; Keilim 1:9
Between *Ulam* and Altar, stairs..Middos 3:6

Betzalel..*see* **Bezalel**, page 56
Beulah leKohen Gadol.............................*see* **Non-virgin woman to *Kohen* Gadol**, page 449
Be'yado
Be'yado, blood of disqualified sacrifice..Zevachim 34b; Menachos 59b
Be'yado, trustworthiness...Yevamos 88a; Gittin 54b
Be'yado, trustworthiness for divorce...Bava Basra 134b-135a

Beyomo..*see* **Same day, paying salary of worker**, page 587
Beyond letter of law
Beyond letter of law, coin..................................Bava Metzia 30b; Berachos 7a, 45b; Kesubos 97a
Beyond letter of law, lost item..Bava Metzia 24b
Beyond letter of law, source..Bava Metzia 30b
Beyond letter of law, workers..Bava Metzia 83a

***Bezachim* of Temple**...Pesachim 64b
Bezalel
Bezalel, his father's age at his birth..Sanhedrin 69b
Bezalel, Tabernacle..Berachos 55a

Bi'ur..*see* **Removing**, page 557
Bichdei sheyaasu.............................*see* **Time necessary to make, Shabbos work**, page 691
Bidding for division of property...Bava Basra 13a-13b
Bigdei kehunah...*see* **Priestly garments**, page 503
Bigmar devarav adam nitfas ....*see* **Contradiction between beginning and end of sentence**, page 126
Bigthan and Teresh..Megillah 13b
Bikkurim...*see* **First fruit**, page 225

Bikur cholim..*see* **Visiting the sick**, page 725
Bilaam...*see* **Balaam**, page 41
Bila..............................*see* **Mixture considered mixed, in tithe of two years** page 418
Bile, diseases ....Bava Kama 92b; Bava Metzia 107b
Bilgah, episode ....Succah 56b
Bilhah, Reuben ....Shabbos 55b; Sotah 7b
Bill
  Bill ....*see also* **Legal document**, page 361
  Bill of sale, "I did not retain anything" ....Bava Basra 61b
  Bill of trust, witnesses' appeal ....Bava Basra 48b-49a; Kesubos 19b
Bimus, Altar ....Avodah Zarah 53b
Binding
  Binding daily offering ....Tamid 31b
  Binding four species................................Succah 11b, 30b-31b, 33a; Sanhedrin 88b; Menachos 27a
  Binding of Isaac ....Sanhedrin 89b
  Bound like a *lulav*, Israel ....Menachos 27a
  Binding *lulav*
    Binding *lulav*...Succah 31a, 33a; Menachos 27a
    Binding *lulav*, how ....Succah 33b
    Binding *lulav*, intervening substance...Succah 36b
Binyamin..*see* **Benjamin**, page 54
Binyamin *Hatzadik*, charity ....Bava Basra 11a
Binyan..*see* **Building**, page 79
Binyan av, *mah matzinu* ....Chullin 115b-116a
Binyan av..*see* **Deduction by comparison**, page 156
***Birah*,** Temple ....Zevachim 104b; Yoma 2a
Bircas
  Bircas Ha'Ilanos ....Berachos 43b; Rosh Hashanah 11a
  Bircas HaChamah...Berachos 59b
  Bircas HaGeshamim..Taanis 6b-7a; Berachos 59b
  Bircas HaLevanah...Sanhedrin 41b-42a
  Bircas HaMinim..Berachos 28b-29a
  Bircos Chasanim..Kesubos 7a-8a
  Bircos HaNehenim, medicine..Berachos 36a, 38a
  Bircos HaNehenim, source......................................Berachos 21a, 35a-35b, 48b
  Bircos HaShachar...Berachos 60b; Menachos 43b
  Bircos Krias Shema...Berachos 11a-12a
  Bircas HaMazon
    Bircas HaMazon, being discharged by wife and children ...Berachos 20b, 45b, 48a-48b; Succah 38a
    Bircas HaMazon, episodes...Berachos 53b
    Bircas HaMazon for mourner ....Berachos 46b
    Bircas HaMazon for volume of an olive....................Berachos 20b; Niddah 70b
    Bircas HaMazon, how ....Berachos 51b
    Bircas HaMazon, in every language...Sotah 33a
    Bircas HaMazon, quantity of food ....Berachos 49b
    Bircas HaMazon, text...Berachos 48b-49a
    Bircas HaMazon, woman ....Berachos 20b
    Bircas HaMazon, Yannai ....Berachos 48a

B

Bircas Kohanim

Bircas Kohanim, aggadah .... Sotah 38b; Chullin 49a
Bircas Kohanim, barefoot .... Sotah 40a; Rosh Hashanah 31b
Bircas Kohanim, cantor .... Berachos 34a
Bircas Kohanim, congregation .... Sotah 38b-39a
Bircas Kohanim, congregation reciting verses during .... Sotah 39b-40a
Bircas Kohanim, disqualified *Kohen* .... Megillah 24b; Berachos 32b
Bircas Kohanim, how .... Sotah 37b-38a; Tamid 7:2
Bircas Kohanim, intoxicated *Kohen* .... Taanis 26b-27a
Bircas Kohanim, minor .... Chullin 24b
Bircas Kohanim, not to add .... Rosh Hashanah 28b
Bircas Kohanim, other congregation .... Rosh Hashanah 28b
Bircas Kohanim, Rabbi Yose .... Shabbos 118b
Bircas Kohanim, requirement .... Sotah 38b; Menachos 44a
Bircas Kohanim, when .... Taanis 26b
Bircas Kohanim with G-d's name in Temple .... Yoma 39b
Bircas Kohanim with G-d's name in Temple, and throughout *Eretz Yisrael* .... Tamid 7:2;
.... Sotah 37b-38a

Bird
see also **Poultry**, page 495

Episodes —

Bird, preventing from resting upon Temple roof .... Shabbos 90a; Menachos 107a
Bird, slaughtering in air .... Chullin 4a, 27b-28a, 85b-86a; Nazir 29a; Kiddushin 71a
Bird, Yonassan ben Uziel .... Succah 28a
Birds, giant, episode .... Bava Basra 73b-74b; Bechoros 57b
Birds of Herod .... Chullin 139b

Kashrus —

Bird, majority are *kosher* .... Chullin 63b
Bird, signs of *kashrus* .... Chullin 61a-62a, 63b, 65a
Bird, slaughtering .... Chullin 27b-28a

Scientific facts —

Bird, more expensive than sheep .... Menachos 107b
Birds, beneficial to sick .... Avodah Zarah 14a
Birds, characteristics .... Chullin 57a; Sanhedrin 108b
Birds, creation .... Chullin 27b; Eruvin 28a
Birds drink by sucking up .... Gittin 86b
Birds, numerous species .... Chullin 62b-63b; Niddah 50b
Birds, work for man .... Sanhedrin 59b; Bava Metzia 91b

Misc. —

Bird, distance from neighbors .... Bava Kama 83a; Bava Basra 23a
Bird, impure and pure .... Chullin 139b-140a
Bird, impurity of utensils .... Keilim 17:14
Bird in sky will bring voice, secret .... Bava Basra 4a
Bird, news of future redemption .... Chullin 63a
Bird, parable about slave .... Menachos 99b

Birds for leper

Birds for leper, benefit .... Kiddushin 57a-57b; Chullin 82a, 140a
Birds for leper, sending away .... Kiddushin 57b
Birds for leper, similar .... Yoma 62b
Birds for leper, talkative man .... Arachin 16b

Birds for leper, which are valid...Chullin 62a, 140a

Bird *neveilah*

Bird *neveilah*, impure bird..Zevachim 69b-70b; Chullin 100b; Niddah 42b

Bird *neveilah*, light impurity...............Taharos 1:1-3; Zevachim 105a-105b; Bechoros 10a; Niddah 50b

Bird *neveilah*, primary and secondary impurities..Zevachim 105b

Bird *neveilah*, sacrifice..Zevachim 68a-69a, 70b; Meilah 3a

Bird *neveilah*, thought.......................Niddah 50b-51a; Zevachim 105b; Bechoros 10a; Krisos 21a;

Taharos 1:1, 8:6; Uktzin 3:3

Bird *neveilah*, throat..Zavim 5:9

Bird *neveilah*, volume of olive..Zevachim 70a

Bird *neveilah*, impurities..Taharos 1:1-3

Bird sacrifice

Bird sacrifice..*see also* **Nests**, page 441

Bird sacrifice, age for *kashrus*...Chullin 22a-22b

Bird sacrifice, crop and feather...Zevachim 65a

Bird sacrifice, disqualified, impurity.........................Zevachim 68a-69a, 70b; Meilah 3a

Bird sacrifice, episode about price.........................Krisos 8a; Bava Basra 166a-166b

Bird sacrifice, exchanged...Zevachim 66a-68a

Bird sacrifice, from which city...Menachos 87a

Bird sacrifice, offering its skin...Shabbos 108a

Bird sacrifice, only one bird for burnt offering..................Zevachim 65a; Krisos 9a

Bird sacrifice, sprinklings...Zevachim 64b

Bird sacrifices etc., essential laws...Avos 3:18

Biris, definition...Shabbos 63b

Birth

Laws —

Birth...*see also* **Pregnancy**, page 500

Birth after mother's conversion, inheritance.................................Kiddushin 17b-18a

Birth, blessing...Berachos 59b

Birth control........................Yevamos 12b, 34b, 100b; Kesubos 39a; Nedarim 35b; Niddah 45a

Birth control, nursing woman..Yevamos 34b

Birth delayed, concern of immorality..Yevamos 80b

Birth, fetus waiting before coming out..Yevamos 71b

Birth, from when...Bechoros 46a-47a

Birth, head coming out...Niddah 42b; Chullin 72a

Birth of stillborn, from when.........................Bechoros 46a-46b; Niddah 28a, 29a

Birth, overrides Shabbos.........................Shabbos 128b-129b; Arachin 7a-7b

Birth without blood, impurity...Niddah 42b

Misc. —

Birth, equal to signs of puberty..Yevamos 12b-13a

Birth, fate..Shabbos 156a

Birth, fetus comes down...Niddah 31a

Birth, key...Taanis 2a-2b; Sanhedrin 113a

Birth of righteous, goodness...Sanhedrin 113b

Birth of righteous, when another is dead..................Kiddushin 72b; Yoma 38b

Birth of twins, interval...Niddah 27a

Birth of twins, Rabbi Chiya...Yevamos 65b; Niddah 27a

Birth of Isaac..................Bava Metzia 87a; Shabbos 156a-156b; Rosh Hashanah 16b

Birth, pain...Sotah 12a

Birth pangs, birth limbs...Bechoros 45a
Birth pangs of Messiah...Sanhedrin 98b
Birth, time when child comes out...Sotah 11b
Birth, woman kneels down...Yevamos 103a

Birthday
Birthday, fate...Shabbos 156a
Birthday, festival of non-Jews...Avodah Zarah 10a

Biryah...*see* **Creature**, page 133
Bishul goy...*see* **Cooking by non-Jew**, page 128
Bitachon BaHashem...*see* **Trust in G-d**, page 704

Bite
Bite, baby...Kesubos 50a
Bite, cure by insects...Shabbos 77b

Bitlu velo bitlu...*see* **Annulled and did not annul**, page 26
Bitter almonds, tithes...Chullin 25b; Eruvin 28b; Maasros 1:4

Bitter herbs
Bitter herbs, blessing...Pesachim 114b-115a
Bitter herbs, disqualified for *s'chach*...Succah 13b
Bitter herbs in present times...Pesachim 28b, 115a; Kiddushin 37b
Bitter herbs, *seder* night...Pesachim 39b
Bitter herbs, species...Pesachim 39a; Succah 13a
Bitter herbs, way of eating...Pesachim 115a, 115b

Bitul...*see* **Annulment**, page 27
Bitul kli mehechano...*see* **Annulment of utensil use**, *muktzeh*, page 27
Bitul melachah lemes...*see* **Cessation of work at someone's death**, page 91
Bitul miktzas...*see* **Mistake, partial**, page 416
Bitul mitzvas yevamin...*see* **Bond before levirate marriage, prohibition to annul**, page 71
Bitul reshus...*see* **Annulment of ownership**, page 28
Bitul Torah...*see* **Refraining from Torah learning**, page 554
Biyah...*see* **Intimate relations**, page 316
Bizuy mitzvah...*see* **Despising commandment**, page 161

Black
"Black heads," wording of vow...Nedarim 30b
Black is a red substance which spoiled, lung...Chullin 47b
Black is of red origin, myrtle...Succah 33b
Black man, blemishes of *Kohen*...Bechoros 44b
Black people, Ham's punishment...Sanhedrin 108b
Black-red, color of blood...Niddah 19a-19b, 20a; Succah 33b; Chullin 47b
Black hair, Red Heifer...Parah 2:1-5; Bechoros 25a

Blackened face, fasts...Chagigah 22b; Nazir 52b

Blank
Blank paper, child's learning...Avos 4:20
Blank paper, divorce certificate...Gittin 19b-20a
Blank paper, signature...Bava Basra 167a; Kesubos 21a

Blasphemer
Blasphemer, desert...Sanhedrin 78b
Blasphemer, Divine Names...Sanhedrin 60a
Blasphemer, explanation...Krisos 7a-7b
Blasphemer, non-Jew...Sanhedrin 56a

Blasphemer, sin offering..Krisos 7a-7b
Blasphemer, with Divine Name and Attribute ....Sanhedrin 55b-56a, 81b; Shevuos 36a
Blasphemer, zealots kill him..Sanhedrin 81b, 82b
Blaspheming, thief's blessing...Sanhedrin 6b; Bava Kama 94a

Blemish

Bodily blemishes —
Blemish, bone...Bechoros 40a, 41a
Blemish, ear...Bechoros 37b
Blemish, eye..Bechoros 3b, 38a-39a, 40a; Niddah 23a
Blemish, genital area..Bechoros 39b, 40a
Blemish, hand..Bechoros 40a
Blemish, horns..Bechoros 44a
Blemish, legs...Bechoros 40b, 44a
Blemish, mouth...Bechoros 35a, 39a, 40a-40b
Blemish, nose...Bechoros 39a
Blemish, split bone...Bechoros 41a
Blemish, tail..Bechoros 40b-41a
Blemish, unequal limbs...Bechoros 3b

Offerings —
Blemish, checking daily offering.................Menachos 49b-50a; Arachin 13a-13b; Succah 42a
Blemish in animals, Rav learned...Sanhedrin 5b
Blemish in sacrifice, in present times..Avodah Zarah 13b
Blemish in sacrifice, prohibition to make.............Menachos 56b; Beitzah 27b; Bechoros 33b-34a
Blemish in tithe, prohibition to make...Temurah 21a
Blemish, non-Jew's sacrifice..................Avodah Zarah 5b-6a, 51a; Zevachim 116a; Temurah 7a
Blemishes, source..Bechoros 43a

Other blemishes —
Blemish after slaughtering.................................Zevachim 25b, 26a; Bechoros 39b
Blemish, blemishing another's animal...Bava Kama 98a
Blemish, *chavarvar* (white flecks)......................................Bechoros 38b; Yevamos 80a
Blemish, flaw..Chullin 17b-18a; Bechoros 37b
Blemish, internal limb missing..Bechoros 39a-39b
Blemish, permanent, boils...Bechoros 41a
Blemish, permanent water...Bechoros 38b-39a; Yevamos 80a
Blemish, second, sacrifice..................................Bechoros 33b; Menachos 56b
Blemish, gender doubtful and androgyny......................Yevamos 83b-84a; Bechoros 42a
Blemish, temporary, was healed...Zevachim 77b
Blemish, wart..Bechoros 40b
Blemishes, frequent...Menachos 101a

Sacrifices —
Blemish, calf whose neck is broken...Sotah 45b-46a
Blemish, goat to Azazel..Temurah 6b-7a
Blemish made to replacing animal, prohibition ....Temurah 21a
Blemish of firstborn, eating................Bechoros 32b-33a; Zevachim 75b; Temurah 24a
Blemish, wheat of meal offerings..Menachos 85b
Blemish, wood which became wormy......................Menachos 85b, 101a; Middos 2:5
Blemishes of tithe, trustworthiness..Bechoros 36b

Misc. —
Blemish in yourself, your friend..Bava Metzia 59b

Blemish, *Leviim* ....Nazir 40a; Chullin 24a
Blemishes, in sale ....Bava Metzia 80a
Blemishes of men, forced to divorce ....Kesubos 77a
Blemishes of slaves ....Kiddushin 11a; Kesubos 57b-58a; Bava Basra 92b

Blemish of a *Kohen*
Blemish of a *Kohen*, being informed of ....Kiddushin 66b; Makos 11b-12a
Blemishes of a *Kohen*, differences ....Bechoros 43a-43b
Blemishes of a *Kohen*, ear ....Bechoros 37b
Blemishes of a *Kohen*, eating ....Zevachim 101b, 102a-102b
Blemishes of a *Kohen*, like that of animals ....Bechoros 43a
Blemishes of a *Kohen*, other blemishes ....Bechoros 43b-45b; Kesubos 75a
Blemishes of a *Kohen,* prohibition to make ....Bechoros 37b; Kiddushin 21b
Blemishes of a *Kohen*, prohibition to serve ....Sanhedrin 84a

Blemishes of women
Blemishes of women, *kesubah* and *kiddushin* ....Kiddushin 50a; Kesubos 72b
Blemishes of women, annulment of *kiddushin* ....Kesubos 74b
Blemishes of women, betrothed girl's *terumah* ....Kesubos 57b-58b; Kiddushin 10b-11a
Blemishes of women, *chazakos* ....Kesubos 75b-76a
Blemishes of women, proof ....Kesubos 75a-76a
Blemishes of women, which ....Kesubos 75a, 76b-77a

Blemished animal
Blemished animal, consecrated items Treasury ....Bechoros 14b; Chullin 130a; Temurah 10b, 33b
Blemished animal, its young ....Bechoros 14a, 15b; Chullin 130a; Temurah 10b, 33b
Blemished animal, non-Jew's sacrifice ....Avodah Zarah 5b-6a, 51a; Zevachim 116a; Temurah 7a
Blemished animal, not to take down animal from Altar ....Zevachim 35b, 84a, 85b
Blemished animal, private altar ....Zevachim 16a; Temurah 7a
Blemished animal, prohibitions ....Temurah 6b-7b
Blemished animal, redeeming ....Temurah 32b; Menachos 101a, 108a-108b; Bechoros 37b
Blemished animal, replacing sacrifice or young ....Bechoros 14b; Nazir 25a; Temurah 17b
Blemished animal, sacrifice ....Bechoros 14b
Blemished animal, sacrificed outside ....Bechoros 16a

Bless
Bless G-d Who is blessed ....Berachos 50a
Blessed are You Who returned our lost verse ....Avodah Zarah 52b
Blessed be G-d every day, Hillel ....Beitzah 16a
Blessed be G-d who did not give him back to the earth ....Berachos 54b
Blessed be G-d who entrusted His world to guardians ....Avodah Zarah 40b
Blessed be G-d who humiliated Avdan ....Yevamos 105b
Blessed be G-d Who killed him ....Shabbos 13b
Blessed be G-d, Jethro ....Sanhedrin 94a
Blessed be He and blessed be His Name ....Yoma 37a
Blessed be He Who heals the sick ....Berachos 60a
Blessed be He who separates, issue of Shabbos ....Shabbos 150b
Blessed be the Judge of truth ....Berachos 60a
Blessed be He Who did not show partiality ....Shabbos 13b

Blessing
   Abundance —
Blessings, benefitting without blessing ....Berachos 35a-35b; Sanhedrin 102a
Blessing, by scholar ....Berachos 42a

Blessing of non-Jews for Israel..Yevamos 63a
Blessing on house when fully inhabited.................Kesubos 103a; Bava Basra 144b
Blessing on produce of field..Yevamos 63a
Blessing on something hidden...Bava Metzia 42a; Taanis 8b
Blessing, only because of wife...Bava Metzia 59a
Blessings lost, figs..Nedarim 50b

Commandments —
Blessing for Rabbinical commandments, *vetzivanu*......................Shabbos 23a; Succah 46a
Blessing on affixing *tzitzis* on garment..Menachos 42a
Blessing on covering blood...Chullin 86b-87a
Blessing on putting on *tzitzis*...Menachos 43a
Blessing on Torah...Berachos 11b, 21a, 48b
Blessing when removing *tefillin*...Niddah 51b
Blessing, You put my lot among those who sit.................................Berachos 28b
Blessings for groom...Kesubos 7a-8a
Blessings for wedding, *bircas nisuin*..Kesubos 7b
Blessings on circumcision..Shabbos 137b; Menachos 42a
Blessings on *megillah*..Megillah 21b
Blessings on redeeming son and donkey...Pesachim 121b
Blessings on wedding...Kesubos 7b

Blessings on commandments
Blessings on commandments, how many..................................Succah 45b-46a
Blessings on commandments, on which ones..........................Menachos 42a-42b
Blessings on commandments, Rabbinical...............Shabbos 23a; Succah 46a
Blessings on commandments, text..Pesachim 7a-7b

Blessing on *tefillin*
Blessings on *tefillin*, how many...............Berachos 60b; Menachos 36a, 42b
Blessings on *tefillin*, touching..Succah 46a
Blessings on *tefillin*, when..Menachos 35b
Blessing when taking off *tefillin*..Niddah 51b

Blessing on Torah
Blessing on Torah...Berachos 11b, 21a, 48b
Blessing on Torah, caused destruction of Temple...........Bava Metzia 85a-85b; Nedarim 81a
Blessings on Torah reading...Megillah 21b, 32a

Enjoyment —
Blessing, *Al Hamichyah*..Berachos 37a-37b, 44a
Blessing, *Al Netilas Lulav*..Succah 37b
Blessing, *Asher Yatzar*..Berachos 60b
Blessing, "Blessed be the owner of this bread".............................Berachos 40b
Blessing, *Borei Minei Mezonos*.......................................Berachos 38a, 42a
Blessing, *Borei Nefashos*...Berachos 44b
Blessing, *Borei Peri Haadama*...Berachos 39a, 40a
Blessing, *Borei Peri Haetz*...................................Berachos 38a, 40a-40b
Blessing, *Hamotzie Lechem*...Berachos 38a-38b
Blessing, *Me'ein Shalosh*...Berachos 37a-37b, 44a
Blessing, *Mezonos*..Berachos 38a, 42a
Blessing, *Sheasa Li Nes*...Berachos 54a-54b
Blessing, *Shehakol*.................Berachos 36a, 38a, 39a, 40b, 44b-45a; Bava Basra 96b; Nedarim 55b
Blessing, water...Berachos 44b-45a

Blessings for enjoyment, medicine..Berachos 36a, 38a
Blessings for enjoyment, source...Berachos 21a, 35a-35b, 48b
Blessings, various foods...Berachos 36a, 36b, 38b-39a, 40b; Eruvin 28b

Blessing, final
Blessing, final......................................Berachos 12a, 37a-37b, 44a, 44b; Niddah 51b-52a
Blessing, final, on seven species..Berachos 37a-37b, 44a
Blessing, final, quantity..Berachos 38b-39a

Episodes —
Blessing of Balaam...Taanis 20a; Sanhedrin 105b-106a
Blessing of blind person, episode..Chagigah 5b
Blessing of Patriarchs, "I shall make you a great people"....................Pesachim 117b
Blessings, Mount Gerizim..Sotah 33b, 37a
Blessings of G-d for Messiah...Sanhedrin 93b
Blessings of Patriarchs...Bava Basra 16b
Blessings said by G-d and by Moses..Bava Basra 88b

Laws —
Blessing, discharging someone else's duty..............................Rosh Hashanah 29a-29b
Blessing in his place only..Pesachim 101a-102a
Blessing, mistake..Berachos 12a
Blessing next to another...Berachos 46a; Pesachim 104b
Blessing, penalty for taking blessing...Chullin 87a
Blessing, precedence...Berachos 39a-39b, 41a-41b, 43b
Blessing, text of end like beginning..Pesachim 104a
Blessing, unnecessary..Berachos 33a
Blessings, how to say..Berachos 47a
Blessings, prohibition to write...Shabbos 115b

Praise —
Blessing, *Chacham Harazim*...Berachos 58a
Blessing, earthquake..Berachos 59a
Blessing, Lot's wife..Berachos 54b
Blessing, *Matziv Gevul Almanah*...Berachos 58b
Blessing, *Meshaneh Habrios*...Berachos 58b
Blessing on lightning...Berachos 59a
Blessing on moon..Sanhedrin 41b-42a
Blessing on rain..Taanis 6b-7a; Berachos 59b
Blessing on sun..Berachos 59b
Blessing on trees.......................................Berachos 43b; Rosh Hashanah 11a
Blessing, *Oseh Maaseh Bereshis*.....................................Berachos 58b-59b
Blessing, *Sheakar Avodah Zarah Meartzenu*.......................Berachos 57b
Blessing, *Shekacha Lo Beolamo*..Berachos 58b
Blessing, *Sheloh Chiser*..........................Berachos 43b; Rosh Hashanah 11a
Blessing, slow to anger...Berachos 57b
Blessing, Who formed with justice..Berachos 58b
Blessings, sixty myriads (persons)...Berachos 58a

Prayer —
Blessing "*Me'ein Sheva*"..Shabbos 24b
Blessing about heretics..Berachos 28b-29a
Blessing before commandment.........................Pesachim 7b; Succah 39a
Blessing before commandment, *tefillin*.............................Menachos 35b

Blessing before immersing..Pesachim 7b
Blessing, *Hagomel*...Berachos 54b
Blessing on *Haftorah, Rosh Chodesh*...Shabbos 24a
Blessing on *Hallel*...Pesachim 119b; Succah 38a, 39a
Blessing, *Sheloh Asani*...Menachos 43b
Blessing, *Velamalshinim*..Berachos 28b-29a
Blessings after *Shema*..Berachos 12a
Blessings before *Shema*...Berachos 11a-12a
Blessings, morning...Berachos 60b; Menachos 43b
Blessings on fast days...Taanis 15a-15b, 16b-17a

Times —
Blessing, *Hamapil*..Berachos 60b
Blessing, *Havdala*...Berachos 52a, 52b
Blessing on Pesach lamb and *chagigah*....................Pesachim 121a; Zevachim 37a
Blessings mutual indispensibility, Rosh Hashanah........................Rosh Hashanah 34b
Blessings on *Chanukah* light...Shabbos 23a; Succah 46a
Blessings on succah...Succah 45b, 56a; Pesachim 7b
Blessing, searching for *chametz*..Pesachim 7a-7b

Wishes —
Blessed will you be in town...Bava Metzia 107a
Blessing, "give us life"...Berachos 16b
Blessing, "May you see your future world in your life"...................Berachos 17a
Blessing it shall come to him!............................Pesachim 32a; Eruvin 29b
Blessing for slave, listening..Sotah 40a
Blessing from Sage...Bava Basra 116a; Taanis 8a
Blessing, *Mechaye Chaim*...Yoma 71a
Blessing of departing watch of *Kohanim*....................Berachos 11b-12a; Tamid 5:1
Blessing of guest for host...Berachos 46a, 55a
Blessing of ordinary person...Megillah 15a
Blessing of righteous, out of curse of wicked.............................Yoma 38b
Blessing that Israel will not be ashamed........................Moed Katan 9b
Blessing unlimited, tithe.....................Makos 23b; Shabbos 32b; Taanis 9a, 22b
Blessings, "also to you"...Megillah 27b
Blessings fall on his head............Megillah 25b; Berachos 33a; Shabbos 31a; Avodah Zarah 60b
Blessings, hidden content...Moed Katan 9b

Misc. —
Blessing, established by Great Assembly........................Berachos 33a H
Blessing, *Shehasimcha Bimeono*..Kesubos 8a

Blessing for mourners
Blessings for mourners...Kesubos 8a-8b
Blessing for mourners, *El Emes Dayan*.................................Berachos 46b
Blessings for mourners, episodes...Kesubos 8b

"Blind my eyes," damage...Bava Kama 91b

Blind
Blind, agent for divorce certificate...Gittin 23a
Blind, blessing to Sages...Chagigah 5b
Blind carrying staff, Yom Tov...Beitzah 25b
Blind, commandments.....................Bava Kama 86b-87a; Kiddushin 31a
Blind comparable to dead...Nedarim 64b

Blind, exile..Makos 9b; Nedarim 87b-88a; Bava Kama 86b-87a
Blind, *Haggadah shel* Pesach...Pesachim 116b
Blind, his wife committed adultery...Kiddushin 66a
Blind, judge..Sanhedrin 34b; Niddah 49b-50a
Blind man in sky-light...Bava Basra 12b; Niddah 20b
Blind person is never satiated...Yoma 74b
Blind, recognizes his wife's voice...Gittin 23a
Blind, slaughtering...Chullin 13b
Blind, testimony..Bava Basra 128a
Blind, torches...Megillah 24b
Blind, *tzitzis*...Menachos 43a
Blind woman, checking for *terumah*..Niddah 13b
Blind, *Yotzer or*...Megillah 24b
Blisters in lung...Chullin 47a
Bliyah...*see* **Absorbed**, page 5
Bliyas isur...*see* **Absorbed forbidden substance, kidney**, page 5
Blood

Impurity —
Blood and fat, intervening substance...Zevachim 98b
Blood, impurity...Niddah 55b-56a
Blood, impurity of food.................Chullin 33a, 35b-36b; Pesachim 16a-16b, 20a, 22b; Krisos 22a
Blood intermingled, during death..............Niddah 71a-71b; Oholos 2:2, 3:5; Zevachim 36a
Blood, interposes on substance during immersion..Menachos 21a
Blood, *mikveh* water..Chullin 84a
Blood of dead, impurity..................Oholos 3:2, 3:3; Bava Kama 101b; Chullin 87b-88a; Niddah 62b-63a;
....Meilah 17a
Blood of dead, two dead persons...Meilah 17a; Oholos 3:3
Blood of *neveilah*, impurity..Menachos 103b-104a
Blood of reptiles...Krisos 4b; Meilah 17a
Blood of sacrifice and animal, impurity of food.................Pesachim 16a-16b; Chullin 33a, 36b
Blood, unwanted..Keilim 8:11

Niddah* and *zavah —
Blood, absorbed in flesh...Chullin 113a
Blood discharge due to intimate relations..Niddah 65b-66a
Blood discharge during intimate relations.................Shevuos 14b, 17b-18b; Niddah 12a, 14b-15a
Blood, green-yellow, considered liquid..Niddah 19b
Blood, green-yellow, self impurity...Niddah 19b
Blood of desire...Niddah 20b
Blood of desire, bride...Niddah 66a
Blood of leprous woman...Niddah 34b
Blood of woman after birth, immersion..Niddah 42a-42b
Blood, pure, woman after birth.................Krisos 10a-11a; Niddah 11a-11b, 35b-36a; Sanhedrin 87b
Blood, redder than another's.........................Pesachim 25a-25b; Yoma 82a-82b; Sanhedrin 74a

Blood of *niddah*
Blood of *niddah*, cesarean birth...Niddah 41a-41b
Blood of *niddah*, chamber pot...Niddah 59b
Blood of *niddah*, doubtful origin.....................................Niddah 17b-18a; Bava Basra 24a
Blood of *niddah*, dripping..Niddah 10b
Blood of *niddah*, episodes about rulings...Niddah 20a-20b

Blood of *niddah*, impurity .... Niddah 35b, 54b-55a; Temurah 34a
Blood of *niddah*, marks .... Niddah 19a-21a; Sanhedrin 87b
Blood of *niddah*, pipe and piece .... Niddah 21b-22a

Prohibitions —
Blood, categories for prohibition .... Krisos 4b, 22a; Pesachim 65a; Chullin 74b
Blood, different kinds .... Krisos 4a, 20b-21a; Chullin 74b
Blood, from which species is forbidden .... Krisos 20b-21a
Blood in different parts of body .... Chullin 93b, 110b-111b
Blood in egg .... Chullin 64b; Krisos 20b
Blood, mixture .... Chullin 87a-87b
Blood of blood-letting, definition .... Krisos 22a
Blood, benefit permitted .... Pesachim 22a-22b
Blood, prohibition to eat .... Menachos 21a; Krisos 4b
Blood, roast meat .... Pesachim 74a-75a; Chullin 93b, 111b-112b

Sacrifices —
Blood, entered in *Heichal* .... Zevachim 10b-11a, 38b, 82a-83a
Blood, guilt offering for leper .... Zevachim 47b
Blood, half on upper part of Altar .... Zevachim 38a-38b
Blood in neck, animal entering *Heichal* .... Zevachim 11a, 92b
Blood, leftover, impure and profaned .... Zevachim 46a
Blood of bird sacrifice, spilled .... Zevachim 92b
Blood of bird sacrifice, squeezing .... Zevachim 52a-52b, 65a, 66a; Meilah 8b-9a
Blood of bull is like the bull .... Yoma 49b-50a; Menachos 16a
Blood of flesh, sprinkling .... Krisos 4b, 22a; Pesachim 65a-65b; Zevachim 25a, 35a
Blood of leper's bird .... Sotah 16b
Blood of redeemed sacrifice .... Chullin 35b
Blood of sacrifice .... *see also* **Sprinkling**, page 651
Blood of sacrifice, becoming *kosher* again .... Chullin 87b
Blood of sacrifice, mixture .... Zevachim 35a, 36a, 77b-79b-82a; Pesachim 65a; Menachos 22a-22a;
.... Chullin 87b; Temurah 5b; Niddah 71b
Blood of sacrifice, spilled .... Zevachim 15a, 25a; Yoma 48a; Menachos 26b
Blood of sacrifice, taken out of Temple Courtyard .... Zevachim 82a-82b
Blood of Yom Kippur, intermingled .... Yoma 57b-58a; Zevachim 42b, 81b; Menachos 16b
Blood of Yom Kippur, spilled .... Yoma 61a-62a
Blood on floor, sprinkling of Pesach lamb .... Pesachim 65a-65b; Zevachim 34b-35a, 60a
Blood, secular use .... Meilah 11a-11b, 12a; Yoma 58b-60a; Berachos 31a; Zevachim 46a-46b; Chullin 117a
Blood, receiving blood from neck of sacrifice .... Zevachim 25a
Blood, remaining at sunset .... Zevachim 56a-56b; Menachos 20b

Blood of sin offering
Blood of sin offering, disqualified .... Zevachim 93a
Blood of sin offering, how to wash .... Zevachim 94a-95a
Blood of sin offering, in what to wash .... Zevachim 95a-95b
Blood of sin offering, lost .... Temurah 22b
Blood of sin offering, place to wash .... Zevachim 94b
Blood of sin offering, washing .... Zevachim 93b-94a
Blood of sin offering, what to wash .... Zevachim 92b-94a
Blood of sin offering, which blood .... Zevachim 38b-39a, 92a-93b, 98b; Meilah 5a

Scientific facts —
Blood, danger of excessive blood .... Bava Basra 58b; Bechoros 44b

Blood, disgusting to man .... Makos 23b
Blood of woman, advantage .... Niddah 64b; Kesuvos 10b
Blood, produces woman's milk .... Niddah 9a; Bechoros 6b
Blood, *reviis* in man .... Sotah 5a; Shabbos 31b

Slaughtering —
Blood, absorbed, covering .... Chullin 87a
Blood into hole, ritual slaughter .... Chullin 17a, 41a-41b
Blood spilled onto flax .... Chullin 85b
Blood stain .... *see* **Stain of *niddah***, page 653
Blood which was exposed, covering .... Chullin 87a; Succah 33a; Avodah Zarah 47a

Misc. —
Blood flowing from fingers, Rava .... Shabbos 88a
Blood of Rava, honor of teacher .... Yoma 53a
Blood of sacrifice and of *tamtzis* ..... Chullin 33a, 36b; Pesachim 16a-16b, 20a, 22b
Blood of scratched finger, atonement .... Chullin 7b
Blood of Zechariah, Nebuzaradan .... Sanhedrin 96a-96b; Gittin 57b

Blood flowing before birth
Blood flowing before birth ..... Niddah 7b, 8b-9a, 36b, 37b, 38b, 41a-41b; Yevamos 83a; Sanhedrin 87b
Blood flowing before birth, annulling purity count .... Niddah 37a
Blood flowing before birth, cesarean birth .... Niddah 41a-41b
Blood flowing before birth, time .... Niddah 37b-38b

Blood of covenant
Blood of covenant, born circumcised .... Shabbos 135a; Yevamos 71a
Blood of covenant, convert .... Shabbos 135a
Blood of covenant, making drip .... Shabbos 135a; Yevamos 71a

Blood-letter
Blood-letter, blame of physician .... Kiddushin 82a
Blood-letter, episode .... Taanis 21b-22a

Bloodletting
Bloodletting .... Pesachim 22b
Bloodletting, harmful foods .... Shabbos 129a-129b; Nedarim 54b; Avodah Zarah 29a; Meilah 20b
Bloodletting, health .... Shabbos 129a-129b; Nedarim 54b
Bloodletting, prayer and thanksgiving .... Berachos 60a
Bloodletting, tasting in store .... Shabbos 129a
Bloodletting, too much is harmful .... Gittin 70a
Bloodletting, washing hands afterwards .... Pesachim 112a

Bloris goy .... *see* **Hair, forelock of non-Jew**, page 264

Blowing
Blowing on cereal peel to separate it from kernel .... Beitzah 12b-14a
Blowing trumpets in Temple .... Rosh Hashanah 27a

Blowing *shofar*
Rosh Hashanah —
Blowing *shofar*, *aggadah* .... Rosh Hashanah 16a-16b
Blowing *shofar* and prayer, preference .... Rosh Hashanah 34b
Blowing *shofar* in Yavneh, decree .... Rosh Hashanah 29b
Blowing *shofar*, individual .... Rosh Hashanah 34b
Blowing *shofar*, interruption .... Rosh Hashanah 34a-34b; Succah 54a; Arachin 10a
Blowing *shofar*, mutual indispensibility .... Rosh Hashanah 34b
Blowing *shofar*, Shabbos .... Rosh Hashanah 29b-30a, 32b-33a; Succah 43a

Blowing *shofar, shevarim teruah* .... Rosh Hashanah 33b-34a; Arachin 10a
Blowing *shofar*, time .... Rosh Hashanah 32b
Blowing *shofar*, who .... Rosh Hashanah 29a, 33a-33b
Blowing *shofar*, year when they did not blow .... Rosh Hashanah 16b

Shabbos —
Blowing *shofar* on Shabbos eve .... Shabbos 35b
Blowing *shofar*, Yom Kippur for Shabbos .... Shabbos 114b; Succah 54b
Blowing *shofar*, Yom Tov for Shabbos .... Chullin 26b; Shabbos 114b

Calamities —
Blowing *shofar* for tragedy on Shabbos .... Bava Kama 80b
Blowing *shofar*, for which sin .... Taanis 14a, 18b-19b, 22a; Bava Basra 91a
Blowing *shofar*, how .... Taanis 14a
Blowing *shofar* on fast days .... Taanis 14a, 22a
Blowing *shofar* on fast for rain .... Taanis 16b-17a

Misc. —
Blowing *shofar*, echo .... Rosh Hashanah 27b-28a
Blowing *shofar*, how .... Rosh Hashanah 33b; Succah 53b-54a; Arachin 10a
Blowing *shofar* in Temple, when .... Succah 54a-55a
Blowing *shofar* is not a work .... Shabbos 117b, 131b; Rosh Hashanah 29b
Blowing *shofar* when filling water for *Succoth* libations .... Succah 51a-51b

Blows
Blows, a hundred were given .... Bava Basra 85b; Kesubos 53a
Blows, Avimi to Rav Chasda .... Menachos 7a; Arachin 22a

Blue dye
Blue dye, chest in sea .... Bava Basra 74a-74b
Blue dye, *chilazon* .... Menachos 44a
Blue dye for *tzitzis*, false .... Menachos 41b
Blue dye, is it an indispensable requirement for white *tzitzis*? .... Menachos 38a-38b
Blue dye, left by Nevuzaradan .... Shabbos 26a
Blue dye, preparation and disqualified persons .... Menachos 42b-43a
Blue dye, sea and Throne of Glory .... Menachos 43b; Sotah 17a; Chullin 89a
Blue dye, wool .... Yevamos 4b
Blue dye, Zebulun .... Megillah 6a

B'nai Braq
B'nai Braq, flowing with milk .... Kesubos 111b
B'nai Braq, Rabbi Akiva .... Sanhedrin 32b

B'nei
B'nei aliyah, righteous .... Succah 45b; Sanhedrin 97b
B'nei Torah, Mechuza .... Shabbos 139a-139b; Avodah Zarah 58a, 59a; Yevamos 46a
B'nei Torah, stringencies .... Shabbos 139a-139b; Avodah Zarah 58a, 59a

B'nei chayei umezonei .... *see* **Life, children and livelihood, fate**, page 369
B'nei Eli .... *see* **Sons of Eli**, page 644
B'nei Haman .... *see* **Sons of Haman**, page 645
B'nei olam haba .... *see* **Destined to World to Come**, page 161
B'nei Yisrael .... *see* **Israel**, page 318

Board
Board and beam, courtyard .... Eruvin 12b
Board and beam, expenses .... Eruvin 80a
Board, large closed alley .... Eruvin 10a-10b

Board turned upside down, impurity .... Menachos 96b
Boards at an angle, determining domains .... Eruvin 17b-18a, 19a-21a, 22a-23a
Boards, *lavud* stringency .... Eruvin 9b
Boards, *muktzeh* .... Shabbos 49b
Boards of Tabernacle .... Shabbos 98a-98b; Yoma 72a; Succah 45b
Boards of Tabernacle, wagons .... Shabbos 49b
Boards, *s'chach* .... Succah 14a-14b, 15a, 17b-18a, 37a

Board for alley
Board for alley, for half closed alley .... Eruvin 14b
Board for alley, passageway .... Shabbos 6a-6b; Eruvin 12b
Board for alley which fell on Shabbos .... Eruvin 95a

Board for *eruv*
Board for *eruv*, animal .... Eruvin 15a-15b
Board for *eruv*, carrying in front of it .... Eruvin 8b-9b
Board for *eruv*, dimension .... Eruvin 14b
Board for *eruv*, distance of three handbreadths .... Eruvin 14b
Board for *eruv*, four cubits .... Eruvin 5a-5b, 10a
Board for *eruv*, Shabbos .... Eruvin 11b-12a, 13a
Board for *eruv*, standing by itself .... Eruvin 15a
Board for *eruv*, why is it effective? .... Eruvin 12b

Boasting, let others praise you .... Nedarim 62a
Boat .... *see* **Ship**, page 616
Boaz
Boaz, allusions to Ruth .... Shabbos 113b; Sanhedrin 93a-93b
Boaz and Joseph, battle against evil urge .... Sanhedrin 19b
Boaz, death of wife and sons .... Bava Basra 91a
Boaz, did not invite Manoah .... Bava Basra 91a

Bodily needs
Laws —
Bodily needs .... *see also* **Toilets**, page 695
Bodily needs, before prayer .... Berachos 15a
Bodily needs, clearing on Shabbos .... Shabbos 81a-81b
Bodily needs in fellow's field .... Bava Kama 81b
Bodily needs, modesty .... Berachos 61b-62b, 23b; Tamid 27b
Bodily needs, not to become abominable .... Makos 16b
Bodily needs, prayer .... Berachos 22b-23a
Bodily needs, waiting .... Shabbos 33a; Makos 16b
Bodily needs, wiping on Shabbos .... Shabbos 81a-81b; Bava Kama 81b; Succah 36b
Misc. —
Bodily needs before eating .... Shabbos 41a, 82a
Bodily needs, cure .... Shabbos 110a
Bodily needs, danger of wiping .... Shabbos 81a, 82a; Berachos 55a
Bodily needs, danger to refrain from relieving oneself .... Bechoros 44b
Bodily needs, morning and evening .... Berachos 62a
Bodily needs, prevent pride .... Bava Basra 75a
Bodily needs, sickness .... Pesachim 118a; Sotah 42b
Body
Body and soul, punishment .... Sanhedrin 91a-91b
Bodies, different, number of sin offerings .... Krisos 2b, 15a

Bodies, different, sacrifices .... Krisos 15b
Body, clean, *tefillin* .... Shabbos 49a, 130a
Body has benefit, three things .... Berachos 57b
Body impurity by eating impure food .... Shabbos 13b-14a; Yoma 80b; Sotah 30a; Chullin 33b-34a; Taharos 2:2; Zavim 5:12

Boel niddah .... *see* **Intimate relations with *niddah*,** page 317
Bogeres .... *see* **Adult girl,** page 12
Boils
Boil and burn, mark of leprosy .... Negaim 9:1-2; Chullin 8a
Boils, abundant blood .... Bechoros 44b
Boils, blemish .... Bechoros 41a
Boils, cure .... Shabbos 67a, 77b
Boils, cutting limbs .... Krisos 15b
Boils, different kinds .... Kesubos 77b
Boils in Egypt .... Bava Kama 80b; Bechoros 41a
Boiled
Boiled, wording of vow .... Nedarim 49a, 51b
Boiling utensil, sacrifice .... Avodah Zarah 76a; Zevachim 97a
Boka de'atma .... *see* **Upper thigh, *treifah*** page 716
Bold, Israel .... Beitzah 25b
Bolt, closing on Shabbos .... Shabbos 126a-126b; Eruvin 101b-102a
Bond before levirate marriage
Bond before levirate marriage .... Yevamos 18b-19a
Bond before levirate marriage, brothers to sisters ... Yevamos 18a, 23b, 26a-26b, 27b; Eduyos 5:500
Bond before levirate marriage, prohibition to annul .... Yevamos 17b-18b, 24a, 26a, 28a
Bond before levirate marriage, to one or two brothers .... Yevamos 29b, 30a-30b; Nedarim 74a
Bond before levirate marriage, vows .... Yevamos 29b; Nedarim 74a
Bond before levirate marriage, widow's relatives ... Yevamos 17b-18b, 26b, 27a, 30a, 41a, 51a-51b, 53a; Megillah 18b
Bone
  Impurity —
  Bone from living animal .... Chullin 129b; Eduyos 6:3
  Bone like barley grain .... Yoma 79a; Nazir 56b-57a; Shabbos 132a; Pesachim 81b
  Bone utensil, impurity .... Chullin 25b
  Bone, whole, less than volume of barley grain .... Nazir 53b-54a
  Bones, impurity .... Nazir 52a-52b; Bechoros 45a; Oholos 2:1
  Bones, impurity of load .... Chullin 126b
  Prohibitions —
  Bone which broke, *treifah* .... Chullin 76b-77a
  Bones, annulling mixture .... Chullin 98b
  Bones for animals, *muktzeh* .... Shabbos 128a
  Bones, *muktzeh* .... Shabbos 143a, 157a; Beitzah 2a
  Bones, worms and reptiles .... Chullin 58a-58b
  Sacrifices —
  Bone, Pesach lamb .... Pesachim 83a, 84a-85a, 95a; Makos 17a; Shevuos 3b, 70a; Zevachim 97b
  Bones of leftover sacrifice .... Pesachim 83a-83b; Chullin 125a
  Bones of sacrifices, offering .... Zevachim 98a
  Bones of sacrifices, profit .... Zevachim 86a, 98a, 103b; Menachos 83a

B

Misc. —

Bone, Rabbi Yochanan kept his son's bone (tooth, see Rashi) .... Berachos 5b; Bava Basra 116a
Bone stuck in throat, whisper .... Shabbos 67a
Bone which broke, marrow .... Chullin 125a
Bones, episode about count .... Bechoros 45a
Bones of corpses
Bones of corpses, episodes .... Niddah 24b
Bones of corpses, impurity of *nazir* .... Nazir 52b-53b
Bones of corpses, picking .... Berachos 18a; Moed Katan 8a
Bones of corpses, sheets .... Niddah 61a
Bones of corpses, volume for impurity .... Eduyos 1:7; Oholos 2:1; Nazir 52b-53a
Bones of corpses, wine .... Niddah 24b
Boneh Yerushalayim, *Amen* .... Berachos 45b
Boneh .... *see* **Building,** page 79
Bonfire on Yom Tov .... Beitzah 21b
Bonias
Bonias, his son's garments .... Eruvin 85b-86a
Bonias, thin garments .... Gittin 59a
Book
Book .... *see also* **Scroll,** page 593
Book not proofread, retention .... Kesubos 19b
Book not proofread, not to use for learning .... Pesachim 112a
Book of Adam .... Bava Metzia 85b-86a
Book of *aggadah,* reading on Shabbos .... Gittin 60a
Book of lineage, *Divrei Hayamim* .... Pesachim 62b
Book of remedies (*refuah*), Hezekiah .... Pesachim 56a; Berachos 10b
Book, reward for lending .... Kesubos 50a
Book, *Shem Olam* .... Sanhedrin 93b
Books, holy .... *see* **Holy books,** page 282
Books of righteous, Rosh Hashanah .... Rosh Hashanah 16b; Berachos 6a
Books, secular, prohibition .... Sanhedrin 100b
Book of Chronicles
Book of Chronicles, episode .... Pesachim 62b
Book of Chronicles, homilies .... Pesachim 62b
Book of Chronicles, who wrote .... Bava Basra 14b-15a
Book of Creation, permission .... Sanhedrin 67b
Book of Ecclesiastes
Book of Ecclesiastes, impurity to hands .... Megillah 7a; Yadayim 3:5; Eduyos 5:3
Book of Ecclesiastes, Sages wanted to conceal .... Shabbos 30b
Book of Judges, who wrote .... Bava Basra 14b
Book of Proverbs
Book of Proverbs, Sages wanted to conceal .... Shabbos 30b
Book of Proverbs, Solomon .... Bava Basra 14b-15a
Boor
Boor, not sin fearing .... Avos 2:5
Boor, seven things .... Avos 5:7
Booty
Booty in the future, consecration .... Pesachim 50a
Booty, king's rights .... Sanhedrin 20b-21a

Booty of Egypt...Berachos 4b, 9a-9b; Bechoros 5b
Booty taken by non-Jews, consecrated money.................Bechoros 50a; Avodah Zarah 52b
Booty taken by non-Jews, returning................................Rosh Hashanah 23a
Bor..*see* **Pit**, page 489
Bordering parts, who..Bava Basra 12b
Borders, closed, Judea and Galilee...Bava Basra 38b
Borders of *Eretz Yisrael*...Gittin 7b-8a; Bechoros 55a
Borei
"*Borei*," past or future tense..Berachos 52b
Borei Meorei Haesh, blessing...Berachos 52a, 52b
Borei Minei Mezonos, blessing..Berachos 38a, 42a
Borei Minei Mezonos.............................*see also* **Wheat, blessing,** page 741
Borei Nefashos, blessing..Berachos 44b
Borei Peri Haadamah, blessing...Berachos 39a, 40a
Borei Peri Haetz, blessing..Berachos 38a, 40a-40b
Borer beshabbos.............................*see* **Selecting on Shabbos,** page 599
Borganim......................................*see* **Hut of leaves,** *techum,* page 289
Born
Born during his father's life, levirate marriage..................Yevamos 9a-9b, 17a-17b, 18b-19b
Born persons are destined to die..Avos 4:22
Borrow
Borrow.............................*see also* **Loan,** page 376, **Custody with owner,** page 138
Borrow on my account and I shall repay.......................................Beitzah 15b
Borrow to eat, advice...Chullin 84a
Borrowed from his wife...Bava Basra 51a-51b
Borrowed or rented animal, died...Bava Metzia 97a-98b
Borrower and lender hold promissory note....................Bava Metzia 7a-7b; Bava Basra 170a
Borrower, appointed Rosh Yeshivah...Sotah 40a
Borrower believes lender...Bava Metzia 35a
Borrower, died because of work...Bava Metzia 96b-97a
Borrower, from when is he responsible...........................Kesubos 34b; Bava Kama 112a
Borrower, liable for unavoidable damage............Bava Metzia 93a, 94b-95a; Shevuos 49a-49b
Borrower, prohibition to lend borrowed item................................Bava Metzia 29b
Borrower, property left to him.......................Bava Metzia 113b-114a; Arachin 23b-24a
Borrower, suffering..Eruvin 41b
Borrower, ways to borrow..Bava Metzia 96a
Borrower who bequeathed.......................................Bava Kama 112a; Kesubos 34b
Borrower who wrote promissory note..............................Gittin 20b-21a; Eduyos 2:3
Borrower, wording to borrow..Bava Metzia 103a
Borrowing, equal to owning...Avodah Zarah 15a
Borrowing his fast and fasting later...Shabbos 11a
Borrowing on Shabbos, "lend me"..Shabbos 148a
Borrowing, ox considered as goring occasionally...............................Bava Kama 40a-40b
Borrowing without owner's consent....................Bava Metzia 41a, 43b; Bava Basra 88a
Borrows and does not pay back...Avos 2:9
Borrows and redeems, redeeming estate..........................Arachin 30b; Kiddushin 20b-21a
"*Bosha imchem,*" sixty myriads non-Jews...............................Berachos 58a, 58b
Boshes..*see* **Shame,** page 609
Bosis..*see* **Basis** page 44

B

Bottle and coin, child..Bava Basra 87b-88a

Bottom
"Bottom of pot," David's enemies...Shabbos 30a
Bottom determines, cooking...Pesachim 75b-76a

Bound...*see* **Binding**, page 57

Boundaries of field, sale..Bava Basra 62a-62b

Bow, *tefillin* knot...Eruvin 97a

Bowing
Bowing...*see also* **Prostrating**, page 508
Bowing at *Modim,* snake..Bava Kama 16a
Bowing during *Shemoneh Esrei*.....................................Berachos 12a-12b, 28b, 34a-34b; Yoma 53b
Bowing, explanation...Berachos 34b; Megillah 22b; Shevuos 16b
Bowing, Levi...Taanis 25a; Succah 53a; Megillah 22b
Bowing, Rabbi Akiva...Berachos 31a

Bowl
Bowl for kneading, split, impurity..Keilim 20:2; Yadayim 4:1
Bowls of Altar...Succah 48a-48b

Box
Box for consecrated money of bird sacrifices...Pesachim 90b
Boxes, consecrated, in Temple...Menachos 104a, 107b-108a; Yoma 55a-55b; Shekalim 6:5; Temurah 23b

Boyi kallah...*see* **Come bride, Shabbos**, page 115

Brace, included in sale...Bava Basra 77b-78a

Braiding hair, Shabbos...Shabbos 94b-95a

Brain
Brain, "he has no brain in his skull"...Yevamos 9a
Brain, checking *treifah*...Chullin 56a-56b
Brain membrane, checking...Chullin 56a-56b
Brain membrane, *treifah*..Chullin 45a-45b, 56a-56b
Brain surgery..Kesubos 77b
Brain, *treifah*..Chullin 45a-45b, 56a-56b
Brains of slain inhabitants of Jerusalem..Gittin 58a

Bran
Bran, collecting damage..Bava Kama 7a-7b, 9a, 10b, 14b
Bran, kneading...Shabbos 155b-156a

Branches
Branches in courtyard, tithes...Maasros 3:8-10
Branches out of *Eretz Yisrael*, tithes...Gittin 22a
Branches, putting down...Shabbos 4b, 7b-8a

Branches of tree
Branches of tree in Jerusalem, second tithe..Makos 12a-12b
Branches of tree, neighbors...Bava Basra 27b, 82b
Branches of tree, refuge city...Makos 12a-12b

Breach
Breach attracts a thief..Succah 26a
Breach in corner of wall, not considered as opening...........................Eruvin 6a, 94a-94b
Breach in closed alley, annulling opening...Eruvin 10b
Breach in partition, closed alley...Eruvin 5b
Breach in partition, in height...Eruvin 16b
Breach in *s'chach*..Succah 15a-15b, 18a

Breach of four cubits in closed alley .... Eruvin 5b-6a
Breach of ten cubits .... Kilayim 4:4; Eruvin 10a
Breach on side of closed alley .... Eruvin 5a

Breached part equal to existing, partition .... Eruvin 5b, 10b, 15b-16b; Kilayim 4:4; Succah 15a-15b

Bread

Advice —

Bread, advice .... Menachos 50b
Bread along with bread .... Nedarim 49b; Beitzah 16a
Bread and porridge, eating .... Nedarim 49b
Bread crumbs .... Chullin 105b; Pesachim 111b
Bread, dark, health .... Pesachim 42a; Eruvin 55b-56a
Bread dipped in salt, eating .... Avos 6:4
Bread, eating small portions .... Shabbos 140b
Bread hanging, poverty .... Pesachim 111b
Bread in basket, feeling satiated .... Yoma 18b, 67a, 74b; Yevamos 37b; Kesuvos 62b, 63ba
Bread in the morning .... Shabbos 10a; Pesachim 12b; Bava Metzia 107b
Bread, white, health .... Pesachim 42a-42b
Bread, without accompaniment, harmful as swords .... Kiddushin 62a
Bread, yours before your family's .... Chullin 84a

Laws —

Bread baked with forbidden wood .... Pesachim 26b-27b, 75a
Bread baked with milk .... Bava Metzia 91a; Pesachim 30a, 36a; Zevachim 95b
Bread, blessing .... Berachos 38a-38b
Bread in small quantity, prison .... Sanhedrin 81b
Bread left on table .... Sanhedrin 92a
Bread, lying down .... Berachos 42b-43a
Bread, moldy, *chametz* .... Pesachim 7a
Bread of poverty, *matzah* .... Pesachim 36a-37a, 115b
Bread, soaked, blessing .... Menachos 75b; Berachos 37b
Bread stuck to another, combining for *challah* .... Pesachim 48b
Bread, two loaves, Shabbos .... Shabbos 117b; Berachos 39b

Sacrifices —

Bread and sacrifice, indispensable requirement .... Menachos 46a-46b
Bread, combining to *piggul* .... Menachos 15a-15b
Bread, considered partner of sheep for Shavuos .... Menachos 15b
Bread of meal offering .... Menachos 59a, 59a, 60a, 63a-63b, 72b, 73a
Bread of thanksgiving .... *see* **Loaves of thanksgiving**, page 376
Bread, ram of *nazir* .... Nazir 24b; Menachos 48b

Misc. —

Bread, Adam's efforts .... Berachos 58a
Bread by weight, curse .... Menachos 87b
Bread, kinds .... Challah 1:8; Eruvin 81a; Beitzah 21a
Bread mixed, Ezekiel .... Eruvin 81a
Bread of high-quality, Daniel .... Yoma 76b
Bread stolen, taste .... Sanhedrin 104b

Bread of non-Jew

Bread of non-Jew, episode to obtain permission .... Avodah Zarah 38b
Bread of non-Jew, permitted .... Avodah Zarah 35b
Bread of non-Jew, renegade .... Chullin 13a

Bread of non-Jew, up to one *parsa* .... Chullin 122b-123a
Bread of non-Jews, made by Cutheans .... Sheviis 8:10

Break
Break barrel and keep its wine .... Bava Basra 16a
Break my jug, damage .... Bava Kama 91b
Breaking barrel on Shabbos .... Beitzah 33b; Shabbos 146a
Breaking bone of Pesach lamb ...... Pesachim 83a-83b, 84a-85a, 95a; Zevachim 97b; Makos 17a; Shevuos 3b
Breaking clay vessels, child .... Yoma 78b
Breaking covenant of Abraham .... Sanhedrin 99a; Avos 3:11
Breaking cup at wedding .... Berachos 31a
Breaking items forbidden to benefit, worker .... Avodah Zarah 63b-64a
Breaking neck, blood .... Chullin 113a
Breaking oven, impurity .... Keilim 5:7-11a; Chullin 123b-124a
Breaking sacrificial utensils in Temple .... Zevachim 94b, 95a
Broke broken utensil .... Bava Kama 26b
Broke by itself, idol .... Avodah Zarah 41b-42b; Meilah 14a
Broke neck, impurity .... Chullin 21a
Broken items .... *see* **Fragments of utensils**, page 238
Broken leg, *treifah* .... Chullin 42b, 54a-54b

Breaking of Tablets
Breaking of Tablets, approved by G-d .... Pesachim 87b
Breaking of Tablets, letters fly in air .... Pesachim 87b
Breaking of Tablets, reason .... Shabbos 87a
Breaking of Tablets, troubles .... Eruvin 54a

Breaking idol
Breaking idol, commandment .... Sanhedrin 55a; Avodah Zarah 45b-46a
Breaking idol, episodes .... Avodah Zarah 41b
Breaking idol, how .... Pesachim 28a; Avodah Zarah 43b-44a
Breaking idol, offering sacrifice .... Avodah Zarah 50b-51a

Breast
Breast and fat, order of offering .... Menachos 62a
Breast, at place of understanding .... Berachos 10a
Breast, definition .... Chullin 45a
Breast like towers, discourses .... Pesachim 87a; Bava Basra 7b-8a
Breast like woman, episode .... Shabbos 53b

Breast and leg
Breast and leg, Jerusalem .... Zevachim 55a
Breast and leg, non-holy animals .... Chullin 130a
Breast and leg, widow .... Yevamos 87a

Breastplate, Aaron's joy .... Shabbos 139a

Breath
Breath, interruption in speech .... Succah 38b-39a
Breath of schoolchildren .... Shabbos 119b

Breirah .... *see* **Retroactive clarification**, page 563

Bribe
Bribe, Chavrei people in Babylon .... Yevamos 63b
Bribe, Divine anger against world .... Bava Basra 9b
Bribe, episode about philosopher .... Shabbos 116a-116b
Bribe, episodes about Sages .... Kesubos 105b-106a; Makos 24a

Bribe, money corresponding to time spent .... Kesubos 105a-105b; Bechoros 29b
Bribe, punishment and care .... Kesubos 105a-105b
Bricks
Bricks, *muktzeh* .... Beitzah 31b; Shabbos 124b
Bricks, wall thickness .... Bava Basra 3a
Bride
Bride and groom, protection .... Berachos 54b
Bride, how to dance before her .... Kesubos 16b-17a
Bride, immersion after intimate relations .... Yevamos 34b
Bride, impatient to come home, commentaries .... Pesachim 87a; Kesubos 71b
Bride, new, death of righteous .... Moed Katan 25b
Bride on shoulders .... Kesubos 17a
Bride, pitiful, golden calf .... Shabbos 88b; Gittin 36b
Bride, prohibition to look at her .... Kesubos 17a
Bride, rejoicing and precedence .... Berachos 6b
Bride, seven days of purity .... Niddah 66a
Bride taken away from marriage canopy .... Yevamos 110a
Bride turns head aside .... Pesachim 86b
Bride, why does she comes under canopy .... Shabbos 33a; Kesubos 8b
Bride with beautiful eyes, no examination necessary .... Taanis 24a
Bridesmaids, virginity .... Kesubos 12a
Bridge
Bridge, danger .... Shabbos 32a
Bridge, dead Sages honoring one to another .... Moed Katan 25b
Bridge for *eruv* .... Eruvin 79a
Bridle, purchase of animal .... Bava Metzia 8a-9b
Brine .... *see* **Sauce of fish**, page 589
Brine of non-Jew .... Avodah Zarah 34b
Bring
"Bring in!," accepting liability .... Bava Kama 48b
Bringing forth, animals .... Bechoros 7b-8a; Bava Basra 16a
Bringing in *tevel* before requirement to give tithe .... Pesachim 9a; Niddah 15b; Berachos 31a; Menachos 67b
Bringing into domain on Shabbos, included in taking out .... Shabbos 2b
Bringing meal offering .... Zevachim 63b; Menachos 60a-61a; Sotah 14b
Bringing peace .... Yevamos 109a-109b; Avos 1:12
Bringing sacrificial blood
Bringing sacrificial blood in Temple .... Zevachim 15a-15b
Bringing sacrificial blood, non-*Kohen* .... Zevachim 14a-14b; Yoma 49a
Bringing sacrificial blood, rectifying disqualification .... Zevachim 15a
Bringing sacrificial blood to Altar, disqualifying thought .... Zevachim 14a
Bringing sacrificial blood, with left hand .... Yoma 48b-49a
Bringing sacrificial blood, without walking .... Zevachim 14b-15a; Menachos 13b
Bris
Bris bein habesarim (Covenant between the parts) .... Megillah 31b; Taanis 27b
Bris melach, suffering .... Berachos 5a
Bris milah .... *see* **Circumcision**, page 106
Broker
Broker, responsibility .... Bava Metzia 81a

Broker, toothless ox..Bava Metzia 42b
Broker for forbidden relations ....Shevuos 47b

Brother
Brother, "he is our brother," inheritance.............................Bava Basra 135a-135b
Brother, "you are our brother," Agrippas.............................Sotah 41b
Brother, after inheritance was shared...................................Bava Basra 106b-107a
Brother from the father, levirate marriage ....Yevamos 17b
Brother, oldest, honor..Kesubos 103a
Brother's wife, during his life...Yevamos 9a-9b, 17a-17b, 18b-19b
Brother's wife, marriage by mistake.....................................Yevamos 95b
Brothers, after sharing..Bava Basra 7a-7b, 65a
Brothers, canceling sharing..Bava Basra 106b-107a; Bava Kama 9a
Brothers, cases of sharing...Bava Basra 172a
Brothers died because of circumcision.................................Yevamos 64b
Brothers from the mother, inheritance.................................Bava Basra 110b, 109b, 142a-142b, 159b
Brothers of mother, her sons will resemble them...............Bava Basra 110a
Brothers of Rava, letter...Kesubos 111a
Brothers of woman, marriage...Bava Basra 109b-110a
Brothers, pool resources...Bava Kama 11b; Bava Basra 139a, 144b
Brothers, sharing..Kiddushin 42a-42b; Yevamos 67b; Kesubos 100a; Gittin 34a
Brothers, tithe of animal...Bechoros 56b
Brothers to sisters, levirate marriage....................................Yevamos 18a, 23b, 26a-26b, 27b, 30a; Eduyos 5:5

Brother of deceased childless husband
Brother of deceased childless husband, annulling *kiddushin*..............Bava Kama 110b-111a
Brother of deceased childless husband, dowry....................Kesubos 66a
Brother of deceased childless husband, inheritance ....Yevamos 38a-39a, 40a; Kesubos 80b-82b;
....Bechoros 52a-52b
Brother of deceased childless husband like husband, wife's vow...........Yevamos 112a-112b
Brother of deceased childless husband, sharing inheritance..............Bava Basra 12b
Brother of deceased childless husband, testimony for inheritance..............Yevamos 117a
Brother of deceased childless husband, who fled................Kesubos 107b

Brothers of Joseph
Brothers of Joseph, dread...Taanis 9a
Brothers of Joseph, Pharaoh..Bava Kama 92a
Brothers of Joseph, why show yourself.................................Taanis 10b

Bruriah
Bruriah, do not speak too much...Eruvin 53b
Bruriah, episode..Avodah Zarah 18b
Bruriah, ruffians..Berachos 10a
Bruriah, three hundred laws...Pesachim 62b
Bruriah, which one to Lod...Eruvin 53b
Bruriah, wife of Rabbi Meir..Avodah Zarah 18b

Brushing hair
Brushing hair, health...Nedarim 81a
Brushing hair, *nazir*..Nazir 42a; Shabbos 50b, 81b
Brushing hair on Shabbos, inevitable act.............................Shabbos 50a-50b

Buckwheat, variety of wheat...Pesachim 35a; Menachos 70a
Bug, reptile..Niddah 58b
Builders, Sages..Shabbos 114a

B

Building

Building and destroying in utensils .... Shabbos 102b-103a, 122b; Eruvin 35a; Beitzah 10a, 11b, 22a
Building causes poverty .... Yevamos 63a; Sotah 11a
Building, cheese on Shabbos .... Shabbos 95a
Building for idolatrous purpose, salary .... Avodah Zarah 19b
Building for rejoicing, fast day .... Taanis 14b; Megillah 5b
Building, minimal, on Shabbos .... Shabbos 102b
Building by children is destruction .... Nedarim 40a
Building by Herod .... Succah 51b; Bava Basra 3b-4a
Building on Sabbatical year .... Moed Katan 4b
Building or finishing work .... Shabbos 102b-103a
Building private altar .... Chagigah 22a
Building, secondary category of work .... Shabbos 73b
Building, smallest on Shabbos .... Shabbos 102b
Building stone, positioning on ground on Shabbos .... Shabbos 102b
Building, temporary, on Yom Tov .... Beitzah 32b
Building then sanctifying .... Meilah 14a-14b; Bava Metzia 57b

Building of Temple

Building of Temple, at night .... Shevuos 15b
Building of Temple, from non-consecrated materials ..... Meilah 14a-14b; Bava Metzia 57b
Building of Temple, on Shabbos .... Yevamos 6a
Building of second Temple .... Rosh Hashanah 3a-4a; Megillah 10a, 12a

Bull

Bull .... see also **Ox**, page 467
Bull for sacrifice, age .... Parah 1:2; Rosh Hashanah 10a
Bull in stadium games, for sacrifice .... Bava Kama 40b
Bull of Yom Kippur, place of standing .... Zevachim 20a; Yoma 35b, 36a
Bull of Yom Kippur, private sacrifice .... Yoma 50a-50b, 51b
Bull, very large, strength of *Kohanim* .... Succah 52b
Bulls and rams, mutually indispensable .... Succah 47a

Bull for *Kohen Gadol*

Bull for *Kohen Gadol*, unintentional transgression .... Horayos 6b-7a
Bull for *Kohen Gadol*, partial mistake .... Horayos 7b; Sanhedrin 62a
Bull for *Kohen Gadol*, who .... Horayos 12a

Bulmus .... see **Hunger, episodes**, page 288
Bunch of grapes, spies .... Sotah 34a
Bundle

Bundle, necessary number to make bundle .... Succah 13a
Bundle, running on Shabbos .... Shabbos 153b
Bundle, *s'chach* .... Succah 12a-13b

Burial .... see also **Grave**, page 256

Episodes —

Burial in mat, episode .... Berachos 18b
Burial of Hezekiah and Asa .... Bava Kama 16b-17a
Burial of Rav Huna .... Moed Katan 25a

Laws —

Burial, "do not fund my burial from my money" .... Kesubos 48a
Burial, delaying, prohibition .... Sanhedrin 46b
Burial of apparatus used for death penalty .... Sanhedrin 45b; Avodah Zarah 62b

Burial of items forbidden to profit .... Temurah 33b-34a; Pesachim 24a
Burial on Yom Tov .... Shabbos 139a-139b; Beitzah 6a, 22a

Rights —
Burial, "someone to bury me," claim .... Yevamos 65b; Kesubos 64a
Burial of one's fiancee .... Kesubos 53a
Burial of one's wife .... Kesubos 48a
Burial of widow awaiting levirate marriage .... Kesubos 80b-81a
Burial of widow, who must pay for it .... Kesubos 95b

Misc. —
Burial, "the way in which they will go" .... Bava Metzia 30b; Bava Kama 100a
Burial, close to whom .... Sanhedrin 47a
Burial in *Eretz Yisrael* .... Kesubos 111a
Burial of righteous, by G-d Himself .... Sotah 9b
Burial, praying even for good burial .... Berachos 8a
Burial, source and reason .... Sanhedrin 46b
Burial, urgent, for whom is it recommended .... Moed Katan 22a

Buried forbidden substances .... Temurah 33b-34a; Pesachim 24a
Burn, leprous mark .... Chullin 8a; Negaim 9:1-3
Burning
Burning a prostitute, episode .... Bechoros 45a
Burning, doubt about impurity .... Taharos 4:5-6; Niddah 33b
Burning fellow's crop .... Sotah 11a
Burning friend's bills .... Bava Kama 33b, 98a-98b
Burning handful of meal offering .... Zevachim 110a
Burning idol .... Avodah Zarah 45b-46a
Burning kings' belongings after death .... Sanhedrin 52b; Avodah Zarah 11a-11b
Burning of items forbidden to profit .... Temurah 33b-34a; Pesachim 24a, 27b
Burning of Torah scroll, Temple destruction .... Yevamos 16b
Burning on Altar, is it considered as eating .... Chullin 81b
Burning one's dish in public, shame .... Berachos 17b
Burning Red Heifer .... Zevachim 113a; Parah 3:9-11
Burning remainder of sacrifice, prohibition .... Menachos 57b; Yoma 47b; Yevamos 100a;
                                                                                                   Sotah 23a; Zevachim 76b
Burning started, sacrifices .... Zevachim 43a-43b, 85b
Burning wood on Altar .... Yoma 24b, 45a
Burnt animal, *treifah* .... Chullin 56b, 57a
Burnt by friend's canopy .... Bava Basra 75a
Burnt by warm water, rebuke .... Berachos 16b
Burnt daughter-in-law with persimmon oil .... Shabbos 26a
Burnt, prohibitions .... Temurah 33b-34a; Pesachim 24a, 27b

Burning disqualified
Burning disqualified sacrifice .... Pesachim 49a, 81b-82a; Berachos 49b
Burning leftover sacrifice .... Yevamos 72b; Zevachim 98a
Burning leftover sacrifice and disqualified Pesach .... Pesachim 73b, 83b-84a
Burning sacrifices, profit .... Shabbos 25a-25b
Burning sacrifices, quantity .... Pesachim 49b-50a; Berachos 49b
Burning sacrifices, starting by day .... Menachos 26b
Burning sacrifices, where .... Shekalim 8:6-7
Burning sacrifices, Yom Tov .... Shabbos 23b-25a; Menachos 46b

Burning impure

Burning impure *terumah*, benefit .... Yevamos 73b, 74a; Shabbos 25a-25b
Burning *terumah*, doubt .... Kiddushin 80a-80b; Taharos 4:5-6; Niddah 33b
Burning *terumah* oil .... Terumos 11:10
Burning *terumah*, profit .... Shabbos 25a-25b; Pesachim 32a; Yevamos 73b, 74a

Burning parts of sacrifices

Burning parts of sacrifices before eating .... Pesachim 59b
Burning parts of sacrifices, how .... Menachos 26b-27a; Pesachim 64b; Zevachim 46b
Burning parts of sacrifices, impurity .... Yoma 46a-46b
Burning parts of sacrifices, Shabbos .... Yoma 46a-46b
Burning parts of sacrifices which are not entirely burned .... Yoma 45a-45b; Zevachim 83b;
Menachos 26b

Burning penalty

Burning penalty, forbidden relations .... Sanhedrin 75a-75b
Burning penalty, how .... Sanhedrin 52a; Pesachim 75a
Burning penalty, relations with daughter .... Sanhedrin 76a
Burning penalty, relations with mother-in-law .... Yevamos 94b; Sanhedrin 75a-75b
Burning penalty, Sadducee *beis din* .... Sanhedrin 52b

Burning sin offerings

Burning sin offerings, where .... Zevachim 104a-104b, 105b-106a
Burning inside sin offerings .... Pesachim 75a-75b; Yoma 67b-68a; Zevachim 50a-50b
Burning invalid inside sin offerings .... Zevachim 82a; Pesachim 83a
Burning dedication sin offering .... Zevachim 16a-16b, 101a-101b; Pesachim 82a-82b

Burnt offering

Burnt offering, age of animal .... Menachos 48b; Temurah 19b
Burnt offering, atonement .... Yoma 36a-36b; Zevachim 5b, 6a-7a
Burnt offering, changing name .... Zevachim 12b-13a
Burnt offering, disqualified, skinning .... Zevachim 85a-85b, 104a
Burnt offering, female, private altar .... Avodah Zarah 24b
Burnt offering for Yom Tov .... *see* **Olas reiyah**, page 457
Burnt offering, gift after repentance .... Zevachim 7b
Burnt offering, money consecrated for unspecified .... Nazir 24b-25a, 25b-26a; Menachos 4b;
Meilah 11a
Burnt offering of bird, burning .... Zevachim 64b-65a
Burnt offering of bird, cutting head .... Zevachim 64b-65a; Menachos 97b
Burnt offering of bird, interruption in slaughtering .... Zevachim 65b
Burnt offering of bird, learned from sin offering .... Chullin 21a-22a
Burnt offering of bird, separating head .... Zevachim 64b-65a; Chullin 21a-22a
Burnt offering of woman after birth, atonement .... Zevachim 5b
Burnt offering, place of sprinklings .... Zevachim 51a-52a
Burnt offering, returning bird .... Bava Kama 78b
Burnt offering, song of *Leviim* .... Arachin 11b
Burnt offerings in desert .... Chagigah 6a-6b; Yevamos 5b; Zevachim 115b
Burnt offerings of Solomon .... Zevachim 59a-60a

Burnt parts of sacrifices

Burnt parts of sacrifices, eating flesh is permitted .... Menachos 26b; Sotah 15a
Burnt parts of sacrifices, *Kohen* who ate .... Menachos 74a-74b
Burnt parts of sacrifices, order of cutting up .... Menachos 77b
Burnt parts of sacrifices, secular use .... Zevachim 85b

Bursif, evil omen for Torah .... Sanhedrin 109a
Burying
Burying like donkey, standing .... Bava Basra 101b
Burying one's sons, forgiveness .... Sotah 48b-49a; Berachos 5b
Burying transgressor among wicked .... Yevamos 32a-33b
Business
Business .... *see also* **Merchandise**, page 405
Business, better helping in business than giving charity .... Shabbos 63a
Business with honesty, wealth .... Niddah 70b
Busy with commandment
Busy with commandment, deceased and burial .... Berachos 19a-19b
Busy with commandment, digging grave .... Berachos 14b
Busy with commandment, exemption .... Succah 25a-26a; Berachos 11a, 16a-16b; Sotah 44b
Busy with commandment, groom .... Succah 25b-26a
Busy with communal needs .... Avos 2:2
Butcher
Butcher, appeasing Rav .... Yoma 87a
Butcher being *Kohen*, priestly gifts .... Chullin 132b
Butcher, days when special meals are prepared .... Chullin 83a
Butcher disqualified, trustworthiness .... Sanhedrin 25a; Chullin 93b
Butcher, firstborn animal .... Bechoros 31b
Butcher, wealth as reward for honoring Shabbos .... Shabbos 119a
Butcher who does not examine .... Beitzah 25b
Butcher who spoiled slaughter, liability .... Bava Kama 99b; Bava Basra 93b
"Butter of Torah," for whom .... Berachos 63b
Buy
Buy and sell, will you be called a merchant? .... Bava Metzia 40b; Bava Basra 90a; Menachos 77a
Buy food with your last coin .... Chullin 84a
Buying .... *see also* **Sell**, page 600, **Sale**, page 585
Buying a master, Hebrew slave .... Kiddushin 22a
Buying a master, prayer not answered .... Bava Metzia 75b
Buying from five persons, doubt .... Bava Kama 103b; Yevamos 118b
Buying from non-Jew who seized from Jew .... Gittin 58b
Buying house in *Eretz Yisrael* .... Bava Kama 80b; Gittin 8b
Buying is earning, selling is losing .... Bava Metzia 51a
Buying item before person interested to buy it .... Kiddushin 59a
Bought from this man, *chazakah* .... Bava Basra 30a-31a
Buying, tithe of animal .... Bechoros 11a, 55b-56b; Bava Kama 110b
Buying from thief
Buying from thief, act of acquisition .... Bava Kama 115a
Buying from thief, collecting increase in value .... Bava Kama 96a; Bava Metzia 14b-15a
Buying from thief, customer knew .... Bava Metzia 15b
Buying from thief, liability .... Bava Basra 44b
Buying from thief, retracting .... Kesubos 92b-93a; Bava Kama 8b; Bava Metzia 14a
Buying from thief, stolen man's claim .... Bava Kama 111b, 115a; Chullin 134a
Buying from thief, who bought afterwards .... Bava Metzia 15b-16a
Buying from suspected thief .... Bava Kama 113a, 113b, 118b-119a; Bava Basra 51b-52a
Buyer
Buyer, argument in defense of buyer .... Bava Basra 23a; Gittin 58b

Buyer criticizes item .... Bava Basra 84a
Buyer, happy .... Berachos 5a
Buyer's floor, act of acquisition by money .... Bava Metzia 49b
Buzzard, long distance vision .... Chullin 63b
By
By heart, Rabbi Meir's Megillah .... Megillah 18b
By heart, Torah .... Gittin 60b; Temurah 14b
By me and you will G-d be praised, teaching .... Sotah 40a
By-pass vineyard, *nazir* .... Avodah Zarah 17a, 58b, 59a; Shabbos 13a; Pesachim 40b; Yevamos 46a;
.... Bava Metzia 92a

B

C

Cabbage

Cabbage, cure..Berachos 44b, 57b; Avodah Zarah 29a
Cabbage, health...Berachos 44b, 57b; Avodah Zarah 29a
Cabbage, medical examination...Nedarim 50b

Caesar

Caesar...*see* **Emperor**, page 195

Cain

Cain and Abel...Sanhedrin 37b; Yevamos 62a
Cain, found pretext..Sanhedrin 101b
Cain, his sister was permitted to him...Sanhedrin 58b

Cakes

Cakes, blessing...Berachos 42a
Cakes, *challah*..Challah 1:5; Pesachim 37a

Calamities

Calamities, two, fast...Taanis 8b
Calamity to whole country, tenant farmer.......................Bava Metzia 103b, 105b-106b

Calculate

Calculate reward for commandment against..Avos 2:1
Calculating time of coming of Messiah, harmful......................................Sanhedrin 97a

Calculation

Calculation of added sum, according to final sum.........................Bava Metzia 53b-54a
Calculations on Shabbos, prohibition..........................Shabbos 150a-150b; Kesubos 5a

Caleb

Caleb, Basiah...Megillah 13a
Caleb married Miriam..Sotah 11b-12a
Caleb, names and lineage..Sotah 11b-12a; Temurah 16a
Caleb, property in *Eretz Yisrael*..Bava Basra 122a-122b
Caleb, spies...Sotah 34b-35a
Caleb's daughter, Achsah...Temurah 16a

Calendar

Calendar, *"lo adu rosh"*......................................Rosh Hashanah 20a-20b; Succah 43b, 54b
Calendar, adding day to *Elul*.............................Rosh Hashanah 19b, 20b, 32a; Beitzah 6a, 22b
Calendar, adding day to month...Arachin 8b-10a
Calendar, avoiding witnesses' testimony................................Rosh Hashanah 20a-20b
Calendar, calculation of appearance of new moon....Rosh Hashanah 20b, 24b-25a; Arachin 9b

Calendar, days of *Adar* ...... Rosh Hashanah 19b-20a; Bechoros 58a; Sanhedrin 11a; Arachin 9b
Calendar, secret of lunar cycle ...... Rosh Hashanah 20b

Calf
Calf for sacrifice, age ...... Rosh Hashanah 10a
Calf, golden ...... *see* **Golden calf**, page 254
Calves of Jeroboam ...... Sanhedrin 101b

Calf whose neck is broken
Calf whose neck is broken, age ...... Parah 1:1
Calf whose neck is broken, *aggadah* ...... Sotah 46a
Calf whose neck is broken, benefit ...... Kiddushin 57a; Avodah Zarah 29b; Zevachim 70b;
...... Krisos 24b-25a
Calf whose neck is broken, breaking neck ...... Sotah 46b; Chullin 23b-24a
Calf whose neck is broken, disqualifying factors ...... Sotah 45b-46a
Calf whose neck is broken, elders ...... Sotah 44b-45a; Sanhedrin 14a-14b; Makos 10b
Calf whose neck is broken, impurity ...... Zevachim 70b
Calf whose neck is broken, measuring ...... Sotah 45a, 45b; Sanhedrin 14b, 88a
Calf whose neck is broken, testimony ...... Sotah 47b
Calf whose neck is broken, when ...... Sotah 45a-45b

Called
Called his master by name, Gehazi ...... Sanhedrin 100a
Called in name of future ...... Kesubos 10b
Called ninth "tenth" ...... Nazir 31b-32a; Bechoros 59a-59b, 60b-61a; Eruvin 50a; Kiddushin 51a
Calling before speaking ...... Yoma 4b
Calling one's fellow "wicked" and "slave" ...... Kiddushin 28a; Bava Metzia 71a
Calling one's teacher by name ...... Sanhedrin 100a

Called up to Torah
Called up to Torah, how many men ...... Megillah 21b-23a
Called up to Torah, longevity ...... Berachos 55a
Called up to Torah, man in disheveled garments ...... Megillah 24a-24b
Called up to Torah, order ...... Gittin 59a-60a
Called up to Torah, who ...... Megillah 23a

Calligraphic ornament of *yud* letter ...... Menachos 29a-29b, 34a
Came to teach and learned ...... Sanhedrin 73a, 74a; Yoma 82a

Camel
Camel, carried and ate a *kur* ...... Shabbos 155b
Camel, cut up, brayed ...... Yevamos 120b
Camel dead, getting back its ear ...... Shevuos 11b
Camel, episode about captives ...... Sanhedrin 104a-104b
Camel flying in the air ...... Shevuos 29a
Camel, illusion ...... Sanhedrin 67b
Camel killed another, proof ...... Sanhedrin 37b; Shevuos 34a; Bava Basra 93a
Camel, miracle to escape it ...... Berachos 54a
Camel, narrow passage ...... Sanhedrin 32b
Camel son of cow ...... Bechoros 6b-7a
Camels, going out on Shabbos ...... Shabbos 54a-54b

Camp
Camp of army, leniencies ...... Eruvin 17a-17b
Camp of Israel in desert ...... Yoma 75b
Camps, desert and Temples ...... Zevachim 116b-117a

Camps, impurity..Pesachim 67a-68a

Camps, journeys of Tabernacle...Menachos 95a-95b; Taanis 21b

Can learn and do not learn..Berachos 5a

Can of worms, appointment of leader..Yoma 22b

Canaan

Canaan, curse...Yoma 75a

Canaan, will to his sons..Pesachim 113b

Canaanite

Canaanite, merchant...Pesachim 50a; Bava Basra 75a

Canaanite women, wives of tribes...Pesachim 50a

Canaanites, accepting their repentance..Sotah 35b

Canaanites, Gebiha's answers...Sanhedrin 91a

Canaanites, marriage...Yevamos 76a

Canal

Canal, banks..Bava Metzia 107b-108a

Canal in courtyard, Shabbos...Eruvin 87a-87b

Canal, Sabbatical year..Moed Katan 4b

Canal, sale and rights...Bava Basra 99b

Canceling

Canceling *kiddushin*, by Rabbinical Decree.........Gittin 33a, 73a; Bava Basra 48b; Yevamos 90b, 110a;

....Kesubos 3a

Canceling non-Jew's loan...Bava Kama 113b

Cancellation in advance

Cancellation in advance about divorce document.....Arachin 21b; Kiddushin 12b; Yevamos 52a

Cancellation in advance, divorce document, gift and sale................Bava Basra 40a-40b, 48b

Cancellation in advance, legal document.........................Bava Basra 49a; Kesubos 19b

Cancellation of debts

Cancellation of debts, at end of year...Arachin 28b

Cancellation of debts, collateral.................Bava Metzia 48b-49a; Shevuos 44b; Gittin 37a; Makos 3b;

....Sheviis 10:2

Cancellation of debts, debt of tithes..Gittin 29b-30a

Cancellation of debts, exemption of oath..Shevuos 49a

Cancellation of debts, in present times.................Gittin 36a; Kiddushin 38b; Moed Katan 2b

Cancellation of debts, *kesubah*..Gittin 18a

Cancellation of debts, loan for ten years...Makos 3a-3b

Cancellation of debts out of *Eretz Yisrael*...Kiddushin 38b

Cancellation of debts, *prozbul*......................Sheviis 10:3-7; Gittin 32b-33a, 36b-37b

Cancellation of debts, returning money.............Gittin 37b; Sheviis 10:8; Shabbos 148b

Cancellation of debts, warranty...Gittin 37a

Cancellation of debts, which debts..Sheviis 10:1-2

Cancellation of sale

Cancellation of sale, fraud in price............Bava Metzia 49b-50b; Kiddushin 42b; Bava Basra 95a

Cancellation of sale, land..Bava Metzia 57a-57b; Temurah 27b

Cancellation of sale, weights and measures..........Bava Metzia 56b; Kiddushin 42b; Bava Basra 90a;

....Menachos 69a

Candles, Bava ben Butha...Nedarim 66b

Candlesticks, *muktzeh*..Shabbos 121b-122a

Cane of Rava..Nedarim 25a; Shevuos 29a-29b , 39a

Cannibals, Resh Lakish...Gittin 47a

Canopies
Canopies for Adam .... Bava Basra 75a
Canopies of righteous .... Bava Basra 75a
Canopy on succah .... Succah 10b-11a, 19b
Canopy, temporary tent .... Shabbos 45b-46a, 138a-138b; Eruvin 102a-102b
Cantillation notes
Cantillation notes of Holy Writings .... Nedarim 37b
Cantillation notes, signs to reader during reading .... Berachos 62a
Cantillation notes, Torah reading .... Megillah 32a
Cantor
Cantor, *aleph ayin* .... Megillah 24b
Cantor, beard .... Chullin 24b
Cantor, concern that he is heretic .... Megillah 24b
Cantor, decent, who .... Taanis 16a-16b
Cantor, fast .... Taanis 16a-16b
Cantor, permission .... Arachin 11b
Cantor, refusing .... Berachos 34a
Caper
Caper, blessing .... Berachos 36a
Caper, *orlah* .... Berachos 36a-36b
Caper, strongest tree .... Beitzah 25b
Capital cases
Capital cases, differences .... Sanhedrin 36b, 32a
Capital cases, fast .... Sanhedrin 63a
Capital cases, fleeing man .... Makos 7a; Gittin 28b, 29a; Sanhedrin 45b
Capital cases, how .... Sanhedrin 46a
Capital cases, wine .... Sanhedrin 42a
Capital
Capital of wife's property .... Kesubos 79a-79b, 101a
Capital or income, dried tree .... Bava Metzia 79a, 109b-110a; Kesubos 95b
Captive
Captive .... *see also* **Redeeming captive**, page 552
Captive, beautiful, David's warriors .... Kiddushin 76b; Sanhedrin 21a
Captive child, sacrifice .... Shabbos 68a-68b
Captive, custodian .... Bava Metzia 38b-39b
Captives, drowned in sea .... Gittin 57b
Captives, episode about trampling .... Sanhedrin 92b
Captives, exploitation of their beauty .... Gittin 58a
Captives, Illish fled .... Gittin 45a
Captives of Jerusalem, wisdom .... Sanhedrin 104a-104b
Captives, Paltihu .... Kiddushin 72b
Captives, Rabbi Meir's sister-in-law .... Avodah Zarah 18a-18b
Captives, Rabbi Yishmael .... Gittin 58a
Captives, Rabbi Yishmael's children .... Gittin 58a
Captive woman
Captive woman, conquered city .... Kesubos 27a-27b; Avodah Zarah 71a
Captive woman, daughter of *Kohen Gadol* .... Gittin 58a
Captive woman, episode about seclusion with one's wife .... Kesubos 27b
Captive woman, married .... Kesubos 26b-27a, 51b; Avodah Zarah 23a

C

Captive woman, mouth who forbade..Kesubos 23a
Captive woman, redeeming one's wife...Kesubos 51b-52b
Captive woman, redeeming widow..Kesubos 52a
Captive woman to *Kohen, kesubah* and penalty ....Kesubos 36b-37a; Gittin 81a; Eduyos 3:6
Captive woman, trustworthiness...Kesubos 23b
Captive woman, trustworthiness of father...Kiddushin 64a
Captive woman, trustworthiness of maidservant...Kesubos 27b
Captivity, harsher than famine ....Bava Basra 8b
Capture, domestic animal ....Shabbos 106a-106b
Caravan
Caravan, expenses...Bava Kama 116b
Caravan, partitions...Eruvin 93a
Caravan, sharing expenses..Bava Kama 116b
Caravans frequent, lost divorce document ....Gittin 27a-28a; Bava Metzia 18a-19a
Caraway seeds, heart disorders..Berachos 40a
Carcass in street, livelihood ....Bava Basra 110a
Carding wool
Carding wool, craft...Bava Kama 119b
Carding wool, measure of span..Shabbos 106a
Cardo, lineage...Yevamos 16a
Care
Care, scribe...Sotah 20a
Care, Torah cares about Jews' money.................Rosh Hashanah 27a; Menachos 76b; Negaim 12:5
Careful in one's answers ....Megillah 25b
Carmel, initials..Menachos 66b; Shabbos 105a
Carmelis ....*see Karmelis,* page 332
Carobs
Carobs of *Eretz Yisrael* ....Bava Basra 91b
Carobs, planting trees...Taanis 23a
Carobs, Rabbi Chanina..Berachos 17b; Taanis 24b; Chullin 86a
Carpenter son of carpenter, answer..Avodah Zarah 50b
Carpets of Nakdimen, episode...Kesubos 66b-67a
Carriage
Carriage for child, impurity of couch......................................Beitzah 23b; Shabbos 66a
Carriage of gold, Rabbi Nachman...Gittin 31b
Carriage of Rabbi Chiya...Bava Metzia 85b
Carriage of *zav*...Eruvin 27a; Keilim 23:2-3; Zavim 5:8
Carried
Carried by oxen, impurity ....Shabbos 83b-84a
Carry my load, only if you also do it in your city..Megillah 28a
Carrying...*see also Muktzeh,* page 429
Carrying in public domain, source of prohibition...Shabbos 96b
Carrying on head, Hutzel city..Shabbos 92a-92b
Carrying on Shabbos, to use item and place........................Shabbos 122b-124b, 141b
Carrying on Yom Tov..Beitzah 12a
Carrying poles, how..Shabbos 92a
Carrying out
Carrying out, accessories of animal..Shabbos 52b-54b, 58a
Carrying out, bandage...Shabbos 50a

Carrying out, between courtyards..Eruvin 98b-99b
Carrying out, camels going out..Shabbos 54a-54b
Carrying out, change from intention..Shabbos 92b
Carrying out, guarding animal...Shabbos 51b-52a
Carrying out higher than ten handbreadths...Shabbos 92a, 97a
Carrying out, how many...Shabbos 2a-3a; Shevuos 2a, 5a-5b
Carrying out, intention of work...Shabbos 11b
Carrying out, intervening substance for immersion....................................Shabbos 57a-57b
Carrying out, jewelry..Shabbos 57b, 59a-60a, 62a-62b, 64b
Carrying out on Shabbos, rolling reed..Shabbos 8b
Carrying out on Yom Kippur...Krisos 14a; Yoma 66b
Carrying out, source...Shabbos 49b, 96a-96b
Carrying out through *karmelis*..Shabbos 5b-6a
Carrying out through *mekom petur*...............Eruvin 9a, 77a, 85b, 98a, 99a, 101b; Shabbos 6a, 8b-9a
Carrying out, with what..Shabbos 57b, 58a, 62a, 63a, 65a
Carriers who broke barrel, episode...Bava Metzia 83a
Carthage, acknowledge G-d..Menachos 110a
Cartilages, Pesach lamb..Pesachim 84a
Case
Case of necessity, Rabbinical Decree...Eruvin 46a; Niddah 9b
Case of transgression, not mentioned..Yevamos 78a
Castor-oil plant, *kikayon*..Shabbos 21a
Castrated man
Castrated man, circumcision...Shabbos 135a
Castrated man, forbidden marriages..Yevamos 75b
Castration
Castration after castration.............................Shabbos 111a; Menachos 56b; Bechoros 33b
Castration, dogs..Chagigah 14b
Castration, fine..Bava Metzia 90a-90b
Castration in eggs...Kiddushin 25b
Castration, rooster..Shabbos 110b
Cat
Cat, danger from snake..Pesachim 112b
Cat, keeping...Bava Kama 80a-80b
Cat, killed by mice...Bava Metzia 97a
Cat, modesty..Eruvin 100b
Cat, recognizes its Creator..Horayos 13a
Cat severed hand, episode...Bava Kama 80b
Catching
Catching cold, man's responsibility....Kesubos 30a; Bava Basra 144b; Bava Metzia 107b; Avodah Zarah 3b
Caught on Yom Tov, doubt...Beitzah 24a-24b
Cattle
Cattle and brace, included in sale..Bava Basra 77b-78a
Cattle and sheep sacrifice, definition..Menachos 90b-91a
Cause of land destruction, Torah...........................Bava Metzia 85a-85b; Nedarim 81a
Causing
Causing another to do a commandment..Sanhedrin 99b
Causing death to Jew..Sanhedrin 37a
Causing extinguishment on Shabbos...Shabbos 120a-120b

Causing extinguishment on Yom Tov..Beitzah 22a
Causing invalidity, sacrifice..Zevachim 75b-76a
Causing invalidity, *terumah*..Zevachim 75b-76a
Causing newly formed substance on Shabbos, hail..Shabbos 51b
Causing public to sin, atonement..Yoma 87a
Causing public to sin, punishment..Avos 5:18

Causing damage
Causing damage..Bava Kama 33b, 48b, 60a, 62a, 98a-98b, 100a-100b
Causing damage, distance..Bava Basra 22b-23a
Causing damage, firstborn animal..Bechoros 28b
Causing damage, mortgage and legal document....................Bava Kama 33b, 98a; Gittin 41a
Causing damage, renouncing repayment of loan..Kesubos 85b-86a
Causing myself damage, payment..Bava Kama 91b, 93a

Causing impurity
Causing impurity, prohibition......................................Niddah 6b; Avodah Zarah 55b-56a
Causing impurity, *terumah*..................Bechoros 33b-34a; Terumos 8:8-11; Pesachim 14b-15b, 20b-21a;
....Menachos 48a-48b
Causing impurity to others..Niddah 35a

Cave
Cave, large, *techum*..Eruvin 44b
Cave of Moses..Megillah 19b
Cave of Rabbi Shimon bar Yochai..Shabbos 33b
Caves for graves..Bava Basra 100b-101b; Moed Katan 8b

Cave of Machpelah
Cave of Machpelah..Eruvin 53a; Bava Metzia 87a
Cave of Machpelah, Eliezer..Bava Basra 58a
Cave of Machpelah, Rabbi Banaah..Bava Basra 58a

Cedar
Cedar and reed, wind..Taanis 20a; Sanhedrin 105b-106a
Cedar, giant, episode..Bechoros 57b
Cedar tree, leper..Sotah 15b
Cedars, eulogy about Rav Ashi..Moed Katan 25b
Cedars, species..Rosh Hashanah 23a; Bava Basra 80b-81a

Ceiling
Ceiling of *Heichal* which caved in..Zevachim 40a
Ceiling, repairs by neighbors..Bava Metzia 117a; Bava Basra 6b-7a
Ceiling which collapsed, tenant's rights..Bava Metzia 116b-117a
Ceiling which opened, sowing..Bava Metzia 117b-118a

Cellar, search for *chametz*..Pesachim 8b

Cemented cistern, Rabbi Eliezer..Avos 2:8

Cemetery
Cemetery..*see also* **Grave**, page 256
Cemetery, blessing..Berachos 58b
Cemetery, prohibitions..Megillah 29a
Cemetery, *tzitzis* and *tefillin*..Berachos 18a

Census
Census of Israel, David..Berachos 62b; Yoma 22b
Census, prohibition..Yoma 22b

Centipede, reptile..Chullin 67b

Certainty, claim requiring oath .... Bava Metzia 2b
Certainty and doubt
    Certainty and doubt, "I do not know" .... Bava Basra 135a-135b; Kesuvos 12b-13a; Bava Kama 118a;
    .... Bava Metzia 97b-98b, 116b
    Certainty and doubt, acquitting oneself from Divine Judgment .... Bava Kama 118a
    Certainty and doubt, lineage of child .... Kesuvos 14a
    Certainty and doubt, vs. *chazakah* .... Kesubos 12b-13a; Bava Metzia 37b, 97b, 116b
    Certainty and doubt, vs. *migo* .... Kesubos 12b-13a
Certificate of freedom
    Certificate of freedom and financial independence, together .... Kiddushin 23a
    Certificate of freedom, like woman .... Gittin 9a-10a
    Certificate of freedom, text .... Gittin 40b, 85b
Cesarea and Jerusalem, destruction .... Megillah 6a
Cesarean birth
    Cesarean birth, animal disqualified for sacrifice ... Niddah 40a-41a; Avodah Zarah 23b; Chullin 51b
    Cesarean birth, blood flowing before birth .... Niddah 41a-41b
    Cesarean birth, circumcision .... Shabbos 135a-135b
    Cesarean birth, firstborn animal .... Bechoros 19a-19b, 47b
    Cesarean birth, firstborn child .... Bechoros 47b
    Cesarean birth, sacrifice of woman after birth .... Krisos 7b
    Cesarean birth, woman after birth .... Niddah 40a
Cessation of work at someone's death .... Moed Katan 27b
Chacham
    Chacham charashim, explanation .... Chagigah 14a
    Chacham Harazim, blessing .... Berachos 58a
Chacham .... *see* **Sage,** page 583, *see also* **Wise,** page 753
Chad Chad nachis bela, whisper .... Shabbos 67a
Chadash .... *see* **New grain,** page 442
Chafetz chaim .... *see* **Desires life, episode,** page 161
Chaff, damage to plants .... Bava Basra 24b
Chafisah, explanation .... Bava Metzia 20b; Gittin 28a
Chagei goyim .... *see* **Idolaters' festivals,** page 295
Chagigah
    Chagigah, from second tithe .... Chagigah 7b-8b
    Chagigah, making up for ... Chagigah 2a, 9a-9b, 17a; Rosh Hashanah 4b; Yoma 3a; Beitzah 20b; Megillah 5a
    Chagigah of Pesach .... Pesachim 69b-70a, 71a; Chagigah 8a
    Chagigah, price .... Chagigah 6a-7a
    Chagigah, public sacrifice .... Yoma 51a
    Chagigah, semichah .... Beitzah 20a
    Chagigah, Shabbos .... Pesachim 69b-70b; Megillah 5a
    Chagigah, source .... Chagigah 10b
    Chagigah, stringencies .... Chagigah 6b
    Chagigah, two days .... Pesachim 71a-71b
Chain
    Chain between legs for virgin, impurity .... Shabbos 63b
    Chains, impurity .... Keilim 14:3
    Chains in Temple *Ulam* .... Middos 3:8
    Chains to Egypt, Jacob .... Shabbos 89b

C

Chair

Chair, carrying out on Yom Tov...Beitzah 25b

Chair, holes, tent of corpse..Eruvin 10b

Chair, three-legged, Moses..Berachos 32a

Chairs before G-d...Chagigah 14a; Sanhedrin 38b

Chairs, receive impurity of couch...Keilim 22:3-7, 23:4; Eduyos 1:11

Chak tochos...Gittin 20a-20b

Chakeku vekavu..*see* **Engraved and established**, *mikveh*, page 197

Chakirah...*see* **Examination of witnesses**, page 205

Chaladah..*see* **Slaughtering by pressing**, page 635

Chalal

Chalal, did not react..Kesubos 14b

Chalal, his disqualification became known................Terumos 8:1-2; Kiddushin 66b; Pesachim 72b;
....Yevamos 34a; Makos 11b-12a

Chalal, in cemetery..Sanhedrin 5b

Chalal, redeeming son..Bechoros 47b

Chalal to *Koheness*...Yevamos 85a; Kiddushin 73a

Chalalah

Chalalah, Aaron's offspring...Yevamos 74b

Chalalah, because of *Kohen's* forbidden marriage...Kiddushin 77b-78a

Chalalah, forbidden relations and excising of soul..Yevamos 44a-44b

Chalalah, her offspring are *chalalim*.....................................Kiddushin 64a, 67a, 74b, 77a

Chalalah, non-virgin to *Kohen Gadol*...Yevamos 60a

Chaldeans, G-d's regret...Succah 52b

Chalifin..*see* **Exchange**, page 206; *see also* **Barter**, page 43

Chalishus hadaas...*see* **Hurt feelings**, page 289

Chalitzah

Chalitzah and levirate marriage, preference.................Yevamos 21a, 39b; Kesubos 64a; Bechoros 13a

Chalitzah, cannot be married by levirate...Yevamos 20a-20b

Chalitzah, convert judge...Yevamos 102a

Chalitzah, erroneous...Yevamos 106a; Kesubos 74a

Chalitzah, explanation..Yevamos 102b

Chalitzah, how...Yevamos 102a-103a, 104a

Chalitzah invalid, all brothers must perform *chalitzah*.................Yevamos 26b-27b, 51b, 53a

Chalitzah invalid, invalidates..Gittin 24b-25a

Chalitzah, knee..Yevamos 103a; Arachin 19b

Chalitzah, man does not inherit..Yevamos 40a

Chalitzah, not effective like divorce document...Kiddushin 3b-4a, 14a

Chalitzah on condition..Yevamos 53a, 106a; Kesubos 74a

Chalitzah on Shabbos...Beitzah 36b-37a

Chalitzah, one-armed woman...Yevamos 105a

Chalitzah, place..Yevamos 101b

Chalitzah, pretended..Yevamos 106a

Chalitzah without intention..Yevamos 102b

Challah

From what —

Challah, dough of consecrated items from Treasury...........................Menachos 67a; Challah 3:3

Challah, exempt in case of partnership...Chullin 135a-136a

Challah from Sabbatical year dough..Bechoros 12b

Challah, from when one must separate ....Challah 3:1
Challah, from which species...Challah 1:3
Challah, kinds of bread.........................Berachos 37b-38a; Challah 1:4-6; Pesachim 37a-37b; Eduyos 5:2
Challah, mixture exempt ....Challah 3:7-10
Challah, non-Jew's dough ....Challah 3:5-6; Menachos 67a-67b
Challah out of *Eretz Yisrael* ....Challah 4:8, 4:10; Chullin 104a-104b; Bechoros 27a-27b
Challah, preparing leaven to sell portions..Challah 1:7
Challah, quantity ....Parah 1:1
Challah, quantity of dough ....Shabbos 15a, 76b; Eruvin 83a-83b; Pesachim 48b; Challah 2:6-7;
....Eduyos 1:2
Challah, second tithe ....Pesachim 37b-38a; Succah 35a-35b; Sanhedrin 112b
Challah, species necessitating ....Menachos 70a-70b; Challah 1:1
Challah, tax..Pesachim 6a
Challah, *terumah* intermingled ....Challah 3:2; Niddah 46b-47a

Separating —
Challah, combining basket ....Pesachim 48b; Challah 2:4; Niddah 8a
Challah, combining dough ....Challah 2:4, 4:1-5; Pesachim 48b
Challah, impure, closeness...Challah 2:8; Sotah 30a-30b
Challah, impure dough ....Challah 3:2; Niddah 6b-7a
Challah like *terumah*, for what ....Challah 1:9
Challah, quantity of dough for separating..Challah 2:6-7; Eruvin 81a
Challah, separated from flour ....Challah 2:5; Kiddushin 46b
Challah, separating on Pesach ....Pesachim 46a-46b, 48a
Challah, separating on Shabbos ....Beitzah 37a
Challah, separating on Yom Tov ....Beitzah 9a

Misc. —
Challah, called *terumah*..Meilah 15b
Challah, causing impurity ....Niddah 6b-7a; Challah 3:2; Sotah 30b; Gittin 53a
Challah, fruit juice ....Challah 2:2
Challah, impurity of dough ....Challah 2:3, 3:2; Niddah 6b
Challah in present times ....Kesubos 25a-25b; Niddah 47a
Challah, owner's money..Kiddushin 53a
Challah, punishment ....Shabbos 32b
Challah which leavened on Pesach ....Pesachim 46a-46b
Challenge, one does not challenge after the fact.................................Rosh Hashanah 29b
Chalutz hanaal, exclamation...Yevamos 101b, 106b; Kiddushin 14a
Chalutzah
Chalutzah and rival, prohibition................................Yevamos 10b-11a, 32a, 40b, 53a
Chalutzah, doubtful, to *Kohen* ....Yevamos 24a
Chalutzah, exempting from levirate marriage ....Yevamos 10b
Chalutzah, her relatives ....Yevamos 27a, 40a-41a, 44a; Kiddushin 45a
Chalutzah to *Kohen* ....Yevamos 24a; Makos 13a; Kiddushin 78a
Chalutzah's relative, like divorced woman's relative .....Yevamos 40b, 41a, 44a-44b; Kiddushin 45a
Cham, son of Noah ....*see* **Ham, son of Noah**, page 267
Chamar gamal ....*see* **Donkey and camel driver, eruv**, page 174
Chamar medinah ....*see* **Popular drink**, page 494
Chamatah merubah mitzalatah ....*see* **Sunlight greater than shade**, page 663
Chamber pot
Chamber pot, *muktzeh* ....Beitzah 21b, 36b; Shabbos 47a, 121b, 143a

Chamber pot, *niddah* blood ....Niddah 59b
Chamber pot, prayer ....Berachos 25b

Chametz
  Elimination —
    Chametz ....*see also* **Searching for *chametz*, page 594**
    Chametz, annuling ....Pesachim 4b, 6b-7a, 10a
    Chametz destined to sit on it ....Pesachim 45b
    Chametz, destroying ....Pesachim 5b, 12b, 21a, 27b-28a; Temurah 34a
    Chametz, found on Pesach ....Pesachim 6a
    Chametz, hidden, eliminating ....Pesachim 5b
    Chametz in cracks of clay pan ....Pesachim 45a-45b
    Chametz in rented house ....Pesachim 4b
    Chametz in store, doubt ....Pesachim 31b
    Chametz, quantity for eliminating ....Pesachim 49b-50a; Beitzah 7b
    Chametz, rat ....Pesachim 9a, 9b
    Chametz, sale by custodian ....Pesachim 13a
    Chametz, time for searching ....Pesachim 4a, 10b
    Chametz, trustworthiness for searching ....Pesachim 4a-4b
    Chametz, under collapsed house ....Pesachim 8a, 31b; Bava Metzia 42a
    Chametz, various places ....Pesachim 10b
  Meal offerings —
    Chametz, disqualified meal offering ....Menachos 52b-53a
    Chametz in meal offering, prohibition ....Menachos 55a-55b; Shabbos 111a; Yevamos 40a;
    ....Sotah 15a; Shevuos 15b; Bechoros 33b
    Chametz, loaves of thanksgiving ....Beitzah 19b; Pesachim 13b; Menachos 53b-54a
  Misc. —
    Chametz, after Pesach ....Pesachim 28a-28b
    Chametz and leaven, quantity ....Beitzah 7b
    Chametz and *matzah*, doubt ....Pesachim 7a
    Chametz, as if in one's possession ....Pesachim 6b
    Chametz, before time ....Pesachim 21a-21b
    Chametz, cases of doubt ....Pesachim 9b-10b
    Chametz, cases of leavening ....Pesachim 39b-41a
    Chametz, combining to obtain quantity ....Pesachim 45b
    Chametz, consecrated, secular use ....Pesachim 29a-29b
    Chametz, transformed ....Pesachim 42b, 43a, 45b
    Chametz in slaughtering of Pesach lamb ....Pesachim 63a-64a; Menachos 78b
    Chametz, *kiddushin* ....Pesachim 7a, 21b
    Chametz, mixture ....Pesachim 29b-30a, 43a
    Chametz on Pesach, excising of soul ....Pesachim 43a
    Chametz, Pesach eve ....Pesachim 4b-5b, 12b, 13a, 21a, 28a-28b
    Chametz, Pesach in Egypt ....Pesachim 28b, 96a-96b
    Chametz, profit ....Pesachim 21b, 23a, 28a-28b, 30a, 32a-32b
    Chametz, wheat immersed in water ....Pesachim 40b
  Chametz of non-Jew
    Chametz of non-Jew, in one's house ....Pesachim 6a
    Chametz of non-Jew, permitted ....Pesachim 5b, 23a, 28b-29a; Eruvin 64b
    Chametz of non-Jew, security ....Pesachim 5b-6a, 31a-31b
Chamishah Asar B'Av ....*see* **Fifteenth of Av, page 221**

Chamishah Asar B'Shevat..*see* **Fifteenth of *Shevat*, page 221**

Chamsan...*see* **Robber, page 570**

Chana

    Chana and her seven sons...Gittin 57b

    Chana, anguish because of Peninnah..Bava Basra 16a

    Chana, Samuel's mother...Berachos 31a-31b

    Chana spoke harshly to G-d...Berachos 31b

    Chana, *Tzevaos*..Berachos 31b

Chanan Bisha

    Chanan Bisha..Bava Kama 37a

    Chanan Bisha, well-known thief...Bava Kama 115a

Chanan Hanechba, rain...Taanis 23b

Chanan the Egyptian, "discussed in front of Sages".........................Sanhedrin 17b

Chanan

    Chanan, Jerusalem judges..Kesubos 104b-105a

    Chanan and Admon, *halacha*...Kesubos 109a

Chananiah ben achi Rabbi Yehoshua, leap year................................Berachos 63b

Chananiah ben Chachinai, "discussed in front of Sages"...................Sanhedrin 17b

Chananiah and his friends

    Chananiah and his friends, castrated..Sanhedrin 93b

    Chananiah and his friends, furnace..................Pesachim 118a-118b; Sanhedrin 92b, 93a

    Chananiah and his friends, had they been beaten................................Kesubos 33b

Chananiah ben Azor...Sanhedrin 89a, 90a

Chananiah ben Chizkiyah, Ezekiel..............Shabbos 13b; Chagigah 13b; Menachos 45a

Change

    Laws —

        Change in gifts for synagogue...Arachin 6b

        Change in lung..Chullin 46b

        Change in quantity, swelled and was reduced.......Menachos 54a-54b; Taharos 3:4; Uktzin 2:8

        Change in Temple, prohibition..Zevachim 33a

        Change of appearance, *esrog*..Succah 35b-36b

        Change of appearance, *mikveh*....................Mikvaos 7:3-5; Eruvin 29b; Makos 3b-4a

        Change of objective, charity money....Bava Basra 8b-9a; Bava Metzia 78b, 106b-107a; Arachin 6a-6b

        Change of place, blessing.............................Pesachim 101a-102a; Berachos 59b

        Change of sacrifice name, before time...Yoma 62b-63a

        Change of use in items whose benefit is forbidden.........................Pesachim 24b-25a

    Change of manner

        Change of manner, cases of works...Shabbos 73b, 74b

        Change of manner in performing work on festival............................Moed Katan 12a-12b

        Change of manner in work, Sabbatical year.....................................Sheviis 8:6

        Change of manner in Yom Tov work.........Shabbos 148a-148b; Beitzah 14a-14b, 29b-30a

        Change of manner, milking a cow....................Kesubos 60a; Yevamos 114a

        Change of manner, ring on finger..Shabbos 62a

        Change of manner to carry out on Shabbos, cases............................Shabbos 92a-92b

        Change of manner, to perform commandment..................................Pesachim 66b

    Monetary matters —

        Change, damages by animal...Bava Kama 20a

        Change in sowing, field...Bava Metzia 107a

        Changes in rights by usage...Bava Basra 6a

Theft —

Change of name, theft.................................Bava Kama 65b, 66b-67a, 96a-96b; Succah 30b-31a
Change of ownership, stolen item..Bava Kama 68a
Change of stolen item........................Bava Kama 66a-67a, 93b-95a; Bava Metzia 43b; Temurah 6a
Change reversible, theft..Bava Kama 93b-94b; Succah 30b-31a

Misc. —

Change in eating habits, Shabbos..Nedarim 37b
Change in eating habits, sickness.......................................Bava Basra 146a; Nedarim 37b, 110b
Change, not to change from custom...Bava Metzia 86b
Change of name, sick...Rosh Hashanah 16b
Change of place, Heavenly decree..Rosh Hashanah 16b
Changing argument in *beis din*..Bava Basra 31a
Changing city of dwelling if unsuccessful...Bava Metzia 75b
Changing eating habits, "days of poor man are bad"..Bava Basra 146a
Changing from owner's will..Bava Metzia 78a-78b
Changing one's mind, lifting item on Shabbos........................Shabbos 5b; Kesubos 31a; Eruvin 20b
Changing Pesach lamb to peace offerings...............................Pesachim 64a, 73a-73b; Chullin 30a
Changing text of blessings..Berachos 40b
Changing text of divorce certificates...............................Gittin 5b, 80a; Bava Metzia 55b

Change of owner

Change of owner, burnt offerings...Zevachim 7b
Change of owner, differences..Zevachim 3b, 7a-7b
Change of owner, sin offering.........................Zevachim 3b, 4b, 7a, 8a-8b, 9b; Pesachim 62a
Change of owner, thought during offering of Pesach lamb...Zevachim 7b
Change of owner, thought during sacrifice......................................Zevachim 3b, 4a-4b, 7a

Change, receiving change from thief...Bava Kama 113a
Changed his mind after death!..Nazir 52b

Changing name

Which sacrifice —

Changing name, guilt offering...Zevachim 5a-5b, 10a-10b
Changing name, guilt offering for leper..Yoma 61b
Changing name, libations and wood..Menachos 89b-90a
Changing name, meal offerings.......................................Zevachim 11a; Menachos 2b
Changing name of burnt offering...Zevachim 12b-13a
Changing name of sacrifice to higher or lower..Zevachim 11b
Changing name, oil for leper..Menachos 28a
Changing name, *omer*...Menachos 5a-5b
Changing name, Pesach..Pesachim 62b; Zevachim 7b, 10b-11b
Changing name renders *kosher*..Menachos 4a-5a
Changing name, sheep for Shavuos..Menachos 49a
Changing name, sin offering..Zevachim 3b, 7b-8b, 10b

Misc. —

Changing name, making sacrifice *kosher*....................Menachos 2b-4a, 47b; Zevachim 114b-115b
Changing name of Pesach and sin offering.........................Zevachim 11a-11b; Pesachim 62b
Changing name of sacrifice, atonement..........................Zevachim 6a, 11b; Menachos 90a
Changing name of sacrifice by mistake...Menachos 49a
Changing name of sacrifice, does not expiate......................Zevachim 2a, 4b-5b; Menachos 2a

Chanina ben Chachinai, heavenly chariot...Chagigah 14b
Chanina My son, carobs.......................................Berachos 17b; Taanis 24b; Chullin 86a

Chanukah
Chanukah, Bircas HaMazon .... Shabbos 24a
Chanukah, camel flax .... Bava Kama 62b
Chanukah, kindling lights .... Shabbos 21a-23b; Succah 46a
Chanukah lamp, dishonoring commandment .... Shabbos 22a
Chanukah, place for kindling lights .... Bava Kama 30a, 62b; Shabbos 21b-22a
Chanukah, story .... Shabbos 21b
Chanukah, Torah reading and *haftorah* .... Megillah 30b-31a
Chaos .... Chagigah 12a
Character traits, wonderful, Rabbi Akiva .... Gittin 67
Charamim .... *see* **Vows of *cherem*,** page 727
Charash umasger .... *see* **Hacharash vehamasger,** exile, page 263
Charash vehamasger, exile .... Gittin 88a; Sanhedrin 38a
Charatah .... *see* **Regret,** page 554
Chariot
Chariot equipment, impurity .... Keilim 14:4-5
Chariot of iron, after Temple destruction .... Sotah 48b
Chariot of Israel and its riders .... Moed Katan 26a
Chariots of Pharaoh and Sisera .... Pesachim 118b
Charitable, Israel .... Yevamos 79a
Charity .... *see also* **Poor,** page 494
 Episodes —
  Charity before death, episode .... Kesubos 67b
  Charity, Binyamin *Hatzadik* .... Bava Basra 11a
  Charity, destruction of charity house .... Berachos 58b
  Charity, episode about dream .... Bava Basra 10a
  Charity, fall in stairs .... Bava Basra 10a
  Charity, house with four doors .... Berachos 58b
  Charity, Ifra Hormuz .... Bava Basra 10b
  Charity, Munbaz .... Bava Basra 11a
  Charity, Nahum Ish Gam Zu .... Taanis 21a
  Charity, saves from snake .... Shabbos 156b
 For whom —
  Charity, examining before giving .... Bava Basra 9a
  Charity, inhabitants of other city .... Megillah 27a-27b
  Charity, poor of other city .... Bava Metzia 31b
  Charity, supporting one's sons .... Kesubos 50a
  Charity, swindlers .... Peah 8:9; Kesubos 67b-68a
  Charity, to decent poor .... Succah 49b; Bava Basra 9b
  Charity to men going bankrupt .... Kesubos 67b
  Charity to non-Jew .... Gittin 61a
  Charity to woman, unobtrusively .... Chagigah 5a
  Charity, wealthy man .... Peah 5:4; Chullin 130b; Bava Kama 7a-7b
 From whom —
  Charity, receiving from suspected persons .... Bava Kama 119a
  Charity, relatives' duty .... Nedarim 65b
 How —
  Charity before prayer .... Bava Basra 10a
  Charity, better to give quickly .... Shabbos 151b

Charity, fast day..Berachos 6b; Sanhedrin 35a
Charity, four attitudes...Avos 5:13
Charity fund, collecting and distributing...................Bava Basra 8b; Peah 8:7; Sanhedrin 17b
Charity, giving to charity collector..Bava Basra 10b
Charity, not to cause humiliation..Kesubos 67b
Charity, "So that my son will live"...........Bava Basra 10b; Pesachim 8a-8b; Rosh Hashanah 4a
Charity, ways to give...Kesubos 67b

Requirement —
Charity, abjured from Sinai..Shevuos 25a
Charity, duty..Gittin 7a-7b
Charity, from when one must pay..Bava Basra 8a
Charity, not to delay giving..Rosh Hashanah 4a, 5b, 6a
Charity, quantity..Bava Basra 9a

Reward and punishment —
Charity given insufficiently, money lost..Kesubos 67a
Charity, greater than sacrifices..Succah 49b
Charity in public, punishment..Chagigah 5a
Charity, protection of one's money..Kesubos 66b
Charity, punishment for forcing community..Bava Basra 8b
Charity, punishment for one who refrains...................................Beitzah 32b; Temurah 16a
Charity, reward...Gittin 7a-7b; Bava Basra 9a-9b
Charity, reward according to kindness within it..Succah 49b
Charity, reward for who does not accept...Peah 8:9
Charity, rich and poor meet..Temurah 16a
Charity saves from death..Bava Basra 9a-9b
Charity, saves from *Gehinnom*...Bava Basra 10a
Charity, sons as a reward...Bava Basra 9b, 10b
Charity to poor when under pressure...Chagigah 5a

Misc. —
Charity at all times, raising an orphan...................................Kesubos 50a; Sanhedrin 19b
Charity, avoid to accept..........................Pesachim 112a, 113a; Shabbos 118a; Sanhedrin 81a
Charity, changing purpose of money....Bava Basra 8b-9a; Arachin 6a-6b; Bava Metzia 78b, 106b-107a
Charity, custodians..Bava Kama 93a
Charity, fifth...Kesubos 50a, 67b; Arachin 28a
Charity, non-Jews' merit..Bava Basra 10b
Charity, poor suffers shame..Berachos 6b
Charity, room for inconspicuous charity in Temple...Shekalim 5:6
Charity, small sum...Bava Metzia 31b
Charity, taking for oneself...Chullin 134b
Charity, what to do with what is left...Shekalim 2:5
Charity, wicked does not merit to give to true poor.....................Bava Kama 16b; Bava Basra 9b

Charity collector
Charity collector, like Rabbi Chananiah ben Teradion......Bava Basra 10b; Avodah Zarah 17b
Charity collectors, "May my lot be with them"..Shabbos 118b
Charity collectors, laws..Bava Basra 8b, 9a

Charity from idolaters
Charity from idolaters, avoid receiving..Bava Basra 4a, 10b
Charity from idolaters, defective.....................................Rosh Hashanah 4a; Bava Basra 10b
Charity from idolaters, disqualified to testify..Sanhedrin 26b

Charon af .... *see* **Anger**, page 23

Charoses, bitter herbs .... Pesachim 115a-116a

Charufasi, wording of *kiddushin* .... Kiddushin 6a

Chasan .... *see* **Groom**, page 259; *see also* **Son-in-law**, page 646

Chaseiros veyeseiros .... *see* **Letters**, page 366

Chashmal, angel .... Chagigah 13a-13b

Chashmonaim .... *see* **Hasmoneans**, page 271

Chashud .... *see* **Suspected**, page 666

Chasidim .... *see* **Pious men**, page 489

Chataos .... *see* **Sin offering**, page 627

Chateh sheyizkeh chavercha .... *see* **Transgress in order that your friend will not**, page 699

Chatichah hareuyah lehiskabed .... *see* **Piece of food suitable for a guest**, page 487

Chatichah mishtei chatichos .... *see* **Piece from two pieces**, page 487

Chatichah naasis neveilah .... *see* **Mixture, permitted piece becomes** *neveilah*, page 418

Chatzav .... *see* **Squill**, page 653

Chatzeir .... *see* **Courtyard**, page 130

Chatzi .... *see* **Half**, page 266

Chatzitzah .... *see* **Intervening substance**, page 316

Chatzos .... *see* **Midnight**, page 409

Chatzotzros, called *shofar* .... Shabbos 36a; Succah 34a

Chav le'acharim .... *see* **Repayment of debt, seizure for fellow**, page 559

Chavah .... *see* **Eve** page 203

Chaverim, destructive angels .... Kiddushin 72a

Chaver .... *see* **Scholar**, page 591

Chavilah, *s'chach* .... *see* **Bundle,** *s'chach*, page 79

Chavitin .... *see* **Meal offering for** *Kohen*, page 397

Chavivah mitzvah beshaatah .... *see* **Commandment in its time, beloved**, page 116

Chavivin yisurim .... *see* **Suffering, beloved**, page 662

Chavrei of Babylon .... Yevamos 63b; Gittin 17a

Chavrusa .... Taanis 7a; Berachos 63b; Makos 10a

Chavrusa .... *see* **Learning partner**, page 359

Chayav bedinei shamayim .... *see* **Liable by Divine Judgment**, page 368

Chayav inish livesumei .... *see* **Drunk, man must get drunk on** *Purim*, page 182

Chayecha kodmim .... *see* **Life, your life comes first**, page 369

Chayei, bonei, umezonei .... *see* **Life, children and livelihood, fate**, page 369

Chayei shaah .... *see* **Life for a few hours, saving a life**, page 370

Chayos Hakodesh .... Chagigah 12b-13a

Chazakah

  Acquisition —

    Chazakah, act of acquisition of hoe .... Bava Basra 53a-54b

    Chazakah, because he bought from a non-Jew .... Bava Basra 35b-36a

    Chazakah, cases of act of acquisition .... Bava Basra 52b, 53a-54b, 57a

    Chazakah of act of acquisition, source .... Kiddushin 26a

    Chazakah on ten lands .... Kiddushin 27a-27b

    Chazakah, purchase for fruit .... Bava Basra 87a

  Chazakah owner —

    Chazakah, bank of river .... Bava Metzia 108a

    Chazakah, craftsman .... Bava Basra 47a

    Chazakah, first owner .... Kesubos 76a-76b

Chazakah, freely grazing animals .... Bava Basra 36a
Chazakah in money matters .... Bava Basra 30a, 159b; Kesubos 20a; Yevamos 31a-31b
Chazakah of damage, cases .... Bava Basra 22b-23a
Chazakah of daughter, monetary rights .... Kesubos 76a
Chazakah of land, tree .... Bava Basra 37a-38a
Chazakah of rock .... Bava Basra 29b
Chazakah of three years, contradiction .... Bava Basra 56b
Chazakah of window .... Bava Basra 59a, 60a
Chazakah on two estates by one act .... Bava Basra 67a-67b
Chazakah, plowing .... Bava Basra 36a-37a
Chazakah vs. *migo* .... Bava Basra 5b; Kesubos 27b; Kiddushin 64b; Bava Metzia 81b; Bechoros 36a

Contrary indication —
Chazakah from prohibition to prohibition .... Chullin 9a
Chazakah, *mikveh* .... Gittin 31b; Kiddushin 66b, 79a; Mikvaos 2:2; Niddah 2b
Chazakah of body vs. money .... Kesubos 75b
Chazakah, problem appeared .... Chullin 10a-10b; Kiddushin 79a; Niddah 2b
Chazakah vs. majority .... Yevamos 119a-119b; Niddah 18a-19a

For whom —
Chazakah, condemned to death .... Gittin 28b-29a
Chazakah, divorced woman .... Bava Basra 47a-47b, 52a
Chazakah, fleeing man's real estate .... Kesubos 17b
Chazakah, from intimidating person .... Bava Basra 36a
Chazakah, heir .... Bava Basra 47a
Chazakah, married woman .... Bava Basra 50b-51a
Chazakah, minor's real estate .... Kesubos 17b; Bava Metzia 39a-39b
Chazakah on land, son .... Bava Basra 47a, 52a
Chazakah, partner .... Bava Basra 42a-42b
Chazakah, tenant farmer .... Bava Basra 46b, 47a
Chazakah, thief .... Bava Basra 47a

How —
Chazakah, "I bought from this man" .... Bava Basra 30a-31a
Chazakah, bought from buyer .... Bava Basra 41b
Chazakah by means of use, which is effective .... Bava Basra 57a-57b
Chazakah, combining possession of three buyers .... Bava Basra 41b-42a
Chazakah in front of claimant, immediately .... Bava Basra 41a
Chazakah of forty years, law of country .... Bava Basra 55a
Chazakah of three years .... Bava Basra 28a-29a
Chazakah on land, immediate .... Bava Basra 35b
Chazakah, use at night .... Bava Basra 29a-29b

Invalid —
Chazakah, busy in market .... Bava Basra 30a
Chazakah, case of bad use .... Bava Basra 29b, 36a
Chazakah for less than three years, land .... Bava Basra 28b, 36b
Chazakah invalid, payment of fruit .... Bava Basra 33b
Chazakah, objection about precedence .... Bava Basra 30b-31a
Chazakah with interval .... Bava Basra 29b
Chazakah without claim .... Bava Basra 28b, 41a

Presumption —
Chazakah, agent fulfills his mission .... Eruvin 31b-32a; Nazir 12a; Gittin 64a-64b; Chullin 12a

Chazakah, drinking from a cup .... Kesubos 75b-76a
Chazakah, estimate, cases .... Kesubos 55a-56a
Chazakah of Rava, hair of puberty .... Niddah 46a, 48b
Chazakah, paying back before due time .... Bava Basra 5a-6a
Chazakah, preparing wedding feast .... Kesuvos 10a; Yevamos 107a
Chazakah, sinning for someone else's benefit .... Bava Metzia 5b
Chazakah that scholar tithed .... Pesachim 4b, 9a; Niddah 15b; Avodah Zarah 41b; Eruvin 32a

Women —
Chazakah, changed in front of us .... Kiddushin 79a-79b; Niddah 2a-3a
Chazakah, marriage and divorce .... Yevamos 30b
Chazakah, mother to daughter .... Kesubos 13a-13b
Chazakah of epilepsy, marriage .... Yevamos 64b
Chazakah of women, permitted to their husbands .... Niddah 15a-15b
Chazakah of *zavah*, examining .... Niddah 7b, 68b

Misc. —
Chazakah about prohibition, contradiction of two sets of witnesses .... Yevamos 31a-31b;
.... Gittin 78b
Chazakah, according place of object .... Kesubos 75b
Chazakah, burning *terumah* .... Kiddushin 80a-80b
Chazakah, death penalty .... Kiddushin 63b, 80a
Chazakah, impurity .... Keilim 9:3; Niddah 4a
Chazakah, lineage of *Kohanim* .... Kiddushin 69b; Kesubos 24b-25a
Chazakah of previous situation, source .... Chullin 10b-11a
Chazakah of living man .... Gittin 28a-28b; Yoma 55b; Succah 23b
Chazakah, *terumah* and discovered vinegar .... Gittin 31a-31b

Chazakah of use
Chazakah of use, cases .... Bava Basra 57a-57b, 58b-59a
Chazakah of use, changes .... Bava Basra 6a
Chazakah of use, protuberance .... Bava Basra 59a-59b
Chazakah of use, succah .... Bava Basra 6b

Chazakah, three times
Chazakah, three times .... Yevamos 26a, 64b-65a; Eruvin 97a; Kesubos 43b; Bava Kama 23b;
.... Bava Metzia 106b; Sanhedrin 81b; Niddah 63b-64a
Chazakah, three times, circumcision .... Yevamos 64b
Chazakah, three times, ox goring regularly .... Bava Kama 23b-24a; Kesubos 64b-65a

Chazarah bitshuvah .... *see* **Repentance**, page 559
Chazarah lekirah .... *see* **Returning pot to stove-top, cooking on Shabbos**, page 564
Chazaras hashatz .... *see* **Repetition by cantor, reason** page 560
Chazaros limud .... *see* **Reviewing one's learning**, page 565
Chazazis, *esrog* .... Succah 35b-36b
Chazeh veshok .... *see* **Breast and leg**, page 76
Chazek vekni .... Bava Basra 52b-53a
Chazeres .... *see* **Horseradish**, page 284
Cheap meat, payment to heir .... Bava Kama 112a; Kesubos 34b
Cheating
Cheating non-Jew, prohibition .... Chullin 94a
Cheating, various utensils .... Bava Basra 89b; Keilim 29:16
Cheek
Cheek of animal, *treifah* .... Chullin 55b

C

Cheeks full, *kiddush* ....Pesachim 107a

Cheese
Cheese, new, quality ....Shabbos 134a
Cheese of non-Jews ....Avodah Zarah 34b-35b
Cheese on Shabbos, building ....Shabbos 95a

Cheftza, vows ....Nedarim 2b
Cheil, Temple ....Middos 2:3; Pesachim 86a; Yoma 16a
Chelbenah in incense, wicked ....Krisos 6b

Cherem
Cherem ....*see also* **Vow of *cherem***, page 727
Cherem, Temple Treasury or *Kohen* ....Arachin 28b-29a; Sanhedrin 88a
Cheresh ....*see* **Deaf**, page 149
Cherev kechalal ....*see* **Sword impure like slain man**, page 667

Cherished
Cherished are Sages' teachings ....Avodah Zarah 35a
Cherished, Torah ....Berachos 63b
Chermon, Siryon ....*see* **Hermon, Siryon** page 277
Cherries, health ....Eruvin 28a

Cherubs
Cherubs, dimensions ....Succah 5b
Cherubs embraced, Temple destruction ....Yoma 54b
Cherubs, faces turned ....Bava Basra 98b-99a
Cherubs, Holy of Holies ....Bava Basra 98b-99a
Cherubs, revealed love ....Yoma 54a-54b
Ches, curved shape ....Menachos 29b
Chesed ....*see* **Kindness**, page 339
Cheshbono shel olam ....*see* **Self-examination**, page 599

Chest
Chest ....*see also* **Heart**, page 273
Chest for blue dye ....Bava Basra 74a-74b
Chet, unwilling ....Yoma 36b
Chetz be'einei haSatan ....*see* **Arrow in eyes of Satan**, page 32
Chevra Kadisha ....Moed Katan 27b
Chiburim letumas mes ....*see* **Connections, impurity of corpse**, page 122

Chick
Chick, from when is it permitted ....Beitzah 4a, 6b; Chullin 64a-64b
Chick, *muktzeh* ....Beitzah 4a, 6a-6b
Chick of *treifah* animal, sacrifice ....Temurah 31a
Chidekel, *chadin* and *kalin* ....Berachos 59b

Chilazon
Chilazon, blue dye ....Menachos 44a
Chilazon, inevitable act ....Shabbos 75a
Chilazon, rain ....Sanhedrin 91a
Chilazon, work on Shabbos ....Shabbos 75a
Child ....*see also* **Baby**, page 39, **Minor**, page 411
Aggadah —
Child and fool, prophecy ....Bava Basra 12b
Child, attracted by money ....Gittin 40a
Child, male, his loaf in hand ....Niddah 31b

Child, schoolteacher's whip .... Succah 29a
Child, when does he start to talk? .... Berachos 40a
Children accountable for sins of generation .... Shabbos 33b
Children, G-d teaches them Torah .... Avodah Zarah 3b
Children, having children depends on fate .... Moed Katan 28a
Children, reward for bringing them to *Hakhel* .... Chagigah 3a

Commandments —
Child, discharging adult .... Berachos 20b; Succah 38a
Child, act of acquisition of *lulav* .... Succah 46b
Child, being counted for Pesach lamb .... Pesachim 88a, 89a; Succah 42b; Nedarim 36a
Child, blowing *shofar* .... Rosh Hashanah 33a-33b; Eruvin 96b; Arachin 2b
Child, educating him to perform commandments .... Succah 42a; Arachin 2b
Child, Pesach lamb .... Succah 42b
Child, reading *megillah* .... Megillah 20a
Child, separating tithe .... Niddah 46b; Terumos 1:3
Child, song in Temple .... Arachin 13b
Child, succah .... Succah 28b

Death —
Child, burial .... Moed Katan 24a-24b
Child, mourning .... Moed Katan 24b
Child, murderer liable .... Sanhedrin 84b; Niddah 44b
Child who died, sins of his generation .... Shabbos 33b
Children die, atonement .... Sotah 48b-49a; Berachos 5b
Children die, because of wicked .... Shabbos 32b
Children die, punishment .... Sanhedrin 27b
Children, eulogy .... Moed Katan 24b

Episodes —
Child, *Avodah Zarah* tractate .... Avodah Zarah 56b
Children depend on him .... Chullin 18a
Children, sheep tails .... Bechoros 35a

Health —
Child, beneficial things .... Yoma 78b
Child, healing wound .... Shabbos 134b
Child, in danger without milk .... Yevamos 114a
Child, medicine .... Shabbos 134a
Child, scorpion and bee .... Kesubos 50a

Impurity —
Child, doubtful impurity .... Kiddushin 80a; Chullin 86a-86b; Taharos 3:8; Niddah 18b
Child, impurities .... Niddah 43b-44a
Child, thought causing impurity .... Keilim 17:15; Chullin 12b-13a
Child, *zivah* and discharge .... Niddah 32b, 43b-44a; Arachin 3a
Children for Red Heifer .... Succah 21a; Zevachim 113a; Parah 3:2-4

Laws —
Child, according to father's command .... Shabbos 121a
Child, asking him about cut letter .... Menachos 29a-29b, 34a
Child, drinking Yom Kippur from a cup .... Eruvin 40b
Child, his acts are carelessly done .... Chullin 86a-86b
Child in his clothes, carrying out .... Shabbos 141b-142a
Child is considered like sinning willingly .... Sanhedrin 55b

Child kept captive, sacrifice .... Shabbos 68a-68b
Child longing for his father, *muktzeh* .... Shabbos 141b-142a
Child of doubtful lineage .... Kiddushin 73a-73b
Child, wine of idolaters .... Avodah Zarah 57a-57b
Monetary matters —
Child, age for business deal .... Gittin 59a, 64b-65a; Bava Basra 155a-156a
Child, damage to saucer .... Bava Basra 87b-88a
Child, gift .... Gittin 59a
Child, his ox caused damage .... Bava Kama 39a-40a
Child, legal transfer of benefits to others .... Gittin 64b-65a
Child, lost item .... Bava Metzia 12a-12b
Child, not liable for damages .... Bava Basra 87b-88a; Bava Kama 87a
Child, oath .... Shevuos 42a-42b, 45a; Bava Kama 106b; Kesubos 94a; Gittin 50a-50b
Child, payment, damage made by ox .... Bava Kama 42a, 48b-49a
Misc. —
Child, "I acted like a child" .... Bava Basra 131a
Child, age to beget children .... Sanhedrin 68b-69b
Child, blank paper .... Avos 4:20
Child, good that he be average .... Berachos 31b
Child, keeping one's promise to child .... Succah 46b
Child looking like adult .... Gittin 89b
Child of doubtful lineage, *Kohen* .... Yevamos 100b
Child who does not need his mother .... Eruvin 82a; Succah 28b
Children died, mother not frightened .... Kesubos 62a
Children know it, evident .... Gittin 29a; Berachos 5a; Chullin 81b
Children, no preferential treatment to one child .... Shabbos 10b
Childless
Childless, excising of soul .... Yevamos 55a
Childless person, considered as dead .... Nedarim 64b
Chileab son of David, Daniel .... Berachos 4a
Chilka and tirgis .... Moed Katan 13b; Nedarim 55b; Machshirin 6:2
Chillul Hashem .... *see* **Desecration of G-d's name,** page 160
Chiltis
Chiltis, cure .... Shabbos 140a
Chiltis, eating .... Chullin 59a
Chiltis of non-Jews .... Avodah Zarah 40b
Chiltis, Shabbos .... Shabbos 140a
Chilul .... *see* **Redeeming,** page 552
Chimneys, tent of dead person .... Oholos 5:2-5, 10:1-5; Succah 18a
Chinuch Kohen .... *see* **Consecration of *Kohen*,** page 124
Chinuch .... *see* **Education,** page 187
Chiram .... *see* **Hiram,** page 279
Chisaron kis .... *see* **Loss of money, *muktzeh*,** page 378
Chiya bar Rav, punishment .... Arachin 16b
Chizkiah son of Rabbi Chiya, prayer .... Bava Metzia 85b
Chocher .... *see* **Lessee,** page 365
Chol HaMoed (intermediate days of Yom Tov)
Connected to land —
Chol HaMoed, building .... Moed Katan 7a, 8b

Chol HaMoed, covering figs .... Moed Katan 13b
Chol HaMoed, irrigating .... Moed Katan 2a-2b, 4a-4b, 6b
Chol HaMoed, land .... Moed Katan 6b-7a, 12b
Chol HaMoed, repairs for water .... Moed Katan 4b-5a
Chol HaMoed, trees .... Moed Katan 4b; Avodah Zarah 50b
Prohibitions —
Chol HaMoed, act needed for festival .... Moed Katan 11a
Chol HaMoed, animals .... Moed Katan 12a
Chol HaMoed, burial .... Moed Katan 8a, 8b
Chol HaMoed, deceased .... Moed Katan 28b
Chol HaMoed, eulogy .... Moed Katan 27b, 28b; Megillah 3b
Chol HaMoed, fingernails .... Moed Katan 17b-18a
Chol HaMoed, laundering .... Moed Katan 13b-14a, 18a-18b; Taanis 29b; Chullin 107b-108a
Chol HaMoed, moving house .... Moed Katan 13a
Chol HaMoed, purchase .... Moed Katan 13b
Chol HaMoed, shaving .... Moed Katan 13b-14b, 17b
Women —
Chol HaMoed, betrothal .... Moed Katan 18b
Chol HaMoed, wedding .... Moed Katan 8b-9a, 18b; Chagigah 8b
Chol HaMoed, women's adornments .... Moed Katan 8b, 9b; Avodah Zarah 6b
Works —
Chol HaMoed, effort .... Moed Katan 2a-2b
Chol HaMoed, necessary for festival .... Moed Katan 10a-11a, 12b
Chol HaMoed, possible loss .... Moed Katan 10b-11a, 12a-12b
Chol HaMoed, pretending .... Moed Katan 12b; Shabbos 139b
Chol HaMoed, prohibition of work .... Chagigah 18a; Moed Katan 11b
Chol HaMoed, sewing .... Moed Katan 10a
Chol HaMoed, utensils from craftsman .... Pesachim 55b; Moed Katan 13a-13b
Chol HaMoed, worker .... Moed Katan 13a
Chol HaMoed, works .... Pesachim 55b; Moed Katan 10a-10b, 12a, 18b-19a
Chol HaMoed, writing .... Moed Katan 18b-19a
Misc. —
Chol HaMoed, *beis din* .... Moed Katan 14b
Chol HaMoed, episodes .... Moed Katan 10b, 12b
Chol HaMoed, non-Jew .... Moed Katan 12a
Chol HaMoed, punishment for disregarding .... Pesachim 118a; Makos 23a
Chol HaMoed, sacrifice .... Temurah 14b
Chol, eternal bird .... Sanhedrin 108b
Chomer, quantity .... Menachos 77a
Chomesh .... see **Fifth**, page 221
Choni Ham'agel, slept seventy years .... Taanis 23a
Chonyo, temple .... Megillah 10a; Avodah Zarah 52b; Menachos 109a, 109b
Choose
Choose a kinder death .... Sanhedrin 45a, 52a; Pesachim 75a; Kesubos 37a; Sotah 8b; Bava Kama 51a
Choosing animal on Yom Tov, *muktzeh* .... Beitzah 25a
Chopped man, *agunah* .... Yevamos 120b
Choser kol, meaning .... Nedarim 41a
Choshed biksheirim .... see **Suspecting innocent**, page 666
Choteh niskar .... see **Sinner, will not gain anything**, page 629

Chozer umagid .... see **Testimony, retracting**, page 684
Chozer veneor .... see **Mixture, reawakens**, page 419; see also **Impurity, reawakens**, page 303
Chronicles .... see **Divrei Hayamim** page 172
Chronological order in Torah .... Pesachim 6b
***Chukah*,** **to make detail indispensable** .... Menachos 19a; Chullin 24a
***Chukim*,** definition .... Kiddushin 37a
Chukos hagoy .... see **Customs of non-Jews**, page 138
Chukosai and ***mishpatai*,** significance .... Yoma 67b
Chulda .... see **Hulda**, page 287
Chullin .... see **Non-holy**, page 447
Chullin baazarah .... see **Non-holy animal in Temple Courtyard**, page 447
Chullin betaharah .... see **Non-holy food**, page 447
Chumah
    Chumah, Abbaye's widow .... Kesubos 65a
    Chumah, married three times .... Yevamos 64b
***Chumashim*,** reading .... Gittin 60a
Chumra .... see **Stringency**, page 659
Chuppah .... see **Wedding canopy**, page 739
Chur, golden calf .... see **Hur, golden calf** page 289
Churban Beis Hamikdash .... see **Destruction of Temple**, page 161
Chut hasikrah .... see **Thread *sikrah***, page 688
Chutz laaretz .... see **Out of *Eretz Yisrael***, page 464
Chutz limkomo .... see **Out of place sacrifices**, page 464
***Chutz*,** exhaustive list .... Eruvin 27a
Cider, apple cider, Rebbi .... Avodah Zarah 40b
Cinnamon, Jerusalem trees .... Shabbos 63a
Circle
    Circle, how to calculate .... Succah 7b-8b; Eruvin 13b, 14a, 76a-76b; Oholos 12:6
    Circle, proportion to square .... Succah 7b-8b; Eruvin 13b, 14a, 76a-76b; Oholos 12:6
Circumcised but not immersed
    Circumcised but not immersed, convert .... Yevamos 46a-46b; Berachos 47b
    Circumcised but not immersed, Pesach lamb .... Yevamos 71a
Circumciser, who .... Avodah Zarah 26b-27a; Menachos 42a
Circumcision .... see also **Uncircumcised**, page 714
    Aggadah —
        Circumcision, "for Your sake we are slaughtered all day" .... Gittin 57b
        Circumcision, "if not for My covenant" .... Shabbos 137b; Nedarim 32a
        Circumcision, covenants .... Nedarim 31b
        Circumcision, importance .... Nedarim 31b, 32a
        Circumcision, in Abraham's lap .... Kiddushin 72b
        Circumcision, joy .... Shabbos 130a
        Circumcision, Moses' neglect .... Nedarim 31b-32a
        Circumcision on eighth day, reason .... Niddah 31b
        Circumcision, Psalm .... Menachos 43b
    Procedure —
        Circumcision, blessings .... Shabbos 137b; Pesachim 7b; Menachos 42a
        Circumcision, dressings .... Shabbos 134a
        Circumcision, necessary knowledge for Sage .... Chullin 9a
        Circumcision, place .... Shabbos 108a

Circumcision, sucking .... Shabbos 133b
Circumcision, washing baby .... Shabbos 86a, 134b

Time —
Circumcision after midnight, how .... Yevamos 71a-71b
Circumcision, cloudy day .... Yevamos 72a
Circumcision, not in time .... Shabbos 133a
Circumcision on eighth day, who .... Shabbos 135a-135b; Yevamos 72a-72b
Circumcision, sick baby .... Shabbos 134a, 137a; Yevamos 71a-71b; Chullin 47b
Circumcision, time .... Megillah 20a

Who —
Circumcision, brothers died .... Yevamos 64b
Circumcision, converts .... Yevamos 46a-46b; Krisos 9a; Berachos 47b
Circumcision, duty on whom .... Kiddushin 29a
Circumcision, household members .... Shabbos 135b
Circumcision, impurity afterwards .... Pesachim 92a; Eduyos 5:2
Circumcision, mother exempt .... Kiddushin 29a
Circumcision of son and slave, Pesach lamb .... Yevamos 71a-71b
Circumcision of son, commandment .... Kiddushin 29a
Circumcision, who is responsible .... Sanhedrin 59b

Misc. —
Circumcision, cutting leprous mark .... Shabbos 132b-133a
Circumcision, episode about castration .... Shabbos 135a
Circumcision, excising of soul .... Krisos 2a
Circumcision, healing powder .... Shabbos 134a
Circumcision in desert .... Yevamos 71b-72a
Circumcision, punishment for who neglects .... Sanhedrin 99a; Avos 3:11

Circumcision on Shabbos
Circumcision on Shabbos, androgyny .... Shabbos 136b-137a
Circumcision on Shabbos, asking a non-Jew .... Eruvin 67b-68a
Circumcision on Shabbos, baby cried before Shabbos .... Niddah 42b
Circumcision on Shabbos, bits of skins .... Shabbos 133b
Circumcision on Shabbos, carrying out knife .... Shabbos 130a-130b
Circumcision on Shabbos, carrying out water .... Eruvin 68a-68b
Circumcision on Shabbos, child born circumcised .... Shabbos 135a
Circumcision on Shabbos, doubt when born .... Shabbos 134b-135a
Circumcision on Shabbos, doubtful stillborn .... Shabbos 134b-136a
Circumcision on Shabbos, episode .... Niddah 42b
Circumcision on Shabbos, making tools .... Shabbos 130a, 131b-132a, 133a
Circumcision on Shabbos, mistake .... Shabbos 137a; Pesachim 72a-72b; Krisos 19b
Circumcision on Shabbos, overrides Shabbos .... Shabbos 132a-132b; Sanhedrin 59b
Circumcision on Shabbos, two foreskins .... Shabbos 135b

Circumspect
Circumspect and rules, Rabbah bar Matnah .... Horayos 14a
Circumspect before marrying .... Yevamos 63a
Circumspect in judgment .... Sanhedrin 7b; Avos 1:1
Circumspect in one's answers .... Megillah 25b
Circumstances point out, *sotah* .... Sotah 2b, 3a; Niddah 3a
Citizen low, foreigner high .... Bava Kama 42a; Eruvin 9a; Yoma 47a
Citron .... *see* **Esrog**, page 201

City
Dwelling —

Cities built by giants..Yoma 10a; Sotah 34b
Cities fortified in Heaven, overstatement ....Chullin 90b; Tamid 29a-29b
Cities of Judea, tearing...Moed Katan 26a
Cities of *Leviim* ....Eruvin 56b-57a; Arachin 33b; Sotah 27b
Cities of *Leviim*, sale ....Arachin 33b
Cities of Solomon and Hiram...Shabbos 54a
Cities of thieves...Chullin 127a
Cities, theft and forbidden relations ....Eruvin 21b
City and town, advantages...Kesubos 110b
City and town, preference...Kesubos 110b
City, horses and dogs...Pesachim 113a
City inhabitants, from when ....Bava Basra 8a, 11a; Sanhedrin 112a
City, its heads are Sages...Pesachim 112a, 113a
City of scoffers, keeping away ....Pesachim 112b
City, slopes ....Eruvin 56a
City, ten things...Sanhedrin 17b

Prohibitions —

City built as an arch...Eruvin 55a-55b, 57b
City close to idolatrous cult...Avodah Zarah 11b-12a
City conquered, *kohanos* ....Kesubos 27a-27b; Avodah Zarah 71a
City, idolatrous, purchase...Avodah Zarah 13b
City, leaving place out of *eruv* ....Eruvin 59a-60a
City of gold, carrying out on Shabbos...........................Shabbos 59a-59b, 138a; Eduyos 2:7

Misc. —

City, definition...Eruvin 26a; Sanhedrin 17b
City dweller who arrived that day, Purim...Megillah 19a
City, included in sale...Bava Basra 68a-68b, 150a
City, new, sins are few ....Shabbos 10b-11a
City of Bursif, evil omen for Torah...Sanhedrin 109a
City, responsibility of Sage...Moed Katan 6a
City, tax for expenses...Bava Metzia 108a; Bava Basra 8a
City, *techum* and outskirts...Nedarim 56b
City, walled...*see* **Walled city**, page 730

Cities of *Eretz Yisrael*

Cities of *Eretz Yisrael*, Shechem...Sanhedrin 102a
Cities of *Eretz Yisrael*, Tiberias and Tzippori ....Megillah 6a
Cities of *Eretz Yisrael*, Joshua...Megillah 6a; Bava Basra 56a

City led to idolatry

City led to idolatry, *beis din* session ....Sanhedrin 112a
City led to idolatry, burning ....Sanhedrin 112a-113a
City led to idolatry, death by sword ....Sanhedrin 52b
City led to idolatry, definition ....Sanhedrin 16b
City led to idolatry, despairing of ownership...Krisos 24a
City led to idolatry, did it exist ....Sanhedrin 71a
City led to idolatry, inciters...Sanhedrin 111b, 67a, 89b
City led to idolatry, unintentional ....Yevamos 9a; Horayos 8a
City led to idolatry, its inhabitants...Sanhedrin 112a

City led to idolatry, number of inhabitants..Sanhedrin 15b
City led to idolatry, one *mezuzah*..Sanhedrin 71a, 113a
City led to idolatry, *Sanhedrin*..Sanhedrin 16b
City led to idolatry, self-incited..Sanhedrin 112a
City led to idolatry, several towns..Sanhedrin 16b
City led to idolatry, tribe..Sanhedrin 15b

City of Refuge
  Exiled man —
    City of Refuge, burial..Makos 12a
    City of Refuge, disciple..Makos 10a
    City of Refuge, exiled man's needs..Makos 10a
    City of Refuge, killed there..Makos 12b
    City of Refuge, *Kohen Gadol*..Makos 11a-11b; Horayos 12b
    City of Refuge, murderer who died..Makos 11b, 12a
    City of Refuge, paying rent..Makos 13a
  Refuge —
    City of Refuge, branches of tree..Makos 12a-12b
    City of Refuge, ineligible inhabitants..Makos 10b
    City of Refuge, Moses..Makos 10a
    City of Refuge, *techum*..Makos 12a
    City of Refuge, where..Makos 12b; Zevachim 117a
    City of Refuge, words of Torah..Makos 10a
  Misc. —
    City of Refuge..Makos 9b-10a; Bava Basra 122b
    City of Refuge, *aggadah*..Makos 10a
    City of Refuge, angel of Rome..Makos 12a
    City of Refuge, Reuben..Makos 10a
    City of Refuge, road posts..Makos 10a-10b
    City of Refuge, Joshua..Makos 11a

Claim
  Claim, *chazakah*..Bava Basra 28b, 41a
  Claim from third person, field purchase..Shevuos 31a
  Claim from third person, retracting from purchase..Kesubos 92b-93a; Bava Kama 8b; Bava Metzia 14a
  Claim of borrower, sale contradicting loan..Kesubos 110a
  Claim of virginity..*see* **Virginity**, page 724
  Claims of litigants..Bava Basra 31a
  Claim proves a right..Shevuos 40b

Claim to collect from fellow
  Claim to collect from fellow, claim..Bava Basra 30a, 159b; Yoma 9, Kesuvos 76b; Sotah 48b; Gittin 48b
  Claim to collect from fellow, doubtful firstborn..Taharos 4:12; Nedarim 19a; Bava Metzia 6b; Bechoros 18a-18b
  Claim to collect from fellow, majority..Bava Kama 46a-46b
  Claim to collect from fellow, sick person..Bava Basra 153a-153b; Kiddushin 79b
  Claim to collect from fellow, Symmachus..Bava Kama 35b, 46a-46b; Bava Metzia 2b, 6a, 98b, 35b, 100a, 100b; Bava Basra 141a
  Claim to collect from fellow, worker's salary..Shevuos 45b-46a

Claimant, heard first in *beis din*..Bava Kama 46b

Claimed

Claimed large utensil..Shevuos 43a
Claimed, oil and jugs...Kesubos 108b
Claiming her *kesubah*, widow's right to alimony.....................Kesubos 54a; Gittin 35a; Arachin 22a
Claiming it was stolen, double payment............................Bava Kama 63b, 106a, 108b; Shevuos 49a

Claimed wheat

Claimed wheat and acknowledged barley..........................Bava Metzia 5a, 100b; Bava Kama 35b-36a;
....Shevuos 38b, 40a-40b
Claimed wheat, barley exempt...Bava Kama 35b-36a; Shevuos 40a
Claimed wheat, pretending...Shevuos 40b

Clapper of bell, impurity...Shabbos 58a-58b

Clapping

Clapping fingers, episode...Yoma 19b
Clapping hands on Shabbos..Beitzah 30a, 36b; Shabbos 148b

Clay

Clay, "took up clay from depths of sea"...Bava Kama 91a
Clay, danger to wipe with it..Shabbos 82a
Clay, *muktzeh*..Shabbos 124b
Clay of Daryani, wine concentrate..Avodah Zarah 32a
Clay vessel, keeping liquids..Taanis 7a
Clay vessels for child...Yoma 78b

Clay utensil

Clay utensil...Keilim 2:7
Clay utensil, absorbing..Avodah Zarah 34a
Clay utensil, container...Keilim 2:3-8, 4:4
Clay utensil, damaged, impurity...Keilim 2:6, 4:2-3
Clay utensil exudes water...Yoma 78a
Clay utensil, fragment..Keilim 2:6, 4, 2-3
Clay utensil, impurity..Shabbos 84a-84b; Eruvin 104b
Clay utensil, intervening substance for impurity of corpse.....Chagigah 22a-22b; Keilim 10:1;
....Oholos 5:3-4; Eduyos 1:14
Clay utensil, plastered...Kesubos 107b; Pesachim 30b; Avodah Zarah 33b-34a
Clay utensil, reptile and purity..Pesachim 20a-20b; Shabbos 138b
Clay utensil, space...................Chullin 24b-25a; Keilim 2:1; Zevachim 3a-3b; Pesachim 20a-20b;
....Shabbos 138b; Bava Basra 20a

Clean body, *tefillin*..Shabbos 49a, 130a

Cleaning

Cleaning garment, rubbing..Shabbos 140a, 141a
Cleaning garments on Shabbos..Shabbos 147a
Cleaning inner Altar...Tamid 30b, 33a, 6:1
Cleaning *menorah*...Yoma 14b-15a; Tamid 30b, 33a
Cleaning substances, blood of sin offering...Zevachim 95a-95b
Cleaning substances, stain of *niddah*..............Niddah 61b-63a; Sanhedrin 49b; Zevachim 95a-95b
Cleaning substances to launder leprous mark...Zevachim 95a

Cleanliness, Sage...Bava Basra 57b-58a

Clear

Clear law, forgotten...Shabbos 139a
Clear teaching, forgotten..Shabbos 139a

Clearing
Clearing out menstruation cycle .... Niddah 64a-64b
Clearing table, *seder* night .... Pesachim 115b
Cleopatra .... Niddah 30b; Shabbos 104b; Chullin 49b
Climbing and going down, health .... Eruvin 56a
Climbing vine on fruit tree .... Bava Metzia 116b
Clips to hold parchment .... Menachos 31b
Cloak of Rabbi Yehudah .... Nedarim 49b-50a
Close
Close, do not get close to authorities .... Avos 1:10
Close to her, divorce document .... Gittin 78a-78b; Yevamos 31a
Close to her, *kiddushin* .... Gittin 78b
Close to him, divorce document .... Gittin 78b
Close to himself and his money, testimony .... Yevamos 25a-25b; Sanhedrin 9b-10a
Close to menstruation .... Shevuos 18b; Niddah 15a-15b, 63b; Yevamos 62b
Close to menstruation, journey .... Yevamos 62b
Close to *mincha*, eating .... Berachos 28b; Shabbos 9b-10a; Succah 38a
Close to *mincha*, prohibitions .... Shabbos 9b-10a
Close to night, carrying on Shabbos .... Shabbos 11a-11b
Close to royal court .... Bava Kama 83a
Close to wall of city, Purim .... Megillah 3b
Closer to death than to life .... Shabbos 129b; Gittin 70a
Closed
Closed, by nearby organ .... Chullin 48b
Closing door before borrowers, ordinary land .... Bava Kama 8a
Closing eyes from seeing evil .... Bava Basra 57b; Makos 24a
Closing eyes of deceased man .... Shabbos 151b
Closed alley
  Shabbos —
  Closed alley, board and beam .... Shabbos 6a-6b; Eruvin 12b
  Closed alley, breach of four cubits .... Eruvin 5b-6a
  Closed alley, breached on side .... Eruvin 5a
  Closed alley, comparable to centipede .... Eruvin 8b
  Closed alley, courtyards opened on it .... Eruvin 12b, 73b-75a
  Closed alley, curved, Shabbos .... Eruvin 6a
  Closed alley, four handbreadths .... Eruvin 5a
  Closed alley, high, beam .... Eruvin 2a-3b; Succah 2a
  Closed alley, larger than ten cubits .... Eruvin 2b, 10a-10b
  Closed alley opened into courtyard, Shabbos .... Eruvin 7a-8b
  Closed alley opened into land .... Eruvin 7a
  Closed alley, smaller than four cubits .... Eruvin 12a, 13a
  Closed alley too high, repair .... Eruvin 4b-5a
  Closed alley, width longer .... Eruvin 5a, 12b
  Closed alley without partnership, Shabbos ...... Shabbos 130b-131a; Eruvin 91b
  Misc. —
  Closed alley, act of acquisition .... Bava Basra 84b-85b
  Closed alley, blocking it in front of one's door .... Bava Basra 11b-12a
  Closed alley, expenses for board and beam .... Eruvin 80a
  Closed alley, opening door .... Bava Basra 11b-12a

Closed alley, wanted to block ....Bava Basra 12a

Closeness
Closeness and majority, doubt ....Bava Basra 23b-24b; Beitzah 10b
Closeness, impure *challah* ....Challah 2:8; Sotah 30a-30b
Closeness to separate first fruit ....Bikkurim 2:5

Cloth
Cloth, act of acquisition by *chalifin* ....Bava Metzia 7a
Cloth, impurity ....Succah 17b; Shabbos 76a, 79a; Meilah 18a; Keilim 16:5-8, 27:1-4, 28:1-3; Eduyos 3:4
Cloth on pitcher, Shabbos ....Shabbos 48a
Cloth on wound, healing ....Shabbos 134b
Cloth, remainder, impurity ....Shabbos 39b-40a, 47a
Cloth rugged, knife ....Chullin 8b
Cloth, to examine *niddah* ....Niddah 14a-14b, 16a-16b, 17a

Cloth partition
Cloth partition in Temple ....Yoma 51b-52a, 54a; Kesubos 106a
Cloth partition of Holy of Holies ....Yoma 51b-52a; Bava Basra 3a-3b; Shekalim 8:4-5
Cloth partition, sacrifice for mistake of *beis din* ....Zevachim 41b
Cloth partition, sprinklings of Yom Kippur ....Yoma 56b-57a; Zevachim 57a
Cloth partition, Treasury in Rome ....Meilah 17b
Cloth partition, worn out ....Megillah 26b

Clothes, clothing ....*see* **Garments**, page 243

Clouds
Clouds, benefit ....Taanis 3b
Clouds, not withheld ....Taanis 3b
Clouds of Glory, Aaron's merit ....Taanis 9a
Clouds, prayer retained ....Berachos 32b
Clouds, scientific facts ....Taanis 9b, 10a; Bava Basra 75b
Cloudy day, prayer ....Berachos 32b
Cloudy day, sun ....Yoma 28b

Clover
Clover, damage to herbs ....Bava Kama 81a
Clover, *terumah* ....Terumos 10:5-6

Cluster of grapes, for the poor ....Peah 7,-6 7:7, 8:1; Taanis 6b
Coarse man, uncivilized ....Kiddushin 40b-41a
Coat, not to sell ....Yevamos 63a

Coated
Coated utensils, impurity ....Chagigah 26b; Menachos 96b-97a; Keilim 22:1
Coating idol ....Temurah 28b
Coating *tefillin* with gold ....Megillah 24b
Coercing, Sodom attitude ....Bava Kama 20a-21a; Eruvin 49a; Kesubos 103a; Bava Basra 12b, 59a, 168a

Coercion
Coercion ....*see also* **Unavoidable circumstances**, page 713
Coercion, idolatry ....Pesachim 25a-25b; Yoma 82a; Sanhedrin 74a
Coercion, punishment for forcing community ....Bava Basra 8b
Coercion to *chalitzah* ....Yevamos 106a

Coffin
Coffin in the street, dead woman ....Moed Katan 27b-28a
Coffin, mourning ....Moed Katan 25a
Coffins, impurity ....Oholos 9:15

Coffins in *Eretz Yisrael*, Gog's horses..Sanhedrin 98b

Coffins, one handbreadth, impurity..Berachos 19b

Cohen...*see* **Kohen**, page 345

Cohen Gadol...*see* **Kohen Gadol**, page 346

Cohen, *mum*...*see* **Blemish of a Kohen**, page 62

Coheness..*see* **Koheness**, page 348

Coheness, *almanah*..*see* **Widow eating *terumah***, page 745

Coheness, *shevuyah*..*see* **Captive woman**, page 87

Coin..*see also* **Money**, page 421

Monetary matters —

Coin, adding to its weight............................Bava Basra 90a-90b; Menachos 77a-77b; Bechoros 5b, 50a

Coin, became void and increased in value...Bava Kama 97a-98a

Coin, fraud...Bava Metzia 51b-52b

Coin, one per week, supporting wife.......................................Kesubos 58b-59a, 64b

Coin, Rav Yosef...Bava Kama 56b

Coin unusable, tasting in store..Shabbos 129a

Coins in staff, oath..Nedarim 25a; Shevuos 29a

Coins, lost..Bava Metzia 25a-25b

Coins of Sages, ordinary currency..........Kiddushin 11a; Bava Kama 36b-37a, 90b, 89b; Bechoros 50b

Coins of Torah, Tyre currency.........................Kiddushin 11a; Bava Kama 36b; Bechoros 50b

Coins written in legal documents, without number.....................Bava Basra 165b-166a

Misc. —

Coin adds up to coin, Divine Judgment...Sotah 8b-9a

Coin, fell from two people..Bava Metzia 26a-26b

Coin from pocket, consecrating..Meilah 21b-22a

Coin in barrel makes noise...Bava Metzia 85b

Coin, looking at its picture.......................................Avodah Zarah 50a; Pesachim 104a

Coin minted, second tithe..Succah 41a; Bava Metzia 47b

Coin of Abraham...Bava Kama 97b

Coin, old, preference...Bava Metzia 45b

Coin to charity, "...so that my son shall live".....Bava Basra 10b; Pesachim 8a-8b; Rosh Hashanah 4a

Coin which fell on sand, despairing..Bava Metzia 26b, 24b

Coins, close-fisted...Bava Metzia 52b

Coins in garment, carrying out on Shabbos.......................................Shabbos 147a

Coins of Jerusalem...Bava Kama 97b

Coins on pillow, *muktzeh*...Shabbos 142b

Colander, Yom Tov..Shabbos 139b

Cold

Cold food in cold food, rinsing..Chullin 107b; Pesachim 76a

Cold food in hot, cooking on Shabbos......................................Shabbos 41a, 42a

Cold water, cure..Shabbos 108b

Cold

Cold, man's responsibility..............Kesubos 30a; Bava Basra 144b; Bava Metzia 107b; Avodah Zarah 3b

Cold, sickness...Bava Metzia 107b

Collapsed house

Collapsed house, annulment of *chametz*.....................Pesachim 8a, 31b; Bava Metzia 42a

Collapsed houses, episodes about rescue.......................................Berachos 60a

Collapsed house, doubt about inheritance...........Bava Basra 157a, 158a-158b, 159b; Yevamos 38b;

....Bava Metzia 37b

Collapsed house, fast .... Taanis 20b
Collapsed house, living people underneath .... Yoma 85a
Collar, Shabbos .... Shabbos 48a; Makos 3b
Collateral
Collateral, cancellation of debts .... Bava Metzia 48b-49a; Shevuos 44b
Collateral, *chametz* of non-Jew .... Pesachim 31a-31b
Collateral, from when .... Pesachim 30b-31b
Collateral, "I do not want my collateral to be kept by another" .... Bava Metzia 36a
Collateral, *kiddushin* .... Kiddushin 8a-8b
Collateral, lost .... Bava Metzia 81b-82b; Shevuos 43b-44b
Collateral, oath about value .... Shevuos 43a-43b; Bava Metzia 34b-35a
Collateral, prohibition and returning .... Bava Metzia 82b, 113a-113b, 115a-116a; Sanhedrin 21a
Collateral, prohibitions .... Bava Metzia 82b, 113a-113b, 115a-116a; Sanhedrin 21a
Collateral, returning .... Bava Metzia 31b, 114b-115a
Collateral, unfit for act of acquisition .... Kiddushin 8b
Collateral, what is its use .... Bava Metzia 114b-115a
Collecting
Collecting debt .... *see also* **Mortgage**, page 423
Collecting from enemy in one payment .... Avodah Zarah 4a
Collecting from heir, partially .... Kesubos 91b; Gittin 30b
Collecting, from one or the other .... Bava Kama 111b, 115a; Chullin 134a
Collecting *kesubah* .... Kesubos 67a
Collecting rain, removing .... Shabbos 5a-5b
Collecting debt from debtor's debtor
Collecting debt from debtor's debtor, acknowledges .... Kesubos 19a
Collecting debt from debtor's debtor, gift to freed slave .... Kiddushin 15a
Collecting debt from debtor's debtor, ox goring regularly .... Bava Kama 40b
Collecting debt from debtor's debtor, *prozbul* .... Gittin 37a
Collecting debt from debtor's debtor .... Pesachim 31a
Collector, tax .... Bava Kama 113a; Bava Basra 54b, 55a
Color
Color of garment, components .... Bava Kama 101a-101b
Color of leprous marks on garments .... Negaim 11:4
Colored
Colored garment, blood stain .... Niddah 61b
Coloring, span, Shabbos .... Shabbos 106a
Comb, impurity .... Yevamos 43a; Keilim 13:8
Combing wool, span .... Shabbos 106a
Combining
Commandments —
Combining air space in succah .... Succah 19a
Combining basket, *challah* .... Pesachim 48b; Challah 2:4; Niddah 8a
Combining dough for *challah* .... Challah 2:4, 4:1-5; Pesachim 48b
Combining for quantity of flour .... Menachos 70b; Shabbos 76b; Challah 2:6
Combining unfit with *kosher* .... Succah 19a
Impurity —
Combining cloths, impurity .... Succah 17b; Shabbos 76a; Meilah 18a; Keilim 27:2-4
Combining for impurity of corpse .... Oholos 2:6, 3:1-3, 8:6, 15:10; Eduyos 3:1; Nazir 52a-52b;
.... Chullin 124b, 125a-125b; Meilah 17a

Combining for impurity of meat..Chullin 117b-122a; Taharos 1:4
Combining for quantity of impurity.....................................Chullin 124b-125b; Meilah 17b
Combining impure *neveilah*..Meilah 15b-16a
Combining mud to *mikveh* water..Succah 19a-19b; Mikvaos 7:1
Combining utensil, impurity....Chagigah 20b, 23b-24a; Eduyos 8:1; Pesachim 19a; Menachos 23b-24a
Combining for quantity of *mikveh*...Mikvaos 6:6-9
Combining foods for impurity..Pesachim 46a; Taharos 1:5-6

Mixture —
Combining, accidental act..Shabbos 41a-42a; Yoma 34b
Combining forbidden substances, mixture....................Orlah 2:1-3, 2:14-17; Shabbos 89b-90a;
....Avodah Zarah 66a; Zevachim 78a-79a; Meilah 15b
Combining, mixture in barrel.....................................Beitzah 3b-4a; Terumos 4:10; Zevachim 73a
Combining permitted substance to mixture..............Pesachim 43b-45a; Nazir 35b-36b, 37a-38a
Combining pot to mixture...Chullin 97b, 98a

Prohibitions —
Combining, carrying out on Shabbos.......................Shabbos 80a; Bava Basra 55b-56a
Combining, derivatives of vineyard to *nazir*......................Pesachim 45a; Nazir 35b, 37a-38a
Combining food left between teeth...Chullin 103b
Combining in Shabbos works..Menachos 57a
Combining, prohibitions.....................Avodah Zarah 66a; Orlah 2:10; Shabbos 89b-90a
Combining, removal of *chametz*...Pesachim 45b
Combining to make quantity, cases...Meilah 15a-18a
Combining to make quantity, vomit..Chullin 103b

Sacrifices —
Combining disqualified sacrifices....................Zevachim 109a-109b; Meilah 15a, 17b
Combining parts of sacrifice...Meilah 15b
Combining thoughts, sacrifice..........Zevachim 31a-31b; Menachos 12b-13a, 15a-15b, 16b
Combining to require sacrifice........................Krisos 4b, 12b; Shabbos 71a-71b
Combining utensil, meal offering..................................Menachos 24a, 24b

Misc. —
Combining judges and *batei din*..................................Bava Basra 165b
Combining possession of three buyers, *chazakah*.........Bava Basra 41b-42a
Combining testimony, one after the other.............Makos 6b; Sanhedrin 30a-30b, 81b
Combining two halves of testimony.............Bava Kama 70a-70b; Bava Basra 56a-56b;
....Sanhedrin 30b-31a, 86a-86b

Come
Come bride, Shabbos..................................Shabbos 119a; Bava Kama 32a-32b
Come down from Altar, which disqualified sacrifices...Zevachim 84a-84b, 27b; Niddah 40a-41a
Comes to purify himself, received Divine help.....Yoma 38b-39a; Shabbos 104a; Avodah Zarah 55a;
....Menachos 29b
Coming from impure, impure.....................................Bechoros 6b-7b
Coming from object of vow, substance.................................Nedarim 52b-53a
Coming into city before night.................Bava Kama 60b; Pesachim 2a; Taanis 10b
Coming into one's possession, consecrated item.....................Arachin 20b-21a
Coming out and in, person guarding.................Chullin 3a; Avodah Zarah 61a, 69a
Coming out of Holy of Holies, *Kohen Gadol*.................................Yoma 53a

Comet...Berachos 58b
Comforted me, Rabbi Yehoshua.................................Rosh Hashanah 25a

Comforting the bereaved
   Episodes —
      Comforting the bereaved, Rabbi Yishmael...Moed Katan 28b
      Comforting the bereaved, Resh Lakish..Kesubos 8b
      Comforting the bereaved, son's bone (Rashi – tooth)..............Berachos 5b; Bava Basra 116a
      Comforting the bereaved, Isaac..Sotah 14a
   Misc. —
      Comforting the bereaved after seven days..Moed Katan 21b
      Comforting the bereaved, deceased in front of him.................................Avos 4:18
      Comforting the bereaved, how...Moed Katan 28b
      Comforting the bereaved, keeping silent...Berachos 6b
      Comforting the bereaved, learning and *aggadah*..............................Moed Katan 23a
      Comforting the bereaved, line.......................................Sanhedrin 19a; Kesubos 8a-8b
      Comforting the bereaved, nodding head..Moed Katan 27b
      Comforting the bereaved on Shabbos..Shabbos 12a-12b
      Comforting the bereaved, sitting...........................Bava Basra 100b; Megillah 23b
      Comforting the bereaved, slaves..Berachos 16b

Commanded
   Commanded and performs.........................Kiddushin 31a; Bava Kama 38a, 87a; Avodah Zarah 3a
   Commanded us, blessing for Rabbinical commandments.............Shabbos 23a; Succah 46a

Commandment
   Aggadah —
      Commandment for which Jews sacrificed their lives............................Shabbos 130a
      Commandment in its time, beloved.............Pesachim 68b, 105b; Kiddushin 33a; Chullin 54b
      Commandment received with joy..Shabbos 130a
      Commandment, testimony and non-Jews in the future.................Avodah Zarah 2a, 4b
      Commandments, annulled in the future..................Avodah Zarah 3a, 4b; Eruvin 22a
      Commandments, deceased...Shabbos 30a, 151b
   Commandments —
      Commandment and pure body..Pesachim 112b
      Commandment to abide by deceased's will.............Gittin 14b-15a, 40a; Kesubos 69b-70a
      Commandment to divorce, whom................Sotah 25a; Gittin 90a-90b; Yevamos 63b
      Commandment to obey, knew *beis din* erred..Horayos 2b
      Commandment to obey Sages..............Yevamos 20a, 53a; Kiddushin 50a; Bava Basra 48a;
                                                                              Sanhedrin 53b; Horayos 2b; Chullin 106a
      Commandment to repay father's debt................Bava Basra 157a; Kesubos 91b
      Commandment to sanctify month, seeing moon.....................................Arachin 9b
      Commandment to say thing which will be heard.....................................Yevamos 65b
      Commandment with monetary reward...Pesachim 112b
      Commandments given in Marah...........................Sanhedrin 56b; Horayos 8b
      Commandments kept by non-Jews..Chullin 92a-92b
      Commandments of non-Jews...................Sanhedrin 56a-57a, 59a-60a, 74b-75a
   How —
      Commandment, on man more than on his agent.............................Kiddushin 41a
      Commandment originating in transgression...........Succah 30a; Bava Kama 94a; Sanhedrin 6b;
                                                                              Berachos 47b; Megillah 32a
      Commandment with item used for commandment............................Berachos 39b
      Commandment, with permitted idolatrous item ....Avodah Zarah 46a-47a

Commandments necessitate intention .... Pesachim 114b; Rosh Hashanah 28a-28b, 33b;
.... Berachos 13a; Eruvin 95b
Commandments performed all together, cups .... Pesachim 102a-102b
Reward —
Commandment leads to commandment .... Avos 4:2
Commandment, one, reward .... Moed Katan 28b
Commandment performed exactly as it was given .... Shabbos 63a
Commandment, tips balance of world .... Kiddushin 40b
Commandment, when must one interrupt learning .... Moed Katan 9a-9b
Commandment with reward at its side .... Chullin 110b-111a
Misc. —
Commandment incumbent on man is greater than voluntary one .... Kiddushin 64b
Commandment, momentary .... Kiddushin 29b
Commandment, payment by one who snatched .... Bava Kama 91b; Chullin 87a
Commandment performed, personal use .... Pesachim 26a; Yoma 59b-60a; Krisos 6a
Commandment with one's money, pleased with it .... Pesachim 4b; Bava Metzia 29b;
.... Bechoros 18b, 58a
Commandments annul one another .... Zevachim 79a; Pesachim 115a
Commandments, not given for benefit .... Rosh Hashanah 28a; Nedarim 16b; Eruvin 31a;
.... Chullin 89a-89b
Commandments not given for personal benefit, vow .... Rosh Hashanah 28a
Commandments, positive, women .... Berachos 20a-20b; Kiddushin 33b-35a; Eruvin 27a, 96a-96b
Commandments, several mitzvos on one cup .... Pesachim 102a-102b
Commemorating Temple destruction
Commemorating Temple destruction, ash for groom .... Bava Basra 60b
Commemorating Temple destruction, breaking cup .... Berachos 31a
Commemorating Temple destruction, crown of grooms .... Gittin 7a; Sotah 49a, 49b
Commemorating Temple destruction, decrees .... Gittin 7a; Bava Basra 60b; Shabbos 80b
Commemorating Temple destruction, prohibitions .... Sotah 48a-48b
Commemorating Temple destruction, Sages did not decree .... Shabbos 62b; Bava Basra 60b
Commemorating Temple destruction, source .... Succah 41a
Commentary, application to other subject .... Yevamos 54b; Zevachim 17a
Commerce in honesty, questions .... Shabbos 31a
Commercial interest, way to permit .... Bava Metzia 68a-69a
Commitment on intangible thing
Commitment on intangible thing, gift .... Bava Metzia 49a-49b
Commitment on intangible thing, not keeping one's word .... Bava Metzia 47b-48a, 49a;
.... Bechoros 13b
Commitment on intangible thing, sharing .... Bava Basra 3a
Commitment on intangible thing, to non-Jew .... Bechoros 13b
Commitment by presumption
Commitment by presumption, "this wine" .... Bava Metzia 73b-74a
Commitment by presumption, is it effective .... Nedarim 27b
Commitment by presumption, paying off debt .... Bava Metzia 66a-66b; Bava Basra 168a
Commitment by presumption, returning sale .... Bava Metzia 67a
Commitment by presumption, tenant farmer who exaggerated .... Bava Metzia 104b, 109a
Commitments, marital, vow .... Kesubos 70a-70b; Nedarim 85a-86b
Communal
Communal leaders, money received for sale of holy items .... Megillah 27a

C

Communal needs, caring for .... Avos 2:2
Communal needs destroy man .... Sanhedrin 17a
Communal peace offerings, eating .... Zevachim 54b-55a, 97b-98a
Communal peace offerings, north .... Zevachim 54b-55a

Communal prayer
Communal prayer, Aramaic language .... Sotah 33a; Shabbos 12b
Communal prayer, freeing slave .... Gittin 38b; Berachos 47b
Communal prayer, importance of its prayer .... Berachos 7b-8a
Communal prayer, missing *Kedushah* and *Modim* .... Berachos 21b
Communal prayer, not to hasten one's prayer .... Berachos 28b
Communal prayer, prayer without concentration .... Taanis 8a
Communal prayer, small courtyard opened to large one .... Eruvin 92b
Communal prayer, ten males .... Berachos 21b; Megillah 23b
Communal prayer, up to where must one go .... Pesachim 46a; Chullin 122b-123a

Communal sacrifice
Communal sacrifice, *chagigah* .... Yoma 51a
Communal sacrifice, *chagigah* on Shabbos .... Pesachim 70b
Communal sacrifice, exempt from sin offering .... Horayos 2b
Communal sacrifice, impurity .... Pesachim 76b-78a; Yoma 6b-7a, 8a, 50a
Communal sacrifice, indispensable .... Menachos 27a, 44b-45a
Communal sacrifice, new *terumah* .... Rosh Hashanah 7a; Yoma 65b; Megillah 29b
Communal sacrifice, Pesach .... Yoma 51a
Communal sacrifice, redeeming .... Shevuos 10b-12a; Zevachim 7a; Menachos 79b
Communal sacrifice, sacrificial animals .... Horayos 9a
Communal sacrifice, sin offering is not disqualified by death .... Horayos 6b; Temurah 16a

Community
Community .... *see also* **Public**, page 509
Community, Divine abundance .... Taanis 9a
Community, *Kohanim* and *Leviim* .... Horayos 6a-6b
Community, sacrifice for mistake of *beis din* .... Horayos 5b

Comparing slave to master .... Bava Kama 79b
Compensate, may G-d compensate your loss .... Berachos 16b

Compensation
Compensation for sick leave, slave .... Bava Kama 85b-86a
Compensations, avoided testifying .... Bava Kama 56a
Compensations, employing false witnesses .... Bava Kama 56a
Compensations, judge and Rebbi who made a mistake .... Sanhedrin 6a; Bechoros 28b

Competition
Competition .... Bava Metzia 60a-60b; Bava Basra 21b
Competition between teachers increases wisdom .... Bava Basra 21a, 22a
Competition in commerce .... Bava Basra 21b-22a
Competition in trade .... Sanhedrin 81a; Makos 24a

Complain
Complain, "Why should a living man complain" .... Kiddushin 80b
Complaining to G-d about someone .... Berachos 55a; Bava Kama 93a; Rosh Hashanah 16b
Complainers in the desert .... Yoma 75a

Completed
Completed by man, *muktzeh* .... Beitzah 27a
Completed item, craftsman's custody .... Bava Metzia 81a

Completion
Completion of Torah, three years..Megillah 29b
Completion of tractate, episodes........................Shabbos 118b-119a; Pesachim 68b
Completion of utensil
Completion of utensil, mat..Keilim 20:7
Completion of clay utensils, impurity.................Keilim 4:4, 5:1-2, 5:4; Beitzah 32a
Completion of iron utensils, impurity......................................Keilim 14:1, 14:5
Completion of utensils, impurity...Keilim 12:8, 27:5
Completion of utensils, wood and leather........Keilim 16:1-4, 20:7; Nedarim 56b; Sanhedrin 20b
Completion of work
Completion of work, similar to water touching food........................Chullin 118a
Completion of work, tithes...Maasros 3:4, 4:4
Completion of work, wine..........Avodah Zarah 56a-56b; Maasros 1:7; Bava Metzia 92b
Complexion of Jews, neither light nor dark.....................................Negaim 2:1
Compromise, *beis din*...Sanhedrin 6a-7a
Concealed
Concealed from all living...Shevuos 5a
Concealing Divine names...Shabbos 61b; Arachin 6a
Concealing face..Chagigah 5a-5b
Concealing her property before marriage............Kesubos 78b-79a; Bava Basra 150b, 151a
Concealing sacred books..Shabbos 115a
Concealing sacred objects...Megillah 26b
Concealment
Concealment of Ark, place..Yoma 54a; Shekalim 6:2
Concealment of Tabernacle and Temple doors.................................Sotah 9a
Concealment of Temple utensils, Josiah............Horayos 12a; Yoma 52b; Krisos 5b
Conceding
Conceding man, reward...............Rosh Hashanah 17a; Megillah 28a, 28a; Yoma 23a, 87b
Conceding to one's opinion, Hillel..Eduyos 1:4
Conceding Sage, healed...Rosh Hashanah 17a
Conceding Sage, Rabbi Akiva...Taanis 25b
Conceding with my money..............................Megillah 28a; Bava Basra 10b
Concentration
Concentration in prayer...Berachos 30b, 34b
Concentration in prayer, behavior..Shabbos 118b
Concentration in prayer, daily sin...Bava Basra 164b
Concentration in prayer, recalls sin..............Berachos 55a; Rosh Hashanah 16b
Concentration in reading *Shema*................Berachos 13a-13b, 16a, 33b-34a
Concubine in Gibeah
Concubine in Gibeah, why did they fall................Sanhedrin 103b; Shevuos 35b
Concubine in Gibeah, Benjamin.................................Bava Basra 116a, 121a
Concubine in Gibeah, husband's anger...Gittin 6b
Condemned to death
Condemned to death, *chazakah*...Gittin 28b-29a
Condemned to death, giving wine to condemned man......................Sanhedrin 43a
Condemned to death, hitting and cursing him........................Sanhedrin 85a-85b
Condemned to death, sacrifice..Arachin 6b-7a

Condition
Conditions —
Condition, consecrating on condition .... Nedarim 28b
Condition to return .... Kiddushin 6b; Bava Basra 137b
Condition to return, *lulav* .... Succah 41b; Kiddushin 6b; Bava Basra 137b
Conditions, deducting positive from negative .... Shevuos 36a-36b

How —
Condition after act .... Bava Metzia 94a
Condition, by agent .... Kesubos 74a
Condition, double .... Kiddushin 61a-62a; Gittin 46b, 75a-75b, 76a; Yevamos 53a; Nedarim 11a
Condition, impossible to fulfill .... Gittin 84a-84b; Bava Metzia 94a
Condition, keeping shoulder for oneself .... Chullin 134a
Condition, renouncing .... Gittin 74b
Condition, rules to make it valid .... Gittin 75a-75b; Kiddushin 61a-62a
Condition, witnesses' appeal .... Kesubos 19b

Marriage —
Condition, "on condition that I possess" .... Kiddushin 60b
Condition, "that you marry so-and-so" .... Gittin 84a
Condition, *chalitzah* .... Yevamos 53a, 106a; Kesubos 74a
Condition for *kiddushin*, marrying without specifying .... Kesubos 72b-74b; Yevamos 110a
Condition for marriage, "that father agrees" .... Kiddushin 63a-63b
Condition, gift to married woman .... Kiddushin 23b-24a
Condition of *kesubah*, like *kesubah* .... Kesubos 54b-55a, 104b
Condition, returning paper for divorce document .... Gittin 20b, 75a-75b
Condition that I possess field, concern he really has .... Kiddushin 60b
Condition to serve one's father, father died .... Gittin 76a
Conditions, wordings, *kiddushin* .... Kiddushin 49a-49b

Monetary matters —
Condition, excluding part of gift .... Bava Basra 148a-148b
Condition, fraud .... Bava Metzia 51a-51b; Kesubos 84a; Makos 3b
Condition, giving to heirs .... Gittin 74a
Condition, rights kept by seller .... Bava Basra 63a-63b
Conditions of workers guilds .... Bava Basra 8b, 9a
Conditions of Joshua .... Bava Kama 80b-81b

Vows —
Condition, commitment to *nezirus* .... Nedarim 19b, 21a; Eruvin 82a; Chagigah 10a;
.... Nazir 34a, 62a; Sanhedrin 25a
Condition in vow, unintentional .... Shevuos 28a-28b
Condition in vow, prohibition because of doubt .... Nedarim 14b-15b
Condition, man forbidding his son-in-law to benefit .... Nedarim 88a-88b
Condition to cause pain to former wife .... Gittin 74b

Misc. —
Condition by *beis din*, coming out in peace .... Tevul Yom 4:7
Condition by *beis din*, redeeming public sacrifice .... Shevuos 11a-12a; Menachos 79b
Condition for Shabbos, tithes .... Demai 7:1-5
Condition made by G-d, accepting Torah .... Shabbos 88a; Avodah Zarah 3a, 5a
Condition that tithe arrives safely .... Tevul Yom 4:7

Condition in divorce document
Condition in divorce document, "except so-and-so" .... Gittin 82a-82b, 85a

Condition in divorce document, "that you marry so-and-so" .... Gittin 84a
Condition in divorce document, before she fulfilled them .... Gittin 84a
Condition in divorce document, cases of disqualification .... Gittin 84b-85a
Condition in divorce document, insufficient breaking off ...... Gittin 21b, 83b; Eruvin 15b;
.... Yoma 13a; Succah 24b; Kiddushin 5a
Condition in divorce document, paper .... Gittin 20b, 75a-75b
Condition in divorce document, second condition .... Gittin 76a
Condition in divorce document, time of application .... Gittin 75b-76a
Condition in divorce document, unavoidable situation .... Gittin 30a, 34a-34b;
.... Kesubos 2b-3a; Nedarim 27a-27b

Condition to annul law
Condition to annul law, cases .... Bava Basra 126b
Condition to annul law, in monetary matters .... Bava Metzia 51a-51b, 94a; Kesubos 56a;
.... Gittin 84b; Kiddushin 19b; Bava Basra 126b
Condition to annul law of Torah .... Kesubos 56a, 83b-84a; Kiddushin 19b;
.... Bava Metzia 51a, 94a; Bava Basra 126b

Confession
Confession, Achan .... Sanhedrin 43b-44a
Confession by man condemned to death .... Sanhedrin 44b
Confession of dying man .... Shabbos 32a; Sanhedrin 43b
Confession of sin, Judah .... Sotah 7b
Confession of Yom Kippur, hindering .... Yoma 40b
Confession on Yom Kippur, how .... Yoma 86b, 87b
Confession for tithe
Confession for tithe, general .... Maaser Sheni 5:1-14
Confession for tithe, in any language .... Sotah 32b
Confession for tithe, reason for annulling .... Sotah 47b-48a
Confession of *Kohen Gadol*
Confession of *Kohen Gadol* on Yom Kippur, *Kohanim* .... Yoma 43b
Confession of *Kohen Gadol* on Yom Kippur, standing .... Yoma 35b-36a, 37a
Confession of *Kohen Gadol* on Yom Kippur, text .... Yoma 36b-37a, 66a
Confidence of Jerusalem wicked .... Shabbos 139a
Confiscated by government, rented donkey .... Bava Metzia 78b-79a
Congealing agents in mixture .... Avodah Zarah 35a
Congregation
Congregation .... *see also* **Communal prayer**, page 118
Congregation of Israel, your mother .... Berachos 35b
Congregation, ten men .... Megillah 23b; Berachos 21b; Sanhedrin 74b
Conjugal relations .... *see* **Marital relations** page 392
Connected
Connected to utensil, impurity ... Keilim 15:4, 20:3, 21:1-3, 29:2; Parah 12:8-10; Shabbos 48b-49a, 58b
Connecting poured water, impurity .... Taharos 8:9; Machshirin 5:9-11; Nazir 50a-50b; Sotah 48b;
.... Gittin 16a; Avodah Zarah 72a-72b

Connected to earth
Impurity —
Connected to earth, impurity .... Keilim 11:2, 12:3, 14:3, 20:4-5; Bava Basra 66a
Connected to earth, impurity of food .... Chullin 127a-127b, 128b; Uktzin 3:8; Nedarim 76a
Connected to earth, impurity of key indentations .... Shabbos 81a
Connected to earth, susceptible to impurity .... Pesachim 16a; Bava Basra 66b; Chullin 16a

Prohibitions —

Connected to earth, cases of idolatry..Avodah Zarah 46a, 47b, 54b
Connected to earth, covering on idol...Avodah Zarah 45a
Connected to earth, feeding animal on Shabbos.................................Shabbos 122a; Eruvin 79a
Connected to earth, idolatrous sacrifice................................Chullin 39b-40a; Avodah Zarah 42b
Connected to earth, sale to non-Jew...*see* **Non-Jew**, page 448
Connected to earth, smelling on Shabbos...Succah 37b
Connected to earth, stones of idolatrous mountain..................................Avodah Zarah 46a, 59a

Misc. —

Connected to earth, divorce document...Gittin 21a-21b
Connected to earth, fraud...Menachos 69a; Bava Metzia 56a
Connected to earth, like earth...Bava Basra 65b-66b
Connected to earth, oath.............Shevuos 43a; Kesubos 51a; Gittin 39a; Sanhedrin 15a; Bava Metzia 100b
Connected to earth, slaughtering..Chullin 15b-16b
Connected to earth, *terumah* when he will pick.......................Kiddushin 62a-62b; Yevamos 93b
Connected to earth, way of eating..Menachos 70a

Connection

Connection in poured liquid, impurity...Nazir 50a-50b
Connection of liquids, counting first and second..Zevachim 105b
Connection of liquids, impurity...................Avodah Zarah 75b; Taharos 1:9, 8:8-9; Tevul Yom 2:6-8
Connection of sacrificial flesh...Zevachim 87b
Connections, impurity...Zavim 5:6-8, 5:10
Connections, impurity of corpse...Avodah Zarah 37b; Nazir 42b
Connections, impurity of *zav*..Zavim 5:1-2
Connections of utensils, impurity...................Keilim 15:4, 20:3, 21:1-3, 29:2; Parah 12:8-10;
....Shabbos 48b-49a, 58b
Connections to impurity, separating...Uktzin 2:5-6

Connection between foods

Connection between foods, cases..Tevul Yom 1:1-5, 2:5
Connection between foods, considered as crumbled.......................Chullin 73a; Pesachim 85a
Connection between foods, egg...Tevul Yom 3:2-3
Connection between foods, holding smaller part...................Tevul Yom 3:1; Chullin 127b-128a
Connections between foods, stuck loaves..Taharos 1:7-8

Connection to *mikveh*

Connection to *mikveh*..Mikvaos 6:7-9
Connection to *mikveh*, about purity of sacrifice..Pesachim 34b
Connection to *mikveh*, *mikveh* and liquid.................Taharos 8:9; Mikvaos 10:6; Pesachim 34b
Connection to *mikveh*, Shabbos..Beitzah 18b-19a
Connection to *mikveh*, wine from residues......................Chullin 26a-26b; Maaser Sheni 1:3
Connection of water to *mikveh*, considered as sowing..Pesachim 34b

Conquest

Conquest, individual, Syria...............................Gittin 8b, 47a-47b; Avodah Zarah 21a
Conquest of Babylon, Sabbatical year...Sheviis 6:1
Conquest of *Eretz Yisrael*, forbidden foods...Chullin 17a

Consecrated

Consecrated for defined time..Nedarim 28b-29b
Consecrated produce, tithes...Peah 4:8; Challah 3:4; Menachos 66b
Consecrated produce, worker's and animal's consumption.......................................Meilah 13a
Consecrated utensil, from which material....................Sotah 14b; Succah 50b; Menachos 28b

C

Consecrated utensil, from which money where they bought .... Kesubos 106b

Consecrated item

Consecrated item, disqualified .... Temurah 17a-17b

Consecrated item, lost, remains consecrated .... Chullin 139a; Rosh Hashanah 6a

Consecrated item, redeeming .... Kiddushin 55a

Consecrated items, their holiness does not disappear without redemption ... Nedarim 29a-29b

Consecrated items Treasury

Consecrated items Treasury which damaged, and/or was damaged ... Bava Kama 37b-38a

Consecrated items Treasury, act of acquisition ... Kiddushin 28b-29a; Maaser Sheni 4:6; Gittin 52a

Consecrated items Treasury, act of acquisition by speech ...... Kiddushin 28b; Bava Metzia 6a;

.... Bava Basra 133b; Avodah Zarah 63a; Temurah 29b

Consecrated items Treasury, collected from which land/field .... Bava Kama 6b-7a

Consecrated items Treasury, custodians .... Bava Metzia 58a

Consecrated items Treasury, fraud .... Bava Metzia 56a-57b; Temurah 27a

Consecrated items Treasury, interest .... Bava Metzia 57b

Consecrated items Treasury, money for *kiddushin* .... Kiddushin 52b-53b

Consecrated items Treasury, *muktzeh* .... Shabbos 127b-128a

Consecrated items Treasury, oath .... Bava Metzia 57b; Shevuos 42b-43a

Consecrated items Treasury, permitted benefits .... Shekalim 7:5-7

Consecrated items Treasury, sale .... Shekalim 4:9

Consecrating

Cases —

Consecrating by mistake .... Nazir 30b-31b; Bava Basra 120b; Arachin 23a

Consecrating consecrated item, when it will be redeemed .... Nedarim 29b-30a

Consecrating doubtful money .... Bava Metzia 6a-6b

Consecrating gift, Beis Horon .... Nedarim 43b, 48a-48b; Bava Basra 134a; Kesubos 71a

Consecrating, non-Jew .... Arachin 5b, 6a; Zevachim 45a-45b; Temurah 2b

Consecrating on condition .... Nedarim 28b

Consecrating one limb of an animal .... Arachin 4b-5a; Temurah 11a-11b; Chullin 69b

Consecrating one's slave, freeing .... Gittin 38b

Consecrating wife's work ... Kesubos 58b-59b, 66a, 70a; Nedarim 85a-86b; Yevamos 93a; Kiddushin 63a

Consecrating without mentioning quantity .... Shabbos 90a; Menachos 106b-107a

How —

Consecrating animal, without explaining .... Menachos 104b-105a

Consecrating, wordings .... Menachos 63a, 108b; Arachin 4b, 19a-19b

Consecration in thought .... Shevuos 26b

In one's possession —

Consecrating item annuls mortgage .... Gittin 40b; Kesubos 59b; Bava Kama 90a;

.... Yevamos 46a, 66b-67a; Nedarim 86b

Consecrating item not his, paying its value .... Arachin 5b

Consecrating, mortgaged field .... Kesubos 59a-59b

Consecrating, stolen money .... Bava Kama 69a-69b

Consecrating, when item will become mine .... Arachin 20b-21a

Laws —

Consecrating goring ox .... Bava Kama 33b

Consecrating, included in field .... Bava Basra 71b-73a, 79a-79b; Meilah 13a

Consecrating limbs to Temple Treasury .... Arachin 4b, 18a; Bava Metzia 114a

Sacrifices —

Consecrating animals, sacrifice or Temple Treasury .... Shekalim 4:6-8; Temurah 31b

Consecrating blemished animal................Bechoros 14a-14b; Chullin 130a; Temurah 10b, 33b
Consecrating fetus................Temurah 10a-11a, 16b, 19a-19b, 25a-25b; Menachos 81a
Consecrating firstborn................Arachin 29a; Nedarim 13a
Consecrating sacrifice, Divine Name................Nedarim 10a-10b
Consecrating sacrifice on Shabbos................Shabbos 148b; Pesachim 66b; Beitzah 36b
Consecrating sacrifice on Yom Tov................Shabbos 148b; Pesachim 66b
Time —
Consecrating after thirty days................Nedarim 28b-29b
Consecrating in present times................Avodah Zarah 13a-13b; Bechoros 53a
Consecrating on Shabbos................Beitzah 36b-37a; Shabbos 148b; Pesachim 66b
Misc. —
Consecrating, *challah*................Menachos 67a; Challah 3:3
Consecrating, pearl in fish................Bava Basra 133b
Consecrating plunder of future................Pesachim 50a
Consecrating, sacrificial skin................Pesachim 57a
Consecrating meal offering
Consecrating meal offering, by halves................Menachos 7b-8b
Consecrating meal offering, handful................Menachos 26a-26b
Consecrating meal offering, handful in utensil................Menachos 13b
Consecrating meal offering, libations................Menachos 79a-79b
Consecrating meal offering, loaves of thanksgiving................Menachos 78b
Consecrating meal offering, on private altar................Zevachim 69a
Consecrating meal offering, source................Sotah 14b
Consecration
Consecration by *beis din*, Shabbos................Nedarim 78a-78b
Consecration, invalid because of presumption................Nedarim 28a-28b
Consecration of Temple................Moed Katan 9a; Shabbos 30a
Consecration of Temple, Ezra................Menachos 45a
Consecration of Temple utensils................Sanhedrin 16b; Shevuos 15a; Menachos 50a; Yoma 12b
Consecration by utensil
Consecration by utensil, air space of Altar................Zevachim 87b
Consecration by utensil, at night................Yoma 29b
Consecration by utensil, disqualified for offering................Menachos 102b
Consecration by utensil in Temple................Zevachim 87a-88a; Menachos 7a-8b, 19b
Consecration by utensil, knife................Menachos 78b
Consecration by utensil, measuring utensil................Menachos 8b, 57b, 90a, 88a-88b
Consecration by utensil, not in its time................Menachos 100a-100b; Yoma 29b; Temurah 14a
Consecration by utensil, oven................Menachos 72b, 95b
Consecration by utensil, ramp of Altar................Zevachim 87a-88a
Consecration by utensil, table in Temple................Menachos 87b, 96a
Consecration by utensil, tenth of *ephah*................Menachos 95b
Consecration by utensil, unintentionally................Succah 49b-50a; Menachos 7a, 78b, 90a; Sotah 14b
Consecration of *Kohen*
Consecration of *Kohanim*, order of dressing................Yoma 5b-6a
Consecration of *Kohen Gadol*................Yoma 5a, 12a-12b
Consecration of *Kohen Gadol*, meal offerings................Menachos 78a
Consecration of *Kohen*, meal offering for *Kohen*................Menachos 51b, 78a
Consent
Consent of owner, *eruv*................Eruvin 46b, 80b, 81b, 81b-82a, 95a

Consent of owners, impurity of food .... Bava Metzia 22a-22b
Consent to vow
  Consent to vow, cases .... Nedarim 79a
  Consent to vow, inwardly .... Nedarim 79a
  Consent to vow, kept silent to upset his wife .... Nedarim 78b-79a
  Consent to vow, permitting .... Nedarim 69a
Consider
  Consider, do not consider you did something great .... Avos 2:8
  Considered as dead .... Nedarim 64b
  Considered as on top and on bottom .... *see Gud asik*, page 261
  Considered identical kind like inexistent .... Avodah Zarah 73a-73b
  Considered like liar, *beis din* .... Bava Metzia 16b-17a
  Considering I already received it .... Nedarim 24a; Gittin 74b
  Considering wine as water .... Zevachim 78b-79a
Considerate in judgment, judge .... Sanhedrin 7b; Avos 1:1
"Consoled me," Rabbi Akiva .... Makos 24b
Conspiracy of wicked, Shevna .... Sanhedrin 26a
Conspiring witnesses
  Cases —
    Conspiring witnesses, contradicted then revealed .... Bava Kama 73b-74b; Kesubos 19b
    Conspiring witnesses, made a mistake .... Pesachim 11b-13a; Sanhedrin 41b, 42a
    Conspiring witnesses, several groups .... Makos 5a-5b
    Conspiring witnesses, *treifah* .... Sanhedrin 78a
    Conspiring witnesses whose plot was revealed .... Sanhedrin 9b-10a
  In which case —
    Conspiring witnesses against Canaanite slave .... Bava Kama 88a
    Conspiring witnesses, penalty for atonement and Hebrew slave .... Makos 2b
    Conspiring witnesses, *kesubah* .... Bava Kama 88b-89a; Makos 3a
    Conspiring witnesses, *Koheness* .... Sanhedrin 90a
  Punishment —
    Conspiring witness, lashes and indemnity .... Makos 4a-4b; Kesubos 32b-33a
    Conspiring witnesses, exempt .... Sanhedrin 41a
    Conspiring witnesses, lashes .... Makos 2a-2b, 4a; Kesubos 32b; Bava Kama 5a, 74b
    Conspiring witnesses, monetary punishment .... Makos 2b-3a, 5a
    Conspiring witnesses, one stage .... Sanhedrin 86a-86b
    Conspiring witnesses, punishment .... Makos 5a
  Misc. —
    Conspiring witness, episode .... Makos 5b; Chagigah 16b
    Conspiring witness, from when is he disqualified .... Bava Kama 72b-73a; Sanhedrin 27a
    Conspiring witnesses, how to prove their plot .... Bava Kama 73b-74b; Makos 5a, 5b
    Conspiring witnesses, place .... Makos 5a
    Conspiring witnesses, warning .... Makos 4a-4b; Kesubos 32b-33a
Container
  Container containing food, carrying out on Shabbos .... Shabbos 62b
  Container, destined to be filled .... Succah 12b
  Container for blessing, peace .... Uktzin 3:12
  Container for libation, *kashering* .... Avodah Zarah 74b-75b; Niddah 65a-65b
  Container, impure, makes liquid important .... Shabbos 17a
  Container of clay .... Keilim 2:7

Container to prepare sprinkling water, which .... Shabbos 95b; Parah 5:5-9; Yadayim 1:2
Container, washing hands .... Chullin 107a; Yadayim 1:2
Container, wine of idolaters .... Avodah Zarah 32a, 33a-34a
Containers, dividing meal offering .... Menachos 103b; Bava Basra 143a-143b
Containers of glass, impurity .... Shabbos 15b-16b; Keilim 2:1, 30:1-4

Container, outer side
Container, outer side, impurity ..... Keilim 25:9; Berachos 52a-52b; Chagigah 22b; Bechoros 38a; Niddah 7b
Container, outer side, non-holy and holy .... Chagigah 22b; Berachos 52a-52b; Bechoros 38a;
.... Keilim 25:6; Niddah 7b
Container, outer side, what does it render impure ... Niddah 7b; Berachos 52a-52b; Chagigah 22b;
.... Bechoros 38a; Keilim 25:1-9; Taharos 8:7
Container, outer side, which containers .... Keilim 25,1-5; Pesachim 17b

Contention by heretics .... Berachos 12a
Contractor, non-Jew, Shabbos .... Moed Katan 12a
Contradicting
Groups of witnesses —
Contradicting about details, monetary matters ..... Sanhedrin 30b-31a; Nazir 20a; Bava Basra 41b
Contradicting about sum .... Bava Basra 41b; Nazir 20a; Sanhedrin 31a
Contradicting, *chazakah* decides .... Yevamos 31a-31b; Gittin 78b
Contradicting, monetary *chazakah* .... Kesubos 20a; Yevamos 31a-31b
Contradicting, *nazir* .... Nazir 20a-20b; Eduyos 4:11
Contradicting, what did he sow .... Bava Basra 56b
Contradicting, witnesses about sacrifice .... Krisos 11b-12b; Bava Metzia 3b; Yevamos 87b-88a;
.... Kiddushin 65b
Contradicting witnesses, additional group .... Makos 5b
Contradicting, witnesses regarding impurity ..... Eruvin 35b-36a; Taharos 5:9; Kiddushin 65b, 75b

Women —
Contradicting about *kiddushin, kesubah* .... Kiddushin 65a
Contradicting, divorce .... Kesubos 22b-23a
Contradicting, *kiddushin* .... Kesubos 22b-23a
Contradicting, testimony about *agunah* ... Yevamos 88a-88b, 117b-118a; Kesubos 22b; Bava Basra 31b
Contradicting, testimony about *sotah* .... Sotah 31b-32a

Misc. —
Contradicting gift and freedom .... Gittin 40b
Contradicting, majority of opinions .... Shevuos 42a
Contradicting teacher .... Sanhedrin 110a; Berachos 27b
Contradicting verses, which determines .... Zevachim 63b; Sotah 14b
Contradicting witnesses, in their presence .... Kesubos 19b-20a

Contradiction
Contradiction between beginning and end of sentence .... Pesachim 59b-60b
Contradiction in Beraisa .... Gittin 73a
Contradiction in text of legal documents .... Bava Basra 166b

Contradiction in speech
Contradiction in speech, consecrating .... Menachos 103a; Temurah 26a
Contradiction in speech, monetary matters .... Bava Basra 104b-105b; Bava Metzia 102a-102b
Contradiction in speech, replacing sacrifice .... Temurah 26a; Zevachim 30b
Contradiction in speech, terms of legal document .... Bava Metzia 102a-102b

Contradiction in Mishnah
Contradiction in Mishnah, how is it possible .... Nedarim 72a

Contradiction in Mishnah, two different cases .... Kiddushin 63b; Sanhedrin 62b; Bava Metzia 41a
Contradiction in Mishnah, two tannaim .... Rosh Hashanah 7b; Kiddushin 63b;
.... Bava Kama 36b, 40b, 47b; Shevuos 5a; Yevamos 13a

Contradictory thought in same sacrifice .... Pesachim 59b-60b
Contrary
Contrary in boor .... Avos 5:7
Contrary is more logical (correct) .... Berachos 45b
Controller over weights and prices .... Bava Basra 89a
Conversation
Conversation, futile, prohibition .... Yoma 19b, 77a
Conversation, futile, Sage .... Succah 21b; Avodah Zarah 19b
Conversation, light, judgment .... Chagigah 5b
Conversation with one's wife .... Chagigah 5b
Conversation with woman .... Nedarim 20a; Eruvin 53b; Avos 1:5
Conversion
Conversion, according to *beis din*'s consent .... Kesubos 11a
Conversion after conception, inheritance .... Kiddushin 17b-18a
Conversion, how .... Yevamos 46a-46b
Conversion of slave, his consent .... Yevamos 47b-48a
Convert
Aggadah —
Convert, observe commandements including minutia .... Pesachim 91b
Converts, *aggadah* .... Kiddushin 70b; Pesachim 87b
Converts, difficult for Israel .... Kiddushin 70b; Yevamos 47b, 109b; Niddah 13b
Converts, epoch of Messiah .... Avodah Zarah 3b, 24a
Converts, Giving of Torah .... Shabbos 146a
Converts, hanging of Saul's sons .... Yevamos 79a
Converts, hinder coming of Messiah .... Niddah 13b
Converts, love one another .... Pesachim 113b
Converts, Naaman and Nebuzaradan .... Gittin 57b; Sanhedrin 96b
Converts, sons of wicked .... Gittin 57b
Laws —
Convert, *Avos* blessing .... Bikkurim 1:4
Convert, death penalty .... Sanhedrin 71b
Convert, gift from sick convert .... Bava Basra 149a
Convert, immersion on Pesach eve .... Pesachim 92a
Convert, impurity for seven days .... Pesachim 92a; Eduyos 5:2
Convert, interest .... Bava Metzia 72a
Convert, judge .... Niddah 49b; Sanhedrin 32a, 36b; Horayos 4b
Convert, not sold to slave .... Bava Metzia 71a
Convert, Pesach lamb .... Yevamos 71a
Convert, position of authority .... Yevamos 45b; Kiddushin 76b; Shabbos 154a
Convert, Rabbinical inheritance .... Kiddushin 17b-18a
Convert, testimony .... Yevamos 22a; Kesubos 28b; Bava Kama 88a
Convert who died
Convert who died, Canaanite slave .... Kiddushin 22b-23a
Convert who died, *eruv* .... Eruvin 70b-71a
Convert who died, libations .... Menachos 51b; Shekalim 7:6
Convert who died, ownerless belongings .... Bava Kama 49b; Yevamos 52b; Bava Basra 142a

C

Marriage —

Convert betrothed, stoning..Kesubos 44a-44b
Convert, father's family...Yevamos 98a
Convert, forbidden relations...........................Yevamos 22a, 97b-98b; Sanhedrin 57b-58a
Convert, *kesubah*..Kesubos 90a
Convert, marrying an illegitimate woman........................Kiddushin 67a, 72b-73a, 75a
Convert, possibility of being illegitimate......................Yevamos 16a-17a; Niddah 56b
Convert, procreation...Bechoros 47a; Yevamos 62a
Convert, renders woman disqualified to marry *Kohen*....................................Kiddushin 78a
Convert to *Koheness*, marriage...Yevamos 85; Kiddushin 73a

Prohibitions —

Convert, bending judgment for..Chagigah 5a
Convert, buying slaves...Bava Metzia 71a
Convert, not to belittle non-Jew in front of..Sanhedrin 94a
Convert, prohibition to cause him pain........................Bava Metzia 59b; Sanhedrin 94a
Convert who inherited idol..Avodah Zarah 64a-64b

Misc. —

Convert, accepting....................................Yevamos 47a-47b, 109b; Bechoros 30b
Convert, like newborn child....................Bechoros 47a; Yevamos 22a, 48b, 62a, 97b
Convert, prohibitions more severe than to non-Jews..Yevamos 22a
Convert, trustworthiness for conversion..................Krisos 8b-9a; Rosh Hashanah 31b
Convert who returned to his former religion...Bechoros 30b

Convert woman

Convert woman, immoral...Kesubos 44a-44b
Convert woman, marrying..................Berachos 8b; Horayos 13a; Pesachim 112b
Convert woman to injured *Kohen*..Yevamos 57a, 76a
Convert woman to *Kohen*..................Yevamos 60b; Kiddushin 74b, 78a, 78b

Convulsing...*see* **Twitching**, page 707

Cooked

Cooked food, blessing..Berachos 38b-39a
Cooked, wording of vow..Nedarim 49a

Cooking

Cooking by non-Jew....................Avodah Zarah 37b-38b, 59a; Yevamos 46a; Beitzah 16a-16b; Shabbos 51a;
....Moed Katan 12b
Cooking on Yom Tov, transgressions......................Makos 21b-22a; Pesachim 47b; Beitzah 12a-12b
Cooking, requirement to give tithes..Maasros 4:1

Cooking on Shabbos

Cooking on Shabbos......................*see also* **Leaving food on fire on Shabbos**, page 360
Cooking on Shabbos, Ben Drusai's dish.......................Shabbos 20a; Menachos 57a
Cooking on Shabbos, bringing next to stove-top...Shabbos 37a
Cooking on Shabbos, cold in hot..Shabbos 41a, 42a
Cooking on Shabbos, cooking after cooking...................................Shabbos 39a, 145b
Cooking on Shabbos, foods that cook quickly...Shabbos 145b
Cooking on Shabbos, hand withdraws at contact....................................Shabbos 40b
Cooking on Shabbos, in hot springs of Tiberias..................Shabbos 40b; Pesachim 41a
Cooking on Shabbos, kinds of kettles..Shabbos 41a
Cooking on Shabbos, oil...Shabbos 40b
Cooking on Shabbos, penalty......Terumos 2:3; Gittin 53b; Chullin 15a; Bava Kama 71a; Kesubos 34a
Cooking on Shabbos, pitch..Shabbos 74b

Cooking on Shabbos, salt..Shabbos 42a
Cooking on Shabbos, second container...Shabbos 40b
Cooking on Shabbos, spice...Shabbos 42a
Cooking on Shabbos, wood...Shabbos 74b

Copper snake
Copper snake..Rosh Hashanah 29a
Copper snake, Hezekiah..Pesachim 56a

Coppersmith, craft...Kesubos 77a

Copy
Copy of legal document..Bava Basra 171a
Copy of lost legal document..Bava Basra 168a-169b

Coral, taking out of sea...Rosh Hashanah 23a

Corner
Corner, breach...Eruvin 6a, 94a-94b
Corner, *karmelis*..Shabbos 7a
Corner of Altar, south, which sacrifice..Zevachim 64a
Corners of beard, place...Negaim 10:9

Corners of head
Corners of head and beard....................Nazir 40b, 57b-58b; Makos 20b-21a; Shevuos 2b-3a
Corners of head, *nazir* and *Kohen*.......................Nazir 41a-41b, 58a-58b; Yevamos 5a
Corners of head, shaving whole head...Nazir 41a-41b, 57b-58a
Corners of head, women..Kiddushin 35b; Nazir 57b

Cornice of Temple utensils..Yoma 72b

Correct
Correct yourself before correcting others.........Bava Metzia 107b; Bava Basra 60b; Sanhedrin 18a, 19a
Correct yourself, episode...Bava Basra 60a-60b
Correcting mistakes in holy parchments..Menachos 29b-30a

Correcting service
Correcting service...Zevachim 34b; Meilah 5b
Correcting service, bringing sacrificial blood..Zevachim 15a
Correcting service, *kemitzah*...Menachos 6b-7a, 26b
Correcting service, receiving sacrificial blood................................Zevachim 26b, 34b

Corridor
"Corridor," majority of head of fetus..Bechoros 46a-46b
"Corridor," *niddah* blood in female body.....................Niddah 17b-18a; Bava Basra 24a

Corrupted
Corrupted child, dreadful...Berachos 7b
Corrupted nations, wicked Jew worse than they are...............................Sanhedrin 39b
Corrupting fellow, punishment..Sanhedrin 55a

Cosmetics
Cosmetics for girls................................Shabbos 80b; Moed Katan 9b; Pesachim 42b-43b
Cosmetics on non-Jewish girl, episode......................Shabbos 80b; Moed Katan 9b
Cosmetics, Shabbos...Shabbos 94b-95a

Cost price sale...Bava Metzia 51b

Cotton wool, mixed species in vineyard..Kilayim 7:2-3

Couch
Couch, impurity after intimate relations with *niddah*............Niddah 32b; Zavim 5:11
Couch, impurity of leprous mark...Niddah 54b
Couch, impurity of *zav*...Zavim 4:6

Count
Count of days without discharge .... Niddah 38a
Count of *zavah*, immersion without count .... Niddah 30a, 69a-69b
Counts of *niddah* and *zavah* .... Arachin 8a-8b; Niddah 53b-54b, 69a-69b

Counted
Counted for tithe, animal becomes exempt .... Bechoros 59b-60a; Bava Metzia 6b
Counting days for months .... Megillah 5a
Counting letters in Torah .... Shabbos 49b
Counting *Omer* .... Menachos 65b; Chagigah 17b; Rosh Hashanah 5a
Counting one's coins, advice .... Bava Basra 9a
Counting, various Mishnayos .... Krisos 2b
Counting Israel, David .... Berachos 62b; Yoma 22b

Couples of *Kohanim* and *Kohanos*
.... Berachos 44a

Courts
.... *see* **Idolaters' courts**, page 294

Courtyard
Acquisition —
Courtyard, cases of acts of acquisition .... Bava Metzia 12a, 102a
Courtyard, hand or agent .... Bava Metzia 10b, 12a; Gittin 21a, 77b
Courtyard, minor boy and girl .... Bava Metzia 10b
Courtyard, moving, act of acquisition .... Bava Kama 12a; Gittin 21a, 78a; Bava Metzia 9b
Courtyard, presence of buyer .... Bava Kama 49b; Gittin 77b; Bava Metzia 11a-12a, 102a
Courtyard, well kept, act of acquisition .... Bava Metzia 11a-12a

Shabbos —
Courtyard and roof, carrying between them .... Eruvin 23b, 35a, 74a, 89a, 90b-92a;
.... Shabbos 147b, 130b; Menachos 72a
Courtyard behind houses .... Eruvin 24a
Courtyard, board and beam .... Eruvin 12b
Courtyard, board for *eruv* .... Eruvin 12a
Courtyard, large, open on small one .... Eruvin 8a, 9b, 92a-92b
Courtyard of Tabernacle, hangings .... Eruvin 2b; Zevachim 59b-60a
Courtyard, whole, *eruv* .... Eruvin 80b
Courtyards, connection by ladder .... Eruvin 59b-60a, 77b-78b
Courtyards, connection for *eruv* .... Eruvin 77b-78b
Courtyards in Temple, measures .... Yoma 16a-16b; Middos 2:6, 5:1-2
Courtyards in Temple, slain person .... Parah 3:3

Misc. —
Courtyard about to become his, divorce document .... Gittin 24a, 63b
Courtyard between two alleys .... Eruvin 49a
Courtyard, divorce .... Gittin 21a, 77a-77b, 79a-79b; Bava Metzia 11b-12a
Courtyard, grazing .... Bava Kama 21a-21b
Courtyard, included in sale .... Bava Basra 67a
Courtyard of grave, impurity .... Sotah 44a; Oholos 15:8
Courtyard of person suffering damage, ox goring occasionally .... Bava Kama 14a-14b,
.... 15b-16a, 18b, 24b-25a
Courtyard of synagogue .... Megillah 25b-26b
Courtyard, requirement to give tithe ...... Beitzah 34b-35b; Bava Metzia 87b-88b; Maasros 3:1, 3:5-6;
.... Terumos 8:3; Berachos 35b; Niddah 47b
Courtyard, shared, damaged .... Bava Kama 13b-14a
Courtyard, walking, divorce document .... Gittin 21a, 78a

Covenant

Covenant between parts .... Megillah 31b; Taanis 27b
Covenant for Oral Torah .... Gittin 60b
Covenant, if not for My covenant, Torah .... Nedarim 32a; Pesachim 68b
Covenant of peace, Phinehas (Pinchas) .... Kiddushin 66b
Covenant of salt, suffering .... Berachos 5a
Covenant sealed on lips .... Moed Katan 18a; Sanhedrin 102a
Covenants for Torah commandments .... Sotah 37a-37b

Cover of Ark

Cover of Ark .... Succah 5a-5b
Cover of Ark, sprinklings of Yom Kippur .... Yoma 54b-55a

Covered

Covered item before it burned, damage .... Bava Kama 56a
Covered yard, Temple .... Pesachim 13b, 52b; Berachos 33b; Succah 45a
Covering excrement, prayer .... Berachos 25b
Covering one's mouth, unclean place .... Berachos 24b

Covered by leprous marks

Covered by leprous marks, garment .... Niddah 19a; Sanhedrin 87b-88a; Zevachim 49b
Covered by leprous marks, man .... Negaim 8:1-10; Arachin 18b
Covered by leprous marks, *nesek* .... Zevachim 49b

Covered parts of body

Covered parts of body, immersion .... Niddah 66b
Covered parts of body, impurities .... Chullin 72b, 129a; Niddah 42b-43a, 44b
Covered parts of body, swallowed object .... Niddah 42b
Covered parts of body, washing .... Niddah 66b

Covering blood

How —

Covering blood, blessing .... Chullin 86b-87a
Covering blood by foot, prohibition .... Chullin 87a; Shabbos 22a
Covering blood, dishonoring commandment .... Shabbos 22a
Covering blood, earth .... Chullin 88a-88b
Covering blood, how .... Chullin 31a, 83b; Beitzah 7b
Covering blood, in air .... Chullin 31a
Covering blood, part of blood .... Chullin 88a
Covering blood which became intermingled .... Chullin 87a-87b; Zevachim 78a
Covering blood, who .... Chullin 87a

Misc. —

Covering blood, act needed for itself .... Beitzah 8a
Covering blood, becoming *kosher* again .... Chullin 87a, 87b
Covering blood, cases .... Chullin 83b, 87a
Covering blood, killing when blood is needed .... Chullin 27b, 85b-86a
Covering blood, learning laws .... Krisos 4b
Covering blood on Shabbos .... Chullin 84b
Covering blood on Yom Tov .... Beitzah 7b-8b; Chullin 84b-85a
Covering blood, sacrificial and consecrated .... Chullin 83b-84a
Covering blood, which animals .... Chullin 84a
Covering blood, wild animal and bird together .... Chullin 86b-87a

Covering head

Covering head, episode about fate .... Shabbos 156b

Covering head, man..Shabbos 118b; Kiddushin 31a
Covering head, married man...Kiddushin 29b
Covering head, married woman...Kesubos 72a-72b
Covering head, non-Jewish women...Sanhedrin 58b
Covering head of married woman, episode..Bava Kama 90b
   Covering pit
Covering pit, became uncovered...Bava Kama 52a
Covering pit, cover became damaged..Bava Kama 52a-52b
Covering pit, fellow's pit...Bava Kama 29b
Covering pit, insufficient weight of camels...Bava Kama 52b
Covering pit with fellow's object...Bava Kama 30a

Covering
Covering...*see also* **Tent**, page 681
Covering of idolatrous mountain...Avodah Zarah 45a
Covering of succah...*see* **S'chach**, page 576
Coverings of books, impurity..Keilim 28:4

Coveting, theft...Bava Metzia 5b

Cow
Cow and *tallis*, mutual damage..Bava Kama 14b
Cow, crouching, kicked...Bava Kama 20a, 24b, 32a
Cow heavy with young, assessment of damage.......................................Bava Kama 47a
Cow of Rabbi Elazar ben Charsum...Beitzah 23a
Cow, red...*see* **Red Heifer**, page 551
Cow wants to nurse..Pesachim 112a
Cows, returned Ark from Philistines..Avodah Zarah 24b
Cows, time for burning *chametz*..Pesachim 14a

Cowboy, herding large animals permitted...Sanhedrin 25b

Cracked object, holding smaller piece........................Chullin 127b-128a; Tevul Yom 3:1

Craft
Craft and not work..Shabbos 117b, 131b; Rosh Hashanah 29b
Craft for son...Kiddushin 30b, 82a-82b; Berachos 63a
Craft for son, Torah..Kiddushin 82b
Craft, G-d beautifies...Berachos 43b
Craft of fathers...Arachin 16b
Crafts, sign of blessing..Pesachim 50b

Craftsman
Craftsman...*see also* **Worker**, page 761
Craftsman, acquires item by improving it.......Bava Kama 98b-99b; Kiddushin 48b; Bava Metzia 112a
Craftsman, items he pretends are his..Bava Basra 45a-46a
Craftsman makes a living even during famine..Sanhedrin 29a
Craftsman, responsibility of custodian..Bava Metzia 80b-81a
Craftsman, way of carrying object on Shabbos..Shabbos 11b-12a
Craftsmen of Alexandria, Temple...Yoma 38a
Craftsmen of Temple, blame..Yoma 38a-38b

Crazy occasionally..Kesubos 20a; Yevamos 31a

Cream, depilatory..Bava Kama 86a; Makos 20b

Created
Created alone, man...Sanhedrin 37a
Created everything for a reason...Shabbos 77b

Created evil urge and Torah as antidote.................................Kiddushin 30b; Bava Basra 16a
Created ox etc., evil urge...Bava Basra 16a
Created Torah as antidote...Bava Basra 16a; Kiddushin 30b
Creating worlds, righteous are able to...Sanhedrin 65b
Creation
Creation of man and animal, *Sefer Yetzirah*.....................................Sanhedrin 65b, 67b
Creations of G-d in His world..Avos 6:10
Creation of world
Creation of world, according to its species.......................................Chullin 60a-60b
Creation of world, according to their unique character.......................Chullin 60a-60b
Creation of world, by G-d's hand and fingers...Kesubos 5a
Creation of world, chaos...Chagigah 12a
Creation of world, first day...Chagigah 12a
Creation of world, from where...Yoma 54b
Creation of world, order of creation.............................Tamid 32a; Chagigah 12a
Creation of world, sky...Chagigah 12a
Creation of world, when..............Rosh Hashanah 8a, 10b-11a, 27a; Avodah Zarah 8a
Creator's honor, does not care about.........................Kiddushin 40a; Chagigah 16a
Creature
"Creatures drown in the sea," not to sing...Sanhedrin 39b
Creature cannot stand next to them...Bava Basra 10b
Creature, whole, lashes for eating negligible quantity..................Nazir 51b-52a; Makos 17a;
....Chullin 96a-96b, 102a
Creature, whole, mixture..Chullin 100a
Creature without bones, length of life...Chullin 58a-58b
Creditor
Creditor, not to act as creditor..Bava Metzia 75b
Creditors, suffering..Eruvin 41b
Cress
Cress, health..Yoma 18b
Cress, health and advice..Moed Katan 11a
Cress, public property...Bava Metzia 107a
Crest of rooster..Shabbos 110b
Cries of Azarah...Pesachim 57a; Krisos 28a-28b
Crime, rebellion...Yoma 36b
Crimson wool
Crimson wool, leper...Yoma 41b-42a; Sotah 15b
Crimson wool, Red Heifer...Yoma 41b-42a
Crimson wool, Yom Kippur...............................Yoma 41b, 67a; Rosh Hashanah 31b
Criticize
Criticize, do not criticize much...Pesachim 113a
Criticizing, one's own flaw..Kiddushin 70a
Crooked thing cannot be corrected, immorality.............................Chagigah 9b-10a
Crop
Crop, bird sacrifice...Zevachim 65a
Crop, strength of *Kohanim*...Zevachim 64a
Crop, *treifah* bird...Chullin 56b
Crossroads, parable...Sotah 21a

Crouching

Crouching, damages made by animal .... Bava Kama 16a
Crouching donkey .... Bava Metzia 31a-33a; Pesachim 113b

Crowding of disciples .... Eruvin 53a

Crown

Crown for groom, prohibition .... Gittin 7a
Crown of David .... Avodah Zarah 44a
Crown of righteous in World to Come .... Megillah 15b; Sanhedrin 111b
Crown of Sages, wealth .... Sotah 49b
Crown of Tiberias .... Bava Basra 8a
Crown of wisdom, Rabbi Elazar bar Ilai .... Sotah 49b
Crown to elevate oneself, Torah .... Avos 4:5
Crown to its ancient glory, "*Hagadol*" .... Yoma 69b
Crowns at Giving of Torah .... Shabbos 88a
Crowns in *Ulam* of Temple .... Middos 3:8
Crowns of groom and bride, prohibition .... Gittin 7a; Sotah 49a, 49b
Crowns of month of *Nissan* .... Shabbos 87b
Crowns of righteous, Divine Presence .... Berachos 17a
Crowns, three .... Avos 2:7, 4:13
Crowns to G-d, *ofanim* angels .... Chagigah 13b

Crown of Torah

Crown of Torah, cornice on table in Temple .... Yoma 72b
Crown of Torah, Rabbi Tarfon .... Nedarim 62a
Crown of Torah, Sages .... Yoma 72b
Crown of Torah, using .... Nedarim 62a; Avos 1:13, 4:5

Crowns of letters

Crowns of letters .... Menachos 29b
Crowns of letters, Moses .... Shabbos 89a; Menachos 29b
Crowns of letters, multitude of laws .... Eruvin 21b

Cruel

Cruel, judge in capital cases .... Sanhedrin 36b
Cruel man, always in good mood .... Bava Basra 145b; Sanhedrin 100b
Cruel, to learn Torah .... Eruvin 21b-22a

Crumbs

Crumbs, poverty .... Pesachim 111b; Chullin 105b
Crumbs, waste of food .... Berachos 52b; Shabbos 143a

Crushing

Crushing idol .... Pesachim 28a; Avodah Zarah 43b-44a
Crushing on Yom Tov .... Beitzah 14a-14b
Crushing pepper on Shabbos .... Shabbos 141a

Crust, baking .... Shabbos 19b-20a, 37b

Crying

Crying about past .... Berachos 60a
Crying for all generations, *Tisha B'Av* .... Taanis 29a; Sotah 35a; Sanhedrin 104b
Crying for dead, episodes .... Shabbos 151b; Sanhedrin 104b
Crying for dead, not excessively .... Moed Katan 27b
Crying for honest man who died .... Moed Katan 25a
Crying of G-d, destruction .... Chagigah 5b
Crying of G-d, man abandoning Torah .... Chagigah 5b

Crying when reading verses .... Chagigah 4b-5a; Yoma 9b; Makos 24a; Sanhedrin 81a
Crying without being answered, who .... Bava Metzia 75b
Crystal cup, use it even if it will break .... Berachos 28a

Cubit
Cubit, "they measure one cubit like their hat" .... Gittin 14b
Cubit, five or six .... Keilim 17:10; Succah 5b; Menachos 97a-98a
Cubit high, beard one cubit, Pharaoh .... Moed Katan 18a
Cubit, measured by step .... Eruvin 42a
Cubit, small and medium .... Menachos 97a-98a; Succah 32b
Cubits, different measures .... Eruvin 3b-4a; Menachos 97a-98; Keilim 17:9-10
Cubits of Shushan .... Menachos 98a; Pesachim 86a; Bechoros 39b-40a; Keilim 17:9

Cunning
Cunning in fear of G-d .... Berachos 17a
Cunning of Sage .... Sotah 21b

Cup
Cup of David in future .... Pesachim 119b; Yoma 76a
Cup of glass, wedding .... Berachos 31a
Cup of mourner and bathhouse .... Nedarim 38b
Cup of teacher, refined person .... Tamid 27b
Cup, pocket and anger .... Eruvin 65b
Cup to become sterile, Rabbi Chiya's wife .... Yevamos 65b
Cup, washing .... Tamid 27b
Cup with two straws, commemorating Temple destruction .... Shabbos 62b

Cup of blessing
Cup of blessing, drinking .... Berachos 51a-51b; Succah 49b
Cup of blessing, forty gold coins .... Chullin 87a
Cup of blessing, generous man .... Sotah 38b
Cup of blessing, how .... Berachos 51a-51b; Pesachim 105b-106a, 107a; Berachos 50b
Cup of blessing, longevity .... Berachos 55a
Cup of blessing, popular drink .... Pesachim 107a
Cup of blessing, requirement .... Berachos 52a; Pesachim 105b, 117b
Cup of blessing, Sadducee .... Chullin 87a
Cup of blessing, wine .... Berachos 50b
Cup of blessing, Yalta .... Berachos 51b

Cupping glass, Shabbos .... Shabbos 66b
Curling hair, improper for a man .... Nazir 3a; Rosh Hashanah 26b; Megillah 18a

Currency
Currency .... Bava Kama 36b-37a, 89b, 90b; Bechoros 50b
Currency, doubt in promissory note .... Kesubos 110b
Currency of Syria or usual currency .... Kiddushin 11a; Bava Kama 36b, 90b; Bechoros 49b-51a
Currency, second tithe .... Bava Kama 97b

Curse
Episodes —
Curse of Ahijah Hashiloni .... Taanis 20a; Sanhedrin 105b-106a
Curse of Rav on Shmuel .... Shabbos 108a; Bava Kama 80b
Curse on Adam .... Pesachim 118a
Curse on judge, episodes .... Gittin 35a; Bava Basra 153a
Curse on Sadducee, Rabbi Yehoshua ben Levi .... Berachos 7a; Sanhedrin 105b; Avodah Zarah 4b
Curses, Karna .... Shabbos 108a; Bava Basra 89a

C

Curses of Abbaye, mistake in law .... Moed Katan 12b
Curses of David to Joab .... Sanhedrin 48b
Curses of Isaiah .... Chagigah 14a
Curses on Eve .... Eruvin 100b
Curses, Rav Adda .... Bava Basra 22a
Curses, Rav Huna's wife .... Bava Kama 80a; Nazir 57b
Curses, river banks .... Bava Metzia 107b

Rebuke —
Curse, bread by weight .... Menachos 87b
Curse for reneging on one's word in business .... *see* **Mi shepara**, page 408
Curse, wife and children discharge him from *Bircas HaMazon* .... Succah 38a; Berachos 20b
Curse, wording of oath .... Shevuos 35b-36a
Curses, cancelled by prophets .... Makos 24a
Curses, from G-d and Moses .... Bava Basra 88b-89a
Curses, modification in reading .... Shevuos 36a
Curses, not to interrupt Torah reading .... Megillah 31b
Curses on Mount Ebal .... Sotah 33b, 37a, 37b
Curses, together with blessing .... Taanis 20a; Berachos 4b

Misc. —
Curse, beginning by small person .... Berachos 61; Taanis 15b
Curse, blessing on food coming from curse .... Berachos 40b
Curse, effect .... Moed Katan 18a; Sanhedrin 49a, 102a
Curse of ordinary person, effect .... Megillah 15a, 28a; Bava Kama 93a
Curse of wicked, from blessing of righteous .... Yoma 38b
Curse on condition, effect .... Makos 11a
Curse on who feeds his father from tithe .... Kiddushin 32a
Curse, worded in third person .... Sotah 11a

Cursed
Cursed, includes vow .... Shevuos 36a
Cursed is he who performs G-d's work carelessly .... Bava Basra 21b
Cursing, doubt if he is his father .... Yevamos 101a; Makos 16a
Cursing father and mother .... Sanhedrin 66a, 85a-85b; Bava Metzia 94b-95b; Shevuos 27a-27b, 36a;
                                                                                        Menachos 90b-91a; Chullin 78b
Cursing, man going to execution .... Sanhedrin 85a-85b
Cursing one's fellow, deduction .... Sanhedrin 66a; Temurah 3b-4a
Cursing one's fellow with Divine Attribute .... Sanhedrin 56a, 66a; Shevuos 35a-36a
Cursing, wicked father .... Sanhedrin 85a

Curtain
Curtain is not closed, theft .... Bava Metzia 59a
Curtain, partition in wind .... Eruvin 8a
Curtain, sin of idolatry .... Bava Metzia 59a
Curtain, temporary tent .... Shabbos 138a; Eruvin 102a-102b
Curtains in Tabernacle .... Shabbos 98b-99a

Curved shape of *ches* letter .... Menachos 29b

Custodian
Custodians —
Custodian, after finishing work .... Bava Metzia 80b-81a
Custodian, land, slave and bill .... Bava Metzia 57b; Shevuos 43a

Custodian of lost item .... Bava Kama 56b-57a; Bava Metzia 29b, 82a-82b; Nedarim 33b-34a;
.... Shevuos 44a-44b
Custodian, paid, craftsman .... Bava Metzia 80b
Custodians .... *see also* **Deposit**, page 159
Custodians, Angel of Death .... Bava Metzia 36b
Custodians, charity .... Bava Kama 93a
Custodians, consecrated items Treasury .... Bava Metzia 58a
Custodians, sacrifice for oath .... *see* **Sacrifice for oath by custodian**, page 581

Liability —
Custodian, animal which lost its value .... Bava Metzia 96b
Custodian, conditions of liability .... Bava Metzia 94a
Custodian, different unavoidable circumstances .... Bava Metzia 93a-94a
Custodian, forgot where deposit is .... Bava Metzia 35a, 42a
Custodian, paid, stolen and lost item .... Bava Metzia 93a-95a; Shevuos 49a
Custodian, shepherds and sticks .... Bava Metzia 93b
Custodians, damages of ox .... Bava Kama 13b-14a, 45a-45b
Custodians, differences in liability .... Bava Metzia 94b-95a
Custodians, numerous, negligence of one of them .... Bava Kama 10a

Orphans —
Custodian, appraises for himself .... Kesubos 98a
Custodian, garments from orphan's money .... Gittin 52b
Custodian, minor's sale .... Kesubos 70a
Custodian, oath .... Gittin 52b
Custodian of orphans, tithe .... Gittin 52a
Custodian, ox which caused damage .... Bava Kama 39a-40a
Custodian, relative .... Bava Metzia 39a-39b
Custodian, sale .... Gittin 52a
Custodian, when is he dismissed .... Gittin 52b
Custodian, who .... Kesubos 109b

Theft —
Custodian, penalty for thief .... Bava Kama 57a, 62b, 63b, 106a, 106b, 107b, 108b; Shevuos 49a
Custodian, thief found .... Bava Kama 108b; Bava Metzia 93b
Custodian who denied deposit, thief .... Bava Kama 105b-106a
Custodian who paid, penalty .... Bava Kama 108a-108b; Bava Metzia 33b-34a, 37a
Custodian who paid, right to increase in value .... Bava Metzia 33b, 37a
Custodian who stole, finished his custody .... Bava Kama 118b

Misc. —
Custodian for adults, captive .... Bava Metzia 38b
Custodian who entrusted deposit to his mother .... Bava Metzia 42a-42b
Custodian who gave to custodian .... Bava Kama 11b, 56b; Bava Metzia 36a-36b
Custodian who lent, profit .... Bava Metzia 35b, 36b-37a, 96b
Custodians .... *see also* **Rent**, page 558, **Borrower**, page 73
Custodians, oath .... Bava Kama 106b-107b; Bava Metzia 5b, 98a-98b
Custodians, subtracting fragments .... Bava Kama 11a

Custody
Custody, "I gave back" .... Bava Basra 45b, 70a-71a
Custody, "place your belongings inside" .... Bava Kama 48b
Custody by deaf-mute, demented, and minor; damages .... Bava Kama 9b
Custody by husband, responsibility .... Bava Metzia 96a-96b

Custody, damages from horn .... Bava Kama 45b-46a, 55b, 99b
Custody of lost item .... Bava Kama 56b-57a; Bava Metzia 29a, 82a-82b; Nedarim 33b-34a; Shevuos 44a-44b
Custody of money .... Bava Metzia 36a, 42a; Pesachim 31b
Custody, permission to bring in .... Bava Kama 47a-48a, 59b
Custody, put into one's domain .... Bava Kama 47a-47b, 48b, 59b; Beitzah 40a; Bava Metzia 81b

Custody with owner

Custody with owner, cases .... Bava Metzia 96a, 98b, 96b
Custody with owner, how is it possible .... Bava Metzia 94a-94b, 95b-96a
Custody with owner, husband .... Bava Metzia 96a
Custody with owner, negligence .... Bava Metzia 95a-95b
Custody with owner, partner .... Bava Basra 43a-43b
Custody with owner, who .... Bava Metzia 81a-81b, 97a; Bava Basra 43b

Custom

Weddings —

Custom of Jerusalem, who will sign .... Sanhedrin 23a
Custom of secluding with one's fiancee .... Kesubos 9b, 12a
Customs of non-Jews .... Bava Kama 83a; Sanhedrin 52b
Customs of non-Jews, burning king's belongings .... Sanhedrin 52b; Avodah Zarah 11a-11a
Customs of weddings .... Berachos 50b
Customs, sum of dowry .... Kesubos 66a-66b; Bava Metzia 104b

Misc. —

Custom and "people used to," difference .... Taanis 26b
Custom, determining law .... Berachos 45a; Eruvin 14b; Pesachim 54a; Menachos 32a, 35b
Custom, everyone follows his custom .... Chullin 18b, 57a
Custom, from place to place .... Pesachim 51a, 51b-52a; Chullin 18b
Custom, not to change .... Pesachim 50b-51a; Bava Metzia 86b
Custom of area, fast .... Taanis 10b
Custom of their father's, idolatry .... Chullin 13b
Custom of work, eve of Pesach .... Pesachim 2b, 50a-50 51b, 55a
Custom of your father's, keep it .... Beitzah 4b
Custom, slander about Rabban Gamliel's sons .... Pesachim 51a

Custom of country

Custom of country, building a wall .... Bava Basra 3a
Custom of country, lessee .... Bava Metzia 103a-103b
Custom of country, worker's meal .... Bava Metzia 86a, 87a

Customs, not to smuggle goods .... Pesachim 112b

Cut off hand, Rav Huna .... Sanhedrin 58b

Cut

Cuts reeds in bogs, common man .... Shabbos 95a; Sanhedrin 32b, 33a
Cuts up tree then claims money .... Bava Basra 24b
Cutting bread .... Berachos 40a; Sanhedrin 102b
Cutting boil, act needed for itself .... Shabbos 107b
Cutting in tiny pieces on Shabbos .... Shabbos 74b
Cutting loaf of bread, host .... Berachos 46a
Cutting on Shabbos .... Shabbos 75b, 74b
Cutting, pulling hair .... Shabbos 94b; Makos 20b; Bechoros 24b
Cutting skin on Shabbos .... Shabbos 94b
Cutting up beetroot, Shabbos .... Shabbos 74b
Cutting wart on Shabbos .... Pesachim 68b; Eruvin 103a-103b

Cutting wound on Shabbos..................................Shabbos 107a, 107b; Kesubos 6b-7a; Eduyos 2:5
Cutting neck of bird
Cutting neck of bird...Zevachim 65a; Chullin 19b-20a
Cutting neck of bird burnt offering..Zevachim 64b-65a
Cutting neck of bird, disqualifications...Chullin 19b-20a
Cutting neck of bird, how.................................Zevachim 64b, 65a; Chullin 19b-20a
Cutting neck of bird, nape of the neck...Chullin 20b-21a
Cutting neck of bird, outside Temple...Nedarim 78a
Cutting neck of bird, slaughtering by pressing..Chullin 20b
Cutting neck of burnt offering, place...Zevachim 64a
Cutting neck of sin offering, place.............Zevachim 63a-63b, 66a, 67a; Menachos 2b
Cutting off
Cutting off end of splinter on Yom Tov...Beitzah 33b
Cutting off spices on Shabbos..Shabbos 128a
Cutting off leprous mark
Cutting off leprous mark, lashes...Shevuos 4a
Cutting off leprous mark, one of three hairs..Shabbos 94b
Cutting off leprous mark, prohibition..................................Negaim 7:4; Shabbos 94b
Cutting off leprous mark, when will he be pure.......Bechoros 34a-34b; Negaim 7, 4-5
Cutting off of soul..*see* **Excising of Soul**, page 207
Cuthean
Prohibitions —
Cuthean, lashes..Makos 8b
Cuthean, slaughtering...Chullin 3a-3b, 5b-6a, 17a
Cuthean, trustworthiness................Gittin 10a; Chullin 3a, 3b-4a; Niddah 56b-57a
Cuthean, wicked, hitting and cursing......................Sanhedrin 85b; Makos 8b
Cutheans, bread...Sheviis 8:10
Cutheans, marriage...Kiddushin 75a-76a
Cutheans, wine...Avodah Zarah 31a-31b; Chullin 6a
Misc. —
Cuthean, annulling his domain for Shabbos...Chullin 6a
Cuthean, circumcision..............................Avodah Zarah 26b-27a; Menachos 42a
Cuthean does not obey...Avodah Zarah 22a
Cuthean, signing on divorce document..Gittin 9a, 10a-10b
Cuthean, tithes and *revai*...Terumos 3:9
Cutheans, blood stains..Niddah 56b
Cutheans, image of a *yonah*..Chullin 6a
Cutheans, impurity..........................Niddah 31b-32a, 33a, 33b; Shabbos 16b; Chagigah 25a
Cutheans, insincere conversion.............Kiddushin 75b; Bava Kama 38b; Sanhedrin 85b; Chullin 3b;
Niddah 56b
Cutheans, penalty on Cutheans' money.....................................Bava Kama 38b-39a
Cutheans, wordings of vows..Nedarim 31a
Cycle of moon, calculation.............................Rosh Hashanah 20b, 24b-25a; Arachin 9b
Cymbal, *Leviim's* song...Arachin 10b
Cyrus
Cyrus, proper king...Rosh Hashanah 3b-4a
Cyrus, second Temple..Rosh Hashanah 3a-3b; Megillah 12a
Cyrus, years of reign..Megillah 11b-12a

D

Da...*see* **Know, page 344**

Daas acheres makneh..*see* **Purchase by receiving from seller's hands, page 511**

Daas be'alim...*see* **Returning stolen item, page 564**

Daas habrios nochah...*see* **People are pleased with him, judge, page 480**

Daas lehashil..*see* **Doubtful impurity, cannot be asked, page 179**

Daas rabo..*see* **Mind of his teacher, forty years page 411**

Daas sovaltan..*see* **Mind cannot tolerate, page 411**

Daas toah...*see* **Mistake possible, fraud, page 416**

Daas Torah, submitting to...Rosh Hashanah 25a-25b

Daas Torah...*see* **Torah outlook, submitting to page 696**

Daato legarshah..*see* **Intention to divorce, intimate relations, page 312**

Daato meureves...*see* **Pleasant behavior, page 492**

Daato shefelah..*see* **Humility, reward, page 288**

Daber, harsh expression...Makos 11a

Dagon, cult at doorstep...Avodah Zarah 41b

Daily offering

  Offering —

    Daily offering, binding...Tamid 31b

    Daily offering, bringing up flesh on to Altar..............................Shekalim 8:8, Succah 54b-55a

    Daily offering, number of *Kohanim*...Yoma 26b, 27a-27b

    Daily offering, order is a requisite...Sanhedrin 49b

    Daily offering, order of offering...Tamid 30b-31b

    Daily offering, place of slaughtering...Tamid 31b

    Daily offering, sprinkling..Yoma 15a-15b, 25b

    Daily offering, time of offering...Berachos 26b

    Daily offering, time of slaughtering...Pesachim 58a-58b

  Misc. —

    Daily offering and *mussaf* sacrifice, preference..................Menachos 49a-49b; Zevachim 90b-91a

    Daily offering, checking for blemish................Arachin 13a-13b; Succah 42a; Pesachim 96a;

    ....Menachos 49b-50a

    Daily offering, first and last..Pesachim 59a-59b, 73b;

    ....Yoma 33b-34a; Bava Kama 111a; Menachos 49a; Tamid 28b

    Daily offering, impurity overridden...Pesachim 66a, 66b

    Daily offering, libations..Yoma 34a-34b

Daily offering, not by private person .... Menachos 65a
Daily offering, penalty for *Kohanim* .... Menachos 50a
Daily offering, sacrifices in desert .... Chagigah 6a-6b; Yevamos 5b
Dakah, *eruv* .... *see* **Eruv, separation with** *dakah*, page 199
Daled **in** *tefillin* .... Shabbos 62a
Dam .... *see* **Blood**, page 66
Dam besulim .... *see* **Virginity**, page 724
Dam bris .... *see* **Blood of covenant**, page 68
Dam korban .... *see* **Sprinkling**, page 651
Dam koshi .... *see* **Blood flowing before birth**, page 68
Dama ben Nesina .... Kiddushin 31a; Avodah Zarah 23b-24a
Damage .... *see also* **Primary categories of damage**, page 504
  Animals —
  Damage by animal .... *see* **Ox**, page 467
  Damage by animals, slaughtering .... Bava Kama 23b
  Damage by man .... *see* **Four indemnities**, page 238
  Damages by ox .... *see* **Horn**, page 284
  Damages, differences between causes of damage .... Bava Kama 3b-4a
  Cases of damage —
  Damage, causing partial damage .... Bava Kama 10a-10b
  Damage done by sight .... Bava Basra 2a-3a, 59b
  Damage, shared, payment .... Bava Kama 13a-13b, 28b, 53a-53b
  Damage to fellow's mortgage .... Bava Kama 33b; Gittin 41a
  Damage to gifts to poor .... Chullin 130b
  Damage to priestly gifts .... Chullin 130b, 131b, 132a
  Damage with permission .... Bava Kama 93a
  Family members —
  Damage, shame and defect, of wife .... Kesubos 65b-66a
  Damage to wife by husband .... Bava Kama 32a
  Damages by married woman, payment .... Bava Kama 89a-89b
  Damages by one's daughter .... Kesubos 43a-43b; Bava Kama 87b-88a
  Damages done by one's son .... Bava Kama 87a-88a
  Misc. —
  Damage, consecrated items from one's best land for the Treasury .... Bava Kama 6b-7a
  Damage, estimate for .... Bava Kama 91a
  Damage, taking oath to collect .... Bava Kama 62a
  Damage to consecrated item Treasury .... Bava Kama 37b-38a; Bava Metzia 99b
  Damage to empty apartment .... Bava Kama 21a
  Damage to public, Shabbos .... Shabbos 42a
  Damages by worker, responsibility .... Bava Kama 99b; Bava Metzia 80a, 80b, 82b-83a
  Damages, non-Jew .... Bava Kama 13b, 38a
  Damage from neighbor
  Damage from neighbor, direct cause .... Bava Basra 22b, 25b-26a; Bava Metzia 117a
  Damage from neighbor, direct damage because of proximity ...... Bava Basra 22b, 25b-26a; Bava Metzia 117a
  Damage from neighbor, distance from pit wall .... Bava Basra 17a-17b
  Damage from neighbor, distance from pit's wall .... Bava Basra 19a-19b, 20b, 22a-22b
  Damage from neighbors, cases when distance is necessary .... Bava Basra 20b, 25b-26a
  Damage from neighbors, distance from birds .... Bava Kama 83a; Bava Basra 23a

D

Damage from neighbors, distance from threshing floor .... Bava Basra 24b-25a
Damage from neighbors, from when must one move away .... Bava Basra 17b-18b

Damage, indirect
Damage, indirect .... Bava Kama 98b
Damage, indirect, oath .... Bava Kama 105b; Shevuos 32a
Damage, indirect, one witness .... Shevuos 32a-32b
Damage, indirect, stealing animal .... Bava Kama 71b

Damage, pain etc
Damage, pain etc., fell from roof .... Bava Kama 27a
Damage, pain etc., hair .... Bava Kama 86a
Damage, pain etc., how .... Bava Kama 32b-33a, 85a-85b
Damage, pain etc., unintentional .... Bava Kama 26a-26b
Damage, pain etc., ox .... Bava Kama 33a

Damaged
Damaged Altar, disqualified .... Zevachim 59a, 60a-60b; Succah 48b-49a; Chullin 18a; Succah 48b-49a
Damaging person must move away .... Bava Basra 18b-19a; Bava Metzia 117a; Bava Kama 23b

Dan
Dan, "judge my judgment" .... Pesachim 4a
Dan, name of idol .... Shabbos 67b
Dan, numerous descendants .... Bava Basra 143b
Dan's sons, Hushim .... Bava Basra 143b

Dance
Dance for righteous in the future .... Taanis 31a
Dances by Sages .... Succah 53a; Kesubos 17a

Dancing
Dancing in front of bride .... Kesubos 16b-17a
Dancing on Shabbos .... Beitzah 30a, 36b; Shabbos 148b

Danger
Danger, more severe than prohibition .... Chullin 9b-10a
Danger of death, sale of field .... Gittin 55b, 58a-58b; Bava Basra 47b, 48a
Danger, ox .... Pesachim 112b; Berachos 33a
Danger, protection .... Shabbos 32a, 129b
Danger, putting oneself in danger to know ruling .... Bava Kama 61a
Danger, severity .... Chullin 9b-10a; Avodah Zarah 30a
Dangers, bridge .... Shabbos 32a
Dangers, fire .... Shabbos 26a
Dangers from animals .... Shabbos 121b
Dangers, glass in pot .... Shabbos 67b
Dangers in city, responsibility of public .... Moed Katan 5a
Dangers, new bathhouse .... Pesachim 112b
Dangers, unstable ladder .... Bava Kama 15b

Daniel son of David .... Berachos 4a
Daniel
Daniel, blessings of praise .... Berachos 57b
Daniel, Gabriel's defense .... Yoma 77a
Daniel, Gabriel's revelation .... Megillah 3a; Sanhedrin 93b-94a
Daniel, hardships .... Yoma 76b
Daniel, lions' pit .... Bava Basra 4a
Daniel, lost high position .... Bava Basra 4a; Megillah 15a

Daniel, Messiah..Sanhedrin 98b
Daniel, Temple destruction...Nazir 32b
Daniel, writing of Belshazzar..Sanhedrin 22a
Daniel's friends
   Daniel's friends, furnace................Pesachim 118a-118b; Sanhedrin 92b, 93a
   Daniel's friends, had they been beaten...............................Kesubos 33b
   Daniel's friends, *serisim*...Sanhedrin 93b
   Daniel's friends, thrown in furnace..................................Sanhedrin 93a
Darius, years of reign..Megillah 11b-12a
Dargash, significance..........Nedarim 56a-56b; Sanhedrin 20a-20b; Moed Katan 27a
Darkei Emori..*see* **Ways of Emorite**, page 737
Darkei shalom...*see* **Peaceful ways**, page 477
Darkness, Talmud Bavli..Sanhedrin 24a
Darko lehimanos....................................*see* **Usually counted**, page 717
Daryavesh..*see* **Darius**, page 143
Das Moshe veYehudis..Kesubos 72a-72b
Dash...*see* **Beating grain**, page 46
Dash, signature..Bava Basra 163a
Dathan and Abiram...Nedarim 64b
Date
   Date on *kiddushin* document.......................................Yevamos 31b
   Date on legal document, on Shabbos or later date...........Bava Basra 171a-172a
   Date on legal document, writing delayed........................Bava Basra 172a
Date
  Episodes —
   Date, delicious, episode...Sotah 49a
   Dates of Babylon, Ulla..............................Pesachim 88a; Taanis 9b
   Dates, palm trees of Babylon...Taanis 29b
   Dates, wine taste...Bava Kama 92a
  Laws —
   Dates, *Bircas HaMazon*..Berachos 12a
   Dates, estimate of damage...Bava Metzia 99b
   Dates for *kiddushin* money, combining...................Kiddushin 44a, 46a
   Dates in bunch, *muktzeh*..Pesachim 56b
   Dates, male palm tree, tithe...Eruvin 28b
   Dates, mashed, blessing...Berachos 38a
   Dates, *muktzeh*..Pesachim 56b
   Dates, retail or wholesale price..................................Bava Metzia 99b
  Quantities —
   Date, two olives...Krisos 14a
   Date, volume..Yoma 78b-79b
   Date, volume of large date...Yoma 78b
  Misc. —
   Date, *perutah* in Medea..Kiddushin 12a
   Dates, bitter, sickness...Bava Metzia 113b
   Dates, health................................Kesubos 10b; Gittin 70a
   Dates, old, inferior...Bava Basra 91b
   Dates, picking..Shabbos 73b

D

Date pits
Date pits, *muktzeh* .... Shabbos 143a
Date pits, size .... Chullin 50b
Date pits, volume .... Yoma 79b

Daughter
Biblical sources —
Daughter, Benjamin's inheritance .... Bava Basra 116a
Daughter of Abraham, *bakol* .... Bava Basra 16b, 141a
Daughter of Nadiv, Abraham .... Succah 49b; Chagigah 3a
Daughter of Pharaoh, Divine anger .... Niddah 70b
Daughter of Pharaoh, Solomon .... Yevamos 76a-76b
Daughter of Jephthah .... Taanis 4a
Daughters of Canaan, Judah .... Pesachim 50a
Daughters of Job .... Bava Basra 16b
Daughters of Midian, atonement .... Shabbos 64a-64b
Daughters of Midian, checking .... Yevamos 60b
Daughters of Moab and Midian .... Sanhedrin 106a; Bechoros 5b
Daughters of Zelophehad, *Eretz Yisrael* .... Bava Basra 118b-119b
Daughters of Zelophehad, Moses .... Sanhedrin 8a; Bava Basra 119a
Daughters of Israel, cry! .... Nedarim 66a

Episodes —
Daughter given to disciple, episode .... Horayos 12b
Daughter of Emperor, spindle .... Chullin 60a
Daughter of Emperor, wine in gold containers .... Nedarim 50b; Taanis 7a-7b
Daughter of Kalba Savua, Rabbi Akiva .... Nedarim 50a; Kesubos 62b-63a
Daughter of Nakdimen .... Kesubos 65a, 66b
Daughter of Nechunya, pit .... Bava Kama 50a; Yevamos 121b
Daughter of Rabbi Akiva and Ben Azzai .... Kesubos 63a
Daughter of Rabbi Akiva, snake .... Shabbos 156b
Daughter of Rabbi Chanina, Rabbi Meir .... Avodah Zarah 18a-18b
Daughter of Rabbi Chiya, death .... Kesubos 62b
Daughter of Rabbi Yishmael, captive .... Gittin 58a
Daughter of Rabbi Yochanan, Zeirei .... Kiddushin 71b
Daughter of Rabbi Yose de'min Yokrat .... Taanis 24a
Daughter of Rami bar Chama .... Beitzah 29b
Daughter of Rav Bibi, cosmetics .... Shabbos 80b; Moed Katan 9b
Daughter of Rav Chisda, marriage .... Bava Basra 12b
Daughters, "would you have also neglected your daughters"? ...... Moed Katan 18a
Daughters of Rabbi Nachman, captivity .... Gittin 45a
Daughters of Shmuel, captivity .... Kesubos 23a
Daughters of Shmuel's father .... Shabbos 65a-65b; Nedarim 40b; Bechoros 55b; Niddah 67a

Forbidden relations —
Daughter and wife's daughter .... Sanhedrin 51a, 75a-75b, 76a, 87b; Chagigah 11b; Yevamos 3a; Krisos 5a
Daughter born from forbidden relations .... Yevamos 22b
Daughter born from forbidden relations, to *Kohen* .... Yevamos 15b, 44a-44b; Niddah 69b-70a
Daughter of daughter, forbidden relations .... Sanhedrin 75a-75b
Daughter of father's wife .... Sotah 43b
Daughter of *Kohen* .... *see* **Koheness**, page 348
Daughter of rape victim .... Sanhedrin 76a

Daughter permitted, widow also .... Kiddushin 74b-75a
Daughters of Cutheans, impurity .... Niddah 31b-32a; Shabbos 16b
Daughters of Jerusalem, immodest behavior .... Shabbos 62b; Yoma 9b

Marriage —
Daughter, duty to marry off one's daughter ..... Sanhedrin 76a-76b; Pesachim 113a; Kiddushin 30b
Daughter has grown up, free your slave .... Pesachim 113a
Daughter of *Kohen* marrying Israelite .... Pesachim 49a
Daughter of Sage and good family, marrying .... Yoma 71a-71b
Daughter of scholar and *Kohen*, marrying .... Pesachim 49a-49b
Daughter of sister, marriage .... Sanhedrin 76b; Yevamos 62b-63a
Daughter of so-and-so to so-and-so .... Sotah 2a; Moed Katan 18b; Sanhedrin 22a
Daughter, young, can she marry without father's consent? .... Kiddushin 43b-44a

Rights —
Daughter, inheritance .... Bava Basra 110a-110b, 113a-113b, 122b
Daughter, living with her mother .... Kesubos 102b-103a
Daughter, mother's inheritance .... Bava Basra 110b-111a
Daughter of one's wife, supporting her .... Kesubos 102b; Gittin 51a
Daughter of son, inheritance .... Bava Basra 115a-116a
Daughter, rebellious .... Sanhedrin 69b-70a

Misc. —
Daughter, agent for divorce .... Kiddushin 44b
Daughter, *aggadah* .... Bava Basra 16b
Daughter, better to sell her than to borrow with interest .... Kiddushin 20a; Arachin 30b
Daughter, damages .... Bava Kama 87a-88a
Daughter, divorce .... Gittin 64b; Kesubos 47a
Daughter, father's rights .... Kiddushin 3b-4a, 10a; Kesubos 43b, 46b-47a; Niddah 47a
Daughter first, good omen .... Bava Basra 141a
Daughter, gift on condition .... Nedarim 88a-88b
Daughter, her father's worry .... Sanhedrin 100b
Daughter, like her mother .... Kesubos 63a
Daughter of *Kohen Gadol*, captive .... Gittin 58a
Daughter, precedence over son .... Bava Basra 141a
Daughter, rights to indemnity for damages .... Kesubos 43a-43b; Bava Kama 87b-88a
Daughter sold as maidservant, no profit .... Megillah 27a
Daughters of Israel were stringent .... Niddah 66a; Berachos 31a; Megillah 28b

Daughters of Lot
Daughters of Lot, precedence for commandment ... Bava Kama 38b; Nazir 23b-24a; Horayos 11a
Daughters of Lot, refined language .... Bava Kama 38b; Nazir 23b; Horayos 10b-11a
Daughters of Lot, reward .... Bava Kama 38b

Daughter-in-law
Daughter-in-law, forbidden relations .... Sanhedrin 54a
Daughter-in-law, hatred .... Yevamos 117a
Daughter-in-law, modest, reward .... Megillah 10b
Daughter-in-law of one's wife, permitted .... Sanhedrin 76a
Daughter-in-law of Rebbi, death .... Kesubos 62b
Daughter-in-law screamed at you, leave .... Eruvin 86a

Davar beito mah tov .... *see* **Thing at its time, how good,** page 687
Davar beshem omro .... *see* **Thing in name of who said it,** page 687
Davar charif .... *see* **Sharp substance, knife,** page 610

Davar haaved .... *see* **Monetary loss**, page 420
Davar haba be'aveirah .... *see* **Resulting from transgression**, page 563
Davar halamed meinyano .... *see* **Deduction from contextual subject**, page 156
Davar hamaamid betaaruvos .... *see* **Congealing agents in mixture**, page 121
Davar mechoar .... *see* **Adultery, signs of misconduct**, page 12
Davar shebe'ervah .... *see* **Testimony concerning forbidden relations, two**, page 684
Davar shebehechshero .... *see* **Deduction, "all the more so" from the outset**, page 156
Davar shebeminyan, gezeiros .... *see* **Rabbinical Decree, when permitted to annul it**, page 533
Davar shebeminyan, taaruvos .... *see* **Mixture, sold by unit**, page 418
Davar shebe'yado .... *see* **Be'yado**, page 56
Davar shebikdushah baasarah .... *see* **Quorum, for which prayers**, page 515
Davar shehayah bichlal .... *see* **Deduction, exceptional law in one element of group**, page 156
Davar sheyesh lo matirin .... *see* **Mixture, temporary prohibition**, page 418

David

Events —

David and Jonathan, love .... Avos 5:16
David, bread from Jonathan .... Sanhedrin 104a
David, bringing Ark .... Pesachim 36b
David, crown .... Avodah Zarah 44a
David, episode about Nabal .... Pesachim 3b; Rosh Hashanah 18a; Megillah 14a-14b
David, episode about Temple foundations .... Succah 53a-53b; Makos 11a
David, hanging of Saul's sons .... Yevamos 78b
David, opening of Temple doors .... Shabbos 30a
David, showbread .... Menachos 95b-96a
David, Temple .... Zevachim 54b, 116b
David, years of reign .... Temurah 14b; Zevachim 118b-119a

Wars —

David, Goliath and his brothers .... Sotah 42b
David, killed eight hundred .... Moed Katan 16b
David, war of Keila .... Eruvin 45a
David, wars .... Sanhedrin 16a-16b
David's warriors .... Kiddushin 76b
David's advisers for war .... Berachos 3b-4a; Sanhedrin 16a-16b

Family —

David, appeased by Tekoah woman .... Menachos 85b
David, decree on his offspring .... Sanhedrin 48b, 95a-95b
David did not marry Avishag .... Sanhedrin 22a
David, Eliab's anger .... Pesachim 66b
David, his wives .... Sanhedrin 19b, 21a
David's son Daniel .... Berachos 4a

Filiation —

David, hint in Torah .... Yevamos 77a
David, his mother's name .... Bava Basra 91a
David, lineage .... Bava Basra 91b
David, Ruth .... Berachos 7b; Bava Basra 14b

Mistakes —

David, argument for repenting people .... Avodah Zarah 4b-5a
David, Bathsheba permitted to him .... Kesubos 9a; Shabbos 56a
David, called G-d "inciter" .... Berachos 62b

David, census .... Berachos 62b
David, do not write my mistake .... Yoma 86b
David, episode with Bathsheba .... Sanhedrin 107a-107b
David, his mistakes .... Yoma 22b
David, Mephibosheth and Tziva .... Shabbos 56a-56b; Yoma 22b
David, poem about Saul's defeat .... Moed Katan 16b
David, repentance accepted .... Shabbos 30a; Pesachim 2b; Moed Katan 9a; Sanhedrin 107b
David wanted to worship idol .... Sanhedrin 107a
David, whoever says he sinned .... Shabbos 56a-56b
David, words of Torah were songs .... Sotah 35a

Piety —
David, behavior .... Berachos 3b-4a
David, charity in judgment .... Sanhedrin 6b
David, evil urge .... Bava Basra 17a
David, humility .... Moed Katan 16b; Megillah 11a; Sotah 10b; Chullin 89a
David, inquiries in monetary matters .... Bava Kama 60b-61a
David, midnight .... Berachos 3b-4a; Sanhedrin 16a
David, purpose of world .... Sanhedrin 98b
David, seven shepherds .... Succah 52b
David, taught Torah to disciples .... Eruvin 53a
David, Torah and greatness .... Gittin 59a
David, Torah learning .... Makos 10a; Shabbos 30a

Suffering —
David, Ahitophel's curse .... Succah 53b; Makos 11a
David and Shimei, curse .... Shabbos 105a
David, Abner's funeral .... Sanhedrin 20a
David, Absalom's revolt .... Berachos 7b, 10a
David, curse to Joab .... Sanhedrin 48b
David, despising garments .... Berachos 62b
David, Doeg's praise .... Yevamos 76b-77a; Sanhedrin 93b
David, his death .... Shabbos 30a-30b
David, his enemies' faces blackened .... Shabbos 30a; Moed Katan 9a; Sanhedrin 107b
David, Mephibosheth .... Berachos 4a
David, mistake by his pursuers .... Sotah 21a
David, wanted to serve idol .... Sanhedrin 107a
David will become his enemies' friend .... Sanhedrin 105a

Misc. —
David, "listen, my brothers and my friends" .... Sotah 40a
David, "*Odecha*" .... Pesachim 119a
David, *Barchi nafshi* .... Berachos 10a
David, circumcised .... Sotah 10b
David, cup in World to Come .... Pesachim 119b; Yoma 76a
David, Messiah's time .... Sanhedrin 98b
David's kingdom, punishment for one who opposes .... Sanhedrin 110a

Dawn
Dawn, announcing in Temple .... Yoma 28a-28b; Menachos 100a
Dawn, commandments .... Megillah 20a-20b
Dawn, day .... Berachos 2b; Megillah 20b
Dawn, reading *Shema* .... Berachos 9b, 25b

D

Dawn, worker going out to work...Bava Metzia 83a-83b

Day

Duration —

Day after night...Chullin 83a

Day after night, animal and its young..Chullin 83a-83b

Day and night, sacrifice..Zevachim 36a

Day cloudy, prayer...Berachos 32b

Day, cloudy, sun...Yoma 28b

Day, counts for two..Nazir 15a-15b

Day employees, we are...Eruvin 65a

Day, from when to when...Berachos 2b; Megillah 20b

Day in month, counts like a month...Rosh Hashanah 10a-10b

Day in year, counts like a year...............Rosh Hashanah 2b, 10a-10b; Chagigah 5b; Niddah 45a

Day is short...Avos 2:15

Day of his heart's rejoicing, Temple...Taanis 26b

Day of vacation, *yoma depagra*...Shabbos 129b

Day passed, sacrifice is disqualified..Berachos 26a

Day walking distance..Pesachim 93b; Sanhedrin 94a

Days, means a year...Kesubos 57b

Days of counting, leper...Bava Basra 9b

Days of female discharge..Niddah 72b-73a; Sanhedrin 87a

Days of poor people, which ones are bad.............Bava Basra 145b-146a; Sanhedrin 100b-101a

Days of purification, Pesach...Krisos 10a

Days of purification, woman after birth.............Krisos 9b-10b; Niddah 11a-11b, 35b-36a, 71b

Days when Rosh Hashanah cannot fall............Rosh Hashanah 20a-20b; Succah 43b, 54b

Misc. —

Day and night, G-d's deeds...Avodah Zarah 3b

Day, last, impurity of *nazir*..Niddah 68b

Day of death, same as day of birth............Sotah 13b; Kiddushin 38a; Rosh Hashanah 11a

Day of gathering, towns...Megillah 2a-2b

Day of his marriage, Giving of Torah..Taanis 26b

Day of impurity, *zav*..Niddah 72a-72b; Zavim 1:1

Day on which man matures..Chullin 7b

Day or two, slave...Bava Kama 90a; Bava Basra 50a-50b

Day, which commandments...Megillah 20a-21a

Day, wording of vow..Nedarim 60a-61a

Days of purity

Days of purity, checking of *zavah*..Niddah 7b, 68b-69a

Days of purity, *zav*..............Pesachim 81a; Niddah 22a, 33a-33b, 37a; Nazir 15b-16a; Zavim 1:2

Days of purity, *zavah*...Niddah 37a-37b, 54a-54b

Days of Tabernacle dedication

Days of Tabernacle dedication, crowns...Shabbos 87b

Days of Tabernacle dedication, G-d's joy..Megillah 10b

Days of Tabernacle dedication, honor to heads of tribes.......................................Horayos 6b

Days of Tabernacle dedication, laws..Yoma 4b-5b

Days of Tabernacle dedication, Moses' garments.............Avodah Zarah 34a; Taanis 11b

Days of Tabernacle dedication, sacrifices...Menachos 78a

Days of Tabernacle dedication, twelve days...Horayos 6b

Dayan Haemes...Berachos 60a, 60b

Dayan .... *see* **Judge**, page 327
Dayan shaatan .... *see* **Niddah** without retroactive impurity, page 444
Dayo, "all the more so" deduction .... Bava Kama 18b, 24b-25a; Bava Basra 111a; Zevachim 69b
Daytiki, significance .... Bava Basra 135b; Bava Metzia 19a-19b
De'alach sni lechavrach lo saavid .... *see* **Hateful, that which is hateful to you**, page 271

Dead

Dead .... *see also* **Death**, page 149; **Deceased person**, page 152
Dead, "your friend died," believe it .... Gittin 30b
Dead animal .... *see* ***Neveilah***, page 442
Dead, family member hurries without thinking .... Shabbos 43b-44a; Yoma 85a
Dead flesh does not feel .... Shabbos 13b
Dead, four are considered as dead .... Nedarim 64b
Dead man came on his two legs .... Bava Kama 74b
Dead, perhaps he changed his mind .... Nazir 52b
Dead Sea, drowning .... Shabbos 108b

Deaf

Deaf and orphan girls, levirate marriage .... Yevamos 110b-111b
Deaf, *chalitzah* .... Yevamos 104b
Deaf, divorce certificate .... Gittin 59a, 71a-71b; Yevamos 110b, 112b, 113b
Deaf, *kesubah* .... Yevamos 113a
Deaf, *kiddushin* .... Yevamos 110b-111a, 112b
Deaf, laws .... Chagigah 2b; Yevamos 113a-113b
Deaf, levirate marriage .... Yevamos 104b, 110a-110b, 112b, 114b
Deaf man and woman, *terumah* .... Gittin 55a; Yevamos 56a, 113a-113b
Deaf, purchase .... Gittin 59a
Deaf, testimony .... Gittin 71a

Deaf-mute, demented and minor

Deaf-mute, demented and minor, cause damage .... Bava Kama 87a
Deaf-mute, demented and minor, custody .... Bava Kama 9b
Deaf-mute, demented and minor, ember .... Bava Kama 9b, 22b, 59b-60a
Deaf-mute, demented and minor, ox which caused damage .... Bava Kama 39a-40a
Deaf-mute, demented and minor, slaughtering animal .... Chullin 12b

Deafness, payment for whole person if caused .... Bava Kama 85b
Deal, rights .... Bava Metzia 69a, 104b-105a; Bava Basra 70b

Death

***Aggadah* —**

Death, a long way .... Kesubos 67b
Death, all knees are bent .... Niddah 30b
Death in the future .... Sanhedrin 91b, 92a
Death, men's feet bring them to .... Succah 53a
Death of young man before old man, proverb .... Sanhedrin 52a
Death, prevents pride .... Bava Basra 75a-75b
Death, sleep after death .... Eruvin 65a
Death, so that another man will reign .... Taanis 5b
Death, wicked pretend not to remember it .... Shabbos 31b

Atonement and punishment —

Death .... *see also* **Men put to death by government**, page 387
Death, "may my death be an atonement" .... Shabbos 32a; Sanhedrin 43b
Death and life, in the power of the tongue .... Arachin 15b

D

D

Death, atonement	Yoma 86a; Sanhedrin 47a-47b
Death of kidnapped person, or of thief, theft	Bava Kama 119a; Bava Metzia 112a
Death, one who does not learn, deserves	Avos 1:13
Death since sin of golden calf	Avodah Zarah 5a
Death, suffering	Moed Katan 28b-29a
Death without sin	Shabbos 55a-55b; Chagigah 5a

Death of one's children

Death of one's children, punishment	Sotah 48b-49a; Sanhedrin 27b; Makos 24a; Berachos 5b, 7a
Death of one's children, sin of generation	Shabbos 33b
Death of one's children, suffering and atonement	Berachos 5a

Biblical sources —

Death in peace, Zedekiah and Josiah	Moed Katan 28b
Death, Moses	Sotah 13b
Death of Aaron's sons	Sanhedrin 52a, 94a; Yoma 53a; Shabbos 113b; Eruvin 63a; Pesachim 75a; Zevachim 115b
Death of David	Shabbos 30a-30b
Death of Elijah the Prophet	Moed Katan 26a
Death of firstborn, "about midnight"	Berachos 3b
Death of Miriam	Moed Katan 28a; Bava Basra 17a
Death of Moses, reading	Menachos 30a
Death of Moses, who wrote it	Bava Basra 15a; Menachos 30a; Makos 11a
Death of Sennacherib's host	Shabbos 113b; Sanhedrin 95b-96a
Death of Solomon's scribes	Succah 53a
Death of Josiah	Taanis 22a-22b

Divine intervention —

Death and poverty, glance of Sages	Nedarim 7b; Chagigah 5b; Sotah 46b
Death by Divine intervention, age	Moed Katan 28a
Death by Divine intervention, for whom	Sanhedrin 83a
Death, disqualified men who performed service	Sanhedrin 83b
Death, drunk *Kohen*	Krisos 13b
Death for commandments of prophet	Sanhedrin 89a-89b
Death for *terumah*, non-*Kohen* and impure	Sanhedrin 83a-83b
Death, non-*Kohen* who performed service	Sanhedrin 84a
Death of hidden illegitimate child	Yevamos 78b
Death of *sotah*	Sotah 20b
Death of *sotah* and her partner	Sotah 9b
Death of wife, reason	Sanhedrin 22a; Rosh Hashanah 6a; Zevachim 29b
Death, Rabbinical prohibition	Berachos 4b
Death, *tevel*	Yevamos 86a; Sanhedrin 83a

Episodes —

Death, city of Luz	Sotah 46b
Death, mule rider	Nedarim 41a
Death of betrothed girl, episode	Kesubos 62b
Death of disciple who rebels against his teachers	Chagigah 5a
Death of father at birth of son	Moed Katan 25b
Death of scoffer	Bava Basra 75a; Sanhedrin 100a
Death of woman who saw her husband suddenly coming	Kesubos 62b

How —

Death, by animals	Nedarim 41a

Death by evil eye .... Bava Metzia 107b
Death of fetus before its mother .... Arachin 7a; Bava Basra 142a-142b; Niddah 44a-44b
Death, sound of soul leaving body .... Yoma 20b-21a
Death, sudden, sick .... Eruvin 41b
Deaths, kinds and hardship .... Berachos 8a; Bava Basra 8b

Righteous —

Death .... *see also* **Dead**, page 149, **Deceased person**, page 152, **Murderer**, page 432
Death, defeated Rabbi Tarfon .... Menachos 68b
Death of Rabbah .... Bava Metzia 86a
Death of Rebbi .... Kesubos 103a-104a
Death of Rabbi Akiva's disciples .... Yevamos 62b
Death of Rabbi Yose de'min Yokrat's daughter .... Taanis 24a
Death of Rav Chisda .... Makos 10a
Death of Sages, harm .... Moed Katan 25b; Sotah 49b
Death of Sages who delayed coming back home .... Kesubos 62b
Death of Yose ben Yoezer, loss of virtues .... Temurah 15b-16a; Sotah 47a
Death, *zimun* with ignoramus .... Berachos 47b

Death of righteous

Death of righteous, atonement .... Moed Katan 28a
Death of righteous, before impending tragedy .... Bava Kama 60a
Death of righteous, for fear he sins .... Chagigah 5a
Death of righteous, like Temple destruction .... Rosh Hashanah 18b
Death of righteous on his birthday .... Sotah 13b; Kiddushin 38a; Rosh Hashanah 11a
Death of righteous, sin of generation .... Shabbos 33b
Death of righteous, trouble .... Sanhedrin 113b
Death of righteous, when another is born .... Kiddushin 72b; Yoma 38b

Misc. —

Death and flight of animal, do we consider the possibility .... Succah 23a-23b
Death is more frequent than wealth .... Gittin 30b
Death, lying down .... Bava Basra 116a
Death of brother of deceased childless husband, permission .... Kiddushin 14a
Death of husband, widow permitted .... Kiddushin 13b
Death of man in power, to leave his place to another .... Taanis 5b
Death, tearing garment .... Moed Katan 25a; Shabbos 105b
Death will disappear, old age in the future .... Pesachim 68a; Sanhedrin 91b

Death of wicked

Death of wicked, G-d's pain .... Sanhedrin 39b
Death of wicked, good .... Sanhedrin 113b; Yevamos 63b
Death of wicked, when does G-d want .... Niddah 70b

Death penalty
How —

Death penalties, order of severity .... Sanhedrin 40b, 49b-50b
Death penalty, announcement .... Sanhedrin 43a, 89a
Death penalty, by sword, how .... Kesubos 37b; Sanhedrin 52b
Death penalty, daytime .... Sanhedrin 34b
Death penalty, impure *Kohen* who performed service ...... Sanhedrin 82b-83b; Shevuos 17a-17b
Death penalty, merciful .... Sanhedrin 45a
Death penalty, place .... Sanhedrin 42b-43a
Death penalty, who pays for the expenses incurred .... Sanhedrin 43a

Death penalty, women..Kiddushin 35b; Bava Kama 15a
Misc. —
Death penalty by mistake, episodes..Sanhedrin 52b; Makos 5b
Death penalty, exile of *Sanhedrin*..................Sanhedrin 41a; Shabbos 15a; Avodah Zarah 8b
Death penalty, in present times..............Sanhedrin 37b, 41a; Kesubos 30a-30b; Sotah 8b
Death penalty, majority..Sanhedrin 69a-69b
Death penalty, other forms of death..Sanhedrin 45b, 53a
Death penalty, Shabbos....................................Yevamos 6b-7a; Sanhedrin 35b-36a
Death penalty, temporary....................................Sanhedrin 46a; Yevamos 90b
Death penalty, trustworthiness of *kiddushin*..............................Kiddushin 63b-64a
Death penalty, two in one act..Krisos 3b
Debasing dead person by examination..Bava Basra 154a
Debate
Debate with disciples, ways to acquire Torah..Avos 6:5
Debates with heretics, answers..Sanhedrin 38b
Deborah
Deborah, Lappidoth's wife..Megillah 14a
Deborah, pride for woman..Megillah 14b
Deborah, prophecy..Megillah 14a-14b
Debt
Debt...*see also* **Creditor**, page 133; **Loan**, page 376
Debt, collecting from debtor's debtor..Pesachim 31a
Debt of married woman..Bava Basra 139a
Debt, other, argument..Shevuos 42a; Kesubos 85a
Debt, repaying to man forbidden by vow to benefit............Nedarim 33a-33b; Kesubos 107b-108b
Debt, suffering..Eruvin 41b
Debt to pay salary, cancellation of debts..Gittin 18a
Decapitating
Decapitating donkey..Bechoros 13a
Decapitating, calf..Chullin 23b-24a
Decay
Decay of bones, jealousy..Shabbos 152b
Decay of dead, impurity....Nazir 50b-51b, 65a; Chullin 126b; Eduyos 6:3; Niddah 27a-27b; Oholos 2:2, 3:2
Decay of dead, order..Shabbos 151b
Deceased..*see* **Death**, page 149
Deceased person..............*see also* **Grave**, page 256, **Impurity of** *Kohen*, page 304, **Funeral**, page 241
Aggadah —
Deceased person, angels welcome him..Kesubos 104a
Deceased person, did not leave a son..Bava Basra 116a, 141a
Deceased person, favorable signs................Shabbos 153a; Kesubos 103b; Sanhedrin 47a
Deceased person, forgotten from heart................Pesachim 54b; Berachos 58b; Moed Katan 8b
Deceased person having no mourners..Shabbos 152a-152b
Deceased person, hears his eulogy..Shabbos 152b
Deceased person, his soul goes up and down..Shabbos 152b-153a
Deceased person, his soul mourns..Shabbos 152a-152b
Deceased person, knows about this world..Berachos 18a-19a
Deceased person, process of putrefaction..Shabbos 151b
Deceased person, putrefaction for society's benefit..Pesachim 54b
Deceased person, replacement..Bava Basra 91a

Care —

Deceased person, care on Shabbos................................Shabbos 43b-44a, 151a-151b
Deceased person, carrying him away from bride................................Kesubos 17a
Deceased person, *chol hamoed*................................Moed Katan 8b
Deceased person, closing his eyes................................Shabbos 151b
Deceased person, protection................................Berachos 17b-18a
Deceased person, turning him on his face................................Avodah Zarah 20b
Deceased person, Yom Tov................................Beitzah 6a, 22a; Shabbos 139a-139b

Episodes —

Deceased person, sheets................................Niddah 61a
Deceased person under Aramean's bed................................Berachos 8b; Pesachim 112b
Deceased person, wolf ate him and evacuated................................Taanis 22b; Menachos 69b
Deceased persons in desert, Rabbah bar bar Chana................................Bava Basra 73b-74a
Deceased persons in desert, who................................Bava Basra 121b
Deceased persons resurrected by Ezekiel................................Sanhedrin 92b
Deceased persons, spirits speaking................................Berachos 18b

Impurity —

Deceased person destroyed, impurity................................Niddah 27b
Deceased person, impurities................................Niddah 55a, 56a
Deceased person, impurity of idolater................................Yevamos 61a; Bava Metzia 114b
Deceased person in body of dog................................Oholos 11:7; Chullin 126a
Deceased person, less than volume of olive................................Nazir 49b-50a
Deceased person, skin................................Chullin 123a
Deceased persons who lived, purity................................Niddah 70b
Deceased person, how much renders impure................................Oholos 1:1-4

Prohibitions —

Deceased person, carrying him out to *karmelis*................................Shabbos 94b
Deceased person, learning in front of................................Berachos 3b
Deceased person, profit from his hair................................Arachin 7b
Deceased person, prohibition of benefit................................Avodah Zarah 29b
Deceased person, prohibition of surgery................................Chullin 11b
Deceased person, prohibition to debase................................Bava Basra 154a
Deceased person, prohibition to delay burial................................Sanhedrin 46b
Deceased person, punishment for desecration of graves................................Yevamos 63b
Deceased person, quantity forbidden to carry out on Shabbos................................Shabbos 94b
Deceased person, walled city................................Keilim 1:7

Women —

Deceased wife, when can he remarry................................Moed Katan 23a
Deceased woman, impurity from womb................................Niddah 71a
Deceased woman, intimate relations................................Yevamos 55b
Decedent's husbands, "*katlonis*"................................Kesubos 43b; Yevamos 26a, 64b

Misc. —

Deceased person, evil urge annulled................................Bava Basra 58a
Deceased person, exempt from commandments................................Shabbos 30a, 151b
Deceased person, gift destined to................................Gittin 14b-15a
Deceased person, hiding his death................................Pesachim 3b
Deceased person, one of the group................................Shabbos 105b-106a

Deceased unburied person

Deceased unburied person, burying him................................Bava Kama 81b; Eruvin 17b

Deceased unburied person, *Kohen* .... Nazir 43b; Eruvin 17b; Yevamos 89b
Deceased unburied person, *Kohen Gadol* .... Nazir 48b, 47b
Deceased unburied person, missing limb .... Sotah 45b
Deceased unburied person, *nazir* ..... Nazir 48a-48b; Berachos 19b-20a; Megillah 3b; Zevachim 100a
Deceased unburied person, overrides .... Sanhedrin 35a-35b
Deceased unburied person, permitted .... Nazir 43b, 47a-48b; Berachos 19b-20a; Megillah 3b;
.... Sanhedrin 35a; Zevachim 100a

Decided
Decided inwardly, consecration .... Shevuos 26b
Decided inwardly, vow .... Shevuos 26b; Nedarim 28a; Chagigah 10a
Deciding by himself, without consulting one's teacher .... Yevamos 109b
Deciding fast day, *nasi* .... Taanis 24a

Decision
Decision in money matters, cancellation of debts .... Gittin 18a
Decision to purchase, fixed price .... Avodah Zarah 72a; Bava Basra 85b-86a
Decisions of sailors and donkey drivers .... Bava Kama 116b
Decisions of workers' guild .... Bava Basra 8b, 9a

Declaration in forced sale .... Bava Basra 40a-40b, 48b

Decline
Decline needed for ascent .... Makos 7a-7b
Decline of generations .... Eruvin 53a
Decline of generations and their consequences .... Sotah 47b
Decline of generations, since Temple destruction .... Sotah 49a-49b

Decorating first fruit .... Bikurim 3:9-11; Bava Kama 92a

Decree
Decree .... *see also* **Rabbinical Decree**, page 533
Decree, "I do not want to benefit from this decree" .... Gittin 77b
Decree, annulling by another *beis din* .... Beitzah 5a-5b; Sanhedrin 59b
Decree, Divine, annulment .... Rosh Hashanah 17b-18a; Yevamos 105a
Decree for commerce, stolen goods .... Bava Kama 115a
Decree for repenting people .... Gittin 55a; Succah 31a
Decree, infrequent matters .... Gittin 5a, 44a; Eruvin 63b; Beitzah 2b, 18a; Yevamos 31a; Kesubos 56b;
.... Nazir 55a; Kiddushin 28b; Bava Metzia 46b, 47a; Bechoros 3a; Niddah 34a
Decree, new .... Avodah Zarah 35a
Decree on *kares* more than on a prohibition .... Yevamos 119a
Decree, one measure for everybody .... Bava Basra 29a; Shabbos 35b; Megillah 18b; Gittin 14a;
.... Chullin 9a, 32a
Decree that public cannot accept .... Bava Basra 60b
Decrees for society's benefit .... Gittin 32a-53a
Decrees, laws .... Kiddushin 37a
Decrees of Ezra, laundering .... Bava Kama 82a-82b
Decrees of Rabbi Yochanan ben Zakai .... Rosh Hashanah 31b-32a
Decrees, Joshua's .... Bava Kama 80b-81b

Decree because of concern
Decree because of concern, drawing water on Shabbos .... Shabbos 125b
Decree because of concern, lest hat falls on Shabbos .... Shabbos 138b; Eruvin 102b
Decree because of concern, lest he cooks more .... Chullin 15b
Decree because of concern, lest he drives nail .... Shabbos 122b, 138b; Eruvin 102b
Decree because of concern, lest he rakes coals .... Shabbos 18b, 20a

Decree because of concern, lest he rakes trough .... Shabbos 140b

Decree because of concern, lest he tilts high lamp .... Shabbos 12b, 149a

Decree because of concern, lest he tilts lamp .... Shabbos 12a, 13b

Decree because of concern, lest he tilts lamp, lice and garments .... Shabbos 12a

Decree because of concern, lest he tilts lamp, permitted cases .... Shabbos 12b-13a, 149a

Decrees of idolaters

Decrees of idolaters are generally annulled .... Kesubos 3b

Decrees of idolaters, candle .... Gittin 17a

Decrees of idolaters, Chavrei nations .... Yevamos 63b

Decrees of idolaters, cruelty .... Gittin 17a

Decrees of idolaters, demonstration .... Rosh Hashanah 19a; Taanis 18a

Decrees of idolaters, episode about midget .... Meilah 17b

Decree of Usha

Decree of Usha, married woman .... Kesubos 50a, 78b; Bava Kama 88a-88b; Bava Metzia 35a, 96b;
.... Bava Basra 50a, 139b

Decrees of Usha, fifth for charity .... Kesubos 50a, 67b; Arachin 28a

Decrees of Usha, learning .... Kesubos 50a

Decree on decree

Decree on decree .... Chullin 104a; Beitzah 3a

Decree on decree, Rabbinical oath .... Bava Metzia 5a-5b

Decree on decree, Shabbos .... Shabbos 11b

Dedication

Dedication in Ezra's time .... Menachos 45a

Dedication of Tabernacle .... *see* **Days of Tabernacle dedication**, page 148

Dedication of Temple .... Moed Katan 9a; Shabbos 30a

Dedication of Temple, Ezra .... Menachos 45a

Deducing

Deducing from renting cost .... Bava Metzia 103b-104a, 105b-106b

Deducing positive from negative, conditions .... Shevuos 36a-36b

Deducing undefined from explicit .... Zevachim 53a; Horayos 6b; Chullin 132a

Deduction .... *see also* **Commentary, application to other subject**, page 117;
.... **General and specific**, page 247

Cases —

Deduction, came to teach and learned .... Sanhedrin 73a, 74a; Yoma 82a

Deduction from Sage's words .... Berachos 11b

Deduction, Rabbinical, precious .... Bava Kama 17b; Yevamos 2b, 71a

Deduction, worker and employee .... Zevachim 82b

Deduction —

Deduction from damage, evaluation .... Bava Kama 59a

Deduction, words implying indispensable requirements .... Yoma 5a

Deduction, *yud* from *ein* .... Kiddushin 4a

Exclusion and inclusion —

Deduction, double exclusion .... Menachos 9b, 67a; Yoma 43a; Megillah 23b; Bava Kama 86b;
.... Bava Basra 14a; Sanhedrin 15a, 46a, 86a; Makos 9b; Shevuos 7b; Chullin 132a

Deduction, double inclusion .... Bava Kama 45b; Pesachim 23a

Deduction, first word of series .... Sanhedrin 3b; Succah 6b

Deduction, inclusion then exclusion .... Shevuos 4b-5a, 26a; Bava Kama 54b, 63a

Juxtaposition —

Deduction according to previous deduction .... Yoma 42b-43b

Deduction from next section .... Zevachim 48a; Menachos 19a-19b; Bava Metzia 95a; Krisos 22b
Deduction, from previous verses ...... Menachos 19a; Zevachim 24b; Shabbos 32b; Rosh Hashanah 9b;
.... Kiddushin 15b Bava Metzia 95a Chullin 118b
Deduction from contextual subject .... Bava Metzia 61a

Principles —
Deduction, exceptional law .... Yevamos 7a; Zevachim 49a-49b; Krisos 2b
Deduction, exceptional law in one element of group ... Yevamos 7a; Zevachim 49a-49b; Krisos 2b
Deduction, exceptional permission .... Pesachim 62a
Deduction, impossible from possible .... Menachos 19a, 82a-82b; Niddah 37b; Succah 50b;
.... Yevamos 46a, 61b-62a; Horayos 6b; Zevachim 98a; Temurah 16b, 18b
Deduction, juxtaposed verses .... Yevamos 4a-4b; Berachos 10a, 21b
Deduction, general and specific, far from one another .... Niddah 33a; Pesachim 6b;
.... Sanhedrin 45b-46a; Bava Kama 85a; Menachos 55b
Deduction, law being exception to rule .... Sanhedrin 84a
Deduction, possible from impossible .... Menachos 19a, 82a-82b; Niddah 37b; Succah 50b;
.... Yevamos 46a, 61b-62a; Horayos 6b; Zevachim 98a; Temurah 16b, 18b
Deduction, prohibition from "all the more so" ...... Yevamos 22b; Zevachim 106b; Pesachim 24a;
.... Makos 5b
Deduction, prohibition from impurity .... Yevamos 103b
Deduction, prohibition from money and penalty ... Kiddushin 3b; Berachos 19b; Bava Metzia 20b
Deduction, ruling needing a detail .... Chullin 88b; Bechoros 19a
Deduction strictly following first law ...... Shevuos 31a; Yevamos 78b; Bava Kama 25b; Sanhedrin 75b;
.... Zevachim 91b; Menachos 62a, 107a; Chullin 120b; Niddah 43b
Deduction, temporary law .... Menachos 19b, 56a, 59a; Chagigah 6a; Sanhedrin 15b
Deduction, Torah from Prophets .... Bava Kama 2b; Chagigah 10b; Niddah 23a
Deduction, when possible .... Pesachim 24b; Bechoros 6b
Deduction, written in Torah despite this .... Zevachim 49b

Sacrificial laws —
Deduction, concerning sacrifices .... Menachos 7b, 8a
Deduction for sacrificial laws .... Zevachim 57a-57b; Yoma 57a; Menachos 78a
Deduction from deduction, sacrifices .... Zevachim 49b-51a, 57a-57b; Yoma 57a; Menachos 78a;
.... Shevuos 10a; Temurah 21b
Deductions concerning sacrifices .... Zevachim 49b-51a; Shevuos 10a; Temurah 21b

Misc. —
Deduction by comparison .... Chullin 115b-116a

Deduction, "all the more so"
Deduction, "all the more so," by oneself .... Niddah 19b
Deduction, "all the more so," contradicting possibilities .... Zevachim 16b-17a
Deduction, "all the more so," *dayo* .... Bava Kama 18b, 24b-25a; Bava Basra 111a; Zevachim 69b
Deduction, "all the more so" from the outset .... Zevachim 51a, 69a, 84b
Deduction, "all the more so," from law .... Nazir 56b-57a; Shabbos 132a; Pesachim 81b
Deduction, "all the more so," indispensable requirement .... Kiddushin 14a; Chullin 24a
Deduction, "all the more so," leniency and stringency .... Avodah Zarah 46b
Deduction, "all the more so," negative commandment .... Yevamos 22b; Zevachim 106b;
.... Pesachim 24a; Makos 5b
Deduction, "all the more so," punishment .... Sanhedrin 76a
Deduction, "all the more so," punishments .... Makos 5b, 14a, 17a, 17b; Zevachim 106b;
.... Sanhedrin 54a, 73a, 74a, 76a; Temurah 9a; Krisos 3a
Deduction, "all the more so," refutation .... Shevuos 9b

Deduction "all the more so," stringency leading to leniency................Succah 36b
Deduction, "all the more so," supplementary inference....Kiddushin 4b; Pesachim 18b, 77b;
....Yoma 43a; Yevamos 22b; Sotah 29a; Bava Metzia 94b; Sanhedrin 40b, 41a; Zevachim 82b, 103b; Chullin 118b
Deduction, "all the more so," will finally lead to leniency................Succah 36b

Deed
Deed...*see also* **Act**, page 7
Deeds, all your deeds are written in a book................................Avos 2:1
Deeds for Heaven's sake, all your deeds...................................Avos 2:12
Deeds for Heaven's sake, stringent disciple...............................Bava Kama 81b

Deenor River...Chagigah 13b-14a

Deep fried, meal offering...Menachos 63a

Deer
Deer bitten by snake, Rav...Chullin 59a
Deer, dropping young..Bava Basra 16a
Deer Debei Ilai...Chullin 59b
Deer, Esther...Yoma 29a
Deer has branched horns..Yoma 29a
Deer, narrow womb................................Bava Basra 16b; Eruvin 54b; Yoma 29a

Defamation..*see* **Slander**, page 633

Defeat begins by flight..Sotah 44b

Defeated
Defeated, "My sons defeated Me," Achnai.....................................Bava Metzia 59b
Defeated and pleased, G-d..Pesachim 119a

Defect, blemish..Chullin 17b-18a; Bechoros 37b

Defender, accuser....................Rosh Hashanah 26a; Berachos 59a; Kiddushin 5a

Defense
Defense, *beis din*..Sanhedrin 42a; Shevuos 31a
Defense, capital cases......................................Sanhedrin 32b-34a, 43a
Defense, death penalty................Sanhedrin 6b, 29a, 32b-34a, 43a; Shevuos 31a
Defense first, death penalty...Sanhedrin 29a

Definite leper..Moed Katan 7b, 14b-15b

Degree of cooking and roasting, Shabbos.................................Menachos 57a

D'ei lo ksiv..................*see* **Case of transgression, not mentioned**, page 89

Delay
Delay, charity..Rosh Hashanah 4a, 5b, 6a
Delay, from when................Beitzah 19b; Rosh Hashanah 4a-4b, 5b, 6a, 6b; Temurah 18b
Delay, gifts for poor..Rosh Hashanah 4a-5b
Delay in payment, rent...Bava Metzia 111b
Delay in payment, salary...Bava Metzia 110b-112a
Delay, in which sacrifices................Rosh Hashanah 5a-6a; Zevachim 29a-29b
Delay, *nazir*...Nedarim 3b-4b
Delay, prohibition to delay sacrifices.........................Rosh Hashanah 6a-6b
Delay, punishment..Rosh Hashanah 6a
Delay, who...Rosh Hashanah 6b

Delaying
Delayed asking for support...Kesubos 96a
Delayed news of death......................................Moed Katan 20a-20b; Eruvin 46a
Delayed to claim *kesubah*.........................Kesubos 104a-104b; Shevuos 48a
Delaying bodily needs, prohibition...Makos 16b

D

Delaying burial, prohibition ....Sanhedrin 46b
Delaying capital cases ....Sanhedrin 35a
Delaying justice, punishment ....Shabbos 33a
Delaying payment of salary ....Bava Metzia 110b-112a
Delaying verdict for one night, capital cases ....Sanhedrin 35a
Deliberation, mistake ....Sanhedrin 6a
Delilah, Samson ....Sotah 9b
Delo ke'asmachta ....*see* Annotation, "*delo ke'asmachta,*" page 26
Delo yalif ketala chayav ....*see* **Death, one who does not learn, deserves,** page 150
Deloskama, storage bin for old people, significance ....Bava Metzia 20b; Gittin 28a
Demai
  Permission —
    Demai, baker ....Yoma 8b-9a; Demai 2:4
    Demai, permitted mixture ....Chullin 6a
    Demai, permitted to whom ....Berachos 47a; Demai 3:1; Shabbos 127b; Eruvin 17b, 31a-31b;
                                                    Pesachim 35b; Succah 35b
    Demai, poor ....Berachos 47a; Demai 3:1
    Demai, cases of exemption ....Demai 1:2-4
    Demai, cases of leniencies ....Bava Metzia 55b-56a; Demai 5:3-4
    Demai, wholesaler ....Demai 2:4-5
  Misc. —
    Demai, bought from ignoramus ....Demai 6:12; Eruvin 37b
    Demai, cases of stumbling-block ....Demai 3:2-3
    Demai, decree ....Sotah 48a; Yoma 8b; Maaser Sheni 5:15
    Demai, from outside *Eretz Yisrael* ....Demai 2:1
    Demai, returning to seller ....Bava Basra 88a
    Demai, tithe for poor ....Demai 4:3; Nedarim 84a-84b; Makos 16b-17a
Demon
  Caution —
    Demon, throwing some of the water drunk by demons ....Chullin 105b
    Demons, dangerous to those who fear them ....Pesachim 110b
    Demons, dangers ....Berachos 3b, 43b; Sanhedrin 101a; Pesachim 110b, 112b
    Demons, protection in toilet ....Berachos 62a
    Demons, shade of moon and tree ....Pesachim 111a-111b
    Demons, *shalom* ....Sanhedrin 44a
  Episodes —
    Demon, Emperor's daughter ....Meilah 17b
    Demon, female, episode ....Pesachim 112b
    Demon, payment of damage ....Chullin 105b
    Demon, spectacular feats ....Bava Basra 73a-73b
    Demon, Joseph, episode ....Eruvin 43a
    Demons, Adam gave birth to ....Eruvin 18b
    Demons, Ashmedai ....Gittin 68a-68b
    Demons, episode about amulet ....Pesachim 111b
    Demons, Sage flew from noblewoman ....Kiddushin 39b-40a
    Demons, sorcery ....Sanhedrin 67b
  Laws —
    Demon, concern in testimony about *agunah* ....Yevamos 122a
    Demon, non-identified command to divorce ....Gittin 66a; Yevamos 122a

Demons, prohibition to burn incense to .... Krisos 3b
Demons, question on Shabbos .... Sanhedrin 101a
Demons, question to demon .... Sanhedrin 101a
Misc. —
Demon, Divine Name in vain .... Sanhedrin 44a
Demons, cure .... Shabbos 67a
Demons, double shadow .... Yevamos 122a; Gittin 66a
Demons, how can they be seen .... Berachos 6a
Demons, how many .... Berachos 6a
Demons, *Ketev* .... Pesachim 111b
Demons, like angel and like man .... Chagigah 16a
Demons, shadow .... Yevamos 122a; Gittin 66a
Demons, what are they permitted to take .... Sanhedrin 67b; Chullin 105b
Demonstration at night .... Rosh Hashanah 19a; Taanis 18a
Denial, necessary sum for oath .... Shevuos 39b-40b
Denouncing hypocrites .... Yoma 86b
Denying
Denying .... *see also* **Contradicting**, page 126
Denying deposit, thief .... Bava Kama 105b-106a
Denying everything, oath .... Shevuos 40b-41a; Bava Metzia 5a, 6a
Denying idolatry, *Yehudi* .... Megillah 13a
Denying penalty, oath .... Kesubos 42a-43a; Shevuos 36b, 38b
Denying theft .... Bava Metzia 43a-43b; Pesachim 32a; Bava Kama 65a-66a, 93b-94b, 96b, 103a
Dependant
Dependant, do not make yourself dependant on people ...... Pesachim 112a, 113a; Shabbos 118a
Dependant on other person, *brairah* .... Gittin 25a-26a
Dependent on time, women .... Berachos 20a-20b; Kiddushin 33b-35a; Eruvin 27a, 96a-96b
Depending on baker, man having no field .... Menachos 103b-104a
Deposit
Deposit .... *see also* **Custody**, page 137
Deposit, act of acquisition .... Kiddushin 8b; Bava Metzia 48b-49a
Deposit, avoid taking .... Yevamos 109b
Deposit belonging to orphans, Shmuel's father .... Berachos 18b
Deposit *chametz*, from non-Jew .... Pesachim 5b-6a
Deposit, custodian's wife and children .... Bava Metzia 36a-36b, 42b
Deposit decaying, sale .... Bava Metzia 38a-38b; Pesachim 13a-13b
Deposit from married woman .... Bava Basra 51b-52a
Deposit, loss of percentage of produce .... Bava Metzia 40a
Depth
Depth of judgment is unrevealed .... Pesachim 54b
Depth of thought, Rabbi Meir .... Eruvin 13b, 53a
Depth of thought, Rabbi Oshiah .... Eruvin 53a
Depth of Torah, Moses' generosity .... Nedarim 38a
DeRabbanan .... *see* **Rabbinical Decree**, page 533
Derara demamona .... *see* **Self-understood monetary claim**, page 599
Derech .... *see* **Road**, page 570; *see also* **Way**, page 737, **Journey**, page 326, **Passageway**, page 475
Derech eretz .... *see* **Proper manners, calling friend**, page 506
Derech gedilasan .... *see* **Four species, as they grow**, page 237
Derech hanaatan .... *see* **Forbidden foods, unusual way of benefit**, page 233

Derech hinuach unefilah...*see* **Lost item, how was it placed**, page 378
Derech ketzarah...*see* **Short way, teaching**, page 620
Derech malbush...*see* **Wearing**, page 739
Derech sheirus..*see* **Service, usual manner, sacrifice**, page 603
Derech yeitzer hara...*see* **Way of evil urge, "do this,"** page 737

Derivates
   Derivates of sun and fire...Shabbos 38b-39a
   Derivates of water, *mikveh*...Zevachim 22a; Mikvaos 7:1

Derogatory
   Derogatory remark about deceased Sage...Berachos 19a
   Derogatory speech in front of three people...Arachin 16a

Derogatory speech
  Cases —
   Derogatory speech, about Sage..Berachos 19a
   Derogatory speech, *beis din* agent..Moed Katan 16a
   Derogatory speech, judge...Sanhedrin 31a; Bava Kama 99b
   Derogatory speech, testifying alone...Pesachim 113b
   Derogatory speech, traces....................................Bava Basra 164b-165a; Arachin 15b-16a
  Episodes —
   Derogatory speech, David's mistakes..Shabbos 56a-56b; Yoma 22b
   Derogatory speech, desiring life..Avodah Zarah 19b
   Derogatory speech, Doeg.....................................Yevamos 76b-77a; Sanhedrin 93b
   Derogatory speech, Gedaliah...Niddah 61a
   Derogatory speech, Jeroboam and Amos...Pesachim 87b
  Punishment —
   Derogatory speech, atonement...Arachin 16a-16b
   Derogatory speech, diphtheria...Shabbos 33a-33b
   Derogatory speech, G-d keeps away..Sotah 5a
   Derogatory speech, groups...Sanhedrin 103a; Sotah 42a
   Derogatory speech, leprous marks..Arachin 16a
   Derogatory speech, punishment..Arachin 15a-16b
   Derogatory speech, to dog.......................................Pesachim 118a; Makos 23a
  Misc. —
   Derogatory speech, daily..Bava Basra 164b-165a
   Derogatory speech, listening to be on one's guard..Niddah 61a
   Derogatory speech, prohibition..............................Bava Basra 164b-165a; Arachin 15b-16a

Derosh vekabel sachar............................*see* **Laws, learning laws not practiced today, reward**, page 355
Derusah...*see* **Trampled animal**, page 699

Desecrating
   Desecrating service, who.................................Kiddushin 66b; Sanhedrin 83b-84a; Zevachim 22b
   Desecrating Shabbos, renegade..Eruvin 69a-69b

Desecration of graves, transgressions..Yevamos 63b

Desecration of G-d's name
   Desecration of G-d's name, definition..Yoma 86a
   Desecration of G-d's name, hidden transgression.................Chagigah 16a; Kiddushin 40a
   Desecration of G-d's Name, honor to teacher....Berachos 19b; Sanhedrin 82a; Eruvin 63a; Shevuos 30b
   Desecration of G-d's Name, hypocrites...Yoma 86b
   Desecration of G-d's name, Sage..Berachos 43b
   Desecration of G-d's name, uprooting commandment.......................................Yevamos 79a

Desecration of G-d's Name, general..Avos 4:4, 5:9
Desecration of G-d's Name, punishment..............Shabbos 33a; Avos 4:4, 5:9; Kiddushin 40a

Desert
Desert, doubt about time of Shabbos...Shabbos 69b
Desert, firstborns...Sanhedrin 17a; Bechoros 4b-5a
Desert, journeys...Taanis 29a; Menachos 95a
Desert, meat for pleasure...Chullin 16b-17a
Desert, public domain..Shabbos 6b
Desert, repaying loan in desert...Bava Kama 118a
Desert, returning deposit...Bava Kama 118a
Desert wanderers, their life...Eruvin 55b

Deshaim, blessing...Berachos 40a
Deshen..*see* **Ash from Altar**, page 32

Desire for Torah, Ben Azzai..Yevamos 63b

Desired
Desired his master's wife..Gittin 58a
Desired what was not his..Sotah 9b
Desires life, episode..Avodah Zarah 19b

Desolation of Judea...Shabbos 145b; Yoma 54a

Despairing
Despairing from ownership, impliedly...Bava Metzia 21b-22b
Despairing, lost item...Bava Metzia 21b-24b
Despairing of finding slave..Gittin 38b-39a
Despairing, stolen item..........................Bava Kama 66a-68b, 114a-114b, 115a
Despairing, stoned ox and city led to idolatry....................................Krisos 24a

Despising
Despising any man...Avos 4:3
Despising commandment..Shabbos 22a, 74b
Despising commandment, covering up blood..................Chullin 87a; Shabbos 22a
Despising G-d's word, soul cut off.........................Sanhedrin 99a; Shevuos 13a
Despising, speaking about Sages..Sanhedrin 99b

Dessert, lupine..Beitzah 25b

Destined
Destined for one's fellow, man does not touch what is....................Yoma 38b; Moed Katan 28a
Destined to World to Come...Pesachim 113a; Sanhedrin 88b

Destroyer
Destroyer of Israel's money!...Chullin 56a; Bechoros 40a
Destroyers of world, Mishnah...Sotah 22a

Destroying
Destroying, bricks without cement..................................Beitzah 31b; Eruvin 34b
Destroying neighbor's wall to build anew.......................................Bava Basra 7a
Destroying to build elsewhere...Shabbos 31b

Destruction
  Temple —
    Destruction, no more Divine Laughter.................................Avodah Zarah 3b
    Destruction of Temple, G-d's crying...Chagigah 5b
    Destruction of Temple, Name *Yud-Heh*......................................Eruvin 18b
    Destruction of Temple, reckoning of years.....................Avodah Zarah 9a-9b
    Destruction of Temple, signs before...Yoma 39b

Destruction of Temple, sin of murder .... Shabbos 33a
Destruction of two Temples, sins .... Yoma 9a-9b
Destruction of two Temples, time .... Taanis 29a; Arachin 12a-13a
Destruction, aftermath .... *see* **Since Temple destruction**, page 629

Destruction of first Temple
Destruction of first Temple, cherubs .... Yoma 54b
Destruction of first Temple, defense of Abraham .... Menachos 53b
Destruction of first Temple, Gabriel .... Yoma 77a
Destruction of first Temple, keys .... Taanis 29a
Destruction of first Temple, Nebuchadnezzar .... Sanhedrin 94b, 96b
Destruction of first Temple, idolaters .... Yevamos 16b; Sanhedrin 103a
Destruction of first Temple, sins .... Shabbos 119b-120a
Destruction of first Temple, verses .... Gittin 57b

Destruction of second Temple
Destruction of second Temple, blessing on Torah .... Bava Metzia 85a-85b; Nedarim 81a
Destruction of second Temple, episode .... Gittin 55b-56b
Destruction of second Temple, forty years before .... Yoma 39b
Destruction of second Temple, Nebuzaradan .... Sanhedrin 96a-96b; Gittin 57b
Destruction of second Temple, prophecies .... Nazir 32b

Misc. —
Destruction of Beitar .... Gittin 58a
Destruction of charitable house .... Berachos 58b
Destruction of elders is construction .... Nedarim 40a; Megillah 31b
Destruction of *Eretz Yisrael*, wilderness .... Berachos 58a; Shabbos 145b; Yoma 54a
Destruction of *Har Hamelech* .... Gittin 57a
Destruction of houses of righteous .... Berachos 58b
Destruction of idol .... Avodah Zarah 45b-46a
Destruction of Jerusalem, transgressions .... Shabbos 119b-120a

Detail, specific, agent .... Gittin 65a-65b; Kiddushin 48b-49a; Bava Basra 76b, 165a
Determining
Determining fruit, separating tithes .... Terumos 3:5; Eruvin 37b
Determining place, *muktzeh* .... Shabbos 45b

Devarim bego .... *see* **Substituting Sage's name, episode**, page 660
Devarim beteilim, prohibition .... Yoma 19b, 77a
Devarim haasuyim lehashil .... *see* **Items usually lent**, page 319
Devarim hanikarim .... *see* **Slander, tangible proofs**, page 633
Devarim haomdim berum olam ...... *see* **Top of the world, neglected things**, page 695
Devarim shebalev .... *see* **Intent**, page 311
Devarim shebichtav .... *see* **Things which are written, orally**, page 687
Devarim .... *see* **Commitment on intangible thing**, page 117
Devarim, *mechusar amanah* ... *see* **Commitment on intangible thing, not keeping one's word**, page 117
Devir, book .... Avodah Zarah 24b
Devorah .... *see* **Deborah**, page 152
Devotion, Israel .... Sanhedrin 64a
Dew
Dew, not withheld .... Taanis 3a-3b
Dew of resurrection of dead .... Shabbos 88b; Chagigah 12b
Dew, susceptible to become impure ..... Eruvin 87b-88a; Machshirin 6:1-2; Chullin 13a
Diadem, carrying out on Shabbos .... Shabbos 57b

Diagonal
Diagonal according to side .... Succah 8a
Diagonal, how to calculate .... Eruvin 57a, 76b; Succah 8a; Bava Basra 101b
Diagonal, private domain .... Eruvin 51a
Diagonal, public domain .... Eruvin 51a
Diagonal, *techum* of city .... Eruvin 56b

Diarrhea, beneficial for sick .... Berachos 57b

Dibrah Torah kivnei adam .... *see* **Torah uses man's speech**, page 697

Dibrah Torah lashon havai .... *see* **Torah speaks inexactly**, page 696

Dibru Neviim, *chachomim, lashon havai* .... *see* **Prophets, sages, speak inexactly**, page 507

Dibur, harsh speech .... Makos 11a

Dice
Dice game, prohibition .... Shabbos 149b; Sanhedrin 24b-25b
Dice play, testimony .... Sanhedrin 24b-25a, 27b; Rosh Hashanah 22a; Eruvin 82a

Die
Die, "better he dies innocent" .... Sanhedrin 71b-72a
Die, "let them die to sanctify Your Name" .... Shabbos 89b
Die during birth, women .... Shabbos 31b-32a
Die, let him die rather than speak to her .... Sanhedrin 75a
Died .... *see also* **Deceased person**, page 152
Died, "my husband died" .... Yevamos 116a-116b
Died, "my son died," levirate marriage .... Yevamos 118b, 119b
Died because of circumcision, brothers .... Yevamos 64b
Died because of primeval snake .... Bava Basra 17a; Shabbos 55b
Died because of work, animal .... Bava Metzia 96b-97a
Died before wedding, parents .... Kesubos 3b-4b
Died children, mother not frightened .... Kesubos 62a
Died in *Eretz Yisrael*, advantage .... Kesubos 111a
Died on the way, mistake in ruling .... Niddah 65a
Died owner .... *see* **Owner died**, page 467
Died, parents before wedding .... Kesubos 3b-4b
Died while performing *mitzvah*, advantage .... Shabbos 118b
Died within year, scoffer .... Berachos 39a

Difference
Difference of opinion .... *see* **Dispute**, page 167
Differences between man and ox, damages .... Bava Kama 34b-35a
Differences in men's faces .... Sanhedrin 38a

Different, sizes cannot be different for everyone .... Bava Basra 29a; Shabbos 35b; Megillah 18b;
Gittin 14a; Chullin 9a, 32a

Difficult
Difficult are converts for Israel .... Kiddushin 70b; Yevamos 47b, 109b; Niddah 13b
Difficult for memory .... Horayos 13a-13b
Difficult is man's livelihood like the splitting of the sea; finding a spouse ...... Pesachim 118a
Sota 2a
Difficult is this day for Israel .... Moed Katan 25b
Difficult to acquire like gold .... Chagigah 15a
Difficult to learn old teachings .... Yoma 29a

Difficulty in learning, solution .... Taanis 8a

Dig with me and I shall dig with you, interest .... Bava Metzia 75a-75b

Digestion, dog and animals .... Oholos 11:7; Shabbos 155b

Digging

Digging grave, exempt from commandments .... Berachos 14b

Digging hole on Shabbos, considered as spoiling .... Chagigah 10a-10b; Shabbos 73b; Beitzah 8a

Digging hole, purposeful work .... Chagigah 10a-10b; Shabbos 73b; Beitzah 8a

Digging in graves, episode .... Bava Basra 58a

Diglas, river .... Berachos 59b

Digon, Greek .... Bava Basra 164b

Dikduk .... *see* **Grammar,** *ches* like *heh*, page 255

Dikduk hadin .... *see* **Precision in Divine Judgment**, page 500

Dikdukei anius .... *see* **Poverty, extreme**, page 496

Diligence

Diligence in house of study .... Shabbos 83b; Beitzah 24b

Diligence in learning, market .... Eruvin 54b

Diligence in learning, wedding canopy .... Berachos 16a

Diligent, Ben Azzai .... Sotah 49b

Dilug bekrias haTorah .... *see* **Omitting section in Torah reading**, page 460

Dilug vestos .... *see* **Interval, unequal, menstruation**, page 316

Din .... *see* **Judgment**, page 329

Din le'atzmo .... *see* **Self-help**, page 599

Dina Demalchusa

Dina demalchusa .... *see* **Law of the land**, page 355

Dina Demalchusa, Persians .... Bava Basra 55a

Dina Demalchusa, tax .... Bava Kama 113a; Nedarim 28a; Bava Basra 54b, 55a

Dinah

Dinah, Job's wife .... Bava Basra 14b-15b

Dinah, Leah's judgment .... Berachos 60a

Dinar

Dinar, forged, episode .... Bava Kama 99b

Dinar, inheritance of *kesubah* .... Kesubos 90b-91b

Dinar, *kiddushin* .... Kiddushin 11a-12a

Dinar, silver and gold, value .... Kiddushin 12a; Bava Metzia 44b

Dinei mamonos .... *see* **Monetary cases**, page 421

Dinei nefashos .... *see* **Capital cases**, page 87

Diofra, Greek origin .... Eruvin 18a

Diomed, Greek origin .... Eruvin 18a

Diomeses river

Diomeses river, forgetting one's learning .... Shabbos 147b

Diomeses river, healing on Shabbos .... Shabbos 147b

Diphtheria

Diphtheria, death .... Berachos 8a

Diphtheria, *havdala* .... Pesachim 100b, 105a

Diphtheria, water and salt .... Berachos 40a

Diphtheria, why .... Shabbos 33a-33b

Dipping food, health .... Gittin 70a

Dirty animal, sacrifice .... Bechoros 41a; Temurah 28b

Dirtying bed, resentment .... Shabbos 46a-46b

Disassembling tent, succah .... Beitzah 30b

Disavowing marriage

Disavowing marriage, avoiding ....Yevamos 109a
Disavowing marriage, how ....Yevamos 25b, 106a, 107b-108a
Disavowing marriage, laws ....Yevamos 108a-108b
Disavowing marriage, penalty ....Kesubos 35b-36a
Disavowing marriage, so as to permit levirate marriage ..... Yevamos 29a, 108b, 109a, 111a-111b;
....Niddah 8a
Disavowing marriage, until when ....Chullin 26b; Niddah 46a, 52a-52b
Disavowing marriage, who ....Yevamos 107a-107b; Gittin 65a
Disavowing marriage with brother of deceased childless husband ....Yevamos 12a-13a,
....107a-107b

Discharges

Discharges other from blessing ....Rosh Hashanah 29a-29b
Discharges other, intention ....Rosh Hashanah 28b-29a, 33b
Discharges towards Heaven, doubt of borrower ....Bava Kama 118a

Discharge

Discharge of woman during pure days ....Niddah 33a-33b, 42a
Discharge of *zavah* ....Krisos 8b; Niddah 52b-53b; Bava Kama 24a

Discharge, male

Discharge, male, annulling count of *zav* ....Niddah 22a, 33a-33b
Discharge, male, cure ....Berachos 57b
Discharge, male, impurity ....Zavim 5:11; Pesachim 67b; Yoma 6a-6b
Discharge, male, *Kohen* in Temple ....Middos 1:9; Tamid 27b
Discharge, male, liquid coming out of *zav* .....Nazir 65b-66a; Bava Kama 25a-25b; Niddah 22a
Discharge, male, occurrence ....Mikvaos 8:2-4; Niddah 22a, 43a; Chagigah 15a
Discharge, male, on Yom Kippur ....Yoma 88a
Discharge, male, prohibitions ....Berachos 20b-22b; Bava Kama 82b
Discharge, male, quantity ....Niddah 43b

Discharge of *zav*

Discharge of *zav* and semen, difference ....Niddah 35b
Discharge of *zav* and semen, quantity ....Niddah 43b
Discharge of *zav*, external circumstances ....Niddah 35a-35b, 37a, 71a; Pesachim 67b;
....Yoma 18a-18b; Nazir 65b; Chullin 51b; Krisos 8b; Zavim 2:2
Discharge of *zav*, first one ....Niddah 72a-72b; Zavim 1:1
Discharge of *zav*, first one, minor ....Niddah 34b-35a
Discharge of *zav*, impurity ....Niddah 43a, 55a-55b
Discharge of *zav*, occurrences or days ....Bava Kama 24a

Disciple

Episodes —

Disciples, from one teacher to another ....Zevachim 96b; Krisos 8a
Disciples, in one cubit ....Eruvin 53a
Disciples of Abraham and Balaam ....Avos 5:19
Disciples of Elisha ....Kesubos 106a
Disciples of Hillel ....Succah 28a; Bava Basra 134a
Disciples of Rabbi Akiva ....Yevamos 62b
Disciples of Rabbi Meir ....Kiddushin 52b; Nazir 49b-50a
Disciples of Rabbi Yochanan ben Zakai ....Avos 2:8
Disciples of Rav Pappa, gestures ....Taanis 9a-9b
Disciples of Shamai and Hillel, cause of disputes ....Sanhedrin 88b; Sotah 47b

Law —
Disciple and teacher, opinions..Sanhedrin 36a-36b
Disciple, defense..Shevuos 31a; Sanhedrin 6b, 42b
Disciple, ignoramus, training course in *beis din*................................Shevuos 30b
Disciple rules like his teacher..Shevuos 13a
Disciple, training course in *beis din*..Horayos 3b

Learning —
Disciple, beneficial for teacher................................Taanis 7a; Makos 10a
Disciple, in the name of his teacher..Yevamos 96b
Disciple rejected his teacher, episode..Chagigah 5a
Disciple, unsuitable................................Chullin 133a; Makos 10a

Misc. —
Disciple, exiled..Makos 10a
Disciple, his teacher needs him................................Bava Metzia 33a
Disciple needing teacher only for his knowledge................................Sanhedrin 36b
Disciple of Sages takes people's garments!................................Shevuos 41a
Disciple, teacher is not jealous of him................................Pesachim 113a
Disciple, who is considered................................Taanis 10b; Kiddushin 49b

Disciple-Sage
Disciple-Sage, Amoraim..Eruvin 63a
Disciple-Sage, Ben Azzai................................Bava Basra 158b
Disciple-Sage, honor................................Berachos 27b
Disciple-Sage, Rav's disciples................................Sanhedrin 36b

Discourse
Discourse, *aggadah* and *halacha*................................Bava Kama 60b
Discourse, episodes about questions................................Taanis 9b; Beitzah 21a; Moed Katan 5a-5b
Discourse, episodes about resentment................................Berachos 28b
Discourse, forcing Amora to come to lecture................................Shabbos 148a
Discourse in Temple shade................................Pesachim 26a
Discourse, Rabbi Eliezer................................Beitzah 15b
Discourse, Sabi Nizonia................................Kiddushin 25a
Discourses on Divine Chariot, stories................................Chagigah 13a, 14b; Shabbos 80b

Discovered
Discovered, something which will be..Bechoros 36a-36b; Rosh Hashanah 22b; Yevamos 93b, 115a, 116b
Discovered that he did not sin................................Krisos 23b-24b; Temurah 34a
Discovering money hidden by his wife................................Bava Basra 51a-51b

Disease, "all diseases of Egypt"................................Sanhedrin 101a
Disgrace of Torah................................Avos 1:13
Disgusting
Disgusting, forbidden foods................................Bechoros 37a
Disgusting others, prohibition................................Shabbos 12a
Disgusting to me, rebellious wife................................Kesubos 63b
Dish
Dish of Ben Drusai................................Shabbos 20a, 36b; Avodah Zarah 38a; Menachos 57a
Dishes, different, numerous transgressions................................Krisos 12b, 15b-16a
Dishun hamenorah................................*see* **Cleaning** *menorah*, page 110
Disinheriting, not recommended................................Bava Basra 133b
Dislodged leg, *treifah* animal................................Chullin 57a-57b
Dismissing butcher................................Sanhedrin 25a; Chullin 93b

Disobedient person, *beis din*..Moed Katan 16a; Bava Kama 112b-113a; Shevuos 41a
Displacing
Displacing *choshen* from *ephod*...Yoma 72a
Displacing fence to steal land, squill..Beitzah 25b
Displacing fence, trade...Bava Basra 21b-22a
Dispute
Law —
Dispute..*see also* **Contradicting**, page 126
Dispute about source of law..Sanhedrin 34a-34b
Dispute, extreme, between tannaim...Shabbos 138a
Dispute on scriptual derivation, not on law............Zevachim 52b; Rosh Hashanah 20b; Yoma 60b;
.............................Moed Katan 7b; Yevamos 94b; Nazir 43a; Bava Metzia 27a; Sanhedrin 75a; Shevuos 19a
Dispute, oven of Achnai...................Bava Metzia 59a-59b; Berachos 19a; Eduyos 7:7; Keilim 5:8
Dispute, possibility to follow either of two opinions..Berachos 27a
Dispute, these and these..Gittin 6b; Eruvin 13b; Chagigah 3b
Disputes, broken post in house of study..Bava Metzia 20b
Disputes, episode about Akavia...Eduyos 5:6
Disputes, from when...Temurah 15b-16a; Sotah 47a
Disputes, Torah scroll was torn..Yevamos 96b
Misc. —
Dispute and division, prohibition.............................Yevamos 13b-14a; Sanhedrin 110a
Dispute, do not add..Bava Basra 158b
Dispute for Heaven's sake..Avos 5:17
Dispute, one anonymous saying v. two anonymous sayings.............Kiddushin 54b; Yevamos 101b
Dispute, standing before Sages, episode..Horayos 13b-14a
Dispute and undisputed
Dispute and undisputed, *Eduyos*..Kiddushin 54b
Dispute and undisputed, Rebbi..Shevuos 4a
Dispute and undisputed, two *mesechtos*.......................Bava Kama 102a; Avodah Zarah 7a
Dispute and undisputed, two Mishnayos, *halacha*.............Yevamos 42b-43a; Avodah Zarah 7a;
....Bava Kama 102a; Niddah 11b
Disqualified
Lineage —
Disqualified families...Kiddushin 71a
Disqualified in congregation, marrying one another............................Kiddushin 74a-74b
Disqualified in congregation...................................*see also* **Forbidden relations**, page 233
Disqualified offspring, laws...Yevamos 22a-22b
Disqualified woman to *Kohen*.........................Yevamos 15b, 44a-44b; Niddah 69b-70a
Sacrifices —
Disqualified animals becoming fit......Temurah 26a-26b; Pesachim 98a; Yoma 64a; Kiddushin 7a-7b ;
....Zevachim 12a, 59a, 73b; Krisos 27a, 28a
Disqualified, becoming valid again...Yevamos 76a
Disqualified item becoming fit afterwards..........Yoma 64a-65a; Krisos 27a, 28a; Pesachim 73b, 98a;
....Zevachim 12a-12b, 59a, 73b; Temurah 26b
Disqualified item becoming fit, commandments..................Succah 33a-33b; Avodah Zarah 47a;
....Chullin 87a, 87b
Disqualified item becoming fit, retroactively............Temurah 26a-26b; Yoma 64a; Kiddushin 7a-7b;
....Zevachim 12a, 59a; Krisos 27a, 28a
Disqualified offspring, *terumah*..Yevamos 70a

Disqualified sacrifice becoming fit, blood of sacrifice ....Zevachim 34b
Disqualified sacrifice becoming fit, cases of sacrifices............Zevachim 12a-12b, 59a, 73b;
............Pesachim 98a; Yoma 64a-65a; Kiddushin 7b; Sanhedrin 47a; Temurah 26b; Krisos 27a, 28a
Disqualified sacrifice becoming fit, holiness of money......Temurah 26a-26b; Kiddushin 7a-7b;
............Zevachim 12a-12b; Krisos 27a, 28a
Disqualified sacrifice becoming fit, intermingled sacrifices............Zevachim 73b-74a
Disqualified sacrifice becoming fit, partners' sacrifice........Temurah 26a-26b; Kiddushin 7a-7b;
............Zevachim 12a; Krisos 27a
Disqualified sacrifice, slaughtering on Shabbos............Pesachim 73a

Misc. —
Disqualified becoming adequate, valid at beginning............Succah 33a-33b; Avodah Zarah 47a;
............Chullin 87a; Pesachim 73b; Yoma 64a

Disqualifying
Disqualifying from eating *terumah*, who............Yevamos 67b-68a
Disqualifying witness of other party............Sanhedrin 23a-24a

Distance
Distance during seven days of purity, death............Shabbos 13a-13b
Distance, fire............Bava Kama 61a, 61b
Distance from fishing net............Bava Basra 21b
Distance from neighbors............*see* **Damage from neighbor**, page 141
Distance from *niddah* wife............Shabbos 13a, 64b; Kesubos 4b, 61a, 65b
Distance necessary for mixed seeds............Pesachim 39b; Kilayim 2:6-10, 3:3-7
Distance to save from damage, individual and public............Bava Basra 24b
Distance, who must move away............Bava Basra 18b-19a; Bava Metzia 117a; Bava Kama 23b

Distortion of justice, punishment............Shabbos 33a

Distribution
Distribution between creditors............Kesubos 93a
Distribution of meal offering, no exchange............Menachos 72b-73a
Distribution of sacrifices, exchanging............Kiddushin 53a; Menachos 72b-73a
Distribution of sacrifices, to whom............Zevachim 98b-99a, 102a-102b

Disturbances
Disturbances, avoiding in house of study............Eruvin 60a; Avodah Zarah 74b
Disturbances in learning, Joseph............Yoma 35b

Disturbing *beis din* twice............Bava Kama 89b; Bava Metzia 110a
Ditch, bridge for *eruv*............Eruvin 79a
"Dived and took up clay from depths of sea"............Bava Kama 91a
Divert eyes from beautiful woman............Yevamos 63b; Sanhedrin 100b
Dividends of commandments in this world............Shabbos 127a-127b; Peah 1:1; Kiddushin 39b-40a, 41a

Dividing
Dividing between people receiving gift............Bava Basra 138a
Dividing between women collecting *kesubah*............Kesubos 93a
Dividing, by partner without permission............Bava Metzia 69a-69b
Dividing field, how............Bava Basra 12a-12b
Dividing partnership, three appraisers............Bava Metzia 31b-32a
Dividing, she lost her *kesubah*............Bava Basra 132a-133a
Dividing speech............Yevamos 25a-25b; Sanhedrin 9b-10a; Bava Basra 134b

Dividing up
Dividing up............*see also* **Sharing**, page 610
Dividing up between partners, size............Bava Basra 12a

Dividing up, doubt in monetary matters .... Bava Basra 34b-35b; Bava Metzia 2a-3a, 62b
Dividing up, Symmachus ....Bava Kama 35b, 46a-46b; Bava Metzia 2b, 6a, 98b, 100a, 100b; Bava Basra 141a

Divine
Divine decree, annulment .... Rosh Hashanah 17b-18a; Yevamos 105a
Divine Judgment, sinner's approval .... Taanis 11a
Divine Name .... *see* **Names of G-d**, page 436
Divine property, second tithe ....Sanhedrin 112b; Pesachim 38a; Succah 35b; Kiddushin 24a, 53a-53b, 54b

Divine help
Divine help, for commerce .... Megillah 6b
Divine help in ruling, episodes .... Bava Metzia 81a; Niddah 65a; Yevamos 121a
Divine help, learning .... Megillah 6b
Divine help to avoid judge's mistake .... Bava Metzia 81a

Divine inspiration
Divine inspiration, Esther .... Megillah 7a
Divine inspiration, Rabban Gamliel .... Eruvin 64b
Divine inspiration, Rebbi .... Kiddushin 72a-72b

Divine Presence
Episodes —
Divine Presence, Babylonians' synagogues .... Megillah 29a
Divine Presence, second Temple .... Yoma 9b-10a
Divine Presence, synagogue .... Berachos 6a
Israel —
Divine Presence in exile .... Megillah 29a
Divine Presence in impurity of exile .... Yoma 56b-57a
Divine Presence in Israel, Moses' request .... Berachos 7a; Bava Basra 15b
Divine Presence in Israel's tragedies .... Taanis 16a
Divine Presence, twenty two thousand .... Bava Kama 83a; Yevamos 64a
Where —
Divine Presence above sick man's bed .... Nedarim 40a; Shabbos 12b
Divine Presence, higher than ten handbreadths .... Succah 5a
Divine Presence in *beis din* .... Berachos 6a
Divine Presence in front of him, prayer .... Sanhedrin 22a
Divine Presence, place .... Bava Basra 25a; Sanhedrin 39a
Who —
Divine Presence among men learning Torah .... Berachos 6a; Avos 3:2-3, 3:6
Divine Presence, husband and wife .... Sotah 17a
Divine Presence, learning at night .... Tamid 32b
Divine Presence, meal with a Sage .... Berachos 64a
Misc. —
Divine Presence among ten Jews .... Sanhedrin 39a
Divine Presence on every Jew .... Sotah 3b
Divine Presence rests, prophecy .... Nedarim 38a; Moed Katan 25a; Shabbos 92a

Divine voice
Low degree of prophecy —
Divine voice, Beis Hillel ....Chullin 43b-44a; Eruvin 6b; Rosh Hashanah 14b
Divine voice, episodes .... Sotah 33a; Sanhedrin 11a
Divine voice, *halacha* .... Berachos 51b-52a
Divine voice in exile .... Bava Basra 74a
Divine voice, Rabbi Chaninah .... Berachos 17b

Divine voice to persons fit for prophecy .... Sanhedrin 11a
Divine voice, Judah .... Makos 23b; Berachos 17b; Taanis 24b; Chullin 86a
Misc. —
Divine voice, *agunah* .... Yevamos 122a
Divine voice, omen .... Megillah 32a

Diviner
Diviner, cases .... Sanhedrin 65b-66a
Diviner, punishment, and reward for abstaining .... Nedarim 32a
Diviner, what is forbidden .... Megillah 32a; Chullin 95b; Krisos 5b-6a

Division of city between two tribes .... Sanhedrin 111b

Division of *Eretz Yisrael*
Division of *Eretz Yisrael*, how .... Bava Basra 121b-122b
Division of *Eretz Yisrael*, in the future .... Bava Basra 122a
Division of *Eretz Yisrael*, men who came out of Egypt .... Bava Basra 116b-119a
Division of *Eretz Yisrael*, places .... Bava Kama 81b; Bava Basra 122a
Division of *Eretz Yisrael*, seven years of conquest .... Arachin 13a
Division of *Eretz Yisrael*, to whom .... Bava Basra 118a, 119a
Division of *Eretz Yisrael*, Joshua and Caleb .... Bava Basra 118b, 122a-122b
Division of *Eretz Yisrael*, Zebulun .... Megillah 6a

Divorce
Divorce, "I divorced my wife," trustworthiness .... Bava Basra 134b-135a; Gittin 64a
Divorce, "You divorced me," trustworthiness .... Kesubos 22b, 23a; Yevamos 116a; Nedarim 91a;
.... Gittin 64b, 89b
Divorce me, women are used to say .... Yevamos 116a
Divorced, doubt, *terumah* .... Gittin 65a-65b
Divorces and takes back, mind cannot tolerate .... Pesachim 113b
Divorcing first wife .... Sanhedrin 22a
Divorcing, who .... Sotah 25a; Gittin 90a-90b; Yevamos 63b

Divorce after levirate marriage .... Yevamos 8b, 39a, 52a-52b; Kesubos 82a

Divorce document
Disqualified —
Divorce document and receipt, exchanged .... Gittin 80b-81a
Divorce document, before child conception .... Gittin 26b, 79b; Eduyos 4:7
Divorce document, connected to earth or to living creature .... Gittin 3b, 21b-22a
Divorce document, divorced but child is illegitimate .... Gittin 5b, 79b-80b, 86a-86b;
.... Yevamos 91b; Bava Metzia 55b
Divorce document, embossing around letter .... Gittin 20a-20b
Divorce document, improper, *Kohen* .... Gittin 24b-25a, 82b; Yevamos 52a, 94a
Divorce document, non-Jewish court .... Gittin 9a-9b, 10b-11a
Divorce document, old, before conception of child .... Gittin 26b, 79b; Eduyos 4:7
Divorce document, said it was a legal document .... Yevamos 113b; Gittin 55a
Divorce document, string held by husband .... Gittin 78b; Bava Metzia 7a
Divorce document to sleeping wife .... Gittin 78a
Divorce document, written in front of me .... *see* **Before me it was written**, page 48
Divorce document written on item forbidden to have benefit thereof .... Gittin 20a
Divorce obtained by coercion .... Gittin 88b; Bava Basra 48a
For whom —
Divorce, *agunah* whose husband came back .... Yevamos 88b-89a
Divorce document, first wife .... Sanhedrin 22a

Divorce document for levirate betrothal...Yevamos 32a, 52b
Divorce document, whom must one divorce ....Sotah 25a; Gittin 90a-90b; Yevamos 63b
Divorce document, young girl...Kesubos 47a; Gittin 64b
Divorce, claim about husband's sterility....................................Yevamos 65b; Kesubos 64a
Divorce for faulty marriage ....Yevamos 94a-94b
Divorce intended, intimate relations..Gittin 90a; Yevamos 37b
Divorce, *kesubah* to discourage divorce...........................Kesubos 11a, 39b, 54a; Yevamos 89a
Divorce obligatory, why..Kesubos 77a; Yevamos 112a
Divorce, sterile man...Yevamos 65a
Divorce without paying *kesubah* ....Yevamos 84a, 85a-85b; Kesubos 72a-72b, 100b, 101a-101b

Giving —
Divorce and financial independence, together ....Gittin 77b
Divorce document, act of acquisition by courtyard........................Gittin 21a, 77a-78a, 79a-79b;
....Bava Metzia 11b-12a
Divorce document, after a certain time ....Gittin 18b, 29b, 76b
Divorce document, agent...Gittin 62b-63a
Divorce document, different acts of acquisition...Gittin 21a, 78a-78b
Divorce document, giving..Gittin 19b, 78b, 84b
Divorce document, revealing intention ....Gittin 30a, 34a-34b
Divorce document, tearing...Kesubos 89b

Intended —
Divorce document, cases of intended act......................Gittin 24a-24b; Sotah 20b; Zevachim 2b
Divorce document exchanged, personal...Gittin 86b
Divorce document, important man present ....Gittin 23a
Divorce document, rewriting to make it personal ....Gittin 20a
Divorce document, tacit intention ....Zevachim 2b-3a

Writing —
Divorce document, agent to write ....Gittin 63b, 66a-67b, 71b-72a
Divorce document, husband says "Say" ....Gittin 66b-67a, 71b-72a
Divorce document, husband's command.....................................Gittin 63b, 65b, 66a, 67b
Divorce document, husband's mental clarity...Gittin 70b
Divorce document of *Kohanim*.........Gittin 81b-82a; Kiddushin 49a; Bava Basra 160a-160b, 164a-164b
Divorce document of *Kohanim*, how ....Bava Basra 160b-161b
Divorce document, on what is it written ....Succah 24b; Eruvin 15b; Gittin 20a, 20b, 21b, 22b
Divorce document, scribe's salary...Gittin 20a; Bava Basra 168a
Divorce document, text ....Gittin 80a, 85a-86a
Divorce document, write and give ....Kesubos 55a; Bava Basra 135b-136a, 152a; Gittin 9b
Divorce document, writing ....Gittin 3a-4a, 6a, 19a, 20a-20b, 23a
Divorce document, written on wife's tablet ....Gittin 20b-21a
Divorce, determining husband's lucidity...Gittin 70b-71a

Misc. —
Divorce document, "when I marry" ....Yevamos 52a-52b
Divorce document, act of acquisition...Gittin 21a, 78a-78b
Divorce document, breaking off.....Gittin 21b, 83b; Eruvin 15b; Yoma 13a; Succah 24b; Kiddushin 5a
Divorce document, conditions..............................*see* **Condition in divorce document**, page 120
Divorce document considered like accepting vow...Nedarim 71b-72a
Divorce document, invalid agents..Gittin 23a-23b, 62b
Divorce document of Uriah, David's wars.......................................Kesubos 9a; Shabbos 56a
Divorce document which was found ....Yevamos 115b-116a; Gittin 27a-28a; Bava Metzia 18a-19a, 20a

D

Divorce document, young girl's agent .... Kiddushin 44b
Divorce document because of illness
Divorce document because of illness, condition .... Gittin 75b
Divorce document because of illness, recovered .... Gittin 72b-73a
Divorce document because of illness, terms .... Gittin 72a, 74b; Kesubos 2b;
.... Kiddushin 59b, 60a; Bava Basra 136a, 137a
Divorce document because of illness, wife's statute .... Gittin 73b-74a
Divorcee
Divorcee, buying back her dowry .... Yevamos 66a-67a
Divorcee, *chazakah* of her property .... Bava Basra 47a-47b, 52a
Divorcee, doubt, found item .... Bava Metzia 12b
Divorcee, doubtful, supporting her .... Kesubos 97a; Gittin 74a; Bava Metzia 12b; Bava Basra 47b
Divorcee, marrying .... Gittin 90b; Pesachim 112a; Sotah 6a
Divorcee, oath .... Gittin 35a
Divorcee of one's brother, forbidden relations .... Yevamos 54b
Divrei chalomos .... *see* **Dream**, page 180
Divrei haRav divrei mi shomim .... *see* **Teacher's and disciple's instructions,**
.... **which must one listen**, page 674
Divrei Hayamim
Divrei Hayamim, episode .... Pesachim 62b
Divrei Hayamim, homilies .... Pesachim 62b
Divrei Hayamim, who wrote .... Bava Basra 14b-15a
Divrei nevius .... *see* **Words of prophecy**, page 760
Divrei shchiv mera .... *see* **Words of sick man**, page 760
Divrei Sofrim .... *see* **Sages' words**, page 584
Divrei Torah .... *see* **Words of Torah**, page 760
D'mei vlados .... *see* **Abortion**, page 3
Do not
"Do not pay me," witnesses .... Shevuos 41a-41b
Do not lift up .... Avodah Zarah 13b, 26a-26b; Sanhedrin 57a
Do not make them a crown .... Nedarim 62a; Avos 4:5
Do not withhold good from its recipient .... Bava Kama 81b
Do your will like His will .... Avos 2:4
Dochak .... *see* **Answer, unsatisfactory, not adopted as law**, page 29
Dochek hashaah .... *see* **Forcing the issue to reign earlier**, page 234
Dochek raglei haShechinah .... *see* **Pushing away Divine Presence**, page 512
Dochsostos, holy parchments .... Shabbos 79b; Menachos 32a-32b
Doctor .... *see* **Physician**, page 486
Doeg
Doeg and David .... Yevamos 76b-77a; Sanhedrin 93b
Doeg, evil in his heart .... Chagigah 15b
Doeg, wisdom and punishment .... Sanhedrin 69b, 106b
Doeg, World to Come .... Sanhedrin 105a
Doeg ben Yosef, famine .... Yoma 38b
Dog
Characteristics —
Dog barks only in its city .... Eruvin 61a
Dog digs under doors .... Bava Kama 23a
Dog, eats anything when hungry .... Bava Kama 92b

Dog, food..Shabbos 155b

Dog, impudent...Beitzah 25b

Dog, particularities....................................Shabbos 155b; Bava Metzia 42a; Pesachim 31b; Horayos 13a

Dog, time it takes to digest...Oholos 11:7; Shabbos 155b

Dogs, hate...Pesachim 113b

Laws —

Dog, ember on stack..Bava Kama 23a

Dog, feeding it on Shabbos...Shabbos 19a, 155b

Dog, forcing it to bite someone..Bava Kama 24b

Dog, prohibition to raise...........................Shabbos 63a-63b; Bava Kama 15b, 46a, 83a; Kesuvos 41b

Dog, prohibition to trade...Bava Kama 80a

Dog, suspicion of widow...Bava Metzia 71a; Avodah Zarah 22b

Dog which ate from flesh of dead...Oholos 11:7; Chullin 126a

Misc. —

Dog, "I am not a dog"..Nedarim 24a

Dog, a live one is better than dead lion...Shabbos 30a

Dog, episode about excommunication..Moed Katan 17a

Dog, intimate relations in Noah's ark..Sanhedrin 108b

Dog licking sea, Rabbi Eliezer's wisdom...................................Sanhedrin 68a

Dog, rabid...Shabbos 121b; Yoma 83b-84a

Dog, woman miscarried...Bava Kama 83a; Shabbos 63b

Dogs, derogatory speech...Pesachim 118a; Makos 23a

Dogs, false testimony..Pesachim 118a; Makos 23a

Dogs, guarding city..Pesachim 113a

Dogs killed wolf..Sanhedrin 105a

Dogs play, Elijah comes..Bava Kama 60b

Dog returns to its vomit...Yoma 86b

Dolphins..Bechoros 8a

Doma ben Nesina...Kiddushin 31a

Domain

Domain of damaged person, ox goring occasionally...Bava Kama 14a-14b, 15b-16a, 18b, 24b-25a

Domain where carrying is permitted by Rabbinical Decree.................*see **Karmelis**, page 332*

Domain where carrying is permitted...................................*see **Mekom petur**, page 403*

Domains, separate, for divorce certificate..Gittin 77b-78a

Domains, tooth and leg..Bava Kama 13b-14a

Domains for doubtful impurity

Domains for doubtful impurity, cases.................................Taharos 5:1-2, 6:3-5, 8:3

Domains for doubtful impurity, changed........................Taharos 6:1; Bava Basra 153b

Domains for doubtful impurity, doubt about place.......................Bava Basra 153b

Domains for doubtful impurity, in two domains...............................Taharos 6:2

Domains for doubtful impurity, places........................Taharos 6:6-9a, 10:8; Shabbos 6a; Pesachim 19b;

Bava Basra 153b

Domains for doubtful impurity, ruling...Avodah Zarah 37b

Domains for doubtful impurity, *sotah's* garment..Niddah 3a

Domains for doubtful impurity, source...Sotah 28a-29a

Domains for doubtful impurity, testimony.......................................Nazir 57a-57b

Domains for doubtful impurity, transferred domain.......................Taharos 6:1

Dominate

Dominate evil urge like man...Avodah Zarah 19a

Dominate their evil urge, reckoning .... Bava Basra 78b

Don minah uminah .... *see* **Deduction strictly following first law**, page 156

Donation

Donation for communal sacrifice, is it permitted .... Rosh Hashanah 7a-7b; Yoma 35b; Bava Metzia 118a

Donations for synagogue, changing for another use .... Arachin 6b

Donations of shekels in desert .... Megillah 29b

Donation valuation

Donation valuation, age .... Arachin 18a, 18b

Donation valuation, heir .... Arachin 20a-20b

Donation valuation, poor .... Arachin 4a, 7b, 17a; Bechoros 10b-11a

Donation valuation, who .... Arachin 4a-5b, 6b

Donation valuations, cases .... Arachin 5a-5b, 20a-20b

Donation valuations, non-Jew .... Nazir 61a-62a; Arachin 5b, 13b

Donation valuations, value of utensil .... Arachin 5a-5b

Donkey

Characteristics —

Donkey, "they called you donkey" .... Bava Kama 92b

Donkey, identified by white stomach .... Gittin 45a

Donkey is cold in summer .... Shabbos 53a

Donkey, signs of quality .... Chullin 60a

Donkey, strength by barley .... Shabbos 51b

Episodes —

Donkey of Abbaye, lost .... Gittin 45a

Donkey of Rabbi Pinchas ben Yair .... Chullin 7a-7b

Donkey of Rav Safra, lion .... Bava Kama 116a

Donkey, precise salary .... Taanis 24a

Donkey rebellious, episode .... Shabbos 51b-52a

Donkey, to entertain son .... Shabbos 154b

Donkeys, booty of Egypt .... Bechoros 5b

Monetary matters —

Donkey and not objects, pit .... Bava Kama 5b, 10a, 28b, 53b-54a

Donkey, child's hand .... Bava Kama 84a

Donkey, died on the way .... Bava Metzia 79a

Donkey, hired, confiscated by government .... Bava Metzia 78b-79a

Donkey hired, loading .... Bava Metzia 79b; Avodah Zarah 65a

Donkey in ship, dangerous .... Bava Kama 117b

Donkey, included in sale .... Bava Basra 78a-78b

Donkey, liability of renter .... Bava Metzia 78a

Donkey, returned according to signs of saddle if lost .... Bava Metzia 27a

Misc. —

Donkey and camel driver, *eruv* .... Eruvin 35a, 52b

Donkey, breeding on *chol hamoed* .... Moed Katan 12a

Donkey, crouched .... Bava Metzia 31a-33a

Donkey crouched, enemy .... Pesachim 113b

Donkey drivers, decisions .... Bava Kama 116b

Donkey of clowns, impurity .... Shabbos 66b

Donkey of Messiah .... Sanhedrin 98a

Donkey, sorcery .... Sanhedrin 67b

Door .... *see also* **Gate**, page 244, **Opening**, page 461
  Monetary matters —
    Door, rights to part of courtyard .... Bava Basra 11a-11b; Succah 3b
    Doors, dog digs under .... Bava Kama 23a
    Doors of Israel, modesty .... Bava Basra 60a
  Prohibitions —
    Door, carrying on Shabbos .... Shabbos 9a
    Door, *mezuzah* .... Yoma 11a-11b; Menachos 33a-34a
    Door, putting back hinge on Shabbos .... Eruvin 102b
    Doors, disassembling and putting back .... Shabbos 122b
    Doors of furniture, *muktzeh* .... Shabbos 122b
    Doors, public domain .... Eruvin 6a-6b, 11b
    Doors, putting back on Shabbos .... Eruvin 101a
  Misc. —
    Door, limit of the room .... Pesachim 85b; Nedarim 56b
    Door of success which closed .... Bava Kama 80b
    Door, to fill and empty .... Shabbos 146a
    Doors of *Heichal* .... Middos 3:7, 4:1-2; Yoma 54a; Eruvin 2a, 3a
    Doors of *Heichal*, sacrifice .... Zevachim 55b; Eruvin 2a; Yoma 62b-63a
    Doors of *Nikanor* .... Yoma 38a; Middos 2:3
    Doors opening before Temple destruction .... Yoma 39b
Doorpost, impurity of corpse .... Oholos 12:8
Doorsill
  Doorsill, impurity of corpse .... Oholos 12:8
  Doorsill, *mekom ptur* .... Shabbos 8b-9a
  Doorsill of Dagon, cult .... Avodah Zarah 41b
  Doorsill, Shabbos .... Shabbos 9a, 124a
  Doorsill, Shabbos domains .... Shabbos 9a, 91b
  Doorsill, synagogue .... Pesachim 85b
  Doorsill, when is it considered as inside .... Pesachim 85b; Nedarim 56b
Dor .... *see* **Generation**, page 248
Dorkati, have no blood .... Kesubos 10b
Dormer windows to repair Holy of Holies .... Pesachim 26a; Middos 4:5
Doros mishaah .... *see* **Deduction, temporary law**, page 156
Doros rishonim .... *see* **First generations**, page 225
Double
  Double condition .... Kiddushin 61a-62a; Gittin 46b, 75a-75b, 76a; Yevamos 53a; Nedarim 11a
  Double doubt to permit certain widow to *Kohen* .... Kesubos 14a; Eduyos 8:3; Kiddushin 75a
  Double exclusion .... Menachos 9b, 67a; Yoma 43a; Megillah 23b; Bava Kama 86b; Bava Basra 14a;
      Sanhedrin 15a, 46a, 86a; Makos 9b; Shevuos 7b; Chullin 132a
  Double inclusion .... Bava Kama 45b; Pesachim 23a
  Double kingship, Moses and Joshua .... Sotah 13b
  Double majority, stringency in lineage .... Kesubos 15a-15b
  Double oath .... *see* **Oath, double**, page 452
Double bequest
  Double bequest, gave to his son .... Bava Basra 137b
  Double bequest, husband .... Kesubos 95b; Bava Basra 125b
  Double bequest, inheritance .... Bava Basra 129b, 133a-133b
  Double bequest, second person died .... Bava Basra 129b, 130a, 133a

Double bequest, sold land afterwards .... Bava Basra 137a; Sotah 21b

Double doubt
Double doubt about impurity, valley .... Pesachim 10a; Bava Basra 55b; Avodah Zarah 70a; Taharos 6:5
Double doubt, lineage of child .... Kesubos 14a
Double doubt, mixture .... Zevachim 74a-74b
Double doubt, saving life .... Yoma 85a
Double doubt, virginity .... Kesubos 9a

Double payment
Double payment, custodian who denied .... Bava Kama 57a, 62b, 63b, 106b, 107b
Double payment, custodian's rights .... Bava Metzia 33b-34a, 37a

Double payment of thief
Double payment of thief, *aggadah* .... Bava Kama 79b
Double payment of thief, firstborn donkey .... Bechoros 11a
Double payment of thief, for which stolen item .... Bava Kama 62b-64b; Bava Metzia 57b;
                                                                                    Shevuos 42b
Double payment of thief, who must pay .... Bava Kama 57a-57b, 63b, 64b, 108b

Double prohibition
Double prohibition .... Yevamos 32a-33b; Shevuos 24b; Chullin 100b-101b, 103a, 113b, 116a
Double prohibition, eating and intimate relations .... Yevamos 34a; Krisos 14a-14b
Double prohibition, more severe .... Krisos 23a-23b
Double prohibition, mother-in-law .... Sanhedrin 81a-81b; Yevamos 32a; Krisos 14b
Double prohibition, *neveilah* .... Meilah 16a; Zevachim 70a; Chullin 37a
Double prohibition, *neveilah* on Yom Kippur .... Shevuos 24a; Pesachim 35b-36a; Nazir 4a;
                                                                                    Kiddushin 77b; Krisos 23a
Double prohibition, sacrifices .... Krisos 23a-23b
Double prohibition, sciatic nerve .... Chullin 89b-90a
Double prohibition, women for *Kohanim* .... Kiddushin 77a-77b

Doubt
Commandments —
Doubt about blessing, Yom Tov out of *Eretz Yisrael* .... Shabbos 23a
Doubt about where one made a mistake, *Shema* .... Berachos 16a
Doubt if excrement, prayer .... Berachos 25a
Doubt if prayed, *nedavah* prayer .... Berachos 21a
Doubt if read *Shema* .... Berachos 21a
Doubt in blessing .... Shabbos 23a
Doubt, washing hands .... Yadayim 2:4

Festivals —
Doubt about *chametz* .... Pesachim 7a
Doubt about day, Yom Kippur .... Rosh Hashanah 21a
Doubt about *eruv chatzeiros* .... Shabbos 34a
Doubt about *Rosh Chodesh*, condition .... Eruvin 40a
Doubt about stillborn child, Shabbos .... Shabbos 134b-136a
Doubt if caught on Yom Tov .... Beitzah 24a-24b
Doubt if surrounded by wall, Purim .... Megillah 5b
Doubt, which day is Shabbos, desert .... Shabbos 69b

Filiation —
Doubt, double .... *see* **Double doubt**, page 176
Doubt if illegitimate child .... Yevamos 37a; Kiddushin 73a, 74a, 75a
Doubt if Jewish, lineage .... Kesubos 15b

Doubt if Jewish, majority..Yoma 84b-85a
Doubt if *Kohen*, lineage ....Yevamos 100b; Kesubos 13b
Doubt if *Kohen*, meal offering...Yevamos 100a
Doubt, which husband is child's father, general ....Yevamos 37a
Doubt, which husband is child's father, inheritance.......Yevamos 37b-38a, 100b; Bechoros 47b

Impurity —
Doubt about stillborn animal, *neveilah*..Shabbos 136a
Doubt, attributing to friend, blood stain ....Niddah 59b-61a
Doubt, attributing to other cause, stain of *niddah* ....Niddah 19b-20a, 58b-59a
Doubt, attributing to wound, *niddah* ....Niddah 16a
Doubt if child touched dough.............Kiddushin 80a; Chullin 86a-86b; Taharos 3:8; Niddah 18b
Doubt, *niddah* or *zavah*............................Niddah 53b-54a, 69a-69b; Arachin 8a-8b
Doubt, reptile found in basket..Niddah 3b-4a
Doubt, reptile in closed alley................................Niddah 3a, 56a-56b
Doubt, burning *terumah*....................Kiddushin 80a-80b; Taharos 4:5-6; Niddah 33b
Doubt about leprous marks, impurity.....Nazir 65b; Kesubos 75b; Bava Metzia 86a; Sanhedrin 87b;
....Negaim 4:11, 5:4-5; Niddah 19a
Doubt about who touched, impurity................Taharos 5:7-8; Eruvin 35b; Niddah 4a
Doubt, two baskets................................Terumos 7:5-7; Pesachim 9b
Doubt about *mikveh* and immersion..........Mikvaos 2:1-3; Eruvin 35b; Gittin 31b; Kiddushin 79a;
....Niddah 2b-3a

Doubt about impurity
Doubt about impurity, miscarriage.................................Niddah 29b-30b
Doubt about impurity, olive press.................Taharos 9:8-9, 10:8; Avodah Zarah 75b
Doubt about impurity, stringency................................Niddah 2a-4a
Doubt about impurity, *terumah*.............Kiddushin 80a-80b; Bechoros 33b-34a; Shabbos 15b;
................Pesachim 15a, 20b; Menachos 48a-48b; Terumos 8:8; Taharos 4:5-6; Niddah 33b

Marriage —
Doubt about divorcee, found item................................Bava Metzia 12b
Doubt about intermingled children, levirate marriage ....Yevamos 98b-99b
Doubt about *kiddushin*, gifts................................Kiddushin 50a-50b
Doubt about *kiddushin*, *kesubah*................................Kiddushin 50b
Doubt about nine months, levirate marriage................Yevamos 100a-100b
Doubt about puberty, *kiddushin*................................Kiddushin 79a
Doubt about who gave *kiddushin*, *kesubah*................Yevamos 118b
Doubt if *chalutzah*, to *Kohen*................................Yevamos 24a
Doubt if father accepted................................Kiddushin 44b-45a, 45b
Doubt if her rival became pregnant, levirate marriage............Yevamos 36a, 119a-119b
Doubt if her rival gave birth, levirate marriage................Yevamos 36a, 119a-119b
Doubts, levirate marriage and *chalitzah*..........Yevamos 23b-24a, 30b-31b; Gittin 86b

Monetary matters —
Doubt about currency of bill................................Kesubos 110b
Doubt about inheritance, collapsed house.......Bava Basra 157a, 158a-158b, 159b; Yevamos 38b;
....Bava Metzia 37b
Doubt about money, consecrating................................Bava Metzia 6a-6b
Doubt about to whom to return loan or deposit................Bava Metzia 37a-37b
Doubt about who gored................................Bava Kama 13b, 35a-36a
Doubt, cow which gored................................Bava Kama 46b-47a
Doubt if placed down, lost item................................Bava Metzia 25b, 37b

Doubt if sick at time of bequest .... Bava Basra 153a-153b; Kiddushin 79b
Doubt in sum of bill .... Bava Basra 165b-167a
Doubt, occurred in his possession .... Kesubos 76a-76b
Doubt, price is proof .... Bava Basra 77b-78a, 92a; Bava Kama 46a
Doubt, shoulder and cheek and stomach to *Kohen* .... Bechoros 18a-18b
Doubt, to whom one owes money .... Bava Kama 103b; Yevamos 118b
Doubt, which bill was repaid .... Bava Basra 173a

Principles —
Doubt about Rabbinical prohibition .... Eruvin 35b-36a; Beitzah 3b; Mikvaos 2:1-2; Yevamos 31a
Doubt about Torah prohibition .... Beitzah 3b; Yevamos 31a; Niddah 46a
Doubt, cases of leniencies .... Taharos 4:12-13
Doubt does not override certainty .... Pesachim 9a-9b; Niddah 15b-16a; Avodah Zarah 41b-42a;
.... Yevamos 19b, 38a; Chullin 10a
Doubt does not override certainty, money matter .... Yevamos 37b-38b
Doubt, forbidden item known but not found .... Chullin 43b
Doubt if slaughtered or immersed, does not override certainty .... Chullin 10a
Doubt in case of danger to life, must be lenient .... Shabbos 129a; Yoma 83a, 84b-85a;
.... Kesubos 15a; Bava Kama 44b, 90a; Bava Basra 50b; Sanhedrin 79a
Doubt in vow, is vow valid? .... Nedarim 18b-19b, 61a-61b; Kiddushin 64b
Doubt, verse cannot apply to doubt .... Yoma 74a-74b; Chullin 22b; Bechoros 41b; Chagigah 4a;
.... Krisos 21a

Prohibitions —
Doubt about *orlah* .... Orlah 1:6, 3:9; Berachos 36a-36b; Gittin 54b; Kiddushin 38b-39a
Doubt about *tevel, chazakah* .... Eruvin 32a-32b; Pesachim 4b, 9a; Niddah 15b; Avodah Zarah 41b
Doubt about widow, *terumah* .... Gittin 28a-28b
Doubt about wine of idolaters, cases .... Bava Basra 24a
Doubt, *eruv techumin* .... Shabbos 34a; Eruvin 35b-36a, 59a
Doubt if divorced, *terumah* .... Gittin 65a-65b
Doubt if husband is dead, *terumah* .... Gittin 28a-28b
Doubt in mixed species in vineyard .... Orlah 3:9; Kiddushin 38b-39a
Doubt in mixture, forbidden by Rabbinical Decree .... Yevamos 82a-82b; Pesachim 9b-10a, 44a;
.... Nazir 36b
Doubt, item between two baskets .... Shekalim 7:1
Doubt, *nezirus* .... Nedarim 18b-19b; Taharos 4:12
Doubt, non-Jew touched wine, cases .... Avodah Zarah 70a-70b
Doubt, substance forbidden by Rabbinical Decree .... Terumos 7:5-7; Pesachim 9b
Doubt, vows .... Nedarim 18b-19b, 61a-61b

Sacrifices —
Doubt about leper, sacrifice .... Zevachim 76a-77a; Nazir 60a-60b; Menachos 105a-105b;
.... Niddah 70a-70b; Negaim 14:13
Doubt about *nazir* and leper, sacrifice .... Nazir 55b-56a, 59b-60b; Niddah 70a-70b
Doubt about sacrifice, bird sin offerings .... Nazir 29a-29b; Krisos 8a, 26b; Bava Basra 166a;
.... Taharos 4:13
Doubt about sacrifice, found not liable .... Krisos 22b, 23b-24b, 26b; Temurah 34a
Doubt about when windpipe became loose in neck .... Chullin 54a
Doubt about who sinned, sacrifice .... Krisos 7b, 22b-23a
Doubt about *zavah* and woman after birth, sacrifice .... Nazir 29a-29b; Krisos 8a-8b, 26b;
.... Bava Basra 166a; Taharos 4:13
Doubt, coins in Jerusalem .... Shekalim 7:2

Doubt from whom one stole .... Bava Metzia 37a-37b; Yevamos 118b; Bava Kama 103b-104a

Doubt, from whom one stole and bought .... Bava Kama 103b-104a; Yevamos 118b; Bava Metzia 37a

Doubt if torn alive, *treifah* .... Chullin 9a, 10a, 50b-51a; Beitzah 25a

Doubt if worm came out during animal's life, lung .... Chullin 49a

Doubt, offering for questionable guilt .... Yevamos 113a; Krisos 19b

Doubt, either/or, impurity .... Shevuos 19a-19b; Krisos 18b-19a; Taharos 5:3-6; Niddah 60a; Kesubos 27a

Doubt, *Pesach Sheni* .... Pesachim 88b-89a

Doubt, sacrifice, either/or .... Krisos 19a, 22b-23a; Shevuos 18b; Horayos 5a

Doubt, transgressing with positive action .... Eruvin 100a-100b

Doubt, which sacrificial animal was found .... Kiddushin 55a-55b; Shekalim 7:4-5

Doubts, animal tithe .... Bava Metzia 6b-7a; Bechoros 58b

Misc. —

Doubt about stillborn .... Shabbos 135b-136b; Yevamos 36b, 80b; Niddah 44b

Doubt about way to read verses .... Yoma 52a-52b

Doubt and doubt, monetary matters .... Bava Metzia 37b, 97b, 116b

Doubt, we forbid even because of minority .... Chullin 6a, 11b, 86a-86b; Yevamos 61b, 119a; Gittin 2b; Avodah Zarah 34b, 40b; Bechoros 19b-20b, 42b; Niddah 31b-32a, 48a

Doubts, died and will die .... Gittin 28a-28b

Doubt about firstborn

Doubt about firstborn animal .... Bechoros 18a, 18b-19a

Doubt about firstborn, mutual authorization .... Bava Basra 127a

Doubt about firstborn, redeeming son .... Bechoros 48a-49a

Doubt about impurity, places .... Bava Basra 55b-56a; Pesachim 10a, 10b

Doubtful owner, staying in deposit .... Bava Metzia 3a, 37b-38a

Doubtful impurity, cannot be asked

Doubtful impurity, cannot be asked, cases .... Taharos 3:6-8

Doubtful impurity, cannot be asked, coming from man .... Niddah 5b; Pesachim 19b-20a

Doubtful impurity, cannot be asked, from when .... Succah 42a

Doubtful impurity, cannot be asked, source .... Sotah 28b-29a

Doubting act of teacher .... Sanhedrin 110a

Dough

Dough, interposing substance in vessel .... Pesachim 45a-46a

Dough of shepherds, bread .... Challah 1:8; Beitzah 21a

Dough to repair vessel, purity .... Pesachim 46a; Chullin 129a

Doughnut, *challah* .... Pesachim 37a; Challah 1:4-5

Dove

Characteristics —

Dove, distance from nest .... Bava Basra 23a, 23b

Dove, fidelity .... Gittin 45a

Dove, pairs born monthly .... Bava Basra 80a

Dove, pursued among birds .... Bava Kama 93a

Dove, sucks .... Gittin 86b

Doves hunter, disqualified for testimony .... Rosh Hashanah 22a; Eruvin 82a; Sanhedrin 24b, 25a-25b, 27b

Doves, teach about forbidden relations .... Eruvin 100b

Misc. —

Dove in animal's womb .... Chullin 69a

Dove is recalled, Rava's son .... Kesubos 63a

Dove of gold, returning to his place for *Bircas HaMazon* .... Berachos 53b

D

Dove, Israel .... Berachos 53b; Shabbos 49a, 130a; Gittin 45a; Sanhedrin 95a

Doves, distance and hunt .... Bava Kama 83a; Bava Basra 23a

Doves for sacrifice, which ones .... Chullin 62a-62b

Doves for sacrifices, age of *kashrus* .... Chullin 22a-22b

Doves, how many to leave in dove-cot .... Bava Basra 80a

Doves of Herod, "*kiri*" .... Chullin 139b

Dovecote, distance from neighbors .... Bava Kama 83a; Bava Basra 23a

Downward from navel, prohibition .... Niddah 13b

Dowry

Dowry .... *see also* **Tenth for dowry, from married woman**, page 681

Dowry, brother of deceased childless husband .... Kesubos 66a

Dowry, customs .... Kesubos 66a-66b; Bava Metzia 104b

Dowry, determining amount, act of acquisition .... Kesubos 102b; Kiddushin 9b; Moed Katan 18b

Dowry, episode about charity .... Taanis 24a

Dowry, episode about determining amount .... Kesubos 52b-53a

Dowry for daughter, source .... Kiddushin 30b; Kesubos 52b

Dowry, how to estimate .... Kesubos 67a

Dowry, husband selling .... Kesubos 79b; Yevamos 66b-67a

Dowry of grooms, inheritance .... Kesubos 47a-47b

Dowry of Nakdimen's daughter .... Kesubos 65a, 66b

Dowry, tenth of father's property .... Kesubos 52b, 68a-68b, 69a; Bava Basra 66b-67a; Gittin 51a

Dowry, went bankrupt .... Kesubos 108b-109a

Dozing .... Taanis 12a-12b; Niddah 63a; Pesachim 120b; Megillah 18b; Yevamos 54a

Drachim, Mishnayos .... Kiddushin 2b-3a

Dragging bench on Shabbos .... Shabbos 22a, 29b, 46b; Pesachim 101a; Beitzah 23b; Menachos 41b

Dragon, idolatry .... Avodah Zarah 42b-43a

Drain

Drain, impurity of corpse .... Oholos 3:7

Drain, repair expenses .... Bava Metzia 108a

Drara demamona .... *see* **Self-understood monetary claim**, page 599

Drasah beshechitah .... *see* **Slaughtering by pressing**, page 635

Drashah .... *see* **Discourse**, page 166

Drawing

Drawing and giving to drink, Eliezer .... Yoma 28b

Drawing water on Shabbos .... Eruvin 104a-104b

Draws heart like water .... Chagigah 14a

Drawings

Drawings on walls, Temple .... Yoma 54a-54b

Drawings, prohibitions .... Avodah Zarah 42b-43b; Rosh Hashanah 24a-24b

Dream

Episodes —

Dream, episode about charity .... Bava Basra 10a

Dream, good *shalom* .... Taanis 24b

Dream, king's garments .... Berachos 56a-56b

Dream of Pharaoh's ministers .... Chullin 92a; Berachos 55b; Sotah 9a

Dream of Jacob .... Chullin 91b

Dream, Rabbi Chanina .... Yoma 87b

Dream, Rabbi Yochanan .... Menachos 84b

Dreams, Bar Hadia .... Berachos 56a-56b

Dreams, episodes .... Berachos 56a-56b
Misc. —
Dream, "broken reed" .... Yevamos 93b
Dream, excommunication .... Nedarim 8a-8b
Dream, fast .... Shabbos 11a; Taanis 12b
Dream, good .... Pesachim 117a
Dream, good, Divine pity .... Berachos 55a
Dream, good for sick .... Berachos 57b
Dream, hanged on palm tree .... Yoma 87b
Dream, interpretations .... Berachos 56b-57b; Bava Kama 55a
Dream, interpreting favorably .... Berachos 55b
Dream, lower level of prophecy .... Berachos 55b
Dream, meaning .... Berachos 55a-56a; Gittin 52a; Sanhedrin 30a; Horayos 13b
Dream, verse .... Chullin 133a
Dressed
Dressed in neglected fashion .... Megillah 24a-24b
Dressing in priestly garments .... Yoma 5b-6a, 24b; Tamid 5:3
Dressing on wound
Dressing on wound, carrying out on Shabbos .... Shabbos 50a
Dressing on wound, circumcision .... Shabbos 134a
Dressing on wound, rubbing .... Eruvin 102b
Dressing on wound, Shabbos .... Eruvin 102b; Beitzah 11b
Dried
Dried reptiles, impurity .... Niddah 56a
Dried up fountain, lessee .... Bava Metzia 103b
Dried up fruit, picking on Shabbos .... Chullin 127b
Drill, size to make *treifah* .... Chullin 57b
Drilling hole on Shabbos .... Menachos 57a; Shabbos 102b-103a
Drink
Health —
Drink, beneficial from forty years old .... Shabbos 152a
Drink, hot, too much is harmful .... Gittin 70a
Drink when thirsty .... Berachos 62b
Misc. —
Drink composed from flour, blessing .... Berachos 38a
Drink, good manners .... Pesachim 86b; Beitzah 25b; Chullin 105b; Tamid 27b; Bechoros 44b
Drink, popular, *havdala* .... Pesachim 107a
Drink, popular, *kiddush* .... Pesachim 107a
Drink to animal before slaughtering .... Beitzah 40a
Drink to guests, reward .... Sanhedrin 103b-104a
Drink which fell into the sea, *mikveh* .... Makos 4a
Drinking
Prohibitions —
Drinking between domains .... Shabbos 11a-11b; Eruvin 20a-20b, 99a
Drinking from gutter on Shabbos .... Eruvin 99b
Drinking in bloodletting bottle .... Makos 16b
Drinking, Yom Kippur .... Yoma 80a-80b
Misc. —
Drinking *alontis*, episode .... Shabbos 140a

D

Drinking from teacher's cup, refined person...Tamid 27b
Drinking in cup, need to check it..Kesubos 75b-76a
Drinking, leech and demon.....................................Avodah Zarah 12b; Pesachim 112a
Drinking like eating....................................Shevuos 22b-23a; Yoma 76a-76b; Chullin 120a
Drinking while standing, weakness...Gittin 70a
Dripping, blood of covenant...Shabbos 135a; Yevamos 71a
Drishah vachakirah..*see* **Witnesses, examination,** page 753
Driving
Driving, act of acquisition..Bava Metzia 8b-9b
Driving mixed species of animals...Kilayim 8:2-4; Bava Metzia 8b
Driving, purchase of ship..Kesubos 85a
Driving, redeemed sacrifice...Makos 22a
Drop
Drop of Angel of Death..Avodah Zarah 20b
Drop of blood like mustard seed.........................Niddah 66a; Berachos 31a; Megillah 28b
Drop of cold water, cure..Shabbos 108b
Drop, wise or unwise, fetus...Niddah 16b
Drops in sea, wisdom..Horayos 10a
Dror, significance..Rosh Hashanah 9b
Drought...*see* **Famine,** page 214
Drowning
Drowning, came up from a pit.............................Bava Kama 50a-50b; Yevamos 121b
Drowning, eulogy for fisherman...Yevamos 121a
Drowning from ship, episodes...Yevamos 121a
Drowning, man who drowned others will be drowned...............................Avos 2:6
Drowning ship, thorn..Niddah 31a
Drowsy....................................Taanis 12a-12b; Niddah 63a; Pesachim 120b; Megillah 18b; Yevamos 54a
Drugs, avoiding...Pesachim 113a
Drunk
  Aggadah —
  Drunk, and not from wine..Eruvin 65a
  Drunk, let him fall by himself..Shabbos 32a
  Drunk, proverb...Shabbos 32a
  Drunk, transgressions seem permitted..Yoma 74b-75a
  Prohibitions —
  Drunk, prayer...Berachos 31b; Eruvin 64a, 65a
  Drunk, priestly blessing...Taanis 26b-27a
  Drunk who performed service, death...Sanhedrin 83b
  Misc. —
  Drunk, considered as sober man..Eruvin 65a
  Drunk, cure on Shabbos..Shabbos 66b
  Drunk, man must get drunk on Purim...Megillah 7b
  Drunk, Noah...Sanhedrin 70a
  Drunk, Purim..Megillah 7b
Drunkenness
Drunkenness, blemishes of *Kohen*..Bechoros 45b
Drunkenness, keeping away from.........................Yoma 74b-75a; Sanhedrin 70a; Berachos 29b
Drunkenness, man is known by..Eruvin 65b
Drunkenness, Rabbi Chiya's sons..Sanhedrin 38a

Drunkenness, ruling..Eruvin 64b; Krisos 13b; Kesubos 10b; Beitzah 4a; Zevachim 18a
Drunkenness, value of avoiding..Pesachim 113b
Dry
Dry, blood of *niddah*..Niddah 35b, 54b-55a; Temurah 34a
Dry, flesh of deceased..Niddah 55a, 56a
Duck
Duck legs..Berachos 41b
Duck walks head down but looks everywhere..Bava Kama 92b; Megillah 14b
Dudaei Reuvein..*see* **Mandrakes, Reuben**, page 388
Duke shook hands with me..Zevachim 96b
Dumah, rest of souls..Shabbos 152b
Dumb..*see* **Mute**, page 433
Dung
Dung, forbidden benefit..Avodah Zarah 34b-35a
Dung, impurities..Menachos 69a-69b; Taanis 22b; Bava Basra 22a
Dung in public domain, damage..Bava Kama 29b
Duration of sickness, sign for dead person..Moed Katan 28a
Dusk
Dusk, Creation..Avos 5:6; Pesachim 54a-54b
Dusk, *eruv chatzeiros*..Shabbos 34a
Dusk, *eruv techumin*..Shabbos 34a
Dusk, its time..Shabbos 34b-35b; Berachos 2b; Niddah 53a-53b
Dusk, one of two things..Shabbos 35b; Krisos 19b
Dusk, stain..Niddah 52b-53b
Dust
  Episodes —
Dust from Rav's grave..Sanhedrin 47b
Dust of Abraham's war..Sanhedrin 108b
Dust of Babylon, curse..Berachos 57b-58a
Dust of Nahum Ish Gam Zu..Taanis 21a; Sanhedrin 108b-109a
Dust of place where Sages of Athens lived..Bechoros 8b-9a
Dust, Taya (Arab merchant) smelled..Bava Basra 73b
  Misc. —
Dust, covering blood..Chullin 88a-88b
Dust for *sotah*..Sotah 15b-16a
Dust for *sotah*, Abraham..Sotah 17a; Chullin 88b
Dust in his mouth..Bava Basra 16a
Dust of dead..Nazir 51b, 65a
Dust of meal offerings semolina..Menachos 85a
Dust seen in sunlight, cure..Nedarim 8b
Dust, sunlight..Yoma 20b
Dust, Israel..Megillah 16a
Dwelling
Dwelling in fellow's courtyard..Bava Kama 20a-21a, 97a; Bava Metzia 64b-65a
Dwelling, married woman..Kesubos 110a, 110b
Dwelling next to one's teacher..Berachos 8a
Dwelling only in a place of Torah..Avos 6:9
Dwelling, orphan with her mother..Kesubos 102b-103a
Dwelling, widow..Kesubos 103a

Dwelling in *Eretz Yisrael*
Dwelling in *Eretz Yisrael* .... Gittin 8b; Kesubos 110b-111a; Arachin 3a-3b
Dwelling in *Eretz Yisrael*, buying house on Shabbos .... Bava Kama 80b; Gittin 8b
Dwelling in *Eretz Yisrael*, dwelling quarters .... Kesubos 110b-111a; Arachin 3a-3b
Dwelling in *Eretz Yisrael*, in present times .... Shabbos 41a; Berachos 24b; Kesubos 110b-111a
Dwelling in *Eretz Yisrael*, longevity .... Berachos 8a
Dwelling place
Dwelling place, behavior .... Pesachim 114a
Dwelling place, changing .... Kesubos 28a; Bava Metzia 75b
Dwelling place for righteous in World to Come .... Shabbos 152a; Bava Metzia 83b
Dwelling place .... *see also* **City**, page 108
Dwelling place, temporary, succah .... Succah 7b, 21b
Dwelling places of non-Jews, impurity .... Oholos 18:7-10; Pesachim 9a
Dye of garment, components .... Bava Kama 101a-101b
Dyeing with *orlah* fruit peels .... Pesachim 22b; Kiddushin 56b; Bava Kama 101a
Dying
Dying animal, signs of twitching .... Avodah Zarah 16b; Chullin 37a, 37b-38b
Dying animal, slaughtering permitted .... Chullin 37a-37b
Dying animal, Ezekiel's stringencies .... Chullin 37b, 44b
Dying man
Dying man, confession .... Shabbos 32a; Sanhedrin 43b
Dying man, endowment valuation and damage .... Arachin 6b
Dying man, examining .... Yoma 85a
Dying man, impurity .... Oholos 1:6
Dying man, majority will die .... Gittin 28a; Kiddushin 71b; Shevuos 33a, 37b; Arachin 18a
Dying man, murderer .... Sanhedrin 78a
Dying man, touching him .... Shabbos 151b

E

Eagle

Eagle, goat bringing forth...Bava Basra 16a

Eagle, king of birds...Chagigah 13b

Eagle, Israel's sin...Kiddushin 70a

Ear

Ear is burned first...Kesubos 5b

Ear like a funnel, *aggadah*...Chullin 89a; Chagigah 3b

Ear lobe is soft...Kesubos 5b

Ears, blocking with pumpkins...Gittin 34a

Early coming to house of study, destruction of enemy...Gittin 7a

Earth

Earth...*see also* **Dust**, page 183

Earth, danger of eating earth...Shabbos 113b

Earth, vow to eat...Shevuos 24a-24b

Earthquake

Earthquake, blessing...Berachos 59a

Earthquake, G-d's pain...Berachos 59a

East

East is illuminated, time of daily offering...Yoma 28a-28b; Menachos 100a

East, *panim*...Yoma 55a; Menachos 27b

East, *Shemoneh Esrei*...Berachos 30a; Bava Basra 25a, 25b

Easily cooked foods...Shabbos 145b

Easy to lose like glass...Chagigah 15a

Eat...*see also* **Meal**, page 395

   Behavior —

   Eat onion etc..Pesachim 114a

   Eating, commandment to keep one's health...Taanis 11b

   Eating, cure for ravenous hunger...Yoma 83b

   Eating during journey...Taanis 10b-11a

   Eating in street, testimony...Kiddushin 40b

   Eating, not to speak while eating...Taanis 5b

   Eating, two hearts...Bava Basra 12b

   Eating, walking and relieving oneself...Shabbos 41a, 82a

   Eating when still hungry...Berachos 62b

Eating while standing, weakness..Gittin 70a
Eating without walking..Bava Metzia 113b

Prohibitions —
Eating a *pras*, interruption...Krisos 12b-13a
Eating after *afikoman*..Pesachim 119b-120a
Eating before examining a *treifah*...Beitzah 25a-25b
Eating before *havdala*..Pesachim 100b, 105a
Eating before performing commandment......................Succah 38a; Shabbos 9b
Eating before prayers................Berachos 10b, 28b; Shabbos 9b-10a; Succah 38a
Eating during fast..Berachos 14a
Eating during fast, ate by mistake...Taanis 10b
Eating hardly edible food, carrying out on Shabbos.......................Shabbos 76a
Eating, inappropriate, oath..Shevuos 23b-24b
Eating more than one's appetite or a planted fruit........Yoma 80b; Yevamos 40a
Eating on pesach eve...Pesachim 99b-100a, 107a-108a
Eating on Shabbos eve..Pesachim 99b-100a
Eating on *Tisha B'Av*..Pesachim 54b
Eating, one, sin offerings............Shevuos 24b-25a; Shabbos 102a; Yevamos 34a; Krisos 13b-14a

Rights —
Eating consecrated produce, worker..Meilah 13a
Eating, servant..Kesubos 61a
Eating with one's wife...Kesubos 65b
Eating, worker.............Bava Metzia 87a-87b, 88b-89b, 91b-93a; Maasros 2:7-8

Sacrifice —
Eating burned parts of sacrifices, prohibition..........................Menachos 74a-74b
Eating disqualified sacrifice..................Pesachim 24a; Makos 18a-18b; Meilah 17b
Eating firstborn animal.............Makos 19a-19b; Bechoros 32b-33a; Zevachim 75b, 60b
Eating, impossibility to eat Pesach lamb.........Pesachim 69b, 78b-79a; Zevachim 100b
Eating of Altar, is it considered as eating...................................Chullin 81b

Eating sacrifice
Eating sacrifice, after being satiated........................Temurah 23a; Menachos 21b
Eating sacrifice, atonement...Pesachim 59b
Eating sacrifice, like kings..............Zevachim 28a, 91a; Sotah 15a; Chullin 132b
Eating sacrifices, time..Zevachim 36a
Eating sacrifices in *Heichal*.............................Zevachim 63a; Menachos 8b-9a
Eating sacrificial flesh after burning parts of sacrifice..................Pesachim 59b
Eating sacrificial flesh before throwing blood.........Pesachim 77b; Sanhedrin 63a; Makos 18b
Eating *shalmei tzibur*..Zevachim 97b-98a
Eating, thought about sacrifice..Zevachim 31a-31b

Misc. —
Eat and drink for tomorrow we shall die.....................................Taanis 11a
Eating a lot, Yochanan ben Nerbai.............................Pesachim 57a; Krisos 28a-28b
Eating after giving food to one's animal.....................Berachos 40a; Gittin 62a
Eating, cow eating on back of another.....................Bava Kama 20a, 21b
Eating for cure, blessing..Berachos 36a, 38a
Eating for one's wife, *Koheness*..Chullin 132a
Eating in succah.............................Succah 27a; Eruvin 23a; Yoma 79b
Eating, considered as if putting down on Shabbos........................Shabbos 102a
Eating *matzah* together with bitter herbs...............................Pesachim 115a

Eating on Yom Kippur eve...Yoma 81b; Rosh Hashanah 9a-9b
Eating one's fill, *Bircas HaMazon*...Berachos 49b
Eating *terumah*, service...Pesachim 72b-73a
Eating, usual, tooth...Bava Kama 15b, 19b-20a
Eating volume of meal, interruption..Krisos 12b-13a
Eating a snack
   Eating a snack, becoming liable to tithe....................Terumos 8:3; Beitzah 35a
   Eating a snack in succah..........................Succah 26b-27a; Yoma 79a-79b
   Eating a snack, tithe...Beitzah 13a
   Eating a snack, tree branches in courtyard..........................Maasros 3:8-10
   Eating a snack, until when..Beitzah 13a-13b
   Eating non tithed produce as a snack, gift................................Maasros 2:1-2
Eaves, beams, *chazakah*...Bava Basra 58b-59a
Ebal Mount, curses...Sotah 37b
Ecclesiastes
   Ecclesiastes, impurity to hands...............Megillah 7a; Yadayim 3:5; Eduyos 5:3
   Ecclesiastes, Sages wanted to conceal....................................Shabbos 30b
Echad befeh ve'echad belev..............................*see* **Hypocrisy,** page 290
Echad hamarbeh ve'echad hamamit.......*see* **One who does more and one who does less,** page 460
Echad mechaburah she'mes....................*see* **One of group who dies,** page 460
Echad, reading *Shema*...Berachos 13b
Echo, sound of *Shofar*...Rosh Hashanah 27b-28a
Echol...*see* **Eat,** page 185
Echteh ve'ashuv..............................*see* **Sin, "I shall sin then I shall repent,"** page 626
Eclipses of sun and moon, astronomy...Succah 29a
Ed..*see* **Witness,** page 753
Ed, *bedikas niddah*............................*see* **Cloth, to examine *niddah*,** page 112
Ed echad..*see* **Single witness,** page 629
Eden, no eye has seen..Berachos 34b; Sanhedrin 99a
Edge of ceiling
   Edge of ceiling, mixed species..Eruvin 93a
   Edge of ceiling, partition.................Eruvin 25a-25b, 90b, 94b; Succah 18a-19a
   Edge of ceiling, succah..Succah 18a-19a
Edom..Megillah 6a-6b
Educate child according to his ways...Kiddushin 30a
Education
   Education, according to his ways..Kiddushin 30a
   Education, from when...Succah 42a; Arachin 2b
   Education, hitting...Moed Katan 17a; Makos 8a
   Education, not to show preference to one child..............................Shabbos 10b
   Education, schoolteacher's blows...Bava Basra 21a
   Education, to which commandments...Chagigah 6a
Edus...*see* **Testimony,** page 683
Eduyos, importance for ruling..Kiddushin 54b
Eee avid mahani........................*see* **Effectiveness of forbidden act,** page 187
Eee efshar beli chidush..................*see* **New teaching in study hall,** page 442
Eee efshar.............................*see* **Impossible to act differently, prohibition,** page 300
Eee efshi betakanah.......*see* **Decree, "I do not want to benefit from this decree,"** page 154
Eee lav hai yoma.......................*see* **If not this day, *Shavuos*,** page 296

E

Eee shamayim .... *see* **Decrees of idolaters, demonstration**, page 155
Effectiveness of forbidden act .... Temurah 4b-6b
Effort
   Effort, "I made an effort and I was successful" .... Megillah 6b
   Efforts for food and clothing .... Berachos 58a
Eged .... *see* **Binding four species**, page 57
Eged be'yado .... *see* **Partial raising of item**, page 473
Eged lulav .... *see* **Binding *lulav***, page 57
Egg
  Health —
    Egg, bad spirit .... Niddah 17a
    Egg, cure .... Yoma 18a
    Egg, digested by egg white .... Shabbos 108b
    Egg, health .... Berachos 44b
    Egg in pickled milk, baby .... Yoma 78b
    Egg, shrunk .... Nedarim 50b
    Egg simmered is better .... Shabbos 38a
    Eggs before meal, danger .... Chullin 59a
  Impurity —
    Egg of *naamit* bird, impurity .... Keilim 17:14
    Egg, size for impurity .... Yoma 80a
    Eggs of *neveilah* .... Beitzah 7a; Menachos 70a
    Eggs of reptile, impurity .... Chullin 64a, 126b
  Prohibitions —
    Egg, blood .... Chullin 64b; Krisos 20b
    Egg, boiled, cooking .... Shabbos 38b-39a
    Egg connected to bird, eating .... Menachos 70a
    Egg, from consecrated hen .... Meilah 12b; Temurah 31b
    Egg in milk, connected to bird .... Beitzah 6b-7a
    Egg in pickled milk, ruling in presence of teacher .... Kesubos 60b
    Egg, *kashrus* .... Chullin 63b-65a
    Egg not fertilized .... Beitzah 7a-7b
    Egg on idolatrous tree .... Meilah 13b-14a; Avodah Zarah 42b
    Egg, taste given off .... Chullin 64b, 97b-98a
    Egg, *treifah* .... Eduyos 5:1; Chullin 57b-58a; Temurah 31a
  Shabbos —
    Egg, came out and went back in .... Beitzah 6b-7a
    Egg found in nest .... Beitzah 7a-7b
    Egg in mother's womb .... Beitzah 2b, 6b-7a
    Egg in mustard, filtering .... Shabbos 139b-140a
    Egg, *muktzeh* .... Beitzah 3a-4a; Eruvin 38b
    Egg, reason for *muktzeh* .... Beitzah 2a-3a
    Egg, to use it and its place .... Beitzah 3b, 4a; Shabbos 43a
    Eggs of fish .... Avodah Zarah 39a, 40a-40b; Chullin 63b-64a
    Eggs of lice .... Shabbos 107b; Avodah Zarah 3b
    Eggs of lice, livelihood .... Shabbos 107b; Avodah Zarah 3b
    Egg volume, quantity .... Yoma 78b-79b
    Egg volume, throat .... Yoma 80a

Misc. —

Egg, collecting payment of "horn" damage	Bava Kama 47a
Egg for mourner	Bava Basra 16b
Egg of giant bird	Bechoros 57b
Egg, scientific facts	Beitzah 6b-7b; Temurah 31a; Niddah 39b
Egg, throat	Yoma 80a
Egg, volume	Yoma 79a-79b
Egg, which animals	Bechoros 7b-8a
Eggs in one's courtyard, act of acquisition	Bava Metzia 102a; Chullin 141b-142a

Eglah arufah .... *see* **Calf whose neck is broken**, page 85
Eglon, king of Moab .... Sanhedrin 60a
Egrof .... *see* **Fist, dimension**, page 228
Egypt

Egypt, beauty of Tzoan	Kesubos 112a
Egypt, end of slavery	Rosh Hashanah 11b
Egypt, how many Hebrews left	Sanhedrin 111a
Egypt in chains, appropriate to go to	Shabbos 89b
Egypt, leaving in haste	Berachos 9a
Egypt, miracle of Hebrew children	Sotah 11a-11b
Egypt, miracles of redemption	Avos 5:4
Egypt, prohibition to return there	Succah 51b
Egypt, reward for hospitality	Berachos 63b
Egypt, slavery	Sotah 11a-11b
Egypt, ten plagues	Avos 5:4; Sanhedrin 67b; Pesachim 53a; Bava Kama 80b; Bechoros 41a
Egypt, time of slavery	Eduyos 2:9
Egypt, twelve months	Eduyos 2:10

Egyptian

Egyptian girl of third generation, to *Kohen*	Yevamos 77a-77b
Egyptian woman to Ammonite, lineage	Kiddushin 67b
Egyptians, Gebiha's answers	Sanhedrin 91a
Egyptians, marriage	Yevamos 77b-78a

Ei shamayim .... *see* **Decrees of idolaters, demonstration**, page 155
Eichah

Eichah, burning scroll	Moed Katan 26a
Eichah, commentaries	Sanhedrin 104a-104b

Eifah

Eifah, Pumbedita's sharp ones	Sanhedrin 17b
Eifah, tested Avimi	Shevuos 28b-29a

Eifah .... *see* **Ephah, quantity**, page 197
Eigel hazahav .... *see* **Golden calf**, page 254
Eight

Age —

Eight days for circumcision, reason	Niddah 31b
Eight days, sacrifice	Parah 1:4
Eight days, slaughter	Shabbos 136a
Eight months old, *neveilah*	Chullin 74a
Eight months old, stillborn	Yevamos 80a-80b
Eight months, stillborn baby	Yevamos 80a-80b
Eight years old, age to beget children	Sanhedrin 69b

Misc. —

Eight mothers, examining .... Kiddushin 76a-76b
Eight princes, righteous .... Succah 52b
Eight reptiles, injuring on Shabbos .... Shabbos 107a-107b
Eight reptiles, skin .... Shabbos 107a-107b; Chullin 122b
Eight sections .... Gittin 60a-60b

Eight last verses

Eight last verses, Moses' death .... Bava Basra 15a; Menachos 30a; Makos 11a
Eight last verses, reading .... Menachos 30a; Bava Basra 15a
Eight last verses, Joshua .... Makos 11a

Eighteen

Eighteen decrees .... Shabbos 15a, 153b
Eighteen thousand rows of righteous surrounding G-d .... Succah 45b; Sanhedrin 97b
Eighteen thousand worlds .... Avodah Zarah 3b

Eighth of eight, arrogance .... Sotah 5a
Eighty years, elderly .... Moed Katan 28a
Eimah bebeiso .... *see* **Fear in one's household,** page 218
Eimasay, lefaresh .... *see* **When, comes to explain,** page 741
Ein adam dar im nachash .... *see* **Man cannot live together with snake,** page 388
Ein adam choteh velo lo .... *see* **Man does not sin for someone else's benefit,** page 387
Ein ani ela bedaas .... *see* **Poor, in intelligence,** page 494
Ein anius bimkom ashirus .... *see* **Poverty, not found in place of wealth,** page 496
Ein apotropus le'arayios .... *see* **There is no guardian against immorality,** page 685
Ein aror pachos shenayim .... *see* **Appeal, two witnesses,** page 30
Ein baal haness makir .... *see* **Miracle, one who experiences it is not aware,** page 413
Ein berachah ela bizechus ishto .... *see* **Blessing, only because of wife,** page 63
Ein beriyah yecholah laamod bemechitzasan .. *see* **Creature cannot stand next to them,** page 133
Ein bo mamash .... *see* **Tangible item, vow and oath,** page 672
Ein bur yerei chet .... *see* **Boor, not sin fearing,** page 72
Ein chadash .... *see* **Nothing new, messianic times,** page 450
Ein chavin laadam .... *see* **Legal transfer of rights in man's absence,** page 363
Ein chavush motzi atzmo .... *see* **Prisoner cannot free himself from prison,** page 504
Ein chochmah le'ishah ela bapelech .... *see* **Wisdom of women, in their spindle,** page 753
Ein darkan lehisbonen .... *see* **Attention when walking, damage,** page 35
Ein davar sheein lo makom .... *see* **Item which has no place,** page 319
Ein dochin nefesh .... *see* **Pregnant woman, pursuer,** page 501
Ein dor yasom… .... *see* **Generation, orphan, Rabbi Elazar ben Azariah,** page 248
Ein esek benistaros .... *see* **Hidden things, not to learn,** page 278
Ein gozrim al hatsibur .... *see* **Decree that public cannot accept,** page 154
Ein habor mismaleh mechulyaso .... *see* **Pit is not filled from its earth,** page 490
Ein hadaas sovlasan .... *see* **Mind cannot tolerate,** page 411
Ein hakometz masbiya ari .... *see* **Handful does not satiate lion,** page 268
Ein hapargod ninal .... *see* **Curtain, sin of idolatry,** page 136
Ein hashoel reshai lehashil .... *see* **Borrower, prohibition to lend borrowed item,** page 73
Ein hekesh lemachatzeh .... *see* **Analogy, all laws included,** page 22
Ein holkhin bemamon achar harov .... *see* **Money matters, majority,** page 421
Ein ishah ela leyofi .... *see* **Woman's purpose is etc.,** page 755
Ein ishah koreses bris .... *see* **Woman makes covenant,** page 757
Ein kategor naaseh sanegor .... *see* **Accuser cannot become defender,** page 6

E

Ein kishuy ela ledaas .... *see* Erection is always voluntary, page 198

Ein lah vesses .... *see* Woman having no menses, page 757

Ein lahem shiur .... *see* Measure, things which have no, page 398

Ein lanu lehishaen ela al Hashem .... *see* Father in Heaven, relying upon, page 217

Ein Lashem ela halacha .... *see* G-d only has four cubits of *halacha*, page 245

Ein lechah ben chorin .... *see* Free man, only by studying Torah, page 239

Ein lechah ela shofet shebeyamecha .... *see* Judge, only those of your generation, page 328

Ein ledayan ela she'einav ro'os .... *see* Judge, what he can see, page 328

Ein lemeidin mehaklalus .... *see Kol*, exhaustive list, page 348

Ein li ela Torah .... *see* Torah, I have only, page 696

Ein lo banim .... *see* Childless person, considered as dead, page 104

Ein lo tov'im .... *see* Money, without claimants, page 421

Ein maavirin al hamitzvos .... *see* Passing by commandments, zeal, page 475

Ein maavirin al haochlin .... *see* Food, not to pass by, page 232

Ein machzikin ovrei aveirah .... *see* Helping sinner, page 276

Ein mafsikin befuranus .... *see* Interrupting, during Torah reading of punishment, page 315

Ein makifin bechilul Hashem .... *see* Desecration of G-d's Name, punishment, page 161

Ein makir beniso .... *see* Miracle, one who experiences it is not aware, page 413

Ein malchus nogaas bechevratah .... *see* Kingdom does not encroach upon another, page 341

Ein mashgichin bevas kol .... *see* Divine voice, page 169

Ein maspidim harugei malchus .... *see* Eulogy, men put to death by government, page 203

Ein mayim ela Torah .... *see* Water, refers to Torah, page 734

Ein mazhirim mehadin .... *see* Deduction, prohibition from "all the more so," page 156

Ein mazkirin maasei nisim .... *see* Miracle, not to rule on a law, page 413

Ein me'arvin simchah besimchah .... *see* Rejoicing, not to mix one with another, page 555

Ein meratzin beshaas kaas .... *see* Appeasing, not when man is angry, page 30

Ein meshivim achar maaseh .... *see* Challenge, one does not challenge after the fact, page 93

Ein mesichin baseudah .... *see* Eating, not to speak while eating, page 185;
                                        see also Talking while eating, page 671

Ein mevatlim isur .... *see* Mixing forbidden food to permit it, page 417

Ein meviim re'ayah mishotim .... *see* Proof, not brought from fools (Cleopatra), page 506

Ein meviin terumah lipsul .... *see* Causing invalidity, *terumah*, page 90

Ein mezarzin ela limezurazin .... *see* Encouraging those who..., page 196

Ein mikra yotzeh mipshuto .... *see* Verse does not lose its simple meaning, page 722

Ein mispalelin al rov tovah .... *see* Prayer to stop abundance, page 498

Ein moach bekadkodo .... *see* Brain, "he has no brain in his skull," page 74

Ein morim ken .... *see* Rule, we do not rule this way, page 574

Ein mukdam umeuchar baTorah .... *see* Before, there is no "before" or "after" in the Torah, page 48

Ein oneshim min hadin .... *see* Punishment, not from "all the more so" deduction, page 510

Ein osher veoni mehaumanus .... *see* Work does not enrich nor impoverish, page 761

Ein pachos... .... *see* No less than etc., no more than etc., page 447

Ein puranos ela me'amei haaretz ... *see* Punishment comes to world because of ignoramus, page 510

Ein reshus leharher .... *see* Prohibition to criticize commandments, page 505

Ein retzoni sheyehei pikdoni ..*see* Collateral, I do not want my collateral be kept by another, page 114

Ein roeh nega atzmo .... *see* Leprous marks, one does not see one's own, page 364

Ein ruach chachamim nochah .... *see* Sages are not pleased with him, page 584

Ein safek motzi mivadai .... *see* Doubt does not override certainty, page 178

Ein shaas hadechak re'ayiah .... *see* Emergency case, no proof, page 195

Ein shaliach lidvar aveirah .... *see* Agent, no agent for sin, page 14

Ein shney neviim besignon echad .... see **Prophets, two using same words**, page 507

Ein simchah ela bemakom seudah .... *see* **Happiness, only by feast**, page 269

Ein somkhim al haness .... see **Relying, not to rely on miracles**, page 556

Ein tinok .... see **Baby, eating wheat**, page 39

Ein tzadik baaretz .... *see* **Righteous man without sin, there is no**, page 569

Ein tzadik niftar .... *see* **Birth of righteous, when another is dead**, page 59

Ein zeh yelud ishah .... see **He is not a human being but an angel**, page 273

Ein, deduction from *yud* .... Kiddushin 4a

Einah lischirus ela basof .... see **Rent, paid at the end**, page 558

Einah tzrichah legufah .... *see* **Necessary for itself, not**, page 439

Eini dar ela bimkom Torah .... see **Dwelling only in a place of Torah**, page 183

Eini melamed ela Torah .... see **Teaching my son only Torah**, page 673

Eini nizones ve'eini osah .... see **Support, "I do not want to be supported,"** page 664

Eini yode'a .... see **I do not know**, page 291

Einin alefin .... see *Aleph, ayin*, page 18

Eino birshuso .... see **Belongings, possibility to consecrate**, page 51

Eino domeh misbayesh me'atzmo .... see **Embarrassed by others**, page 194

Eino min hayishuv .... see **Coarse man, uncivilized**, page 112

Eino miskavein .... *see* **Unintentionally**, page 715

Eirev rav .... see **Amalgam of nations, do not have compassion**, page 20

Eis laasos Lashem .... see **"Time to act," from beginning to end**, page 692

Eishel Avraham .... *see* **Inn, Abraham**, page 310

Eishes chaver .... see **Wife of scholar**, page 747

Eishes ish .... see **Woman guilty of forbidden relations**, page 758

Either/or

   Either/or, impurity .... Shevuos 19a-19b; Taharos 5:3-6; Niddah 60a; Kesubos 27a

   Either/or, money matters .... Yevamos 37b

   Either/or, sacrifice .... Krisos 19a, 22b-23a; Shevuos 18b; Horayos 5a

   Either/or, twilight .... Krisos 19b

Eivas goy .... see **Loathing, idolater**, page 376

Eizehu mekoman shel zevachim .... see **Place of sacrifices**, page 491

Eizehu .... see **Who is**, page 742

El

   El emes dayan, mourner's blessing .... Berachos 46b

   El Melech Ne'eman, Amen .... Shabbos 119b; Sanhedrin 111a

Ela, *tnai o chutz* (condition or exception) .... Avodah Zarah 18a-18b

Elaha DeMeir Aneni .... Avodah Zarah 18a-18b

Elazar ben Durdaya .... Avodah Zarah 17a

Elazar from Birtha, dowry .... Taanis 24a

Elazar, his wife's lineage .... Sotah 43a; Bava Basra 109b-110a; Sanhedrin 82b

Eldad and Medad .... Sanhedrin 17a

Elder

   Elder already ruled, episode .... Shabbos 51a; Sanhedrin 24a, 29b

   Elder and sitting in *yeshivah*, Patriarchs .... Yoma 28b

   Elder, fit for *yeshivah* .... Chagigah 14a

   Elder, rebellious, death .... Sanhedrin 89a

   Elder, rebellious, forgiving .... Sanhedrin 88b; Sotah 25a

   Elder ruled .... Shabbos 51a; Yevamos 105b; Sanhedrin 24a, 29b

   Elder sitting in *yeshivah* .... Yoma 78a

Elder who forgot his learning..Berachos 8b
Elders, episodes about Sages...Shabbos 152a; Megillah 28a
Elders of Nizonia, discourse..Kiddushin 25a
Elders of Nizonia, Rav Hamnuna...Kiddushin 25a
Elders of Pumbedisa, Heavenly Chariot...Chagigah 13a
Elders of the South...........................Zevachim 22b-23a Yevamos 45a Chullin 132b
Elders, Rebbi's maidservant...Shabbos 152a
Eldest brother, levirate marriage.................Yevamos 24a, 39a-39b; Beitzah 37a
Elephant
Elephant, act of acquisition...Kiddushin 25b-26a
Elephant, blessing..Berachos 58b
Elephant having swallowed basket.......................Menachos 69a-69b; Bava Basra 22a
Elephant in hole of needle...Bava Metzia 38b
Elevated matters...Berachos 6b
Eli lamah azavtani...................................*see* **G-d, why did You forsake me**, page 246
Eli
Eli, curse on his sons..Yevamos 105a; Rosh Hashanah 18a
Eli's sons, protests in Temple Courtyard...Pesachim 57a
Eliab, angry at David...Pesachim 66b
Eliezer
Eliezer and Rebecca, Divination..Chullin 95b
Eliezer, drawing and giving to drink...Yoma 28b
Eliezer, episode with Rebecca..Taanis 4a; Sanhedrin 95a
Eliezer, Machpelah Cave..Bava Basra 58a
Eliezer Zeira, black shoes..Bava Kama 59a-59b
Elijah
  Prophets' deeds —
  Elijah, angry..Sanhedrin 113a-113b
  Elijah, death..Moed Katan 26a
  Elijah, meat from Ahab...Chullin 5a; Sanhedrin 113a
  Elijah, Mount Carmel...Berachos 6b, 9b
  Elijah, ravens...Chullin 5a
  Elijah, served Patriarchs..Bava Metzia 85b
  Elijah spoke harshly to G-d..Berachos 31b
  Elijah, withholding rain...Sanhedrin 113a
  Sages' deeds —
  Elijah closed gatehouse...Bava Basra 7b
  Elijah, cured from snake bite..Shabbos 109b
  Elijah, higher than ten handbreadths..Succah 5a
  Elijah, leaves from Gan Eden...Bava Metzia 114b
  Elijah, lion devoured man...Makos 11a
  Elijah, men destined for World to Come.................................Taanis 22a
  Elijah, Rabbah bar Avua...Bava Metzia 114b
  Elijah Rabbah, Elijah Zuta...Kesubos 106a
  Elijah, Rabbi Chiya's prayer...Bava Metzia 85b
  Elijah, Rabbi Yehoshua ben Levi..Sanhedrin 98a
  Elijah, Rabbi Yose's ruin...Berachos 3a
  Elijah rules like Shmuel...Kiddushin 72b
  Elijah saved Rav Kahana..Kiddushin 40a

Elijah, servant's food .... Kesubos 61a
Elijah, sins committed on Yom Kippur .... Yoma 19b-20a
Misc. —
Elijah, flying .... Berachos 4b
Elijah, four craftsmen .... Succah 52b
Elijah, princes of mankind .... Succah 52b
Elijah still living .... Bava Basra 121b
Elijah the Prophet, redemption .... Eduyos 8:7; Eruvin 43b; Kiddushin 71a; Pesachim 13a
Elijah will explain it .... Menachos 45a
Elil .... *see* **Idol**, page 292
Elimelech
Elimelech did not pray for his generation .... Bava Basra 91b
Elimelech left *Eretz Yisrael* .... Bava Basra 91a, 91b
Elimelech, son of Nachshon .... Bava Basra 91a
Elimelech went out of *Eretz Yisrael* .... Bava Basra 91a
Elisha
Elisha, bears .... Sotah 46b-47a
Elisha, bird wings in his hands .... Shabbos 49a, 130a
Elisha, disciples .... Kesubos 106a
Elisha, iron axe floated .... Sotah 13a
Elisha, Naaman .... Sanhedrin 107b
Elisha, resurrection .... Chullin 7b
Elisha, Shunamite woman .... Berachos 10b
Elisha the prophet, Elijah's death .... Moed Katan 26a
Elisha ben Abuyah
Elisha ben Abuyah .... Chagigah 15a-15b; Chullin 142a
Elisha ben Abuyah, Pardes .... Chagigah 14b
Elisheba .... Zevachim 102a
Elkanah .... Megillah 14a
Elohai
Elohai ad shelo notzarti .... Yoma 87b; Berachos 17a
Elohai neshamah .... Berachos 60b
Elohai netzor .... Berachos 17a
Elohei Abraham, "I shall make you a great people" .... Pesachim 117b
Eloheihem soneh zimmah .... *see* **G-d, their G-d hates immorality**, page 245
Eloheinu Vehohei Avoseinu .... Berachos 30a
Elohim, Attribute of Judgment .... Berachos 60b
Elu ve'elu divrei Elohim chaim .... *see* **These and those are words of the living G-d**, page 686
Elul male vechaser (full and missing) .... Rosh Hashanah 19b, 20b, 32a; Beitzah 6a, 22b
Elyonim lematah... .... *see* **"Great ones are down and small ones are up,"** page 257
Elyono shel zav .... *see* **Upper blanket of *zav*, impurity**, page 716
Em lemikra velimasores .... *see* **Pronunciation or written text, which determines**, page 506
Embarrassed
Embarrassed by others .... Taanis 15b-16a; Sanhedrin 42a
Embarrassed, value .... Nedarim 20a; Yevamos 79a
Embellishment of commandment .... Shabbos 133b; Succah 11b; Nazir 2b
Ember
Ember, carrying out on Shabbos .... Beitzah 39a
Ember, damage to slave .... Bava Kama 27a

Ember given to deaf-mute, demented and minor .... Bava Kama 9b, 22b, 59b-60a
Ember like fire .... Beitzah 39a; Pesachim 75a-75b; Chullin 8a
Ember which fell from Altar .... Zevachim 108b
Embers for incense .... Yoma 44b; Tamid 29a, 32b-33a, 5:5; Pesachim 75b; Zevachim 58a-58b
Embers of destruction, Gabriel .... Yoma 77a
Embers of *retama*, episode .... Bava Basra 74b
Embers of *retama*, for who stops learning .... Avodah Zarah 3b; Chagigah 12b
Embers of Sages .... Avos 2:10
Embers, raking on Shabbos .... Krisos 20a-20b
Embossing around letter .... Gittin 20a-20b
Embracing idol .... Sanhedrin 63a
Embroidery in garment, annulled in mixture .... Temurah 34a
Embryo .... *see* **Fetus** page 220
Emergency case
Emergency case, no proof .... Niddah 9b
Emergency case, ruling leniently .... Berachos 9a; Shabbos 45a; Gittin 19a; Niddah 6a
Emes Veyatziv, to link .... Berachos 14a-14b
Emetic on Shabbos .... Shabbos 123a-123b, 147a
Emigration of Ezra
Emigration of Ezra, dependence on Persia .... Berachos 4a; Sotah 36a; Sanhedrin 98b
Emigration of Ezra, *Leviim* .... Yevamos 86b
Emigration of Ezra, sacrifices .... Horayos 6a; Temurah 15b
Emigration of Ezra, sanctification .... Arachin 32b; Megillah 10a-10b; Shevuos 16a
Emigration of Ezra, when .... Arachin 13a; Rosh Hashanah 3b
Emigration of Ezra, who participated .... Horayos 6a
Emigration to *Eretz Yisrael*
Emigration to *Eretz Yisrael*, episodes .... Kesubos 112a-112b
Emigration to *Eretz Yisrael* in present times .... Shabbos 41a; Berachos 24b; Kesubos 110b-111a; Arachin 3a-3b
Emigration to *Eretz Yisrael*, Rabbi Abba .... Berachos 24b
Emigration to *Eretz Yisrael*, Rabbi Zeira .... Shabbos 41a
Emor me'at vaaseh harbeh .... *see* **Say little and do much,** page 584
Emorite ways
Emorite ways .... Shabbos 67a-67b; Chullin 77b-78a
Emorite ways, burning .... Avodah Zarah 11a-11b
Emperor
Emperor and Onkelos .... Avodah Zarah 11a
Emperor and Shvor Malka .... Shevuos 6b
Emperor, dream .... Berachos 56a-56b
Emperor, his daughter ruined his wine .... Nedarim 50b; Taanis 7a-7b
Emperor, lion Debei Ilai .... Chullin 59b
Emperor, Nahum Ish Gam Zu .... Taanis 21a; Sanhedrin 108b-109a
Emperor, Rabbi Tanchum .... Sanhedrin 39a
Emperor, Rabbi Yehoshua .... Chullin 59b-60a
Emperor, Rabbi Yehoshua's allusions .... Chagigah 5b
Emperor, Sages of Athens .... Bechoros 8b-9a
Emperor, spice of Shabbos .... Shabbos 119a
Emperor's daughter, spindle .... Chullin 60a
Emperor's daughter, wine in gold containers .... Nedarim 50b; Taanis 7a-7b

Employees by day
"Employees by day, we are"..Eruvin 65a
Employees by day, incident..Taanis 23a
Employing workers, loss..Bava Metzia 29b-30a
Empty ones, full of commandments like pomegranate...Sanhedrin 37a; Berachos 57a; Eruvin 19a;
....Megillah 6a; Chagigah 27a

Empty land
Empty land added to city...Eruvin 57a-57b
Empty land and *karmelis*, between them..Eruvin 67b
Empty land breached on courtyard...Eruvin 25b
Empty land, definition..Eruvin 23a-23b, 26a
Empty land, domain..Eruvin 67b; Shabbos 7a
Empty land, fenced as a dwelling..Eruvin 26a
Empty land, flooded...Eruvin 24a-24b
Empty land, less than two *seah*..Eruvin 25a
Empty land, new partition...Eruvin 24a
Empty land, planted or sown...Eruvin 23b-24a; Bava Basra 24b
Empty land, roofed...Eruvin 25a-25b
Empty land, tree..Eruvin 15a, 99b-100a; Succah 24b-25a
Emunah..*see* **Faith,** page 213
Emurin...*see* **Burnt parts of sacrifices,** page 81
Encircling
Encircling Altar, service...Zevachim 64a-64b; Succah 48b
Encircling Temple Mount..Middos 2:2
Encompassed History..Bava Basra 121b
Encounter, deaf-mute, demented and minon, better not to, bad result...........Bava Kama 87a
Encouragement, four things...Berachos 32b
Encouraging
Encouraging non-Jew on Sabbatical year...Gittin 62a
Encouraging those who...Makos 23a
End
End because of beginning..Nedarim 72a
End, in the end honor will come...Nedarim 62a
End of blessing, for which blessings..................Berachos 11a, 46a; Pesachim 104b-105a; Kesubos 7b
End of blessing, how...Berachos 49a; Pesachim 104a
End of day, *eruv*...Eruvin 36a-36b, 38b
End of intimate relations...Yevamos 55b-56a
End of man is death...Berachos 17a
End of Mishnah, added because of beginning...................Zevachim 91b; Eruvin 16a; Yevamos 102a;
....Nedarim 28b, 72a
End of Mishnah, Rebbi and Rabbi Nassan..Bava Metzia 86a
End of ruling, Rav Ashi and Ravina...Bava Metzia 86a
End of Shabbos, meal...Shabbos 119b
End of Shabbos, work..Pesachim 50b
End of summer hotter than summer..Yoma 28b-29a
End of Torah, last eight verses................................Bava Basra 15a; Menachos 30a; Makos 11a
End of Torah, three years...Megillah 29b
End proves
End proves, divorce certificate...Gittin 66a, 65b

End proves intention..Chullin 39b
End proves, protested..Bava Basra 138a
Ending with praise and prayer..Berachos 31a
Endowment...*see* **Donation**, page 174
Enemies
Enemies fall, do not rejoice..Megillah 16a
Enemies, women, trustworthiness for divorce certificate ....Gittin 23b-24a, 62b
Enemy, advice and fall...Gittin 7a; Megillah 16a
Enemy destroyed, coming early to house of study........................Gittin 7a
Enemy, donkey crouched..................................Pesachim 113b; Bava Metzia 32b
Enemy, enemy's fall...Megillah 16a
Enemy, exile and death...Makos 6b, 9b
Enemy, judge...Kesubos 105b
Enemy, paid back in one payment ....Avodah Zarah 4a
Enemy, testimony..Sanhedrin 29a
Enemy's kisses, Balaam's blessing...Sanhedrin 105b
Enforcement, coercing by *beis din*.....................................Bava Basra 34b
Engraved
Engraved and established, *mikveh*............Bava Basra 65b-66b; Bava Kama 67a; Parah 5:7
Engraving around letter...Gittin 20a-20b
Enhancement of commandment...............Shabbos 133b; Succah 11b; Nazir 2b
Enlarging mind..Berachos 57b
Enlighten
Enlighten my eyes..Berachos 28b
Enlightening one's teacher, ways to acquire Torah........................Avos 6:6
Entering
Entering body, benefit...Berachos 57b
Entering house suddenly............................Niddah 16b; Pesachim 112a
Entering in *Eretz Yisrael*, how...Sotah 33b
Entering in Holy of Holies to perform repairs................Pesachim 26a; Middos 4:5
Entering in unusual way, house afflicted with leprosy...................Shevuos 17b
Entering partly in Temple..............................Zevachim 32a; Yoma 31a
Entering Temple and *Heichal*......................Menachos 27b; Keilim 1:8-9
Entering Temple, shoes................................Shabbos 66b; Chagigah 4b
Ephah, quantity..Menachos 77a
Ephod..Sotah 36a-36b
Ephraim and Menashe, number of tribes.................................Horayos 6b
Ephron, Machpelah Cave...Bava Metzia 87a
Epileptic
Epileptic, blemishes of women..Kesubos 76b-77a
Epileptic, naked in front of lamp..Pesachim 112b
Epileptics, modesty during intimate relations...........................Pesachim 112b
Episode
Episode about pious man..........................Temurah 15b; Bava Kama 103b
Episode of Tamar...............................Sotah 10a-10b; Makos 23b; Megillah 10b
Episode of Zimri..Sanhedrin 82a-82b
Episode which happened was thus.... Kesubos 7a, 27a; Eruvin 65b; Rosh Hashanah 14b; Kiddushin 76a;
                                                                 Bava Basra 155b; Avodah Zarah 38a
Episodes of history.............................Avodah Zarah 8b-9a; Shabbos 15a

Epoch of Messiah .... Kesubos 112b; Sanhedrin 97a, 98a-98b
Equipment of chariot, impurity .... Keilim 14:4-5
Er and Onan .... Yevamos 34b
Erased
  Erased legal document, copy .... Bava Basra 168a-169b
  Erased space in document, how to avoid forging .... Bava Basra 163b-164a
  Erasing Amalek .... Megillah 7a; Bava Basra 21a-21b
  Erasing on Shabbos .... Shabbos 75b
  Erasing Divine Names
    Erasing Divine Names, legal document .... Rosh Hashanah 18b
    Erasing Divine Names, source .... Sanhedrin 56a; Makos 22a
    Erasing Divine Names, washing oneself .... Shabbos 120b; Yoma 8a, 28a
    Erasing Divine Names, which Names .... Shevuos 35a-35b
Erech af, blessing .... Berachos 57b
Erech .... see **Donation valuation**, page 174
Erect standing .... Kiddushin 31a; Berachos 43b; Sanhedrin 81a
Erection is always voluntary .... Yevamos 53b
Eretz Shinar, eulogy .... Moed Katan 25b
Eretz Tzvi .... Kesubos 112a
Eretz Yisrael
  Aggadah —
    Eretz Yisrael, curse on festivals .... Shabbos 145b
    Eretz Yisrael, deer skin .... Gittin 57a
    Eretz Yisrael, deserted .... Yoma 54a; Shabbos 145b
    Eretz Yisrael, destined to World to Come .... Pesachim 113a
    Eretz Yisrael, high .... Kiddushin 69a-69b; Sanhedrin 87a; Zevachim 54b
    Eretz Yisrael, redemption .... Kesubos 75a
    Eretz Yisrael, rivers and seas .... Bava Basra 74b
    Eretz Yisrael, suffering .... Berachos 5a
  Commandment to dwell —
    Eretz Yisrael, buying house .... Bava Kama 80b; Gittin 8b
    Eretz Yisrael, buying house on Shabbos .... Gittin 8b
    Eretz Yisrael, Canaanite slave .... Kesubos 110b
    Eretz Yisrael, dwelling in present times .... Shabbos 41a; Kesubos 110b-111a
    Eretz Yisrael, House .... Kesubos 110b; Arachin 3a-3b; Shabbos 41a; Berachos 24b
    Eretz Yisrael, longevity .... Berachos 8a
    Eretz Yisrael, married woman living in .... Kesubos 110b; Gittin 44b; Arachin 3a-3b
  Generation of desert —
    Eretz Yisrael, from when it belongs to Jews .... Bava Basra 119a-119b
    Eretz Yisrael, how to enter .... Sotah 33b
    Eretz Yisrael, Moses .... Sotah 14a
  Misc. —
    Eretz Yisrael and Babylon, hate .... Yoma 66b; Menachos 100a
    Eretz Yisrael, borders .... Gittin 7b-8a; Bechoros 55a
    Eretz Yisrael, burial .... Kesubos 111a
    Eretz Yisrael, holiness .... Keilim 1:6-8
    Eretz Yisrael, lineage .... Kiddushin 69b, 71a-71b; Kesubos 111a
    Eretz Yisrael, Rabbi Elazar's joy .... Kesubos 112a
    Eretz Yisrael, rain .... Taanis 10a

E

***Eretz Yisrael*, purity**

Eretz Yisrael, purity after flood...Zevachim 113a
Eretz Yisrael, purity by pretext..Kesubos 20b; Nazir 65b
Eretz Yisrael, purity of towns..Oholos 18:9

Erev Pesach...*see* **Eve of Pesach**, page 203
Erev Shabbos...*see* **Eve of Shabbos**, page 203
Erroneous purchase, expenses...Kesubos 91b-92a
Erusin...*see* **Betrothal**, page 55
Eruv

Eruv......................*see also* **Annulment of ownership**, page 28; **Renting domain for Shabbos**, page 558
Eruv, by air...Eruvin 85a-85b, 88a
Eruv, carrying out on Yom Kippur...Krisos 14a; Yoma 66b
Eruv, carrying out on Yom Tov...Beitzah 12a
Eruv, damaged on Shabbos..Eruvin 17a, 93b-94a
Eruv, for closed alley..Eruvin 85b; Succah 3b
Eruv partnership, courtyard permitted....................................Eruvin 73a-73b, 71b-72a
Eruv partnership, open courtyards...Eruvin 73b
Eruv, platform between two courtyards..Eruvin 77b
Eruv, rights in rented house...Eruvin 86a
Eruv, separation with *dakah*...Eruvin 59b
Eruv, shared house...Eruvin 72a-72b

Eruv chatzeiros

How —

Eruv chatzeiros, act of acquisition from baker...Eruvin 81a-81b
Eruv chatzeiros, collecting..Eruvin 31b, 49b
Eruv chatzeiros, how...Eruvin 49a-49b
Eruv chatzeiros, husband's consent...Eruvin 80a
Eruv chatzeiros, invalidated by person refusing to share it.........................Eruvin 49a, 68a
Eruv chatzeiros, legal transfer of benefits...............Eruvin 73b, 79b; Nedarim 88b; Gittin 64b
Eruv chatzeiros, owner's consent............................Eruvin 46b, 80b, 81b, 81b-82a, 95a
Eruv chatzeiros, place............................Eruvin 75b-76a, 85b; Succah 3b; Gittin 60b

With which item —

Eruv chatzeiros, bread for blessing...Berachos 39b
Eruv chatzeiros, dimension...Eruvin 80b
Eruv chatzeiros, forbidden food..Eruvin 30a-30b
Eruv chatzeiros, shared wine...Eruvin 71b
Eruv chatzeiros, two drinks...Eruvin 71a-71b, 73b
Eruv chatzeiros, two utensils...Eruvin 48b, 49a
Eruv chatzeiros, with which item..............................Eruvin 26b, 80b; Kiddushin 34a

Misc. —

Eruv chatzeiros, division of city *chatzeiros*...Eruvin 59b
Eruv chatzeiros, dusk...Shabbos 34a
Eruv chatzeiros, episode about refraining..Eruvin 68a
Eruv chatzeiros, from one courtyard to another...............Eruvin 48a-49a, 46b, 71a, 72b, 73a
Eruv chatzeiros, leaving part of town without..Eruvin 59a-60a
Eruv chatzeiros, leniencies during war...Eruvin 17a-17b
Eruv chatzeiros, reason for effectiveness...Eruvin 49a-49b
Eruv chatzeiros, Yom Tov...................................Eruvin 38a-39a; Beitzah 16b-17a
Eruv, passageway between courtyards...................................Eruvin 59b, 65b, 75a-75b

E

Eruv tavshilin

Eruv tavshilin, cooked unlawfully...Beitzah 17a-17b
Eruv tavshilin, did not make ....Beitzah 17a-17b
Eruv tavshilin, how to make ....Beitzah 16a-16b
Eruv tavshilin, keeping food warm ....Beitzah 22a
Eruv tavshilin, legal transfer of benefits....................Eruvin 80a; Beitzah 15b, 16b, 21b-22a
Eruv tavshilin, quantity...Beitzah 17b
Eruv tavshilin, was eaten ....Beitzah 17b
Eruv tavshilin, when ....Beitzah 6a, 17a

Eruv techumin

Disqualified —

Eruv techumin, camel driver...Eruvin 35a, 52b
Eruv techumin, disqualified ....Eruvin 35a-35b
Eruv techumin, doubt..Shabbos 34a; Eruvin 35b-36a
Eruv techumin, dusk...Shabbos 34a
Eruv techumin, end of day ....Eruvin 36a-36b, 38b
Eruv techumin, in town ....Eruvin 61a-61b
Eruv techumin, lost key ....Eruvin 34b-35a
Eruv techumin, out of populated area ....Eruvin 33b-34a
Eruv techumin, placed outside of two thousand *mil* ....Eruvin 60a-60b

How —

Eruv techumin, agent...Eruvin 31b; Meilah 21a
Eruv techumin, by prohibited things ....Eruvin 30a, 31a-31b
Eruv techumin, by speech ....Eruvin 51a-52a
Eruv techumin, components ....Eruvin 27a, 28a-28b
Eruv techumin, distance.....................Eruvin 28b-30a, 82b-83a; Kesubos 64b; Keilim 17:11
Eruv techumin, fit for consumption...Eruvin 36a-36b, 38b
Eruv techumin, legal transfer of benefits...Eruvin 80a
Eruv techumin, place...Eruvin 30b-31a, 32b-34b
Eruv techumin, started to walk...Eruvin 51b, 52a-52b
Eruv techumin, tree...Eruvin 49b-50b, 50b
Eruv techumin, walking person...Eruvin 51a

Misc. —

Eruv techumin, child by his mother's...Eruvin 82a-82b; Kesubos 65b
Eruv techumin, for *mitzvah*..Eruvin 31a, 82a
Eruv techumin, on Yom Tov...Beitzah 16b-17a
Eruv techumin, strict laws..Eruvin 46a-46b
Eruv techumin, Yom Tov *Sheni*...Beitzah 17a

Es

Es, meant to include ....Bava Kama 41b; Pesachim 22b; Kiddushin 57a; Bechoros 6b
Es vahev, Arnon river...Berachos 54a-54b

Esau

Esau, death..Sotah 13a
Esau, five sins...Bava Basra 16b
Esau, found pretext ....Sanhedrin 101b
Esau, is not Abraham's seed ....Nedarim 31a; Sanhedrin 59b
Esau, lived among righteous men ....Yoma 38b
Esau, meeting with Jacob..Sotah 41b
Esau, sorting Patriarchs' offspring ....Shabbos 146a

Esau, will fall by Joseph's offspring .... Bava Basra 123b
Esau, Isaac's request .... Megillah 6a
Escape from doubt .... Avos 1:16
Esnan .... *see* **Prostitute's fee**, page 507
Esrog
  Episodes —
    Esrog, episode about excessively refined speech .... Kiddushin 70a
    Esrog, *kashering* knife .... Avodah Zarah 76b
    Esrog, pelting Sadducee .... Succah 48b
  Sabbatical year —
    Esrog, bonus on Sabbatical year .... Succah 39a; Bechoros 31b
    Esrog, Sabbatical year .... Rosh Hashanah 15a-15b
    Esrog tree, spoils on Sabbatical year .... Rosh Hashanah 15a
  Succos —
    Esrog, beautiful tree .... Succah 35a
    Esrog, binding .... Succah 34b
    Esrog, change of appearance .... Succah 35b-36b
    Esrog, *chazazis* .... Succah 35b-36b
    Esrog, disqualified .... Succah 31b, 35a-36b
    Esrog, *menumar* .... Succah 35b-36b
    Esrog, not to bring another fruit .... Succah 31a
    Esrog, second tithe .... Pesachim 38a; Succah 35a
    Esrog, smelling on Succos .... Succah 37b
  Misc. —
    Esrog, as tree and as vegetable ... Bikurim 2:6; Rosh Hashanah 14b-15b; Succah 39b-40a; Kiddushin 2b-3a
    Esrog for pregnant woman .... Kesubos 60b-61a
    Esrog on tree, Shabbos .... Succah 37b
    Esrog, peel .... Shabbos 108b
    Esrog, small, tithe .... Succah 36a; Maasros 1:4
Esther
  Megillah —
    Esther, "they readily accepted it" .... Shabbos 88a
    Esther, accusation against Israel .... Megillah 12a
    Esther, impurity to hands .... Megillah 7a; Yadayim 3:5
    Esther, introductions and commentaries .... Megillah 10b-11a
    Esther, miracle could be written .... Yoma 29a
    Esther, story of Megillah .... Megillah 12a-16b
    Esther, written with Divine inspiration .... Megillah 7a
  Misc. —
    Esther appeared before king .... Megillah 15b
    Esther, beauty .... Megillah 15a
    Esther, compared to hind .... Yoma 29a
    Esther, hinted in the Torah .... Chullin 139b
    Esther invited Haman .... Megillah 15b
    Esther, Mordechai and Ahasuerus .... Megillah 13a
    Esther, names .... Megillah 13a
    Esther, prophecy .... Megillah 14b
Estimate
  Estimate, annulling deal .... Kesubos 97a

E

Estimate, donation by sick man .... Bava Basra 146b-147a
Estimate for damage .... Bava Kama 91a
Estimate, man's capacity to bear lashes .... Makos 22a-22b
Estimate of consecrated item, cases .... Arachin 19b-20a
Estimate of consecrated item, who .... Sanhedrin 14b-15a, 88a; Megillah 23b
Estimate, others will estimate .... Avodah Zarah 72a
Estimate, promissory note .... Bava Basra 169a
Estimate, settling .... Bava Basra 107a-107b; Avodah Zarah 72a
Estimate, testimony .... Sanhedrin 37b; Shevuos 34a
Estimate, value of *kiddushin* .... Kiddushin 7b-8a, 9a
Estimate vs. *chazakah* .... Bava Basra 93a

Estimate for tithes
Estimate for tithes, do not tithe excessively .... Avos 1:16
Estimate for tithes, how .... Terumos 1:7
Estimate for tithes, *terumas maaser* ...... Gittin 31a; Beitzah 13b; Menachos 54b-55a; Bechoros 58b-59a

Estimate of damage
Estimate of damage, according to land of person who damaged .... Bava Kama 84a
Estimate of damage, cases .... Bava Kama 47a
Estimate of damage, deaf .... Bava Kama 85b
Estimate of damage, deduction .... Bava Kama 59a
Estimate of damage, palm tree .... Bava Kama 58b-59b
Estimate of damage, price changed .... Bava Metzia 99b
Estimate of damage, tooth .... Bava Kama 6b, 20a, 58b-59b

Etching line
Etching line, before writing verse .... Gittin 6b
Etching lines for holy parchments .... Menachos 32b; Megillah 18b
Etching lines, Shabbos .... Shabbos 75b

Eternal life, learning .... Shabbos 10a, 33a; Beitzah 15b; Taanis 21a

Eternity of Israel
Eternity of Israel, like winds .... Taanis 3b; Avodah Zarah 10b
Eternity of Israel, tribes .... Bava Basra 115b

Ethics .... *see* **Suffering**, page 662; *see also* **Punishment**, page 510, **Reward**, page 566, **Self-examination**, page 599, **Evil urge**, page 204

Ethrog .... *see* **Esrog**, page 201

***Etz hadar**, esrog* .... Succah 35a

Eulogizer will be eulogized .... Moed Katan 28b; Kesubos 72a; Nedarim 83b

Eulogy
Episodes —
Eulogy for living fisherman .... Yevamos 121a
Eulogy for Moses .... Sotah 13b
Eulogy for Rabbi Yishmael .... Nedarim 66a
Eulogy of Mashiach ben Joseph .... Succah 52a
Eulogy, pilgrimage .... Moed Katan 8a
Eulogy, warming up audience .... Shabbos 153a

Sayings —
Eulogy, "I have no one to ask my questions" .... Sanhedrin 68a
Eulogy, "*Nitzchu areilim es hametzukim*" .... Kesubos 104a
Eulogy, atonement for generation .... Moed Katan 28a
Eulogy, by sin of generation .... Shabbos 33b

Eulogy, like a new bride .... Moed Katan 25b
Eulogy, like burning of Temple .... Rosh Hashanah 18b
Eulogy, like losing a diamond .... Megillah 15a
Eulogy, other sayings .... Moed Katan 25b, 28b; Megillah 6a
Eulogy, the man whom I feared .... Moed Katan 24a
Eulogy, there is no one like him .... Horayos 13a
Eulogy, what a humble man! .... Berachos 6b
Eulogy, what a pity for those who left us .... Sanhedrin 111a
Eulogy, woe to the ship! .... Bava Basra 91a-91b

When —
Eulogy close to Yom Tov .... Moed Katan 8a-8b
Eulogy, days of rejoicing .... Moed Katan 28b
Eulogy for Sage, until when .... Yevamos 78b
Eulogy on *chol hamoed* .... Moed Katan 27b, 28b; Megillah 3b
Eulogy on *Pesach Sheni* .... Chullin 129b

Who and how —
Eulogy in front of coffin .... Shabbos 153a
Eulogy for children .... Moed Katan 24b
Eulogy, quality the deceased did not have .... Berachos 62a
Eulogy, whose honor .... Sanhedrin 46b-47a

Misc. —
Eulogy, good omen if deceased is not eulogized .... Sanhedrin 47a
Eulogy, men put to death by government .... Sanhedrin 11a
Eulogy, punishment for who neglects .... Shabbos 105b
Eulogy, reward .... Berachos 6b; Sanhedrin 108b
Eulogy shows deceased's value .... Shabbos 153a

Euphrates, course and reason for its name .... Bechoros 55a-55b
Evaluation of fragments, stolen item .... Bava Kama 11a, 94a

Eve
Eve, beauty .... Bava Basra 58a
Eve, creation .... Berachos 61a; Eruvin 18a-18b; Sanhedrin 39a
Eve, curse .... Shabbos 145b-146a; Eruvin 100b; Yoma 75a
Eve, G-d was usher .... Berachos 61a; Shabbos 95a; Eruvin 18b
Eve, pleasing to Adam .... Yevamos 63a
Eve's note .... Sotah 12a
Eve of Yom Kippur, *Kohen Gadol* .... Yoma 18a-19b

Eve of Pesach
Eve of Pesach, *chametz* .... Pesachim 4b-5b
Eve of Pesach, custom about work .... Pesachim 51b, 55a
Eve of Pesach, eating .... Pesachim 99b-100a, 107a-108a
Eve of Pesach on Shabbos .... Pesachim 13a, 20b, 49a
Eve of Pesach, prohibition to work .... Pesachim 2b, 50a-50b, 51b, 55b; Moed Katan 13a; Yevamos 13b
Eve of Pesach, works .... Pesachim 55a-55b; Moed Katan 13a

Eve of Shabbos
Eve of Shabbos, "did you separate tithes" .... Shabbos 34a; Gittin 6b
Eve of Shabbos, eating .... Pesachim 99b-100a
Eve of Shabbos, quarrel .... Gittin 52a
Eve of Shabbos, running .... Bava Kama 32a-32b
Eve of Shabbos, things created .... Pesachim 54a-54b; Avos 5:6

Eve of Shabbos, three *parsaos* .... Succah 44b
Eve of Shabbos, tithe .... Yevamos 93a-93b
Eve of Shabbos, work .... Pesachim 50b

Eved .... *see* **Slave**, page 636
Eved ivri .... *see* **Hebrew slave**, *terumah*, page 275
Even
Even maskis, prostrating upon .... Megillah 22b
Even mesama .... Niddah 69b, 71a
Even mesama, impurity of idolatry .... Shabbos 82b-83a
Even shesia, Creation .... Yoma 54b
Even shesia, incense .... Yoma 52b
Even toen .... Bava Metzia 28b; Taanis 19a

Evening prayer .... *see* **Maariv**, page 382
Events of History .... Avodah Zarah 8b-9a; Shabbos 15a
Ever min hachai, limb from a live animal .... *see* **Limb**, page 370
Every day, *kashering* utensils for fellow .... Avodah Zarah 76a; Zevachim 97a
Everybody needs men rich in Torah knowledge ..... Bava Basra 145b; Berachos 64a; Horayos 14a
Everyone would build private altar .... Chagigah 22a
Everything
Everything comes from G-d's hand, Temple .... Zevachim 33a
Everything comes from Heaven .... Kesubos 30a
Everything for Heaven's sake, Rav Acha .... Kiddushin 82a
Everything G-d does is for the best, Rabbi Akiva .... Berachos 60b
Everything is firm and valid .... Bava Basra 160b
Everything is in G-d's hands, fear of G-d .... Berachos 33b; Berachos 33b; Megillah 25a; Niddah 16a
Everything was created in G-d's honor .... Avos 6:11
Everything will man give to save his life .... Bava Basra 16a
Everywhere
Everywhere etc., list .... Chullin 26b
Everywhere, G-d's humility .... Megillah 31a
Evil
Evil comes about by guilty man .... Shabbos 32a; Bava Basra 119b; Sanhedrin 8a
Evil in their heart, Doeg and Ahitophel .... Chagigah 15b
Evil eye
Evil eye, amulet on Shabbos .... Shabbos 57b
Evil eye, damage .... Bava Metzia 30a, 107a-107b; Bava Basra 118a-118b
Evil eye, fish .... Berachos 20a, 55b; Sotah 36b; Bava Metzia 84a; Bava Basra 118b
Evil eye, may it burst .... Avodah Zarah 65a
Evil eye, *segulah* .... Berachos 55b
Evil eye, Joseph's offspring .... Bava Basra 118a-118b; Sotah 36b; Berachos 20a, 55b; Bava Metzia 84a
Evil urge
Evil urge, "do this" .... Shabbos 105b
Evil urge, after death .... Bava Basra 58a
Evil urge, alien god .... Shabbos 105b
Evil urge assaulted him, married by transgression .... Bechoros 46a
Evil urge, created by G-d .... Berachos 32a; Succah 52b
Evil urge, David .... Bava Basra 17a
Evil urge dominates .... Sotah 8a
Evil urge, elimination in Ezra's days .... Sanhedrin 64a; Yoma 69b; Arachin 32b

Evil urge, episodes about its annulment .... Sanhedrin 64a; Yoma 69b; Arachin 32b
Evil urge for forbidden relations .... *see* **Forbidden relations**, page 233
Evil urge forced her, widow having forbidden relations .... Kesubos 54a
Evil urge, from when .... Sanhedrin 91b
Evil urge, future .... Succah 52a
Evil urge, G-d's regret .... Succah 52b
Evil urge, how .... Berachos 61a
Evil urge, left hand pushes away .... Sotah 47a; Sanhedrin 107b
Evil urge, names .... Succah 52a-52b
Evil urge overcomes, modesty .... Chagigah 16a; Kiddushin 40a
Evil urge, Patriarchs .... Bava Basra 17a
Evil urge, safeguarding oneself from it .... Avodah Zarah 5b
Evil urge, submitting him .... Berachos 5a
Evil urge, traps .... Nedarim 32b
Evil Merodach, years of reign .... Megillah 11b
Ewe, female ram .... Menachos 107b
Examination
Examination by Haggai .... Pesachim 16b-17a
Examination, Eifa examined Avimi .... Shevuos 28b-29a; Zevachim 26a
Examination, how .... Sanhedrin 41b
Examination, Karna of Rav .... Shabbos 108a
Examination, Rav Dimi .... Bava Basra 22a
Examinations and checking, difference .... Sanhedrin 41b
Examinations with sheets .... Niddah 61a
Examination of witnesses
Examination of witnesses, *agunah* .... Yevamos 122a-122b
Examination of witnesses, denying .... Sanhedrin 41a
Examination of witnesses, how .... Sanhedrin 40b
Examination of witnesses in monetary matters .... Sanhedrin 2b-3a, 29a, 30b-31a, 32a-32b;
                                                                            Yevamos 122b; Pesachim 12a
Examination of witnesses, source .... Sanhedrin 40a-40b
Examine witnesses thoroughly .... Avos 1:9
Examining
  Animals —
Examining and comparing, *treifah* .... Chullin 50a
Examining blemish in firstborn .... Beitzah 27a; Bechoros 28a-28b, 36b-37a
Examining brain membrane .... Chullin 56a-56b
Examining by slaughterer from the outset .... Chullin 3a
Examining clawed animal .... Chullin 53b-54a
Examining daily offering for blemish .... Menachos 49b-50a; Arachin 13b; Pesachim 96a; Succah 42a
Examining gullet, *treifah* .... Chullin 28a-28b, 43a-43b
Examining Pesach lamb, in other generations .... Pesachim 96a
Examining signs, slaughtering .... Chullin 9a
Examining, slaughtering while relying on future examining .... Chullin 3a
Examining *treifah* before eating .... Beitzah 25a-25b
  Men —
Examining converts .... Yevamos 47a-47b; Bechoros 30b
Examining hairs as signs of puberty .... Bava Basra 156a
Examining *Kohanim* .... Middos 5:4

Examining person in death throes .... Yoma 85a
Examining witnesses, denying .... Sanhedrin 41a
Examining witnesses in monetary matters ...... Sanhedrin 2b-3a, 30b-31a, 32a-32b; Yevamos 122b
Examining witnesses of new moon .... Rosh Hashanah 23b-24a

Niddah —
Examined on first day, *zavah* .... Niddah 68b
Examining, cloth .... Niddah 14a-14b, 16a-17a
Examining, exempt .... Niddah 11a-11b, 38b-39a
Examining, for her husband .... Niddah 11b-12b, 15a, 16b
Examining, Jewish women .... Niddah 4b, 12a
Examining young girls, by women .... Niddah 10b, 13b; Chullin 31b

Women —
Examining hair, women .... Niddah 48b-49a
Examining husband's lucidity, divorce certificate .... Gittin 70b-71a
Examining lineage of eight mothers .... Kiddushin 76a-76b
Examining Midianite women .... Yevamos 60b
Examining virgins, wine .... Yevamos 60b; Kesubos 10b
Examining woman's brothers .... Bava Basra 109b-110a
Examining, we do not examine married women .... Yevamos 42a

Misc. —
Examined and did not find .... Pesachim 10a; Bechoros 25b; Niddah 61a
Examining before giving charity .... Bava Basra 9a
Examining, book not examined .... Kesubos 19b
Examining *mezuzah* .... Yoma 11a
Examining one's actions .... Eruvin 13b
Examining pockets before Shabbos .... Shabbos 12a
Examining pockets, lost item .... Bava Metzia 21b
Examining Temple Courtyard, morning .... Tamid 28a-28b
Examining Torah scroll, *tefillin* and *mezuzah* .... Eruvin 96b-97a

Examining knife
Examining knife for slaughtering .... Chullin 10b, 17a-18a
Examining knife in front of teacher .... Eruvin 62b-63a
Examining knife of renegade .... Chullin 3a-3b, 4a-4b

Example
Example of teacher, ruling ...... Bava Basra 83a, 130b; Shabbos 21a, 126b; Pesachim 51a-51b; Niddah 65b
Examples in this world, messianic times .... Shabbos 30b

Except So-and-so
Except So-and-so, divorce certificate .... Gittin 82a-83b, 85a
Except So-and-so, *kiddushin* .... Gittin 82b

Exceptional law, meat with milk .... Nazir 37a

Exchange
Exchange, act of acquisition by cloth .... Bava Metzia 7a
Exchange, act of acquisition of slave .... Kiddushin 22b
Exchange, *kiddushin* .... Kiddushin 3a-3b
Exchange of item forbidden for benefit .... Nedarim 47a-47b, 52b, 57a, 59a
Exchange of items forbidden to profit .... Kiddushin 58a; Avodah Zarah 71a, 71b
Exchange of Sabbatical year produce ...... Succah 40b-41a; Avodah Zarah 54b; Sheviis 8:7-8;
.... Kiddushin 58a; Bechoros 9b
Exchange .... *see also* **Substituted**, page 660; **Barter**, page 43

Exchange, tithe and *terumah* .... Bava Metzia 11b

Exchanged

Exchanged donkey with cow .... Bava Metzia 47a

Exchanged items in bathhouse .... Bava Basra 46a

Exchanged wives at wedding .... Yevamos 33b

Exchanged wives, exile .... Shabbos 62b; Kiddushin 71b

Excising of Soul

For which sin —

Excising of soul, deduction from blasphemer .... Sanhedrin 64b

Excising of soul, for which sin .... Krisos 2a, 3a-3b

Excising of soul, Pesach lamb .... Pesachim 93a-93b

Excising of soul, sacrifice in impurity .... Zevachim 43b

Excising of soul without act, sacrifice .... Krisos 3b-4a; Sanhedrin 65a-65b

Misc. —

Excising of soul, "he will bear his sin" .... Pesachim 93b

Excising of soul, age .... Moed Katan 28a

Excising of soul, childless .... Yevamos 55a

Excising of soul, lashes .... Megillah 7b; Makos 23a-23b

Excising of soul, more severe than negative commandment, decree .... Yevamos 119a

Excising of soul, repentance .... Sanhedrin 90b; Shevuos 13a

Excising of soul, sin offering .... Yevamos 8b-9a; Horayos 8a; Shabbos 68b-69a

Excising of soul, two in one act .... Krisos 3b

Exclusion, double .... Menachos 9b, 67a; Yoma 43a; Megillah 23b; Bava Kama 86b; Bava Basra 14a;
.... Sanhedrin 15a, 46a, 86a; Makos 9b; Shevuos 7b; Chullin 132a

Excommunicated, encircling Temple Mount .... Middos 2:2

Excommunication

Episodes —

Excommunication and forgiveness, episode .... Niddah 36b-37a

Excommunication, caused conversion from Judaism .... Kiddushin 72a

Excommunication, dog stealing shoes .... Moed Katan 17a

Excommunication, forgiveness after death .... Niddah 36b-37a

Excommunication of Meroz by Barak .... Shevuos 36a; Moed Katan 16a

Excommunication of woman who humiliated Shmuel .... Nedarim 50b

Excommunication, permission to marry given to *agunah* .... Yevamos 121a

Excommunication, Yom Tov in Diaspora .... Pesachim 52a

Heavenly —

Excommunication, Divine, for which sin .... Pesachim 113b

Excommunication, feast for commandment .... Pesachim 113b

Excommunication for going barefoot .... Pesachim 112a, 113b

Excommunication, procreation .... Pesachim 113b

How —

Excommunication, disciple .... Moed Katan 17a

Excommunication, expressions .... Moed Katan 17a

Excommunication in dream .... Nedarim 8a-8b

Excommunication on condition .... Makos 11b

Who —

Excommunication, for which sin .... Berachos 19a

Excommunication, hitting one's grown son .... Moed Katan 17a

Excommunication, man refusing to obey *beis din* ... Moed Katan 16a; Bava Kama 112b; Shevuos 41a

Excommunication, mentioning Divine Name in vain .... Nedarim 7b
Excommunication, non-Jewish courts .... Bava Kama 113b-114a
Excommunication, ruling about *muktzeh* .... Shabbos 19b
Excommunication, selling to non-Jew .... Bava Kama 114a
Excommunication, unstable ladder .... Bava Kama 15b
Excommunication, work on Pesach eve .... Pesachim 50b

Misc. —
Excommunication, contrary to law .... Moed Katan 17a
Excommunication, death of excommunicated man .... Moed Katan 17a-17b
Excommunication, laws of excommunicated man .... Moed Katan 14b-15b
Excommunication of one's wicked father .... Sanhedrin 85a
Excommunication, permitting it .... Moed Katan 16a, 17a; Nedarim 7b, 8b
Excommunication, time .... Moed Katan 16a
Excommunication, wording of vow .... Nedarim 7a-7b

Excrement
Excrement, burning, transgression of Rabbinical Decree .... Eruvin 21b
Excrement, covering one's mouth .... Berachos 24b
Excrement, distance .... Berachos 22b
Excrement edible by dog, *muktzeh* .... Shabbos 121a-121b
Excrement, four cubits .... Berachos 26a
Excrement in house .... Berachos 25b
Excrement, liquid .... Pesachim 20a
Excrement of animals, prayer .... Berachos 25a
Excrement of baby, prayer .... Succah 42b
Excrement on one's body .... Berachos 25a; Yoma 30a
Excrement, passing by .... Berachos 25a
Excrement, prayer .... Berachos 22b, 25b; Eruvin 92b
Excrement, sin for who reads *Shema* .... Berachos 24b
Excrement, three reasons .... Shabbos 140b

Excuse to purify *Eretz Yisrael* .... Kesubos 20b; Nazir 65b
Execution .... *see* **Condemned to death**, page 119
Exempt
Exempt according to *beis din* law, cases .... Bava Kama 55b-56a
Exempt but forbidden .... Shabbos 3a, 107a
Exempt on behalf of one who is obligated, separating *terumah* .... Demai 5:3-8, 5:9-11;
.... Yevamos 89a-89b; Bava Metzia 56a
Exempt place .... *see* ***Mekom petur***, page 403
Exerted
Exerted, "I exerted myself and I was successful" .... Megillah 6b
Exerting oneself in prayer .... Sanhedrin 44b
Exhaustive list ...... Kiddushin 40a; Eruvin 29a; Succah 54a; Taanis 14a; Yevamos 21b, 73a, 84b; Kesubos 41a;
.... Kiddushin 34a; Nazir 38b; Sotah 16a; Bava Kama 10a, 15a, 43b, 62b; Makos 21b
Exilarch .... *see* **Reish *Galusa***, page 554
Exile .... *see also* **City of Refuge**, page 109
***Aggadah* —**
Exile, angel's hint to Jacob .... Chullin 92a
Exile, G-d did not reject Israel .... Megillah 11a
Exile, G-d's pain .... Berachos 3a; Bava Basra 74a
Exile, G-d's pity .... Pesachim 87b; Chagigah 5b; Berachos 9b; Megillah 11a

E

Exile, G-d's regret .... Succah 52b
Exile of Israel, Divine Presence .... Megillah 29a; Yoma 56b-57a
Exile, reasons .... Pesachim 118b
Exile, to add converts .... Pesachim 87b
Exile, Israel's existence among nations .... Yoma 69b

Babylon —

Exile, *Hacharash vehamasger* .... Gittin 88a; Sanhedrin 38a
Exile in Babylon, first .... Gittin 88a; Sanhedrin 38a
Exile in Babylon, preference .... Menachos 110a
Exile of Jehoiachin .... Sanhedrin 38a
Exile of Jehoiachin and Zedekiah .... Gittin 88a; Sanhedrin 38a

Murderer —

Exile, blind .... Nedarim 87b-88a; Makos 9b; Bava Kama 86b-87a
Exile, enemy .... Makos 6b, 9b
Exile, hastened his death .... Yevamos 120b-121a
Exile, in the same inn .... Makos 10b
Exile, iron slipped from handle .... Makos 7b
Exile, kinds of death .... Bava Kama 26b; Makos 8a
Exile, murderer by indirect act .... Sanhedrin 77b-78a; Makos 8a
Exile, non-Jew or resident non-Jew .... Makos 9a
Exile, of man who killed unintentionally .... Makos 12b
Exile, return to previous function .... Makos 13a
Exile, voluntary murderer .... Makos 10b
Exile, when murderer is exempt .... Bava Kama 32b-33a; Makos 7a-8b

Misc. —

Exile atones .... Sanhedrin 37b; Berachos 56a
Exile, for which sins .... Avos 5:9
Exile, nations who stayed in their country .... Megillah 12b
Exile of *Sanhedrin* .... Shabbos 15a; Rosh Hashanah 31a-31b; Avodah Zarah 8b
Exile of ten tribes .... Yevamos 16b-17a; Shabbos 147b; Sanhedrin 94a; Arachin 33a
Exile to learn Torah .... Avos 4:14; Berachos 63b

Exile yourself to a place of Torah .... Avos 4:14

Existing already

Existing already, cases .... Bava Metzia 16a-16b
Existing already, gift .... Gittin 13b; Bava Basra 131a, 141b
Existing already, habitual things .... Bava Basra 79b
Existing already, is it effective .... Gittin 13b, 42b-43a; Bava Basra 79b, 131a, 141b, 157a; Yevamos 92b-93a;
.... Kesubos 58b-59b; Kiddushin 62a-63a; Bava Metzia 16b, 33b
Existing already, tithe .... Yevamos 93a-93b
Existing already, vow .... Nedarim 85b

Exodus

Exodus, date .... Shabbos 87b-88a
Exodus, end of enslavement .... Rosh Hashanah 11b
Exodus, haste .... Berachos 9a
Exodus, in *Shema* .... Berachos 12b, 14b
Exodus, *kiddush* .... Pesachim 117b
Exodus, mentioned in commandments .... Bava Metzia 61b
Exodus, mentioning .... Berachos 21a
Exodus, miracles of redemption .... Avos 5:4

Exodus, number of people who participated .... Sanhedrin 111a
Exodus, section of Balak .... Berachos 12b

Expecting Redemption, questions .... Shabbos 31a

Expenses
Expenses, behavior .... Chullin 84a, 84b
Expenses for mistaken sale .... Kesubos 91b-92a
Expenses for Shabbos, borrow on My account .... Beitzah 15b
Expenses for wife's property .... Kesubos 79b-80a; Bava Metzia 39a
Expenses of caravan, sharing .... Bava Kama 116b
Expenses of poor, advice .... Shabbos 140b

Experience
Experience for doubt about impurity .... Niddah 5b
Experience repeated, stain of *niddah* .... Niddah 58a

Experiment
Experiment contrary to Torah, fools .... Niddah 30b
Experiments, do not contradict law .... Chullin 57b
Experiments, Rabbi Shimon ben Chalafta .... Chullin 57b

Expert
Expert, blemishes of firstborn .... Yoma 78a; Bechoros 28b-29a
Expert, buying holy parchments from .... Menachos 42b
Expert in divorce certificates .... Kiddushin 6a, 13a-13b
Expert physician, curing by non-Jew .... Avodah Zarah 28a
Expert, slaughtering .... Chullin 3b, 9a, 12a-12b
Expert, trustworthiness about forbidden items .... Avodah Zarah 39b

Expert judge
Expert judge, alone .... Sanhedrin 5a, 8a
Expert judge, consecrating new month .... Rosh Hashanah 25b
Expert judge, mistake .... Sanhedrin 5a
Expert judge, permitting vow .... Yevamos 25b; Nedarim 78a-78b; Bava Basra 120b
Expert judges .... Bava Kama 15b, 84a-84b; Sanhedrin 2b-3b; Gittin 88b
Expert judges, conversion .... Yevamos 46b

Expertise in agriculture, ancient Sages .... Shabbos 85a

Expiring, righteous men .... Bava Basra 16b

Explains his opinion, Rabbi Yose .... Gittin 67a

Explicit law, not to rely on .... Niddah 7b; Bava Basra 130b

Expression .... *see also* **Verbal expression**, page 721

Marriage —
Expression in text of divorce certificate .... Gittin 85a-86a
Expression of divorce .... Kiddushin 5b, 6a-6b; Gittin 85b
Expression of *kiddushin* .... Kiddushin 5b-6a

Monetary matters —
Expression by sick man .... Bava Basra 148b-149a
Expression in gift of field .... Gittin 40b
Expression, lending .... Bava Metzia 103a
Expression meaning gift .... Bava Basra 62b-63a
Expression, movable goods .... Bava Basra 150a
Expression of rent .... Rosh Hashanah 7b

Vows and oaths —
Expression made-up by Sages, vows .... Nedarim 3a, 10a-10b

Expression, doubles *nezirus'* days .... Nazir 8b
Expression, oath .... Shevuos 20a-20b
Expression of vow, intention .... Nedarim 20a
Expression of vows, inaccurate .... Nedarim 4b-5a, 7a-7b, 10a-10b; Nazir 3a
Expressions of oath, intention .... Nedarim 25a; Shevuos 29a

Misc. —
Expression, first, is principal .... Temurah 26a
Expression, last, is effective .... Bava Basra 105b
Expression of legal document, analyzing .... Bava Metzia 104a-104b
Expression of teacher, precision .... Berachos 33b, 38b, 47a; Shabbos 15a; Pesachim 52b; Eduyos 1:3;
.... Bechoros 5a
Expression of teacher, requirement .... Eduyos 1:3
Expression, superfluous, gift .... Bava Basra 138a-138b
Expression used by Rav, law .... Pesachim 114b
Expression of consecration .... Arachin 19a-19b
Expression of wisdom, poetic phrases .... Eruvin 53b
Expression to replace and redeem sacrifice .... Temurah 26b-27a

Extinction, act needed for itself .... Shabbos 31b, 42a; Zevachim 91b-92a

Extinguishing
Extinguishing, causing .... Shabbos 120a-120b
Extinguishing fire on Altar .... Yoma 46b; Zevachim 91b-92a
Extinguishing lamp for sick, Shabbos .... Shabbos 29b-30b
Extinguishing, non-Jew .... Shabbos 121a
Extinguishing on Shabbos, episode .... Shabbos 121a

Eye
Health —
Eye, cure by firstborn's saliva .... Bava Basra 126b
Eye, depends on heart .... Avodah Zarah 28b
Eye, drawing poison from eye .... Niddah 55b
Eye, eating fish .... Nedarim 54b
Eye, evil .... *see* **Evil eye**, page 204
Eye, fruit are beneficial .... Sanhedrin 17b
Eye, *gargir* .... Yoma 18b
Eye, harmful things .... Pesachim 111b
Eye, *kchol* .... Shabbos 151b
Eye, lung is beneficial .... Chullin 49a
Eye, tears .... Shabbos 151b
Eye, things beneficial to .... Shabbos 108b-109a
Eyes of deceased man, closing .... Shabbos 151b
Eyes revolving, obscurity .... Berachos 59b

Scientific facts —
Eyes of grasshoppers and roosters .... Shabbos 77b
Eyes of grasshoppers, dew .... Shabbos 106b
Eyes of Tarmudim, round .... Shabbos 31a

Misc. —
Eye, desecrating Shabbos to save eye .... Avodah Zarah 28b
Eye for eye, money .... Bava Kama 83b-84a
Eye, good, virtue .... Avos 2:9
Eye has not seen .... Berachos 34b; Sanhedrin 99a

E

Eye of Absalom, episode ....Niddah 24b
Eye of deceased, episode ....Tamid 32b
Eye seeing, meditation ....Avos 2:1
Eye sees, sixteen *mil* ....Bechoros 54b
Eyes down, prayer ....Yevamos 105b
Eyes of disciple, resentment ....Chagigah 3b
Eyesight, health ....Pesachim 111b
Eyn Eitam
Eyn Eitam, height ....Yoma 31a-31b, Zevachim 54b
Eyn Eitam, Jerusalem ....Shabbos 145b, Zevachim 54b
Eytan
Eytan Haezrachi, Abraham ....Bava Basra 15a
Eytan, significance ....Sotah 46a-46b; Rosh Hashanah 11a
Ezekiel
Ezekiel, resurrected dead ....Sanhedrin 92b
Ezekiel, *halacha* to Moses from Sinai ....Sanhedrin 22b; Moed Katan 5a; Taanis 17b; Yoma 71b;
....Zevachim 18b; Chagigah 13a
Ezekiel, mixed bread ....Eruvin 81a
Ezekiel, stringencies ....Chullin 37b, 44b
Ezekiel, suffering ....Sanhedrin 39a
Ezekiel, surprising verses ....Menachos 45a; Shabbos 13b; Chagigah 13a
Ezekiel, villager seeing king ....Chagigah 13b
Ezekiel, who authored Book of ....Bava Basra 15a
Ezov, explanation ....Shabbos 109b
Ezra
Ezra, decree on laundering ....Bava Kama 82a
Ezra, elimination of evil urge ....Sanhedrin 64a; Yoma 69b
Ezra, his righteousness ....Sanhedrin 21b
Ezra, Malachi ....Megillah 15a
Ezra, penalty on first tithe ....Yevamos 86b; Kesubos 26a; Chullin 131b
Ezra, second sanctification ....Arachin 32b; Megillah 10a-10b; Shevuos 16a
Ezra, selecting people forbidden to marriage ....Kiddushin 69b-70a, 71b
Ezra, taught Torah which had been forgotten ....Succah 20a
Ezra, Torah and greatness ....Gittin 59a
Ezra, ten decrees ....Bava Kama 82a-82b
Ezra, when did he go to *Eretz Yisrael* ....Arachin 13a; Rosh Hashanah 3b
Ezras Nashim
Ezras Nashim, Simchas Beis Hashoevah ....Succah 51b-52a; Middos 2:5
Ezras Nashim, Temple ....Middos 2:5; Yoma 16a

F

Face

Face, "your face is resplendent" ....Nedarim 49b

Face, blackened by fasts ....Chagigah 22b; Nazir 52b

Face of generation like face of dog ....Sanhedrin 97a

Face of man, prohibition ....Avodah Zarah 42b, 43b; Rosh Hashanah 24b

Face of Moses comparable to sun ....Bava Basra 75a

Face, permitting *agunah* ....Yevamos 120a; Bava Metzia 27b; Bechoros 46b

Face upwards, woman ....Niddah 31b

Faces are not similar ....Sanhedrin 38a

Fair, idolatrous

Fair, idolatrous ....Avodah Zarah 32b-33a

Faith

Faith, "this too is for the best" ....Berachos 60b-61a

Faith and obedience to Sages ....Rosh Hashanah 25a-25b

Faith, weak ....Sotah 48b

Faithful to come to synagogue, G-d asks about him

Faithful to come to synagogue, G-d asks about him ....Berachos 6b

Fall of enemies, do not rejoice

Fall of enemies, do not rejoice ....Megillah 16a

Fallen

Fallen animal, *treifah* ....Bava Kama 50b-51a; Chullin 51a-52a, 56b, 57a

Falling down ladder, charity ....Bava Basra 10a

Falling from a roof, unavoidable circumstances ....Bava Kama 27a; Yevamos 54a

Falling from high roof down to pit ....Chagigah 5b

Falling from ten handbreadths, death ....Bava Kama 50b-51a

Falling on one's face, important man ....Taanis 14b; Megillah 22b

Falling star, blessing ....Berachos 58b

Fell from ten handbreadths, *treifah* ....Bava Kama 50b-51a; Chullin 51a-52a, 56b, 57a

Fell in fire, *treifah* ....Chullin 56b, 57a

Fell in garden, tooth ....Bava Kama 57b-58a

Fell in pit, atonement payment ....Bava Kama 44a, 48b

False

False is charm, reference to Joseph, generaton of Moses, Joshua etc. ....Sanhedrin 20a

False Messiah, Bar Kochba ....Sanhedrin 93b

False testimony, prohibition ....Makos 23a; Shevuos 31a; Kesubos 19a

False witnesses, compensation by those who hired them ....Bava Kama 56a

False prophet
False prophet inciting to idolatry...Sanhedrin 67a
False prophets, Nebuchadnezzar..Sanhedrin 93a
False prophets, spirit of Navos..Sanhedrin 89a
False prophets, wonders..Sanhedrin 90a
Falsified your Torah! Cutheans..Sotah 33b
Families
Families, disqualified, not to publicize...Kiddushin 71a
Families, their lineage will be revealed in the future...................................Kiddushin 70b-71a
Family flaw, sells his tomb..................................Bava Basra 100b; Kesubos 84a; Bechoros 52b
Family members, do not ignore..................................Kesuvos 52b, 86a; Shevuos 39a
Family, man is accustomed to visit father, father's family..............................Yevamos 21a
Family, marriage...Yevamos 64b
Family name, divorce certificate...Gittin 88a
Family of mother is not family..Bava Basra 109b, 110b
Family of sinner, punishment...Shevuos 39a
Family of tax collector, all tax collectors...Shevuos 39a
Family ties, strange...Yevamos 97b
Famine
Episodes —
Famine, ate her son..Yoma 38b
Famine, episodes...Bava Basra 91b; Taanis 19b
Famine, Jehoram's time...Taanis 5a
Famine, Joel...Taanis 5a
Famine, Rebbi supported scholars..Bava Basra 8a
Famine, Rav Yehudah..Taanis 24b
Misc. —
Famine, fast...Taanis 18b-19b
Famine, for which sin...Avos 5:8
Famine, G-d proclaims..Berachos 55a
Famine, gifts to only one *Kohen*..Eruvin 63a
Famine, harsher than sword..Bava Basra 8b
Famine in town, protection...Bava Kama 60b
Famine, livelihood for craftsman...Sanhedrin 29a
Famine, separating from one's wife..Taanis 11a
Famous names, Sages...Yevamos 37b
Fanning fire together with wind...Bava Kama 60a
Farech, *peh rach*, soft tongue..Sotah 11b
Fast
Communal —
Fast, accepting wicked..Krisos 6b
Fast, cantor...Taanis 16a-16b
Fast, charity...Berachos 6b; Sanhedrin 35a
Fast, custom of region..Taanis 10b
Fast day, *nasi* decides..Taanis 24a
Fast of Gedaliah..Rosh Hashanah 18b
Fast, program of day...Taanis 12b-13a; Megillah 30b
Fast, Torah reading...Megillah 30b, 31b
Fast, washing..Megillah 5b

Episodes —

Fast, "perhaps he changed his mind after his death" .... Nazir 52b

Fast, honor of Beis Shamai .... Chagigah 22b

Fast of Yom Kippur, whispering .... Yoma 82b-83a

Fast, *tefillin* strap .... Moed Katan 25a

Fasts, all year long .... Pesachim 68b

Fasts of Rabbi Tzaddok .... Gittin 56a

Fasts of Sages .... Bava Metzia 85a

Hardships —

Fast, calamity passed .... Taanis 10b

Fast, communal, hardships .... Taanis 12b, 13a

Fast, communal, in Babylon .... Taanis 11b, 12b

Fast for dangers .... Taanis 21a-21b, 22b

Fast for two calamities .... Taanis 8b

Fast, collapsed houses .... Taanis 20b

Fast, when decree will be abolished .... Taanis 8b

Fast for rain

Fast for rain, blessings .... Taanis 13b, 15a-15b, 16b-17a

Fast for rain, blowing *shofar* .... Taanis 16b-17a

Fast for rain, episodes .... Taanis 24b, 25b

Fast for rain, it rained .... Taanis 25b

Fast for rain, prayer .... Taanis 15a-15b

Fast for rain, prohibitions .... Taanis 14b

Fast for rain, quantity of rain .... Taanis 6b, 25b

Fast for rain, repentance .... Taanis 16a

Fast for rain, Sages .... Taanis 10a-10b

Fast for rain, thirteen fasts .... Taanis 14a-14b

Fast for rain, who is exempt .... Taanis 14a

Private —

Fast, borrowing and fasting later .... Shabbos 11a

Fast for bad dream .... Shabbos 11a; Taanis 12b

Fast of a few hours .... Taanis 11b-12a; Avodah Zarah 34a

Fast, private, severity of communal fast .... Taanis 12b

Fast to atone for improper fast .... Berachos 31b; Taanis 12b

When —

Fast, night .... Taanis 12a-12b

Fast on days of rejoicing .... Taanis 18b

Fast on Shabbos .... Berachos 31b

Fast on Sunday, difficult .... Taanis 27b

Fast, Shabbos eve .... Eruvin 40b-41b; Rosh Hashanah 19a; Taanis 18b

Misc. —

Fast, ate by mistake .... Taanis 10b

Fast, capital cases .... Sanhedrin 63a; Moed Katan 14b

Fast, going to cemetery .... Taanis 16a

Fast, Rav Sheishes' prayer .... Berachos 17a

Fast, tasting dish .... Berachos 14a

Fast, value .... Berachos 32b

Fasts of *Anshei Maamad* .... Taanis 27b

Fastidious person
Fastidious person, "poor man's life is difficult" .... Bava Basra 145b; Sanhedrin 100b
Fastidious person, claim of disturbance, neighbor .... Bava Basra 22b
Fastidious person, drinking from teacher's cup .... Tamid 27b
Fastidious person, mourner .... Berachos 16b
Fastidious persons have no life .... Pesachim 113b

Fat
Prohibition —
Fat, blemished animal .... Pesachim 43b
Fat, forbidden, care .... Chullin 8b-9a
Fat, forbidden, sending meat .... Chagigah 5a
Fat of beast and bird .... Krisos 4a
Fat of fetus .... Chullin 74a-74b, 92b
Fat of non-holy animals .... Pesachim 43b
Fat of sciatic nerve .... Chullin 91a-92b; Pesachim 83b
Fat of stillborn and fetus .... Chullin 75a
Fat, benefit permitted .... Pesachim 23a-23b
Fats .... Chullin 49a-49b, 75a, 92b-93a; Krisos 4a

Misc. —
Fat and breast, order of offering .... Menachos 62a
Fat of leftover sacrifice, *perutah* .... Krisos 23a
Fat of sacrificial fetus .... Chullin 75a
Fat, purity .... Pesachim 23a-23b; Zevachim 69b-70b
Fat stuffing hole, *treifah* .... Chullin 49b-50a

Fat meat
Fat meat, different parts .... Yoma 25b
Fat meat in *Eretz Yisrael* .... Bava Basra 91b

Fate
Fate, birth and Israel .... Shabbos 156a-156b
Fate caused .... Bava Metzia 106a
Fate, children, life and money .... Moed Katan 28a
Fate, covering head to avoid fate of thief .... Shabbos 156b
Fate, for man and not for animal .... Bava Kama 2b; Shabbos 53b
Fate has seen .... Sanhedrin 94a
Fate, items not lent because of fate .... Bava Metzia 27b
Fate of owner, wine .... Bava Basra 98a
Fate of partners, preferable .... Bava Metzia 105a
Fate of Israel in *Adar* .... Taanis 29a-29b
Fate, Sage or schoolteacher .... Yevamos 21b
Fate, two persons with same fate .... Bava Basra 12a
Fate, Isaac's birth .... Shabbos 156a-156b; Nedarim 32a

Father-in-law
Father-in-law, mourning .... Kesubos 4b; Moed Katan 20b
Father-in-law, tearing garment .... Moed Katan 26b

Father
"Father, give us rain!" .... Taanis 23b
"Fathers ate unripe fruit," Rabbi Meir .... Sanhedrin 38b-39a
Father accompanied bride, wedding .... Kesubos 48b-49a; Nedarim 89a; Sanhedrin 66b
Father agrees, condition for marriage .... Kiddushin 63a-63b

Father, commandments concerning son .... Kiddushin 29a, 30b
Father, crossed animals .... Chullin 79b-80a, 132a
Father dishonored scholar, episode .... Bechoros 30b
Father does not give merit to his son .... Sanhedrin 104a
Father, Father, Israel's chariot! .... Moed Katan 26a
Father, gives character traits to his son .... Eduyos 2:9
Father in Heaven, relying upon .... Sotah 49a
Father, compensation for his daughter's rape and seduc .... Kesubos 41b-42a
Father is alive, Rav's father .... Pesachim 4a
Father, *kiddushin* for his son .... Kiddushin 45a-45b
Father, making his son his agent .... Kiddushin 45b
Father of non-Jew, lineage .... Yevamos 62a; Kiddushin 67b
Father of numerous peoples, Abraham .... Shabbos 105a
Father who hit, refuge .... Makos 8a-8b
Father whose son finds a lost item .... Bava Metzia 12a-12b
Father wicked, disgrace .... Sanhedrin 85a
Father's rights, *kesubah* .... Kesubos 43b
Father's rights in his daughter .... Kesubos 43b, 46b-47a; Kiddushin 3b-4a, 10a; Niddah 47a
Fathers of men in Tanach .... Megillah 15a
Fathers say: "We lost blessings" .... Nedarim 50b

Father and mother
Father and mother .... *see also* **Honor of father**, page 283
Father and mother, baby .... Berachos 40a
Father and mother, cursing them .... Sanhedrin 85b
Father and mother, hitting them .... Sanhedrin 84b, 85b
Father and mother, mourning them .... Moed Katan 20b, 22a-22b

Father, precedence
Father, precedence for inheritance .... Bava Basra 108b-109b
Father, precedence for returning lost item .... Bava Metzia 33a

Father, trustworthiness
Father, trustworthiness about his firstborn, inheritance .... Kiddushin 78b; Yevamos 47a;
.... Bava Basra 126b, 127b, 128b
Father, trustworthiness about his son .... Kiddushin 74a, 78b; Yevamos 47a; Bava Basra 127a
Father, trustworthiness about his son's age .... Kiddushin 63b-64a
Father, trustworthiness about marriage and captive woman .... Kiddushin 64a; Kesubos 22a

Father's wife
Father's wife, forbidden relations .... Sanhedrin 53a-54a
Father's wife, his children's enemy .... Yevamos 63b; Berachos 56a
Father's wife, orphans' suffering .... Yevamos 63b; Berachos 56a

Fattened
Fattened livestock on festival, Rebbi .... Avodah Zarah 16a
Fattened swans, Solomon .... Bava Metzia 86b

Favor
Favor of wicked is bad for righteous .... Yevamos 103a-103b; Nazir 23b; Horayos 10b
Favors, throw them on thorns ...Shabbos 63b; Beitzah 29b; Kesubos 53b; Bava Kama 83a; Bava Metzia 63b

Favorable
Favorable Divine word is not revoked .... Berachos 7a; Shabbos 55a
Favorable time, choosing partner .... Pesachim 112a, 113a
Favorite food, precedence for blessing .... Berachos 39a

F

Favoritism towards Israel...Berachos 20b; Rosh Hashanah 17b; Niddah 70b
Fear
   Fear, "do not fear any man"..Sanhedrin 6b
   Fear your G-d..Kiddushin 32b; Bava Metzia 58b
   Fearing Sages..Shabbos 23b
Fear
   Fear, accessories for *beis din*..Sanhedrin 7b
   Fear and worry..Berachos 60a
   Fear, cause and putting an end to..Pesachim 111b-112a; Sanhedrin 94a
   Fear causes weakness..Gittin 70a
   Fear in one's household..Gittin 6b-7a
   Fear, instilling in household...Shabbos 105b
   Fear of father and mother...Kiddushin 31b-32a
   Fear of government.......................................Zevachim 102a; Avodah Zarah 4a; Avos 3:2; Menachos 98a
   Fear of judge..Sanhedrin 8a
   Fear of judgment...Chagigah 4b
   Fear of man upon animals..Shabbos 151b
   Fear of public, source...Sotah 40a
   Fear of sin, Rebbi..Sotah 49b
   Fear of sin, Rabbi Nachman...Sotah 49b
   Fear of teacher, equal to fear of Heaven..Avos 4:12
   Fear of Temple..Yevamos 6a-6b; Berachos 54a, 62b-63a
   Fear of weak animals among the strong..Shabbos 77b
   Fear, punishment of leader..Rosh Hashanah 17a
   Fear stops menstruation...Niddah 9a, 71a, 39a; Sotah 20b
   Fear that he will break my skull, Beis Shamai..Yevamos 15b
Fear of G-d
   Fear of G-d and love, preference...Sotah 31a
   Fear of G-d and Torah, parables..Shabbos 31a-31b
   Fear of G-d, effort to acquire..Berachos 33b
   Fear of G-d, including Sage.................................Kiddushin 57a; Pesachim 22b; Bava Kama 41b; Bechoros 6b
   Fear of G-d, not in Heavens' hand..................................Berachos 33b; Megillah 25a; Niddah 16b
   Fear of G-d, parables...Berachos 33b
   Fear of G-d preceding wisdom..Avos 3:9, 3:17
   Fear of G-d, Torah learning..Yoma 72b; Shabbos 30b, 31a-31b
   Fear of G-d, with cunning...Berachos 17a
   Fear of Heaven, equal to that of man..Berachos 28b
Fearful and soft of heart, war...Sotah 43a-43b, 44a-44b
Feast..*see also* **Meal**, page 395
   Behavior —
   Feast, non-holy..Pesachim 49a
   Feast, non-holy, Rav..Chullin 95b
   Feast of uninhibited people, preventing wife from going..Kesubos 72a
   Feast, Sage keeps away..Berachos 43b; Pesachim 49a; Niddah 16b
   Feasts for commandments —
   Feast for commandment, punishment for avoiding..Pesachim 113b
   Feast for completion of tractate...Shabbos 118b-119a; Pesachim 68b
   Feast for Sages, recovery..Berachos 46a
   Feast for wedding...Pesachim 49a; Succah 25b; Chullin 83a

Feast of Purim .... Megillah 7b
Feast of righteous, wicked .... Shabbos 153a
Feast of thanksgiving, recovery .... Berachos 46a
Feast, sixty years old .... Moed Katan 28a

Kings —
Feast of Ahasuerus .... Megillah 12a-12b
Feast of Emperor, to G-d .... Chullin 59b-60a
Feast of king, episode .... Kesubos 61a-61b
Feast of king, parables .... Shabbos 153a; Sanhedrin 108a
Feasts of Solomon .... Bava Metzia 86b

Misc. —
Feast in the next world .... Bava Basra 73b
Feast, lamp is a sign of feast .... Sanhedrin 32b
Feast of wedding, certainly not to divorce immediately .... Kesubos 10a; Yevamos 107a

Feather
Feather, bird sacrifice .... Zevachim 65a
Feather, Shabbos works .... Shabbos 74b
Feather, shining, bird sacrifice .... Chullin 22a-22b
Feather, strength of *Kohanim* .... Zevachim 64a
Feathers of bird, *treifah* .... Chullin 58b

Fee
Fee for dog, for sacrifice .... Temurah 30a-30b; Yevamos 59b; Sotah 26b
Fee for prostitute .... *see* **Prostitute's fee**, page 507
Fee for scribe, divorce certificate .... Gittin 20a; Bava Basra 168a

Feet of men lead them to place of death .... Succah 53a

Female
Female animal in place of male, young .... Temurah 18b-19b, 20b-21a
Female for burnt offering, private altar .... Avodah Zarah 24b
Female in place of male, sacrifice .... Temurah 19b-20b, 27b-28a
Female lamb for Pesach, young .... Pesachim 97b-98a
Female, time of formation .... Niddah 30b
Female, which sacrifices .... Temurah 14a

Femur
Femur, covered impurity .... Chullin 124b-125a, 126b
Femur of Og, episode .... Niddah 24b

Fence
Fence .... *see also* **Safety fence**, page 582
Fence, act of acquisition .... Bava Basra 52b
Fence and small hill, combining .... Eruvin 93b; Gittin 15b
Fence for Torah etc., *Pirkei Avos* .... Avos 1:1, 3:13
Fence for wisdom, silence .... Avos 3:13
Fence of roses, *niddah* .... Sanhedrin 37a
Fence of thorns, damage .... Bava Kama 30a
Fence, thought on Shabbos about repairing, episode .... Shabbos 150b

Fenced as a dwelling, free land .... Eruvin 26a

Festival
Festival .... *see also* **Yom Tov**, page 771
Festival, visiting one's teacher .... Succah 27b
Festivals in *Eretz Yisrael* and in Babylon .... Shabbos 145b

F

Festivals of idolaters .... *see* **Idolaters' festivals**, page 295

Festival on which moon is covered .... Rosh Hashanah 8a, 11a, 34a; Beitzah 16a, Sanhedrin 96b

Fetus

Birth —

Fetus, leg extended outside .... Chullin 69a

Fetus, miscarriage .... Niddah 24b

Fetus, put out limbs .... Chullin 68b-69a

Fetus, withdrew leg back in .... Chullin 68a-68b

Damages —

Fetus, ox goring occasionally .... Bava Kama 41b-42b

Fetus, payment .... Bava Kama 42b-43a, 49a-49b

Fetus, payment, damage made by ox .... Bava Kama 42a, 48b-49a

Laws —

Fetus, abortion .... Sanhedrin 57b

Fetus, bequeathing inheritance to .... Bava Basra 141b-142b

Fetus completed, hair and nails .... Yevamos 80a-80b

Fetus, danger to its mother .... Oholos 7:6; Sanhedrin 72b

Fetus discernable, after how much time .... Sanhedrin 69a; Yevamos 37a, 42a; Niddah 8b

Fetus, freedom for maidservant's fetus .... Gittin 23b; Kiddushin 69a; Temurah 25a-25b

Fetus, his mother's conversion .... Yevamos 78a-78b

Fetus, inheritance .... Bava Basra 142a-142b; Arachin 7a; Niddah 44a-44b

Fetus, *kiddushin* when she will be born .... Kiddushin 62b

Fetus, mother killed by *beis din* .... Arachin 7a

Prohibitions —

Fetus, causes *terumah* to be forbidden to slave .... Yevamos 67a-67b; Bava Basra 141b; Niddah 44a

Fetus, dead, impurity .... Chullin 70b

Fetus, disqualifies from *terumah* .... Yevamos 67b; Niddah 44a

Fetus, dissolved, impurity .... Bechoros 21b-22a, 23a-23b; Niddah 27b

Fetus in mother's womb, slaughtering .... Chullin 74a

Fetus, resembling man .... Niddah 23b

Fetus which put a leg out and in, animal .... Chullin 68a-68b

Fetus, without cloven hooves, in cow's womb .... Chullin 69a

Sacrifices —

Fetus consecrated, its mother slaughtered outside Temple .... Temurah 12a

Fetus, consecrating .... Zevachim 98a; Temurah 10a-11b, 16b, 19a-19b, 25a-25b; Yevamos 78a;

Menachos 81a, 83a; Chullin 90a; Krisos 23b; Niddah 41a

Fetus of slaughtered sacrifice .... Chullin 75a

Characteristics —

Fetus, characteristics .... Niddah 16b, 25a-25b

Fetus, died before its mother .... Arachin 7a; Bava Basra 142a-142b; Niddah 44a-44b

Fetus, formation and *aggadah* .... Berachos 10a; Megillah 14a; Yoma 85a; Niddah 30b-31a

Fetus, soul .... Sanhedrin 91b

Misc. —

Fetus, like mother's femur ...... Nazir 51a; Temurah 10b, 11a, 19a, 25a-25b, 30b, 31a; Yevamos 78a-78b;

Gittin 23b; Bava Kama 78b; Sanhedrin 80b; Chullin 58a

Fetus, prayers .... Berachos 60a

Fetus, whispering to it on Yom Kippur .... Yoma 82b

Fever

Fever, sick .... Nedarim 41a-41b; Sanhedrin 108b

Fever *yerakon*, cure .... Shabbos 110a-110b

Field

Agriculture —

Field .... *see also* **Land**, page 352

Field, advice about agriculture .... Bava Metzia 107a; Bava Basra 24b

Field, irrigated or dependant only on rain .... Moed Katan 2a

Field, ownership .... Yevamos 63a; Sanhedrin 58b; Menachos 103b-104a

Field, plowing .... Bava Kama 30a; Bava Basra 12a; Menachos 85b, 87a

Field, Sage's knowledge of .... Shabbos 85a

Monetary matters —

Field, buying from non-Jew .... Bava Basra 54b-55a

Field, how to divide .... Bava Basra 12a-12b

Field of fellow, using .... Bava Kama 80b-81b

Field of patrimony .... *see* **Patrimony**, page 476

Field, plowed, *chazakah* .... Bava Basra 36a-37a

Field, sale, filled with rocks .... Kiddushin 61a; Bava Basra 102b-103b

Field, size for dividing up .... Bava Basra 12a

Field stolen .... Bava Kama 116b

Fields, act of acquisition of several .... Kiddushin 27a-27b; Bava Kama 12a; Bava Basra 67a-67b

Prohibitions —

Field and plot of land, towns in *Eretz Yisrael* .... Arachin 33b

Field, doubtful impurity, repair .... Oholos 18:1, 18:4-6; Niddah 57a

Field, gifts for poor .... Chullin 131a-131b

Field kept on Sabbatical year .... Sheviis 9:1; Maasros 5:8; Succah 39b

Field where deceased is eulogized, impurity .... Oholos 18:4

Misc. —

Field of apples, Jacob .... Taanis 29b

Field of lazy man .... Sanhedrin 103a

Field, doubtful impurity

Field, doubtful impurity .... Oholos 13:6, 17:5

Field, doubtful impurity, cases .... Oholos 18:2-4; Moed Katan 5b

Field, doubtful impurity, checking .... Chagigah 25b; Bechoros 29a; Oholos 18:4-5

Field, doubtful impurity, how .... Oholos 17:4; Moed Katan 5b-6a; Temurah 12b-13a

Field, doubtful impurity, *Kohen* .... Avodah Zarah 13a

Field, doubtful impurity, size .... Oholos 17:1-3; Moed Katan 5b-6a; Niddah 57a

Fifteen

Fifteen, Succos learned from Pesach .... Succah 27a

Fifteen women, levirate marriage .... Yevamos 2a-3b

Fifteenth of *Av* .... Bava Basra 121a-121b; Taanis 30b-31a

Fifteenth of *Shevat* .... Rosh Hashanah 14a-14b

Fifth

Temple Treasury —

Fifth, addition during auction .... Arachin 27b-28a

Fifth, endowment valuation and field redemption .... Arachin 14b

Fifth, person atoned is exempt .... Temurah 2b, 9b-10a; Yoma 50b; Nedarim 36b; Zevachim 6a

Fifth, secular use .... Bava Kama 111a; Bava Metzia 99b; Krisos 27a

Fifth, Rabbinical secular use .... Meilah 2b

Fifth, second redeeming .... Temurah 9b-10a; Bava Metzia 54b

F

Misc. —

Fifth, according to total sum..Bava Metzia 53b-54a

Fifth added to fifth..Bava Metzia 54b; Temurah 9b

Fifth, charity..Kesubos 50a, 67b; Arachin 28a

Fifth, does not invalidate payment........................Bava Metzia 54a; Berachos 47b; Bava Kama 111a

Fifth, first fruit and *challah*..Meilah 15b

Fifth, for what..Bava Metzia 55b

Fifth inferior to *perutah*, redeeming................................Arachin 27a; Bava Metzia 53b-54a

Fifth, like capital..Bava Metzia 54a-54b

Fifth of *terumah*, non-holy food................................Bava Metzia 54a; Terumos 6:4

Fifth, redeeming revai................................Maaser Sheni 5:1, 5:5; Eduyos 4:5; Kiddushin 54b

Fifth, redeeming second tithe..Shabbos 127b

Fifth, *terumah*................................Terumos 7:1-4; Shabbos 69b; Pesachim 32a

Fifty gates of understanding................................Rosh Hashanah 21b; Nedarim 38a

Fifty shekels

Fifty shekels, redeeming field..Arachin 14a-14b

Fifty shekels, rocks................................Kiddushin 61a; Bava Basra 102b-103a; Arachin 25a

Fifty shekels, stones..Arachin 14b

Fifty shekels, trees................................Bava Basra 72a-72b; Arachin 14a

Fig

Fig, hidden fruit..Eruvin 54a-54b

Fig, makes drunk................Nazir 4a; Yoma 76a-76b; Sanhedrin 70b-71a; Shevuos 23a; Bechoros 45b; Krisos 13b

Figs, beautiful beams..Tamid 29b-30a

Figs, fallen, *demai*..Berachos 40b-41a; Demai 1:1

Figs in the east..Yoma 83b

Figs on dried figs, tithes..Menachos 54b-55a

Figs, thousand foods..Nedarim 50b

Figs, tithes..Niddah 50a

Figs to idolater, idolatrous cult................................Avodah Zarah 13b-14b

Figs, unripe, tithe..Eruvin 28b

Figs, unripe, transport..Chagigah 5a

Fig-tree, give me your fruit..Taanis 24a

Fig, dried

Fig, dried, amount..Keilim 17:7

Fig, dried, size of *sela* coin..Shabbos 78b

Figs, dried, *muktzeh*................................Shabbos 45a-45b; Beitzah 40a-40b

Figs, dried, nine in a meal..Eruvin 80b

Figs, dried, Rav Dimi..Bava Basra 22a

Filling

Filling and pouring, wine container..Avodah Zarah 74b-75a

Filling water for sprinkling................................Pesachim 34b-35a; Sotah 16b

Filling water, *techum*..Beitzah 39a-39b

Fills righteous man's years................................Sotah 13b; Kiddushin 38a; Rosh Hashanah 11a

Filter, uncovered................................Succah 50a; Bava Kama 115b; Bava Basra 97b

Filtering

Filtering on Shabbos................................Shabbos 138a, 139b-140a, 109a

Filtering on Yom Tov..Shabbos 139b

Final

Final blessing................................Berachos 12a, 37a-37b, 44a, 44b; Niddah 51b-52a

Final blessing, quantity .... Berachos 38b-39a
Final letters .... Megillah 2b-3a; Shabbos 104a
Final touch, cases .... Shabbos 48a-48b, 75b, 102b-103a

Find
Prohibitions —
Found *chametz* on Pesach .... Pesachim 6a
Found, doubt if it is this item .... Pesachim 10a
Found its kind and reawakens .... Avodah Zarah 73a; Eruvin 9a; Bechoros 22a-23a
Found its kind, *karmelis* .... Eruvin 9a
Found sacrificial animal .... Kiddushin 55a-55b; Shekalim 7:4-5
Found slaughtered meat .... Chullin 12a-12b; Bava Metzia 24b
Found woman, found goodness .... Yevamos 63b
Misc. —
Find more bitter than death, bad woman .... Yevamos 63a-63b
Finding good or bad wife .... Yevamos 63b; Berachos 8a
Found differently from way one left it ...... Maaser Sheni 4:12; Beitzah 10b; Pesachim 10b; Gittin 51a
Found item
Found item .... *see also* **Lost item**, page 378
Found item, by daughter .... Kesubos 46b-47a; Niddah 47a
Found item, by Hebrew maidservant .... Kiddushin 16b
Found item, by lapse of attention .... Sanhedrin 97a
Found item, by slave .... Bava Metzia 12b
Found item, by widow .... Kesubos 96a
Found item, by wife .... Kesubos 65b-66a; Yevamos 90b
Found item, by worker .... Bava Kama 116b; Bava Metzia 12b
Found item, picked up for friend .... Beitzah 39b; Bava Metzia 8a, 9a-10a
Fine flour .... *see* **Semolina**, page 601
Finger
"Finger between teeth," responsibility .... Kesubos 52a, 59b, 71a-71b
Finger, dimension for which items .... Bechoros 39b-40a
Finger in wax, decline of generations .... Eruvin 53a
Finger of G-d, magicians .... Sanhedrin 67b
Fingers clapping, episode .... Yoma 19b
Fingers, eating porridge .... Nedarim 49b
Fingers, handbreadth .... Menachos 41b
Fingers, names and use .... Kesubos 5b; Menachos 11a
Fingers of Greek man, revenge .... Taanis 18b
Fingers resembling stakes, reason .... Kesubos 5b
Fingernails .... *see* **Nails**, page 434
Finish
Finish work is not your responsibility .... Avos 2:96-16
Finished his custody .... Bava Kama 118b
Finishing, amount for Shabbos violation .... Krisos 17a, 19b; Shabbos 104b, 105a
Fins and scales, why did both need to be written .... Chullin 66a-66b; Niddah 51b
Fire pan
Fire pan containing ashes, *muktzeh* .... Shabbos 47a
Fire pan of incense, taking out .... Yoma 47a

Fire

Aggadah —
Fire, creation .... Pesachim 54a
Fire, different kinds .... Yoma 21b
Fire, Divine immersion .... Sanhedrin 39a
Fire, expressions .... Bava Kama 60a
Fire, one sixtieth of *Gehinnom* .... Berachos 57b
Fire, religion of fire for Israel .... Beitzah 25b
Fire, second Temple .... Yoma 21b
Fire sparks, Rebbi and Rav .... Chullin 137b

Damages —
Fire, atonement payment in case of death .... Bava Kama 43b
Fire, cases of no liability .... Bava Kama 60a
Fire, compared to arrows .... Bava Kama 22a-23a, 60b
Fire, damage caused to hidden item .... Bava Kama 23a, 60a, 61b-62a
Fire, distance .... Bava Kama 61a, 61b
Fire, fanned with wind .... Bava Kama 60a

Episodes —
Fire by Amram's house! .... Kiddushin 81a
Fire, Rabbi Zeira .... Bava Metzia 85a
Fire, Sages' funerals .... Kesubos 17a, 77b
Fire, saved by merit of deeds of kindness .... Taanis 21b
Fire, to escape sin with noblewoman .... Kiddushin 40a

Prohibitions —
"Fire near straw," *niddah* .... Sanhedrin 37a
Fire for incense and *menorah* .... Yoma 45b-46a
Fire on Altar .... Yoma 21b, 45a; Zevachim 61b; Menachos 22a
Fire on Altar, putting out .... Yoma 46b; Zevachim 91b-92a

Misc. —
Fire, concern of *treifah* .... Chullin 56b, 57a
Fire on righteous men's canopy .... Bava Basra 75a
Fires to announce sanctifying of month .... Rosh Hashanah 22b-23a; Beitzah 4b

Fire on Shabbos
Fire on Shabbos, carrying out on Shabbos .... Beitzah 39a
Fire on Shabbos in Temple, Shabbos eve .... Shabbos 20a-20b
Fire on Shabbos, kindling on Shabbos eve .... Shabbos 20a-20b
Fire on Shabbos, child .... Shabbos 121a
Fire on Shabbos, episode .... Shabbos 121a
Fire on Shabbos, holy writings .... Shabbos 115a-117b
Fire on Shabbos, *muktzeh* .... Shabbos 46b-47a
Fire on Shabbos, non-Jew .... Shabbos 121a
Fire on Shabbos, saving .... Shabbos 117b, 120a-120b; Eruvin 95b
Fire on Shabbos, Shabbos desecration .... Shabbos 119b

Firm and valid .... Bava Basra 160b
Firmaments
Firmaments, dimensions .... Pesachim 94a-94b
Firmaments, general .... Chagigah 12b

First
"First," commandments about which "first" is written .... Pesachim 5a

F

First expression determining ....Temurah 26a
First fleece ....Chullin 135a, 136a-138b; Berachos 22a
First group to perform commandment, better ....Pesachim 65a
First, means previous ....Pesachim 5a
First one gains, penalty ....Bava Kama 30b
First owner, *chazakah* ....Kesubos 76a-76b
First purchase, unfavorable sign ....Kiddushin 59a
First ruling is mistaken ....Beitzah 16b
First Sages did not give reason ....Bava Basra 81b
First sanctification of *Eretz Yisrael* ....Megillah 10a-10b; Shevuos 16a; Zevachim 60b, 107b
First speaker, Rabbi Yehudah ....Shabbos 33b; Berachos 63b
First thing first, wise man ....Avos 5:7
First to come to house of study, Sage ....Berachos 43b
First to keep commandment, preference ....Yoma 62a, 64a
First to thank G-d, Leah ....Berachos 7b
First use, impurity ....Keilim 16:1
First word of series, deduction ....Sanhedrin 3b; Succah 6b

First generations
First generations, humility ....Sanhedrin 11b
First generations, importance ....Berachos 35b; Shabbos 112b; Eruvin 53a; Yoma 9b
First generations like angels ....Shabbos 112b
First generations, self-sacrifice ....Berachos 20a
First generations, stringencies ....Gittin 81a; Berachos 35b

First fruit
From which field —
First fruit, all one's field ....Bikkurim 2:4
First fruit, close to fellow's ....Bava Basra 26b-27b
First fruit, doubt ....Bava Basra 81b
First fruit, field not his ....Gittin 47b
First fruit, places ....Menachos 84a-85a; Bikurim 1:3; Challah 4:11; Pesachim 53a
First fruit, cases of exemption ....Bikurim 1:1-3, 1:10; Pesachim 53a; Menachos 84a-84b
First fruit, buyer ....Bikurim 1:6, 1:10-11; Bava Basra 27a, 81a-82a; Gittin 48a
How —
First fruit, addition ....Bikurim 3:9-11; Bava Kama 92a
First fruit, bringing ....Bikurim 3:2-8; Kiddushin 33a; Chullin 54b
First fruit, does not read ....Bikkurim 1:4-7, 1:8-9
First fruit, *Kohen* ....Bikurim 3:12; Chullin 131a
First fruit, proximity ....Bikkurim 2:5
First fruit, reading ....Bikurim 3:6-7; Sotah 33a; Bava Basra 81b
First fruit, separating tithes ....Bikurim 3:1
First fruit, song ....Arachin 11a
First fruit, time ....Challah 4:10
First fruit, waving ....Succah 47b; Makos 18b-19a; Menachos 61a-61b
First fruit, what is an indispensable requirement ....Makos 17a, 18b-19a
Misc. —
First fruit, agent ....Bava Basra 81b-81b; Gittin 47b
First fruit, are called *terumah* ....Meilah 15b; Pesachim 36b; Yevamos 73b; Makos 17a; Chullin 120b
First fruit, eliminating ....Bikkurim 2:2; Yevamos 73a-73b
First fruit, from when are they forbidden ....Makos 18b-19a

F

First fruit, gift to Sage..Kesubos 105b
First fruit, lashes..Makos 17a-17b, 18b
First fruit, *matzah* for first day of Pesach..Pesachim 36a-36b
First fruit, misleading government..Taanis 28a
First fruit, *onein*...Bikurim 2:2; Pesachim 36b; Yevamos 73a-73b
First fruit, responsibility...Bikkurim 1:8-9

Firstborn
  Inheritance —
Firstborn, after death...Bava Basra 142b; Niddah 44a-44b
Firstborn, after stillborn...Bechoros 46a, 47b
Firstborn and brother, were mixed...Bava Basra 127a
Firstborn, before sharing...Bava Basra 126a-126b
Firstborn, contiguous parcels of land...Bava Basra 12b
Firstborn, foolish, father's declaration...Bava Basra 126b
Firstborn, double portion...Bava Basra 122b-123a
Firstborn, father disinherits..Bava Basra 130a
Firstborn, increase in value of inheritance ....Bava Metzia 110b; Bava Basra 123b-124b, 126a;
                                                                                        Bava Kama 95b; Bechoros 51b-52b
Firstborn, inheritance of future property ...Bechoros 51b-52b; Bava Basra 55a, 119a, 123b, 124b-126a
Firstborn, inheritance of future property and increase in value.................Bechoros 51b-52b
Firstborn, mother's inheritance......................................Bava Basra 111a-111b; Bechoros 51b-52a
Firstborn, renouncement..Bava Basra 124a, 126a-126b
  Redeeming —
Firstborn, caesarian birth...Bechoros 47b
Firstborn, convert...Bechoros 47a
Firstborn of mother, redeeming..Kiddushin 29b
Firstborn, two heads..Menachos 37a-37b
  Misc. —
Firstborn devil, daughter's rival...Yevamos 16a
Firstborn, foolish..Bava Basra 126b
Firstborn, father's trustworthiness......Bava Basra 126b, 127b, 128b; Kiddushin 74a, 78b; Yevamos 47a
Firstborn in desert...Sanhedrin 17a; Bechoros 4b-5a
Firstborn, its spit cures...Bava Basra 126b
Firstborn, levirate marriage...Yevamos 24a
Firstborn rights of Joseph...Bava Basra 123a
Firstborn, service..Zevachim 115b
Firstborn, trustworthiness...Kiddushin 73b-74a

Firstborn animal
  Blemishes —
Firstborn animal, androgyny..Bechoros 41b
firstborn animal, *Ayalah*, expert in blemishes.................................Bechoros 29a
Firstborn animal, blemished, eating...Bechoros 32b-33a
Firstborn animal, *muktzeh*.......................................Shabbos 46b; Beitzah 25b-26b
Firstborn animal, in present times, blemish ....Bechoros 3b, 35a, 53a-53b; Temurah 24b
Firstborn animal, resembling to another species.............Bechoros 3b, 5b, 6b, 12a, 16b, 17a;
                                                                                                                            Bava Kama 78a
Firstborn animal, gender doubtful..Bava Basra 126b
Firstborn animal, *treifah*..Zevachim 104a
Firstborn animal, visible and permanent blemish.............................Bechoros 37a-37b

Checking and trustworthiness —

Firstborn animal, blemish on Yom Tov ......Beitzah 25b-26b, 27a-27b; Shabbos 136a; Chullin 51b
Firstborn animal, checking blemish ....Beitzah 27a; Bechoros 28a-28b, 36b-37a
Firstborn animal, expert judge ....Bechoros 28b-29a
Firstborn animal, giving authority to check blemishes ....Yoma 78a
Firstborn animal, trustworthiness about blemish.............Shabbos 145a-145b; Bechoros 28a, 36a
Firstborn animal, trustworthiness of *Kohen* ....Yoma 78a; Bechoros 36a-36b
Firstborn donkey, lamb...Chullin 74b; Bechoros 4b, 10b-12b
Firstborn donkey, redeeming ....Bechoros 5b, 9a-9b, 11a, 12b-13a

Laws —

Firstborn animal, a year......Zevachim 29a-29b; Rosh Hashanah 5b-7a; Bechoros 27b, 28a; Temurah 21b
Firstborn animal, blemished, to *Kohen*..Bechoros 28a
Firstborn animal, caring ....Bechoros 26b; Temurah 8b
Firstborn animal, eating ....Makos 19a-19b; Bechoros 32b-33a; Zevachim 60b
Firstborn animal, fine for who causes a blemish...Bechoros 34a-34b
Firstborn animal, hair ....Bechoros 25a-26b; Eduyos 5:6
Firstborn animal, prohibition to cause a blemish....................................Bechoros 33b-34a
Firstborn animal, redeemed sacrifices...Bechoros 15a
Firstborn animal, sale ....Zevachim 75b; Temurah 5b, 7b-9a; Bechoros 31b-32a; Maaser Sheni 1:2;
....Bava Kama 12b-13a
Firstborn animal, sanctity by speech ....Nazir 4b; Nedarim 12b-13a
Firstborn animal, skin..Bechoros 33a; Temurah 24a
Firstborn animal, time for eating ....Zevachim 57a; Bechoros 27b-28a
Firstborn animal, ways to cause a blemish....................................Bechoros 33b-34a, 35a
Firstborn animal, whose property...Temurah 7b-8b

Misc. —

Firstborn animal, consecrating...Arachin 29a; Nedarim 13a
Firstborn animal, avoiding in present times ....Bechoros 3b, 35a, 53a-53b; Temurah 10b, 24b
Firstborn animal, birth ....Chullin 69b-70a
Firstborn animal, blemished, eating.....................Bechoros 32b-33a; Zevachim 75b; Temurah 24a
Firstborn animal, doubt ....Bechoros 17a-20b, 21b, 24a-24b, 41b; Niddah 29a
Firstborn animal, exempt....................................Chullin 135b; Bechoros 19a-19b, 47b
Firstborn animal, non-Jew .....Pesachim 6a; Bava Metzia 70b; Bechoros 3a-3b, 16a-17a, 9b; Chullin 135b
Firstborn animal, in present times...Bechoros 35a
Firstborn animal, outside *Eretz Yisrael*.............................Temurah 21a-21b; Challah 4:11
Firstborn animal, sacrifice....................Zevachim 37a, 56b; Bechoros 5b; Pesachim 64b-65a

Fish

Episodes —

Fish caught on Shabbos, excommunication...Kiddushin 72a
Fish, episode about diamond..Bava Basra 133b
Fish, episode about Rabbi Shimon b'Rebbi...Beitzah 28a
Fish for Shabbos, diamond..Shabbos 119a
Fish, giant...Bava Basra 73b-74b
Fish, impure, saved from eating...Avodah Zarah 39a

Health —

Fish and meat, leprosy...Pesachim 76b
Fish, eye disease...Nedarim 54b
Fish, health...Horayos 12a
Fish, health and advice...Berachos 44b; Moed Katan 11a

Fish, little, health .... Berachos 40a
Prohibitions —
Fish eggs .... Avodah Zarah 39a, 40a-40b; Chullin 63b-64a
Fish, eggs and innards .... Avodah Zarah 39a, 40a-40b; Chullin 63b-64a
Fish, ground, *kashrus* .... Avodah Zarah 39b-40a
Fish, impure, liquid permitted .... Chullin 99b; Terumos 10:8
Fish in milk .... Chullin 111b-112a
Fish, *kashrus* .... Succah 18a; Avodah Zarah 39a; Bechoros 7b
Fish, killing .... Shabbos 107b
Fish prepared by non-Jew .... Avodah Zarah 34b
Fish, ritual slaughter .... Chullin 27b
Fish salted together with poultry .... Chullin 112b-113a
Fish scales .... Avodah Zarah 39a; Chullin 66a-66b; Niddah 51b
Fish, signs .... Avodah Zarah 39a-40a; Chullin 66a-66b; Niddah 51b
Fish, vowing to refrain from male and female .... Nedarim 51b, 52b
Scientific facts —
Fish, big fish eats small one .... Avodah Zarah 4a
Fish, numerous species .... Chullin 63b
Fish, old, strength .... Shabbos 77b; Avodah Zarah 30b
Fish, characteristics .... Bava Metzia 79b; Avodah Zarah 40a
Fish, work for man .... Sanhedrin 59b; Bava Kama 55a
Misc. —
Fish, breaded .... Pesachim 112a-112b
Fish, distance from net .... Bava Basra 21b
Fish, evil eye .... Berachos 20a, 55b; Sotah 36b; Bava Metzia 84a; Bava Basra 118b
Fish, impurity .... Chullin 75a
Fish, parable for man .... Avodah Zarah 3b-4a
Fish, parable for two answers .... Bava Kama 41b-42a
Fisherman
Fisherman at sea, ownerless .... Bava Kama 81b
Fisherman, fish tunnel .... Yevamos 121a
Fisherman, moving net away .... Bava Basra 21b
Fishing
Fishing net, moving away .... Bava Basra 21b
Fishing trap .... Sanhedrin 81b
Fist, dimension .... Bechoros 37b
Fit
Fit, firstborn .... Bechoros 51b-52b; Bava Basra 55a, 119a, 123b, 124b-126a
Fit for dog, impurity of food .... Pesachim 45b; Taharos 8:6; Krisos 21a
Fit for dog, *muktzeh* .... Shabbos 121a-121b; Beitzah 33a
Fit for dogs, impurity of *neveilah* .... Bechoros 23a-23b; Nazir 50a; Chullin 71a
Fit for seven days, succah .... Succah 23a, 27b
Fit, sacrifice outside .... Zevachim 108a
Fit to receive but does not have .... Bava Kama 35b-36a
Fit to receive Divine Presence .... Sanhedrin 11a
Fitting, poverty for Israel .... Chagigah 9b
Five
Five *chumashin* .... Bava Metzia 55b
Five dead sin offerings .... Pesachim 97a-97b; Temurah 21b-22a; Meilah 10b-11a

Five nations from one couple..Yevamos 99a
Five oxen goring occasionally...Bava Kama 15b
Five *sela*, redeeming...Kiddushin 8a
Five voices, groom..Berachos 6b
Five years old, Mishnah..Avos 5:21

Fixed
Fixed price, purchase..Avodah Zarah 72a; Bava Basra 85b-86a
Fixed times for Torah study..Eruvin 54b
Fixing single time for everybody...Sheviis 2:1

Flag, synagogue in Alexandria..Succah 51b

Flame
Flame, carrying out on Shabbos...Beitzah 39a
Flame, not like fire...Beitzah 39a

Flask of manna, concealed...............................Horayos 12a; Yoma 52b; Krisos 5b

Flat
Flat cakes, meal offerings...............................Menachos 59a, 59a, 60a, 63a-63b, 72b, 73a
Flat cakes of *nazir*..Menachos 19a, 27a, 76a, 78a

Flat utensils
Flat utensils, glass...Shabbos 16a; Keilim 2:1
Flat utensils, immersion...Shabbos 84b
Flat utensils, impurity...Keilim 2:1, 15:1
Flat utensils, impurity of couch...Bava Kama 25b

Flatterers
Flatterers, desecrate G-d's name...Yoma 86b
Flatterers, groups...Sanhedrin 103a; Sotah 42a

Flattery
Flattery, Babylon...Sanhedrin 24a; Kiddushin 49b
Flattery, in this world...Sotah 41b
Flattery, Korah's assembly..Sanhedrin 52a
Flattery, prohibition..Sotah 41b-42a
Flattery to King Agrippas, punishment...Sotah 41b

Flaw
Flaw of family, sells his tomb..........................Bava Basra 100b; Kesubos 84a; Bechoros 52b
Flaw of virgin, acknowledgment...Kesubos 41a

Flax
Flax..*see also* **Linen,** page 371
Flax, non intermingled fiber.......................................Yoma 71b; Zevachim 18b
Flax of Babylon...Taanis 29b
Flax on lamp of storekeeper..Bava Kama 62b
Flax, tree...Shabbos 27b

Flea
Flea, *niddah* stains...Niddah 58b-59a
Flea, reptile...Niddah 58b

Fled
Fled, husband supporting his wife..Kesubos 48a, 106b-107b
Fled, landowner, *chazakah* by use..Kesubos 17b
Fleeing from power...Eruvin 13b
Fleeing man, death penalty...............................Makos 7a; Gittin 28b, 29a; Sanhedrin 45b

F

Fleece

Fleece of animal partly destined to be sacrificed .... Temurah 11b
Fleece of firstborn .... Bechoros 24b-26b; Eduyos 5:6
Fleece of fit sacrifice .... Bechoros 26a-26b, 14a
Fleece of redeemed sacrifice .... Bechoros 6b, 15a, 25a; Chullin 137a; Temurah 31a

Flesh

Flesh .... *see also* **Meat**, page 398
Flesh dangling, eating .... Chullin 73b-74a
Flesh dangling, *neveilah* .... Chullin 73a-74a
Flesh of dead, olive volume, impurity .... Chullin 129b
Flesh of sacrifices .... *see also* **Burnt parts of sacrifices**, page 81
Flesh, putrefied, of dead .... Nazir 50a
Flesh to be cut by veterinary, *treifah* .... Chullin 53b

Flies

Flies, sayings .... Chullin 58b
Fly, cure for hornet .... Shabbos 77b
Fly, longevity .... Chullin 58b
Fly of Egypt, danger .... Shabbos 121b

Flight is beginning of defeat .... Sotah 44b

Flock which value is fixed

Flock which value is fixed, buying back after divorce or death .... Yevamos 66a-67a
Flock which value is fixed, firstborn .... Bava Metzia 70b; Bechoros 16a-17a
Flock which value is fixed, interest .... Bava Metzia 70b

Flood

Flood, Babylon .... Zevachim 113b
Flood, *Eretz Yisrael* .... Zevachim 113a-113b
Flood, reason .... Sanhedrin 107b-108a
Flood, stars .... Berachos 59a
Flood, twelve months .... Eduyos 2:10
Flood, when and how .... Rosh Hashanah 11b-12a
Flood, who was saved .... Zevachim 113b

Floor

"Floor," *niddah* blood in female body .... Niddah 17b-18a; Bava Basra 24a
Floor above Holy of Holies and *Heichal* .... Middos 4:5; Pesachim 86a
Floor, changes in building .... Bava Metzia 116b, 117b
Floor for me, gift .... Bava Basra 148a-148b
Floor in Temple, holiness .... Pesachim 86a
Floor of buyer, act of acquisition .... Bava Metzia 49b
Floor of Temple Courtyard, height .... Yoma 31a-31b
Floor of Temple Courtyard, offering .... Zevachim 59a-60a
Floor, upper, leaving right to .... Bava Basra 63a-63b, 64a, 148a
Floor which caved in, tenant's rights .... Bava Metzia 116b-117a
Floor, who must repair .... Bava Metzia 117a; Bava Basra 6b-7a

Flour

Flour .... *see also* **Semolina**, page 601
Flour, blessing .... Berachos 36a
Flour from sand, episode .... Taanis 24b
Flour, ground, you ground .... Sanhedrin 96b
Flour separated for *challah* .... Challah 2:5; Kiddushin 46b

Flow
Flow, continuous, *zavah* .... Nazir 16a
Flowing water, *mikveh* .... Chullin 31b
Flowing with milk, *Eretz Yisrael* .... Kesubos 111b-112a

Flowing liquid
Flowing liquid, connection to *mikveh* .... Taharos 8:9
Flowing liquid, *mikveh* .... Gittin 16a; Avodah Zarah 72a
Flowing liquid, wine of idolaters .... Avodah Zarah 72a

Flower pot
Flower pot, act of acquisition .... Gittin 22a
Flower pot, divorce certificate .... Gittin 21b-22a
Flower pot, *Eretz Yisrael* .... Gittin 7b-8a
Flower pot, hole on bottom, like soil .... Shabbos 95a-95b, 108a; Gittin 7b-8a
Flower pot, impurity of food .... Uktzin 2:9-10; Chullin 128a; Shabbos 95a-95b
Flower pot in vineyard, mixed species .... Kilayim 7:8; Pesachim 25a; Chullin 116a
Flower pot, mixed seeds .... Menachos 70a
Flower pot, Shabbos .... Shabbos 81b
Flower pot, tithes .... Kiddushin 46b; Yoma 83b; Demai 5:10; Yevamos 89b; Menachos 70a
Flowerbed, mixed species .... Shabbos 84b-85a; Kilayim 3:1-2; Pesachim 39a-39b; Kiddushin 39b
Flute in Temple .... Arachin 10b
Foam in cup, dangerous .... Chullin 105b
Folded
Folded garment, Shabbos .... Shabbos 58a, 142a, 147a
Folding garments on Shabbos .... Shabbos 113a
Following teacher and not disciple! .... Niddah 14b
Food .... *see also* **Support**, page 664

Behavior —
Food at home, otherwise woman shouts .... Temurah 16a
Food, buying food with last coin .... Chullin 84a
Food, enjoyable, keep away .... Gittin 70a
Food in the house, be mindful of .... Bava Metzia 59a
Food missing at home, poverty .... Bava Metzia 59a
Food needed for journey .... Pesachim 113a
Food, tasty, there is always room for it .... Megillah 7b; Eruvin 82b
Foods harmful like swords .... Kiddushin 62a

Forbidden food —
Food of non-Jew, concern .... Avodah Zarah 31b-32a, 34b, 35b-36a, 38b-39b, 40b
Food of non-Jew, theft .... Avodah Zarah 34b-35b
Foods, forbidden, conquest of *Eretz Yisrael* .... Chullin 17a
Foods, forbidden, fraud .... Bechoros 37a

Impurity —
Food, considered impure .... Machshirin 6:2-3
Food forbidden to non-Jew, impurity .... Chullin 129a-129b; Menachos 101b; Bechoros 9b
Food impurity, combining for meat .... Taharos 1:4; Chullin 117b
Food impurity, fit for dog .... Krisos 21a; Pesachim 45b; Taharos 8:6
Food impurity, forbidden to non-Jew .... Chullin 129a-129b; Menachos 101b; Bechoros 9b
Food impurity, mixed and divided .... Taharos 1:5-6; Zevachim 31a
Food impurity, mixture .... Zevachim 31a; Taharos 1:5
Food, rendering impure .... Pesachim 18a-18b

Food touching food, impurity..Pesachim 14a
Food, combining for impurity by eating
Food, combining for impurity by eating..............................Mikvaos 10:7; Krisos 13a
Food, combining for impurity by eating, quantity.............Chullin 33b-35a; Taharos 2:2
Food, combining for impurity by eating, Rabbinical.............Shabbos 13b-14a; Yoma 80b
Prohibitions —
Food for animal, cutting off end of wood splinter............................Beitzah 33b
Food for rare animal, *muktzeh*..Shabbos 128a
Food, not to pass by...Eruvin 64b; Bava Metzia 23a
Food on Yom Tov, *muktzeh*..Beitzah 31b
Food on Yom Tov...*see* **Yom Tov**, page 771
Food to animal on Shabbos.......................................Shabbos 155a-155b, 156b
Food, wording of vow..Eruvin 30a; Berachos 35b
Foods that cook quickly..Shabbos 145b
Misc. —
Food coming from curse, blessing..Berachos 40b
Food, considered separated..Chullin 73a
Food, debasement and spoiling...............................Berachos 50b, 52b; Shabbos 50b
Food for servant..Kesubos 61a
Food, garments, marital relations..Kesubos 47b-48a
Food of Ben Drusai.............Shabbos 20a, 36b; Avodah Zarah 38a; Menachos 57a
Foods for Rosh Hashanah.......................................Horayos 12a; Krisos 6a
Fool
Fool...*see also* **Deaf-mute, demented and minor**, page 149
Fool all one's life, better...Eduyos 5:6
Fool, does not say always same nonsense...Gittin 68b
Fool is not hurt...Shabbos 13b
Fool jumps first...Megillah 12b
Fool, no solution for him..Niddah 13b
Fool walks in darkness...................Eruvin 6b-7a; Rosh Hashanah 14b; Chullin 43b-44a
Fool, who is a...Chagigah 3b-4a
Fool, demented
Fool, demented, and deaf-mute, sanctifying water for sprinkling................Parah 5:4;
....Shabbos 137a; Yoma 43a
Fool, demented, checking for *terumah*..Niddah 13b
Fool, demented, commandments and laws....................................Chagigah 3b-4a
Fool, demented, prophecy...Bava Basra 12b
Fool, demented, Sages did not refer to him.....................................Bava Basra 7a
Fool, demented, supporting his wife...Kesubos 48a
Fool, demented, who was cured, sacrifice.......Sanhedrin 47a; Nedarim 36a; Zevachim 12b
Fool, demented, woman, divorce certificate...........................Yevamos 113b; Gittin 71b
Fools demented, no *kiddushin*..Yevamos 112b
Foolishness, man's foolishness misleads him..................................Taanis 9a
Foot
Foot of Bar Kipok..Moed Katan 25b
Foot, right, first...Yoma 11b; Menachos 34a
Footsteps of Messiah.................................Kesubos 112b; Sanhedrin 97a, 98a-98b
For
"For Your sake we are killed," captives...Gittin 57b

For Heaven's sake, Peninnah..Bava Basra 16a
For Heaven's sake, service...Pesachim 50b
For me was the world created...Sanhedrin 37a

Forbidden...*see also* **Prohibition**, page 505
  Women —
    Forbidden jobs...Kiddushin 82a
    Forbidden, wife without *kesubah*...Kesubos 7a, 57a
    Forbidden women..*see* **Forbidden relations**, page 233
    Forbidden women by Rabbinical Decree...Yevamos 20a; Sanhedrin 53a-53b
  Misc. —
    Forbidden act, forbidden foods..Chullin 114b
    Forbidden act, is it effective..Temurah 4b-6b
    Forbidden act on Shabbos, prohibition to use...................Chullin 15a; Bava Kama 71a; Kesubos 34a;
    ....Terumos 2:3; Gittin 53b
    Forbidden fat, care..Chullin 8b-9a
    Forbidden fat, sending meat...Chagigah 5a
    Forbidden, fellow's money...Bava Metzia 117b
    Forbidden item known but not found...Chullin 43b
    Forbidden substances annul one another...Zevachim 78a-79b
    Forbidden things, permitted for holy purposes...Menachos 5b
    Forbidden to non-Jew but permitted to Jew...Chullin 33a
    Forbidden to non-Jew, impurity.......................Chullin 129a-129b; Menachos 101b; Bechoros 9b
    Forbidden use, without law of secular use..Meilah 12b
  Forbidden food
    Forbidden food, fell in and was taken out..Chullin 97b
    Forbidden foods, coming from forbidden act..Chullin 114b
    Forbidden foods for sick, least forbidden...Yoma 83a-83b
    Forbidden foods, unusual way of benefit..Pesachim 24b-25a
  Forbidden benefit
    Forbidden benefit, animals...Kiddushin 57a
    Forbidden benefit, commandments.......................Succah 31b; Rosh Hashanah 28a; Chullin 89a-89b
    Forbidden benefit, exchange...Kiddushin 58a; Avodah Zarah 71a, 71b
    Forbidden benefit, fire...Temurah 33b-34a; Pesachim 24a
    Forbidden benefit, general..Pesachim 21b-24a; Avodah Zarah 34b-35a
    Forbidden benefit, *kiddushin*...Temurah 30b; Pesachim 7a; Kiddushin 56b
    Forbidden benefit, kindling oven...Pesachim 26b-27b, 75a
    Forbidden benefit, money..Kiddushin 58a
    Forbidden benefit, non-Jew...Avodah Zarah 63b-64a, 71a, 71b
    Forbidden benefit, non-Jewish worker...Avodah Zarah 63a-63b
    Forbidden benefit, substance considered as dust..Yevamos 103b

Forbidden relations
  Episodes —
    Forbidden relations, Abbaye's pain...Succah 52a
    Forbidden relations, Elijah and Rav Kahana...Kiddushin 40a
    Forbidden relations, going into oven...Kiddushin 40a
    Forbidden relations, let him die rather than speak to her..Sanhedrin 75a
    Forbidden relations, Sages' trials..Kiddushin 81a-81b
    Forbidden relations, saved from harmful forces..Kiddushin 39b-40a

Who —

Forbidden relations .... *see also* **Secondary category of forbidden relations**, page 596
Forbidden relations, convert .... Yevamos 22a, 97b-98b; Sanhedrin 57b-58a
Forbidden relations, from father's and mother's sides .... Yevamos 54b-55a
Forbidden relations, non-Jew .... Sanhedrin 56a-57a, 57b-58b
Forbidden relations, non-Jewish woman .... Avodah Zarah 36b; Kiddushin 68b
Forbidden relations, slave .... Sanhedrin 58b
Forbidden relations to all brothers, six .... Yevamos 3b, 13a

Misc. —

Forbidden relations and theft, man is attracted by .... Chagigah 11b; Makos 23b
Forbidden relations, explicating before three people .... Chagigah 11b
Forbidden relations, doves .... Eruvin 100b
Forbidden relations, exile .... Shabbos 33a
Forbidden relations, *kiddushin* .... Kiddushin 67b-68a
Forbidden relations, rather be killed than transgress .... Pesachim 25a-25b;
                                        Sanhedrin 74a-74b; Kiddushin 39b-40a; Yoma 82a
Forbidden relations, levirate marriage .... Yevamos 3b-8b
Forbidden relations, not to change meaning of verses .... Megillah 25a
Forbidden relations, repentance .... Avodah Zarah 17a

Forbidding

Forbidding by air space, *eruv* .... Eruvin 85a-85b, 88a
Forbidding other man's belongings, idolatry .... Chullin 40a-41a; Avodah Zarah 54a-54b
Forbidding other man's item .... Yevamos 83b
Forbidding substance is not forbidden .... Menachos 15a-15b

Force

Marriage —

Forced .... *see also* **Coercion**, page 112
Forced, "as if forced by demon" .... Nedarim 20b; Rosh Hashanah 28a
Forced acceptance by suspending mountain like a dome ...... Shabbos 88a; Avodah Zarah 2b
Forced "I was," *Kohen* and *terumah* .... Nedarim 90b, 90b-91b; Yevamos 112a
Forced marriage .... Bava Basra 48b
Forced sale .... Bava Kama 62a; Bava Basra 47b-48b
Forced sale, declaration .... Bava Basra 40a-40b, 48b
Forced to sell .... Bava Basra 48a
Forced to sign, witnesses' appeal .... Kesubos 18b-19a
Forcing one to divorce .... Yevamos 65b, 112a; Kesubos 63a, 77a-77b; Gittin 88b; Bava Basra 48a
Forcing one to divorce, vows .... Kesubos 52a, 61b, 70a, 71a-71b
Forcing one to levirate marriage .... Yevamos 4a, 8b; Makos 23a
Forcing one to perform *chalitzah* .... Yevamos 106a
Forcing one to perform *chalitzah* and levirate marriage .... Yevamos 39b

Misc. —

Forcing, *beis din* .... Bava Basra 34b
Forcing by hitting .... Kesubos 77a
Forcing for sacrifices, which ones .... Arachin 21a; Bava Kama 40a, 102b
Forcing, Sodom trait (*midas Sodom*) .... Bava Kama 20a-21a; Eruvin 49a; Kesubos 103a;
                                                        Bava Basra 12b, 59a, 168a
Forcing an event to occur earlier .... Berachos 64a; Eruvin 13b
Forcing to offer sacrifice, "I want" .... Rosh Hashanah 6a; Arachin 21a; Yevamos 106a; Kiddushin 50a;
                                                        Bava Basra 48a

Forcing to repay debt .... Kesubos 86a-86b

Forehead-plate

Forehead-plate, for which sins .... Pesachim 77a-78b; Shevuos 9b; Menachos 25b

Forehead-plate, for Israel's benefit .... Yevamos 60b

Forehead-plate, holy to G-d .... Succah 5a; Gittin 20a-20b; Shabbos 63b

Forehead-plate, makes valid impure sacrifice .... Yoma 7a-7b; Menachos 25a

Forehead-plate, makes valid when on forehead .... Yoma 7b-8a

Forehead-plate, Treasury in Rome .... Sukka 5a

Forehead-plate, when does it make sacrifice valid .... Menachos 25a-26a; Pesachim 80b; Yevamos 90a; Yoma 7b Gittin 54a Zevachim 45a-45b

Forehead-plate, width .... Succah 5a; Shabbos 63b

Forehead-plate, wool skullcap .... Chullin 138a

Foreskin

Foreskin pulled, *terumah* .... Yevamos 72a

Foreskin re-covers member, relations with non-Jew .... Eruvin 19a

Foresworn at Mount Sinai .... Shevuos 21b, 22b, 23b, 25a-25b, 27a-27b; Yoma 73b; Nedarim 8a; Nazir 4a; Makos 22a

Forger

Forger, tried to forge his legal document .... Kesubos 36b

Forgers, episodes .... Bava Basra 167a

Forgetfulness

Forgetfulness and memory .... Horayos 13a-13b

Forgetfulness, tower of Babylon .... Sanhedrin 109a

Forgetting

Forgetting dead .... Berachos 58b; Moed Katan 8b

Forgetting, impure man in Temple .... Shevuos 18b-19a; Niddah 28b

Forgetting laws, Moses' death .... Temurah 15b-16a

Forgetting, necessitating sacrifice if knew beforehand .... Shevuos 5a

Forgetting, not paying attention .... Sanhedrin 29b

Forgetting oath and object .... Shevuos 26a

Forgetting *omer*, then remembering .... Bava Metzia 11a

Forgetting only one principle, idolatry .... Sanhedrin 62a, 63a; Shabbos 72b

Forgetting Shabbos and prohibited labors, sin offerings .... Shabbos 69b-71a

Forgetting, twelve months .... Berachos 58b

Forgot his vow about meal offering .... Menachos 104b-106b

Forgot location of collateral, negligence .... Bava Metzia 35a, 42a

Forgot, Moses acknowledged he forgot .... Zevachim 101a

Forgot parts of prayer .... Berachos 29a-29b

Forgot to say blessing .... Berachos 50b-51a

Forgot what one consecrated .... Menachos 104b-105a

Forgot when Shabbos occurs .... Shabbos 69b

Forgotten olives .... Peah 7:1-2

Forgetting Torah

Forgetting Torah, breaking of Tablets .... Eruvin 54a

Forgetting Torah, how .... Taanis 7b

Forgetting Torah, prohibition .... Menachos 99b; Yoma 38b; Avos 3:8

Forgetting Torah, punishment .... Avos 3:8

Forgetting Torah, Sages taught it anew .... Succah 20a

F

Forgot his learning
Forgot his learning, Avimi .... Menachos 7a

Forgot his learning, Rabbi Nehorai .... Shabbos 147b

Forgot his learning, Rav Yosef ...Nedarim 41a; Eruvin 10a, 41a, 66b, 73a, 89b; Makos 4a; Niddah 39a, 63b

Forgotten sheaves
Forgotten sheaves, sheaves and standing grain .... Peah 5:7-8, 6:1-11; Eduyos 4:3-4

Forgotten sheaves, two *seah* .... Bava Basra 72b

Forgotten sheaves, vine .... Peah 7:7

Forgotten sheaves, which sheaves .... Sotah 45a

Forged legal document
Forged legal document, cases .... Bava Basra 167a; Kesubos 21a

Forged legal document, *migo* .... Bava Basra 32a-32b

Forged legal document, signature .... Gittin 10b

Forging, legal document which can be forged
.... Gittin 22a-22b

Forgiveness
Forgiveness after death, episode .... Niddah 36b-37a

Forgiveness before going to sleep .... Megillah 28a

Forgiveness, episode about gutter .... Yoma 87a

Forgiveness, episode about rebellious donkey .... Shabbos 51b-52a

Forgiveness for sins .... *see* **Atonement**, page 35

Forgiveness from lecturer, *aggadah* .... Sotah 40a

Forgiveness from one's fellow .... Yoma 87a-87b; Bava Kama 92a; Bava Basra 173b; Makos 10b

Forgiveness from Sages, episodes .... Yoma 87a, 87b

Forgiveness from Saul's remains .... Yoma 22b

Forgiveness, Rav and butcher .... Yoma 87a

Forgiveness, Rava asking from Rav Yosef .... Nedarim 55a-55b; Eruvin 54a

Form
Form .... *see also* **Mold**, page 420

Form inside of form, fetus .... Berachos 10a; Megillah 14a

Forms, forbidden .... Avodah Zarah 42b-43b; Rosh Hashanah 24a-24b

Forms of divorce certificates .... Gittin 26a-26b; Zevachim 3a

Forms of idolatry .... Avodah Zarah 40b-41a, 42b-43b; Rosh Hashanah 24b

Formation of embryo
.... Chullin 69a

Former wife
Former wife, keeping distance .... Kesubos 27b-28a

Former wife, not to remarry .... Gittin 45b-46b; Yevamos 25a; Kesubos 74b-75a

Former wife, remarrying .... Yevamos 11b; Kiddushin 78a

Former wife, seclusion .... Gittin 73a-73b, 81a-81b; Eduyos 4:7

Forsake, do not forsake your mother's Torah
.... Chullin 93b

Fortress, theft and distance
.... Gittin 60b-61a

Forty
Forty days, Moses' stay on Mount Sinai .... Yoma 4a-4b

Forty *seah, mikveh* ....Pesachim 109a-109b; Eruvin 4b, 14a; Yoma 31a; Succah 6a; Chagigah 11a; Avodah Zarah 75b

Forty *seah*, utensil .... Keilim 15:1, 18:1-2; Shabbos 35a

Forty times, reviewing .... Kesubos 50a

Forty days
Forty days, match .... Sotah 2a; Moed Katan 18b; Sanhedrin 22a

Forty days, pregnancy .... Niddah 30b

Forty days, stillborn baby .... Niddah 25b

Forty days without suffering..Arachin 16b-17a
Forty years
Forty years, halachic inquiry..Succah 44b
Forty years, preferred diet..Shabbos 152a
Forty years, ruling................................Avodah Zarah 19b; Sotah 22a-22b
Forty years, teacher's thought................................Avodah Zarah 5b
Forty nine, *omer* count................................Menachos 65b; Chagigah 17b
Foundation
Foundation, inside Altar..Zevachim 50a
Foundation of Altar................Zevachim 53b-54b, 62a, 108b, 120a; Middos 3:1
Four
Four categories of damages................................Bava Kama 4b-5a
Four craftsmen, righteous..Succah 52b
Four days, butcher................................Chullin 83a; Eruvin 81b
Four days, special meal..Chullin 83a
Four deaths................................*see* **Death penalty**, page 151
Four doors, charity..Berachos 58b
Four faces, making shape................................Avodah Zarah 43b
Four fast days..Rosh Hashanah 18b
Four groups, Divine Presence................Sanhedrin 103a; Sotah 42a
Four hours of the day, heat................................Berachos 27a
Four kinds of disciples..Avos 5:15
Four letters together, writing................................Yoma 38b
Four Matriarchs only..Berachos 16b
Four men died because of the snake................................Bava Basra 17a
Four passages read in *Adar*................................Megillah 30a-30b
Four people need to thank................................Berachos 54b
Four questions, *Seder* night................................Pesachim 115b, 116a
Four Sages came into Pardes................................Chagigah 14b, 15b-16a
Four services in meal offerings................................Zevachim 13b
Four services, thought................................Zevachim 4a-4b
Four species..Succah 29b-42b
Four species, as they grow..Succah 45b
Four things need encouragement................................Berachos 32b
Four things................................*see* **Four indemnities**, page 238
Four times, learning................................Eruvin 54b-55a
Four traits, in man..Avos 5:10
Four traits, charity..Avos 5:13
Four winds blowing................................Bava Basra 25a-25b
Four cubits
Four cubits, act of acquisition................................Bava Metzia 10a-10b
Four cubits, corpse................................Sotah 44a; Oholos 15:8
Four cubits, *eruv techumin*................................Eruvin 32b, 35a, 52a
Four cubits, excrement................................Berachos 26a
Four cubits, house..Succah 3a-3b
Four cubits in *Eretz Yisrael*................................Kesubos 111a
Four cubits of *halacha*................................Berachos 8a
Four cubits of praying man................................Berachos 31b
Four cubits, ox and harnessing................................Bava Basra 83a

F

Four cubits without *tefillin* .... Yoma 86a

Four cups
Four cups, general .... Pesachim 108a-108b, 99b, 117b; Nazir 38a
Four cups, pairs .... Pesachim 109b-110a
Four cups, poor .... Pesachim 112a
Four cups, sickness .... Nedarim 49b

Four hundred
Four hundred captives .... Gittin 57b
Four hundred chapters on idolatry .... Avodah Zarah 14b
Four hundred times, reviewing .... Eruvin 54b
Four hundred Torah scrolls .... Bava Basra 14a
Four hundred vineyards .... Bava Basra 14a

Four indemnities
Four indemnities, cases .... Bava Kama 32b-33a, 85a-85b
Four indemnities, falling from a roof .... Bava Kama 27a; Yevamos 54a
Four indemnities, unintentional .... Bava Kama 26a-26b
Four indemnities, ox .... Bava Kama 33a
Four indemnity payments, hair .... Bava Kama 86a

Fourth
Fourth level of impurity for sacrifices ... Pesachim 18b-19a; Chagigah 24a; Sotah 29a-30a; Taharos 2:5-7
Fourth of *log* .... *see* **Reviis**, page 566

Fox
Fox and fish, parable .... Berachos 61b
Fox at his hour, prostrate yourself before him .... Megillah 16b
Fox, characteristics .... Sotah 10a
Fox, does not die in his den .... Nedarim 81b
Fox in Temple, Rabbi Akiva .... Makos 24b
Foxes, parables .... Berachos 61b; Sanhedrin 38b-39a

Fragments
Fragments of clay utensil .... Keilim 2:2, 2:6, 4:1-3; Chullin 54b-55a
Fragments of container, impurity .... Keilim 19:7-10, 20:1
Fragments of containers, split .... Keilim 12:6
Fragments of idol .... Avodah Zarah 41b-42b, 49b; Meilah 14a
Fragments of metal utensil .... Keilim 13:1-5, 14:1, 14:6-7
Fragments of stolen item .... Bava Kama 11a, 94a
Fragments of Tablets in Ark .... Menachos 99a; Berachos 8b; Bava Basra 14b
Fragments of wood utensil .... Keilim 16:1, 22:1-8
Fragments, payment of custodian .... Bava Kama 11a

Fragments of utensils
Fragments of utensils, impurity .... Keilim 14:8, 20:2
Fragments of utensils, *muktzeh* .... Shabbos 28b, 29a, 124b-125a, 143a; Beitzah 32a; Chullin 14b
Fragments of utensils, *s'chach* .... Succah 15b-16a

Fragrant spices
Fragrant spices .... *see also* **Perfume**, page 481
Fragrant spices before *Bircas HaMazon* .... Berachos 43a
Fragrant spices, blessing .... Berachos 43a-43b, 53a
Fragrant spices for *havdala* .... Berachos 52b-53b
Fragrant spices for mourner .... Moed Katan 27a
Fragrant spices, good for intelligence .... Sanhedrin 70a; Yoma 76b

Fragrant spices, *havdala* on Yom Tov...Pesachim 102b-103a
Fragrant spices, Jerusalem..Shabbos 63a
Fragrant spices, last blessing...Niddah 51b-52a
Fragrant spices, speech enhances them...Krisos 6b
Frame of table..Menachos 96b
Frankincense
Frankincense, burning bowls..Zevachim 58a-58b
Frankincense, for which meal offerings...Menachos 59a-59b
Frankincense, impurity....................Pesachim 24b; Chagigah 35a; Zevachim 34a, 46b; Chullin 36b
Frankincense, indispensable requirement for meal offering.............................Menachos 8a-8b
Frankincense, invalidating thought...Menachos 13a-13b
Frankincense, is it offered as donation...Menachos 104b
Frankincense, man let to execution..Sanhedrin 43a
Frankincense, meal offering for *Kohen*..Menachos 52a
Frankincense, missing quantity..Menachos 11a-11b
Frankincense, non-*Kohen*..Menachos 13b
Frankincense offered to Temple, quantity..Menachos 106b
Frankincense, rare...Menachos 101a
Frankincense, separated two handfuls...Menachos 11b
Frankincense, undefined gift to Altar...Menachos 106b
Fraud..*see* **Overcharging** page 466
Free
Free bird, does not accept master...Shabbos 106b
Free man, only by studying Torah..Avos 6:2
Free of charge, teaching Torah...Nedarim 36b-37b; Bechoros 29a
Freed
Freed maidservant, marriage..Horayos 13a
Freeing half maidservant...Gittin 38a-38b, 43b; Yevamos 66a
Freeing slave, advantage...Gittin 12b-13a; Bava Metzia 19a
Freeing slave, for quorum..Gittin 38b; Berachos 47b
Freeing slave, prohibition...Berachos 47b; Gittin 38a-38b; Sotah 3b
Freeing slave, property to two slaves..Gittin 42a, 87a
Freeing slave, sick...Gittin 40a, 9a
Freeing slave, terms.......................................Gittin 40b, 85b, 86a; Kiddushin 6b
Freedom, fetus.....................................Gittin 23b; Kiddushin 69a; Temurah 25a-25b
Frequent sacrifices, order of precedence..Zevachim 91a
Friend
Friend...*see also* **Love**, page 379
Friend, "our friend," Rav Huna's resentment..Kesubos 69a-69b
Friend, "your friend died," believe it...Gittin 30b
Friend, "your friend has a friend".......Bava Basra 28b, 29a, 38b-39a; Kesubos 109b, 110a; Arachin 16a
Friend and enemy, judge...Kesubos 105b
Friend, good..Avos 2:9
Friend, look for one greater than you..Yevamos 63a
Friend of G-d..Bava Basra 16a; Berachos 34a; Megillah 25a
Friend punished because of him..Shabbos 149b; Bava Kama 93a
Friend, testimony...Sanhedrin 29a
Friend's misfortune, "I did not rejoice"..Megillah 28a
Friends, adages beginning with "Come"..Menachos 53a-53b

F

Friends in one's house, not to have many .... Berachos 63a
Friends of wicked, disappear when he is punished .... Megillah 16a
Friends, tolerant in learning .... Shabbos 63a
Friendship or death .... Bava Basra 16b; Taanis 23a
Friezes above *Ulam* door .... Middos 3:7; Eruvin 3a
Frightening fellow and making him deaf ...... Bava Kama 56a, 91a; Kiddushin 24b
Frogs, Egypt .... Pesachim 53b; Sanhedrin 67b
From
From all your meal, can't you give me a slice .... Berachos 31b
From His mouth, knowledge and intelligence .... Niddah 70b
From Jericho, incense .... Yoma 39b; Tamid 30b
From now on, act of acquisition after thirty days .... Kesubos 82a, 86b
From now on, *kiddushin* .... Kiddushin 59b-60a
From sun to shade, *muktzeh* .... Shabbos 123b-124a
From Tyre to Carthage .... Menachos 110a
From today
From today till after death, divorce certificate ...Gittin 72a-74b; Kiddushin 59b, 60a; Bava Basra 136a
From today till after death, doubt .... Bava Basra 136a, 138b-139a
From today, time of legal document ...Gittin 72a-72b, 76b-77a, 85b; Bava Basra 136a; Avodah Zarah 37a
Fruit
Monetary matters —
Fruit about to be picked...Shevuos 43a; Kesubos 50b-51a; Gittin 39a; Sanhedrin 15a; Bava Metzia 100b
Fruit after harvest .... Nedarim 62a
Fruit, barter .... Kiddushin 28a, 28b; Bava Metzia 46b, 47a
Fruit between fields .... Bava Metzia 107a
Fruit, buying from thief .... Bava Metzia 14b-15a
Fruit from stolen field .... Gittin 50b-51a
Fruit in ownerless field .... Pesachim 6b
Fruit, invalid *chazakah* .... Bava Basra 33a-33b
Fruit, sale of produce .... Kesubos 79a, 101a
Fruit scattered, found .... Bava Metzia 21a
Prohibitions —
Fruit of first three years of tree .... see **Orlah**, page 463
Fruit which dried up on tree .... Chullin 127b
Fruit which fell from tree, egg .... Beitzah 2b-3a; Eruvin 39b
Fruit which fell from tree, *muktzeh* .... Pesachim 56b
Fruit, wording of vow .... Nedarim 55b; Berachos 40b
Fruit, ripeness, tithes .... Maasros 1:1-4
Misc. —
Fruit at *Gan Eden* door .... Eruvin 19a
Fruit, cooked, blessing .... Berachos 38b-39a
Fruit does not fall far from the tree .... Avodah Zarah 31a
Fruit, healthy .... Sanhedrin 17b
Fruit of *Eretz Yisrael* .... Bava Basra 91b
Fruit of Ginosar, episode .... Berachos 44a; Eruvin 30a
Fruit of Ginosar, Jerusalem .... Pesachim 8b
Fruit of woman, blessed by man .... Berachos 51b
Fruit, since Temple destruction .... Sotah 49a
Fruit, time of growth .... Bechoros 8a; Rosh Hashanah 11a

Fruits of transgression .... Kiddushin 40a

Fruit juice
Fruit juice, blessing .... Berachos 38a
Fruit juice, impurity .... Terumos 11:2
Fruit juice, leavening .... Pesachim 35a-36a
Fruit juice, *mikveh* .... Mikvaos 7:3-5; Shabbos 144b; Makos 3b; Chullin 26a
Fruit juice, washing hands .... Zevachim 22a

Full
Full and empty, impurity .... Megillah 26b
Full cheeks, *kiddush* .... Pesachim 107a
Full cheeks, quantity of drink on Yom Kippur .... Yoma 80a-80b
Full contains, learning .... Berachos 40a; Succah 46a-46b
Full measure .... Sotah 9a; Arachin 15a
Full of commandments like pomegranate ...Sanhedrin 37a; Berachos 57a; Eruvin 19a; Megillah 6a; Chagigah 27a

Fundraising, what to do with surplus .... Shekalim 2:5

Funeral
Funeral, requirement and reward .... Berachos 18a
Funeral, time for reading *Shema* .... Berachos 19a
Funeral, wasting time from Torah learning .... Megillah 3b, 29a; Kesubos 17a-17b
Funeral, women .... Sanhedrin 20a

Furnace, Daniel's friends
Furnace, Daniel's friends .... Pesachim 118a-118b; Sanhedrin 92b, 93a
Furnace, Daniel's friends, blessing .... Berachos 57b

Furniture, assembling on Shabbos .... Shabbos 47a-47b, 138a

Fury
Fury .... *see also* **Anger,** page 23
Fury, G-d's behavior .... Avodah Zarah 4a
Fury over poured, resembling idolaters .... Sanhedrin 105a

Future
Future, abundance in *Eretz Yisrael* .... Kesubos 111b; Shabbos 30b
Future, addition to Jerusalem .... Pesachim 50a
Future and hope, Torah .... Kiddushin 82a
Future, clarification of verses .... Sanhedrin 91b
Future, evil urge .... Succah 52a
Future, G-d will reveal lineage of families .... Kiddushin 70b-71a
Future, G-d's knowledge .... Sanhedrin 90b
Future, G-d's Name, reffered to as Jerusalem .... Bava Basra 75b
Future, illegitimate children will become pure .... Kiddushin 72b
Future, Jerusalem for those destined .... Bava Basra 75b
Future, pearls in Jerusalem .... Bava Basra 75a; Sanhedrin 100a
Future, prohibition to ask about future .... Pesachim 113b
Future, sharing *Eretz Yisrael* .... Bava Basra 122a
Future, Torah will be forgotten .... Shabbos 138b-139a
Future, Torah written for .... Kesubos 10b
Future world, commandments .... Avodah Zarah 3a, 4b; Eruvin 22a

Future property
Future property, inheritance of *yavam* .... Bechoros 52a-52b
Future property, *kesubah* and support for daughters .... Bechoros 52a
Future property, relative bequeathing to one's wife .... Bava Basra 113a, 125a; Bava Kama 42b

G

Gaal Yisrael, *Shema* and *Hallel* .... Pesachim 117b

Gaavah .... *see* **Pride**, page 503

Gabachas and ***karachas,*** leprous marks .... Negaim 10:10

Gabai tzedakah .... *see* **Charity collector**, page 98

Gabriel
   Gabriel and Michael .... Berachos 4b
   Gabriel, defense of Daniel .... Yoma 77a
   Gabriel, Divine voice .... Sotah 33a
   Gabriel, revelation to Daniel .... Megillah 3a; Sanhedrin 93b-94a
   Gabriel, stands up for Israel .... Yoma 77a
   Gabriel, stood up for Abraham and Sarah .... Sanhedrin 44b

Gad, name of idol .... Shabbos 67b

Gadlehu me'echav .... *see* **Raise him above his brothers**, page 535

Gadol al gabav .... *see* **Adult supervising**, page 12

Gadol bechochmah uveminyan .... *see* **Greater in wisdom and number,** *beis din*, page 258

Gadol hamalbin shinayim .... *see* **Smiling to fellow, importance**, page 640

Gadol mechavero .... *see* **Greater than his fellow, evil urge**, page 258

Gadol .... *see* **Greater is**, page 258

Gain, so that transgressor will not gain .... Yevamos 92b

Galgal chozer .... *see* **Vicious circle**, page 723

Galilee
   Galilee and Judea, value .... Bava Basra 122a
   Galilee, stuttering .... Eruvin 53b

Gall bladder, *treifah* .... Chullin 43a, 48a

Galmudah, *niddah* .... Rosh Hashanah 26a; Sotah 42a

Galus .... *see* **Exile**, page 208

Gam zu letovah
   Gam zu letovah .... *see also* **Nahum Ish Gam Zu**, page 434; **Best, this also is for the best**, page 55
   Gam zu letovah, episode .... Taanis 21a; Sanhedrin 108b-109a
   Gam zu letovah, faith .... Berachos 60b-61a

Gambling, lots .... Shabbos 149b; Sanhedrin 24b-25b

Game of dice
   Game of dice, prohibition .... Shabbos 149b; Sanhedrin 24b-25b

Game of dice, testimony .... Sanhedrin 24b-25a, 27b; Rosh Hashanah 22a; Eruvin 82a

Gan Eden

Gan Eden, Adam .... Bava Basra 75a

Gan Eden, dimensions .... Pesachim 94a; Taanis 10a

Gan Eden, door .... Eruvin 19a

Gan Eden, no eye has seen .... Berachos 34b; Sanhedrin 99a

Gan Eden, Raba bar Abuah .... Bava Metzia 114b

Gan is different from *Eden* .... Berachos 34b

Ganav .... *see* **Thief**, page 686

Garbage

Garbage, concern that it be collected .... Eruvin 8a, 99b

Garbage, lost item found in garbage .... Bava Metzia 24a, 25b

Garbage, throwing through window .... Eruvin 8a, 99b

Garden

Garden, dimensions .... Bava Basra 98b

Garden surrounded by vine plants .... Eduyos 2:4

Garinin, with *aleph* or *ayin* .... Shabbos 77b

Garlic

Garlic, bad spirit .... Niddah 17a

Garlic, crushed, uncovered .... Beitzah 7b

Garlic, eating a second time .... Shabbos 31b

Garlic, eating from side of leaves .... Beitzah 25b

Garlic, health .... Eruvin 56a; Bava Kama 82a

Garlic on Shabbos, decree .... Bava Kama 82a

Garlic peel, Sages compared to Ben Azzai .... Bechoros 58a

Garlic, preventing humiliation .... Sanhedrin 11a

Garlic to stop barrel, Shabbos .... Shabbos 139b

Garments

Aggadah —

Garments during era of resurrection of dead .... Sanhedrin 90b

Garments for those who are demented, parable .... Shabbos 152b

Garments he has not but shoes he has .... Kesubos 65b; Sotah 8b

Garments of high position, not to remove .... Sanhedrin 92b

Garments, patched, Isaiah .... Yoma 77a

Commandments —

Garments, beautiful, for prayer .... Berachos 30b

Garments for Shabbos .... Shabbos 113a

Garments for taking out ashes .... Yoma 23b-24a; Shabbos 114a, 119a

Garments for Yom Tov .... Pesachim 71a, 109a

Garments of *Kohen Gadol* on Yom Kippur .... Yoma 12b, 35a-35b

Garments worn when cooking for one's master .... Shabbos 114a

Episodes —

Garment, Adam's efforts .... Berachos 58a

Garment, one for six disciples .... Sanhedrin 20a

Garment, red, episode .... Berachos 20a

Garments of king, worms .... Berachos 56a-56b; Bava Metzia 78b

Garments of leather .... Sotah 14a

Garments of wealthy men, Rebbi .... Eruvin 85b-86a

Garments, precious and fine .... Gittin 59a

Impurity —

Garment afflicted with leprosy, impurity .... Yevamos 103b
Garment, impurity .... Keilim 16:5-8, 27:1, 28:1-3; Succah 17b; Eduyos 3:4
Garment, impurity through touching .... Niddah 55b
Garment, impurity of mat .... Keilim 28:9-10
Garment, wool and linen .... Shabbos 26a-27a
Garments, began to tear, impurity .... Chullin 123a

Monetary matters —

Garment .... see also **Wearing**, page 739
Garment, concern of falling down on Shabbos .... Shabbos 147a, 147b
Garment I wear, guarantee .... Bava Kama 11b; Bava Basra 44b, 157a
Garment of widow, deduction .... Kesubos 54a
Garments as a present, for whom .... Bava Basra 143b
Garments for sons, spending more than one's means .... Chullin 84b
Garments for wife .... Kesubos 47b-48a
Garments of brothers, inheritance .... Bava Kama 11b; Bava Basra 139a
Garments of custodian .... Gittin 52b
Garments, worker's salary .... Kesubos 54a

Prohibitions —

Garment carried out by wearing it, Shabbos .... Shabbos 142a
Garment, colored, blood stain .... Niddah 61b
Garment, folded, Shabbos .... Shabbos 58a, 142a, 147a
Garments, colored, impure thoughts .... Avodah Zarah 20a
Garments, intermingled .... Orlah 3:1; Bava Kama 101b
Garments of dead man, *agunah* .... Bava Metzia 27b
Garments of *Kohanim* .... see **Priestly garments**, page 503
Garments of *niddah* .... Kesubos 65b
Garments of wife, consecrating .... Bava Kama 102b; Kesubos 54a; Arachin 24a
Garments, saving from fire .... Shabbos 120a

Misc. —

Garments, behavior .... Bava Metzia 52a; Shabbos 114a
Garments, eighteen .... Shabbos 120a
Garments, expenses .... Chullin 84b
Garments handed by servant .... Berachos 51a
Garments, spend more for garments than for food .... Bava Metzia 52a
Garments, vow, what is included .... Nedarim 55b

Garments of Sages

Garments of Babylonian Sages .... Shabbos 145b
Garments of Sage, behavior .... Bava Basra 57b
Garments of Sage for ignoramus .... Bava Basra 98a
Garments of Sage, stain .... Shabbos 114a

Garmi .... see **Damage, indirect**, page 142

Gas

Gas, intestinal, distance .... Berachos 24b
Gas, intestinal, *tefillin* .... Shabbos 49a, 130a

Gas ruach .... see **Arrogance**, page 32

Gate

Gate, "great," opening .... Tamid 30b
Gate of Ashpos, two weavers .... Shabbos 15a

Gate of *Gan Eden*, place...Eruvin 19a
Gate of her father, stoning..Kesubos 45a
Gate of Nikanor...Middos 2:3; Yoma 38a
Gate of Shushan...Menachos 98a; Middos 1:3
Gates of *Heichal*...Middos 3:7, 4:1-2; Eruvin 2a, 3a
Gates of prayer...Berachos 32b; Bava Metzia 59a
Gates of tears...Berachos 32b; Bava Metzia 59a
Gates of understanding, Moses............Rosh Hashanah 21b; Nedarim 38a

Gates of Temple
   Gates of Temple, how many................Tamid 27a; Yoma 19a; Middos 1:4-5
   Gates of Temple, names and place.........Middos 1:3-5, 2:6; Shekalim 6:3; Yoma 19a, 25b; Tamid 27a
   Gates of Temple, prostrating.................Shekalim 6:1-3; Middos 2:3

Gatehouse
Gatehouse, Eijah the prophet..Bava Basra 7b
Gatehouse, *eruv*..............................Eruvin 72b, 75b, 85b; Succah 3b
Gatehouse, expenses..Bava Basra 7b
Gatehouse, *mezuzah*...Succah 8b
Gatehouse, poor..Bava Basra 7b

Gatekeeper who sang, death penalty..Arachin 11b

Gathering
Gathering, death of righteous men................................Bava Basra 16b
Gathering fruit on Shabbos, work of weekdays.................Shabbos 143b
Gathering fruit, secondary category of Shabbos labors..........Shabbos 73b
Gathering of righteous, benefit...Sanhedrin 72a
Gathering, vegetables..Rosh Hashanah 14a

Gathering bones of corpse
   Gathering bones of corpse, eating sacrifices..................Pesachim 92a
   Gathering bones of corpse, honor.......................................Berachos 18a
   Gathering bones of corpse, mourning.............................Moed Katan 8a
   Gathering bones of corpse on *Chol HaMoed*..................Moed Katan 8a

***Gavra* and *cheftza*,** oath...Nedarim 2b
***Gavra vecheftza*...*see* **Man and object, oath**, page 388
***Gazlan*..*see* **Thief**, page 686

G-d
   Attributes —
      G-d, defeated and pleased...Pesachim 119a
      G-d, *Hashem*, Attribute of Mercy......................................Berachos 60b
      G-d outlives His creatures..Berachos 10a
      G-d, their G-d hates immorality...Sanhedrin 93a
      G-d's attributes, different from man's...............................Berachos 10a
   Behavior —
      G-d, does He cover or bear sin............Arachin 8b; Rosh Hashanah 17a
      G-d does not punish without reason......................................Berachos 5b
      G-d gave, G-d took away...Bava Basra 16a
      G-d, immersion in fire...Sanhedrin 39a
      G-d is lenient, punishment...Bava Kama 50a
      G-d is not exacting towards His creatures.....................Avodah Zarah 3a
      G-d only has four cubits of *halacha*.................................Berachos 8a
      G-d proclaims..Pesachim 113a

G

G-d proclaims, which righteous .... Berachos 55a
G-d teaches children .... Avodah Zarah 3b
G-d's deeds, various hours .... Avodah Zarah 3b
G-d's strength, humility .... Megillah 31a

Israel —
G-d did not abandon us, answer to heretic .... Yevamos 102b
G-d, our eyes are turned to G-d .... Succah 53b
G-d purifies Israel .... Yoma 85b
G-d saw that righteous are few .... Yoma 38b
G-d wanted to give merit to Israel .... Makos 23b
G-d will lift His countenance, to Israel .... Berachos 20b; Rosh Hashanah 17b; Niddah 70b

Service —
G-d desires heart (piety) .... Sanhedrin 106b
G-d's house, let's go with emotion .... Yoma 24b
G-d's Name beloved thanks to disciples .... Yoma 86a
G-d-fearing, fulfilling both opinions .... Berachos 39b; Shabbos 61a
G-d-fearing man, his words are heard .... Berachos 6b

Verses —
G-d made things happen this way .... Makos 10b
G-d, open my lips .... Berachos 4b, 9b
G-d, why did You forsake me .... Megillah 15b
G-d, words of the living G-d .... Gittin 6b; Eruvin 13b

Misc. —
G-d, may He compensate your loss .... Berachos 16b
G-d, Name explicit .... Sanhedrin 101b
G-d, non-Jews acknowledge G-d .... Menachos 110a
G-d of Israel, permitting vow .... Nedarim 22b
G-d save me from shame, Shimi's questions .... Taanis 9b
G-d save us .... Shabbos 84b; Kesubos 45b; Bava Kama 65b
G-d's span .... Eruvin 21a

Gedaliah, murder .... Niddah 61a
Gedi, young of cow and ewe .... Chullin 113b
Gedidah usritah .... see **Scratching skin for dead, mourning,** page 246
Gedolei hador .... see **Great men of generation, to submit to,** page 258
Gedulah le'adam .... see **Greatness,** page 258
Gedulas Hashem .... see **Greatness of G-d, humility,** page 258

Geese
Geese, in the next world .... Bava Basra 73b
Geese, white, impure thoughts .... Berachos 20a

Gehazi
Gehazi, called his teacher by name .... Sanhedrin 100a
Gehazi, sins .... Sanhedrin 107b
Gehazi, Shunammite woman .... Berachos 10b
Gehazi, World to Come .... Sanhedrin 105a
Gehazi, Jeroboam's calves .... Sotah 47a

Gehinnom
Gehinnom, acknowledging justice of judgment .... Eruvin 19a
Gehinnom, dimensions .... Pesachim 94a; Taanis 10a
Gehinnom, Jews .... Chagigah 27a; Eruvin 19a

Gehinnom, Korah's followers .... Nedarim 39b; Bava Basra 74a; Sanhedrin 110a-110b
Gehinnom on Shabbos .... Sanhedrin 65b
Gehinnom, openings .... Eruvin 19a; Succah 32b
Gehinnom, place .... Tamid 32b
Gehinnom, punishment for wicked .... Rosh Hashanah 16b-17a
Gehinnom, Refaim .... Bava Basra 79a
Gehinnom .... *see also* **Kaf hakela, punishment after death,** page 331
Gehinnom, sixty times hotter than fire .... Berachos 57b
Gehinnom, terrifying .... Menachos 99b-100a
Gehinnom, time of creation .... Pesachim 54a; Nedarim 39b
Gehinnom, two, Torah without fear of G-d .... Yoma 72b
Gehinnom, who will escape .... Sanhedrin 111a
Geir .... *see* **Convert,** page 127
Geir toshav .... *see* **Resident non-Jew,** page 562
Geirus .... *see* **Conversion,** page 127
Gelilas Sefer Torah .... *see* **Torah scroll, rolling up,** page 697
Gemar din .... *see* **Verdict,** page 722
Gemar kli .... *see* **Completion of utensil,** page 119
Gemar melachah .... *see* **Completion of work,** page 119
Gemara, Babylon is mixed with .... Sanhedrin 24a
Gematria
Gematria, Abraham .... Nedarim 32b
Gematria, delicacies to wisdom .... Avos 3:18
Gematria, Judea uninhabited .... Shabbos 145b; Yoma 54a
Gematria, *nazir "yihye"* .... Nazir 5a
Gematria of wine, *yayin* .... Eruvin 65a; Sanhedrin 38a
Gemi herb, healing .... Zevachim 19a
Gemiah, with *aleph* or *ayin* .... Shabbos 77a
Gender doubtful
Gender doubtful, blemish .... Yevamos 83b-84a
Gender doubtful, can he procreate .... Yevamos 83b
Gender doubtful, doubt .... Bava Basra 140b-141a; Bechoros 41b-42b
Gender doubtful, eating *terumah* .... Yevamos 72a
Gender doubtful, firstborn .... Bava Basra 126b
Gender doubtful, impurity after giving birth to ...... Niddah 28a, 40a; Bava Basra 127a
Gender doubtful, laws .... Bava Basra 126b-127a
Gender doubtful, sterility and levirate marriage .... Bechoros 42b-43a; Yevamos 72a, 81a, 83b
Gender doubtful, white and red discharge .... Niddah 28a-28b; Zavim 2:1
General
General custom, lessee .... Bava Metzia 103a-103b
General law, not explicit .... Zevachim 4b
General rule, wording of Mishnayos .... Shabbos 67b-68a
General and specific
General and specific, and general .... Bechoros 51a; Shevuos 5a; Chullin 66a
General and specific, deduction .... Chullin 88b; Bechoros 19a
General and specific, deduction .... Eruvin 28a
General and specific far from one another .... Niddah 33a; Pesachim 6b; Sanhedrin 45b-46a;
.... Bava Kama 85a; Menachos 55b
General and specific, how .... Nazir 35a-35b; Eruvin 28a; Bava Kama 63a, 64a

General and specific, *kol* to add laws .... Bava Kama 54b, 63a; Niddah 33a
General and specific, or include and exclude .... Shevuos 4b-5a, 26a; Bava Kama 64b; Chullin 67a;
.... Bechoros 51a
General and specific, positive and negative commandments .... Moed Katan 3a; Sanhedrin 113a
General and specific, when .... Zevachim 4b

Generation
Episodes —
Generation of Babylon, tower .... Sanhedrin 109a
Generation of Hezekiah .... Sanhedrin 20a
Generation of desert, World to Come .... Sanhedrin 110b
Generation of the Flood .... Sanhedrin 107b-108b
Generation of Rav Yehudah, laws of damages .... Berachos 20a
Generations, first .... *see* **First generations**, page 225

Misc. —
Generation according to leader .... Arachin 17a
Generation, each generation and its leaders .... Sanhedrin 38b; Avodah Zarah 5a
Generation, new one better than previous one .... Yevamos 39b; Chullin 93b
Generation, not well developing .... Taanis 24b
Generation, orphan, Rabbi Elazar ben Azariah .... Chagigah 3b
Generations before creation .... Chagigah 13b-14a
Generations, commandments .... Bava Basra 120a
Generations, last, leniencies .... Gittin 81a; Berachos 35b
Generations preceding Torah, kindness .... Avos 5:2; Pesachim 118a

Generosity
Generosity, barrel .... Shabbos 146a
Generosity, consecrating to Temple .... Bava Basra 71b-72b; Nazir 31b; Menachos 108b; Arachin 14a
Generosity, Moses .... Nedarim 38a
Generosity, quantity of *terumah* .... Chullin 137b; Terumos 4:3
Generosity, sale and gift .... Bava Basra 53a, 64a-65b, 71a, 72a, 82b

Geneivah .... *see* **Theft**, page 685

Geneivas daas .... *see* **Misleading**, page 415

Genital
Genital area, non-Jew .... Berachos 25b; Shabbos 150a
Genital area seen by other limbs .... Berachos 25b
Genital member relaxed, intimate relations .... Shevuos 18a; Yevamos 55b; Sanhedrin 55a
Genital member, starve it .... Succah 52b; Sanhedrin 107a

Geniva
Geniva, chained .... Gittin 65b
Geniva, dispute with Mar Ukva .... Gittin 7a
Geniva, greetings to Sages .... Gittin 62a
Geniva, quarrel .... Gittin 7a

Genizah
Genizah .... *see also* **Concealed**, page 119
Genizah, carrying on Shabbos .... Shabbos 90a

Geometry
Geometry, measures .... Eruvin 43b
Geometry of circle .... Succah 7b-8b; Eruvin 13b, 14a, 76a-76b; Bava Basra 14b; Oholos 12:6
Geometry of diagonal .... Eruvin 57a, 76b; Succah 7b-8a; Bava Basra 101b. Zevachim 74a

Ger .... *see* **Convert**, page 127

Gerus .... *see* **Conversion,** page 127

Ger toshav .... *see* **Resident non-Jew,** page 562

Gerizim Mount .... Sotah 33b, 37a

German, leprous mark (*Germani*) .... Negaim 2:1

Germination for *orlah,* time .... Rosh Hashanah 9b-10b; Yevamos 83a

Gerushaso .... *see* **Former wife,** page 236

Gerushin .... *see* **Divorce,** page 170

Gestation

   Gestation of animals, duration .... Bechoros 8a-8b, 19b-20b, 20b-21a; Niddah 24b

   Gestation of various animals .... Beitzah 7a; Bechoros 7b-8a

Get .... *see* **Divorce certificate,** page 170

Get shichrur .... *see* **Certificate of freedom,** page 91

Getting up early, difficulty .... Yoma 22a

Geulah **juxtaposed to** *Shemoneh Esrei,* journey .... Berachos 30a

Geulah .... *see* **Redemption,** page 553

Geulas eved vaamah .... *see* **Redeeming Hebrew slave and maidservant, coercion,** page 553

Geulas Mitzrayim .... *see* **Redemption from Egypt,** page 553

Geulas sdeh mikneh .... *see* **Redeeming field which was bought,** page 552

Gever, rooster .... Yoma 20b

Gevias chov .... *see* **Collecting debt,** page 114; *see also* **Repayment of debt,** page 558

Geviha ben Pesisa .... Sanhedrin 91a

Gevini Kruz, Temple officers .... Shekalim 5:1-2; Yoma 20b; Tamid 30b

Geviyah .... *see* **Impurity of body by eating,** page 304

Gevuros shemonim shanah .... *see* **Old age, eighty years,** page 458

Gezeirah shavah

   Gezeirah shavah, cases .... Krisos 5a

   Gezeirah shavah, festivals .... Succah 27a

   Gezeirah shavah from *gezeirah shavah,* sacrifice .... Bava Kama 2b; Chagigah 10b; Niddah 23a

   Gezeirah shavah from one's teacher .... Niddah 19b; Pesachim 66a

   Gezeirah shavah from tradition .... Bava Kama 2b; Chagigah 10b; Niddah 23a

   Gezeirah shavah, general deduction .... Krisos 22b

   Gezeirah shavah, general deduction and preference .... Zevachim 48a; Menachos 4a

   Gezeirah shavah, how .... Yevamos 17b; Shevuos 31a

   Gezeirah shavah, superfluous word ... Yevamos 70b, 74a; Niddah 22b-23a; Shabbos 64a, 131a; Bava Kama 25b

   Gezeirah shavah, two verses .... Zevachim 57a; Arachin 14b

   Gezeirah shavah, when .... Sanhedrin 84a

Gezeiros deRabbanan .... *see* **Rabbinical Decrees,** page 533

Gezeiros goyim .... *see* **Decrees of idolaters,** page 155

Gezel .... *see* **Theft,** page 685

Gezel ha'ger .... *see* **Stolen item, from convert,** page 655

Giant

   Giant man .... Yoma 10a

   Giants, Ahiman and his brothers .... Yoma 10a; Sotah 34b

   Giant animals

      Giant animals, episodes .... Bava Basra 73b-74b; Zevachim 113b

      Giant animals, feast for righteous .... Bava Basra 74b-75a

      Giant animals, *Re'em* .... Bava Basra 73b; Zevachim 113b

Gibor, vast knowledge .... Chagigah 14a

Gid hanasheh .... *see* **Sciatic nerve,** page 592

Gideon, exceptional permission..Temurah 28b-29a
Gift
  Aggadah —
    Gift in My treasure house, Shabbos...............................Shabbos 10b; Beitzah 16a
    Gift to heir...........................Bava Basra 129a-131a, 133a; Yevamos 36a-36b
    Gift to Sage, first fruit...Kesubos 105b
    Gift to son during one's life, prays and is not heard...............Bava Metzia 75b
    Gift to son, support...Kesubos 49b-50a
    Gift, will, change of price...................................Kesubos 54a-54b
    Gifts given with suffering..Berachos 5a
    Gifts to poor..Megillah 7a-7b
  Examples —
    Gift..*see also* **Bequeathing**, page 54
    Gift, child..Gittin 59a
    Gift from healthy man, for after his death........Bava Basra 135b; Bava Metzia 19a-19b
    Gift, hidden..Bava Basra 40b-41a
    Gift, impossible to consecrate.........Nedarim 43b, 48a-48b; Bava Basra 134a; Kesubos 71a
    Gift, in life and in death..Bava Basra 153a
  How —
    Gift intended for man who died.................................Gittin 14b-15a
    Gift, expressions......................................Bava Basra 62b-63a
    Gift, generous.............................Bava Basra 53a, 64a-65a, 71a
    Gift of field, expressions..Gittin 40b
    Gift, seizing debt from..Gittin 50b
  Prohibitions —
    Gift, requirement to give tithes..Maasros 4:2
    Gift, small, not to retract..Bava Metzia 49a-49b
    Gift to and from non-Jew.....Avodah Zarah 20a, 64a; Pesachim 21b, 23b; Bava Kama 41a; Chullin 114b
    Gift to and from non-Jew on his holiday...................Avodah Zarah 6b, 64b-65a
  Refusal —
    Gift, denying..Gittin 40b
    Gift, episodes concerning refusal.............Kiddushin 59a; Chullin 44b-45a; Megillah 28a
    Gift, expressions of refusal.........................Krisos 24a-24b; Gittin 32a
    Gift of Beis Horon, episode...................................Nedarim 48a-48b
  Women —
    Gift, given to whomever marries my daughter.............................Beitzah 20a
    Gift on condition, daughter..Nedarim 88a-88b
    Gift on condition to return, cases..Kiddushin 6b
    Gift on condition to return, consecrated item.........................Bava Basra 137b
    Gift on condition to return, four species..........Succah 41b; Kiddushin 6b; Bava Basra 137b
    Gift on condition to return, redeeming son..Bechoros 51b
    Gift, she lost her *kesubah*.................Bava Basra 132a-133a, 150a; Peah 3:7
    Gift to married woman, on condition.........................Kiddushin 23b-24a
    Gifts, concern of *kiddushin*.........................Kiddushin 50a-50b
    Gifts for wedding, by heirs.........................Bava Basra 144b-145b
    Gifts for wedding, replacing *kiddushin*.........................Kesubos 73b
    Gifts to bride, returning.........................Bava Basra 145a-146b
  Misc. —
    Gift from Heaven is not taken back.........................Taanis 25a

Gift, must let one know..Shabbos 10b; Beitzah 16a
Gift to freed slave..........................Kiddushin 15a, 16b-17b; Bava Metzia 31b
Gift, total..*see* **Administrator**, page 12
Gifts from non-Jews to Messiah.....................................Pesachim 118b-119a
Gifts to *Kohanim*..*see* **Priestly gifts**, page 503
Gifts for poor
   Gifts for poor, causing damage..Chullin 130b
   Gifts for poor, doubt...Chullin 134a-134b
   Gifts for poor, requirement of poor......................................Chullin 131a-131b
   Gifts for poor, tithe...Sotah 43b; Berachos 40b
   Gifts for poor, which ones...Chullin 131a-131b
Gilead, murderers..Makos 9b-10a
Gilgul shevuah..........*see* **Oath, included in obligatory oath**, page 452
Giluy...*see* **Uncovered**, page 714
Giluy daas begittin.......*see* **Revealing intention, divorce certificate**, page 565
Giluy milsa...*see* **Deduction**, page 155
Giluy panim baTorah.......................*see* **Misinterpreting Torah**, page 415
Giluy rosh...........................*see* **Bareheaded, prohibition for man**, page 42
Ginger
   Ginger, blessing..Berachos 36b
   Ginger, health..Pesachim 42b
Ginosar
   Ginosar, fruits...Berachos 44a; Eruvin 30a
   Ginosar, Jerusalem...Pesachim 8b
Ginosia, non-Jews...Avodah Zarah 10a
Gira be'einei satan....................*see* **Arrow in eyes of *Satan***, page 32
Gireh dilei..................*see* **Damage from neighbor, direct cause**, page 141
Girl
   Girl from another tribe, marrying......................Bava Basra 120a; Taanis 30b
   Girl, little, *niddah*...Niddah 32a-32b, 44a
   Girl, not level-headed..Menachos 110a
   Girl, prayer..Sotah 22a
   Girl seduced by one's father, forbidden relations.............Yevamos 4a-4b, 97a
   Girl, three years old.............................*see* **Three years old girl**, page 689
   Girls are quick............................Pesachim 89a; Nedarim 37a; Gittin 25a
   Girls, sleeping together...Shabbos 65a-65b
Gittin.......................................*see* **Divorce certificate**, page 170
Giulei goyim.....................*see* **Utensils of non-Jews, absorbed food**, page 718
Give
   "Give him, and he will marry my daughter"..............................Beitzah 20a
   "Give one shekel to my son," bequest...........Kesubos 69b-70a; Bava Basra 129a
   "Give to So-and so and afterwards to others"........Bava Basra 143a-143b; Yoma 17b; Sanhedrin 21a;
   Avodah Zarah 10b
   "Give," directive by one who is on deathbed...........Gittin 13a-13b, 65b-66a; Bava Basra 148b-149a
   Give Him from what is His...Avos 3:7
   Give, like "make an act of acquisition".....................................Gittin 11b
   Give me your daughter, Rav...Yevamos 45a
   Give our share in Your Torah...Avos 5:20
   Give us long life..Berachos 16b

G

Give your hand, healing .... Berachos 5b
Given by one "Shepherd," Torah .... Chagigah 3b
Given wholly to heart, you will fear .... Kiddushin 32b; Bava Metzia 58b
Gives a bad taste .... Avodah Zarah 65b, 67a-68b
Gives father quail to eat .... Kiddushin 31a
Giving birth, equated to signs of puberty .... Yevamos 12b-13a
Giving by coercion .... Gittin 74b-75a; Arachin 31b-32a
Giving charity secretly .... Bava Basra 10b
Giving divorce certificate .... Gittin 19b, 78b, 84b
Giving nickname to friend, *Gehinnom* .... Bava Metzia 58b
Giving *treifos* to Jews to eat .... Chullin 56a; Bechoros 40a
Giving up sin, reward .... Kiddushin 39b-40a
Giving wife all of one's property, *kesubah* .... Bava Basra 132a, 150a
Giving merit to multitude
Giving merit to multitude, bringing them near to Torah .... Avos 1:12
Giving merit to multitude, fathers' merit .... Avos 2:2
Giving merit to multitude, merit of their deeds .... Sanhedrin 99b
Giving merit to multitude, saved from sin .... Avos 5:18
Giving merit to multitude, their merit depends on him .... Avos 5:18
Giving of Torah
Giving of Torah, converts .... Shabbos 146a
Giving of Torah, covenants .... Sotah 37a-37b
Giving of Torah, existence of world ...... Shabbos 88a, 129b; Avodah Zarah 3a
Giving of Torah, for all generations .... Bava Basra 120a
Giving of Torah, G-d's joy .... Berachos 5a; Taanis 26b
Giving of Torah, Mount Tabor .... Megillah 29a
Giving of Torah, mountain like a barrel ...... Shabbos 88a; Avodah Zarah 2b
Giving of Torah, non-Jews refused .... Avodah Zarah 2b
Giving of Torah, non-Jews' fear .... Zevachim 116a
Giving of Torah, oath .... Nedarim 25a; Shevuos 29a-29b
Giving of Torah, story .... Shabbos 86b-87a, 88b; Yoma 4b; Taanis 28b
Giving of Torah, when .... Shabbos 86b-88a
Giving of Torah, Written and Oral .... Berachos 5a; Megillah 19b
Giyores .... *see* **Convert woman**, page 128
Giyur .... *see* **Conversion**, page 128
Gizzard, *treifah* .... Chullin 43a
Glass
Glass containers, impurity .... Shabbos 15b-16b; Keilim 2:1, 30:1-4
Glass cup, use it even if it will break .... Berachos 28a
Glass cup, wedding .... Berachos 31a
Glass, forgetting Torah .... Chagigah 15a
Glass in pot, danger .... Shabbos 67b
Glass of Tiberias .... Niddah 21a
Glass utensils, flat .... Shabbos 16a; Keilim 2:1
Glass, white, after Temple destruction .... Sotah 48b
Glass, white, loss .... Bava Metzia 29b
Glass, Zebulun .... Megillah 6a
Gloves of *Kohen Gadol*, episode .... Krisos 28b
Glowing coals, Sages .... Avos 2:10

Glue of bookbinder, *chametz* .... Pesachim 42b
Go
  "Go back to earth," episode .... Taanis 24a
  Go "in" peace and "to" peace .... Berachos 64a; Moed Katan 29a
  Go away from the vineyard, *nazir* .... Avodah Zarah 17a, 58b, 59a; Shabbos 13a; Pesachim 40b;
                                                  Yevamos 46a; Bava Metzia 92a
  Go down a level, marriage .... Yevamos 63a
  Go out and say your teaching outside .... Bava Kama 34b
  Go up a level to find a friend .... Yevamos 63a
  Go up to the sky, Israel .... Megillah 16a
  Goes before man, commandment .... Avodah Zarah 5a; Sotah 3b
  Going bankrupt .... Kesubos 108b-109a
  Going out backwards .... Chullin 10b
  Going out from one's teacher .... Yoma 53a-53b
  Going out of *Eretz Yisrael* .... Moed Katan 14a; Bava Basra 91a, 91b; Kesubos 111a
  Going out on a journey, intimate relations .... Yevamos 62b
  Gone is the man whom I feared .... Moed Katan 24a
Go'el hadam .... *see* **Avenger**, page 37
Go'el Yisrael, prayer .... Pesachim 117b
Goat
  Goat and sheep, preference .... Pesachim 57a-57b; Krisos 28a
  Goat for idolatry .... Horayos 7b
  Goat, healing of pious man .... Bava Kama 80a; Temurah 15b
  Goat, most impudent animal .... Beitzah 25b
  Goat, mountain-goat, bringing forth young .... Bava Basra 16a-16b
  Goats, he-goat and she-goat .... Menachos 107b
  Goats of Bala, wild animal .... Chullin 80a
  Goats of festivals, atonement .... Shevuos 2a-2b, 9a-10b; Zevachim 6b
  Goats of Rabbi Chanina ben Dosa .... Taanis 25a
  Goats of Yom Kippur, dead .... Yoma 40a, 64a-65a; Temurah 22a, 23a
  Goats of Yom Kippur, resembling .... Yoma 62a-62b; Shevuos 13b
  Goats, precedence in herd .... Shabbos 77b
Goat to Azazel
  Goat to Azazel, benefit .... Yoma 67a-67b; Meilah 11b
  Goat to Azazel, blemish .... Temurah 6b-7a
  Goat to Azazel, died .... Yoma 63b, 65a; Zevachim 34b, 74a; Temurah 6b
  Goat to Azazel, from when are we discharged .... Yoma 68b
  Goat to Azazel, from when did they go .... Yoma 68b
  Goat to Azazel, how did they know it arrived .... Yoma 68b
  Goat to Azazel, huts .... Yoma 66b-67a
  Goat to Azazel, impurity .... Yoma 67b; Zevachim 105a
  Goat to Azazel, must stay alive .... Yoma 40b, 65a, 71a
  Goat to Azazel, outside .... Zevachim 113b; Yoma 63a-63b; Temurah 6b
  Goat to Azazel, overrides .... Yoma 66a-66b
  Goat to Azazel, place .... Yoma 67b
  Goat to Azazel, sacrifices slaughtered outside .... Yoma 63a-64a
Goatskin
  Goatskin, hide of firstborn .... Bechoros 33a
  Goatskin, redeemed sacrifices .... Bechoros 33a-33b

God .... *see* **G-d**, page 245

Godesh, quantity .... Shabbos 35a; Eruvin 14b

Godros .... *see* ***Chazakah,*** **freely grazing animals**, page 100

Gog, written next to Absalom .... Berachos 10a

Gog and Magog

Gog and Magog, Messiah .... Sanhedrin 98b; Avodah Zarah 3b

Gog and Magog, more miraculous than Exodus .... Berachos 13a

Gog and Magog, twelve months .... Eduyos 2:10

Gold

Gold, coin or fruit .... Bava Metzia 44a-44b

Gold, estimate of dowry .... Kesubos 67a

Gold, protection .... Meilah 19a

Gold, redeeming second tithe .... Bava Metzia 44b-45b; Maaser Sheni 2:7

Gold, treasure of Egypt .... Pesachim 87b, 119a

Gold, treasures of Egypt .... Pesachim 87b, 119a

Gold, varieties .... Yoma 44b-45a

Gold, walls of *Heichal* .... Middos 4:1

Golden

Golden sheet for time of *Shema* reading .... Yoma 37b

Golden trees in Temple .... Yoma 21b, 39b

Golden calf

Golden calf, "who took you out of Egypt" .... Sanhedrin 63a

Golden calf, Aaron and Hur .... Sanhedrin 7a

Golden calf, checking like *sotah* .... Avodah Zarah 44a

Golden calf, deaths .... Yoma 66b

Golden calf, defense of Moses .... Berachos 32a; Pesachim 119a; Sanhedrin 102a, 111b; Yoma 86b

Golden calf, G-d's love for Israel .... Shabbos 88b

Golden calf, idolatry in *Eretz Yisrael* .... Avodah Zarah 53b

Golden calf, punishment for all generations ... Sanhedrin 102a; Avodah Zarah 5a

Golden calf, satan .... Shabbos 89a

Golden calf, tribe of Levi .... Yoma 66b

Golel vedofek .... *see* **Tombstones, impurity**, page 695

Golem .... *see* **Boor, seven things**, page 72

Golem, *Sefer Yetzirah* ... *see* **Creation of man and animal**, *Sefer Yetzirah*, page 133

Goliath and David .... Sotah 42b

Good

Righteous —

Good deeds, standing before man performing .... Kiddushin 33b

Good eye, Moses .... Nedarim 38a

Good for righteous and for world .... Avos 6:8

Good for righteous man, good for his neighbor .... Succah 56b

Good for the world, birth of righteous man .... Sanhedrin 113b

Good, righteous .... Chagigah 12a; Yoma 38b

Good to Heaven and to men .... Kiddushin 40a

Misc. —

Good eye, virtue .... Avos 2:9

Good friend .... Avos 2:9

Good health, house of study .... Berachos 53a

Good heart .... Avos 2:9

Good, poverty for Israel...Chagigah 9b

Good thing, Abijah son of Jeroboam instituted..Moed Katan 28b

Good urge, forgotten..Nedarim 32b

Good heart

Good heart, continuous feast.................................Bava Basra 145b-146a; Sanhedrin 100b-101a

Good heart, good wife...Bava Basra 145b

Good heart, learning..Bava Basra 145b

Goral...*see* **Lots**, page 379

Gorem lemamon..*see* **Indirect damage**, page 308

Gorin umosifin..................................*see* **Removing letter from verse and adding it**, page 557

Goring

Goring..*see also* **Horn**, page 284, **Ox**, page 467

Goring, sacrifice.....................................Bava Kama 40b; Bechoros 41a; Temurah 28b

Gosess...*see* **Dying man**, page 184

Gossip...*see* **Derogatory speech**, page 160

Government

Government....................................*see also* **Men put to death by government**, page 387

Government, causing death of one sixth of its citizens...Shevuos 35b

Government does not rescind its plan..Bava Basra 3b

Government, if not for fear of government..............................Avodah Zarah 4a; Avos 3:2

Government, wicked, Edom..Bava Basra 60b

Governor

Governor, episode about prayer...Berachos 32b-33a

Governor, questions to Rabban Gamliel...Chullin 27b

Goy...*see* **Non-Jew**, page 448

Goyah..*see* **Idolatrous woman**, page 295

Grab and eat...Eruvin 54a

Grace after meal...*see* ***Bircas HaMazon***, page 57

Grace

Grace, fear of G-d...Succah 49b

Grace in idolaters, prohibition to find...........................Avodah Zarah 20a; Arachin 14a

Grace of man learning Torah...Kesubos 77b

Grace of wife, of place, and of purchase..Sotah 47a

Graf shel re'i...*see* **Chamber pot**, page 93

Grafting

Grafting, mixed species.................................Kilayim 1:4, 1:7-8; Sotah 43b; Eruvin 34b

Grafting, mixed species in vineyard.................................Kilayim 7:1-2; Bava Basra 19b

Grafting palm trees..Pesachim 56a

Grafting seeds, mixed species..Chullin 60a-60b

Grain

Grain of wheat, whole, blessing..Berachos 37a

Grain, tithe from third of growth..........................Rosh Hashanah 12b-13b; Maasros 1:3

Gram...*see* **Causing**, page 89

Grama...*see* **Damage, indirect**, page 142

Grama vegarmi..*see* **Causing damage**, page 90

Gramia of Edom..Megillah 6b

Grammar, *ches* like *heh*..Megillah 24b

Grandchild

Grandchild, teaching...Kiddushin 30a

Grandchildren are like children .... Yevamos 62b; Bava Basra 143b
Grandchildren, inheritance .... Bava Basra 115a-116a, 158b-159b
Grandchildren, peace upon Israel .... Kesubos 50a
Granddaughter
Granddaughter, betrothed, on his lap .... Kiddushin 81b
Granddaughter of Antoninus gave birth .... Niddah 45a
Grandfather, inheritance .... Bava Basra 116a-116b
Grandmother, relations forbidden by Rabbinical Decree .... Sanhedrin 75b-76a
Grandson
Grandson permitting widow to eat *terumah* .... Yevamos 70a
Grandsons are like sons .... Yevamos 62b
Grandsons, converts .... Gittin 57b
Grandsons, peace from levirate marriage .... Kesubos 50a
Grape
Grape seed and skin, *nazir* .... Nazir 34a-35a, 38b-39a; Pesachim 41b
Grapes about to be picked .... Shevuos 43a; Gittin 39a; Sanhedrin 15a; Bava Metzia 100b
Grapes, absorbing forbidden substance .... Avodah Zarah 65b
Grapes bunch, spies .... Sotah 34a
Grapes fallen, for poor .... Peah 7,-68:1; Taanis 6b
Grapes, harvest .... Shabbos 73b
Grapes of vineyard, daughter of scholar .... Pesachim 49a
Grapes, parable for scholar .... Chullin 92a
Grapes, susceptible to become impure .... Shabbos 17a; Taharos 10:4-5; Avodah Zarah 39b;
   Machshirin 5:11; Chullin 36b
Grapes to winepress, non-Jew .... Avodah Zarah 59a-59b
Grapevine
Grapevine climbing on fig tree, smell of tree .... Bechoros 17a
Grapevine, dream of chief butler .... Chullin 92a
Grapevine, low, mixed species .... Sotah 43b
Grapevine of gold in Temple .... Middos 3:8; Tamid 29a-29b; Chullin 90b
Grapevine, parable for Israel .... Chullin 92a
Grapevine, prohibitions to *nazir* .... Nazir 34a-35a, 38b-39a
Grasping depth of thought, Rabbi Oshaiah .... Eruvin 53a
Grass, Shabbos .... Eruvin 100b
Grasshopper
Grasshopper, living, eating .... Shabbos 90b
Grasshoppers, dew .... Shabbos 106b
Grasshoppers, numerous species .... Chullin 63b
Grasshoppers, signs .... Avodah Zarah 37a-37b; Chullin 65a-66a
Gratitude
Gratitude .... Avodah Zarah 5a-5b; Kesubos 53a; Bava Kama 92b
Gratitude for eating Sabbatical fruit .... Sheviis 4:2
Gratitude to Golden Calf, idolaters .... Avodah Zarah 5a
Grave .... *see also* **Burial**, page 79
  Episodes —
  Grave of father, episode concerning prayers .... Taanis 23b
  Graves, "Did you prepare your graves?," repentance .... Taanis 25b
  Graves, episode about digger .... Bava Basra 58a
  Graves, episode about spirits .... Berachos 18b

Graves, Og's femur .... Niddah 24b
Graves, Rabbi Banaah .... Bava Basra 58a
Graves, Rabbi Shimon .... Shabbos 33b-34a
Graves, Rav Achai .... Shabbos 152b

Impurity —

Grave, closed, impurity .... Bava Basra 12a; Shabbos 146b
Grave, different forms .... Oholos 9:15
Grave, doubt .... Bechoros 25b
Grave, evacuated, impurity .... Sanhedrin 47b
Grave in mound, doubt .... Kesubos 20b; Oholos 16:2
Grave unknown under Temple .... Parah 3:3
Graves, checking area .... Nazir 64b-65b; Bava Basra 101b-102b; Oholos 16:3-5

Misc. —

Grave, calculation of shadow .... Eruvin 43b
Grave, marking .... Moed Katan 5a-6a; Bava Kama 69a
Grave, sale, family's refusal .... Bava Basra 100b; Kesubos 84a; Bechoros 52b
Graves, blessing .... Berachos 58b
Graves, communal fast .... Taanis 16a
Graves, how .... Bava Basra 100b-101b
Graves, sorcery .... Niddah 17a; Sanhedrin 65b

Grazing

Grazing, animal could have not eaten .... Bava Kama 47b
Grazing, animal fell in garden .... Bava Kama 57b-58a
Grazing animal on neighbor's grain .... Bava Kama 56a-56b
Grazing, atonement payment penalty .... Bava Kama 44b
Grazing, benefit .... Bava Kama 23b
Grazing, cow ate atop another .... Bava Kama 20a, 21b
Grazing, eating .... Bava Kama 15b, 19b-20a
Grazing, evaluation of damage .... Bava Kama 6b, 20a, 58b-59b
Grazing, mouth of cow .... Bava Kama 23a-23b
Grazing, place intended to public .... Bava Kama 21a-21b
Grazing, secondary categories .... Bava Kama 3a
Grazing, shared domain .... Bava Kama 13b-14a
Grazing, sidewalk .... Bava Kama 21a-21b
Grazing, source .... Bava Kama 2b-3a

Great

"Great ones are down and small ones are up" .... Bava Basra 10b; Pesachim 50a
Great are Chiya's acts .... Bava Metzia 85b
Great are righteous men in death .... Chullin 7b
Great are righteous men's deeds .... Kesubos 5a
Great is circumcision .... Nedarim 31b, 32a
Great is drinking together .... Sanhedrin 103b-104a
Great is he who makes a living by working .... Berachos 8a
Great is Torah .... Avos 6:7
Great is value of serving a Sage .... Kesubos 96a; Berachos 7b
Great is work because it warms .... Gittin 67b
Great man, expressions .... Berachos 19b; Gittin 55b; Niddah 50b
Great man, praise about Amora .... Bava Kama 40a
Great man, this disciple served a great man .... Eruvin 54a

G

Great men listen to small ones .... Rosh Hashanah 25b
Great men of generation, to submit to .... Rosh Hashanah 25a-25b
Great Assembly
Great Assembly, ancient glory .... Yoma 69b
Great Assembly, blessings .... Berachos 33a
Great Assembly, Torah tradition .... Avos 1:1
Greater
Greater are righteous men than angels .... Sanhedrin 93a
Greater in one thing, honor .... Bava Metzia 33a; Pesachim 113b
Greater in wisdom and number, *beis din* ..... Avodah Zarah 36a; Megillah 2a; Moed Katan 3b; Gittin 36b;
.... Eduyos 1:5
Greater is he who encourages others to do .... Bava Basra 9a
Greater is he who is commanded .... Kiddushin 31a; Bava Kama 38a, 87a; Avodah Zarah 3a
Greater is he who lends money .... Shabbos 63a
Greater is prayer than etc. .... Berachos 32b
Greater than his fellow, evil urge .... Succah 52a-52b
Greater the man, greater his evil urge .... Succah 52a
Greater was the removing of ring .... Megillah 14a
Greatness
Greatness, after atonement of sins .... Sanhedrin 14a
Greatness, beginning by great person .... Berachos 61a; Taanis 15b
Greatness, given from Heaven .... Megillah 13b; Zevachim 102a
Greatness of G-d, humility .... Megillah 31a
Greece
Greece, enslavement of Israel .... Yoma 77a
Greece, years of kingship .... Avodah Zarah 9a-10a
Greek
Greek letters, C and Π, anointing .... Horayos 12a; Krisos 5b
Greek man, fingers cut off .... Taanis 18b
Greek, numbers .... Bava Basra 164b
Greek, preferable language .... Bava Kama 83a
Greek, Torah scroll .... Megillah 8b-9b
Greek, words .... Bava Basra 164b; Shabbos 31b; Moed Katan 28a; Sanhedrin 76b
Greek wisdom
Greek wisdom, episode .... Sotah 49b; Bava Kama 82b; Menachos 64b
Greek wisdom, prohibition .... Menachos 99b
Greek wisdom, prohibition to learn .... Bava Kama 82b-83a
Greet
Greet, being the first to greet others and to answer .... Berachos 6b
Greeting by Divine name, source .... Berachos 63a; Makos 23b
Greeting in divorce certificate .... Gittin 87a; Bava Basra 176a
Greeting one's teacher .... Berachos 27b
Greeting teacher .... *see also* **Visiting teacher**, page 725
Greeting
  Episodes —
    Greeting .... *see also* **Shalom**, page 609
    Greet every man with cheerful countenance .... Avos 1:15, 3:12
    Greeting fellow first .... Berachos 6b
    Greeting from Heaven, episodes .... Taanis 21b-22a

Greeting governor, during prayer .... Berachos 32b-33a
Greeting, mistake .... Chullin 94b
Greeting, Rabbi Yochanan ben Zakai's behavior .... Berachos 17a
Greeting Sages, Geniva .... Gittin 62a

Prohibitions —
Greeting before prayer .... Berachos 14a
Greeting during *Shema* and prayer .... Yoma 19b
Greeting during *Shema*, *Hallel* and *megillah* .... Berachos 13b-14a
Greeting to woman .... Kiddushin 70a-70b; Bava Metzia 87a

Misc. —
Greeting, to living and to deceased .... Berachos 64a; Moed Katan 29a
Greeting to non-Jew, *shalom* .... Gittin 62a
Greeting to Sages and king .... Gittin 62a

Grievance
Grievance against workers' agent .... Bava Metzia 76a-76b
Grievance, payment little by little .... Bava Metzia 77b
Grievance, renting ship .... Bava Metzia 79b

Grill, roasting Pesach lamb .... Pesachim 75a

Grind
Grind, makes father grind at grindstone .... Kiddushin 31a-31b
Grinding, continuing on Shabbos .... Shabbos 18a
Grinding, cutting in tiny pieces on Shabbos .... Shabbos 74b
Grinding idol .... Pesachim 28a; Avodah Zarah 43b-44a
Grinding on Shabbos, pepper .... Shabbos 141a
Grinding on Yom Tov .... Beitzah 14a-14b
Ground flour you ground .... Sanhedrin 96b

Grindstone
Grindstone, flour given as payment .... Kesubos 103a
Grindstone, from Shabbos eve to Shabbos .... Shabbos 18a
Grindstone, impurity .... Beitzah 23b
Grindstone on neck .... Kiddushin 29b
Grindstone, sign of circumcision feast .... Sanhedrin 32b

Griss
Griss, size of blood stain .... Niddah 58b-59a
Griss, size of leprous marks .... Negaim 6:1-4

Grogros .... *see* **Fig**, page 222

Groom
Groom .... *see also* **Wedding**, page 739
Groom and bride, protection .... Berachos 54b
Groom, atonement .... Yevamos 63b
Groom, *Shema* .... Berachos 17b; Succah 25b-26a
Groom sits at head of table .... Moed Katan 28b
Groom, waiting to see his leprous mark .... Negaim 3:2; Moed Katan 7b; Bechoros 34b
Grooms whose wives were exchanged .... Yevamos 33b, 34a

Gross speech, punishment .... Shabbos 33a; Kesubos 8b

Group
Group, not to stay out of .... Berachos 49b-50a
Group, one, in the world .... Chagigah 3a; Berachos 6a
Group, particular about their money .... Bava Metzia 75a

Group, Torah learning..Avos 4:15; Nedarim 81a
Group, Israel is cherished when united.................................Menachos 27a
Groups not seeing Divine Presence....................................Sanhedrin 103a
Groups, not to separate into groups...................................Yevamos 13b-14a
Group for Pesach lamb
Group for Pesach lamb, how many......................................Pesachim 64b
Group for Pesach lamb, single...Pesachim 86a-86b
Group for Pesach lamb, taking out....................................Pesachim 85a-86a, 119b
Group for Pesach lamb, who...Pesachim 91a-91b
Group for Pesach lamb, withdrawing..................................Pesachim 99a
Guarantee
Guarantee..*see also* **Warranty**, page 732
Guarantee, "*kablan*"..Bava Basra 173a-174a
Guarantee, act of acquisition by third person.......................Kiddushin 7a
Guarantee for *kesubah*, episode..Bava Basra 174b
Guarantee for non-Jew, first one asked to pay......................Bava Basra 174b
Guarantee, *kiddushin* money...Kiddushin 7a
Guarantee, prohibition of interest.......................................Bava Metzia 75b
Guarantee, when is commitment valid.........Gittin 49b-50a; Bava Basra 173a-174b, 176a-176b;
                                                                              Arachin 23a-23b
Guarantor
Guarantor, avoid becoming..Yevamos 109b
Guarantor for interest...Bava Metzia 71a-71b
Guarantor needs another guarantor...................................Gittin 28b; Succah 26a
Guarantor, orphans..Bava Basra 174a-174b
Guard
Guard..*see also* **Keep**, page 333
Guard My guard..Yevamos 21a
Guarding *challah* from impurity...Niddah 6b-7a
Guarding deceased.................................Berachos 17b-18a; Shabbos 151b
Guarding fire, distance..Bava Kama 61a, 61b
Guarding from harmful forces, three..................................Berachos 54b
Guarding from impurity.............*see* **Protection concerning impurity**, page 508
Guarding, light purity to severe purity................Chullin 35a-35b; Chagigah 18b
Guarding, like active worker...Bava Metzia 93a
Guarding non-Jew's foods.........................Avodah Zarah 39a-39b; Chullin 3a, 3b
Guarding one's eyes, episode...Pesachim 113b
Guarding one's eyes, evil urge cannot dominate....................Sotah 8a
Guarding poorly, damages...Bava Kama 55b
Guarding Temple, source...Tamid 25b-26b
Guarding Temple, where.............................Tamid 25b-27a; Middos 1:1-2
Guarding water for sprinkling...........................Parah 6:1, 7:1-12, 8:1, 7:10
Guardian
Guardian..*see also* **Custodian**, page 136
Guardian of prison, episode...Taanis 22a
Guardian, sleeping with *tefillin*..Succah 26a-26b
Guardian who slept in Temple...........................Tamid 27b-28a; Middos 1:2
Gud achis
Gud achis and fold...Eruvin 87a

Gud achis, partition .... Shabbos 101a-101b; Eruvin 87a

Gud asik

Gud asik and *gud achis*, *Halacha* to Moses from Sinai .... Succah 6b
Gud asik for *mikveh* .... Chagigah 19a-19b
Gud asik, roof .... Eruvin 89a-90a
Gud asik, succah .... Succah 4b

Gud o agud .... Bava Basra 13a-13b
Gud o agud .... *see* **Bidding for division of property**, page 56

Guess

Guess, cases .... Sanhedrin 65b-66a
Guess, first sale .... Kiddushin 59a
Guess, permitted and forbidden .... Megillah 32a; Chullin 95b; Krisos 5b-6a; Horayos 12a
Guess, Rav .... Chullin 95b
Guess, reward and punishment .... Nedarim 32a

Guest

Episodes —

Guests, Abraham .... Sotah 10a-10b
Guests, Rabban Gamliel .... Kiddushin 32b
Guests, stories of embarrassment .... Chullin 94a

Guest's behavior —

Guest, blessing for host .... Berachos 46a
Guest bringing in another guest .... Bava Basra 98b
Guest, marital relations .... Kesubos 65a
Guest, eating eggs .... Yoma 12a, 18b
Guest, garment for laundering .... Shabbos 140b
Guest, good and bad .... Berachos 58a
Guest, greeting host .... Bava Metzia 87a
Guest, leaving things to host .... Yoma 12a
Guest, obeying host .... Pesachim 86b
Guest, share for host's son .... Chullin 94a
Guest, sleeping in his clothes .... Yoma 12a, 18b

Misc. —

Guest arrives in town, wife .... Bava Kama 92a; Makos 9b
Guest, escorting .... Berachos 31a; Sotah 46b
Guest must obey his host .... Pesachim 86b
Guest, possession of his food share .... Nedarim 34b
Guest, stinginess .... Chullin 7b
Guest who is a Sage, commandment .... Berachos 10b
Guests, behavior .... Berachos 46a; Shabbos 140b
Guests, behavior at the table .... Berachos 43a, 46b-47b
Guests, hospitality .... Avos 1:5, 1:15, 3:12
Guests, wife is stingy towards .... Bava Metzia 87a
Guests, woman understands their character .... Berachos 10b

Gufei

Gufei halachos .... Avos 3:18
Gufei Torah, commentaries .... Chagigah 11a-11b
Gufei Torah, consecrated items and tithe .... Shabbos 32a-32b

Gufim mechulakim .... *see* **Bodies, different, sacrifices**, page 71
Guild, decisions .... Bava Basra 8b, 9a

G

Guilt offering
  Offering —
    Guilt offering, atonement...Krisos 22b
    Guilt offering, changing name...Zevachim 5a-5b, 10a-10b
    Guilt offering, north...Zevachim 49a-49b
    Guilt offering, place of sprinkling..Zevachim 10b
    Guilt offering, *semichah*..Zevachim 33a
  Guilt offering for doubtful culpability
    Guilt offering for doubtful culpability, atonement.................Yoma 85b; Krisos 25a, 26b
    Guilt offering for doubtful culpability, discovered he did not sin...............Krisos 23b-24b
    Guilt offering for doubtful culpability, discovered he sinned.....................Krisos 26b
    Guilt offering for doubtful culpability, endowment...........Krisos 18a, 25a-25b; Zevachim 77a;
    ....Chullin 41b
    Guilt offering for doubtful culpability, for which sin...............................Horayos 8b
    Guilt offering for doubtful culpability, impurity.........................Krisos 7a; Horayos 9b
    Guilt offering for doubtful culpability, *Kohen Gadol*...........................Horayos 7a, 8a
    Guilt offering for doubtful culpability, secular use...........Krisos 16a, 22a-22b; Zevachim 48a
    Guilt offering for doubtful culpability, Yom Kippur.............Yoma 85b; Krisos 7a, 25b-26b
  Guilt offering for *nazir*
    Guilt offering for *nazir*.....................................*see also* **Sacrifice for *nazir***, page 581
    Guilt offering for *nazir*, Shimon Hatzaddik.....................................Nazir 4b
    Guilt offering for *nazir*, without purpose.......................................Krisos 27a
  Guilt offering for theft
    Guilt offering for theft, acknowledged.....Bava Kama 65a-65b, 106a; Bava Metzia 3b; Shevuos 37b
    Guilt offering for theft, convert..Bava Kama 110b-111a
    Guilt offering for theft, for which sin..Shevuos 37b-38a
    Guilt offering for theft, in which case..Bava Metzia 48a
  Misc. —
    Guilt offering, age...........Kiddushin 55b; Zevachim 90b; Menachos 48b; Temurah 19b
    Guilt offering for leper.................................Zevachim 47b; Yoma 61b; Yevamos 7a-7b
    Guilt offering for secular use.............Bava Kama 111a; Krisos 22b, 26b-27a; Kiddushin 12a
    Guilt offering, rare..Kiddushin 55b
    Guilt offering, two shekels.............................Krisos 22b, 27a; Zevachim 90b
    Guilt offerings for warranty..Krisos 24a
Guilty man acknowledges, legal document.........................Bava Metzia 12b-14a
Gullet
  Gullet and windpipe, torn..Chullin 20a-20b
  Gullet, checking *treifah*...................................Chullin 28a-28b, 43a-43b
  Gullet, place for slaughtering..Chullin 43b-44b
Gums, health..Yoma 84a
Gutter
  Gutter, *chazakah*..Bava Basra 59a
  Gutter, clearing on Shabbos...Kesubos 60a
  Gutter, Shabbos domains..Eruvin 99b
Gviyah..*see* **Impurity of body by eating**, page 304

Haaraah..*see* **Penetration, male,** page 480

Haaramah..*see* **Pretending,** page 502

Haazinu, division of Torah reading..Rosh Hashanah 31a

Hacharash vehamasger, exile..Gittin 88a; Sanhedrin 38a

Hachnasas orchim........................*see* **Guest,** page 261; *see also* **Hospitality,** page 285

Hachrazah.......................*see* **Announcement,** page 26; *see also* **Auction,** page 36

Hachzakas Torah...*see* **Supporting Torah,** page 665

Hadar dina...........................*see* **Judgment, contradictory, re-examining,** page 329

Hadar

   Hadar, esrog...Succah 31a-31b

   Hadar, lulav...Succah 29b, 31a

Hadar...*see* **Beautiful,** page 46

Hadas...*see* **Myrtle,** page 433

Ha'el Hagadol, prayer...Yoma 69b

Hafarah..*see* **Annulling vow,** page 27

Hafrashas maaser...*see* **Separating tithe,** page 602

Haftorah

   Haftorah, Book of Haftaros..Gittin 60a

   Haftorah, festivals..Megillah 31a-31b

   Haftorah, how many verses...Megillah 23a-23b

   Haftorah, maftir's commandments....................................Megillah 24a-24b; Sotah 39b

   Haftorah, mincha of Shabbos...Shabbos 24a

   Haftorah scroll, Shabbos...Gittin 60a

Hagadol

   Hagadol, Ezra called G-d...Yoma 69b

   Hagadol Hagibor, prayer...Yoma 69b

Hagalah...*see* **Kashering** clay utensil, page 332

Hagbaah veglilah.........................*see* **Raising and rolling up Torah scroll,** page 535

Hagbahah and gelilah...Megillah 32a

Hagbahah..*see* **Purchase by raising,** page 370

Hagbalah, Giving of Torah..Shabbos 87a

Haggadah of Pesach.......................................Pesachim 116a-116b, 117b-118a

Haggai, examination..Pesachim 16b-17a

Haggle, do not haggle if you do not have money...............Pesachim 112b; Bava Metzia 58b

Hagiographs, prohibition on Shabbos .... Shabbos 116b
Hagomel, blessing .... Berachos 54b
Hagramah .... *see* **Slaughtering in partially wrong place**, page 634
Hair
   Consecrated —
      Hair, black, Red Heifer .... Parah 2:1-5; Bechoros 25a
      Hair, donation valuation .... Sanhedrin 15a
      Hair falling from offering .... Bechoros 26a-26b
      Hair of firstborn .... Bechoros 24b-26b; Eduyos 5:6
      Hair, personal use .... Gittin 39a; Sanhedrin 15a
   Leprosy —
      Hair in old leprous mark, new mark .... Negaim 5:3
      Hair, leprous mark on head .... Negaim 10:1-4, 10:8
      Hair that separates, leprous mark .... Negaim 10:6-7
      Hair, white, leprous marks .... Negaim 4:1-4, 4:1-11
   Prohibitions —
      Hair, brushing .... Nedarim 81a
      Hair, mourner .... Moed Katan 14b, 17b, 19b, 24a, 22b
      Hair of body, prohibition to shave .... Nazir 58b-59a
      Hair of dead woman, profit .... Arachin 7b
      Hair of *Kohanim,* long .... *see* **Long hair of *Kohanim***, page 377
      Hair of woman, nakedness .... Berachos 24a
      Hair, shaving on Shabbos .... Shabbos 94b; Makos 20b; Bechoros 24b
      Hair, successive periods of mourning .... Moed Katan 17b; Taanis 13a
      Hair, white, prohibition to tear out .... Shabbos 94b
   Scientific facts —
      Hair, from where does it grow .... Nazir 39a-39b
      Hair, its place is insignificant .... Negaim 4:4
      Hair, Jewish women .... Sanhedrin 21a
      Hair, measure of length .... Nazir 39b
      Hair, special hole (pore) .... Niddah 52a-52b
   Misc. —
      Hair, blood of *niddah* .... Niddah 21a, 22a-22b, 54b, 54b
      Hair, forelock of non-Jew, prohibition to Jewish barber .... Avodah Zarah 29a
      Hair, four payments .... Bava Kama 86a
      Hair, improper for man to curl his hair .... Nazir 3a; Rosh Hashanah 26b; Megillah 18a
      Hair, intervening substance .... Succah 6a-6b; Eruvin 4b
      Hair of armpit, episode .... Nazir 59a
      Hair of leper .... Moed Katan 15a
      Hair of *sotah,* uncovering .... Sotah 8a; Sanhedrin 45a
      Hair unkempt, sickness .... Nedarim 81a
   Hair of *nazir*
      Hair of *nazir,* benefit .... Kiddushin 57b; Pesachim 23a
      Hair of *nazir,* burning .... Nazir 45b
      Hair of *nazir,* meat broth .... Nazir 45b
   Hair of puberty
      Hair of puberty .... Niddah 45b-46a, 48b
      Hair of puberty, pores .... Niddah 52a-52b

Hair of puberty, minor girl disavowing marriage................Chullin 26b; Niddah 46a, 52a-52b;
....Yevamos 12b; Kesubos 36a; Bava Basra 156a
Hair of puberty, quantity..Niddah 52a
Hairs of puberty, checking..Bava Basra 156a

Haircut
Haircut..*see also* **Shaving**, page 610
Haircut, king...Sanhedrin 22b; Taanis 17a
Haircut, *Kohen Gadol*..Sanhedrin 22b; Taanis 17a
Haircut of *Kohen Gadol*, Ben Elassa..........................Nedarim 51a; Sanhedrin 22b
Hairnet, impurity of couch..Keilim 28:9-10
Hakadosh Baruch Hu..*see* **G-d**, page 245
Hakafas harosh vehazakan..................................*see* **Shave, head and beard**, page 611
Hakamah...*see* **Approving vow**, page 30
Hakdamas maos..*see* **Payment in advance**, page 476
Hakhel
Hakhel, bringing children...Chagigah 3a
Hakhel, Torah reading by king.....................................Sotah 41a-41b
Hakol
Hakol in Mishnayos, what does it teach.......................Arachin 2a-4a
Hakol, teaching of Mishnah..Chullin 2a-2b
Hakol min hashamayim..*see* **Everything comes from Heaven**, page 204
Hakol sharir vekayam..*see* **Everything is firm and valid**, page 204
Haktarah..*see* **Burning parts of sacrifices**, page 81
Halacha
Decision —
Halacha..*see also* **Law**, page 355, *see also*; **Ruling**, page 574
Halacha according to lenient opinion in *eruv*..............Eruvin 46b, 81b, 80a
Halacha according to lenient opinion in *techum*...........Eruvin 46a-46b
Halacha, from the Torah and Rabbinical.......................Avodah Zarah 7a
Halacha like Rebbi, general rules.................................Eruvin 46b-47b
Misc. —
Halacha, according to intermediate opinion.............Bava Kama 116a; Pesachim 21a; Nazir 53a;
....Chullin 137a
Halacha and *aggadah*, episode..................................Bava Kama 60b
Halacha, four cubits for G-d.......................................Berachos 8a
Halacha from Heaven...Temurah 16a
Halacha from source and reasoning, preference............Zevachim 96b
Halacha MiSinai
Halacha MiSinai annuls verse.....................................Sotah 16a
Halacha MiSinai, deduction "all the more so".........Nazir 56b-57a; Shabbos 132a; Pesachim 81b
Halacha MiSinai, details for Torah reading..................Nedarim 37b
Halacha MiSinai, greater part of Torah.......................Gittin 60b
Halacha MiSinai, measures and quantities............Yoma 80a; Eruvin 4a; Succah 5b
Halacha leMoshe, myrtle and libations.............Succah 34a, 44a; Moed Katan 3b; Zevachim 110b
Halacha MiSinai, partitions..Succah 6b
Halachic query, Sage sent questioner to Sage who was lenient..............Chullin 48a, 99b
Halanah..*see* **Delaying**, page 157
Halbanas panim..*see* **Humiliating**, page 287

H

Half

Half damage payment, penalty or compensatory payment	Kesubos 41a-41b; Bava Kama 15a-15b; Shevuos 33a
Half field, wording of sale	Bava Basra 107b
Half guilty half innocent	Kiddushin 40b
Half *issaron*, consecrating	Menachos 8a
Half like majority	Yevamos 82b; Chullin 28b-29a
Half maidservant, episode about freedom	Gittin 38a-38b, 43b; Yevamos 66a
Half measure, prohibitions	Yoma 73b-74a
Half of five, thief	Bava Kama 71b-72a
Half of permitter, intent	Zevachim 41b-42b, 110a; Menachos 13a, 14b, 16a, 17a; Pesachim 63a
Half olives volumes, combining for impurity of dead	Oholos 3:1, 8:6, 15:10; Chullin 125a-125b
Half *perutah*, returning stolen item	Bava Kama 105a
Half roasted, Pesach lamb	Pesachim 41a-41b; Bava Metzia 115b
Half sin offering, half burnt offering	Temurah 26a
Half testimony	Bava Kama 30b, 70a-70b; Bava Basra 56a-56b; Sanhedrin 30a-31a, 86a-86b
Half their days, murderers will not live	Sanhedrin 106b
Half to G-d, Yom Tov	Pesachim 68b; Beitzah 15b
Halves equivalent to whole	Kesubos 109b
Halves on upper and lower part of Altar, blood	Zevachim 38a-38b

Half shekel

Half shekel, adding a little coin	Bechoros 56b; Shekalim 1, 6-7; Beitzah 39b; Chullin 25b
Half shekel, agent who made a mistake	Shekalim 2:2
Half shekel, coins	Shekalim 2:4
Half shekel, giving from consecrated items Treasury	Shekalim 2:2
Half shekel, *Kohanim*	Shekalim 1:4; Arachin 4a; Menachos 21b
Half shekel, money value	Bechoros 51a
Half shekel, reckoning in desert	Bechoros 5a
Half shekel, stolen shekels	Shekalim 2:1; Bava Metzia 57b-58a; Yoma 65a
Half shekel, when	Megillah 13b, 29a-29b; Shekalim 1, 3-4

Half slave

Half slave, payment of atonement for goring by an ox	Gittin 42a-42b, 43a
Half slave, freeing	Eduyos 1:13; Gittin 23b, 41a-41b; Bava Basra 13a; Chagigah 2a-2b; Pesachim 88a-88b; Arachin 2b; Temurah 25b
Half slave, *kiddushin*	Gittin 43a-43b
Half slave, *reiyah* sacrifice	Chagigah 2a-2b, 4a
Half slave, sounding *shofar*	Rosh Hashanah 29a

Hall

Hall, dimensions	Bava Basra 98b
Hall of Temple	*see* **Heichal**, page 275

Hallel

Hallel, after *Shacharis*	Rosh Hashanah 32b
Hallel, blessing	Pesachim 119b; Succah 38a, 39a
Hallel, commentaries on verses	Pesachim 117a, 118b; Megillah 14a
Hallel, days	Taanis 28b; Arachin 10a-10b
Hallel, different reading customs	Succah 38a-39a
Hallel, eating Pesach lamb	Pesachim 85b
Hallel, greeting	Berachos 14a
Hallel Hagadol, Pesach	Pesachim 117b-118a

Hand, literally .... Bava Metzia 56b
Hand of G-d, creation .... Kesubos 5a
Hand of idol, Temple .... Taanis 28b-29a
Hand of *Kohen* sprinkling blood, cut off .... Zevachim 15a
Hand on forehead, sleep .... Pesachim 112a
Hand touching etc., better be cut off .... Shabbos 108b-109a
Hands are always "busy" .... Shabbos 14a; Succah 26b; Niddah 58a; Taharos 7:8
Hands of Esau .... Gittin 57b

Handbreadth
Handbreadth, coffins .... Berachos 19b
Handbreadth, impurity of dead .... Oholos 3:6-7, 13:1-4
Handbreadth in woman, nakedness .... Berachos 24a
Handbreadth, size .... Menachos 41b
Handbreadth, which matters .... Niddah 26a-26b

Handful
Handful does not satiate lion .... Berachos 3b; Sanhedrin 16a
Handful of incense of Yom Kippur .... Yoma 47a-49b
Handful of semolina (fine flour) .... *see* **Kemitzah**, page 334

Handing over
Handing over man to save a community .... Terumos 12a
Handing over, ship .... Bava Basra 76a-76b
Handing over slave, prohibition .... Gittin 45a
Handing over to wedding canopy .... Kesubos 48b-49a; Sanhedrin 66b; Nedarim 89a
Handing over, two persons necessary .... Bava Metzia 8b
Handing over, way to purchase animal .... Kiddushin 25b; Bava Kama 11b; Bava Basra 86b

Handle
Impurity —
Handle, cases of impurity .... Chullin 128a-128b
Handle for impurity, domestic animal .... Chullin 127b
Handle for impurity of corpse .... Oholos 3:4
Handle, impurity of food .... Chullin 117b-120a; Uktzin 1:1
Handle of oven, impurity .... Keilim 5:2; Niddah 26a
Handle of utensil, impurity .... Keilim 29:1, 29:3-8
Handle, to receive impurity .... Chullin 118b, 128a
Misc. —
"Handles" for Torah, Solomon .... Eruvin 21b; Yevamos 21a
Handle, coverings .... Shabbos 125a, 126b
Handle on clay jar, impurity .... Keilim 25:6
Handle, sponge .... Shabbos 143a
Handles of Temple utensils, Munbaz .... Yoma 37a-37b
Handle for food
Handle for food, accessory to fruit .... Uktzin 1:2-6, 2:1-2
Handle for food, hair .... Chullin 119b-120a
Handle for food, produce .... Succah 13b-14a
Handle for food, succah .... Succah 13b

Handwriting
Handwriting, disqualified divorce certificate .... Gittin 86a-86b
Handwriting, mortgage .... Bava Basra 175b
Hane'elavim ve'einam olvim .... *see* **Offended but do not offend**, page 455

Hanging
Hanging, death penalty, woman...Sanhedrin 45b-46a; Sotah 23a
Hanging fish, family of hanged man...Bava Metzia 59b
Hanging, *hokaah*...Sanhedrin 34b
Hanging, how...Sanhedrin 46a-46b
Hanging *Kohen*, sacrificial services...Zevachim 26a
Hanging letters of holy parchments...Menachos 30a-30b
Hanging, Saul's sons...Yevamos 78b
Hanging *tefillin*, prohibition...Berachos 24a
Hanging Torah scroll, prohibition...Berachos 24a

Hangings
Hangings in building of second Temple.......Megillah 10a; Shevuos 16a; Eduyos 8:6; Zevachim 107b
Hangings of Tabernacle...Eruvin 2b; Zevachim 59b-60a

Hanukah...*see* **Chanukah** page 97
Hapeh she'assar...*see* **Migo**, page 409; *see also* **Mouth which forbade**, page 428
Happiness...*see also* **Rejoicing**, page 555

On which occasion —
Happiness by meat and wine...Pesachim 71a, 109a
Happiness in learning...Shabbos 30b
Happiness in performing commandment, circumcision...Shabbos 130a
Happiness in suffering...Taanis 8a
Happiness of commandment and not of commandment...Shabbos 30b
Happiness of heart, wife...Shabbos 152a
Happiness of man repaying his debt...Berachos 7b
Happiness, only by feast...Succah 25b
Happiness when being defeated in *beis din*...Sanhedrin 6b, 7a
Happiness when boy is born...Niddah 31b

Misc. —
Happiness at death of righteous...Moed Katan 25b
Happiness before prayer...Berachos 31a
Happiness, Divine Presence...Pesachim 117a; Shabbos 30b
Happiness, forbidden to mourner...Moed Katan 22b
Happiness intermingled with joy...Moed Katan 8b-9a
Happiness of his heart, Temple...Taanis 26b
Happiness of upright men, reward...Taanis 15a
Happiness turned to sadness...Moed Katan 25b

Happy
Biblical sources —
Happy is he whose master concedes to him, Moses...Berachos 32a
Happy is the generation, king's sin...Horayos 10b
Happy is the man, Abraham...Avodah Zarah 18b-19a
Happy is the man who fears...Berachos 60a

Learning —
Happy are you, scholars!...Menachos 18a
Happy are you who are all Sages...Eruvin 53b
Happy are you who were arrested, Torah...Berachos 61b
Happy is he who labors in Torah...Berachos 17a
Happy is his father who taught him Torah...Yoma 86a
Happy, knowing well his learning.......Kesubos 77b; Pesachim 50a; Moed Katan 28a; Bava Basra 10b

Righteous —
Happy are you who earned a good reputation..Yevamos 16a
Happy is he who dies with a good reputation......................................Berachos 17a
Happy is he who is wrongly suspected........................Shabbos 118b; Moed Katan 18b
Happy is he who never sinned..Succah 53a
Happy is he who repents while still a man (in his prime – strength, see Rashi)........
....Avodah Zarah 19a
Happy is our youth which did not shame our old age...............................Succah 53a
Happy is righteous, woe to wicked..Horayos 10b
Happy is she who gave birth to him..Avos 2:8
Happy is the generation whose great men listen to smaller ones...........Rosh Hashanah 25b
Happy with commandments, Rav Brona...Berachos 9b

Misc. —
Happy are you whose net is spread..Pesachim 3b
Happy are you, Israel, before Whom do you purify.................................Yoma 85b
Happy is he whose children are males...Kiddushin 82b
Happy is the perfumer, woe to the tanner.....................................Kiddushin 82b
Happy is the King praised thus in His house.....................................Berachos 3a
Happy with one's lot, rich...Avos 4:1

Har
Har Eival, curses...Sotah 37b
Har Gaash, explanation..Shabbos 105b
Har Gerizim and Eival...Sotah 33b, 37a
Har Hamelech, bounty..Berachos 44a
Har Hamelech, destruction..Gittin 57a
Har habayis...*see* **Temple Mount**, page 679
Har Sinai...*see* **Mount Sinai**, page 426
Haran and Abraham, birth..Sanhedrin 69b
Harchakos..*see* **Damage from neighbor**, page 141
Harchakos m'niddah.......................*see* **Distance from** *niddah* **wife**, page 168
Hard as iron, Sage...Taanis 4a
Hardened
Hardened lung..Chullin 55b
Hardening iron, unintentionally...........................Shabbos 41a-42a; Yoma 34b
Harei Choshech, *Gehinnom*...Tamid 32b
Harei shelecha lefanecha.................................*see* **Returning**, page 378
Hareini kaparas mishkavo.........*see* **Honor of father, before and after death**, page 283
Hareini keilu hiskabalti..............*see* **Considering I already received it**, page 125
Hareini mochel, *hamapil*............*see* **Forgiveness before going to sleep**, page 236
Harmful
Harmful creatures, killing on Shabbos.......................................Shabbos 121b
Harmful forces, protection..Berachos 54b
Harmful like swords, foods..Kiddushin 62a
Harmful like swords, squash.....................Berachos 57b; Avodah Zarah 11a, 29a
Harmful to memory..Horayos 13a-13b
Harmful to them and to world..Sanhedrin 72a
Harotzeh lehachkim.....................................*see* **Wants to become wise**, page 730
Harp
Harp in Temple and in the future..Arachin 13b

Harp of David .... Berachos 3b-4a; Sanhedrin 16a-16b

Harpania, disqualified lineage .... Yevamos 17a

Harsh words towards G-d .... Taanis 25a; Succah 53a; Megillah 22b

Harvest of grapes .... Shabbos 73b

Harvesting

Harvesting for hay, *peah* .... Menachos 71b-72a; Peah 2:1

Harvesting, secondary category of work .... Shabbos 73b

Hasagas gevul bemischar .... *see* **Competition in commerce,** page 118

Hasagas gevul .... *see* **Displacing fence,** page 167

Haseivah .... *see* **Reclining,** page 551

Hashaka .... *see* **Connection to** *mikveh,* page 122

Hashkiveinu, between mention of redemption and prayer .... Berachos 4b, 9b

Hashavas aveidah .... *see* **Lost item,** page 378

Hashchasah, explanation, immorality .... Sanhedrin 57a; Avodah Zarah 23b; Chullin 23a;

.... Bechoros 57a; Temurah 28b

Hashem .... *see* **G-d,** page 245

Hashlamas tefilah .... *see* **Making up, prayer,** page 386

Hasmoneans

Hasmoneans, *Chanukah* .... Shabbos 21b

Hasmoneans, Herod .... Bava Basra 3b-4a

Hasmoneans, revenge on Greek man .... Taanis 18b

Hasmoneans, years of reign .... Sanhedrin 97b; Avodah Zarah 9a

Hasraah .... *see* **Warning,** page 731

Haste in Egypt .... Berachos 9a

Hastened his death, slaughtered man .... Yevamos 120b-121a

Hat

Hat, carrying out on Shabbos .... Shabbos 138b; Eruvin 102b

Hat, one cubit like them .... Gittin 14b

Hatarah .... *see* **Permitting vows,** page 482

Hatavas chalom .... *see* **Interpreting dreams favorably,** page 315

Hated

Hated by G-d, hated by people .... Sanhedrin 103b

Hated wife, marital relations .... Nedarim 20b

Hates theft in burnt offering .... Succah 30a

Hating gifts, episodes .... Chullin 44b; Megillah 28a

Hating gifts, turning over loaf of bread .... Kiddushin 59a

Hating position of authority .... Avos 1:10; Tamid 32a

Hate one another, women, trustworthiness for divorce certificate ...... Gittin 23b-24a, 62b

Hate one another, who .... Yevamos 117a

Hate, do not hate your brother in your heart .... Arachin 16b

Hateful, that which is hateful to you .... Shabbos 31a

Hatfassah .... *see* **Vow by comparison,** page 727

Hatmanah .... *see* **Keeping food warm,** page 333

Hatov Vehametiv

Hatov Vehametiv, Bircas HaMazon, burial, corpses at Beitar .... Berachos 46a-46b, 48b-49a

Hatov Vehametiv, in World to Come .... Pesachim 50a

Hatov Vehametiv, thanksgiving .... Berachos 59b

Hatov Vehametiv, wine .... Berachos 59b; Pesachim 101b

Hatred

Enemies —
Hatred .... *see also* **Enemies**, page 197
Hatred, between dogs etc. .... Pesachim 113b
Hatred, female relatives .... Yevamos 117a
Hatred of ignoramus .... Pesachim 49b
Hatred of judge and Sage .... Kesubos 105b
Hatred of Mishnah learners towards Gemara learners .... Bava Metzia 33b

Prohibition —
Hatred, as severe as three capital transgressions .... Yoma 9b
Hatred, baseless, Jerusalem .... Yoma 9b
Hatred, baseless, punishment .... Shabbos 32b
Hatred of judge .... Kesubos 105b
Hatred, prohibition .... Arachin 16b

Misc. —
Hatred overrides one's better judgement .... Sanhedrin 105b
Hatred towards heretics .... Shabbos 116a
Hatred towards wicked .... Pesachim 113b

Hatzalah .... *see* **Saving from fire, Shabbos**, page 590

Haughtiness, women .... Megillah 14b

Haughty
Haughty man loses prophecy and wisdom .... Pesachim 66b
Haughty men, differences of opinion .... Sotah 47b; Chullin 7a
Haughty men, marriage .... Sotah 47b
Haughty ones of Israel, troubles .... Shabbos 139a

Hav lan unevarech .... Berachos 42a

Havaas shalom .... *see* **Bringing peace**, page 77

Havchanah .... *see* **Three months before remarrying**, page 689

Havdala
Havdala after meal, wine .... Pesachim 102b, 105b; Berachos 52a
Havdala, ate before .... Pesachim 105b, 106b-107a
Havdala before end of Shabbos .... Berachos 27a
Havdala, destined to World to Come .... Pesachim 113a
Havdala, diphtheria .... Pesachim 100b, 105a
Havdala in prayer, forgot .... Berachos 26b, 29a
Havdala in prayer, where .... Niddah 8a-8b; Berachos 29a, 33a
Havdala late, Shabbos not seen as burden .... Berachos 52a; Pesachim 105b
Havdala, learning text .... Pesachim 104b
Havdala light, torch .... Pesachim 8a, 103b
Havdala light, which kind .... Berachos 52b-53b
Havdala, on popular drink .... Pesachim 107a
Havdala on Yom Tov, *Vatodieinu* .... Berachos 33b
Havdala, prayer and wine .... Berachos 33a-33b; Shabbos 150b; Pesachim 105b, 107a
Havdala, reward .... Shevuos 18b
Havdala, seven mentions in Holy Writings .... Pesachim 104a
Havdala, text .... Berachos 51b, 52a, 52b; Pesachim 102b-105a
Havdala, until when .... Pesachim 105a, 106a, 107a
Havdala, Yom Tov .... Chullin 26b
Havdala, Yom Tov outside *Eretz Yisrael* .... Beitzah 4b

H

Havineinu..Berachos 29a, 30a

Havlaah...*see* **Included**, page 306

Havraah meal

Havraah meal, cups of wine..Kesubos 8b

Havraah meal, how..Moed Katan 27b

Havraah meal, lentils and eggs...................................Bava Basra 16b

Havraah meal, men condemned by *beis din*...................Sanhedrin 63a

Hay

Hay at beginning of word.....................Horayos 12a; Chullin 134b

Hay at end of word, *lamed* at beginning.......................Yevamos 13b

Hay, creation of this world.......................................Menachos 29b

Hay to include or exclude..Sotah 17a

Hayman, Moses..Bava Basra 15a

Hazaah...*see* **Sprinkling**, page 651

Hazamah...*see* **Conspiring witness**, page 125

Hazmanah ledin........................*see* **Summoning to judgment**, page 663

Hazmanah.........................*see* **Preparation**, *muktzeh*, page 501

He is not a human being but an angel...........................Niddah 13a

He'elem...*see* **Forgetting**, page 235

He'elem tzibur................*see* **Sacrifice for mistake of** *beis din*, page 581

Head

Head, birth..........................Bechoros 46a-46b; Niddah 28a, 29a

Head cover bought for thirteen dinar............................Kiddushin 8a

Head, impurity after birth......................Niddah 42b; Chullin 72a

Head, king of organs..Shabbos 61a

Head near tail, rebuke...Shabbos 119b

Head of Babylonians, round..Shabbos 31a

Head of sacrifice with fat...............Chullin 27a-27b; Yoma 25b-26a

Head sold, wordings of sale...Arachin 4b

Headache

Headache, like chains to neck..Shabbos 32a

Headache, painful...Shabbos 11a

Headache, Torah...Eruvin 54a

Headdress, carrying out on Shabbos.............................Shabbos 57b

Healthy flesh in leprous mark.................Negaim 4:2-3, 4:10, 6:5-6

Heaped

Heaped container, quantity.......................Shabbos 35a; Eruvin 14b

Heaped measure in offerings, consecration....................Menachos 88a

Heard

Hearing...*see also* **Listening**, page 373

Heard that his son was dead, bequest...............Bava Basra 132a, 146b

Hearing, annulling vows..Nedarim 72b-73a

Hearing from teacher, never said what he did not hear.........Berachos 27b

Hearing oneself, reading of *Shema*.........Berachos 13a, 15a-15b; Megillah 17b, 19b-20a; Sotah 32b

Heart

Heart beats and he desists..Niddah 3b

Heart, cure..Shabbos 140a; Eruvin 29b

Heart depends on eye...Avodah Zarah 28b

Heart disorders, caraway seeds......................................Berachos 40a

Heart does not absorb .... Pesachim 74b
Heart, good .... Avos 2:9
Heart knows its own pain .... Yoma 83a
Heart knows, lie .... Sanhedrin 26a
Heart like flesh, prayer .... Sotah 5a
Heart of first Sages, large as *Ulam* opening .... Eruvin 53a
Heart of king is in G-d's hand .... Berachos 55a
Heart of palm, blessing .... Berachos 36a; Eruvin 28b
Heart of palm, impurity of food .... Uktzin 3:7; Eruvin 28b
Heart sees genital area .... Berachos 24b, 25b
Heart towards Heaven, prayer .... Yevamos 105b
Heart, *treifah* .... Chullin 45b
Heart turned to G-d, prayer .... Berachos 30a, 31a
Heart understands .... Berachos 61a

Heartache, very painful .... Shabbos 11a

Heating
Heating knife until white-hot and slaughtering .... Chullin 8a
Heating *mikveh* of *Kohen Gadol* .... Yoma 34b
Heating until white-hot, clay utensil .... Pesachim 30b; Zevachim 95b-96b
Heating until white-hot, utensils .... Pesachim 30b; Avodah Zarah 75b-76b

Heaven
Heaven does not take back .... Taanis 25a
Heaven, Torah is not in Heaven .... Temurah 16a
Heaven, Torah not in Heaven, ways to remember learning .... Eruvin 55a
Heaven's sake, commandments .... Nedarim 62a
Heaven-sent item, never impure .... Sanhedrin 59b

Heavenly
Heavenly greeting, episodes .... Taanis 21b-22a
Heavenly Host, stronger than sorcery .... Chullin 7b; Sanhedrin 67b
Heavenly Yeshivah .... Berachos 18b; Bava Metzia 85b

Heavenly Chariot
Heavenly Chariot and Throne of Glory .... Chagigah 12b-13a
Heavenly Chariot, episodes .... Chagigah 13a, 14b; Shabbos 80b
Heavenly Chariot, interruption during learning .... Berachos 21b

Hebrew
Hebrew, *chalitzah* .... Sotah 33a-33b
Hebrew, preferable language .... Bava Kama 83a
Hebrew, readings .... Sotah 32a-33a; Berachos 40b; Shevuos 39a

Hebrew maidservant
Hebrew maidservant, acts of acquisition .... Kiddushin 9b, 11b-12a
Hebrew maidservant, father's death .... Kiddushin 16a-16b; Bava Metzia 12b
Hebrew maidservant, found item .... Kiddushin 16b
Hebrew maidservant, her mother .... Sotah 23b
Hebrew maidservant, second sale .... Kiddushin 18a-18b; Bechoros 34a
Hebrew maidservant, to relatives .... Kiddushin 18b, 19b-20a, 44b
Hebrew maidservant, young and adolescent .... Kiddushin 4a-4b

Hebrew slave
Freedom —
Hebrew slave, freedom .... Kiddushin 15b-16a, 17b

Hebrew slave, Jubilee .... Rosh Hashanah 8b; Kiddushin 15a-16a; Arachin 29a
Hebrew slave, making up for sick leave .... Kiddushin 16b-17a
Hebrew slave, returning to his position .... Makos 13a
Hebrew slave, tooth and eye .... Kiddushin 20a
Hebrew slave with pierced ear, freedom .... Kiddushin 21b

Laws —

Hebrew slave, *kiddushin* .... Kiddushin 7a
Hebrew slave *Kohen*, maidservant .... Kiddushin 21b
Hebrew slave, maidservant .... Kiddushin 15a, 20a; Temurah 30a
Hebrew slave, *terumah* .... Kiddushin 4a; Yevamos 70a-70b; Zevachim 82b

Misc. —

Hebrew slave, acts of acquisition .... Kiddushin 16a, 14b
Hebrew slave, buys master .... Kiddushin 22a
Hebrew slave, his value equivalent to his theft .... Kiddushin 18a
Hebrew slave, second sale .... Kiddushin 18a
Hebrew slave, selling himself .... Kiddushin 14b-15a
Hebrew slave, tax .... Bava Metzia 73b

Hebron compared to Tzoan .... Kesubos 112a

Heichal (Holy Sanctuary)

Heichal, ceiling caved in .... Zevachim 40a
Heichal, different from *Ulam* .... Yoma 44b
Heichal, dimensions and structure .... Middos 4:6-7; Yoma 52a
Heichal, leaving during service .... Yoma 43b-44b; Keilim 1:9
Heichal, painting and repairing .... Middos 3:4
Heichal, ravens, spiked roof .... Shabbos 90a; Menachos 107a; Middos 37a
Heichal .... see also **Temple**, page 678

Hechsher l'tumah .... see **Susceptible to becoming impure**, page 665

Hechsher mitzvah .... see **Accessories for commandment**, page 5

Hechsher .... see *Kashering*, page 332

Hediot yachol lehachziro .... see **Utensil, reparable, impurity**, page 718

"Hee," punishment of wicked .... Eruvin 21a

Hefker, mafkir .... see **Abandon**, page 704

Hefker .... see **Ownerless**, page 467

Hefsed merubeh .... see **Important loss**, page 300

Hefsed mitzvah keneged secharah .... see **Loss occasioned by commandment...**, page 378

Hefsek .... see **Interrupting**, page 315; see also **Interruption**, page 315

Hefsek taharah .... Niddah 33a, 68a-68b

Hegeh, reward of righteous .... Eruvin 21a

He-goat and she-goat .... Menachos 107b

Height

Height of *Eretz Yisrael* .... Bava Metzia 118b-119a; Gittin 22a
Height of man, beauty .... Bechoros 45b
Height of righteous men in World to Come .... Bava Basra 75a
Height of Sages .... Bava Metzia 84a; Niddah 24b
Height of Saul, beauty .... Berachos 48b
Height of succah .... Succah 2a-3a, 7b; Eruvin 2a
Height of Temple .... Kiddushin 69a-69b; Sanhedrin 87a; Zevachim 54b
Height of Torah scroll .... Bava Basra 14a

Heilech .... see **"Here it is"** page 276

H

Heir

Monetary matters —

Heirs..*see also* **Inheritance**, page 309
Heir, arguments on his behalf...Bava Basra 23a, 41a, 52a; Gittin 58b
Heir, *chazakah*...Bava Basra 47a
Heir, deceased not rich...Kesubos 85b
Heirs, collecting......Kesubos 91b, 92a; Arachin 6b-7a; Bava Basra 5b, 70b, 157a; Pesachim 31a; Gittin 30b
Heirs, oath......Kesubos 87a, 88a, 94a; Bava Basra 5b, 33a; Gittin 34b, 50a; Shevuos 42b, 45a, 47a, 48a
Heirs of borrower..Bava Kama 112a; Kesubos 34b
Heirs of stolen item...............................Bava Kama 111b-112a, 113a; Bava Metzia 70a
Heirs, paying to fulfill condition...Gittin 74a
Heirs, received their father's debt......................Kesubos 92a, 110a; Bava Basra 125a-125b; Pesachim 31a
Heirs, what does one collect from them...............Gittin 50a-50b; Kesubos 91b, 94a; Shevuos 42b

Misc. —

Heir, annulling ownership on Shabbos..Eruvin 70a-71a
Heir, father's loins..Eruvin 70b
Heir, Pesach lamb...Pesachim 98a
Heir, sacrifice for *nazir*...Nazir 27b, 30a-30b; Sotah 23a
Heir, sacrifices..Zevachim 5b-6a
Heir, tithe of animal...Bechoros 56b
Heirs murdered their brother...Kesubos 102b
Hekdesh...*see* **Consecrating**, page 123
Hekef gvil...*see* **Perimeter of scroll**, page 481
Hekesh..*see* **Analogy**, page 22

Helen

Helen, Queen, golden chandelier..Yoma 37b
Helen, Queen, *nezirus*..Nazir 20a
Helen, Queen, righteousness...Succah 2b
Helen, Queen, *sotah* tablet...Yoma 37b
Hell...*see* **Gehinnom**, page 246

Helping

Helping a non-Jew, sick on Shabbos..Beitzah 22a
Helping her husband..Yevamos 63a
Helping in granary to receive *terumah*..Bechoros 26b-27a
Helping non-Jew..Gittin 62a
Helping, not considered as working......................................Shabbos 93a-93b; Beitzah 22a
Helping sinner..Gittin 61a; Sheviis 5:9
Helping transgressors...Sheviis 5:6-10; Gittin 61a
Hem amah vekovan amah..........................*see* **Hat, one cubit like them**, page 271

Hen

Hen of Rabbi Abba...Shabbos 145b
Hen you took out of your house..Shabbos 151b
Hen, one in Greek...............................Shabbos 31b; Moed Katan 28a; Sanhedrin 76b
Henpeik..*see* **Attestation of legal document**, page 35
Herbs sticking, desert...Bava Basra 74b

Here

"Here it is," partially acknowledging..Bava Metzia 4a-5a
Here is a table set, no mouth to eat...Kiddushin 46a

Heresy
Heresy, body made by two idols .... Sanhedrin 39a
Heresy, repentance .... Avodah Zarah 17a
Heretic
Heretic, *apikores*, answers .... Avos 2:14; Sanhedrin 38b
Heretic, burying holy parchments .... Shabbos 116a
Heretic, distance and hate .... Shabbos 116a
Heretic, laws .... Chullin 13a
Heretic, prohibition to learn from them .... Shabbos 75a
Heretic, questions on verses .... Berachos 7a; Avodah Zarah 4a
Heretic, who is considered .... Sanhedrin 99b-100a
Heretic who slaughtered, idolatry .... Chullin 13a-13b
Heretics and informers, blessing in *Shemoneh Esrei* .... Berachos 28b-29a
Heretics, answers .... Sanhedrin 39a; Bava Basra 91a; Avodah Zarah 4a
Heretics, contention .... Berachos 12a
Heretics, Sasson and Simcha .... Succah 48b
Hero, vast knowledge in Torah .... Chagigah 14a
Hermon, Siryon .... Chullin 60b
Herod
Herod, abundance in his days .... Taanis 23a
Herod, birds .... Chullin 139b
Herod, episodes .... Bava Basra 3b-4a
Herod, Temple .... Succah 51b; Bava Basra 3b-4a
Herod, years of reign .... Sanhedrin 97b; Avodah Zarah 9a
Hesech hadaas .... *see* **Inattentive**, page 305
Hesger .... *see* **Quarantine**, page 514
Hesped .... *see* **Eulogy**, page 202
Hesped, tipuach, kilus .... Moed Katan 27b
Hesset .... *see* **Moving item**, page 428
Hester panim .... *see* **Concealing face**, page 119
Heter horaah .... *see* **Semichah**, page 600
Heter iska .... *see* **Commercial interest, way to permit**, page 117
Heter iska, interest .... Bava Metzia 68a-69a, 70a, 70b; Bechoros 15b
Hevei az kanamer .... *see* **Be strong as a leopard**, page 45
Hevei dan lechaf zechus .... *see* **Judging favorably, episodes** page 328
Hevei goleh limkom Torah .... *see* **Exile yourself to a place of Torah**, page 209
Hevei marbeh lachkor edim .... *see* **Examine witnesses thoroughly**, page 205
Hevei mechashev sechar mitzvah .... *see* **Calculate reward for commandment against**, page 84
Hevei mekabel besever panim yafos ...... *see* **Greet every man with cheerful countenance**, page 258
Hevei memaet be'esek .... *see* **Reduce your commerce**, page 553
Hevei misabek be'avak chachamim .... *see* **Roll yourself in dust of Sages' feet**, page 571
Hevei mischamem be'esh chachamim .... *see* **Warm yourself at Sages' light**, page 731
Hevei mispalel lishlom malchus .... *see* **Prayer for welfare of government**, page 497
Hevei mitalmidav shel Aaron .... *see* **Be among Aaron's disciples**, page 45
Hevei shakud lilmod .... *see* **Be diligent to learn**, page 45
Hevei zahir .... *see* **Be careful**, page 45
Hevei zanav laarayos .... *see* **Be tail to lions**, page 45
Hevel pi tashbar .... *see* **Breath of schoolchildren**, page 76
Hezek reiyah .... Bava Basra 2a-3a, 59b

Hezek reiyah .... *see* **Damage done by sight**, page 141

Hezekiah

Sins and troubles —

Hezekiah, Ravshakeh's blasphemy .... Sanhedrin 60a

Hezekiah, sickness and marriage .... Berachos 10a-10b

Hezekiah, adding month .... Pesachim 56a; Sanhedrin 12a-12b; Berachos 10b

Hezekiah, episode about Shevna .... Sanhedrin 26a-26b

Hezekiah, premature death .... Pesachim 87b

Hezekiah, sun returned .... Sanhedrin 96a

Hezekiah, Merodach's emissaries .... Sanhedrin 104a

Hezekiah, unintentional sins .... Pesachim 56a; Sanhedrin 104a; Berachos 10b

Misc. —

Hezekiah, blood of salamander .... Sanhedrin 63b

Hezekiah, funeral .... Bava Kama 16b-17a

Hezekiah, his names .... Sanhedrin 94a

Hezekiah, learning and being satisfied with little .... Sanhedrin 94b

Hezekiah, Messiah .... Sanhedrin 94a

Hezekiah, messianic times .... Sanhedrin 98b, 99a

Hezekiah, prevented non-Jews from idolatry .... Menachos 109b-110a

Hezekiah, Sages approved of him .... Pesachim 56a; Berachos 10b

Hezekiah, song .... Sanhedrin 94a

Hezekiah, Torah and greatness .... Gittin 59a

Hezekiah welcomed deceased .... Berachos 28b

Hezekiah, *yeshivah* at his door .... Eruvin 26a

Hidden

Hidden from the eye, blessing .... Bava Metzia 42a; Taanis 8b

Hidden goods, claims he bought them .... Shevuos 46b

Hidden item, damage by fire .... Bava Kama 23a, 60a, 61b-62a

Hidden things, not to learn .... Chagigah 13a

Hiding face .... Chagigah 5a-5b

Hide

Hide .... *see also* **Leather**, page 359

Hide, animal, different layers .... Gittin 22a; Shabbos 79a

Hide, destined to a certain usage, impurity .... Keilim 26:7-9; Zevachim 94a

Hide, impurity .... Pesachim 46a; Chullin 122a-124a

Hide, *muktzeh* .... Shabbos 49a-49b

Hide of sheep, impurity .... Chullin 55b-56a, 122a-122b; Pesachim 84a; Zevachim 28a

Hide offered to idolatry .... Avodah Zarah 32a-32b

Hides, different stages of preparation .... Gittin 22a; Shabbos 79a

Hides, tanner .... Kesubos 77a

Hiddur

Hiddur, beauty of Torah scroll .... Yoma 70a

Hiddur, best of the flock .... Yoma 34b, 70b; Megillah 28a

Hiddur, binding *lulav* .... Succah 33a

Hiddur for commandment, up to a third .... Bava Kama 9a-9b

Hiddur, sacrificial animals .... Menachos 87a; Sotah 34b

Hiddur, which commandments .... Shabbos 133b; Nazir 2b

Hiel, Jericho .... Sanhedrin 113a

Hierarchy in Roman nobility .... Shevuos 6b

H

High up place in private domain..Shabbos 9a; Eruvin 89a, 90b

High Priest..*see* ***Kohen Gadol***, page 346

Higher than the sun...Shabbos 30b

Higher than ten handbreadths

Higher than ten handbreadths, carrying out.................................Shabbos 92a, 97a

Higher than ten handbreadths, *mekom petur*.......................................Shabbos 7a

Higher than ten handbreadths, throwing to garbage........................Eruvin 8a, 99b

Hikdiach tavshilo.........................*see* **Burning one's dish in public, shame**, page 80

Hilchasa belo taama...................*see* **Law given without reason, his son**, page 355

Hillel

Hillel, a hundred years before Temple destruction................................Shabbos 15a

Hillel and Shamai, differences of opinion..Shabbos 15a

Hillel and Shamai, sword planted...Shabbos 17a

Hillel and Shevna (his brother) "partnering" in Torah.................................Sotah 21a

Hillel compels poor..Yoma 35b

Hillel, concise teaching...Pesachim 3b

Hillel, disciples...Succah 28a; Bava Basra 134a

Hillel, episode about converts...Shabbos 31a

Hillel, honoring Shabbos...Beitzah 16a

Hillel, like disciple in front of Shamai...Shabbos 17a

Hillel, no personal use with his burnt offering..................Nedarim 9b; Pesachim 66b

Hillel, poverty...Yoma 35b

Hillel, Shemayah and Avtalyon..Yoma 35b

Hillel, sons of Beseira...................................Pesachim 66a; Bava Metzia 85a

Hillel, taught Torah when it became forgotten.......................................Succah 20a

Hillel, test to anger him..Shabbos 30b-31a

Hillel, worthy of Divine Presence..Sanhedrin 11a

Hin, twelve *log*..Menachos 89a

Hindering (*me'akeiv*)........................*see* **Indispensable requirement**, page 308

Hinge of door, Shabbos..Eruvin 102b

Hinted in the Torah, where..Chullin 139b

Hiram

Hiram, pride...Bava Basra 75a-75b

Hiram, rebuke about his pride...Chagigah 13a

Hiram, towns given by Solomon...Shabbos 54a

Hire

Hire...*see also* **Rent**, page 558

Hired ship, sank...Bava Metzia 79a-79b

Hiring false witnesses, compensation..Bava Kama 56a

Hiring oneself to idolatrous cult...Bava Basra 110a

Hishtachavaah, explanation.................Berachos 34b; Megillah 22b; Shevuos 16b

History..Avodah Zarah 8b-9a; Shabbos 15a

Hit his head, because of mistake in learning.....................................Megillah 19b

Hitting

Fellow Jew —

Hitting, compared to cursing..................Sanhedrin 85b; Yevamos 101a; Makos 9a

Hitting fellow, cut off hand...Sanhedrin 58b; Niddah 13b

Hitting, fixed payments..Bava Kama 27b, 36b, 90a-90b

Hitting man led to execution..Sanhedrin 85a-85b

Hitting, pays and does not receive lashes .... Kesubos 32b, 33a-33b
Hitting, seriousness and punishment .... Sanhedrin 58b
Hitting wicked Cuthean .... Sanhedrin 85b; Makos 8b

Misc. —
Hitting myrtle and fronds .... Succah 43b-44a, 45b
Hitting on anvil, Shabbos .... Shabbos 103a
Hitting one's grown son, excommunication .... Moed Katan 17a
Hitting one's son .... Makos 8a
Hitting pupils, incident .... Gittin 36a
Hitting Rav Chisda, Avimi .... Menachos 7a; Arachin 22a
Hitting sacrifice to slaughter it .... Sotah 48a
Hitting until he dies .... Kesubos 86a
Hitting with blacksmith hammer .... Berachos 34a

Hitting one's father
Hitting one's father, doubt .... Yevamos 101a; Makos 16a
Hitting one's father, illegitimate child .... Yevamos 22b
Hitting one's father, is he really his father .... Chullin 11b
Hitting one's father, pulling a thorn .... Sanhedrin 84b-85a
Hitting one's father, punishment .... Bava Kama 86a
Hitting one's wicked father .... Sanhedrin 85a
Hitting one's father and mother .... Sanhedrin 84b, 85b

Hizharu .... *see* **Be careful**, page 45
Ho'il .... *see* **Because**, page 47
Hodisa, *kinyan* .... *see* **Acknowledgement, verbal, act of acquisition**, page 7
Hoe, act of acquisition by *chazakah* .... Bava Basra 53a-54b

Hogras
Hogras refused to teach his skill .... Yoma 38a-38b
Hogras, singer in Temple .... Shekalim 5:1-2; Yoma 38a, 38b

Hokaah, significance .... Sanhedrin 34b
Holachah .... *see* **Bringing sacrificial blood**, page 77
Holachas dam korban .... *see* **Bringing sacrificial blood in Temple**, page 77

Holding
Holding a holy item, oath .... Shevuos 38b
Holding objects during prayer .... Succah 41b; Berachos 23b
Holding smaller piece of cracked object .... Chullin 127b-128a; Tevul Yom 3:1
Holding Torah scroll without its covering .... Shabbos 14a; Megillah 32a
Holds lender at the expense of another .... Gittin 11b; Kesuvos 84b-85a

Hole
Purity —
Hole in ceiling, tent of corpse .... Oholos 12:4
Hole in container to prepare sprinkling water .... Shabbos 95b
Hole in vessels, sizes .... Shabbos 95b-96a; Keilim 3:1-2, 17:1-4; Niddah 49a-49b
Hole, liquid can run from it .... Shabbos 95b-96a; Niddah 49a-49b
Hole, plugged, then new hole .... Shabbos 112b

Shabbos —
Hole in *karmelis*, equivalent to *karmelis* .... Eruvin 87b
Hole in public domain, Shabbos .... Shabbos 8a-8b
Hole, minimal, putting down on Shabbos .... Shabbos 7b, 100a
Hole of barrel, Shabbos .... Shabbos 146b

Hole on Shabbos, dimension .... Menachos 57a; Shabbos 102b
Holes of private domain .... Shabbos 7b
Holes of public domain .... Shabbos 7b

Treifah —
Hole, closed by nearby organ .... Chullin 48b
Hole during slaughtering .... Chullin 32b-33a
Hole, fat, plugging up .... Chullin 49b-50a
Hole in lung .... Chullin 45b, 46a-46b, 47b, 49a
Hole in lung, torn wing .... Chullin 57a
Hole like a drill, *treifah* .... Chullin 57b
Holes in skull, *treifah* .... Chullin 57b

Misc. —
Hole close to letter, sign .... Gittin 27b; Bava Metzia 18b
Hole, damage to public domain .... Bava Kama 50a; Bava Basra 27b, 60a
Hole, half of it closed .... Bava Kama 105a
Hole, holy writings parchment .... Shabbos 108a; Chullin 119b
Hole is the "thief," not the mouse .... Gittin 45a
Holes, dimensions .... Bechoros 37b-38a
Holes for foundations, digging in public domain .... Bava Kama 50a
Holes, puberty hair .... Niddah 52a-52b

Holech kizechi .... *see* **Agent for gift, beneficiary died**, page 14
Holiday .... Shabbos 129b
Holiness
Holiness, damage to holy covenant .... Niddah 13a-14a, 16b, 43a; Berachos 13b
Holiness insufficient to be redeemed .... Bechoros 15b
Holiness of *Heichal* and *Ulam* .... Yoma 44b
Holiness of Jerusalem .... Pesachim 85b-86a
Holiness of money, becoming valid again ..... Temurah 26a-26b; Kiddushin 7a-7b; Zevachim 12a-12b;
.... Krisos 27a, 28a
Holiness of synagogue .... Megillah 27b, 28a-29a
Holiness, one, two days of Rosh Hashanah .... Eruvin 39a-39b; Beitzah 4b-5a, 22a
Holiness, one, Yom Tov .... Eruvin 38a, 39b; Beitzah 4b

Holiness of Temple
Holiness of Temple, earth .... Zevachim 24a
Holiness of Temple, rooms .... Pesachim 86a; Yoma 25a; Maaser Sheni 3:8
Holiness of Temple, rooms and roofs .... Pesachim 86a
Holiness of Temple, rooms and wall .... Zevachim 55b-56a
Holiness of Temple, levels .... Yoma 44b; Keilim 1:6-8
Hollowing out wall to complete dimension ... Shabbos 7b, 100a; Eruvin 11b, 33b, 101b; Yoma 11b
Holy
Holy of Holies, dimensions .... Bava Basra 98b-99a
Holy of Holies, entering to perform repairs .... Pesachim 26a; Middos 4:5
Holy parchments, bought from expert .... Menachos 42b
Holy to G-d, forehead-plate .... Gittin 20a-20b
Holy tongue .... *see* **Hebrew**, page 274
Holy Writings in foreign language .... Shabbos 115a-115b
Holy Writings, saving .... Shabbos 115a-115b, 116b-117b
Holy! to righteous .... Bava Basra 75b

H

Holy Ark

Holy Ark called Arna, death punishment..Shabbos 32a-32b
Holy Ark, impurity..Megillah 26b
Holy Ark, worn out..Megillah 26b

Holy books

Holy books, honor...Eruvin 98a
Holy books, intimate relations..Berachos 25b-26a
Holy books, saving..Shabbos 115a-117b

Homosexuality

Homosexuality, age...Sanhedrin 54b-55a
Homosexuality, father..Sanhedrin 54a; Krisos 3a
Homosexuality, penetration...Sanhedrin 55a; Yevamos 54b
Homosexuality, prohibition and sin offerings..............................Sanhedrin 54a-54b; Krisos 3a
Homosexuality, self-penetration...Sanhedrin 55a

Honest

Honest "yes," keeping one's word...Bava Metzia 49a
Honest man who died...Moed Katan 25a
Honest man who died, tearing garment..............................Moed Katan 24b-25a; Shabbos 105b

Honesty

Honesty, giving one's word....................................Bava Metzia 47b-48a, 49a; Bechoros 13b
Honesty in business, questions..Shabbos 31a
Honesty in business, wealth...Niddah 70b
Honesty, reward and importance..Taanis 8a

Honey

Prohibitions —

Honey, forbidden on Altar...Menachos 57b-58b
Honey from bees, impurity..Bava Basra 80a-80b
Honey from dates, blessing...Berachos 38a
Honey from dates, liquid...Terumos 11:2
Honey made by non-Jews...Avodah Zarah 39b
Honey, permitted...Bechoros 7b; Machshirin 6:4
Honey, picking up on Shabbos..Shabbos 95a
Honey which came out on Shabbos...Shabbos 145b

Misc. —

Honey and milk, drunkenness....................Nazir 4a; Yoma 76a-76b; Sanhedrin 70b-71a; Shevuos 23a;
....Bechoros 45b; Krisos 13b
Honey and sweet foods, injury..Bava Kama 85a
Honey, bees castration..Bava Basra 80a
Honey, considered a liquid...Uktzin 3:11
Honey of *zipim*..Sotah 48b; Nazir 50a; Machshirin 5:9
Honey, one sixtieth of manna..Berachos 57b
Honey, spoiled..Bava Metzia 38a-38b

Honeycombs, two..Beitzah 36a

Honor

Honor, disciple's and friend's..Avos 4:12
Honor of congregation, *Chumashim*...Gittin 60a
Honor of congregation, man dressed in tattered garments............................Megillah 24a-24b
Honor of husband despised husband, wife..Megillah 12b
Honor of disciple in front of teacher...................Bava Basra 119b; Sotah 40b, 41b; Yoma 69a

Honor of holy books .... Eruvin 98a
Honor of host, reward .... Berachos 63b
Honor of host, Yavneh .... Berachos 63b
Honor of husband, commandment .... Kiddushin 31a; Krisos 28a
Honor of judge .... Sanhedrin 8a
Honor of king .... Sanhedrin 19b, 22a; Sotah 41b; Kesubos 17a; Kiddushin 32b
Honor of king and teacher, renouncing .... Kiddushin 32a-32b
Honor of man occupying high position .... Sanhedrin 92b
Honor of princess, inside .... Yevamos 77a
Honor of sons, spending more than one's means .... Chullin 84b
Honor of synagogue .... Megillah 28a-29a
Honor of wealthy people .... Eruvin 86a
Honor of wife .... Bava Metzia 59a; Sanhedrin 76b; Chullin 84b
Honor, your friend's as important as yours .... Avos 2:10, 4:12

Honor of father
Honor of father and commandment .... Kiddushin 32a
Honor of father and mother, and reverence .... Kiddushin 31b-32a
Honor of father and mother, episodes .... Kiddushin 31b
Honor of father and mother, precedence .... Kiddushin 31a; Krisos 28a
Honor of father and Torah learning .... Megillah 16b-17a
Honor of father, Baladan .... Sanhedrin 96a
Honor of father, before and after death .... Kiddushin 31b
Honor of father, does not override .... Bava Metzia 32a; Yevamos 5b-6a
Honor of father, from whose money .... Kiddushin 31b-32a
Honor of father, making him toil at grindstone .... Kiddushin 31a-31b
Honor of father, Red Heifer .... Kiddushin 31a; Avodah Zarah 23b-24a
Honor of father, renouncing .... Kiddushin 32a
Honor of father, returning his stolen item .... Bava Kama 113a
Honor of father, supporting him with second tithe .... Kiddushin 32a
Honor of father, Tablets .... Kiddushin 31a
Honor of father, wicked .... Yevamos 22b, 94b; Bava Metzia 62a
Honor of father, woman .... Kiddushin 30b

Honor of human beings
Honor of human beings, died on Shabbos .... Shabbos 94b
Honor of human beings, *muktzeh* .... Shabbos 81a-81b; Succah 36b
Honor of human beings, overrides prohibitions .... Berachos 19b-20a
Honor of human beings, *tzitzis* .... Menachos 37b-38a

Honor of Sage
Honor of Sage remains unaffected .... Bechoros 30b
Honor of Sages, precedence .... Megillah 3b; Bava Basra 120a
Honor of Sages, reward .... Shabbos 23b; Avos 4:6
Honor of Sages, Jehoshaphat .... Kesubos 103b

Honor of teacher
Honor of teacher and father, precedence .... Krisos 28a
Honor of teacher, festival .... Chagigah 3a
Honor of teacher, greater in one thing .... Bava Metzia 33a; Pesachim 113b
Honor of teacher, Mar Ukva .... Moed Katan 16b
Honor to teacher, desecration of G-d's Name .... Berachos 19b; Eruvin 63a; Sanhedrin 82a;
.... Shevuos 30b

H

Honor of Torah
Honor of Torah, did not convert...Berachos 17b
Honor of Torah, giving seat to Sage...Shevuos 30b
Honor of Torah, individual..Megillah 3b
Honor of Torah, learning while standing....................................Megillah 21a
Honor of Torah, non-Jews..Chullin 92b
Honor of Torah, wealth..Shabbos 119a

Honored
Honored through fellow's humiliation..Megillah 28a
Honoring when entering and going out...................................Berachos 46b-47a
Honoring wife, blessing...Bava Metzia 59a
Honoring wife more than oneself...Chagigah 5b

Hoodlums, repentance..Berachos 10a; Sanhedrin 37a
Hoof, sign of *kosher* animal...Chullin 59a
Hope of man is worm..Avos 4:4
Horaah...*see* **Ruling,** page 574
Horaas shaah...*see* **Temporary ruling, Gideon,** page 679
Hordos..*see* **Herod,** page 277

Hormiz
Hormiz bar Lilis...Bava Basra 73a-73b
Hormiz, upper part of body..Sanhedrin 39a

Horn
Horn...*see also* **Shofar,** page 619, **Ox (Goring),** page 468
Horn, damage by ox...Bava Kama 2b
Horn, damage from, guarding......................................Bava Kama 45b-46a, 55b, 99b
Horn, definition and secondary category...Bava Kama 2b
Horn, dividing ox..Bava Kama 34a-34b
Horn, exemption if ox was ownerless...Bava Kama 13b
Horn in eye, episode..Shabbos 108a; Bava Basra 89a
Horns of animal, blemish..Bechoros 44a
Horns of antelope, livelihood....................................Shabbos 107b; Avodah Zarah 3b
Horns, signs of wild animal...Chullin 59a-59b

Hornet
Hornet, conquest of *Eretz Yisrael*..Sotah 36a
Hornet, danger of swallowing...........................Avodah Zarah 12b; Gittin 70a
Hornet of Ninveh, danger...Shabbos 121b

Horoscope, prohibition..Pesachim 113b

Horse
Horse, characteristics..Pesachim 113b
Horse on Shabbos, episode..Sanhedrin 46a
Horse to rich man who became poor..Kesubos 67b
Horses, guarding city...Pesachim 113a
Horses, king...Sanhedrin 21b
Horses of Solomon..Sanhedrin 21b

Horseradish
Horseradish, health..Avodah Zarah 11a
Horseradish, Pesach...Pesachim 39a
Horseradish, soft in the beginning..Pesachim 39a

Hoshana Rabba
   Hoshana Rabba..................Succah 34a, 43b-45b; Taanis 3a; Moed Katan 3b; Zevachim 110b
   Hoshana Rabba on Shabbos..................Succah 43b
Hosea the prophet..................Pesachim 87a-87b; Bava Basra 14b
Hospitality
   Hospitality, Abraham..................Sotah 10a-10b
   Hospitality, Micah..................Sanhedrin 103b
   Hospitality, more important than…..................Shabbos 127a; Shevuos 35b
   Hospitality, reward..................Berachos 55a
Host
   Host, accepting gift from Egypt..................Pesachim 118b
   Host cuts up bread..................Berachos 46a
   Host, do everything he asks (except "leave")..................Pesachim 86b
   Host house, behavior..................Arachin 16b; Yoma 12a
   Host house, courtyard..................Bava Basra 11b
   Host of Rav Adda, high position..................Kiddushin 76b
   Host of Rav, *beis din*..................Sanhedrin 7b-8a
   Host of Sennacherib..................Shabbos 113b; Sanhedrin 95b-96a
   Host of Zeiri, deceased..................Berachos 18b
   Host, Sages' discourses..................Berachos 63b
Hot
   Hot drink, too much is harmful..................Gittin 70a
   Hot in part, hot in whole..................Pesachim 74a
   Hot pepper, proverb..................Megillah 7a; Chagigah 10a; Yoma 85b
   Hot, sun..................Berachos 27a
   Hot springs
      Hot springs of Tiberias, cooking on Shabbos..................Shabbos 40b; Pesachim 41a
      Hot springs of Tiberias, heat..................Shabbos 39a
      Hot springs of Tiberias, Jerusalem..................Pesachim 8b
   Hot water
      Hot water, danger..................Shabbos 40b
      Hot water on Motzaei Shabbos..................Shabbos 119b
      Hot water, washing child..................Chullin 24b
Hot-tempered man, his life is no life..................Pesachim 113b
Hotzaah..................*see* **Carry**, page 88
Hotzaah beShabbos..................*see* **Carrying out on Shabbos, rolling reed**, page 89
Hour
   Hour before praying..................Berachos 32b
   Hour of birth, fate..................Shabbos 156a
   Hours, age of sacrifice..................Zevachim 25b
   Hours, G-d's deeds..................Avodah Zarah 3b
   Hours, man makes a mistake about..................Pesachim 11b-13a; Sanhedrin 40b
   Hours written in Jerusalem, legal documents..................Kesubos 94b
House
   Aggadah —
      House, nice, mind at ease..................Berachos 57b
      House of G-d, let us go..................Yoma 24b
      Houses of Edom, study houses..................Megillah 6a
      Houses of righteous, destruction..................Berachos 58b

Commandments —

House, *mezuzah* .... Yoma 10a-11b; Menachos 33a-34a
House of mourner, learning .... Moed Katan 23a
House, requirement for tithes .... Bava Metzia 87b-88b; Berachos 35b; Maasros 2:1-3, 3:6-7
House vineyard and marriage, order .... Sotah 44a

Definition —

House, and not hut .... Kesubos 54a, 103a
House, expressions of vows .... Nedarim 56a
House is considered as filled .... Eruvin 76b
House like four cubits .... Berachos 25b; Eruvin 42b
House, measures .... Bava Basra 7a, 98b
House, summer and winter .... Yoma 10a

Men —

House of Aaron, *Kohanim* .... Shevuos 14a
House of Abidan, dispute with heretics .... Shabbos 116a
House of Eli, *semicha* .... Sanhedrin 14a
House of Hillel, *halacha* .... Eruvin 13b; Beitzah 11b; Yevamos 15b; Chullin 43b-44a; Berachos 11a
House of Nebuchadnezzar .... Berachos 57b
House of Rabban Gamliel, incense on Yom Tov .... Beitzah 22b

House of Shamai

House of Shamai, did they apply their opinion .... Yevamos 14a-16a
House of Shamai, leniency .... Eduyos 4:1-12, 5:1-4; Shabbos 77a; Zevachim 38b; Menachos 104a
House of Shamai, not considered as Mishnah .... Beitzah 11b; Berachos 36b; Yevamos 9a
House of Shamai, *semichah* .... Beitzah 20a-20b
House of Shamai, sharp-minded .... Yevamos 14a
House of Shamai, stricter .... Berachos 11a

Monetary matters —

House among my houses, sale .... Menachos 108b; Nedarim 56a
House and attic, changes in building .... Bava Metzia 116b, 117b
House and attic, repair .... Bava Metzia 117a; Bava Basra 6b-7a
House and field to non-Jew .... *see* **Non-Jew**, page 448
House in which one married his son .... Bava Basra 144a; Gittin 14a
House, included in sale .... Bava Basra 61a, 63b-64a, 65a-65b, 69a
House not checked before Pesach, retracting .... Pesachim 4b
House, small, found only large one .... Bava Basra 71a
Houses in open city, return on Jubilee .... Arachin 33a

Shabbos —

House, houses necessitating *eruv* .... Eruvin 72b
House impure, size to carry out on Shabbos .... Shabbos 91a-91b
House in *Eretz Yisrael*, Shabbos .... Bava Kama 80b; Gittin 8b
House in which *eruv* was put .... Eruvin 49a
House less than ten handbreadths, Shabbos .... Shabbos 7a-7b
House used to get fresh air .... Eruvin 22a
Houses, one inside the other, *eruv* .... Eruvin 75a-75b

Misc. —

House, "my house is in front of you," responsibility to watch .... Bava Metzia 49b
House, cases of damage .... Sotah 48a; Bava Kama 21a
House, coming in suddenly .... Niddah 16b; Pesachim 112a
House in air, Sages of Athens .... Bechoros 8b

House, in Eretz Yisrael................................Kesubos 110b; Arachin 3a-3b; Shabbos 41a; Berachos 24b
House in open city, consecrated items to Treasury.................................Arachin 33a
House is maintained up thanks to its occupants..................................Bava Kama 21a
House, leprous, impurity.........................Yevamos 103b; Negaim 13,3-4; Moed Katan 8a
House without openings, defilement by corpse..................................Bava Basra 12a

House in walled city
House in walled city, usury..................................Arachin 31a-31b
House in walled city, Jubilee..................................Arachin 29a
House in walled city, redeeming..................................Arachin 31a-31b

House of study
House of study, "great house"..................................Megillah 27a
House of study, avoiding disturbances.................Eruvin 60a; Avodah Zarah 74b
House of study, being the first to arrive................Megillah 27b; Succah 28a
House of study, cherished by G-d..................Berachos 8a, 30b; Megillah 29a
House of study, learning..................................Avos 5:14
House of study, locking oneself in.................Shabbos 120a; Chagigah 14a
House of study, studying out of..................................Chullin 86b
House of study without new interpretation..................................Chagigah 3a

How
"How many Yosef already exist!"..................................Pesachim 68b
How beloved is Your Torah, Yosef Habavli..................................Menachos 18a
How good are your tents..................................Bava Basra 60a
How great are Your works..................................Chullin 127a
How to acquire wisdom..................................Niddah 70b
How to dance before a bride..................................Kesubos 16b-17a

How beautiful
How beautiful are this girl's steps..................................Avodah Zarah 18a
How beautiful are your steps..................................Succah 49b; Chagigah 3a
How beautiful, interrupting learning..................................Avos 3:7

Hu, means from beginning to end..................................Megillah 11a

Huchzak kafran.........................*see* **Considered like liar,** *beis din*, page 125

Hulda
Hulda, pride for woman..................................Megillah 14b
Hulda, prophecy..................................Megillah 14a-14b
Hulda, Josiah..................................Megillah 14b

Human intervention
Human intervention, pouring sacrificial blood..................................Zevachim 60a
Human intervention, sanctification of Red Heifer ash..................................Parah 6:1
Human intervention, washing hands..................................Chullin 107a; Yadayim 1:5

Humble
Humble and knee bent, World to Come..................................Sanhedrin 88b
Humble, judge..................................Sanhedrin 88b
Humble man, moves back before others................Taanis 16a; Megillah 29a
Humble, what a humble man!..................................Berachos 6b

Humiliating
Humiliating a Sage, and a man in front of a Sage...............Shabbos 119b; Sanhedrin 99b
Humiliating clothes, David cut Saul's cloak..................................Berachos 62b
Humiliating food..................Berachos 50b, 52b; Shabbos 50b, 143a
Humiliating, *Gehinnom*..................................Bava Metzia 58b

H

Humiliating, hot furnace..Berachos 43b; Kesubos 67b
Humiliating one's wife in *beis din*.............................Kesubos 74b-75a, 97b; Gittin 46a
Humiliating, severity...Bava Metzia 58b-59a
Humiliating, Shmuel, punishment...Berachos 19a
Humiliating, World to Come...Sanhedrin 99a

Humility
  Episodes —
  Humility, "be very very humble"...Avos 4:4, 4:10
  Humility, Abraham...Chullin 88b-89a; Sotah 17a
  Humility, Beseira's sons...Bava Metzia 85a
  Humility, David....................Moed Katan 16b; Megillah 11a; Sotah 10b; Chullin 89a
  Humility, episodes about forgiveness...Sotah 40a
  Humility, first generations...Sanhedrin 11b
  Humility, Hillel..Shabbos 30b-31a
  Humility, Moses and Aaron...Chullin 89a
  Humility, Rabban Gamliel...Sanhedrin 11b
  Humility, Rabban Shimon ben Gamliel................................Bava Metzia 84b-85a
  Humility, Rebbi and Rav Yosef..Sotah 49b
  Humility, Rav, repeated loudly, Rabbi Shila's lecture...........................Yoma 20b
  Humility, reward..Sanhedrin 43b; Sotah 5b
  Misc. —
  Humility, atonement............................Rosh Hashanah 17a; Megillah 15b; Sanhedrin 111b
  Humility, disappeared since Sages died...Sotah 49b
  Humility, G-d's..Megillah 31a
  Humility, G-d's proximity to humble man...Sotah 5a
  Humility, greater than all virtues.............................Avodah Zarah 20b; Arachin 16a
  Humility of Israel, G-d gave them greatness..Chullin 89a
  Humility, reward..Sanhedrin 43b; Sotah 5b
  Humility, Sage's..Yoma 71a
  Humility, Torah learning..Bava Metzia 85b; Eruvin 55a
  Humility, value...Sotah 4b-5b
  Humility, world stands on humble person..Chullin 89a
Hump, blemish...Bechoros 43b
Huna bar Nassan
  Huna bar Nassan, belt...Zevachim 19a
  Huna bar Nassan, roasting meat in desert...Bava Basra 74b
Hundred
  Hundred and one times, reviewing...Chagigah 9b
  Hundred, annulling *terumah*........................Terumos 4:7-13, 5:1-9; Avodah Zarah 69a
  Hundred blessings..Menachos 43b
  Hundred blows were given..Bava Basra 85b; Kesubos 53a
  Hundred years old, detached from world...Avos 5:21
Hunger, episodes..Yoma 83a, 83b
Hungry soul, bitter seems sweet...Bava Kama 92b
Hunter
  "Hunter swindler," way of learning.......................Eruvin 54b; Avodah Zarah 19a
  Hunter of doves, disqualified for testimony.....................Rosh Hashanah 22a; Eruvin 82a;
....Sanhedrin 24b, 25a-25b, 27b

Hunting
Hunting harmful creatures on *Chol HaMoed* .... Moed Katan 6b-7a
Hunting on Shabbos, act needed for itself .... Shabbos 107b
Hunting on Shabbos, cases .... Shabbos 106a-107a
Hunting on Shabbos, which species .... Beitzah 23b-24a; Shabbos 106b
Hunting weapons, impurity .... Keilim 15:6, 23:5
Hur, golden calf .... Sanhedrin 7a
Hurry
Hurry, transgression when in hurry .... Pesachim 10b-11b
Hurry, worried for one's money .... Pesachim 11a-11b
Hurt feelings
Hurt feelings .... *see also* **Resentment**, page 562
Hurt feelings, rain .... Taanis 24b
Hurt feelings, Rav Pappa .... Taanis 9a-9b
Hurting
Hurting convert's feelings .... Bava Metzia 59b
Hurting feelings by speech .... Berachos 43b; Bava Metzia 58b-59a
Hurting wife's feelings .... Bava Metzia 59a
Husband .... *see also* **Inheritance of wife**, page 309
Aggadah —
Husband and wife, if they merit .... Sotah 17a
Husband, demanding wife's modesty .... Gittin 90a-90b
Husband died, his wife's pain .... Sanhedrin 22b
Laws —
Husband included in "people," vow .... Nedarim 83b-84a
Husband like his wife, testimony .... Sanhedrin 28a-28b
Husband missing .... *see* **Agunah**, page 15
Husband who permitted .... Nedarim 77b-78a
Husband's consent, woman's vow .... Nedarim 73b, 74a; Shabbos 46b; Yevamos 29b; Gittin 83b;
.... Niddah 46b
Husbands died, *"katlonis"* .... Kesubos 43b; Yevamos 26a, 64b
Monetary matters —
Husband, authorization .... Gittin 48b
Husband, custody .... Bava Metzia 96a-96b
Husband, custody with owner .... Bava Metzia 96a
Husband like heir or like customer .... Bava Basra 139a-139b
Husband, rights to indemnity for wife's shame .... Kesubos 65b-66a
Husband who employed tenant farmers .... Kesubos 80a
Husband who ran away, supporting his wife .... Kesubos 48a, 106b-107b
Husband's rights, parallel to wife's .... Kesubos 47b
Misc. —
Husband, honoring one's husband .... Megillah 12b; Kiddushin 31a; Krisos 28a
Husband of mother, honoring .... Kesubos 103a
Husband's will, episode .... Nedarim 66b
Hut
Hut dwellers, their life .... Eruvin 55b
Hut is not like a house .... Kesubos 54a, 103a
Hut of leaves, *techum* .... Eruvin 21a
Hutar miklalo .... *see* **Deduction, exceptional permission**, page 156

H

Hybrid animal

Hybrid animal, covering blood on Yom Tov .... Beitzah 8a-8b; Chullin 84b-85a

Hybrid animals and beasts .... Chullin 78a-78b, 79b-80a, 83b, 132a; Bikurim 2:8-10; Yoma 74a-74b;

.... Beitzah 8a; Nazir 34a; Kiddushin 3a; Krisos 21a

Hypocrisy .... Pesachim 113b; Bava Metzia 49a

Hypocrites

Hypocrites, denouncing .... Yoma 86b

Hypocrites, keep away from .... Sotah 22b

Hypocrites, world destroyers .... Sotah 22b

Hyssop

Hyssop for leper .... Negaim 14:6; Succah 13a-13b; Chullin 62b; Parah 11:7; Sotah 15b

Hyssop for sprinkling .... Succah 13a-13b; Shabbos 109b; Chullin 62b; Niddah 26a; Negaim 14:6;

.... Parah 11:7-9

Hyssop impure, sprinkling .... Parah 12:6

Hyssop used for sprinkling, leftovers .... Succah 13a-13b; Parah 11:9

<dd>x</dd>

I

I also, accepting *nezirus* .... Nazir 13a-13b
I am G-d your healer .... Sanhedrin 101a
I borrowed from you .... Bava Basra 172a-172b
I deserve it because I transgressed Rav's words .... Shabbos 135a
I did not borrow, I did not pay .... Shevuos 41b; Kesubos 88a; Bava Basra 6a
I did not hear, wise man .... Avos 5:7
I have set G-d before me always .... Sanhedrin 22a
I merit a reward for my behavior .... Shabbos 118b-119a
I renounce the debt, Sabbatical year .... Gittin 37b; Sheviis 10:8; Shabbos 148b
I shall not eat, oath .... Nedarim 16a; Shevuos 19b-20a
I tried and I found, believe him .... Megilah 6b
I want, by coercion .... Rosh Hashanah 6a; Yevamos 106a; Kiddushin 50a; Bava Basra 48a; Arachin 21a
I do not know
    I do not know, certain and uncertain ...... Bava Basra 135a-135b; Bava Kama 118a; Kesubos 12b-13a;
    .... Bava Metzia 97b-98b, 116b
    I do not know, judge .... Sanhedrin 17a
    I do not know, maybe wrong .... Berachos 4a
    I do not know, oath .... Bava Metzia 97b-98b, 116b; Shevuos 47a
    I do not know, so as not to make a mistake .... Berachos 4a
    I do not know, negligence .... Bava Metzia 35a, 42a
I paid
    I paid, claim .... Bava Basra 5a-6a, 45b, 70a-71a; Shevuos 41b-42a
    I paid, considered like liar in *beis din* .... Bava Metzia 16b-17a
    I paid, oath .... Shevuos 41a
    I paid, ruling of *beis din* .... Bava Metzia 17a-17b
    I paid you, tenant .... Bava Metzia 102b-103a
Ibdah kesuvasah .... *see* **Lost her *kesubah***, page 378
Ibud ochlim .... *see* **Crumbs, waste of food**, page 134
Ibur hachodesh .... *see* **Adding a month**, page 11
Ibur ir .... *see* **Outskirts of city**, page 464
Ibur shanah .... *see* **Adding a month**, page 11
Ibur tzurah .... *see* **Leaving sacrificial flesh until its time for consumption is over**, page 359
Iddo the prophet .... Sanhedrin 89b

Identification of item, concern of theft .... Bava Basra 46a-46b
Idis .... *see* **Best land,** page 55
Idle men fill the streets .... Berachos 17b; Pesachim 51b, 55a
Idleness
  Idleness .... Avos 3:2
  Idleness causes mental illness .... Kesubos 59b
Idol
  Connected to land —
    Idol, connected to earth .... Avodah Zarah 46a, 47b, 54b; Chullin 16a; Meilah 20a
    Idol, connected water .... Avodah Zarah 58b-59a
    Idol, land .... Avodah Zarah 54b
    Idol, mobile item placed in the ground .... Avodah Zarah 47b
  Idols —
    Idol, Maacah's monster .... Avodah Zarah 44a
    Idol, *Markolis* .... Avodah Zarah 49b-50a; Bava Metzia 25b; Sanhedrin 64a
    Idol, Peor .... Sanhedrin 64a
  Laws —
    Idol, blessing .... Berachos 57b
    Idol broke hand .... Taanis 28b-29a
    Idol, destroying .... Pesachim 28a; Avodah Zarah 43b-44a, 45b-46a; Sanhedrin 55a
    Idol, giving a degrading name .... Avodah Zarah 45b-46a
    Idol, names .... Sanhedrin 63b; Avodah Zarah 11b
    Idol, Sages avoided passing by .... Avodah Zarah 17a-17b
  Profit —
    Idol, accessories .... Temurah 28b
    Idol, broke by itself .... Avodah Zarah 41b-42b; Meilah 14a
    Idol, coating .... Temurah 28b
    Idol, ornament .... Avodah Zarah 51b
    Idols, exchange .... Demai 6:10; Kiddushin 17b; Avodah Zarah 54b, 64a-64b
    Idols, forbidden for benefit from when .... Avodah Zarah 46a, 51b-52a, 53b
  Misc. —
    Idol, shapes .... Avodah Zarah 40b-41a, 42b-43b; Rosh Hashanah 24b
    Idols, worthless .... Chullin 121a
Idolater
  Aggadah —
    Idolater eating Pesach lamb, episode .... Pesachim 3b
    Idolaters, giving of the Torah .... Avodah Zarah 2b
    Idolaters, looking for merit .... Avodah Zarah 4a
    Idolaters, impurity of snake .... Shabbos 145b-146a; Yevamos 103b; Avodah Zarah 22b
    Idolaters, too heavy subjugation .... Kesubos 111a
  Commandments —
    Idolater, charity .... Bava Basra 10b
    Idolater, circumcision .... Avodah Zarah 26b-27a; Menachos 42a
    Idolater, holy parchments in his possession .... Gittin 45a-45b
    Idolater, *nazir* .... Nazir 61a-62a
    Idolater, punishment for seven commandments .... Bava Kama 38a
    Idolater, shoulder and cheek of animal .... Chullin 133a-133b
    Idolater who kept Shabbos .... Sanhedrin 58b-59a

Death —
Idolater, death for unintentional sin...Makos 9a-9b
Idolater, for which sin is he killed...Sanhedrin 57a-57b
Idolater, less than a *perutah*...Avodah Zarah 71b; Eruvin 62a; Yevamos 47b
Idolater who hit, death...Sanhedrin 58b
Marriage —
Idolater, his son from a Jewish woman...Yevamos 44b-45b, 70a, 99a
Idolater, lineage...Yevamos 62a; Kiddushin 67b
Monetary matters —
Idolater, act of acquisition...Avodah Zarah 71a-72a; Bechoros 13a-13b
Idolater, inheritance...Kiddushin 17b-18a; Nazir 61a
Idolater, lost item...Bava Kama 113b; Sanhedrin 76b
Idolater, receiving his rights by buying his property...Bechoros 11b
Idolater, repayment from guarantor...Bava Basra 174b
Idolater, right because he bought from him...Bava Basra 35b-36a
Idolaters, damages...Bava Kama 13b, 38a
Idolaters, their courts.................................Gittin 10b-11a, 19b, 88b; Bava Kama 113b-114a
Prohibitions —
Idolater, learning Torah.................................Chagigah 13a; Bava Kama 38a; Sanhedrin 59a; Avodah Zarah 3a
Idolater, impurity.........................Nazir 61a-61b; Avodah Zarah 36b-37a; Niddah 34a-34b; Shabbos 17b; Eduyos 5:1
Idolater, impurity of corpse...Yevamos 61a
Idolater, sinning with animal.................................Avodah Zarah 14b-15b, 22a-23a
Prohibitions for Jews —
Idolater, cheese made by...Avodah Zarah 34b-35b
Idolater, concern about food he prepared.........Avodah Zarah 31b-32a, 34b, 35b-36a, 38b-39b, 40b
Idolater, gift on his festival...Avodah Zarah 64b-65a
Idolater giving gift...Avodah Zarah 6b
Idolater, giving *tzitzis* to...Menachos 41b
Idolater, his wine...*see* **Wine of idolaters**, page 751
Idolater unclothed, praying in front of him.................................Berachos 25b; Shabbos 150a
Idolater, loan with interest...Bava Metzia 70b-71b
Idolater, meat in his possession...Chullin 94b-95a
Idolater, prohibition of gift.................................Pesachim 21b; Chullin 114b; Avodah Zarah 20a
Idolater, spinning *tzitzis*...Menachos 42b
Idolater, Yom Tov...Beitzah 21a-21b
Prohibitions in deals —
Idolater, acquiring land to make excavations...Gittin 47a
Idolater, buying field from him...Bava Basra 54b-55a
Idolater, buying field in *Eretz Yisrael*...Bava Metzia 101a; Gittin 47a-47b; Menachos 31a; Bechoros 11b
Idolater, buying slaves...Gittin 37b-38a
Idolater, *chazakah* on property he sold...Bava Basra 35b-36a
Idolater, excommunication, one who sells to him...Bava Kama 114a
Idolater, forbidden sales...Avodah Zarah 15b; Nedarim 62b
Idolater, keeping one's word...Bechoros 13b
Idolater, partnership...Sanhedrin 63b; Bechoros 2b
Idolater, selling and renting him land...Avodah Zarah 20b-21b
Idolater, selling him after he took by force...Gittin 44a
Idolater, selling him an animal.................................Avodah Zarah 14b-16a, 20b; Bechoros 2b-3a
Idolater, selling him field, source...Avodah Zarah 19b-21b

Idolater, selling him tree so that he can cut it down .... Avodah Zarah 20b
Idolater, selling him *tzitzis* .... Menachos 43a
Idolater who took from buyer .... Bava Basra 45a

Sacrifice —
Idolater, accepting his sacrifice ...... Chullin 13b; Nazir 62a; Menachos 73b; Temurah 2b; Shekalim 1:5
Idolater, concern of sacrificial animal which sinned with man ... Avodah Zarah 14b-15a, 22a-22b
Idolater, endowment valuation .... Nazir 61a-62a; Arachin 5b, 13b
Idolater, libations .... Menachos 51b, 73b; Shekalim 7:6
Idolater, secular use of item he consecrated .... Temurah 3a; Zevachim 45a; Arachin 5b
Idolater, sacrifice in present times .... Zevachim 116b
Idolater waving sacrifice .... Menachos 61a-61b
Idolater, which sacrifices .... Menachos 73b; Nazir 62a; Chullin 13b; Temurah 2b
Idolater, which sacrificial laws apply to them .... Zevachim 45a-45b; Temurah 3a
Idolaters, consecrating item .... Arachin 5b, 6a; Zevachim 45a-45b; Temurah 2b

Separating tithe —
Idolater, *challah* .... Challah 3:5-6; Menachos 67a-67b
Idolater, shoulder and cheek of animal .... Chullin 133a-133b
Idolater, tithe of his sale .... Bechoros 11a
Idolater who finished work, tithe .... Menachos 66b-67a
Idolater who tithed .... Terumos 3:9; Gittin 23b; Kiddushin 41b; Arachin 6a

Trustworthiness —
Idolater, trustworthiness about *agunah* .... Yevamos 121b-122a
Idolater, trustworthy when freely speaking .... Yevamos 122a
Idolaters, not trustworthy .... Chullin 133b

Misc. —
Idolater, being agent .... Bava Metzia 71b-72a; Kiddushin 41b; Gittin 23b
Idolater, charity .... Bava Basra 10b
Idolater, disqualified to testify .... Bava Kama 15a
Idolater of sun, tax .... Nedarim 62b
Idolater, Jew's idol .... Avodah Zarah 46a, 53b
Idolater, not to provoke .... Pesachim 113a
Idolater, slaughtering .... Chullin 13a-13b
Idolaters, snake venom .... Avodah Zarah 31b; Shabbos 86b
Idolaters, thieves .... Bava Basra 45a; Chullin 133b
Idolaters, wording of vows .... Nedarim 31a
Idolaters, dangers .... Avodah Zarah 25a-26a, 27a-28a; Berachos 61a
Idolaters, Divine Fury .... Avodah Zarah 4a
Idolaters, haircut .... Avodah Zarah 29a
Idolaters, how does G-d punish them .... Sotah 9a
Idolaters, keeping distance .... Avodah Zarah 20a, 26a; Gittin 62a
Idolaters, loss for who approves them .... Bava Basra 91b
Idolaters, slaves in the future .... Eruvin 43b
Idolaters, will convert in the future .... Avodah Zarah 24a

Idolaters' courts
Idolaters' courts, *agunah* .... Gittin 28b-29a
Idolaters' courts, divorce certificate .... Gittin 9a-9b, 10b-11a
Idolaters' courts, judges without proofs .... Bava Kama 114a
Idolaters' courts, legal document .... Gittin 19b, 10b-11a
Idolaters' courts, prohibition .... Bava Kama 113b-114a; Gittin 88b

Idolaters' courts, saving oneself from idolater .... Gittin 44a

Idolaters' festivals
Idolaters' festivals, birthday .... Avodah Zarah 10a
Idolaters' festivals, dependant city .... Avodah Zarah 8a
Idolaters' festivals, episode .... Avodah Zarah 65a
Idolaters' festivals, gentile feasts .... Avodah Zarah 2a
Idolaters' festivals, Ginosia .... Avodah Zarah 10a
Idolaters' festivals, present .... Avodah Zarah 6b, 64b-65a
Idolaters' festivals, private ones .... Avodah Zarah 8a, 11b
Idolaters' festivals, trade .... Avodah Zarah 5b-6b, 7b, 11b

Idolatrous
Idolatrous Altar, annulment .... Avodah Zarah 53b-54a
Idolatrous animal, permitted for secular use .... Temurah 29a
Idolatrous customs, burning king's belongings .... Sanhedrin 52b; Avodah Zarah 11a-11a
Idolatrous woman, impurity by intimate relations ...... Niddah 34a-34b; Shabbos 86b; Mikvaos 8:4
Idolatrous woman, *kiddushin* .... Kiddushin 68b
Idolatrous woman, prohibition and punishment .... Sanhedrin 81b-82a; Avodah Zarah 36b;
.... Eruvin 19a; Kiddushin 68b

Idolatrous sacrifice
Idolatrous sacrifice, bird .... Chullin 23a
Idolatrous sacrifice, cases .... Avodah Zarah 32b, 51a, 51b
Idolatrous sacrifice, connected to earth .... Chullin 39b-40a; Avodah Zarah 42b
Idolatrous sacrifice, considered like dead .... Avodah Zarah 32b
Idolatrous sacrifice, impurity .... Avodah Zarah 32b, 48b; Chullin 13b
Idolatrous sacrifice, prohibition .... Avodah Zarah 29b
Idolatrous sacrifice, slaughtering performed by idolater ... Chullin 13a-13b, 38b, 116b; Gittin 45a;
.... Avodah Zarah 32b
Idolatrous sacrifice, tent .... Chullin 13b; Avodah Zarah 32b, 48b

Idolatry
Aggadah —
Idolatry, all commandments .... Horayos 8a-8b
Idolatry, distant, lie .... Sanhedrin 61b
Idolatry, exile .... Shabbos 33a
Idolatry, G-d is slow to anger .... Avodah Zarah 54b-55a
Idolatry, *Gehinnom* .... Taanis 5a
Idolatry in purity .... Avodah Zarah 8a
Idolatry, didn't act even like *turmus* plant .... Beitzah 25b
Idolatry, pagans clung to it .... Sanhedrin 63b-64a
Idolatry, to permit forbidden relations .... Sanhedrin 63b
Idolatry, wonders .... Sanhedrin 90a
Idolatry, Israel exchanged .... Taanis 5b

Episodes —
Idolatry, doorstep of Dagon .... Avodah Zarah 41b
Idolatry, embracing idol .... Sanhedrin 63a
Idolatry, false wonders .... Avodah Zarah 54b-55a
Idolatry, human sacrifice .... Sanhedrin 63b
Idolatry in *Eretz Yisrael,* prohibition .... Avodah Zarah 53b
Idolatry in Temple, Rabbi Yochanan's tears .... Yoma 9b
Idolatry, Kings of Judah .... Sanhedrin 102b

Idolatry, Kings of Israel...Sanhedrin 102a-102b
Idolatry, money exchanged...Avodah Zarah 64a-64b
Idolatry, permitting in part...Horayos 7b

Prohibitions —
Idolatry, appearance..Avodah Zarah 12a-12b
Idolatry, fellow's animal...Avodah Zarah 54a-54b
Idolatry, from one service to another.........Sanhedrin 60b-61a; Chullin 39a-39b; Avodah Zarah 34b;
....Zevachim 10a
Idolatry, let yourself be killed but do not transgress..............Pesachim 25a-25b; Yoma 82a;
....Sanhedrin 74a
Idolatry, sin offerings...Sanhedrin 62a, 63a; Shabbos 72b
Idolatry, slaughtering performed by non-Jew.........Chullin 13a-13b, 38b, 116b; Gittin 45a;
....Avodah Zarah 32b

Misc. —
Idolatry, because of fear.............................Sanhedrin 61b-62a; Shabbos 72b; Krisos 3a
Idolatry, impurity...Shabbos 82a-83b
Idolatry, invalidates *Kohen*...Menachos 109a-109b
Idolatry, *muktzeh*..Temurah 28b-29a
Idolatry, out of *Eretz Yisrael*...Chullin 13b

If
Aggadah —
If among cedars, eulogy about Rav Ashi...................................Moed Katan 25b
If I am here, everything is here..Succah 53a
If I am not for myself...Avos 1:14
If I were not afraid…..Shevuos 17b
If like sons, if like slaves..Bava Basra 10a
If not for a verse, impossible...Rosh Hashanah 17b
If not for fear of government, men would devour one another.......Avodah Zarah 4a; Avos 3:2
If seas were ink..Shabbos 11a
If there is no… there is no…..Avos 3:17
If they had not sinned, Holy Writings..Nedarim 22b
If Israel kept, Shabbos...Shabbos 118b
If you come to My house, Temple..Succah 53a

Conditions —
If father agrees, condition for marriage......................................Kiddushin 63a-63b
If I die, divorce certificate, meanwhile.......................................Gittin 73b-74a
If I die, divorce certificate of sick man......................................Gittin 75b
If I do not come, divorce certificate..................Gittin 72a, 76b-77a; Avodah Zarah 37a; Kesubos 2b

Learning —
If not for My covenant, Torah...Nedarim 32a; Pesachim 68b
If not now, when..Avos 1:14
If not this day, Shavuos..Pesachim 68b
If this vile one approaches you, pull him to house of study........Kiddushin 30b
If you learned much Torah...Avos 2:8
If you listen to old teaching...Berachos 40a; Succah 46b
If you neglected Torah...Avos 4:10

Misc. —
If I forget you, Jerusalem...Succah 41a
If I had come only for this, it would be sufficient......................Shabbos 41a

If I had known… ....Bava Kama 110b-111a

If not for My covenant, circumcision ....Shabbos 137b; Nedarim 32a

Ifcha mistabra...*see* **Contrary is more logical (correct)**, page 127

Ifra Hormiz

Ifra Hormiz, blood of *niddah*..Niddah 20b

Ifra Hormiz, charity ....Bava Basra 10b

Ifra Hormiz, sacrifice ....Zevachim 116b

Igeres bikores..................................*see* **Announcement by *beis din*, sale**, page 26

Ignoramus

Avoiding —

Ignoramus, avoiding daughter's marriage to ....Pesachim 49a-49b

Ignoramus, keeping away from ....Pesachim 49b; Nedarim 20a

Ignoramus pious, distance..Shabbos 63a

Ignoramus, Sage keeps away from party of ....Berachos 43b

Impurity —

Ignoramus, avoiding because of impurity ....Shabbos 13a

Ignoramus, concern of touch ....Taharos 7:1-7, 7:9, 8:1-5; Chagigah 26a; Kesubos 24b

Ignoramus, found close to ritually pure items ....Avodah Zarah 70b

Ignoramus, guarding ritual purity of his produce ....Gittin 62a

Ignoramus, his workers' ritual purity ....Taharos 10:1-3; Berachos 62a

Ignoramus, ritual impurity..Demai 6:6

Ignoramus, ritual impurity of deposit ....Taharos 8:1-2

Ignoramus, ritual impurity of pots ....Kesubos 24b

Laws —

Ignoramus, helping ....Gittin 61a-62b; Demai 3:6; Sheviis 5:9

Ignoramus, the majority separate tithes ......Beitzah 35b; Shabbos 13a, 23a; Kesubos 24a; Gittin 61a;

....Menachos 31a

Ignoramus, maybe he will exchange ....Gittin 61b-62a; Demai 3:4-6; Chullin 6a-6b; Bechoros 11b

Ignoramus, prohibition to perform a wedding ceremony ....Kiddushin 6a, 13a-13b

Ignoramus, servant ....Berachos 52b

Ignoramus, *terumah* ....Sanhedrin 90b; Chullin 130b

Ignoramus, intentional like unintentional ....Bava Metzia 33b

Ignoramus, vow ....Nedarim 20a

Misc. —

Ignoramus, crown of Tiberias ....Bava Basra 8a

Ignoramus is not pious ....Avos 2:5

Ignoramus men ruined commandment to appoint king...........................Sanhedrin 20b

Ignoramus, resurrection ....Kesubos 111b

Ignoramus, Sage's garment ....Bava Basra 98a

Ignoramus, scorn towards Sage ....Sanhedrin 52b

Ignoramus, who ....Berachos 47b; Sotah 22a; Gittin 61a

Ignoramus, trustworthiness

Ignoramus, trustworthiness and testimony ....Shabbos 32a-32b; Chagigah 22a

Ignoramus, trustworthiness for purity ....Chagigah 22a-22b, 24b-26a; Taharos 9:4

Ignoramus, trustworthiness for tithe..............Shabbos 32a-32b; Demai 4:1-2, 4:5-7; Chullin 75b;

....Bechoros 36a-36b

Ignoramus, trustworthiness of poor ....Peah 8:2-4

Ignoramus, trustworthiness on festival ....Beitzah 11b; Chagigah 26a; Niddah 34a

Ignoramus, trustworthy about food having sacrificial sanctity.............Chagigah 22a-22b

Ilan bameh avarechecha .... *see* **Tree, "how shall I bless you?,"** page 701

Ilani

Ilani, Queen, golden chandelier .... Yoma 37b

Ilani, Queen, *nezirus* .... Nazir 20a

Ilani, Queen, *sotah* tablet .... Yoma 37b

Ilfa, went for business .... Taanis 21a

Ill person .... *see* **Sick person,** page 623

Illegitimate woman, marriage to convert .... Kiddushin 72b-73a, 67a, 75a

Illegitimate child

Filiation —

Illegitimate child by Rabbinical Decree, invalid divorce certificate .... Gittin 5b, 86a;

.... Bava Metzia 55b

Illegitimate child did not respond, disqualified .... Kesubos 14b

Illegitimate child, doubt .... Yevamos 37a; Kiddushin 73a, 74a, 75a

Illegitimate child forgotten, permitted .... Kiddushin 71a

Illegitimate child, from which forbidden unions .... Yevamos 44a, 49a-49b; Kesubos 29b-30a;

.... Kiddushin 64a, 68a, 74b

Illegitimate child, permitting offspring by marrying maidservant .... Kiddushin 69a;

.... Yevamos 78a

Illegitimate child, ten generations .... Yevamos 78b

Illegitimate child, will be pure in the future (eligible to marry) .... Kiddushin 72b

Laws —

Illegitimate child being a scholar, precedence .... Horayos 13a

Illegitimate child giving *terumah* to eat .... Yevamos 70a

Illegitimate child, inheritance and prohibitions .... Yevamos 22a-22b

Illegitimate child, judge .... Niddah 49b; Sanhedrin 32a, 36b; Kiddushin 76b; Horayos 4b

Illegitimate child, levirate marriage .... Yevamos 22a-22b

Illegitimate child who hit his father .... Yevamos 22b

Misc. —

Illegitimate child, "crooked thing cannot be corrected" .... Chagigah 9b-10a

Illegitimate child, calling one's fellow .... Kiddushin 28a

Illegitimate child, hidden, death .... Yevamos 78b

Illegitimate children in Alexandria, episode .... Bava Metzia 104a

Illish, flee! .... Gittin 45a

Illness *hadrokan*, danger and punishment .... Bechoros 44b; Shabbos 33a

Ilmalei .... *see* **If,** page 296

Ilule demistafina .... *see* **If I were not afraid...,** page 296

Im .... *see* **If,** page 296

Im eino inyan .... *see* **Commentary, application to other subject,** page 117

Im rishonim kemalachim .... *see* **First generations like angels,** page 225

***Im*,** means a plea .... Avodah Zarah 5a

Image, looking at .... Shabbos 149a

Imahos .... *see* **Matriarchs,** page 393

Imanu hayisem .... *see* **Conspiring witnesses, place,** page 125

Immersed

Immersed and not circumcised .... Yevamos 45b

Immersed in water for 24 hours .... *see* **Pickled food,** page 6

Immersing while holding dead reptile .... Taanis 16a

I

Immersed that day

Immersed that day, announcing ....Beitzah 19a
Immersed that day, desecrating service ....Zevachim 17a
Immersed that day, impurity for sacrifices ....Sotah 29b-30a; Meilah 8a-8b
Immersed that day, impurity of mixed dish ....Pesachim 44a; Nazir 36a; Tevul Yom 2:3-4
Immersed that day, incense ....Shevuos 10b
Immersed that day, Red Heifer .....Yoma 2a, 43b; Yevamos 73a; Zevachim 17b, 21a; Chagigah 23a-23b;
....Parah 3:7-8
Immersed that day, second tithe ....Yevamos 74b, 75a
Immersed that day, sprinkling and preparing water ....Yevamos 73a
Immersed that day, terumah ....Berachos 2a-2b; Yevamos 74a-75a
Immersed that day, what does he forbids ....Niddah 71b
Immersed that day, mixture of terumah ....Tevul Yom 2:3-5, 3:4-5; Pesachim 44a; Nazir 36a-36b
Immersed that day, produce about to become terumah ....Tevul Yom 4:1-4; Niddah 7a
Immersed that day, connection to impurity ....Tevul Yom 1:1-5, 2:5-8

Immersion
Festivals —

Immersion for Yom Tov ....Rosh Hashanah 16b
Immersion of utensil on Shabbos ....Beitzah 17b-19a
Immersion on Shabbos, penalty ....Terumos 2:3; Beitzah 17b
Immersion on Tisha B'Av ....Niddah 68a
Immersion on Yom Tov ....Beitzah 18a-18b
Immersions of Kohen Gadol, on Yom Kippur ....Yoma 19a, 29a, 30a-31b, 34b-35a, 71a;
....Zevachim 19b

Who —

Immersion after discharge, on Yom Kippur ....Yoma 88a
Immersion after seminal discharge ....Berachos 22a-22b, 26a; Gittin 16a; Chullin 24b
Immersion, impurity preceding sacrifice ....Chagigah 24b
Immersion of converts ....Yevamos 45b-46b, 47b; Krisos 9a
Immersion of converts, fetus ....Yevamos 78a-78b
Immersion, onein ....Chagigah 24b

Women —

Immersion ....see also **Intervening substance**, page 316
Immersion, became niddah when she came out of mikveh ....Niddah 66a
Immersion, meeting a woman after her immersion ....Pesachim 111a
Immersion of doubtful zavah and niddah ....Niddah 69a-69b
Immersion of niddah and zavah by day ....Niddah 67b
Immersion of niddah, intention ....Chullin 31a-31b
Immersion of women, episodes ....Berachos 20a; Bava Metzia 84a
Immersion, white geese ....Berachos 20a
Immersion with blood in body ....Niddah 42a-42b

Misc. —

Immersion, Benaiah ben Jehoiada ....Berachos 18b
Immersion, flat utensils ....Shabbos 84b
Immersion for each sprinkling ....Zevachim 93b; Menachos 7b
Immersion for Temple ....Yoma 30a-31a
Immersion, how ....Niddah 66b-67a
Immersion in Temple, when ....Zevachim 20b; Yoma 28a
Immersion into object ....Mikvaos 6:2; Chagigah 22a

Immersion of G-d in fire .... Sanhedrin 39a
Immersion of new utensil for Temple .... Chagigah 23a-23b
Immersion of non-Jew's utensil .... Avodah Zarah 75b
Immersion of Temple utensils .... Chagigah 26a-26b
Immersion on time is a *mitzvah* .... Shabbos 120b-121a; Yoma 8a, 88a; Niddah 30a
Immersion, thought for *terumah* and sacrifice .... Chagigah 19a
Immersion upon utensil .... Niddah 66b
Immigrants from Babylon, lineage .... Kiddushin 69b-70a, 71b
Immoral woman
Immoral woman, chooses her partner .... Kesubos 14a
Immoral woman, her children's lineage .... Sotah 27a
Immorality of wicked men of Jerusalem .... Shabbos 62b-63a
Impatient to answer, boor .... Avos 5:7
Imperfection in yourself, your friend .... Bava Metzia 59b
Important
Important loss, Rabbinical Decree .... Eruvin 46a
Important substance, mixture .... Orlah 3:6-8; Beitzah 3b-4a; Yevamos 81a-81b; Zevachim 72a-72b
Important things, neglected .... Berachos 6b
Important person
Important person, food cooked by non-Jew .... Shabbos 51a
Important person, *kiddushin* .... Kiddushin 7a
Important person, lawyers .... Kesubos 52b
Important person, *nefilas apayim* .... Taanis 14b; Megillah 22b
Important person, stringencies .... Shabbos 51a, 142b; Pesachim 110a; Megillah 22b;
.... Moed Katan 11b-12b; Kesubos 52b, 86a; Bava Metzia 73a; Avodah Zarah 8b, 48b
Imposing upon the community .... Bava Basra 8b; Shekalim 5:2
Imposing upon the congregation
Imposing upon the congregation, prayer .... Berachos 31a
Imposing upon the congregation, section of Balak .... Berachos 12b
Impossible from possible, deduction .... Menachos 19a, 82a-82b; Niddah 37b; Succah 50b;
.... Yevamos 46a, 61b-62a; Horayos 6b; Zevachim 98a; Temurah 16b, 18b
Impossible
Impossible to act differently, prohibition .... Pesachim 25b-26b; Shabbos 29b
Impossible to hear, will finally be heard .... Avos 2:4
Imprisonment
Imprisonment, black shoes .... Bava Kama 59b
Imprisonment, Rabbi Akiva .... Yevamos 105b, 108b
Imprisonment, Rabbi Eliezer .... Avodah Zarah 16b-17a
Improper requests .... Taanis 4a
Impudence
Impudence, insolence .... Sanhedrin 105a
Impudence, picking neighbor's dates .... Bava Basra 33b, 36a
Impudent
Impudent animals .... Beitzah 25b
Impudent men in generation .... Chagigah 14a
Impudent to *Gehinnom* .... Avos 5:20
Impudent, wicked .... Taanis 7b
Impudent, Israel .... Beitzah 25b

Impure

Impure animal born of pure one, eating .... Bechoros 6a-6b
Impure animal, sacrifice .... Zevachim 34a
Impure place, passing over .... Zevachim 93a; Parah 10:5
Impure, rendering, damage .... Gittin 52b-53a; Chullin 41a
Impure water, mixture .... Machshirin 2:3-4

Impure person
see also **Impurity**, page 718

Sacrifice —

Impure person, offering his sacrifice .... Zevachim 22b-23b; Pesachim 69a, 80b, 81a, 90a-90b
Impure person who ate sacrifice, excising of soul .... Zevachim 43b
Impure person who ate sacrifice, prohibition ...... Zevachim 33b-34a; Yevamos 75a; Makos 14b
Impure person who ate sacrifice, punishment .... Zevachim 33b-34a; Yevamos 75a; Makos 14b
Impure person who ate sacrifice, when .... Zevachim 34a
Impure person who ate sacrifice, which one .... Zevachim 36b, 46b, 108a; Yevamos 7a;
Menachos 25b
Impure person who ate sacrifice, who .... Zevachim 99a-99b

Temple service —

Impure *Kohen* who performed service, death .... Sanhedrin 82b-83a
Impure person, communal sacrifice .... Zevachim 16b-17a
Impure person, desecrating service .... Zevachim 17a-17b, 19b, 22b-23b
Impure person, *Kohen Gadol* .... Zevachim 16b-17a
Impure person, private altar .... Zevachim 16a
Impure person, *semichah* .... Zevachim 32a-33a
Impure person, services exempt from penalty .... Zevachim 112b
Impure person, slaughtering sacrifice .... Zevachim 31b-32b, 33b; Chullin 2b-3a
Impure person, zealous ones kill him .... Sanhedrin 82b-83a

Temple —

Impure person, Eastern Gate .... Pesachim 82a; Tamid 5:6
Impure person, entering from Temple roof .... Shevuos 17b
Impure person entering Temple, who .... Keilim 1:8-9
Impure person in Temple, immersed that day .... Pesachim 92a; Nazir 44b-45a
Impure person in Temple, punishment .... Makos 14b; Shevuos 16b-17b
Impure person, partly entered in Temple .... Zevachim 32a-33a; Yoma 31a
Impure person, sent out of camps .... Zevachim 116b-117a
Impure person, Tabernacle journeyed .... Menachos 95a-95b; Taanis 21b
Impure person, three camps .... Pesachim 67a-68a

Misc. —

Impure person eating *terumah*, death .... Sanhedrin 83a-83b
Impure person on Pesach .... *see* **Impurity of community on Pesach**, page 304
Impure person, prohibitions about *terumah* ...... Makos 14b; Yevamos 75a; Shevuos 7a
Impure person, purity of sacrifices .... Chullin 2b
Impure person, second tithe .... Makos 19b; Yevamos 73b; Zevachim 43b
Impure person stands and pure one passes by .... Taharos 6:2; Eduyos 3:7
Impure person, *terumah* from outside *Eretz Yisrael* .... Niddah 32a; Bechoros 27a-27b

Impurity
see also **Purity**, page 511

Communal sacrifice —

Impurity for communal sacrifice, permitted .... Pesachim 76b-78a; Yoma 6b-7a, 8a, 50a
Impurity of meat, Pesach lamb .... Pesachim 62a-62b
Impurity of utensils, Pesach lamb .... Pesachim 70a-70b; Shekalim 8:3

Impurity overridden, daily offering .... Pesachim 66a, 66b
Impurity, *Pesach Sheni* .... Yoma 51a; Pesachim 95b

Corpse —
Impurity eventually goes out .... Oholos 7:3; Eruvin 68a; Beitzah 10a, 36a, 37b; Chullin 125b-126a
Impurity of corpse, goes through .... Chullin 125b; Succah 4a; Eruvin 78b-79a; Oholos 15:6-7
Impurity of living, man torn like fish .... Chullin 21a
Impurity of tents .... Shabbos 27b, 28a; Oholos 7:2
Impurity on wall .... Oholos 6:3-7, 7:1, 11:9, 15:4-7
Impurity under one of the tree branches .... Nazir 54a-54b; Niddah 57a

Doubts —
Impurity, checking marketplace .... Shabbos 33b-34a
Impurity, checking sheets .... Niddah 61a
Impurity, doubt, from place to place .... Niddah 4a
Impurity, doubt, when discovered .... Taharos 3:5, 5:7, 9:9; Niddah 4a
Impurity floating, doubt .... Nazir 63b-64a; Taharos 4:7-8; Chullin 127a
Impurity, lost .... Bechoros 25b; Niddah 61a
Impurity, no one to ask .... Niddah 4b, 5b; Sota 28b
Impurity of abyss .... Pesachim 81b; Nazir 63a, 63b
Impurity of abyss, permitted to whom .... Pesachim 80b-81b; Nazir 63b, 64b; Zevachim 23a
Impurity of item thrown in air .... Taharos 4:1-4
Impurity of Temple, *treifah* .... Chullin 73a, 123b

Food —
Impurity of eater greater than impurity of food .... Chullin 34a
Impurity of food .... *see* **Susceptible to becoming impure**, page 665
Impurity of food, washing without owner's consent .... Bava Metzia 22a-22b
Impurity of liquids .... *see* **Liquid (Impurity)**, page 372
Impurity, second tithe .... Makos 19b; Yevamos 73b; Zevachim 43b
Impurity, supplementary, *terumah* .... Pesachim 14a-15b; Eduyos 2:1

Primary source —
Impurities coming from man's body .... Keilim 1:5
Impurity after birth, pure period .... Krisos 9b-10b; Niddah 11a-11b, 35b-36a, 71b
Impurity and sacrifice after birth .... Niddah 28a, 40a, 42b
Impurity of reptile .... Chullin 21a
Impurity of vehicle .... Eruvin 27a; Keilim 23:2-3; Zavim 5:8
Impurity of womb .... Niddah 16a, 22a, 41b, 66a, 71a
Impurity, predisposed to primary source impurity .... Chullin 121a

Rabbinical Decree —
Impurity of convert .... Pesachim 92a; Eduyos 5:2
Impurity of Cutheans .... Niddah 31b-32a, 33a, 33b; Chagigah 25a; Shabbos 16b
Impurity of hands, impurity of liquids .... Shabbos 14b
Impurity of *madaf*, Rabbinical .... Niddah 4b
Impurity of non-Jews .... Nazir 61a-61b; Avodah Zarah 36b-37a; Niddah 34a-34b; Eduyos 5:1; Shabbos 17b
Impurity of wine of idolaters .... Avodah Zarah 30b-31a
Impurity outside *Eretz Yisrael* .... Shabbos 15a-15b; Oholos 18:6; Gittin 8b
Impurity outside *Eretz Yisrael*, air .... Shabbos 15b; Nazir 19b-20a, 54b-55a; Gittin 8b
Impurity, recycled metal .... Keilim 11:1-4; Shabbos 16a-16b; Avodah Zarah 52a
Impurity, Sages did not want to expand too much .... Beitzah 7a

Sacrifices —
Impurity, bones of left-over sacrifice .... Pesachim 83a-83b; Chullin 125a

Impurity, burning of sacrifices .... Pesachim 14a, 15b; Eduyos 2:1
Impurity, exception, inedible sacrifices .... Chullin 36a-37a
Impurity, frankincense .... Pesachim 24b; Chagigah 35a; Zevachim 34a, 46b; Chullin 36b
Impurity, leftover burned parts of sacrifices .... Yoma 46a-46b
Impurity, non-Jew's sacrifice .... Zevachim 15b, 45a; Menachos 25a-25b; Temurah 3a; Arachin 5b
Impurity of goat to Azazel .... Yoma 67b; Zevachim 105a
Impurity of *onein*, for sacrifice .... Zevachim 99a-99b; Chagigah 21a
Impurity of owner, offering sacrifice .... Zevachim 22b-23b; Moed Katan 15b-16a
Impurity, of part of sacrifice .... Menachos 14b-15a
Impurity of Red Heifer .... Parah 4:4; Bava Kama 77a-77b; Chullin 29b
Impurity of sacrifice, from when .... Zevachim 45b-46a; Meilah 8a-10a
Impurity of sacrifice, item permitting another .... Zevachim 45b-46a
Impurity of sin offerings inside *Heichal* .... Yoma 68a-68b; Zevachim 83a, 104b-106a
Impurity, sacrificial blood .... Zevachim 46a
Impurity, thought about sacrifice .... Zevachim 36b
Impurity, Yom Tov goats .... Shevuos 2a-2b, 9a-10b; Zevachim 6b
Misc. —
Impurity, absorbed .... Chullin 71a-72a; Keilim 9:4-6; Mikvaos 10:8; Niddah 42b, 62b-63a; Oholos 3:2;
.... Bava Kama 101b
Impurity, added to another .... Menachos 24a-24b
Impurity and *muktzeh*, differences .... Shabbos 123a
Impurity, primary source impurity annulled, lesser one annulled .... Keilim 19:9-10, 20:1
Impurity of hands .... *see* **Hand**, page 267
Impurity of hidden parts of body .... Chullin 72b, 129a; Niddah 42b-43a
Impurity of *nazir* .... *see* **Nazir**, page 437
Impurity of *niddah* .... *see* **Niddah**, page 444
Impurity of sprinkling water .... *see* **Water for sprinkling**, page 736
Impurity of utensils .... *see* **Utensil (Impurity)**, page 718
Impurity, reawakens .... Bechoros 22a-23a
Impurity, receiving when being separated .... Krisos 15b
Impurity, remainder of cloth .... Shabbos 39b-40a, 47a
Impurity, rotten .... Bechoros 23a-23b; Nazir 50a; Chullin 71a
Impurity, wood of Altar .... Pesachim 24b; Chagigah 35a; Zevachim 34a, 46b; Chullin 36b
Impurity through connections
Impurity through connections, dead .... Avodah Zarah 37b; Nazir 42b
Impurity through connections, general .... Zavim 5:6-8, 5:10
Impurity through connections, *zav* .... Zavim 5:1-2
Impurity through intimate relations
Impurity through intimate relations, inside body .... Niddah 41b-42a
Impurity through intimate relations, non-Jews ...... Niddah 34a-34b; Shabbos 86b; Mikvaos 8:4
Impurity through intimate relations, until when .... Shabbos 86a-86b; Mikvaos 8:3-4;
.... Niddah 41b-42a
Impurity through intimate relations, with sponge .... Yevamos 12b, 100b; Kesubos 39a;
.... Nedarim 35b; Niddah 45a
Impurity in Temple
Impurity in Temple .... Eruvin 104b-105a
Impurity in Temple, leniencies .... Pesachim 19a-19b
Impurity in Temple, realizing duty to offer sacrifice .... Shevuos 5a, 14a-14b, 18b-19b;
.... Niddah 28b

Impurity, primary source

Impurity, primary source, bird..Niddah 51a

Impurity, primary source, food...Chullin 129a

Impurity, primary source, *neveilah*...Krisos 21a-21b

Impurity, primary source, susceptible to become impure..........Chullin 73b; Uktzin 3:3, 3:9;
....Zevachim 105a

Impurity of body by eating

Impurity of body by eating, how...............Chullin 33b-35a; Taharos 2:2; Shabbos 14a; Sotah 30a

Impurity of body by eating, quantity.....................Chullin 120a; Mikvaos 10:7; Krisos 13a

Impurity of body by eating, Rabbinical.................................Shabbos 13b-14a; Yoma 80b

Impurity of *Kohen*

Impurity of *Kohen*, abandoned corpse................................Nazir 43b, 47a-47b, 48b

Impurity of *Kohen*, adding connections...Nazir 42b

Impurity of *Kohen* for his sister...Yevamos 60a-60b

Impurity of *Kohen* for illegitimate relative...............................Yevamos 22b

Impurity of *Kohen* for relative, requirement.........................Sotah 3a; Zevachim 100a

Impurity of *Kohen* for relative with missing limb.............Nazir 43b-44a; Sotah 3a

Impurity of *Kohen*, his minor wife...Yevamos 89b

Impurity of *Kohen*, man in death throes.....................................Nazir 43a

Impurity of *Kohen*, minor..Yevamos 114a-114b

Impurity of *Kohen*, other impurities...Nazir 48a

Impurity of *Kohen*, Rabbinical.........................Avodah Zarah 13a; Berachos 19b

Impurity of community on Pesach

Impurity of community on Pesach, ate.............................Pesachim 95b-96a

Impurity of community on Pesach, came in...........Pesachim 67b, 95b; Menachos 95b

Impurity of community on Pesach, half..............Pesachim 79a-79b; Chullin 29a

Impurity of community on Pesach, impure persons.............Pesachim 90a-90b

Impurity of community on Pesach, tribe...................Pesachim 80a; Menachos 15a

Impurity of community on Pesach, utensils........................Pesachim 79a

Impurity of community on Pesach, *zav*.....Pesachim 66b-67a, 95b; Zevachim 32b; Bechoros 33a;
....Krisos 10a

Impurity of idolatrous

Impurity of idolatrous sacrifice.........................Avodah Zarah 32b, 48b; Chullin 13b

Impurity of idolatry..Shabbos 82a-83b

Impurity of idolatry, annulment.....................................Avodah Zarah 52a-52b

Impurity of Temple and sacrifices

Impurity of Temple and sacrifices...............................Nazir 56b; Shevuos 6b-10b

Impurity of Temple and sacrifices, variable guilt offering.................Shevuos 6b-7b

Impurity of Temple and sacrifices, guilt offering for doubtful culpability............Krisos 7a;
....Horayos 9b

Impurity preceding sacrifice

Impurity preceding sacrifice, after daily offering...................Pesachim 59a-59b

Impurity preceding sacrifice, concerning sacrifices.............Yevamos 74b; Zevachim 17b;
....Meilah 8a-10a

Impurity preceding sacrifice, desecrating service.............Zevachim 17a-17b, 19b

Impurity preceding sacrifice, eating sacrifice............Zevachim 99a-99b; Chagigah 21a

Impurity preceding sacrifice, immersion.....................................Chagigah 24b

Impurity preceding sacrifice, impurity from first source.................Sotah 30a

Impurity preceding sacrifice in Temple...........................Nazir 44b-45a

Impurity preceding sacrifice, knowledge...Krisos 7b
Impurity preceding sacrifice, Pesach offering.....................................Pesachim 90a-90b
Impurity preceding sacrifice, *terumah*.........................Berachos 2a-2b; Yevamos 74a-75a
Impurity preceding sacrifice, who...Krisos 8b

Imurim..*see* **Burnt parts of sacrifices**, page 81
In
In all your ways know Him...Berachos 63a
In front of him..*see* **Before him** page 48
In front of me it was written.................................*see* **Before me it was written** page 48
In its time, I shall hasten it...Sanhedrin 97b
In life and in death, gift...Bava Basra 153a
In which way, death..Berachos 28b
In the name of
In the name of his teacher, teaching..Sanhedrin 99b
In the name of *Reish Galusa*, bill...Bava Kama 102b-103a
In the name of Sage who said it................Megillah 15a; Chullin 104b; Avos 6:6; Niddah 19b
In the name of who said it, episode........................Bechoros 31b; Yevamos 96b-97a
In chatfi vedidi chatfi..............................*see* **Oath, witness was not contradicted**, page 452
Inaccurate wording of vows.................................Nedarim 4b-5a, 7a-7b, 10a-10b; Nazir 3a
Inadvertant
Inadvertant, damages done by man...Bava Kama 26a-26b
Inadvertant, idolatrous sacrifice...........Krisos 3a-3b; Shabbos 72b; Sanhedrin 61b-62a
Inadvertant, in sacrifice and in excising of soul..Shabbos 69a-69b
Inadvertant like intentional, Sage..Bava Metzia 33b
Inadvertant, oath..Shevuos 26b
Inadvertant, rebel due to his desires.................Horayos 2a, 11a; Shabbos 69a; Yoma 80a; Chullin 5b
Inadvertant sin, close to voluntary..Bava Kama 32b-33a
Inadvertant sinner because of voluntary one, penalty...............Gittin 53b-54b; Bava Kama 95a
Inadvertant transgressions, non-Jew should have learned........................Bava Kama 92a
Inadvertant transgressor lashed, replacing sacrifice.............................Temurah 13a, 17a
Inadvertant, would have transgressed even if he knew..............................Shevuos 26b
Inadvertant, would not have sinned if he had known......Shevuos 26b; Shabbos 69a; Yoma 80a;
Horayos 2a, 11a; Chullin 5b

Inattentive
Impurity —
Inattentive, how........................Chagigah 20a-20b; Zevachim 99a-99b; Taharos 7:8
Inattentive, impurity..............Pesachim 34a-34b; Yoma 30b; Zevachim 99a-99b; Chagigah 20a
Inattentive, Red Heifer...Yoma 42a-42b
Inattentive, sprinkling water...Parah 6:1, 7:1-12, 8:1
Misc. —
Inattentive, blessing............Berachos 40a, 42a; Pesachim 103a-103b; Chullin 86b-87a, 107b
Inattentive, *tefillin*.....................................Menachos 36b; Yoma 7b-8a; Shabbos 12a
Inattentive, three...Sanhedrin 97a
Inattentive, washing hands...Pesachim 115b; Yoma 30a
Inattentive when walking..Bava Kama 27b
In-breadth learning before in-depth...Shabbos 63a
Incense
How —
Incense, Beis Avitnas...Yoma 38a

Incense, embers .... Yoma 44b; Tamid 32b-33a, 5:5; Pesachim 75b
Incense, secret ingredient, straight smoke .... Yoma 53a
Incense, order of burning .... Tamid 32b-33a, 5:4-5, 33; a 6:2-3
Incense, preparation .... Krisos 6a-6b
Incense, quantity .... Zevachim 109b

Prohibitions —
Incense, donated, prohibition .... Menachos 50a-50b
Incense, missing ingredients, prohibition .... Yoma 53a; Krisos 6a
Incense, prohibition to prepare non-holy incense .... Krisos 5a, 6a
Incense, prohibition to smell .... Krisos 6a

Misc. —
Incense, atones for derogatory speech .... Zevachim 88b; Arachin 16a; Yoma 44a
Incense, blessing .... Berachos 43a
Incense, consecrated item .... Shevuos 10b
Incense in Jericho and Shiloh .... Yoma 39b; Tamid 30b
Incense on Yom Tov .... Beitzah 22b-23a; Eduyos 3:11
Incense, wealth .... Yoma 26a
Incense which burst from Altar .... Yoma 45a-45b; Zevachim 83b; Menachos 26b

Incense of Yom Kippur
Incense of Yom Kippur, changes .... Yoma 44b
Incense of Yom Kippur, place .... Yoma 52b
Incense of Yom Kippur, Sadducees .... Yoma 19b, 53a
Incense of Yom Kippur, taking a handful .... Yoma 47a-49b
Incense on Yom Kippur, how .... Yoma 47a

Incident, cause of decree .... Yevamos 116b; Chagigah 23a
Incision .... *see* **Cutting** page 138
Inciter to idolatry
Inciter to idolatry, condemned city .... Sanhedrin 67a, 89b
Inciter to idolatry, finding extenuating circumstances .... Sanhedrin 29a, 33b
Inciter to idolatry, inciting individual .... Sanhedrin 63b
Inciter to idolatry, prophet .... Sanhedrin 67a, 84a, 89b
Inciter to idolatry, witnesses concealed .... Sanhedrin 67a

Inciting
Inciting people to worship him .... Sanhedrin 61a
Inciting to bite, dog which damaged .... Bava Kama 24b

Included
Included, domains .... Eruvin 44b-45a
Included, *esrog* on Sabbatical year .... Succah 39a; Bechoros 31b
Included in gift, by generosity .... Bava Basra 64a-65a, 71a
Included in sale, accessories .... Bava Basra 78b
Included in two hundred, one hundred .... Bava Basra 41b; Nazir 20a; Sanhedrin 31a
Included, payment for work on Shabbos .... Nedarim 37a-37b; Bava Metzia 58a
Included, purchase from second tithe .... Maaser Sheni 1:3-4, 3:12-13; Eruvin 27a-28a

Inclusion
Inclusion, double .... Bava Kama 45b; Pesachim 23a
Inclusion then exclusion .... Shevuos 4b-5a, 26a; Bava Kama 54b, 63a

Increase in value
Collecting —
Increase in value, collecting from thief .... Bava Kama 96a; Bava Metzia 14b-15a

Increase in value, fruit ready to be sold..................Bava Kama 95b-96a; Bava Metzia 15a-15b, 110b
Increase in value, *kesubah* and daughters...Bechoros 52a
Increase in value, seizure from buyers...........Bava Kama 95b-96a; Bava Metzia 14b, 15a-15b, 110b;
....Bava Basra 157b; Bechoros 52a
Increase in value, trustworthiness and *chazakah*..Bava Metzia 110a-110b

Damaging ox —
Increase in value, fetus..Bava Kama 42b-43a, 49a-49b
Increase in value of *neveilah*, ox goring occasionally...Bava Kama 34b

Inheritance —
Increase in value, firstborn............Bava Metzia 110b; Bava Basra 123b-124b, 126a; Bechoros 51b-52b;
....Bava Kama 95b
Increase in value, heirs...Bava Metzia 39b-40a; Bava Basra 143b-144a
Increase in value, inheritance of brother of deceased childless husband...Bechoros 52a-52b
Increase in value of wife's property...................................Kesubos 79b-80a; Bava Metzia 39a

Rights —
Increase in value, land improvements..Bava Metzia 109a-109b
Increase in value of stolen item...............................Bava Metzia 43a-43b; Pesachim 32a;
....Bava Kama 65a-66a, 93b-94b, 95a-95b, 96b, 103a
Increase of value by thief, interest...Bava Metzia 14b

Misc. —
Increase in value of consecrated items, atonement...Menachos 80a, 81a; Temurah 25b; Krisos 27a
Increase in value of consecrated items, for guilt offering.......................................Krisos 27a
Increase in value resulting from work, *kiddushin*...Kiddushin 48b
Increase of value of item, craftsman............Bava Kama 98b-99b; Kiddushin 48b; Bava Metzia 112a

Increasing holiness of item but not lowering it..................Menachos 39a, 99a; Berachos 28a;
....Shabbos 21b; Yoma 12b, 73a; Megillah 9b, 21b; Horayos 12b; Tamid 31b

Increasing
Increasing peace, behavior..Berachos 17a
Increasing peace, Sages.............Berachos 64a; Yevamos 122b; Nazir 66b; Krisos 28b; Tamid 32b

Indecency
Indecency..*see also* **Modesty**, page 420
Indecency, commandment to divorce...Gittin 90a-90b
Indecency, girls of Jerusalem...Shabbos 62b; Yoma 9b

Indemnities
Indemnities..*see also* **Four indemnities**, page 238
Indemnity, warranty of caterer...Bava Basra 93b

Indentation
Indentation of Altar, disqualified..Zevachim 59a, 60a-60b
Indentation of Altar, size...Chullin 18a; Succah 48b-49a

Indentation in knife
Indentation in knife, checking...Chullin 10b, 17b-18a
Indentation in knife, doubt...Chullin 10a-10b, 43b
Indentation in knife, slaughtering knife...Chullin 17a-18a

In-depth learning
In-depth learning and in-breadth, order.............Shabbos 63a; Succah 28b-29a; Avodah Zarah 19a
In-depth learning and in-breadth, preference...Horayos 14a
In-depth learning and in-breadth, source...Bechoros 52b
In-depth learning from several Sages...Avodah Zarah 19a
In-depth learning, too much hinders learning...Eruvin 48a

Indirect strength..*see* **Strength, indirect**, page 659
Indirect damage
Indirect damage...Bava Kama 98b
Indirect damage, oath...Bava Kama 105b; Shevuos 32a
Indirect damage, one witness..Shevuos 32a-32b
Indirect damage, stealing animal...Bava Kama 71b
Indispensable requirement
Indispensable requirement, bulls and rams..Succah 47a
Indispensable requirement, communal sacrifice.........................Menachos 27a, 44b-45a
Indispensable requirement detail, source........................Menachos 19a-19b; Zevachim 23a
Indispensable requirement, details of commandments......Sanhedrin 45b, 71a-71b; Makos 10b
Indispensable requirement, parts of meal offering..........................Menachos 27a
Indispensable requirement, sheep and loaves on Shavuos...............Menachos 45b-46b
Indispensable requirement, words implying..Yoma 5a
Individual
Individual and majority opinion, *halacha*...........................Avodah Zarah 7a; Eduyos 5:7
Individual and numerous Rabbinical Decrees.....................................Eruvin 46a
Individual, daily offering..Menachos 65a
Individual, Divine abundance..Taanis 9a
Individual opinion, Shmuel is stringent..............................Yevamos 83a; Megillah 18b
Individual opinion, why do we mention.........................Eduyos 1:5-6; Yevamos 122a
Indulgent, G-d loves him...Pesachim 113b
Inedible because of salt...Pesachim 76a; Chullin 112a
Inevitable act
Inevitable act, plugging up barrel..Shabbos 111a-111b
Inevitable act, Shabbos.................Shabbos 75a, 103a, 111a-111b, 117a, 120b, 133a, 143a; Succah 33b;
....Beitzah 36a; Kesubos 6a; Bechoros 25a
Inevitable act, sponge...Shabbos 143a
Inevitable act, virgin on Shabbos..Kesubos 5b
Infidelity, man in whom I trusted was unfaithful..........................Sanhedrin 7a
Informer
Informer, caused damage...Bava Kama 116b-117b
Informer, episode about Rav Kahana...................................Bava Kama 117a-117b
Informer, ruining his money...Bava Kama 119a
Informer, taking oath to collect..Bava Kama 62a
Infrequent matters, Sages did not decree................Gittin 5a, 44a; Eruvin 63b; Beitzah 2b, 18a;
.......................Yevamos 31a; Kesubos 56b; Nazir 55a; Kiddushin 28b; Bava Metzia 46b, 47a; Bechoros 3a; Niddah 34a
Ingathering of exiles..Pesachim 88a
Ingratitude
Ingratitude...Avodah Zarah 5a-5b; Kesubos 53a; Bava Kama 92b
Ingratitude of Israel, Giving of Torah.....................................Avodah Zarah 5a
Ingredient thickening food, mixture..................................Avodah Zarah 35a
Inhabitants
Inhabitants of Jericho, six things............................Menachos 71a-71b; Pesachim 55b-56b
Inhabitants of Mechuza, character traits................................Berachos 59b
Inhabitant of city
Inhabitant of city, from when...Bava Basra 11a, 8a
Inhabitants of city, from when..Bava Basra 11a, 8a
Inhabitants of city, from when..Sanhedrin 112a

Inhabiting world, procreation...Gittin 41b
Inheritance......................*see also* **Heir,** page 276; **Firstborn, inheritance of future property,** page 226,
....**Will,** page 747, **Bequeathing,** page 54

Who —

Inheritance, automatic, fetus...Bava Basra 141b-142a
Inheritance, daughter.......................Bava Basra 110a-111a, 113a-113b, 115a, 122b
Inheritance, grandchildren.........................Bava Basra 115a-116a, 158b-159b
Inheritance, grandfather..Bava Basra 116a-116b
Inheritance, non-Jew..Kiddushin 17b-18a; Nazir 61a
Inheritance of betrothed girl..Kesubos 47a-47b
Inheritance of brother of deceased childless husband, *agunah*..............Yevamos 117a
Inheritance of convert.................Bava Kama 49b; Yevamos 52b; Bava Basra 142a
Inheritance of convert, his father.................................Kiddushin 17b-18a
Inheritance of illegitimate child..Yevamos 22a-22b
Inheritance of woman, taking away from tribe................Bava Basra 112a-113a
Inheritance, order.................Bava Basra 110a-110b, 113a-113b, 115a
Inheritance, precedence of father.................................Bava Basra 108b-109b
Inheritance, who...Bava Basra 108a-108b

Misc. —

Inheritance, a few vegetables, Resh Lakish...............................Gittin 47a
Inheritance and dwelling, deduction...............................Kiddushin 37a-38a
Inheritance, blessing...Berachos 59b
Inheritance cannot be interrupted.................Bava Basra 129b, 133a-133b
Inheritance, cases of doubt...Yevamos 37b-38b
Inheritance, doubt, collapsed house.............Bava Basra 157a, 158a-158b, 159b; Yevamos 38b;
....Bava Metzia 37b
Inheritance from one tribe to another, Benjamin................Bava Basra 116a
Inheritance, giving more to one son.............Bava Basra 129a-131a, 133a; Yevamos 36b
Inheritance, idolatry..Avodah Zarah 64a-64b
Inheritance, increase in value.............Bava Metzia 39b-40a; Bava Basra 143b-144a
Inheritance of G-d, children...Shabbos 152a
Inheritance, retroactive...Bechoros 56b-57a
Inheritance, sale before death.......................................Bava Metzia 16a-16b
Inheritance without limits, Jacob..Shabbos 118b

Inheritance of mother

Inheritance of mother...Bava Basra 114b-115a
Inheritance of mother, firstborn................................Bava Basra 111a-111b
Inheritance of mother in grave.............................Bava Basra 114b, 159b

Inheritance of mother's *kesubah*

Inheritance of mother's *kesubah*, customers.....................Kesubos 55a, 90b
Inheritance of mother's *kesubah*, general.............Kesubos 52b, 53a, 90b-91b; Bava Kama 89b
Inheritance of mother's *kesubah*, how did they buy................Bava Basra 131a

Inheritance of wife

Inheritance of wife.................Kesubos 84a; Bava Basra 109b, 111b-113a; Bava Kama 42b
Inheritance of wife, examined his wife inside a ruin................Bava Basra 146a-146b
Inheritance of wife, future property.............Bava Basra 113a, 125a; Bava Kama 42b
Inheritance of wife, parallel to which right........................Kesubos 47b
Inheritance of wife, which rights................................Bava Kama 42b-43a

Inheritance of *yavam*
Inheritance of *yavam*, during father's life .... Yevamos 40a
Inheritance of *yavam*, future property .... Bechoros 52a-52b
Inheritance of *yavam*, increase in value .... Bechoros 52a-52b
Inheritance of *yavam*, property .... Yevamos 38a-39a; Kesubos 80b-82a

Inheriting
Inheriting sacrifice, atonement .... Nazir 27b-28a; Krisos 27b
Inheriting *tevel*, tithe .... Bechoros 11a

Initials
Initials, *Adam* .... Sotah 5a
Initials, *BaSaR* .... Sotah 5a
Initials, *Carmel* .... Menachos 66b; Shabbos 105a
Initials, *pachaz kamayim* .... Shabbos 55b
Initials, *vateragnu* .... Shevuos 47b
Initials, words explained by their initials .... Shabbos 77b, 105a; Kesubos 10b-11a; Menachos 66b
Initials, *zaken* .... Kiddushin 32b

Injured
Injured by staff, *kesubah* .... Kesubos 11a-12a, 13a
Injured *Kohen*, female convert .... Yevamos 57a, 76a
Injured man, wife's *terumah* .... Yevamos 56b-57a, 75a
Injured, swears and collects .... Shevuos 46b
Injuring on Shabbos, damage .... Shabbos 106a; Bava Kama 34b
Injuring oneself .... Bava Kama 91a-91b

Ink
Ink, divorce certificate .... Gittin 19a
Ink, holy parchments .... Shabbos 23a; Megillah 18b-19a; Sotah 20a-20b
Ink, invisible, divorce certificate .... Gittin 19b-20a
Ink, prepared with gum .... Eruvin 13a
Ink, quantity and addition, Shabbos .... Shabbos 79b-80a
Ink, writing like putting down .... Shabbos 80a

Inn
Inn, Abraham .... Sotah 10a-10b
Inn, unintentional and willful murderers in same inn .... Makos 10b

Innocent will atone for the guilty .... Shevuos 14a

Inquiries
Inquiries .... *see also* **Mistake in ruling**, page 416
Inquiries about *treifah*, episodes .... Sanhedrin 7b; Horayos 3b
Inquiries, circumcision on Shabbos .... Niddah 42b
Inquiries concerning *niddah*, rulings .... Niddah 20a-20b
Inquiries, human snake .... Niddah 24b
Inquiries in ruling, straight inquirer .... Succah 44b
Inquiries, of lenient Sage .... Chullin 99b
Inquiries of teacher .... Berachos 63b; Eruvin 67b; Chullin 6a; Niddah 27a
Inquiry from Rav, law .... Avos 1:16
Inquiry to cause laughter, episode .... Niddah 23a

Inquiring from dead .... Sanhedrin 65b

Insides
Insides he ate, and peel he discarded, Rabbi Meir .... Chagigah 15b
Inside like outside, impurities .... Niddah 42a-42b

Inside like outside, personality .... Yoma 72b; Berachos 28a
Insolence .... Sanhedrin 105a
Installments, interest .... Bava Metzia 65b
Instigator, city led to idolatry .... Sanhedrin 63b
Instruments for circumcision, Shabbos .... Shabbos 131b-132a
Instruments, musical .... *see* **Musical instruments,** page 432
Insulted but do not insult .... Gittin 36b; Shabbos 88b; Yoma 23a
Intelligence .... *see* **Knowledge,** page 344
Intelligent, he is so intelligent .... Berachos 58b
Intend
Intend .... *see* **Prepare,** page 501
Intended, bill of *kiddushin* .... Kiddushin 9a-9b, 48a
Intended for commandment, succah .... Succah 8b
Intended for commandment, *tzitzis* .... Menachos 42b; Succah 9a
Intended for different kind of sacrifice .... Zevachim 3a
Intended for Heaven's sake, Holy Names .... Gittin 20a, 54b
Intended for non-holy purpose, differences .... Zevachim 3a-3b
Intended for non-holy purpose, sin offering .... Zevachim 46b
Intended for other sin offering .... Zevachim 7a, 9b
Intended for this sacrifice, acts prove .... Menachos 2b-4a, 49a; Zevachim 9b
Intended, parchment for holy parchments .... Gittin 54b
Intended, scroll of *sotah* .... Eruvin 13a-13b; Sotah 20b
Intended divorce certificate
Intended divorce certificate, adult supervising .... Gittin 23a
Intended divorce certificate, cases .... Gittin 24a-24b; Sotah 20b; Zevachim 2b
Intended divorce certificate, intermingled .... Gittin 86b
Intended divorce certificate, express intention .... Zevachim 2b-3a
Intended divorce certificate, writing and signing .... Gittin 3a-4a, 23a
Intended for idolatry
Intended for idolatry and worshipped .... Bechoros 41a; Temurah 28b-29a; Bava Kama 40b;
.... Zevachim 85b; Niddah 41a
Intended for idolatry, bird sacrifice .... Chullin 23a
Intended for idolatry, from when .... Avodah Zarah 44b
Intended for idolatry, Gideon's sacrifice .... Temurah 28b-29a
Intended for idolatry, non-holy use .... Temurah 29a
Intended for idolatry, permission .... Avodah Zarah 44b
Intent .... *see also* **Want,** page 730
Damages —
Intention, atonement payment penalty .... Bava Kama 44a-44b
Intention, ox to be stoned .... Bava Kama 44b
Intention to damage, horn .... Bava Kama 2b
Commandments —
Intent considered like speech .... Berachos 20b; Shabbos 150a
Intent, separating tithe .... Beitzah 13b; Gittin 30b, 31a; Bechoros 58b-59a; Menachos 54b-55a
Intent to perform commandment, reward .... Kiddushin 40a; Berachos 6a; Shabbos 63a
Intent to require tithe .... Niddah 51a
Intent, vow to consecrate .... Shevuos 26b; Chagigah 10a
Intention in performing commandments .... Pesachim 114b; Rosh Hashanah 28a-28b, 33b;
.... Berachos 13a; Eruvin 95b

Intention to discharge fellow .... Rosh Hashanah 29a, 33b

How —

Intent from one "permitter" to another .... Menachos 13b, 14b, 16a

Intent from one service to another .... Zevachim 9b-10a; Chullin 39a-39b

Intent in half of a "permitter" .... Zevachim 41b-42b, 110a; Menachos 13a, 14b, 16a, 16b, 17a;

.... Pesachim 63a

Intent in part of sacrifice .... Menachos 13b-14b

Intentions annulling *piggul* .... Zevachim 13b, 29b

Intentions not invalidating sacrifice .... Zevachim 35b-36a

Impurity —

Intent, annulling connection to impurity .... Succah 13b-14a

Intent for impurity .... Uktzin 3:1-3, 3:9; Bechoros 10a; Krisos 21a; Niddah 50b-51a

Intent, impurity of utensils ...... Kiddushin 59a-59b; Shabbos 52b, 58b; Succah 13b-14a; Zevachim 94a;

.... Menachos 69a; Keilim 25:9

Intent of child, causing impurity .... Keilim 17:15; Chullin 12b-13a

Intent of owner .... Zevachim 47a; Chullin 38b-39a

Intent of thief, impurity .... Bava Kama 66b, 114a-114b; Keilim 26:8

Intention in immersion .... Chagigah 18b-19a; Chullin 31a-31b

Intention in washing hands .... Chagigah 18b-19a

Prohibitions —

Intent about Torah in bathhouse .... Avodah Zarah 44b; Berachos 24b; Shabbos 40b, 150a;

.... Kiddushin 33a; Zevachim 102b

Intent about work on Shabbos .... Shabbos 113b, 150a

Intent about work on Shabbos, episode .... Shabbos 150b

Intent from one service to another, idolatry .... Sanhedrin 60b-61a

Intent of non-Jew for idolatry .... Chullin 13a, 38b-39a, 116b; Gittin 45b; Avodah Zarah 32b

Intent, permitting *muktzeh* .... Shabbos 49b-50a, 125b, 126b

Intention to throw on Shabbos, change .... Shabbos 73a; Bava Kama 26b

Relations —

Intention in *chalitzah* .... Yevamos 102b

Intention, revealing, divorce certificate .... Gittin 30a, 34a-34b

Intention to cause pain to former wife, by condition .... Gittin 74b

Intention to divorce, intimate relations .... Gittin 90a; Yevamos 37b

Sacrifices —

Intent, because of .... Pesachim 62a, 62b

Intent, bringing blood to Altar .... Zevachim 14a

Intent, cases of eating .... Zevachim 31a-31b

Intentions, combining .... Zevachim 31b; Menachos 12b-13a, 14b-15b, 16b

Intentions, continuing service .... Zevachim 2a-2b, 7b; Menachos 2a-2b

Intent, contradictory in same sacrifice .... Pesachim 59b-60b

Intent for sacrifice, on lost .... Meilah 7a; Zevachim 26b

Intent, four services .... Zevachim 4a-4b, 13b

Intent in burning frankincense .... Menachos 13a-13b

Intent in fellow's sacrificial service .... Zevachim 47a; Chullin 38b-39a

Intent in sacrifice, source .... Zevachim 14a, 28a-29a

Intent, in which service .... Zevachim 13a-13b

Intent invalidating sacrifice, when .... Zevachim 26b; Menachos 5b

Intent, inside (Altar) sin offerings .... Zevachim 13b-14a, 44b-45a

Intent of eater, prohibition .... Chullin 102b

Intent of transgression, daily sin..Bava Basra 164b

Intent of transgression, impurity at night...Chullin 44b

Intent of transgression, Midianite women...Shabbos 64a-64b

Intent of transgression, more serious than transgression...Yoma 29a

Intent of transgression, punishment..Kiddushin 40a, 39b, 49b

Intent, part of sacrifice destined to be burned...Zevachim 28a, 31b, 35a;
Menachos 12b-13a, 17a-17b; Chullin 81b

Intent, Pesach offering...Zevachim 7b, 10b; Pesachim 61a-63a, 78b

Intent, sprinklings..Zevachim 38b

Intent to leave over for tomorrow..Zevachim 27a, 35b-36a; Menachos 17b-18a

Intent to take blood into *Heichal*..Zevachim 82a-82b

Intent, unspecified intent like specified...Zevachim 2b

Intent, which sacrifices...Menachos 48b

Intent when eating flesh of sacrifice...Zevachim 12b, 13b, 17a-17b, 27b-28a, 31b, 35a;
Menachos 12b-13a, 17a-17b; Chullin 81b

Intent, Yom Kippur incense...Yoma 48a-48b

Intention for *terumah* and sacrifice...Chagigah 19a

Intention during act..Zevachim 41b-42a; Menachos 16a-16b

Intention, forbidden acts..*see* **Unintentionally**, page 715

Intention in slaughtering..Chullin 12b, 31a

Intention in slaughtering sacrifice...Chullin 13a, 31b; Zevachim 46b-47a; Menachos 110a

Intention, unspecified like specified..Zevachim 2b-3a

Intentions, for meal offerings...Menachos 11b-12a

Intentions intermingled, sacrifice..Zevachim 29b-31b; Meilah 4a

Intentions, six, Temple service..Zevachim 2b, 46b

Vows —

Intention of G-d, oath...Nedarim 25a; Shevuos 29a-29b

Intention of man making vow, explaining..Nedarim 20a

Intention of man making vow, judging..Nedarim 55b-56a, 63b

Intention when swearing, explaining...Nedarim 25a; Shevuos 29a

Misc. —

Intent, grasping Rabbi Oshaia's depth...Eruvin 53a

Intent in depth, Rabbi Meir..Eruvin 13b, 53a

Intent, is not valid..Kiddushin 49b-50a; Nedarim 28a; Meilah 21a

Intent makes place important...Eruvin 99a

Intent of minor..Chullin 12b-13a; Taharos 8:6

Intent, vow..Nedarim 28a; Shevuos 26b; Chagigah 10a

Intention, not realized, Shabbos labors..Shabbos 72a-73a; Sanhedrin 62b; Krisos 19b

Intentions of friend, not revealed..Pesachim 54b

Intentional sin

Intentional sin, liable to sacrifices...Krisos 9a; Shevuos 25b, 37a

Intentional sin like unintentional, ignoramus..Bava Metzia 33b

Intentional sin, sacrifice for *nazir*..Krisos 9a

Intentional sin, sacrifice of testimony...Shevuos 25b, 31b, 35a; Krisos 9a

Intentional work

Intentional work..*see also* **Unintentionally**, page 715

Intentional work, cases..Bava Kama 26b; Shabbos 73a

Intentional work, hole..Chagigah 10a-10b; Shabbos 73b; Beitzah 8a

Interceding
Interceding for host .... Kiddushin 76b
Interceding, one among a thousand .... Shabbos 32a

Interest
In commerce —
Interest, decided to sell then sold to another .... Bava Kama 103a
Interest, fixed price of merchandise .... Bava Metzia 62b-63b, 65b, 72b
Interest, house in walled city .... Arachin 31a-31b
Interest in commerce .... Bava Metzia 65b
Interest, merchandise .... Bava Metzia 64a-65b, 68a, 72b-73b
Interest, paying produce in advance .... Bava Metzia 64a, 73a
Interest, paying wine in advance .... Bava Metzia 73b
Interest, possessing same matter .... Bava Metzia 63b, 74a-74b

Permitted —
Interest, claiming lent money belongs to non-Jew .... Kesubos 86a
Interest for orphans .... Bava Metzia 70a
Interest, *heter iska* .... Bava Metzia 68a-69a, 70a, 70b; Bechoros 15b
Interest in commerce, way to permit .... Bava Metzia 68a-69a
Interest permitted .... Bava Metzia 14b, 57b, 69b, 70a, 75a; Gittin 30a
Interest to consecrated items Treasury .... Bava Metzia 57b

Prohibition —
Interest, *aggadah* .... Kiddushin 20a; Bava Metzia 71a, 75b
Interest, disqualified to testify .... Sanhedrin 24b-25a, 27b; Rosh Hashanah 22a; Eruvin 82a
Interest, negative commandments .... Bava Metzia 60b-61a, 62a, 75b
Interest, prohibition .... Bava Metzia 61a
Interest, salary for money kept .... Bava Metzia 63b

Rabbinical Decree —
Interest, disguised .... Bava Metzia 62b-63a
Interest, group particular about their money .... Bava Metzia 75a
Interest, measure for measure .... Shabbos 148b; Bava Metzia 44b, 45a, 74b-75a
Interest, non-Jew .... Bava Metzia 70b-71b
Interest on mortgage .... Bava Metzia 67b-68a
Interest, possibility .... Megillah 27b; Bava Metzia 63a, 65b
Interest, Rabbinical .... Bava Metzia 62b-63a, 64b-65a, 75a-75b
Interest, small .... Bava Metzia 75a

Misc. —
Interest, bill .... Bava Metzia 72a; Bava Kama 30b; Bava Basra 94b
Interest, cases .... Bava Metzia 46a
Interest, convert .... Bava Metzia 72a
Interest, *kiddushin* money .... Kiddushin 6b
Interest, purchase to return .... Megillah 27b; Bava Metzia 63a
Interest, renting .... Bava Metzia 65a, 69b-70a, 73a
Interest, renting money .... Bava Metzia 69b
Interest, resident non-Jew .... Bava Metzia 71a
Interest, returning .... Bava Metzia 61b-62b, 65a, 65b, 67a-67b; Bava Kama 112a; Temurah 6a-6b
Interest, taking increase in value from thief .... Bava Metzia 14b
Interest, worker's salary .... Bava Metzia 73a; Bava Basra 86b-87a
Interested by its existence, forbidden benefit .... Avodah Zarah 63b, 64a

Intermediary
Intermediary, decedent's will..Kesubos 69b
Intermediary for divorce certificate, trustworthiness..Gittin 64a-64b
Intermediary for forbidden relations..Shevuos 47b
Intermediary, trustworthiness..Sanhedrin 31a-31b; Gittin 64a

Intermediate days of festival..*see **Chol HaMoed**, page 104*

Intermingled
Men —
Intermingled children, levirate marriage..Yevamos 98b-99b
Intermingled Jews and non-Jews...Yoma 84b-85a
Intermingled men or oxen condemned to death..Sanhedrin 79b-80b

Sacrifices —
Intermingled disqualified sacrifices.........................Zevachim 70b-71b, 74b-75b; Temurah 28a
Intermingled libations...Menachos 89a-89b
Intermingled meal offerings..Menachos 22b-23a, 89a-89b, 106a
Intermingled Pesach lamb and sacrifices..Pesachim 98a-98b
Intermingled sacrificial animals..............................Zevachim 70b-71b, 74b-75b; Temurah 28a
Intermingled sacrificial fats...Menachos 89b; Pesachim 64b
Intermingled sacrificial limbs.....................Zevachim 74a, 77a-77b; Yoma 64a; Menachos 48a

Misc. —
Intermingled animals..Zevachim 72a-72b
Intermingled garment with leprous marks...Negaim 11:12
Intermingled threads...Orlah 3:2-3; Temurah 34a
Intermingled garments...Orlah 3:1-3; Bava Kama 101b
Intermingled coins of second tithe.................Maaser Sheni 2:5-6; Beitzah 10b; Bava Metzia 55b-56a

Interpretation, piece of clay instead of pearl...Yevamos 94a

Interpreting dreams
Interpreting dreams..Gittin 52a; Sanhedrin 30a
Interpreting dreams favorably..Berachos 55b

Interrupting
Interrupting between milk and meat..Chullin 104b-105a
Interrupting during *Shema*, *Hallel* and *megillah*..Berachos 13b-14a
Interrupting, during Torah reading of punishment...Megillah 31b
Interrupting learning for *Shema* and prayer..Shabbos 11a
Interrupting learning Heavenly Chariot...Berachos 21b
Interrupting learning, punishment...Avos 3:7
Interrupting learning to perform commandment...Moed Katan 9a-9b
Interrupting meal to perform commandment..Succah 38a; Shabbos 9b
Interrupts friend's words...Avos 5:7

Interruption
Interruption between blowing of *shofar* etc...Rosh Hashanah 34b
Interruption, blessing..Berachos 40a
Interruption during blowing of *shofar*.........................Rosh Hashanah 34a-34b; Succah 54a; Arachin 10a
Interruption in bird burnt offering...Zevachim 65b
Interruption in middle of verse.....................................Taanis 27b; Megillah 22a; Berachos 12b
Interruption in slaughtering..Chullin 9a, 32a
Interruption in Torah reading, middle of passage..............Berachos 12b; Taanis 27b; Megillah 22a
Interruption in verse, *Hallel*..Succah 38b-39a

Interruption in prayer
Interruption in prayer, governor .... Berachos 32b-33a
Interruption in prayer, prohibition .... Yoma 19b
Interruption in prayer, snake .... Yerushalmi Berachos 38a
Interruption in prayer, unavoidable circumstances .... Berachos 32b-33a

Interval
Interval, *Nissan* and *Tishrei* .... Berachos 35b
Interval, unequal, menstruation .... Niddah 64a; Bava Kama 37b

Intervening item, carrying out on Shabbos .... Shabbos 57a-57b

Intervening substance
Immersion —
Intervening substance, immersion of utensils .... Mikvaos 10:1-5
Intervening substance, *Halacha* to Moses from Sinai .... Succah 6a-6b; Eruvin 4a-4b
Intervening substance, in same substance .... Yoma 58a
Intervening substance, mud .... Mikvaos 7:7
Intervening substance, which utensils .... Mikvaos 9:5-7
Intervening substances, fastidious person .... Succah 6b; Eruvin 4b; Niddah 67b
Intervening substances for man's immersion .... Shabbos 57a-57b; Menachos 21a;
.... Mikvaos 8:5, 9:1-4; Niddah 67a-67b

Temple —
Intervening substance, between *Kohen's* feet and Temple Floor .... Zevachim 24a; Shabbos 93b
Intervening substance, blood in bowl .... Yoma 58a
Intervening substance in priestly garments .... Eruvin 103b-104a; Zevachim 19a-19b
Intervening substance, salt on ramp .... Eruvin 104a
Intervening substance, Temple Floor .... Chullin 83b

Misc. —
Intervening substance, garments .... Shabbos 114a; Zevachim 98b
Intervening substance in *lulav* .... Succah 37a-37b
Intervening substance, in permeable substance .... Yoma 58a
Intervening substance, washing hands .... Chullin 106a-106b

Intestines
Intestines deteriorated by heat, *treifah* .... Chullin 56b, 57a
Intestines, episode about trickery .... Chullin 56b-57a
Intestines, exempt from salting .... Chullin 113a
Intestines of bird, *treifah* .... Chullin 56b
Intestines to non-Jew .... Chullin 33a
Intestines, *treifah* .... Chullin 48b

Intimate relations .... *see also* **Marital relations**, page 392
Impurity —
Intimate relations .... *see also* **Impurity through intimate relations**, page 303
Intimate relations, relaxed genital member .... Shevuos 18a; Yevamos 55b; Sanhedrin 55a
Intimate relations with *zav* .... Niddah 71b, 73a
Intimate relations with *zavah* of one day .... Niddah 73a

Prohibitions —
Intimate relations, forbidden and maidservant .... Krisos 11a-11b
Intimate relations, forbidden to mourner .... Moed Katan 23a-24a
Intimate relations, man does not want relations without marriage .... Kesubos 73a;
.... Yevamos 107a; Gittin 81b
Intimate relations, numerous, maidservant .... Krisos 9a

Intimate relations, relaxed member .... Yevamos 55b; Shevuos 18a
Intimate relations with dead woman .... Yevamos 55b
Intimate relations with non-Jewish woman .... Eruvin 19a; Avodah Zarah 36b; Sanhedrin 81b-82a
Intimate relations with *sotah*, death .... Sotah 9b, 27b-28a
Intimate relations with wife after he decided to divorce her .... Gittin 90a; Yevamos 37b

Intimate relations with *niddah*
  Intimate relations with *niddah*, episode .... Niddah 25b
  Intimate relations with *niddah*, impurity .... Niddah 32b; Zavim 5:11
  Intimate relations with *niddah*, rebuke .... Beitzah 25b
  Intimate relations with *niddah*, time for his immersion .... Yoma 6a-6b

Misc. —
  Intimate relations, concern of *kiddushin* .... Gittin 73b, 81a-81b; Eduyos 4:7
  Intimate relations, *kiddushin* .... Kiddushin 4b, 9b
  Intimate relations, latter part makes *kiddushin* .... Kiddushin 10a-10b
  Intimate relations, nine-year-old boy, levirate marriage .... Yevamos 96a, 96b, 111b;
                                                        Niddah 45a-45b; Bava Basra 156a; Sanhedrin 55b
  Intimate relations, penetration .... Yevamos 54a-56a; Sotah 26b
  Intimate relations, pregnancy from first .... Yevamos 34a
  Intimate relations, second time .... Eruvin 100b; Niddah 31b
  Intimate relations with three-year-old girl ...... Niddah 44b-45a; Yevamos 57b; Kiddushin 10a-10b;
                                                                        Sanhedrin 55b, 69a
  Intimate relations without blood .... Kesubos 6b, 10a
Intimidating
  Intimidating before oath .... Shevuos 38b-39a
  Intimidating witnesses .... 32b, 40b; Sotah 8a; Sanhedrin 29a
  Intimidating witnesses in capital cases .... Sanhedrin 37a-37b
Inuy hadin .... *see* **Delaying justice, punishment**, page 158
Invei hagefen .... *see* **Grapes of vineyard, daughter of scholar**, page 256
Inverted Tannaim, opinions, Mishnayos .... Beitzah 9b-10a
Investments
  Investments, advice .... Bava Metzia 42a
  Investment, divided in three .... Bava Metzia 42a
Invitation to meal refused, episodes .... Chullin 7b; Megillah 28a
Inviting non-Jew, prohibition .... Avodah Zarah 8a-8b; Sanhedrin 104a
Ipcha mistabra .... *see* **Contrary is more logical (correct)**, page 127
Ir chomah .... *see* **Walled city**, page 730
Ir hanidachas .... *see* **City led to idolatry**, page 108
Ira Hayeiri, Torah and greatness .... Gittin 59a
Iron
  Iron, disqualified for Altar .... Middos 3:4
  Iron in Temple .... Tamid 26b
  Iron, murder by .... Sanhedrin 76b
  Iron pieces to heat *mikveh* for *Kohen Gadol* .... Yoma 34b
  Iron, prohibition to sell iron to robbers and non-Jew .... Avodah Zarah 15b-16a
  Iron, Sage .... Taanis 4a
  Iron, used to reduce man's life .... Middos 3:4
  Iron utensil
    Iron utensil, bell .... Shabbos 58a-58b
    Iron utensil, chains .... Shabbos 63b

Iron utensil, fragments .... Keilim 13:1-5, 14:1, 14:6-7
Iron utensil, impurity of corpse .... Nazir 53b
Iron utensil, needles .... Shabbos 52b, 60a, 123a; Keilim 13:5
Iron utensil, other utensils .... Keilim 11:5-9, 12:1-2, 12:7-8, 14:2-3
Iron utensil, rings .... Shabbos 52a-52b, 59b-60a; Keilim 11:8, 12:1, 13:6

Irrigating
Irrigating field, Abbaye .... Gittin 60b
Irrigating on Sabbatical year .... Moed Katan 6b
Irrigating, secondary category of work .... Moed Katan 2b
Irrigation holes for grapevines, *Chol HaMoed* .... Moed Katan 4b
Irritable man, comes away only with his irritation (anger) .... Kiddushin 40b-41a

Isaac
Isaac and Abraham, upright men .... Avodah Zarah 25a
Isaac, birth .... Bava Metzia 87a; Shabbos 156a-156b; Rosh Hashanah 16b
Isaac, bound on Altar .... Sanhedrin 89b
Isaac, comforted Abraham .... Sotah 14a
Isaac, may Esau be pardoned .... Megillah 6a
Isaac .... *see also* **Patriarchs**, page 475

Isaiah
Isaiah, Amaziah's nephew .... Megillah 10b
Isaiah, death .... Yevamos 49b
Isaiah, naked and barefoot .... Yoma 77a
Isaiah, wicked men's answer .... Sanhedrin 105a

Ish
Ish .... *see* **Man**, page 386
Ish Haeshkolos, Yose ben Yoezer .... Temurah 15b; Sotah 47a, 47b
Ish milchamah, Torah .... Chagigah 14a
Ish ploni atah chayav .... *see* **Ruling of** *beis din*, page 574
Ishbi in Nov, David .... Sanhedrin 95a

Ishmael
Ishmael, not Abraham's seed .... Nedarim 31a; Sanhedrin 59b
Ishmael, repentance .... Bava Basra 16b
Ishmael, sorting Patriarchs' offspring .... Shabbos 146a

Ishmaelites
Ishmaelites, demons of toilets .... Kiddushin 72a
Ishmaelites, G-d's regret .... Succah 52b
Ishmaelites, Gebiha's debate .... Sanhedrin 91a
Ishtabesh cahanei .... *see* **Mistake of** *Kohanim*, examination, page 416
Ishto kegufo .... *see* **Wife like oneself**, page 747
Ishus .... *see* **Marital relations**, page 392
Isi ben Akavia, names .... Pesachim 113b; Yoma 52b
Isi ben Yehudah, meat and milk .... Pesachim 24b; Nidah 36b
Islands, *Eretz Yisrael* .... Gittin 8a
Ispaklaria hameirah .... *see* **Aspaklaria meira**, page 34
Israel .... *see also* **Eretz Yisrael**, page 198

Aggadah —
"Israel by whom I shall be glorified" .... Yoma 86a
Israel, holy people, give even when they do not have .... Chullin 7b
Israel, nation more cherished than angels .... Chullin 91b-92a

Israel, one group in the world .... Chagigah 3a; Berachos 6a

Israel resembling idolaters over pouring, exceeded G-d's anger .... Sanhedrin 105a

Israel, sons of kings .... Shabbos 128a, 67a, 111a; Bava Metzia 113b

Israel, suffering .... Yevamos 47a

Israel who sinned, Divine Presence .... Yoma 56b-57a

Israel who sinned, still Israel .... Sanhedrin 44a

Israel, Jacob .... Berachos 13a

Misc. —

Israel and non-Jews, majority .... Yoma 84b-85a

Israel does not keep Shabbos .... Avodah Zarah 70a

Israel, going in *ezras Kohanim* .... Keilim 1:8

Israel, if they kept two Shabbosos .... Shabbos 118b

Israel, responsible for each other .... Sotah 37b; Bava Metzia 31a; Sanhedrin 43b

Israel, wordings of vows .... Nedarim 31a

Isru Chag .... Succah 45b

Issacher

Issacher, his birth and his wisdom .... Eruvin 100b; Niddah 31a

Issacher, ruling Rabbis .... Yoma 26a

Issar

Issar, coin .... Kiddushin 12a; Bava Metzia 44b

Issar, vow .... Shevuos 20a-20b

Issaron ha'ephah .... *see* **Tenth of *ephah***, page 681

Issued from impure, impure .... Bechoros 6b-7b

Issur .... *see* **Prohibition**, page 505

Issur bemakom kares .... *see* ***Assur*, said where excising of soul is concerned**, page 34

Issur chal al isur .... *see* **Double prohibition**, page 176

Issur cheftza .... *see* **Vow, prohibition of item**, page 726

Issur hanaah .... *see* **Forbidden benefit**, page 233

Issur nechasim .... *see* **Tenth for daughter's dowry, during father's life**, page 681

Issurei biyah .... *see* **Forbidden relations**, page 233

Issurei maachal .... *see* **Forbidden food**, page 233

Issurim deRabbanan .... *see* **Rabbinical Decrees**, page 533

Istinis .... *see* **Fastidious person**, page 216

Istra belegina .... *see* **Coin in barrel makes noise**, page 113

Isur Giora, episode .... Bava Basra 149a

Italy of Greece .... Megillah 6b

Item

Item .... *see also* **Object**, page 455

Item easily sold .... Nedarim 31a-31b

Item left in custody .... *see* **Custody**, page 137

Item, limited, oath .... Shevuos 43a

Item thrown, considered like put down .... Shabbos 4a-5a, 97a-98a; Gittin 79a; Bava Kama 70b

Item which has no place .... Avos 4:3

Items suitable, couch and other uses, impurity .... Niddah 49b; Shabbos 59a; Chagigah 23b

Items usually lent .... Shevuos 46b; Bava Metzia 116a; Bava Basra 52b

Items forbidden for benefit, throwing to Dead Sea .... Avodah Zarah 49b

Item situated in place of doubt, majority

Item situated in place of doubt, majority, cases ...... Pesachim 9b; Bava Kama 44b; Sanhedrin 79a;
Yevamos 16b; Kesubos 15a; Chullin 95a; Niddah 18a

Item situated in place of doubt, majority, sacrifices .... Pesachim 9b
Item situated in place of doubt, majority, saving life .... Yoma 84b
Item taken out of place of doubt, majority
Item taken out of place of doubt, majority, cases .... Kesubos 15a; Pesachim 9b; Yoma 84b;
.... Yevamos 16b; Kiddushin 73a; Chullin 95a; Niddah 18a
Item taken out of place of doubt, majority, sacrifices .... Zevachim 73a-73b
Item taken out of place of doubt, majority, will return .... Nazir 12a
Iter .... *see* **Left-handed**, page 360
Itran, resin waste .... Shabbos 20b
Itztadin .... *see* **Bull in stadium games, for sacrifice**, page 79
Itztagninus Abraham .... *see* **Astrology, Abraham**, page 34
Itzteva .... *see* **Platform**, page 492
Itztinus .... *see* **Fastidious person**, page 216
Iyov .... *see* **Job**, page 324
Iyum .... *see* **Intimidating**, page 317
Iyun .... *see* **In-depth learning**, page 307
Iyun tefilah .... *see* **Concentration in prayer**, page 119
Izgadar .... Zevachim 19a

I

J

Jacob

Jacob .... *see also* **Patriarchs**, page 475
Jacob, apple orchard .... Taanis 29b
Jacob, Abraham's seed .... Nedarim 31a; Sanhedrin 59b
Jacob, beauty .... Bava Metzia 84a; Bava Basra 58a
Jacob, bowed before Joseph .... Megillah 16b
Jacob, camped facing city .... Shabbos 33b
Jacob, difficulties in raising his children .... Sanhedrin 19b
Jacob, events .... Sanhedrin 95b; Chullin 91a-92a
Jacob, first sickness .... Bava Metzia 87a; Sanhedrin 107b
Jacob, funeral and burial .... Sotah 13a
Jacob, G-d called him "El" .... Megillah 18a
Jacob, going to Egypt in chains .... Shabbos 89b
Jacob, holiness .... Yevamos 76a
Jacob is not dead .... Taanis 5b
Jacob, meeting with Esau .... Sotah 41b
Jacob, power of prayer .... Gittin 57b
Jacob, revelation of end of days .... Pesachim 56a
Jacob, saw Shem son of Noah .... Bava Basra 121b
Jacob, sciatic nerve .... Chullin 91a
Jacob, seven shepherds .... Succah 52b
Jacob, years of separation from Joseph .... Megillah 16b-17a
Jacob, Israel .... Berachos 13a

Jacob's sons

Jacob's sons, "why should you show yourselves" .... Taanis 10b
Jacob's sons, before Pharaoh .... Bava Kama 92a
Jacob's sons, compared to various animals .... Sotah 11b
Jacob's sons, dread of Joseph .... Taanis 9a
Jacob's sons, married Canaanite women .... Pesachim 50a

Jael

Jael, beauty .... Megillah 15a
Jael, episode with Sisera .... Yevamos 103a-103b; Nazir 23b; Horayos 10b
Jael, may she be blessed among women .... Sanhedrin 105b
Jael, transgression for Heaven's sake .... Nazir 23b; Horayos 10b

Japheth..*see* **Yefes, in tents of Shem**, page 768
Jealousy
  Jealousy, between sons...Shabbos 10b
  Jealousy between teachers increases wisdom..Bava Basra 21a, 22a
  Jealousy, desire and pursuit of honor..Avos 4:21
  Jealousy, non-Jew, snake and pupil...Pesachim 113a
  Jealousy of woman, of her rival...Megillah 13a; Avodah Zarah 55a
  Jealousy, punishment..Sotah 9a-9b
  Jealousy, decomposition of bones after death...Shabbos 152b
  Jealousy, toward son and disciple...Sanhedrin 105b
Jechoniah
  Jechoniah, exile..Gittin 88a; Sanhedrin 38a
  Jechoniah, Nehemiah's mother's conception..Sanhedrin 37b
Jehoahaz ben Josiah...Horayos 11b; Krisos 5b
Jehoiakim
  Jehoiakim, G-d's anger..Sanhedrin 103a
  Jehoiakim, scroll burning...Moed Katan 26a
  Jehoiakim, skull...Sanhedrin 82a, 104a
  Jehoiakim the king..Sanhedrin 103a, 103b
  Jehoiakim, World to Come...Sanhedrin 104a
  Jehoiakim skull..Sanhedrin 82a
Jehoiachin, exile..Arachin 12a
Jehonathan ben Manasseh..Bava Basra 109b, 110a
Jehonathan, *Av Beis Din*...Moed Katan 26a
Jehoshaphat
  Jehoshaphat, Ahab..Chullin 4b-5a
  Jehoshaphat, honor of Sages..Kesubos 103b
Jehu
  Jehu, anointed from oil flask..Horayos 12a
  Jehu, reason for his moral decline...Sanhedrin 102
Jephthah
  Jephthah and his daughter...Taanis 4a
  Jephthah in his generation like Shmuel in his...Rosh Hashanah 25b
Jeremiah
  Jeremiah, slander...Bava Kama 16b
  Jeremiah, stumbling-block of charity for his enemies...............Bava Basra 9b; Bava Kama 16b
  Jeremiah, Temple destruction...Nazir 32b
  Jeremiah, Josiah...Megillah 14b
Jericho
  Jericho, collapse of wall..Berachos 54b
  Jericho, Hiel..Sanhedrin 113a
  Jericho, incense..Yoma 39b; Tamid 30b
  Jericho, six things......................................Menachos 71a-71b; Pesachim 55b-56b
Jeroboam
  Jeroboam, "who will be first"...Sanhedrin 102a
  Jeroboam, calves..Sanhedrin 101b
  Jeroboam, episode...Sanhedrin 101b-102a
  Jeroboam, his names...Sanhedrin 101b
  Jeroboam, pilgrimage...Gittin 88a; Sanhedrin 101b

J

Jeroboam, rebuke to Solomon...Sanhedrin 101b
Jeroboam, wisdom in Torah...Sanhedrin 102a, 103b
Jeroboam, World to Come...Sanhedrin 104b
Jeroboam's calves, Gehazi..Sotah 47a

Jerusalem

Aggadah —

Jerusalem and Cesarea, destruction..Megillah 6a
Jerusalem, fruit of Ginosar...Pesachim 8b
Jerusalem in its glory..Succah 51b
Jerusalem, institutions..Kesubos 105a
Jerusalem, judges..Kesubos 104b-105a
Jerusalem, men of pure mind...Sanhedrin 23a
Jerusalem, minor girl to adult boy..Sanhedrin 104a
Jerusalem, miracles..Yoma 21a; Avos 5:5
Jerusalem, powerful men...Pesachim 57a
Jerusalem, three *parsaos*..Bava Basra 75b
Jerusalem, wicked............................Yoma 76b-77a; Kiddushin 72b; Succah 51b
Jerusalem, wisdom of captives..................................Sanhedrin 104a-104b

Jerusalem in the future

Jerusalem in the future, addition..Pesachim 50a
Jerusalem in the future, diamonds..................Bava Basra 75a; Sanhedrin 100a
Jerusalem in the future, Divine Name...Bava Basra 75b
Jerusalem in the future, only people invited............................Bava Basra 75b

Law —

Jerusalem, annexing area..Shevuos 15a-16a
Jerusalem, commandment to dwell.......................Kesubos 110b; Arachin 3b
Jerusalem, custom of *lulav*..Succah 41b
Jerusalem, custom of meal..Sanhedrin 23a
Jerusalem, holiness...Pesachim 85b-86a
Jerusalem, impurity.......................................Pesachim 19b; Shekalim 8:1-3
Jerusalem, married woman dwelling in.................Kesubos 110b; Arachin 3b
Jerusalem, mourning...Moed Katan 26a; Bava Basra 60b
Jerusalem, private domain......................................Eruvin 6b, 22a, 101a
Jerusalem, second tithe..Maaser Sheni 3:7; Temurah 21b
Jerusalem, ten sanctities..Bava Kama 82b

Misc. —

Jerusalem, immodest girls...Shabbos 62b; Yoma 9b
Jerusalem, simplified pronounciation..Bava Kama 6b
Jerusalem, *nachalah*...Zevachim 119a-119b
Jerusalem of Above...Taanis 5a
Jerusalem, other city...Arachin 32b
Jerusalem to Tribes...Yoma 12a

Jesse

Jesse, David's father...Berachos 58a
Jesse, princes of mankind..Succah 52b

Jesters, World to Come...Taanis 22a

Jethro

Jethro, Blessed be G-d..Sanhedrin 94a
Jethro, hospitality...Berachos 63b

Jethro, Pharaoh's counsel .... Sanhedrin 106a; Sotah 11a
Jethro, when did he come .... Zevachim 116a; Avodah Zarah 24a-24b
Jethro's sons, wine .... Bava Basra 91b
Jew
   Jews .... *see also* **Israel**, page 318
   Jew, denies idolatry .... Megillah 13a
   Jews, prophets or sons of prophets .... Pesachim 66a
Jewelry
   Jewelry, carrying out on Shabbos .... Shabbos 57b, 59a-60a, 62a-62b, 64b
   Jewelry, decree concerning peddlers .... Bava Kama 82b; Bava Basra 22a
   Jewelry for woman .... Kesubos 65a
   Jewelry, impurity .... Keilim 11:8-9
   Jewelry, names .... Shabbos 63b, 64a
   Jewelry of Midian, thoughts .... Shabbos 64a-64b
   Jewelry when going out, Shabbos .... Shabbos 64b
Jezebel, Ahab's wife .... Sanhedrin 39b
Joab
   Joab, Amalek .... Bava Basra 21a-21b
   Joab ben Tzeruyah .... Sanhedrin 48b-49a
   Joab, David's curses .... Sanhedrin 48b
   Joab, David's nephew .... Shabbos 55b
   Joab, his death .... Sanhedrin 48b-49a; Makos 12a
Jochebed
   Jochebed, marriage to Amram .... Bava Basra 119b-120a; Sotah 12a; Sanhedrin 58b
   Jochebed, seventy souls .... Bava Basra 120a, 123b; Sotah 12a
Job
   Job for son .... Kiddushin 30b, 82a-82b; Berachos 63a
   Jobs, forbidden .... Kiddushin 82a
Job
   Job, advice to Pharaoh .... Sanhedrin 106a; Sotah 11a
   Job, daughters .... Bava Basra 16b
   Job, debate .... Bava Basra 16a-16b
   Job, episode .... Bava Basra 15b-16a
   Job, love and fear .... Sotah 31a
   Job, twelve months .... Eduyos 2:10
   Job, who was he .... Bava Basra 14b-15b
Joel the prophet, drought .... Taanis 5a
Joke
   Joke .... *see also* **Laughter**, page 354
   Joke, answering in jest .... Bava Kama 17b
   Joke, before learning .... Shabbos 30b
Jolly face because you won .... Menachos 68b
Jonah
   Jonah the prophet, Ninveh .... Taanis 16a
   Jonah, third prophecy .... Yevamos 98a
   Jonah, wealth .... Nedarim 38a
Jonathan, bread to David .... Sanhedrin 104a
Jordan
   Jordan, course .... Bava Basra 74b; Bechoros 55a

Jordan, land of Canaan .... Bechoros 55a
Jordan, stones .... Sotah 33b-34b, 34a

Joseph

Egypt —
Joseph, abstained from wine .... Shabbos 139a
Joseph and Boaz, battle against evil urge .... Sanhedrin 19b
Joseph, bowing .... Megillah 16b
Joseph, exiled to Egypt .... Chullin 60b
Joseph, feast for his brothers .... Chullin 91a
Joseph, his brothers introduced to Pharaoh .... Bava Kama 92a
Joseph, Pharaoh's astrologers .... Sotah 13b
Joseph, Potiphar .... Sotah 13b
Joseph, Potiphar's wife .... Sotah 36b; Yoma 35b; Zevachim 118b; Shabbos 49b

Sale —
Joseph and his brothers .... Megillah 16a-16b; Yevamos 88a; Kesubos 27b; Bava Metzia 39b
Joseph, pit .... Shabbos 22a; Chagigah 3a
Joseph, punishment for details .... Sotah 13b
Joseph, sale .... Sotah 11a
Joseph, saved by Judah .... Sanhedrin 6b
Joseph, time of release .... Rosh Hashanah 11a-11b
Joseph, tunic .... Shabbos 10b; Megillah 16b
Joseph, years of separation .... Megillah 16b-17a

Misc. —
Joseph, blessing for his offspring ..... Sotah 36b; Berachos 20a, 55b; Bava Metzia 84a; Bava Basra 118b
Joseph, burial .... Sotah 13a-13b
Joseph compels wicked .... Yoma 35b
Joseph, dread of judgment .... Chagigah 4b
Joseph, Esau .... Bava Basra 123b
Joseph, evil eye .... Sotah 36b; Bava Basra 118a-118b; Berachos 20a, 55b; Bava Metzia 84a
Joseph, firstborn right .... Bava Basra 123a
Joseph's brothers .... *see* **Jacob's sons**, page 321

Joshua
Joshua and Moses, Shabbos of double kingship .... Sotah 13b
Joshua, annulling evil urge .... Arachin 32b
Joshua, decrees .... Bava Kama 80b-81b
Joshua, did not leave a son .... Eruvin 63a
Joshua had said, I would not have accepted .... Chullin 124a
Joshua, his face like the moon .... Bava Basra 75a
Joshua loved Jews .... Eruvin 22b
Joshua, met angel .... Sanhedrin 44a-44b
Joshua, order of Holy Writings .... Bava Basra 14b-15a
Joshua, righteousness and audacity .... Sanhedrin 44a
Joshua, share in *Eretz Yisrael* .... Bava Basra 118b, 122a
Joshua, signs for boundaries of *Eretz Yisrael* .... Bava Basra 56a
Joshua, sun stayed still .... Avodah Zarah 25a; Taanis 20a
Joshua, Torah and greatness .... Gittin 59a
Joshua, ways of *Eretz Yisrael* .... Eruvin 22b
Joshua's decrees .... Bava Kama 80b-81b

J

Josiah

Josiah, "you will die in peace" .... Moed Katan 28b
Josiah, his death .... Taanis 22a-22b
Josiah, his righteousness .... Shabbos 56b
Josiah, his sons .... Horayos 11b; Krisos 5b
Josiah, repented .... Shabbos 56b
Josiah, Ten Tribes .... Arachin 33a
Josiah, Hulda the prophetess .... Megillah 14b

Jotham

Jotham, king .... Succah 45b
Jotham, premature death .... Pesachim 87b

Journey

Journey causes weakness .... Gittin 70a
Journey dissipates wine .... Eruvin 64b; Taanis 17b; Sanhedrin 22b
Journey, distance of day walking .... Taanis 10b; Yoma 21a; Bava Kama 60b
Journey, eating .... Taanis 10b-11a
Journey, food needed .... Pesachim 113a
Journey, large steps .... Taanis 10b
Journey, learning during journey .... Taanis 10b; Eruvin 54a; Sotah 46b, 49a
Journey, nightfall approaching, Shabbos .... Shabbos 17b, 153a-153b
Journey, too much is harmful .... Gittin 70a
Journeys in desert, dates .... Taanis 29a
Journeys in desert, night .... Menachos 95a
Journeys of Divine Presence .... Rosh Hashanah 31a

Joy
Joy .... *see* **Happiness** page 269

Jubilee

Jubilee, consecrated land .... Arachin 24a-26b, 29a, 33a
Jubilee, estate .... Arachin 24a, 29b-30a; Gittin 44b-45a
Jubilee, from when does it cancel debts .... Arachin 28b; Kiddushin 40b
Jubilee, how to reckon .... Nedarim 61a
Jubilee, in which case property returns .... Bechoros 52b, 57a; Bava Basra 139a-139b;
.... Gittin 25a, 48a, 48a; Bava Kama 69b; Beitzah 37b
Jubilee, increase in value by buyer .... Bava Metzia 109a
Jubilee, laws depending on it .... Arachin 29a
Jubilee, prayer .... Rosh Hashanah 27a
Jubilee, slave and maidservant .... Rosh Hashanah 8b; Kiddushin 15a-16a; Arachin 29a
Jubilee, temporary purchase .... Bava Metzia 79a
Jubilee, what is necessary .... Rosh Hashanah 9b
Jubilees in time of Temple, reckoning .... Arachin 12b, 32b-33a

Judah

Judah, daughter of Canaanite .... Pesachim 50a
Judah, episode with Tamar .... Sotah 10a-10b; Megillah 10b; Makos 23b
Judah, kingship .... Sotah 37a
Judah, Moses' prayer .... Makos 11b
Judah, *Reish Galusa* .... Horayos 11b; Sanhedrin 5a
Judah, sale of Joseph .... Sanhedrin 6b
Judah, thanksgiving to G-d .... Berachos 7b
Judah the legislator, Sages .... Yoma 26a

Judea

Judea and Galilee, closed frontiers .... Bava Basra 38b

Judea, as additional proof to verse .... Kiddushin 6a

Judea, better land than Galilee .... Bava Basra 122a

Judea, destruction .... Shabbos 145b; Yoma 54a

Judea, precision in speech .... Eruvin 53b

Judea, seclusion with one's fiancée .... Kesubos 9b, 12a

Judge .... *see also* **Beis din**, page 50

Disqualified —

Judge, blind .... Sanhedrin 34b; Niddah 49b-50a

Judge, convert .... Yevamos 102a

Judge, dishonest .... Sanhedrin 7b

Judge, disqualified, accepted .... Sanhedrin 23a-23b, 24a-24b, 25b; Bava Basra 128a

Judge, friend and enemy .... Kesubos 105b; Sanhedrin 29a

Judge, implicated .... Bava Basra 43a

Judge in capital cases, disqualified .... Sanhedrin 36b

Judge, relative disqualified .... Sanhedrin 27b

Judge, trustworthiness even if unacceptable .... Sanhedrin 23a-24b

Judge, who .... Sanhedrin 7b, 88b; Bava Basra 58b; Bechoros 35b

Episodes —

Judge and prophet, in every tribe .... Succah 27b

Judge, boor, episode .... Sanhedrin 7b

Judge, Rabbi Nassan .... Bava Metzia 117b; Bava Kama 39a, 53a

Judges, "come to judge!" .... Shabbos 10a

Judges in desert, number .... Sanhedrin 18a

Judges of decrees, Jerusalem .... Kesubos 104b-105a

Judges of Diaspora, who are they .... Sanhedrin 17b

Judges of Sodom .... Sanhedrin 109a-109b

Judges, *Reish Galusa* .... Bava Basra 65a

For which cases —

Judge expert .... *see* **Expert judge**, page 210

Judge or witness, gift .... Bava Basra 113b-114a; Sanhedrin 34b

Judges, adding to number .... Sanhedrin 42a

Judges for *chalitzah* .... Yevamos 101a-102a, 104a, 105b-106a

Judges for sanctification of month .... Rosh Hashanah 25b-26a

Mistake —

Judge, distinguished one is absent, mistake of *beis din* .... Horayos 4b

Judge knowing that *beis din* made a mistake .... Horayos 2b

Judge must only consider that which seems clear to him .... Bava Basra 131a; Sanhedrin 6b;
.... Niddah 20b

Judge perceives that case is misleading .... Sanhedrin 32a

Judge who made a mistake .... Bava Kama 100a, 117b; Sanhedrin 5a, 6a, 30a, 33a-33b;
.... Kesubos 84b, 100a; Bechoros 28b

Reward and punishment —

Judge, delaying and distorting judgment .... Shabbos 33a

Judge, did not consult his teacher .... Yevamos 109b

Judge, did not save victim of theft .... Shabbos 55a

Judge, reward and punishment .... Sanhedrin 7a-7b

J

Judge, reward for truthful judgment .... Peah 8:9; Shabbos 10a; Megillah 15b; Bava Basra 8b; Sanhedrin 7a

Judges, wicked, punishment .... Shabbos 139a

Warnings —

Judge, "open your mouth to one who is mute" .... Kesubos 36a; Gittin 37b; Bava Basra 41a

Judge, clarifying law .... Sanhedrin 7b

Judge, derogatory speech .... Sanhedrin 31a; Bava Kama 99b

Judge, duty-bound to judge .... Sanhedrin 6b

Judge, helping litigant .... Avos 1:8-9

Judge, listening to arguments .... Sanhedrin 7b; Shevuos 31a

Judge, moral teachings .... Sanhedrin 6b

Judge, not to be obstinate .... Shevuos 30b

Judge, one *perutah* like a hundred .... Sanhedrin 8a

Judge, soft to one .... Kesubos 46a

Judge, what his eyes can see .... Sanhedrin 6b; Bava Basra 131a; Niddah 20b

Judge, warnings .... Avos 1:1, 1:8-9, 4:7-8; Sanhedrin 6b

Judge, who judges with him .... Sanhedrin 23a

Who —

Judge, only those of your generation .... Rosh Hashanah 25b

Judge, people are pleased with him .... Sanhedrin 88b

Judges of the diaspora, who were called thus .... Sanhedrin 17b

Judges, ordained .... Bava Kama 15b, 84a-84b; Sanhedrin 2b-3b; Gittin 88b

Judges today, agents of expert judges .... Bava Kama 84b; Gittin 88b

Misc. —

"Judge my judgment," member of Dan tribe .... Pesachim 4a

Judge alone, expert .... Sanhedrin 5a, 8a

Judge believes him .... Kesubos 85a; Yevamos 101b

Judge, do not judge before being in other's place .... Avos 2:4

Judge, inferior speaks first .... Sanhedrin 36a; Gittin 58b-59a

Judge, inferior to him .... Kiddushin 70a

Judge, king and *Kohen Gadol* .... Sotah 45a

Judge, loved or hated .... Kesubos 105b

Judge of truth .... Berachos 60a, 60b

Judges altogether condemning, capital case .... Sanhedrin 17a

Judges, commandment to appoint .... Sanhedrin 16b

Judges, how many .... Sanhedrin 2a-3b, 5b-6a, 10a; Gittin 32b-33a, 30a, 87b; Kesubos 22a

Judges, selecting .... Sanhedrin 23a-24b, 31b

Judged because of future .... Sanhedrin 68b, 71b-72a

Judging favorably, episodes .... Shabbos 127b

Judging fellow favorably .... Avos 2:4; Shabbos 127b; Shevuos 30a

Judging impartially, equally presenting litigants .... Shevuos 30a, 31a

Judging judges .... Bava Basra 15b

Judging man according to his present actions .... Rosh Hashanah 16b

Judge certifying legal document

Judge certifying legal document, appeal .... Kesubos 21b-22a

Judges certifying legal document, considered as one .... Kesubos 21a-21b

Judges certifying legal document, dead .... Bava Basra 165b

Judges, who wrote this Book .... Bava Basra 14b

Judgment
Beis din —

Judgment "became old" .... Sanhedrin 42a
Judgment, appeal .... Sanhedrin 33b
Judgment at night .... Sanhedrin 34b
Judgment, contradictory, re-examining .... Yevamos 37b
Judgment for penny like for hundred .... Sanhedrin 8a
Judgment in presence of accused, ox .... Bava Kama 45a
Judgment, not against three litigants .... Pesachim 112b
Judgment on Shabbos .... Beitzah 36b
Judgment, preventing from questioning .... Bava Kama 96b
Judgment, re-examining, sharing of heirs .... Bava Basra 106b
Judgment, true .... Peah 8:9; Shabbos 10a; Bava Basra 8b

Judgment, monetary cases

Judgment, monetary cases, like fountain .... Berachos 63b; Bava Basra 175b
Judgment, monetary cases, ordained judges .... Bava Kama 15b, 84a-84b; Sanhedrin 2b-3b
Judgment, monetary cases, women .... Kiddushin 35a-35b; Bava Kama 15a

Heavenly judgment —

Judgment at resurrection of dead .... Rosh Hashanah 17a
Judgment, capital cases, differences .... Sanhedrin 36b, 32a
Judgment, capital cases, fast .... Sanhedrin 63a
Judgment, capital cases, how .... Sanhedrin 46a
Judgment, capital cases, wine .... Sanhedrin 42a
Judgment, *Elohim* .... Berachos 60b
Judgment, fear of Divine Judgment .... Chagigah 4b
Judgment in the future .... Sanhedrin 111b
Judgment of idolaters in the future .... Avodah Zarah 2a-3b
Judgment of poor and rich in World to Come .... Yoma 35b
Judgment of wicked .... Eduyos 2:10; Shabbos 33b; Rosh Hashanah 17a
Judgment, Rosh Hashanah .... Rosh Hashanah 8a-8b, 16a, 16b
Judgment without judgment .... Berachos 5b
Judgment, worry of mourner .... Moed Katan 27b

Misc. —

Judgment and charity, David .... Sanhedrin 6b
Judgment, Divine, precise .... Bava Kama 50a-50b; Chagigah 5a; Eruvin 22a; Yevamos 121b
Judgment, Divine, sinner's approval .... Taanis 11a
Judgment for oneself .... Bava Kama 27b-28a

Jug

Jug and barrel, explanation and purchase .... Bava Kama 27a-27b
Jug of oil, *Chanukah* .... Shabbos 21b
Jugs, *kashering* .... Avodah Zarah 74b-75a
Jugs, small, precious .... Chullin 91a
Jugs, wordings of sale .... Bava Basra 93b-94a, 97b

Juice

Juice from fruit .... *see also* **Fruit juice**, page 241
Juice from fruit, blessing .... Berachos 38a
Juice from fruit, considered liquid .... Terumos 11:2-3
Juice of olives, liquid .... Shabbos 144b; Taharos 9:1-3, 9:5-7; Meilah 21a

Jumped
Jumped and became menstruated .... Niddah 11a
Jumped from Altar, parts of sacrifice from Altar .... Zevachim 83b, 86a-87a, 108b;
.... Yoma 20a-20b, 45b; Menachos 26b

Junction of sinews, *tereifah* .... Chullin 76a-76b

Just
Just as fish eat little ones .... Avodah Zarah 3b-4a
Just as He is merciful etc. .... Shabbos 133b

Justice
Justice .... *see also* **Judgment**, page 329
Justice and compassion .... Rosh Hashanah 17b

Justification
Justification, rumor .... Gittin 89b
Justification to purify *Eretz Yisrael* .... Kesubos 20b; Nazir 65b
Justification, trustworthiness .... Kesubos 22a-22b

Juxtaposing mention of redemption
Juxtaposing mention of redemption and prayer .... Berachos 4b, 9b
Juxtaposing mention of redemption, during journey .... Berachos 30a

J

K

Kabalah merabo .... *see* **Tradition from teacher, ruling, page 699**
Kabalah .... *see* **Heavenly Chariot, page 274**
Kabalas hadam .... *see* **Receiving blood of sacrifice, correcting mistakes, page 550**
Kabalas lashon hara .... *see* **Believing derogatory speech, page 51**
Kabalas panim .... *see* **Greeting, page 258**
Kabalas pnei rabo .... *see* **Visiting teacher, page 725**
Kabalas Shabbos .... *see* **Welcoming Shabbos, page 740**
Kaddish
  Kaddish, answering during prayer .... Berachos 21b
  Kaddish, Divine voice expressing pain .... Berachos 3a
  Kaddish, maintains world .... Sotah 49a
  Kaddish, reward .... Shabbos 119b
Kadi, name of Amora .... Bava Metzia 2a
***Kaf hakela*,** punishment after death .... Shabbos 152b
Kaf veki yevani .... *see* **Greek letters, C and Π, annointing, page 258**
Kaf zechus .... *see* **Judging fellow favorably, page 328**
Kaftorim people, from Avim .... Chullin 60b
Kahal .... *see* **Community, page 118**
Kal vachomer .... *see* **Deduction, "all the more so," page 156**
Kala ilan .... *see* **Blue dye for *tzitzis*, false, page 69**
Kalba Savua
  Kalba Savua, wealth .... Gittin 56a
  Kalba Savua's daughter, Rabbi Akiva .... Nedarim 50a; Kesubos 62b-63a
Kalei habishul .... *see* **Easily cooked foods, page 185**
Kallah .... *see* **Bride, page 77;** *see also* **Daughter-in-law, page 145**
Kam dina .... *see* **Judgment, re-examining, sharing of heirs, page 329**
Kam lei .... *see* **Penalty (Severest), page 479**
Kama kama batil .... *see* **Mixture annulled drop by drop, page 418**
Kamah Yosef ika beshuka .... *see* **"How many Yosef already exist!," page 287**
Kamiah .... *see* **Amulet, page 21**
Kamtza and Bar Kamtza .... Gittin 55b-56b
Kan nimtzeu .... *see* **Place of object, *chazakah*, page 491**
Kania d'Rava .... *see* **Cane of Rava, page 86**
***Kankantom*,** Rabbi Meir .... Eruvin 13a; Sotah 20a

Kantrin, shekel of Prophets...Bechoros 50a

Kanunya..*see* **Kesubah, concern about conspiracy,** page 335

Kaparah..*see* **Atonement,** page 35

Kapores haaron..*see* **Cover of Ark,** page 131

Kapos temarim, lulav..Succah 32a

Kashering

   Kashering clay utensil...Pesachim 30b; Avodah Zarah 34a

   Kashering from wine of idolaters..........Avodah Zarah 60b, 74b-75b; Niddah 65a-65b

   Kashering sacrificial utensils..................Zevachim 93a, 94b, 95b, 96b, 97a

   Kashering, sacrificial vessel..................Zevachim 93a, 94b, 95b, 96b-97a

   Kashering utensils..................Avodah Zarah 75b-76b; Zevachim 96b

   Kashering, various utensils..Pesachim 30b

   Kashering wine press, episode....................................Avodah Zarah 74b

   Kashering wine press from impurity.........Avodah Zarah 75a-75b; Taharos 10:8

Karachas and gabachas, leprous marks...Negaim 10:10

Kares..*see* **Excising of soul,** page 207

Karfaf..*see* **Empty land,** page 196

Karkov of Altar..Zevachim 62a

Karmelis

   Karmelis, cases..Shabbos 6b-7a; Eruvin 87a

   Karmelis, strength of man..................Shabbos 100b-101a, 141a

   Karmelis to empty land, carrying......................................Eruvin 67b

   Karmelis, up to ten handbreadths..................................Shabbos 7a-7b

Karna

   Karna, horn in his eye..........................Shabbos 108a; Bava Basra 89a

   Karna, judges of the diaspora....................................Sanhedrin 17b

   Karna, test of Rav...Shabbos 108a

Karnuna, Rav Hamnuna..Kiddushin 25a

Karov le'atzmo ulemamono................*see* **Relative to himself and his money,** page 555

Karpaf..*see* **Empty land,** page 196

Karpas on Seder night..Pesachim 114a-114b

Karshinim, health..Berachos 44b; Shabbos 110a

Kasheh leshikchah..*see* **Harmful to memory,** page 270

Kashim mezonosav..................................*see* **Difficult is man's livelihood,** page 163

Katafras......................................*see* **Flowing liquid, connection to** *mikveh,* page 231

Katan......................................*see* **Minor,** page 411; *see also* **Child,** page 102

Katina, *tzitzis*..Menachos 41a

Katlei kanei be'agma........................*see* **Cuts reeds in bogs, common man,** page 138

Katlonis........................*see* **Woman whose two husbands died, episode of Abbaye,** page 756

Kav hakite'a..................................*see* **Prosthesis of leg,** *chalitzah,* page 507

Kav, amount..Bava Basra 89b-90a

Kav"an, theft..Rosh Hashanah 26b

Kavanah..................................*see* **Intent,** page 311; *see also* **Concentration,** page 119

Kavul, Hiram's towns..Shabbos 54a

Kavush kimevushal......................................*see* **Pickled food, like cooked,** page 487

Kchol, eyes..Shabbos 151b

Kebeitzah..*see* **Egg volume,** page 188

Kechatzos, death of firstborn..Berachos 3b

Kedar-laomer, writing..Chullin 65a

Ke'dei achilas pras .... *see* **Eating volume of meal, interruption,** page 187
Ke'dei klipah .... *see* **Peeling slice,** page 478
Ke'dei lakuf leikaro .... *see* **Hair, measure of length,** page 264
Ke'dei netilah .... *see* **Removing prohibited thickness of food,** page 557
Ke'dei sheyaasu .... *see* **Work on Shabbos, result forbidden until when,** page 761
Kedeirah bas yoma .... *see* **Pot used within day,** page 495
Kedeirah debei shutfei .... *see* **Pot of two partners,** page 495
Ke'di, name of Amora .... Bava Metzia 2a
Kedushah

  Kedushah .... *see also* **Holiness,** page 281
  Kedushah Desidra, maintains world .... Sotah 49a
  Kedushah and *Modim,* arriving late .... Berachos 21b
  Kedushah, in congregation .... Berachos 21b; Megillah 23b
  Kedushah, song of angels .... Chullin 91b-92a
Kedushah rishonah .... *see* **First sanctification of** *Eretz Yisrael,* page 225
Kedushas guf vedamim .... *see* **Consecrated,** page 122; *see also* **Holiness,** page 281
Keep

  Keep silent to G-d, enemy .... Gittin 7a
  Keep silent! Thus came this thought before Me .... Menachos 29b
  Keeping a Jew alive .... Sanhedrin 37a
  Keeping away bad smell from city .... Bava Basra 25a
  Keeping away from bad neighbor .... Avos 1:7
  Keeping away from bad rumor, suspicion .... Chullin 44b
  Keeping contact, carrying out basket on Shabbos .... Shabbos 91b-92a
  Keeping from leavening, *matzos* for Pesach night .... Pesachim 40a-40b
  Keeping fruit to raise prices .... Bava Basra 90b
  Keeping mouth closed during argument .... Chullin 89a
  Keeping one's money in land .... Bava Metzia 42a
  Keeping one's word, honest "yes" .... Bava Metzia 49a
  Keeping one's word, gift .... Bava Metzia 49a-49b
  Keeping silent, concern about illegitimate child .... Kesubos 14b
  Keeping silent to annoy wife, permitting vows .... Nedarim 78b-79a
  Keeping strength in old age .... Kesubos 62a
  Kept field on Sabbatical year .... Sheviis 9:1; Maasros 5:8; Succah 39b
Keeping food warm

  Keeping food warm, adding warmth .... Shabbos 39b, 47b-48a, 49a, 51b; Bava Basra 19a
  Keeping food warm, displacing *muktzeh* .... Shabbos 48a, 50b
  Keeping food warm, how is it permitted .... Shabbos 51a-51b, 146b
  Keeping food warm in rocks .... Bava Basra 19a
  Keeping food warm in sand and in pipe .... Shabbos 39a-39b
  Keeping food warm on Shabbos, reason of decree .... Shabbos 34a
Keeping wine

  Keeping wine, advice .... Bava Metzia 44a; Krisos 6b
  Keeping wine, barrel .... Avodah Zarah 69b
  Keeping wine, cases .... Avodah Zarah 61a-61b
  Keeping wine, porter .... Avodah Zarah 60a
  Keeping wine, seal .... Avodah Zarah 31a-31b; Shabbos 122a
Kefel .... *see* **Double payment,** page 176
Kefiah .... *see* **Force,** page 234

Keila, David's war..Eruvin 45a

Keitzad merakdin lifnei hakallah..............................*see* **How to dance before bride,** page 287

Kele'achar yad..*see* **Change of manner,** page 95

Keilim................................*see* **Container,** page 125; *see also* **Utensil,** page 718

Kemitzah

Kemitzah, by hand..Menachos 19b

Kemitzah, cases of disqualification................................Menachos 10b-11a

Kemitzah, container on floor................................Menachos 7a-7b

Kemitzah, divided meal offering................................Menachos 24a

Kemitzah, how................................Yoma 47a-47b; Menachos 11a

Kemitzah, invalid, correcting................................Menachos 6b-7a, 8b

Kemitzah, one of most difficult services in Temple................Menachos 11a, 54a

Kemitzah, place................................Menachos 6b, 8b; Zevachim 63a

Kemitzah, quantity................Menachos 26b, 58a-58b; Pesachim 44a; Nazir 36a

Kemitzah without frankincense................................Zevachim 110a

Kenaanim..*see* **Canaanites,** page 86

Kenaan..*see* **Canaan,** page 86

Kenunya..*see* **Plot,** page 492

Kerem revai..*see* **Revai,** page 565

Keren..*see* **Horn, damage by ox,** page 284

Keri..*see* **Discharge, male,** page 165

Kerosene

Kerosene and persimmon, parable................................Yoma 38b-39a

Kerosene, danger..Shabbos 26a

Kerosene, wasting..Shabbos 67b

Ke'rus shafcha, significance................................Yevamos 75b

Kesar..*see* **Emperor,** page 195

Kesem niddah..*see* **Stain of *niddah*,** page 653

Keshem shenichnas lebris, blessing on circumcision................Shabbos 137b; Menachos 42a

Kesitah, explanation................................Rosh Hashanah 26a

Kesubah..*see also* **Support,** page 664

Collecting —

Kesubah, best land................................Gittin 49b; Bava Kama 7b

Kesubah, collecting during life................................Kesubos 81a-81b

Kesubah, decree of warranty................................Kesubos 82b; Shabbos 16b

Kesubah, dividing between sons................................Bava Basra 132a-133a

Kesubah from consecrated item................................Arachin 23a

Kesubah, from slaves................................Yevamos 99a

Kesubah, from which coin................................Kesubos 110b

Kesubah, gave his property to his wife................Bava Basra 132a-133a, 150a; Peah 3:7

Kesubah, increase in value................................Bechoros 52a

Kesubah, leaving for husband after seizure................Nedarim 65b-66a

Kesubah, movable goods................................Kesubos 67a; Nedarim 65b

Kesubah on golden tray, paying................................Gittin 20b

Kesubah partially paid, oath................................Kesubos 87a-87b; Shevuos 45a

Kesubah, seizure from orphans................................Kesubos 84a

Kesubah, several women................................Kesubos 93a

Kesubah, warranty of betrothal................................Kesubos 43b

K

For whom —

Kesubah, agunah .... Yevamos 116b-117a
Kesubah, betrothed girl .... Kesubos 89b, 47a-47b, 54b; Bava Metzia 17b
Kesubah, forbidden women .... Yevamos 84a, 85a-85b; Kesubos 100b, 101a-101b
Kesubah of widow awaiting levirate marriage .... Yevamos 52a; Kesubos 82b
Kesubah, orphan girl and deaf .... Yevamos 113a
Kesubah, she did not have relations .... Kesubos 56a
Kesubah, they do not have .... Kesubos 101a-101b
Kesubah, transgressors .... Kesubos 72a-72b, 101a-101b; Sotah 25a
Kesubah, violated girl .... Kesubos 39b
Kesubah, violated *Koheness* .... Nedarim 90b-91a
Kesubah, woman injured by piece of wood .... Kesubos 11a-12a, 13a

Trustworthiness —

Kesubah, claiming without *kesubah* .... Kesubos 16b, 88b-89b; Bava Metzia 17b
Kesubah, concern about conspiracy .... Arachin 23a-23b; Bava Basra 173b, 174b
Kesubah, contradicting about *kiddushin* .... Kiddushin 65a
Kesubah, lost .... Bava Metzia 17b-18a; Kesubos 88b-89b
Kesubah, lost, returning .... Bava Metzia 7b
Kesubah, oath .... Gittin 34b-35a
Kesubah of virgin, proof .... Kesubos 15b-16a
Kesubah of virgin, trustworthiness .... Kesubos 28a

Misc. —

Kesubah, advice to divorce and remarry .... Bava Basra 174b
Kesubah, delayed to claim .... Kesubos 104a-104b; Shevuos 48a
Kesubah, designing items .... Kesubos 7a, 81b
Kesubah, from the Torah .... Kesubos 10a, 56a-56b
Kesubah given to males, idolaters .... Chullin 92b
Kesubah, Nakdimen's daughter .... Kesubos 65a, 66b
Kesubah, conspiring witnesses .... Bava Kama 88b-89a; Makos 3a
Kesubah, possibility of *kiddushin* .... Kiddushin 50b
Kesubah, prohibition to stay without .... Kesubos 7a, 57a
Kesubah, quarrel .... Shabbos 130a
Kesubah, reducing sum .... Kesubos 51a-51b, 56b-57a, 54b
Kesubah, to discourage divorce .... Kesubos 11a, 39b, 54a; Yevamos 89a
Kesubas benin dichrin .... *see* **Inheritance of mother's *kesubah*, page 309**
Kesuvim, prohibition on Shabbos .... Shabbos 116b
Keter Torah .... *see* **Crown of Torah, page 134**
Ketev Meriri, demon .... Pesachim 111b
Ketia bar *Shalom* .... Avodah Zarah 10b
Ketina deAbbaye .... *see* **Collecting from heir, partially, page 114**
Ketores .... *see* **Incense, page 305**
Kettles, different, cooking on Shabbos .... Shabbos 41a
Kever .... *see* **Grave, page 256**
Kevod ha... .... *see* **Honor, page 282**

Key

Key, act of acquisition .... Bava Kama 51b-52a
Key, impurity of notches .... Shabbos 81a
Key, ways to carry out .... Eruvin 101a-101b
Keys, not given to agent .... Taanis 2a-2b; Sanhedrin 113a

Keys of pit in fellow's property .... Bava Basra 99a-99b

Keys of Temple, destruction .... Taanis 29a

Keys, Torah and fear of G-d .... Shabbos 31a-31b

Kezayis .... *see* **Olive volume**, page 459

Ki

Ki, four meanings .... Gittin 90a; Rosh Hashanah 3a; Taanis 9a; Shevuos 49b

Ki *kol*, to include .... Pesachim 43b

Ki *Tov*, daytime .... Bava Kama 60b; Pesachim 2a; Taanis 10b

Kibud av va'em .... *see* **Honor of father and mother**, page 283

Kibush yachid .... *see* **Conquest, individual, Syria**, page 122

Kicked

Kicked, crouched cow .... Bava Kama 20a, 24b, 32a

Kicking at his teachers .... Sotah 22a-22b

Kicking at his teachers, episode .... Chagigah 5a

Kid

Kid, roasted whole on Pesach .... Pesachim 53a-53b, 74a; Beitzah 23a; Berachos 19a

Kid, young of goat .... Menachos 107b

Kids accountable for sins of generation .... Shabbos 33b

Kids annul partition .... Shabbos 101a-101b

Kids have become goats .... Berachos 63a

Kida, definition .... Berachos 34b; Megillah 22b; Shevuos 16b

Kiddush beis din .... *see* **Consecration by** *beis din*, **Shabbos**, page 124

Kiddush haChodesh .... *see* **Sanctifying month**, page 588

Kiddush Hashem .... *see* **Self-sacrifice**, page 599

Kiddush kli Mikdash .... *see* **Consecration by utensil**, page 124

Kiddush levanah .... Sanhedrin 41b-42a

Kiddush mincha .... *see* **Consecrating meal offering**, page 124

Kiddush yadayim .... *see* **Sanctifying hands**, page 588

Kiddush

Episodes —

Kiddush by Rebbi after his death .... Kesubos 103a

Kiddush, episodes .... Megillah 27b

Kiddush in the morning, episode .... Pesachim 106a

Kiddush, merit for rain .... Taanis 24a

How —

Kiddush, at place of meal .... Pesachim 100b-101a

Kiddush, blessing on wine and on day .... Berachos 51b-52a; Pesachim 114a; Succah 56a

Kiddush on bread .... Pesachim 106b

Kiddush, popular drink .... Pesachim 107a

Kiddush, quantity to eat .... Pesachim 107a

Kiddush, spreading tablecloth .... Pesachim 100a-100b

Kiddush, text .... Pesachim 117b

Kiddush, wines .... Bava Basra 97a-97b

Time —

Kiddush at night, preference .... Pesachim 105a-105b

Kiddush before Shabbos .... Berachos 27a

Kiddush, interrupting meal .... Pesachim 100a-100b, 102a-102b, 105a

Kiddush, night and day .... Pesachim 106a

Kiddush, replacing by day .... Pesachim 105a-105b, 107a

Kiddush, welcoming Shabbos earlier..Pesachim 105b; Berachos 52a
Misc. —
Kiddush, ate before by mistake..Pesachim 106b-107a
Kiddush in synagogue..Pesachim 100b-101a
Kiddush on Shabbos, woman..Berachos 20b; Shevuos 20b
Kiddush, reward..Shabbos 23b
Kiddush, washing hands..Pesachim 106a-106b

Kiddushin..*see also* **Marriage**, page 390
Cases —
Kiddushin, annulment of conditions at wedding canopy..........Kesubos 72b-74b; Yevamos 110a
Kiddushin, except So-and-so..Gittin 82b
Kiddushin, forced..Bava Basra 48b
Kiddushin, gave more value than she thought..Kiddushin 48b
Kiddushin, give me an item..Kiddushin 8b-9a
Kiddushin, non verbal, discussing this matter..Kiddushin 6a
Kiddushin of father for his son..Kiddushin 45a-45b
Kiddushin, said and gave..Kiddushin 5b, 4b
Kiddushin, silence after receiving..Kiddushin 12b-13a
Kiddushin, wordings..Kiddushin 5b-6a
Forbidden women —
Kiddushin, brother's fiancee in error..Yevamos 95b
Kiddushin, forbidden relations..Kiddushin 67b-68a
Kiddushin, forbidden relations in error..Yevamos 94a-94b
Kiddushin, maidservant..Kiddushin 68b
Kiddushin, negative commandments and positive one..Kiddushin 68a
Kiddushin, *niddah*..Kiddushin 68a; Yevamos 49b
Kiddushin, non-Jewess..Kiddushin 68b
Kiddushin, relations impractical..Kiddushin 51a-52a
Kiddushin, *sotah*..Yevamos 49b
Kiddushin, two sisters..Kiddushin 50b
Kiddushin, when relations will be possible..Kiddushin 62a-62b
Daughter —
Kiddushin by way of forbidden to benefit items..........Temurah 30b; Pesachim 7a; Kiddushin 56b
Kiddushin by way of fruit of Sabbatical year..Kiddushin 52a, 53a
Kiddushin by way of loan..Kiddushin 6b, 19a-19b, 46a, 47a-48b
Kiddushin by way of loan and interest..Kiddushin 6b
Kiddushin by way of loan and *perutah*..Kiddushin 46a
Kiddushin by way of salary of work..Kiddushin 48a-48b, 63a
Kiddushin, by way of several dates..Kiddushin 46a, 47a
Kiddushin by way of stolen item..Kiddushin 52a-52b, 13a
Kiddushin, by way of this article and what is inside..Kiddushin 48b
Kiddushin by way of tithe and consecrated item..Kiddushin 53b
Kiddushin, way of collateral..Kiddushin 8a-8b
Kiddushin, copper dinar..Kiddushin 8a
Kiddushin, dinar according to Beis Shamai..Kiddushin 11a-12a
Kiddushin, doubt if woman was adult..Kiddushin 79a
Kiddushin, estimation of value..Kiddushin 7b-8a, 9a
Kiddushin for young girl, who..Kiddushin 43b-44a
Kiddushin, maneh less a dinar..Kiddushin 8a, 47a

K

Kiddushin, maybe father accepted .... Kiddushin 44b-45a, 45b
Kiddushin of daughter, father's right .... Kiddushin 3b-4a; Kesubos 46b-47a
Kiddushin, one of his daughters .... Kiddushin 64b-65a
Kiddushin, *perutah* .... Kiddushin 12a
Kiddushin, *perutah* in Medea .... Kiddushin 12a
Kiddushin, trustworthiness of father .... Kiddushin 64a; Kesubos 22a
Kiddushin, two by a *perutah* .... Kiddushin 7b
Kiddushin with *chametz* .... Pesachim 21b

Who —
Kiddushin, deaf man and woman .... Yevamos 110b-111a, 112b
Kiddushin, demented one .... Yevamos 112b
Kiddushin given by woman .... Kiddushin 4b, 5b
Kiddushin, minor .... Sanhedrin 52b; Yevamos 112b
Kiddushin, non-Jew .... Sanhedrin 52b
Kiddushin, one's maidservant .... Gittin 39b-40a

Doubts —
Kiddushin, contradiction between them .... Kiddushin 65a
Kiddushin of agent who died, doubt .... Nazir 11b-12a
Kiddushin of agent, who received first .... Kiddushin 78b-79a
Kiddushin, one of five .... Yevamos 118b
Kiddushin, rumor .... Kiddushin 12b; Gittin 88b-89b
Kiddushin, trustworthiness of mother .... Kiddushin 12a-12b

Act of acquisition —
Kiddushin, act of acquisition by barter .... Kiddushin 3a-3b
Kiddushin, act of acquisition by way of wedding canopy .... Kiddushin 5a-5b, 3a
Kiddushin after thirty days .... Kiddushin 59a-60a
Kiddushin, beginning of intimate relations .... Kiddushin 10a-10b
Kiddushin, by half .... Kiddushin 7a-7b
Kiddushin by intimate relations, concern .... Gittin 73b, 81a-81b
Kiddushin, guarantee and Canaanite slave .... Kiddushin 7a
Kiddushin, important man .... Kiddushin 7a
Kiddushin, intimate relations .... Kiddushin 4b, 9b
Kiddushin, money, contract and intimate relations .... Kiddushin 3b, 4b-5a
Kiddushin, money close to her .... Gittin 78b

Misc. —
Kiddushin, according to Sages' will .... Gittin 33a, 73a; Yevamos 90b; Kesubos 3a
Kiddushin, cases of lashes .... Kiddushin 12b; Yevamos 52a
Kiddushin returned, fiancee .... Bava Basra 144b-145a
Kiddushin returned, sister .... Kiddushin 46b
Kiddushin, testimony .... Kiddushin 65a-65b
Kiddushin to shelter wine, episode .... Bava Metzia 101b
Kiddushin to sister .... Kiddushin 46b; Bava Metzia 15b; Arachin 30a; Gittin 45a

Kiddushin for levirate marriage
Kiddushin for levirate marriage .... Yevamos 52a
Kiddushin for levirate marriage, agreement .... Yevamos 19b; Kiddushin 43b-44a
Kiddushin for levirate marriage, second act .... Yevamos 52b-53a
Kiddushin for levirate marriage, useful for what purpose .... Yevamos 29a-29b, 39a, 51b;
.... Nedarim 74a, 74b
Kiddushin for levirate marriage, young girl .... Kiddushin 43b-44a

Kidnapping

Kidnapping .... Sanhedrin 85b-86a

Kidnapping at wedding canopy, Alexandria .... Bava Metzia 104a

Kidney

Kidney, absorbing forbidden food .... Chullin 97a

Kidney, cases of *treifah* .... Chullin 42b, 55a-55b

Kidney, only one, from birth .... Bechoros 39a

Kidneys, counsel .... Berachos 61a; Shabbos 33b; Chullin 11a

Kidor, episode .... Yoma 83b

***Kikar* of Temple,** double .... Bechoros 5a

Kikar .... see **Loaf of bread, quantity,** page 375

Kikayon .... Shabbos 21a

Kilaei beheimah .... see **Mixed species of animals,** page 417

Kilayim .... see **Mixed species,** page 417

Killed

Killing .... see also **Murderer,** page 432

Killed by government .... see **Men put to death by government,** page 387

Killed, let yourself be killed but do not transgress .... Pesachim 25a-25b; Yoma 82a-82b;

.... Sanhedrin 74a-74b

Killed man came on his two legs .... Bava Kama 74b

Killing animal, to exempt from covering its blood .... Chullin 27b, 85b-86a

Killing harmful creatures on Shabbos .... Shabbos 121b

Killing louse in front of friend .... Shabbos 12a; Chagigah 5a

Killing man in death throes .... Sanhedrin 78a

Killing on Shabbos .... Shabbos 107b

Killing one's evil urge .... Sanhedrin 43b

Killing oneself for Torah .... Shabbos 83b; Gittin 57b; Berachos 63b

Killing oneself to live .... Tamid 32a

Kilus, significance .... Moed Katan 27b

Kim leh .... see **Penalty (Severest),** page 479

Kimchis, modesty .... Yoma 47a

Kind one towards the other, Sages .... Taanis 8a; Megillah 32a

Kindling

Kindling fire on Yom Tov .... Beitzah 21b, 33b; Pesachim 5b

Kindling on Shabbos, damage .... Shabbos 106a; Bava Kama 34b-35a

Kindling on Shabbos, to differentiate it from other works .... Shabbos 70a

Kindling Shabbos lamp .... see **Lamp for Shabbos,** page 352

Kindness

Kindness .... see also **Charity,** page 97

Kindness, *aggadah* .... Succah 49b; Sotah 14a; Avodah Zarah 17b

Kindness, birth pangs of Messiah .... Sanhedrin 98b

Kindness, Divine Attribute .... Rosh Hashanah 17b

Kindness, long life .... Yevamos 105a; Rosh Hashanah 18a

Kindness of idolaters, sin .... Bava Basra 10b

Kindness of Israel's scattering, exile .... Pesachim 87b

Kindness, Rav Huna .... Taanis 20b

Kindness, reward .... Bava Kama 17a

Kindness, Torah .... Succah 49b

K

Kindness and Torah

Kindness and Torah, Eli's sons .... Yevamos 105a; Rosh Hashanah 18a
Kindness and Torah, order .... Sotah 44a
Kindness and Torah, protection from evil urge .... Avodah Zarah 5b
Kindness and Torah, Joseph .... Bava Kama 17a

Kinei ofos .... *see* **Nests**, page 441

King .... *see also* **Prince**, page 504

Aggadah —

King, G-d's name .... Shevuos 35b
King, good, Divine pity .... Berachos 55a
King like Haman, repentance .... Sanhedrin 97b
King, parables .... Zevachim 41b
King, parables about meal .... Shabbos 153a; Sanhedrin 108a
King, slave to his subjects .... Horayos 10a
King who sinned, happy is his generation .... Horayos 10b
King's fall before Messiah .... Sanhedrin 38a

Commandments —

King and Temple, order .... Sanhedrin 20b
King, haircut .... Sanhedrin 22b; Taanis 17a
King, Torah scroll .... Sanhedrin 21b, 22a
Kings, blessing .... Berachos 58a

Episodes —

King, new, Pharaoh .... Sotah 11a
King, Rav Sheishes and Sadducee .... Berachos 58a
King, request from Shmuel .... Sanhedrin 20b
Kings of nations, Messiah .... Taanis 14b-15a
Kings, reckoning years of reign .... Rosh Hashanah 2a-2b, 8a; Avodah Zarah 9b-10a
Kings who ruled whole world .... Megillah 11a-11b

Laws —

King .... *see also* **Men put to death by government**, page 387
King, burning his belongings after his death .... Avodah Zarah 11a-11b
King, horses .... Sanhedrin 21b
King inciter, not to listen to him .... Sanhedrin 49a
King, judge .... Sanhedrin 18b
King, levirate marriage .... Sanhedrin 19b
King, looking at .... Chagigah 16a
King, silver and gold .... Sanhedrin 21b
King who died .... Moed Katan 22b-23a
King, women .... Sanhedrin 21a

Rights —

King, booty .... Sanhedrin 20b-21a
King breaching fence .... Bava Kama 60b; Yevamos 76b; Bava Basra 100b; Sanhedrin 20b
King, fear .... Zevachim 102a; Menachos 98a
King, his rights .... Sanhedrin 20b
King, honor .... Sanhedrin 19b, 22a
King, precedence at judgment .... Rosh Hashanah 8b, 16a; Avodah Zarah 2b
King who waived his honor .... Kiddushin 32b

Sacrifices —

King, animals for sacrifice .... Horayos 9a-9b; Yevamos 9a

King, exemptions from sacrifice..........................Yevamos 8b-9a; Horayos 8a, 11a
King, sinned and transgressed...Horayos 9b-10a
King, sinned before his appointment...............Horayos 10a; Kesubos 45a
Who —
King, leprosy..Horayos 10a
King, slave disqualified to become king...........................Bava Kama 88a
King son of king, Rome..Avodah Zarah 10a
King, throne hereditary..........................Kesubos 103b; Horayos 11b
King, who is chosen...Kiddushin 82a
Misc. —
King, Divine punishments...Sotah 9a
King, I am not..Nedarim 24a
Kings, our Sages..Gittin 62a
Kings of Israel
Kings of Israel, days reduced...Pesachim 87b
Kings of Israel, discourses of commentaries.........Sanhedrin 102a-102b
Kings of Israel, field of lazy man................................Sanhedrin 103a
Kings of Israel, wickedness...Sanhedrin 103b
Kings of Israel, wisdom...Sanhedrin 103b
Kings of Israel, World to Come.............................Sanhedrin 104b-105a
King Agrippas
King Agrippas, bride...Kesubos 17a
King Agrippas, flattery..Sotah 41b
King Amaziah, Josiah's uncle...Megillah 10b
King Amon..Sanhedrin 103a, 103b
King Asa..Sotah 10a
King Izgadar...Zevachim 19a
King Jotham...Succah 45b
Kingdom
Kingdom does not encroach upon another..........Yoma 38b; Taanis 5b; Berachos 48b; Shabbos 30a;
....Moed Katan 28a
Kingdom, economic reckonings...Shabbos 11a
Kingdom, lowly..Gittin 80a
Kingdom of Greece, years................................Avodah Zarah 9a, 10a
Kingdom on earth like that of Heaven, Rav Sheishes........Berachos 58a
Kingdom...*see also* **Government**, page 255
Kingship
Kingship, text of blessing..Berachos 40b, 49a
Kingship, thirty elements to achieve..Avos 6:5
Kinim, *hegeh, hee,* significance..Eruvin 21a
Kinite, Kenizite and Kadmonite...................................Bava Basra 56a
Kinneres, names and praises..Megillah 6a
Kintrin, shekel of Prophets...Bechoros 50a
Kinuy..*see* **Warning to** *sotah*, page 731
Kinyan agav
Kinyan agav, act of acquisition by bill.........................Bava Basra 77b
Kinyan agav, act of acquisition of coins.....................Bava Basra 77b
Kinyan agav, carrying on Shabbos..Shabbos 62b
Kinyan agav, cases of acquisition.......................................Kiddushin 27a

Kinyan agav, place of objects...Kiddushin 26a-27a
Kinyan agav, slave...Bava Kama 12a
Kinyan agav, source...Kiddushin 26a-27a
Kinyan peiros..*see* **Property through right of earnings**, page 506
Kinyan...*see* **Act of acquisition**, page 338
Kipah
Kipah...*see* **Covering head**, page 131
Kipah, Kohen Gadol..Chullin 138a
Kipah, significance...Chullin 120a
Kirah
Kirah..*see* **Stove-top**, page 658
Kirah, expression of sale.......................................Rosh Hashanah 26a; Sotah 13a; Chullin 92a
Kiri, Herod's birds..Chullin 139b
Kirias Arba..Eruvin 53a; Sotah 13a
Kisei Hakavod.....................................Chagigah 12b-13a; Pesachim 54a; Nedarim 39b
Kisei Hakavod...*see* **Throne of Glory**, page 690
Kiss
Kiss, death..Berachos 8a
Kiss, Miriam's death...Moed Katan 28a; Bava Basra 17a
Kiss on hand..Berachos 8b
Kisses of enemy, Balaam's blessing...Sanhedrin 105b
Kissing
Kissing earth of *Eretz Yisrael*...Kesubos 112a-112b
Kissing rocks of Akko...Kesubos 112a
Kisuy dam...*see* **Covering blood**, page 131
Kisuy rosh...*see* **Covering head**, page 131
Kitz mizbeach...*see* **Sacrifices** *kitz mizbeach*, **which ones**, page 580
Kiymo velo kiymo.....................................*see* **Annulled and did not annul**, page 26
Kiyor in Temple.......................................Zevachim 21b-22a, 58b-59a; Yoma 37a
Kiyum neder..*see* **Consent to vow**, page 125
Kiyum shtar..*see* **Attestation of legal document**, page 35
Klaf...*see* **Parchment**, page 472
Klal uprat..*see* **General and specific**, page 247
Klalah...*see* **Curse**, page 135
Klalah nimretzes, initials...Shabbos 105a
Klalos, *kol vechutz*.......................................*see* **Negative commandment including several**, page 440
Klei Mikdash...*see* **Temple utensils**, page 679
Kli..*see* **Container**, page 125, *see also;* **Utensil**, page 718
Kli golah, meaning...Nedarim 40b-41a
Kli kibul..*see* **Container**, page 125
Kli mateches...*see* **Iron utensil**, page 317
Kli mechubar..*see* **Utensil connected to ground**, page 719
Kli midras..*see* **Items suitable, couch and other uses, impurity**, page 319
Kli shares..*see* **Consecrated utensil**, page 122
Kli shem'lachto l'issur.....................................*see* **Utensil whose use is forbidden**, page 719
Klipah..*see* **Peel**, page 478
Klutah kemi shehunchah.....................................*see* **Item thrown, considered like put down**, page 319
Knass..*see* **Penalty**, page 479
Knei lecha chaver..*see* **Acquire a friend**, page 7

K

Kneading
Kneading, adding liquid on Shabbos..Shabbos 140a
Kneading, bran...Shabbos 155b-156a
Kneading dough, *challah* requirement..Challah 3:1
Kneading, flax in water...Zevachim 94b
Kneading *matzah*..Pesachim 37a
Kneading on Shabbos, possible to make dough.....................Shabbos 18a, 155b-156a

Knee
Knee bent, World to Come..Sanhedrin 88b
Knee, *chalitzah*..Yevamos 103a; Arachin 19b
Knee, *treifah*..Chullin 42b, 57a-57b, 76a

Knesses Hagdolah
Knesses Hagdolah, blessings...Yoma 69b; Berachos 33a
Knesses Hagdolah, Torah tradition...Avos 1:1

Knesses Yisrael...................................*see* **Congregation of Israel, your mother**, page 121

Knew and accepted, marriage..Kesubos 70b

Knife
Knife, *kashering*..Pesachim 30b; Chullin 8b
Knife, *kashering* by cutting turnip...Chullin 111b-112a
Knife, planting..Avodah Zarah 76b
Knife, rinsing..Chullin 111b
Knife, sharp substance..Avodah Zarah 39a
"Knife, sharpened, to cut verses".................Bava Basra 111b; Menachos 74a; Arachin 26a
Knife, consecrates sacrifice without intention.................................Menachos 78b
Knife for circumcision, Shabbos...Shabbos 131b-132a
Knife of Angel of death, episode...Kesubos 77b
Knife on Yom Tov...Beitzah 28a-28b
Knife planted in wall or reeds, Shabbos..Shabbos 50b
Knife, purity of Pesach lamb...Pesachim 70a-70b; Shekalim 8:3
Knife, sacrifices...Zevachim 97b
Knife, sacrificial, lifting and cleaning...Zevachim 25a
Knife, sharp, ruling...Yevamos 122a; Chullin 77a

Knife for slaughtering
Knife for slaughtering, discharging..Chullin 111b
Knife for slaughtering, absorbed forbidden substance.......................Chullin 8a-8b
Knife for slaughtering, connected to earth.......................................Chullin 15b-16b
Knife for slaughtering, dent..Chullin 17a-18a
Knife for slaughtering, doubtful nick..Chullin 10a-10b, 43b
Knife for slaughtering, examining...Chullin 10b, 17b-18a
Knife for slaughtering, heating up..Chullin 8a, 17b
Knife for slaughtering, idolatrous..Chullin 8a-8b
Knife for slaughtering on Yom Tov...Beitzah 28b
Knife for slaughtering, size...Chullin 31a
Knife for slaughtering, teacher...Eruvin 62b-63a
Knife for slaughtering, under neck..Chullin 16b

Knock
Knock your head against the wall...Chullin 39b
Knocked on father's grave..Bava Basra 58a
Knocking one's finger...Chullin 7b

Knot

Knot in *tefillin* .... Eruvin 97a; Menachos 35b
Knot of *tefillin*, Moses .... Berachos 7a; Menachos 35b

Knot on Shabbos

Knot on Shabbos, bucket .... Pesachim 11a
Knot on Shabbos, cases .... Shabbos 111b-113a; Eruvin 97a, 102b-103a; Pesachim 11a; Succah 33b
Knot on Shabbos, rope of weaver .... Shabbos 113a
Knot on Shabbos, Temple .... Shabbos 74b; Eruvin 102b-103a, 105a

Know

Know .... *see also* **I do not know**, page 291
Know before whom you stand .... Berachos 28b
Know from where you came, meditation .... Avos 3:1
Know that G-d will bring you to judgment .... Shabbos 63b
Know what to answer .... Avos 2:14
Known by cup, purse and anger .... Eruvin 65b
Known that he did not sin .... Krisos 23b-24b; Temurah 34a
Known, true words .... Sotah 9b
Knows how to purify reptile .... Eruvin 13b

Knowledge

Knowledge .... *see also* **Wisdom**, page 752
Knowledge from one teacher .... Avodah Zarah 19a-19b
Knowledge in Torah, everybody needs him .... Bava Basra 145b; Berachos 64a; Horayos 14a
Knowledge, learning Mishnayos .... Sanhedrin 42a
Knowledge, no intelligence in his brain .... Yevamos 9a; Menachos 80b
Knowledge, no pity for one deprived of knowledge .... Sanhedrin 92a
Knowledge of being impure, impurity preceding sacrifice .... Krisos 7b
Knowledge of G-d, future .... Sanhedrin 90b
Knowledge, precise, in one's learning .... Niddah 14b
Knowledge, written between two Divine Names .... Berachos 33a

Knowledge and in-depth study

Knowledge and in-depth study, order .... Shabbos 63a; Succah 28b-29a; Avodah Zarah 19a
Knowledge and in-depth study, preference .... Horayos 14a
Knowledge and in-depth study, source .... Bechoros 52b

Knowledgeable

Knowledgeable in Tanach, future reward .... Bava Metzia 33b
Knowledgeable Sage, deserves to teach .... Makos 10a; Horayos 13b
Knowledgeable Sage, divorce certificates and *kiddushin* .... Kiddushin 6a, 13a-13b
Koach beis din .... *see* **Authority of *beis din***, page 36
Koach chachamim .... *see* **Authority of Sages**, page 36
Koach gavra .... *see* **Human intervention**, page 287
Kocho .... *see* **Strength, indirect**, page 659
Kodesh Kodashim .... *see* **Holy of Holies**, page 281
Kodesh Lashem .... *see* **Holy to G-d, forehead-plate**, page 281
Kodshei Kodashim .... *see* **Sacrifices, highest degree of holiness**, page 582
Kodshim Kalim .... *see* **Sacrifices of moderate holiness, place**, page 580
Kodshim lebeis hapsul .... *see* **Sacrifices, causing them to become invalid**, page 580
Kofer .... *see* **Penalty for atonement**, page 480

Koheles

Koheles, impurity to hands .... Megillah 7a; Yadayim 3:5; Eduyos 5:3

Koheles, Sages wanted to conceal..Shabbos 30b
Kohen, *mum* ....*see* **Blemish of a** *Kohen*, page 62
Kohen Tzedek, one of the four craftsmen..Succah 52b
Kohen..*see also* **Non-***Kohen*, page 449

Disqualified —
Kohanim, examining...Middos 5:4
Kohen, age for service...Chullin 24b
Kohen deprived of priesthood...*see* **Chalal**, page 92
Kohen, doubtful lineage...Yevamos 100b
Kohen, drinking wine in present times..Taanis 17a-17b; Sanhedrin 22b
Kohen, idolater...Menachos 109a-109b
Kohen, injured, wife's *terumah*...Yevamos 56b-57a, 75a
Kohen, missing garments and washing..Zevachim 112b; Sanhedrin 83b
Kohen, uncircumcised and rebellious.....Sanhedrin 83b-84a; Yoma 71b; Taanis 17b; Moed Katan 5a;
....Zevachim 18b, 22b
Kohen uncircumcised, *onein* and sitting..................................Sanhedrin 83b-84a; Zevachim 23b
Kohen unwashed, death..Sanhedrin 83b
Kohen unwashed, which services..Zevachim 112b
Kohen watches in Temple, wine...Taanis 17a-17b
Kohen who does not believe in Temple service...Menachos 18b; Bechoros 30b; Chullin 132b-133a
Kohen who served and then was then found disqualified.........Kiddushin 66b; Pesachim 72b;
....Makos 11b-12a

Episodes —
Kohanim, Abbaye..Chullin 133a
Kohen helps *Kohen*..Chullin 49a
Kohen, murder in Temple..Yoma 23a-23b
Kohen, Shem and Abraham..Nedarim 32b
Kohen son of *Kohen* will sprinkle blood..Berachos 28a
Kohen thief, episode...Kiddushin 53a

Gifts —
Kohen being butcher, shoulder, cheek, and stomach..Chullin 132b
Kohen, blemish of firstborn...Bechoros 35a-36b
Kohen, exempt from redemption..Bechoros 3b-4b, 13a
Kohen habitually receiving priestly gifts..Chullin 133a
Kohen helping during harvest, *terumah* outside *Eretz Yisrael*....................Bechoros 27a
Kohen helping during harvest to receive *terumah*.................................Bechoros 26b-27a
Kohen helps, firstborn...Temurah 8b-9a
Kohen, precedence.......................Gittin 59b; Megillah 28a; Moed Katan 28b; Nedarim 62a; Horayos 12b, 13a
Kohen, trustworthiness of firstborn..Bechoros 35b-36b

Laws —
Kohanim and *Leviim*, self-understood..Arachin 3b
Kohanim, looking at...Chagigah 16a
Kohanim, sacrifice for mistake of *beis din*...Yoma 50a
Kohanim, suspected about Sabbatical year...Sanhedrin 26a
Kohen, impure, *terumah* from outside *Eretz Yisrael*...................Niddah 32a; Bechoros 27a-27b
Kohen, lost item in cemetery...............................Bava Metzia 30a-30b; Berachos 19b; Sanhedrin 18b
Kohen, proofs about his being *Kohen*.............................Kiddushin 69b; Kesubos 24b-26a, 28b
Kohen, seeing leprous mark..................................Negaim 2:3, 3:1; Niddah 50a; Moed Katan 8a
Kohen, Torah reading...Gittin 59a-60a

Kohen, trustworthiness for priesthood .... Kesubos 24a, 24b-26a, 28b; Kiddushin 69b

Marriage —
Kohanim to *Kohanos*, episode .... Berachos 44a
Kohen, forcing to divorce .... Yevamos 88b
Kohen, injured, female convert .... Yevamos 57a, 76a
Kohen, prohibitions concerning marriage .... Kiddushin 78a; Makos 13a
Kohen who married divorced woman .... Bechoros 45b-46a; Gittin 35b-36a

Temple service —
Kohanim, Haggai's examination .... Pesachim 16b-17a
Kohanim eat, and owners receive atonement .... Pesachim 59b
Kohanim, G-d's agents .... Nedarim 35b-36a; Kiddushin 23b; Yoma 19a-19b
Kohanim, negligent, daily offering .... Menachos 50a
Kohanim on watch, gifts .... Arachin 28a-28b
Kohanim, share in sacrifices .... Zevachim 98b-99a, 102a-102b
Kohanim, sleeping in Temple .... Tamid 26b
Kohanim's pants, shape .... Niddah 13b
Kohen, his meal offering for sinner .... Menachos 73b-74a; Yevamos 100a; Sotah 23a-23b
Kohen, his sacrifices .... Bava Kama 109b-110a; Menachos 74a
Kohen who burns Red Heifer .... Yoma 42b
Kohen, whole meal offering .... Menachos 51b, 74a

Kohen, drunk
Kohen, drunk, definition of drinking .... Krisos 13b
Kohen, drunk, desecrates service .... Zevachim 17b-18a
Kohen, drunk, other causes of drunkenness .... Nazir 4a; Yoma 76a-76b; Sanhedrin 70b-71a;
.... Shevuos 23a; Bechoros 45b; Krisos 13b

Kohen, long-haired
Kohen, long-haired, death .... Sanhedrin 83b
Kohen, long-haired, desecration of service .... Sanhedrin 22b
Kohen, long-haired, in present times .... Taanis 17a-17b
Kohen, long-haired, size .... Taanis 17a

Kohen performing service without priestly garments
Kohen performing service without priestly garments, death .. Sanhedrin 83b; Zevachim 17b
Kohen performing service without priestly garments, desecration .... Zevachim 17b-18a
Kohen performing service without priestly garments, which services ...... Zevachim 112b

Misc. —
Kohanim are zealous .... Shabbos 20a, 114b; Eruvin 103a; Pesachim 59b, 65a; Beitzah 18a;
.... Bava Basra 90a; Zevachim 35a; Chullin 123b
Kohanim, atonement on Yom Kippur .... Yoma 50b, 51b, 61a; Shevuos 13b-14a; Menachos 92a
Kohanim, called *Leviim* .... Yevamos 86b; Chullin 24b; Bechoros 4a-4b; Tamid 27a
Kohanim, judges .... Bechoros 35b
Kohanim, number of tribes .... Horayos 6b
Kohanim, quarrelling .... Kiddushin 70b
Kohanim .... *see also* **Impurity of _Kohen_**, page 304
Kohanim, separated from rest of people .... Pesachim 104a
Kohen anointed with *terumah* oil, non-priest .... Krisos 7a
Kohen becoming impure through contact with corpse .... Bechoros 46a

Kohen Gadol
Laws —
Kohen Gadol, dismissed .... Megillah 9b; Yoma 73a; Horayos 12b

K

Kohen Gadol, funeral and comforting .... Sanhedrin 19a
Kohen Gadol, laws .... Sanhedrin 18a-18b
Kohen Gadol married to non-virgin, *chalalah* .... Yevamos 60a
Kohen Gadol, murderer returning home .... Sanhedrin 18a-18b; Makos 11a, 11b; Horayos 12b
Kohen Gadol, sinned and was dismissed .... Horayos 9b-10a
Kohen Gadol, sinned before appointment .... Horayos 10a; Kesubos 45a
Kohen Gadol takes first .... Yoma 17b-18a
Kohen Gadol, tearing garment for dead .... Horayos 12b

Temple service —
Kohen Gadol, animals for sacrifice .... Horayos 9a-9b
Kohen Gadol, atonement by communal sacrifice .... Horayos 7a-7b
Kohen Gadol, consecration .... Yoma 5a, 12a-12b
Kohen Gadol, exempt from sacrifice .... Horayos 6b-7a, 11a
Kohen Gadol, garments .... Yoma 12b, 35a-35b
Kohen Gadol, guilt offering for doubtful culpability .... Horayos 8a, 7a
Kohen Gadol, *onein* ... Yoma 13b-14a; Moed Katan 14b; Bava Kama 110a; Horayos 12b; Zevachim 16b-17a, 99a
Kohen Gadol, service .... Yoma 17b; Tamid 7:1, 7:3; Menachos 94a
Kohen Gadol, walking in Temple .... Yoma 51b-52a, 53a

Yom Kippur —
Kohen Gadol .... *see also* **Bull for *Kohen Gadol*, page 79**
Kohen Gadol anointed for war .... Yoma 72b-73a; Horayos 12a-12b
Kohen Gadol anointed for war, "who is the man" .... Sotah 42a-42b
Kohen Gadol, changes on Yom Kippur .... Yoma 45a
Kohen Gadol, died on Yom Kippur .... Yoma 49b-50a
Kohen Gadol, oath .... Yoma 19a-19b
Kohen Gadol on Yom Kippur, prayer .... Yoma 53b; Taanis 24b
Kohen Gadol on Yom Kippur, weakness .... Zevachim 20a
Kohen Gadol, only he can serve on Yom Kippur .... Yoma 32b, 73a; Horayos 12b; Chullin 29b
Kohen Gadol, second, Yom Kippur .... Yoma 13a-13b
Kohen Gadol, separation from wife .... Yoma 2a-4a, 6a, 8b
Kohen Gadol, sprinklings on him .... Yoma 4a, 8a-8b, 14a-14b; Pesachim 78a; Parah 3:1
Kohen Gadol, wife on Yom Kippur .... Yoma 13a-13b
Kohen Gadol, Yom Kippur eve .... Yoma 18a-18b
Kohen Gadol, Yom Kippur night .... Yoma 18a, 19b

Misc. —
Kohen Gadol disqualifies someone from *terumah*, how .... Yevamos 70a
Kohen Gadol, haircut .... Sanhedrin 22b; Taanis 17a
Kohen Gadol, wealth and virtues .... Yoma 18a
Kohen Gadol, who is chosen .... Kiddushin 82a

Kohanim Gedolim
Kohanim Gedolim, differences .... Megillah 9b; Horayos 12a-12b
Kohanim Gedolim, gloves .... Krisos 28b
Kohanim Gedolim, ignoramus .... Yoma 18a
Kohanim Gedolim, Kimchis' modesty .... Yoma 47a
Kohanim Gedolim, Pinchas .... Zevachim 101b
Kohanim Gedolim, Sadducee .... Yoma 19b
Kohanim Gedolim, screams .... Pesachim 57a; Krisos 28a-28b
Kohanim Gedolim, second Temple .... Yoma 9a
Kohanim Gedolim who burned Red Heifers .... Parah 3:5

K

Kohanim Gedolim, Yehoshua ben Gamla .... Yevamos 61a; Yoma 18a

Koheness
  Marriage —
    Koheness as collateral (captive) .... Kesubos 26b-27a; Avodah Zarah 23a; Eduyos 8:2
    Koheness born from forbidden marriage .... *see* **Chalalah**, page 92
    Koheness, marriage .... Pesachim 49a
    Koheness, conspiring witnesses .... Sanhedrin 90a
    Koheness, rape victim .... Yevamos 35a, 56b
    Koheness raped, *kesubah* .... Nedarim 90b-91a
    Koheness, to convert .... Yevamos 85a; Kiddushin 73a
    Koheness to disqualified man, *terumah* .... Yevamos 56b-57a, 75a, 81a
    Koheness to man disqualified for marriage .... Kiddushin 73a, 76a; Yevamos 84b-85a
    Koheness who had forbidden relations, burning .... Sanhedrin 51b, 66b; Terumos 7:2
    Koheness who had forbidden relations, disgrace to his father .... Sanhedrin 52a
  Misc. —
    Koheness, differences from *Kohen* .... Sotah 23b
    Koheness, dividing *terumah* .... Yevamos 86a, 99b-100a
    Koheness, exemption from redeeming son .... Bechoros 47a
    Koheness, husband possibly dead .... Gittin 28a-28b
    Koheness like innkeeper .... Yevamos 122a
    Koheness, meal offering .... Sotah 23a-23b; Chullin 131b-132a
    Koheness, conspiring witnesses .... Sanhedrin 90a; Makos 2a
    Koheness, Rav Kahana .... Chullin 132a
    Koheness, Rav Pappa .... Chullin 132a
    Koheness, shoulder, cheek, and stomach .... Chullin 131b-132a
Koheness, *almanah* .... *see* **Widow eating** *terumah*, page 745
Koheness, *shevuyah* .... *see* **Captive woman**, page 87
Kohl for eyes .... Shabbos 151b
Kol .... *see* **Voice**, page 725
Kol
  Kol .... *see also* **Rumor**, page 575
  Kol comes to add laws, deduction .... Niddah 33a
  Kol, deduction to include .... Pesachim 43b; Bava Kama 54b, 63a; Niddah 33a
  Kol, exhaustive list .... Eruvin 27a
Kol de'avid .... *see* **Everything G-d does is for the best, Rabbi Akiva**, page 204
Kol de'parish .... *see* **Item taken out of place of doubt, majority**, page 320
Kol ha'omed... .... *see* **About to**, page 3
Kol haposel bemumo posel .... *see* **Criticizing, one's own flaw**, page 133
Kol kavua .... *see* **Item situated in place of doubt, majority**, page 319
Kol mah sheomer baal habayis .... *see* **Guest must obey his host**, page 261
Kol mezonosav meRosh Hashanah .... *see* **Livelihood, fixed on** *Rosh Hashanah*, page 374
Kol Nidrei .... Nedarim 23a-23b
Kol shehu .... *see* **Negligible quantity**, page 440
Kol Yisrael .... *see* **Israel**, page 318
Kolel, *shevuah* .... *see* **Oath, double, adding detail**, page 452
Konam, *konamos* .... *see* **Vow**, page 725
Koneis mashkeh .... *see* **Hole, liquid can run from it**, page 280
Korah
  Korah, his quarrel .... Sanhedrin 109b-110a

Korah, his wife..Sanhedrin 109b-110a
Korah, luminaries complained..............................Nedarim 39b; Sanhedrin 110a
Korah, Moses is true..................................Bava Basra 74a; Sanhedrin 110a
Korah, Moses suspected..Sanhedrin 110a
Korah, punishment.............Nedarim 39b; Bava Basra 74a; Sanhedrin 52a, 109b-110a
Korah, Samuel...Megillah 14a
Korah, treasures of Egypt...Pesachim 119a
Korah, voices of his clan...Sanhedrin 110a-110b
Korah, wealth.....................................Sanhedrin 110a; Pesachim 119a
Korban tzibur...............................*see* **Communal sacrifice**, page 118
Korban, korbanos...................................*see* **Sacrifice**, page 578
Kore'a...*see* **Tearing**, page 674
Korech, *matzah* and bitter herbs...............................Pesachim 115a
Koreh....................................*see* **Beam for closed alley**, page 45
Koresh..*see* **Cyrus**, page 139
Kortov, amount...Bava Basra 90a
Kos berachah.................................*see* **Cup of blessing**, page 135
Kosem................................*see* **Magician, episodes**, page 383
Kosem, king..Chagigah 14a
Koseves hagasah.................................*see* **Date, volume**, page 143
Kosher
   Kosher and improper, confusion between them.....................Gittin 85a
   Kosher animal..................................*see* **Treifah**, page 702
   Kosher for this, invalid for that.............................Chullin 19b-24a
Koshi samuch leleidah................*see* **Blood flowing before birth**, page 68
Kovesh schar sachir................*see* **Retaining worker's salary**, page 563
Kovim lemaaser................*see* **Requirement to give tithes**, page 561
Koy, kvi.......................................*see* **Hybrid animal**, page 290
Kri ksiv...............................Megillah 25b; Nedarim 37b-38a
Kri uchtiv...............................*see* **Read and written**, page 547
Krias hagever, significance.....................................Yoma 20b
Krias HaTorah..............................*see* **Torah reading**, page 697
Kriyah, explanation...............Berachos 34b; Megillah 22b; Shevuos 16b
Kriyah...............................*see* **Tearing garment**, page 675
Kriyas Yam Suf.....................*see* **Splitting of Red Sea**, page 651
Krum, bird...Berachos 6b
Krus shafchah................................*see* **Castrated man**, page 89
Kruvim meurim............*see* **Cherubs embraced, Temple destruction**, page 102
Kruz, announcement in Temple...................................Yoma 20b
Kshot atzmecha................................*see* **Correct yourself**, page 129
Kula..*see* **Leniencies**, page 363
Kulei hai veulay...........*see* **"All these troubles for an uncertainty,"** page 19
Kumaz, explanation...Shabbos 64a
Kupas sheratzim............*see* **Can of worms, appointment of leader**, page 86
Kushi, meaning a praise...Moed Katan 16b
Kushiyos......................................*see* **Question**, page 514
Kushta city, episode...Sanhedrin 97a
Kusim...*see* **Cuthean**, page 139
Kutach......................................*see* **Milk, pickled**, page 411

K

K

L

Laav .... *see* **Negative commandment**, page 440

Lachash .... *see* **Whisper**, page 742

La'chem, borrowed or shared succah .... Succah 27b

Lachmei todah .... *see* **Loaves of thanksgiving**, page 376

Laban, Balaam's father .... Sanhedrin 105b

Ladder

　Ladder, between courtyards .... Eruvin 59b-60a, 77b-78b

　Ladder, *chazakah* .... Bava Basra 58b-59a

　Ladder of Jacob .... Chullin 91b

　Ladder on Yom Tov .... Beitzah 9a-9b

　Ladder, roof close to public domain .... Eruvin 84b

　Ladder, unstable .... Bava Kama 15b

Lahat, sorcery .... Sanhedrin 67b

Laimor

　Laimor, negative commandment .... Pesachim 42a

　Laimor, so that he tells Israel .... Yoma 4b

Lamb

　Lamb, sheep species .... Menachos 107b

　Lambs, unblemished, daily offering .... Menachos 49b-50a; Arachin 13a-13b

***Lamed* at beginning of word,** *heh* at end .... Yevamos 13b

Lamed vav tzadikim .... *see* **Thirty six righteous**, page 687

Lamentations

　Lamentations, burning scroll .... Moed Katan 26a

　Lamentations, commentaries .... Sanhedrin 104a-104b

Lamp

　Commandments —

　　Lamp for Yom Kippur .... Pesachim 53b-54a

　　Lamp for searching for *chametz* .... Pesachim 7b-8a

　　Lamp, middle, *menorah* .... Menachos 98b

　　Lamp of *menorah*, extinguished before Temple destruction .... Yoma 39b

　　Lamp of *menorah*, extinguished, disqualified .... Menachos 88b

　　Lamp for *Chanukah*

　　　Lamp for *Chanukah*, benefit .... Shabbos 21a-22b

　　　Lamp for *Chanukah*, lighting .... Shabbos 21a-23b; Succah 46a

Lamp for *Chanukah*, place .... Bava Kama 30a, 62b; Shabbos 21b-22a

Prohibitions —
Lamp, modesty during intimate relations .... Pesachim 112b
Lamp on palm tree, Yom Tov .... Shabbos 45a
Lamp, waste .... Shabbos 67b

Shabbos prohibitions —
Lamp behind door .... Shabbos 120b
Lamp, oil dripping .... Shabbos 29b; Pesachim 11a
Lamp, Shabbos prohibitions .... Shabbos 120b
Lamp, wick in another container .... Shabbos 29b

Shabbos —
Lamp, cases when reading is permitted .... Shabbos 12b-13a
Lamp, decree because of possibility of tilting .... Shabbos 12a, 13b
Lamp for *Havdala* .... Pesachim 53b
Lamp for *Havdala*, torch .... Pesachim 8a, 103b
Lamp, high, possibility of tilting .... Shabbos 12b, 149a
Lamp, moving on Shabbos .... Shabbos 45b-46a; Beitzah 22a
Lamp, moving table to make it fall on Shabbos .... Shabbos 120b
Lamp, *muktzeh* because repulsive .... Shabbos 46a-46b
Lamp, possibility of tilting on Shabbos, cases .... Shabbos 12b-13a, 149a

Lamp for Shabbos
Lamp for Shabbos, commandment .... Shabbos 25b
Lamp for Shabbos, oils .... Shabbos 20b-21a, 26a
Lamp for Shabbos or *Chanukah* .... Shabbos 23b
Lamp for Shabbos, read and tilted it .... Shabbos 12b
Lamp for Shabbos, reward .... Shabbos 23b
Lamp for Shabbos, *terumah* oil .... Shabbos 23b-24a
Lamp for Shabbos, time for kindling .... Shabbos 23b, 35b
Lamp for Shabbos, flammable oil .... Shabbos 25b-26a
Lamp for Shabbos, wick flickering .... Shabbos 28b-29a
Lamp for Shabbos, wicks .... Shabbos 20b-21a

Misc. —
Lamp before torch, righteous .... Pesachim 8a
Lamp for one, lamp for a hundred .... Shabbos 122a
Lamp in mother's womb .... Niddah 30b
Lamp, western, of *menorah* .... Shabbos 22b; Menachos 86b; Tamid 6:1
Lamp of storekeeper, flax .... Bava Kama 62b
Lamp of Israel, you saw right! .... Menachos 88b
Lamp, suggestions .... Shabbos 67b
Lamps at *Simchas Beis Hashoevah* .... Succah 52b

Land
Monetary matters —
Land, custodians not liable .... Bava Metzia 57b; Shevuos 43a
Land, fraud .... Bava Metzia 57a-57b; Temurah 27b
Land, included in sale .... Bava Basra 61b, 68b-69a
Land, loss .... Bava Metzia 31a
Land, one third of one's investments .... Bava Metzia 42a
Land, *prozbul* .... Gittin 37a; Sheviis 10:6
Land, purchase by contract .... Kiddushin 26a

Land, theft .... Bava Kama 116b, 117b-118a; Shevuos 37b
Land of worst quality
Land of worst quality, *kesubah* .... Gittin 49b; Bava Kama 7b
Land of worst quality, orphans .... Gittin 50a
Land of worst quality, paying a little more .... Bava Kama 7b
Land of worst quality, repayment of debt .... Gittin 49b, 50a; Bava Kama 8a
Misc. —
Land, idolatry .... Avodah Zarah 54b
Land, mind at ease .... Tamid 32a
Land of Shinar, eulogy .... Moed Katan 25b
Land of the deer .... Kesubos 112a
Land of Israel .... *see **Eretz Yisrael**, page 198*
Land, ownership .... Yevamos 63a; Sanhedrin 58b; Menachos 103b-104a
Land, personal use .... Meilah 18b
Landlord, preoccupied with his workers .... Shevuos 45a-45b; Bava Metzia 112b-113a
Language
Language, simplified pronounciation, in Jerusalem .... Bava Kama 6b
Language of men, Torah ...... Bava Metzia 31b, 94b; Berachos 31b; Yevamos 71a; Kesubos 67b; Nedarim 3a;
.... Gittin 41b; Kiddushin 17b; Sanhedrin 56a, 64b, 85b, 90b; Makos 12a;
.... Avodah Zarah 27a; Zevachim 108b; Arachin 3a; Krisos 11a
Language, prayer in every language .... Sotah 33a
Language, readings in every language .... Sotah 32a-33a; Berachos 40b; Shevuos 39a
Language, *Sursis* and Persian .... Bava Kama 83a
Lashes
For whom —
Lashes and payment, conspiring witness .... Makos 4a-4b; Kesubos 32b-33a
Lashes, first fruit .... Makos 17a-17b, 18b
Lashes for impurity of Temple .... Zevachim 32b-33b
Lashes for unintentional transgressor, replacing sacrifice .... Temurah 13a, 17a
Lashes for making sacrifice *piggul* .... Zevachim 29b
Lashes for conspiring witnesses .... Makos 2a-2b, 4a; Kesubos 32b; Bava Kama 5a, 74b
Lashes, for whom .... Makos 13a
How —
Lashes, evaluating a man's capacity to bear .... Makos 22a-22b
Lashes, for fear he dies .... Sanhedrin 10a-10b
Lashes, how is it performed .... Makos 22b-23a; Bava Kama 32b; Krisos 11a
Lashes, how many .... Makos 22a-22b
Lashes, number of judges .... Sanhedrin 10a
Rabbinical Decree —
Lashes by Rabbinical Decree, for which sin .... Kiddushin 12b; Yevamos 52a
Lashes, slanderous testimony .... Pesachim 113b
Lashes for seclusion (with prohibited person) .... Kiddushin 81a; Kesubos 13a
Lashes, for various kinds of *kiddushin* .... Kiddushin 12b; Yevamos 52a
Lashes, men serving in Temple .... Yoma 23a
Lashes, rumor of bad conduct .... Kiddushin 81a
Lashes for one who lives with his mother-in-law .... Kiddushin 12b; Yevamos 52a
Lashes, until he dies .... Kesubos 86a; Chullin 132b
Misc. —
Lashes, episode about armpit hair .... Nazir 59a

Lashes exempt from excising of soul .... Megillah 7b; Makos 23a-23b
Lashes, like death .... Sanhedrin 10a-10b
Lashes, more severe than death .... Kesubos 33a-33b
Lashon bnei adam .... *see* **Speech of men**, page 649
Lashon hakodesh .... *see* **Hebrew**, page 274
Lashon harah .... *see* **Derogatory speech**, page 160
Lashon hediot .... *see* **Expression of legal document, analyzing**, page 211
Lashon nekiyah .... *see* **Proper speech**, page 506
Lashon rishon ikar .... *see* **Expression, first, is principal**, page 211
Last
Last day, impurity of *nazir* .... Niddah 68b
Last expression determining .... Bava Basra 105b; Bava Metzia 102b
Last generations, leniencies .... Gittin 81a; Berachos 35b
Last line, legal document .... Bava Basra 161b-162a
Last use, resolving doubt .... Pesachim 7a; Bava Metzia 26a
Lateihem, demons' sorcery .... Sanhedrin 67b
Laughter
  Episodes —
Laughter at Rabbi Abba's prayer .... Beitzah 38a-38b
Laughter, inquiry about wedding of animal .... Niddah 23a
Laughter, jesters' reward .... Taanis 22a
Laughter, Rabbi Akiva .... Makos 24a-24b
  Misc. —
Laughter, about idolatry .... Sanhedrin 63b
Laughter at wedding, restrained .... Berachos 31a
Laughter, city of jokers .... Pesachim 112b
Laughter, forbidden to mourner .... Moed Katan 26b
Laughter, G-d's .... Avodah Zarah 3b
Laughter, good and bad .... Shabbos 30b
Laughter, prohibition to fill one's mouth .... Berachos 30b-31a
Laughter, punishments .... Avodah Zarah 18b
Launderer, colored garment .... Shabbos 19a
Laundering
Laundering and life of others, precedence .... Nedarim 80b-81a
Laundering before Shabbos .... Shabbos 19a
Laundering colored garments, episode .... Shabbos 19a
Laundering, health .... Nedarim 81a
Laundering leprous mark, ingredients .... Zevachim 95a
Laundering, mourner .... Taanis 13a-13b; Moed Katan 15a, 17b
Laundering on *Chol HaMoed* .... Moed Katan 13b-14a, 18a-18b; Taanis 29b; Chullin 107b-108a
Laundering on Thursday .... Bava Kama 82a
Laundering, price and checking .... Shabbos 19a
Laundering priestly garments .... Zevachim 88a-88b
Laundering, retroactive purity .... Niddah 56b
Laundering, Sabbatical year .... Succah 40a-40b; Bava Kama 101b-102a
Laundering, shared courtyard .... Bava Basra 57a-57b
Laundering, successive periods of mourning .... Moed Katan 17b; Taanis 13a
  Laundering on Shabbos
Laundering on Shabbos, leather .... Zevachim 94a-94b; Shabbos 142b

Laundering on Shabbos, rubbing..Shabbos 140a, 141a
Laundering on Shabbos, shaking out...Shabbos 147a
Laundering on Shabbos, soaking..Zevachim 94b

Laundering sacrificial blood
Laundering sacrificial blood, how..Zevachim 94a-95a
Laundering sacrificial blood, in which detergent.........................Zevachim 95a-95b
Laundering sacrificial blood, place...Zevachim 94b
Laundering sacrificial blood, what must be laundered................Zevachim 92b-94a
Laundering sacrificial blood, which sacrifice............Zevachim 38b-39a, 92a-93b, 98b

Lavud
Lavud, cases...Kilayim 4:4; Eruvin 16b
Lavud in *s'chach*..Succah 18a
Lavud, putting down..................Shabbos 5a, 80a, 92a, 97a, 100a-100b; Eruvin 98b
Lavud, size...................Eruvin 9a-9b, 14a, 16a-16b, 76a, 79b, 87b; Succah 22a-22b
Lavud, source..Shabbos 97a; Succah 6b
Lavud, stringency..Eruvin 9b
Lavud, succah..Succah 19a
Lavud, tent of corpse...Succah 18a
Lavud, upside down beehive...Shabbos 8a

Law
Law, clear, forgotten..Shabbos 139a
Law, custom and "people used to"...Taanis 26b
Law, explicit, not to rely on...........................Niddah 7b; Bava Basra 130b
Law for himself, Sage...............Yevamos 77a, 98a; Bechoros 31a, 38b; Kiddushin 70b
Law from source and reasoning, preference..................................Zevachim 96b
Law given without reason, his son..Bava Basra 144a
Law, in messianic times...Zevachim 45a; Sanhedrin 51b
Law in messianic times, Moses..Niddah 70b
Law in mourning, according to lenient opinion...........Moed Katan 18a, 19b, 20a, 22a, 26b;
                                                    Eruvin 46a; Chullin 50a; Bechoros 49a
Law is according to you, Rav Nachman...Bava Basra 65a
Law, learning before prayer...Berachos 31a
Law, monetary, amazing...Bava Basra 158b-159b
Law not settled...Berachos 27a
Law of Jewesses, covering hair...Kesubos 72a-72b
Law of the land.................................see also **Idolaters' courts** page 294
Law of the land, Persians...Bava Basra 55a
Law of the land, tax...................Bava Kama 113a; Nedarim 28a; Bava Basra 54b, 55a
Law, opinion but not to rule..Gittin 19a, 37a
Law, practical..............Bava Basra 130b; Shabbos 54a; Beitzah 29b; Avodah Zarah 74a; Niddah 7b
Law without given reason.............................Gittin 14a; Bava Basra 144a
Laws during festival and before festival.........Pesachim 6a-6b; Megillah 32a
Laws forgotten, Moses..Temurah 15b-16a
Laws, learning laws not practiced today...........Zevachim 45a; Sotah 44a; Sanhedrin 51b, 71a
Laws of equal weight, deduced together.......Zevachim 4b; Nazir 58b; Bava Kama 3a; Arachin 4b

Law, but we do not rule in this manner
Law, but we do not rule in this manner, closed alley........................Eruvin 7a
Law, but we do not rule in this manner, doubtful impurity........Avodah Zarah 37b
Law, but we do not rule in this manner, dung rendered public property...Bava Kama 30b

L

Law, but we do not rule in this manner, Shabbos lamp .... Shabbos 12b-13a
Law, but we do not rule in this manner, *tefillin* at night .... Menachos 31a-31b
Law, but we do not rule in this manner, *Yom Tov* .... Beitzah 28b

Lawyer
Lawyer, avoid being .... Avos 1:8; Shevuos 31a
Lawyer, lie .... Shabbos 139a
Lawyer, proxy .... Bava Kama 70a
Lawyers, Rabbi Yochanan .... Kesubos 52b

Layering, *orlah* .... Sotah 43b
Laying eggs, cycle .... Niddah 39b
Laziness
Laziness for Torah and commandments .... Berachos 63a
Laziness, proverb .... Sanhedrin 7a
Lazy men on festival, praise .... Succah 27b
"Le'es metzo," requests .... Berachos 8a
Lead
Lead drowns noise .... Yoma 69b; Sanhedrin 64a
Lead, hot, death penalty by burning .... Sanhedrin 52a; Pesachim 75a
Leader
Leader according to generation .... Arachin 17a
Leader, acting with strength .... Kesubos 103b
Leader, resoluteness .... Sanhedrin 8a
Leader, working in public .... Kiddushin 70a
Leaders, Sages or physicians .... Pesachim 112a, 113a
Leader of community
Leader of community, appointed if can of worms is trailing behind him .... Yoma 22b
Leader of community, arrogant, mind cannot tolerate .... Pesachim 113b
Leader of community, consulting community .... Berachos 55a
Leader of community, G-d proclaims .... Berachos 55a
Leader of community, haughtiness .... Chagigah 5b
Leader of community imposing fear .... Rosh Hashanah 17a
Leader of community, reward .... Sanhedrin 92a
Leader of community, wealth .... Yoma 22b
Leadership
Leadership, convert .... Yevamos 45b; Kiddushin 76b; Shabbos 154a
Leadership, difficult to quit .... Menachos 109b
Leadership given by Heaven .... Bava Basra 91b; Berachos 58a
Leadership, guiding community .... Sanhedrin 8a; Kesubos 103b
Leadership, hating .... Tamid 32a
Leadership, needy disciples .... Horayos 10a-10b
Leadership, not to remove special garments .... Sanhedrin 92b
Leadership, prohibition to work in public .... Kiddushin 70a
Leadership, Rabbi Adda's host .... Kiddushin 76b
Leadership, Sage .... Shabbos 114a; Taanis 10b
Leadership, two men .... Bava Basra 8b; Shekalim 5:2
Leah
Leah, birth of Issacher .... Niddah 31a
Leah placated Jacob .... Eruvin 100b
Leah, Rachel's signs .... Bava Basra 123a; Megillah 13b

Leah, soft eyes...Bava Basra 123a
Leah, thanksgiving..Berachos 7b
Leaning like standing..Zevachim 19b
Leap
Leap, damages by animal...Bava Kama 19b-20a, 21b-22a
Leap ("shortening") of road, for whom...Sanhedrin 95a
Leap ("shortening") of road, Jacob...Sanhedrin 95a-95b; Chullin 91b
Leap year
Leap year...*see* **Adding a month**, page 11
Leap year, rent..Bava Metzia 102a-102b; Bava Basra 105a
Learning.........*see also* **Deduction**, page 155; **Refraining from Torah learning**, page 554; **Torah**, page 695
Aggadah —
Learning, brings peace to Heavenly Host...Sanhedrin 99b
Learning, Divine Presence...Berachos 6a; Avos 3:2-3, 3:6
Learning, encouragement..Berachos 32b
Learning, first question on Day of Judgment...............................Sanhedrin 7a; Kiddushin 40b
Learning from elder, parable..Avos 4:20
Learning, greater than deed...Kiddushin 40b; Megillah 27a; Bava Kama 17a
Learning in mother's womb..Niddah 30b
Learning like Moses learned from G-d..Yevamos 72b
Learning, more important than daily offerings...Sanhedrin 44b
Learning, preferable to sacrifice...Megillah 3a-3b; Eruvin 63b; Sanhedrin 44b
Learning, success in business...Avodah Zarah 19b
Learning Torah continually, World to Come...Sanhedrin 88b
Episodes —
Learning in toilets, episode...Zevachim 102b
Learning of David...Makos 10a; Shabbos 30a
Learning of non-Jews, episode..Bava Kama 38a
Learning, subsistence from reeds..Eruvin 22a
How —
Learning amidst difficulties..Sanhedrin 100a
Learning, clearly in your mouth..Kiddushin 30a-30b
Learning, how...Eruvin 54a; Megillah 32a; Shabbos 30b
Learning in fear..Shabbos 30b; Berachos 22a; Moed Katan 15a
Learning in upper part of city...Pesachim 112a
Learning, pleasant day...Megillah 28b
Learning to teach or to perform..Avos 4:5
Learning, tolerant friends..Shabbos 63a
Learning while standing...Megillah 21a
Learning with excessive meticulousness..Eruvin 48a
Learning, with fear of G-d...Shabbos 31a-31b; Yoma 72b
Livelihood —
Learning and working for livelihood.....................Berachos 35b; Avos 2:2, 2:5, 4:10; Kiddushin 29b
Learning in poverty, reward...Avos 4:9
Learning is good with an occupation...Avos 2:2
Learning trade...Bava Metzia 30b; Bava Kama 99b-100a
Precedence —
Learning and honoring father..Megillah 16b-17a
Learning and prayer, preference...Shabbos 10a

Learning and time to marry..Kiddushin 29b-30a; Menachos 110a; Yoma 72b
Learning, separation from wife...Kesubos 61b-62a

Prohibitions —
Learning, bathhouse...............Shabbos 40b, 41a, 150a; Berachos 24b; Kiddushin 33a; Avodah Zarah 44b;
....Zevachim 102b
Learning, distance from excrement...Berachos 24b
Learning in front of deceased and in cemetery..Berachos 3b
Learning in front of ignoramus...Pesachim 49b
Learning, mourner...Moed Katan 15a, 21a-21b
Learning, non-Jew...............................Chagigah 13a; Bava Kama 38a; Sanhedrin 59a; Avodah Zarah 3a

Reviewing —
Learning..see also **Teach**, page 673
Learning and forgetting..Sanhedrin 99a
Learning difficult as iron..Taanis 8a
Learning four times...Eruvin 54b
Learning in one's hand.....................................Kesubos 77b; Pesachim 50a; Moed Katan 28a; Bava Basra 10b
Learning unclear, diligence...Taanis 8a
Learning without reviewing..Sanhedrin 99a-99b

Warnings —
Learned and forsook...Chagigah 9b
Learning is not the most important...Avos 1:17
Learning, one who does not learn merits death...Avos 1:13

When —
Learning a little at a time..Avodah Zarah 19a; Eruvin 54b
Learning before prayer..Berachos 31a
Learning by day, quality..Eruvin 65a
Learning, completing at night...Eruvin 65a
Learning during journey..Taanis 10b; Eruvin 54a; Sotah 46b, 49a
Learning during meal...Avos 3:3; Sanhedrin 101a
Learning during Shabbos meal...Megillah 12b
Learning during Torah reading...Berachos 8a
Learning from deduction, only the minimum..Succah 5b
Learning irregularly, fool...Sanhedrin 99b
Learning law before prayer...Berachos 31a
Learning on Shabbos, punishment for neglecting..Gittin 38b

Which subjects —
Learning, dividing one's time in three parts...........................Kiddushin 30a; Avodah Zarah 19b
Learning, educating child..Succah 42a
Learning laws, importance...Berachos 8a
Learning laws, World to Come...Megillah 28b; Niddah 73a
Learning of her son, mother...Kiddushin 29a-29b
Learning, reading *Shema*...Nedarim 8a; Menachos 99b
Learning superficially or by rote before in-depth..Avodah Zarah 19a
Learning what one desires...Avodah Zarah 19a
Learning, woman...Sotah 21b

Misc. —
Learning insufficiently, cause of disputes...Sanhedrin 88b; Sotah 47b
Learning laws not practiced today, reward....................................Zevachim 45a; Sotah 44a; Sanhedrin 51b, 71a
Learning learned in childhood...Shabbos 21b

Learning, not to learn hidden things .... Chagigah 13a
Learning to decide law .... Sanhedrin 106b
Learning traits from animals .... Eruvin 100b
Learning without disturbance, Abbaye .... Eruvin 65a

Learning at night
Learning at night, "you will meditate on it" .... Menachos 99b
Learning at night, Divine Presence .... Tamid 32b
Learning at night, from 15th *Av* .... Bava Basra 121b
Learning at night, punishment for neglecting .... Eruvin 18b; Sanhedrin 92a
Learning at night, reward .... Bava Basra 10a; Menachos 99b-100a; Avodah Zarah 3b

Learning partner
Learning partner .... Taanis 7a; Berachos 63b; Makos 10a
Learning partner, source .... Berachos 63b; Makos 10a
Learning partners without teacher, when .... Shabbos 63a

Leasing, interest .... Bava Metzia 67b-68a
Least Sage among you resurrects dead .... Avodah Zarah 10b
Leather
Leather .... *see also* **Hide**, page 278, **Skin**, page 632
Leather garments .... Sotah 14a
Leather, laundering on Shabbos .... Zevachim 94a-94b; Shabbos 142b
Leather of hair with holes, tent of corpse .... Eruvin 10b
Leather utensil, impurity .... Shabbos 28a; Sanhedrin 68a; Keilim 17:15, 23:1, 26:1-6

Leaven
Leaven and honey, sacrifice .... Menachos 57b-58b; Pesachim 43b
Leaven, *chametz* .... Pesachim 43a, 48b; Menachos 53a; Chullin 23b
Leaven, *chametz* in thanksgiving loaves .... Menachos 53b-54a
Leaven in dough, evil urge .... Berachos 17a
Leaven, meal offering .... Chullin 23b
Leaven prepared to be sold in portions, *challah* .... Challah 1:7
Leaven, quantity for burning .... Beitzah 7b; Yoma 79b
Leaven, *terumah* and non-holy, mixed .... Avodah Zarah 68a; Orlah 2:8-9, 2:11
Leaven, too much is harmful .... Berachos 34a
Leaven used as chair, purity .... Chullin 129a

Leavening
Leavening, cases .... Pesachim 39b-41a
Leavening of loaves of thanksgiving .... Menachos 53b-54a
Leavening, wheat submerged in river .... Pesachim 40b

Leaves of *Gan Eden*, episode .... Bava Metzia 114b

Leaving
Leaving city during daytime .... Bava Kama 60b; Pesachim 2a; Taanis 10b
Leaving forbidden food, stumbling-block .... Bava Kama 115b-116a; Pesachim 20b, 33b-34a;
.... Chullin 53b
Leaving friend, law .... Berachos 31a; Eruvin 64a
Leaving *Heichal* during service .... Yoma 43b-44b; Keilim 1:9
Leaving one's animal under the sun .... Bava Kama 56a
Leaving one's teacher, parting from him .... Moed Katan 9a
Leaving sacrificial flesh until its time for consumption is over ...... Pesachim 34a-34b, 73b, 82b
Leaving synagogue to come in house of study .... Berachos 64a; Moed Katan 29a
Leaving Torah learning, punishment .... Bava Basra 79a

Left his possession, vow..Nedarim 42a-42b, 47a

Leaving food on fire on Shabbos

Leaving food on fire on Shabbos, maybe someone will rake coals...........Shabbos 18b, 20a

Leaving food on fire on Shabbos, oven and stove-top..............................Shabbos 38b

Leaving food on fire on Shabbos, penalty..Shabbos 37b-38a

Leaving food on fire on Shabbos, stove-top..................................Shabbos 20a, 36b, 37a, 37a

Leaving minimum to live

Leaving minimum to live, donation valuation.....Bava Metzia 113b-114a; Arachin 7b-8a, 23b-24a

Leaving minimum to live, payment of *kesubah*...Nedarim 65b-66a

Leaving minimum to live, seizure...........Bava Metzia 113b-114a; Arachin 23b-24a; Bava Kama 11b

Lech lech amrinan nezira...*see* **Go away from vineyard, *nazir*, page 253**

"*Lecha*," from your property only..Yoma 3a-3b; Avodah Zarah 44a

Lechaf zechus...*see* **Judging favorably, page 328**

***Lechah Dodi*,** commentary...Eruvin 21b

***Lechaim*,** drinking wine...Shabbos 67b

Lechem..*see* **Bread, page 75**

Lechem Hapanim..*see* **Showbread, page 621**

Lechi...*see* **Board for *eruv*, page 70**

Lecture...*see* **Discourse, page 166**

Lee velo leyorshi...........................*see* **Heirs, giving them to keep condition, page 276**

Leech, drinking water...Avodah Zarah 12b

Leek, health...Eruvin 56a

Lees of wine, like wine...Bava Basra 96b-97a

Lefi tumo..*see* **As if by accident, Shabbos, page 32**

Left hand

Left hand casting away...Sotah 47a; Sanhedrin 107b

Left hand, *Kohanim* service...Zevachim 24a-25a; Menachos 9b-10b, 26a

Left hand, oath...Nazir 3b

Left-handed

Left-handed, blemish..Bechoros 45b

Left-handed, writing..Shabbos 103a

Leftover

Leftover..*see also* **Remainder, page 556**

Leftover blood, sunset...Zevachim 56a-56b; Menachos 20b

Leftover of non-Jew's sacrifice...Zevachim 45a; Temurah 3a

Leftover of Pesach lamb, burning....................Pesachim 73b, 83b-84a; Shabbos 24b, 133a; Temurah 4b

Leftover sacrificial blood...Zevachim 46a

Leftovers of Pesach lamb, parts...Pesachim 83b

Leftovers to craftsman...Bava Kama 119a-119b

Leftover sacrifice

Leftover sacrifice, application of *piggul* law..Meilah 8a-10a

Leftover sacrifice, burning..Yevamos 72b; Zevachim 98a

Leftover sacrifice, impurity...Pesachim 85a, 120b-121a

Leftover sacrifice, impurity of bones.......................................Pesachim 83a-83b; Chullin 125a

Leftover sacrifice, item permitting another...Zevachim 45b-46a

Leftover sacrifice, two days...Zevachim 56b

Lefum churfa shabashta...............................*see* **Sharpness of mind causes mistakes, page 610**

Lefum tzaara agra...*see* **Reward according to effort, page 566**

Leg

Animals —

Leg, atonement payment penalty .... Bava Kama 26a, 41a, 44b
Leg damage .... *see* **Trampling underfoot**, page 699
Leg, included in purchase of head .... Bava Basra 83b
Leg of bird, *treifah* .... Chullin 57a-57b
Leg, secondary categories .... Bava Kama 2b-3a
Leg, source .... Bava Kama 2b-3a, 55b
Leg, *treifah* .... Chullin 42b, 54a-54b, 57a-57b, 76a

Episodes —

Leg, nakedness of woman .... Berachos 24a
Leg of table, Rabbi Chanina .... Taanis 25a
Leg of Africans, large .... Shabbos 31a

Man —

Leg .... *see also* **Foot**, page 232
Leg, ankle .... Yevamos 103a
Leg, *chalitzah* .... Yevamos 103a; Arachin 19b
Leg, cure .... Shabbos 65a
Leg, up to where .... Arachin 19b

Misc. —

Leg, "on one leg" .... Shabbos 31a
Leg of stove-top, Shabbos .... Shabbos 138b
Leg, decomposed from inside .... Sanhedrin 39b
Leg, shared domain .... Bava Kama 13b-14a
Legs of duck .... Berachos 41b

Legal document

Acquisition —

Legal document, act of acquisition from when .... Bava Metzia 13a
Legal document, act of acquisition, order to write it .... Kiddushin 65b; Bava Basra 40a
Legal document of land, *kinyan agav* .... Bava Basra 77b
Legal document, purchase of land .... Kiddushin 26a; Bava Metzia 99b; Bava Basra 51a, 86a, 150b
Legal document, rescinding purchase .... Bava Basra 169b
Legal document without payment, act of acquisition .... Bava Basra 51a

Invalid —

Legal document, appearing false .... Kesubos 21b, 85a-85b; Gittin 26b
Legal document containing interest .... Bava Metzia 72a; Bava Kama 30b; Bava Basra 94b
Legal document, forged, cases .... Bava Basra 167a; Kesubos 21a
Legal document, forged, rumor .... Kesubos 36b
Legal document, invalid witness signed .... Bava Basra 162b
Legal document of courts and in Persian .... Gittin 19b, 10b-11a
Legal document, torn by *beis din* .... Bava Basra 168b
Legal document which can be forged .... Gittin 22a-22b
Legal documents contradicting .... Kesubos 94a; Bava Basra 34b-35a
Legal documents, two, concerning one matter .... Kesubos 43b-44a, 89b

Laws —

Legal document .... *see also* **Promissory note**, page 505
Legal document, additional copy .... Bava Basra 171a
Legal document erased, copy .... Bava Basra 168a-169b
Legal document, who must pay .... Bava Basra 168a

Legal document, without guarantee .... Kesubos 51a-51b, 104b; Bava Metzia 13a, 14a, 15b;
Bava Basra 169b; Bava Kama 95a

Legal documents —
Legal document about claims and arbitration .... Bava Basra 168a; Bava Metzia 20a
Legal document, *adrachta* .... Kesubos 104b; Bava Kama 112b; Bava Metzia 17b; Bava Basra 169a
Legal document attesting that girl renounced marriage .... Yevamos 107b-108a
Legal document, not made for sale of fruit .... Bava Basra 33b
Legal document of *beis din* decision .... Sanhedrin 30a
Legal document of *chalitzah* .... Yevamos 39b, 106a, 106b
Legal documents for seizure .... Bava Basra 169a

Slave —
Legal document, release of slave, like divorce certificate .... Gittin 9a-10a
Legal document, release of slave, text .... Gittin 40b, 85b
Legal document, sale of slave .... Gittin 86a

Text —
Legal document with witnesses signed on one line .... Bava Basra 163b
Legal document, command was not written .... Bava Basra 40a; Sanhedrin 29b
Legal document, contradiction in text .... Bava Basra 166b
Legal document, place of writing .... Bava Basra 172a
Legal document, text according to seller .... Kiddushin 9a
Legal document, too refined style .... Bava Basra 69b
Legal document, writing G-d's name .... Rosh Hashanah 18b

Time —
Legal document, date corresponding to Shabbos .... Bava Basra 171a
Legal document, later date .... Bava Basra 171a-172a
Legal document, predated, payment .... Bava Metzia 72a-72b; Bava Basra 17a, 157b, 171b; Rosh Hashanah 2a, 8a; Sanhedrin 32a; Sheviis 10:5
Legal document, predated, signed at night .... Gittin 18a-18b
Legal document, writing delay .... Bava Basra 172a
Legal document, years of kings .... Rosh Hashanah 2a-2b, 8a; Avodah Zarah 9b-10a

Misc. —
Legal document, avoid .... Pesachim 113a
Legal document, episodes about falsification .... Bava Basra 167a
Legal document, gift which became lost .... Bava Metzia 19a-19b
Legal document given to two persons .... Pesachim 78a
Legal document of *beis din* to bothersome persons .... Bava Basra 153a, 168b
Legal document, one *zuz* .... Bava Basra 155b
Legal documents, blank, seem false .... Gittin 26b
Legal documents, forbidden to keep .... Kesubos 19a-19b

Legal document in name of
Legal document in name of administrator .... Bava Basra 52a-52b
Legal document in name of one another .... Bava Basra 173a
Legal document, in name of *Reish Galusa* .... Bava Kama 102b-103a

Legal document, lost
Legal document, lost, certified .... Bava Metzia 17a
Legal document, lost, "I paid" .... Bava Metzia 7b
Legal document, lost, cases .... Bava Metzia 16b, 20a-20b
Legal document, lost, concern .... Bava Metzia 12b-13a, 14a, 16b, 17a, 19a
Legal document lost, copy .... Bava Basra 168a-169b

Legal document, lost, possibility that it fell .... Bava Basra 172b
Legal document of *kiddushin*
Legal document of *kiddushin*, date .... Yevamos 31b
Legal document of *kiddushin*, intended .... Kiddushin 9a-9b, 48a
Legal document of *kiddushin*, text .... Kiddushin 9a
Legal transfer of rights
Legal transfer of rights, *eruv chatzeiros* .... Nedarim 88b; Eruvin 73b, 79b; Gittin 64b
Legal transfer of rights, *eruv techumin* .... Eruvin 80a
Legal transfer of rights in man's absence .... Kiddushin 23a, 42a; Eruvin 81b; Yevamos 118b;
.... Kesubos 11a; Gittin 11b; Bava Metzia 12a; Chullin 83a
Legal transfer of rights of divorce certificate, for a woman .... Yevamos 118b; Gittin 11b
Legal transfer of rights, *peah* .... Bava Metzia 9b-10a; Peah 4:9; Gittin 11b-12a
Legal transfer of rights to found object .... Bava Metzia 8a, 9a, 9b-10a; Beitzah 39b
Legumes, year of tithe .... Rosh Hashanah 13b-14a
Legislator
Legislator, Moses .... Bava Basra 15a
Legislator, Judah .... Horayos 11b
Lehachis .... *see* **Rebel, with intention to rebel**, page 549
Leil haSeder .... *see* **Seder** night, page 597
Leil shimurim .... *see* **Night of protection**, page 445
Leimor
Leimor, negative commandment .... Pesachim 42a
Leimor, so that he tells Israel .... Yoma 4b
Leka delo remizei beOraisa .... *see* **Nothing that is not alluded in Torah**, page 450
Leket .... *see* **Sheaves left for poor**, page 612
Lemafre'a .... *see* **Retroactively**, page 564
Lend
Lend me and then I shall keep something for you .... Bava Metzia 81a
Lending .... *see also* **Borrow**, page 73
Lending books .... Kesubos 50a
Lending, commandment .... Bava Metzia 71a; Sanhedrin 76b; Shabbos 63a
Lending lent item .... Bava Metzia 29b
Lending to poor in time of need .... Sanhedrin 76b
Lent, items usually lent, *chazakah* .... Shevuos 46b
Lent, items usually lent, seizing .... Bava Metzia 116a
Lender
Lender and borrower .... *see also* **Loan**, page 376
Lender and borrower seize promissory note .... Bava Metzia 7a-7b; Bava Basra 170a
Lender, last, seizure .... Kesubos 90a-90b, 94a; Bava Kama 34a; Arachin 7b
Lender, wanted to gather or divide promissory notes .... Bava Basra 172a
Lender who seized property from heir .... Bava Kama 9a; Bava Basra 107a
Length of days in its right hand .... Shabbos 63a, 88b
Leniencies
Leniencies, impurity in Temple .... Pesachim 19a-19b
Leniencies, military camp .... Eruvin 17a-17b
Leniencies of Beis Shamai .... Eduyos 4:1-12, 5:1-4; Shabbos 77a; Zevachim 38b; Menachos 104a
Leniencies, Shabbos coming in during journey .... Shabbos 17b, 153a-153b
Leniency, his "cane" will tell him .... Pesachim 52b
Leniency, mixed species in *Eretz Yisrael* .... Shabbos 139a; Berachos 36a

Leniency, more difficult than stringency............Berachos 60a; Beitzah 2b; Eruvin 72b; Gittin 41b, 74b;

Kiddushin 60b; Chullin 58a; Niddah 59b

Leniency or stringency, analogy.................Yevamos 8a; Shabbos 83b; Kiddushin 68a; Avodah Zarah 46b

Leniency, *orlah* outside *Eretz Yisrael*...Berachos 36a

Leniency, Rabbinical divergence of opinions ....Avodah Zarah 7a

Lenient, pretending G-d is lenient...Bava Kama 50a

Lenient commandment is like stringent

Lenient commandment is like stringent, attention ....Avos 2:1, 4:2

Lenient commandment is like stringent, Divine Judgment...Chagigah 5a

Lentil

Lentil, size..Keilim 17:8

Lentil volume, piece of dead reptile........................Nazir 52a; Meilah 16b-17a; Chagigah 11a

Lentils for mourner..Bava Basra 16b

Lentils, to prevent diphtheria...Berachos 40a

Leper

Leper, definite..Moed Katan 7b, 14b-15b

Leper, hair and garments...Moed Katan 15a

Leper in quarantine.................................Megillah 8b; Sanhedrin 106b; Arachin 15b

Leper, Pesach lamb...Pesachim 66b-67a

Leper, purification...Negaim 14:1-6

Leper, *semichah* on guilt offering...Zevachim 33a

Leper, sending him out of camp...............................Pesachim 67a-68a; Zevachim 117a

Leprosy

Causes —

Leprosy, derogatory speech..Arachin 16a-16b

Leprosy, harmful things...Pesachim 76b, 112b

Leprosy, increase of semen...Bechoros 44b

Leprosy, miserliness..Arachin 16a

Episodes —

Leprosy of Aaron..Shabbos 97a

Leprosy of Miriam..Zevachim 101b-102a

Leprosy of Moses...Shabbos 97a

Misc. —

Leprosy, Babylon..Kesubos 77b

Leprosy comparable to death...Nedarim 64b

Leprosy, king..Horayos 10a

Leprosy, not to show on oneself...Gittin 57b

Leprosy with *nezirus*..Nazir 55a-56b, 17b

Leprosy, woman..Sotah 23b; Arachin 3a; Krisos 8b

Leprous mark

Aggadah —

Leprous marks, atonement Altar..Berachos 5b

Leprous marks, charity and judgment..Arachin 8b

Leprous marks, for Israel's benefit..Horayos 10a

Leprous marks, one does not see one's own...Negaim 2:5

Leprous marks, punishment for which transgressions......Arachin 16a; Sotah 15a; Shevuos 8a;

Krisos 26a

Leprous marks, spreading..Negaim 4:1-2, 4:10

Looking at —

Leprous mark, time to look at ..... Moed Katan 7a-8a; Negaim 1:4, 2:2, 3:2
Leprous marks, black and white men ..... Negaim 2:1
Leprous marks, how to stand ..... Negaim 2:4; Niddah 67a
Leprous marks, *Kohen* looking at ..... Negaim 2:3, 3:1; Niddah 50a; Moed Katan 8a

Misc. —

Leprous mark, altered ..... Negaim 1:5-6, 4:7-10, 7:1-3
Leprous mark *nesek*, woman ..... Kiddushin 35b
Leprous marks, colors ..... Negaim 1:1-2, 1:4; Shevuos 2a, 5b-6b; Shabbos 2b; Zevachim 88b
Leprous marks, combining ..... Negaim 1:3, 4:5
Leprous marks, covered whole body ..... Negaim 8:1-10; Arachin 18b; Niddah 19a; Sanhedrin 87b-88a; Zevachim 49b
Leprous marks, garments ..... Negaim 11:4-6; Zevachim 49b, 95a; Niddah 19a; Sanhedrin 87b-88a
Leprous marks, *nesek* ..... Negaim 10:1-5
Leprous marks, pure ..... Horayos 10a
Leprous marks, which garments ..... Negaim 11:1-4, 11:7-10, 11:11
Leprous marks, widely discussed in Torah ..... Chagigah 11a

Leprous marks on houses

Leprous marks on houses, attic ..... Nedarim 56a
Leprous marks on houses, how ..... Sanhedrin 71a
Leprous marks on houses, looking at and quarantine ..... Nedarim 56b-57a; Negaim 12:6-7, 13:1, 13:5
Leprous marks on houses, idolater ..... Gittin 82a
Leprous marks on houses, number of walls ..... Negaim 12:1-4; Bava Basra 164b; Nazir 8b
Leprous marks on houses, painted house ..... Nedarim 56a
Leprous marks on houses, size ..... Negaim 12:3-4; Sanhedrin 71a, 87b; Niddah 19a
Leprous marks on houses, size and how ..... Negaim 12:3-4; Sanhedrin 71a, 87b; Niddah 19a
Leprous marks on houses, taking out stones and destroying house ..... Negaim 12:6-7, 13:2-3; Chullin 128b
Leprous marks on houses, it never happened ..... Sanhedrin 71a
Leprous marks on houses, which houses ..... Negaim 12:1-4; Yoma 11b-12a

Lesbian to *Kohen* ..... Yevamos 76a; Shabbos 65a-65b
Le'shem chullin ..... see **Intended for non-holy purpose**, page 311
Le'shem matzas mitzvah ..... see **Matzah, for sake of commandment**, page 394
Le'shem shamayim ..... see **For Heaven's sake**, page 233

Less

Less than four cubits, carrying out ..... Eruvin 97b
Less than a *perutah*, returning stolen item ..... Bava Kama 105a
Less than a *perutah*, redeeming ..... Arachin 27a; Bava Metzia 53b-54a

Lessee

Lessee ..... see also **Tenant farmer**, page 680
Lessee, general custom ..... Bava Metzia 103a-103b
Lessee, payment by his fruit ..... Bava Metzia 106b
Lessee, sown other species ..... Bava Metzia 106b-107a
Lessee, unsuccessful crop ..... Bava Metzia 103b-104a, 105b-106b
Lessee, weeding ..... Bava Metzia 105a

Let

Let drunken man fall by himself ..... Shabbos 32a
Let him be, he is scrupulous in *mitzvos* ..... Nazir 59a

Let my share be with etc., behavior...Shabbos 118b

Letakunei shedartich.......................................*see* **Agent who caused damage**, page 14

Lete'avon...*see* **Personal interest, renegade**, page 482

Letter

Letter about rebellious wife...Kesubos 64a

Letter, eve of Shabbos...Shabbos 19a

Letter from Rava's brothers...Kesubos 111a

Letter in secret code, episode...Sanhedrin 12a

Letter on utensil, mark..Maaser Sheni 4:9-11; Yevamos 115b

Letter, Rava..Shabbos 115a

Letter, written in coded language...Sanhedrin 12a

Letters

Letters, *aggadah*...Shabbos 104a; Succah 52b

Letters, combining in Creation..Berachos 55a

Letters, final...Megillah 2b-3a; Shabbos 104a

Letters fly up in air, breaking of Tablets...Pesachim 87b

Letters fly up in air, Rabbi Chanina ben Teradyon...................................Avodah Zarah 18a

Letters, missing or additional, forgotten..Kiddushin 30a

Letters of Rabban Gamliel...Sanhedrin 11b

Letters, precision in pronunciation...Megillah 24b

Letters recognizable, erased legal document..Bava Basra 169b

Letters, sale of promissory note.............Bava Basra 76a, 169a-169b, 173a; Kiddushin 47b; Sanhedrin 31a

Letters, see name of letter..Sotah 17a

Letters in holy parchments

Letters in holy parchments, change...Shabbos 103b-104a

Letters in holy parchments, cut...Menachos 29a-29b

Letters in holy parchments, missing and superfluous..................Sotah 20a; Eruvin 13a

Letters in holy parchments, shape...Menachos 29b

Letzorech gufo......................................*see* **Muktzeh**, to use item and place, page 431

Letzorech hamoed..........................*see* **Chol HaMoed**, act needed for festival, page 105

Letzorech mekomo.............*see* **To use its place, carrying together with permitted item**, page 694

Levanon, Temple...Yoma 39b

Levayah...*see* **Funeral**, page 241

Leveling

Leveling by non-Jew, tithe...Menachos 66b-67a; Bechoros 11a-11b

Leveling grain, obligation to give tithes...Maasros 1:5-8

Leveling holes

Leveling holes, barrel..Shabbos 141a

Leveling holes on Shabbos, nuts...Eruvin 104a

Leveling holes, removing mud from shoe...Shabbos 141a

Leveling holes, trough...Shabbos 140b

Leveling holes, weaving..Shabbos 113a

Levels in purity, stringencies...Chullin 35a-35b

Levi son of Rav Huna, donkey overtook..Shabbos 51b-52a

Levi

Levi, "discussed in front of Rebbi"...Sanhedrin 17b

Levi did not come to Rav Afes' lecture...Berachos 18b

Levi, Divine Presence in synagogue..Megillah 29a

Levi, episode about lameness...........................Taanis 25a; Succah 53a; Megillah 22b

L

Levi, Heavenly Yeshivah .... Berachos 18b
Levi, juggling .... Succah 53a
Levi, mistake in date of Yom Kippur .... Rosh Hashanah 21a
Levi, Rebbi's lecture .... Avodah Zarah 19a
Levi, teaching in the name of the majority .... Gittin 20a

Leviathan
Leviathan .... Bava Basra 74b-75a; Chullin 67b
Leviathan, Divine Laughter .... Avodah Zarah 3b

Leviim
Laws —
Leviim, exempt from redeeming .... Bechoros 3b-4b, 13a
Leviim, field and houses .... Arachin 33b
Leviim, fitness to serve .... Chullin 24a
Leviim, guarding Temple .... Tamid 25b-26b; Middos 1:1
Leviim, redemption in their cities .... Arachin 27a
Leviim, tithe of their crops .... Chullin 131b
Leviim, Torah reading .... Gittin 59b
Leviim, unintentional murder .... Makos 12b; Zevachim 117a
Misc. —
Leviim, community and tribe .... Horayos 6b
Leviim, emigration of Ezra .... Yevamos 86b
Leviim, gatekeeper who sang, death penalty .... Arachin 11b
Leviim, Golden Calf .... Yoma 66b
Leviim, height .... Shabbos 92a
Leviim, *Kohanim* .... Yevamos 86b; Chullin 24b; Bechoros 4a-4b; Tamid 27a
Leviim, number of tribes .... Horayos 6b
Leviim, people .... Chullin 131a-131b
Leviim, policemen .... Yevamos 86b
Leviim, reckoning in desert .... Bechoros 5a
Leviim, ruling rabbis .... Yoma 26a
Leviim, shaving .... Nazir 40a; Negaim 14:4

Levirate marriage
Levirate marriage, *agunah* .... Yevamos 92a-92b, 93b-94a, 114b, 118b; Shevuos 32b; Eduyos 1:12
Levirate marriage and *chalitzah*, preference .... Yevamos 21a, 39b; Kesubos 64a; Bechoros 13a
Levirate marriage for forbidden marriages .... Yevamos 20a-21a, 61a
Levirate marriage, forcing .... Yevamos 4a, 8b, 39b
Levirate marriage, giving decedent's name to firstborn .... Yevamos 24a
Levirate marriage, good advice .... Yevamos 44a
Levirate marriage, king .... Sanhedrin 19b
Levirate marriage, not for sake of commandment .... Yevamos 39b
Levirate marriage of betrothed girl, *Kohen Gadol* .... Sanhedrin 18b-19a; Yevamos 20a-20b, 61a
Levirate marriage on Shabbos .... Beitzah 36b-37a
Levirate marriage outside *Eretz Yisrael*, episode .... Kesubos 111a
Levirate marriage, prohibition to annul .... Yevamos 17b-18b, 24a, 26a, 28a
Levirate marriage, several women .... Yevamos 43b-44a
Levirate marriage, she cannot undergo *chalitzah* .... Yevamos 20a-20b
Levirate marriage, *sotah* .... Sotah 5b-6a; Yevamos 11a-11b
Levirate marriage, two sisters to one brother of deceased childless husband ..... Yevamos 19a, 28a-29a, 50b-51b

Levirate marriage, unintentional .... Yevamos 53b-54a

Levites .... *see* **Leviim**, page 367

Leviyah
Leviyah, exemption from redeeming son .... Bechoros 4a-4b, 47a; Chullin 132a
Leviyah who had forbidden relations, tithe .... Yevamos 91a; Bechoros 47a

Levonah .... *see* **Frankincense**, page 239

Liable
Liable by Divine Judgment, cases .... Bava Kama 55b-56a
Liable by Divine Judgment, testimony .... Bava Kama 56a
Liable etc. not liable etc., list .... Chullin 25b

Liar
Liar in *beis din* .... Bava Metzia 16b-17a
Liar, not believed even when tells truth .... Sanhedrin 89b
Liars, groups .... Sanhedrin 103a; Sotah 42a

Libations
Disqualified —
Libations, changing name .... Menachos 89b-90a
Libations, disqualified sacrifice .... Menachos 79a-79b
Libations missing .... Menachos 27a
Libations, mixture .... Menachos 89a-89b
Libations, *piggul* .... Menachos 15b; Zevachim 44a

How and how many —
Libations, consecration .... Menachos 44b, 79a-79b
Libations, for each animal .... Menachos 91b-92a
Libations for young sheep .... Menachos 91b-92a; Chullin 23a-23b; Parah 1:3
Libations, receipts .... Shekalim 5:3-5

Sacrifices —
Libations, daily offering .... Yoma 34a-34b
Libations, oil for *omer* .... Menachos 89b
Libations, *omer* .... Menachos 89b
Libations, sin offering .... Sotah 15a
Libations, which sacrifices .... Menachos 9-91b

Misc. —
Libation, may be offered as donation .... Menachos 104b
Libations, adding to sacrifice .... Meilah 15b; Pesachim 79a; Zevachim 109a-109b; Menachos 9b, 26a; Krisos 16a
Libations, deceased convert and non-Jew .... Menachos 51b; Shekalim 7:6
Libations, *Leviim's* song .... Arachin 11a, 12a; Berachos 35a
Libations, non-Jew .... Zevachim 45a; Temurah 3a; Menachos 51b, 73b; Shekalim 7:6
Libations on private altar .... Zevachim 111a
Libations, preferences .... Menachos 45a-45b

Libation of water
Libation of water, angel of rain, calls .... Taanis 25b
Libation of water, blessing of abundance .... Rosh Hashanah 16a
Libation of water by Sadducee .... Succah 48b
Libation of water, disqualified because remained overnight .... Succah 49b-50a
Libation of water, order .... Succah 48a-48b, 53b
Libation of water, outside .... Zevachim 110b-111a
Libation of water, secular use .... Meilah 13b

Libation of water, quantity .... Succah 49b-50a; Zevachim 110b; Meilah 13b
Libation of water, Shabbos .... Succah 49b-50a
Libation of water, *shofar* .... Succah 53b, 54a
Libation of water, source .... Taanis 2b-3a; Shabbos 103b; Succah 34a, 44a; Moed Katan 3b;
.... Zevachim 110b
Libation of water, when .... Yoma 26b; Taanis 2b-3a; Succah 42b, 48b
Libation of wine
Libation of wine, how .... Succah 49b
Libation of wine, order of precedence .... Menachos 44b
Libation of wine, time .... Temurah 14a-14b; Zevachim 8a, 84a; Menachos 44b, 52a
Libo nokfo uforesh .... *see* **Heart beats and he desists**, page 273
Libun keilim .... *see* **Heating until white-hot**, page 274
Lice
Lice, birth and eggs .... Shabbos 107b; Avodah Zarah 3b
Lice, disgusting to one's friend .... Shabbos 12a; Chagigah 5a
Lice, disturbing one's learning .... Eruvin 65a
Lice in Egypt, magicians .... Sanhedrin 67b
Lice, killing on Shabbos .... Shabbos 12a, 107b
Lice, *niddah* stains .... Niddah 58b-59a
Lice, searching for on Shabbos .... Shabbos 12a, 13b
Lice, sorcery .... Chullin 105b; Shabbos 81b-82a
Lid
Lid of utensil and well, Shabbos .... Shabbos 125a, 126b
Lid of utensils, impurity .... Keilim 12:3, 12:6, 14:3, 16:7; Eduyos 3:9
Lie
Episodes —
Lie, bad wife's dish .... Yevamos 63a
Lie, episode about city named Kushta .... Sanhedrin 97a
Lie, to avoid Rav Nachman .... Bava Kama 11b
Lie to escape robbers .... Avodah Zarah 25b-26a
Lie, to rule like Rebbi .... Pesachim 27a
Misc. —
Lie, begins with truth .... Sotah 35a
Lie does not have permanence .... Shabbos 104a
Lie, ignoramus on Shabbos .... Demai 4:1-2; Chullin 75b
Lie in *beis din*, prohibition .... Shevuos 31a
Lie to prevent transgression .... Shabbos 115a
Lies, idolaters .... Bava Basra 45a
Lies permitted .... Yevamos 65b; Bava Metzia 23b-24a, 87a
Lien .... *see* **Mortgage**, page 423
Life
Life .... *see also* **Longevity**, page 377
Life and wine to Sages' mouths .... Shabbos 67b
Life, children and livelihood, fate .... Moed Katan 28a
Life of others and laundering, precedence .... Nedarim 80b-81a
Life, your life comes first .... Bava Metzia 62a
Life, your life comes first, wife and children .... Chullin 84a
Life for a few hours
Life for a few hours, non-Jewish physician .... Avodah Zarah 27b

Life for a few hours, prayer .... Shabbos 10a
Life for a few hours, saving a life .... Yoma 85a
Life is no life
Life is no life, bad wife .... Beitzah 32b
Life is no life, character traits .... Pesachim 113b
Life is no life, suffering .... Beitzah 32b
Lifnei iver .... *see* **Stumbling-block**, page 660
Lifnei mi atah amel .... *see* **Before Whom you are toiling**, page 48
Lifnim mishuras hadin .... *see* **Beyond letter of law**, page 56
Lifting found object for friend .... Bava Metzia 8a, 9a-10a; Beitzah 39b
Lifting to purchase
Lifting to purchase, *eruv* .... Eruvin 79b-80a
Lifting to purchase, generally raised .... Bava Basra 86a-86b
Lifting to purchase, high place .... Bava Metzia 9a
Lifting to purchase, partially in one's hand .... Bava Metzia 7a
Lifting to purchase, slave .... Kiddushin 22b
Light
Light and darkness, order of creation .... Tamid 32a
Light for righteous, reward .... Taanis 15a
Light for the bat, parable .... Sanhedrin 98b
Light, G-d does not need it .... Menachos 86b; Shabbos 22b
Light is Torah .... Megillah 16b
Light, modesty during intimate relations .... Pesachim 112b
Light, night or day .... Pesachim 2a-3a
Light of righteous .... Chagigah 12a
Light of the Diaspora, Rabbi Achay .... Chullin 59b
Lighting
Lighting *Chanukah* lamps .... Shabbos 21a-23b; Succah 46a
Lighting with *orlah* oil .... Pesachim 22b; Kiddushin 56b; Bava Kama 101a
Lighting the menorah
Lighting the *menorah*, lamp which became extinguished .... Menachos 88b
Lighting the *menorah*, middle lamp .... Shabbos 22b
Lighting the *menorah*, non-*Kohen* .... Yoma 24b
Lighting the *menorah*, preparation .... Yoma 14b-15a; Menachos 88b, 107a; Tamid 30b, 33a
Lightning
Lightning, blessing .... Berachos 59a
Lightning, origin .... Berachos 59a
Like
Like all nations, appointing a king .... Sanhedrin 20b
Like Moses, *nazir* .... Nazir 14a
***Liknos*, wording of acquisition** .... Bava Metzia 9b
Likut atzamos .... *see* **Gathering bones of corpse**, page 245
Lilis, sleeping alone .... Shabbos 151b
Limb
Limb, additional, impurity .... Bechoros 45a; Niddah 49b
Limb gives birth to limb .... Chullin 69a
Limb missing, sacrifice for non-Jew .... Avodah Zarah 5b-6a, 51a; Zevachim 116a
Limb, whole, lashes penalty .... Chullin 96a-96b, 102a
Limbs, according to majority .... Chullin 70a; Krisos 14a

L

Limbs, final parts, leprous marks .... Negaim 6:7-8; Kiddushin 25a
Limbs, freedom to slave .... Kiddushin 24b-25a
Limbs, impurity of corpse .... Eduyos 6:2-3; Oholos 1:7
Limbs inside mother animal .... Chullin 69a
Limbs of fetus, birth .... Chullin 68b-69a
Limbs smashed, *treifah* .... Bava Kama 50b-51a; Chullin 51a-52a, 56b, 57a
Limbs unequal, blemish .... Bechoros 3b

Limb nearly severed
Limb nearly severed, eating .... Chullin 73b-74a
Limb nearly severed, impurity .... Chullin 127a-127b; Krisos 15a-15b
Limb nearly severed, *neveilah* .... Chullin 73a-74a, 127b

Limb torn from living animal
Limb torn from living animal, eating .... Chullin 101b-102a, 102b-103a
Limb torn from living animal, impurity .... Chullin 129b; Eduyos 6:3
Limb torn from living animal, minimal quantity .... Chullin 102a-102b
Limb torn from living animal, *neveilah* .... Chullin 128b
Limb torn from living animal, non-Jew .... Sanhedrin 59a-59b; Chullin 33a
Limb torn from living animal, benefit .... Pesachim 22b
Limb torn from living animal, severed .... Chullin 103b
Limb torn from living animal, slaves .... Gittin 7a, 67b-68a
Limb torn from living animal, twitching .... Chullin 121b

Lime, to whiten skin of girls .... Shabbos 80b; Moed Katan 9b; Pesachim 42b-43b
Limited item, oath .... Shevuos 43a
Limud zechus al chaveiro .... *see* **Judging fellow favorably**, page 328
Limud zechus b'din .... *see* **Defense,** *beis din*, page 157
Limud .... *see* **Learning**, page 357; *see also* **Deduction**, page 155
Linah .... *see* **Overnight off the Altar**, page 466
Line, comforting the bereaved .... Sanhedrin 19a; Kesubos 8a-8b

Lineage
Lineage acceptable, marriage .... Kiddushin 71b
Lineage according to country .... Kiddushin 70b, 71b-72a
Lineage for marriage, episode .... Kiddushin 71b
Lineage, G-d will reveal in the future .... Kiddushin 70b-71a
Lineage, marriage .... Yoma 71a-71b
Lineage of Babylonians, discourse .... Kiddushin 71a
Lineage of child from forbidden relations .... Kiddushin 66b-67b
Lineage of child from non-Jew and Jewess .... Yevamos 44b-45b, 70a, 99a
Lineage of convert .... Yevamos 98a
Lineage of nations according to male .... Yevamos 78b; Kiddushin 67a-67b
Lineage of non-Jew .... Yevamos 62a, 78b; Kiddushin 67b
Lineage of slave .... Yevamos 62a
Lineage, places and families .... Yevamos 17a; Kiddushin 69b, 70b-72b
Lineage, Rabbinical stringency .... Kesubos 15a-15b
Lineage, riddles .... Yevamos 97b, 99a
Lineage, silence and quarrel .... Kiddushin 71b
Lineage, Temple and community officers .... Kiddushin 76b
Lineage without wisdom .... Menachos 53a

Linen
Linen .... *see also* **Flax**, page 229

Linen and wool, *shatnez* .... Yevamos 4b; Shabbos 26b, 27a; Menachos 39b
Linen, does not absorb color .... Niddah 61b
Linen or wool, impurity .... Shabbos 26a-27a
Linen, priestly garments .... Yoma 71b-72a
Linen, worms .... Chullin 85b

Lining, impurity of garment .... Keilim 28:7; Shabbos 29a

Lion
  Damages —
    Lion, "I did not borrow a lion," goring ox .... Bava Kama 40a
    Lion in hiding, cure .... Bava Kama 85a; Bava Metzia 101b; Bava Basra 168a
    Lion, whole damage .... Bava Kama 16b
  Episodes —
    Lion, Elijah and Rabbi Yehudah ben Levi .... Makos 11a
    Lion, Iddo the prophet .... Sanhedrin 89b
    Lion, Rav Safra .... Bava Kama 116a
    Lions, Daniel .... Berachos 57b; Bava Basra 4a
    Lions pit, Daniel .... Berachos 57b; Bava Basra 4a
    Lions pit, Rabbi Tanchum .... Sanhedrin 39a
    Lions, Rabbi Tanchum .... Sanhedrin 39a
  Sages —
    Lion became fox .... Bava Kama 117a
    Lion came up from Babylon .... Bava Kama 117a
    Lion of the group .... Shabbos 111b; Kiddushin 48b; Bava Basra 88a; Sanhedrin 8b
    Lion son of lion, Rabbi Elazar ben Rabbi Shimon .... Bava Metzia 84b
  Misc. —
    Lion *Debei Ilai* .... Chullin 59b
    Lion, devours two people .... Shabbos 151b
    Lion, dead, live dog is better .... Shabbos 30a
    Lion, his names .... Sanhedrin 95a
    Lion, king of beasts .... Chagigah 13b
    Lion lies on it .... Eruvin 78b; Shevuos 22b
    Lion roaring, meat .... Berachos 32a
    Lion, working with .... Avodah Zarah 16b

Lips move in tomb .... Bechoros 31b; Yevamos 97a; Sanhedrin 90b

Liquid
  Impurity —
    Liquid .... *see also* **Drink**, page 181
    Liquid absorbed, impurity .... Oholos 3:2; Bava Kama 101b; Niddah 62b-63a
    Liquid, already when enclosed in fruit, *zav* .... Pesachim 33b
    Liquid coming from man who immersed that day .... Niddah 71b
    Liquid, congealed .... Taharos 3:1-3
    Liquid, connected to *mikveh* .... Taharos 8:9; Mikvaos 10:6
    Liquid, impure animal or reptile .... Bechoros 6b; Chullin 112b, 120a
    Liquid, impure, susceptible to make impure .... Tevul Yom 3:6
    Liquid, impurity from the Torah .... Pesachim 14b, 15b-16a, 17b-18b; Nedarim 19a; Avodah Zarah 37b
    Liquid, impurity of first source .... Shabbos 14b
    Liquid of reptiles, source .... Chullin 112b
    Liquid of Temple, purity .... Pesachim 16a, 17a-17b, 20a; Avodah Zarah 37b; Chullin 36b
    Liquid, receiving impurity .... Tevul Yom 2:1-2

Liquid, rendering impure..Pesachim 18a-18b, 20a

Liquid used for food, considered like food..Shabbos 144b-145a

Liquid, water of *mikveh*..Chullin 84a; Mikvaos 7:1-2

Liquid, wetting, *mikveh*..Gittin 15b-16a; Avodah Zarah 72a

Liquids in body, dead man..Chullin 87b-88a

Liquids of leper..Niddah 28b, 34b

Liquids, pure, in Temple.................Pesachim 16a, 17a-17b, 20a; Avodah Zarah 37b; Chullin 36b

Liquids, very susceptible to become impure..Pesachim 18b

Liquids, which make impure............Machshirin 2:1-3, 6:4-7; Niddah 55b-56a; Uktzin 3:11

Liquids of zav

Liquids of *zav*, chamber pot, shard, fragment..................................Zevachim 79b

Liquids of *zav*, definition...Krisos 13a-13b; Niddah 55b-56a

Liquids of *zav*, differences..Chullin 87b-88a

Liquids of *zav*, seminal discharge............Nazir 65b-66a; Bava Kama 25a-25b; Niddah 22a

Misc. —

Liquid coming from object of vow..Nedarim 52b-53a

Liquid in lung...Chullin 55b

Liquid, *reviis*, equal to volume of olive..Shabbos 77a

Liquid soaking, wine of idolaters...Avodah Zarah 72a

Liquid which came out on Shabbos.......Shabbos 19a-19b, 143b-144b, 145b; Eduyos 2:6; Beitzah 3a;
....Chullin 14b

Liquids, definition and different kinds.............Terumos 11:2-3; Pesachim 24b; Berachos 38a;
....Chullin 120b-121a

Liquids which run, egg..Beitzah 3a

Liquor...*see* **Alcoholic beverage, page 18**

Lishkah, lishkos...*see* **Room in Temple, page 571**

Lishkas HaGazis

Lishkas HaGazis, checking of *Kohanim*..Middos 5:4

Lishkas HaGazis, order for inquiry..Sanhedrin 88b

Lishkas HaGazis, Sanhedrin..Yoma 25a; Sanhedrin 88b

Lishkos Mikdash..*see* **Rooms in Temple, page 572**

Lishmah...*see* **Intended, page 311**

Lishmah beget..*see* **Intended divorce certificate, page 311**

Lishmo..................................*see* **Changing name of sacrifice to higher or lower, page 96**

Lishmor chukav, removing *tefillin*..Niddah 51b

List in Mishnah, non exhaustive..............Eruvin 27a; Taanis 13b; Kiddushin 16a-16b

Listening

Listening forbidden, finger into ear..Kesubos 5a-5b

Listening greater than seeing..Rosh Hashanah 25b

Listening is like answering...Succah 38b

Listening to Sages...Yevamos 20a

Listening to someone blessing you..Sotah 40a

Litigant

Litigant, answering him only....................Kesubos 92b; Bava Kama 8b; Bava Metzia 14a

Litigant claiming having documents and witnesses...........Bava Basra 169b-170b; Sanhedrin 23b

Litigant, loss...Sanhedrin 6b, 7a

Litigants, considered wicked...Avos 1:8

Litigants, forbidden things.................Bava Metzia 39b; Kesubos 27b; Shevuos 30a, 31a

Litrin, shekel of prophets...Bechoros 50a

L

Little
Little man with burned legs, Rabbi Zeira.. Bava Metzia 85a
Little profit from close source better than big profit from afar.................... Pesachim 113a

Live
"Live by them," saving life........................ Yoma 85b; Sanhedrin 74a; Avodah Zarah 27b, 54a
Live until half my days, blessing... Megillah 28a
Lived among righteous men and did not learn... Yoma 38b

Living
Living in fellow's courtyard........................ Bava Kama 20a-21a, 97a; Bava Metzia 64b-65a
Living in town whose leaders are Sages or physicians....................... Pesachim 112a, 113a
Living only in a place of Torah... Avos 6:9
Living with snake... Kesubos 72a, 77a, 86b

Livelihood
Aggadah —
Livelihood, depends on fate.. Moed Katan 28a
Livelihood, difficult because of my sins... Kiddushin 82b
Livelihood, encouragement... Berachos 32b
Livelihood, fixed on Rosh Hashanah............................... Beitzah 16a; Bava Basra 10a
Livelihood, for community.. Taanis 9a
Livelihood, for each creature............... Shabbos 107b; Pesachim 118a; Avodah Zarah 3b
Livelihood from one's work, value.. Berachos 8a
Livelihood, key... Taanis 2a-2b; Sanhedrin 113a
Livelihood, man does not know.. Pesachim 54b
Livelihood, more difficult for man than for animal............................. Kiddushin 82b
Livelihood, more difficult than miracle... Shabbos 53b
Livelihood, when do others do it for you... Berachos 35b
Livelihood, Who gives livelihood gives life... Taanis 8b

Episodes —
Livelihood and learning, Hillel... Yoma 35b
Livelihood, Rabbi Yochanan and Ilfa... Taanis 21a
Livelihood, Rabbi Yose... Shabbos 49b
Livelihood, Rava's disciples... Horayos 10b

How —
Livelihood, by work.................................. Avos 1:10; Gittin 67b; Bava Basra 110a
Livelihood, craft....................... Berachos 43b; Pesachim 50b; Arachin 16b; Kiddushin 30b
Livelihood, effort............... Berachos 8a, 35b; Kiddushin 29b; Avos 2:2, 2:5, 4:10; Bava Metzia 30b
Livelihood, reward for what.. Shabbos 119a
Livelihood, teaching craft to one's son... Kiddushin 30b, 82b
Livelihood, trade... Yevamos 63a; Pesachim 113a
Livelihood, trading in wine... Pesachim 113a
Livelihood, wealth in commerce............................... Niddah 70b; Pesachim 112a

Misc. —
Livelihood, hinders learning.. Eruvin 55a
Livelihood, prayer... Kiddushin 82b

Liver
Liver, absorption................................. Terumos 10:11-12; Chullin 110b-111a
Liver gets angry.. Berachos 61b
Liver, impurity of corpse's blood... Bechoros 55a
Liver, prohibition of blood... Chullin 110b-111b

Liver, *treifah* .... Chullin 43a, 46a, 48a
Living
Living creature lifts itself .... Shabbos 94a, 141b; Yoma 66b; Eruvin 103a
Living, instilling fear in animals .... Shabbos 151b
Living man does not contradict living man .... Berachos 27b
Living person in his clothes, carrying out .... Shabbos 141b-142a
Living water, *zav* and leper .... Parah 8:8-11
Living waters, fountain .... Mikvaos 1:7
Livuy parsah .... *see* **Accompanying on a *parsah*, crouched donkey**, page 6
Lizard
Lizard during king's meal .... Pesachim 88b
Lizard, lentil size .... Chagigah 11a
Lo am haaretz chasid .... *see* **Ignoramus is not pious**, page 297
Lo ba laolam .... *see* **Existing already**, page 209
Lo bashamayim hee .... *see* **Heaven, Torah is not in Heaven**, page 274
Lo kedarkah .... *see* **Sodomy, marital relations**, page 641
Lo
Lo lanu, who said .... Pesachim 117a
Lo taguru, significance .... Sanhedrin 7a
Lo lishmah baavodas Hashem .... *see* **Ulterior service of G-d**, page 713
Lo lishmo .... *see* **Changing name**, page 96
Lo maalim velo moridim .... *see* **Do not lift up**, page 172
Lo nitnah Torah lemalachei shares .... *see* **Torah not given to angels**, page 696
Lo ra'inu einah re'ayah .... *see* **"We did not see" is not proof**, page 737
Lo saaseh .... *see* **Negative commandment**, page 440
Lo sachmod .... *see* **Coveting, theft**, page 132
Lo sassur deRabbanan .... *see* **Source from Torah for Rabbinical Decrees**, page 648
Lo sechonem .... *see* **Grace in idolaters, prohibition to find**, page 255
Lo sisgodedu .... *see* **Separate into groups, prohibition**, page 601
Lo sonu .... *see* **Hurting feelings by speech**, page 289
Lo yilbash gever .... *see* **Wearing woman's dress**, page 739
Load
Load, cases .... Zavim 4:4-7, 5:2-5; Shabbos 93a-93b
Load, *even mesama* .... Shabbos 82b-83a; Niddah 69b, 71a
Load, forbidden to hold during prayer .... Bava Metzia 105b
Load, impurity of corpse .... Zavim 4:6
Load, impurity of discharge .... Niddah 55a-55b
Load, impurity, who .... Chullin 124b, 126b; Keilim 1:1-3
Load of rented donkey .... Bava Metzia 79b, 80a-80b; Avodah Zarah 65a
Load, parts of dead .... Oholos 2:1-4
Loaded
Loaded and not loaded .... Sanhedrin 32b
Loading, crouching donkey .... Bava Metzia 31b-33a
Loading wood, episode .... Bava Metzia 30b
Loaf
Loaf and child, *muktzeh* .... Shabbos 30b, 43b, 142b
Loaf of bread, quantity .... Eruvin 82b-83a; Kesubos 64b
Loaf stuck to another, combining for *challah* .... Pesachim 48b
Loaves stuck during baking, connections for impurity .... Taharos 1:7-8

Loaves of thanksgiving
Loaves of thanksgiving, *chametz*..Beitzah 19b
Loaves of thanksgiving, disqualified sacrifice ..... Menachos 78b-79a; Temurah 18b; Pesachim 13b
Loaves of thanksgiving, doubtful..Menachos 80b-81a
Loaves of thanksgiving, exempt.......................................Menachos 46a, 79b-80a; Krisos 27a
Loaves of thanksgiving, four loaves ....Menachos 76a-76b; Nedarim 12b; Niddah 6b
Loaves of thanksgiving, leavening...Menachos 53b-54a
Loaves of thanksgiving, number and quantity...Menachos 76b-78a
Loaves of thanksgiving, *piggul* with it..Menachos 15a
Loaves of thanksgiving, remainder...Menachos 80a-80b
Loaves of thanksgiving, sanctifying...Menachos 78b
Loaves of thanksgiving, species...Menachos 77a-77b
Loaves of thanksgiving, *terumah*...Menachos 77b
Loaves of thanksgiving, time for eliminating *chametz*..........................Pesachim 13b-14a
Loaves of thanksgiving, unfit...Menachos 78b
Loaves of thanksgiving, vow...Menachos 81b
Loan
Loan and *perutah*, *kiddushin*...Kiddushin 46a, 48b
Loan, avoiding..Pesachim 113a
Loan, commandment...Bava Metzia 71a; Sanhedrin 76b; Shabbos 63a
Loan, destined to be used...Kiddushin 47a, 47b
Loan, episode about Isur Giora..Bava Basra 149a
Loan, I gave back..Bava Basra 5a-6a; Shevuos 41b-42a
Loan, interest..Bava Metzia 64a-64b
Loan, *kiddushin*.............Kiddushin 6b, 19a-19b, 46a, 47a-48b; Bava Kama 99a-99b; Sanhedrin 19b
Loan, repayment..*see* **Repayment of debt**, page 558
Loan, Sabbatical year..Sheviis 10:1-2
Loan to buy back tithes..Gittin 30a-30b
Loan to *Levi* and poor, subtracting tithe from repayment........................Gittin 30a-30b
Loan, verbal, mortgage...Bava Basra 41b-42a
Loan without date, time...Makos 3b
Loan without witnesses...Bava Metzia 75b
Loathing
Loathing, delivery of non-Jewish woman...Avodah Zarah 26a
Loathing, idolater..Avodah Zarah 6b
Lobe
Lobe of liver, inside (Altar) sin offerings...Zevachim 41a-41b
Lobe of liver, sacrifice for mistake of *beis din*..Zevachim 41b
Lobe of lung...Chullin 47a-47b
Locking, act of acquisition..Bava Basra 52b
Locusts, fast day..Taanis 21b
Loeg larash...*see* **Scoffing at pauper**, page 592
Log, quantity..Bava Basra 89b-90a
Logic
Logic and source, preference...Zevachim 96b
Logic in learning...Berachos 6b
Logical deduction, does not need verse..Bava Kama 46b
Lonely, *niddah* is called..Rosh Hashanah 26a; Sotah 42a

Long
Long life, lengthening prayer..Berachos 54b-55a
Long prayer..Berachos 32b, 54b-55a
Long hair of *Kohanim*
Long hair of *Kohanim*, death..Sanhedrin 83b
Long hair of *Kohanim*, desecrating service..Sanhedrin 22b
Long hair of *Kohanim*, in present times..Taanis 17a-17b; Sanhedrin 22b
Long hair of *Kohanim*, size..Taanis 17a; Sanhedrin 22b
Longer than earth, dimension..Eruvin 21a
Longevity
Longevity..*see also* **Old age**, page 458
Longevity, *Eretz Yisrael*..Berachos 8a
Longevity, how..Berachos 54b-55a; Rosh Hashanah 18a; Megillah 27b-28a; Tamid 32a
Longevity, like father..Eduyos 2:9
Longevity, Rabbi Preida..Eruvin 54b
Longevity, Sages..Shabbos 152a; Megillah 28a
Longevity, seven elders..Bava Basra 121b
Longevity, *tefillin*..Menachos 44a-44b
Longing
Longing, baby..Shabbos 141b-142a
Longing, cure..Shabbos 66b
Look
Look at three things..Avos 3:1
Look at what is inside pitcher..Avos 4:20
Look for, do not look for wealth..Avos 6:4
Look of Sages, curse..Nedarim 7b; Chagigah 5b; Sotah 46b
Looked into Torah, Creation..Avos 3:14
Looking at bride, prohibition..Kesubos 17a
Looking at mating animals..Bava Metzia 91a-91b
Looking at forbidden women, severity..Yoma 74b
Looking at one's wife, modesty..Nedarim 20a
Looking at owneless item, act of acquisition..Bava Metzia 2a, 118a
Looking at, *sotah* and stoned woman..Sanhedrin 44b-45a; Sotah 8a-8b
Looking at wicked..Megillah 28a
Looking, prohibitions..Chagigah 16a
Looks at what is not his..Sotah 9a-9b
Looking at women
Looking at women, choosing another way..Bava Basra 57b
Looking at women, prohibition..Avodah Zarah 20a-20b; Shabbos 64b; Berachos 24a
Looking at women, punishment..Berachos 61a; Eruvin 18b
Looking at women, severity..Yoma 74b; Nedarim 20a; Shabbos 64b
Look, reproving
Look, reproving, episode about Ulla..Pesachim 53b
Look, reproving, Resh Lakish..Kesubos 25b; Makos 5b
Look, reproving, Shmuel..Niddah 26b
Loom
Loom, impurity..Keilim 21:1
Loom, work on Shabbos..Shabbos 75b

L

Lose

Lose hope, do not lose hope of retribution .... Avos 1:7
Lose mind, because of non-Jews .... Eruvin 41b
Losing one's money, how .... Bava Metzia 29b
Lost and did not find, doubt .... Niddah 61a; Pesachim 10a; Bechoros 25b
Lost children, mother not frightened .... Kesubos 62a
Lost her *kesubah* .... Bava Metzia 17b-18a; Kesubos 88b-89b
Lost her *kesubah*, gift to one's wife .... Bava Basra 132a-133a, 150a; Peah 3:7
Lost his way .... Kesubos 109b; Yevamos 37b

Loss

Loss, attributed to whom, proof .... Kesubos 75a
Loss cannot be estimated .... Chagigah 9b; Berachos 26a
Loss, important, Rabbinical Decree .... Eruvin 46a
Loss, may G-d compensate your loss .... Berachos 16b
Loss occasioned by commandment against its benefit .... Bava Basra 78b; Avos 2:1
Loss of *kesubah* .... Yevamos 84a, 85a-85b; Kesubos 72a-72b, 100b, 101a-101b
Loss of money, *muktzeh* .... Shabbos 123a, 123b, 157a
Loss of percentage of produce, deposit .... Bava Metzia 40a
Loss of value of *neveilah*, ox goring occasionally .... Bava Kama 10b-11a, 34a-34b
Loss, Sages did not decree in case of loss .... Kesubos 60a

Lost item

Returning —

Lost item, announcement .... Bava Metzia 28a-28b
Lost item, mark of place .... Bava Metzia 22b-23b, 25b-26a
Lost item, mark on utensil .... Bava Metzia 25a
Lost item, marks .... Bava Metzia 22b-24a, 27a-28a; Yevamos 120a-120b
Lost item, payment for returning .... Bava Kama 116a-116b; Bava Metzia 31b
Lost item, place .... Bava Metzia 26b-27a
Lost item, recognizing .... Gittin 23a; Bava Metzia 23b-24a; Chullin 95b-96a
Lost item, returning .... Bava Kama 57a; Bava Metzia 26b, 30a-31a, 33a
Lost item, trustworthiness to return .... Bava Metzia 28a, 28b

Which —

Lost item, animal .... Bava Metzia 27a, 28b, 30b-31a, 32a
Lost item, coin .... Bava Metzia 25a-25b
Lost item, despairing of recovering .... Bava Metzia 21a-24b, 26b, 27a
Lost item, fell from two people .... Bava Metzia 26a-26b
Lost item, how was it placed .... Bava Metzia 25b, 23a
Lost item, lost willingly .... Bava Metzia 21b-22b
Lost item, put down .... Bava Metzia 23a, 25a-25b
Lost item, worth less than *perutah* .... Bava Metzia 26b, 27a

Who —

Lost item, forbidden benefit from reward .... Kesubos 108a; Nedarim 33b-34a
Lost item found by household members .... Bava Kama 116b; Bava Metzia 12a-12b
Lost item found by worker .... Bava Kama 116b; Bava Metzia 10a, 12b
Lost item of ignoramus .... Pesachim 49b
Lost item of non-Jew .... Bava Kama 113b; Sanhedrin 76b
Lost item of rebel .... Avodah Zarah 26b

Misc. —

Lost item, episode about donkey .... Gittin 45a

Lost item, G-d proclaims poor man who found .... Pesachim 113a

Lost item, guarding .... Bava Kama 56b-57a; Bava Metzia 29a, 82a-82b; Nedarim 33b-34a; Shevuos 44a-44b

Lost item to king, Persians .... Bava Metzia 28b

Lost item, two heads .... Chullin 95b

Lost item, using .... Bava Metzia 29b, 30a

Lot

Lot and his wife, blessing .... Berachos 54b

Lot, flaw and offspring .... Nazir 23a-23b

Lot's wife, impurity .... Niddah 70b

Lots

Lots, act of acquisition .... Bava Basra 106b

Lots casting on Shabbos .... Shabbos 149a-149b

Lots, *Eretz Yisrael* .... Bava Basra 121b-122a

Lots for elders in desert .... Sanhedrin 17a

Lots for firstborn in desert .... Sanhedrin 17a; Bechoros 4b-5a

Lots, goats of Yom Kippur .... Yoma 37a, 39a, 40b

Lots in book, guess .... Chullin 95b

Lots on left hand before Temple destruction .... Yoma 39b

Lots on Yom Kippur, indispensable requirement .... Yoma 39b-41a, 63b

Lots, prohibition .... Shabbos 149b; Sanhedrin 24b-25b

Lots in Temple

Lots in Temple .... Yoma 22a, 23a, 24b-26b, 27b

Lots in Temple, decree .... Tamid 28a

Lots in Temple for daily sacrifice .... Tamid 30a; Yoma 14b

Lots in Temple for incense .... Tamid 32b-33a, 5:2

Lots in Temple, how .... Yoma 23a

Love

Love .... *see also* **Friend**, page 239

Love and fear, Job .... Sotah 31a

Love and fear, preference .... Sotah 31a

Love depending on something .... Avos 5:16

Love of commandments, custom of *lulav* .... Succah 41b

Love of *Eretz Yisrael*, episodes .... Kesubos 112a-112b

Love of G-d to Israel .... Avos 3:14

Love of judge and Sage .... Kesubos 105b

Love of peace and people .... Avos 1:12

Love of Torah, Rabbi Elazar .... Eruvin 54b

Love overrides one's better judgement .... Sanhedrin 105b

Love, proverb .... Sanhedrin 7a

Love through Torah war .... Kiddushin 30b

Love each other, Sages .... Shabbos 51a; Sanhedrin 24a

Love work .... Avos 1:1, 1:10

Love your neighbor, kind death .... Sanhedrin 45a, 52a; Pesachim 75a; Kesubos 37b; Sotah 8b;
Bava Kama 51a

Loved Above .... Berachos 17a

Loved by men and G-d .... Avos 3:1

Loved by men and G-d .... Avos 3:10

Loved by people, loves others .... Berachos 17a

Loving one another .... Pesachim 113b

L

Loving one's neighbors .... Sanhedrin 76b; Yevamos 62b-63a
Loving one's wife like oneself .... Sanhedrin 76b; Yevamos 62b-63a
Loving peace, Aaron .... Sanhedrin 6b; Avos 1:12
Loving Sages .... Shabbos 23b
Loving sufferings of exile .... Shabbos 13b

Low
Low rate, sale .... Bava Metzia 74b
Low voice in prayer, source .... Berachos 31a

Lowering prices, episode .... Pesachim 30a; Succah 34b; Krisos 8a

Luach .... *see* **Calendar,** page 84

Luchos .... *see* **Tablets,** page 670

Ludeans, Resh Lakish .... Gittin 47a

Ludkiya, episode about oil .... Menachos 85b

Lukewarm, making lukewarm is cooking .... Shabbos 40b

Lukus and Lus .... Gittin 11a

Lulav

Kashrus —
Lulav, "yours" .... Succah 41b; Pesachim 38a; Bava Basra 137a-137b
Lulav, dimension .... Succah 29b, 32b; Niddah 26a
Lulav, disqualified .... Succah 32a; Bava Kama 96a-96b
Lulav, dry .... Succah 29b
Lulav, not to add to commandment .... Sanhedrin 88b; Succah 31a-31b
Lulav, second tithe .... Pesachim 38a
Lulav, stolen .... Succah 27b, 29b-30a

Shaking —
Lulav, at daytime .... Succah 43a; Shabbos 131b
Lulav, binding, intervening substance .... Succah 36b
Lulav, blessing .... Pesachim 7b; Succah 37b, 45b
Lulav, blessing before performing commandment ...... Succah 42a
Lulav, custom showing love .... Succah 41b
Lulav, educating child .... Succah 42a; Arachin 2b
Lulav, first day .... Succah 43a
Lulav, how to take .... Succah 31b, 37b, 45b
Lulav in Temple .... Succah 44b-45a
Lulav, seven days .... Succah 41a; Rosh Hashanah 30a
Lulav, Shabbos .... Succah 42b-43a, 44a
Lulav, shaking .... Succah 37b-38a

Misc. —
Lulav, a thousand *zuz* .... Succah 41b
Lulav, binding .... Menachos 27a; Succah 11a, 33b
Lulav, kapos .... Succah 31b-32b
Lulav, keeping in water .... Succah 42a
Lulav, like building an Altar .... Succah 45a-45b
Lulav, merit for rain .... Taanis 2b
Lulav, muktzeh .... Succah 46b
Lulav to child .... Succah 46b
Lulav, Israel united like a bunch .... Menachos 27a

Lulianus and Papus .... Taanis 18b

Luminaries, prohibition to represent .... Avodah Zarah 42b-43b; Rosh Hashanah 24a-24b

L

Lunar cycle .... Rosh Hashanah 20b
Lung
    Treifah —
      Lung, adhesions .... Chullin 46b-47a, 48a
      Lung, blister .... Chullin 47a
      Lung, cases of *treifah* .... Chullin 46b, 47b-48a
      Lung, change in lobes .... Chullin 47a-47b
      Lung, change of appearance .... Chullin 47b
      Lung, collapsing .... Chullin 53b
      Lung, containing clear water .... Chullin 55b
      Lung, hardened .... Chullin 55b
      Lung, hole .... Chullin 45b, 46a-46b, 49a, 57a
      Lung, liquid in lung .... Chullin 55b
      Lung, lobe .... Chullin 47a-47b
      Lung, pimples .... Chullin 48a-48b
      Lung, stuck to thorax .... Chullin 48a
      Lung, worm coming out .... Chullin 49a
    Misc. —
      Lung pumps liquids .... Berachos 61b
      Lung, remedy for eye .... Chullin 49a
Lupine
    Lupine, preparing it .... Beitzah 25b
    Lupine, rebuke against idolatry .... Beitzah 25b
Lust, their G-d hates lust .... Sanhedrin 93a
Luz
    Luz, its advantages .... Sotah 46b
    Luz, reward for Canaanite .... Sotah 46b
Lying
    Lying down, means death .... Bava Basra 116a
    Lying on back .... Berachos 13b; Niddah 14a
    Lying on back, reading *Shema* .... Berachos 13b; Niddah 14a
Lying, comparable to idolatry .... Sanhedrin 92a

L

Ma yisron la'adam..*see* **Under the sun, no profit**, page 714

Ma'is alei..*see* **Disgusting to me, rebellious wife**, page 166

Maabarta, *tefillin* boxes..Menachos 35a

Maachah, Asa's mother, idol...Avodah Zarah 44a

Maah, value...Kiddushin 12a

Maakeh...*see* **Safety fence**, page 582

Maaleh ashan, incense...Yoma 53a

Maaleh bachutz.......................................*see* **Offering sacrifice outside Temple**, page 455

Maamad shloshtan..............................*see* **Three men, act of acquisition of debt**, page 689

Maamad umoshav le'mes...............................*see* **Comforting the bereaved, sitting**, page 116

Maamad Yisrael

   Maamad Yisrael, fasts..Taanis 27b

   Maamad Yisrael, prayer..Taanis 27b-28b; Yoma 37b

   Maamad Yisrael, prohibitions...Taanis 17a

   Maamad Yisrael, Torah reading..Taanis 27b-28a

   Maamad Yisrael, why..Taanis 27a

Maamar...*see* **Kiddushin** **for levirate marriage**, page 338

Maamid betaaroves..*see* **Ingredient**, page 308

Maamid..*see* **Support**, page 664

Maaminim bnei maaminim..............................*see* **Believers sons of believers**, page 51

Maarachos mizbeach.............................*see* **Piles of wood on Altar**, page 488

Maariv

   Maariv, importance..Berachos 6b

   Maariv, voluntary..Berachos 27b; Shabbos 9b; Yoma 87b

   Maariv, time...Berachos 27a

Maasav garmu...............................*see* **Pit, movable item causing damage**, page 490

Maasav merubim..*see* **Acts, numerous**, page 8

Maaseh

   Maaseh...*see* **Act**, page 7

   Maaseh beis din...*see* **Ruling of beis din**, page 574

   Maaseh bereshis..*see* **Creation of world**, page 133

   Maaseh Merkavah..*see* **Heavenly Chariot**, page 274

   Maaseh nissim...*see* **Miracle**, page 413

   Maaseh Rav...*see* **Act of teacher, ruling**, page 7

Maaseh rokem and choshev, definition .... Yoma 72b

Maaseh uman .... *see* **Work of expert,** *Chol HaMoed,* page 760

Maaser ani .... *see* **Tithe for poor,** page 694

Maaser beheimah .... *see* **Tithe of animal,** page 694

Maaser sheni .... *see* **Second tithe,** page 595

Maaseros .... *see* **Tithe,** page 693

Maavir al hamitzvos .... *see* **Passing by commandments,** page 475

Maavir birshus harabim .... *see* **Carrying in public domain, source of prohibition,** page 88

Maavir midaas baal habayis .... *see* **Changing from owner's will,** page 96

Maavir midosav .... *see* **Conceding Sage,** page 119

Maavirim al daato .... *see* **Make one lose his mind,** page 386

Maayan .... *see* **Well,** page 740

Maayanos .... *see* **Liquids,** page 373

Mabul .... *see* **Flood,** page 230

Machanos .... *see* **Camp,** page 85

Machatzis hashekel .... *see* **Half** *shekel,* page 266

Machlokes .... *see* **Dispute,** page 167; *see also* **Quarrel,** page 514

Machlon and Kilyon .... Bava Basra 91a, 91b

Machpelah Cave

    Machpelah Cave .... Eruvin 53a; Sotah 13a; Bava Basra 58a

    Machpelah Cave, Eliezer .... Bava Basra 58a

    Machpelah Cave, Rabbi Banaah .... Bava Basra 58a

Machshavah .... *see* **Intent,** page 311

Machshirei mitzvah .... *see* **Accessories for commandment,** page 5

Machshirei ochel nefesh .... *see* **Accessories to prepare food, work on Yom Tov,** page 5

Machshirin .... *see* **Accessories,** page 5

Machzir grushaso .... *see* **Remarrying one's former wife,** page 556

Madaf, Rabbinical impurity .... Niddah 4b; Zavim 4:6

Madhevah, Babylon .... Shabbos 149b-150a

Mafik, significance .... Eruvin 65a

Mafkiin she'arim .... *see* **Raising prices,** page 535

Mafkir nezakav .... *see* **Abandoning broken item which caused damage,** page 1

Mafraatah, *treifah* .... *see* **Meat of stomach,** *treifah,* page 399

Maftir

    Maftir, cantor for blessings of *Shema* .... Megillah 24a-24b

    Maftir, is he counted among men called up to Torah .... Megillah 23a

Magen

    Magen Avos Bidvaro, Shabbos .... Shabbos 24b

    Magen David, Haftorah .... Pesachim 117b

Magic, sleight of hand .... Sanhedrin 65b, 67b; Chullin 56b-57a

Magician, episodes .... Sanhedrin 67b; Chullin 56b-57a

Magnet, Jeroboam's calves .... Sotah 47a

Magog, nation .... Yoma 10a

Mah nefshach .... *see* **One of two things, dusk,** page 460

Mah nishtanah .... Pesachim 115b, 116a

Mai shier dehai shier .... *see* **Non exhaustive list, which law was omitted as well,** page 447

Maidservant

  Marriage —

    Maidservant, *kiddushin* .... Kiddushin 68b

Maidservant, married one's maidservant .... Gittin 39b-40a
Maidservant, promised, lashes for intimate relations .... Krisos 10b-11a
Maidservant, promised, sacrifice .... Shabbos 71b-72a; Krisos 9a, 10b-11a; Gittin 41b, 43a
Maidservant, shame and marriage .... Niddah 47a
Maidservant to Hebrew slave .... Kiddushin 15a
Maidservant to *Kohen* slave .... Kiddushin 21b
Maidservant to unmarried Hebrew slave .... Kiddushin 20a; Temurah 30a

Misc. —
Maidservant, episode about freedom .... Gittin 43b, 38a-38b; Yevamos 66a
Maidservant for slave, non-Jew .... Sanhedrin 57a, 58b
Maidservant of Rabban Gamliel, impurity .... Niddah 6b
Maidservant, son born to Jew from .... Yevamos 23a; Kiddushin 68b
Maidservant, woman who stole .... Sotah 23b
Maidservants of wife .... Kesubos 80b
Maidservants, work by married woman .... Kesubos 59b, 61a, 61b

Maidservant, Hebrew
Maidservant, Hebrew, acts of acquisition .... Kiddushin 9b, 11b-12a
Maidservant, Hebrew, father's death .... Kiddushin 16a-16b; Bava Metzia 12b
Maidservant, Hebrew, found item .... Kiddushin 16b
Maidservant, Hebrew, her mother .... Sotah 23b
Maidservant, Hebrew, second sale .... Kiddushin 18a-18b; Bechoros 34a
Maidservant, Hebrew, to relatives .... Kiddushin 18b, 19b-20a, 44b
Maidservant, Hebrew, young and adolescent .... Kiddushin 4a-4b

Maidservant of Rebbi
Maidservant of Rebbi, explanation of words .... Rosh Hashanah 26b
Maidservant of Rebbi, old age .... Shabbos 152a
Maidservant of Rebbi, poetic phrases .... Eruvin 53b
Maidservant of Rebbi, Rebbi's death .... Kesubos 104a
Maidservant of Rebbi, reproved man who curled his hair ..... Nazir 3a; Rosh Hashanah 26b;
.... Megillah 18a

Majority
Animals —
Majority of animals are impure .... Chullin 63b
Majority of birds are pure .... Chullin 63b
Majority of limb, connection of sacrificial flesh .... Zevachim 87b
Majority of limb, firstborn .... Chullin 70a; Krisos 14a
Majority of signs, sacrifice .... Chullin 29a
Majority of thickness or of circumference .... Chullin 44a-44b

Beis din —
Majority, death penalty .... Sanhedrin 69a-69b
Majority, judges .... Sanhedrin 3b
Majority, judges for capital cases .... Sanhedrin 17a
Majority of *Sanhedrin*, Yair .... Bava Basra 121b

Cases —
Majority experts, slaughtering .... Chullin 3b, 12a-12b
Majority of brides are virgins .... Kesubos 16a-16b; Bava Basra 92b
Majority of child's acts are carelessly done .... Chullin 86a-86b
Majority of ignoramus separate tithes .. Beitzah 35b; Shabbos 13a, 23a; Kesubos 24a; Gittin 61a; Menachos 31a
Majority of men in death throes die .... Gittin 28a; Kiddushin 71b; Shevuos 33a, 37b; Arachin 18a

M

Majority of sick people live...Gittin 28a; Kiddushin 71b; Bava Basra 153b
Majority of women conceive and give birth..Yevamos 119a
Jews —
Majority, doubt if Jewish..Yoma 84b-85a
Majority of Jews, lineage...Kesubos 15b
Majority of thieves are Jews.....................................Avodah Zarah 70a; Beitzah 15a
Principles —
Majority and closeness...Bava Basra 23b-24b; Beitzah 10b
Majority, because of change...Bechoros 42b
Majority considered as obvious, cases...Niddah 18a-19a
Majority depending on act...Bechoros 20a
Majority, double, stringency in lineage..Kesubos 15a-15b
Majority like whole.......................Nazir 42a; Horayos 3b; Chullin 19a, 70a; Niddah 29a
Majority, not in front of us..............Yevamos 119a-119b; Chullin 11a-12a; Bechoros 19b
Majority, in place of doubt and in other place..........Kesubos 15a; Bava Kama 44b; Sanhedrin 79a;
....Pesachim 9b; Yevamos 16b; Niddah 18a
Majority to collect money......................Bava Basra 92a-93b; Bava Kama 27a-27b, 46a-46b
Majority vs. *chazakah*...Yevamos 119a-119b; Niddah 18a-19a
Majority, we forbid even because of minority........Chullin 6a, 11b, 86a-86b; Yevamos 61b, 119a;
..............Gittin 2b; Avodah Zarah 34b, 40b; Bechoros 19b-20b, 42b; Niddah 31b-32a, 48a
Misc. —
Majority, burning *terumah*..Kiddushin 80a-80b
Majority in mixture...*see* **Mixture**, page 410
Majority, mixture of impurity...Machshirin 2:3-11
Majority obvious, *zimun*..Berachos 48a-48b
Majority of bones, impurity.........................Bechoros 45a; Oholos 2:1; Eduyos 1:7; Nazir 52b
Majority of community, sacrifice for public error.........................Horayos 3a-3b, 4b-5a
Majority of people sin by theft...Bava Basra 165a
Majority of signs properly slaughtered..Chullin 30b
Majority of sons, resemble mother's brothers...Bava Basra 110a
Majority, saving a life..Yoma 84b-85a
Majority, wordings of vows...Nedarim 53a
Majority of opinions
Majority of opinions, decision...Shevuos 42a
Majority of opinions, disqualified witnesses.................Yevamos 88b, 117b; Sotah 31b-32a, 47b
Majority of opinions, Rabbinical Decree..Eruvin 46a
Majority of opinions, rule..........Avodah Zarah 7a; Eduyos 5:7; Berachos 9a, 37a; Shabbos 60b, 130b;
............Yoma 36b; Beitzah 11a; Yevamos 40a, 45a, 46b, 47a; Bava Kama 102a; Bava Basra 36b;
....Bechoros 37a; Niddah 30b, 49a
Majority of Sages
Majority of Sages, concerning Rabbinical Decree, like individual...........................Eruvin 46a
Majority of Sages, difference of opinion not decided.............Eduyos 5:7; Avodah Zarah 7a
Majority of Sages, taking into consideration individual opinion...Yevamos 83a; Megillah 18b
Majority of Sages, to accept his words...Gittin 20a, 77a
Makdim refuah lamakah.................................*see* **Preparing cure before illness**, page 501
Makdim shelom chavero.......................................*see* **Greeting fellow first**, page 258
Makdish..*see* **Consecrating**, page 123
Make
Make but not from what is already made, succah.............Succah 11a-11b, 12a-12b, 15a, 16a

M

Make but not from what is already made, *tzitzis* .... Succah 11a-11b
Make do with little .... Avos 6:4
Make for yourself a Rav .... Avos 1:6, 1:16
Make one lose his mind .... Eruvin 41b
Make your Shabbos a weekday, charity .... Pesachim 112a, 113a; Shabbos 118a
Make your Torah a fixed duty .... Avos 1:15
Makes as if His eye cannot see .... Bava Kama 79b
Making bed, *niddah* .... Kesubos 4b, 61a
Making merry every day .... Shabbos 151b
Making oneself as mute .... Chullin 89a
Making one sit in house of study, behavior .... Shabbos 118b
Making up, prayer .... Berachos 26a-26b
Making valid, changing name .... Menachos 4a-5a
Makeh aviv .... *see* **Hitting one's father**, page 280
Makeh bepatish .... *see* **Final touch, cases**, page 223
Make-up, Shabbos .... Shabbos 94b-95a
Makir tovah .... *see* **Gratitude**, page 256
Makirei kehunah .... *see* ***Kohen*** **habitually receiving priestly gifts**, page 345
Makkas mardus .... *see* **Lashes (Rabbinical Decree)**, page 353
Makom .... *see* **Place**, page 490
Makom petur .... *see* ***Mekom petur***, page 403
Makos, order of *mesechtos* .... Shevuos 2b-3a
Makos Mitzraim .... *see* **Egypt, ten plagues** page 189
Makpid, *chatzitzah* .... *see* **Intervening substances, fastidious person**, page 316
Malachi the prophet .... Megillah 15a; Sanhedrin 11a; Yoma 9b
Malach .... *see* **Angel**, page 22
Malbin panim .... *see* **Humiliating**, page 287
Malchus, text of blessing .... Berachos 40b, 49a
Malchuyos
   Malchuyos, Rosh Hashanah .... Rosh Hashanah 16a, 32a-32b, 34b
   Malchuyos, war .... Taanis 16b-17a
Male
   Male child, born with his loaf in hand .... Niddah 31b
   Male child, reward for wooing wife .... Bava Basra 10b
   Male for certain, androgyny *zav* .... Niddah 28b
   Male, sacrifice .... Temurah 14a
   Male, seclusion .... Kiddushin 82a
   Male will receive, will .... Bava Basra 141a-141b
Malkosh, rain .... Taanis 5a, 6a
Malkus .... *see* **Lashes**, page 353
Maluah kerote'ach .... *see* **Salted, like boiling**, page 587
Mamon be'alim .... *see* **Owner's money**, page 467
Mamon gavoah .... *see* **Divine property, second tithe**, page 169
Mamon she'ein lo tov'im .... *see* **Money, without claimants**, page 421
Mamzer .... *see* **Illegitimate child**, page 298
Man
   ***Aggadah* —**
      Man, "you are called Man" .... Yevamos 61a; Bava Metzia 114b; Krisos 6b
      Man and animal, shows his inferiority .... Chullin 5b

M

Man, compared to fish..Avodah Zarah 3b-4a
Man, honest, who died...Moed Katan 25a
Man honors his place...Taanis 21b
Man is born to toil...Sanhedrin 99b
Man is not judged when in pain...Bava Basra 16b
Man, like angel and like beast...Chagigah 16a
Man's foolishness misleads him..Taanis 9a
Men are like grass...Eruvin 54a
Men knowing Scripture, future reward................................Bava Metzia 33b

Characteristics —
Man, damages from pit..Bava Kama 53b-54a
Man, damaging, different from ox......................................Bava Kama 34b-35a
Man does not sin for someone else's benefit............Kiddushin 63b; Bava Metzia 5b; Shevuos 42b;
....Arachin 23a
Man does not envy etc...Sanhedrin 105b
Man does not abandon his money, Shabbos.................Shabbos 153a; Sanhedrin 72a; Yoma 85b
Man habitually checks his pockets...Bava Metzia 21b
Man, has his hour..Avos 4:3
Man has *mazal*...Bava Kama 2b; Shabbos 53b
Man hurries without thinking when his dear one is dead................Shabbos 43b-44a; Yoma 85a
Man is forever responsible for damage.............................Bava Kama 26a-26b
Man, known by his cup, purse, and anger..................................Eruvin 65b
Man sitting, measures a cubit..Succah 7b
Man who damaged, unavoidable situation........................Bava Kama 28b-29a

Death —
Man condemned to death penalty, his sacrifice....................Arachin 6b-7a
Man condemned to death penalty, intermingled..................Sanhedrin 80b
Men who must be killed and not saved..........Avodah Zarah 26a-26b; Chullin 13b; Sanhedrin 57a

Men put to death by government
Men put to death by government, eulogy...........................Sanhedrin 11a
Men put to death by government, possessions.................Sanhedrin 48b
Men put to death by government, prophecies.............Sanhedrin 11a, 68a
Men put to death by government, their worth.....................Bava Basra 10b

Episodes —
Man, found one out of a thousand...Gittin 45a
Man picking up wood in desert........................Shabbos 96b; Sanhedrin 78b
Man picking up wood in desert, Moses did not know....Sanhedrin 78b; Bava Basra 119a-119b
Man, this is a man....................Shabbos 112b; Eruvin 24a; Avodah Zarah 10b
Man was created alone...Sanhedrin 38a
Man whom I feared is gone...Moed Katan 24a
Men destined for World to Come..Taanis 22a

Forbidden relations —
Man guilty of forbidden relations, "crooked thing cannot be corrected"..Chagigah 9b-10a
Man guilty of forbidden relations, episode about slander.................Berachos 23a
Man guilty of forbidden relations, his wife also...............................Sotah 10a
Man guilty of forbidden relations, indigent......................................Sotah 4b
Man guilty of forbidden relations, punishment.................................Sotah 4b
Man guilty of forbidden relations, stumbling-block.....................Yevamos 37b
Man guilty of forbidden relations warned about snake.................Nedarim 91b

Man guilty of forbidden relations who fled and who saved .... Nedarim 91b

Impurity —

Man having had discharge .... *see **Zav**, page 775*

Man, impurities coming from his body .... Keilim 1:5

Man, impurity from primary source .... Bava Kama 2b

Man, impurity of food .... Krisos 21a-21b; Uktzin 3:2

Marriage —

Man, agent to receive divorce certificate .... Gittin 62b

Man cannot live together with snake .... Kesubos 72a, 77a, 86b

Man dies only for his wife .... Sanhedrin 22b

Man does not accept his wife's blemishes .... Kesubos 75b-76a

Man does not allow his wife to be humiliated .... Kesubos 74b-75a, 97b; Gittin 46a

Man does not make wedding feast, trustworthiness .... Kesuvos 10a; Yevamos 107a

Man looks for a wife .... Kiddushin 2b; Niddah 31b

Man produces sperm, female .... Niddah 25b, 28a, 31a; Berachos 60a

Testimony —

Man considered like his own relative .... Yevamos 25b; Sanhedrin 9b-10a, 25a

Man does not find any wrong in himself .... Kesubos 105b; Shabbos 119a

Man is believed about himself .... Krisos 12a-12b

Man makes a mistake, how many hours .... Pesachim 11b-13a; Sanhedrin 40b

Man pretending to be wicked .... Yevamos 25b; Sanhedrin 9b-10a

Vows —

Man forbidden by vow to benefit, advice .... Nedarim 43a; Kesubos 70b

Man forbidden by vow to benefit, cases of sale .... Nedarim 31a-31b

Man forbidden by vow to benefit from food, prohibitions .... Megillah 8a; Nedarim 32b-33a

Man forbidden by vow to benefit, healing .... Nedarim 41b

Man forbidden by vow to benefit, out of his possession .... Nedarim 42a-42b, 46a, 47a

Man forbidden by vow to benefit, prohibitions .... Nedarim 38a-38b, 41b

Man forbidden by vow to benefit, Rabbinical Decrees .... Nedarim 42b-43a

Man forbidden by vow to benefit, rent .... Nedarim 46b

Man forbidden by vow to benefit, repaying debt .... Nedarim 33a-33b; Kesubos 107b-108b

Man forbidden by vow to benefit, returning lost item .... Nedarim 33b-34a

Man forbidden by vow to benefit, Sabbatical year .... Nedarim 42a

Man forbidden by vow to benefit, visiting the sick .... Nedarim 38b-39b

Misc. —

Man and object, oath .... Nedarim 2b

Man does not prohibit item not his .... Yevamos 83b

Man having animal form, can he live .... Niddah 23a-23b

Man is hard as iron .... Menachos 95b

Man performing good deeds, standing before .... Kiddushin 33b

Man, scholars .... Yoma 71a

Man who dies in tent, Torah .... Gittin 57b; Berachos 63b; Shabbos 83b

Men of pure mind, behavior .... Sanhedrin 23a

Mandrakes, Reuben .... Sanhedrin 99b

***Maneh* of Temple,** double .... Bechoros 5a-5b; Bava Basra 90a-90b; Menachos 77a

Manesseh

Manesseh, derogatory commentaries .... Sanhedrin 99b

Manesseh found pretext .... Sanhedrin 101b

Manesseh, his wisdom and wickedness .... Sanhedrin 102b-103b

Manesseh killed Isaiah .... Yevamos 49b

Manesseh, place to cut bread .... Sanhedrin 102b

Manesseh, repentance .... Sanhedrin 101a-101b, 102b-103a

Manesseh, World to Come .... Sanhedrin 104b

Manichim chayei olam .... *see* **Abandoned eternal life, page 1**

Manichim divrei haRav! .... *see* **Following teacher and not disciple!, page 231**

Manna

Manna, "to test you" .... Yoma 74b

Manna, date .... Shabbos 87b

Manna in desert .... Yoma 75a-76a

Manna, period when it fell .... Kiddushin 38a

Manna, sixty times sweeter than honey .... Berachos 57b

Manna, through Moses' merit .... Taanis 9a

Manna, when did it dissolve .... Berachos 27a

Manoah

Manoah, Boaz's feasts .... Bava Basra 91a

Manoah, ignoramus .... Berachos 61a; Eruvin 18b

Manure

Manure, abundant, damage to field .... Bava Basra 24b

Manure in courtyard .... Bava Basra 11b

Manure, non-Jew on Shabbos .... Moed Katan 12a

Manure, Sabbatical year .... Sheviis 3:1-4; Moed Katan 4b

Many daughters have accomplished, Israel .... Sanhedrin 20a

Maos konos .... *see* **Money as an act of acquisition, price of ox, page 421**

Mar bar Rav Ashi

Mar bar Rav Ashi, demon had to pay .... Chullin 105b

Mar bar Rav Ashi, kerchief .... Kiddushin 8a

Mar Bar Rav Ashi, Rosh Yeshivah .... Bava Basra 12b

Mar bar Ravina

Mar bar Ravina, fasts .... Pesachim 68b

Mar bar Ravina, miracles .... Berachos 54a

Mar bar Yosef, dispute at Bei Avidan .... Shabbos 116a

Mar Ukva

Mar Ukva and his brother, two sisters .... Berachos 44a

Mar Ukva, charity before his death .... Kesubos 67b

Mar Ukva, dispute with Geniva .... Gittin 7a

Mar Ukva, distance from bribe .... Kesubos 105b

Mar Ukva entered an oven .... Kesubos 67b

Mar Ukva, honoring his teacher .... Moed Katan 16b

Mar Ukva, preventing humiliation .... Kesubos 67b

Mar Ukva, trial .... Sanhedrin 31b

Mar Yehudah, Shvor (Shapor) Malka .... Avodah Zarah 76b

Mar Zutra son of Rabbi Nachman, personal mistake .... Chullin 94b

Mar Zutra

Mar Zutra, excommunication of butcher .... Chullin 18a

Mar Zutra, meal for king .... Kesubos 61a-61b

Mar Zutra, moral teachings to himself .... Yoma 87a; Sanhedrin 7b

Mar Zutra, prayer with congregation .... Berachos 30a

Mar Zutra, tenant farmer's fruit .... Bava Metzia 22a

M

Mar Zutra, wiping hands on someone's garment .... Bava Metzia 24a

Mara de'asra .... *see* **Rav of city**, page 543

Mara kama .... *see* **First owner, *chazakah***, page 225

Mara likvurah .... *see* **Burial, "someone to bury me," claim**, page 80

Marah, commandments given in .... Sanhedrin 56b; Horayos 8b

Marbeh beshiurim .... *see* **Adding to permitted quantity**, page 10

Marbeh nechasim marbeh daagah .... *see* **More possessions, more worry**, page 423

Marcheshes, container or meal offering .... Menachos 63a

Marcheshes .... *see* **Deep fried, meal offering**, page 157

Mareh makom .... *see* **Detail, specific, agent**, page 162

Marei deAbraham .... *see* **Master of Abraham**, page 393

Mareimar, prayer with congregation .... Berachos 30a

Maris ayin .... *see* **Appearance**, page 30

Mark

Mark on utensil, deposit .... Yevamos 115b, 116a

Marks, leprosy .... Negaim 10:10

Marks on measuring utensil, in Temple .... Menachos 87b-88a; Shabbos 80b; Bava Basra 86b

Marketplaces

Marketplaces, judgment of non-Jews .... Avodah Zarah 2b

Marketplaces, lands of the living .... Yoma 71a

Marketplaces of Tzipori .... Bava Basra 75b

Marking

Marking grave and *orlah* .... Bava Kama 69a

Marking graves .... Moed Katan 5a-6a

Marking graves, Rabbi Benaah .... Bava Basra 58a

Marking graves, Rabbi Shimon .... Shabbos 33b-34a

Marking *revai*, how .... Maaser Sheni 5:1; Bava Kama 69a

Markolis

Markolis .... Avodah Zarah 49b-50a, 51a; Bava Metzia 25b

Markolis, debasing cult .... Sanhedrin 64a

Maror .... *see* **Bitter herbs**, page 60

Marriage

Advice —

Marriage .... *see also* **Forbidden relations**, page 233; ***Kiddushin***, page 337; **Wedding**, page 739

Marriage and learning Torah .... Kiddushin 29b-30a; Yoma 72b; Menachos 110a

Marriage, four women .... Yevamos 44a

Marriage, free your slave for your aging daughter .... Pesachim 113a

Marriage, go down a level .... Yevamos 63a

Marriage, her eyes are beautiful .... Taanis 24a

Marriage, house and vineyard .... Sotah 44a

Marriage, prohibition to marry before seeing her .... Kiddushin 41a

Aggadah —

Marriage, *aggadah* .... Moed Katan 18b; Sotah 2a

Marriage, as if he gave birth to her .... Sotah 12a

Marriage, concern if someone else precedes him .... Moed Katan 18b

Marriage, man looks for wife .... Kiddushin 2b; Niddah 31b

Marriage, of more distinguished lineage than the first .... Bechoros 8b

Marriage, prayer .... Moed Katan 18b

Marriage, prayer "*le'es metzo*" .... Berachos 8a

Marriage, pure body .... Pesachim 112b

Episodes —
Marriage, advancing wedding date .... Kesubos 62b
Marriage, Ben Azzai .... Kesubos 63a
Marriage, daughter to disciple .... Horayos 12b
Marriage, Rabbi Akiva .... Kesubos 62b-63a; Nedarim 50a
Marriage, Rav Chisda's daughter .... Bava Basra 12b
Marriage, refusal of Zeirei .... Kiddushin 71b
Marriage, refused proposal of non-Jew's son .... Yevamos 45a
Marriage, tax collector's wife .... Bechoros 30b; Avodah Zarah 39a

Prohibitions —
Marriage between tribes .... Bava Basra 120a; Taanis 30b
Marriage during thirty days mourning period .... Yevamos 43a-43b
Marriage for limited period .... Yoma 18b
Marriage, forbidden with non-Jews .... Avodah Zarah 36b; Kiddushin 68b
Marriage, suspicion .... Yevamos 24b-26a
Marriage, wife died .... Moed Katan 23a
Marriages in two places .... Yevamos 37b

With whom —
Marriage, checking her brothers .... Bava Basra 109b-110a
Marriage, convert, woman .... Berachos 8b; Horayos 13a; Pesachim 112b
Marriage, daughter of scholar .... Pesachim 49a-49b; Yoma 71a-71b
Marriage, epileptics and lepers .... Yevamos 64b
Marriage, freed maidservant .... Horayos 13a
Marriage, identical names of bride's and groom's parents .... Berachos 42a
Marriage, mediocre husband .... Kesubos 75a; Yevamos 118b
Marriage, prostitute's daughter .... Sotah 26b-27a
Marriage, sister's daughter .... Sanhedrin 76b; Yevamos 62b-63a
Marriage, two strange persons .... Bechoros 45b
Marriage, widow and divorcee .... Pesachim 112a-112b; Gittin 90b; Sotah 6a
Marriage, woman of good family .... Bava Basra 109b-110a
Marriage, young girl to old man .... Yevamos 44a; Sanhedrin 76a-76b

Misc. —
Marriage by decree of Edom .... Bava Basra 60b
Marriage, causes levirate marriage .... Yevamos 13a, 30b
Marriage, changing dwelling .... Kesubos 110a-110b; Gittin 44b; Arachin 3a-3b
Marriage contract .... *see* **Kesubah**, page 334
Marriage, for limited periods of time .... Yoma 18b; Yevamos 37b
Marriage for one's son .... Kiddushin 30b
Marriage for one's son and daughter, from when .... Sanhedrin 76a-76b
Marriage, second, sons' troubles .... Yevamos 63b; Berachos 56a
Marriage without match .... Kiddushin 12b; Yevamos 52a
Marriage, woman wants to marry .... Yevamos 113a; Kesubos 319 49b, 86a

Married woman
Married woman, *chazakah* .... Bava Basra 50b-51a
Married woman, consecrating her property .... Bava Metzia 96b
Married woman, damages .... Bava Kama 89a-89b
Married woman, *Gehinnom* .... Bava Metzia 58b
Married woman, rights .... Kesubos 65a-65b

Married woman, wants to divorce in order to marry another ....Nedarim 91b
Married women who sold ....Kesubos 50a, 78a-78b; Bava Kama 88a-88b

Marry
Married by mistake, is marriage effective ....Yevamos 91b
Marry my daughter, condition ....Beitzah 20a
Marrying girl from another tribe ....Bava Basra 120a; Taanis 30b
Marrying, like giving birth to wife ....Sotah 12a
Marrying one's daughter to ignoramus ....Pesachim 49a
Marrying one's daughter to Sage ....Kesubos 111b; Berachos 34b
Marrying one's son in one's house, gift of room ....Gittin 14a; Bava Basra 144a
Marrying sister's daughter, reward ....Sanhedrin 76b; Yevamos 62b-63a

Marrying Hebrew maidservant
Marrying Hebrew maidservant ....Kiddushin 18a, 19a-20a
Marrying Hebrew maidservant, like betrothal ....Kiddushin 18b-19a
Marrying Hebrew maidservant, preference ....Bechoros 13a

Marital relations
How —
Marital relations, care for pregnant woman ....Yevamos 42a; Niddah 31a
Marital relations, modesty ....Niddah 16b-17a; Nedarim 20a-20b; Kesubos 65b
Marital relations, physical closeness ....Kesubos 48a
Marital relations, seducing husband ....Nedarim 20b; Eruvin 100b
Marital relations, seducing wife ....Eruvin 100b; Bava Basra 10b
Prohibitions —
Marital relations, annulling vow ....Nedarim 81b-82a
Marital relations, cases of prohibition ....Nedarim 20a-20b; Gittin 90a; Yevamos 37b
Marital relations, close to menstruation ....Shevuos 18b; Yevamos 62b; Niddah 63b
Marital relations during famine ....Taanis 11a
Marital relations, holy books ....Berachos 25b-26a
Marital relations, mourner ....Moed Katan 15b, 21a
Marital relations, vow to abstain ....Nedarim 15b, 81b-82a; Kesubos 71b
Time —
Marital relations, not at prescribed times ....Yevamos 62b; Pesachim 72b
Marital relations, Shabbos ....Kesubos 62a-62b, 65b
Marital relations, time ....Kesubos 62a-62b
Marital relations, time for pious men ....Niddah 38a
Misc. —
Marital relations, cases of sickness ....Gittin 70a; Pesachim 112b; Kesubos 77b; Niddah 17a
Marital relations, preventing others from ....Eruvin 63b
Marital relations, Sages separated from their wives ....Kesubos 62b; Gittin 6b
Marital relations, too much is harmful ....Shabbos 152a

Marrow, fracture ....Chullin 125a
Marta
Marta, appointment of *Kohen Gadol* ....Yevamos 61a; Yoma 18a
Marta, relinquished her property ....Gittin 56a
Marzach, mourner ....Kesubos 69b
Masa Mechasia
Masa Mechasia, dwelling ....Horayos 12a
Masa Mechasia, indifferent towards Sages ....Kiddushin 33a
Masa Mechasia, strong hearted non-Jew ....Berachos 17b

Masa, *tumah*..*see* **Load, impurity,** page 375

Maseches...*see* **Loom, impurity,** page 377

Maseches Avodah Zarah, Abraham ....Avodah Zarah 14b

Mashach Tura, Torah reading on Pesach ....Megillah 31a

Mashiach...*see* **Messiah,** page 406

Mashiv Haruach

Mashiv Haruach, forgot...Berachos 26b, 29a

Mashiv Haruach, mistake...Taanis 3b

Mashiv Haruach, optional...Taanis 3a-3b

Mashiv Haruach, second blessing...Berachos 33a

Mashiv Haruach, when..Taanis 2b, 3a, 4a-5a

Mashkanta..*see* **Mortgage,** page 423

Mashkeh...*see* **Liquid,** page 372

Mashkon...*see* **Collateral,** page 114

Mashlah ha'or...*see* **Burning started, sacrifices,** page 80

Mashma motzei mimashma ....*see* **Deduction according to previous deduction,** page 155

Mashmaous dorshin.................................*see* **Dispute on scriptual derivation, not on law,** page 167

Masneh levatel hakasuv baTorah ....*see* **Condition to annul law of Torah,** page 121

Masig gevul...*see* **Displacing fence to steal land, squill,** page 167

Masig gevul bemischar..*see* **Competition in commerce,** page 118

Masiin, fire ....Rosh Hashanah 22b

Masks, impurity...Shabbos 66b

Master

Master, Abraham called G-d..Berachos 7b

Master of Abraham.................................Kesubos 2a; Shabbos 22a; Eruvin 75b; Bava Basra 134b

Master, will be judged by cold water..Shabbos 55a

Masturbation...Niddah 13b

Mat

Mat, impurity ....Succah 19b-20b; Keilim 17:3, 17:17; Eduyos 3:4

Mat, impurity of couch...Keilim 20:7

Mat, *s'chach* and impurity...Succah 16a, 19b-20b

Mat upon beehive, hunting on Shabbos ....Beitzah 36a-36b

Mats spread on Shabbos...Shabbos 101b

Matan beseser...*see* **Giving charity secretly,** page 252

Matan secharah betzidah................*see* **Reward explicit in Torah, resurrection of dead,** page 566

Matan Torah...*see* **Giving of Torah,** page 252

Matanah lehachzir..*see* **Gift on condition to return,** page 250

Matanos Laevyonim ....Megillah 7a-7b

Matar (MTR), meaning according to initials ....Kesubos 10b

Matateh, significance ....Rosh Hashanah 26b

Matatron...Sanhedrin 38b

Matchmaking on Shabbos...Shabbos 12a

Matirin lekorban...*see* **Permitting for sacrifice,** page 481

Matirin letaaruvos ....*see* **Prohibition, temporary, mixture,** page 505

Matnos aniim...*see* **Gifts for poor,** page 251

Matnos chatas ....*see* **Sprinkling blood of sin offering, place,** page 652

Matnos kehunah...*see* **Priestly gifts,** page 503

Matriarchs

Matriarchs, hills...Rosh Hashanah 11a

M

Matriarchs, only four .... Berachos 16b
Matriarchs, sterile .... Yevamos 64a-64b
Matriarchs, when did they conceive .... Rosh Hashanah 11a
Matters of city, Sage .... Moed Katan 6a
Matun matun .... see **Patience, episode about red garment**, page 475
Matun matun, red garment .... Berachos 20a
Maturity .... see **Adulthood**, page 12
Matza es mino .... see **Found its kind**, page 223
Matza ishah matza tov .... see **Found woman, found goodness**, page 223
Matza o motzeh .... see **Finding good or bad wife**, page 223
Matza o motze, marriage .... Yevamos 63b; Berachos 8a
Matzah
   Commandment —
    Matzah baked in pot .... Pesachim 37a; Menachos 78b
    Matzah, bread of poverty .... Pesachim 36a-37a, 115b
    Matzah, crumbs .... Berachos 37b
    Matzah, disqualified .... Pesachim 36a-36b
    Matzah for *seder* night, eating .... Pesachim 115a, 115b
    Matzah in present times .... Pesachim 28b, 115a, 116b, 120a; Kiddushin 37b
    Matzah made with juice, leavening .... Pesachim 35a-36a, 38b
    Matzah made with juice, *seder* night .... Pesachim 35a, 36a
    Matzah, meal offering for *nazir* .... Menachos 78a
    Matzah of thanksgiving, Pesach .... Pesachim 38a-38b
    Matzah, ownership .... Pesachim 38a
    Matzah, second tithe .... Pesachim 36b, 37b-38a; Succah 35a
    Matzah soaked, *seder* night .... Pesachim 35a, 41a; Berachos 38b
    Matzah together with bitter herbs .... Pesachim 115a
    Matzah, whole and cut .... Berachos 39b
   Misc. —
    Matzah, different kinds of bread .... Berachos 37b
    Matzah, filaments stretching .... Pesachim 37a
    Matzah for other days of Pesach, preventing leavening .... Pesachim 48b
    Matzah, for sake of commandment .... Pesachim 40a-40b
    Matzah, forbidden to eat .... Pesachim 35b-36a
    Matzah, keeping it from leavening .... Pesachim 40a-40b
    Matzah, kneading and baking .... Pesachim 42a, 48b
    Matzah, quantity of dough .... Pesachim 48a-48b
    Matzah, scalded .... Yevamos 40a
    Matzah, species .... Pesachim 35a
    Matzah, spiced .... Menachos 23b
    Matzah, thickness .... Pesachim 36b-37a; Beitzah 22b
    Matzah, warm water .... Pesachim 36a
    Matzos of Baithus .... Pesachim 37a
Matzah, means leather .... Gittin 22a; Shabbos 79a
Matziv gevul almanah, blessing .... Berachos 58b
Matzmiach Keren, prayer .... Pesachim 117b
Matzran .... see **Neighbor**, page 441
Maav'eh, damaging .... Bava Kama 3b-4b
Mavoi .... see **Closed alley**, page 111

M

Mavriach ari .... *see* **Preventing a loss**, page 502

Maxims, Dan and Zebulun tribes .... Pesachim 4a

May

    May blessing come to him! .... Pesachim 32a; Eruvin 29b

    May G-d compensate your loss .... Berachos 16b

    May G-d save us .... Shabbos 84b; Kesubos 45b; Bava Kama 65b

    May his memory be a blessing .... Kiddushin 31b

    May it be His will that my words be accepted .... Beitzah 38a

    May it be His will that you permit forbidden fat! .... Shabbos 136b

    May it be His will, with congregation .... Berachos 30a

    May it be Your will, prayers .... Berachos 16b-17a; Avos 5:20

    May there be more like you in Israel .... Yevamos 16a

    May this action be a remedy for me .... Berachos 60a

Mayan pasuach .... *see* **Opening of womb, stays open and blood flows**, page 461

Mayanos hazav .... *see* **Liquids of *zav***, page 373

Mayim acharonim .... *see* **Washing hands after meal**, page 733

Mazal .... *see* **Fate**, page 216

M'deRabbanan .... *see* **Rabbinical Decree**, page 533

Me'abed atzmo ladaas .... *see* **Suicide, prohibition**, page 663

Me'akev .... *see* **Indispensable requirement**, page 308

Me'amer .... *see* **Gathering fruit**, page 245

Me'amtzin, with *aleph* or *ayin* .... Shabbos 77b

Me'aras HaMachpelah .... *see* **Machpelah Cave**, page 383

Me'aras Rashbi .... *see* **Cave of Rabbi Shimon bar Yochai**, page 90

Me'aseh chaveiro lemitzvah .... *see* **Causing another to do a commandment**, page 89

Me'ein haprat .... *see* **General and specific**, page 247

Me'ein olam haba .... *see* **World to Come (Semblance)**, page 763

Me'ein

    Me'ein shalosh, blessing .... Berachos 37a-37b, 44a

    Me'ein Shemoneh Esrei .... Berachos 29a

    Me'ein sheva, Shabbos .... Shabbos 24b

Me'ein Shemoneh Esrei .... *see* **Short *Shemoneh Esrei***, page 620

Me'es le'es .... *see* **Twenty four hours, concerning which laws**, page 706

Me'es le'es, *shanim* .... *see* **Year, complete or not**, page 767

Me'igra rama lebira .... *see* **Falling from high roof down to pit**, page 213

Me'ilah .... *see* **Personal use**, page 483

Meager food, removing thickness having been absorbed .... Chullin 97a

Meal

    Behavior —

        Meal, behavior of servant .... Chullin 107b

        Meal, customs in Jerusalem .... Sanhedrin 23a

        Meal, enjoyable, keep away .... Gittin 70a

        Meal, good manners .... Berachos 43a, 46b-47b

        Meal, salt and soup .... Berachos 44a

        Meal, special, four days in year .... Chullin 83a

        Meal, words of Torah .... Avos 3:3; Sanhedrin 101a

        Meals during day .... Shabbos 10a; Pesachim 12b; Bava Metzia 107b; Berachos 2b

    Meals for commandments —

        Meal .... *see also* **Feast**, page 218

M

Meal before fast, *Tisha B'Av* .... Taanis 29b, 30a-30b; Sanhedrin 70a
Meal before fast, Yom Kippur .... Yoma 81b; Rosh Hashanah 9a-9b
Meal for adding a month .... Sanhedrin 70b
Meal for mourners .... *see* **Havraah** meal, page 273
Meal, blessings .... Berachos 41b-42a
Meal by *kav*, how many .... Kesubos 64b
Meal, nine figs .... Eruvin 80b
Meal of non-Jew, prohibition .... Avodah Zarah 8a-8b; Sanhedrin 104a
Meal of workers .... Bava Metzia 86a-87a
Meal shared, canceling partnership .... Pesachim 89b
Meal with a Sage, Divine Presence .... Berachos 64a
Meal with ignoramus, Sage must keep away .... Berachos 43b
Meals, two, *eruv* .... Eruvin 82b-83a; Kesubos 64b; Keilim 17:11
Meals on Shabbos
Meals on Shabbos, how many .... Shabbos 117b-118a, 118b; Kesubos 64b
Meals on Shabbos, learning .... Megillah 12b
Meals on Shabbos, night .... Shabbos 119b
Meals on Shabbos, pleasure .... Shabbos 118a-118b
Meals on Shabbos, preparing .... Shabbos 117b
Meals on Shabbos, reward .... Shabbos 118a-118b
Meals on Shabbos, songs .... Megillah 12b
Meals on Shabbos, time .... Shabbos 119a-119b
Meals on Shabbos, unusual eating habits .... Nedarim 37b
Meal offering
 Disqualified —
Meal offering, barley disqualified .... Menachos 60b
Meal offering, brought leaven .... Chullin 23b
Meal offering from barley, consecrating .... Menachos 103a-103b; Nazir 9b-10a; Pesachim 53b;
 .... Arachin 20a
Meal offering, other than that he vowed .... Menachos 3a, 102b-103a
Meal offering, one and a half amount .... Menachos 24b
Meal offering, prohibition of *chametz* .... Menachos 55a-55b; Shabbos 111a; Yevamos 40a; Sotah 15a;
 .... Shevuos 15b; Bechoros 33b
Meal offering which leavened .... Menachos 52b-53a
Meal offering which leavened by itself .... Menachos 56b-57a
Meal offerings, changing name .... Zevachim 11a; Menachos 2b
Meal offerings, mixture .... Menachos 22b-23a, 89a-89b, 106a
Meal offerings, thoughts invalidating .... Menachos 7a, 11b-12a, 13b, 17a; Zevachim 13b
Meal offerings, wheat among dung .... Menachos 69a
 Temple services —
Meal offering, bringing .... Zevachim 63b; Sotah 14b; Menachos 19b, 60a-61a
Meal offering, burning handful .... Menachos 26b
Meal offering, consecrating in utensil .... Menachos 13b
Meal offering, consecration, source .... Sotah 14b
Meal offering, crumbling .... Menachos 18a-18b, 75a-75b
Meal offering, crushing .... Menachos 18a-18b, 75a-75b
Meal offering, four services .... Zevachim 13b
Meal offering, half consecration .... Menachos 7b, 8a-8b
Meal offering, how was it consecrated .... Menachos 26a-26b

M

Meal offering, indispensable services..Menachos 19b-20a
Meal offering, kneading with water..Menachos 57b
Meal offering, mixing..Menachos 9a
Meal offering, possible ways of consecration....................Yoma 48a; Menachos 11a
Meal offering, pouring oil..................................Menachos 18a-18b, 20a, 74b-75b
Meal offering, rubbing and pounding..Menachos 76a
Meal offering, sacred utensil...Menachos 96a
Meal offering, services concerning oil..Menachos 74b-75a
Meal offering, sources for various services..Sotah 14b-15a
Meal offering, warm water....................................Pesachim 36a; Menachos 53a, 55a

Various meal offerings —
Meal offering, deep fried...Menachos 63a
Meal offering for doubtful *Kohen*..Yevamos 100a
Meal offering for *Koheness*..Sotah 23a-23b; Chullin 131b-132a
Meal offering for pauper..Menachos 104b
Meal offering, half bread half *matzos*................Menachos 59a, 60a, 63a-63b, 72b, 73a
Meal offering of *nazir*......................................Menachos 19a, 27a, 76a, 78a
Meal offering of Tabernacle dedication...Menachos 78a
Meal offering, pan fried..Menachos 63a
Meal offering, *revuchah*..Zevachim 50a
Meal offering, ways of cooking..............................Menachos 59a, 63a-63b

Meal offering for *Kohen*
Meal offering for *Kohen*, completely burned....................Menachos 51b, 74a
Meal offering for *Kohen*, consecration by *Kohen*................Menachos 51b, 78a
Meal offering for *Kohen*, frankincense................................Menachos 52a
Meal offering for *Kohen*, half remained...............................Menachos 50b
Meal offering for *Kohen*, how....................................Menachos 50b-51a
Meal offering for *Kohen*, *Kohen Gadol* died....................Menachos 51b-52b
Meal offering for *Kohen*, offered by halves........................Menachos 8a
Meal offering for *Kohen*, oil..Menachos 51a
Meal offering for *Kohen*, overriding Shabbos..............Menachos 50b-51a, 96a
Meal offering for *Kohen*, tenth of *ephah*....................Menachos 50b, 87b
Meal offering for *Kohen*, warm water..................................Tamid 28b

Meal offering for sinner
Meal offering for sinner, disqualifying elements....................Menachos 6a-6b
Meal offering for sinner, frankincense....................Menachos 23a, 59b-60a
Meal offering for sinner, *Kohen*............Menachos 73b-74a; Yevamos 100a; Sotah 23a-23b
Meal offering for sinner, oil and frankincense......Sotah 15a; Menachos 23a, 59b-60a
Meal offering for sinner, thought....................................Menachos 4a
Meal offering for sinner, water......................................Menachos 54a

Meal offering for *sotah*
Meal offering for *sotah*, *aggadah*................................Sotah 15a-15b
Meal offering for *sotah*, burning..............................Sotah 6a-6b, 22b-23a
Meal offering for *sotah*, numerous men..............................Krisos 9b
Meal offering for *sotah*, waving................Sotah 19a; Succah 47b; Kiddushin 36b

Misc. —
Meal offering, eating remainder....................................Yevamos 39b-40a
Meal offering given to *Kohen* offering it............................Yevamos 39b-40a
Meal offering in two containers............Menachos 103b; Bava Basra 143a-143b

Meal offering, individual only..Menachos 104b
Meal offering, leftovers to *Kohanim*.................................Menachos 72b-73a
Meal offering, number of loaves..Menachos 76a
Meal offering, sixty one *issaron*...Menachos 103b
Meal offering, worth a *perutah*...Krisos 10b
Meal offerings given to *Kohen*, source...........Zevachim 44b; Menachos 73a
Meal offerings, number of *seah*...Menachos 76b
Meal offerings, wording of vow...Menachos 105a
Meal offering, missing
Meal offering, missing, burning.....................Menachos 9a, 12a-12b, 26a
Meal offering, missing, disqualified................Menachos 8a, 9a-9b, 12a-12b, 26a, 27a, 106a-106b;
....Meilah 8b-9a; Yoma 47b
Meal offering missing, source..Menachos 27a
Measure
Measures —
Measure according to each one...........Eruvin 30b, 48a; Bava Basra 29a; Keilim 17:11-12
Measure, according to large or small reference.....................Keilim 17:11-12
Measure, missing, prohibition.............Bava Metzia 61a-61b; Bava Basra 89b-90a
Measure, missing, punishment.............Bava Basra 88b, 90b; Yevamos 21a
Measure, new, Rav Pappa...Bava Basra 90b
Measure, things which have no................Peah 1:1; Chagigah 6b-7a; Chullin 137b
Measures, adding to specified measures..............Bava Basra 90a-90b; Menachos 77a
Measures of Sages, precision..Rosh Hashanah 13a
Measures of storekeeper, episode...Beitzah 29a
Measures of volume.............................Menachos 77a; Bava Basra 89b-90a
Measures for commandments —
Measure of succah, correcting...Succah 3b-4b
Measure, perhaps it will change..Yoma 80a
Measures, *Halacha* from Sinai............Yoma 80a; Eruvin 4a; Succah 5b
Measures of liquid in Temple............Menachos 8b, 19b, 87b-89a, 90a; Zevachim 88a
Measures of solids in Temple.......................................Menachos 57b, 90a
Misc. —
Measure for measure.............Sotah 8b-9a; Megillah 12b; Sanhedrin 90a-90b, 100a-100b
Measure is full..Sotah 9a; Arachin 15a
Measure one uses, same one is used for him....................Sanhedrin 90a-90b
Measuring
Measuring, care..Bava Basra 87a-87b
Measuring for breaking neck of calf...........Sotah 45a; Sanhedrin 14b
Measuring kerosene, by yourself..Yoma 38b-39a
Measuring on Shabbos..Shabbos 157b
Measuring on Yom Tov..Beitzah 29a-30a
Measuring, precision.............Bava Metzia 61b, 107b; Bava Basra 89a-89b
Measuring, stick to level..Bava Basra 89b
Measuring utensils, Temple............Menachos 8b, 57b, 87a-88b, 90a
Meat
Behavior —
Meat, at night and at torch light...Yoma 75b
Meat, before skinning..Beitzah 25a-25b
Meat, days when special meals are prepared..........................Chullin 83a

M

Meat, not to cut on one's hand .... Berachos 8b
Meat, not to eat before death of animal .... Sanhedrin 63a
Meat, roasting it out of eater's presence .... Sanhedrin 39a
Meat to ignoramus .... Pesachim 49b

Health —

Meat and fish, leprosy .... Pesachim 76b
Meat, cure .... Berachos 44b, 57b; Avodah Zarah 29a
Meat, entire creature .... Berachos 44b
Meat, fat, health .... Pesachim 42a-42b
Meat, neck .... Berachos 44b; Chullin 33a
Meat of fowl, for sick person .... Avodah Zarah 14a
Meat of neck, three reasons .... Shabbos 140b
Meat, who is fit to eat .... Chullin 84a

Kashrus —

Meat about which Sage ruled .... Chullin 44b
Meat, Adam .... Sanhedrin 59b
Meat belonging to non-Jew .... Chullin 94b-95a
Meat, fat, different parts .... Yoma 25b
Meat, fat, health .... Pesachim 42a-42b
Meat, fat, in *Eretz Yisrael* .... Bava Basra 91b
Meat for pleasure, in the desert .... Chullin 16b-17a
Meat found in street, doubt .... Chullin 12a-12b; Bava Metzia 24b
Meat from Heaven, permitted .... Sanhedrin 59b
Meat from living animal .... Eduyos 6:3
Meat from living animal, *neveilah* .... Chullin 128b
Meat in Temple Courtyard, doubt .... Shekalim 7:3
Meat of dying animal .... Chullin 37b, 44b
Meat of fetus which came out in Temple Courtyard .... Chullin 69a
Meat of limb dangling, eating .... Chullin 73b-74a
Meat of stomach, *treifah* .... Chullin 50b, 52b
Meat thrown by bird .... Bava Metzia 24b
Meat which disappeared .... Chullin 95a-95b; Beitzah 40a; Bava Metzia 24b

Meat and milk

Meat and milk, at the same table .... Chullin 104a-104b, 107b-108a; Shabbos 13a; Eduyos 5:2
Meat with milk, benefit .... Kiddushin 57b; Menachos 101b; Chullin 114b-116a
Meat with milk, does milk itself become forbidden .... Chullin 108b-109a
Meat with milk, episodes of mistakes .... Pesachim 43a; Chullin 110a
Meat with milk, even not its mother's milk .... Chullin 114a-114b
Meat with milk, exceptional law .... Nazir 37a
Meat with milk, which meat .... Chullin 113a-114a
Meat with milk, which milk .... Chullin 113a-114a

Laws —

Meat, "This meat is for Pesach" .... Pesachim 53a-53b
Meat and wine, rejoicing on Yom Tov .... Pesachim 71a, 109a
Meat, cheap, payment to heir .... Bava Kama 112a; Kesubos 34b
Meat left on skin .... Chullin 121a-122a, 124a
Meat, roast, Pesach night .... Beitzah 23a; Berachos 19a; Pesachim 53a-53b, 74a

Misc. —

Meat, bringing Holy Ark .... Pesachim 36b

Meat, during famine in Jehoram's time...Taanis 5a
Meat, ground, wording of vow...Nedarim 52b
Meat of ox, Sage's mistake...Bava Kama 72a
Meat, raw, Alexandrians...Menachos 100a
Meat, what is included..Meilah 20a-20b; Nedarim 54a
Mechaah..*see* **Protest**, page 508
***Mechabetz* on Shabbos**..Shabbos 95a
Mechaleh mamon Yisrael.................................*see* **Destroyer of Israel's money!**, page 161
Mechalel Shabbos................................*see* **Desecrating Shabbos, renegade**, page 160
Mechalelei avodah..................................*see* **Desecrating service, who**, page 160
Mechamer...*see* **Working animal on Shabbos**, page 763
Mechaye
   Mechaye Chaim, blessing..Yoma 71a
   Mechaye Hamesim, seeing friend..Berachos 58b
Mechilah.....................................*see* **Atonement**, page 35; *see also* **Forgiveness**, page 236
Mechilas zechus...............*see* **Renouncing**, page 557; *see also* **Releasing by mistake**, page 555
Mechilos...*see* **Underground passages**, page 715
Mechitzah...*see* **Partition**, page 473
Mechokek
   Mechokek, Moses...Bava Basra 15a
   Mechokek, Judah...Horayos 11b
Mechubar..*see* **Connected to earth**, page 121
Mechusar zman..*see* **Before time**, page 48
Mechussar amanah...*see* **Keeping one's word, gift**, page 333
Mechussar begadim.............*see* ***Kohen*** **performing service without priestly garments**, page 346
Mechussar ever..................................*see* **Limb missing, sacrifice for non-Jew**, page 370
Mechussar kapparah.............................*see* **Impurity preceding sacrifice**, page 304
Mechuza
   Mechuza, characteristics...Berachos 59b
   Mechuza, lazy women..Shabbos 32b-33a; Pesachim 50b
Mechzei..*see* **Appearing**, page 30
Mechzei keshikra................................*see* **Legal document, appearing false**, page 361
Medea
   Medea, customs...Berachos 8b
   Medea, nation..Yoma 10a
   Medea, returning stolen item..................Bava Kama 103a-104a, 105a; Bava Metzia 55a
Mediach.......................................*see* **Instigator, city led to idolatry**, page 311
Medicine..................................*see also* **Treatment**, page 701; **Remedy**, page 556
   Beneficial things —
   Medicine, beneficial things...Berachos 57b
   Medicine, blessing on food...Berachos 36a, 38a
   Medicine, Diomeses (name of salty river, Rashi; see Isaiah 28)..............Shabbos 147b
   Medicine, sun in the future...Sanhedrin 91b
   Medicine, time..Bechoros 39a
   Episodes —
   Medicine, conceding Sage..Rosh Hashanah 17a
   Medicine, episode about noblewoman.................Yoma 84a; Avodah Zarah 28a
   Medicine, extending hand to Rabbi Yochanan, she was healed...............Berachos 5b
   Medicine, Rebbi..Bava Metzia 85a

M

Medicine, Rabbi Chanina ben Dosa...Yoma 49a

Medicines —
Medicines, avoiding...Pesachim 113a
Medicines, barley..Nedarim 41b
Medicines, different illnesses.....................................Shabbos 66b-67a, 110a-110b; Gittin 67b, 68b-70a, 86a;
....Avodah Zarah 28a-28b
Medicines, food..Berachos 40a, 44b, 57b; Avodah Zarah 29a
Medicines, fowl meat...Avodah Zarah 14a
Medicines, from animals...Shabbos 77b
Medicines, mouth smells.....................................Berachos 40a; Shabbos 65a; Kesubos 75a
Medicines, salt for teeth...Shabbos 65a
Medicines, semolina and eggs..Yoma 18a
Medicines, wine...Bava Basra 58b

Prohibitions —
Medicine by non-Jewish physician..Avodah Zarah 27a-28a
Medicine, man forbidden to benefit...Nedarim 41b
Medicine on Yom Tov...Beitzah 22a
Medicine, Sabbatical year produce...........................Sheviis 8:1; Succah 40a-40b; Bava Kama 102a
Medicine with verse...Sanhedrin 101a

Medicine on Shabbos
Medicine on Shabbos..Shabbos 108b
Medicine on Shabbos, animal..Shabbos 53a-53b
Medicine on Shabbos, *anumlin*....................................Shabbos 140a; Avodah Zarah 30a
Medicine on Shabbos, besmear intestines.......................Shabbos 147b; Sanhedrin 101a
Medicine on Shabbos, baby..Shabbos 66b, 123a-123b, 147b
Medicine on Shabbos, began before...Shabbos 140a
Medicine on Shabbos, *chiltis*...Shabbos 140a
Medicine on Shabbos, drunkenness...Shabbos 66b
Medicine on Shabbos, eye.......................................Shabbos 108b; Sanhedrin 101a
Medicine on Shabbos, intestines.................................Shabbos 66b; Sanhedrin 101a
Medicine on Shabbos, limbs..Shabbos 147b-148a
Medicine on Shabbos, not tested...Yoma 84a-84b
Medicine on Shabbos, rose oil.........................Shabbos 111b, 128a; Bava Metzia 113b
Medicine on Shabbos, throat...Yoma 84a-84b
Medicine on Shabbos, vertebra...Shabbos 66b
Medicine on Shabbos, vinegar for tooth................Shabbos 111a; Beitzah 18b; Avodah Zarah 28a
Medicine on Shabbos, vomiting...Shabbos 123b, 147b
Medicine on Shabbos, washing...Shabbos 109a-109b
Medicine on Shabbos, wine and oil...Shabbos 134b
Medicine on Shabbos, wine and vinegar...Shabbos 109a
Medicine on Shabbos, wound...Shabbos 134b

Misc. —
Medicine expenses for widow...Kesubos 52b
Medicine for Canaanite slave...Gittin 12b
Medicine, permission and source..............................Bava Kama 85a; Berachos 60a
Medicine, since Elisha...Bava Metzia 87a; Sanhedrin 107b
Medicine, time..Shabbos 147b; Pesachim 42b; Bechoros 39a

Meditation before prayer..Berachos 32b
Mediterranean Sea, blessing..Berachos 59a

M

Medras .... *see* **Items suitable, couch and other uses, impurity**, page 319

Meeting .... *see* **Encounter**, page 196

Meeting place for Sages .... Avos 1:4

Mefagel .... *see* **Piggul**, page 487

Mefaneh libo levatalah .... *see* **Idleness**, page 292

Mefarek kele'achar yad .... *see* **Beating grain, unusual manner**, page 46

Mefarkeses .... *see* **Twitching animal in death throes**, page 707

Mefateh .... *see* **Seducer**, page 598

Mefuraas, *shechitah* .... *see* **Slaughtering, non gaping cut on windpipe**, page 634

Megadeif .... *see* **Blasphemer**, page 60

Megadeif, explanation .... Krisos 7a-7b

Megalgelim zechus vechovah .... *see* **Merit brought about by meritorious person**, page 405

Megillas sotah .... *see* **Scroll of** *sotah*, page 593

Megillas starim, laws .... Shabbos 6b, 96b; Bava Metzia 92a

Megillas Esther
  Reading —
    Megillas Esther, blessings .... Megillah 21b
    Megillas Esther, from where do we read .... Megillah 18b, 19a
    Megillas Esther, greeting .... Berachos 14a
    Megillas Esther, how to read .... Megillah 18a, 21a
    Megillas Esther, in other languages .... Megillah 18a
    Megillas Esther, innovation of Sages .... Megillah 14a
    Megillas Esther, minor reading .... Megillah 20a
    Megillas Esther, overrides commandments .... Megillah 3a-3b; Arachin 4a
    Megillas Esther, quorum .... Megillah 5a
    Megillas Esther, reading Haman's sons' names .... Megillah 16b
    Megillas Esther, reading in sequence .... Megillah 17a, 18a-18b
    Megillas Esther, Shabbos .... Megillah 4b
    Megillas Esther, time .... Megillah 4a, 20a
    Meguillah, reading for villagers .... Megillah 2a-2b, 4b-5a; Yevamos 13b
  Misc. —
    Megillas Esther by heart, Rabbi Meir .... Megillah 18b
    Megillas Esther, etching lines .... Megillah 16b
    Megillas Esther, one *zuz* .... Bava Basra 155b
    Megillas Esther, proper .... Megillah 18b-19b
    Megillas Esther, writing Haman's sons' names .... Megillah 16b
    Megillas Taanis
      Megillas Taanis, days .... Taanis 17b-18b
      Megillas Taanis, in present times .... Rosh Hashanah 18b-19b
      Megillas Taanis, who wrote .... Shabbos 13b

Megis kederah beShabbos .... *see* **Stirring pot on Shabbos**, page 656

Mehapech bachararah .... Kiddushin 59a

Mehapech bachararah .... *see* **Buying item before person interested to buy it**, page 82

Mehayom ul'achar misah .... *see* **From today till after death**, page 240

Mei Merivah, Moses .... Shabbos 55b

Meidiach .... *see* **Instigator, city led to idolatry**, page 311

Meifer bris Avraham .... *see* **Breaking covenant of Abraham**, page 76

Meinekes chaveiro .... *see* **Nursing woman**, page 451

Meis echad mehachaburah .... *see* **Deceased person, one of the group**, page 153

M

Meis mitzvah .... see **Deceased unburied person**, page 153

Meisah machmas melachah .... see **Died because of work, animal**, page 163

Meisha, offered his father as sacrifice .... Taanis 4a; Sanhedrin 39b

Meishiv aveidah .... see **Returning lost item, oath**, page 564

Meisiach lefi tumo .... see **Speaking without intention to testify**, page 649

Meisim atzmo rasha .... see **Testimony, pretending to be wicked**, page 683

Meisis .... see **Inciter to idolatry**, page 306

Meisu be'alav .... see **Owner died**, page 467

Meitav .... see **Best**, page 55

Meizid .... see **Intentional sin**, page 313

Mekach taus .... see **Erroneous purchase**, page 199; *see also* **Cancellation of sale**, page 86

Mekadeish

   Mekadeish .... see *Kiddushin*, page 337

   Mekadeish Hashabbos, prayer .... Pesachim 117b

   Mekadeish Yisrael Vehazemanim .... Pesachim 117b; Beitzah 17a; Berachos 49a

Mekalel .... see **Cursing**, page 136

Mekalkel .... see **Ruining**, page 573

Mekaneh sheim lechaveiro .... see **Nickname to friend**, *Gehinnom*, page 444

Mekasheh atzmo ladaas .... see **Masturbation**, page 393

Mekaven melachto bamoed .... see **Penalty, leaving one's work for** *Chol HaMoed*, page 479

Mekayem nefesh miYisrael .... see **Saving a life**, page 590

Mekom petur

   Mekom petur, carrying out on Shabbos .... Eruvin 9a, 77a, 87a-87b, 101b; Shabbos 8b

   Mekom petur, carrying out through .... Shabbos 6a, 8b-9a; Eruvin 9a, 77a, 85b, 98a, 99a, 101b

   Mekom petur, cases .... Shabbos 7a

   Mekom petur, in *karmelis* .... Eruvin 9a

Mekor ishah .... see **Womb of woman, impurity**, page 759

Mekosheish eitsim bamidbar .... see **Man picking up wood in desert**, page 387

Melachah she'einah tzrichah legufah .... see **Necessary for itself, not**, page 439

Melamed tinokos .... see **Schoolteacher**, page 591

Melave d'Malkah

   Melave d'Malkah, episode .... Shabbos 119b

   Melave d'Malkah, meal .... Shabbos 119b

Meleches machsheves .... see **Intentional work**, page 313

Melichas bassar .... see **Salting meat**, page 587

Melikah .... see **Cutting neck of bird**, page 139

Melo lugmav .... see **Full cheeks**, page 241

Melt liquid, drinking forbidden substances .... Chullin 120a-120b

Melumad benisim .... see **Used to miracles**, page 717

Mem and samekh in Tablets .... Shabbos 104a; Megillah 2b-3a

Mema'enes .... see **Disavowing marriage**, page 165

Memale mekom aviv .... see **Replacing one's father, position of authority**, page 560

Member of household, oath .... Shevuos 48b

Membrane blocking, lung .... Chullin 47b, 48a; Yevamos 76a

Memory

   Memory and forgetfulness .... Horayos 13a-13b

   Memory in learning, Heavenly help .... Megillah 6b

   Memory of righteous for a blessing .... Yoma 38b

Memucan, Haman .... Megillah 12b

M

Menachos ....*see* **Meal offering**, page 396
Menahem, pairs of Sages ....Chagigah 16a-16b
Menashe ....*see* **Manesseh** page 388
Mene mene, Belshazzar ....Sanhedrin 22a
Menorah
  Kindling —
    Menorah, kindling by non-*Kohen* ....Yoma 24b
    Menorah, kindling from middle lamp ....Shabbos 22b
    Menorah, lamp extinguished ....Menachos 88b
  Temple —
    Menorah, cleaning lamps ....Yoma 14b-15a; Menachos 88b, 107a; Tamid 30b, 33a
    Menorah, cleaning lamps with utensil ....Menachos 107a
    Menorah, middle lamp ....Menachos 98b
    Menorah, shown to Moses ....Menachos 29a
    Menorah, Temple ....Menachos 28a-29a, 88b, 98b-99a
    Menoros of Solomon ....Menachos 98b-99a
  Misc. —
    Menorah, prohibition to make ....Avodah Zarah 43a; Rosh Hashanah 24a-24b
Menstruating woman ....*see* **Niddah**, page 444
Menstruation
  Menstruation, average period ....Niddah 9b
  Menstruation, body and food ....Niddah 63a-63b
  Menstruation, caused by jumping ....Niddah 11a
  Menstruation, cancelled ....Niddah 64a-64b
  Menstruation, checking ....Niddah 9a, 16a
  Menstruation comes at its time, *chazakah* ....Niddah 16a, 64b
  Menstruation, fear ....Niddah 9a, 71a, 39a; Sotah 20b
  Menstruation, fixing ....Niddah 11a, 39a-39b, 63a-63b, 68b
  Menstruation, husband going out on a journey ....Yevamos 62b
  Menstruation, intermittent intervals ....Niddah 64a; Bava Kama 37b
  Menstruation, non-menstruating woman ....Niddah 12b, 39a
  Menstruation, separating before ....Shevuos 18b; Yevamos 62b; Niddah 15a-15b, 63b
  Menstruation, source ....Niddah 15a-16a
Mentioning
  Mentioning for praise and criticism ....Yoma 37a-38b
  Mentioning G-d's name in vain, superfluous blessing ....Berachos 33a
Menuchah, Shiloh ....Zevachim 119a-119b; Megillah 10a
Menuchas hanefesh ....*see* **Peace of mind**, page 477
Menudeh ....*see* **Excommunication, laws of excommunicated man**, page 208
Menumar, spotted *esrog* ....Succah 35b-36b
Meonen, sorcery ....Sanhedrin 65b
Meor Hagolah, Rabbi Achai ....Chullin 59b
Mephiboshet
  Mephiboshet and David ....Berachos 4a
  Mephiboshet, David and Tziva ....Shabbos 56a-56b; Yoma 22b
  Mephiboshet, David's mistakes ....Shabbos 56b; Yoma 22b
Merab, David's wife ....Sanhedrin 19b
Meraglim ....*see* **Spies**, page 650
Merapson igrey, amazing ....Kiddushin 63b

Merchandise
Merchandise indispensable to life .... Bava Basra 90b-91a

Merchandise, one third of one's investments .... Bava Metzia 42a
Merchant
Merchant, fraud .... Bava Metzia 51a

Merchants of Lud, fraud .... Bava Metzia 50a-50b
Merciful
Merciful, belongs to Abraham's seed .... Shabbos 151b; Beitzah 32b

Merciful, his life is no life .... Pesachim 113b

Merciful, Israel .... Yevamos 79a

Merciful man, his life is bad .... Bava Basra 145b; Sanhedrin 100b
Mercy
Mercy, Divine Attribute .... Rosh Hashanah 17b

Mercy, Divine Name .... Berachos 60b

Mercy for others, Divine Pity in reward .... Beitzah 32b; Shabbos 151b

Mercy of father towards his son .... Sotah 49a

Mercy on other's young, animal .... Bechoros 24a
Merit
Commandments —
Merit at time of judgment, G-d remembers .... Yevamos 78b

Merit, delaying punishment of sinner .... Shevuos 39a

Merit for deceased, Torah in his name .... Bechoros 31b; Yevamos 96b-97a; Sanhedrin 90b

Merit of commandments, protection .... Sotah 21a

Merit of fathers, until when .... Shabbos 55a

Merit of Torah, protection .... Sotah 21a

Merit, saving *sotah* .... Sotah 6a-6b, 20b-21a, 22b
Episodes —
Merit, delivered by righteous women's merit .... Sotah 11b

Merit of deeds of kindness, episodes .... Taanis 21b

Merit of *Eretz Yisrael*, Isaac's birth .... Rosh Hashanah 16b

Merit of rain, episodes .... Taanis 24a

Merit of righteous, episodes .... Berachos 17b; Chullin 86a

Merit of teacher, disciple ate, episodes .... Yoma 75b
Misc. —
Merit brought about by meritorious person ...... Bava Basra 119a-119b; Shabbos 32a; Sanhedrin 8a

Merit, if they merit Divine Presence is between them .... Sotah 17a
Merit of multitude
Merit of multitude, bringing them close to Torah .... Avos 1:12

Merit of multitude, merit of fathers .... Avos 2:2

Merit of multitude, merit of their deeds .... Sanhedrin 99b

Merit of multitude, saving from sin .... Avos 5:18

Merit of multitude, their merit depends on him .... Avos 5:18
Merkavah .... *see* **Heavenly Chariot**, page 274

Meroz, excommunication .... Shevuos 36a; Moed Katan 16a

Mes echad mehachaburah .... *see* **Deceased person, one of the group**, page 153

Mes mitzvah .... *see* **Deceased unburied person**, page 153

Mesah machmas melachah .... *see* **Died because of work, animal**, page 163

Mesarvin lekatan .... *see* **Refusing, an important and ordinary person**, page 554

Mesaye'a .... *see* **Helping**, page 276

M

Mesechtos, order...Nazir 2a; Sotah 2a; Shevuos 2b-3a

Meshameshes...*see* Impurity through intimate relations, page 303

Meshamshei avodah zarah..............................*see* Accessories of idolatrous cult, page 5

Meshaneh Habrios, blessing...Berachos 58b

Meshaneh Habrios...*see* Blessing, *Meshaneh Habrios*, page 64

Meshaneh matbe'a berachos..........................*see* Changing text of blessings, page 96

Meshaseh kelev hamazik................................*see* Inciting to bite, dog which damaged, page 306

Meshateh..*see* Answering elusively, acknowledging debt, page 29

Meshichah...*see* Pulling to purchase, page 510

Meshichah...*see* Anointment, page 28

Meshiv aveidah..*see* Returning lost item, oath, page 564

Meshuach milchamah......................................*see Kohen Gadol* anointed for war, page 347

Mesiach lefi tumo..*see* Speaking without intention to testify, page 649

Mesim atzmo rasha...*see* Testimony, pretending to be wicked, page 683

Mesirah...*see* Handing over, page 268

Mesirus nefesh...*see* Self-sacrifice, page 599

Mesis...*see* Inciter to idolatry, page 306

Mesivta derakiya...*see* Heavenly *Yeshivah*, page 274

Mesores haTorah..*see* Tradition of Torah, page 699

Messiah
  Qualities —

    Messiah, expecting Tzion...Kesubos 75a

    Messiah, four craftsmen..Succah 52b

    Messiah, G-d's name..Bava Basra 75b

    Messiah, G-d's spirit..Sanhedrin 93b

    Messiah, his names..Sanhedrin 96b, 98b

    Messiah, how will he judge..Sanhedrin 93b

    Messiah, like whom...Sanhedrin 98b

    Messiah, princes of mankind..Succah 52b

    Messiah, purpose of world...Sanhedrin 98b

    Messiah, Shabbos observance..Shabbos 118b

    Messiah son of Joseph..Succah 52a

    Messiah, suffering...Sanhedrin 93b, 98a, 98b

  When —

    Messiah, "may he come and may I not see him"...................................Sanhedrin 98b

    Messiah, "when will you come"..Sanhedrin 98a

    Messiah, calculating end of times...Sanhedrin 97a

    Messiah, comes during lapse of attention..Sanhedrin 97a

    Messiah, false, Bar Kochba...Sanhedrin 93b

    Messiah, in which month..Rosh Hashanah 11b

    Messiah, news by bird...Chullin 63a

    Messiah, prayer...Sanhedrin 94a

    Messiah, repentance...Sanhedrin 94a, 97b-98a

    Messiah, six thousand years.....................................Sanhedrin 97a-97b; Avodah zara 9a

    Messiah, time of coming.........................Sanhedrin 94a, 97b, 99a; Avodah Zarah 9b

    Messiah, when souls will be used up...Yevamos 62a

    Messiah, who holds him back..Niddah 13b

  Misc. —

    Messiah, being saved from birth pangs of his coming...........................Sanhedrin 98b

M

Messiah, expecting him .... Sanhedrin 97a, 98b-99a, 105a
Messiah, fall of king .... Sanhedrin 38a
Messiah, gifts from non-Jews .... Pesachim 118b-119a
Messiah, more miraculous than Exodus .... Berachos 12b-13a
Messiah, on cloud or on donkey .... Sanhedrin 98a
Messianic times
Messianic times and World to Come .... Sanhedrin 91b, 98b, 99a; Berachos 34b; Shabbos 63a, 151b;
.... Pesachim 68b
Messianic times, change in world ...... Shabbos 63a, 151b; Berachos 34b; Pesachim 68a; Sanhedrin 91b, 99a
Messianic times, examples in this world .... Shabbos 30b
Messianic times, honor of Israel .... Taanis 14b-15a
Messianic times, no desire .... Shabbos 151b
Messianic times, plenty and birth .... Shabbos 30b
Messianic times, trees .... Kesubos 112b
Messianic times, war .... Shabbos 63a
Mesurah, amount .... Bava Basra 89b
Metal, partly hot .... Pesachim 74a
Metaltelin .... see **Movable property**, page 428
Methusaleh
Methusaleh, eulogy about righteous .... Sanhedrin 108b
Methusaleh, men who encompassed History .... Bava Basra 121b
Methusaleh, seven shepherds .... Succah 52b
Meticulous
Meticulous, hair breadth .... Taanis 11a
Meticulous in one's deeds, episodes .... Shabbos 37b; Beitzah 29b; Chullin 110a
Metoch she'eino yachol lishava .... see **Oath, "I do not know,"** page 453
Metoch shehutra .... see **Work permitted on Yom Tov**, page 760
Metoch shelo lishmah .... see **Ulterior goal leads to Heaven's sake**, page 713
Metzar shehichziku rabim .... see **Passageway used by the public**, page 475
Metzitzas hamilah .... see **Sucking, circumcision**, page 662
Metzora .... see **Leper**, page 364
Metzulah, Babylon .... Zevachim 113b; Shabbos 113b
Metzuveh veoseh .... see **Commanded and performs**, page 116
Meuberes chaveiro .... see **Pregnant woman, fellow's wife**, page 500
Meukav shichrur .... see **Slave, before certificate of freedom**, page 637
Meuvas .... see **Crooked thing cannot be corrected, immorality**, page 133
Mevalei olam .... see **Destroyers of world**, page 161
Mevashel .... see **Cooking on Shabbos**, page 128
Mezakeh harabim .... see **Giving merit to multitude**, page 252
Mezakeh lachaveiro .... see **Legal transfer of rights**, page 363
Mezaneh .... see **Man guilty of forbidden relations**, page 387
Mezid .... see **Intentional sin**, page 313
Mezigas Kisri, episode .... Moed Katan 26a
Mezonos .... see **Support**, page 664
Mezonos, blessing .... Berachos 38a, 42a
Mezonos, berachah .... see **Blessing, Mezonos**, page 63
Mezuzah
Requirement —
Mezuzah, doors .... Yoma 11a-11b; Menachos 33a-34a; Eruvin 11b

Mezuzah, four by four handbreadths .... Succah 3a
Mezuzah, gatehouse .... Succah 8b
Mezuzah, houses .... Yoma 10a-11b; Menachos 33a-34a
Mezuzah, partnership .... Chullin 135-136a
Mezuzah, rented house .... Menachos 44a
Mezuzah, tenant .... Bava Metzia 101b-102a; Pesachim 4a
Mezuzah, woman .... Berachos 20b

Writing —
Mezuzah, margins .... Menachos 31b
Mezuzah, on two scrolls .... Menachos 33a
Mezuzah, parchment .... Menachos 34a
Mezuzah, what must be written .... Berachos 15b
Mezuzah, writing .... Menachos 31b-32a

Misc. —
Mezuzah, checking .... Yoma 11a
Mezuzah, death punishment .... Shabbos 32b
Mezuzah, episode about government decree .... Yoma 11a
Mezuzah, episode about Onkelos .... Avodah Zarah 11a
Mezuzah, guarding .... Avodah Zarah 11a
Mezuzah, how to roll .... Menachos 31b
Mezuzah, position on door .... Menachos 32b-33b
Mezuzah, protection through its merit .... Menachos 43b
Mezuzah, punishment for one who removes .... Bava Metzia 102a
Mezuzah, putting hand on .... Avodah Zarah 11a
Mezuzah, reward .... Shabbos 23b

Mezuyaf mitocho .... *see* **Forged legal document, signature, page 236**
Mi berosh .... *see* **Jeroboam, "who will be first," page 322**
Mi gilah raz zeh .... *see* **Who revealed this secret, page 742**
Mi she'achal shum .... *see* **Garlic, eating a second time, page 243**
Mi shepara
Mi shepara, cases of rescinding .... Bava Metzia 63b, 74b
Mi shepara, how .... Bava Metzia 48b
Mi shetarach be'erev Shabbos .... *see* **Whomever worked before Shabbos, page 742**
Micah
Micah, idol .... Sanhedrin 103b
Micah, Nebat .... Sanhedrin 101b
Mice
Mice, characteristics .... Horayos 13a-13b; Chullin 126b-127a
Mice killed cat .... Bava Metzia 97a
Mouse did not steal, hole did .... Kiddushin 56b
Mouse, doubts for *chametz* .... Pesachim 9b-10a
Mouse formed from earth .... Sanhedrin 91a
Mouse, guarding corpse from mice .... Shabbos 151b
Mouse, in alcoholic beverage .... Avodah Zarah 68b-69a
Mouse laying on gold coins, miserliness .... Sanhedrin 29b
Mouse of sea and of earth, impurity .... Chullin 126b-127a
Mouse, taste in dish .... Avodah Zarah 69a
Michael
Michael and Gabriel .... Berachos 4b

M

Michael offers, place of Altar..Zevachim 62a

Michael, offers sacrifice in Heaven..Chagigah 12b; Menachos 110a

Michal

Michal, beauty...Megillah 15a

Michal, David's disgrace...Sanhedrin 21a

Michal, David's wife...Sanhedrin 19b

Michiah, leprous mark...Negaim 4:2-3, 4:10, 6:5-6

Michlal lav

Michlal lav, deducting positive from negative...Shevuos 36a-36b

Michlal lav, wording of vows...Nedarim 11a-11b, 13b

Michlal lav...*see* **Negative form, wording of vows,** page 440

Michzei...*see* **Appearing,** page 30

Midas bassar v'dam..................................*see* **G-d's attributes, different from man's,** page 245

Midas chasidus, fraud..Bava Metzia 52b

Midas chasidus...*see* **Attribute of piety, fraud,** page 36

Midas hadin..*see* **Attribute of justice,** page 36

Midas Sodom......................*see* **Attribute of Sodom, refusing when not losing,** page 36

Middah keneged midah...*see* **Measure for measure,** page 398

Middah tovah merubah.............................*see* **Reward, greater than punishment,** page 566

Middle

Middle, advantage..Berachos 31b

Middle of the night, parable..Sotah 21a

Middle of Torah...Kiddushin 30a

Middle of world, Sages of Athens..Bechoros 8b

Middle one is most important..Menachos 98b

Midget

Midget, blemishes of *Kohen*..Bechoros 43b

Midget, blessing...Berachos 58b

Midian and Moab, hate..Sanhedrin 105a

Midnight

Midnight, "about midnight," death of firstborn...Berachos 3b

Midnight, *afikoman*...Pesachim 120b

Midnight, Pesach lamb...............................Berachos 9a; Pesachim 120b; Megillah 21a; Zevachim 57b

Midnight, time for *Shema*..Berachos 4a-4b, 9a

Midnight, time of Divine Favor...Yevamos 72a

Midos shebeMikdash..................................*see* **Measures of liquid in Temple,** page 398

Midos, who arranged this Tractate...Yoma 16a-17a

Midras..............................*see* **Items suitable, couch and other uses, impurity,** page 319

Midwife

Midwife, non-Jewish..Avodah Zarah 26a

Midwife, trustworthiness about lineage...Kiddushin 73b-74a

Migo

Trustworthiness —

Migo, "I gave back," custodian...Bava Basra 45b, 70a-71a

Migo, "why should I lie"...Bava Basra 5b

Migo, captive to *Kohen*...Kesubos 27a-27b

Migo, forged legal documents...Bava Basra 32a-32b

Migo, exempt from oath.......................................Bava Basra 70b; Shevuos 45b

Migo, trustworthiness of *agunah*..Yevamos 114b-115a

M

Migo, virginity .... Kesubos 16a
Migo vs. "we are witnesses" .... Bava Metzia 81b; Kesubos 27b; Bechoros 36a
Migo vs. rumor .... Bava Basra 32b-33a
Migo vs. witnesses .... Bava Basra 31a, 33b
  Misc. —
    Migo, from succah to Shabbos .... Succah 7a-7b
    Migo, *muktzeh* extended to next day .... Succah 46b
    Migo, suspected about oath .... Bava Metzia 5b-6a
Migufo .... *see* **Payment by ox which gored occasionally**, page 476
Mikdash vekodashav .... *see* **Impurity of Temple and sacrifices**, page 304
Miklat .... *see* **City of Refuge**, page 109
Mikra nidrash lefanav .... *see* **Deduction, from previous verses**, page 156
Mikra umasores .... *see* **Writing or pronunciation, which determines**, page 765
Miktzas... .... *see* **Part of...**, page 472
Mikveh
  Mikveh .... *see also* **Immersion**, page 299
  Mikveh considered *kosher*, doubt .... Mikvaos 8:1
  Mikveh, calculation of its dimension ...... Pesachim 109a-109b; Eruvin 4b, 14a; Yoma 31a; Chagigah 11a
  Mikveh, *chazakah* .... Gittin 31b; Kiddushin 66b, 79a; Mikvaos 2:2; Niddah 2b
  Mikveh divided by basket .... Chagigah 22a
  Mikveh gates, episodes .... Bava Metzia 84a; Berachos 20a
  Mikveh, low water, raising .... Mikvaos 7:7
  Mikveh of *Kohen Gadol*, heating .... Yoma 34b
  Mikveh, pumped water which flowed horizontally .... Temurah 12a-12b; Mikvaos 4:4
Mil
  Mil, distance .... Pesachim 46a; Megillah 2b
  Mil, time of leavening .... Pesachim 46a
Milah .... *see* **Circumcision**, page 106
Military camp, leniencies .... Eruvin 17a-17b
Milk
  Impurity —
    Milk, liquid .... Shabbos 143b-144a; Niddah 55b-56a
    Milk, liquid coming out of body, impurity .... Krisos 13a-13b; Keilim 8:11
    Milk which flowed by itself, impurity .... Machshirin 6:8; Keilim 8:11; Shabbos 143b-144a;
    .... Krisos 13a-13b
  Mixture —
    Meat with milk, episode about guest .... Pesachim 43a
    Milk after meat .... Chullin 104b-105b
    Milk close to salt and vinegar .... Chullin 112a
    Milk, meat with milk .... Chullin 113a-114a
  Prohibitions —
    Milk, limb taken from a living animal .... Bechoros 6b
    Milk of non-Jew .... Avodah Zarah 35b, 39b
    Milk of woman .... Kesubos 60a; Krisos 22a
    Milk, produce of consecrated animal .... Meilah 12b; Temurah 31b
    Milk, proof that cow already has firstborn .... Bechoros 20b, 24a-24b
  Misc. —
    Milk and honey, *Eretz Yisrael* .... Megillah 6a
    Milk before birth .... Bechoros 20b

M

Milk coming from blood..Niddah 9a; Bechoros 6b

Milk, drunkenness............Nazir 4a; Yoma 76a-76b; Sanhedrin 70b-71a; Shevuos 23a; Bechoros 45b; Krisos 13b

Milk, health and advice...Moed Katan 11a

Milk of animal to baby..Yevamos 114a

Milk of redeemed sacrifices...Bechoros 15a

Milk, Torah...Taanis 7a-7b

Milk, pickled

    Milk, pickled, close to salt and vinegar...Chullin 112a

    Milk, pickled, health...Horayos 12a; Krisos 6a

    Milk, pickled, repulsive or tasty...Shabbos 145b

Milking on Shabbos..Shabbos 95a; Pesachim 65a

Millet

    Millet, exempt from *challah*...Menachos 70a-70b

    Millet, final blessing...Berachos 37a

Milsa debedichusa...*see* **Joke**, page 324

Miluy ve'iruy...*see* **Filling and pouring, wine container**, page 222

Milveh...*see* **Loan**, page 376

Mimah nefshach..*see* **Either/or**, page 192

Min...*see* **Heretic**, page 277

Min bemino ubeshe'eino mino...*see* **Mixture of same substance and of different substance**, page 419

Min bemino...*see* **Mixture of same substance**, page 419

Min Haolam, in Temple..Berachos 63a; Sotah 40b; Taanis 16b

Min hashamayim yerachmu.............*see* **Women, using sponge during intimate relations**, page 757

Mincha

    Mincha..*see also* **Meal offering**, page 396; **Semolina**, page 601

    Mincha, eating before...Shabbos 9b-10a; Berachos 28b; Succah 38a

    Mincha, importance of this prayer...Berachos 6b

    Mincha of Shabbos, Torah reading...Megillah 31b-32a; Bava Kama 82a

    Mincha, time..Berachos 26b-27a, 29b; Yoma 28b; Shabbos 118b

    Mincha, what is forbidden before...Shabbos 9b-10a

Mind

    Mind cannot tolerate...Pesachim 113b

    Mind of his teacher, forty years..Avodah Zarah 5b

Mine

    "Mine and yours are hers"...Nedarim 50a; Kesubos 63a

    Mine is yours, yours is yours...Avos 5:10

Minhag...*see* **Custom**, page 138

Minimum only can be learned from deduction..Succah 5b

Minister

    Minister before king, Rabbi Chanina ben Dosa...Berachos 34b

    Minister of world, young man...Yevamos 16b

Minor..*see also* **Child**, page 102; **Education**, page 187; **Deaf**, page 149

    Commandments —

    Minor and slave, counted for quorum...Berachos 47b

    Minor, collecting bread for *eruv*..Eruvin 31b, 49b

    Minor in last year of minority, tithe...Niddah 46b

    Minor, priestly blessing...Chullin 24b

    Minor, real estate, *chazakah* of use..............................Kesubos 17b; Bava Metzia 39a-39b

    Minor, *zimun*..Berachos 47b-48b; Arachin 3a

M

Impurity —
Minor, act and intention..Chullin 12b-13a; Taharos 8:6
Minor *Kohen*, impurity..Yevamos 114a-114b
Minor, sprinkling and sanctification..............Yevamos 72b; Yoma 43a-43b; Arachin 3a; Parah 5:4
Marriage —
Minor, his wife's *kesubah*...Kesubos 90a
Minor, homosexuality...Sanhedrin 54b-55a
Minor, levirate marriage........Yevamos 61b, 96a, 96b, 111b, 119a; Bechoros 19b; Niddah 32a, 45a-45b;
                                                                                            Bava Basra 156a; Sanhedrin 55b
Minor, no *kiddushin*.......................................Yevamos 112b; Sanhedrin 52b; Kiddushin 19a
Minor, not of age to marry...Sanhedrin 76b
Minor, renders disqualified for marriage with *Kohen*..Sanhedrin 69b
Minors, *chalitzah*...Yevamos 105b; Bechoros 19b
Monetary matters —
Minor, act of acquisition..Gittin 52a-52b
Minor, *eruv* made by his mother...Eruvin 82a-82b; Kesubos 65b
Minor, forbidden to slaughter animal..Succah 42b; Chullin 12b
Minor, legal transfer of benefits by others..Bava Basra 157a
Minor, sale according to the Torah...Bava Metzia 12a-12b
Minors, act of acquisition by courtyard..Bava Metzia 10b
Prohibitions —
Minor, transgressions.............................Yevamos 114a-114b; Shabbos 121a; Gittin 55a
Minor, vow...Niddah 45b
Minor who consecrated, lashes...Niddah 46a-46b
Minor, Yom Kippur fast..Yoma 82a
Trustworthiness —
Minor, testimony..Kesubos 28a-28b; Bava Basra 155b-156a
Minor, testimony in his presence...Bava Kama 112a-112b
Minor, trustworthiness about *agunah*...Yevamos 121b
Minor, trustworthiness for inspecting...Pesachim 4a-4b
Misc. —
Minor, *challah* outside *Eretz Yisrael*...Bechoros 27a
Minor, conversion...Kesubos 11a
Minor, *terumah* in granary...Succah 42a
Minors, World to Come...Sanhedrin 110b
Minor girl
Kiddushin **—**
Minor girl..*see also* **Orphan girl**, page 464
Minor girl, her *kiddushin* grew.................................Yevamos 109b-110a; Kesubos 73a-74a
Minor girl, *kiddushin* by father's command...Kiddushin 19a
Minor girl, *kiddushin* given to mother..Sotah 23b
Minor girl, married on her own..Kiddushin 44b-45b, 46a
Minor girl, prohibition to give her *kiddushin*.......................................Kiddushin 41a, 81b
Minor girl, Rabbinical *kiddushin*...Gittin 65a
Marriage —
Minor girl, disavowing marriage......................................Yevamos 25b, 101b, 107b
Minor girl, disqualified to marry *Kohen*...Niddah 45a
Minor girl, divorce...Gittin 64b, 65a; Kiddushin 43b-44a
Minor girl, husband's rights....................................Yevamos 89b, 108a; Kesubos 101a

M

Minor girl, intimate relations..Niddah 44b-45a
Minor girl, *kesubah*..Kesubos 100b-101a
Minor girl, rapist and seducer................................Kesubos 29a, 36a, 40b; Chullin 26b
Minor girl, renders impure by relations..Niddah 32a
Minor girl, seduced considered like raped................................Yevamos 33b, 61b
Minor girl, time to marry..Kesubos 57b
Minor girl to *Kohen*..Yevamos 61b
Misc. —
   Minor girl, father's rights..Kesubos 43b
   Minor girl, giving birth..........Niddah 45a; Yevamos 12b-13a; Kesubos 39a; Nedarim 35b; Sanhedrin 69b
   Minor girl, *niddah* and *zavah*................................Niddah 9b-10b, 32a-32b, 43b-44a
   Minor girl, pre-menstrual..Niddah 7a-7b, 8b, 10b
   Minor girl to adult man, Jerusalem..Sanhedrin 104a
   Minor girl who married, *terumah*..Kiddushin 45b-46a
Minority
   Minority, added to *chazakah*................Chullin 86a-86b; Kiddushin 80a; Yevamos 119b; Niddah 18b
   Minority added to half, majority..Chullin 77b
   Minority, do we consider................Chullin 6a, 11b, 86a-86b; Yevamos 61b, 119a; Gittin 2b; Kiddushin 80a;
                                 Avodah Zarah 34b, 40b; Bechoros 19b-20b, 42b; Niddah 18b, 31b-32a, 48a
   Minority of minority..Yevamos 119b; Avodah Zarah 34b
   Minority of signs improperly slaughtered..Chullin 30b
   Minority sin in forbidden relations..Bava Basra 165a
   Minority, wordings of vows..Nedarim 53a
Minuy..*see* **Participating in Pesach lamb**, page 473
Minyamin bar Ihi, food for servant..Kesubos 61a
Minyamin Saksnaah, mistake in ruling..Niddah 65a
Minyan..*see* **Quorum**, page 515
Mipnei she'anu medamin................................*see* **Law, opinion but not to rule**, page 355
Miracle
  Episodes —
   Miracle in vain, Rava..Taanis 24b
   Miracle of *Chanukah*..Shabbos 21b
   Miracle of place of Ark................................Bava Basra 98b-99a; Yoma 21a; Megillah 10b
   Miracle of showbread................................Yoma 21a; Chagigah 26b; Menachos 29a, 96b
   Miracles, conquest of *Eretz Yisrael*..Sotah 36a
   Miracles, false, by idols..Avodah Zarah 54b-55a
   Miracles in Temple and Jerusalem................Yoma 21a-21b, 39a-39b; Avos 5:5
   Miracles of deliverance in desert..Berachos 54a-54b
   Miracles of Egypt and Red Sea..Avos 5:4
  Misc. —
   Miracle, benefitting without being aware..Niddah 31a
   Miracle, blessing..Berachos 54a-54b
   Miracle, deduction of rights..Shabbos 32a
   Miracle more frequent than livelihood..Shabbos 53b
   Miracle, not to rely on..Pesachim 64b; Megillah 7b
   Miracle, not to rule on a law................Berachos 60a; Yevamos 121b; Chullin 43a
   Miracle, one who experiences it is not aware..Niddah 31a
   Miracle performed by prophet..Sanhedrin 89b
   Miracle, trial of forbidden relations..Kiddushin 40a

Miracle, women participated..Megillah 4a
Miracles, avoiding...Taanis 24b
Miracles, to prove..Berachos 60a; Yevamos 121b; Chullin 43a
Miracle within miracle
    Miracle within miracle, Daniel's friends.......................................Pesachim 118b
    Miracle within miracle, staff..Shabbos 97a
    Miracle within miracle to punish...Chullin 127a
Miriam
    Miriam, death...Moed Katan 28a; Bava Basra 17a
    Miriam, leprosy..Zevachim 101b-102a
    Miriam *Magdela Nashia*..Chagigah 4b-5a
    Miriam, married Caleb...Sotah 11b-12a
    Miriam, Moses' prophecy.......................................Sotah 12b-13a; Megillah 14a
    Miriam's well, Carmel...Shabbos 35a
Mirror
    Mirror, impurity...Keilim 14:6
    Mirror, looking at on Shabbos...Shabbos 149a
Miruach...*see* **Leveling**, page 366
Misah b'dei Shamayim....................*see* **Death by Divine intervention**, page 150
Misas beis din...*see* **Death penalty**, page 151
Misasek..*see* **Accidentally**, page 6
Miscarriage
    Miscarriage, crushed fetus...Niddah 25b-26a
    Miscarriage cut limb, impurity..Niddah 28a
    Miscarriage, disintegrated fetus...Niddah 27b
    Miscarriage, doubt..Niddah 18b, 29b-30a, 69a-69b
    Miscarriage, firstborn animal....................Chullin 77b, 69b-70a; Bechoros 20a, 21b
    Miscarriage, impurity and sacrifice..Niddah 28a
    Miscarriage, impurity of dead..Oholos 7:4-5
    Miscarriage, piece of flesh.....................................Niddah 18b-19a, 21a-22a, 22b
    Miscarriage, placenta..................Bava Kama 11a-11b; Niddah 26b-27a; Chullin 77b
    Miscarriage, sacrifice.............Nazir 64b; Krisos 7b-8a, 9b; Pesachim 3a; Eduyos 4:10
    Miscarriage, subhuman creatures..Niddah 22b-24b
    Miscarriage, time before new conception...........................Bechoros 19b-20a, 21a
    Miscarrying a snake, episode...Niddah 24b
Miscarrying woman, *kesubah*..Yevamos 65b
Mischar...*see* **Trade**, page 699
Misconduct, married woman...Yevamos 24b-25a
Miserliness
    Miserliness, leprosy..Arachin 16a
    Miserliness, not to benefit from it....................................Sotah 38b; Chullin 7b
    Miserliness, shortcoming..Sotah 38b
Misfortune
    Misfortune of friend, "I did not rejoice"..Megillah 28a
    Misfortune suffices in its time..Berachos 9b
Mishenichnas Adar, joy...Taanis 29a
Mishenichnas Adar v'Av.........................*see* **Beginning of** *Adar* **and of** *Av*, page 49
Misherabu........................*see* **Decline of generations and their consequences**, page 154
Mishkan..*see* **Tabernacle**, page 669

Mishkav zachar..*see* **Homosexuality**, page 282
Mishkav...*see* **Items suitable, couch and other uses, impurity**, page 319
Mishlei
   Mishlei or *Tehillim*, lecture...Avodah Zarah 19a
   Mishlei, Sages wanted to conceal..Shabbos 30b
   Mishlei, Solomon..Bava Basra 14b-15a
Mishloach Manos
   Mishloach Manos..Megillah 7a-7b
   Mishloach manos, episode..Megillah 7a-7b
Mishloach manos..*see* **Sending gifts of food on *Purim***, page 601
Mishmar...*see* **Watches of *Kohanim***, page 734
Mishmoros halaylah...*see* **Night, parts**, page 445
Mishnah *berurah*..*see* **Clear teaching, forgotten**, page 110
Mishnah
   Mishnah, according to two Sages.............Bava Kama 40b, 47b, 47b; Yevamos 13a
   Mishnah and Gemara, learning..........................Sotah 44a; Kiddushin 30a
   Mishnah, preference for learning.........................Bava Metzia 33a-33b
   Mishnah, punishment of one who neglects Mishnah...................Sanhedrin 99a
   Mishnah, Rebbi and Rabbi Nassan........................Bava Metzia 86a
   Mishnah, Tosefta, etc., author............Sanhedrin 86a; Eruvin 96b; Gittin 4a
   Mishnah, unnecessary..Yevamos 50a
   Mishnah was not changed........Yevamos 30a, 32a; Kiddushin 25a; Shevuos 4a; Avodah Zarah 35b;
   ....Chullin 32b, 116b
   Mishnayos forgotten..Chagigah 14a
   Mishnayos, war of Torah..Sanhedrin 42a
Mishpachos meyuchasos........*see* **Families, their lineage will be revealed in the future**, page 214
***Mishpatai vechukosai*, significance**..Yoma 67b
***Mishpatim*, laws**...Kiddushin 37a
***Mishtachaveh*, explanation**..Megillah 22b
Misinterpreting Torah.......................................Sanhedrin 99a, 99b; Avos 3:11
Miskabed bekalon chavero...........*see* **Honored through fellow's humiliation**, page 284
Miskaven..*see* **Intended**, page 311
Misleading
   Misleading act of tearing garment......................................Moed Katan 26b
   Misleading non-Jew...Chullin 94a
   Misleading, prohibition..Chullin 94a, 94b
   Misleading in greeting, episode...Chullin 94b
Missing
   Missing and superfluous letters, in holy parchments...........Sotah 20a; Eruvin 13a
   Missing limb, sacrifice for non-Jew.........Avodah Zarah 5b-6a, 51a; Zevachim 116a
   Missing part in Mishnah, reason...Nedarim 23b
Mission returned to husband, divorce certificate......................Gittin 24a, 63b
Mistake
   ***Beis din* —**
      Mistake about date, conspiring witnesses..............................Sanhedrin 41b
      Mistake about hours, conspiring witnesses.......Pesachim 11b-13a; Sanhedrin 42a
      Mistake in death penalty...........Sanhedrin 52b; Makos 5b; Chagigah 16b
      Mistake in deliberation...Sanhedrin 6a
      Mistake in testimony, slave...................Kesubos 28b; Yevamos 99b

M

Mistake of judge or of ruling......Sanhedrin 5a, 6a, 30a, 33a-33b; Bechoros 28b; Bava Kama 100a, 117b
Mistake, ruling contradictory to Mishnah...Bechoros 28b

Episodes —
Mistake in examination, episode...Shevuos 28b; Zevachim 26a
Mistake in what I said yesterday, lecture...........Eruvin 16b, 104a; Shabbos 63b; Yevamos 20b, 76a;
....Bava Basra 127a; Chullin 56a; Niddah 68a
Mistake of *Kohanim*, examination...Pesachim 17a
Mistake before ruler, fatal....................Moed Katan 18a; Kesubos 23a, 62b; Bava Metzia 68a
Mistakes, because of sharpness of mind...............Bava Metzia 96b; Eruvin 90a; Niddah 33b

Monetary matters —
Mistake, act of acquisition for another...Gittin 14a
Mistake in conceding something...Bava Basra 41a-41b
Mistake of non-Jew...Bava Kama 113b
Mistake possible, fraud..Bava Basra 78a

Prayer —
Mistake in *Avos* blessing..Berachos 34b
Mistake in blessing about heretics...Berachos 28b-29a
Mistake in prayer, from where one must repeat..Berachos 34a

Sacrifices —
Mistake of *beis din*..*see* **Sacrifice for mistake of *beis din*, page 581**
Mistake, partial, communal bull...Horayos 4a-4b, 7b
Mistake, partial, *Kohen Gadol*'s bull...Horayos 7b; Sanhedrin 62a
Mistake, thought for sacrifice...Menachos 49a

Misc. —
Mistake in blessing..Berachos 12a
Mistake in commandment, transgression................Shabbos 137a; Pesachim 71b-72b; Succah 42a;
....Yevamos 34a
Mistake in consecration.................................Nazir 30b-31b; Bava Basra 120b; Arachin 23a
Mistake in higher value, *kiddushin*...Kiddushin 48b
Mistake in holy parchments, correcting...Menachos 29b
Mistake in speech, *terumah*...Terumos 3:8; Pesachim 63a
Mistake, *niddah* and *zavah*.........................Arachin 8a-8b; Niddah 53b-54a, 69a-69b
Mistake, no misleading in greeting...Chullin 94b
Mistake, welcoming Shabbos...Berachos 27b
Mistakes in holy parchments, correcting...Menachos 29b-30a

Mistake in ruling
Mistake in first ruling...Beitzah 16b
Mistake in ruling, egg water...Sanhedrin 5b
Mistake in ruling, G-d prevented...Bava Metzia 81a; Niddah 65a
Mistake in ruling, meat of ox...Bava Kama 72a
Mistake in ruling, nursing woman...Kesubos 60b
Mistake in ruling, one judge knows that they erred..Horayos 2b
Mistake in ruling, Resh Lakish...Avodah Zarah 58b
Mistake in ruling, turning face away...Yoma 73a
Mistake in ruling, Yom Tov...Beitzah 4a

Mistress stricken, maidservant all the more so...Taanis 21b

Mitoch she'eino yachol lishava..........................*see* **Oath, "I do not know," page 453**
Mitoch shehutra...*see* **Work permitted on Yom Tov, page 760**
Mitoch shelo lishmah......................*see* **Ulterior goal leads to Heaven's sake, page 713**

Mitznefet...*see* **Turban of Kohen**, page 706
Mitzri umitzris..*see* **Egyptian**, page 189
Mitztaer besuccah..*see* **Painful**, *succah*, page 470
Mitzvah..*see* **Commandment**, page 116
Mitzvas aseh..*see* **Positive commandment**, page 495
Mitzvas lo taaseh..*see* **Negative commandment**, page 440
Mitzvas yevamin.......................*see* **Bond before levirate marriage, prohibition to annul**, page 71
Mivta, oath..Shevuos 20a-20b
Mixed species
  Distance —
    Mixed species, flowerbed................Shabbos 84b-86a; Kilayim 3:1-2; Pesachim 39b; Kiddushin 39a-39b
    Mixed species, keeping away.............................Kilayim 2:6-10, 3:3-7; Pesachim 39b
    Mixed species, low grapevine..Sotah 43b
    Mixed species, outline of opening..Eruvin 11a-11b, 16a
    Mixed species, quantity...........Kilayim 1:9, 2:1-2; Bava Basra 94a-94b; Moed Katan 6a-6b
    Mixed species, tree branches..Kilayim 2:11
  Misc. —
    Mixed species, agents of *beis din*.................Moed Katan 6a-6b; Shekalim 1:1-2
    Mixed species, covering with earth or keeping...........................Makos 21b
    Mixed species in vineyard..................................*see* **Vineyard**, page 723
    Mixed species, non-Jew...Sanhedrin 60a
    Mixed species outside *Eretz Yisrael*...................Kiddushin 38a-39b; Bava Kama 55a
    Mixed species, permitted new growths...................Menachos 69b; Nedarim 57b
    Mixed species, two species and seed........Kiddushin 39a; Berachos 22a; Kilayim 1:9; Bechoros 54a;
    ....Chullin 82b, 136b
    Mixed species, uprooting before sowing.......................Kilayim 2:3-4
    Mixed species, which species..............................Kilayim 1:1-5; Pesachim 39a
  Mixed species of animals
    Mixed species of animals, do they procreate........................Bechoros 7a, 8a
    Mixed species of animals, keeping them...............................Kilayim 8:1
    Mixed species of animals, permitted.....................Kilayim 2:5; Bava Kama 81a
    Mixed species of animals, same enclosure........................Bava Metzia 91a-91b
    Mixed species of animals, sheep and goat.........................Bava Kama 77b-78a
    Mixed species of animals, species from father....Chullin 79a-79b; Kilayim 8:4-5; Kesubos 111b
    Mixed species of animals, which species...................Kilayim 1:6; Bava Kama 54b, 55a
Mixing
  Mixing forbidden food to permit it..Beitzah 4b
  Mixing meal offering....................Menachos 9a, 18a-19a, 74b-75a; Pesachim 36a
  Mixing preservative ingredient in wheat, parable.................................Shabbos 31a
Mixture
  Combining —
    Mixture, became mixed a second time................Terumos 5:5-6; Temurah 12a; Zevachim 74a-74b
    Mixture, combining bones...Chullin 98b
    Mixture, combining forbidden substances..................Orlah 2:1-3, 2:14-17; Shabbos 89b-90a;
    ....Avodah Zarah 66a; Meilah 15b; Zevachim 78a-79a
    Mixture, combining pot...Chullin 97b, 98a
    Mixture, forbidden substances cancel one another.......................Zevachim 78a-79b
    Mixture in barrel, combining...................Beitzah 3b-4a; Terumos 4:10; Zevachim 73a
    Mixture of second forbidden substance.......................................Terumos 5:7-8

M

Mixture of several spices .... Orlah 2:10; Avodah Zarah 66a, 68b
Mixture, permitted piece becomes *neveilah* .... Chullin 100a-100b, 108a-109a

Food —

Mixture .... *see* also **Absorption**, page 5, *see also* **Intermingled**, page 315
Mixture, bad taste .... Avodah Zarah 65b, 67a-68b
Mixture, forbidden food taken out .... Chullin 97b
Mixture in liquid, considered mixed .... Rosh Hashanah 13b-14a; Zevachim 80a-81a
Mixture, ingredient thickening .... Avodah Zarah 35a
Mixture, liquid, cases .... Terumos 10:11-12
Mixture, name and taste .... Avodah Zarah 66a-66b
Mixture permitted to *Kohen* .... Yevamos 82a
Mixture, produce of Sabbatical year .... Sheviis 7:7, 9:5; Pesachim 52a; Nedarim 58a

Mixture of impure foods

Mixture of impure foods .... Zevachim 31a; Taharos 1:5
Mixture of impure foods, majority .... Machshirin 2:3-11
Mixture of impure foods, melted .... Bechoros 21b-22a
Mixture of impure foods, same substance .... Orlah 2:4-5

Principles —

Mixture annulled drop by drop .... Avodah Zarah 73a; Chullin 87b
Mixture, commandments cancel each other .... Zevachim 79a; Pesachim 115a
Mixture, common element between the two substances .... Menachos 23a-23b; Beitzah 38b
Mixture, defined by last substance .... Pesachim 26b-27a; Orlah 2:11; Avodah Zarah 49a, 73b;
.... Temurah 12a
Mixture, equal quantity of components .... Zevachim 80a-81a; Rosh Hashanah 13b-14a
Mixture forbidden by Rabbinical Decree, attributing .... Yevamos 82a-82b; Pesachim 9b-10a, 44a;
.... Nazir 36b-37a
Mixture, important thing .... Orlah 3:6-8; Beitzah 3b-4a; Yevamos 81a-81b
Mixture in its place .... *see* **Item situated in place of doubt, majority**, page 319
Mixture of something counted .... Avodah Zarah 74a
Mixture, part of it was lost .... Zevachim 74a, 74b, 77b
Mixture, Rabbinical prohibitions, leniencies .... Yevamos 81a, 82a
Mixture, sold by unit .... Avodah Zarah 74a; Beitzah 3b-4a
Mixture, temporary prohibition .... Beitzah 3b, 39a; Nedarim 58a, 59a; Bava Metzia 53a

Prohibitions —

Mixture, *chametz* .... Pesachim 29b-30a, 43a
Mixture, food for idolatry .... Avodah Zarah 49b
Mixture, *orlah* .... Orlah 1:6, 3:4-5; Pesachim 26a-27a; Gittin 54b
Mixture, vowed food .... Nedarim 52a-52b
Mixture, wine of idolaters .... Avodah Zarah 49b, 56b, 71b, 73a-74a
Mixture, wine of *nazir* .... Pesachim 45a; Nazir 35b, 37a-38a

Quantity —

Mixture, *kezayis* in *pras* .... Nazir 36b-37a; Pesachim 44a-44b; Avodah Zarah 67a
Mixture which swelled up or was reduced .... Terumos 5:9
Mixture, liquid, quantity .... Orlah 2:6-7; Chullin 97a-99b; Avodah Zarah 69a

Separating tithes —

Mixture considered mixed, in tithe of two years .... Rosh Hashanah 13b
Mixture, leniencies for *terumah* out of *Eretz Yisrael* .... Bechoros 27a
Mixture of *demai* .... Chullin 6a
Mixture of second tithe .... Maaser Sheni 2:1; Bava Metzia 53a

M

Mixture of tithe, cases .... Demai 7:7-8

Mixture of tithe, in Jerusalem .... Bikkurim 2:1

Mixture of *terumah*

Mixture of *terumah, challah* .... Challah 3:2; Niddah 46b-47a

Mixture of *terumah,* combining .... Terumos 4:7-13

Mixture of *terumah,* dry .... Terumos 5:1, 5:4

Mixture of *terumah,* immersed that day ...... Tevul Yom 2:3-5, 3:4-5; Pesachim 44a; Nazir 36a-36b

Mixture of *terumah,* Shabbos .... Shabbos 142a-142b

Mixture of *terumah,* taste .... Terumos 10:1-2

Mixture of *terumah,* two baskets .... Terumos 7:5-7; Pesachim 9b, 44a; Yevamos 82a-82b;

.... Nazir 36b-37a

Mixture of *terumah,* separating .... Terumos 5:2-3; Bechoros 22a-23a

Mixture of *tevel*

Mixture of *tevel,* cases .... Demai 7:7; Challah 3:9

Mixture of *tevel,* how to correct .... Menachos 31a

Mixture of *tevel,* negligible quantity .... Avodah Zarah 73b; Challah 3:10

Misc. —

Mixture, barrel which opened .... Zevachim 74b

Mixture of blood, cases .... Chullin 87a-87b

Mixture of sacrificial blood ..... Zevachim 35a, 36a, 77b-78a, 79a-82a; Pesachim 65a; Menachos 22a-22b;

.... Chullin 87a-87b; Temurah 5b; Niddah 71b

Mixture, reawakens, ... Avodah Zarah 73a; Eruvin 9a; Bechoros 22a, 23a

Mixture, two *techumim* .... Beitzah 38a-39a

Mixture of same substance

Mixture of same substance and of different substance .... Avodah Zarah 73a-73b

Mixture of same substance, cases ..... Orlah 2:4-5, 2:6-7; Chullin 99a-99b; Challah 3:1; Zevachim 78b

Mixture of same substance, intervening ..... Yoma 58a; Succah 37b; Zevachim 110a; Bechoros 9b;

.... Rosh Hashanah 27b

Mixture of same substance, negligible quantity .... Yevamos 81b-82a; Menachos 22b;

.... Avodah Zarah 73b; Pesachim 29b-30a

Miyut achar miyut .... *see* **Double exclusion,** page 175

Mizbeach .... *see* **Altar,** page 19

Mizbeach, meaning according to initials .... Kesubos 10b

***Mizmor* about Absalom** .... Berachos 10a

Mizrach .... *see* **East,** page 185

***Mizrakim* of Temple** .... Pesachim 64b

Moab

Moab and Midian, hate .... Sanhedrin 105a

Moab, Ruth .... Bava Kama 38a-38b

Moabite

Moabite man who married Egyptian woman .... Kiddushin 67b

Moabites, disqualified to marry into Jewish people ...... Yevamos 76b-77a; Nazir 23b; Horayos 10b

Moabites, Sennacherib .... Berachos 28a; Yadayim 4:4

Mobile item placed in the ground, idolatry .... Avodah Zarah 47b; Chullin 16a; Meilah 20a

Mocheis .... *see* **Tax collector,** page 673

Modaah .... *see* **Cancellation in advance,** page 86

Modeh .... *see* **Acknowledged,** page 7

Modest, Rabbinical commandment .... Niddah 12a

Modestly walking .... Succah 49b; Makos 24a

M

Modesty
  Episodes —
    Modesty, Medes and Persians .... Berachos 8b
    Modesty, Rabbi Eliezer .... Nedarim 20b
    Modesty, Rabbi Yose .... Shabbos 118b
    Modesty, Saul .... Berachos 62b; Megillah 13b
  Marriage —
    Modesty, behavior of married woman .... Shabbos 140b
    Modesty, *Kohanim gedolim* .... Yoma 47a
    Modesty, looking at one's wife .... Nedarim 20a
  Women —
    Modesty, "return to dust" .... Taanis 24a
    Modesty, girl's steps .... Avodah Zarah 18a
    Modesty, granddaughter on his lap .... Kiddushin 81b
    Modesty, husband's demand for .... Gittin 90a-90b
    Modesty in *Eretz Yisrael* .... Bava Basra 91b
    Modesty, Kimchis, *Kohanim gedolim* .... Yoma 47a
    Modesty, one-armed woman .... Shabbos 53b
    Modesty, punishment by *beis din* .... Sanhedrin 46a
    Modesty, Rachel .... Bava Basra 123a; Megillah 13b
    Modesty, red garment .... Berachos 20a
    Modesty, shoes for immoral women .... Pesachim 113b
    Modesty, Tamar, reward .... Megillah 10b
  Misc. —
    Modesty, doors of Israel .... Bava Basra 60a
    Modesty in bathhouse .... Shabbos 41a
    Modesty in learning .... Succah 49b; Moed Katan 16a-16b
    Modesty in toilet .... Berachos 61b-62b
    Modesty, learned from cat .... Eruvin 100b
    Modesty when performing commandments .... Succah 49b; Makos 24a

Modim
  Modim deRabbanan .... Sotah 40a
  Modim Modim, silencing .... Berachos 33b; Megillah 25a
  Modim, punishment for who does not bow .... Bava Kama 16a

Mofes hador .... *see* **Wonder of generation**, page 759

Molad .... *see* **New moon**, page 443

Mold
  Mold for shoe, *muktzeh* .... Shabbos 141b
  Mold for showbread .... Menachos 94a

Mole, reptile .... Chullin 63a

Molech, idolatry .... Sanhedrin 64a-64b

Monarchy, synonyms .... Sanhedrin 99b

Monday and Thursday
  Monday and Thursday, days of *beis din* sessions .... Bava Kama 82a
  Monday and Thursday, Torah reading .... Megillah 31b-32a; Bava Kama 82a

Monetary
  Monetary loss, festival .... Moed Katan 10b-11a
  Monetary loss, mourner .... Moed Katan 11b

M

Monetary cases

Monetary cases, like fountain .... Berachos 63b; Bava Basra 175b

Monetary cases, ordained judges .... Bava Kama 15b, 84a-84b; Sanhedrin 2b-3b

Monetary cases, women .... Kiddushin 35a-35b; Bava Kama 15a

Money .... *see also* **Coin**, page 113; *see also* **Price**, page 502

Acquisition —

Money, act of acquisition from the Torah .... Bava Metzia 47b-48b; Eruvin 81b; Kiddushin 28b;

.... Chullin 83a; Bechoros 13a-13b

Money, act of acquisition of land .... Kiddushin 26a; Bava Metzia 99b; Bava Basra 86a, 150b

Money as an act of acquisition, price of ox .... Bava Metzia 46b; Kiddushin 28b

Money, barter .... Bava Metzia 45b-46b, 47a; Kiddushin 28a-28b

Money, buyer returning purchase .... Bava Metzia 47b, 49b, 74b

Money, finished after thirty days .... Kiddushin 59a

Money, fruit in buyer's attic .... Bava Metzia 49b

Money to and from non-Jew .... Avodah Zarah 71a-71b; Bechoros 13a-13b

Aggadah —

Money, more precious than oneself .... Berachos 61b; Pesachim 25a; Yoma 82a; Sanhedrin 74a

Money of righteous, more precious than body .... Chullin 91a; Sotah 12a

Money puts back on one's legs (Rashi – "makes a man happy") .... Pesachim 119a

Money spent, society's benefit .... Pesachim 54b

Claims —

Money, "my money is with you" .... Yevamos 37b

Money and lashes, severest penalty .... Kesubos 31b-33a; Makos 4b, 13b

Money for nothing, purchase .... Bava Metzia 14a

Money for one and death for the other .... Sanhedrin 9b-10a

Money in hand, better legal position .... Bava Metzia 49b

Money, man does not give up on his money .... Sanhedrin 72a-72b

Money matters, majority .... Bava Basra 92a-93b; Bava Kama 27a-27b, 46a-46b

Money returned, buying from thief .... Bava Metzia 15b

Money, without claimants .... Chullin 130b

Commandments —

Money given on Purim, changing .... Bava Metzia 78b, 106b-107a

Money of owner, *challah* .... Kiddushin 53a

Money of owner, *terumah* .... Kiddushin 53a-53b

Money of synagogue, holiness .... Megillah 27a

Custodians —

Money, custody .... Bava Metzia 36a, 42a; Pesachim 31b

Money left in custody, using .... Bava Metzia 43a; Meilah 21b

Money, lost item value .... Bava Metzia 28b-29b

Money of sale, custody .... Bava Metzia 49a

Episodes —

Money, improper, destroyed proper money .... Kesubos 66b

Money in staff, oath .... Nedarim 25a; Shevuos 29a

Money of Jerusalem .... Bava Kama 97b

Money of orphans, episode .... Berachos 18b

Prohibitions —

Money from sale of idolatrous item .... Avodah Zarah 64a-64b

Money, from sale of items forbidden to profit .... Kiddushin 58a

Money of fellow, forbidden to profit .... Bava Metzia 117b

Money of orphans, investing it in business .... Bava Metzia 70a
Money of sale of item forbidden to have benefit thereof .... Kiddushin 58a
Money of second tithe, exchange .... Maaser Sheni 2:7-9; Eduyos 1:9-10; Bava Metzia 44b-45b
Money of second tithe which became intermingled .... Maaser Sheni 2:5-6; Beitzah 10b;
.... Bava Metzia 55b-56a
Money plundered from Temple .... Bechoros 50a; Avodah Zarah 52b

Sacrifices —
Money consecrated for unspecified sacrifice .... Nazir 24b-25a, 25b-26a
Money for participation in Pesach lamb .... Pesachim 89b-90a
Money for secular use of sin offering .... Meilah 9b
Money of *nazir*, changed use .... Nazir 26b-27b
Money of *nazir*, designed for his three sacrifices .... Nazir 26a-26b
Money of owner, sacrifice ...... Bava Kama 12b-13a; Kiddushin 52b-53a; Pesachim 90a; Bava Basra 123b;
.... Sanhedrin 112b; Zevachim 114a; Bechoros 53b
Money of sin offering after owners' atonement .... Temurah 23b-24a
Money unspecified, sin offering .... Nazir 24b-25a; Menachos 4b; Meilah 11a

Women —
Money contract and intimate relations, *kiddushin* .... Kiddushin 3b, 4b-5a
Money does not substitute divorce certificate ... Kiddushin 5a; Eruvin 15b; Succah 24b; Gittin 21b
Money of sale of maidservant, *kiddushin* .... Kiddushin 19a
Money ready for household needs .... Kesubos 80b
Money, women .... Kiddushin 35a-35b; Bava Kama 15a

Misc. —
Money, child is attracted to .... Gittin 40a
Money, fixed, leniency and stringency .... Arachin 13b-15a
Money lost in synagogue .... Bava Metzia 24a
Money matters, not learned from penalties and prohibition .... Kiddushin 3b; Kesubos 40b, 46b
Money of poor, investing .... Kesubos 106b
Money purifies, disqualified lineage .... Kiddushin 71a

Money-changer
Money-changer, transfer of rights .... Bava Metzia 112a
Money-changer who made a mistake, liability .... Bava Kama 99b

Monkey
Monkey, blessing .... Berachos 58b
Monkey compared to man, Sarah and Eve .... Bava Basra 58a
Monkey, Rav Gamda's treasure .... Nedarim 50b

Month
Month added, rent .... Bava Metzia 102a-102b; Bava Basra 105a
Month added to year .... *see* **Adding a month**, page 11
Month of *Adar* .... *see* **Adar**, page 10
Month of *Elul*, full and missing .... Rosh Hashanah 19b, 20b, 32a; Beitzah 6a, 22b
Month, wording of vow .... Nedarim 60a-60b
Months, counting days .... Megillah 5a
Months, defective and full .... Arachin 8b-10a
Months of checking before remarrying .... Yevamos 34a-35a, 41b-43b; Kesubos 37; Gittin 18a
Months of pregnancy .... Sanhedrin 69a; Niddah 38a; Yevamos 37a
Months of pregnancy, concern of forbidden relations .... Yevamos 80b

Moon
Moon, calculations of new moon .... Rosh Hashanah 20b, 24b-25a; Arachin 9b

Moon, learning by its light .... Eruvin 65a
Moon, light straight like stick .... Yoma 28b
Moon, reduced .... Chullin 60b
Moon, sun never saw its missing part .... Rosh Hashanah 23b
Moon, time when seen .... Rosh Hashanah 21a

More than
More than a man wishes to marry, a woman wishes to marry .... Yevamos 113a; Kesubos 86a;
.... Gittin 49b
More than is written here .... Yoma 68b; Megilla 34b
More than the calf wishes to nurse .... Pesachim 112a

Mora ravcha .... *see* **Fear of teacher, equal to fear of Heaven, page 218**

Mordechai
Mordechai, episode of *Megillah* .... Megillah 15a
Mordechai hinted in the Torah .... Chullin 139b
Mordechai, interprets allusions .... Menachos 64b-65a
Mordechai, Malachi .... Megillah 15a
Mordechai, means pure frankincense .... Megillah 10b; Chullin 139b
Mordechai, names and lineage .... Megillah 12b-13a
Mordechai, *Sanhedrin* separated from him .... Megillah 16b
Mordechai, Temple officers .... Shekalim 5:1-2; Menachos 65a

More possessions, more worry .... Avos 2:7
Mored bemalchus .... *see* **Rebel against government, belongings, page 549**
Mored umoredes .... *see* **Rebel in marital relations, husband and wife, page 549**
Moriah Mount .... Taanis 16a

Morid Hageshem
Morid Hageshem and *Morid Hatal* .... Berachos 33a; Taanis 2a
Morid Hageshem, when .... Taanis 2b, 3a, 4a-5a

Morning
Morning, beginning journey .... Yoma 21a
Morning blessings .... Berachos 60b; Menachos 43b
Morning, first or second .... Pesachim 71a-71b, 120b
Morning prayer .... *see* **Shacharis, page 608**
Morning, sow your seed .... Yevamos 62b

Mortgage
Mortgage .... *see also* **Seizure, page 598**
Mortgage, "property that I will buy" .... Bava Basra 44b, 157a-157b
Mortgage annulled, promissory note annulled .... Bava Metzia 17a; Kesubos 85a-85b; Gittin 26b
Mortgage, bought from non-Jew .... Bava Metzia 73b
Mortgage, collecting from consecrated items Treasury .... Arachin 23b
Mortgage, damage .... Gittin 41a
Mortgage, dry tree .... Bava Metzia 109b-110a; Kesubos 95b
Mortgage, for what .... Gittin 50b-51a; Kiddushin 13b; Bava Basra 41b-42a, 175b-176a
Mortgage, from the Torah .... Bava Basra 175b
Mortgage, from whom do we collect .... Bava Basra 42a, 157a, 175a-176a
Mortgage, interest .... Bava Metzia 67b-68a
Mortgage, loan .... Bava Metzia 67b-68a; Pesachim 112b
Mortgage, movable items .... Bava Basra 44b
Mortgage of Sura .... Bava Metzia 67b, 110a; Bava Basra 35b38a
Mortgage, slaves .... Bava Kama 11b; Bava Basra 128a-128b

Mortgage, trustworthiness and *chazakah* .... Bava Metzia 110a

Mortgage, verbal loan .... Kiddushin 13b; Bava Basra 41b-42a, 157a, 175b-176a; Bava Kama 104b;
.... Bechoros 48b; Arachin 6b-7a, 20a

Mortification, sinner .... Taanis 11a-11b, 22b; Nedarim 10a; Nazir 19a, 22a; Sotah 15a; Bava Kama 91b;
.... Shevuos 8a; Krisos 26a

Mosar mezonos .... *see* **Remainder of support money, page 556**

Mosaros hekdesh vekorban .... *see* **Remainders of consecrated item and sacrifice, page 556**

Moser .... *see* **Informer, page 308**

Moshav leitzim .... *see* **Sitting-place of scoffers, page 631**

Moses

   Character traits —

     Moses, acknowledged without shame .... Zevachim 101a

     Moses, face comparable to sun .... Bava Basra 75a

     Moses, gates of understanding .... Rosh Hashanah 21b; Nedarim 38a

     Moses, generosity .... Nedarim 38a

     Moses, humility .... Chullin 89a

     Moses, purpose of world .... Sanhedrin 98b

     Moses, reward .... Sotah 14a

     Moses, seven shepherds .... Succah 52b

   Divine Presence —

     Moses, "may my sin be written" .... Yoma 86b

     Moses, burning bush .... Berachos 7a

     Moses, cave .... Megillah 19b

     Moses, defense .... Berachos 32a

     Moses, G-d approved .... Shabbos 87a; Yevamos 62a

     Moses, G-d's ways .... Berachos 7a

     Moses, G-d's word .... Yoma 4b; Berachos 63b; Bava Basra 121a-121b

     Moses, knot of *tefillin* .... Berachos 7a; Menachos 35b

     Moses, requests from G-d .... Berachos 7a; Bava Basra 15b

     Moses spoke harshly to G-d .... Berachos 32a

     Moses, vision .... Yevamos 49b

     Moses, why did You mistreat .... Sanhedrin 111a

   Giving of Torah —

     Moses, answer to angels .... Shabbos 88b-89a

     Moses, climbing on mountain .... Shabbos 89a; Yoma 4a-4b; Sanhedrin 111a

     Moses, enterings in cloud .... Yoma 4b

     Moses from Sinai, Rabbinical commandments .... Megillah 19b

     Moses, his decrees are kept .... Shabbos 30a

     Moses, learning on Mount Sinai .... Megillah 21a; Nedarim 38a

     Moses, Rabbi Akiva's prophecy .... Menachos 29b

     Moses, received from Sinai .... Chagigah 6a-6b; Sotah 37b; Zevachim 115b

     Moses, taller than ten cubits .... Succah 5a

     Moses, was shown *kosher* species .... Chullin 42a

   His life —

     Moses, allusions in verses about Nile river .... Sotah 11a

     Moses, death and burial .... Sotah 13b-14a; Kiddushin 38a; Megillah 13b

     Moses, *Eretz Yisrael* .... Sotah 14a

     Moses, eulogy .... Sotah 13b-14a

     Moses' face similar to sun .... Bava Basra 75a

M

Moses, feared Og .... Niddah 61a
Moses, fell on his face when spies came back .... Taanis 14b
Moses found difficult, three things .... Menachos 29a
Moses, his birth and being pulled out of river .... Sotah 12a-13a
Moses, his height .... Bechoros 44a; Shabbos 92a; Nedarim 38a
Moses, his names .... Megillah 13a; Sotah 12a; Bava Basra 15a
Moses, his son's circumcision .... Nedarim 31b-32a
Moses is true, Korah .... Bava Basra 74a; Sanhedrin 110a
Moses, Joseph's grave .... Sotah 13a-13b
Moses, kingship to his sons .... Zevachim 102a
Moses, leprosy .... Shabbos 97a
Moses, looked after him .... Kiddushin 33b
Moses, numerous offspring .... Berachos 7a
Moses, Pharaoh .... Zevachim 102a
Moses, prayer for Judah .... Makos 11b
Moses, priesthood .... Zevachim 101b-102a
Moses, putting tent back in camp .... Berachos 63b
Moses, suspected by Korah .... Sanhedrin 110a
Moses, was he a hunter .... Chullin 60b
Moses, Waters of Dispute .... Shabbos 55b
Moses, wealth .... Nedarim 38a
Moses, Zelophehad and wood gatherer .... Sanhedrin 8a; Bava Basra 119a
Misc. —
Moses and Aaron, resurrection .... Yoma 5b
Moses, announcement to Patriarchs .... Berachos 18b
Moses, Cities of Refuge .... Makos 10a
Moses hinted in the Torah .... Chullin 139b
Moses, sun stood still .... Avodah Zarah 25a; Taanis 20a
Moses, Tabernacle dedication .... Avodah Zarah 34a; Taanis 11b
Moses! What you say is true .... Shabbos 101b; Succah 39a; Beitzah 38b
Mosif gore'a .... see **Adding equivalent to subtracting**, page 10
Mosif hevel .... see **Adding warmth**, page 10
Mosquito, cure for snake bite .... Shabbos 77b
Most .... see **Majority**, page 384
Mother
Forbidden relations —
Mother, forbidden relations .... Sanhedrin 53a-54a
Mother, her daughter's *kiddushin* .... Sotah 23b
Mother of mother-in-law, forbidden relations .... Sanhedrin 76b; Yevamos 94b
Mother, trustworthiness for *kiddushin* .... Kiddushin 12a-12b
Mother's mother, Rabbinical prohibition .... Sanhedrin 75b-76a
Misc. —
Mother does not forget her son .... Bava Basra 36a
Mother, family .... Bava Basra 109b, 110b
Mother, firstborn's inheritance .... Bava Basra 111a-111b
Mother, inheritance .... Bava Basra 114b-115a
Mother of Nehemiah, pregnancy .... Sanhedrin 37b
Mother of sick, text of whispers .... Shabbos 66b
Mother said to me, Abbaye .... Kiddushin 31b

M

Mother who lost her mind, episode .... Kiddushin 31b
Mothers, examination .... Kiddushin 76a-76b
Mothers of men in Tanach .... Bava Basra 91a

Mother-in-law
Mother-in-law burned her daughter-in-law .... Shabbos 26a
Mother-in-law, distance to avoid forbidden relations .... Pesachim 113a; Kiddushin 12b;
.... Yevamos 52a; Bava Basra 98b
Mother-in-law, forbidden relations .... Yevamos 94b; Sanhedrin 76b
Mother-in-law, hatred .... Yevamos 117a
Mother-in-law, mourning .... Kesubos 4b
Mother-in-law's and husband's daughter, hatred .... Yevamos 117a
Mother-in-law's mother, forbidden relations .... Sanhedrin 76b; Yevamos 94b

Motza, willows .... Succah 45a

Motzaei Shabbos
Motzaei Shabbos, meal .... Shabbos 119b
Motzaei Shabbos, work .... Pesachim 50b

Motzaei Shabbos .... *see* **End of Shabbos**, page 196
Motzi chavero bivrachah .... *see* **Discharges other from blessing**, page 165
Motzi mechavero .... *see* **Taking from other, proof**, page 671
Motzi shem ra .... *see* **Slander**, page 633
Mound, impurity .... Kesubos 20b; Oholos 16:2

Mount
Mount Hermon .... Chullin 60b
Mount Eibal, curses .... Sotah 37b
Mount Gerizim and Eibal .... Sotah 33b, 37a
Mount Moriah .... Taanis 16a
Mount of Temple .... *see* **Temple Mount**, page 679
Mount Sinai .... *see* **Sinai**, page 628
Mount Tabor, giant animal .... Bava Basra 73b; Zevachim 113b
Mount Tabor, Giving of Torah .... Megillah 29a

Mountain
Mountain, idolatrous sacrifice .... Chullin 39b-40a; Avodah Zarah 42b
Mountain like a barrel .... Shabbos 88a; Avodah Zarah 2b
Mountain, signs .... Pesachim 53a
Mountain, who is stronger than .... Bava Basra 10a
Mountains, blessing .... Berachos 59a
Mountains hanging by a hair .... Chagigah 10b-11a
Mountains of Darkness, *Gehinnom* .... Tamid 32b

Mourner
Prohibitions —
Mourner after wife's death, when can he remarry .... Moed Katan 23a
Mourner being a refined person, washing .... Berachos 16b
Mourner, betrothal and marriage .... Yevamos 43a-43b
Mourner, cleaning house .... Moed Katan 27a
Mourner, eating sacrifice .... Zevachim 99b-101a
Mourner, forbidden closeness to wife .... Kesubos 4b
Mourner, forbidden to have marital relations .... Moed Katan 15b, 21a, 24a
Mourner, going to synagogue .... Moed Katan 23a
Mourner, greeting .... Moed Katan 15a

M

Mourner, holding a baby .... Moed Katan 26b
Mourner, ironed and new garment .... Moed Katan 23a
Mourner, laughter .... Moed Katan 26b
Mourner, nails and mustache .... Moed Katan 17b-18a
Mourner, part of day .... Moed Katan 17b, 19b; Nazir 15b
Mourner, Pesach lamb .... Zevachim 99b-101a; Pesachim 91b-92a
Mourner, rule according to lenient opinion .... Eruvin 46a; Moed Katan 18a, 19b, 20a, 22a, 26b;
.... Chullin 50a; Bechoros 49a
Mourner, shaving .... Moed Katan 14b, 17b, 19b, 22b, 24a
Mourner, shoe .... Moed Katan 15b, 20b
Mourner, successive periods of mourning .... Moed Katan 17b; Taanis 13a
Mourner, *tefillin* .... Succah 25a, 25b; Berachos 11a, 16b; Moed Katan 15a, 21a; Kesubos 6b
Mourner, wine .... Sanhedrin 70a; Eruvin 65a
Mourner, work .... Moed Katan 11b, 15b, 21b, 26b-27a
Misc. —
Mourner, adult woman .... Taanis 13b
Mourner, bed turned upside down .... Moed Katan 15a, 26b-27a
Mourner before funeral .... *see* **Onein**, page 460
Mourner cannot speak .... Bava Basra 16b
Mourner, comforting .... *see* **Comforting the bereaved**, page 116
Mourner, encircling Temple Mount .... Middos 2:2
Mourner, guarding .... Berachos 54b
Mourner, is called "*marzach*" .... Kesubos 69b
Mourner, not told to sit .... Moed Katan 27b
Mourner, tearing garment .... *see* **Tearing garment**, page 675
Mourner, worrying .... Moed Katan 27b
Mourners' meal .... *see* **Havraah meal**, page 273
Mourning
Other —
Mourning, definite leper .... Moed Katan 14b-15b
Mourning, excommunicated person .... Moed Katan 14b-15b
Mourning for Jerusalem, black shoes .... Bava Kama 59b
Mourning for Jerusalem, general .... Bava Basra 60b; Moed Katan 26a; Taanis 30b
Mourning for Jerusalem, groom .... Bava Basra 60b
Mourning of *omer* period .... Yevamos 62b
When —
Mourning, counting from when .... Moed Katan 21b-22a; Chullin 50a
Mourning, festivals .... Moed Katan 19a-20a, 24b; Nazir 15a-15b
Mourning, for man deceased on Yom Tov .... Moed Katan 19b-20a
Mourning on Shabbos .... Moed Katan 23a-24a
Mourning on Yom Tov .... Moed Katan 14b
Who —
Mourning, betrothed girl .... Kesubos 53a
Mourning, for father and mother .... Moed Katan 22a-22b
Mourning for father-in-law and mother-in-law .... Moed Katan 20b; Kesubos 4b
Mourning for stillborn .... Bechoros 49a; Niddah 44b; Shabbos 136a
Mourning, relatives .... Moed Katan 20b
Misc. —
Mourning before wedding .... Kesubos 3b-4b

M

Mourning, episodes about weeping .... Shabbos 151b; Sanhedrin 104b
Mourning learned from the Torah .... Zevachim 99b, 100b-101a; Berachos 16b; Pesachim 92a
Mourning, learning, *tefillin* and going out .... Moed Katan 15a, 21a-21b
Mourning of seven days, source .... Moed Katan 20a
Mourning revolves in the world .... Bava Basra 16b
Mourning, washing body and clothes .... Moed Katan 15a-15b, 17b; Taanis 13a-13b

Mouse, not the thief, hole is .... Gittin 45a

Mouth
Mouth, "a holy mouth would say this?" .... Sanhedrin 24a
Mouth and heart equal .... Pesachim 63a; Terumos 3:1
Mouth did not stop learning, David's death .... Shabbos 30b
Mouth of cow, domain of victim .... Bava Kama 23a-23b
Mouth of dog, putting down on Shabbos .... Shabbos 102a; Eruvin 99a
Mouth of pork, considered like excrement .... Berachos 25a
Mouth of Satan, not to provoke .... Berachos 19a, 60a; Kesubos 8b
Mouth opened with wisdom, David .... Berachos 10a
Mouth which emitted diamonds, Rabbi Chutzpis .... Chullin 142a

Mouth which falsified
Mouth which falsified, against witness .... Bechoros 36a; Kesubos 27b; Bava Metzia 81b
Mouth which falsified, firstborn .... Bechoros 36a; Shabbos 145b

Mouth which forbade
Mouth which forbade, captive woman .... Kesubos 23a
Mouth which forbade, ignoramus .... Demai 6:11
Mouth which forbade, general .... Kesubos 17b-18b, 22a, 23a-24a; Bechoros 36a
Mouth which forbade, source .... Kesubos 22a

Movable property
Movable property, expressions .... Bava Basra 150a
Movable property, facilitates impurity .... Shabbos 16b-17a; Oholos 16:1-2
Movable property, payment of *kesubah* .... Kesubos 67a
Movable property together with real estate .... Bava Basra 44b

Moved
Moved from his place and received object, Shabbos .... Shabbos 5a
Moving barrel, responsibility .... Bava Metzia 82b-83a
Moving breastplate from *ephod* .... Yoma 72a
Moving courtyard, act of acquisition .... Bava Kama 12a; Gittin 21a, 78a; Bava Metzia 9b
Moving for man is more difficult than for woman .... Kesubos 28a; Sanhedrin 26a
Moving from city if unsuccessful .... Bava Metzia 75b

Moving item
Moving item, cases .... Zavim 3:1-3; Bava Metzia 105b; Niddah 7a
Moving item, different from corpse .... Zavim 4:6
Moving item, impurity of idolatry .... Shabbos 82a-83b
Moving item, *niddah* .... Gittin 61b
Moving item on Shabbos .... *see* **Muktzeh**, page 429
Moving item, shaking, trembling .... Eruvin 35a; Zavim 4:3
Moving item, tent .... Eruvin 35a; Zavim 4:3
Moving item, *zav* carried by weak man or beast .... Bava Metzia 105b; Zavim 3:1, 4:3
Moving item, *zav* standing on unstable support .... Bava Metzia 105b; Zavim 3:1, 4:3
Moving item, *zav* who knocked .... Zavim 4:1-3; Eruvin 35a

Muad .... *see* **Ox goring regularly**, page 469

Muchan laadam.. *see* **Prepared for man,** *muktzeh***,** page 501
Muchlat... *see* **Definite leper,** page 157
Muchni lekiyor...*see* **Supports for basin in Temple,** page 665
Muchni, impurity of corpse ....Oholos 4:3; Keilim 18:2; Shabbos 44b, 46a
Mucus, damage.. Bava Kama 3b
Mud
  Mud, intervening substance ....Mikvaos 9:1-4
  Mud, *mikveh*.....................................Zevachim 22a; Mikvaos 2:10; Succah 19a-19b
  Mud on garment, Shabbos...Shabbos 141a
  Mud on shoe, Shabbos ....Shabbos 141a-141b
  Mud, standing on mud on Shabbos ....Shabbos 147b
  Mud, washing hands ....Zevachim 22a
  Mud, wiping foot on Shabbos...Shabbos 141a
Mudar..................................... *see* **Man forbidden by vow to benefit,** page 388
Mufla beis din...................... *see* **Judge, distinguished one is absent, mistake of** *beis din***,** page 327
Mufla samuch le'ish.................... *see* **Minor in last year of minority, tithe,** page 411
Mufneh ligzeirah shavah....................*see* **Superfluous word, similar words,** page 664
Mukaf..*see* **Closeness,** page 112
Muktzeh
  Animals —
    Muktzeh, animal which died ....Beitzah 2a, 6b, 27b; Shabbos 45b, 156b; Chullin 14a
    Muktzeh, animals grazing............................Beitzah 40a-40b; Shabbos 45b, 157a
    Muktzeh, bones for animal.............................Shabbos 143a, 157a; Beitzah 2a
    Muktzeh, designing chicken for Yom Tov ....Beitzah 9b, 10a-11a; Chullin 142a
    Muktzeh, prepared for dogs.............................Beitzah 6b; Pesachim 56b
    Muktzeh, slaughtered animal...Chullin 14a-15a
    Muktzeh, unloading animal...Shabbos 154b
  Basis —
    Muktzeh, at dusk...Shabbos 44b-45a
    Muktzeh, basis for forbidden and permitted item ....Shabbos 117a
    Muktzeh, instances of basis...Shabbos 44b-45a, 142b
    Muktzeh, lamp as basis for fire...Shabbos 46b-47a
  Food —
    Muktzeh, bones ....Shabbos 143a
    Muktzeh, date pits ....Shabbos 143a
    Muktzeh, dates ....Pesachim 56b
    Muktzeh, designing fruit for Yom Tov.........................Beitzah 26b; Shabbos 45a
    Muktzeh, edible food combined with waste.................................Beitzah 14b
    Muktzeh, falling fruit..Pesachim 56b
    Muktzeh, fruit peels...Shabbos 143a
    Muktzeh, oil in lamp.........................Shabbos 44a, 46b; Beitzah 30b
    Muktzeh, raisins...................Beitzah 26b, 40a-40b ; Shabbos 45a-45b
    Muktzeh, *tevel*.......................................Beitzah 34b, 35a; Shabbos 43a
    Muktzeh, *tevel* and tithes..Shabbos 127b-128a
    Muktzeh, wine in non-Jew's cup...Beitzah 21b
  Items —
    Muktzeh, basket on tree...Shabbos 155a
    Muktzeh, candlesticks...Shabbos 121b-122a
    Muktzeh, coins on bed..Shabbos 44b-45a

M

Muktzeh, doors of furniture .... Shabbos 122b
Muktzeh, inserted stick .... Shabbos 140a-140b
Muktzeh, large beehive .... Shabbos 35a
Muktzeh, mold for shoe .... Shabbos 141b
Muktzeh, *shofar* and trumpets .... Shabbos 35b-36a
Muktzeh, stone on barrel .... Shabbos 125b, 142b
Muktzeh, sword for barrel .... Shabbos 146a
Muktzeh, torn shoe .... Shabbos 112a
Muktzeh, wagon .... Shabbos 122a
Muktzeh, weaving machine .... Shabbos 113a, 140b

Other cases —

Muktzeh, animal hides .... Shabbos 49a-49b
Muktzeh, ash of stove-top .... Beitzah 8a-8b
Muktzeh, boards .... Shabbos 49b
Muktzeh, bricks .... Beitzah 31b; Shabbos 124b
Muktzeh, clay .... Shabbos 124b
Muktzeh, consecrated items .... Shabbos 127b-128a
Muktzeh for rich people .... Shabbos 47a
Muktzeh, four species .... Succah 46b; Beitzah 30b
Muktzeh, heating on Yom Tov .... Shabbos 28b-29a, 124b, 143a; Beitzah 32a, 33a
Muktzeh, keeping food warm .... Shabbos 48a, 50b
Muktzeh, stillborn child .... Shabbos 135a; Yevamos 80a-80b; Bava Basra 20a
Muktzeh, succah .... Beitzah 30b; Succah 9a, 10a-10b, 46b; Shabbos 22a, 45a

Permissions —

Muktzeh, baby longing for his father .... Shabbos 141b-142a
Muktzeh, food fit for dog .... Shabbos 121a-121b; Beitzah 6b, 33a
Muktzeh for food .... Beitzah 31b-32a
Muktzeh, moving with loaf and child .... Shabbos 142b
Muktzeh, moving by one's body .... Shabbos 50a, 141a
Muktzeh, moving indirectly .... Shabbos 43b, 123a, 141a
Muktzeh, moving with permitted object .... Shabbos 47a, 141b-142a; Beitzah 21b
Muktzeh, permission to wipe .... Shabbos 81a-81b; Succah 36b
Muktzeh, shaking table .... Shabbos 143a

Types —

Muktzeh, annulling use of utensil .... Shabbos 43a, 47b, 128b, 154b
Muktzeh because of disgust .... Shabbos 44a, 46a-46b; Yevamos 14a
Muktzeh because of its weight .... Shabbos 35a, 123b, 128a; Eruvin 102a
Muktzeh because of monetary loss .... Shabbos 123a, 123b, 157a; Eruvin 35a
Muktzeh because of prohibition .... Shabbos 44a; Yevamos 14a
Muktzeh, determining place .... Shabbos 45b
Muktzeh even to use item and place .... Shabbos 124a
Muktzeh for a commandment .... Shabbos 45a-45b
Muktzeh, fragments of utensils .... Shabbos 28b, 29a, 124b-125a, 143a; Beitzah 32a; Chullin 14b
Muktzeh, its work is forbidden .... Shabbos 122b-124b, 141b; Beitzah 11a
Muktzeh, moving utensil for *muktzeh* item .... Beitzah 36a-36b; Shabbos 43a
Muktzeh, newly formed on Shabbos .... Beitzah 2a-2b; Shabbos 45b
Muktzeh, prohibition extended to next day .... Shabbos 43a
Muktzeh, rare article, saving .... Shabbos 42b-43a
Muktzeh, storehouse .... Shabbos 126b-127a

Muktzeh, tree .... Eruvin 100a-100b

Wood —

Muktzeh, beams .... Beitzah 2b, 31a-31b; Shabbos 157a

Muktzeh, lamp on palm tree .... Shabbos 45a

Muktzeh, tree roots .... Eruvin 100a

Muktzeh, using wood .... Beitzah 33a; Shabbos 143a

Muktzeh, wood annulled by non-*muktzeh* wood .... Beitzah 4b; Shabbos 29a

Muktzeh, wood in field .... Beitzah 31a

Muktzeh, wood which fell .... Beitzah 4b; Shabbos 29a

Misc. —

Muktzeh, according to Rabbi Shimon .... Shabbos 45a-45b, 46b

Muktzeh and impurity, differences .... Shabbos 123a

Muktzeh, cases of dispute .... Shabbos 19b

Muktzeh, decree .... Shabbos 123b-124b

Muktzeh, destined to be permitted .... Beitzah 30b

Muktzeh, episode about excommunication .... Shabbos 19b

Muktzeh for half of Shabbos .... Beitzah 26b-27a

Muktzeh, from sun to shade .... Shabbos 123b-124a

Muktzeh lavodah zarah .... *see* **Intended for idolatry**, page 311

Muktzeh, law according to whom .... Shabbos 45a-46a, 128a, 142b-143a, 156b-157a

Muktzeh, preparation and intent .... Shabbos 49b-50a, 125b, 126b

Muktzeh, preparing before Shabbos .... Beitzah 2b, 4a-4b; Eruvin 38b

Muktzeh, sides of animal .... Shabbos 154b-155a; Chagigah 16b-17a

Muktzeh, source .... Pesachim 47b-48a

Muktzeh, to use item and place .... Shabbos 124a

Muktzeh, Yom Tov .... Beitzah 30a, 31b-32a; Shabbos 124a

Mule

Mule, characteristics .... Chullin 79a; Bechoros 8b

Mule, death of rider .... Nedarim 41a

Mule, injury .... Chullin 7b; Yoma 49a

Mule, who brossbred the first one .... Pesachim 54a

Mules, mixed species .... Chullin 79a-79b

Multitude

Multitude, king's glory .... Yoma 70a; Berachos 53a; Zevachim 14b; Menachos 62a

Multitude, offering Pesach lamb .... Pesachim 64b

Mum .... *see* **Blemish**, page 61

Mumar .... *see* **Rebel**, page 549

Mumcheh .... *see* **Expert**, page 210

Munbaz

Munbaz, charity .... Bava Basra 11a

Munbaz, donors for Temple .... Yoma 37a-37b

Murder

Murder, angry man on the way to *Eretz Yisrael* .... Nedarim 22a-22b

Murder by a snake .... Sanhedrin 78a

Murder, destruction .... Shabbos 33a

Murder, Gilead and Shechem .... Makos 9b-10a

Murder in Temple, incident .... Yoma 23a-23b

Murder, let yourself be killed but do not transgress .... Pesachim 25a-25b; Yoma 82a-82b;

Sanhedrin 74a

Murder of man in death throes .... Sanhedrin 78a
Murder, with what .... Sanhedrin 76b
Murderer
  Episodes —
    Murderer, episode about witness who stole .... Sanhedrin 27a-27b
    Murderer, punished by snake .... Sanhedrin 37b; Shevuos 34a
    Murderers, episode about Rabbi Tarfon .... Niddah 61a
    Murderers, Gilead and Shechem .... Makos 9b-10a
    Murderers, killed their brother .... Kesubos 102b
    Murderers will not live half their days .... Sanhedrin 106b
  How —
    Murderer, causing death .... Bava Kama 27a; Sanhedrin 77a-77b
    Murderer, intended to kill someone else .... Sanhedrin 78b-79b; Kesubos 15a; Bava Kama 44b
    Murderer, ten men killed one .... Sanhedrin 78a; Bava Kama 10b, 26b-27a
    Murderer, threw from roof .... Bava Kama 26b-27a
  Misc. —
    Murderer, death by sword .... Sanhedrin 52b
    Murderer, found after calf's neck was broken .... Sotah 47a-47b; Kesubos 37b
    Murderer, his victim is dangerously ill ...... Sanhedrin 78a-78b; Kesubos 33b; Nazir 65b
    Murderer, intermingled Jews with non-Jews .... Bava Kama 44b
    Murderer, stillborn .... Sanhedrin 84b
    Murderer, *treifah* man .... Chullin 11b
Mursheh .... *see* **Power of attorney**, page 496
Mushroom
  Mushroom, uprooting it from its place of growth .... Shabbos 107b-108a
  Mushrooms, blessing .... Berachos 40b
Music
  Music, Divine Presence .... Pesachim 117a; Shabbos 30b
  Music, since Temple destruction .... Sotah 48a-48b; Gittin 7a
  Musical instruments
    Musical instruments, impurity .... Keilim 15:6
    Musical instruments in Temple, craft .... Arachin 10b-11a
    Musical instruments in Temple, number .... 13b; Arachin 10b
    Musical instruments in Temple, Shabbos .... Succah 50b-51a
    Musical instruments in Temple, who can play .... Arachin 11a
Mussaf **of Rosh Hashanah,** verses .... Rosh Hashanah 16a, 34b
Mussaf **sacrifice**
  Mussaf sacrifice and daily offering, preference .... Menachos 49a-49b; Zevachim 90b-91a
  Mussaf sacrifice and *Mincha*, precedence .... Berachos 27a, 28a
  Mussaf sacrifice, atonement .... Shevuos 2a-2b, 9a-10b
  Mussaf sacrifice, blame of who delays .... Berachos 28a
  Mussaf sacrifice, eating before .... Berachos 28b; Shabbos 9b-10a
  Mussaf sacrifice, from one festival to another .... Shevuos 2b, 12b
  Mussaf sacrifice, nine hours .... Berachos 26b
  Mussaf sacrifice of Succos, outside *Eretz Yisrael* .... Succah 55a
  Mussaf sacrifice of Yom Kippur, *avodah* text .... Yoma 56b
  Mussaf sacrifice, past its time .... Temurah 14a
  Mussaf sacrifice, prayer of community .... Berachos 30a-30b
  Mussaf sacrifice, similar sheep .... Yoma 62b

Mussaf sacrifice, time of prayer .... Berachos 30a-30b
Mussaf sacrifice, verses about *mussaf* sacrifices .... Rosh Hashanah 35a
Mussaf sacrifice of Rosh Hashanah
   Mussaf sacrifice of Rosh Hashanah, blessings .... Rosh Hashanah 32a
   Mussaf sacrifice of Rosh Hashanah, *malchuyos* .... Rosh Hashanah 32a-32b
   Mussaf sacrifice of Rosh Hashanah, *Rosh Chodesh* .... Eruvin 40a-40b
   Mussaf sacrifice of Rosh Hashanah, Shabbos .... Eruvin 40a-40b
   Mussaf sacrifice of Rosh Hashanah, when .... Avodah Zarah 4b
Mussar .... *see* **Rebuke**, page 550; *see also* **Punishment**, page 510; **Reward**, page 566;
                                       Self-examination, page 599; **Evil urge**, page 204
Mustache
   Mustache, shaving during mourning .... Moed Katan 17b-18a
   Mustache, shaving on *Chol HaMoed* .... Moed Katan 18a
Mustard
   Mustard and bees, distance .... Bava Basra 18a-18b, 25b
   Mustard, health .... Berachos 40a
Mutav sheyihyu shogegim .... *see* **Better they sin involuntarily**, page 56
Mute
   Mute, *chalitzah* .... Yevamos 104b
   Mute, laws .... Chagigah 2b; Terumos 1:2; Niddah 13b
   Mute scholars, Rebbi's prayer .... Chagigah 3a
   Mute, testimony .... Gittin 71a
Mutual attestation, trustworthiness .... Kesubos 24a; Avodah Zarah 61b
Muzzling
   Muzzling cow, receives lashes and pays .... Bava Metzia 91a
   Muzzling ox, consecrated produce .... Meilah 13a
   Muzzling ox, prohibition .... Bava Metzia 88b-89a, 90a-92a
Myrtle
  Succos —
   Myrtle, concern about stolen myrtle .... Succah 30a-31a
   Myrtle, dimension .... Succah 32b
   Myrtle, disqualified .... Succah 32b-33a
   Myrtle, disqualifying berries .... Succah 11b, 33a-33b
   Myrtle, smelling on Succos .... Succah 37b
   Myrtle, top cut off .... Succah 33a, 34b
   Myrtle, what is it .... Succah 32b-33a
   Myrtles, how many .... Succah 34b
  Misc. —
   Myrtle among thorns .... Sanhedrin 44a
   Myrtle at virgin's wedding .... Kesubos 17b
   Myrtle connected to soil, Shabbos .... Succah 37b
   Myrtle for Shabbos, episode .... Shabbos 33b
   Myrtle for wedding, punishment .... Shabbos 110a
   Myrtle in desert, teaching .... Rosh Hashanah 23a
   Myrtle, righteous are called .... Megillah 13a; Sanhedrin 93a
   Myrtle to gladden, cheer up bride .... Kesubos 17a
Mysticism .... *see* **Heavenly Chariot**, page 274

N

Na, implies request .... Berachos 9a

Naalsa, interpretation by initials .... Menachos 66b

Naat bar Naat .... *see* **Absorption in food giving taste to another food**, page 5

Naaman

Naaman, conversion .... Gittin 57b; Sanhedrin 96b

Naaman, Elisha .... Sanhedrin 107b

Naarah .... *see* **Young girl**, page 774

Naaseh venishma .... Shabbos 88a

Naaseh venishma .... *see* **We shall do and we shall listen**, page 738

Naboth, Jeroboam's father .... Sanhedrin 101b

Nachalei Arnon .... *see* **River Arnon, miracle for Israel**, page 570

Nachas asisi lebaali .... *see* **Agreement to sell husband's property**, page 15

Nachmani (Abbaye) .... Gittin 34b; Meilah 20b; Shabbos 33a

Nadab and Abihu

Nadab and Abihu, burning sin offering .... Zevachim 16a-16b, 101a-101b; Pesachim 82a-82b

Nadab and Abihu, episode .... Sanhedrin 52a, 94a; Zevachim 115b; Yoma 53a; Shabbos 113b;

.... Pesachim 75a; Eruvin 63a

Naeh doresh umekayem .... *see* **Well speaks and well applies**, page 740

Nagid Shema avad shemei .... *see* **Rabbinate, avoid**, page 533

Nahshon

Nahshon, his sons .... Bava Basra 91a

Nahshon, Red Sea .... Sotah 36b-37a

Nahum Ish Gam Zu

Nahum Ish Gam Zu, earth .... Taanis 21a; Sanhedrin 108b-109a

Nahum Ish Gam Zu, episodes .... Taanis 21a

Nahum Ish Gam Zu, Rabbi Akiva .... Chagigah 12a

Nahum the Mede

Nahum the Mede, judge .... Kesubos 105a

Nahum the Mede, ruling .... Avodah Zarah 7b

Nail

Nail of first Sages better than etc. .... Yoma 9b

Nails, *Chol HaMoed* .... Moed Katan 17b-18a

Nails, danger .... Moed Katan 18a; Niddah 17a

Nails, mourner .... Moed Katan 17b-18a

Nails, Shabbos .... Shabbos 94b
Nails, washing hands after cutting .... Pesachim 112a
Nails, words of Torah .... Chagigah 3b

Nakdimen

Nakdimen, episode about water .... Taanis 19b-20a
Nakdimen, his daughter's dowry .... Kesubos 65a, 66b
Nakdimen, wealth .... Kesubos 66b-67a; Gittin 56a

Naked

Naked, blessing .... Bava Metzia 114b
Naked in front of Divine Name .... Shabbos 120b
Naked in front of lamp, epilepsy .... Pesachim 112b
Naked in street, non-Jews .... Yevamos 63b
Naked, patched garments .... Yoma 77a
Naked, prayer .... Succah 10b-11a

Nakedness

Nakedness covered by glass .... Berachos 25b
Nakedness, prayer and learning .... Berachos 24a
Nakedness, which part of body .... Berachos 24a

Nakeh lo yenakeh, which sins .... Yoma 86a

Name

Name, by your name they will call you etc. .... Yoma 38a-38b
Name, good, crown .... Avos 2:7, 4:13
Name, good name better than good oil .... Berachos 17a

Idols —

Name of idol, mentioning .... Sanhedrin 63b
Names of idols .... Sanhedrin 63b; Avodah Zarah 11b
Names of idols, debasing .... Avodah Zarah 45b-46a

Marriage —

Name of family, divorce certificate .... Gittin 88a
Name, sign in divorce certificate .... Yevamos 115b-116a
Name, testimony of *agunah* .... Yevamos 115b-116a
Names, divorce certificates .... Gittin 24b, 34b, 88a; Bava Basra 167b

Men's names —

Name and father's name, men in Tanach .... Megillah 15a
Name, episode about Kidor .... Yoma 83b
Names, famous, Sages .... Yevamos 37b
Name influences .... Berachos 7b
Name of one's teacher, prohibition .... Sanhedrin 100a
Name of son, same as name of father .... Moed Katan 25b
Name of wicked will rot .... Yoma 38b
Name of wicked, giving to son .... Yoma 38b
Name significance, episode about Rabbi Meir .... Yoma 83b
Names of Messiah .... Sanhedrin 96b, 98b
Names of Moses .... Megillah 13a; Sotah 12a; Bava Basra 15a
Names of non-Jews .... Gittin 11a

Name of Sages

Name of Sages teaching law, citing .... Nazir 56b
Name of Sages teaching law, preciseness .... Bava Kama 96b; Chullin 18b
Names of Sages, substituted, inquiry .... Bava Kama 11b

N

Names of Sages substituted, episode .... Kiddushin 44b

Name of sick

Name of sick, changing.. Rosh Hashanah 16b

Name of sick man's mother .... Shabbos 66b

Name of sick, prayer... Berachos 34a

Misc. —

"Name, he sold him only a name"... Bava Metzia 104a; Bava Basra 7a

Name added, different species .... Succah 13a; Chullin 62b; Parah 11:7

Name of impurity, sons of Keturah.. Sanhedrin 91a

Names identical, legal document...................... Bava Basra 172b-173a; Gittin 24b; Bechoros 48a

Names of items, changed by generations ....Shabbos 36a; Succah 34a

Names of Temple .... Pesachim 88a; Taanis 16a; Zevachim 104b; Yoma 2a

Names, separate, sin offerings .... Krisos 2b-3a

Names, similar, concern .... Yevamos 115b-116a

Names of G-d

Names —

Name and Kingship, blessing... Berachos 12a, 40b, 49a

Name of G-d, *E-hye*.. Berachos 9b

Name *Yud-Heh*, since Temple destruction... Eruvin 18b

Names of G-d, four, twelve and forty two letters .... Kiddushin 71a

Names of G-d, *Hagadol* .... Yoma 69b

Names of G-d, in the future .... Pesachim 50a

Names of G-d, *Sha-dai*... Chagigah 12a

Names of G-d, *Shalom* and *Ne'eman* .... Shabbos 10b

Names of G-d, *Tze-vaos*... Berachos 31b

Names of G-d, which are holy .... Shevuos 35b

Misc. —

Name of G-d and Attributes in Ark... Bava Basra 14b

Name of G-d, beloved thanks to disciples .... Yoma 86a

Name of G-d, concealing... Shabbos 61b; Arachin 6a

Name of G-d, explicit, in Temple... Yoma 39b, 69b; Sanhedrin 101b

Name of G-d in bathhouse.. Shabbos 10a-10b

Name of G-d in vain.. Nedarim 7b, 8b-9a, 10a-10b; Sanhedrin 56a

Name of G-d in vain, excommunication.. Nedarim 7b

Name of G-d, *Kohen Gadol* on Yom Kippur..Yoma 39b

Name of G-d, mentioning and erasing.. Sanhedrin 56a

Name of G-d on clay, David .... Succah 53a-53b; Makos 11a

Name of G-d on righteous.. Bava Basra 75b

Name of G-d, replaced by name of idolatry...Sanhedrin 102b

Name of G-d, respect in front of... Shabbos 120b

Name of G-d, sections concerning sacrifices .... Menachos 110a

Name of G-d, writing for His sake .... Gittin 20a, 54b

Names of G-d, writing.. Menachos 30b

Nanfi, explanation ....Rosh Hashanah 26a

Naomi

Naomi.. Bava Basra 91a

Naomi, daughter of Nahshon's son .... Bava Basra 91a

Nape of the neck, cutting...Chullin 20b-21a

Nard, thanksgiving for wind ....Bava Metzia 86a

N

Nasa venasan beyad .... *see* **Payment by judge who made a mistake**, page 476
Nasal secretions, sickness .... Bava Metzia 107b
Nassan Detsutsita, repentance .... Shabbos 56b
Nassan einav... .... *see* **Desired...**, page 161
Nassan einav bo .... *see* **Scoffer, death**, page 592
Nasata devareicha leshiurim .... *see* **Sizes cannot be different for everyone**, page 632
Nasata Toras kol echad be'yado .... *see* **Fixing single time for everybody**, page 229
Nascha deRabbi Abba .... *see* **Oath, witness was not contradicted**, page 452
Nashim, order of *mesechtos* .... Sotah 2a
Nashim .... *see* **Woman**, page 755
Nasi

   Nasi .... *see also* **King**, page 340; **Prince**, page 504
   Nasi, adding a month .... Sanhedrin 11a
   Nasi, deciding fast day .... Taanis 24a
   Nasi, pairs of Sages .... Chagigah 16a-16b
   Nasi, Rabban Gamliel .... Berachos 27b-28a
   Nasi, sacrifices .... Horayos 11a
Nation

   Nation, inferior, Arabs .... Kesubos 66b
   Nations, lineage according to male .... Kiddushin 66a, 67b; Yevamos 78b
Nations of the world

   Nations of the world, did not learn Torah .... Sotah 35b
   Nations of the world, Divine Laughter .... Avodah Zarah 3b
   Nations of the world, judgment in the future .... Avodah Zarah 2a-3b, 4b
   Nations of the world, prophecy .... Bava Basra 15b
   Nations of the world, seventy bulls offered on Succos .... Succah 55b
   Nations of the world, succah in the future .... Avodah Zarah 3a
Natzal hames .... *see* **Flesh, putrefied, of dead**, page 230
Naval Hakarmeli

   Naval Hakarmeli, Abigail .... Pesachim 3b; Megillah 14a-14b
   Naval Hakarmeli, death .... Rosh Hashanah 18a
Navi .... *see* **Prophets**, page 507
Navi sheker .... *see* **False prophet inciting to idolatry**, page 214
Navon lachash, significance .... Chagigah 14a
Naboth and Ahab .... Sanhedrin 89a
Nazarene, *Gehinnom* .... Gittin 57a
Nazir

  Cases —

   Nazir, difference with woman .... Sotah 23b
   Nazir, eternal .... Nazir 8b
   Nazir like Samson .... Nazir 4a-4b
   Nazir like Samson, permitting vows .... Makos 22a
   Nazir, non-Jew .... Nazir 61a-62a; Menachos 73b

  Commitment —

   Nazir "from this cup" .... Nazir 11a
   Nazir, birth of son .... Nazir 12b-13b
   Nazir, condition contrary to law .... Nazir 11a
   Nazir, conditional .... Nedarim 19b, 21a; Eruvin 82a; Chagigah 10a; Nazir 34a, 62a; Sanhedrin 25a
   Nazir, contradiction of witnesses .... Nazir 20a-20b; Eduyos 4:11

N

Nazir, doubt..Nedarim 18b-19b; Nazir 8a, 33a-34a; Taharos 4:12

Nazir, from one food..Nazir 9a-9b, 10a; Menachos 81b, 103a

Nazir, from one prohibition..Nazir 3b-4a, 11b, 38a; Nedarim 4a

Nazir, if this is a hybrid animal..Nazir 34a

Nazir, if this one is so-and-so ....Nazir 32b-33a, 62a; Eruvin 82a; Chagigah 10a; Nedarim 19b, 21a;
....Sanhedrin 25a

Nazir, must vow be evident................Nedarim 19b, 21a; Eruvin 82a; Chagigah 10a; Nazir 34a, 62a;
....Sanhedrin 25a

Nazir, one of his limbs..Nazir 21a-21b

Impurity —
Nazir, became impure at end of his *nezirus*................................Nazir 6a-6b, 16a-16b, 39b, 47a, 63b

Nazir, became impure on last day..Nazir 5a-7a

Nazir, becoming impure before end of vow................................Nazir 16b, 39b, 47a, 63a-63b

Nazir, commitment when impure..Nazir 16b-17a, 18a, 19a-19b

Nazir, impure, from when does he count................................Nazir 17b, 18a-19a, 54a; Pesachim 59a

Nazir, impurities..Nazir 52b-53b

Nazir, impurity added..Nazir 42a-43a

Nazir, impurity occurred before sacrifice..Nazir 14b-15a, 47a

Nazir, *meis mitzvah*................................Nazir 48a-48b; Berachos 19b-20a; Megillah 3b; Zevachim 100a

Nazir, outside *Eretz Yisrael*..Nazir 19b-20a; Eduyos 4:11

Nazir, permitted impurities..Nazir 43a, 48a

Nazir, prohibition to become impure..Nazir 48a-49b

Nazir, Rabbinical impurity..Niddah 68b

Shaving —
Nazir, annulling count because of shaving..Nazir 40a

Nazir, annulling days because of shaving..Nazir 44a

Nazir like Absalom, shaving..Nazir 4b-5a

Nazir, rendering him impure and shaving him..Nazir 44a

Nazir, shaving..*see also* **Shaving (*Nazir*)**, page 611

Misc. —
Nazir, beginning count anew, cases..Nazir 14a-14b

Nazir, considered before time..Chagigah 9b

Nazir, differences between three prohibitions..Nazir 44a

Nazir, is it recommended..Nedarim 9b-10a; Sotah 2a

Nazir, not to postpone..Nedarim 3b-4b

Nazir, Order of Nashim..Nazir 2a

Nazir, period of time................Nazir 5a-7a, 39a; Taanis 17a; Moed Katan 19b; Nedarim 4b; Sanhedrin 22b

Nazir, permitting his vow..Nazir 9a

Nazir, sacrifice without purpose..Krisos 27a

Nazir, sinner................Nedarim 9b-10a; Nazir 2b-3a, 19a, 22a; Sotah 15a; Bava Kama 91b; Taanis 11a-11b;
....Shevuos 8a; Krisos 26a

Nazir, stay away from vineyard................Avodah Zarah 17a, 58b, 59a; Shabbos 13a; Pesachim 40b;
....Yevamos 46a; Bava Metzia 92a

Ne'elavim ve'einam olvim..*see* **Insulted but do not insult**, page 311

Ne'eman baal melachtecha..*see* **Trustworthy is your Employer**, page 705

Ne'eman, adjective for G-d..Shabbos 10b

Ne'emanus..*see* **Trustworthiness**, page 704

Ne'evad..*see* **Idolatrous sacrifice**, page 295

Ne'ilas deles..*see* **Closing door before borrowers, ordinary land**, page 111

Nearby produce, tithes..Eruvin 30b, 32b; Gittin 30b; Chullin 7a; Niddah 71b
Nebuchadnezzar
Nebuchadnezzar, burning gold poured in his mouth ....Sanhedrin 92b
Nebuchadnezzar, false prophets..Sanhedrin 93a
Nebuchadnezzar, for Israel..Chagigah 13b
Nebuchadnezzar, hare..Nedarim 65a
Nebuchadnezzar, his soldiers' strength..Sotah 42b
Nebuchadnezzar, praise to G-d...Sanhedrin 92b
Nebuchadnezzar, pride.............................Chullin 89a; Chagigah 13a; Pesachim 94a-94b
Nebuchadnezzar, reward for his steps...Sanhedrin 96a
Nebuchadnezzar ruled the whole world...Megillah 11a-11b
Nebuchadnezzar, Temple destruction...Sanhedrin 94b
Nebuchadnezzar, wickedness and power..Shabbos 149b-150a
Nebuchadnezzar, years of reign..Megillah 11b
Nebuzaradan
Nebuzaradan, conversion..Gittin 57b
Nebuzaradan, Temple destruction...Gittin 57a-57b, 58a
Nebuzaradan, Zechariah's blood..Sanhedrin 96a-96b; Gittin 57b
Necessary to study this problem..Bava Metzia 16a
Necessary for itself, not
Necessary for itself, not, abscess..Shabbos 107b
Necessary for itself, not, covering blood...Beitzah 8a
Necessary for itself, not, damage to public.......................Shabbos 42a; Zevachim 91b-92a
Necessary for itself, not, extinguishing..Shabbos 31b
Necessary for itself, not, Shabbos labor...........Shabbos 42a, 94a-94b; Zevachim 91b-92a
Necessary for itself, not, to avoid being soiled..Shabbos 11b
Necessity of times
Necessity of times, episodes..Sanhedrin 46a; Krisos 8a
Necessity of times, forbidden thing permitted, prophet...........Yevamos 90b; Sanhedrin 89b, 90a
Necessity of times, Gideon..Temurah 28b-29a
Necessity of times, punishments...Sanhedrin 46a
Nechemiah...*see* **Nehemiah**, page 441
Nechsei melog...*see* **Wife's property**, page 747
Nechunya the pit digger
Nechunya the pit digger, episode...Bava Kama 50a; Yevamos 121b
Nechunya the pit digger, Temple officers..Shekalim 5:1-2
Nechunya's daughter fell in pit..Bava Kama 50a
Neck
Neck breaking, blood..Chullin 113a
Neck broken, impurity...Chullin 21a
Neck, choice meat..Berachos 44b
Neck upon knife...Chullin 16b
Nedavah **prayer**...Berachos 21a-21b; Pesachim 54b
Neder...*see* **Vow**, page 725
Nedunyah...*see* **Dowry**, page 180
Need encouragement...Berachos 32b
Needle
Needle, impurity...Shabbos 52b, 60a, 123a; Keilim 13:5
Needle in flesh of living..................Berachos 18b; Shabbos 13b, 152a; Sotah 10a; Sanhedrin 48b

N

Needle in windpipe..Chullin 48b-49a

Needle, *muktzeh*...Shabbos 123a

Needle, *treifos*...Chullin 48b-49a, 50b-51a; Shabbos 36a; Succah 34a; Kesubos 76b

Needs of public, theft..Bava Kama 94b; Beitzah 29a

Nefel..*see* **Stillborn**, page 656

Nefesh raah..*see* **Coins, close-fisted**, page 113

Nefilah al panav..*see* **Falling on one's face, important man**, page 213

Nefilas apayim..Megillah 22b-23a; Berachos 34b

Negaim...*see* **Leprous mark**, page 364

Negative commandment

Negative commandment from positive......Pesachim 41b-42a; Makos 18b; Zevachim 34a; Chullin 81a

Negative commandment, *hishamer, pen* and *al*..Menachos 36b

Negative commandment including several.....Pesachim 24a, 41b; Bava Metzia 115b; Menachos 58b;
....Sanhedrin 63a; Temurah 7b

Negative commandment including several, blemished animal.............................Temurah 7b

Negative commandment, lashes..Menachos 36b

Negative commandment, more rigorous than positive..................................Yevamos 7a

Negative commandment, warning of death penalty.......Makos 13b; Bava Kama 74b; Sanhedrin 86b;
....Shabbos 154a-154b; Eruvin 17b; Shevuos 4a

Negative commandment without act, sacrifice................................Krisos 3b-4a; Sanhedrin 65a-65b

Negative commandments concerning reptiles....................Makos 16b; Eruvin 28a; Pesachim 24a

Negative commandments in one act.....Makos 21b-22a; Krisos 14b-15a; Pesachim 47b; Beitzah 12a-12b

Negative commandments, two..Pesachim 24a-24b; Bechoros 6b

Negative commandments, women...Kiddushin 35a-35b; Bava Kama 15a

Negative commandment completed by positive

Negative commandment completed by positive...Makos 13b

Negative commandment completed by positive, annulled.........Makos 16a-16b; Chullin 141a

Negative commandment completed by positive, cases.................Temurah 4b; Pesachim 67a

Negative commandment completed by positive, how................Chullin 141a-141b; Yoma 36b

Negative commandment preceded by positive...Makos 14b-15b

Negative form, wordings of vows..Nedarim 11a-11b, 13b

Negid shemei avad shemei..................................*see* **Rabbinate, avoid**, page 533

Neglected

Neglected dress, Torah reading...Megillah 24a-24b

Neglected things...Berachos 6b

Neglecting eulogy, punishment...Shabbos 105b

Neglecting, proverb...Sanhedrin 7a

Neglecting Torah..Avos 4:10

Neglecting Torah and commandment...Berachos 63a

Negligence

Negligence, forgot place of deposit...Bava Metzia 35a, 42a

Negligence, with owner...Bava Metzia 95a-95b

Negligible quantity

Negligible quantity, important substance..............Orlah 3:6-8; Beitzah 3b-4a; Yevamos 81a-81b;
....Zevachim 72a-72b

Negligible quantity, lashes....................Makos 17a; Meilah 18a; Nazir 4a; Shevuos 21b, 24a

Negligible quantity, mixture of same substance................Yevamos 81b-82a; Menachos 22b;
....Avodah Zarah 73b; Pesachim 29b-30a

Negligible quantity, mixture of *tevel*........................Avodah Zarah 73b; Challah 3:10

Negligible quantity, oath..Shevuos 21b-22b
Negligible quantity, whole creature...Chullin 100a
Nehemiah
Nehemiah, miracle of conception..Sanhedrin 37b
Nehemiah, satisfied with his own deeds...Sanhedrin 93b
Nehemiah, second Temple...Rosh Hashanah 3a-3b
Neheneh..*see* **Benefitting without blessing**, page 54
Nehirin shvilei dishmaya....................................*see* **Astrology, he knows paths of Heaven**, page 34
Neighbor
Neighbor..*see also* **Damage from neighbor**, page 141
Neighbor, bad, keeping away...Avos 1:7
Neighbor, better than distant brother...Kesubos 85b; Bava Metzia 108b
Neighbor, good, importance..Bava Metzia 108b; Avos 2:9; Kesubos 85b
Neighbor opposing repairs...Bava Basra 7a
Neighbor, priority rights...Bava Metzia 108a-108b; Bava Basra 5a, 12b
Neighbor, priority rights in sharing..Bava Basra 12b
Neighborhood, three inhabitants...Avodah Zarah 21a
Neilah, Yom Kippur...Yoma 87b-88a
Neither eye shadow
Neither eye shadow, bride...Kesubos 17a
Neither eye shadow, *semichah*...Sanhedrin 14a
Nekiim...*see* **Days of purity**, page 148
Nemushos, explanation..Taanis 6b; Peah 8:1; Bava Metzia 12a, 21b
Ner...*see* **Lamp**, page 351
Neron, converted to Judaism...Gittin 56a
Nes..*see* **Miracle**, page 413
Nesachim...*see* **Libations**, page 368
Nesech..*see* **Wine of idolaters**, page 751
Nesek
Nesek, leprous mark..Negaim 10:1-4
Nesek, woman..Kiddushin 35b
Neshamah...*see* **Soul**, page 647
Neshef, explanation...Berachos 3b
Neshikah..*see* **Kiss, death**, page 342
Nesias kapayim..*see* **Bircas Kohanim**, page 58
Nesichei adam..*see* **Princes of Israel, eight**, page 504
Nesinim
Nesinim, episode about David..Yevamos 78b
Nesinim, prohibition...Yevamos 78b-79b
Nesinite woman to injured *Kohen*...Yevamos 76a
Nest
Nest of bird in idolatrous tree..Meilah 13b-14a; Avodah Zarah 42b
Nest of bird, Your mercy..Berachos 33b; Megillah 25a
Nests, birds flying from one to another...Kinin 2:1-5; Nazir 12a
Nests, deciding which is sin offering............Krisos 28a; Yoma 41a-41b; Eruvin 37a-37b; Nazir 26b
Nests, doubts..Kinin 1:2-4, 2:5, 3:6; Zevachim 73b
Nests, episode about Rabbi Shimon ben Gamliel..Krisos 8a
Nests etc., essential laws...Avos 3:18
Nests, intermingled..Kinin 22b-23a, 1:2-4

Nests, obligatory and endowment .... Kinin 22a-22b, 1:1

Nests of bird sacrifices, mistake of *Kohen* .... Kinin 3:1-4; Zevachim 67b-68a, 73b

Nesu panim, significance .... Chagigah 14a

Net spread up to Jerusalem, Rabbi Yehudah ben Beseira .... Pesachim 3b

Neta revai .... *see* **Revai**, page 565

Netilas lulav, blessing .... Succah 37b

Netilas yadayim .... *see* **Washing hands**, page 733

Netirah unekamah .... *see* **Revenge and grudge**, page 565

Netulah min hayehudim .... *see* **Vow, to be forbidden to all Jews**, page 726

Netz hachama .... *see* **Sunrise**, page 663

Netzach Yisrael .... *see* **Eternity of Israel**, page 202

Netzach, explanation .... Eruvin 54a

Netzel hames .... *see* **Putrefied flesh of dead**, page 512

Neveilah

   Impurity —

     Neveilah and impure animal, adding up prohibition .... Meilah 16a

     Neveilah, combining for impurity .... Meilah 15b-16a

     Neveilah, impurity in volume of olive .... Niddah 42b

     Neveilah, impurity of food .... Krisos 21a-21b

     Neveilah, load impurity .... Keilim 1:2

     Neveilah of bird .... *see* **Bird *neveilah***, page 59

     Neveilah when living, Azazel .... Zevachim 105a

     Neveilah, while still living .... Chullin 20b-21a, 30a, 84a, 117b, 121a-121b; Oholos 1:6

   Prohibitions —

     Neveilah, bird sin offering .... Zevachim 44b; Menachos 73a

     Neveilah given to non-Jew .... Pesachim 21b, 23b; Chullin 114b; Avodah Zarah 20a

     Neveilah given to resident non-Jew .... Pesachim 21b, 23b; Chullin 114b; Avodah Zarah 20a

     Neveilah, rotten, impurity .... Bechoros 23a-23b; Nazir 50a; Chullin 71a

     Neveilah, seven years of conquest .... Chullin 17a

     Neveilah, slaughtering by disqualified persons .... Chullin 86a-86b

   Misc. —

     Neveilah, ox which caused damage .... Bava Kama 10b-11a, 34a-34b, 15b, 53b

Never existed, city led to idolatry and rebellious son .... Sanhedrin 71a

Neviim and Kesuvim, order .... Bava Basra 14b-15a

Nevuah .... *see* **Prophecy**, page 507

New

   New decree .... Avodah Zarah 35a

   New king, Pharaoh .... Sotah 11a

   New teaching in study hall .... Chagigah 3a

   New faces

     New faces, acquisition of stolen item .... Bava Kama 96a-96b

     New faces, *sheva berachos* .... Kesubos 7b-8a

     New faces, utensils .... Shabbos 112b

   New grain

     New grain, benefit permitted .... Pesachim 23a

     New grain, eating grain .... Menachos 70b-71a; Krisos 5a

     New grain, for a commandment .... Menachos 72a

     New grain, forbidden new growths .... Menachos 69b

     New grain, harvesting for hay .... Menachos 71b; Pesachim 23a

N

New grain, harvesting from valley .... Menachos 68a, 71a; Pesachim 11a, 56a-56b
New grain in Temple .... Menachos 5b, 68b
New grain, outside Israel .... Kiddushin 37a, 38b; Menachos 68b
New grain, permitted from when .... Succah 41a-41b; Rosh Hashanah 30a-30b; Menachos 5b, 68a-68b;
.... Eruvin 32a
New grain, permitted since it took root .... Menachos 70b-71a
New grain, planted a second time .... Menachos 69a-69b, 70a; Bava Metzia 56a
New grain, sown a second time .... Menachos 69a

New moon
New moon, calculation .... Rosh Hashanah 20b, 24b-25a; Arachin 9b
New moon, from *Tishrei* .... Rosh Hashanah 8a, 12a
New moon, place of moon .... Rosh Hashanah 23b
News of death, delayed .... Moed Katan 20a-20b; Eruvin 46a

New year
New year for trees .... Rosh Hashanah 14a-14b; Eruvin 7a; Yevamos 15a
New years, four days of judgment .... Rosh Hashanah 16a
New years, which ones .... Rosh Hashanah 7b-8a

Newly formed on Shabbos
Newly formed on Shabbos, hail .... Shabbos 51b
Newly formed on Shabbos, *muktzeh* .... Beitzah 2a-2b; Shabbos 45b

News
News, bad, rending garment .... Moed Katan 26a
News, blessing .... Berachos 59b
News, no bad news by merit of learning .... Berachos 14a
News of death, father and mother .... Pesachim 4a
News of death, how .... Pesachim 3b

Nezek .... *see* **Damage**, page 141
Nezifah ....*see* **Rebuke**, page 550
Nezikin
Nezikin .... *see* **Damages**, page 6
Nezikin, Rav Yehudah's generation .... Berachos 20a
Nezikin, three *Bavos* are one *mesechta* .... Bava Kama 102a

Nezirus
Nezirus during *nezirus* .... Nazir 13b-14a, 15a
Nezirus, long .... Nazir 7a, 8a-8b
Nezirus, making one's son *nazir* .... Nazir 24b, 28b-29a, 29b-30a, 61b; Sotah 23a, 23b
Nezirus, numerous .... Nedarim 17a-18a; Nazir 7a-7b, 8a-8b
Nezirus of Absalom .... Temurah 14b
Nezirus of Shmuel .... Nazir 66a
Nezirus, Queen Helen .... Nazir 20a
Nezirus, second .... Nedarim 3b, 18a
Nezirus, Shimon Hatzaddik .... Nazir 4b
Nezirus, slave .... Nazir 61a, 62b
Nezirus with leprosy .... Nazir 55a-56b, 17b

Nice house, mind at ease .... Berachos 57b
Nicha leinish leme'avad mitzvah .... *see* **Pleased that commandment is performed**
.... **with one's money**, page 492
Nichfeh .... *see* **Epileptic**, page 197
Nichnas ledivrei chavero .... *see* **Interrupts friend's words**, page 315

N

Nichnas yayin yatza sod................................*see* **Wine goes in, secret comes out**, page 749
Nichtav bayom venechtam balailah...........*see* **Written at daytime and signed at night**, page 765
Nichum...*see* **Comforting the bereaved**, page 116
Nichush...*see* **Guess**, page 261
Nichvah mechupas chaveiro...............................*see* **Burnt by friend's canopy**, page 80
Nickname to friend, *Gehinnom*..Bava Metzia 58b
Nidche.................................*see* **Disqualified becoming adequate, valid at beginning**, page 168
Niddah

   Niddah...*see also* **Blood of** *niddah*, page 66; ***Zavah***, page 775
   Niddah, "I am pure"..Niddah 11b
   Niddah, changing garments..Kesubos 65b
   Niddah, death of disciple...Shabbos 13a-13b
   Niddah, distance...Shabbos 13a-13b, 64b; Kesubos 4b, 61a
   Niddah, fence of roses..Sanhedrin 37a
   Niddah, immersion during daytime...Niddah 67b
   Niddah, investigation by Shmuel..Niddah 25b
   Niddah is called "lonely"...Rosh Hashanah 26a; Sotah 42a
   Niddah, kiddushin..Kiddushin 68a; Yevamos 49b
   Niddah, not to appear unattractive..Shabbos 64b
   Niddah or *zavah,* calculations about doubt............Arachin 8a-8b; Niddah 38a, 53b-54b, 69a-69b
   Niddah, ornaments permitted..Shabbos 64b
   Niddah, sensation..Niddah 57b
   Niddah, sleeping in husband's room..Eruvin 63b
   Niddah, to endear herself to her husband..Niddah 31b
   Niddah when coming out of *mikveh,* episode...Niddah 66a
   Niddah, women reveal it to their husband...Pesachim 87a

  Niddah without retroactive impurity

   Niddah without retroactive impurity, becoming like every woman...........Niddah 10b-11a
   Niddah without retroactive impurity, blood stain.......................................Niddah 4b-5a
   Niddah without retroactive impurity, convert...Kesubos 37a
   Niddah without retroactive impurity, minor...Niddah 8b
   Niddah without retroactive impurity, old woman...Niddah 9a-9b
   Niddah without retroactive impurity, pregnant woman...................................Niddah 8b-9a
   Niddah without retroactive impurity, time of menstruation...............................Niddah 4b
   Niddah without retroactive impurity, who...Niddah 7a-7b

Nidmeh...*see* **Resembling**, page 561
Nidon al shem sofo..*see* **Judged because of future**, page 328
Nidon bichvodo.......................................*see* **Consecrating limbs to Temple Treasury**, page 123
Nidui...*see* **Excommunication**, page 207

Night

  Commandments —
   Night, learning...*see* **Learning at night**, page 359
   Night of *Seder*..*see Seder* **night**, page 597
   Night of Yom Kippur, *Kohen Gadol*...Yoma 18a, 19b
   Night, slaughtering..Chullin 13b
   Night, sprinkling and sanctification...Yoma 42b
   Night, succah..Succah 43a-43b; Shabbos 131b
   Night, *tefillin*..Menachos 36a-36b; Eruvin 96a; Zevachim 19a
   Night, *tzitzis*...Menachos 43a; Shabbos 27b; Zevachim 18b

N

Temple service —

Night after day, sacrifice .... Chullin 83a; Temurah 14a
Night, building Temple .... Shevuos 15b
Night, burning sacrifices, starting by day .... Menachos 26b
Night, parts .... Berachos 3a-3b
Night, service for Red Heifer .... Yoma 42b
Night, time for sacrifice .... Yoma 29a-29b; Menachos 100a; Megillah 20b-21a

Misc. —

Night and day, G-d's deeds .... Avodah Zarah 3b
Night before fast .... Taanis 12a-12b
Night, *beis din* .... Sanhedrin 34b; Yevamos 104a; Bava Basra 113b-114a; Niddah 50a
Night, created for learning Torah .... Eruvin 65a
Night, journey .... Yoma 21a
Night of protection, future Redemption .... Rosh Hashanah 11b
Night of protection, Pesach .... Pesachim 109b
Night, permitting vow .... Nedarim 77a-77b, 76b
Night, session for inheritance .... Bava Basra 113b-114a; Sanhedrin 34b
Night, sleep .... Eruvin 65a
Night, sound is better heard .... Yoma 20b
Nights as days, eulogy .... Moed Katan 25b

Nightfall approaching, leniencies .... Shabbos 17b, 153a-153b
Nikanor
Nikanor, door of Temple Courtyard .... Yoma 38a; Middos 2:3
Nikanor Gate .... Middos 2:3; Yoma 38a
Nikar bekoso kiso vekaaso .... see **Known by cup, purse and anger,** page 344
Nikur .... see **Removing forbidden parts,** page 557
Nim velo nim .... see **Drowsy,** page 182
Nimlach bepamaliaso .... see **Took advice from His angels,** page 695
Nimlach lehotzi .... see **Changing one's mind, lifting item on Shabbos,** page 96
Nimretzes, initials .... Shabbos 105a
Nimrod
Nimrod, Amraphel .... Eruvin 53a
Nimrod, his tower is permitted to benefit .... Avodah Zarah 53b
Nimrod, pride .... Chullin 89a
Nimuko imo .... see **Explains his opinion,** page 210
Nine
Nine days, laundering .... Taanis 29b
Nine days, mourning .... Yevamos 43a-43b; Taanis 26b
Nine *kabin* water poured on man having discharge .... Berachos 22a-22b; Gittin 16a
Nine months of pregnancy .... Yevamos 37a
Nine months old from first marriage
Nine months old from first marriage, general .... Yevamos 37a
Nine months old from first marriage, inheritance .... Yevamos 37b-38a; Bechoros 47b
Nine months old from first marriage, levirate marriage .... Yevamos 100a-100b
Nine years old
Nine years old, bestiality .... Sanhedrin 54b-55a
Nine years old, brother of deceased childless husband .... Yevamos 96a; Niddah 45a-45b;
.... Bava Basra 156a; Sanhedrin 55b
Nine years old, disqualified from priesthood .... Sanhedrin 69b

Nine years old, homosexuality...Sanhedrin 54b-55a

Ninth
Ninth, animal tithe..............................Bechoros 59a-59b, 60b-61a; Nazir 31b-32a; Eruvin 50a; Kiddushin 51a
Ninth of *Av*...*see* **Tisha B'Av**, page 692

Nineveh
Nineveh, nation...Yoma 10a
Nineveh, repentance...Taanis 16a

Nirdaf...*see* **Pursuer**, page 512

Nireh kemasuy..*see* **Havdala** late, **Shabbos not seen as burden**, page 272

Nireh mibachutz...*see* **Visible from outside**, page 724

Nireh venidcheh.....................................*see* **Disqualified becoming adequate, valid at beginning**, page 168

Nirim, Shabbos work...Shabbos 105a

Nirtza...*see* **Pierced ear, slave**, page 487

Nirva...*see* **Sinning with male**, page 629

Nisalsa, interpretation by initials...Menachos 66b

Nisayon...*see* **Trial**, page 703

Nischapru be'alav...*see* **Atoned owner**, page 35

Nishba venotel..*see* **Swears and collects**, page 666

Nishmas, Pesach night...Pesachim 117b-118a

Nishtaka hadavar...*see* **Nachum the Mede, ruling**, page 434

Niskal...*see* **Stoning**, page 657; *see also* **Ox to be stoned**, page 469

Niskal, peshiyah...*see* **Stumbling-block**, page 660

Nismalah se'aso..*see* **Full measure**, page 241

Nissan
Nissan and *Tishrei*, intersession...Berachos 35b
Nissan, Creation..Rosh Hashanah 11a; Avodah Zarah 8a
Nissan, crowns...Shabbos 87b
Nissan, first month..Rosh Hashanah 2b-3a, 7a
Nissan, future redemption...Rosh Hashanah 11b
Nissan, Kings of Israel...Rosh Hashanah 2a-2b; Avodah Zarah 10a

Nisuch...*see* **Libation**, page 368

Nisuin...*see* **Marriage**, page 390; *see also* **Wedding**, page 739

Nitai Haarbeili, pairs...Chagigah 16a

Nitak le'aseh..*see* **Transformed into positive commandment, anulled**, page 699

Nitak lereiyah...*see* **Sacrifices, unfit, transferred to graze**, page 580

Nitkal...*see* **Stumbling-block**, page 660

Nitzchu Arelim Es Hametzukim...Kesubos 104a

Nitzchu erelim metzukim.............................*see* **Eulogy, "Nitzchu areilim es hametzukim,"** page 202

Nitzchuni baanai..*see* **Defeated, "My sons defeated Me," Achnai**, page 157

Nitzok..*see* **Poured liquid**, page 496

Nitztadek, initials...Shabbos 105a

Nivlas oaf...*see* **Bird** *neveilah*, page 59

Nivul hames bivdikah.................................*see* **Debasing dead person by examination**, page 152

Nivul peh..*see* **Gross speech, punishment**, page 259

Nizak..*see* **Damage**, page 141

Nizdaken hadin...*see* **Judgment "became old,"** page 329

No
No bears and no forest...Sotah 47a
No desire, messianic times...Shabbos 151b

No less than etc., no more than etc...Arachin 7b-13b

No litigant, unnecessary to answer him ....Kesubos 92b; Bava Kama 8b; Bava Metzia 14a

No no, wording of oath...Shevuos 36a

Noah shelo nivra..*see* **Better not to have been created**, page 56

Noah sheyapil atzmo lekivshan...........*see* **Better jump into furnace than humiliate fellow**, page 56

Noah

Noah, episode about Ham...Sanhedrin 70a-70b

Noah, labor to feed animals...Sanhedrin 108b

Noah, righteous man...Sanhedrin 108a-108b

Noah, sent birds...Sanhedrin 108b

Noblemen in Rome, hierarchy..Shevuos 6b

Noblewoman

Noblewoman, episode about public demonstration and protest..............Rosh Hashanah 19a;

....Taanis 18a

Noblewoman, sorcery...Shabbos 81b-82a; Chullin 105b

Nodding head, suffering...Yevamos 121a

Nofes tzufim, explanation...Sotah 48b

Noge'a bedavar...*see* **Affected by trial, judge**, page 13

Nogi, explanation...Berachos 28a

Noise

Noise..*see also* **Voice**, page 725

Noise of clapping fingers, episode..Yoma 19b

Noise of clouds, Providence..Bava Basra 16a

Noise of rake in Temple...Tamid 5:6

Noise of water, sleep..Eruvin 104a

Noises, various...Yoma 20b-21a

Nokef etzbao..*see* **Knocking one's finger**, page 343

Nokev, meaning...Sanhedrin 56a

Nolad..*see* **Newly formed on Shabbos**, page 443

Nomad, Rabbah bar bar Chana...Bava Basra 73b

Non exhaustive list, which law was omitted as well...Gittin 33a

Non-holy

Non-holy animal, consecrating sacrifice.........Beitzah 19b-20a; Menachos 82a-82b; Zevachim 50a, 98a

Non-holy animal, for sacrifices..Chullin 41b-42a

Non-holy animal in Temple Courtyard

Non-holy animal in Temple Courtyard, bird sin offering...Nazir 29b

Non-holy animal in Temple Courtyard, fetus..Temurah 11b-12a

Non-holy animals in Temple Courtyard, burning...Krisos 24b

Non-holy animals in Temple Courtyard, from the Torah..................Pesachim 23b; Chullin 85b

Non-holy animals in Temple Courtyard, impurity............................Chullin 85b; Kiddushin 58a

Non-holy animals in Temple Courtyard, benefit.....................Kiddushin 57b-58a; Pesachim 22a

Non-holy animals in Temple Courtyard, prohibition.........Kiddushin 57b-58a; Pesachim 22a, 23b;

....Nazir 29a; Bava Kama 72a-72b

Non-holy food

Non-holy food before separating *challah,* purity ....Niddah 6b-7a, 71b

Non-holy food in purity.....................................Pesachim 46a; Avodah Zarah 55b-56a; Chullin 122b-123a

Non-holy food in Temple Courtyard ....Menachos 48a, 106a

Non-holy food in Temple purity ....Niddah 71b; Taharos 2:8; Chagigah 19b-20a; Chullin 2b, 34b-35b

Non-holy food in Temple purity, category of purity..Chagigah 19b-20a

N

Non-holy food in *terumah* purity..Niddah 71b; Taharos 2:8
Non-holy food in third category purity................Chullin 33b-34b; Niddah 7a; Chagigah 19b-20a
Non-holy foods, pure, since destruction..............................Chagigah 25a; Niddah 6b

Non-Jew..*see also* **Asking a non-Jew**, page 34

Aggadah —
Non-Jew, episode about honoring father.................Kiddushin 31a; Avodah Zarah 23b-24a
Non-Jews, commandments they perform...Chullin 92a-92b
Non-Jews, for Israel..Yevamos 63a
Non-Jews, nations of the world acknowledge Ten Commandments.............Kiddushin 31a
Non-Jews, righteous, in every generation..Chullin 92a
Non-Jews, World to Come...Sanhedrin 105a
Non-Jews' decrees..*see* **Decrees of idolaters**, page 155

Death —
Non-Jew, Noahide, abortion..Sanhedrin 57b
Non-Jew should have learned...Bava Kama 92a
Non-Jew who studies Torah..Sanhedrin 59a; Avodah Zarah 3a

Food —
Non-Jew, eating from twitching animal..Chullin 121b
Non-Jew, meat from living animal...Chullin 33a
Non-Jew, taste of mixture...Chullin 97a-97b, 111b

Prohibitions —
Non-Jew, *chametz*...Pesachim 5b-6a
Non-Jew, entering Temple...Keilim 1:8
Non-Jew, his son from a Jewish woman..........................Yevamos 44b-45b, 70a, 99a
Non-Jew, impurity of utensils.....................................Taharos 7:1-7, 7:9, 8:3-4
Non-Jew, *kiddushin*...Sanhedrin 52b
Non-Jew, prohibition not stricter than for Jew..............................Chullin 33a, 121b
Non-Jews, lineage according to male..........................Yevamos 78b; Kiddushin 67a-67b
Non-Jews, Noahide, forbidden relations..Sanhedrin 57b-58b
Non-Jews, Noahide, seven commandments..........Sanhedrin 56a-57a, 59a-60a, 74b-75a

Sacrifice —
Non-Jew, noahide, blemished sacrifice.......Avodah Zarah 5b-6a, 51a; Zevachim 116a; Temurah 7a
Non-Jew, noahide, circumcised, Pesach..Yevamos 71a
Non-Jew, noahide, peace offering..Zevachim 116a
Non-Jew, noahide, sacrifice of impure animal...Zevachim 116a
Non-Jew, partnership, firstborn animal.........Bava Metzia 70b; Bechoros 16a-16b
Non-Jew, sacrifice with missing limb.................Zevachim 116a; Avodah Zarah 5b, 51a

Separating tithe —
Non-Jew, partnership for tithes...Chullin 135a-136a
Non-Jew, separating tithe...Temurah 3a

Shabbos —
Non-Jew, acting by self-interest...Shabbos 121a
Non-Jew, animals fertilizing field on Shabbos.................................Moed Katan 12a
Non-Jew, building on Shabbos..Moed Katan 12a
Non-Jew, carrying close to Shabbos..Shabbos 18b
Non-Jew, coming from out of *techum*..................Eruvin 39b-40a; Beitzah 24b-25a
Non-Jew doing something for a Jew on Shabbos..Shabbos 151a
Non-Jew doing something for himself on Shabbos.............................Shabbos 122a-122b
Non-Jew, *eruv chatzeiros*................*see* **Renting domain for *eruv*, permission to use**, page 558

N

Non-Jew, food in his courtyard, Shabbos..Shabbos 19a
Non-Jew, hint for end of Shabbos..Shabbos 150a
Non-Jew, hunting on Shabbos..Beitzah 24b
Non-Jew, Shabbos eve..Shabbos 19a
Non-Jew, spent Shabbos out of his courtyard..Eruvin 47a, 62b, 86a
Non-Jew, *techumin*..Eruvin 47b

Misc. —
Non-Jew, being agent................................Bava Metzia 71b-72a; Kiddushin 41b; Gittin 23b
Non-Jew, exempt in case of partnership..Chullin 135a-136a
Non-Jews outside *Eretz Yisrael*, idolatry..Chullin 13b
Non-Jews, paying wages on time................................Bava Metzia 111b; Sanhedrin 57a

Non-Jewish
Non-Jewish customs................................Bava Kama 83a; Sanhedrin 52b
Non-Jewish woman, son born to Jew from................................Yevamos 23a; Kiddushin 68b
Non-Jewish woman to *Kohen*, prohibition................................Bechoros 56b; Temurah 29b
Non-Jewish woman, zealots kill him, Jewish man................................Sanhedrin 81b-82a; Avodah Zarah 36b

Non-*Kohen*
Temple services —
Non-*Kohen*, bringing sacrificial blood to Altar................................Zevachim 14a-14b; Yoma 49a
Non-*Kohen*, burning parts of sacrifices..Shevuos 17b
Non-*Kohen*, lighting *menorah*..Yoma 24b
Non-*Kohen*, mixing meal offering................................Menachos 9a, 18b-19a; Pesachim 36a
Non-*Kohen*, permitted services..Yoma 26b-27a
Non-*Kohen*, picking frankincense of meal offering................................Menachos 13b
Non-*Kohen*, pouring oil of meal offering................................Menachos 18a-18b, 20a
Non-*Kohen*, Red Heifer................................Yoma 42a-43b; Zevachim 14b, 68b; Menachos 6b
Non-*Kohen*, services exempt from punishment................................Zevachim 112b
Non-*Kohen*, slaughtering on Yom Kippur..Yoma 42a
Non-*Kohen*, slaughtering sacrifice................................Zevachim 14b, 31b-32a; Menachos 19a; Yoma 27a; Chullin 2b
Non-*Kohen*, which services................................Yoma 24a-24b, 27b-28a; Zevachim 112b
Non-*Kohen* who cut off neck of bird, *neveilah*................................Zevachim 68a-69a

Misc. —
Non-*Kohen*, benefitting from *terumah* oil used by *Kohen*................................Krisos 7a
Non-*Kohen*, burnt offering outside................................Makos 17b-18b
Non-*Kohen*, not to take down from Altar................................Zevachim 69a
Non-*Kohen*, source for disqualifying sacrifice................................Zevachim 15b-16a
Non-*Kohen* who performed service in Temple, death................................Sanhedrin 84a; Zevachim 17a

Non-*Kohen* eating terumah
Non-*Kohen* eating *terumah*, cases................................Yoma 80b-81a
Non-*Kohen* eating *terumah*, death................................Sanhedrin 83b
Non-*Kohen* eating *terumah*, quantity................................Pesachim 32b-33a

Non-virgin woman
Non-virgin woman, *kesubah*................................Kesubos 11b-12a, 13a
Non-virgin woman to *Kohen Gadol*................................Chagigah 14b-15a
Non-virgin woman to *Kohen Gadol*, *chalalah*................................Yevamos 60a

Noose on Shabbos................................Shabbos 111b, 113a; Eruvin 97a, 102b-103a, 105a; Pesachim 11a; Succah 33b

North
North and south, bed................................Berachos 5b
North, communal peace offerings................................Zevachim 54b-55a

North, how to find..Eruvin 56a; Pesachim 94a

North of Temple Courtyard, limits.................................Zevachim 14a, 20a, 33a; Yoma 36a

North of Temple Courtyard, services.........................Zevachim 48a-49b; Menachos 55b-56a

Nose, physiognomy...................................Yevamos 120a; Bava Metzia 27b; Bechoros 46b

Noshchos....................................*see* **Loaves stuck during baking, connections for impurity,** page 375

Nossar...*see* **Leftover sacrifice,** page 360

Nossen einav be'eino shelo...*see* **Looks at what is not his,** page 377

Nossen eino bekoso.....................................*see* **Drunk, transgressions seem permitted,** page 182

Nossen taam bar Naat......................*see* **Absorption in food giving taste to another food,** page 5

Nossen taam lifgam...*see* **Gives a bad taste,** page 252

Not

Not in Heaven, Torah..Temurah 16a

Not in Heaven, ways to remember learning...Eruvin 55a

Not to receive a reward...Avos 1:3; Avodah Zarah 19a

Notarikon...*see* **Initials,** page 310

Nothing

Nothing new, messianic times...Shabbos 63a

Nothing new under the sun, scoffer...Shabbos 30b

Nothing that is not alluded in Torah...Taanis 9a

Nov

Nov, decree on David's offspring...Sanhedrin 95a-95b

Nov, Saul...Berachos 12b

Nov and Giveon

Nov and Giveon, private altar...Megillah 9b

Nov and Giveon, Tabernacle...Zevachim 119a

Nov and Giveon, years of existence...Zevachim 118b-119a

Nowadays...*see* **Present times,** page 501

Noy mitzvah..*see* **Embellishment of commandment,** page 194

Noy succah...*see* **Ornaments of *succah*,** page 463

Number

Number and money, expenses..Bava Basra 7b

Number of blessings in *Shemoneh Esrei*, reason.................................Berachos 28b-29a

Number of bones, experiment to count them...Bechoros 45a

Number of commandments, reduced by Prophets.................................Makos 23b-24a

Number of drops in sea...Horayos 10a

Number of inhabitants, *Eretz Yisrael*..Bava Metzia 28a

Number of Jews offering Pesach lamb...Pesachim 64b

Number of Jews, prohibition...Yoma 22b

Number of *Kohanim*, daily offering...Yoma 26b, 27a-27b

Number of letters and words...Kiddushin 30a

Number of letters in Torah...Shabbos 49b; Kiddushin 30a

Number of organs..Bechoros 45a; Oholos 1:8

Number of tribes, how...Horayos 6b

Number, sign for lost item...Bava Metzia 23b, 24a

Numbers in Greek...Bava Basra 164b

Numerical value...*see* ***Gematria,*** page 247

Numerous slain she made fall.........................Avodah Zarah 19b; Sotah 22a-22b

Nun

Nun inversed, marks...Shabbos 115b-116a

N

Nun, omitted in *Ashrei* .... Berachos 4b

Nursing

Nursing, advice .... Shabbos 134a

Nursing calf, more than the calf wishes to nurse .... Pesachim 112a

Nursing, episode about miracle .... Shabbos 53b

Nursing from impure woman .... Krisos 13a-13b

Nursing from mother, consecrated young animal .... Meilah 13a

Nursing from *treifah* animal, sacrifice .... Temurah 31a

Nursing other animal's young .... Bechoros 24a

Nursing, place of understanding .... Berachos 10a

Nursing, sign of adulthood .... Bechoros 20b, 24a-24b

Nursing, until when .... Kesubos 60a

Nursing woman

Nursing woman .... *see also* **Wet nurse**, page 740

Nursing woman, birth control .... Yevamos 34b

Nursing woman, divorced .... Kesubos 59b-60a

Nursing woman, episode .... Kesubos 60b

Nursing woman, fast .... Taanis 14a

Nursing woman, food and wine .... Kesubos 65b

Nursing woman, foods .... Kesubos 60b

Nursing woman killed her son .... Kesubos 60b

Nursing woman, retroactive impurity .... Niddah 7a-7b, 9a, 10b-11a

Nursing woman, waiting time before remarriage .... Yevamos 36b-37a, 42a, 43a; Kesubos 60a-60b

Nut

Nut, inside does not become soiled .... Chagigah 15b

Nut on garment, Shabbos .... Shabbos 65b

Nut on water, putting down .... Shabbos 5b, 99b-100a

Nuts for children, storekeeper .... Bava Metzia 60a; Bava Basra 21b

Nuts, playing on Shabbos .... Eruvin 104a

N

O

"O"
"O," deduction, including or excluding .... Bava Kama 77b-78a
"O," to differentiate .... Chullin 78b
"O," to differentiate, negative commandments .... Sanhedrin 65a

Oath
Aggadah —
Oath, episode about death of son .... Gittin 35a
Oath of fetus .... Niddah 30b-31a
Oath of woman after birth, sacrifice .... Niddah 31b; Shevuos 8a; Krisos 26a
Oath, punishment .... Shabbos 33a
Oaths of exile .... Kesubos 111a

Beis din —
Oath .... see also **Swears**, page 666
Oath, "only you are trustworthy" .... Bava Metzia 36b; Bava Kama 11b
Oath, "take invalid oath!" .... Sanhedrin 24a-24b
Oath exempts from paying .... Bava Kama 106a-106b
Oath for one and for a hundred .... Kesubos 94a
Oath, imposing on other litigant .... Bava Metzia 5a; Shevuos 41a
Oath, included in obligatory oath .... Kiddushin 27b-28a; Bava Metzia 4b, 100b;
                                                                              Shevuos 38b, 40b, 48b-49a
Oath, included in obligatory oath, *sotah* .... Sotah 18b
Oath, man suspected of lying .... Bava Metzia 5b-6a; Shevuos 46b-47a
Oath, *migo* .... Bava Basra 70b
Oath not accepted when witnesses are present .... Bava Metzia 83a
Oath, to you and you .... Shevuos 23a-23b, 38a-38b
Oath, witness was not contradicted .... Shevuos 32b, 47a-47b; Bava Basra 33b-34a
Oaths, contradictory .... Bava Metzia 2b; Shevuos 45a

Oath, double
Oath, double, adding detail .... Shevuos 23b-24a, 28b-29a
Oath, double, cases .... Shevuos 3b-4a, 21a, 27b; Temurah 3b
Oath, double, episode about examination .... Shevuos 28b-29a
Oath, double, first was permitted .... Nedarim 18a; Shevuos 27b

Oath, false
Oath, false, explanation .... Shevuos 20b-21b

O

Oath, false, lashes..Temurah 3b; Shevuos 3b, 20b-21b
Oath, false, seriousness..Shevuos 39a-39b; Gittin 35a

Oath for testimony
Oath for testimony, *beis din*..Shevuos 31a-32a
Oath for testimony, cases..Shevuos 32a-33a
Oath for testimony, demand..Shevuos 31b-32a, 33b, 35a
Oath for testimony, different from other oaths..Shevuos 25b
Oath for testimony, for the future..Shevuos 35a
Oath for testimony, invalid witness..Shevuos 31a, 35a; Yoma 74a
Oath for testimony, money..Shevuos 33b-34a, 35a
Oath for testimony, one witness..Bava Kama 105b
Oath for testimony, penalty..Shevuos 33a-33b, 34a
Oath for testimony, text..Shevuos 35a
Oath for testimony, when..Shevuos 31b

Deposit —
Oath, collateral is not in one's possession................................Bava Metzia 5b, 34b-35a; Shevuos 43b
Oath for deposit...........Bava Kama 106b-107b; Bava Metzia 5b, 98a-98b; Krisos 9a; Shevuos 34a; Sotah 33a
Oath, value of collateral..Shevuos 43a-43b; Bava Metzia 34b

Exempt —
Oath, connected to earth produce..Shevuos 43a
Oath, consecrated item and slave..Bava Metzia 57b; Shevuos 42b-43a
Oath, indirect damage..Bava Kama 105b; Shevuos 32a
Oath, minor..Shevuos 42a-42b; Bava Kama 106b
Oath, slave and land................................Bava Metzia 57b, 100b; Shevuos 42b-43a; Bava Kama 63a
Oath, sown wheat..Menachos 69a; Bava Metzia 56a

How —
Oath, according to intention of *beis din*................................Nedarim 25a; Shevuos 29a-29b, 39a
Oath, forcing..Shevuos 41a
Oath, holding a holy item..Shevuos 38b
Oath, in any language..Sotah 33a
Oath in front of people knowing his lie..Kesubos 85a
Oath, perhaps it will prove a lie..Bava Metzia 34b-35a
Oath, threat..Shevuos 38b-39a

Loan —
Oath "*heses*," denying everything..Shevuos 40b-41a; Bava Metzia 5a, 6a
Oath, "I do not know"..Bava Metzia 97b-98b; Shevuos 47a
Oath, acknowledging partly..*see* **Acknowledging in part**, page 7
Oath, *bari* and *drara demamona*..Bava Metzia 2b-3a
Oath, cancellation of debts..Shevuos 49a
Oath, coins in staff..Nedarim 25a; Shevuos 29a
Oath, defined item..Shevuos 43a
Oath, minimal sum................................Shevuos 39b-40a, 40b; Kiddushin 11b; Bechoros 50b
Oath, paid promissory note..Shevuos 41a
Oath, single witness..Kesubos 87b; Shevuos 40a
Oath, witnesses testifying about part of sum..Bava Metzia 3a-4a, 5a

Oath for vow —
Oath, eating earth..Shevuos 24a-24b
Oath, explaining one's intention..Nedarim 25a; Shevuos 29a
Oath, impossible................................Nedarim 15a; Succah 53a; Yevamos 121b; Shevuos 25a

Oath includes vow .... Nedarim 80b
Oath, mentioning several things .... Shevuos 23a-23b, 38a
Oath, negation possible as affirmation .... Shevuos 25a-26a
Oath on name of idol .... Sanhedrin 63b
Oath, permitting vows .... Nedarim 28a
Oath, prohibition applying on man .... Nedarim 2b
Oath, since Mount Sinai .... Shevuos 21b, 22b, 23b, 25a-25b, 27a-27b; Yoma 73b; Nedarim 8a;
.... Nazir 4a; Makos 22a
Oath to annul commandment .... Nedarim 16b-17a; Shevuos 25a, 27a-27b
Oath to damage fellow .... Shevuos 27a-27b
Oath to perform commandment .... Nedarim 8a; Shevuos 25b, 27a-27b; Chagigah 10a; Temurah 3b

Other swearing people —
Oath, "swear and collect" .... Bava Basra 128a
Oath, "we did not receive" .... Shevuos 48a
Oath by custodian .... Gittin 52b
Oath, collecting from heir .... Kesubos 87a, 88a, 94a; Bava Basra 5b, 33a; Gittin 34b, 50a-50b;
.... Shevuos 42b, 45a, 47a, 48a
Oath of worker .... Shevuos 45a-46a, 47b; Bava Metzia 3a, 6a, 103a, 112b-113a
Oath of worker, *migo* .... Shevuos 45b-46a
Oath, storekeeper with his account book .... Shevuos 47b; Bava Metzia 3a, 6a
Oath, swears and is not liable .... Shevuos 45a; Bava Kama 106a
Oath, swears and takes .... Shevuos 44b-45a
Oath to sons, inheritance .... Shevuos 47a, 48a-48b
Oath, two men hold garment .... Bava Metzia 5b

Women —
Oath for rival of wife, *kesubah* .... Kesubos 93b-94a
Oath, *kesubah* from consecrated item .... Arachin 23a
Oath of *sotah*, how .... Sotah 18a; Yevamos 58a; Kiddushin 27b
Oath of widow, *kesubah* .... Kesubos 55a, 87a, 88b, 98a; Gittin 34b-36a
Oath of widow to sell .... Kesubos 98a
Oath of wife, for which claim .... Kesubos 86b
Oath, one witness for *kesubah* .... Kesubos 87b-88a
Oath, partially paid *kesubah* .... Kesubos 87a-87b; Shevuos 45a

Misc. —
Oath, cannot take an oath .... Shevuos 32b, 47a-47b; Bava Metzia 98a-98b; Bava Basra 34a
Oath, Giving of Torah .... Nedarim 25a; Shevuos 29a-29b
Oath of *Kohen Gadol* on Yom Kippur .... Yoma 19a-19b
Oath of non-Jew, partnership .... Sanhedrin 63b; Bechoros 2b
Oath, stories .... Gittin 35a
Oath that thus said Rav .... Yevamos 32b; Shevuos 26a
Oath to noblewoman .... Yoma 84a; Avodah Zarah 28a
Oath, unnecessary and false .... Shevuos 20b-21b, 29a, 29b
Oath, unnecessary and false, lashes .... Temurah 3a-3b; Shevuos 21a
Oaths by mistake .... Nedarim 25b; Shevuos 26a-26b, 28a-28b; Shabbos 69b
Oats, variety of barley .... Pesachim 35a; Menachos 70a
Obadiah
Obadiah, among wicked .... Yoma 38b; Sanhedrin 39b
Obadiah, righteousness and prophecy .... Sanhedrin 39b
Obed Edom, Holy Ark .... Berachos 63b-64a

Obeying *beis din*, person..Bava Basra 40a
Object
   Object...*see also* **Item**, page 319
   Object about to rest from fall................................Zevachim 25b; Bava Metzia 12a, 102a
   Object which use is forbidden............................Shabbos 122b-124b, 141b; Beitzah 11a
   Object which use is permitted..Shabbos 123b-124a
   Objects, holy...Megillah 26b, 32a
Obstruction of heart, transgression..Yoma 39a
Ocean, rain...Taanis 9b; Eruvin 45b
Ochazei einayim...*see* **Camel, illusion,** page 85
Ochel nefesh, food on Yom Tov.......................................*see* **Yom Tov,** page 771
Ochel..*see* **Eat,** page 185; *see also* **Food,** page 231
Ochel peiroiseihem baolam hazeh..........*see* **Dividends of commandments in this world,** page 168
Odisa..........................*see* **Acknowledgement, verbal, act of acquisition,** page 7
Ofanei merkavah...*see* **Angel, *Ofan*,** page 22
Ofanim, crowns to G-d...Chagigah 12b-14a
Offended but do not offend.............................Gittin 36b; Shabbos 88b; Yoma 23a
Offense
   Offense...*see also* **Transgression,** page 700
   Offense, intentional sin..Yoma 36b; Krisos 25b
Offering
   Offering animal for communal sacrifice...............................Rosh Hashanah 7a-7b
   Offering fellow's wine to idol...Chullin 41a
   Offering parts of sacrifices not destined to be offered...Menachos 57b; Yoma 47b; Yevamos 100a;
   ....Sotah 23a; Zevachim 76b
   Offering wood...........................Menachos 20b-21a, 106b; Shekalim 6:6
Offering sacrifice outside Temple
   Offering sacrifice outside Temple, cases...........................Zevachim 108b
   Offering sacrifice outside Temple, combining.........Zevachim 107b-108a, 109a; Menachos 23a
   Offering sacrifice outside Temple, prohibition..............Zevachim 107a-107b; Sanhedrin 34b
   Offering sacrifice outside Temple, quantity..................Zevachim 107b-108a, 109b-110a
   Offering sacrifice outside Temple, what is included......Zevachim 35b, 109a, 110a, 113b, 115b
   Offering sacrifices when there is no Temple..................Megillah 10a-10b; Shevuos 16a;
   ....Zevachim 60b, 62a, 107b; Makos 19a; Eduyos 8:6; Temurah 21a
Offerings...*see* **Sacrifices,** page 578
Offspring
   Offspring...*see also* **Son,** page 642
   Offspring, disqualified, laws...Yevamos 22a-22b
   Offspring, disqualified, *terumah*..Yevamos 70a
   Offspring of Abraham, Jacob..............................Nedarim 31a; Sanhedrin 59b
   Offspring of *Kohen* marrying forbidden woman...............*see* ***Chalal,*** page 92
   Offspring of Noah...*see* **Non-Jew,** page 448
   Offspring of wicked, learned Torah...Gittin 57b
   Offspring, *terumah*...Niddah 44a
Offspring of father
   Offspring of father, animal and its young...........................Chullin 78b-79a
   Offspring of father, crossbred animals...........................Chullin 79b-80a, 132a
   Offspring of father, mixed species of animals...........................Chullin 79a-79b
   Offspring of father, two causes...Chullin 58a

O

Og

Og, flood .... Zevachim 113b

Og, miracle of his death .... Berachos 54b

Og, Moses' fear .... Niddah 61a

Og stones .... Berachos 54b

Ohel .... *see* **Tent**, page 681

Oil

Commandments —

Oil before *Bircas HaMazon* .... Berachos 53b

Oil before *Bircas HaMazon*, inattention .... Berachos 42a

Oil, blessing .... Berachos 35b-36a

Oil for kings anointment .... Horayos 11b; Krisos 5b

Oil for meal offering for *Kohen* .... Menachos 51a

Oil for *Simchas Beis Hashoevah* .... Succah 52b

Oil, fragrant, blessing .... Berachos 43a

Oil of second tithe .... Maaser Sheni 2:1-4

Oil for anointing

Oil for anointing, anointing oneself .... Horayos 11b; Krisos 5a, 6b-7a

Oil for anointing, concealed .... Horayos 12a; Yoma 52b; Krisos 5b

Oil for anointing, man preparing .... Krisos 5a

Oil for anointing, preparation .... Horayos 11b; Krisos 5a-5b

Oil for anointing, personal use .... Krisos 6b; Meilah 19a-19b

Oil for menorah

Oil for *menorah*, disqualified .... Shabbos 21a

Oil for *menorah*, quality and preparation .... Menachos 86a-86b

Oil for *menorah*, quantity .... Menachos 89a; Pesachim 59a; Yoma 15a; Zevachim 11b

Impure —

Oil, burned, using it on Yom Tov .... Shabbos 23b-24a, 24b

Oil, impure and pure, absorbed .... Orlah 2:13

Oil of *terumah*, kindling .... Terumos 11:10

Oil of *terumah*, Shabbos lamp .... Shabbos 23b-24a

Prohibitions —

Oil of non-Jews .... Avodah Zarah 35b-36a, 38b; Shabbos 17b

Oil, waste .... Shabbos 67b

Oil, wording of vow .... Nedarim 53a-53b

Sacrifices —

Oil, is it offered as donation .... Menachos 104b; Zevachim 77a, 91a

Oil, libations for *Omer* .... Menachos 89b

Oil of donation, how is it offered .... Zevachim 91a-91b

Oil of donation, quantity .... Zevachim 91a; Menachos 107a

Oil, quantity for libations .... Menachos 89a

Oil and frankincense

Oil and frankincense, meal offering for sinner .... Sotah 15a; Menachos 59b-60a, 23a

Oil for meal offering, became impure .... Yevamos 73b

Oil for meal offering, change in measure .... Menachos 11a

Oil for meal offering, for this meal offering .... Menachos 79b

Oil for meal offering, how .... Menachos 86a-86b

Oil for meal offering, indispensable requirement ..... Menachos 8a-8b

Oil for meal offering, kinds .... Menachos 86a-86b

Oil for meal offering, large .... Menachos 89a, 106b
Oil for meal offering of *nazir* .... Menachos 78a
Oil for meal offering, on wood .... Menachos 23a
Oil for meal offering, quantity .... Menachos 89a
Oil for meal offering, services .... Menachos 9a, 18a-18b, 74b-75a
Oil for meal offering, unfit .... Menachos 86a
Oil for meal offering, which offerings .... Menachos 59a-59b
Oil for meal offerings, became mixed .... Menachos 22b-23a

Shabbos —
Oil, cooking on Shabbos .... Shabbos 40b
Oil for woman giving birth, Shabbos .... Shabbos 128b
Oil in hair, squeezing on Shabbos .... Shabbos 128b
Oil in lamp, *muktzeh* .... Shabbos 44a, 46b; Beitzah 30b
Oil of rose, Shabbos .... Shabbos 111b, 128a; Bava Metzia 113b
Oil of *tzori*, Shabbos lamp .... Shabbos 25b-26a
Oil on wine, putting down on Shabbos .... Shabbos 5b, 100a
Oil, Shabbos lamp .... Shabbos 20b-21a, 26a

Oils —
Oil, different kinds .... Shabbos 26a
Oil of Anfaknon .... Menachos 86a; Shabbos 80b; Pesachim 43a; Megillah 13a; Moed Katan 9b
Oil of myrrh .... Shabbos 80b; Moed Katan 9b; Pesachim 42b-43b; Megillah 13a; Menachos 86a
Oil of olive, wisdom .... Menachos 85b

Misc. —
Oil floats, wine is absorbed .... Sanhedrin 104b
Oil of Ludkiya .... Menachos 85b
Oil press and bathhouse, sale .... Bava Basra 67b-68a, 78b
Oil, residues found in oil which was sold .... Bava Metzia 40b
Oil, spoiled .... Bava Metzia 38a-38b

Oil for leper
Oil for leper, changing name .... Menachos 28a
Oil for leper, hindrance in application .... Yoma 61a
Oil for leper, *piggul* and permitter .... Zevachim 15b, 44a-44b
Oil for leper, place of application .... Menachos 9b-10a
Oil for leper to *Kohen*, source .... Zevachim 44b; Menachos 73a
Oil for leper, was spilled .... Yoma 61a

Ointment, depilatory .... Bava Kama 86a; Makos 20b
Oker davar migidulo .... *see* **Uprooting matter from its place of growth**, page 716
Oker harim .... *see* **Uproots mountains**, page 716
Ol Torah .... *see* **Yoke of Torah, reward**, page 770
Olah .... *see* **Burnt offering**, page 81
Olam haba .... *see* **World to come**, page 763
Olam hazeh .... *see* **World, this world**, page 763
Olas reiyah
Olas reiyah, in desert .... Chagigah 6a-6b
Olas reiyah, price .... Chagigah 6a-7a; Bechoros 51a
Olas reiyah, sacrifice .... Chagigah 7a
Olas reiyah, semichah .... Beitzah 20a
Olas reiyah, stringencies .... Chagigah 6b
Olas reiyah, who .... Chagigah 2a-3a, 4a-4b

O

Old

Old animal, sacrifice .... Bechoros 41a; Temurah 28b
Old animals, stronger .... Shabbos 77b; Avodah Zarah 30b
Old, blessing .... Bava Basra 91b
Old, choicest .... Bava Basra 91b
Old grain .... *see* **New grain**, page 442
Old teaching, more difficult to learn than new .... Yoma 29a

Old age

Old age, by which merit .... Megillah 27b-28a; Rosh Hashanah 18a
Old age, crown of nettles .... Shabbos 152a
Old age, eighty years .... Moed Katan 28a
Old age in future .... Pesachim 68a; Sanhedrin 91b
Old age jumped on him .... Taanis 5b
Old age, learning in one's old age .... Yevamos 62b
Old age, living after a hundred years .... Gittin 28a
Old age, Rav Yosef's feast .... Moed Katan 28a
Old age, seventy .... Moed Katan 28a
Old age, since Abraham .... Bava Metzia 87a; Sanhedrin 107b

Old man
see also **Elder**, page 192

Episodes —

Old men in desert .... Sanhedrin 17a
Old men, Rabbi Chanina .... Chullin 24b
Old men who encompassed history .... Bava Basra 121b

Laws —

Old man and Sage, precedence .... Bava Basra 120a
Old man, disqualified *Kohen* .... Chullin 24b
Old man, standing .... Kiddushin 32b-33b
Old man, urinating before immersing .... Chullin 24b; Mikvaos 8:4

Sages —

Old man and man exempt due to his honor .... Bava Metzia 30a-30b; Berachos 19b; Sanhedrin 18b
Old men, Sages .... Shabbos 152a; Megillah 28a

Misc. —

Old man adulterer, mind cannot tolerate .... Pesachim 113b
Old man, after a hundred years .... Gittin 28a
Old man and old woman in house .... Arachin 19a
Old man, importance of learning from elder .... Avos 4:20
Old man, livelihood .... Niddah 65a
Old man, marriage .... Sanhedrin 76a-76b
Old men, scholars and ignoramus .... Kinin 3:6; Shabbos 152a

Old woman

Old woman, adorning herself like young girl .... Moed Katan 9b
Old woman, giving birth .... Bava Basra 119b
Old woman in house, treasure .... Arachin 19a
Old woman, retroactively *niddah* .... Niddah 9a-9b
Old woman, running to festivities .... Moed Katan 9b
Old woman to young man, marriage .... Yevamos 44a
Old women, Rebbi's maidservant .... Shabbos 152a

Older than one year, Pesach
.... Pesachim 97b-98a

Oleh veyored
.... *see* **Variable guilt offering**, page 720

Olelos, vineyard .... Peah 7,-6 7:7, 8:1; Taanis 6b

Olive

Olive oil, wisdom .... Menachos 85b

Olive, suffering of Israel .... Menachos 53b

Olive tree does not lose its leaves .... Menachos 53b

Olive trees carried away by overflowing .... Bava Metzia 100b-101a

Olive trees sold for their wood .... Bava Metzia 100b-101a

Olives and grapes, squeezing .... Shabbos 145a

Olives, bad, impurity .... Bava Metzia 105a; Uktzin 3:6

Olives, gathering .... Shabbos 73b

Olives given to teacher, episode .... Yevamos 15b

Olives, impurity ..... Shabbos 144b; Taharos 9:1-3, 9:5-7; Pesachim 3b; Eduyos 4:6; Yevamos 15b; Meilah 21a

Olives, requirement for tithes .... Beitzah 35a

Olive volume

Olive volume, amounts of Torah .... Yoma 80a

Olive volume, eating *terumah* .... Pesachim 32b-33a

Olive volume, equal to *reviis* dry .... Shabbos 77a

Olive volume, half of date .... Krisos 14a

Olive volume, half of throat .... Krisos 14a

Olive volume in *pras*, mixture .... Nazir 36b-37a; Pesachim 44a-44b; Avodah Zarah 67a

Olive volume of flesh of dead, impurity .... Chullin 129b

Olive volume of *neveilah* .... Niddah 42b

Olive volume, possibility of change .... Yoma 80a

Olive volume, quantity for giving .... Krisos 7a

Omasum, *treifah* .... Chullin 50b-51a

Omed .... *see* **Estimate,** page 201

Omed... .... *see* **About to,** page 3

Omed merubeh .... *see* **Breach in partition,** page 74

Omemos, with *aleph* or *ayin* .... Shabbos 77b; Berachos 53b; Pesachim 75b

Omen

Omen for deceased, not eulogized .... Sanhedrin 47a

Omen, good, guess .... Krisos 5b-6a; Horayos 12a

Omer imru .... *see* **Divorce certificate, husband says "Say,"** page 171

Omer mutar .... *see* **Saying "permitted,"** page 584

Omer

Meal offering —

Omer, barley meal offering .... Menachos 68b, 84a

Omer, blessing by its merit .... Rosh Hashanah 16a

Omer, from which produce .... Menachos 72a, 83b-84a

Omer, harvesting .... Menachos 72a-72b

Omer, how did they harvest .... Menachos 63b, 65a

Omer, libations .... Menachos 89b

Omer, offering as another sacrifice .... Menachos 5a-5b

Omer, permitting new grain ..... Succah 41a-41b; Menachos 5b, 68a-68b; Rosh Hashanah 30a-30b; Eruvin 32a

Omer, reaping on Shabbos ..... Makos 8b; Menachos 63b, 65a, 72a-72b; Sheviis 1:4; Rosh Hashanah 9a

Omer, roasting .... Menachos 66a-66b

Omer, Sabbatical year .... Bava Metzia 118a-118b; Shekalim 4:1; Menachos 84a

Omer, when is it eaten .... Menachos 5a-5b

Omer, when they entered *Eretz Yisrael* .... Rosh Hashanah 13a

Omer, where to reap it .... Menachos 64b

Misc. —

Omer, counting .... Menachos 65b; Chagigah 17b; Rosh Hashanah 5a

Omer, measure .... Eruvin 83b

Omer, quantity to eat daily .... Eruvin 83b

Omer, Rabbi Akiva's disciples .... Yevamos 62b

Omitting

Omitting components of incense .... Yoma 53a; Krisos 6a

Omitting section in Torah reading .... Yoma 69b-70a; Megillah 24a; Sotah 41a

Omri, town in *Eretz Yisrael* .... Sanhedrin 102b

On

"On this mortar he sat" .... Yevamos 16a

On the same day, paying salary .... Bava Metzia 110b-112a

On ben Peles' wife .... Sanhedrin 109b-110a

Onaah .... *see* **Overcharging**, page 466

Onaah ribis vegezel .... *see* **Overcharging, interest and theft**, page 466

Onah beinonis .... *see* **Menstruation, average period**, page 404

Onah, equal to twelve hours .... Niddah 65a-65b

Onah .... *see* **Marital relations**, page 392

One

One commandment, reward .... Moed Katan 28b

One of a town and two of a family .... Sanhedrin 111a

One of group who dies .... Shabbos 105b-106a

One of my daughters, *kiddushin* .... Kiddushin 51b, 64b-65a

One of two things, dusk .... Krisos 19b

One part of sixty .... Berachos 57b

One part of sixty, mixture .... Avodah Zarah 69a; Chullin 97a-99b

One reason among several .... Zevachim 10b, 90a, 94b; Yoma 79b; Yevamos 48b; Sotah 8a;
.... Bava Kama 106b; Menachos 89b; Krisos 3b

One Sage forbids and one permits .... Gittin 83b

One sign, slaughtering of bird .... Chullin 27b-28a

One *tallis* for two Sages .... Sotah 49a

One, the best in the flock .... Yoma 34b, 70b; Megillah 28a

One thing with difficulty better than a hundred .... Avos deRav Nosson 3:6

One who does more and one who does less .... Menachos 110a

One witness, like two when Torah requires only one ..... Sotah 31b-32a, 47b; Yevamos 88b, 117b;
.... Kesubos 22b

One-armed woman, *chalitzah* .... Yevamos 105a

One-armed woman, episode .... Shabbos 53b

Onein

Onein, Aaron and his sons .... Zevachim 115b

Onein, bringing his sacrifice .... Zevachim 99b; Moed Katan 15b

Onein, desecrates service .... Sanhedrin 83b-84a; Zevachim 16a-16b

Onein, disqualified for service .... Zevachim 16a-16b

Onein, eating sacrifice .... Zevachim 99b-101a

Onein, exempt from commandments .... Berachos 17b-18a; Moed Katan 23b

Onein, first fruit .... Bikurim 2:2; Pesachim 36b; Yevamos 73a-73b

Onein, impurity for sacrifice .... Zevachim 99a-99b; Chagigah 21a

O

Onein, Kohen Gadol........................Yoma 13b-14a; Moed Katan 14b; Bava Kama 110a; Horayos 12b;
....Zevachim 16b-17a, 99a
Onein, Pesach lamb..Pesachim 91b-92a; Zevachim 99b-101a
Onein, purity of sacrifice..Chagigah 24b
Onein, sacrifice on private altar..Zevachim 16a
Onein, terumah..Yevamos 68b, 70b-71a
Oneiss........................*see* **Forced**, page 234; *see also* **Unavoidable circumstances**, page 713
Oneiss besulah..*see* **Rapist**, page 536
Oneness of G-d, questions on verses..Sanhedrin 38b
Onion
Onion, bad spirit..Niddah 17a
Onion, danger of leaves..Eruvin 29a-29b
Onion, eating it from the leaves..Beitzah 25b
Onion, health..Kiddushin 62a
Onion, rooted in attic..Maasros 5:2
Onkelos, stories..Gittin 56b-57a; Avodah Zarah 11a
Only you, Israel's suffering..Avodah Zarah 4a
Open
Open on Temple and outside................................Pesachim 86a; Yoma 25a; Maaser Sheni 3:8
Open your mouth and let your words illuminate..Berachos 22a
Opening boil, act needed for itself..Shabbos 107b
Opening doors, noise..Yoma 39b; Tamid 30b
Opening doors of *Heichal,* sacrifice................................Zevachim 55b; Eruvin 2a; Yoma 62b-63a
Opening mouth to Satan................................Berachos 19a, 60a; Kesubos 8b
Opening stitches on collar, Shabbos..Shabbos 48a; Makos 3b
Opening wound on Shabbos................................Shabbos 107a, 107b; Kesubos 6b-7a; Eduyos 2:5
Opening
Opening, creating on Shabbos, virgin..Kesubos 5b-7a
Opening, damage done by sight..Bava Basra 59b
Opening in *mikveh,* utensil inside another................................Chagigah 22a; Mikvaos 6:2
Opening in roof of Holy of Holies, repairs................................Pesachim 26a; Middos 4:5
Opening less than four cubits..Eruvin 12a, 13a
Opening of *Gehinnom*..Eruvin 19a; Succah 32b
Opening of Tabernacle Courtyard..Eruvin 23b
Opening to closed alley and empty land..Eruvin 67b
Opening to closed alley, preventing..Bava Basra 11b-12a
Opening, to fill and empty..Shabbos 146a
Openings, impurity of corpse................................Eruvin 30a; Oholos 3:6-7, 13:1-4
Openings of Temple..Middos 4:2
Opening of womb
Opening of womb, blood of *niddah*................................Niddah 21b, 22b, 38a, 66a; Krisos 10a
Opening of womb, firstborn animal..Chullin 70a
Opening of womb, impurity of corpse................................Bechoros 22a; Oholos 7:4
Opening of womb, stays open and blood flows..Pesachim 112b
Opening to legally annul vow
Opening to legally annul vow..Nedarim 65b
Opening to legally annul vow, cases..Nedarim 22b-23a
Opening to legally annul vow, regret..Nedarim 21b-22a, 77b

Opinion
Opinion of other Sages, "I never transgressed it" .... Shabbos 118b
Opinions, different, about Amora's opinion .... Kesubos 57a
Or vechoshech .... *see* **Light and darkness, order of creation**, page 370
Oral
Oral Torah, covenant .... Gittin 60b
Oral Torah, writing .... Temurah 14b; Gittin 60b
Oral tradition, forbidden to be written .... Temurah 14b; Gittin 60b
Orbit of sun and planets .... Eruvin 56a
Orchard
Orchard, "he sold him a name" .... Bava Metzia 104a; Bava Basra 7a
Orchard, hoeing good trees .... Sanhedrin 39b
Orchard, keeping from outside .... Yevamos 21a
Orchei milchamah .... *see* **War, Jewish soldiers returning**, page 730
Orchos chaim .... *see* **Wills, ethical, from Sages**, page 748
Ordained judges .... Bava Kama 15b, 84a-84b; Sanhedrin 2b-3b; Gittin 88b
Order .... *see also* **Precedence**, page 499
Temple service —
Order, according to wisdom .... Sanhedrin 69b; Bava Basra 16b
Order of cutting up burned parts of sacrifices .... Yoma 25b; Menachos 77b; Chullin 27a-27b;
.... Shabbos 116b
Order of *Kohen Gadol*'s service on Yom Kippur .... Yoma 30a-71b
Order of offering, sacrifices .... Horayos 12b-13a; Zevachim 89a-90b; Pesachim 59a
Order of precedence, regular and sacred .... Zevachim 89a, 90b-91a; Horayos 12b
Order of Temple service, Abbaye .... Pesachim 58b-59a; Yoma 33a-34a
Order of Yom Kippur, taking out spoon and sin offering .... Yoma 32a, 70b-71a
Misc. —
Order for putting shoes on .... Shabbos 61a
Order for washing .... Shabbos 61a
Order, judges heard .... Sanhedrin 36a; Gittin 58b-59a
Order of events of history .... Avodah Zarah 8b-9a; Shabbos 15a
Order of *mesechtos* .... Nazir 2a; Sotah 2a; Shevuos 2b-3a
Order of Mishnah, preference of Tanna .... Yevamos 2b-3a, 30a, 32a; Rosh Hashanah 12a;
.... Nedarim 3a; Nazir 2b; Bava Kama 17b; Bava Basra 108b; Zevachim 48a; Bechoros 13a
Order of Nach .... Bava Basra 14b-15a
Order, requisite .... Sanhedrin 49b
Order, separating *terumos* and tithes .... Terumos 3:6-7; Temurah 5b
Order to write legal document, act of acquisition .... Kiddushin 65b; Bava Basra 40a
Order of inheritance
Order of inheritance, daughter .... Bava Basra 110a-110b, 113a-113b, 115a, 122b
Order of inheritance, father .... Bava Basra 108b-109b
Order of inheritance, relatives .... Bava Basra 115a
Ordinary
Ordinary person "jumps" to the fore .... Megillah 12b
Ordinary persons permitting firstborn animals .... Bechoros 36b-37a
Ore'ach .... *see* **Guest**, page 261
Orech yamim biyeminah .... *see* **Length of days in its right hand**, page 363
Orez .... *see* **Rice**, page 567
Organs of man and woman .... Bechoros 45a; Oholos 1:8

Orion and Pleiades .... Berachos 58b-59a

Orlah

  In which case —

    Orlah, caper and fennel .... Berachos 36a-36b

    Orlah, hanging saplings .... Sotah 43b

    Orlah, non-Jewish partner .... Avodah Zarah 22a

    Orlah, permitted new growths .... Menachos 69b; Nedarim 57b; Sotah 43b

    Orlah, where and for whom does it apply .... Orlah 1:1-2

    Orlah, in which saplings .... Orlah 1:1-2; Pesachim 23a; Sotah 43b

    Orlah, trees .... Orlah 1:3-5, 1:9; Bava Metzia 119a; Sotah 43b

  Prohibition —

    Orlah, doubt .... Orlah 3:9; Berachos 36a-36b; Kiddushin 38b-39a

    Orlah, intermingled in orchard .... Orlah 1:6

    Orlah, mixture .... Orlah 1:6, 3:4-5; Gittin 54b; Pesachim 26a-27a

    Orlah, outside *Eretz Yisrael* .... Orlah 3:9; Berachos 36a-36b; Kiddushin 38a-39a

    Orlah, prohibition to profit .... Pesachim 22b; Kiddushin 56b; Bava Kama 101a

    Orlah, source .... Kiddushin 56b

    Orlah, whoever is lenient .... Berachos 36a

  Misc. —

    Orlah, counting years .... Rosh Hashanah 9b-10b; Yevamos 83a

    Orlah, marking .... Bava Kama 69a

    Orlah, rebuke for relations with *niddah* .... Beitzah 25b

    Orlah, suspected of transgressing Sabbatical year .... Rosh Hashanah 9b

Ornament

  Ornament, idolatrous .... Avodah Zarah 51b

  Ornaments of succah, dishonoring commandment .... Shabbos 22a

  Ornaments of succah, *s'chach* .... Succah 10a-10b; Shabbos 22a, 45a; Beitzah 30b

Orpah

  Orpah, how was she killed .... Sanhedrin 95a

  Orpah, misconduct .... Sotah 42b

Orphan .... *see also* **Custodian**, page 136; **Minor**, page 411

  Monetary matters —

    Orphans, *beis din* .... Bava Kama 36b-37a

    Orphans, city expenses .... Bava Metzia 108a; Bava Basra 8a

    Orphans, expenses for well .... Bava Basra 8a

    Orphans, investing their money in business .... Bava Metzia 70a

    Orphans, dividing estate by *beis din* .... Kiddushin 42a-42b; Yevamos 67b; Kesubos 100a; Gittin 34a

    Orphans, Shmuel's father .... Berachos 18b

    Orphans' property, announcement .... Kesubos 100b; Arachin 21b-22b

    Orphans' property, collecting and selling .... Kesubos 110a, 100b; Bava Kama 39a-39b;

    .... Arachin 22a-22b

  Misc. —

    Orphan generation, Rabbi Elazar ben Azariah .... Chagigah 3b

    Orphan, merit of raising an orphan .... Kesubos 50a; Sanhedrin 19b; Megillah 13a

    Orphan, merit of teaching him Torah .... Sanhedrin 19b

    Orphan, sacrifice .... Chullin 38b

    Orphan! Did your teacher do thus .... Avodah Zarah 13b; Chullin 111b

    Orphans, Amoraim .... Kiddushin 31b

    Orphans, commandments .... Gittin 52a

Orphans, interest .... Bava Metzia 70a

Orphans, living with their mother .... Kesubos 102b-103a

Orphans, suffering at hand of father's wife .... Yevamos 63b; Berachos 56a

Orphan girl

Orphan girl and deaf girl, levirate marriage .... Yevamos 110b-111b

Orphan girl and widow, insufficient inheritance .... Bava Basra 139b-140b; Kesubos 43a

Orphan girl, brothers' rights .... Kesubos 43a-43b

Orphan girl, husband's rights .... Yevamos 89b, 108a; Kesubos 101a

Orphan girl, *kesubah* .... Kesubos 100b-101a; Yevamos 113a

Orphan girl, *kiddushin* grow with her .... Yevamos 109b-110a; Kesubos 73a-74a

Orphan girl, Rabbinical *kiddushin* .... Gittin 65a

Orphan girl, supported from movable property .... Kesubos 50b-51a

Orphan girl, supporting her after her betrothal .... Kesubos 53b

Orphan girl, who must support her .... Bava Basra 122b

Oseh Maaseh Bereshis, blessing .... Berachos 58b-59b

Oseh maaseh Zimri .... *see* **Acts like Zimri,** page 8

Osek bemitzvah .... *see* **Busy with commandment,** page 82

Osios .... *see* **Letters,** page 366

Oso ha'ish .... *see* **Nazarene,** *Gehinnom,* page 437

Oso ve'es beno .... *see* **Animal and its young,** page 26

Other way, distance from women .... Bava Basra 57b

Othniel

Othniel, taught measures for commandments .... Yoma 80a

Othniel, Yaavetz .... Temurah 16a

Otzar yiras shamayim .... *see* **Treasure of fear of Heaven,** page 700

Otzarei peiros .... *see* **Keeping fruit to raise prices,** page 333

Otzem einav mer'os bera .... *see* **Closing eyes from seeing evil,** page 111

Out

Out of house of study, learning .... Chullin 86b

Out of time sacrifice .... *see* ***Piggul,*** page 487

Outer side of container, impurity .... Keilim 25:9; Berachos 52a-52b; Chagigah 22b; Bechoros 38a;

.... Niddah 7b

Outline of opening

Outline of opening .... Eruvin 11a-11b, 16a

Outline of opening, succah .... Succah 7a

Outlives His creatures, G-d .... Berachos 10a

Outside *Eretz Yisrael*

Commandments —

Outside *Eretz Yisrael, challah* .... Challah 4:8, 4:10; Chullin 104a-104b; Bechoros 27a-27b

Outside *Eretz Yisrael,* commandments .... Kiddushin 36b-37a, 38a-39b; Chullin 138b

Outside *Eretz Yisrael,* firstborn .... Temurah 21a-21b; Challah 4:11

Outside *Eretz Yisrael, mussaf* sacrifice of Succos .... Succah 55a

Outside *Eretz Yisrael,* tithe of animal .... Bechoros 53a

Outside *Eretz Yisrael,* Yom Tov *Sheni* .... Beitzah 4b

Impurity —

Outside *Eretz Yisrael,* air .... Shabbos 15b; Nazir 54b-55a

Outside *Eretz Yisrael,* impurity .... Shabbos 15a-15b; Nazir 19b-20a, 54b-55a; Eruvin 30b;

.... Chagigah 25a; Gittin 8b; Oholos 18:6

Outside *Eretz Yisrael,* Kohen .... Avodah Zarah 13a

Outside *Eretz Yisrael, nazir* .... Nazir 19b-20a; Eduyos 4:11

Prohibitions —

Outside *Eretz Yisrael*, episodes about men leaving *Eretz Yisrael* .... Kesubos 111a;

.... Bava Basra 91a

Outside *Eretz Yisrael*, first grain .... Kiddushin 37a, 38b; Menachos 68b

Outside *Eretz Yisrael*, going out .... Moed Katan 14a; Bava Basra 91a, 91b

Outside *Eretz Yisrael*, idolatry .... Chullin 13b

Outside *Eretz Yisrael*, idolatry in state of purity .... Avodah Zarah 8a

Outside *Eretz Yisrael*, like idolatry .... Kesubos 110b

Outside *Eretz Yisrael*, mixed species in vineyard .... Shabbos 139a; Orlah 3:9; Kiddushin 38b-39a;

.... Berachos 36a

Outside *Eretz Yisrael, orlah* .... Orlah 3:9; Berachos 36a-36b; Kiddushin 38a-39a

Outside *Eretz Yisrael*, vegetable .... Sanhedrin 12a; Nedarim 53b

Misc. —

Outside *Eretz Yisrael, beis din* .... Makos 7a

Outside *Eretz Yisrael*, prophecy .... Moed Katan 25a

Outside *Eretz Yisrael*, resurrection .... Kesubòs 111a-111b

Outside *Eretz Yisrael*, Syria .... Gittin 8a-8b

Outside place sacrifice

Outside place sacrifice, like in its place .... Zevachim 26b-27a

Outside place sacrifices, not taken down from Altar .... Menachos 79a

Outside place sacrifices, partially .... Zevachim 25b-26a

Outskirts of city

Outskirts of city .... *see also* **Techum**, page 675

Outskirts of city, like city .... Nedarim 56b

Outskirts of city, seventy cubits .... Eruvin 57a-57b

Ov

Ov does not understand .... Sotah 12b

Ov on Shabbos .... Sanhedrin 65b

Ov, sorcery .... Sanhedrin 65a, 65b; Krisos 3b

Oven

Episodes —

Oven, not to cause humiliation to poor .... Kesubos 67b

Oven of Achnai, dispute .... Bava Metzia 59a-59b; Berachos 19a; Eduyos 7:7; Keilim 5:8

Oven, Rabbi Zeira .... Bava Metzia 85a

Oven, to escape noblewoman's seduction .... Kiddushin 40a

Impurity —

Oven, accessories .... Keilim 5:3-5; Niddah 26a

Oven, covering with mortar .... Eduyos 7:8

Oven, different kinds .... Keilim 8:9

Oven, fell in oven .... Keilim 8:4-5

Oven, filling with earth .... Keilim 5, 6

Oven on pit .... Shabbos 125a; Keilim 5:6

Oven, partition .... Keilim 8:1-3; Zevachim 3a-3b

Oven, reptile found in it .... Keilim 8:7-8

Oven, shattering .... Keilim 5:7-11a; Chullin 123b-124a

Oven, sizes .... Keilim 5:1-3; Niddah 26a-26b; Chullin 124a

Oven, stone and metal .... Keilim 5:11

Oven, tent of corpse .... Keilim 10:7; Oholos 5:1, 12:1-3

Oven, utensils inside its wall .... Keilim 9:1

Prohibitions —
Oven, keeping food warm during Shabbos .... Shabbos 38b
Oven kindled with forbidden wood .... Pesachim 26b-27b, 75a
Oven, *kashering* clay oven .... Pesachim 30b
Oven on Yom Tov .... Beitzah 32b
Oven, preparation for use on Shabbos .... Shabbos 20a, 36b-37a

Misc. —
Oven consecrates .... Menachos 72b, 95b
Oven, distance from neighbors .... Bava Basra 20b
Oven, metallic, Temple .... Zevachim 96a-96b

Over le'asiasan .... *see* **Blessing before commandment**, page 64
Overes das .... *see* **Wife transgressing law, divorce**, page 745

Overcharging
In which case —
Overcharging, coin .... Bava Metzia 51b-52b
Overcharging, consecrated items .... Bava Metzia 55a, 57a-57b; Arachin 29a; Temurah 27b
Overcharging, forbidden foods .... Bechoros 37a
Overcharging, land .... Bava Metzia 56a-57b; Temurah 27a
Overcharging, market price changed .... Bava Basra 83b-84a
Overcharging, quality of merchandise .... Bava Metzia 60b
Overcharging, rental .... Bava Metzia 56b
Overcharging, sale without knowing quantity .... Bava Metzia 47a
Overcharging, size of field .... Bava Basra 103b-104b
Overcharging, slave .... Kiddushin 11a; Kesubos 57b-58a; Bava Metzia 56a-56b; Temurah 27a, 57a;
                                                                                                                              Bava Basra 92b
Overcharging, specific field .... Bava Basra 106a-106b
Overcharging, wheat planted .... Menachos 69a; Bava Metzia 56a
Overcharging, which items .... Bava Metzia 56a-56b, 58b
Overcharging, wine and fruit .... Bava Metzia 59b-60a

Misc. —
Overcharging, agent .... Kesubos 99b-100a
Overcharging, amount .... Bava Metzia 50a-50b; Kiddushin 42b; Bava Basra 95a
Overcharging, canceling sale .... Bava Metzia 51a; Bava Basra 95a
Overcharging, compensation for expenses .... Bava Basra 93b
Overcharging, condition .... Bava Metzia 51a-51b; Kesubos 84a; Makos 3b
Overcharging, for whom .... Bava Metzia 50b-51a
Overcharging, interest and theft .... Bava Metzia 61a
Overcharging, seller retracting from sale .... Bava Metzia 50b-51a
Overcharging, smallest (amount) .... Bava Metzia 56b, 61b

Overnight off the Altar
Overnight off the Altar, incense .... Shevuos 10b
Overnight off the Altar, inside sin offerings .... Zevachim 104b
Overnight off the Altar, leftover sacrifice .... Pesachim 71a; Zevachim 87a; Meilah 8a-10a
Overnight off the Altar, libations water .... Succah 49b-50a
Overnight off the Altar, sacrificial blood .... Zevachim 46a
Overnight off the Altar, washing hands .... Zevachim 19b-20b, 21b; Pesachim 2b; Yoma 22a
Overnight off the Altar, water of Temple washbasin .... Zevachim 20a, 21a-21b

O

Overnight stay in Jerusalem, sacrifice........................Succah 47a-47b; Rosh Hashanah 5a; Bikurim 2:4;
....Pesachim 95b; Chagigah 17a-17b

Overstatement
Overstatement, in Torah expressions and Sages' assertions............Chullin 90b; Tamid 29a-29b
Overstatement in vows..Nedarim 24b-25a

Owner
Owner..*see also* **Change of owner**, page 96
Owner, intent during sacrifice..Zevachim 3b, 7a
Owner of beam, first implied..Berachos 64a
Owner of ox is exonerated..Bava Kama 41b-42b
Owner, presence during sacrifice..Sotah 8a; Taanis 27a
Owner, redeeming consecrated item..Arachin 27a; Bechoros 13a
Owner, requirement to redeem..Arachin 27b-28a
Owner with him..*see* **Custody with owner**, page 138
Owner's consent, *eruv*..Eruvin 46b, 80b, 81b, 81b-82a, 95a
Owners' consent, impurity of food..Bava Metzia 22a-22b

Owner died
Owner died, guilt offering....................................Pesachim 73a; Shevuos 12a; Temurah 20b
Owner died, permitting of atonement sacrifices................................Menachos 4b
Owner died, sacrifice..Zevachim 5b-6a

Owner's money
Owner's money, *challah*..Kiddushin 53a
Owner's money, sacrifice........Bava Kama 12b-13a; Kiddushin 52b-53a; Pesachim 90a; Bava Basra 123b;
....Sanhedrin 112b; Zevachim 114a; Bechoros 53b
Owner's money, *terumah*..Kiddushin 53a-53b

Ownerless
Tithe —
Ownerless for three days..Nedarim 43b-44a
Ownerless, fruit exempt from *demai*................................Berachos 40b-41a; Demai 1:1; Eruvin 18a
Ownerless, fruit exempt from tithe..Demai 1:1
Ownerless to avoid *tevel*..Bava Kama 69a-69b
Ownerless, vegetables exempt from tithe..Maasros 5:8

Misc. —
Ownerless, damaging ox..Bava Kama 13b
Ownerless, declared by *beis din*............................Bava Kama 96b; Gittin 36b; Yevamos 89b
Ownerless field, fruit after harvest..Nedarim 62a; Pesachim 6b
Ownerless, giving to man forbidden by vow to benefit......................Kesubos 70b-71a
Ownerless item, acquiring by staring, looking..................................Bava Metzia 2a, 118a
Ownerless on Sabbatical year..Sheviis 4:2; Kiddushin 52a, 53a
Ownerless, ox about to be stoned and condemned city......................Krisos 24a
Ownerless, when is it effective..Nedarim 43a-45a; Peah 6:1

Ownership of domains, *eruv*..Eruvin 84b, 88a

Ox
Consecrated —
Ox among my oxen, consecrated items..Menachos 108b
Ox for sacrifice, age..Parah 1:2; Rosh Hashanah 10a
Ox in stadium games, sacrifice..Bava Kama 40b
Ox, not all are destined to Altar..Bava Kama 98a

O

Damages —

Ox, consecrated, caused a damage .... Bava Kama 37b-38a
Ox, crouching .... Bava Kama 16a
Ox, damage in custodian's house .... Bava Kama 13b-14a
Ox damaged courtyard .... Bava Kama 48a
Ox, jumping .... Bava Kama 21b-22a
Ox, protection from damage .... Bava Kama 45b-46a, 55b
Ox, wagging tail .... Bava Kama 19b

Episodes —

Ox called "field," Rabbi Yose .... Shabbos 118b; Gittin 52a
Ox drank alcoholic beverage .... Bava Kama 35a
Ox of Adam .... Chullin 60a; Shabbos 28b; Avodah Zarah 8a
Ox without teeth, custodian (*apotropus*) .... Bava Metzia 42b

Goring —

Ox, cases of exemption .... Bava Kama 44b
Ox, different from man who damaged .... Bava Kama 34b-35a
Ox goring, doubt .... Bava Kama 13b, 35a-36a
Ox goring, sold .... Bava Kama 46a
Ox which gored, belonging to deaf-mute, demented or minor .... Bava Kama 39a-40a
Ox which gored heifer, doubt .... Bava Kama 46b-47a
Oxen gore generally or not .... Kesubos 41a; Bava Kama 15b

Pit —

Ox and not man, pit .... Bava Kama 53b-54a
Ox dug pit .... Bava Kama 48a, 51a
Ox fell, sharpen your knife .... Shabbos 32a
Ox fouled water in pit .... Bava Kama 48b, 53a
Ox which fell in pit .... Bava Kama 44a, 48b
Ox, wild, fell into pit .... Bava Kama 52b, 54a-54b

Scientific facts —

Ox, a day old .... Bava Kama 65b
Ox, choicest domestic animal .... Bava Metzia 86b
Ox, danger .... Pesachim 112b; Berachos 33a
Ox fattened, work .... Avodah Zarah 16a
Ox fell and slaughterer sharpens his knife .... Sanhedrin 98b
Ox, king of animals .... Chagigah 13b
Ox, whisper .... Pesachim 112b
Oxen, color and quality .... Nazir 31b; Chullin 60a

Misc. —

Ox on Sinai, how many judges .... Sanhedrin 15b
Ox, other animals .... Bava Kama 54b
Ox slaughtered, *migo* .... Kesubos 16a
Ox, wild, fats and covering of blood requirement .... Chullin 80a

Ox goring occasionally

Collecting —

Ox goring occasionally, collecting from calf and egg .... Bava Kama 47a
Ox goring occasionally, damage precedes loan .... Bava Kama 33b-34a
Ox goring occasionally, damaged several times .... Bava Kama 36a-36b
Ox goring occasionally, loss and gain of value .... Bava Kama 15a, 34a
Ox goring occasionally, *neveilah* .... Bava Kama 10b-11a, 15b, 53b, 34a-34b

Ox goring occasionally, pay for plowing .... Bava Kama 91a
Ox goring occasionally, serving as payment .... Bava Kama 15a, 16b
Ox goring occasionally, way of paying .... Bava Kama 33a-33b, 34a, 36a
Misc. —
Ox goring occasionally, half payment for atonement for human death .... Bava Kama
.... 41b-42b, 48b
Ox goring occasionally, in damaged person's property .... Bava Kama 14a-14b,
.... 15b-16a, 18b, 24b-25a
Ox goring occasionally, leniencies .... Bava Kama 41b-42b
Ox goring occasionally, sacrifice .... Bava Kama 13a-13b
Ox goring occasionally which gored regularly, custodian .... Bava Kama 40a-40b
Ox goring occasionally, which injured man .... Bava Kama 5a, 33a; Arachin 14b

Ox goring regularly
Ox goring men regularly, how is it possible .... Bava Kama 41a
Ox goring regularly, change of status by new custodian .... Bava Kama 39b, 40b
Ox goring regularly, *chazakah* of three times .... Bava Kama 23b-24a; Kesubos 64b-65a
Ox goring regularly, claims of custodian .... Bava Kama 40a-40b
Ox goring regularly, other species and intermittent .... Bava Kama 2b, 37a-37b, 45b
Ox goring regularly, ox or owner .... Bava Kama 24a-24b, 41a
Ox goring regularly, pebbles flung .... Bava Kama 18a-19a
Ox goring regularly, retains half-sum payment .... Bava Kama 18a, 39b, 45b
Ox goring regularly, returning to normal .... Bava Kama 37a
Ox goring regularly, testimony .... Bava Kama 24a-24b

Ox to be stoned
Ox to be stoned, before verdict .... Bava Kama 44b-45a, 98b
Ox to be stoned, belonging to woman and orphan .... Bava Kama 44b
Ox to be stoned, benefit .... Pesachim 22b; Kiddushin 56b-57a; Bava Kama 41a-41b
Ox to be stoned, children .... Bava Kama 43b-44a
Ox to be stoned, despairing of ownership .... Krisos 24a
Ox to be stoned, in custodian's house .... Bava Kama 45a-45b
Ox to be stoned, in domain of damaged person .... Bava Kama 23b
Ox to be stoned, intention .... Bava Kama 44b
Ox to be stoned, intermingled with others .... Sanhedrin 79b-80a
Ox to be stoned, judgment .... Sanhedrin 36b
Ox to be stoned, killed and damaged .... Bava Kama 90b-91a
Ox to be stoned, owner not liable .... Sanhedrin 15a-15b
Ox to be stoned, ownerless and consecrated .... Bava Kama 13b, 44b
Ox to be stoned, *Sanhedrin* .... Sanhedrin 15a
Ox to be stoned, *treifah* .... Sanhedrin 78a
Oxen goring occasionally and regularly, five .... Bava Kama 15b
Oy .... *see* **Woe**, page 754
Oznayim laTorah .... *see* **"Handles for Torah,"** Solomon, page 268

P

Paced backwards, forgot..Berachos 29b

Pachaz kamayim, initials...Shabbos 55b

Pachin ketanim..*see* **Jugs, small, precious,** page 329

Pack saddle, animal carrying on Shabbos..Shabbos 52b-53a, 54b

Paid

Paid back in one payment, enemy...Avodah Zarah 4a

Paid bill, oath..Shevuos 41a

Paid but did not swear...Bava Metzia 33b-34b, 37a

Paying back before due time...Bava Basra 5a-6a

Paying back in his own coin, swindler...Bava Metzia 101b

Paying employee on same day...Bava Metzia 110b-112a

Paying on time, rent...Bava Metzia 111b

Paying on time, salary...Bava Metzia 110b-112a

Paying to escape trial...Bava Basra 30b

Pail goes to river, whole, not broken..Berachos 58a

Pain

Pain...*see also* **Suffering,** page 662

Pain, associating G-d's Name...Berachos 63a

Pain, dispensation concerning decree of Yom Tov..Yevamos 114a

Pain during birth..Sotah 12a

Pain, evaluation...Bava Kama 84b-85b

Pain, expressions..Berachos 28a

Pain in raising children, Abraham...Sanhedrin 19b

Pain in raising children, curses..Eruvin 100b

Pain of animals...Bava Metzia 32b-33a; Shabbos 128b, 154b

Pain of G-d when punishing wicked...Sanhedrin 46b; Chagigah 15b

Pain of Rabbi Chiya's sons...Berachos 18b

Pain of raped or seduced girl..Kesubos 39a-39b; Bava Kama 59a

Pain, Sages did not decree in case of pain..Kesubos 60a

Pain, with loud voice..Sotah 32b

Painful, succah...Succah 25b

Painting

Painting *Heichal* and Altar..Middos 3:4

Painting tree whose fruit fall prematurely...................................Shabbos 67a; Chullin 77b-78a

Pairs
Pairs, danger..Pesachim 110a-111a; Berachos 51b
Pairs, death of Rabbah..Bava Metzia 86a
Pairs, *Nasi* and *Av Beis Din*..Chagigah 16a-16b
Pairs of divorcee, episode...Pesachim 110b
Palginan dibura...*see* **Dividing speech, page 168**
Palm frond...*see* *Lulav*, page 380
Palm tree
Palm tree, dream...Yoma 87b
Palm tree, evaluation of damage...Bava Kama 58b-59b
Palm tree, Israel...Succah 45b
Palm tree, only one heart...Megillah 14a
Palm tree, two halves...Kesubos 109b
Palm trees, dangers...Pesachim 111a-111b
Palm trees, graft..Pesachim 56a
Palm trees of Babylon...Taanis 29b
Palm trees of Babylon, Gog's horses...Sanhedrin 98b
Palm trees, taste of wine...Bava Kama 92a
Palm trees, valleys..Pesachim 53a
Paltiel, Michal...Sanhedrin 19b-20a
Paltihu, captives..Kiddushin 72b
Pamalya shel maalah.......................*see* **Heavenly Host, stronger than sorcery, page 274**
Pan fried meal offering...Menachos 63a
Panim chadashos...*see* **New faces, page 442**
Panther, full responsibility for damages..Bava Kama 16a
Pants
Pants, destruction of semen...Niddah 13b
Pants of *Kohanim*, atonement..Zevachim 88b; Arachin 16a
Pants of *Kohanim*, shape...Niddah 13b
Pappa bar Aba, bunk...Bava Kama 10b
Paper
Paper, blank, divorce certificate..Gittin 19b-20a
Paper, blank, signature..Bava Basra 167a; Kesubos 21a
Paper, impurity of utensils..Keilim 17:15
Paper of divorce certificate, condition...Gittin 20b, 75a-75b
Papus
Papus and Lilianus..Taanis 18b
Papus, Rabbi Akiva...Berachos 61b
Par mashiach..*see* **Bull for *Kohen Gadol*, page 79**
Parable
Parable, dead resurrected by Ezekiel...Sanhedrin 92b
Parable, Job's story...Bava Basra 15a-16b
Parable, what can son do...Berachos 32a
Parables of Rabbi Meir...Sanhedrin 38b-39a
Parables of Solomon...Eruvin 21b
Parable for Israel
Parable for Israel, apple tree...Shabbos 88a
Parable for Israel, dove..Berachos 53b
Parable for Israel, olive tree...Menachos 53b

P

Parable for Israel, palm tree..Succah 45b

Parah adumah..*see* **Red Heifer**, page 551

Parati.....................................*see* **I paid, considered like liar in** *beis din*, page 291

Parchment

Parchment, bird and fish..Shabbos 108a

Parchment, for its use...Gittin 54b

Parchment, hole...Shabbos 108a; Chullin 119b

Parchment, *kosher*..Shabbos 108a

Parchment, which is used for which holy parchments................Shabbos 79b

Parchments of Torah scroll, size..Menachos 30a

Pardes, four Sages came into..Chagigah 14b, 15b-16a

Parech..*see* ***Farech, peh rach,*** **soft tongue**, page 214

Parents

Parents...*see also* **Father and mother**, page 217

Parents died before wedding..Kesubos 3b-4b

Pargod...*see* **Curtain**, page 136

Parhedrin Room, Temple...Yoma 8b

Parnasah...*see* **Livelihood**, page 374

Parnas..*see* **Leader of community**, page 356

Paroches..*see* **Cloth partition**, page 112

Paroh...*see* **Pharaoh**, page 486

Parsah, time...Pesachim 46a; Chullin 122b-123a

Parshah..*see* **Section**, page 597

Parshas

Parshas Hachodesh..Megillah 30a-30b

Parshas Parah..Megillah 30a-30b

Parshas Shekalim..Megillah 29b-30b

Parshas Zachor..Megillah 18a, 30a-30b

Parshtavina, height...Niddah 24b

Parsiim...*see* **Persians**, page 482

Part of

Part of awareness, impurity..Shevuos 19b

Part of damage...Bava Kama 10a-10b

Part of fruit purchase, act of acquisition....................Bava Basra 86b-87a, 106b

Part of man's praise in his presence..Eruvin 18b

Part of tree in ground, tithes...Gittin 22a

Part of womb, intervening substance......................................Bechoros 9b

Part of work, Shabbos...Shabbos 103a-103b

Part of year, like whole year........Rosh Hashanah 2b, 10a-10b; Chagigah 5b; Makos 3b; Niddah 44b-45a

Parts of the night..Berachos 3a-3b

Part of day

Part of day, like whole day.................................Pesachim 55a; Bechoros 21b-21a

Part of day like whole, in which case...................................Nazir 15a-15b

Part of day, mourning............................Moed Katan 17b, 19b; Nazir 15b; Pesachim 4a

Part of day, *nezirus*...Nazir 5b-6a, 15a-15b

Part of day, *zavah*..Nazir 15b-16a

Part of sacrifice

Part of sacrifice, impurity..Menachos 14b-15a

Part of sacrifice, out of place....................................Zevachim 25b-26a

P

Part of sacrifice, thought .... Menachos 13b-14b

Partial raising of item .... Bava Metzia 7a

Participating in Pesach lamb

Participating in Pesach lamb, money .... Pesachim 89b-90a

Participating in Pesach lamb, withdrawing .... Pesachim 99a

Particular with His creatures .... Avodah Zarah 3a

Parting from one's teacher .... Moed Katan 9a

Partition

How —

Partition, breached part equal to existing .... Eruvin 5b, 10b, 15b-16b; Kilayim 4:4; Succah 15a-15b

Partition hanging .... Eruvin 12a, 16b, 48a, 86b; Succah 16a-16b; Shabbos 97a, 101a-101b

Partition, height .... Succah 4b-5b

Partition, men standing .... Eruvin 44a-44b

Partition, not made by man .... Succah 24a-24b

Partition removable by wind .... Eruvin 8a

Partition standing by itself .... Eruvin 15a-15b

Partition standing in air .... Succah 23a, 24a

Impurity —

Partition, impurity of tent .... Succah 13b; Oholos 7:2, 8:1-5

Partition in utensil, purity .... Shabbos 15b; Keilim 4:4, 10:7-8; Oholos 8:1-3; Zevachim 3a

Partition on window, tent .... Bava Basra 19b-20b; Oholos 13:5-6

Partition, receiving impurity .... Oholos 6:1-2, 11:8-9; Bava Basra 19b

Partition, sky-light .... Oholos 5:2-5

Shabbos —

Partition for Shabbos, episode about removal .... Eruvin 11b, 74a-74b

Partition for stringency .... Eruvin 92b-93a

Partition made on Shabbos .... Shabbos 101b

Partition, making on Shabbos .... Eruvin 43b-44b

Partition, not for dwelling .... Eruvin 26a

Partition of ropes .... Eruvin 93a

Partition of woof or warp .... Eruvin 16b-17a

Partition, private domain .... Eruvin 11b, 12b, 95a

Partition upon partition, empty land .... Eruvin 25a

Partition which fell on Shabbos .... Eruvin 95a

Misc. —

Partition, between men and women .... Kiddushin 81a; Succah 51b

Partition, division or fence .... Bava Basra 2a-3a

Partition for *chametz* on Pesach .... Pesachim 6a

Partition for lamp, intimate relations .... Pesachim 112b

Partition for mixed species .... Eruvin 92a-93a

Partition, *Halacha* from Sinai .... Succah 6b

Partition of four handbreadths, succah .... Succah 16b

Partition of iron, since Temple destruction .... Berachos 32b

Partition of succah, how many .... Succah 7a

Partition on partition, act of acquisition .... Eruvin 25a

Partner

Commandments —

Partners, exemption from commandments .... Chullin 135a-136a

Partners, separating tithes .... Terumos 3:3; Temurah 13a

P

Partners, shoulder, cheek, and stomach .... Chullin 133a-133b
Partners, tithes .... Chullin 135a-136a

Damages —
Partner, custody with owner .... Bava Basra 43a-43b
Partner, making pit .... Bava Kama 51b
Partners in damage .... Bava Kama 10a-10b, 13a, 28b, 51a-51b, 53a-53b
Partners who stole, penalty .... Shabbos 93b; Bava Kama 78b; Bava Metzia 8a

Monetary matters —
Partner, appeal against decision .... Kesubos 94a
Partner, established rights on land .... Bava Basra 42a-42b
Partner, like worker with permission .... Bava Basra 42b
Partner, vow .... Shevuos 48b
Partner who saved money, for whom .... Bava Kama 116b
Partner, withdrawing from partnership to testify .... Bava Basra 43a
Partners in courtyard, approved use .... Bava Basra 57a-57b
Partners, prohibition of testimony .... Shevuos 31a

Sacrifices —
Partner, Jewish, firstborn .... Chullin 135b
Partner, non-Jewish, firstborn ..... Pesachim 6a; Bava Metzia 16a-17a, 70b; Chullin 135b; Bechoros 3a-3b, 9b
Partners, invalidating sacrifice .... Temurah 26a-26b; Kiddushin 7a-7b; Zevachim 12a; Krisos 27a
Partners, sacrifices .... Menachos 104b
Partners, tithe of animal .... Bechoros 56b
Partners, waving sacrifice .... Menachos 62b, 93b-94a

Sharing —
Partner, sharing without three appraisers .... Bava Metzia 31b-32a
Partner, when will he sell .... Gittin 31b
Partner who shared without permission .... Bava Metzia 69a-69b
Partners for meal, canceling partnership .... Pesachim 89b
Partners, sharing profits .... Kesubos 93a-93b
Partners, size for sharing .... Bava Basra 12a

Misc. —
Partner in learning .... Taanis 7a; Berachos 63b; Makos 10a
Partners, joint venture .... Bava Metzia 105a
Partners for learning without teacher, when .... Shabbos 63a
Partners in man, fetus .... Niddah 31a
Partners who vowed .... Nedarim 45b-46b; Bava Basra 57b; Beitzah 39b; Bava Kama 51b

Partnership
Partnership for *eruv*, courtyard permitted .... Eruvin 73a-73b, 71b-72a
Partnership for *eruv*, open courtyards .... Eruvin 73b
Partnership in Sage's Torah .... Sotah 21a
Partnership with man who goes through favorable times .... Pesachim 112a, 113a

Partnership with non-Jew
Partnership with non-Jew, firstborn .... Bava Metzia 70b; Bechoros 16a-16b
Partnership with non-Jew, oath .... Sanhedrin 63b; Bechoros 2b
Partnership with non-Jew, *orlah* .... Avodah Zarah 22a
Partnership with non-Jew, Shabbos .... Avodah Zarah 22a

Parutz ke'omeid .... *see* **Breached part equal to existing, partition**, page 75
Pas besalo .... *see* **Bread in basket, feeling satiated**, page 75
Pas goy .... *see* **Bread of non-Jew**, page 75

P

Pas kisnim..*see* **Cakes, blessing,** page 84
Pasei biraos..................*see* **Boards at an angle, determining domains,** page 70
Pashat lo haregel..*see* **Bankrupt,** page 41

Passageway
Passageway, act of acquisition.......................................Bava Basra 100a
Passageway between courtyards, *eruv*.......................Eruvin 59b, 65b, 75a-75b
Passageway, decisions about *Eretz Yisrael*.........................Bava Kama 80b
Passageway for public in his field, displaced......Bava Basra 99b-100a; Bava Kama 28a
Passageway in fellow's courtyard, right................................Bava Basra 64a
Passageway, one of two things....................Kesubos 109b; Yevamos 37b
Passageway used by the public.....................Bava Basra 12a, 26b, 60b
Passageway where difficult to walk, Shabbos...............Shabbos 8b, 100b

Passing
Passing between women...Pesachim 111a
Passing by commandments, *tefillin*..............................Yoma 33b
Passing by commandments, zeal....Yoma 33a-33b, 58b; Pesachim 64b; Megillah 6b; Menachos 64b
Passing from one subject to another, *kiddushin*.................Kiddushin 6a
Passing in front of praying man..................................Berachos 27a
Passing over impure place, impurity..............................Zevachim 93a
Passing through fire, idolatry...............................Sanhedrin 64a-64b

Passover...*see* **Pesach,** page 484

Past its time
Past its time, after slaughtering..................................Zevachim 25b
Past its time, *mussaf* sacrifice..................................Temurah 14a
Past its time, sacrifice is disqualified............................Berachos 26a

***Pasul* or correction,** wording of Mishnayos........................Succah 2a

Path
Path, breadth dimensions..Bava Basra 100a
Path in storehouse, Shabbos.....................................Shabbos 127a
Path in vineyard, *chazakah*....................................Bava Basra 100a
Path in vineyards, road...Eruvin 24b-25a
Paths of Heaven are known to him as those of my city.............Berachos 58b

Patience, episode about red garment...............................Berachos 20a

Patiently waiting for one's hour..................Berachos 64a; Eruvin 13b

Patriarchs
Patriarchs, "passes over the mountains".......................Rosh Hashanah 11a
Patriarchs, "run like horses"...................................Sanhedrin 96a
Patriarchs, "Your sons sinned"...................................Shabbos 89b
Patriarchs, Elijah served them.................................Bava Metzia 85b
Patriarchs, heavenly judgment....................................Arachin 17a
Patriarchs learned in *yeshivah*..................................Yoma 28b
Patriarchs, month of birth....................................Rosh Hashanah 11a
Patriarchs, not ruled by evil urge..............................Bava Basra 17a
Patriarchs, only three..Berachos 16b
Patriarchs, received blessings.................................Bava Basra 16b
Patriarchs spread G-d's name...................................Menachos 53a
Patriarchs, sterile...Yevamos 64a-64b
Patriarchs, upright...Avodah Zarah 25a

P

Patrimony

Patrimony, bought field from his father .... Arachin 14a-14b, 26b-27a; Bava Basra 72b; Gittin 48a
Patrimony, half redeemed .... Arachin 30b-31a
Patrimony, increase in value by buyer .... Bava Metzia 109a
Patrimony, Jubilee year .... Bechoros 52b; Arachin 24a-26b, 29a, 33a; Bava Metzia 79a
Patrimony, *Kohen* .... Arachin 26a, 27a, 29a, 34a
Patrimony, redeeming .... Arachin 30b
Patrimony, redeeming according to years .... Bava Metzia 106a; Arachin 24b, 25a
Patrimony, rocks .... Kiddushin 61a; Bava Basra 102b-103a; Arachin 25a
Patrimony, sold in Jubilee year .... Arachin 29a, 34a
Patrimony, stones .... Arachin 14b
Patrimony, trees .... Bava Basra 72a; Arachin 14a-14b
Patrimony, two years .... Bava Metzia 106a; Arachin 14b, 29b, 30a

Patur aval asur .... *see* **Exempt but forbidden**, page 208
Patur midinei adam .... *see* **Exempt according to *beis din* law, cases**, page 208
Patzua daka, explanation .... Yevamos 75a-76a; Chullin 77a
Pay .... *see* **Salary**, page 585
Payment .... *see also* **Indemnities**, page 307

Payment, accept even bran .... Bava Kama 46b
Payment attributed to other debt .... Shevuos 42a; Kesubos 85a
Payment, bad, reimbursing little by little .... Bava Metzia 77b
Payment by conspiring witnesses .... Makos 2b-3a, 5a
Payment by false witnesses .... Bava Kama 56a
Payment by field, value of damaged field .... Bava Kama 7b-8a; Kesubos 110a
Payment by informer who made a mistake .... Bava Kama 117a, 117b
Payment by judge who made a mistake .... Bechoros 28b; Bava Kama 117b; Sanhedrin 33a
Payment by one who did not testify .... Bava Kama 56a
Payment by ox which gored occasionally .... Bava Kama 15a, 16b
Payment for damage brought about by two causes .... Bava Kama 13a, 28b, 53a-53b
Payment for fellow, non claimable .... Kesubos 107b-108a; Nedarim 33a-33b
Payment for sick leave, slave .... Bava Kama 85b-86a
Payment for working without permission .... Bava Metzia 101a-101b; Kesubos 80a
Payment, found more than necessary .... Bava Metzia 63b-64a
Payment of deposit in desert .... Bava Kama 118a
Payment of married woman's debt .... Bava Basra 139a
Payment of theft, subtracting value of depreciated carcass .... Bava Kama 11a, 94a
Payment to be exempt according to Divine Judgment, cases .... Bava Kama 55b-56a

Payment in advance

Payment in advance, donkey drivers .... Bava Metzia 72b-73a
Payment in advance, having same merchandise .... Bava Metzia 63b, 73a-74b
Payment in advance in store, non-Jewish worker .... Avodah Zarah 63a-63b
Payment in advance, interest .... Bava Metzia 65a-65b, 68a
Payment in advance, orphans .... Bava Basra 174a-174b
Payment in advance, produce .... Bava Metzia 64a, 73a
Payment in advance, sold to fellow .... Bava Kama 103a
Payment in advance, supporting .... Kesubos 102b, 106b-107b; Gittin 51a
Payment in advance, wine .... Bava Metzia 73b
Payment of debt .... *see* **Repayment of debt**, page 558

Pe'ah nochris .... *see* **Wig**, page 747

Pe'os harosh .... *see* **Corners of head**, page 129

Peace

   Aggadah —

      Peace, Aaron .... Sanhedrin 6b

      Peace, Aaron's disciples .... Avos 1:12

      Peace, Sages increase peace .... Berachos 64a; Yevamos 122b; Nazir 66b; Krisos 28b; Tamid 32b

      Peace, utensil to "contain" blessing .... Uktzin 3:12

   Peace, domestic

      Peace, domestic, Bava ben Buta .... Nedarim 66b

      Peace, domestic, Divine Presence between them .... Sotah 17a

      Peace, domestic, Shabbos eve .... Gittin 52a

   Misc. —

      Peace, "I am older" .... Yevamos 65b

      Peace, effort and reward .... Yevamos 109a-109b

      Peace in Heavenly Host, learning .... Sanhedrin 99b

      Peace of government, prayer .... Avodah Zarah 4a; Avos 3:2

      Peace of mind, learning .... Eruvin 65a

      Peace, permitted to lie .... Yevamos 65b; Bava Metzia 87a

      Peace to my soul, separating from community .... Taanis 11a

   Peace offerings

      Peace offerings, communal, eating .... Zevachim 54b-55a, 97b-98a

      Peace offerings, communal, north .... Zevachim 54b-55a

      Peace offerings, eating time .... Zevachim 56b; Pesachim 3a

      Peace offerings, remainder of Pesach lamb .... Pesachim 96b-97b; Zevachim 8b-9b; Menachos 83b

      Peace offerings, second tithe .... Kiddushin 56a; Menachos 82a; Zevachim 50a

Peaceful ways

   Peaceful ways, non-Jews .... Gittin 61a

   Peaceful ways, theft .... Gittin 60b-61a

   Peaceful ways, Torah .... Gittin 59b

Peah

   Exempt —

      Peah, abandoned his field .... Nedarim 44b; Bava Kama 28a, 94a; Chullin 134b; Temurah 6a; Niddah 51a

      Peah, convert and consecrated items Treasury .... Peah 4:6-7

      Peah, harvesting for hay .... Menachos 71b-72a; Peah 2:1

      Peah, partnership .... Chullin 135a-136a

      Peah, poor did not come .... Peah 8:1

      Peah, there are no poor .... Chullin 134b

   Giving —

      Peah, size .... Chullin 137b-138a; Peah 1:2

      Peah, end of field .... Shabbos 23a-23b

      Peah, end of harvest .... Peah 1:5

      Peah, entire field .... Nedarim 6b

      Peah, giving and taking .... Peah 4:1-5, 4:9; Bava Metzia 9b-10a

      Peah, harvesting .... Peah 2:7

      Peah, helping and preventing .... Peah 5:6

      Peah, poor coming into field .... Sheviis 9:7

      Peah, until when .... Bava Kama 94a; Sanhedrin 88a; Makos 16b; Temurah 6a

      Peah, who is entitled to take .... Peah 5:5-6; Bava Metzia 12a

P

Misc. —

Peah, poor took another .... Bava Kama 28a
Peah, size of land .... Peah 3:6; Kiddushin 26a; Bava Basra 27a, 150a
Peah, two fields .... Bava Kama 61a-61b; Bava Basra 55a-55b; Peah 2:1-6, 3:1-5; Menachos 71b
Peah, which produce requires .... Peah 1:3-5; Shabbos 68a; Pesachim 56b-57a; Niddah 50a

Pearl

Pearl, "you wanted me to lose it" .... Chagigah 3a
Pearl in fish, consecration .... Bava Basra 133b
Pearl in fish, episode .... Shabbos 119a
Pearl in sand keeps its name .... Megillah 15a
Pearl, Rav Chisda's daughters .... Shabbos 140b
Pearls, taking out of sea .... Rosh Hashanah 23a

Pebbles in wheat, damage by selecting .... Bava Basra 93b-94a; Beitzah 38b

Pebbles, flung

Pebbles, flung, cases .... Bava Kama 17b-18a
Pebbles, flung, indirect strength .... Bava Kama 18a, 19a
Pebbles, flung, ox goring regularly .... Bava Kama 18a-19a
Pebbles, flung, payment .... Bava Kama 3b, 17b-19a
Pebbles, flung, place .... Bava Kama 19a-19b

Peddler

Peddler, elixir of life .... Avodah Zarah 19b
Peddler knows other peddlers .... Avodah Zarah 22b
Peddlers, villages .... Bava Kama 82b; Bava Basra 22a

Peddling

Peddling, episode .... Sanhedrin 31a
Peddling, gossip .... Kesubos 46a

Pedestal for blood of Yom Kippur .... Yoma 55b, 56b

Peel

Peel, absorption of forbidden substance .... Pesachim 75b-76a
Peel, adding it to attain quantity .... Menachos 70b
Peel of garlic, Sages compared to Ben Azzai .... Bechoros 58a
Peel of roast .... Pesachim 76a; Chullin 96b-97a, 97b, 112a
Peel, *orlah* .... Berachos 36b
Peels, blood of *niddah* .... Niddah 21a, 22a-22b, 54b
Peels, digestion .... Shabbos 108b
Peels of fruit, considered as fruit .... Orlah 1:8; Berachos 36b
Peels of fruit, *muktzeh* .... Shabbos 143a
Peels of *orlah* fruit, dyeing .... Pesachim 22b; Kiddushin 56b; Bava Kama 41a

Peeling

Peeling, *kashering* wine press .... Avodah Zarah 74b
Peeling slice, absorption .... Pesachim 75b-76a
Peeling slice, roasted food .... Pesachim 76a; Chullin 96b-97a, 112a
Peeling wheat on Shabbos .... Beitzah 13b

Peg

Peg which will not move, affirmation .... Gittin 17a
Pegs, impurity .... Keilim 14:3

Peiros .... see **Fruit**, page 240
Peiros ishto .... see **Wife, support**, page 747
Pelican .... see **Stork**, page 658

Pelimo, arrows to Satan, episode .... Kiddushin 81a-81b
Penalty
 Prohibitions —
  Penalty for field cultivated on Sabbatical year .... Sheviis 4:2; Moed Katan 13b; Gittin 44b
  Penalty for son, redeeming slave .... Gittin 44a-44b; Bechoros 3a
  Penalty for transgressing *nezirus* .... Nedarim 20a; Nazir 31b-32a
  Penalty, leaving one's work for *Chol HaMoed* .... Moed Katan 12b
  Penalty of a fifth, took false oath .... Bava Kama 104b-105a, 107b-108a
  Penalty of judge to transgressor .... Bava Kama 117a
  Penalty of *Kohanim*, daily offering .... Menachos 50a
  Penalty of unintentional sinner because of willful one .... Gittin 53b-54b
  Penalty, transgressor's son .... Moed Katan 12b-13a; Bechoros 34b-35a; Gittin 44a-44b
 Penalty for Shabbos
  Penalty for Shabbos, for whom is it forbidden .... Chullin 15a; Bava Kama 71a; Kesubos 34a;
   .... Terumos 2:3; Gittin 53b
  Penalty for Shabbos, leaving food on fire .... Shabbos 37b-38a
  Penalty for Shabbos, source .... Chullin 15a; Bava Kama 71a; Kesubos 34a
  Penalty for Shabbos, transgression of Rabbinical Decree .... Beitzah 17a-17b
  Penalty for Shabbos works ...... Gittin 53b-54a; Terumos 2:3; Shabbos 38a; Beitzah 17b; Kesubos 34a;
   .... Bava Kama 71a; Chullin 15a
 Penalty for virgin
  Penalty for virgin, died or became engaged .... Kesubos 29b, 38b-39a
  Penalty for virgin, fifty .... Kesubos 38a-38b
  Penalty for virgin, girl having broken off betrothal .... Kesubos 38a-38b, 40a, 70a
  Penalty for virgin having bad reputation .... Kesubos 36b
  Penalty for virgin, heirs .... Kesubos 42b
  Penalty for virgin, inheritance .... Kesubos 42b
  Penalty for virgin, minor girl .... Kesubos 29a, 36a, 40b; Chullin 26b
  Penalty for virgin, pain .... Kesubos 39a-39b
  Penalty for virgin, pursuer .... Sanhedrin 73b-74a
  Penalty for virgin, to father .... Kesubos 41b-42a
  Penalty for virgin, to whom .... Kesubos 11a, 29a-36b; Bava Kama 38b; Sanhedrin 73b
 Severest —
  Penalty, committed involuntarily .... Kesubos 34b-35b; Bava Kama 35a; Sanhedrin 79a-79b, 84b;
   .... Chullin 81b
  Penalty, conspiring witness .... Makos 4a-4b; Kesubos 32b-33a
  Penalty, excising of soul .... Kesubos 30a-30b
  Penalty, for underground (*machteres* – cellar) thief .... Sanhedrin 72a
  Penalty, how .... Kesubos 30b-31b
  Penalty, lashes death and money .... Kesubos 37a-37b; Bava Kama 83b; Makos 4b, 13b
  Penalty, money and lashes .... Kesubos 31b-33a; Makos 4b, 13b
  Penalty, muzzling cow .... Bava Metzia 91a
  Penalty, two acts .... Kesubos 38a
  Penalty, two death penalties .... Sanhedrin 81a
 Thief —
  Penalty, custodian who lied .... Bava Kama 57a, 62b, 63b, 106a, 106b, 107b, 108b; Shevuos 49a
  Penalty, custodian's rights .... Bava Metzia 33b-34b, 37a
  Penalty for married woman's stolen items, to whom .... Kesubos 79a
  Penalty for veteran thief .... Bava Kama 96b

P

Penalty for thief, *aggadah* ....Bava Kama 79b

Misc. —

Penalties, city decisions ....Bava Basra 8b

Penalty, excising of soul ....*see* **Excising of soul**, page 202

Penalty, deduced from prohibitions or monetary laws ....Kiddushin 3b

Penalty, must he sort everything ....Bava Basra 94a-95a

Penalty of death by Divine Intervention, age ....Moed Katan 28a

Penalty on capital, because of increase in value ....Bava Kama 30b

Penalty on Cutheans' money ....Bava Kama 38b-39a

Penalty, sacrifice for oath ....Kesubos 42a-43a; Shevuos 36b, 38b

Penalty, seizure ....Bava Kama 15b, 84a

Penalty for atonement

Penalty for atonement, animal coupled to man ....Bava Kama 40b-41a

Penalty for atonement, does not exempt from death ....Arachin 6b; Kesubos 37b

Penalty for atonement, fell in pit ....Bava Kama 44a, 48b

Penalty for atonement, fire ....Bava Kama 43b

Penalty for atonement for ox, general ....Bava Kama 40a

Penalty for atonement for ox, when ....Bava Kama 43a-43b

Penalty for atonement, half slave ....Gittin 42a-42b

Penalty for atonement, intention ....Bava Kama 44a-44b

Penalty for atonement, leg ....Bava Kama 26a, 41a, 44a-44b

Penalty for atonement of murderer ....Kesubos 37b-38a; Arachin 6b; Bava Kama 83b

Penalty for atonement of slave, when ....Bava Kama 43a-43b

Penalty for atonement, ox goring occasionally ....Bava Kama 41b-42b, 48b

Penalty for atonement, slave gored before being freed ....Gittin 42b

Penalty for atonement, tooth ....Bava Kama 44b

Penalty for atonement, women ....Kiddushin 35a-35b; Bava Kama 15a

Penetration, male ....Sanhedrin 55a; Yevamos 54b

Peninnah, sake of Heaven ....Bava Basra 16a

Pentagon, Greek ....Bava Basra 164b

People

People are pleased with him ....Avos 3:10

People are pleased with him, judge ....Sanhedrin 88b

People, impulsive, Rava ....Shabbos 88a

People, Levi included ....Chullin 131a-131b

People of Chavrei, Babylon ....Yevamos 63b; Gittin 17a

People resembling donkey ....Yevamos 62a

People use to, law ....Taanis 26b

Peor

Peor, *batei dinim* ....Sanhedrin 35a

Peor, debasing cult ....Sanhedrin 64a

Pepper

Pepper against bad smell ....Shabbos 65a

Pepper, blessing ....Berachos 36b

Pepper, hot, proverb ....Megillah 7a; Chagigah 10a; Yoma 85b

Pepper, long, health ....Pesachim 42b

Pepper on Shabbos, crushing ....Shabbos 141a

Pepper, *orlah* ....Berachos 36b

Peras, Euphrates, its course and reason for its name ....Bechoros 55a-55b

P

Perat uklal .... *see* **Specific and general**, page 649
Percentage according to final sum .... Bava Metzia 53b-54a
Peret .... *see* **Grapes fallen, for poor**, page 256
Performed
   Performed, "this one performed what is written here" .... Bava Kama 17a
   Performed and accepted .... Shabbos 88a; Shevuos 39a; Makos 23b; Megillah 7a
Perfume
   Perfume .... *see also* **Fragrant spices**, page 238
   Perfume according to dowry .... Kesubos 66b
   Perfume, carrying out .... Shabbos 62a-62b; Avodah Zarah 35b
   Perfume, disgrace for Sage .... Berachos 43b
Perfumer and tanner, trader .... Kiddushin 82b
Perhaps sin will cause .... Berachos 4a; Sanhedrin 98b
Perimeter
   Perimeter, compared with side .... Succah 8a
   Perimeter of scroll .... Menachos 29a-29b, 34a
Permission
   Permission, "you gave permission to leave the lecture" .... Avodah Zarah 19a
   Permission, damages by man .... Bava Kama 48a-48b
   Permission for who violates his vow .... Shevuos 27b-28a; Nazir 31b-32a; Nedarim 20a
   Permission of *beis din*, damage .... Bava Kama 6a, 30a-30b, 62b, 81b; Bava Metzia 118b
   Permission of second act, to perform first .... Beitzah 11b
   Permission or requirement, deduction .... Sotah 3a-3b
   Permission to bring in, custody .... Bava Kama 47a-48a, 59b
   Permission to bring in, worker suffering damage .... Bava Kama 33a
   Permission to marry given to *agunah*, excommunication .... Yevamos 121a
   Permission to put down, who will guard ... Bava Kama 47a-47b, 48b, 59b; Beitzah 40a; Bava Metzia 81b
Permitted
   Permitted after being forbidden, widow awaiting levirate marriage .... Yevamos 27b-28a,
   .... 30a, 32a, 41a, 109a
   Permitted for holy purposes, prohibitions .... Menachos 5b
   Permitted in part, vow .... Nedarim 25b-27a, 66a
   Permitted substance combining, wine of *nazir* .... Pesachim 45a; Nazir 35b, 37a-38a
   Permitted substance combining with forbidden .... Nazir 35b-38a; Pesachim 43b-45a
   Permitted things corresponding to forbidden ones .... Chullin 109b
   Permitted to intermarry between tribes .... Bava Basra 120a
   Permitted to marry one another, disqualified persons .... Kiddushin 74a-74b
   Permitted you are, sin offering .... Horayos 2a
Permitting
   Permitting, more difficult than forbidding ..... Berachos 60a; Beitzah 2b; Eruvin 72b; Gittin 41b, 74b;
   .... Kiddushin 60b; Chullin 58a; Niddah 59b
   Permitting partially, idolatry .... Horayos 7b
   Permitting *treifah* for oneself, suspicious .... Chullin 44b
Permitting for sacrifice
   Permitting for sacrifice, impurity of sacrifice .... Meilah 10a-10b; Zevachim 34a, 45b-46a
   Permitting for sacrifice, left-over sacrifice .... Zevachim 45b-46a
   Permitting for sacrifice, *piggul* .... Zevachim 41b-42b, 44a-44b; Menachos 13a-13b, 14b, 16b, 17a;
   .... Chullin 117b

P

Permitting vow..*see also* **Annulling vow**, page 27
  In which case —
    Permitting vow, separating tithe..Nedarim 59a
    Permitting vows, consecration.............................Nedarim 78a; Bava Basra 121a; Nazir 9a
    Permitting vows, *nezirus*...Nazir 9a
    Permitting vows, oath...Nedarim 28a
  Who and how —
    Permitting vow, drunk and sitting.............................Eruvin 64b; Nedarim 77b
    Permitting vow, expert judge and three judges....Yevamos 25b; Nedarim 78a-78b; Bava Basra 120b
    Permitting vow, explaining it to Rav...........................Gittin 35b; Bechoros 45b
    Permitting vow, for oneself...............................Negaim 2:5; Nedarim 81b
    Permitting vow, in front of him...Nedarim 65a
    Permitting vow, night and relative and standing................Nedarim 77a-77b, 76b
    Permitting vow, vowed from permitting person..........................Nedarim 90a
    Permitting vow, which three...Bechoros 36b-37a
    Permitting vows in front of one's teacher...............................Nedarim 8b
  Women —
    Permitting vow, episodes concerning women.............................Nedarim 66a-66b
    Permitting vow in place of annulling it.................................Nedarim 77b-78a
    Permitting vow of one's wife...Negaim 2:5
  Misc. —
    Permitting vow made in G-d's Name...................................Nedarim 22b
    Permitting vow on Shabbos..Nedarim 77a
    Permitting vow, Rabban Gamliel...........................Eruvin 64b; Nedarim 77b
    Permitting vows, after applying.......................................Nedarim 89b-90b
    Permitting vows, source.................................Chagigah 10a; Nazir 62a
    Permitting vows, unforeseeable situation................Nedarim 64a-64b; Nazir 32a-32b
Persecutes Israel, becomes leader..Sanhedrin 104b
Persia
  Persia and Rome.............................Yoma 10a; Shevuos 6b; Avodah Zarah 2b
  Persia, domination over Israel...Yoma 77a
  Persia, years of reign...Avodah Zarah 9a
Persian, better language..Bava Kama 83a
Persians
  Persians, bear.........................Kiddushin 72a; Megillah 11a; Avodah Zarah 2b
  Persians, customs...Berachos 8b
  Persians, lost item to king.......................................Bava Metzia 28b
Persimmon
  Persimmon, blessing..Berachos 43a
  Persimmon, burning daughter-in-law.......................................Shabbos 26a
  Persimmon, Divine promise..Taanis 25a
  Persimmon, episode about thieves......................................Sanhedrin 109a
  Persimmon, Nebuzaradan..Shabbos 26a
Personal
  Personal interest, rebel...........................Avodah Zarah 26b; Horayos 11a
  Personal Providence, knocking finger.......................................Chullin 7b
  Personal Providence, orchard..Sanhedrin 39b

Personal use
  Cases —
    Personal use, agent .... Meilah 21a; Chagigah 10b; Kiddushin 50a
    Personal use, avoiding stumbling-block .... Nedarim 9a-10a
    Personal use, cases .... Meilah 18a-20a; Bava Metzia 48a, 99b
    Personal use, combining .... Meilah 15a, 18b; Krisos 18b
    Personal use, damage by use .... Meilah 18a-19a
    Personal use, damaging .... Bava Metzia 99b
    Personal use, from when .... Meilah 8a-10a
    Personal use, from which value .... Pesachim 32b-33a
    Personal use, inadvertantly .... Kiddushin 53b-54b
    Personal use, lending .... Bava Metzia 99a
    Personal use, married woman .... Bava Metzia 96b
    Personal use, ownerless .... Nedarim 34b
    Personal use, Rabbinical .... Meilah 2b-3a, 12a-12b
    Personal use, voluntary .... Sanhedrin 83a, 84a; Kiddushin 54b; Pesachim 32b-33a; Krisos 22b
  Disqualified sacrifice —
    Personal use in bird sacrifice, mistake in offering .... Zevachim 66b-68a; Meilah 3a
    Personal use of dead sin offerings .... Arachin 5b; Temurah 21b-22a; Meilah 3a, 10b-11a
    Personal use of disqualified sacrifices .... Meilah 2a, 3a, 15a; Zevachim 66b, 120a; Menachos 102a
    Personal use of impure meat .... Meilah 10a
    Personal use of sacrifice before time .... Meilah 12a
    Personal use, sacrifices which died .... Meilah 2a, 2b-3a, 12a, 15a, 18a
  For which matter —
    Personal use, ash of Altar .... Meilah 9a-9b
    Personal use, commandment performed .... Pesachim 26a; Yoma 59b-60a; Krisos 6a
    Personal use, connected to earth .... Meilah 18b
    Personal use, consecrated ash .... Temurah 34a
    Personal use in *konam* vow .... Yevamos 88a; Nedarim 35a; Shevuos 22a-22b
    Personal use of anointing oil .... Krisos 6b; Meilah 19a-19b
    Personal use of *chametz* .... Pesachim 29a-29b
    Personal use of consecrated seeds .... Pesachim 56b; Temurah 31b; Bava Basra 79a-79b; Meilah 12b, 13a
    Personal use of ember and fire .... Beitzah 39a
    Personal use of *Kohen's cherem* .... Temurah 32a-32b
    Personal use of priestly garments .... Yoma 68b-69a; Kiddushin 54a; Tamid 27a
    Personal use of slave's hair .... Gittin 39a; Sanhedrin 15a
  Sacrifices —
    Personal use, about to throw .... Meilah 5a-6a
    Personal use, before and after throwing blood .... Meilah 7b-8a; Zevachim 85b
    Personal use of blood .... Chullin 116b-117b; Yoma 58b-60a; Zevachim 46a-46b; Berachos 31a;
                                                                                 Meilah 11a-11b, 12a-12b
    Personal use of eggs and dung .... Meilah 12b
    Personal use of money for sacrifice .... Meilah 11a
    Personal use of non-Jew's sacrifice .... Zevachim 45a; Temurah 3a; Arachin 5b
    Personal use of parts of sacrifice .... Chullin 116b-117b; Meilah 12b
    Personal use of parts of sacrifices taken to Altar .... Meilah 10a
    Personal use of sacrifices, source .... Meilah 15a; Chullin 117a; Temurah 32b; Krisos 23b
    Personal use of sin offering, Dead Sea .... Meilah 9b

P

Misc. —

Personal use, annuls consecration............Pesachim 27b; Bava Metzia 99a; Meilah 19b; Kiddushin 55a
Personal use, death..Sanhedrin 83a
Personal use, like mountains hanging by a hair..Chagigah 10b-11a
Personal use, payment..Bava Metzia 55b, 99b; Meilah 9b-10a

Perutah

Perutah chamurah, second tithe..Bava Metzia 52b-53a
Perutah, eating *terumah*..Pesachim 32b-33a
Perutah from pocket, consecrating..Meilah 21b-22a
Perutah, guarding lost item..Bava Kama 56b
Perutah in Medea..Kiddushin 12a
Perutah, *kiddushin*..Kiddushin 12a
Perutah, lost item..Bava Metzia 26b, 27a
Perutah, Rav Yosef..Bava Kama 56b
Perutah, redeeming..Arachin 27a
Perutah, redeeming in present times..Arachin 29a
Perutah, redeeming second tithe..Bava Metzia 53b, 55a; Arachin 27a
Perutah, sitting of *beis din*..Bava Metzia 55a-55b
Perutah, use it to buy food..Chullin 84a
Perutah, value..Kiddushin 12a; Bava Metzia 44b; Eduyos 4:7
Perutah, which substances..Bava Metzia 55a
Perutah worth, *kiddushin*..Kiddushin 12a
Perutah worth, which..Bava Metzia 55a

Pesach *pasuach*............................*see* **Virginity not found, wife could be forbidden**, page 724

Pesach

Pesach..*see also* **Chametz**, page 94; **Pesach lamb**, page 484
Pesach to Shavuos, cure..Shabbos 147b; Pesachim 42b
Pesach, Torah reading and *Haftorah*..Megillah 30b-31a

Pesach lamb

Disqualified —

Pesach lamb, cases of doubt..Pesachim 88b
Pesach lamb, cases of uncircumcised men..Yevamos 71a-71b
Pesach lamb, disqualifying thought..Zevachim 7b, 10b
Pesach lamb, intended for impure man..Pesachim 61b
Pesach lamb, intended for others than those who will eat it............Pesachim 60a, 61a, 62b, 78b;
....Zevachim 23a
Pesach lamb, intended for uncircumcised..Pesachim 61b-63a
Pesach lamb, leaving sacrificial flesh..Pesachim 73b
Pesach lamb, mourner and *onein*......................................Pesachim 91b-92a; Zevachim 99b-101a
Pesach lamb not in its time, peace offerings..Zevachim 8b-9b
Pesach lamb not in its time, intent................................Pesachim 60b-61a; Zevachim 11b-12a
Pesach lamb which became lost..Pesachim 96b-97b
Pesach lambs which became intermingled..Pesachim 88b, 98a-99a

Eating —

Pesach lamb, "roofs caved in"..Pesachim 85b
Pesach lamb and *chagigah*, blessing..Pesachim 121a; Zevachim 37a
Pesach lamb, eating during daytime..Pesachim 41b; Bava Metzia 116a
Pesach lamb, Hillel..Pesachim 85b
Pesach lamb, impossibility to eat..Pesachim 69b, 78b-79a; Zevachim 100b

P

Pesach lamb, parts eaten..Pesachim 84a; Chullin 76b-77a
Pesach lamb, place of eating...Pesachim 85b-86a
Pesach lamb, prohibition of cooking...Pesachim 41a-41b
Pesach lamb, roasting...Pesachim 41a-41b, 74a, 75a
Pesach lamb, sleeping during eating...Pesachim 120a-120b
Pesach lamb, time for eating..............Berachos 9a; Pesachim 120b; Megillah 21a; Zevachim 57b

Lamb —
Pesach lamb, female and older than one year.............................Pesachim 97b-98a
Pesach lamb, heir..Pesachim 98a
Pesach lamb, price of sale..Pesachim 89b-90a
Pesach lamb, sale..Pesachim 90a; Temurah 30b
Pesach lamb, second tithe...Menachos 82a-82b

Offering —
Pesach lamb and daily offering, order...Pesachim 58b-59a
Pesach lamb, blood on floor.............................Pesachim 65a-65b; Zevachim 34b-35a, 60a
Pesach lamb, carrying from Temple..Pesachim 65b
Pesach lamb in impurity.....................*see* **Impurity of community on Pesach**, page 304
Pesach lamb, offering..Zevachim 37a, 56b; Pesachim 64b-65a
Pesach lamb, offering until morning..Pesachim 59b
Pesach lamb, order of offering..Pesachim 64a-64b, 65b
Pesach lamb, overrides Shabbos....................Pesachim 65b-66b, 68a-69a; Eruvin 103a
Pesach lamb, skinning on Shabbos................Shabbos 116b-117a, 133b; Menachos 63b-64a
Pesach lamb, sprinkling.....................Pesachim 64b-65a; Zevachim 34b-35a, 37a, 56b-57a
Pesach lamb, swiftness of *Kohanim*...Pesachim 64a-64b

Participating —
Pesach lamb, being associated with two.......................................Pesachim 98b; Kiddushin 41b
Pesach lamb, counting children......................Pesachim 89a; Nedarim 36a; Gittin 25a
Pesach lamb, counting married woman...Pesachim 87a, 88a
Pesach lamb, counting one's slave...Pesachim 88a
Pesach lamb, doubt in teacher's order...Pesachim 88b
Pesach lamb for one person............................Pesachim 91a, 95a, 99a; Yoma 51a; Kiddushin 42a
Pesach lamb, groups..Pesachim 91a-91b
Pesach lamb in two groups..Pesachim 86a-86b
Pesach lamb, members of group withdrew....................................Pesachim 99a
Pesach lamb, number of participants...Pesachim 64b
Pesach lamb, one for all Israel........................Pesachim 78b; Kiddushin 41b-42b

Misc. —
Pesach lamb, *chagigah* sacrifice....................Pesachim 69b-70a, 71a; Chagigah 8a
Pesach lamb, changing name of remainder....................................Pesachim 64a, 73a-73b
Pesach lamb in Egypt..Pesachim 28b, 96a-96b
Pesach lamb in Egypt and for all generations................................Pesachim 96a
Pesach lamb, long way..Pesachim 92b-94b
Pesach lamb, make oneself ready to offer.....................................Pesachim 69a-69b
Pesach lamb, non-Jew ate Pesach lambs.......................................Pesachim 3b
Pesach lamb, prisoner and man searching for survivors.............Pesachim 91a
Pesach lamb, public sacrifice..Yoma 51a
Pesach lamb, remainder for peace offering....................Menachos 83b; Zevachim 7b, 8b-9b;
                                                                                          Pesachim 70b, 96b-97b
Pesach lamb, *semichah* on remainder...Pesachim 89a

Pesach lamb, women..Pesachim 79b, 91a-91b; Sanhedrin 12b

Pesach Sheni

Pesach Sheni, desert...Succah 25a-25b

Pesach Sheni, doubt..Pesachim 88b-89a

Pesach Sheni, eulogy...Chullin 129b

Pesach Sheni, excising of soul...Pesachim 93a-93b

Pesach Sheni, Hallel...Pesachim 95b

Pesach Sheni, impurity..Yoma 51a; Pesachim 95b

Pesach Sheni, like first Pesach..Pesachim 95a-95b

Pesach Sheni, who..Pesachim 67a, 93a; Challah 4:11

Pesha, rebellion...Yoma 36b

Peshiah..*see* **Negligence**, page 440

Pesichas kever..*see* **Opening of womb**, page 461

Pesik reisha..*see* **Inevitable act**, page 308

Pestilence in town, protection..Bava Kama 60b

Pestle of Temple..Arachin 10b

Petirah...*see* **Death**, page 149

Petter-chamor...*see* **Firstborn donkey**, page 227

Petter-rechem..*see* **Opening of womb, firstborn animal**, page 461

Petumei milei ....*see* **Speaking without commitment, condition at one's disadvantage**, page 649

Pharaoh

Pharaoh, "Who is G-d"...Chullin 89a

Pharaoh, accompanied Abraham..Sotah 46b

Pharaoh, decree on males...Sotah 11a, 12a-12b; Sanhedrin 106a

Pharaoh, Moses..Zevachim 102a

Pharaoh Neco, Josiah...Taanis 22a-22b

Pharaoh, new king..Sotah 11a

Pharaoh, short..Moed Katan 18a

Pharaoh's chariots and Sisera...Pesachim 118b

Pharaoh's daughter

Pharaoh's daughter, Divine anger..Niddah 70b

Pharaoh's daughter, Solomon..Yevamos 76a-76b

Philistine chiefs cited in Tanach...Chullin 60b

Philosopher, bribe..Shabbos 116a-116b

Phinehas

Phinehas, cut *vav* letter...Kiddushin 66b

Phinehas, episode of Zimri..Sanhedrin 82a-82b

Phinehas, Joseph's revenge..Sotah 43a

Phinehas, lineage......................................Sotah 43a; Bava Basra 109b-110a; Sanhedrin 82b

Phinehas, priesthood..Zevachim 101b

Phinehas, shoulder and priestly gifts..Chullin 134b

Phinehas, Torah and greatness...Gittin 59a

Phylacteries...*see* **Tefillin**, page 677

Physical closeness, intimate relations...Kesubos 48a

Physician

Physician, "by this physician"...Avodah Zarah 55a

Physician expert, curing by non-Jew...Avodah Zarah 28a

Physician, for free and impostor..Bava Kama 85a

Physician, heretic, Ben Dama...Avodah Zarah 27b

P

Physician, heretic, dangerous remedy .... Avodah Zarah 28a
Physician, non-Jewish .... Avodah Zarah 27a-28a
Physician, permitted to heal .... Bava Kama 85a; Berachos 60a
Physician, stranger from afar or for free .... Bava Kama 85a
Physician, worthless .... Chullin 121a
Pi tikra .... *see* **Edge of ceiling**, page 187
Picking
  Picking .... *see also* **Gathering**, page 245
  Picking dates .... Shabbos 73b
  Picking, dried fruit on tree .... Chullin 127b
  Picking, mushroom .... Shabbos 107b-108a
  Picking neighbor's dates, impudence .... Bava Basra 33b, 36a
  Picking olives .... Shabbos 73b
  Picking up honey on Shabbos .... Shabbos 95a
Pickled food
  Pickled food, cases of absorption .... Terumos 10:7-10
  Pickled food, like cooked .... Chullin 111b
  Pickled food, wording of vow .... Nedarim 51b
  Pickling foods on Shabbos .... Shabbos 108b
Pidyon haben .... *see* **Redeeming son**, page 553
Piece
  Piece from two pieces .... Krisos 17a-18b, 23a; Yevamos 113a; Chullin 43b; Niddah 14b
  Piece, *menorah* in one piece .... Menachos 28a
  Piece of food suitable for a guest .... Chullin 100a
Pierced ear, slave .... Kiddushin 14b-15a, 21b-22b
Piercing slave's ear
  Piercing slave's ear, for whom .... Kiddushin 21b, 22a, 14b-15a
  Piercing slave's ear, how .... Kiddushin 21b, 22b, 15a; Bechoros 37b
  Piercing slave's ear, when .... Kiddushin 22a
  Piercing slave's ear, reason of commandment .... Kiddushin 22b
Piety, greater level of all .... Avodah Zarah 20b
Pig
  Pig attached to ewe .... Bechoros 24a
  Pig, his food .... Shabbos 155b
  Pig, intestines similar to man's .... Taanis 21b
  Pig, like excrement .... Berachos 25a
  Pig, old, strength .... Shabbos 77b; Avodah Zarah 30b
  Pig, prohibition to trade in pigs .... Bava Kama 80a
  Pig, raising .... Bava Kama 82b
  Pig, siege of Hasmoneans .... Sotah 49b; Bava Kama 82b; Menachos 64b
Piggul (beyond designated time and place for sacrificial services)
  In which case —
    Piggul, bread .... Menachos 15a
    Piggul, guilt offerings .... Zevachim 56b
    Piggul, inside sin offerings .... Zevachim 44a
    Piggul, libations and oil .... Menachos 15b
    Piggul, matters which permit .... Zevachim 44a-44b; Chullin 117b
    Piggul, non-Jew's sacrifice .... Zevachim 45a; Temurah 3a
    Piggul, oil for leper .... Zevachim 44b

P

Piggul, which parts .... Zevachim 35a-35b

Misc. —

Piggul, application of *piggul* law .... Meilah 8a-10a

Piggul, applying when blood is thrown .... Meilah 3b-4a

Piggul causing, lashes .... Zevachim 29b

Piggul, enabling sacrificial flesh to become *piggul* .... Menachos 16b; Zevachim 28b, 42b

Piggul, impurity .... Pesachim 15b, 85a, 120b-121a

Piggul, leaving sacrificial flesh .... Pesachim 82b

Piggul, payment of damage .... Gittin 53a, 54b

Pikuach nefesh .... *see* **Saving a life**, page 590

Pile

Pile of bones .... Berachos 58a; Shabbos 34a; Bava Basra 75a; Sanhedrin 100a

Pile of nuts, Rabbi Tarfon .... Gittin 67a

Piles of wood on Altar

Piles of wood on Altar, arranging .... Tamid 29a

Piles of wood on Altar, incense .... Zevachim 58a-58b; Tamid 29a

Piles of wood on Altar, number .... Yoma 45a

Piles of wood on Altar, *sovev* .... Zevachim 65a

Piles of wood on Altar, space on array .... Tamid 30a

Pilegesh begivah .... *see* **Concubine in Gibeah**, page 119

Pilegesh, explanation .... Sanhedrin 21a

Pilgrimage

Pilgrimage and redeeming .... Kiddushin 29b

Pilgrimage, Jeroboam .... Gittin 88a; Sanhedrin 101b

Pilgrimage, Jeroboam's son .... Moed Katan 28b

Pilgrimage, kings who prevented .... Gittin 88a

Pilgrimage, protection .... Pesachim 8b; Chullin 142a

Pilgrimage, who .... Chagigah 2a-3a, 4a-4b, 5b-6a, 7a-7b; Pesachim 8b; Yevamos 103a; Arachin 19b

Pillar

Episodes —

Pillar broke in house of study .... Bava Metzia 20b

Pillar of fire, deceased .... Kesubos 17a, 77b

Pillar of fire, Rabbi Chiya's son .... Kesubos 62b

Shabbos —

Pillar, carrying higher than ten handbreadths .... Shabbos 99b

Pillar of *eruv*, sitting next to .... Shabbos 141a, 148b; Beitzah 30a

Pillar of nine handbreadths, domain .... Shabbos 8a; Eruvin 33a

Pillar on Shabbos, stakes .... Eruvin 78a

Pillars to skin animals, near Altar .... Middos 3:5

Misc. —

Pillar from *Asheirah* .... Eruvin 80b

Pillar of cloud completes pillar of fire .... Shabbos 23b

Pillar of cloud, seeing inside barrel .... Shabbos 22b

Pillars of foundation of earth .... Chagigah 12b

Pillars of Tabernacle .... Shabbos 98a-98b

Pillars of Torah scroll .... Bava Basra 14a

Pilpul .... *see* **Depth of Torah, Moses' generosity**, page 159

Pimples

Pimples, cure .... Shabbos 133b-134a

Pimples on lung..Chullin 48b

Pin...*see* **Needle**, page 439

Pinchas...*see* **Phinehas**, page 486

Pinchas, Shmuel's brother, slip of the tongue.......................................Moed Katan 18a

Pinchas Hamalbish, Temple officers..Shekalim 5:1-2

Pious

Pious fool..Sotah 21b

Pious ignorant, avoiding to be his neighbor...Shabbos 63a

Pious man

Pious man, closed gatehouse..Bava Basra 7b

Pious man, episode about goat.......................................Bava Kama 80a; Temurah 15b

Pious man, episode about judging favorably..Shabbos 127b

Pious man, fence on Shabbos..Shabbos 150b

Pious man, humble man!...Sanhedrin 11a; Berachos 6b

Pious man, interruption in prayer..Berachos 32b-33a

Pious man, night in cemetery...Berachos 18b

Pious man, Rabbi Yehudah...Temurah 15b; Bava Kama 103b

Pious man threw stones out on public way...Bava Kama 50b

Pious men, Abba Yose..Sotah 49b

Pious men, care..Bava Kama 30a

Pious men, meditated before praying...Berachos 32b

Pious men of Babylon and tough ones of *Eretz Yisrael*.....Taanis 23b; Chullin 122a; Megillah 28b

Pious men, time for intimate relations...Niddah 38a

Pipe

Pipe, blood of *niddah*...Niddah 21b

Pipe, clearing on Shabbos...Kesubos 60a

Pipe, container...Keilim 2:3

Pipe, curved, law of water...Avodah Zarah 72b

Pipe, *mikveh*...Bava Basra 65b; Mikvaos 4:3

Pipe of Tiberias, keeping food warm..Shabbos 39a-39b

Pipe receiving impurity, water of *mikveh*...Mikvaos 5:5-6

Pipe to courtyard, *chazakah*...Bava Basra 59a

Pipe, wine of idolaters..Avodah Zarah 72b-73a

Pirchei kehunah...*see* **Young** *Kohanim*, page 774

Pirtzah korah laganav.......................................*see* **Breach calls to thief**, page 74

Piryah verivyah..*see* **Procreation**, page 505

Pisayon negaim...*see* **Leprous marks, spreading**, page 364

Pischei nedarim..*see* **Opening to legally annul vow**, page 461

Pischei niddah vezavah...........................*see* *Niddah* or *zavah*, **calculations about doubt**, page 444

Pishpeshei haMikdash......................................*see* **Openings of Temple**, page 461

Piskah shel Chavah...*see* **Eve's note**, page 203

Pit

Damages —

Pit, damage by its air space or by fall...........................Bava Kama 50b, 53a, 54a

Pit, distance from neighbor...Bava Basra 17a-17b

Pit, distance from tree..Bava Basra 25b

Pit, domains..Bava Kama 21a-21b, 29b, 49b-50a

Pit dug by animal...Bava Kama 48a, 51a

Pit, enlarging fellow's pit..Bava Kama 51b

P

Pit, movable item causing damage .... Bava Kama 6a, 19b
Pit, not liable .... Bava Kama 52b, 53b-54a
Pit of partners .... Bava Kama 51a-51b
Pit, ox fell backwards .... Bava Kama 53a
Pit, ox fouled the water .... Bava Kama 48b, 53a
Pit, size .... Bava Kama 3a, 51b
Pit, source of damage from the beginning .... Bava Kama 9b-10a

Episodes —
Pit and rat, promise .... Taanis 8a
Pit, cemented, Rabbi Eliezer .... Avos 2:8
Pit of lions, Daniel .... Berachos 57b; Bava Basra 4a
Pit of lions, Rabbi Tanchum .... Sanhedrin 39a
Pit of Joseph .... Shabbos 22a; Chagigah 3a
Pit, stories of drowning .... Bava Kama 50a-50b; Yevamos 121b
Pits of Nechunya .... Bava Kama 50a

Shabbos —
Pit between courtyards .... Eruvin 85a
Pit, combining with surrounding wall .... Shabbos 99a-99b; Eruvin 78a, 99b
Pit, full, canceling partition .... Shabbos 100a
Pit in public domain, Shabbos .... Shabbos 8a-8b
Pit, partition in middle .... Eruvin 86a-86b; Succah 16a-16b

Misc. —
Pit and cistern, difference .... Bava Basra 64a
Pit from which you drank .... Bava Kama 92b
Pit in fellow's property, keys .... Bava Basra 99a-99b
Pit is not filled from its earth .... Berachos 3b; Sanhedrin 16a
Pit, thickness of wall .... Bava Basra 17b
Pit, water included in sale .... Bava Basra 79b

Pitch
Pitch, cooking on Shabbos .... Shabbos 74b
Pitch, tree resin .... Shabbos 20b

Pitcher, look at what is inside .... Avos 4:20
Pithom and Rameses .... Sotah 11a
Pits of dates .... see **Date pits**, page 144
Pitum Haketores .... Krisos 6a-6b
Pitum haketores .... see **Preparation of incense**, page 501
Pitumei milei .... see **Speaking without commitment, condition at one's disadvantage**, page 649
Pity, no pity for one deprived of knowledge .... Sanhedrin 92a
Piv velibo shavim .... see **Mouth and heart equal**, page 428
Place .... see **Put**, page 512
Place

Aggadah —
Place for Sage to innovate in Torah .... Chullin 7a
Place, man honors place .... Taanis 21b
Place of Divine Presence .... Bava Basra 25a
Place predestined to punishment .... Sanhedrin 102a
Place where repented men stand .... Berachos 34b
Place where there is no man .... Avos 2:5

P

Commandments —

Place, final blessing	Pesachim 101a-102a
Place for prayer, importance	Berachos 6b, 7b
Place for slaughtering	Chullin 18a-19b, 27a-27b, 43b-45a
Place for two *tefillin*	Eruvin 95b; Avodah Zarah 44a
Place of burning sin offerings	Zevachim 104a-104b, 105b-106a
Place of Red Heifer service	Zevachim 113a
Place of Torah, dwelling	Kesubos 111a
Place of Torah, Rabbi Yose ben Kisma	Avos 6:9
Place to put on *tefillin*	Menachos 36b-37b; Berachos 13b; Eruvin 95b; Arachin 19b

Prohibitions —

Place, high, in private domain	Shabbos 9a; Eruvin 89a, 90b
Place of object, *chazakah*	Kesubos 75b; Chullin 51a
Place of slaughtering on neck, boiling	Chullin 8b
Place of slaughtering on windpipe	Chullin 18b-19a
Place, unclean, covering one's mouth	Berachos 24b
Place, unclean, Sage	Berachos 24b
Place, unclean, sin to read	Berachos 24b

Temple —

Place of Ark, miracle	Bava Basra 98b-99a; Yoma 21a; Megillah 10b
Place of Ark, sprinkling	Menachos 27b
Place of Temple	Zevachim 54b

Misc. —

Place for stoning	Sanhedrin 42b-43a
Place impure, passing over	Zevachim 93a; Parah 10:5
Place, mark for lost item	Bava Metzia 22b-23b, 25b-26a
Place of eating, *eruv*	Eruvin 72b-73a, 73a, 74b
Place of eating, *techum*	Eruvin 73a
Place of items, *kinyan agav*	Kiddushin 26a-27a
Place of sacrifices	Zevachim 47a-47b
Place of sitting, measurement, for man	Succah 7b
Place of writing, divorce certificates	Gittin 80a
Place, text of legal documents	Bava Basra 172a; Yevamos 116a; Gittin 80a

Placed

Placed in pocket, reviewing	Kesubos 50a; Berachos 28a; Pesachim 72a; Megillah 7b
Placing barrel on earth, Shabbos	Shabbos 141a

Placenta

Placenta, impurity	Niddah 27a; Bechoros 7b
Placenta, is there a fetus	Chullin 77b; Niddah 26a-27a
Placenta of donkey, eating	Bechoros 7b
Placenta of firstborn animal	Chullin 77b
Placenta, permitted after slaughtering	Chullin 77a
Placenta, shape and size	Niddah 26a
Placenta, without fetus	Niddah 18a, 26a; Bechoros 22a
Placenta, woman giving birth and miscarrying	Bava Kama 11a-11b; Niddah 26b-27b

Plag Haminchah .... Berachos 26b-27a

Plague

Plague, fast	Taanis 21a-21b, 22b
Plague, merit of deeds of kindness	Taanis 21b

Plain, signs ....Pesachim 53a
Plank
Plank of ship, rescue..Yevamos 121a
Planks, disqualified for *s'chach*..Succah 15a
Plant
Plant turning to sun..Shabbos 35b
Plants growing quickly..Avodah Zarah 38b
Plants from sown *tevel* and tithe .... Menachos 69b-70a; Nedarim 57b-60a; Terumos 9:6; Pesachim 34a
Plants from sown tithe............................Bikurim 2:2; Nedarim 57b-59b; Menachos 70a
Plants, medicinal..Gittin 68b-70a, 86a
Plants of impure *terumah*..Pesachim 34a; Terumos 9:7
Plants of Sabbatical year ....Nedarim 58a-59b; Sheviis 6:3
Plants of *terumah* ....Shabbos 17b; Terumos 9:5-7; Pesachim 34a; Nedarim 59b-60a
Plants of that year, vow ....Nedarim 55b
Plants, vow ....Nedarim 47a, 52b, 57a-60a
Planting
Planting, consecrated seeds....................Bava Basra 79a-79b; Temurah 31b; Meilah 12b, 13a
Planting, consecrated seeds, personal use ....Temurah 31b
Planting, forbidden seeds ....Menachos 69b-70a; Nedarim 57b-60a; Shabbos 17b; Pesachim 34a;
                                                    Terumos 9:4-7; Sotah 43b
Planting knife into earth to *kasher* it ....Avodah Zarah 76b
Platform, *karmelis* ....Shabbos 7a
Playing
Playing *paspasin,* "hopscotch"..Kiddushin 21b
Playing with dice, testimony................Sanhedrin 24b-25a, 27b; Eruvin 82a; Rosh Hashanah 22a
Playing with nuts, Shabbos..Eruvin 104a
Pleasant
Pleasant behavior..Kesubos 17a
Pleasant smell, sacrifice owner's intention..Zevachim 46b
Pleasant ways of Torah
Pleasant ways of Torah............................Succah 32a; Nedarim 62a; Gittin 59b
Pleasant ways of Torah, four species..Succah 32a
Pleasant ways of Torah, levirate marriage..Yevamos 15a, 87b
Pleased
Pleased that commandment is performed with one's money .... Pesachim 4b; Bava Metzia 29b;
                                                    Bechoros 18b, 58a
Pleased with him ....Sanhedrin 88b; Avos 3:10; Sheviis 10:9
Pleased with him, judge..Sanhedrin 88b
Pleasing countenance..Avos 1:15, 3:12
Pledge ....*see* **Collateral**, page 114
Pliers were made with pliers ....Pesachim 54a
Ploni, Nachshon's sons ....Bava Basra 91a
Plot
Plot against consecrated items Treasury................Bava Basra 174b; Shevuos 42b; Arachin 23a
Plot conceded to public domain..Bava Basra 60b
Plot in cities in *Eretz Yisrael*..Arachin 33b
Plot of land and field, towns in *Eretz Yisrael*....................................Arachin 33b
Plot, payment of *kesubah*................................Arachin 23a-23b; Bava Basra 173b, 174b

Plow

Plow, responsibility of worker..Bava Metzia 80a

Plowing, advice...Bava Kama 30a; Menachos 85b, 87a

Plowing before Sabbatical year...Moed Katan 3b-4a

Plowing, *chazakah*...Bava Basra 36a-37a

Plowing during one day, quantity...Bava Basra 12a

Plowing furrow on Yom Tov, transgressions.....................Makos 21b-22a; Pesachim 47a

Plowing on Shabbos, quantity...Shabbos 103a

Plowing, payment of ox goring occasionally...Bava Kama 91a

Plowing, secondary category of labor..Shabbos 73b

Plucking off hair, Shabbos............................Shabbos 94b; Makos 20b; Bechoros 24b

Plugging up barrel

Plugging up barrel, squeezing on Shabbos...Shabbos 141a

Plugging up barrel, unintentionally.............Shabbos 111a-111b; Kesubos 6a; Bechoros 25a

Plugging up barrel with grease...Shabbos 146b

Pnei hador kekelev..............................*see* **Face of generation like face of dog,** page 213

Pnei, east...Yoma 55a; Menachos 27b

Pocket

Pocket for *tefillin*, holiness..Berachos 23b-24a

Pockets, checking...Bava Metzia 21b

Poel batel...*see* **Worker unemployed,** page 762

Polar star..Pesachim 94a; Eruvin 56a

Pole

Pole, private domain...Shabbos 7b-8a

Poles, bearing...Shabbos 92a

Poles of Ark

Poles of Ark, protruded...Yoma 54a; Menachos 98a-98b

Poles of Ark, revealed love...Yoma 54a

Poles of Ark, taking out and putting in..Yoma 72a

Poletes.............................*see* **Impurity through intimate relations, inside body,** page 303

Policemen

Policemen, commandment to appoint...Sanhedrin 16b

Policemen in war...Sotah 44b

Policemen, *Leviim*..Yevamos 86b

Polishing

Polishing floor on Shabbos...Shabbos 40b

Polishing old items, fraud...Bava Metzia 60b

Polluted air in pit..Bava Kama 50b, 53a, 54a

Pomegranate

Pomegranate, empty ones of Israel.............Sanhedrin 37a; Berachos 57a; Eruvin 19a; Megillah 6a;

....Chagigah 27a

Pomegranate, episode of coercion to marry...Kesubos 61b

Pomegranate, knocking with stick..Uktzin 2:6

Pomegranate of *Kohen Gadol's* robe...Zevachim 88b

Pomegranate, quantity...Keilim 17:5

Pomegranates of Baadan, why were they mentioned.......................................Keilim 17:5

Pool

Pool for immersion..*see* **Mikveh,** page 410

Pool resources...Bava Kama 11b; Bava Basra 139a, 144b

P

Poor
Aggadah —
Poor comparable to dead..Nedarim 64b
Poor does not know his hunger..Megillah 7b
Poor, importance of his meal offering...Menachos 104b
Poor, in intelligence..Nedarim 41a
Poor needing charity, suffers shame..Berachos 6b
Poor, proverbs...Bava Kama 92a-92b
Poor punished by his egg, suffering...Pesachim 118a
Poor, slice from every meal..Berachos 31b
Poor who returns lost item, G-d proclaims...Pesachim 113a
Assisting —
Poor, decent..Succah 49b; Bava Basra 9b
Poor, how much to give him.........Peah 8:5-7; Shabbos 118a; Eruvin 29a; Kesubos 67a-67b; Bava Basra 9a
Poor of another town..Bava Metzia 31b
Poor of your city, loan...Bava Metzia 71a
Poor, sale of his household items before asking for charity...Kesubos 68a
Poor, tithe of his gifts...Sotah 43b; Berachos 40b
Episodes —
Poor, Hillel, learning...Yoma 35b; Sotah 21a
Poor, Rabbi Chanina...Berachos 17b
Poor, Rabbi Yehudah..Nedarim 49b-50a
Poor, Rabbi Yehudah's disciples..Sanhedrin 20a
Poor turning over loaf of bread, episode..Kiddushin 59a
Misc. —
Poor, his requirement to give gifts for poor...Chullin 131a-131b
Poor, property left to borrower.................Bava Metzia 113b-114a; Arachin 23b-24a; Bava Kama 11b
Poor, proud, mind cannot tolerate him..Pesachim 113b
Poor shaking olive-tree, act of acquisition..Gittin 61a
Poor waiting to be invited, suffering...Beitzah 32b
Poor, wheat shortage..Bava Metzia 59a
Poor who estimated for donation.............Bava Metzia 113b-114a; Arachin 7b-8a, 17a, 23b-24a
Poplar
Poplar, parable for Israel..Succah 34a
Poplar, signs..Succah 33b-34a
Popular drink
Popular drink, *havdala*...Pesachim 107a
Popular drink, *kiddush*...Pesachim 107a
Population of *Eretz Yisrael*
....Bava Metzia 28a
Porch
Porch for water, Shabbos...Eruvin 84b, 86b-87a
Porches, connection to *eruv*..Eruvin 79a
Porches, did not make *eruv*..Eruvin 88a
Porches, *eruv*...Eruvin 72b, 84b, 88a
Poreik ol Torah
....*see* **Removing yoke of Torah, punishment**, page 557
Pork, episode about eating
....Chullin 106a
Porridge
Porridge, *chilka*...Moed Katan 13b; Nedarim 55b; Machshirin 6:2
Porridge, eating...Nedarim 49b

Portion of other, World to Come..Chagigah 15a
Poshei Yisrael...*see* **Sinners, Jewish**, page 629
Position of leadership given by Heaven.........................Bava Basra 91b; Berachos 58a
Positioning
   Positioning Altar...Tamid 28b-29a
   Positioning showbread...Menachos 97a, 99b
Positive commandment
   Positive commandment, atonement through burnt offering....................Yoma 36a-36b
   Positive commandment, atonement through sin offering.....................Zevachim 7a-7b
   Positive commandment, exempt from lashes.......................................Makos 13b
   Positive commandment, less severe than negative.............................Yevamos 7a
   Positive commandment, punishment...Menachos 41a
   Positive commandments, women..............Berachos 20a-20b; Kiddushin 33b-35a; Eruvin 27a, 96a-96b
Positive commandment overrides
   Positive commandment overrides, accessory for commandment.................Yevamos 6a
   Positive commandment overrides, at time of transgression of negative.....Shabbos 132b
   Positive commandment overrides, excising of soul.............................Yevamos 3b-7a
   Positive commandment overrides, fellow's money..............................Bava Metzia 30a
   Positive commandment overrides, in Temple.....................................Zevachim 97b
   Positive commandment overrides negative............................Zevachim 97b; Yevamos 7a
   Positive commandment overrides negative, source.............................Nazir 41b-42a, 58a
   Positive commandment overrides, possible to perform both......Yevamos 20b; Shabbos 133a;
   ....Nazir 41a, 58a; Menachos 40a
Possession
   Possession of heir like buyer..............................Bava Kama 111b-112a; Bava Basra 44a
   Possession of one's portion of food, guest..Nedarim 34b
   Possession which changed, status of goring ox..........................Bava Kama 39b, 40b
Possible from impossible, deduction.....................Menachos 19a, 82a-82b; Niddah 37b; Succah 50b;
   ....Yevamos 46a, 61b-62a; Horayos 6b; Zevachim 98a; Temurah 16b, 18b
Possible
   Possible to act differently, unintentional act.................Pesachim 25b-26b; Shabbos 29b
   Possible to squeeze, absorption.......................................Chullin 108a-109a
Postman, eve of Shabbos..Shabbos 19a
Postponing fast...Shabbos 11a
Pot
   Pot, adding to mixture..Chullin 97b, 98a
   Pot, chamber, *niddah* blood...Niddah 59b
   Pot, chamber, prayer...Berachos 25b
   Pot close to non-Jew's pot..Avodah Zarah 11b-12a
   Pot, cold, set on pot, Shabbos...Shabbos 48a
   Pot of two partners, neither hot nor cold..Bava Basra 24b
   Pot used within day..................................Avodah Zarah 67b, 75b-76a; Pesachim 44b
   Pot, wording of vow...Nedarim 51a
Potiphar
   Potiphar...Sotah 13b; Zevachim 118b
   Potiphar, his wife...Sotah 36b; Shabbos 49b; Yoma 35b
Potters, damages..Bava Kama 31a-31b
Poultry
   Poultry and milk, same table.............................Chullin 104a-104b; Shabbos 13a; Eduyos 5:2

P

Poultry, designating for Yom Tov ...... Beitzah 9b, 10a-11a; Chullin 142a
Poultry in milk ...... Chullin 103b-104a, 113a, 116a; Shabbos 130a
Poultry, slaughtering ...... Chullin 4a, 27b-28a, 85b-86a; Nazir 29a; Kiddushin 71a

Pounding meal offering ...... Menachos 76a
Poured
Poured his own wine to save ...... Bava Kama 81b
Pouring, bottom determines and peel ...... Pesachim 75b-76a
Pouring drink, *niddah* ...... Kesubos 4b, 61a
Pouring in cup, impurity ...... Berachos 52a-52b
Pouring in place of throwing ...... Pesachim 89a, 121a; Zevachim 37a
Pouring oil, meal offering ...... Menachos 18a-18b, 20a, 74b-75b
Pouring sacrificial blood, human strength ...... Zevachim 60a
Pouring sacrificial food, *kashering* ...... Zevachim 93a, 95b, 96b

Poured liquid
Poured liquid, connecting impurity ...... Taharos 8:9; Machshirin 5:9-10; Nazir 50a-50b; Sotah 48b; Gittin 16a; Avodah Zarah 72a-72b
Poured liquid, *mikveh* ...... Gittin 16a; Avodah Zarah 72a
Poured liquid, wine of idolaters ...... Avodah Zarah 56b, 71b, 72a-72b

Poverty
Poverty, cases ...... Beitzah 32b; Bava Metzia 59a
Poverty, causes ...... Shabbos 62b; Pesachim 111b
Poverty, difficulty ...... Bava Basra 116a
Poverty, extreme ...... Eruvin 41b
Poverty in Torah, arrogance ...... Sanhedrin 24a; Kiddushin 49b
Poverty, Israel ...... Sotah 49a; Chagigah 9b; Bava Metzia 59a
Poverty, not found in place of wealth ...... Shabbos 102b; Kesubos 106b; Zevachim 88b; Menachos 89a; Tamid 29a, 31b
Poverty, poor man's days ...... Bava Basra 145b-146a; Sanhedrin 100b-101a
Poverty pursues pauper ...... Bava Kama 92a; Bava Basra 174b; Chullin 105b; Arachin 23a
Poverty, Sage does not beg at doors ...... Shabbos 151b
Poverty, suffering ...... Eruvin 41b
Poverty, wheel ...... Shabbos 151b

Power of attorney
Power of attorney, avoid ...... Avos 1:8; Shevuos 31a
Power of attorney, his wife's property ...... Gittin 48b
Power of attorney, lie ...... Shabbos 139a
Power of attorney, proxy ...... Bava Kama 70a; Shevuos 33b; Bechoros 49a
Power of attorney, seizure ...... Bava Kama 70a

Praise
Praise all nations, commentary on verse ...... Pesachim 118b
Praise it in his eyes, purchase ...... Kesubos 17a
Praising a teaching, prohibition ...... Eruvin 64a
Praising friend, derogatory speech ...... Bava Basra 164b; Arachin 16a

Praise
Praise, low voice ...... Sotah 32b
Praise of Amora, great man ...... Bava Kama 40a
Praise of donators to Temple ...... Yoma 37a
Praise of fellow, slander ...... Bava Basra 164b; Arachin 16a
Praise of non-Jew, prohibition ...... Avodah Zarah 20a; Arachin 14a

P

Praise of righteous, blessings fall on his head .... Megillah 25b
Praise of Tannaim, parables .... Gittin 67a
Praise of wicked, prohibition .... Sotah 42b
Praise, only part of it before man praised .... Eruvin 18b
Praises of G-d, "For You, silence is praise" .... Megillah 18a
Praises of G-d before prayer .... Berachos 32a; Avodah Zarah 7b-8a

Pras
  Pras, measure .... Eruvin 82b-83a
  Pras, time for interruption .... Krisos 12b-13a
Pras .... *see* **Persia**, page 482
Prayer
  Aggadah —
    Prayer accepted, humble man .... Sanhedrin 43b; Sotah 5b
    Prayer, blame of who delays .... Berachos 28a
    Prayer, diminution of reward .... Berachos 16b
    Prayer, encouragement .... Berachos 32b
    Prayer, Jacob's voice .... Gittin 57b
    Prayer, greater than good deeds and sacrifices .... Berachos 32b
    Prayer of G-d .... Berachos 7a
    Prayer of righteous, G-d desires .... Yevamos 64a
    Prayer, serving G-d .... Bava Metzia 107b
    Prayer, since Temple destruction .... Eruvin 65a
    Prayers, corresponding to sacrifices .... Berachos 26b
    Prayers, instituted by Patriarchs .... Berachos 26b
    Praying for mercy, blame .... Makos 11a
  Episodes —
    Prayer, "Yishmael bless Me!" .... Berachos 7a
    Prayer, disciples who shortened and who lengthened .... Berachos 34a
    Prayer, episode about snake .... Yerushalmi Berachos 55a
    Prayer, father's grave .... Taanis 23b
    Prayer of Chana .... Berachos 31a-31b
    Prayer of Patriarchs, Elijah .... Bava Metzia 85b
    Prayer of Rabbi Chiya .... Bava Metzia 85b
    Prayer of Rabbi Nechunya .... Berachos 28b
    Prayer of Rebbi, sterile woman .... Kesubos 62b
    Prayer, Rava's requests .... Moed Katan 28a
  Exempt —
    Prayer and learning, preference .... Shabbos 10a
    Prayer, funeral .... Berachos 19a-19b
    Prayer, interrupting learning .... Shabbos 11a
    Prayer, woman .... Berachos 20b
  For which matter —
    Prayer, even for a good burial .... Berachos 8a
    Prayer for journey .... Berachos 29b-30a, 60a
    Prayer for over-abundance .... Taanis 22b
    Prayer for sick, benefit .... Rosh Hashanah 16a, 18a
    Prayer for success in learning .... Niddah 70b
    Prayer for tree with falling leaves .... Shabbos 67a
    Prayer for welfare of government .... Avodah Zarah 4a; Avos 3:2

P

Prayer, revokes decree..Rosh Hashanah 17b-18a; Yevamos 105a
Prayer, sharp sword...Berachos 10a
Prayer to marry so-and-so..Moed Katan 18b
Prayer, wealth...Niddah 70b
Prayer, when wife is pregnant...Berachos 60a

Prayer for one's
Prayer for one's fellow, answered before him...Bava Kama 92a
Prayer for one's fellow, name...Berachos 34a
Prayer for one's fellow, sick...Berachos 12b
Prayer for one's fellow's punishment.................Berachos 7a, 55a; Bava Kama 93a; Sanhedrin 105b;
Avodah Zarah 4b
Praying for one's generation...Bava Basra 91b; Makos 11a

How —
Prayer accepted, when...Eruvin 54a
Prayer before sickness...Shabbos 32a
Prayer before trouble..Sanhedrin 44b
Prayer, beginning with praises of G-d......................................Berachos 32a; Avodah Zarah 7b-8a
Prayer by way of supplication..Berachos 29b; Avos 2:13
Prayer, earnest preparation..Berachos 30b
Prayer easily said, accepted...Berachos 34b
Prayer, heart like flesh..Sotah 5a
Prayer, long...Berachos 32b, 54b-55a
Prayer not to become sick...Shabbos 32a
Prayer, praying abundantly..Yoma 29a
Prayer, service of the heart...Taanis 2a
Prayer, synagogue..Rosh Hashanah 17b-18a
Prayer, tears...Bava Metzia 59a
Prayer, turning one's face..Berachos 30a; Bava Basra 25a, 25b
Prayer, until one is answered...Berachos 32b, 54b-55a
Prayers, abounding in prayer..Yoma 29a
Prayers, exerting oneself...Sanhedrin 44b
Prayers, when are they accepted...Eruvin 54a

Laws —
Prayer, fluent..Berachos 34b
Prayer, intestinal gas...Berachos 24b
Prayer, no separation between man and wall...Berachos 5b
Prayer to stop abundance..Taanis 22b

Prohibitions —
Prayer behind teacher...Berachos 27a-27b
Prayer, holding objects...Succah 41b; Berachos 23b
Prayer immediately before or after urinating...Megillah 27b
Prayer in bathhouse..Shabbos 10a; Berachos 26a
Prayer in open place..Berachos 34b
Prayer, lifting load...Bava Metzia 105b
Prayer, saying *shalom* before...Berachos 14a

Shemoneh Esrei —
Prayer during journey, how..Berachos 30a
Prayer, establishing text...Megillah 17b-18a; Berachos 28b
Prayer, *nedavah*..Berachos 21a-21b; Pesachim 54b

P

Prayer, reason for number of blessings....................Berachos 28b-29a
Prayer, *Shemoneh Esrei*, personal requests.........Berachos 31a, 34a; Avodah Zarah 7b-8a
Prayer, *Shemoneh Esrei*, short.................................Berachos 29a
Prayer, silent, reason...................................Rosh Hashanah 34b-35a; Sotah 32b
Prayer, three daily, source..Berachos 31a

Supplications —
Prayer before bodily needs.......................................Berachos 60b
Prayer of virgin...Sotah 22a
Prayers *"le'es metzo"*...Berachos 8a
Prayers in *Shemoneh Esrei*......................Berachos 31a, 34a; Avodah Zarah 7b-8a
Prayers of Sages.....................................Berachos 16b-17a; Avos 5:20
Prayers, text..Berachos 60a

Times —
Prayer for tragedy on Shabbos.............................Bava Kama 80b
Prayer of *Kohen Gadol*, Yom Kippur..............Yoma 53b; Taanis 24b
Prayer of Rosh Hashanah..Eruvin 40b
Prayer of Sages during Yom Tov discourse.............Berachos 30a
Prayers of Shabbos, *Mekadesh Hashabbos*.........Pesachim 117b
Prayers of Shabbos, mistake...................................Berachos 21a
Praying for one's needs on Shabbos.....................Bava Kama 80b

Undesirable —
Prayer all day, destroying world..............................Sotah 22a
Prayer as a burden...Berachos 29b
Prayer as a fixed duty..Berachos 29b
Prayer not answered, whose.................................Bava Metzia 75b
Prayer, useless, about past......................................Berachos 60a

Misc. —
Prayer, *atirah*.................................Succah 14a; Yevamos 64a
Prayer, strengthening..Berachos 32b
Prayer of *Anshei Maamad*.......................................Yoma 37b
Prayer of *Kohanim* in Temple..........Berachos 11b-12a; Yoma 37b; Tamid 5:1
Prayer of people in Temple.....................................Succah 53a
Prayer on cloudy day...Berachos 32b
Prayer, personal, adding to *Shemoneh Esrei*.......Berachos 29b
Prayer, short.......................................Berachos 3a, 29a-30a

Preceded
Preceded me in house of study.............Megillah 27b; Succah 28a
Preceded world, Creation.....................Pesachim 54a; Nedarim 39b
Precedes man, commandment..............Avodah Zarah 5a; Sotah 3b
Preceding prayer to illness....................................Shabbos 32a
Precedence..*see also* **Order**, page 462
Commandments —
Precedence between blessings.........Berachos 39a-39b, 41a-41b, 43b
Precedence between commandments.....................Yoma 33a-33b
Precedence for loan...Bava Metzia 71a
Precedence of *Kohen*.......Gittin 59b; Moed Katan 28b; Nedarim 62a; Horayos 12b, 13a
Precedence of woman for charity........................Kesubos 67a-67b
Monetary matters —
Precedence between people receiving gift.......Bava Basra 138a; Gittin 50b

Precedence in *beis din* .... Bava Kama 46b; Shevuos 30a; Yevamos 100a
Precedence, returning lost item .... Bava Metzia 33a; Sanhedrin 64b

Precedence in collecting debt
   Precedence in collecting debt .... Kesubos 84a, 86a
   Precedence in collecting debt, apportioning .... Kesubos 93a
   Precedence in collecting debt, seizure .... Kesubos 90a-90b, 94a; Gittin 11b-12a;
   .... Bava Kama 34a; Arachin 7b

Misc. —
   Precedence at judgment, Rosh Hashanah .... Rosh Hashanah 8b, 16a; Avodah Zarah 2b
   Precedence between men .... Horayos 13a
   Precedence for entrance, episode .... Bava Kama 80a-80b
   Precedence, Lot's older daughter before younger .... Bava Kama 38b
   Precedence, one's food before family's .... Chullin 84a

Precious stone
   Precious stone, sun .... Bava Basra 16b
   Precious stones, Jerusalem .... Bava Basra 75a; Sanhedrin 100a

Precise knowledge of one's learning .... Niddah 14b

Precision
   Precision in Divine Judgment .... Bava Kama 50a-50b; Chagigah 5a; Eruvin 22a; Yevamos 121b
   Precision in Sage's name .... Chullin 18b
   Precision in speech, Babylon .... Gittin 65b
   Precision in speech, Judea .... Eruvin 53b
   Precision in teaching, Amoraim .... Berachos 33b; Pesachim 52b
   Precision, is it possible .... Bechoros 9a-9b, 17a-18a; Yevamos 19a, 28a; Shevuos 32a
   Precision, measures of Sages .... Rosh Hashanah 13a
   Precision, teachers' words .... Berachos 33b, 47a; Eduyos 1:3

Predator, impure bird .... Chullin 65a
Preference, no preferential treatment to one child .... Shabbos 10b
Preferring one's own produce .... Bava Metzia 38a

Pregnancy
   Pregnancy, close to menstruation or immersion .... Niddah 31b; Sotah 27a
   Pregnancy, first intimate relations .... Yevamos 34a
   Pregnancy, second during first .... Niddah 27a
   Pregnancy through bath .... Chagigah 15a
   Pregnancy when standing .... Sanhedrin 37b

Pregnant woman
  Marriage —
   Pregnant woman, marital relations .... Pesachim 72b
   Pregnant woman, effects of intimate relations .... Niddah 31a
   Pregnant woman, levirate marriage .... Yevamos 35b-36a, 41b
  Prohibitions —
   Pregnant woman, fast for rain .... Taanis 14a
   Pregnant woman, fellow's wife .... Yevamos 36b-37a, 42a-42b
   Pregnant woman from Jew, *terumah* .... Yevamos 69a-69b
   Pregnant woman, menstruation .... Niddah 9a
   Pregnant woman on Yom Kippur, episodes .... Yoma 82b-83a
   Pregnant woman, retroactive impurity .... Niddah 7a-7b, 8b-9a, 10b-11a, 36a
   Pregnant woman, whispering to her on Yom Kippur .... Yoma 82b

P

Misc. —

Pregnant woman, fetus visible .... Yevamos 37a; Sanhedrin 69a; Niddah 8b

Pregnant woman, nails .... Moed Katan 18a; Niddah 17a

Pregnant woman, prayers .... Berachos 60a

Pregnant woman, pursuer .... Oholos 7:6; Sanhedrin 72b

Pregnant woman, trustworthiness about her fetus .... Kesubos 13a-14a, 16a; Kiddushin 74a

Premature baby .... *see* **Stillborn**, page 656

Preparation

Preparation before lecture, episode .... Taanis 8a

Preparation before listening to lecture .... Horayos 12a; Krisos 6a

Preparation before prayer .... Berachos 15a

Preparation, *muktzeh* .... Shabbos 49b-50a, 125b, 126b

Preparation of incense .... Krisos 6a-6b

Prepare

Prepare a chair, Hezekiah .... Berachos 28b

Prepare yourself in hallway .... Avos 4:16

Prepare yourself, prayer .... Berachos 15a

Prepare yourself to learn Torah .... Avos 2:12

Prepared for dogs, *muktzeh* .... Shabbos 121b; Beitzah 6b; Pesachim 56b

Prepared for man, *muktzeh* .... Beitzah 6b

Prepared for rare animals, *muktzeh* .... Shabbos 128a

Preparing animal food, Shabbos .... Shabbos 155a-155b, 156b

Preparing animal on Yom Tov, *muktzeh* .... Beitzah 25a

Preparing anointing oil, prohibition .... Krisos 5a

Preparing chicken, *muktzeh* .... Beitzah 9b, 10a-10b; Chullin 142a

Preparing cure before illness .... Megillah 13b

Preparing food, Shabbos .... Shabbos 109a

Preparing for weekdays on Shabbos .... Eruvin 38b-39a

Preparing for Yom Tov .... Beitzah 25a

Preparing, makes item forbidden .... Sanhedrin 47b-48b; Megillah 26b; Berachos 23b; Menachos 34b

Preparing from Yom Tov to Shabbos .... Pesachim 46b

Preparing fruit, *muktzeh* .... Beitzah 26b

Preparing poultry, *muktzeh* .... Beitzah 10a-11a

Preparing pure ingredients in time of Amoraim .... Niddah 6b

Preparing signature of witnesses .... Gittin 19a-19b, 9b

Preparing, to permit *muktzeh* .... Shabbos 49b-50a, 125b, 126b

Preparing wick, Yom Tov .... Beitzah 32a-32b

Presence of owner, sacrifice .... Sotah 8a

Present .... *see* **Gift**, page 250

Present tense, verse .... Bava Kama 54b

Present times

Present times, *challah* .... Kesubos 25a-25b; Niddah 47a

Present times, Chonyo's temple .... Megillah 10a

Present times, commandments .... Shekalim 8:8; Kiddushin 37b; Chullin 138b

Present times, consecrating .... Avodah Zarah 13a-13b; Bechoros 53a

Present times, death penalty .... Sanhedrin 37b, 41a; Kesubos 30a-30b; Sotah 8b

Present times, firstborn animal .... Bechoros 26b

Present times, *matzah* and bitter herbs .... Pesachim 28b, 115a, 116b, 120a; Kiddushin 37b

Present times, Sabbatical year .... Gittin 36a; Kiddushin 38b; Moed Katan 2b

P

Present times, sacrifices...............Megillah 10a-10b; Shevuos 16a; Makos 19a; Zevachim 60b, 62a, 107b;
....Eduyos 8:6; Temurah 21a
Present times, sanctity of *Eretz Yisrael*.................Megillah 10a-10b; Shevuos 16a; Makos 19a;
.....................Zevachim 60b, 62a, 107b; Eduyos 8:6; Chagigah 3b; Chullin 7a; Arachin 32b; Temurah 21a
Present times, tithe of animal...Bechoros 53a-53b, 61a
Present times, tithes...Kesubos 25a; Niddah 46b-47a

Preserved
Preserved food, like cooked..Chullin 111b
Preserving ingredient for wheat, parable...Shabbos 31a
Preserving vegetable in pot.................................Taharos 2:1; Berachos 20a; Taanis 24b

Pressing
Pressing hands on head of sacrifice...*see* **Semichah**, page 600
Pressing wine in purity..Pesachim 33b, 34b; Taharos 3:3
Pressing wine, non-Jew..Avodah Zarah 56b

Presumption
Presumption about vows of consecration..Nedarim 28b
Presumption, invalid acquisition.................Bava Metzia 66a-66b; Bava Basra 168a, 173b
Presumption, no reason to suspect problem...Chullin 56b

Pretending
Pretending, carrying on Shabbos...Shabbos 65b
Pretending, how it is permitted on Shabbos.............................Shabbos 117b, 139b
Pretending on Shabbos, penalty...Beitzah 17a-17b
Pretending, permitted, cases...Shabbos 117b
Pretending to avoid tithe.................Pesachim 9a; Niddah 15b; Berachos 31a; Menachos 67b
Pretending, Yom Tov.........................Beitzah 37a; Shabbos 117b, 124a, 139b

Pretext, Cain and Esau...Sanhedrin 101b

Prevent
Prevent your sons from philosophy...Berachos 28b
Preventing forbidden act, bathhouse.................................Shabbos 40b, 41a
Preventing from getting soiled on Shabbos...Shabbos 11b

Preventing a loss.................Bava Kama 58a; Nedarim 33a-33b; Kesubos 107b-108a; Bava Basra 53a

Price
  Interest —
    Price, fixed, purchase.................................Avodah Zarah 72a; Bava Basra 85b-86a
    Price of merchandise fixed, interest.............................Bava Metzia 62b-63b, 65b, 72b
    Prices going up and down, interest..Bava Metzia 64a-64b
  Sacrifices —
    Price of dog..Temurah 30a-30b; Bechoros 57a
    Price of guilt offering for secular use...Kiddushin 12a
    Price of guilt offerings..........................Krisos 22b, 27a; Zevachim 90b
    Price of meal offering..Krisos 10b
    Price of *reiyah* and *chagigah* sacrifices.................................Chagigah 6a-7a
    Price of sacrificial animals.........................Krisos 27a; Menachos 107b
  Misc. —
    Price control...Bava Basra 89a
    Price, is it a proof.................................Bava Basra 77b-78a; Bava Kama 46a
    Price of commandments, episode about lowering ....Pesachim 30a; Succah 34b; Krisos 8a
    Price of field redemption...Arachin 30a
    Price of legal document by *beis din*.................................Bava Basra 155b

Price of merchandise, episodes ... Bava Metzia 40a-40b
Price, sixth for profit ... Bava Metzia 40b; Bava Basra 90a; Menachos 77a
Prices reducing, episode ... Pesachim 30a; Succah 34b; Krisos 8a

Pride

Pride about Divine gifts, punishment ... Sotah 10a
Pride, because prayer was accepted ... Taanis 8a
Pride, differences of opinion ... Sotah 47b; Chullin 7a
Pride, fall from greatness ... Megillah 13b; Zevachim 102a
Pride, G-d humiliates the proud ... Eruvin 13b, 54a; Zevachim 102a; Megillah 13b; Nedarim 55a
Pride, loss of one's learning ... Eruvin 55a
Pride, marriage ... Sotah 47b
Pride of Hiram ... Chagigah 13a
Pride, proud stricken ... Sotah 10a
Pride, punishment of leprosy ... Arachin 16a
Pride, unsuited for woman ... Megillah 14b

Priest

Priest ... see also **Kohen**, page 345
Priest, idolatrous, episodes ... Sanhedrin 63b

Priestly blessing ... see **Bircas Kohanim**, page 58

Priestly garments

Priestly garments, atonement ... Yoma 72a-72b; Zevachim 88b
Priestly garments, benefit ... Yoma 25a, 35b
Priestly garments, disqualified ... Zevachim 18a-18b, 35a; Pesachim 65b; Yoma 35b
Priestly garments, donning ... Yoma 5b-6a, 24b; Tamid 5:3
Priestly garments, *Kohen Gadol* on Yom Kippur ... Yoma 12b, 35a-35b
Priestly garments, laundering ... Zevachim 88a-88b
Priestly garments, lottery ... Yoma 24b-25a
Priestly garments, making ... Yoma 71b-72b; Zevachim 18b
Priestly garments, secular use ... Kiddushin 54a
Priestly garments, *shatnez* ... Yoma 69a; Tamid 27a-27b
Priestly garments, superfluous ... Eruvin 103b-104a; Zevachim 19a-19b
Priestly garments, tearing ... Yoma 72a

Priestly garments, performing service without

Priestly garments, performing service without, death ... Sanhedrin 83b; Zevachim 17b
Priestly garments, performing service without, desecration ... Zevachim 17b-18a
Priestly garments, performing service without, which services ... Zevachim 112b

Priestly gifts

Priestly gifts ... see also **Shoulder, cheek and stomach**, page 620
Priestly gifts before granting ... Makos 20a; Nedarim 85a; Kiddushin 58b; Bava Basra 123b; Chullin 130b; Bechoros 11a
Priestly gifts, doubt ... Chullin 134a-134b
Priestly gifts, ignoramus ... Sanhedrin 90b; Chullin 130b
Priestly gifts, in case of sale ... Chullin 131a, 132a, 138a-138b; Bava Kama 115a
Priestly gifts, new teaching from Rav ... Shabbos 10b
Priestly gifts, ordinary use ... Chullin 131a; Bikurim 3:12
Priestly gifts, Sabbatical year ... Bechoros 12b
Priestly gifts, thief ... Chullin 134a; Bava Kama 115a
Priestly gifts, to only one *Kohen* ... Eruvin 63a
Priestly gifts, to which *Kohen* ... Chullin 132b-133a

Priestly gifts, twenty four .... Chullin 133b; Bava Kama 110b

Primary
Primary and accessory, blessing .... Berachos 35b-36a, 41a, 44a
Primary and secondary Shabbos labors, sin offerings ...... Krisos 16a-16b; Shabbos 68a, 75b, 96b, 97b;
.... Bava Kama 2a
Primary impurities, levels .... Keilim 1:1-4; Bava Kama 2a-2b
Primary Shabbos labors, list .... Shabbos 73a
Primary Shabbos labors, number .... Shabbos 49b

Primary categories of damage
Primary categories of damage, differences .... Bava Kama 5b-6a, 9b-10a, 25b-26a
Primary categories of damages, how many .... Bava Kama 4b-5a
Primary categories of damages, similarities .... Bava Kama 5a-6a

Prince
Prince .... *see also* **Nasi**, page 437
Prince before king, Rabbi Chanina ben Dosa .... Berachos 34b
Prince of Rome, city of refuge .... Makos 12a
Prince of the sea, episode .... Bava Basra 74b
Prince, standing before him .... Horayos 13b
Prince, who is considered prince concerning sacrifices .... Horayos 11a-11b
Princes of Israel, eight .... Succah 52b

Prison
Prison, black shoes .... Bava Kama 59b
Prison, death .... Sanhedrin 81b, 82b; Yevamos 64b
Prison, Rabbi Akiva .... Yevamos 105b, 108b
Prison, Rabbi Eliezer .... Avodah Zarah 16b-17a

Prisoner cannot free himself from prison .... Sanhedrin 95a

Pritzus .... *see* **Indecency**, page 307

Private altar
Private altar, Altar .... Zevachim 108b
Private altar, consecrating meal offering .... Zevachim 69a
Private altar, Elijah at Mount Carmel .... Berachos 9b
Private altar, Gideon .... Temurah 28b-29a
Private altar, laws .... Zevachim 117b-118a, 119b-120b
Private altar, libations .... Zevachim 111a
Private altar, Nov and Giveon .... Zevachim 119a
Private altar, slaughtering outside .... Zevachim 106a, 119b; Avodah Zarah 51b; Meilah 3b
Private altar, time when permitted .... Zevachim 112b; Megillah 10a; Bechoros 4b
Private altar, which sacrifices .... Zevachim 69a, 112b, 117a-118a, 119b; Megillah 9b; Pesachim 38b;
.... Avodah Zarah 24b; Temurah 14b
Private altar, who offers .... Zevachim 16a, 118a
Private domain, basket .... Eruvin 33b; Shabbos 5a, 101a
Private domain, basket in the street .... Shabbos 8a
Private domain, beehive .... Shabbos 8a
Private domain covered by roof .... Shabbos 5a

Private domain
Private domain for Shabbos, height .... Shabbos 7b-8a
Private domain, high place .... Shabbos 9a; Eruvin 89a, 90b
Private domain, partitions .... Eruvin 11b, 12b, 95a

Priyah, circumcision .... Yevamos 71b

Problem after doubt, *chazakah* .... Chullin 10a
Proclaiming that earth belongs to G-d .... Sanhedrin 39a
Procreation
Procreation .... *see also* **Marital relations,** page 392
Procreation, commandment .... Yevamos 61b-62b
Procreation, convert .... Bechoros 47a; Yevamos 62a
Procreation, in one's old age .... Yevamos 62b
Procreation, punishment .... Yevamos 63b-64a; Pesachim 113b
Procreation, pure body .... Pesachim 112b
Procreation, purpose of world .... Gittin 41b
Procreation, women .... Yevamos 65b-66a; Shabbos 111a; Gittin 43b; Kiddushin 35a
Produce
Produce, kept during Sabbatical year .... Sheviis 9:1; Maasros 5:8; Succah 39b
Produce, third of growth .... Sanhedrin 69a
Produce, third of growth, tithes .... Rosh Hashanah 12b-13b; Maasros 1:3
Produce, time for growth .... Bechoros 8a
Produce, wording of vow .... Nedarim 55a
Profiteering .... Bava Basra 90b
Prohibition
Prohibition, double .... *see* **Double prohibition,** page 176
Prohibition gives it importance, item forbidden to have benefit thereof .... Bechoros 10a-10b
Prohibition, idolatry in *Eretz Yisrael* .... Avodah Zarah 53b
Prohibition, not learned from impurity .... Yevamos 103b
Prohibition, not learned from money and penalty .... Kiddushin 3b; Berachos 19b; Bava Metzia 20b
Prohibition permitted, second also .... Yevamos 7b-8a
Prohibition to criticize commandments .... Yoma 67b
Prohibition to marry before seeing future wife .... Kiddushin 41a
Prohibitions add up one to another .... Avodah Zarah 66a; Orlah 2:10; Shabbos 89b-90a
Prohibitions, trade .... Sheviis 7:3-4; Pesachim 23a; Bava Kama 80a
Prohibitions, unfounded sale .... Bechoros 37a
Prohibition, temporary
Prohibition, temporary, mixture .... Beitzah 3b, 39a Nedarim 58a, 59a; Bava Metzia 53a
Prohibition, temporary, mixture of second tithe .... Bava Metzia 53a
Prohibition, temporary, permitting in case of doubt .... Beitzah 3b-4a
Promise
Promise to sell .... Avodah Zarah 72a
Promise to women .... Berachos 17a
Promissory note
Promissory note about to be collected, like collected .... Sotah 25a-25b; Yevamos 38b;
.... Kesubos 81a; Gittin 37a; Bava Metzia 62a; Shevuos 48b
Promissory note, custodians not liable .... Bava Metzia 57b; Shevuos 43a
Promissory note, doubt about currency .... Kesubos 110b
Promissory note, doubt in sum .... Bava Basra 165b-167a
Promissory note, false .... Kesubos 19a-19b
Promissory note, fraud .... Bava Metzia 56a-56b, 57a; Temurah 27a
Promissory note, its sale .... Bava Basra 76a, 173a
Promissory note, lender wanted to gather or divide .... Bava Basra 172a
Promissory note, liable, man acknowledges .... Bava Metzia 12b-14a
Promissory note not in presence of lender .... Bava Metzia 12b; Bava Basra 167a-167b

P

Promissory note, oath...Bava Metzia 4b, 57b; Shevuos 37b, 42b-43a; Bava Kama 63a
Promissory note, ordinary, Shabbos...Shabbos 148b-149a
Promissory note, to replace lid...Bava Kama 49b
Promissory note written by borrower on his paper...Gittin 20b-21a; Eduyos 2:3

Promissory note, paid
Promissory note, paid, doubt about which...Bava Basra 173a
Promissory note, paid, forbidden to keep...Kesubos 19b; Shabbos 78b
Promissory note, paid, mortgage annulled.................Bava Metzia 17a; Kesubos 85a-85b; Gittin 26b
Promissory note, paid, Shabbos..Shabbos 78b-79a

Pronouncing G-d's name as written..Sanhedrin 101b
Pronunciation
Pronunciation of letters, precision...Megillah 24b
Pronunciation or written text, which determines...........Sanhedrin 4a-4b; Makos 7b-8a; Succah 6b;
....Kiddushin 18b; Pesachim 86b; Zevachim 37b-38a; Bechoros 34a; Krisos 17b
Pronounciation, simplified, in Jerusalem...Bava Kama 6b

Proof
Proof about forbidden relations.....................................Kesubos 13a-13b; Chullin 11b; Niddah 30b
Proof, last...Sanhedrin 31a
Proof, not brought from fools (Cleopatra)...................Niddah 30b; Shabbos 104b; Chullin 49b
Proof, not from emergency case..Niddah 9b
Proof of trustworthiness..*see* **Migo**, page 409
Proofs to show that sale is false...Kesubos 109a-109b

Proper
Proper manners, calling friend...Yoma 4b
Proper requests..Taanis 4a
Proper speech...Pesachim 3a-3b
Proper speech, episodes..Pesachim 3b

Property
Property, "My property will go to Tuviah"...Kesubos 85b
Property and woman, claims..Kiddushin 65b
Property as guarantee, seizure...Bava Basra 174a
Property, Divine, second tithe.........Sanhedrin 112b; Pesachim 38a; Succah 35b; Kiddushin 24a, 53a-53b, 54b
Property given to son during one's life, crying out..Bava Metzia 75b
Property of Bar Sisin, claim...Bava Basra 30a, 159b
Property of captive, custodian...Bava Metzia 38b-39b
Property of heir like of buyer...Bava Kama 111b-112a; Bava Basra 44a
Property of orphans..*see* **Orphan**, page 463
Property of orphans, announcement..Kesubos 100b; Arachin 21b-22b
Property of widow awaiting levirate marriage............................Yevamos 38a-39a; Kesubos 80b
Property, possibility to consecrate..Bava Kama 69a-69b; Arachin 20b-21a
Property, small..............................Kesubos 43a, 103a, 108b; Yevamos 67b; Bava Basra 139b-140b
Property to two slaves...Gittin 42a, 87a
Property, what is included................................Bava Basra 61b-62a, 150b-151a; Arachin 24a
Property which changed, status of goring ox..Bava Kama 39b, 40b

Property through right of earnings
Property through right of earnings, cases............Bava Basra 50a-50b, 136a-137b; Gittin 47b-48a;
....Shabbos 135b; Yevamos 36b; Bava Kama 88b, 90a; Bava Metzia 96b; Arachin 26b
Property through right of earnings, ruling...Yevamos 36a-36b
Property through right of earnings, slave ....Bava Basra 50a-50b; Shabbos 135b; Bava Kama 89b-90a

Property through right of earnings, son who sold...Bava Kama 88b

Prophecy

Prophecy...*see also* **Divine inspiration**, page 169

Prophecies, visions of G-d..Chagigah 14a

Prophecy in dream..Chagigah 5b

Prophecy of Hosea...Pesachim 87a-87b; Bava Basra 14b

Prophecy, out of *Eretz Yisrael*..Moed Katan 25a

Prophecy rests, Divine Presence......................Shabbos 92a; Nedarim 38a; Moed Katan 25a

Prophecy, second Temple..Yoma 21b

Prophecy to cancel commandment................Shabbos 104a; Yevamos 90b; Sanhedrin 89b, 90a

Prophecy, to cancel decree..Sanhedrin 89b

Prophecy to several prophets..Sanhedrin 89a, 89b

Prophecy, transgressions hinder...Sanhedrin 65b

Prophecy was taken from prophets..Bava Basra 12a-12b

Prophecy, words of..Eruvin 60b; Bava Basra 12a; Bechoros 45a

Prophesied without knowing what he prophesied.............................Bava Basra 119b

Prophet

Prophet, acknowledged...Sanhedrin 89b

Prophet, cases of capital penalties..Sanhedrin 89a-90a

Prophet, false..*see* **False prophet**, page 214

Prophet not allowed to innovate.................Shabbos 104a; Yoma 80a; Megillah 2b-3a; Temurah 16a-16b

Prophet, "not a prophet nor son of a prophet".................Yevamos 121b; Berachos 34b; Eruvin 63a;

....Nedarim 38a; Bava Kama 50a

Prophets, Jewish, number..Megillah 14a

Prophets, non-Jewish..Bava Basra 15b

Prophets or sons of prophets, Jews...Pesachim 66a

Prophets, Rabbinical commandments..Megillah 14a

Prophets, sages, speak inexactly..Tamid 29a

Prophets, two using same words..Sanhedrin 89a

Prophets, wealth..Nedarim 38a

Prophets' teachings as Torah teaching...Rosh Hashanah 19a

Prophetesses, who...Megillah 14a-14b

Prophetic vision, clear..Succah 45b

Prophets

Prophets and Hagiographs, order...Bava Basra 14b-15a

Prophets scroll, writing together with Torah scroll....................................Bava Basra 13b-14a

Prosthesis

Prosthesis, impurity of *zav*..Shabbos 66a

Prosthesis of leg, *chalitzah*...Shabbos 66a

Prosthesis, Shabbos...Shabbos 65b-66a; Yoma 78b; Yevamos 103b

Prostitute

Prostitute..*see also* **Woman guilty of forbidden relations**, page 758;

....**Misconduct, married woman**, page 414

Prostitute and her daughter..Sotah 26b-27a

Prostitutes, hate one another..Pesachim 113b

Prostitutes or idolatry, episode..Avodah Zarah 17a-17b

Prostitutes, scorned even by their customers...Avodah Zarah 70a

Prostitute's fee

Prostitute's fee, act of acquisition...Pesachim 90a

P

Prostitute's fee, changed..Bava Kama 65b-66a, 93b-94a; Temurah 30b
Prostitute's fee, excessive sum...Temurah 29a-29b
Prostitute's fee, Red Heifer...Temurah 30b; Avodah Zarah 46b
Prostitute's fee, time of giving.........................Avodah Zarah 62b-63a; Temurah 29a-29b
Prostitute's fee, without claim...Bava Kama 70b

Prostrating
Prostrating, bowing..Megillah 22b
Prostrating, episode about Levi...Taanis 25a
Prostrating in Temple..Shekalim 6:1-3
Prostrating, prohibition...Megillah 22b
Prostrating, Rabbi Akiva...Berachos 31a
Prostrating to idol..Sanhedrin 63a
Prostrating with ample space, Temple...Yoma 21a; Avos 5:5

Protecting from becoming dirty, Shabbos...Shabbos 11b

Protects the innocent
Protects the innocent, circumcision...Yevamos 72a
Protects the innocent, dangers..Shabbos 129b
Protects the innocent, pad.................Yevamos 12b, 100b; Kesubos 39a; Nedarim 35b; Niddah 45a
Protects the innocent, pregnant woman...Niddah 31a
Protects the innocent, uncovered drink..Avodah Zarah 30b

Protection
Protection, merit of commandment...Menachos 43b
Protection of *orlah* fruit...Berachos 36b
Protection, Sages..Bava Basra 7b

Protection concerning impurity
Protection concerning impurity, accessory to fruit.................................Uktzin 1:2-6, 2:1-4
Protection concerning impurity, food............Chullin 117b-118b, 119b; Menachos 70b; Uktzin 1:1
Protection concerning impurity, hair..Chullin 119b-120a
Protection concerning impurity, leaves...Uktzin 2:7 ·
Protection concerning impurity, when...............Chullin 118b-119b, 123b; Uktzin 2:5-6

Protest
Protest against *chazakah*, cases..Bava Basra 35b
Protest against *chazakah*, wording..Bava Basra 38b-39a
Protest against division by *beis din*........Kiddushin 42a-42b; Yevamos 67b; Kesubos 100a; Gittin 34a
Protest against transgression..*see* **Rebuke,** page 550
Protest, blame on righteous who did not protest......................Shabbos 55a, 56b; Sanhedrin 20a
Protest, damage done by sight...Bava Basra 59b
Protest, in front of how many persons...Bava Basra 39a-39b
Protest of owner from afar, *chazakah*..Bava Basra 38a-39a
Protest, second, when..Bava Basra 39b
Protest, selling to other..Bava Basra 30b-31a, 42a
Protest to defend Sage's honor, episode...Bava Metzia 84b

Protuberance
Protuberance between courtyards...Eruvin 78a
Protuberance, *chazakah* and use..Bava Basra 59a-59b
Protuberance in public domain..Eruvin 98b
Protuberance in ship, Shabbos..Shabbos 100b-101a
Protuberances in public domain, harm..Bava Basra 27b, 60a-60b
Protuberances, tent of corpse..Oholos 12:3, 14:1-4, 14:5-7

P

Proud poor, mind cannot tolerate him .... Pesachim 113b
Proved
Proved its end, divorce certificate .... Gittin 66a, 65b
Proves first intention by end .... Chullin 39b; Nedarim 48a; Gittin 66a; Zevachim 2b
Proving argument, legal document and witnesses .... Bava Basra 169b-170b; Sanhedrin 23b
Proverbs and their sources .... Sanhedrin 7a; Bava Kama 92a-92b
Proverbs
Proverbs, by Solomon .... Bava Basra 14b-15a
Proverbs, Sages wanted to conceal this Book .... Shabbos 30b
Providence
Providence, knocking finger .... Chullin 7b
Providence, orchard .... Sanhedrin 39b
Provoking
Provoking, non-Jew, snake and pupil .... Pesachim 113a
Provoking wicked man .... Berachos 7b; Megillah 6b
Proximity
Proximity .... *see also* **Closeness**, page 112
Proximity of verses, deduction .... Yevamos 4a-4b; Berachos 10a, 21b
Proxy
Proxy to lawyer .... Bava Kama 70a; Gittin 48b
Proxy, text .... Gittin 66a
Prozbul, document permitting collection of debt during Sabbatical year .... Sheviis 10:3-7;
.... Gittin 32b-33a, 36a-37b; Kesubos 89a; Bava Kama 36b-37a
Pruning, secondary category of work .... Shabbos 73b
Psak din .... *see* **Ruling of** *beis din*, page 574
Psak halacha .... *see* **Ruling**, page 574
Psalms .... *see* **Tehillim**, page 678
Pshita, Kohanim and *Leviim* .... Arachin 3b
Pshutei Keilim .... *see* **Flat utensils**, page 229
Psik reisha .... *see* **Inevitable act**, page 308
Psok li psukcha .... *see* **Tell me your verse**, page 678
Psukei Dezimra, reward .... Shabbos 118b
Psulei mukdashin .... *see* **Redeemed sacrifices**, page 551
Puberty, signs .... Niddah 47a-47b
Public
Public .... *see also* **Community**, page 118
Public, canceling partition .... Eruvin 8a, 10b, 22a-22b
Public remind one another .... Shabbos 147b
Public domain
Public domain, acts of acquisition .... Bava Basra 76b
Public domain, banners in desert .... Shabbos 5a, 98a
Public domain, board and beam .... Shabbos 6a-6b, 117a; Eruvin 6a-6b, 12b, 22a, 59b, 95a
Public domain, cases .... Shabbos 6b; Eruvin 94a, 22b
Public domain, covered by roof .... Shabbos 5a, 98a
Public domain, damaging use .... Bava Basra 8a, 27b, 60a-60b; Sheviis 3:10
Public domain, desert .... Shabbos 6b
Public domain, doors .... Eruvin 6a-6b, 11b
Public domain, Jerusalem .... Eruvin 6b, 101a
Public domain, Shabbos .... Eruvin 6b, 101a

P

Public domain, wagons...Shabbos 98a, 99a
Publicizing disqualified families..Kiddushin 71a
Puk tani libra...*see* **Go out and say your teaching outside**, page 253
Pulling thread in stitch, Shabbos...Shabbos 75a
Pulling to purchase
Pulling to purchase, act of acquisition by slave..Kiddushin 22b
Pulling to purchase, its entire length..Bava Basra 75b-76a
Pulling to purchase, animal to buy utensils....................................Bava Metzia 9b
Pulling to purchase, by custodians..................Bava Kama 79a; Bava Metzia 99a; Kiddushin 47b
Pulling to purchase, item generally raised...Bava Basra 86a-86b
Pulling to purchase, purchase of ship.......................Bava Basra 75b-76b; Kesubos 85a
Pulling to purchase, source..................Bava Metzia 47b-48b; Bechoros 13a-13b; Chullin 83a
Pulling to purchase, to and from non-Jew..........Avodah Zarah 71a-72a; Bechoros 13a-13b
Pumbedisa
Pumbedisa, dwelling..Horayos 12a; Krisos 6a
Pumbedisa, thieves...Chullin 127a
Pumpkin
Pumpkin, better than squash.............................Kesubos 83b; Succah 56b; Temurah 9a
Pumpkin, bitter inside...Bava Basra 143a
Pumpkin, qualities recognizable from beginning.................................Berachos 48a
Pumpkins, harmful for sick..Nedarim 49a
Pumpkins to block ears..Gittin 34a
Pundion, value...Kiddushin 12a
Punish
Punish your son and he will give you pleasure..Makos 8a
Punishing child, Torah learning..Kesubos 50a
Punishment
Punishment by *beis din*, misdeed for misdeed..Kesubos 86a
Punishment, closeness to idolaters..Pesachim 118b
Punishment comes to world because of ignoramus.................................Bava Basra 8a
Punishment, cut off hand..Sanhedrin 58b; Niddah 13b
Punishment exceptional, times require it..........................Sanhedrin 46a; Yevamos 90b
Punishment for judge...Sanhedrin 7a-7b
Punishment for positive commandment in time of anger.............................Menachos 41a
Punishment for traits, more severe than forbidden relations..........Yevamos 21a; Bava Basra 88b
Punishment for white threads more than for blue.................................Menachos 43b
Punishment, measure is full.......................................Sotah 9a; Arachin 15a
Punishment, not from "all the more so" deduction..............Sanhedrin 54a, 73a, 74a, 76a;
....Makos 5b, 14a; Temurah 9a; Krisos 3a
Punishment of generation, leader..Bava Kama 52a
Punishment of Rabbi Elazar, barley...Kesubos 77a
Punishment of righteous..Bava Kama 92a
Punishment of righteous in this world...Taanis 11a
Punishment, one does not begin by mentioning.............................Gittin 18a, 75b
Punishment, only for prohibition...Sanhedrin 56a
Punishment to idolaters......................................*see* **Idolaters (Death)**, page 293
Punishment to idolaters for Israel..Yevamos 63a
Punishment, Torah reading, not to interrupt......................................Megillah 31b
Punishment, we do not begin with...Bava Basra 14b, 108a

Punishments and sacrifices .... Krisos 4a-4b
Punishments, parables .... Yoma 86b

Purchase

Purchase .... *see also* **Act of acquisition**, page 338
Purchase by receiving from seller .... Bava Metzia 11b
Purchase by receiving from seller's hands .... Bava Metzia 8b
Purchase by speech .... Kesubos 102b; Kiddushin 9b; Moed Katan 18b
Purchase, concern of idolatry .... Avodah Zarah 12b-14b, 32b-33a
Purchase, erroneous, expenses .... Kesubos 91b-92a
Purchase from non-Jew, additional right .... Bava Basra 35b-36a
Purchase, money is not given for nothing .... Bava Metzia 14a
Purchase, praising it to buyer .... Kesubos 17a
Purchase, requirement to give tithes .... Maasros 2:5-6; Beitzah 35b; Bava Metzia 89b
Purchase without knowing if it is good .... Kesubos 93a; Bava Kama 8b; Bava Metzia 14a

Pure

"Pure I am," *niddah* .... Niddah 11b
Pure days, female discharge .... Niddah 33a-33b, 42a
Pure etc. impure etc., list .... Chullin 24b-25a
Pure person, passing through impure place .... Zevachim 93a
Pure person stands and impure one passes by .... Taharos 6:2; Eduyos 3:7

Purgatory .... *see Gehinnom*, page 246

Purification

Purification of *Eretz Yisrael*, pretext .... Kesubos 20b; Nazir 65b
Purification of leper .... Negaim 14:1-6
Purification of Tiberias, episode .... Shabbos 33b-34a

Purim

Purim, city dweller who went to walled city .... Megillah 19a
Purim, commandment to rejoice .... Pesachim 68b
Purim, commandments .... Megillah 7a-7b
Purim *Demukafim* .... Megillah 2b, 3b-4a, 5b
Purim, doubt about walled cities .... Megillah 5b
Purim, *Hallel* .... Megillah 14a
Purim, joy and feast .... Megillah 7b
Purim, leap year .... Megillah 6b-7a; Rosh Hashanah 19b
Purim money, changing .... Bava Metzia 78b, 106b-107a
Purim on Shabbos .... Megillah 4a
Purim, Torah reading and *haftorah* .... Megillah 30b-31a
Purim, towns .... Megillah 2a-2b, 4b-5a; Yevamos 13b
Purim, women .... Megillah 4a
Purim, work .... Megillah 5a-5b

Purity

Purity .... *see also* **Impurity**, page 301
Purity absorbed .... Chullin 71a-72a; Mikvaos 10:8
Purity and piety .... Avodah Zarah 20b
Purity, episodes about keeping pure .... Chagigah 25a; Bechoros 30b
Purity for Red Heifer .... Parah 5:1, 5:4, 10:1-6, 12:6-8; Chagigah 23b
Purity in time of Amoraim .... Chagigah 25a; Niddah 6b
Purity of *Eretz Yisrael*, from which source of impurity .... Zevachim 113a
Purity of *Eretz Yisrael*, towns .... Oholos 18:9

P

Purity of reptile, a hundred and fifty reasons .... Eruvin 13b
Purity of sacrifices and *terumah*, non-holy food .... Chagigah 19b-20a; Niddah 71b; Taharos 2:8
Purity of sacrifices, impure man .... Chullin 2b
Purity of Temple, secondary impurity .... Chullin 35a-35b
Purity of Temple utensils .... Chagigah 26a-27a
Purity, olives given to teacher .... Yevamos 15b
Purity on festival .... Rosh Hashanah 16b

Purpose
Purpose, guilt offering of *nazir* .... Krisos 27a
Purpose of wisdom, good deeds .... Berachos 17a

Pursued
Pursued but not pursuer .... Bava Kama 93a
Pursued, pigeon and dove .... Bava Kama 93a
Pursuing high position .... Eruvin 13b

Pursuer
Pursuer, coming surreptitiously .... Pesachim 2a-2b
Pursuer, donkey in ship .... Bava Kama 117b
Pursuer, fetus .... Oholos 7:6; Sanhedrin 72b
Pursuer, idolatry and Shabbos .... Sanhedrin 73b, 74a
Pursuer, murder and forbidden relations .... Sanhedrin 73a-73b
Pursuer, saving him and law about his money .... Sanhedrin 57a-57b, 74a; Bava Kama 117b

Pushing away Divine Presence .... Berachos 43b; Chagigah 16a; Kiddushin 31a

Put
Put darkness, World to Come .... Bava Metzia 83b
Put down in front of me, custody .... Bava Metzia 81b
Putting back limb on Shabbos .... Shabbos 147b-148a
Putting next to pot, Shabbos .... Shabbos 48a
Putting next to stove-top on Shabbos .... Shabbos 37a
Putting one's money on deer horn .... Kesubos 107b; Nedarim 33b; Gittin 58b

Put out
Put out hand, Shabbos .... Shabbos 3b-4a
Put out head, birth .... Bechoros 46a-47a
Put out leg, embryo .... Chullin 69a

Put down
Put down two and found one .... Beitzah 10b; Pesachim 10a
Putting down and falling, lost item .... Bava Metzia 25b, 23a
Putting down and lifting, taking out Pesach lamb .... Pesachim 85b
Putting down in removing partition, on Shabbos .... Shabbos 99b-100a
Putting down ink, writing .... Shabbos 80a
Putting down on Shabbos, absorption .... Shabbos 102a
Putting down on Shabbos, dog mouth .... Shabbos 102a; Eruvin 99a
Putting down on Shabbos, hand considered as four handbreadths .... Shabbos 5a
Putting down on Shabbos, inclined wall .... Shabbos 5a-5b; Eruvin 98a-98b
Putting down on Shabbos, item dragged .... Pesachim 85b
Putting down on Shabbos, minimal hole .... Shabbos 7b, 100a
Putting down on Shabbos, nut on water .... Shabbos 5b, 99b-100a
Putting down on Shabbos, oil on wine .... Shabbos 5b, 100a
Putting down on Shabbos, three handbreadths ...Shabbos 5a, 80a, 92a, 97a, 100a-100b; Eruvin 98b

Putrefied flesh of dead .... Nazir 50a

Q

Quails

Quails in desert..Yoma 75a-75b; Arachin 15b
Quails, Sages..Yoma 75b
Quails, serve to father...Kiddushin 31a

Quantity
....*see also* **Size**, page 631; **Volume**, page 725; **Measure**, page 398

Commandments —
Quantity for *eruv techumin*..............Eruvin 28b-30a, 82b-83a; Kesubos 64b; Keilim 17:11
Quantity of bread, *Bircas HaMazon*...Berachos 49b
Quantity of charity...Bava Basra 9a
Quantity of food, final blessing...Berachos 38b-39a, 49b
Quantity of food to eat for *kiddush*..Pesachim 107a
Quantity of meal offerings...Menachos 89a
Quantity of water for washing hands..........Yadayim 1:1, 2:1; Nazir 38a; Gittin 15b; Chullin 107a

Eating —
Quantity concerning transgression of oath...................................Shevuos 21b-22b
Quantity of daily food...Eruvin 82b-83a, 83b
Quantity of daily food, *omer*...Eruvin 83b
Quantity of food forbidden on Yom Kippur...Yoma 78b
Quantity of food, oath..Shevuos 27b

General —
Quantities, proof...Succah 5b-6a; Eruvin 4a-4b
Quantity, food with air bubble...Uktzin 2:8
Quantity which swelled and was reduced.............Menachos 54a-54b; Taharos 3:4; Uktzin 2:8

Impurity —
Quantities for impurity of corpse...Oholos 2:5-7
Quantity for impurity of liquids..Krisos 13b
Quantity of discharges, *zav* and *baal keri*......................Niddah 22a, 43b; Pesachim 67b
Quantity of food impurity...Eruvin 83a; Yoma 80a

Monetary matters —
Quantity, dividing up between partners...Bava Basra 12a
Quantity of sum necessary, oath in *beis din*....Shevuos 39b-40a, 40b; Kiddushin 11b; Bechoros 50b
Quantity, to make a mound...Bava Metzia 105a

Prohibitions —
Quantity of *chametz* and leaven..Beitzah 7b

Q

Quantity of dough for *matzah* ....Pesachim 48a-48b
Quantity of leaven to burn...Beitzah 7b; Yoma 79b
Quantity of liquid mixture ....Orlah 2:6-7; Chullin 97a-99b; Avodah Zarah 69a
Quantity of wine concerning *nazir* ....Nazir 38b
Quantity, carrying out on Shabbos
Quantity, carrying out on Shabbos, animal fodder...Shabbos 76a-76b
Quantity, carrying out on Shabbos, combining..Shabbos 80a
Quantity, carrying out on Shabbos, corpse...Shabbos 94b
Quantity, carrying out on Shabbos, drinks..Shabbos 77a-78a
Quantity, carrying out on Shabbos, impure house...Shabbos 91a-91b
Quantity, carrying out on Shabbos, item put aside.................Shabbos 75b-76a, 78a, 90b-91a;
Zevachim 47a
Quantity, carrying out on Shabbos, legal document...Shabbos 78b-79a
Quantity, carrying out on Shabbos, other.....................Shabbos 78a-78b, 80a-81a, 82a, 89b-90b
Quantity, carrying out on Shabbos, quantity after processing.................................Shabbos 79a
Quantity, carrying out on Shabbos, two uses..Shabbos 78a
Quantity, carrying out on Shabbos, writing utensils...........................Shabbos 79a-80a; Gittin 22a
Separating —
Quantity for requirement to separate *challah* ....Challah 2:6-7; Eduyos 1:2; Shabbos 15a, 76b;
Eruvin 83a-83b; Pesachim 48b
Quantity of *terumah*...........................Terumos 4:3-5; Kesubos 99b-100a; Kiddushin 41a-41b; Chullin 137b
Quantity of *terumah*, agent..Terumos 4:3-5
Misc. —
Quantities of *reviis*..Bava Basra 58b
Quantity of donations to consecrated items, Treasury................................Menachos 106b-107a
Quantity of hair, puberty..Niddah 52a
Quantity, *reviis*..*see* **Reviis**, page 566
Quarantine
Quarantine, leprous garment...Negaim 11:5-6
Quarantine, leprous house ....Negaim 13:1
Quarantine of leper ....Megillah 8b; Negaim 3:3-8; Sanhedrin 106b; Arachin 15b
Quarrel
Quarrel, Ahitophel's will...Bava Basra 147a
Quarrel between Geder and Chamas..Eruvin 61a
Quarrel, families disqualified by lineage ....Kiddushin 71b
Quarrel, domestic, because of lack of food ....Bava Metzia 59a
Quarrel, grows like hole made by water...Sanhedrin 7a
Quarrel, prohibition...Yevamos 13b-14a; Sanhedrin 110a
Quarrel, trustworthiness of *agunah*..Yevamos 116a-116b
Quarrels, episode about Geniva ....Gittin 7a
Quarrels, haughty men..Sotah 47b; Chullin 7a
Quarrels of *Kohanim*..Kiddushin 70b
Queen
Queen Helen, righteousness..Succah 2b
Queen of Sheba..Bava Basra 15b
Question..*see also* **Inquiries**, page 310
Episodes —
Question than no carpenter can answer..Avodah Zarah 50b
Question to Rav Pappa, episode ....Niddah 33b

Questions in lecture, episodes..Beitzah 21a; Taanis 9b; Moed Katan 5a-5b
Questions of inhabitants of Alexandria..Niddah 69b
Questions of Shimi, challenge for Rav Pappa...Taanis 9b
Misc. —
   Question to demon..Sanhedrin 101a
   Questions about teacher's ruling...Bava Basra 130b-131a
   Questions, defiance...Sanhedrin 41b
   Questions in *beis din*, avoid...Bava Kama 96b
   Questions to one's teacher.......................Berachos 63b; Eruvin 67b; Chullin 6a; Niddah 27a
   Questions to teacher on other tractate...Shabbos 3b
Questioning considered like challenging..Bava Basra 39a
Quorum
   Quorum...*see also* **Communal prayer**, page 118
   Quorum, Divine Presence...Sanhedrin 39a
   Quorum, for which prayers...Megillah 23b; Berachos 21b
   Quorum, freeing slave..Gittin 38b; Berachos 47b
   Quorum, *megillah*..Megillah 5a
   Quorum, up to one *parsah*...Pesachim 46a; Chullin 122b-123a
   Quorum, who and what can be counted...Berachos 47b-48b

Q

R

Raasan, sickness .... Kesubos 77b

Rabbah

Ruling —

Rabbah and Abbaye, long life .... Yevamos 105a; Rosh Hashanah 18a

Rabbah and Rav Yosef, ruling .... Bava Basra 114b, 143b

Rabbah created human form .... Sanhedrin 65b

Rabbah, death .... Bava Metzia 86a

Rabbah gave cracked vessels to his son .... Yoma 78b

Rabbah, his brother's letter .... Kesubos 111a

Rabbah, his son played with a donkey .... Shabbos 154b

Rabbah, lie to prevent stumbling block .... Shabbos 115a

Rabbah like Shmuel, law .... Shabbos 22a, 40a; Pesachim 101a; Menachos 41b

Rabbah, pillar fell .... Bava Metzia 20b

Rabbah refrained from making *eruv* .... Eruvin 68a

Rabbah, *Rosh Yeshivah* .... Berachos 64a

Rabbah, Shvor Malka .... Bava Basra 115b; Pesachim 54a

Rabbah slaughtered Rabbi Zeira .... Megillah 7b

His life —

Rabbah and Abbaye, Eli's descendants .... Yevamos 105a; Rosh Hashanah 18a

Rabbah, his generation is not fit .... Taanis 24a-24b

Rabbah, unusual occurrences at his death .... Moed Katan 25b

Misc. —

Rabbah, "Amora from Pumbedisa" .... Sanhedrin 17b

Rabbah, careful about *tzitzis* .... Shabbos 118b

Rabbah, fate .... Moed Katan 28a

Rabbah, only to sharpen Abbaye he wished .... Niddah 4b; Berachos 33b

Rabbah, preparations for Shabbos .... Shabbos 119a

Rabbah, uprooting mountains .... Berachos 64a; Horayos 14a

Rabbah bar Avuah, *Gan Eden* .... Bava Metzia 114b

Rabbah bar bar Channah

Miracles —

Rabbah bar bar Channah, camel .... Yevamos 120b

Rabbah bar bar Channah, dead men in desert .... Bava Basra 73b-74a

Rabbah bar bar Channah, episode about Taya .... Bava Basra 73b-74a

Rabbah bar bar Channah, episodes..Bava Basra 73a
Rabbah bar bar Channah, giant animals.....................Bava Basra 73b-74b; Zevachim 113b
Rabbah bar bar Channah, golden dove...Berachos 53b
Misc. —
Rabbah bar bar Channah, angry stare...Pesachim 53b
Rabbah bar bar Channah, authorization from Rebbi...................................Sanhedrin 5a-5b
Rabbah bar bar Channah, beyond letter of law...Bava Metzia 83a
Rabbah bar bar Channah, forced to come to discourse......................................Shabbos 148a
Rabbah bar bar Channah, non-Jew took his candle..Gittin 17a
Rabbah bar bar Channah saved from eating impure fish..............................Avodah Zarah 39a
Rabbah bar Matnah, "deliberate"...Horayos 14a
Rabbah bar Rav Huna
Rabbah bar Rav Huna, beyond letter of law...Bava Metzia 83a
Rabbah bar Rav Huna, curse...Bava Metzia 107b-108a
Rabbah bar Rav Huna, curse to a judge...Gittin 35a
Rabbah bar Rav Huna, donkey overtook Sage...Shabbos 51b-52a
Rabbah bar Rav Huna, episode about date..Sotah 49a
Rabbah bar Rav Huna, episode about witch.........................Shabbos 81b-82a; Chullin 105b
Rabbah bar Rav Huna, honor to his coffin.......................................Moed Katan 25a-25b
Rabbah bar Rav Nachman
Rabbah bar Rav Nachman, curse...Bava Metzia 108a
Rabbah bar Rav Nachman, Shabbos meals.....................Shabbos 119a; Chullin 111a
Rabbah bar Rav Shiloh, a prayer for the day of death...................................Berachos 8a
Rabbah bar Simi, they came to fight..Megillah 24a
Rabbah bar Ulah, loans for Yom Tov..Shabbos 148b
Rabban Gamliel
Learning —
Rabban Gamliel and ruler...Chullin 27b
Rabban Gamliel, answers to heretic...Sanhedrin 39a
Rabban Gamliel wept because of a verse..Makos 24a
Praises —
Rabban Gamliel, Divine inspiration..Eruvin 64b
Rabban Gamliel, humility...Sanhedrin 11b
Rabban Gamliel, replaced his father..Kesubos 103b
Rabban Gamliel, strong ones of first generations.......................................Sanhedrin 11b
Ruling —
Rabban Gamliel, adding a month...Rosh Hashanah 25a-25b
Rabban Gamliel, dismissal from presidency..Berachos 27b-28a
Rabban Gamliel, incense on Yom Tov..Beitzah 22b
Rabban Gamliel, letters...Sanhedrin 11b
Rabban Gamliel, lizard at king's meal...Pesachim 88b
Rabban Gamliel, permitting vow...Eruvin 64b; Nedarim 77b
Rabban Gamliel, woman who miscarried snake..Niddah 24b
Rabban Gamliel, Yavneh...Sanhedrin 32b
Misc. —
Rabban Gamliel, blinded his slave..Bava Kama 74b
Rabban Gamliel, bribe to philosopher..Shabbos 116a-116b
Rabban Gamliel, decree of death..Taanis 29a
Rabban Gamliel heard bereaved woman's weeping.......................................Sanhedrin 104b

R

Rabban Gamliel, high position to his disciples..Horayos 10a-10b
Rabban Gamliel, *lulav*..Succah 41b
Rabban Gamliel, Rabbi Yehoshua's pain...Bechoros 36a
Rabban Gamliel served his guests...Kiddushin 32b
Rabban Gamliel, ship...............Horayos 10a; Bava Metzia 11a-11b; Kiddushin 26b-27a; Maaser Sheni 5:9
Rabban Gamliel, shrouds...Moed Katan 27b
Rabban Gamliel survived among his father's family...Sotah 49b
Rabban Gamliel the Elder, his time...Shabbos 15a
Rabban Gamliel, tithe..Bava Metzia 11a-11b

Rabban Shimon ben Gamliel
  Episodes —
Rabban Shimon ben Gamliel, dance...Succah 53a
Rabban Shimon ben Gamliel, permitting vow about woman...............................Nedarim 66b
Rabban Shimon ben Gamliel, price of birds..................Bava Basra 166a-166b; Krisos 8a
Rabban Shimon ben Gamliel, standing...Horayos 13b-14a
  Misc. —
Rabban Shimon ben Gamliel, his time...Shabbos 15a
Rabban Shimon ben Gamliel, humility...Bava Metzia 84b-85a
Rabban Shimon ben Gamliel, law..Sanhedrin 31a
Rabban Shimon ben Gamliel, prophecy about his death....................................Sanhedrin 11a
Rabban Shimon ben Gamliel, troubles after his death.......................................Sotah 49b

Rabbanan...*see* **Sage**, page 583
Rabbanus...*see* **Rabbinate**, page 533
Rabbeinu Achai, *Meor Hagolah*...Chullin 59b
Rabbeinu Hakadosh...*see* **Rebbi**, page 548

Rabbi Abba
Rabbi Abba appeased Rabbi Yirmiyah..Yoma 87a
Rabbi Abba bought field desired by other Sage...Kiddushin 59a
Rabbi Abba, emigration to *Eretz Yisrael*..Berachos 24b
Rabbi Abba, episodes about forgiveness...Sotah 40a
Rabbi Abba, exibited anger...Shabbos 105b
Rabbi Abba, love for *Eretz Yisrael*..Kesubos 112a
Rabbi Abba, our teachers in *Eretz Yisrael*..Sanhedrin 17b
Rabbi Abba, preparations for Shabbos..Shabbos 119a
Rabbi Abba from Akko, *Rosh Yeshivah*..Sotah 40a
Rabbi Achai, episode about returning deposit..Gittin 14a-14b
Rabbi Afes, *Rosh Yeshivah*...Kesubos 103b

Rabbi Akiva
  Episodes —
"Rabbi Akiva, you have consoled us"..Makos 24a-24b
Rabbi Akiva, "everything G-d does is for the best"..Berachos 60b
Rabbi Akiva, "wine for our Sages' mouth"...Shabbos 67b
Rabbi Akiva, laughter..Makos 24a-24b
Rabbi Akiva, plank of ship..Yevamos 121a
Rabbi Akiva, test of forbidden relations...Kiddushin 81a
Rabbi Akiva, visits sick man..Nedarim 40a
Rabbi Akiva, washing hands..Eruvin 21b
Rabbi Akiva's daughter and Ben Azai..Kesubos 63a
Rabbi Akiva's daughter, snake...Shabbos 156b

R

His life —

Rabbi Akiva, "when I was an ignoramus" ....Pesachim 49b
Rabbi Akiva, B'nai Braq ....Sanhedrin 32b
Rabbi Akiva, death ....Berachos 61b; Menachos 29b; Pesachim 69a
Rabbi Akiva, eulogy ....Moed Katan 21b
Rabbi Akiva, generation preceding Rebbi ....Kiddushin 72b
Rabbi Akiva, his daughter saved due to charity ....Shabbos 156b
Rabbi Akiva, imprisonment ....Yevamos 105b, 108b
Rabbi Akiva, Kalba Savua's daughter ....Kesubos 62b-63a
Rabbi Akiva, men put to death by government ....Bava Basra 10b
Rabbi Akiva, outdoor bathroom ....Berachos 62a
Rabbi Akiva, Pappus ....Berachos 61b
Rabbi Akiva, prophecy of his death ....Sanhedrin 68a
Rabbi Akiva, Turnus Rufus ....Sanhedrin 65b; Avodah Zarah 20a
Rabbi Akiva, wealth ....Nedarim 50a-50b; Kesubos 63a

Learning —

Rabbi Akiva, "Torah arm" ....Sotah 49b
Rabbi Akiva, "whoever separates from you" ....Kiddushin 66b; Zevachim 13a
Rabbi Akiva, came into Pardes ....Chagigah 14b, 15b-16a
Rabbi Akiva, disciples ....Yevamos 62b
Rabbi Akiva, *halacha* ....Eruvin 46b; Kesubos 84b
Rabbi Akiva, Heavenly Chariot ....Chagigah 14b
Rabbi Akiva, his learning ....Nedarim 50a; Kesubos 62b-63a
Rabbi Akiva, his teacher ....Chagigah 12a
Rabbi Akiva, Rabbi Eliezer ....Sanhedrin 101a; Pesachim 69a
Rabbi Akiva, Rabbi Tarfon ....Kesubos 84b
Rabbi Akiva taught Rabbi Shimon ....Pesachim 112a

Praises —

Rabbi Akiva, conciliatory ....Taanis 25b
Rabbi Akiva, "mine and yours are hers," ....Kesubos 63a
Rabbi Akiva, praises ....Gittin 67a
Rabbi Akiva, reputation and humility ....Yevamos 16a
Rabbi Akiva, springs of wisdom ....Sotah 49b
Rabbi Akiva, wisdom ....Zevachim 13a

Misc. —

Rabbi Akiva, Adam ....Sanhedrin 38b; Avodah Zarah 5a
Rabbi Akiva, Moses' prophecy ....Menachos 29b
Rabbi Akiva, prayer ....Berachos 31a
Rabbi Akiva, rebuke ....Arachin 16b

Rabbi Alexandri

Rabbi Alexandri, "desires life" ....Avodah Zarah 19b
Rabbi Alexandri, death of disciple who rejected his teacher ....Chagigah 5a

Rabbi Ami

Rabbi Ami and Rabbi Asi ....Gittin 59b
Rabbi Ami, charity from Ifra Hormiz ....Bava Basra 10b
Rabbi Ami, disciple divulged secret ....Sanhedrin 31a
Rabbi Ami, judges of *Eretz Yisrael* ....Sanhedrin 17b
Rabbi Ami, lecture on *aggadah* and *halacha* ....Bava Kama 60b
Rabbi Ami, love for *Eretz Yisrael* ....Kesubos 112a-112b

Rabbi Ami, numerous Torah scrolls..Bava Basra 14a
Rabbi Ami, preparations for Shabbos..Shabbos 119a
Rabbi Ami, *semichah*..Kesubos 17a; Sanhedrin 14a
Rabbi Ami sent questioners to a lenient Sage...Chullin 99b
Rabbi Ami turned away from Sage who made a mistake..................................Yoma 73a
Rabbi Ami wept because of a verse...Chagigah 4b

Rabbi Asi
Rabbi Asi, Heavenly Chariot..Chagigah 13a
Rabbi Asi, judges of *Eretz Yisrael*..Sanhedrin 17b
Rabbi Asi, lecture on *aggadah* and *halacha*..Bava Kama 60b
Rabbi Asi, love for *Eretz Yisrael*...Kesubos 112a-112b
Rabbi Asi, preparations for Shabbos...Shabbos 119a
Rabbi Asi, *semichah*...Kesubos 17a; Sanhedrin 14a
Rabbi Asi, unusual occurrences at his death..Moed Katan 25b
Rabbi Asi wept because of a verse..Chagigah 4b
Rabbi Asi, wonder of generation..Chullin 103b

Rabbi Avuhu
Rabbi Avuhu appeased lecturer...Sotah 40a
Rabbi Avuhu, beauty...Bava Metzia 84a; Bava Basra 58a
Rabbi Avuhu, episodes about humility...Sotah 40a
Rabbi Avuhu, healing by heretic..Avodah Zarah 28a
Rabbi Avuhu, honoring father...Kiddushin 31b
Rabbi Avuhu, house collapse...Berachos 60a
Rabbi Avuhu, *melaveh malkah* meal..Shabbos 119b
Rabbi Avuhu, preparations for Shabbos...Shabbos 119a
Rabbi Avuhu, Rav of city..Shabbos 46a; Yevamos 14a
Rabbi Avuhu, song..Kesubos 17a; Sanhedrin 14a
Rabbi Avuhu, thanksgiving meal...Berachos 46a
Rabbi Avuhu, unusual occurrences at his death...Moed Katan 25b
Rabbi Avina, Geniva's bequest...Gittin 65b-66a
Rabbi Avtilas, Rabbi Yose's son...Shabbos 118b

Rabbi Banaah
Rabbi Banaah, episodes...Bava Basra 58a-58b
Rabbi Banaah, tombs...Bava Basra 58a
Rabbi Binyamin bar Yefes, student of Rabbi Yochanan...............................Berachos 38b
Rabbi Chalafta, Rabbi Yose's son...Shabbos 118b
Rabbi Chama bar Chanina, rain...Taanis 25a
Rabbi Chanania ben Teradion
Rabbi Chanina ben Teradion...Avodah Zarah 17b-18a
Rabbi Chanania ben Teradion, Sichni...Sanhedrin 32b
Rabbi Chanina bar Pappa, death..Kesubos 77b
Rabbi Chanina ben Antignos, pure utensils..Bechoros 30b
Rabbi Chanina
  His life —
  Rabbi Chanina, did not weep for his daughter..Shabbos 151b
  Rabbi Chanina, dream about Rav...Yoma 87b
  Rabbi Chanina, his daughter's severe punishment....................................Avodah Zarah 18a
  Rabbi Chanina, measure of carobs................................Berachos 17b; Taanis 24b; Chullin 86a
  Rabbi Chanina, strength in his old age...Chullin 24b

R

Learning —
Rabbi Chanina, "I am certain he will rule" ....Nazir 29b
Rabbi Chanina, Heavenly Yeshivah ....Bava Metzia 85b
Rabbi Chanina, *Rosh Yeshivah* ....Kesubos 103b
Rabbi Chanina ruled according to his own opinion ....Niddah 20a

Miracles —
Rabbi Chanina, "give your hand" ....Berachos 5b
Rabbi Chanina, "the times need him" ....Eruvin 29b
Rabbi Chanina ben Dosa, miracles ....Taanis 24b-25a
Rabbi Chanina, noblewoman ....Kiddushin 39b-40a
Rabbi Chanina, prostitutes fled ....Avodah Zarah 17a-17b
Rabbi Chanina, rain ....Yoma 53b
Rabbi Chanina, revived his wife ....Kesubos 62b
Rabbi Chanina, sick ....Berachos 34b
Rabbi Chanina, sorcery ....Sanhedrin 67b
Rabbi Chanina, wild donkey ....Berachos 33a

Misc. —
Rabbi Chanina, adding month outside *Eretz Yisrael* ....Berachos 63a-63b
Rabbi Chanina, *anshei maaseh* ....Sotah 49b
Rabbi Chanina, healing ....Yoma 49a
Rabbi Chanina, limb from living animal ....Gittin 7a
Rabbi Chanina, love for *Eretz Yisrael* ....Kesubos 112a
Rabbi Chanina, Rabbi Yochanan rent his garment ....Moed Katan 24a
Rabbi Chanina, welcoming Shabbos ....Shabbos 119a; Bava Kama 32a-32b
Rabbi Chanina, world sustained by his merit ....Berachos 17b
Rabbi Chaninah ben Dosa, this one lives and this one dies ....Brachos 34b
Rabbi Chaninah bar Pappa, the Angel of Death ....Kesubos 77b
Rabbi Chaninah Segan Hakohanim, the welfare of the kingdom ....Avos 3:2
Rabbi Chaviva, sick sheep ....Chullin 51a
Rabbi Chelbo, heed carefully the *Mincha* prayer ....Berachos 7b
Rabbi Chiya
Episodes —
Rabbi Chiya, bad advice, coin ....Bava Kama 99b
Rabbi Chiya, blind man's blessing ....Chagigah 5b
Rabbi Chiya, chariot ....Bava Metzia 85b
Rabbi Chiya, episode about oath ....Yevamos 32b
Rabbi Chiya, foolish man attacked his family ....Shabbos 30b
Rabbi Chiya, *Kohen* in cemetery ....Sanhedrin 5b
Rabbi Chiya, *kashering* winepress ....Avodah Zarah 74b
Rabbi Chiya, prayer ....Bava Metzia 85b
Rabbi Chiya, rebuke from Rebbi ....Moed Katan 16b
Rabbi Chiya, sides of the road ....Bava Kama 81b
Rabbi Chiya, troubles ceased ....Chullin 86a
His life —
Rabbi Chiya and Rebbi, match ....Kesubos 62b
Rabbi Chiya, Angel of Death appeared like poor man ....Moed Katan 28a
Rabbi Chiya, bad wife ....Yevamos 63a
Rabbi Chiya, his wife and children ....Niddah 27a, 40a; Yevamos 65b-66a
Rabbi Chiya, his wife became sterile ....Yevamos 65b

R

Rabbi Chiya, news of death..Pesachim 4a
Rabbi Chiya, Rav's uncle...................................Sanhedrin 5a; Pesachim 4a; Moed Katan 20a
Rabbi Chiya, unusual occurrences at his death..Moed Katan 25b
Rabbi Chiya's daughter, death..Kesubos 62b

Rabbi Chiya's sons
Rabbi Chiya's sons, drunkenness...Sanhedrin 38a
Rabbi Chiya's sons, learning..Berachos 18b
Rabbi Chiya's sons, prayer...Bava Metzia 85b

Learning —
Rabbi Chiya, Beraisos..Chullin 141a-141b
Rabbi Chiya restored Torah when it became forgotten..................................Succah 20a
Rabbi Chiya, Tanna and can oppose...Bava Metzia 5a
Rabbi Chiya, teaching children...Bava Metzia 85b
Rabbi Chiya, teaching in name of majority...Gittin 77a

Misc. —
Rabbi Chiya, Heavenly Yeshivah..Bava Metzia 85b
Rabbi Chiya, height...Niddah 24b
Rabbi Chiya, *kiddush hachodesh*...Rosh Hashanah 25a
Rabbi Chiya, mispronounciation of ches letter..Megillah 24b

Rabbi Chiya bar Abba
Rabbi Chiya bar Abba, "give your hand"..Berachos 5b
Rabbi Chiya bar Abba, *"tov"* written on Tablets...Bava Kama 55a
Rabbi Chiya bar Abba reviewed his learning..Berachos 38b
Rabbi Chiya bar Abba, urge for forbidden relations..Kiddushin 81b

Rabbi Chiya bar Ashi, evil urge..Kiddushin 81b
Rabbi Chiya bar Avin, loss of meat..Chullin 95b
Rabbi Chiya bar Gamda, love for *Eretz Yisrael*...Kesubos 112b
Rabbi Chiya bar Lulyani, rain..Taanis 25a
Rabbi Chiya bar Zarnoki, plowing on Sabbatical year...............................Sanhedrin 26a
Rabbi Chutzpis, Acher...Chullin 142a
Rabbi Dosa, levirate marriage of rival..Yevamos 16a
Rabbi Dostai, returning deposit..Gittin 14a-14b

Rabbi Elazar
Episodes —
Rabbi Elazar, "give your hand"..Berachos 5b
Rabbi Elazar, Angel of Death...Moed Katan 28a
Rabbi Elazar, invitation from House of Nasi...........................Chullin 44b; Megillah 28a
Rabbi Elazar praised Rabbi Yosi...Chullin 103b
Rabbi Elazar, snake in outdoor bathroom...Berachos 62b
Rabbi Elazar, standing up for Sage..Shabbos 31b

Learning —
Rabbi Elazar, "letter sent from *Eretz Yisrael*"...........................Sanhedrin 17b; Gittin 73a
Rabbi Elazar, careful to cite Sage's name in teaching....................Kesubos 25b; Makos 5b
Rabbi Elazar, preparation of his wedding canopy..Berachos 16a
Rabbi Elazar saw Rabbi Yochanan in a dream..Menachos 84b
Rabbi Elazar wept because of a verse..Chagigah 4b

Misc. —
Rabbi Elazar, "Rav of *Eretz Yisrael*".............................Niddah 20b; Yoma 9b; Gittin 19b
Rabbi Elazar, a great man...Zevachim 5a

Rabbi Elazar, barley..Kesubos 77a
Rabbi Elazar, celebrated as excellent Sage...............................Gittin 26b; Kesubos 40a; Krisos 13b
Rabbi Elazar, diligence..Berachos 16a
Rabbi Elazar, Heavenly Chariot...Chagigah 13a
Rabbi Elazar, joy...Kesubos 112a
Rabbi Elazar, learns in market..Eruvin 54b
Rabbi Elazar, Rabbi Yochanan's beauty...Berachos 5b
Rabbi Elazar, scroll was torn...Yevamos 96b

Rabbi Elazar ben Arach
Rabbi Elazar ben Arach, forgot his learning...Shabbos 147b
Rabbi Elazar ben Arach, fountain..Avos 2:8
Rabbi Elazar ben Arach, Heavenly Chariot..Chagigah 14b

Rabbi Elazar ben Azariah
Rabbi Elazar ben Azariah, "crown of wisdom"..Sotah 49b
Rabbi Elazar ben Azariah, basket of spices..Gittin 67a
Rabbi Elazar ben Azariah, discourses..Sotah 27b
Rabbi Elazar ben Azariah, his cow...Beitzah 23a
Rabbi Elazar ben Azariah, lineage...Berachos 27b
Rabbi Elazar ben Azariah, Nasi...Berachos 27b-28a
Rabbi Elazar ben Azariah, wealth...Beitzah 23a
Rabbi Elazar ben Azariah, wisdom...Berachos 27b; Chagigah 3b

Rabbi Elazar ben Charsum
Rabbi Elazar ben Charsum...Yoma 35b
Rabbi Elazar ben Charsum obligates wealthy men...Yoma 35b
Rabbi Elazar ben Charsum, High Priest..Yoma 9a

Rabbi Elazar ben Durdaya..Avodah Zarah 17a
Rabbi Elazar ben Pedas, bad fate...Taanis 25a
Rabbi Elazar ben Rabbi Shimon
Rabbi Elazar ben Rabbi Shimon...Bava Metzia 84b
Rabbi Elazar ben Rabbi Shimon, beauty..Bava Metzia 84a
Rabbi Elazar ben Rabbi Shimon, fled to cave..Shabbos 33b-34a
Rabbi Elazar ben Rabbi Shimon, guarding one's mouth.....................................Bava Metzia 83b
Rabbi Elazar ben Rabbi Shimon, his son's repentance..Bava Metzia 85a
Rabbi Elazar ben Rabbi Shimon, learning in bathroom..Zevachim 102b
Rabbi Elazar ben Rabbi Shimon, suffering...Bava Metzia 84b
Rabbi Elazar ben Rabbi Shimon, thieves..Bava Metzia 83b
Rabbi Elazar ben Rabbi Shimon, ugly man..Taanis 20a-20b
Rabbi Elazar ben Rabbi Shimon, worm out of his ear...Bava Metzia 84b

Rabbi Elazar ben Rabbi Tzadok
Rabbi Elazar ben Rabbi Tzadok, inquiry about Sabbatical year...................................Succah 44b
Rabbi Elazar ben Rabbi Tzadok, olives..Yevamos 15b

Rabbi Elazar ben Rabbi Yose...Shabbos 118b
Rabbi Elazar ben Rabbi Yose Haglili, begin (speaking) by honoring the host...Berachos 63b
Rabbi Elazar ben Shamua
Rabbi Elazar ben Shamua, old age..Megillah 27b
Rabbi Elazar ben Shamua, *semichah*......................................Sanhedrin 13b-14a; Avodah Zarah 8b
Rabbi Elazar ben Shamua, six disciples in one cubit...Eruvin 53a

Rabbi Elazar ben Yaakov
Rabbi Elazar ben Yaakov, *"kav venaki"*..Gittin 67a

Rabbi Elazar ben Yaakov, "vineyard in Yavneh" .... Berachos 63b
Rabbi Elazar ben Yaakov, testimony about priesthood .... Kesubos 28b
Rabbi Elazar Chasma
Rabbi Elazar Chasma, high position .... Horayos 10a-10b
Rabbi Elazar Chasma, wisdom .... Horayos 10a
Rabbi Elazar Hachorani, olives .... Yevamos 15b
Rabbi Elazar of Hagrunia, "Good peace" .... Taanis 24b
Rabbi Elazar Hakapar, jealousy, lust, and honor .... Avos 4:21
Rabbi Eliashiv, unusual occurrences at his death .... Moed Katan 25b
Rabbi Eliezer
  Character traits —
  Rabbi Eliezer, "Torah scroll was buried" .... Sotah 49b
  Rabbi Eliezer, cemented cistern .... Avos 2:8
  Rabbi Eliezer, wisdom .... Sanhedrin 68a
  Episodes —
  Rabbi Eliezer, "did you prepare graves" .... Taanis 25b
  Rabbi Eliezer, "take back your eyes" .... Chagigah 3b
  Rabbi Eliezer, death .... Sanhedrin 68a
  Rabbi Eliezer freed his slave .... Gittin 38b; Berachos 47b
  Rabbi Eliezer, imprisonment .... Avodah Zarah 16b-17a
  Rabbi Eliezer, oven of Achnai .... Bava Metzia 59a-59b; Berachos 19a
  Rabbi Eliezer, prophecy at time of death .... Sanhedrin 68a
  Rabbi Eliezer, visiting the sick .... Sanhedrin 101a
  Learning —
  Rabbi Eliezer, disciple of Beis Shamai .... Shabbos 130b
  Rabbi Eliezer, discourse .... Beitzah 15b
  Rabbi Eliezer, his teacher's teachings .... Yoma 66b; Succah 27b-28a
  Rabbi Eliezer, ruling .... Niddah 7b-8b
  Misc. —
  Rabbi Eliezer, behavior .... Succah 27b-28a
  Rabbi Eliezer, lengthening and shortening prayer .... Berachos 34a
  Rabbi Eliezer, Lud .... Sanhedrin 32b
  Rabbi Eliezer, merit of disciple who served him .... Eruvin 54a
  Rabbi Eliezer, modesty .... Nedarim 20b
  Rabbi Eliezer, Rabbi Akiva .... Sanhedrin 101a; Pesachim 69a
Rabbi Eliezer ben Parta .... Avodah Zarah 17b
Rabbi Eliezer ben Yaakov, *halacha* .... Gittin 67a
Rabbi Eliezer Hamodai .... Bava Basra 10b
Rabbi Evyatar .... Gittin 6b
Rabbi Hoshaia, Rabbi Chiya .... Krisos 8a
Rabbi Ilai .... Menachos 18a
Rabbi Ilai, Rabbi Eliezer's disciple .... Menachos 18a
Rabbi Levi, the *Aron* was not measurable .... Yoma 21a
Rabbi Mani, prayer .... Taanis 23b
Rav Mani ben Patish, whoever becomes angry .... Pesachim 66b
Rabbi Masia, Rome .... Sanhedrin 32b
Rabbi Meir
  Episodes —
  Rabbi Meir, episode about drowning .... Yevamos 121a

R

Rabbi Meir from behind .... Eruvin 13b
Rabbi Meir, gum .... Eruvin 13a
Rabbi Meir, hoodlums .... Berachos 10a
Rabbi Meir, marital harmony .... Gittin 52a
Rabbi Meir, name signification .... Yoma 83b
Rabbi Meir ransomed his sister-in-law .... Avodah Zarah 18a-18b
Rabbi Meir, standing up in front of Nasi .... Horayos 13b-14a
Rabbi Meir, test regarding forbidden relations .... Kiddushin 81a

Ruling —
Rabbi Meir, annoying disciples .... Kiddushin 52b; Nazir 49b-50a
Rabbi Meir, depth of thought .... Eruvin 13b, 53a
Rabbi Meir, discourses .... Sanhedrin 38b
Rabbi Meir, *halacha* .... Eruvin 46b-47a, 52a; Kesubos 57a, 60b; Sanhedrin 27a
Rabbi Meir, parables .... Sanhedrin 38b-39a
Rabbi Meir, tithe in Beis She'an .... Chullin 6b-7a

Wisdom —
Rabbi Meir, "uproots mountains" .... Sanhedrin 24a
Rabbi Meir, *megillah* by heart .... Megillah 18b
Rabbi Meir, Sage and scribe .... Gittin 67a
Rabbi Meir, wisdom .... Eruvin 53a

Misc. —
Rabbi Meir, Acher .... Chagigah 15a-15b
Rabbi Meir, Bruriah .... *see* **Bruriah**, page 78
Rabbi Meir, height .... Niddah 24b
Rabbi Meir, his colleagues' words .... Shabbos 134a
Rabbi Meir, his names .... Eruvin 13b
Rabbi Meir, his teachers .... Eruvin 13a; Sotah 20a
Rabbi Menachem, son of Rabbi Yosi .... Shabbos 118b
Rabbi Menachem, unusual occurrences at his death .... Moed Katan 25b
Rabbi Menachem bar Simai, "holy man" .... Avodah Zarah 50a; Pesachim 104a
Rabbi Mori, Jehoshaphat .... Kesubos 103b
Rabbi Nassan
Rabbi Nassan, end of Mishnah .... Bava Metzia 86a
Rabbi Nassan, judge .... Bava Metzia 117b
Rabbi Nassan, precise speech .... Gittin 65b
Rabbi Nassan, standing up in front of Nasi .... Horayos 13b-14a
Rabbi Nassan, *yesh omrim* .... Horayos 13b-14a
Rabbi Nechemiah
Rabbi Nechemiah, Heavenly Chariot .... Shabbos 80b
Rabbi Nechemiah, lentils to poor man .... Kesubos 67b
Rabbi Nechemiah, *semichah* .... Sanhedrin 13b-14a; Avodah Zarah 8b
Rabbi Nechemiah, vineyard in Yavneh .... Berachos 63b
Rabbi Nechunia, prayer before learning .... Berachos 28b
Rabbi Nechunia ben Hakaneh
Rabbi Nechunia ben Hakaneh .... Shevuos 26a
Rabbi Nechunia ben Hakaneh, old age .... Megillah 28a
Rabbi Nechunia the Great, old age .... Megillah 28a
Rabbi Nehorai forgot his learning .... Shabbos 147b

R

Rabbi Oshiah
Rabbi Oshiah BeRibbi...Eruvin 53a
Rabbi Oshiah, four disciples in one cubit...Eruvin 53a
Rabbi Oshiah, wisdom...Eruvin 53a
Rabbi Pedas, do not draw close to immorality...Shabbos 13a
Rabbi Pinchas ben Yair
Rabbi Pinchas ben Yair, asceticism..Chullin 7b
Rabbi Pinchas ben Yair, episodes...Chullin 7a
Rabbi Pinchas ben Yair, his donkey..Chullin 7a
Rabbi Pinchas gave a lecture and fled..Kiddushin 71a
Rabbi Preida
Rabbi Preida, old age...Megillah 27b-28a
Rabbi Preida, patience..Eruvin 54b
Rabbi Samlai, *Divrei Hayamim*...Pesachim 62b
Rabbi Shila
Rabbi Shila, appointed judge...Berachos 58a
Rabbi Shila, Rav was his speaker...Yoma 20b
Rabbi Shimon bar Yochai
Rabbi Shimon, "great is work"..Nedarim 49b
Rabbi Shimon, cave..Shabbos 33b
Rabbi Shimon, dais..Bava Metzia 119a
Rabbi Shimon, episode about demon...Meilah 17b
Rabbi Shimon, excommunication of disciple who ruled according to his opinion...Shabbos 19b
Rabbi Shimon, exempting world...Succah 45b
Rabbi Shimon, fasts...Nazir 52b
Rabbi Shimon, grinds a lot...Gittin 67a
Rabbi Shimon, law............Berachos 9a; Shabbos 45a; Eruvin 46b-47a; Beitzah 27a; Gittin 19a; Bechoros 11a
Rabbi Shimon, learned from Rabbi Akiva..Pesachim 112a
Rabbi Shimon, may every mother have a son like him...Makos 17b
Rabbi Shimon, *nasi*...Gittin 15a
Rabbi Shimon, permitting vow regarding married woman..Nedarim 66b
Rabbi Shimon, purified Tiberias...Shabbos 33b-34a
Rabbi Shimon, Rebbi's teacher...Menachos 72a
Rabbi Shimon ben Chalafta
Rabbi Shimon ben Chalafta, did not visit his teacher...Shabbos 152a
Rabbi Shimon ben Chalafta, experiment..Chullin 57b
Rabbi Shimon ben Chalafta, lions..Sanhedrin 59b
Rabbi Shimon ben Chalafta, meat from Heaven..Sanhedrin 59b
Rabbi Shimon ben Elazer, do not appease one during his anger.................................Avos 4:18
Rabbi Shimon b'R' Yose ben Lekuniah, worthwhile to rely on Rabbi Shimon (bar Yochai)...
....Pesachim 51a
Rabbi Shimon ben Menasia, God braided Eve's hair.........................Shabbos 95a; Berachos 61a
Rabbi Shimon ben Nesanel
Rabbi Shimon ben Nesanel..Avos 2:8
Rabbi Shimon ben Rebbi, lion son of fox...Bava Metzia 84b
Rabbi Shimon ben Rebbi, renouncing..Beitzah 28a
Rabbi Shimon ben Rebbi, resentment..Kiddushin 32b, 33a
Rabbi Shimon ben Rebbi, throaty voice...Megillah 24b
Rabbi Shimon ben Rebbi, wisdom...Kesubos 103b

R

Rabbi Shimon ben Shetach..*see* **Shimon ben Shetach**, page 616

Rabbi Shimon Chasidah, Judah and Joseph sanctified God's name........................Sotah 10b

Rabbi Shimon ben Zirod, *semichah*..Sanhedrin 14a

Rabbi Shimon Shazuri, law........................Menachos 30b-31b; Kesubos 55a-55b; Chullin 75b

Rabbi Shmuel ben Nachmeini, wife of one's youth........................Sanhedrin 22a

Rabbi Shimon ben Yehotzedek, plowing during Sabbatical year........................Sanhedrin 26a

Rabbi Simon, standing up in front of Sage........................Shabbos 31b

Rabbi Tanchum, lions pit........................Sanhedrin 39a

Rabbi Tanchum bar Chiya, unusual occurrences at his death........................Moed Katan 25b

Rabbi Tanchum ben Chanilai, do not change one's custom........................Bava Metziah 86b

Rabbi Tarfon

Rabbi Tarfon and Rabbi Akiva........................Kesubos 84b

Rabbi Tarfon, episode in orchard........................Nedarim 62a

Rabbi Tarfon, height........................Niddah 24b

Rabbi Tarfon, his grandson's repentance........................Bava Metzia 85a

Rabbi Tarfon, honoring mother........................Kiddushin 31b

Rabbi Tarfon, pile of nuts........................Gittin 67a

Rabbi Tarfon, punishment of one of his disciples........................Menachos 68b

Rabbi Tarfon, saving murderers........................Niddah 61a

Rabbi Tzaddok

Rabbi Tzaddok, Temple destruction........................Gittin 56a

Rabbi Tzadok entered oven........................Kiddushin 40a

Rabbi Vardimas, Rabbi Yose's son........................Shabbos 118b

Rabbi Yaakov, unusual occurrences at his death........................Moed Katan 25b

Rabbi Yaakov bar Iddi, perhaps the sin caused it........................Berachos 4a

Rabbi Yannai

Rabbi Yannai, "broken reed"........................Yevamos 93b

Rabbi Yannai abandoned his vineyard........................Moed Katan 12b

Rabbi Yannai, cutting tree........................Bava Basra 60a-60b

Rabbi Yannai, four hundred vineyards........................Bava Basra 14a

Rabbi Yannai, Heavenly Yeshivah........................Bava Metzia 85b

Rabbi Yannai, questions during lecture........................Moed Katan 5a-5b

Rabbi Yannai, red shrouds........................Shabbos 114a; Niddah 20a

Rabbi Yannai, welcoming Shabbos........................Shabbos 119a; Bava Kama 32b

Rabbi Yehoshua ben Karchah, castrated man........................Shabbos 152a

Rabbi Yehoshua ben Levi

Rabbi Yehoshua ben Levi and Rabbi Chanina ben Dosa........................Yoma 49a

Rabbi Yehoshua ben Levi, Angel of death........................Kesubos 77b

Rabbi Yehoshua ben Levi, curse........................Berachos 7a; Sanhedrin 105b; Avodah Zarah 4b

Rabbi Yehoshua ben Levi, Elijah........................Makos 11a

Rabbi Yehoshua ben Levi, *Gan Eden*........................Kesubos 77b

Rabbi Yehoshua ben Levi, learned with sick people........................Kesubos 77b

Rabbi Yehoshua ben Levi, Messiah........................Sanhedrin 98a

Rabbi Yehoshua ben Perachiah and the Nazarene........................Sotah 47a

Rabbi Yehoshua

Emperor —

Rabbi Yehoshua, "lion Debei Ilai"........................Chullin 59b

Rabbi Yehoshua, Emperor's daughter........................Nedarim 50b; Taanis 7a-7b; Chullin 60a

Rabbi Yehoshua, Emperor's dream........................Berachos 56a-56b

R

Rabbi Yehoshua, Emperor's feast .... Chullin 59b-60a
Rabbi Yehoshua, Sages of Athens .... Bechoros 8b-9a
Rabbi Yehoshua, Shabbos spice for Emperor .... Shabbos 119a

His life —
Rabbi Yehoshua, Alexandria .... Niddah 69b
Rabbi Yehoshua, dwelling place .... Sanhedrin 32b
Rabbi Yehoshua, Pekiin .... Sanhedrin 32b
Rabbi Yehoshua, ship .... Horayos 10a

Wisdom —
Rabbi Yehoshua, "advice is gone" .... Sotah 49b
Rabbi Yehoshua, *Av Beis Din* .... Bava Kama 74b
Rabbi Yehoshua, defeated me .... Eruvin 53b
Rabbi Yehoshua, hand signs .... Chagigah 5b
Rabbi Yehoshua, happy is she who gave birth to him .... Avos 2:8
Rabbi Yehoshua, Heavenly Chariot .... Chagigah 14b

Misc. —
Rabbi Yehoshua, adding a month .... Rosh Hashanah 25a-25b
Rabbi Yehoshua and Rabban Gamliel .... Bechoros 36a
Rabbi Yehoshua, Bei Avidan .... Shabbos 152a
Rabbi Yehoshua, episode about judging favorably .... Shabbos 127b
Rabbi Yehoshua, fasts .... Chagigah 22b
Rabbi Yehoshua ransomed Rabbi Yishmael .... Gittin 58a
Rabbi Yehoshua, visit on festival .... Chagigah 3a-3b

Rabbi Yehudah
Behavior —
Rabbi Yehudah, cloak .... Nedarim 49b-50a
Rabbi Yehudah, dance with myrtle branch .... Kesubos 17a
Rabbi Yehudah, great is work .... Nedarim 49b
Rabbi Yehudah, satisfied with little .... Nedarim 49b-50a
Rabbi Yehudah, Shabbos eve .... Shabbos 25b
Rabbi Yehudah, sickness after drinking four cups .... Nedarim 49b

Learning —
Rabbi Yehudah became angry with Symmachus .... Kiddushin 52b; Nazir 49b-50a
Rabbi Yehudah, *halacha* .... Eruvin 46b-47a, 52a; Beitzah 27a; Bechoros 11a
Rabbi Yehudah, one *tallis* for six disciples .... Sanhedrin 20a
Rabbi Yehudah, retroactive clarification .... Yoma 55b-56b; Chullin 14a-14b; Eruvin 36b-37a;
                                                                                                                         Succah 23b-24a; Gittin 25a-26a; Bava Kama 69a-69b; Meilah 22a
Rabbi Yehudah, *semichah* .... Sanhedrin 13b-14a; Avodah Zarah 8b
Rabbi Yehudah, vineyard in Yavneh .... Berachos 63b
Rabbi Yehudah, wise when he wants .... Gittin 67a

Misc. —
Rabbi Yehudah, first speaker .... Shabbos 33b; Berachos 63b
Rabbi Yehudah, *muktzeh* .... Shabbos 142b-143a; Beitzah 33a
Rabbi Yehudah, permitting vow regarding married woman .... Nedarim 66b
Rabbi Yehudah, pious man .... Temurah 15b; Bava Kama 103b
Rabbi Yehudah, ravenous hunger .... Yoma 83b
Rabbi Yehudah, seriousness of Sabbatical year .... Gittin 54a; Bechoros 30a
Rabbi Yehudah ben Bava, *semichah* .... Sanhedrin 13b-14a; Avodah Zarah 8b

R

Rabbi Yehudah ben Beseira
Rabbi Yehudah ben Beseira, episode .... Pesachim 3b
Rabbi Yehudah ben Beseira, Netzivin .... Sanhedrin 32b
Rabbi Yehudah ben Geirim, blessings .... Moed Katan 9a-9b
Rabbi Yehudah ben Kenusa, sides of roads .... Bava Kama 81b
Rabbi Yehudah Hanasi .... *see* **Rebbi,** page 548
Rabbi Yehudah Nesiah
Rabbi Yehudah Nesiah .... Bava Basra 111a-111b
Rabbi Yehudah Nesiah, oil .... Avodah Zarah 37a
Rabbi Yehudah Nesiah, hurt feelings .... Taanis 24a
Rabbi Yehudah ben Rav Shmuel bar Shilas, fear of Heaven .... Succah 47a
Rabbi Yeshaivav, *neveilah* and *treifah* .... Chullin 32a
Rabbi Yirmiyah
Rabbi Yirmiyah, "they say in *Eretz Yisrael*" .... Sanhedrin 17b
Rabbi Yirmiyah, emigration to *Eretz Yisrael* .... Kesubos 75a
Rabbi Yirmiyah, gutter .... Yoma 87a
Rabbi Yirmiyah, joke to Rabbi Zeira .... Niddah 23a
Rabbi Yirmiyah, sent away .... Bava Basra 23b, 165b
Rabbi Yirmiyah bar abba, veins of the sinews .... Chullin 57a
Rabbi Yishmael
Episodes —
Rabbi Yishmael, blessing to G-d .... Berachos 7a
Rabbi Yishmael, captivity .... Gittin 58a
Rabbi Yishmael, comforted at his sons' death .... Moed Katan 28b
Rabbi Yishmael, far from bribe .... Kesubos 105b; Makos 24a
Rabbi Yishmael, his sons' captivity .... Gittin 58a
Rabbi Yishmael, Jewish daughters .... Nedarim 66a
Rabbi Yishmael tilted lamp .... Shabbos 12b
Rabbi Yishmael, wicked doctor .... Avodah Zarah 27b
Rabbi Yishmael's daughter, captive .... Gittin 58a
Misc. —
Rabbi Yishmael, "those who go to Usha" .... Bava Basra 28b
Rabbi Yishmael, his teacher .... Shevuos 26a
Rabbi Yishmael, skin of his face .... Chullin 123a
Rabbi Yishmael ben Elisha, "Yishmael, my 'son', bless me!" .... Berachos 7a
Rabbi Yishmael ben Rabbi Yose
Rabbi Yishmael ben Rabbi Yose and Avdan .... Yevamos 105b
Rabbi Yishmael ben Rabbi Yose, beauty .... Bava Metzia 84a
Rabbi Yishmael ben Rabbi Yose, distance from bribe .... Kesubos 105b
Rabbi Yishmael ben Rabbi Yose, his father's place .... Shabbos 51a
Rabbi Yishmael ben Rabbi Yose, loading .... Bava Metzia 30b
Rabbi Yishmael ben Rabbi Yose, permitted vow regarding woman .... Nedarim 66b
Rabbi Yishmael ben Rabbi Yose, thieves .... Bava Metzia 83b-84a
Rabbi Yishmael, Rabbi Yose's son .... Shabbos 118b
Rabbi Yitzchak, his names .... Pesachim 113b-114a
Rabbi Yitzchak bar Elyashiv, Chana become beautiful! .... Taanis 23b
Rabbi Yitzchak bar Ami, a woman fertilizes first, male .... Nidah 25b
Rabbi Yitzchak bar Avidami, secondary utensil .... Shabbos 40b
Rabbi Yitzchak bar Yosef, daughters are supported from movable property ... Kesubos 50b

R

Rabbi Yitzchak Nafcha, *aggadah* and *halacha* .... Bava Kama 60b
Rabbi Yochanan ben Beroka, "Be fruitful and multiply" commanded to women ..... Yevamos 65b
Rabbi Yochanan ben Gudgoda
   Rabbi Yochanan ben Gudgoda, high position .... Horayos 10a-10b
   Rabbi Yochanan ben Gudgoda, wisdom .... Horayos 10a
Rabbi Yochanan ben Nuri, "basket of peddler" .... Gittin 67a
Rabbi Yochanan ben Zakai
   Episodes —
      Rabbi Yochanan ben Zakai, blessing for fear of Heaven .... Berachos 28b
      Rabbi Yochanan ben Zakai, charity by his family members .... Bava Basra 10a
      Rabbi Yochanan ben Zakai, death .... Berachos 28b
      Rabbi Yochanan ben Zakai, decrees .... Rosh Hashanah 31b-32a
      Rabbi Yochanan ben Zakai, events of his life .... Sanhedrin 41a-41b
      Rabbi Yochanan ben Zakai, greetings .... Berachos 17a
      Rabbi Yochanan ben Zakai, Heavenly Chariot .... Chagigah 14b
      Rabbi Yochanan ben Zakai, shadow of *Heichal* .... Pesachim 26a
      Rabbi Yochanan ben Zakai, *shofar* .... Rosh Hashanah 29b
      Rabbi Yochanan ben Zakai, *shofar* in Yavneh .... Rosh Hashanah 29b
      Rabbi Yochanan ben Zakai, Temple destruction .... Gittin 56a-56b
      Rabbi Yochanan ben Zakai, wisdom .... Succah 28a; Bava Basra 134a
   Misc. —
      Rabbi Yochanan ben Zakai, behavior .... Succah 28a
      Rabbi Yochanan ben Zakai, Beror Chail .... Sanhedrin 32b
Rabbi Yochanan
   Character traits —
      Rabbi Yochanan, "this is a man!" .... Shabbos 112b; Eruvin 24a
      Rabbi Yochanan, beauty .... Bava Metzia 84a; Berachos 5b
      Rabbi Yochanan, fire sparks .... Chullin 137b
      Rabbi Yochanan, Heavenly Yeshivah .... Bava Metzia 85b
      Rabbi Yochanan, rav of city .... Shabbos 46a; Yevamos 14a
   Disciples —
      Rabbi Yochanan and Rav Kahana .... Bava Kama 117a-117b
      Rabbi Yochanan, concise teaching .... Pesachim 3b
      Rabbi Yochanan, disciple who scoffed .... Bava Basra 75a; Sanhedrin 100a
      Rabbi Yochanan, four disciples in one cubit .... Eruvin 53a
      Rabbi Yochanan, in the name of who said it .... Yevamos 96b-97a
      Rabbi Yochanan, *semichah* for disciple .... Sanhedrin 30b
      Rabbi Yochanan, *semichah* for Eli's descendants .... Sanhedrin 14a
      Rabbi Yochanan washed hands before learning .... Bava Kama 17a
   Episodes —
      Rabbi Yochanan, "give your hand" .... Berachos 5b
      Rabbi Yochanan, bathhouse collapse .... Kesubos 62a
      Rabbi Yochanan, noblewoman .... Avodah Zarah 28a
      Rabbi Yochanan, ravenous hunger .... Yoma 83b
      Rabbi Yochanan, troubles from non-Jews .... Yevamos 63b
      Rabbi Yochanan, wonders on ship .... Bava Basra 74a-74b
      Rabbi Yochanan's daughter, Zeirei .... Kiddushin 71b
   Learning —
      Rabbi Yochanan, "wisdom is gone" .... Sotah 49b

Rabbi Yochanan, *Divrei Hayamim* .... Pesachim 62b
Rabbi Yochanan, exchange .... Succah 4b
Rabbi Yochanan, Heavenly Chariot .... Chagigah 13a
Rabbi Yochanan in a dream, answer .... Menachos 84b
Rabbi Yochanan, number of letters in Torah .... Shabbos 49b
Rabbi Yochanan, *Toras Kohanim* .... Yevamos 72b
Rabbi Yochanan went back on his words .... Megillah 19b
Rabbi Yochanan wept because of a verse .... Chagigah 5a

Resh Lakish —
Rabbi Yochanan and Resh Lakish .... Kesubos 54b
Rabbi Yochanan, Resh Lakish's death .... Bava Metzia 84a
Rabbi Yochanan, Resh Lakish's mistake .... Avodah Zarah 58b
Rabbi Yochanan, Resh Lakish's son .... Taanis 9a

Sages —
Rabbi Yochanan, Ilfa .... Taanis 21a
Rabbi Yochanan, praised Rav .... Chullin 54a
Rabbi Yochanan, Rabbi Oshiah .... Eruvin 53a
Rabbi Yochanan rent his garment at Rabbi Chanina's death .... Moed Katan 24a
Rabbi Yochanan, Shmuel .... Chullin 95b

Misc. —
Rabbi Yochanan, "*bar* Nafcha" .... Bava Metzia 85b
Rabbi Yochanan, behavior .... Yoma 86a
Rabbi Yochanan, gates of *mikveh* .... Berachos 20a; Bava Metzia 84a
Rabbi Yochanan, his daughter to Zeiri .... Kiddushin 71b
Rabbi Yochanan, his son's bone (tooth) .... Berachos 5b; Bava Basra 116a
Rabbi Yochanan, lawyers .... Kesubos 52b
Rabbi Yochanan, orphan .... Kiddushin 31b
Rabbi Yochanan, whispering on Yom Kippur .... Yoma 82b

Rabbi Yonah
Rabbi Yonah, rain .... Taanis 23b
Rabbi Yonah, strong men of *Eretz Yisrael* .... Taanis 23b

Rabbi Yonassan
Rabbi Yonassan, prostitutes fled .... Avodah Zarah 17a-17b
Rabbi Yonassan wept because of a verse .... Yoma 9b

Rabbi Yonassan ben Asmai, blessings .... Moed Katan 9a-9b

Rabbi Yose

Episodes —
Rabbi Yose, Elijah in a ruin .... Berachos 3a
Rabbi Yose, Elijah's resentment .... Sanhedrin 113a-113b
Rabbi Yose, lamp in blind man's hand .... Megillah 24b
Rabbi Yose, respected by Rebbi .... Sanhedrin 24a
Rabbi Yose submitted to Rebbi's ruling .... Shabbos 51a

His life —
Rabbi Yose, his sons .... Shabbos 118b
Rabbi Yose, ravenous hunger .... Yoma 83b
Rabbi Yose, *semichah* .... Sanhedrin 13b-14a; Avodah Zarah 8b
Rabbi Yose, tanning hides .... Shabbos 49b
Rabbi Yose, Tzipori .... Sanhedrin 32b
Rabbi Yose, unusual occurrences at his death .... Moed Katan 25b; Sanhedrin 109a

R

Learning —
Rabbi Yose, explains his opinion...Gittin 67a
Rabbi Yose, *halacha*..Eruvin 46b-47b; Sanhedrin 27a-27b
Rabbi Yose, Rebbi's teacher...Niddah 14b
Rabbi Yose, ruling according to Rabbi Yehudah...Pesachim 100a
Rabbi Yose, sayings..Shabbos 118b
Rabbi Yose, scroll was torn...Yevamos 96b
Rabbi Yose, *Seder Olam*..Yevamos 82b
Rabbi Yose, vineyard in Yavneh...Berachos 63b

Misc. —
Rabbi Yose, behavior...Shabbos 118b
Rabbi Yose, priestly blessing...Shabbos 118b

Rabbi Yose bar Chanina
Rabbi Yose bar Chanina, "laughter in *Eretz Yisrael*"...Sanhedrin 17b
Rabbi Yose bar Chanina, Heavenly Yeshivah..Bava Metzia 85b
Rabbi Yose bar Chanina is an expert judge..Bava Kama 39a
Rabbi Yose bar Chanina, *semichah*..Sanhedrin 30b

Rabbi Yose bar Kippar
Rabbi Yose bar Kippar, adding month outside *Eretz Yisrael*................................Berachos 63a-63b
Rabbi Yose bar Kippar, returning deposit...Gittin 14a-14b

Rabbi Yose ben Durmaskis, Leviathan..Chullin 67b

Rabbi Yose ben Kisma..Avos 6:9

Rabbi Yose ben Yehudah, two Heavenly angels..Shabbos 119b

Rabbi Yose ben Zimra and Rebbi, nuptial...Kesubos 62b

Rabbi Yose de'min Yokrat..Taanis 24a

Rabbi Yose Haglili, three mitzvos during the Holiday...Chagigah 6b

Rabbi Yose Haglili and Bruriah..Eruvin 53b

Rabbi Yose HaKohen
Rabbi Yose HaKohen..Avos 2:8
Rabbi Yose HaKohen, Heavenly Chariot..Chagigah 14b

Rabbi Yoshiah, foundation of world...Gittin 61a

Rabbi Zakai, merit of *kiddush*...Megillah 27b

Rabbi Zechariah protected his wife...Kesubos 27b

Rabbi Zechariah bar Avkolus, modesty..Gittin 57b

Rabbi Zeira
Episodes —
Rabbi Zeira, appeasement..Yoma 87a
Rabbi Zeira, emigration to *Eretz Yisrael*..Kesubos 112a; Shabbos 41a
Rabbi Zeira, invitation from House of Nasi.......................................Chullin 44b; Megillah 28a
Rabbi Zeira, *semichah*..Kesubos 17a; Sanhedrin 14a
Rabbi Zeira, slaughtering on Purim...Megillah 7a-7b
Rabbi Zeira , violent persons, (*bryonei*) repentence..Sanhedrin 37a

Misc. —
Rabbi Zeira, inquiry to cause laughter..Niddah 23a
Rabbi Zeira, eulogy...Megillah 6a
Rabbi Zeira, fasts..Bava Metzia 85a
Rabbi Zeira, Heavenly Yeshivah...Bava Metzia 85b
Rabbi Zeira, his father was tax collector..Sanhedrin 25b-26a
Rabbi Zeira, old age...Megillah 28a

R

Rabbi Zeira, oven .... Bava Metzia 85a
Rabbi Zeira, pious ones of Babylon .... Chullin 122a
Rabbi Zeira, preparations for Shabbos .... Shabbos 119a
Rabbi Zeira, sharp-minded .... Horayos 14a
Rabbi Zeira, standing before Sage .... Berachos 28a
Rabbi Zerika, *berachah* on *lulav* .... Succah 37b
Rabbinate
Rabbinate .... *see also* **Authority**, page 36
Rabbinate, avoid .... Avos 1:10
Rabbinate buries those who enter it .... Pesachim 87b
Rabbinate, harmful .... Avos 1:10
Rabbinate, reduces days .... Berachos 55a
Rabbinical
Rabbinical court .... *see* **Beis din**, page 50
Rabbinical, deduction, precious .... Bava Kama 17b; Yevamos 2b, 71a; Bava Basra 108b
Rabbinical Decree
Rabbinical Decree .... *see also* **Decree**, page 154
Rabbinical Decree, according to lenient opinion .... Avodah Zarah 7a
Rabbinical Decree, cancels Torah commandment .... Pesachim 92a-92b
Rabbinical Decree, in Temple .... Zevachim 79b
Rabbinical Decree, individual and numerous .... Eruvin 46a
Rabbinical Decree, leniencies in mixture .... Yevamos 81a, 82a
Rabbinical Decree, not accepted among people .... Avodah Zarah 36a-36b
Rabbinical Decree, possibility to exchange .... Yoma 55b
Rabbinical Decree, when permitted to annul it .... Beitzah 5a-5b; Sanhedrin 59b
Rabbinical Decrees, "your elders and they will tell you" .... Shabbos 23a
Rabbinical Decrees, because of event .... Yevamos 116b; Chagigah 23a
Rabbinical Decrees, Divine approval .... Makos 23b
Rabbinical Decrees, do not deviate .... Berachos 19b; Shabbos 23a
Rabbinical Decrees, from Sinai .... Megillah 19b
Rabbinical Decrees, guarding orchard .... Yevamos 21a
Rabbinical Decrees, handles for Torah .... Yevamos 21a; Eruvin 21b
Rabbinical Decrees, not to appear peculiar .... Eruvin 68b
Rabbinical Decrees, precious .... Avodah Zarah 35a
Rabbinical Decrees, source .... Eruvin 21b-22a
Rabbinical prohibition for Shabbos
Rabbinical prohibition for Shabbos, at dusk .... Eruvin 30b, 32b, 34b, 35a
Rabbinical prohibition for Shabbos, even for *mitzvah* .... Eruvin 103a; Pesachim 65b-66a;
.... Chagigah 16b; Beitzah 36b-37a
Rabbinical prohibition for Shabbos, frequent need .... Shabbos 114b; Pesachim 47a
Rabbinical prohibition for Shabbos in Temple .... Pesachim 47a, 65a-65b; Eruvin 102a-104a;
.... Beitzah 11b
Rabbit of Nebuchadnezzar .... Nedarim 65a
Rabid dog .... Shabbos 121b; Yoma 83b-84a
Rabim .... *see* **Majority of Sages**, page 385
Rach kekaneh .... *see* **Soft like reed, Rabbi Elazar ben Shimon**, page 641
Rachamim .... *see* **Mercy, Divine Attribute**, page 405
Rachav umanhig .... *see* **Driving, act of acquisition**, page 182

R

Rachel

Rachel, gave signs to Leah .... Bava Basra 123a; Megillah 13b
Rachel, when did she conceive .... Rosh Hashanah 11a
Rachmana (lit. Hakb'h) liba bayi .... *see* **G-d desires heart (piety)**, page 246
Rachmana litzlan .... Shabbos 84b; Kesubos 45b; Bava Kama 65b
Rachmana litzlan .... *see* **G-d save me**, page 6

Radish

Radish and horseradish, Rebbi and Antoninus .... Avodah Zarah 11a; Berachos 57b
Radish, blessing .... Eruvin 28b; Berachos 36a
Radish, digestion .... Avodah Zarah 11a
Radish, health .... Eruvin 56a
Radish, moving *muktzeh* indirectly .... Shabbos 123a, 141a
Radish, sharpness and peel .... Shabbos 108b

Rag, impurity

.... Shabbos 28b-29b, 39b, 47a; Keilim 27:11-12, 28:1-3

Rahab

Rahab, beauty .... Megillah 15a
Rahab, if he knows her .... Megillah 15a; Taanis 5b
Rahab, prophets descend from her .... Megillah 14b
Rahab, spies .... Zevachim 116a-116b

Rain

Aggadah —

Rain, blessing .... Taanis 6b-7a, 23a, 25b-26a; Berachos 59b
Rain, Divine Judgment .... Taanis 8b; Rosh Hashanah 17b
Rain for one person, episodes .... Taanis 9a-9b
Rain, four species .... Taanis 2b
Rain, importance of rainy day .... Taanis 7a, 8b; Berachos 33a
Rain, merit .... Taanis 7b, 25b
Rain, power .... Taanis 2a
Rain, prayer to stop it .... Taanis 8b

Episodes —

Rain, Abba Chilkia .... Taanis 23a-23b
Rain, Adam's prayer .... Chullin 60b
Rain, Chanan Hanechba .... Taanis 23b
Rain, Choni Ham'agel .... Taanis 23a
Rain, Elijah .... Sanhedrin 113a
Rain, episodes of merit .... Taanis 24a
Rain for one person, episodes .... Taanis 9b; Chullin 60b
Rain in its time, Shimon ben Shetach .... Taanis 23a
Rain in summer, Rava .... Taanis 24b
Rain, Rabbi Akiva .... Taanis 25b
Rain, Rabbi Chanina .... Taanis 24b; Yoma 53b
Rain, Rabbi Yonah .... Taanis 23b
Rain, spoke harshly towards G-d .... Taanis 25a
Rain, Joel .... Taanis 5a

Prayer —

Rain and dew, mentioning .... Berachos 33a; Taanis 3a-5a
Rain and dew, when to mention .... Taanis 2b, 3a, 4a-5a, 6a; Bava Metzia 28a
Rain on fast day, praise for congregation .... Taanis 25b
Rain, source for mentioning .... Taanis 2a

R

Scientific facts —

Rain, bad .... Bava Basra 25b; Berachos 59a; Taanis 8b
Rain, different rainfalls .... Taanis 3b-4a
Rain, difficult .... Taanis 6b, 8b, 22b
Rain, drought .... Taanis 7b, 8b; Shabbos 32b
Rain, excessive .... Taanis 10a
Rain, how .... Taanis 19b; Megillah 15a
Rain, husband of the earth .... Taanis 6b
Rain in *Eretz Yisrael* .... Taanis 10a
Rain, key .... Taanis 2a-2b; Sanhedrin 113a
Rain, origin .... Taanis 8b, 9b-10a; Eruvin 45b
Rain, *revi'yos* .... Nedarim 62b-63a; Taanis 6a-6b
Rain, wonders of Divine providence .... Bava Basra 16a
Rains, different seasons .... Taanis 5a, 6a

Misc. —

Rain, good omen for deceased .... Sanhedrin 47a
Rain on Succos .... Succah 29a
Rain, *techum* .... Eruvin 45b-46a
Rain, worker employed to irrigate .... Bava Metzia 76b-77b

Rainbow

Rainbow, blessing and prostrating to .... Berachos 59a
Rainbow, looking at .... Chagigah 16a; Kiddushin 40a
Rainbow, sun never saw its curve .... Rosh Hashanah 23b-24a

Raise

Raise him above his brothers, *Kohen Gadol* .... Yoma 18a; Horayos 9a; Chullin 134b
Raise him above his brothers, Sage .... Chullin 134b
Raise numerous disciples .... Avos 1:1
Raising a slave, act of acquisition .... Kiddushin 22b
Raising an orphan .... Kesubos 50a; Sanhedrin 19b; Megillah 13a
Raising and putting down, Pesach lamb .... Pesachim 85b
Raising and rolling up Torah scroll .... Megillah 32a
Raising hand, wicked .... Sanhedrin 58b
Raising prices .... Bava Basra 90b
Raising, purchase .... *see* **Lifting to purchase**, page 370

Raising item

Raising item, changing one's mind .... Shabbos 5b; Kesubos 31a; Eruvin 20b
Raising item, collecting rain .... Shabbos 5a-5b
Raising item from its place, received .... Shabbos 5a
Raising item, hand considered as four handbreadths .... Shabbos 5a
Raising item, someone else put it on him .... Shabbos 3a-3b
Raising item when making and canceling partition .... Shabbos 99b

Raisins, *muktzeh* .... Beitzah 26b
Rak, to exclude .... Sanhedrin 49a
Rake in Temple, uses .... Tamid 5:6
Raking

Raking embers on Shabbos .... Krisos 20a-20b
Raking feeding trough on Shabbos .... Shabbos 140b-141a

Ram

Ram, a day old .... Bava Kama 65b

Ram, age .... Parah 1:3
Ram and ewe .... Menachos 107b
Ram of *nazir*, bread .... Nazir 24b; Menachos 48b
Ram of *nazir*, to Israelite .... Zevachim 55a
Rams, head near tail .... Shabbos 119b
Ramatayim, Elkanah .... Megillah 14a
Rami bar BeRabbi, "Neharbelians teach" .... Sanhedrin 17b
Rami bar Abba, building a synagogue .... Megillah 26b
Rami bar Chama
Rami bar Chama, last will .... Bava Basra 151a-151b
Rami bar Chama, reason for his death .... Berachos 47b
Rami bar Chama went to another teacher .... Zevachim 96b
Rami bar Chama's daughter .... Beitzah 29b
Rami bar Tamari, udder .... Chullin 110a-110b
Rami bar Yechezkel, pools that King Solomon built .... Eruvin 14b; Yoma 58b
Ramp
Ramp for goat to Azazel .... Yoma 66b
Ramp for Red Heifer .... Parah 3:6
Ramp in Temple wall .... Middos 4:5
Ramps of Altar .... Eruvin 104a; Zevachim 54a, 62a-63a, 108b, 120a; Middos 3:3
Raos rabos vetzaros .... Chagigah 5a
Rape victim
Rape victim, *kesubah* .... Nedarim 90b-91a
Rape victim, marriage by mistake .... Yevamos 91b
Rape victim, marriage to *Kohen* .... Yevamos 35a, 56b
Rape victim of *Kohen Gadol* .... Yevamos 59b-60a
Rape victim of one's father, forbidden relations .... Yevamos 4a-4b, 49a, 97a
Rape victim of one's father, levirate marriage .... Yevamos 9a-10b
Rape victim, relatives .... Yevamos 26a, 94b-95b, 97a
Rape victim, stringency in lineage .... Kesubos 14b-15b
Rapist
Rapist and seducer, acknowledges .... Kesubos 41a
Rapist and seducer, pain .... Kesubos 39a-39b; Bava Kama 59a
Rapist and seducer .... *see also* **Penalty for virgin,** page 479
Rapist, heirs .... Kesubos 42b
Rapist, *kesubah* .... Kesubos 39b
Rapist, voluntary erection .... Yevamos 53b
Rapist who divorced, required to remarry her .... Makos 15a; Gittin 90a; Temurah 5a
Rasha .... *see* **Wicked,** page 743
Rat
Rat and cat, unfortunate man .... Sanhedrin 105a
Rat and pit, promise .... Taanis 8a
Rat, dragged *chametz* .... Pesachim 9a
Rat, is it a prophet? .... Pesachim 9b
Rat, on land and not in sea .... Chullin 127a
Rate
Rate fixed, retracting from sale, *mi shepara* .... Bava Metzia 63b
Rate, low, for a sale .... Bava Metzia 74b
Ratza Hashem lezakos es Yisrael .... *see* **G-d wanted to give merit to Israel,** page 246

Rauy..*see* **Fit**, page 228; *see also* **Future property**, page 241
Rauy lekelev..*see* **Fit for dog**, page 228
Rav

Rav...*see also* **Teacher**, page 674
Rav of *Eretz Yisrael*...Niddah 20b; Yoma 9b; Gittin 19b

Rav

Episodes —
Rav appeased Rabbi Chanina...Yoma 87b
Rav, beyond letter of law..Bava Metzia 83a
Rav, dream that he was hanged on palm tree..Yoma 87b
Rav, episode about *Adarchan*..Avodah Zarah 10b
Rav, episode about butcher...Yoma 87a
Rav, episode about omens and signs...Chullin 95b
Rav honored Sage at the door..Bava Kama 80a-80b
Rav, non-holy meal..Chullin 95b
Rav, protection from plague...Taanis 21b
Rav, Rav Huna's wealth..Megillah 27b
Rav, repeating Rabbi Shila's lecture in a loud voice..Yoma 20b

Family —
Rav, "give me your daughter"..Yevamos 45a
Rav, bad wife...Yevamos 63a
Rav, his father and mother......................Pesachim 4a; Moed Katan 20a-20b; Sanhedrin 5a
Rav, Rabbi Chiya's nephew..........................Sanhedrin 5a; Pesachim 4a; Moed Katan 20a
Rav, taught trade to his son...Pesachim 113a
Rav, temporary marriage...Yevamos 37b
Rav, visit to son-in-law..Chullin 95b

Praises —
Rav, fire sparks...Chullin 137b
Rav, height...Niddah 24b
Rav, our masters from Babylon...Sanhedrin 17b; Shevuos 47a
Rav, Rabbi Yochanan praised him...Chullin 54a

Ruling —
Rav, betrothal through initmate relations..Kiddushin 12b
Rav "made a decree in a valley"..Chullin 110a
Rav and Shmuel, law..............Shabbos 22a, 40a; Bechoros 49b; Pesachim 101a; Menachos 41b; Niddah 24b
Rav, authorization from Rebbi..Sanhedrin 5a-5b
Rav, cowherds..Sanhedrin 5b
Rav died and we did not know this law...Berachos 42b-43a
Rav is a *Tanna* and can oppose.................Gittin 38b; Eruvin 50b; Kesubos 8a; Bava Basra 42a;
                                                                                         Sanhedrin 83b; Chullin 122b
Rav, *kashering* winepress...Avodah Zarah 74b
Rav, law...Eruvin 90b; Bechoros 49b
Rav, moral teachings when went to judge...Yoma 86b; Sanhedrin 7b
Rav, one strict ruling with two consequences...Bava Kama 99b
Rav, *Rabbeinu Hagadol*...Succah 33a-33b, 35b
Rav turned his face away...Eruvin 94a
Rav's teaching is dear to you..Shabbos 10b

Shmuel —
Rav and Shmuel, excommunication..Yevamos 121a

R

Rav came to *Eretz Yisrael*, Shmuel .... Shabbos 108a
Rav, curse to Shmuel .... Bava Kama 80b
Rav, disciples-colleagues .... Sanhedrin 36b
Rav, Shmuel rent his garment at his death .... Moed Katan 24a
Misc. —
Rav, "stir the audience with your eulogy" .... Shabbos 153a
Rav, Bei Avidan .... Shabbos 116a
Rav, careful to use proper speech .... Pesachim 3b
Rav, no music after his death .... Shabbos 110a
Rav Abba
Rav Abba, "may my words be accepted" .... Beitzah 38a
Rav Abba raised his grandson .... Sotah 49a
Rav Abba bar Kahana, words of Torah before a corpse .... Berachos 3b
Rav Abba bar Mammel, insulting a sleeping person or one who has died ... Bava Kama 86b
Rav Abba bar Yaakov, witness who is a thief .... Sanhedrin 27a-27b
Rav Acha
Rav Acha and Ravina .... Pesachim 74b
Rav Acha danced in front of bride .... Kesubos 17a
Rav Acha bar Abba, his granddaughter on his lap .... Kiddushin 81b-82a
Rav Acha bar Yaakov
Rav Acha bar Yaakov, exhibited anger .... Shabbos 105b
Rav Acha bar Yaakov, great man .... Bava Kama 40a
Rav Acha bar Yaakov, snake .... Kiddushin 29b
Rav Acha bar Yaakov, writing Torah scroll .... Bava Basra 14a
Rav Acha ben Rav Ika, knife used to slaughter .... Eruvin 63a
Rav Acha of Dafti, *Rosh Yeshivah* .... Bava Basra 12b
Rav Achadvoi .... Bava Basra 9b
Rav Achai was found perfect .... Shabbos 152b
Rav Achi excommunicated fishermen .... Kiddushin 72a
Rav Adda bar Abba
Rav Adda bar Abba, cause of his death .... Bava Basra 22a
Rav Adda bar Abba, test .... Bava Basra 22a
Rav Adda bar Ahavah
Rav Adda bar Ahavah, behavior .... Taanis 20b
Rav Adda bar Ahavah, curse to Chuba .... Bava Kama 80a; Nazir 57b
Rav Adda bar Ahavah obtained position for his host .... Kiddushin 76b
Rav Adda bar Ahavah, old age .... Taanis 20b
Rav Adda bar Ahavah, Rav's funeral .... Berachos 42b-43a
Rav Adda bar Ahavah, red garment .... Berachos 20a
Rav Adda bar Ahavah reviewed his learning numerous times .... Taanis 8a
Rav Adda bar Ahavah, wound to genital organ .... Shabbos 135a
Rav Adda bar Minyomi, judges of Nehardea .... Sanhedrin 17b
Rabbi Ada bar Masna, Torah learning through deprivation .... Eruvin 22a
Rav Afes, Levi did not come to his lecture .... Berachos 18b
Rav Aaron, Amora .... Bava Kama 109b; Menachos 74b
Rav Ami, judge .... Shabbos 10a
Rav Amram
Rav Amram, dominating evil urge .... Kiddushin 81a
Rav Amram, pillar broke down .... Bava Metzia 20b

Rav Amram, Reish Galusa's slaves .... Gittin 67b

Rav Anan

Rav Anan, distance from bribe .... Kesubos 105b-106a

Rav Anan, Elijah .... Kesubos 106a

Rav Anan, episode about partition removed .... Eruvin 74b

Rav Anan, preparations for Shabbos .... Shabbos 119a

Rav Anan wrote "our colleague" to Rav Huna .... Kesubos 69a-69b

Rav Ashi

Ruling —

Rav Ashi, Abbaye's curse .... Moed Katan 12b

Rav Ashi examined knife in his teacher's city .... Eruvin 63a

Rav Ashi, end of ruling .... Bava Metzia 86a

Rav Ashi, excommunication of ritual slaughterer .... Chullin 18a

Rav Ashi gathered butchers to rule on *treifah* .... Sanhedrin 7b; Horayos 3b

Rav Ashi, last version .... Bava Basra 157b

Misc. —

Rav Ashi, Angel of Death .... Moed Katan 28a

Rav Ashi, building of synagogue .... Bava Basra 3b

Rav Ashi, eulogy .... Moed Katan 25b

Rav Ashi, *Kidusha Rabba* .... Pesachim 106a

Rav Ashi, meal for king .... Kesubos 61a-61b

Rav Ashi, public prayer .... Berachos 30a

Rav Ashi, Rami bar Chama's daughter .... Beitzah 29b

Rav Ashi, ruler's mistake .... Bava Metzia 68a

Rav Ashi tasted Rav Kahana's dish .... Kesubos 61a

Rav Ashi, Torah and greatness .... Gittin 59a; Sanhedrin 36a

Rav Ashi was born after Rava .... Kiddushin 72b

Rav Ashi's wife, her father was scrupulous in his deeds .... Beitzah 29b

Rav Asi

Rav Asi and Shila, excommunication .... Niddah 36b-37a

Rav Asi, collecting teachings .... Kiddushin 13a

Rav Asi honored Sage at the door .... Bava Kama 80a-80b

Rav Asi, honoring his mother .... Kiddushin 31b

Rav Asi inspected his property .... Chullin 105a

Rav Asi, judge .... Shabbos 10a

Rav Asi, Rav .... Sanhedrin 36b

Rabbi Avira, ate from a gigantic peach .... Kesubos 112a

Rav Aviya

Rav Aviya, dirtying bed, Rava .... Shabbos 46a-46b

Rav Aviya, Rav Yosef's discourse, Rava .... Berachos 28b

Rav Aviya, resentment, Rava .... Shabbos 46a-46b

Rav bar Sheva, boiled liver .... Chullin 111a

Rav Bibi

Rav Bibi, high position .... Kiddushin 76b

Rav Bibi, ointment on his daughter .... Shabbos 80b; Moed Katan 9b

Rav Bibi's daughter, cosmetics .... Shabbos 80b; Moed Katan 9b

Rav Brona, happy with commandments .... Berachos 9b

Rav Chaga never had seminal discharge .... Moed Katan 25a

R

Rav Chama
Rav Chama, "*Amoraei deNehardea*" .... Sanhedrin 17b
Rav Chama, neighbors' and brothers' rights .... Bava Basra 7a
Rav Chama stood up in front of his son .... Kesubos 62b
Rav Chama bar Tuviah, burning of daughter of *Kohen* .... Sanhedrin 52b
Rav Chana bar Bisna, sitting in the succah .... Succah 47a
Rav Chanan bar Rava, resentment .... Shabbos 121a-121b
Rav Chanin died at his son's birth .... Moed Katan 25b
Rav Chanina
Rav Chanina, forgiveness .... Yoma 87b
Rav Chanina guarded his eyes .... Pesachim 113b
Rav Chanina, *Sefer Yetzirah* (Book of Creation) .... Sanhedrin 65b, 67b
Rav Chanina, they stared at him .... Berachos 58b
Rav Chinana bar Shila, badge .... Shabbos 58a
Rav Chisda
Episodes —
Rav Chisda dismissed his tenant farmer .... Bava Kama 119a
Rav Chisda, Elders of Nizonia .... Kiddushin 25a
Rav Chisda, Elders of Sura .... Sanhedrin 17b
Rav Chisda, episode about cow's udder .... Chullin 110a-110b
Rav Chisda, episode about witch .... Shabbos 81b-82a; Chullin 105b
Rav Chisda, quail .... Yoma 75b
Rav Chisda, trees blocked .... Bava Kama 92a
His life —
Rav Chisda, Angel of Death .... Moed Katan 28a
Rav Chisda, astrologers .... Yevamos 21b
Rav Chisda, death .... Makos 10a
Rav Chisda, fate .... Moed Katan 28a
Rav Chisda married his daughter to Rava .... Bava Basra 12b
Rav Chisda married his daughters to brothers .... Berachos 44a
Learning —
Rav Chisda, "Your words are pleasant" .... Gittin 7a
Rav Chisda, blows from Avimi .... Menachos 7a; Arachin 22a
Rav Chisda, his teacher needs him .... Bava Metzia 33a
Rav Chisda, learning Rav's new teachings .... Shabbos 10b
Rav Chisda, serving Sage to learn .... Bava Kama 20b
Rav Chisda, sharpness .... Eruvin 67a
Misc. —
Rav Chisda, "Pious ones of Babylon" .... Taanis 23b
Rav Chisda, destruction of charitable house .... Berachos 58b
Rav Chisda ruled in his teacher's city .... Eruvin 63a
Rav Chisda, sleep after death .... Eruvin 65a
Rav Daniel, rain .... Taanis 9b
Rav Dimi, figs .... Bava Basra 22a
Rav Eyna, Elders of Pumbedisa .... Sanhedrin 17b; Eruvin 79b
Rav Gamda, wealth due to monkey .... Nedarim 50b
Rav Gidal
Rav Gidal, doors of ritual bath .... Berachos 20a
Rav Gidal, intended to buy field .... Kiddushin 59a

R

Rav ha'ir .... *see* **Rav of city**, page 543

Rav Hamnuna

Rav Hamnuna, "*amrei bei Rav*" .... Sanhedrin 17b

Rav Hamnuna excommunicated disciple who ruled like Rabbi Shimon .... Shabbos 19b

Rav Hamnuna, honor to his coffin .... Moed Katan 25a-25b

Rav Hamnuna, *Karnuna* (as in the marketplace) .... Kiddushin 25a

Rav Hamnuna ruled in his teacher's city .... Eruvin 63a

Rav Hamnuna, unusual occurrences at his death .... Moed Katan 25b

Rav Huna

Episodes —

Rav Huna, carrying his burden .... Megillah 28a

Rav Huna caused pain to Chiya bar Rav .... Arachin 16b

Rav Huna, curse to Chuba .... Bava Kama 80a; Nazir 57b

Rav Huna, deeds of kindness .... Taanis 20b

Rav Huna, Elders of Sura .... Sanhedrin 17b

Rav Huna, episode about date .... Sotah 49a

Rav Huna, fingers clapping .... Yoma 19b

Rav Huna, meal of thanksgiving .... Berachos 46a

Rav Huna, numerous Torah scrolls .... Bava Basra 14a

Rav Huna, resentment toward Rav Anan .... Kesubos 69a-69b

Rav Huna, *tefillin* strap .... Moed Katan 25a

Rav Huna, tore garment .... Kiddushin 32a

Rav Huna, vinegar .... Berachos 5b

Greatness —

Rav Huna, merit of *kiddush* .... Megillah 27b

Rav Huna, pious ones of Babylon .... Taanis 23b

Rav Huna, protection from fire .... Taanis 21b

Rav Huna, Rabbi Ami presented to him .... Gittin 59b; Megillah 22a

Rav Huna, wealth .... Megillah 27b

Ruling —

Rav Huna, "Raven, fly away" .... Beitzah 21a; Chullin 124b

Rav Huna, cut off hand .... Sanhedrin 58b; Niddah 13b

Rav Huna did not explain his rationale .... Succah 14b

Rav Huna ruled in his teacher's city .... Eruvin 63a

Misc. —

Rav Huna, "his teacher needs him" .... Bava Metzia 33a

Rav Huna, funeral .... Moed Katan 25a

Rav Huna, his disciples became sterile .... Yevamos 62b, 64b

Rav Huna, preparations for Shabbos .... Shabbos 119a

Rav Huna wept because of a verse .... Chagigah 4b

Rav Huna bar Chiya, tax collector .... Bechoros 31a

Rav Huna bar Nassan .... Pesachim 86b

Rav Huna ben Rabbi Yehoshua

Rav Huna ben Rabbi Yehoshua, recovery .... Rosh Hashanah 17a

Rav Huna ben Rabbi Yehoshua rejects his own explanation .... Sanhedrin 30b

Rav Idi Avuah D'Rav Yaakov bar Iddi, a student of the academy for a certain day ... Chagigah 5b

Rav Idi bar Avin, *Koheness* .... Chullin 132a

Rav Ilash, a great man .... Bava Metzia 68b

R

Rav Kahana

Rav Kahana, beauty .... Bava Metzia 84a; Bava Basra 58a
Rav Kahana, episode about informer .... Bava Kama 117a-117b
Rav Kahana gave food to taste to Rav Ashi .... Kesubos 61a
Rav Kahana judged Rav's host .... Sanhedrin 7b-8a
Rav Kahana, *Koheness* .... Chullin 132a
Rav Kahana, news of his death .... Pesachim 3b
Rav Kahana, Rav .... Sanhedrin 36b
Rav Kahana, test of forbidden relations .... Kiddushin 40a
Rav Kahana, under Rav's bed .... Berachos 62a
Rav Kahana, vast knowledge of Shas .... Shabbos 63a
Rav Katina, angel .... Menachos 41a
Rav Malchio and Rav Malchia ... Beitzah 28b; Kesubos 61b; Makos 21a; Avodah Zarah 29a; Niddah 52a
Rav Masneh, Esther's name is found where in the Torah? .... Chullin 139b
Rav Matnah, "*shelanu*" water for *matzos* .... Pesachim 42a
Rav Menashe, deceived robbers .... Avodah Zarah 25b-26a
Rav Menashia bar Tachlifa, *zimun* .... Berachos 47b
Rav Meri bar Rochel, his mother is an Israelite .... Yevamos 45b
Rav Mesharshiya, gaze upon your Sages .... Horayos 12a

Rav Nachman

Episodes —

Rav Nachman and Rav Yehudah .... Kiddushin 70a-70b
Rav Nachman, Angel of Death .... Moed Katan 28a
Rav Nachman, golden carriage .... Gittin 31b
Rav Nachman, hurt feelings .... Taanis 24a
Rav Nachman, ox meat .... Bava Kama 71b-72a
Rav Nachman, temporary marriage .... Yevamos 37b
Rav Nachman's wife, mock forbidden food .... Chullin 109b

Ruling —

Rav Nachman, "I made a mistake" .... Eruvin 16b
Rav Nachman explained his rationale .... Succah 14b
Rav Nachman, questions in *beis din* .... Bava Kama 96b
Rav Nachman, ruling .... Bava Basra 65a
Rav Nachman, ordered judges to rescind their ruling .... Bava Kama 12a
Rav Nachman, shouting woman .... Succah 31a
Rav Nachman stood up before Sage's widow .... Shevuos 30b
Rav Nachman, taking partition away .... Eruvin 11b

Misc. —

Rav Nachman, "basket full of books" .... Megillah 28b
Rav Nachman, covering head .... Shabbos 156b
Rav Nachman, his daughters' sin .... Gittin 45a
Rav Nachman, Messiah .... Sanhedrin 98b
Rav Nachman, sin fearing .... Sotah 49b
Rav Nachman, wisdom .... Shevuos 41b
Rav Nachman bar Pappa, rain .... Chullin 60b
Rav Nachman bar Rav Chisdah, maneh the son of maneh .... Taanis 21b
Rav Nachman bar Yitzchak
Rav Nachman bar Yitzchak, careful in his deeds .... Shabbos 37b
Rav Nachman bar Yitzchak, preparations for Shabbos .... Shabbos 119a

R

Rav Nachman bar Yitzchak surpassed his father .... Taanis 21b
Rav of city
  Rav of city, Rabbi Elazar .... Niddah 20b; Yoma 9b; Gittin 19b
  Rav of city, Shmuel .... Eruvin 94a; Chullin 53b
  Rav of city, stringencies .... Shabbos 46a; Yevamos 14a
Rav Oshaya
  Rav Oshaya, Book of Creation .... Sanhedrin 65b, 67b
  Rav Oshaya guarded his eyes .... Pesachim 113b
Rav Pappa bar Shmuel
  Rav Pappa bar Shmuel, judges of Pumbedisa .... Sanhedrin 17b
  Rav Pappa bar Shmuel, measure .... Bava Basra 90b
  Rav Pappa bar Shmuel, slave dyed his hair .... Bava Metzia 60b
Rav Pappa
  Episodes —
    Rav Pappa, corpse under his bed .... Berachos 8b; Pesachim 112b
    Rav Pappa, demon .... Chullin 105b
    Rav Pappa, dowry .... Kesubos 52b-53a
    Rav Pappa, hurt feelings .... Taanis 9a-9b
    Rav Pappa, ox prepared in his honor .... Niddah 33b
    Rav Pappa stared at him .... Berachos 58b
    Rav Pappa, they stared at his parents .... Yevamos 106a
  Ruling —
    Rav Pappa, mistake in ruling .... Bava Metzia 81a
    Rav Pappa, money belonging to Jews .... Chullin 49b
    Rav Pappa postponed his ruling .... Beitzah 4a
    Rav Pappa, Rav Shimi's questions .... Taanis 9b
  Misc. —
    Rav Pappa, charity .... Bava Basra 10a
    Rav Pappa, his wife's earnings .... Sanhedrin 14b
    Rav Pappa, *Koheness* .... Chullin 132a
    Rav Pappa married off his daughter to he who solved his doubt .... Horayos 12b
    Rav Pappa, preparations for Shabbos .... Shabbos 119a
Rav Pappi, gave udders to guests .... Chullin 110a
Rav Pealim, Benaiah .... Berachos 18a-19a
Rav Rechumi came home late .... Kesubos 62b
Rav Safra
  Rav Safra, preparations for Shabbos .... Shabbos 119a; Kiddushin 41a
  Rav Safra, questions of heretics .... Avodah Zarah 4a
  Rav Safra, truth .... Chullin 94b; Makos 24a; Bava Basra 88a
  Rav Safra, verse in dream .... Chullin 133a
Rav Sechorah, a great man .... Nedarim 22b
Rav Seorim, Angel of Death .... Moed Katan 28a
Rav Shamen bar Abba, *semichah* .... Sanhedrin 14a
Rav Sheisha b'erai d'Rav Iddi, enactment was permitted for immediate needs ... Shabbos 114b
Rav Sheishess
  Rav Sheishess, Angel of Death .... Moed Katan 28a
  Rav Sheishess, disciple went to another teacher .... Zevachim 96b
  Rav Sheishess, Divine Presence in synagogue .... Megillah 29a
  Rav Sheishess, episode about partition taken away .... Eruvin 11b

R

Rav Sheishess, exhibited anger .... Shabbos 105b
Rav Sheishess, king .... Berachos 58a
Rav Sheishess, *Reish Galusa's* slaves .... Gittin 67b
Rav Sheishess, rejoice my soul .... Pesachim 68b
Rav Sheishess, wisdom .... Eruvin 67a; Shevuos 41b
Rav Shimi
Rav Shimi, questions to Rav Pappa .... Taanis 9b
Rav Shimi, snake .... Shabbos 109b
Rav Shizbi, born due to the merit of the Shabbos candles .... Shabbos 23b
Rav Shmuel bar Shilas
Rav Shmuel bar Shilas .... Bava Basra 8b
Rav Shmuel bar Shilas, schoolteacher .... Bava Basra 8b
Rav Shmuel
Rav Shmuel danced in front of bride .... Kesubos 17a
Rav Shmuel prepared an ox in Sage's honor .... Niddah 33b
Rabbi Simai, two crowns, *naaseh venishma* .... Shabbos 88a
Rav Simi bar Chiya, hastened to join a zimun .... Berachos 47a
Rav Tachlifa, mistake in ruling .... Beitzah 16b
Rav Tovi bar Matnah, wicked man's beard .... Bava Basra 58a
Rav Tuvyomi, city of Kushta .... Sanhedrin 97a
Rav Ukva bar Chama, last will .... Bava Basra 151a-151b
Rav Yaakov bar Acha, standing up in front of ben Torah .... Shabbos 31b
Rav Yehoshua bar Idi, news of death .... Pesachim 3b
Rav Yehudah
Episodes —
Rav Yehudah, emigration to *Eretz Yisrael* .... Berachos 24b
Rav Yehudah, excommunicating Sage .... Moed Katan 17a
Rav Yehudah, exhibited anger .... Shabbos 105b
Rav Yehudah, famine .... Taanis 24b
Rav Yehudah, quail .... Yoma 75b
Rav Yehudah, rebuke .... Moed Katan 16b
Learning —
Rav Yehudah and Rav Nachman .... Kiddushin 70a-70b
Rav Yehudah, Elders of Pumbedisa .... Sanhedrin 17b; Eruvin 79b
Rav Yehudah, forced to come to discourse .... Shabbos 148a
Rav Yehudah, four Orders .... Berachos 20a
Rav Yehudah, learning text of *havdala* .... Pesachim 104b
Rav Yehudah precisely cited name of Sage .... Chullin 18b
Misc. —
Rav Yehudah, angel .... Niddah 13a
Rav Yehudah, bad wife .... Yevamos 63b; Sanhedrin 22b
Rav Yehudah died on Rava's day of birth .... Kiddushin 72b
Rav Yehudah, height .... Niddah 24b
Rav Yehudah, same name as his son-in-law's father .... Berachos 42a
Rav Yehudah, storekeeper .... Bava Metzia 40a-40b
Rav Yimar, *Koheness* .... Chullin 132a
Rav Yirmiyah's father, repentance .... Shabbos 56b
Rav Yitzchak bar Bisna, no music after Rav's death .... Shabbos 110a

Rav Yitzchak bar Yehudah
Rav Yitzchak bar Yehudah, learning text of *havdala*..................................Pesachim 104b
Rav Yitzchak bar Yehudah went to another teacher.................................Zevachim 96b
Rav Yitzchak Nafcha..Chullin 110a
Rav Yochanan ben Beroka, discriminating between sons for inheritance........Bava Basra 130a
Rav Yonassan ben Achmai, *semichah*...Sanhedrin 14a
Rav Yosef
   Behavior —
   Rav Yosef, fasts..Bava Metzia 85a
   Rav Yosef, honor to father..Kiddushin 31b
   Rav Yosef, humility..Sotah 49b
   Rav Yosef, preparations for Shabbos..Shabbos 119a
   Rav Yosef, Shavuos...Pesachim 68b
   Learning —
   Rav Yosef, Heavenly Chariot...Chagigah 13a
   Rav Yosef, lecture..Berachos 28b
   Rav Yosef, sharp rulings..Yevamos 122a
   Misc. —
   Rav Yosef, Amora of Pumbedisa..Sanhedrin 17b
   Rav Yosef, charity from Ifra Hormiz...Bava Basra 8a
   Rav Yosef, drink..Shabbos 140a
   Rav Yosef, forgot his learning.......Nedarim 41a; Eruvin 10a, 41a, 66b, 73a, 89b; Makos 4a; Niddah 39a, 63b
   Rav Yosef, high position for a convert..Kiddushin 76b
   Rav Yosef, resentment..................................Nedarim 55a-55b; Eruvin 54a
   Rav Yosef, *Rosh Yeshivah*...Berachos 64a
   Rav Yosef, ruling...Bava Basra 114b, 143b
   Rav Yosef, Sinai...Berachos 64a; Horayos 14a; Moed Katan 12a
   Rav Yosef, sixty years old...Moed Katan 28a
   Rav Yosef, unusual occurrences at his death....................................Moed Katan 25b
   Rav Yosef wept because of a verse..Chagigah 4b
Rav Yosef ben Rabbi Yehoshua, "upside down" world.............Bava Basra 10b; Pesachim 50a
Rav Zavid died because of vinegar..Avodah Zarah 38b
Rava bar Chinana, excommunication of butcher..................................Chullin 18a
Rava
   Episodes —
   Rava, capsizing of his ship..Bava Basra 153a
   Rava, chicken to poor man..Kesubos 67b
   Rava created a human form..Sanhedrin 65b
   Rava, dirtying the bed, Rav Aviya...Shabbos 46a-46b
   Rava, dreams interpretation..Berachos 56a-56b
   Rava, fasted two days of Yom Kippur..Rosh Hashanah 21a
   Rava, government taxed him..Chagigah 5b
   Rava, Heavenly blame..Chullin 133a
   Rava, impulsive people...Shabbos 88a
   Rava, Isur Giora's inheritance..Bava Basra 149a
   Rava, present to minister on his holiday...Avodah Zarah 65a
   Rava, quail...Yoma 75b
   Rava, rain in summer..Taanis 24b
   Rava, slave dyed his beard..Bava Metzia 60b

R

Rava, verse in dream .... Chullin 133a

Family —
Rava, Abbaye's widow .... Kesubos 65a
Rava, anger towards his son who came home .... Kesubos 63a
Rava, Rav Chisda's daughter .... Bava Basra 12b

Greatness —
Rava, received Heavenly greeting .... Taanis 21b-22a
Rava, unusual occurrences at his death .... Moed Katan 25b
Rava, wisdom and wealth .... Moed Katan 28a

Learning and disciples —
Rava appeased Rav Yosef .... Nedarim 55a-55b; Eruvin 54a
Rava, Bei Avidan .... Shabbos 116a
Rava, came out walking backwards before his teacher .... Yoma 53a
Rava, disciples .... Bava Basra 22a
Rava rejoiced when disciples found a livelihood .... Horayos 10b
Rava, they did not stand up in front of him .... Kiddushin 32b

Queen —
Rava, charity received from Ifra Hormiz .... Bava Basra 10b
Rava, Ifra Hormiz .... Niddah 20b
Rava, Ifra Hormiz's sacrifice .... Zevachim 116b

Ruling —
Rava, coins in swindler's walking stick .... Nedarim 25a; Shevuos 29a
Rava examined knife in his teacher's city .... Eruvin 63a
Rava, inquiry about circumcision on Shabbos .... Niddah 42b
Rava, mistake in ruling .... Bava Metzia 81b
Rava, money belonging to Jews .... Chullin 49b
Rava, moral teachings when he went to judge .... Sanhedrin 7b
Rava, *Resh Gelusa's eruv* .... Eruvin 25b-26a
Rava, scribes of judges .... Bava Basra 136a; Sanhedrin 29b

Misc. —
Rava, "Rav Acha is a great man" .... Bava Kama 40a
Rava, Angel of Death .... Moed Katan 28a
Rava, coded letter .... Sanhedrin 12a
Rava, generation preceding Rav Ashi .... Kiddushin 72b
Rava, preparations for Shabbos .... Shabbos 119a; Kiddushin 41a
Rava, protection in outdoor bathroom .... Berachos 62a

Raven
Raven, flew away .... Beitzah 21a; Chullin 124b
Raven, hates its young .... Kesubos 49b
Raven, liar .... Gittin 45a
Raven, sits at night .... Shabbos 35b
Raven, spits into beak of female .... Sanhedrin 108b
Ravens, Elijah .... Chullin 5a; Sanhedrin 113a
Ravens love one another .... Pesachim 113b
Ravens, roof of *Heichal*, spikes .... Shabbos 90a; Menachos 107a; Middos 37a

Ravin, preceded Abbayeh .... Berachos 47a

Ravina
Ravina and Rav Acha .... Pesachim 74b
Ravina, end of ruling .... Bava Metzia 86a

R

Ravina, eulogy..Moed Katan 25b

Ravina examined knife in his teacher's city ....Eruvin 63a

Ravina, sale on Chol HaMoed..Moed Katan 10b

Ravine to guard field..Bava Basra 107b-108a

Ravshakeh, blasphemy...Sanhedrin 60a

Raw, Pesach lamb..Pesachim 41a-41b; Bava Metzia 115b

Razor

Razor, *nazir*...Nazir 39b-40a

Razor, prohibition of shaving ....Makos 21a; Nazir 40b

Re'ach ra...*see* **Bad smell**, page 40

Re'em, giant animal...Bava Basra 73b; Zevachim 113b

Re'eyah...*see* **Olas reiyah**, page 457

Read

Read and tilted lamp on Shabbos, episode ....Shabbos 12b

Read and written ....Megillah 25b; Nedarim 37b-38a

Reading by brother of deceased childless husband and by widow (*chalitzah*)................

....Yevamos 104a-104b, 106b; Sotah 33a-33b

Reading differently from written words, which determines? .....Sanhedrin 4a-4b; Makos 7b-8a;

............................Succah 6b; Kiddushin 18b; Pesachim 86b; Zevachim 37b-38a; Bechoros 34a; Krisos 17b

Reading divorce certificate...Gittin 19b

Reading in Torah scroll...*see* **Torah reading**, page 697

Reading in Torah scroll, longevity ....Berachos 55a

Reading legal documents, witnesses ....Gittin 19b

Reading *megillah*...*see* **Megillas Esther**, page 402

Reading secular books...Sanhedrin 100b

Reading, prohibitions on Shabbos ....Shabbos 148b-149a

Reading *Shema*...*see* **Shema**, page 614

Reads letter, responsible to accomplish it ....Sanhedrin 82a, 96a; Bava Metzia 83b

Real estate..*see* **Connected to earth**, page 121

Realizing

Realizing at half quantity, sacrifice....................Shabbos 71b, 102a, 105a; Krisos 12b, 17a

Realizing beforehand, sacrifice necessary ....Shevuos 5a

Realizing, doubt, sacrifice...Shevuos 19b; Krisos 18b-19a

Realizing, requirement to offer sacrifice...Shabbos 71b

Reaping new grain.............................Menachos 68a, 71a-72a; Pesachim 11a, 23a, 56a-56b

Reaping the *omer*

Reaping the *omer*, from where...Menachos 64b

Reaping the *omer*, how...Menachos 63b, 65a

Reaping the *omer*, Shabbos............Makos 8b; Rosh Hashanah 9a; Moed Katan 3b; Menachos 72a

Reason

Reason for his rulings, Sage ....Niddah 24b

Reason for new decree ....Avodah Zarah 35a

Reason for prohibition of *niddah*..Niddah 31b

Reason for rulings, explanation given, in order not to forget ....Niddah 24b

Reason for verdict, explaining ....Bava Metzia 69a-69b; Sanhedrin 31b

Reason of law in Torah...Bava Metzia 115a; Sanhedrin 21a

Reason, one among several ....Zevachim 10b, 90a, 94b; Yoma 79b; Yevamos 48b; Sotah 8a;

....Bava Kama 106b; Menachos 89b; Krisos 3b

Reason to suspect, presumption ....Chullin 56b

R

Reasons for commandments, concealing .... Sanhedrin 21b
Reasons to purify reptile .... Eruvin 13b

Reasoning "all the more so," punishment .... Sanhedrin 76a

Rebeccah
Rebeccah, Eliezer's guess .... Chullin 95b
Rebeccah, episode with Eliezer .... Taanis 4a; Sanhedrin 95a; Chullin 95b
Rebeccah, sterile .... Yevamos 64a
Rebeccah, when did she conceive .... Rosh Hashanah 11a

Rebbi
  Character traits —
    Rebbi, "I did not benefit from this world" .... Kesubos 104a
    Rebbi, fear of sin .... Sotah 49b
    Rebbi, fire sparks .... Chullin 137b
    Rebbi, height .... Niddah 24b
    Rebbi, holy behavior .... Shabbos 118b
    Rebbi, humility .... Sotah 49b

  Episodes —
    Rebbi, "I am only your daughter's son" .... Sotah 49a
    Rebbi and Antoninus .... Avodah Zarah 10a-10b
    Rebbi, blind man's blessing .... Chagigah 5b
    Rebbi, cup to Sadducee .... Chullin 87a
    Rebbi, prayer for mute scholars .... Chagigah 3a
    Rebbi, reading of *Shema* .... Berachos 13b
    Rebbi, rebuke .... Moed Katan 16a-16b
    Rebbi, sacrifice of fattened livestock .... Avodah Zarah 16a
    Rebbi, supporting ignoramus .... Bava Basra 8a
    Rebbi, thin garments .... Gittin 59a
    Rebbi, walking at road sides .... Bava Kama 81b
    Rebbi was not visited because of Sage's old age .... Shabbos 152a
    Rebbi, wealthy man's son's garments .... Eruvin 85b-86a
    Rebbi's son-in-law, haircut .... Nedarim 51a; Sanhedrin 22b

  His life —
    Rebbi and Rabbi Chiya, match .... Kesubos 62b
    Rebbi and Rabbi Shimon son of Rebbi, disciples .... Bava Metzia 84b
    Rebbi, Beis Shearim .... Sanhedrin 32b
    Rebbi, belongs to David's offspring .... Shabbos 56a
    Rebbi, apple juice, cider .... Avodah Zarah 40b
    Rebbi, disciples reminded him of his learning .... Nedarim 41a
    Rebbi, dwelling place .... Megillah 5b
    Rebbi, generation preceding Rav Yehudah .... Kiddushin 72b
    Rebbi, his death .... Kesubos 103a-104a
    Rebbi, his funeral .... Kesubos 103b
    Rebbi, Levi's alcoholic beverage .... Pesachim 107a
    Rebbi, made *Kiddush* after his death .... Kesubos 103a
    Rebbi prayed for his sterile daughter-in-law .... Kesubos 62b
    Rebbi, prophecy before death .... Kiddushin 72a-72b
    Rebbi, radish and horseradish .... Avodah Zarah 11a; Berachos 57b
    Rebbi, rumor spread by foolish people .... Shabbos 30b
    Rebbi, suffering and recovery .... Bava Metzia 85a-85b

Rebbi, troubles after his death..Sotah 49b

Ruling —

Rebbi, authorization to disciples..Sanhedrin 5a-5b

Rebbi, elder ruled..Shabbos 51a

Rebbi, end of Mishnah...Bava Metzia 86a

Rebbi, inquiry about double-headed man.......................................Menachos 37a

Rebbi, law.................Bava Basra 124b; Eruvin 46b; Pesachim 27a; Kesubos 21a, 51a; Niddah 14b

Rebbi, lecture on *Tehillim*..Avodah Zarah 19a

Rebbi, permitted Beis She'an..Chullin 6b-7a

Rebbi, quarrel between two villages..Eruvin 61a

Rebbi, Sages are always near him..Niddah 14b

Rebbi, *semichah* to Shmuel..Bava Metzia 85b

Rebbi, six in one cubit..Eruvin 53a

Sages —

Rebbi and Bar Kappara..Nedarim 50b-51a

Rebbi and Rabbi Chiya's sons...Sanhedrin 38a

Rebbi and Rabbi Elazar ben Rabbi Shimon....................................Bava Metzia 84b

Rebbi and Rabbi Pinchas ben Yair..Chullin 7b

Rebbi respected Rabbi Yose..Sanhedrin 24a

Rebbi, Rabbi Elazar ben Shamua..Yevamos 84a

Rebbi, Rabbi Shimon's disciple...Menachos 72a

Rebbi, saw Rabbi Meir from behind..Eruvin 13b

Misc. —

Rebbi, Messiah...Sanhedrin 98b

Rebbi, minor judge heard first................................Sanhedrin 36a; Gittin 58b-59a

Rebbi, not considered Prince concerning sacrifice................................Horayos 11b

Rebbi, Rabbi Yehudah Hanasi....................Kiddushin 63a; Shabbos 32b; Yevamos 45a

Rebbi, subordinate to *Reish Galusa*...Horayos 11b

Rebbi, Rabbi Yehudah Hanasi...*see* **Rebbi**, page 548

Rebel

Rebel against government, belongings..Sanhedrin 48b

Rebel against one *mitzvah* for personal benefit, unintentional......Horayos 2a, 11a; Shabbos 69a;

....Yoma 80a; Chullin 5b

Rebel, examining knife..Chullin 3a-3b, 4a

Rebel, definition..Avodah Zarah 26b; Horayos 11a

Rebel, disqualified sacrifice.......................................Chullin 5a-5b, 13b; Eruvin 69b

Rebel, disqualifies service..Zevachim 22b

Rebel, his lost item..Avodah Zarah 26b

Rebel in marital relations, husband and wife..................................Kesubos 63a-64a

Rebel in marital relations, levirate marriage.......................................Kesubos 64a

Rebel renting domain, *eruv*..Eruvin 68b

Rebel, rejected sacrifice..........................Zevachim 12b; Sanhedrin 47a; Horayos 11a; Krisos 7a

Rebel, testimony..Sanhedrin 27a-27b

Rebel, transgresses without benefit..Chullin 4b

Rebel, trustworthiness..Chullin 4b-5a

Rebel, with intention to rebel......................................Avodah Zarah 26b; Horayos 11a

Rebellion

Rebellion against nations, oath...Kesubos 111a

Rebellion of Absalom...............................Berachos 7b; Temurah 14b-15a; Nazir 5a

Rebellious daughter..Sanhedrin 69b-70a

Rebellious elder
Rebellious elder, death..Sanhedrin 89a
Rebellious elder, for which sin..Sanhedrin 86b-88b
Rebellious elder, forgiving..Sanhedrin 88b; Sotah 25a

Rebellious son
Rebellious son, daughter..Sanhedrin 69b-70a
Rebellious son, did not exist..Sanhedrin 71a
Rebellious son, eating..Sanhedrin 70a, 71a
Rebellious son, elders of his city..Makos 10b
Rebellious son, exempt..Sanhedrin 45b, 71a-71b
Rebellious son, forgiveness..Sanhedrin 88b; Sotah 25a
Rebellious son, lashes..Sanhedrin 71b
Rebellious son, warning..Sanhedrin 63a
Rebellious son, when..Sanhedrin 68b-69a; Niddah 52a
Rebellious son, why..Sanhedrin 71b-72a

Rebuke
Rebuke..Moed Katan 16a
Rebuke, "you yourself do worse than I"..Arachin 16b; Bava Basra 15b
Rebuke, correct yourself..Bava Metzia 107b; Bava Basra 60b; Sanhedrin 18a, 19a
Rebuke, difficult to accept..Arachin 16b
Rebuke, episodes..Moed Katan 16a-16b
Rebuke, how many..Bava Kama 92b; Bava Metzia 31a
Rebuke, Jerusalem..Shabbos 55a
Rebuke, lighter prohibition..Sotah 48a
Rebuke, one's teacher..Bava Metzia 31a
Rebuke, punishment..Shabbos 54b-55a, 119b; Sanhedrin 27b; Shevuos 39a-39b
Rebuke, thorn and beam..Bava Basra 15b
Rebuke to Rabbi Akiva..Arachin 16b
Rebuke, value..Tamid 28a
Rebuke, when to keep silent..Yevamos 65b

Rebuked by G-d, Rava..Chullin 133a

Recall sins, three..Berachos 55a; Rosh Hashanah 16b

Receipt
Receipt, do we write..Kesubos 16b, 89a; Bava Basra 169a, 171b-172a
Receipt for *kesubah*..Kesubos 16b, 89a
Receipt for *kesubah*, lost..Bava Metzia 19b-20a
Receipt found in lender's possession..Bava Metzia 20b-21a
Receipt, orphans' promissory note..Bava Basra 7b
Receipt, partial repayment..Bava Basra 170b-171a; Kesubos 56a
Receipts for libations..Shekalim 5:3-5

Receive
Receive your divorce certificate and your *kesubah*..Gittin 20b
Receiving Torah, condition..Shabbos 88a

Receiving blood
Receiving blood from neck of sacrifice..Zevachim 25a
Receiving blood, guilt offering for leper..Zevachim 47b; Yoma 61b
Receiving blood, intervening substance in bowl..Yoma 58a
Receiving blood of sacrifice, correcting mistakes..Zevachim 26b, 34b

R

Receiving blood of sacrifice, laws .... Zevachim 4a, 13a; Chagigah 11a; Kiddushin 36a-36b
Receiving blood, stood outside .... Zevachim 26a
Receiving blood, vessel cracked open .... Zevachim 25b
Receiving all the blood .... Zevachim 25a

Rechayim al tzavaro .... *see* **Grindstone on neck**, page 259

Reclining
Reclining at table, how .... Berachos 43a, 46b-47b
Reclining on Pesach night .... Pesachim 108a
Reclining to be exempt (individually) from a blessing .... Berachos 42b-43a

Recognizes
Recognizes his goods, stolen .... Bava Kama 114b-115a
Recognizing G-d's justice, blessing in cemetery .... Berachos 58b
Recognizing G-d's justice, text .... Berachos 19a
Recognizing, reliable proof .... Gittin 23a; Bava Metzia 23b-24a; Chullin 95b-96a
Recognizing, which Sage is trustworthy .... Shabbos 114a

Recovery, meat and wine .... Taanis 13b

Recumbence, damages made by animal .... Bava Kama 2b, 16a

Red Heifer
Red Heifer .... *see also* **Ash of Red Heifer**, page 33
Red Heifer, age .... Parah 1:1
Red Heifer, came into field to trample .... Pesachim 26a-26b; Bava Metzia 30a
Red Heifer, children .... Succah 21a; Zevachim 113a; Parah 3:2-4
Red Heifer, coming out alone .... Yoma 42b-43a; Parah 3:7
Red Heifer, honoring father, episode .... Kiddushin 31a; Avodah Zarah 23b-24a
Red Heifer, how to take it out .... Parah 3:6-8
Red Heifer, impurity .... Parah 4:4; Bava Kama 77a-77b; Chullin 29b
Red Heifer, impurity of food .... Bava Kama 77a-77b; Shevuos 11b; Menachos 101b; Chullin 81b
Red Heifer, impurity of person immersed that day .... Chagigah 23a-23b; Yoma 2a; Zevachim 21a;
.... Parah 3:7-8
Red Heifer, *Kohen* .... Yoma 42a, 42b, 43b
Red Heifer, night .... Yoma 42b
Red Heifer, other disqualifications .... Avodah Zarah 23b
Red Heifer, stringencies .... Parah 5:1, 5:4, 10:1-6, 12:6-8; Chagigah 23b
Red Heifer, things disqualifying service .... Parah 2:1-5Bava Metzia 30a; Pesachim 26a-26b
Red Heifer, washing hands .... Zevachim 20b
Red Heifer, which works .... Sotah 46a

Red Sea
Red Sea, miracles .... Avos 5:4
Red Sea, Nachshon .... Sotah 37a
Red Sea, Sisera .... Pesachim 118b

Redeemed sacrifices
Redeemed sacrifices, blood .... Chullin 35b
Redeemed sacrifices, firstborn .... Bechoros 31b
Redeemed sacrifices, laws .... Makos 22a
Redeemed sacrifices, mating .... Moed Katan 12a
Redeemed sacrifices, milk .... Bechoros 15a
Redeemed sacrifices, pit .... Bava Kama 53b-54a
Redeemed sacrifices, sale .... Bechoros 31a-31b, 33b; Beitzah 28a; Chullin 133b; Temurah 8a, 21a, 24a
Redeemed sacrifices, shearing .... Bechoros 6b, 15a, 25a; Temurah 31a; Chullin 137a

R

Redeemed sacrifices, skin .... Bechoros 15a, 33a-33b; Temurah 24a

Redeeming

Property —

Redeeming, borrows and sells .... Arachin 30b
Redeeming by relatives .... Kiddushin 20b-21b
Redeeming field .... Arachin 14b, 29b, 30a
Redeeming half inheritance .... Kiddushin 20b-21b; Arachin 30b-31a
Redeeming, houses in open cities .... Arachin 33a
Redeeming, Levite cities .... Arachin 33b

Redeeming field

Redeeming field, rocks and crevices .... Kiddushin 61a; Bava Basra 102b-103b; Arachin 25a
Redeeming field, stones .... Arachin 14b
Redeeming field, trees .... Bava Basra 72a; Arachin 14a
Redeeming field which was bought .... Arachin 14a-14b

Sacrifice —

Redeeming after slaughtering .... Meilah 19b
Redeeming blemished animal .... Temurah 32b; Menachos 101a, 108a-108b; Bechoros 37b
Redeeming dead sacrifice .... Bechoros 14b-15a; Temurah 31a, 32b-33b; Pesachim 29a-29b
Redeeming, expressions and doubts .... Temurah 26b-27a
Redeeming public sacrifice .... Shevuos 10b-12a; Zevachim 7a; Menachos 79b
Redeeming Red Heifer .... Shevuos 11b
Redeeming sacrifice, expressions .... Temurah 26b-27a
Redeeming sacrifice without blemish .... Kiddushin 55a
Redeeming second tithe .... *see* **Second tithe**, page 595
Redeeming two loaves of Shavuos .... Menachos 48a

Misc. —

Redeeming books from non-Jew .... Gittin 45a-45b
Redeeming donkey, lamb .... Chullin 74b; Bechoros 4b, 10b-12b; Yoma 49b; Bava Kama 78a
Redeeming, donation valuation .... Bava Basra 72b; Arachin 18a, 24a
Redeeming firstborn of donkey .... Bechoros 5b, 9a-9b, 11a, 12b-13a
Redeeming produce of fourth year .... Maaser Sheni 5:1-5
Redeeming produce of Sabbatical year .... Succah 40b-41a
Redeeming *tefillin*, episode .... Gittin 45b

Redeeming captive

Redeeming captive, having sold himself .... Gittin 46b-47a
Redeeming captive, more than his value .... Gittin 45a
Redeeming captive, synagogue .... Bava Basra 3b
Redeeming captive, value .... Bava Basra 8a-8b
Redeeming captive, widow .... Kesubos 52a
Redeeming captive, wife .... Kesubos 51b-52b

Redeeming consecrated item

Redeeming consecrated item, assessment .... Sanhedrin 14b-15a, 88a; Arachin 19b-20a
Redeeming consecrated item, auction .... Arachin 21b-22a, 27a-27b
Redeeming consecrated item, bought field .... Arachin 14a-14b
Redeeming consecrated item for money, pure .... Menachos 100b-101a
Redeeming consecrated item, fraud .... Bava Metzia 57a-57b; Kiddushin 11b; Bechoros 25a, 50b;
.... Arachin 29a; Temurah 27a-27b; Meilah 14b
Redeeming consecrated item, rocks and cracks .... Kiddushin 61a; Bava Basra 102b-103a;
.... Arachin 25a

Redeeming consecrated item, stones .... Arachin 14b
Redeeming consecrated item, trees .... Bava Basra 72a; Arachin 14a
Redeeming consecrated item with contract and land .... Bechoros 51a-51b

Redeeming Hebrew slave
Redeeming Hebrew slave and maidservant, coercion .... Kiddushin 18a
Redeeming Hebrew slave, half .... Kiddushin 20b
Redeeming Hebrew slave, relatives .... Kiddushin 21a-21b
Redeeming Hebrew slave, value .... Kiddushin 20a-20b; Arachin 30a-30b

Redeeming *revai*
Redeeming *revai*, source .... Berachos 35a
Redeeming *revai*, thief .... Bava Kama 69b
Redeeming *revai*, to avoid transgression .... Bava Kama 69a-69b

Redeeming son
Redeeming son, blessing .... Pesachim 121b
Redeeming son, *chalal* .... Bechoros 47b
Redeeming son, commandment .... Kiddushin 29a
Redeeming son, doubtful firstborn .... Bechoros 48a-49a
Redeeming son, episode about cat .... Bava Kama 80b
Redeeming son, gift on condition to return .... Kiddushin 6b; Bechoros 51b
Redeeming son, *Kohanim* and *Leviim* .... Bechoros 3b-4b, 13a, 47a-47b
Redeeming son, mother .... Kiddushin 29a
Redeeming son, precedence .... Kiddushin 29a-29b; Bechoros 49b
Redeeming son, responsibility .... Bechoros 51b
Redeeming son, several *Kohanim* .... Bechoros 51b
Redeeming son, thirty days .... Bava Kama 11b; Bechoros 12b, 49a-49b
Redeeming son, with what .... Bechoros 51a, 51b
Redeeming son, women .... Bechoros 47a; Kiddushin 29a

Redemption
Redemption by observing Shabbos .... Shabbos 118b
Redemption close to prayer, mentioning .... Berachos 4b, 9b
Redemption, Divine Presence leaves Jacob .... Pesachim 56a
Redemption for those who look forward to Zion .... Kesubos 75a

Redemption from Egypt
Redemption from Egypt, end of servitude .... Rosh Hashanah 11b
Redemption from Egypt, how many left .... Sanhedrin 111a
Redemption from Egypt, left in haste .... Berachos 9a
Redemption from Egypt, miracles .... Avos 5:4

Reduce
Reduce your commerce .... Avos 4:10
Reduced and swelled, quantity .... Menachos 54a-54b; Taharos 3:4; Uktzin 2:8
Reducing commandments to one .... Makos 23b-24a
Reducing prices to attract customers .... Bava Metzia 60a-60b; Bava Basra 21b
Reducing sleep, ways to acquire Torah .... Avos 6:5
Reducing sum of *kesubah* .... Kesubos 51a-51b, 54b, 56b-57a

Reed
"Reed broken," dream .... Yevamos 93b
Reed, carrying out by rolling on Shabbos .... Shabbos 8b
Reed, laws .... Chullin 16b
Reed, *muktzeh* .... Eruvin 34b

R

Reeds and cedar, wind .... Taanis 20a; Sanhedrin 105b-106a

Reeds, streams .... Pesachim 53a

Reed pen

Reed pen, engraving on marble .... Avodah Zarah 22b

Reed pen on Shabbos, considered work .... Shabbos 74b

Reed pen, to write holy parchments .... Taanis 20a-20b; Sanhedrin 106a

Refaim, *Gehinnom* .... Bava Basra 79a

References and signs to remember Torah .... Eruvin 53a

Refidim .... Bechoros 5b; Sanhedrin 106a

Refined speech, Lot .... Bava Kama 38b; Nazir 23b; Horayos 10b-11a

Refined person .... *see* **Fastidious person**, page 216

Refraining from Torah learning

Refraining from Torah learning, for bride .... Kesubos 17a

Refraining from Torah learning, for funeral .... Megillah 3b, 29a; Kesubos 17a-17b

Refraining from Torah learning in public .... Berachos 53a

Refraining from Torah learning in public for a Sage's death .... Moed Katan 22b-23a

Refraining from Torah learning, punishments .... Berachos 5a; Shabbos 32b-33b; Sanhedrin 99a

Refraining from Torah learning to learn better afterwards .... Menachos 99a

Refuah .... *see* **Medicine**, page 622

Refuge city .... *see* **City of Refuge**, page 109

Refuses

Refuses ruling, sacrifice .... Horayos 2b

Refusing, an important and ordinary person .... Bava Metzia 87a; Pesachim 86b

Refusing gift, kept silent then refused .... Bava Basra 137b-138a; Krisos 24a-24b

Refusing to give *eruv*, invalid .... Eruvin 49a, 68a

Refusing to obey *beis din* .... Moed Katan 16a; Bava Kama 112b; Shevuos 41a

Refuted

Refuted by wisp of straw, Rabbi Yosef .... Niddah 26b

Refuting analogy .... Menachos 82b; Bava Kama 63b, 106b

Refuting for minimal difference, deduction .... Chullin 115b-116a

Regel .... *see* **Leg**, page 361

Regret, vows .... Nedarim 21b, 22b-23a, 77b

Regrets

Regrets He created .... Succah 52b

Regretting one's performance of commandment .... Kiddushin 40b

Regretting sins .... Chagigah 5a

Regular commandment is first .... Zevachim 89a, 90b-91a; Horayos 12b

Reish Galusa

Reish Galusa, *chazakah* by strong person .... Bava Basra 36a

Reish Galusa, debt .... Shabbos 121b; Yevamos 120a

Reish Galusa, *eruv* .... Eruvin 25b-26a

Reish Galusa, fall before Messiah .... Sanhedrin 38a

Reish Galusa, judges .... Bava Basra 65a

Reish Galusa, lineage .... Horayos 11b; Sanhedrin 5a

Reish Galusa, Rebbi submitted to him .... Horayos 11b

Reish Galusa, seal .... Shabbos 58a

Reisha demasnisin .... *see* **Beginning of *Mishnah***, page 49

Reiusa delo chazinan .... *see* **Presumption, no reason to suspect problem**, page 502

Reiyah .... *see* **Olas reiyah**, page 457

R

Reiyas niddah .... *see* **Blood of** *niddah*, page 66
Reiyas zav .... *see* **Discharge of** *zav*, page 165
Rejoicing
  Rejoicing from Shavuos to Succos .... Pesachim 36b
  Rejoicing on festivals in Babylon .... Shabbos 145b
  Rejoicing on Shavuos .... Pesachim 68b
  Rejoicing on Yom Tov, half to G-d .... Pesachim 68b; Beitzah 15b
  Rejoicing on Yom Tov, how .... Pesachim 71a, 109a
  Weddings —
    Rejoicing bride, episodes .... Kesubos 17a
    Rejoicing days, wedding of virgins and widows .... Kesubos 7a-7b
    Rejoicing, husband cheers his wife .... Kiddushin 34b; Rosh Hashanah 6b
    Rejoicing, not to mix one with another .... Moed Katan 8b-9a
    Rejoicing of groom and bride .... Berachos 6b
  Misc. —
    "Rejoice sterile woman," Sadducees .... Berachos 10a
    Rejoice with trembling, prayer .... Berachos 30b
    Rejoice, young man! .... Shabbos 63b
    Rejoices his wife before marital relations .... Eruvin 100b; Bava Basra 10b
Rekev hames .... *see* **Decay of dead**, page 152
Rekikin .... *see* **Flat cakes, meal offerings**, page 229
Relative
  Forbidden relations —
    Relative (female) of *chalutzah's* rival .... Yevamos 41a
    Relatives (female) of *chalutzah* .... Yevamos 27a, 40a-41a, 44a; Kiddushin 45a
    Relatives (female) of convert .... Yevamos 22a, 97b-98b; Sanhedrin 57b-58a
    Relatives (female) of suspected girl .... Yevamos 26a, 94b-95b, 97a
    Relatives (female) of woman refusing marriage .... Yevamos 108a-108b; Kesubos 101a
  Testimony —
    Relative of guarantee, testimony .... Makos 7a
    Relative to himself and his money .... Yevamos 25b; Sanhedrin 9b-10a, 25a
    Relatives, cases of testimony .... Sanhedrin 27b-28a; Makos 7a
    Relatives, testimony .... Bava Basra 159a; Sanhedrin 27b-28a; Bava Kama 88a
    Relatives, testimony about rights and money .... Sanhedrin 27b-28a
    Relatives, testimony for attestation .... Bava Basra 57a
    Relatives, who is invalid .... Bava Basra 128a, 129a; Sanhedrin 28a-29a
  Misc. —
    Relative, property of captive .... Bava Metzia 38b-39b
    Relatives, disqualified to judge .... Sanhedrin 27b
    Relatives, mourning .... Moed Katan 20b
    Relatives, permitting vow .... Nedarim 77a-77b, 76b
    Relatives, reward for those who maintain good relations ...... Sanhedrin 76b; Yevamos 62b-63a
    Relatives, unusual intimate relations .... Yevamos 97b
Releasing rights to land in error .... Bava Metzia 66b-67a; Bava Basra 41a-41b
Reliable men .... Taanis 8a
Religion
  Religion of fire for Israel .... Beitzah 25b
  Religion of Jewish women, covering hair .... Kesubos 72a-72b
  Religion of Moses and Yehudis .... Kesubos 72a-72b

R

Religious persecution, self-sacrifice..Sanhedrin 74a-74b
Relying
Relying, not to rely on miracles.............................Pesachim 64b; Megillah 7b
Relying upon our Father in Heaven...Sotah 49a
Remainder
Remainder for Altar, from when ....Pesachim 71a; Zevachim 87a; Meilah 8a-10a
Remainder, night of third day......................................Zevachim 56b; Pesachim 3a
Remainder of libations, *kitz mizbeach* sacrifices...........................Menachos 90a-90b
Remainder of libations, sacrifices *kitz mizbeach*.............Menachos 90a-90b; Kesubos 106b
Remainder of loaves of thanksgiving...Menachos 80a-80b
Remainder of sacrifice, day and night ....Zevachim 36a
Remainder of sin offering and guilt offering...............Shevuos 12a-12b; Pesachim 73a; Temurah 20b
Remainder of support money..Kesubos 65b
Remainder of Temple funds..................Shekalim 4:2-3; Kesubos 106b; Kiddushin 54a
Remainder of Temple funds, secular use...Kiddushin 54a
Remainders of consecrated item and sacrifice.............Shekalim 2:3, 4:3-5; Menachos 108a
Remainders of sacrifice, what to do with them...............................Temurah 13b
Remainder of meal offering
Remainder of meal offering, doubtful *Kohen* ....Yevamos 100a
Remainder of meal offering, from when can one eat.......................Zevachim 110a
Remainder of meal offering, *Kohanim*...Menachos 72b-73a
Remainder of meal offering, *Koheness*.............Sotah 23a-23b; Chullin 131b-132a
Remainder of meal offering, permitted from when ....Menachos 26b; Sotah 15a
Remainder of meal offering, to *Kohen* offering it ....Yevamos 39b-40a
Remainder of Pesach lamb
Remainder of Pesach lamb, changing...............Pesachim 64a, 73a-73b; Chullin 30a
Remainder of Pesach lamb, peace offerings...............Zevachim 7b, 8b-9b; Pesachim 70b, 96b-97b;
....Menachos 83b
Remainder of Pesach lamb, *semichah* ....Pesachim 89a
Remainder of Pesach lamb, which part..Pesachim 83b
Remainder of sacrificial blood
Remainder of sacrificial blood, a few cups...............Zevachim 34b, 112a; Yoma 57b; Temurah 22b
Remainder of sacrificial blood, inside sin-offering........Zevachim 42b, 52a-52b, 111a; Yoma 60b;
....Menachos 16b
Remainder of sacrificial blood, not indispensable requirement ....Zevachim 39a-40a
Remainder of sacrificial blood on finger..................Zevachim 93b; Menachos 7b
Remainder of sacrificial blood, place..............Yoma 59a; Zevachim 51a, 53a-53b, 81a
Remainder of sacrificial blood, source.....................................Zevachim 37a, 51a-52a
Remarrying one's former wife
Remarrying one's former wife after her betrothal to another...............Yevamos 11b
Remarrying one's former wife, cases when forbidden...............Yevamos 25a; Gittin 45b-46b
Remarrying one's former wife, *chalalah* ....Yevamos 44a-44b, 15b; Niddah 69b-70a
Remarrying one's former wife, *kesubah* ....Kesubos 89b-90a
Remarrying one's former wife, levirate marriage...............Yevamos 11b-12b, 108b
Remarrying one's former wife, mind cannot tolerate...............Pesachim 113b
Remarrying one's former wife who remarried...............................Kiddushin 78a
Remedy
Remedy before illness..Megillah 13b
Remedy, Sabbatical year...........................Succah 40a-40b; Bava Kama 101b-102a

Remember

Remember and observe in one expression................Shevuos 20b; Rosh Hashanah 27a

Remember and observe, juxtaposed to learn law of *Kiddush*......................Berachos 20b

Remembered before placing down on Shabbos........................Shabbos 102a

Remembered fish in Egypt..Yoma 75a

Remembered for the good, commentaries on Book of Ezekiel...............Menachos 45a

Remembered he already prayed................................Berachos 21a-21b

Remembering learning, Heavenly help.................................Megillah 6b

Remembers mercy, anger...Pesachim 87b

Remembers righteous, anger...Berachos 54b

Remorse, better than a hundred lashes.............................Berachos 7a

Removal of shoe under Levirate law........................*see Chalitzah*, page 92

Removing

Sabbatical year —

Removing, distributing Sabbatical year fruit..........................Sheviis 9:8

Removing, fruit exempt..Niddah 51b

Removing, mixture.....................Pesachim 52a; Sheviis 7:7, 9:5; Nedarim 58b

Removing, produce to different countries............Sheviis 9:2-3; Pesachim 52a-52b

Removing, time....................................Sheviis 9:4-6; Pesachim 52a-53a

Removing, went outside Israel.......................................Pesachim 52b

Removing, who eats..Sheviis 9:8

Misc. —

Remove man from world.............................Avos 2:11, 3:10, 4:21

Removing bread from oven on Shabbos, not considered work.........Shabbos 117b, 131b;
....Rosh Hashanah 29b

Removing bread from oven, saving..................................Shabbos 117b

Removing first fruit....................................Bikkurim 2:2; Yevamos 73a-73b

Removing letter from verse and adding it...........Bava Metzia 54b; Bava Basra 111b; Yoma 48a;
....Zevachim 25a; Bechoros 44b

Removing prohibited thickness of food.................................Chullin 97a

Removing tithes...Maaser Sheni 5:6-10

Removing yoke of Torah, punishment......................................Avos 3:5

Removing *chametz*

Removing *chametz*, blessing.......................................Pesachim 7a-7b

Removing *chametz*, how.............Pesachim 5b, 12b, 21a, 27b-28a; Temurah 34a

Removing *chametz*, time..Pesachim 13a-14a

Removing forbidden parts

Removing forbidden parts, fat......................................Chullin 133a

Removing forbidden parts of cheek.................................Chullin 133a

Removing forbidden parts, sciatic nerve.....................Chullin 92b, 96a-96b

Rending to sew, Shabbos...Shabbos 74b-75a

Renegade...*see* **Rebel** page 549

Renewing of world, Future......................................Sanhedrin 92b

Renouncing

Renouncing a condition..Gittin 74b

Renouncing, beyond letter of law..................................Bava Metzia 30b

Renouncing honor of king and teacher..........................Kiddushin 32a-32b

Renouncing *kesubah*, support.......................................Kesubos 53a

Renouncing, man forbidden to benefit.......Nedarim 32b-33a, 48b; Megillah 8a; Bava Basra 57b

R

Renouncing payment, hand bitten by donkey .... Bava Kama 84a
Renouncing rights, husband .... Kesubos 83a-83b; Bava Basra 49a-49b
Renouncing sold debt .... Kesubos 85b-86a; Kiddushin 48a; Bava Kama 89a; Bava Basra 147b
Renouncing wife's property .... Kesubos 83a-83b, 102b; Bava Basra 49a-49b

Rent
Rent, act of acquisition .... Bava Kama 79a-79b
Rent, act of acquisition of courtyard .... Bava Metzia 102a
Rent equal to sale, fraud .... Bava Metzia 56b
Rent, month added to year .... Bava Metzia 102a-102b; Bava Basra 105a
Rent, paid at end of rental period .... Bava Metzia 65a
Rent, paid at the end of term .... Bava Metzia 65a, 73a, 110b; Kiddushin 48a-48b, 63a
Rent, searching for *chametz* .... Pesachim 4a-4b

Rented
Rented donkey, died .... Bava Metzia 79a
Rented or borrowed animal, died .... Bava Metzia 97a-98b
Renting domain for *eruv*, permission to use .... Eruvin 63b
Renting, equal to owning .... Avodah Zarah 15a
Renting land to non-Jew .... Avodah Zarah 20b-21b
Renting, man forbidden by vow to benefit from someone .... Nedarim 46b
Renting, not to delay payment .... Bava Metzia 111b
Renting place to buy ship .... Bava Basra 76b
Renting to non-Jew on Friday .... Shabbos 19a
Renting to non-Jew on Shabbos .... Avodah Zarah 21b-22a

Renting domain for Shabbos
Renting domain for Shabbos, cases .... Eruvin 67a-67b, 74b-75a
Renting domain for Shabbos, from whom .... Eruvin 65b-66a, 68b, 80a
Renting domain for Shabbos, how .... Eruvin 62a, 65b-66a
Renting domain for Shabbos, non-Jew's worker .... Eruvin 64a
Renting domain for Shabbos, when .... Eruvin 61b-62b, 65b
Renting domain for Shabbos, why .... Eruvin 62a-62b

Renting house
Renting house, became leprous .... Arachin 20b
Renting house, claims .... Bava Metzia 102b-103a
Renting house, departure .... Bava Metzia 101b; Rosh Hashanah 7b
Renting house, fell .... Bava Metzia 103a
Renting house, for one year .... Rosh Hashanah 7b
Renting house, *mezuzah* .... Bava Metzia 101b-102a; Pesachim 4a
Renting house, usages .... Bava Basra 6a-6b
Renting warehouse to swindler, clearing wine .... Bava Metzia 101b

Repairing
Repairing sacred utensils .... Zevachim 88a
Repairing utensils, impurity .... Keilim 3:3-8, 18:6-9; Berachos 50b
Repairs in Temple, entrance .... Eruvin 105a; Pesachim 26a; Middos 4:5
Repaying good with evil .... Kesubos 53a
Repayment of debt
Repayment of debt, appraising quality of field .... Gittin 49b; Bava Kama 7b-8a; Kesubos 110a
Repayment of debt, *beinonis* and *ziboris* .... Kesubos 110a; Gittin 49b, 50a; Bava Kama 8a, 7b-8b
Repayment of debt, best land .... Bava Metzia 66b
Repayment of debt, in part .... Bava Basra 170b-171a; Kesubos 56a

Repayment of debt, joy...Berachos 7b
Repayment of debt, precedence..Kesubos 84a, 86a, 90a-90b, 93a; Gittin 11b-12a
Repayment of debt, seizing from orphan.............................Kesubos 84a-85a, 110a; Bava Kama 14b
Repayment of debt, seizure by second creditor ......Kesubos 90a-90b, 94a; Bava Kama 34a; Arachin 7b
Repayment of debt, seizure for fellow...Gittin 11b-12a

Repeated
Repeated at Sinai, non-Jews...Sanhedrin 59a-59b
Repeated section in Torah, new law...............Sotah 3a-3b; Bava Kama 64b; Shevuos 19a; Menachos 10a
Repeating Torah section to make as indispensable requirement...............................Zevachim 23a;
....Yevamos 40a; Pesachim 61a, 78b; Yoma 51b; Shevuos 14a; Menachos 19a-19b
Repeats transgression, seems permitted.......................Kiddushin 20a, 40a; Yoma 86b; Moed Katan 27b;
....Sotah 22a; Arachin 30b

Repentance
Cases —
Repentance, burnt offering..Zevachim 7b
Repentance, levels...Yoma 86a-86b
Repentance, regret..Chagigah 5a
Repentance, suspected...Sanhedrin 25a-25b; Bechoros 31a
Repentance when offering sacrifice...Berachos 23a
Episodes —
Repentance, bandits (*bryonei*)...Berachos 10a; Sanhedrin 37a
Repentance, golden calf...Avodah Zarah 4b-5a
Repentance of David..Sanhedrin 107a-107b
Repentance of King Manasseh..Sanhedrin 101a-101b, 102b-103a
Repentance of Ninveh inhabitants...Taanis 16a
Repentance, Resh Lakish..Bava Metzia 84a
Transgressions —
Repentance, excising of soul..Sanhedrin 90b; Shevuos 13a
Repentance difficult, for whom...Bava Kama 94b
Repentance from forbidden relations...Avodah Zarah 17a
Repentance from heresy..Avodah Zarah 17a
Repentance from theft, difficult...Chullin 89a
Repentance, profaned of G-d's name...Yoma 86a
When —
Repentance before death, atonement..Kiddushin 40b
Repentance before Redemption..Sanhedrin 97b-98a
Repentance, confession before death.............................Shabbos 32a; Sanhedrin 43b
Repentance on fast for rain...Taanis 16a
Repentance, one day before death...Shabbos 153a
Repentance, while still a man (prime of his life).................................Avodah Zarah 19a
Repentance, Yom Kippur.......................Yoma 85b, 87a; Shevuos 12b-13b; Krisos 7a
Misc. —
Repentance, annuls decree...Rosh Hashanah 17b-18a; Yoma 86b
Repentance, atonement...Yoma 85b-86a
Repentance, G-d's hand is stretched out ....Pesachim 119a
Repentance, intentional sins like unintentional sins.............................Yoma 36b, 86b

Repenting
Repenting people, golden calf...Avodah Zarah 4b-5a
Repenting people, virtue...Berachos 34b

R

Repetition

Repetition by cantor, reason..Rosh Hashanah 34b-35a
Repetition on last line of legal document ....Bava Basra 161b-162a

Replacing one's father, position of authority

....Kesubos 103b

Replacing sacrifice

How —

Replacing *chagigah* sacrifice ....Chagigah 2a, 9a-9b, 17a; Rosh Hashanah 4b; Yoma 3a; Beitzah 20b;
....Megillah 5a
Replacing *chagigah* sacrifice of Shevuos ....Rosh Hashanah 4b-5a; Moed Katan 24b; Chagigah 17a-18a
Replacing sacrifice, cases ....Temurah 13a, 14a, 31b
Replacing sacrifice, expressions ....Temurah 26b-27a
Replacing sacrifice, how...Temurah 17a
Replacing sacrifice, one by two..Temurah 9a-9b
Replacing sacrifice, second time ....Temurah 9a-9b, 13b
Replacing sacrifice, two by one.................Zevachim 30a-30b; Temurah 9a-9b, 25b-26a; Nedarim 69b;
....Bava Kama 73b
Replacing sacrifice, who can replace ....Temurah 2a-3a, 9a, 10a; Yoma 50b; Nedarim 36b;
....Zevachim 6a; Menachos 93a; Arachin 2a

In which matter —

Replacing firstborn, laws ....Zevachim 75b
Replacing sacrifice, blemished..Bechoros 14a-14b; Temurah 9a
Replacing sacrifice, bull of *Kohen Gadol*...Yoma 50b
Replacing sacrifice, by what ....Temurah 13a-13b
Replacing sacrifice, disqualified ....Temurah 17a
Replacing sacrifice, limbs and fetus ....Chullin 69a-69b; Temurah 10a
Replacing sacrifice, non-Jew's sacrifice ....Zevachim 45a; Temurah 3a
Replacing sacrifice, on which animal..Temurah 9a
Replacing sacrifice, Pesach lamb.....................................Pesachim 96b-97b; Zevachim 37b
Replacing sacrifice, sacrifice of heir....................................Zevachim 5b-6a; Temurah 2a-2b

Misc. —

Replacing sacrifice, animal tithe...Temurah 13b
Replacing sacrifice, differences..Yoma 50b-51a
Replacing sacrifice, first animal was not holy ....Nazir 32a
Replacing sacrifice, lashes ....Temurah 3a, 17a
Replacing sacrifice, must die and not be eaten ....Bechoros 16a
Replacing sacrifice, not offered...................Zevachim 37b; Temurah 17b-18a, 21a; Pesachim 96b-97b
Replacing sacrifice, prohibition..Temurah 2a, 9a; Bava Metzia 91a
Replacing sacrifice, remainders of sacrifice ....Temurah 13b
Replacing sacrifice, resulting from transgression..Temurah 20b
Replacing sacrifice, which are offered ......Temurah 17b-18a, 20b-21a; Nazir 25a-25b; Bechoros 14b
Replacing thanksgiving sacrifice, intermingled ....Menachos 80b-81a

Representatives of expert judges

....Bava Kama 84b; Gittin 88b

Reprove (rebuke)

Reprove, do not reprove scoffer...Arachin 16b
Reprove Sage and he will love you ....Arachin 16b

Reproving look

Reproving look, episode about Ulla...Pesachim 53b
Reproving look, Resh Lakish ....Kesubos 25b; Makos 5b
Reproving look, Shmuel..Niddah 26b

R

Reptile
see also **Worm**, page 764

Impurity —
Reptile, a hundred and fifty reasons to declare it pure...............Eruvin 13b
Reptile, dead, lentil volume.................Chagigah 11a; Nazir 52a; Meilah 16b-17a
Reptile, dried or burned...............................Niddah 4a, 56a; Taharos 9:9
Reptile found in basket, doubt.......................................Niddah 3b-4a
Reptile, impurity..Chullin 21a
Reptile in oil press...Taharos 9:8-9
Reptile in Temple Courtyard.....................................Eruvin 104b-105a
Reptile, pure when carried...Keilim 1:1

Misc. —
Reptile, number of negative commandments.........Makos 16b; Eruvin 28a; Pesachim 24a-24b
Reptiles, injuring on Shabbos.................................Shabbos 107a-107b
Reptiles, poison..Avodah Zarah 31b
Reptiles, punishment...Bava Metzia 61b
Reptiles, repulsion...Bava Metzia 61b
Reptiles, shown to Moses...Menachos 29a
Reptiles, various species...Chullin 67b

Repulsive acts
Repulsive acts, bloodletting utensil.....................................Makos 16b
Repulsive acts, bodily needs..Makos 16b
Repulsive acts, eating living grasshopper..............................Shabbos 90b

Reputation
Reputation, bad, not to remarry her after divorce.......Gittin 45b-46b; Yevamos 25a; Kesubos 74b
Reputation, good, better than good oil................................Berachos 17a
Reputation, good, crown...Avos 2:7, 4:13

Requests
Requests...*see also* **Prayer**, page 497
Requests, heart like flesh..Sotah 5a
Requests of Othniel..Temurah 16a
Requests on Shabbos...Bava Kama 80b
Requests, proper and improper...Taanis 4a

Requirement or permission, deduction
....Sotah 3a-3b

Requirement to give tithes
Requirement to give tithes, cooking...................................Maasros 4:1
Requirement to give tithes, drinking in wine press.........Eruvin 99b; Maasros 4:4; Shabbos 11b
Requirement to give tithes, gift.......................................Maasros 4:2
Requirement to give tithes, little storehouse..........................Maasros 4:1
Requirement to give tithes, salt............Maasros 4:3; Beitzah 35a; Bava Metzia 89b
Requirement to give tithes, Shabbos.......Beitzah 33b, 34b-35a; Maasros 4:2; Terumos 8:3; Eduyos 4:10
Requirement to give tithes, *terumah*.............Beitzah 35a-35b; Maasros 2:4
Requirement to give tithes, courtyard............Beitzah 34b-35b Terumos 8:3; Maasros 3:1, 3:5-6;
....Bava Metzia 87b-88b Niddah 47b Berachos 35b
Requirement to give tithes, house............Maasros 2:3, 3:6-7; Bava Metzia 88a-88b
Requirement to give tithes, by which act.................Maasros 2:3-8, 3:1-3
Requirement to give tithes, worker.....................Maasros 2:7-8, 3:1-3
Requirement to give tithes, sale............Maasros 2:5-6; Beitzah 35b; Bava Metzia 89b

Resembling
Resembling, first born animal..........Bechoros 3b, 5b-6b, 12a, 16b, 17a; Bava Kama 78a

R

Resembling, odd animal..Bechoros 3b, 5b-7a, 17a, 24a; Niddah 23b; Chullin 69a

Resentment

Resentment, "catch your eyes!," episode...Chagigah 3b

Resentment, "our friend"...Kesubos 69a-69b

Resentment, dirtying bed..Shabbos 46a-46b

Resentment, disciple who blessed and scoffed...Berachos 39a

Resentment during discourses, episodes...Berachos 28b

Resentment, by author not quoted by name....Bechoros 31b; Yevamos 96b-97a; Kesubos 25b; Makos 5b

Resentment, my teacher needs me..Bava Metzia 33a

Resentment, Rav Yosef..Nedarim 55a-55b; Eruvin 54a

Resentment, taught mistaken teaching to his son.................................Shabbos 121a-121b

Resentment, two heads...Menachos 37a

Reserved field for her support...Kesubos 54b

Resh Galusa...*see* **Reish Galusa** page 554

Resh Lakish

His life —

Resh Lakish, cannibals...Gittin 47a

Resh Lakish, death...Bava Metzia 84a

Resh Lakish, repentance...Bava Metzia 84a

Resh Lakish, strong ones of *Eretz Yisrael*...Chullin 122a

Resh Lakish's son...Taanis 9a

Learning —

Resh Lakish, called "My colleague" by Rabbi Yochanan.................................Kesubos 54b

Resh Lakish, careful to cite Sage's name in teaching...................Kesubos 25b; Makos 5b

Resh Lakish respected Rabbi Meir...Sanhedrin 24a

Resh Lakish, mistake in ruling...Avodah Zarah 58b

Resh Lakish, plowing on Sabbatical year...Sanhedrin 26a

Resh Lakish, reviewed his learning numerous times...Taanis 8a

Resh Lakish, ruling......................................Yevamos 36a-36b; Bava Basra 129b; Chullin 77a

Resh Lakish, uproots mountains...Sanhedrin 24a

Misc. —

Resh Lakish, behavior...Yoma 9b; Gittin 47a

Resh Lakish, comforting the bereaved..Kesubos 8b

Resh Lakish, episode about ignorant judge..Sanhedrin 7b

Resh Lakish, eulogy of Sage...Megillah 28b

Resh Lakish, praises by Rav..Chullin 54a

Resh Lakish, throw me into the water...Megillah 28b

Reshus hanizak.......................*see* **Domain of damaged person, ox goring occasionally**, page 173

Reshus harabim..*see* **Public domain**, page 509

Reshus hayachid..*see* **Private domain**, page 504

Resident non-Jew

Resident non-Jew coming from two nations......................Yevamos 78b; Kiddushin 67a-67b

Resident non-Jew, commandment to give him charity...........Pesachim 21b, 23b; Chullin 114b;
....Avodah Zarah 20a

Resident non-Jew, exile and death...Makos 9a

Resident non-Jew, general................................Pesachim 21b; Chullin 114b; Gittin 45a; Arachin 29a

Resident non-Jew, interest...Bava Metzia 71a

Resident non-Jew, Shabbos...Yevamos 48b; Krisos 9a

Resident non-Jew who annulled idolatrous item...Avodah Zarah 64b

Resident non-Jew, wine and *eruv*..Avodah Zarah 64b
Residing among their impurity...Yoma 56b-57a
Responsibility
Responsibility for breaking utensil.....................Nedarim 31a-31b; Bava Basra 87b
Responsibility for swindlers.................................Bava Kama 69a; Demai 3:5
Responsibility, mutual, of Jews.............Sotah 37b; Bava Metzia 31a; Sanhedrin 43b
Rest
Rest for Sage, World to come............................Berachos 64a; Moed Katan 29a
Rest of souls...Shabbos 152b
Rest, Shiloh.......................................Zevachim 119a-119b; Megillah 10a
Resting place, item about to rest from fall...........Zevachim 25b; Bava Metzia 12a, 102a
Resulting from transgression...Temurah 20b
Resurrection of dead
  Episodes —
    Resurrection of dead, Elisha..Chullin 7b
    Resurrection of dead, Ezekiel...Sanhedrin 92b
    Resurrection of dead, Giving of Torah............................Shabbos 88b
    Resurrection of dead, Sages..Avodah Zarah 10b
  Misc. —
    Resurrection of dead, death...Sanhedrin 91b-92a
    Resurrection of dead, dressed.................Kesubos 111b; Sanhedrin 90b
    Resurrection of dead, key............................Taanis 2a-2b; Sanhedrin 113a
    Resurrection of dead, ordinary persons................Rosh Hashanah 16b-17a
    Resurrection of dead, out of *Eretz Yisrael*................Kesubos 111a, 111b
    Resurrection of dead, reward involved............Chullin 142a; Kiddushin 39b
    Resurrection of dead, sources.......Pesachim 68a; Berachos 15b; Sanhedrin 90b-91b, 92a
Retaining
Retaining one's prophecy...Sanhedrin 89a-89b
Retaining one's testimony........................Pesachim 113b; Bava Kama 56a
Retaining worker's salary...Bava Metzia 61a
Reticulum
Reticulum, change of name.........................Shabbos 36a; Succah 34a
Reticulum *treifah*.............Chullin 48b-49a, 50b-51a; Shabbos 36a; Succah 34a; Kesubos 76b
Retracting
Retracting, Amora...Bava Basra 131a
Retracting from bequest, sick man...............Bava Basra 148b, 151a, 152a-153a
Retracting from gift..Bava Metzia 49a-49b
Retracting from part of purchase...............Bava Basra 86b-87a, 105a, 106b-107a
Retracting from purchase, legal document...........................Bava Basra 169b
Retracting from purchase, until when...........................Bava Basra 114a-114b
Retracting from testimony.......Kesubos 18b; Bava Metzia 28b; Bava Basra 167b-168a; Sanhedrin 44b; Makos 3a
Retracting from writing legal document.............................Bava Basra 77a-77b
Retracting, worker...Bava Kama 116b
Retroactive clarification
Retroactive clarification, cases.......................................Eruvin 36b-37b
Retroactive clarification, dependant on other person................Gittin 25a-26a
Retroactive clarification, *eruv* in barrel..............................Eruvin 68a
Retroactive clarification, heir...Bechoros 56b-57a

R

Retroactive clarification, Rabbi Yehudah .... Yoma 55b-56b; Chullin 14a-14b; Eruvin 36b-37a;
.... Succah 23b-24a; Gittin 25a-26a; Bava Kama 69a-69b; Bava Basra 37b; Meilah 22a
Retroactive clarification, Scriptural and Rabbinical ..... Beitzah 10a, 37b-38a, 39b; Eruvin 36b-38a;
.... Yoma 55b-56b; Chullin 14a-14b, 135b
Retroactive clarification, separating *terumah* and tithes .... Eruvin 37b-38a; Succah 23b-24a

Retroactive impurity of *niddah*
Retroactive impurity of *niddah*, concerning what .... Niddah 5b-7a
Retroactive impurity of *niddah*, examination .... Niddah 5a-5b
Retroactive impurity of *niddah*, how much time .... Niddah 36a
Retroactive impurity of *niddah*, immediately .... Niddah 60b
Retroactive impurity of *niddah*, Shamai .... Niddah 2a, 3a-3b
Retroactive impurity of *niddah*, stain .... Niddah 15a, 53b, 56b
Retroactive impurity of *niddah*, who .... Kesubos 37a
Retroactive impurity of *niddah*, why .... Niddah 36a
Retroactive impurity of *niddah*, woman after birth .... Niddah 4b
Retroactive impurity of *niddah*, woman without menses .... Niddah 4b, 7a-7b, 9a-9b, 10b-11a,
.... 39a, 68b

Retroactively
Retroactively collects, lender .... Pesachim 30b-31b
Retroactively, doubtful impurity .... Niddah 3b-4a

Return
Return man to his senses, which things .... Berachos 57b
Return, rebellious children .... Bechoros 31a
Returned my lost object, Yosef Habavli .... Menachos 18a
Returning bride's and groom's gifts .... Bava Basra 145a-146b
Returning collateral .... Bava Metzia 31b, 114b-115a
Returning crown to its ancient glory .... Yoma 69b
Returning debt, commandment .... Kesubos 86a-86b; Bava Basra 174a; Arachin 22a
Returning deposit in desert .... Bava Kama 118a
Returning from Jewish war .... Sotah 43a-43b, 44a
Returning item having lost its value, rented donkey .... Bava Metzia 78b-79a
Returning lost item .... *see* **Lost item**, page 378
Returning lost item, oath .... Kesubos 18a-18b; Gittin 51a-51b; Shevuos 42a
Returning pot to stove-top, cooking on Shabbos .... Shabbos 38a
Returning seizure in case of payment .... Bava Metzia 35a-35b
Returning to *techum* armed, Shabbos .... Eruvin 45a
Returning Torah scroll to ark .... Sotah 39b
Returning wedding presents .... Bava Basra 145a-146b

Returning stolen item
Returning item stolen by father .... Bava Kama 111b-112a, 113a; Bava Metzia 70a; Arachin 22a
Returning stolen item, decree for repentant people .... Gittin 55a; Succah 31a
Returning stolen item, doubt from whom .... Yevamos 118b; Bava Kama 103b-104a; Bava Metzia 37a
Returning stolen item, fragments .... Bava Kama 11a, 94a
Returning stolen item, from whom one must not receive .... Bava Kama 94b-95a
Returning stolen item, informing owner .... Bava Kama 118a-118b; Bava Metzia 40b-41a, 64a
Returning stolen item, less than a *perutah* .... Bava Kama 105a
Returning stolen item, Mede .... Bava Kama 103a-104a, 105a; Bava Metzia 55a
Returning stolen item, sacrifice .... Bava Kama 78b
Returning stolen item, *tevel* .... Nedarim 84b-85a; Kiddushin 58b

R

Returning stolen item, when it lost its value..Bava Kama 45a, 97a, 98b

Retzeih, *Bircas HaMazon*...Berachos 48b

Retzias eved..*see* **Piercing slave's ear, page 487**

Reuben

Reuben, first city of refuge...Makos 10a

Reuben, firstborn right..Bava Basra 123a

Reuben, mandrakes...Sanhedrin 99b

Reuben, significance of his name..Berachos 7b

Reuben, sin concerning Bilhah...Shabbos 55b; Sotah 7b

Revai

Revai, Divine property...................................Kiddushin 53a-53b, 54b; Sanhedrin 112b-113a

Revai, from non-Jew and Cuthean...Terumos 3:9

Revai, from where does one bring to Jerusalem..................Maaser Sheni 5:2; Rosh Hashanah 31b;

....Beitzah 5a-5b

Revai, gifts to poor..Peah 7:6

Revai, like second tithe..Bava Kama 69b

Revai, marking..Maaser Sheni 5:1; Bava Kama 69a

Revai, other trees...Berachos 35a

Revai, redeeming...Maaser Sheni 5:1-5; Berachos 35a

Revai, redeeming thief...Bava Kama 69b

Revai, redeeming to avoid transgression..Bava Kama 69a-69b

Revealing intention, divorce certificate..Gittin 30a, 34a-34b

Revealed secret

Revealed secret...Sanhedrin 31a

Revealing secret, one out of a thousand............................Yevamos 63b; Sanhedrin 100b

Revealing secret, one's wife..Sanhedrin 100b

Revealing secret, prohibition...Yoma 4b; Sanhedrin 31a, 100b

Revealing secret, verses...Yevamos 63b; Bava Basra 4a

Revenge

Revenge and bearing grudge, Sage...Shabbos 63a

Revenge and grudge...Yoma 23a

Revenge, general..Yoma 23a; Sanhedrin 92a, 102b

Revenge of righteous on idolaters...Rosh Hashanah 23a

Revenge on Greek man, episode...Taanis 18b

Revenge, Sage...Shabbos 63a

Revenge, sayings...Sanhedrin 39b, 95b

Revenge, written between two Divine Names...Berachos 33a

Reverse alphabet, *At Bash*...Shabbos 104a

Revi'yos of rain..Sheviis 9:7; Taanis 6a-6b; Nedarim 62b-63a

Reviewing one's prayer before praying...Rosh Hashanah 35a

Reviewing one's learning

Reviewing one's learning, Abbaye considered man trustworthy.........................Yevamos 64b

Reviewing one's learning, commentaries..Eruvin 54a

Reviewing one's learning, four hundred times...Eruvin 54b

Reviewing one's learning, four times..Eruvin 54b

Reviewing one's learning, learning little by little...............................Avodah Zarah 19a; Eruvin 54b

Reviewing one's learning, learns and forgets..Sanhedrin 99a-99b

Reviewing one's learning, one hundred and one times..Chagigah 9b

Reviewing one's learning, preparation..Taanis 8a

Reviewing one's learning, Roman hunter .... Eruvin 54b
Reviewing one's learning, thirty days .... Berachos 38b; Chullin 86b; Krisos 27a

Reviis
Reviis, amount .... Bava Basra 58b
Reviis, carrying out on Shabbos .... Shabbos 77a
Reviis dry food, equal to volume of olive .... Shabbos 77a
Reviis, impurity of liquids .... Krisos 13b
Reviis of blood, dead .... Chullin 72a
Reviis of blood in man .... Sotah 5a; Shabbos 31b
Reviis of blood, *nazir* .... Nazir 53a
Reviis, utensils and calculation .... Pesachim 109a-109b
Reviis, washing hands .... Yadayim 1:1, 2:1; Nazir 38a; Gittin 15b; Chullin 107a
Reviis, which substances .... Nazir 38a
Reviis, wine of *nazir* .... Nazir 38b

Revolution of stars, calculating .... Shabbos 75a; Eruvin 56a; Rosh Hashanah 8a, 12a
Revuchah, meal offering .... Zevachim 50a

Reward
Aggadah —
Reward according to effort .... Avos 5:23
Reward and punishment, non-Jews .... Bava Kama 38a
Reward during one's life, without suffering .... Sanhedrin 101a
Reward, entrance to Beth El .... Sotah 46b
Reward explicit in Torah, resurrection of dead .... Chullin 142a; Kiddushin 39b
Reward for transgression against loss .... Bava Basra 78b; Avos 2:1
Reward, greater than punishment .... Sotah 11a; Sanhedrin 100a-100b; Yoma 76a
Reward in this world .... Menachos 44a
Reward in this world, non-existent .... Kiddushin 39b
Reward of commandments in this world .... Shabbos 127a-127b; Peah 1:1; Kiddushin 39b-40a, 41a
Reward of creatures is not retained .... Bava Kama 38b
Reward of righteous, deduced from reward of wicked .... Makos 24b

Commandments —
Reward for bringing children, *Hakhel* .... Chagigah 3a
Reward for details in certain commandments .... Berachos 6b
Reward for good deeds customarily performed .... Shabbos 23b
Reward for learning, understanding .... Berachos 6b
Reward for retracting on a teaching .... Bava Kama 41b; Pesachim 22b; Kiddushin 57a; Bechoros 6b
Reward for saying blessing to discharge others .... Nazir 66b; Berachos 53b
Reward for steps, synagogue .... Sotah 22a; Bava Metzia 107a
Reward for tithe .... Taanis 9a
Reward for *tzitzis* .... Menachos 43b-44a
Reward for who gives up sin .... Kiddushin 39b-40a; Makos 23a-23b
Reward of communal leader .... Sanhedrin 92a

Future —
Reward in the future, as opposed to non-Jew .... Avodah Zarah 65a
Reward in the future, for whom .... Berachos 34b; Bava Metzia 33b
Reward in the future, immense .... Sanhedrin 96a; Nedarim 39b; Makos 24b
Reward in World to Come, "You put darkness" .... Bava Metzia 83b
Reward in World to Come, capacity to receive it .... Sanhedrin 100a-100b
Reward of Messiah and future .... Sanhedrin 99a

R

Reward of schoolteacher in the future .... Bava Basra 8b
Misc. —
Reward, "I merit a reward for my behavior" .... Shabbos 118b-119a
Reward comes quickly .... Shabbos 97a
Reward explicit in Torah, forcing .... Chullin 110b-111a
Reward for teaching Torah .... *see* **Teach,** page 673; *see also* **Schoolteacher,** page 591
Reward, Sages' wives .... Yoma 77a
Ribbis .... *see* **Interest,** page 314
Ribon Haolamim, fast day .... Berachos 17a
Ribs, *treifah* .... Chullin 42b, 52a
Rice
Rice and millet, blessing .... Berachos 37b
Rice, *chametz* .... Pesachim 35a, 114b; Berachos 37a
Rice, exempt from *challah* .... Menachos 70a-70b
Rice, final blessing .... Berachos 37a
Rich
Rich .... *see* **Wealthy,** page 738
Rich and poor meet, charity .... Temurah 16a
Rich, who is .... Avos 4:1
Riddles about relatives and lineage .... Yevamos 97b, 99a
Riders of female donkeys .... Eruvin 54b
Ridiculing
Ridiculing, abundance in the future .... Shabbos 30b
Ridiculing, resentment .... Berachos 39a
Ridiculing Sages' words .... Bava Basra 75a; Sanhedrin 100a
Riding
Riding, act of acquisition .... Bava Metzia 8b-9b
Riding animal on Shabbos .... Beitzah 36b
Riding, destruction of semen .... Niddah 14a
Riding horse on Shabbos, episode .... Sanhedrin 46a
Right
Right and left, oath .... Nazir 3b
Right foot first .... Yoma 11b; Menachos 34a
Right hand drawing close .... Sotah 47a; Sanhedrin 107b
Right hand, service of *Kohen* .... Zevachim 24a-25a; Menachos 9b-10b, 26a
Right side first, washing .... Shabbos 61a
Right, turning .... Zevachim 62b; Yoma 15b, 17b, 45a, 58b; Sotah 15b
Right way, *Pirkei Avos* .... Avos 2:1, 2:9
Right
Right because he bought from a non-Jew .... Bava Basra 35b-36a
Right of non-Jew, firstborn .... Bava Metzia 70b; Bechoros 16a-16b
Rights of father, *kesubah* .... Kesubos 43b
Rights of father towards his daughter .... Kesubos 43b, 46b-47a; Kiddushin 3b-4a, 10a; Niddah 47a
Rights of husband, parallel to wife's .... Kesubos 47b
Rights of married woman, necessary items .... Kesubos 70b
Rights of Sage in *beis din* .... Shevuos 30a-30b
Right to grant
Right to grant, act of acquisition .... Bava Metzia 11b
Right to grant, gift of poor .... Chullin 131a-131b

R

Right to grant, monetary matters .... Kiddushin 58a-58b; Nedarim 84b-85a; Pesachim 46b;

.... Bava Metzia 11b

Right to grant, separating tithe for someone else .... Nedarim 36b; Yoma 50b; Zevachim 6a;

.... Temurah 2b-3a, 10a

Right to grant, *terumah* .... Bechoros 26b-27a

Right to grant, tithe for poor .... Nedarim 84a-84b

Righteous

Aggadah —

Righteous are few .... Yoma 38b

Righteous enjoy radiance of Divine Presence .... Berachos 17a

Righteous man decrees and G-d carries out .... Shabbos 59b; Moed Katan 16b

Righteous man, equal to whole world .... Shabbos 30b; Berachos 6b; Sanhedrin 103b

Righteous man, expectation of his birth .... Niddah 31a

Righteous man greater than angel .... Sanhedrin 93a

Righteous man, merit for Israel .... Eruvin 101a; Yoma 38b; Berachos 27b; Shabbos 30b

Righteous, reward in the future .... Berachos 34b

Righteous will blossom like palm tree .... Taanis 25a-25b; Bava Basra 80b

Righteous, world exists for him .... Berachos 6b

Death —

Righteous in death .... Chullin 7b; Berachos 18a

Righteous man, buried by G-d Himself .... Sotah 9b

Righteous man dies because of impending tragedy .... Bava Kama 60a

Righteous man dies only when another is born .... Kiddushin 72b; Yoma 38b

Righteous man is gone, eulogy .... Sanhedrin 113b

Righteous man, wordings for his death .... Bava Basra 16b

Righteous, no righteous man on earth .... Sanhedrin 101a

Righteous, their corpse does not putrefy .... Shabbos 152b

Righteous welcoming deceased .... Berachos 28b; Bava Kama 111b; Bava Metzia 62b

Righteous man who died

Righteous man who died, atonement .... Moed Katan 28a

Righteous man who died, like a new bride .... Moed Katan 25b

Righteous man who died, like Temple destruction .... Rosh Hashanah 18b

Righteous man who died, loss for his generation .... Megillah 15a

Righteous man who died, sins of his generation .... Shabbos 33b

Suffering —

Righteous man, imperfect, punished with wicked .... Avodah Zarah 4a

Righteous men, punished with wicked .... Bava Kama 60a, 92a

Righteous, severity of judgment .... Bava Kama 50a-50b; Taanis 11a; Zevachim 115b; Eruvin 22a;

.... Yevamos 121b

Righteous, sickness of intestines .... Shabbos 118b; Kesubos 103b

Righteous man afflicted with troubles

Righteous man afflicted with troubles .... Yoma 87a

Righteous man afflicted with troubles, for their benefit .... Shabbos 30b

Righteous man afflicted with troubles, we are not concerned .... Avos 4:15

Righteous man afflicted with troubles, why .... Kiddushin 39b, 40b; Berachos 7a

Misc. —

Righteous can create worlds .... Sanhedrin 65b

Righteous, do not be too righteous .... Yoma 22b

Righteous man, blessing for sick person .... Bava Basra 116a; Taanis 8a

R

Righteous man, can he become wicked ....Berachos 29a
Righteous man, his servants ....Chullin 4b
Righteous man without sin, there is no ....Sanhedrin 101a
Righteous men who encompassed history ....Bava Basra 121b
Righteous men will follow them ....Nazir 23a; Horayos 10b
Righteous non-Jews ....Chullin 92a
Righteous son of righteous, prayer ....Yevamos 64a
Righteous, their animals are protected from forbidden foods ....Chullin 5b-6a, 7a;
....Yevamos 99b; Kesubos 28b; Gittin 7a
Rim of utensil, liquid ....Keilim 25:6
Rimah ....*see* **Worm,** page 764
Ring
Ring, large, slaughtering ....Chullin 18a-19a
Ring on finger, unusual way ....Shabbos 62a
Rings, impurity ....Shabbos 52a-52b, 59b-60a; Keilim 11:8, 12:1, 13:6
Rings near Altar ....Middos 3:5
Rinsing
Rinsing, cold food in cold food ....Chullin 107b; Pesachim 76a
Rinsing in cold water ....Zevachim 96b
Rinsing knife in cold water ....Chullin 111b
Rinsing, non-Jew's utensil ....Avodah Zarah 75b-76b
Ripe fruit, tithes ....Maasros 1:1-4
Ripening, fruit ....Rosh Hashanah 15b
Ripui ....*see* **Treatment,** page 701
Rise in status upon marriage, wife ....Kesubos 61a
Rishon, means previous ....Pesachim 5a
Rishonim kemalachim ....*see* **First generations like angels,** page 225
Rishumo nikar ....*see* **Letters recognizable, erased legal document,** page 366
Rishumo nikar, kisuy hadam ....*see* **Visible blood traces, covering blood,** page 724
Risma (coals of rosem wood)
Risma, for who stops learning ....Avodah Zarah 3b; Chagigah 12b
Risma in desert, episode ....Bava Basra 74b
Riss, distance ....Bava Metzia 33a
Ritual
Ritual articles ....Megillah 26b, 32a
Ritual bath ....*see* **Mikveh,** page 410
Ritual slaughter ....*see* **Slaughtering,** page 633
Rival
Levirate marriage —
Rival of daughter, Rabbi Dosa ....Yevamos 16a
Rival of forbidden woman, levirate marriage ....Yevamos 13a-13b, 14b-15a, 27a
Rival of sterile woman, levirate marriage ....Yevamos 3b, 12a-12b, 20a
Rival, one, levirate marriage ....Yevamos 44a; Yoma 13b
Rival outside *Eretz Yisrael,* levirate marriage ....Yevamos 36a, 119a-119b
Misc. —
Rival *chalutzah's* relative ....Yevamos 41a
Rival, jealousy ....Megillah 13a; Avodah Zarah 55a
Rival, marriage ....Yevamos 65a
Rival, not to marry two wives ....Pesachim 113a

R

Rival of *chalutzah*, prohibition .... Yevamos 10b-11a, 40b, 53a
Rival of forbidden woman, permitted .... Yevamos 3b, 8a-8b
Rival, trustworthiness for *agunah* .... Yevamos 117a-118a, 119b-120a

River
  Monetary matters —
  River bank, *chazakah* .... Bava Metzia 108a
  River banks, clearing them to make public way .... Bava Metzia 107b-108a
  River, precedence and diverting .... Gittin 60b
  Rivers —
  River, Diglath .... Berachos 59b
  River Diomeses, cure .... Shabbos 147b
  River Diomeses, forgetting .... Shabbos 147b
  River in Temple, in the future .... Yoma 77b-78a; Menachos 98a; Sanhedrin 100a
  River, *techum* .... Eruvin 61a
  Rivers of balsam, episode .... Taanis 25a
  Rivers of *Eretz Yisrael* .... Bechoros 55a; Bava Basra 74b
  Rivers of world .... Bechoros 44b, 55a-55b; Berachos 59b; Shabbos 145b; Nedarim 40a
  Misc. —
  River Arnon, miracle for Israel .... Berachos 54a-54b
  River, blessing .... Berachos 59a-59b
  River, danger .... Yoma 77b
  River Deenor .... Chagigah 13b-14a
  River, Rabbi Pinchas ben Yair .... Chullin 7a
  Rivers, immersion .... Nedarim 40a-40b; Bechoros 55b; Shabbos 65b; Niddah 67a

Road
  Road, path between vineyards .... Eruvin 24b-25a
  Roads, breadth dimensions .... Bava Basra 100a-100b
  Roads in *Eretz Yisrael*, since Temple destruction .... Rosh Hashanah 23b
  Roads, responsibility of *beis din* .... Shekalim 1:1

Roah machmas tashmish .... *see* **Blood discharge due to intimate relations**, page 66

Roast
  Roast, absorption .... Pesachim 76a; Chullin 96b-97a, 97b, 112a
  Roast meat, blood .... Pesachim 74a-75a; Chullin 111b-112b
  Roast meat on Pesach .... Pesachim 53a-53b, 74a; Beitzah 23a; Berachos 19a

Roasted
  Roasted cereals, cure for heart disease .... Eruvin 29b
  Roasted cereals, leavening .... Pesachim 40a
  Roasting in embers .... Bava Basra 74b
  Roasting Pesach lamb .... Pesachim 41a-41b, 74a, 75a

Robber
  Robber .... *see also* **Thief**, page 686
  Robber, "do not covet" .... Bava Metzia 5b
  Robber, armed .... Bava Kama 57a-57b; Bava Metzia 22a, 95a
  Robber, claiming that one travels a long way .... Avodah Zarah 25b-26a
  Robber, definition .... Bava Kama 62a
  Robber, disqualified for testimony .... Sanhedrin 25b
  Robbers, escaping them by lying about one's destination .... Avodah Zarah 25b-26a
  Robbers like yourself leveled it .... Eruvin 53b

Robe of *Kohen Gadol* .... Zevachim 88b

R

Rocks
Rocks, consecrated field .... Kiddushin 61a; Bava Basra 102b-103b; Arachin 25a
Rocks, sale of field .... Kiddushin 61a; Bava Basra 102b-103b
Rodeif .... *see* **Pursuer**, page 512
Roe .... Avodah Zarah 39a, 40a-40b; Chullin 63b-64a
Roeh chovah le'atzmo .... *see* **Man does not find any wrong in himself**, page 388
Roeh es hanolad .... *see* **Seeing the future**, page 591

Roll
Roll yourself in dust of Sages' feet .... Avos 1:4
Rolling after being placed down, Shabbos .... Shabbos 100a-100b
Rolling spices between fingers on Shabbos .... Shabbos 128a
Rolling up Torah scroll .... Megillah 32a
Rolling up Torah scroll towards middle .... Bava Basra 14a
Rolling wheat between one's fingers on Yom Tov .... Beitzah 12b
Rolling wood splinter between fingers on Yom Tov .... Beitzah 33b
Rolls into courtyard, act of acquisition .... Bava Metzia 12a

Romans set up marketplaces for their own interest .... Shabbos 33b; Avodah Zarah 2b

Rome
Rome, agents sent to learn Torah .... Bava Kama 38a
Rome and Persia .... Yoma 10a; Shevuos 6b; Avodah Zarah 2b
Rome and Israel, agreement .... Avodah Zarah 8b
Rome, events .... Shabbos 15a; Avodah Zarah 8b; Yoma 10a; Sanhedrin 98b
Rome, Jerusalem and Cesarea .... Megillah 6a
Rome, lowly people .... Gittin 80a; Avodah Zarah 10a
Rome, noise .... Yoma 20b
Rome, treasures of Egypt .... Pesachim 87b, 119a
Rome, treasures of the Holy Temple, *paroches* and *tzitz* .... Meilah 17b; Suka 5a

Roof
Roof and courtyard, carrying between them .... Eruvin 23b, 35a, 74a, 89a, 90b-92a; Shabbos 130b,147b; Menachos 72a
Roof, considered as walled .... Eruvin 89a-90a
Roof, cracked, tent of corpse .... Oholos 11:1-2
Roof of Temple, sanctity .... Pesachim 86a; Shevuos 17a-17b
Roofs, carrying on Shabbos .... Eruvin 84b
Roofs caved in, Pesach offering .... Pesachim 85b
Roofs of Jerusalem, holiness .... Pesachim 85b-86a

Room
Room for preparation of sacrifices, Temple .... Middos 3:5
Room for tasty food .... Megillah 7b; Eruvin 82b
Room in apartment, sale .... Bava Basra 61b
Room of husband and wife, prohibition .... Eruvin 63b

Room in Temple
Room in Temple, "*Beis Hamokad*" .... Yoma 15b-16a, 17a-17b; Middos 1:5-9
Room in Temple, "*Beis Hamokad*," sleep .... Tamid 26b
Room in Temple, bull for mistake of *beis din* .... Menachos 52a
Room in Temple, for inconspicuous charity .... Shekalim 5:6
Room in Temple, for lambs .... Yoma 17a; Menachos 49b-50a; Arachin 13a-13b
Room in Temple, for utensils .... Shekalim 5:6
Room in Temple, new taking .... Rosh Hashanah 7a

Room in Temple, Parhedrin .... Yoma 8b
Room in Temple, Stone room for Red Heifer .... Yoma 2a
Room in Temple, taking .... Shekalim 3:1-4, 4:1-2; Kesubos 106a-106b; Moed Katan 6a
Room of Hewn Stone .... *see* **Lishkas HaGazis**, page 373
Rooms in Temple, holiness .... Zevachim 56a; Pesachim 86a
Rooms in Temple, in *Ezras Nashim* .... Yoma 16a
Rooms in Temple, Nikanor .... Yoma 19a; Middos 1:4
Rooms in Temple, six rooms .... Yoma 19a; Middos 5:3-4
Rooms in Temple wall .... Middos 4:3-5; Bava Basra 61a
Rooms open on Temple and outside .... Pesachim 86a; Yoma 25a; Maaser Sheni 3:8

Rooster
Rooster, beneficial to sick .... Avodah Zarah 14a
Rooster, caused damage .... Bava Kama 19b
Rooster, characteristics .... Shabbos 35b, 110b; Eruvin 100b; Beitzah 7a-7b
Rooster, choicest bird .... Bava Metzia 86b
Rooster, doubtful impurity .... Kiddushin 80a
Rooster, *gever* .... Yoma 20b
Rooster, hate .... Pesachim 113b
Rooster, impudent .... Beitzah 25b
Rooster, slaughtering .... Shabbos 128b
Rooster, starting journey .... Yoma 21a
Rooster stoned, episode .... Eduyos 6:1

Rooted
Rooted in sin, penalty .... Bava Kama 67b
Rooting, legumes .... Rosh Hashanah 13b-14a; Sheviis 2:7

Roots
Roots, agriculture .... Bava Basra 19a, 26b-27b
Roots of plants, extending .... Bava Basra 26b-27b
Roots of tree, *muktzeh* .... Eruvin 100a

Ropes
Ropes, partition .... Eruvin 93a
Ropes, thick, difference of opinion .... Bava Basra 31b; Beitzah 27a; Avodah Zarah 7b

Rose oil, Shabbos .... Shabbos 111b, 128a; Bava Metzia 113b

Rosh Chodesh
Rosh Chodesh, blessing on *Haftorah* .... Shabbos 24a
Rosh Chodesh, called *Moed* .... Shevuos 10a
Rosh Chodesh, deceased, mourning .... Moed Katan 28b
Rosh Chodesh, from the Torah .... Taanis 17b
Rosh Chodesh in *mussaf* sacrifice of Rosh Hashanah .... Eruvin 40a-40b
Rosh Chodesh, mentioning because of doubt .... Eruvin 40a
Rosh Chodesh, mistake in song in Temple .... Rosh Hashanah 30b; Beitzah 4b-5a
Rosh Chodesh, Torah reading .... Megillah 21b-22a, 29b; Yoma 70a; Sotah 41a
Rosh Chodesh, work .... Rosh Hashanah 23a; Arachin 10b
Rosh hamedabrim .... *see* **First speaker, Rabbi Yehudah**, page 225

Rosh Hashanah
Rosh Hashanah, days when it cannot occur .... Rosh Hashanah 20a-20b; Succah 43b, 54b
Rosh Hashanah, judgment .... Rosh Hashanah 8a-8b, 16a-16b, 18a; Avodah Zarah 2b
Rosh Hashanah, livelihood .... Beitzah 16a; Bava Basra 10a
Rosh Hashanah, omen for coming year .... Bava Basra 147a

R

Rosh Hashanah, *Shehecheyanu*..Eruvin 40b
Rosh Hashanah, special foods..................................Horayos 12a; Krisos 6a
Rosh Hashanah, Torah reading....................................Megillah 30b-31a
Rosh Hashanah, women who conceived.......................Rosh Hashanah 11a
Rosh Hashanah, *Zeh Hayom Techilas Maasecha*...............Rosh Hashanah 27a
Rosh Yeshivah
Rosh Yeshivah, Abbaye...Horayos 14a
Rosh Yeshivah, Mar BeRav Ashi..Bava Basra 12b
Rosh Yeshivah, Rabbah...Berachos 64a
Rosh Yeshivah, Rabbi Avuhu...Sotah 40a
Rosh Yeshivah, Rabbi Afes...Kesubos 103b
Rosh Yeshivah, Rabbi Chanina..Kesubos 103b
Rosh Yeshivah, Rabbi Elazar ben Azariah.....................................Sotah 27b
Rosh Yeshivah, Rav Yosef...Berachos 64a
Rotev, significance...Chullin 120a
Rotting, society's benefit..Pesachim 54b
Rotzeh adam bekav shelo...................*see* **Preferring one's own produce,** page 500
Rotzeh bekiumo...................*see* **Interested by its existence, forbidden profit,** page 314
Rov...*see* **Majority,** page 384
Rov deos...*see* **Majority of opinions,** page 385
Rov hahodaos, blessing for rain.......................Taanis 6b-7a; Berachos 59b
Rova atzamos.......................................*see* **Bones of corpses,** page 72
Rove'a zachar...*see* **Sinning with male,** page 630
Rovea...*see* **Sinning with animal,** page 629
Rows of righteous before G-d..........................Succah 45b; Sanhedrin 97b
Ruach habrios nochah.................................*see* **Pleased with him,** page 492
Ruach Hakodesh..*see* **Divine inspiration,** page 169
Ruach metzuyah..*see* **Wind, usual,** page 748
Ruach raah..*see* **Bad spirit,** page 40
Ruach shtus...........................*see* **Spirit of folly, transgression,** page 650
Ruach tzefonis...*see* **Wind, Northern,** page 748
Rubbing
Rubbing during prayer..Nazir 59a
Rubbing garment on Shabbos..Shabbos 140a
Rubble, searching for survivors, Pesach lamb...........................Pesachim 91a
Ruchos meisim...................................*see* **Spirits of dead, episode,** page 650
Rude
Rude, making one's father agent...Kiddushin 45b
Rude, oath...Shevuos 42b; Kesubos 18a; Gittin 51b
Ruffians, repentance................................Berachos 10a; Sanhedrin 37a
Ruin
Ruin between houses...Eruvin 88a
Ruin, Elijah and Rabbi Yose..Berachos 3a
Ruin, going into...Berachos 3a-3b
Ruins between courtyards...................................Eruvin 85a-85b, 92a
Ruining
Ruining, digging hole on Shabbos.........Chagigah 10a-10b; Shabbos 73b; Beitzah 8a
Ruining on Shabbos.........................Shabbos 106a; Bava Kama 34b-35a
Ruining, slaughtering on Shabbos..Pesachim 73a

R

Ruining, tearing on Shabbos..Shabbos 105b
Ruining by wound, virgin bride..Kesubos 5b
Rule necessitating a detail...*see* **General and specific,** page 247
Rule
Rule, he will rule, *semichah*..Sanhedrin 5a-5b
Rule, we do not rule this way...Beitzah 28b
Ruled entire world...Megillah 11a-11b
Ruling as nameless Mishnah...*see* **Dispute and undisputed,** page 167
Ruling in money matters, cancellation of debts...Gittin 18a
Ruling in teacher's place...........................Eruvin 62b-63a; Berachos 31b; Kesubos 60b; Sanhedrin 5b
Ruling like Abbaye, in which case......Kiddushin 52a; Bava Metzia 22b; Bava Kama 73a; Sanhedrin 27a
Ruling rabbis, tribe of Levi..Yoma 26a
Ruling, Rav competent to rule..Avodah Zarah 19b; Sotah 22a-22b
Ruling in teacher's presence
Ruling in teacher's presence, Aaron's sons...Yoma 53a
Ruling in teacher's presence, episodes..Eruvin 62b-63a
Ruling in teacher's presence, Shmuel...Berachos 31b
Ruling
Beis din —
Ruling attestation by *beis din*, "I paid"...Bava Metzia 17a-17b
Ruling depends on *beis din*...Horayos 5b
Ruling, episodes about bothersome persons..Bava Basra 153a, 168b
Ruling, guarantee...Bava Basra 175b
Ruling of *beis din*, explaining..Bava Metzia 69a-69b; Sanhedrin 31b
Ruling of *beis din*, majority..Sanhedrin 3b
Ruling, text...Sanhedrin 30a, 6b
Ruling, trustworthiness..Kiddushin 74a
Law according to whom —
Ruling, Abbaye and Rava....................Kiddushin 52a; Bava Metzia 22b; Bava Kama 73a; Sanhedrin 27a
Ruling, according to Tanna deciding between two opinions.......................Bava Kama 116a;
....Shabbos 39b-40a; Pesachim 21a; Nazir 53a; Chullin 137a
Ruling is according to you, Rav Nachman...Bava Basra 65a
Ruling, Nachum the Mede...Avodah Zarah 7b
Ruling, Rabbah and Rav Yosef...Bava Basra 114b, 143b
Ruling, Rabbi Eliezer...Niddah 7b-8b
Ruling, Rav Yosef..Bava Basra 114b, 143b
Ruling, Resh Lakish...Yevamos 36a-36b; Bava Basra 129b; Chullin 77a
Misc. —
Ruling, did not reach ruling...Avodah Zarah 19b; Sotah 22a-22b
Ruling, exempts from sin offering..Yevamos 87b, 92a; Horayos 2a-4b
Ruling from elder.......................................Shabbos 51a; Yevamos 105b; Sanhedrin 24a, 29b
Ruling from Sage...Chullin 44b
Ruling, learning to decide law...Sanhedrin 106b
Ruling, making light of...Avos 4:8
Ruling, mistake....................................Bechoros 28b; Bava Kama 100a, 117b; Sanhedrin 5a, 33a-33b
Ruling of Sage for himself...................Yevamos 77a, 98a; Bechoros 31a, 38b; Kiddushin 70b
Ruling, questions...Eruvin 67b
Ruling, taught in name of numerous Sages..Gittin 20a, 77a

R

Ruling, temporary

Ruling, temporary, prophet .... Yevamos 90b; Sanhedrin 89b, 90a
Ruling, temporary, punishments .... Sanhedrin 46a; Yevamos 90b
Ruling, temporary, stories .... Sanhedrin 46a; Krisos 8a

Rumor

Rumor about forged document .... Kesubos 36b
Rumor about marriage .... Kiddushin 12b; Gittin 88b-89b
Rumor of bad conduct, lashes .... Kiddushin 81a
Rumor of misconduct, married woman .... Yevamos 24b-25a; Gittin 89a; Kesubos 36b
Rumor of witnesses, captive woman .... Kesubos 23a
Rumor, permitting *agunah* .... Yevamos 122a
Rumor, prohibition of *agunah* .... Yevamos 91b-92a
Rumor vs. *migo* .... Bava Basra 32b-33a
Rumor, when it is effective to prohibit .... Gittin 81a, 88b-89b; Yevamos 25a; Moed Katan 18b

Running

Running man who caused damage .... Bava Kama 32a-32b
Running, prohibition on Shabbos .... Shabbos 113b
Running to do a *mitzvah*, even on Shabbos .... Berachos 6b
Running to Mishnah .... Bava Metzia 33a-33b
Running to synagogue .... Berachos 6b
Running with one's sack, Shabbos .... Shabbos 153b

Rushing .... *see* **Hurry**, page 289

Ruth

Ruth, Balak's sacrifices .... Nazir 23b
Ruth, Boaz's allusions .... Shabbos 113b; Sanhedrin 93a-93b
Ruth, comes into Abraham's offspring .... Yevamos 63a
Ruth, David would descend from her .... Bava Basra 91b
Ruth, death of Boaz's wife .... Bava Basra 91a
Ruth, impurity to hands .... Megillah 7a; Yadayim 3:5
Ruth, long life .... Bava Basra 91b
Ruth, reason for her name .... Berachos 7b; Bava Basra 14b
Ruth, saving Moab .... Bava Kama 38a-38b
Ruth, warnings before conversion .... Yevamos 47b
Ruth, wisdom and modesty .... Shabbos 113b

Ruts

Ruts, consecrated field .... Kiddushin 61a; Bava Basra 102b-103a; Arachin 25a
Ruts, sale of field .... Kiddushin 61a; Bava Basra 102b-103b

R

S

S'chach

S'chach, air space, *lavud* .... Succah 18a
S'chach, arrows .... Succah 12b, 15a
S'chach, boards .... Succah 14a-15a, 17b-18a, 37a
S'chach, breach in *s'chach* .... Succah 15a-15b, 18a
S'chach, broken items .... Succah 15b-16a
S'chach, bundle .... Succah 12a-13b
S'chach coming out of succah .... Succah 19a
S'chach, double .... Succah 22a-22b
S'chach, flax .... Shabbos 27b; Succah 12b-13a
S'chach for succah, from which plants .... Succah 11b-12a, 13b, 36b-37a
S'chach improper and air space .... Succah 19a
S'chach improper, dimension .... Succah 17a-18a
S'chach, mat .... Succah 16a, 19b-20b
S'chach, smelling and falling .... Succah 12b-13a
S'chach, sunlight more abundant .... Succah 7b, 19a, 22b
S'chach, support .... Succah 21b
S'chach susceptible to become impure by leprosy .... Shabbos 27b
S'kilah .... *see* **Stoning**, page 657
Sabbatical year .... *see also* **Removing**, page 557

Aggadah —
Sabbatical year, earth belongs to G-d .... Sanhedrin 39a
Sabbatical year, episode of inquiry .... Succah 44b
Sabbatical year, exile .... Shabbos 33a
Sabbatical year, punishment .... Kiddushin 20a-20b; Succah 40b; Arachin 30b

Fruit —
Sabbatical year, buying after that year .... Sheviis 6:4
Sabbatical year, *esrog* .... Rosh Hashanah 15a-15b; Succah 39a; Bechoros 31b
Sabbatical year, exporting produce .... Sheviis 6:5
Sabbatical year, fruit coming in or out of year ...... Sheviis 2:7-10, 5:3-5, 6:3; Nedarim 58a-59b
Sabbatical year, thanksgiving .... Sheviis 4:2
Sabbatical year, inheriting and receiving produce .... Sheviis 9:9
Sabbatical year, kept produce .... Sheviis 9:1; Maasros 5:8; Succah 39b
Sabbatical year, onion kept in earth .... Sheviis 5:2-5

Sabbatical year, ownerless..Sheviis 4:2; Kiddushin 52a, 53a
Sabbatical year, plants...Nedarim 58a-59b; Sheviis 6:3
Sabbatical year, profit and destruction simultaneous...........Succah 40a; Bava Kama 101b-102a
Sabbatical year, self-seeded produce...Sheviis 9:1; Pesachim 51b
Sabbatical year, time of picking fruit...Sheviis 4:7-9
Sabbatical year, which fruit.........Sheviis 7:1-3, 7:5-6; Shabbos 68a; Bava Kama 101b-102a; Niddah 51b

Holiness —
Sabbatical year, borrowing produce...Avodah Zarah 62b
Sabbatical year, exchange..Succah 40b-41a; Avodah Zarah 54b
Sabbatical year, food without roots...................Niddah 62a; Shabbos 90a; Avodah Zarah 14a
Sabbatical year, holiness of initial fruit.............Succah 40b-41a; Sheviis 8:7-8; Kiddushin 58a;
....Avodah Zarah 54b; Bechoros 9b
Sabbatical year, man forbidden by vow to benefit from someone.....................Nedarim 42a
Sabbatical year, prohibition to spoil produce...................Sheviis 4:7-10; Pesachim 52b-53a
Sabbatical year, redeeming..Succah 40b-41a
Sabbatical year, sale of fruit..Sheviis 7:3, 8:3
Sabbatical year, sale to ignoramus...Succah 39a-39b

Prohibited labors —
Sabbatical year, building..Moed Katan 4b
Sabbatical year, caring for fruit.....................................Sheviis 2:5; Avodah Zarah 50b
Sabbatical year, improving tree................Avodah Zarah 50b; Succah 44b; Moed Katan 3a
Sabbatical year, irrigating...Moed Katan 6b
Sabbatical year, irrigating rice..Sheviis 2:4, 2:10
Sabbatical year, labors prohibited from the Torah..................................Moed Katan 2b-3b
Sabbatical year, manure.......................................Sheviis 3:1-4; Moed Katan 4b
Sabbatical year, modification in work...Sheviis 8:6
Sabbatical year, penalty for cultivated field....Sheviis 4:2; Moed Katan 13b; Gittin 44b; Bechoros 34b
Sabbatical year, pruning tree...................Pesachim 52b-53a; Berachos 36b; Sheviis 4:10
Sabbatical year, roots of vineyard.................Succah 44b; Moed Katan 3a; Avodah Zarah 50b
Sabbatical year, stones..Sheviis 3:5-10
Sabbatical year, unintentional labors in field...Sheviis 4:1
Sabbatical year, work in field done by others..Avodah Zarah 15b
Sabbatical year, work on tree..........Sheviis 4:4-6; Avodah Zarah 50b; Succah 44b; Moed Katan 3a

Separating tithes —
Sabbatical year, *challah* from its dough.................................Sheviis 9:9; Bechoros 12b
Sabbatical year, in *terumah* oil..Sheviis 8:7; Zevachim 76a
Sabbatical year, mixing *terumah*...Zevachim 75b-76a
Sabbatical year, priestly gifts..Bechoros 12b
Sabbatical year, tithe...Rosh Hashanah 15a
Sabbatical year, tithes of Ammon and Moab.........Yadayim 4:3; Chagigah 3b; Yevamos 16a

Time and place —
Sabbatical year, calculation of years..Avodah Zarah 9b
Sabbatical year, conquest of Babylon..Sheviis 6:1
Sabbatical year, from Rosh Hashanah..Rosh Hashanah 8b
Sabbatical year in time of Temple, count..Arachin 12b
Sabbatical year, in present times................Gittin 36a; Kiddushin 38b; Moed Katan 2b
Sabbatical year, Rabbi Yehudah's dwelling place.....................Gittin 54a; Bechoros 30a
Sabbatical year, Syria...Sheviis 6:2; Challah 4:7

S

Sabbatical year, work done before.............Sheviis 1:1-8, 2:1-6; Yevamos 83a; Rosh Hashanah 9b, 10b;
.............Succah 34a, 44a; Taanis 3a; Moed Katan 3b-4a; Bava Basra 26b-27a; Zevachim 110b

Use —
Sabbatical year, anointing with oil.............Sheviis 8:2
Sabbatical year, bathhouse.............Sheviis 8:11
Sabbatical year, feeding animal.............Sheviis 8:1
Sabbatical year, *kiddushin* with produce.............Kiddushin 52a, 53a
Sabbatical year, laundering.............Succah 40a-40b; Bava Kama 101b-102a
Sabbatical year, medicines.............Sheviis 8:1; Succah 40a-40b; Bava Kama 102a
Sabbatical year, money.....Succah 40b-41a; Sheviis 8:7-8; Kiddushin 58a; Avodah Zarah 54b; Bechoros 9b
Sabbatical year, oil on leather.............Sheviis 8:8-9
Sabbatical year, repaying debt from its produce.............Avodah Zarah 62a
Sabbatical year, using its money.............Sheviis 8:8-9
Sabbatical year, wood.............Succah 40a-40b; Bava Kama 101b-102a
Sabbatical year, worker's salary.............Sheviis 8:4-5; Avodah Zarah 62a-62b

Misc. —
Sabbatical year, added time.............Sheviis 1:1-8, 2:1-6; Yevamos 83a; Rosh Hashanah 9b, 10b;
.............Succah 34a, 44a; Taanis 3a; Moed Katan 3b; Bava Basra 26b-27a; Zevachim 110b
Sabbatical year, coming into field.............Nedarim 42b
Sabbatical year, *esrog* tree spoils.............Rosh Hashanah 15a
Sabbatical year, forced because of taxes.............Sanhedrin 26a
Sabbatical year, leasing from non-Jew.............Sheviis 4:3
Sabbatical year, *omer* offering.............Bava Metzia 118a-118b; Shekalim 4:1; Menachos 84a
Sabbatical year, redeeming field.............Bava Metzia 106a
Sabbatical year, suspicion about *Kohanim*.............Sanhedrin 26a
Sabbatical year, years of *orlah*.............Rosh Hashanah 9b
Sabbatical year, years of sale for field.............Bava Metzia 106a; Arachin 29b
Sabbation, Shabbos.............Sanhedrin 65b
Sabei Nizonia
Sabei Nizonia, discourse.............Kiddushin 25a
Sabei Nizonia, Rav Hamnuna.............Kiddushin 25a
Sachar.............*see* **Reward**, page 566; *see also* **Salary**, page 585
Sachnya, episodes.............Gittin 57a
Sackcloth
Sackcloth, from goats hair.............Shabbos 64a
Sackcloth, important man.............Taanis 14b
Sackcloth, impurity.............Keilim 27:1
Sacrifice.............*see also* **Consecrated (Sacrifices)**, page 123; **Redeemed sacrifices**, page 551
***Aggadah* —**
Sacrifices, intending for Heaven's sake.............Menachos 110a; Shevuos 15a
Sacrifices, merit of learning.............Megillah 31b; Taanis 27b; Menachos 110a
Sacrifices of Succos, *aggadah*.............Succah 55b
Sacrifices uphold the world.............Megillah 31b; Taanis 27b
Disqualified —
Sacrifice, blemished, not taken down from Altar.............Zevachim 35b, 84a, 85b
Sacrifice, disqualified, not to eat.............Pesachim 24a; Makos 18a-18b; Meilah 17b
Sacrifice, disqualified, slaughtering on Shabbos.............Pesachim 73a
Sacrifice, night of third day, remainder.............Zevachim 56b; Pesachim 3a
Sacrifice, night of third day, intention.............Zevachim 56b

S

Sacrifice, non-holy animal for sacrifice ....Chullin 41b-42a
Sacrifice of bird, disqualified, impurity...Zevachim 68a-69a, 70b; Meilah 3a
Sacrifice, only from *kosher* food.................Menachos 5a-6a; Pesachim 48a; Chullin 90b; Temurah 29a
Sacrifice, ox goring occasionally who gored ....Bava Kama 13a-13b
Sacrifice, service disqualifies animal...Sotah 46a; Bechoros 14a
Sacrifice, too old after slaughtering ....Zevachim 25b
Sacrifice which went out of courtyard after slaughtering and returned...Zevachim 26a, 92b
Sacrifice with permitted idolatrous item..Avodah Zarah 46a-47a
Sacrifice whose money value will be offered for *korban olah*....Shevuos 12a; Pesachim 73a, 97b;
.............................Yoma 62a; Bava Kama 110a; Menachos 12b; Temurah 18b-23a; Krisos 23a-24a, 26b-27a
Sacrifices having spent night on Altar, not taken down..Zevachim 87a
Sacrifices, intermingled, annul one another...Menachos 22a-22b
Sacrifices, intermingled, becoming *kosher* again.....................................Zevachim 73b-74a
Sacrifices, Rabbinical Decree...Zevachim 79b
Sacrifices which became intermingled.............Zevachim 70b-71b, 74b-75b, 77a-77b; Temurah 28a;
....Menachos 48a

Episodes —
Sacrifice, Ifra Hormiz..Zevachim 116b
Sacrifice, *muktzeh*, Gideon..Temurah 28b-29a
Sacrifice of Adam..Chullin 60a; Shabbos 28b; Avodah Zarah 8a
Sacrifice of Arona, place of Temple...Zevachim 116b
Sacrifice of bird, episode about Rabbi Shimon ben Gamliel...Krisos 8a; Bava Basra 166a-166b
Sacrifice of fattened livestock on idolaters' festival.................................Avodah Zarah 16a
Sacrifices, human, episodes...Sanhedrin 63b
Sacrifices in desert....................Chagigah 6a-6b; Yoma 52b; Zevachim 115b; Yevamos 5b
Sacrifices of Babylonian immigrants...Horayos 6a; Temurah 15b
Sacrifices of Balak, Ruth...Nazir 23b
Sacrifices of Solomon...Zevachim 59a-60a

Festivals —
Sacrifice *chagigah* ....*see* **Chagigah**, page 91
Sacrifice for Pesach..*see* **Pesach lamb**, page 484
Sacrifice of *mussaf*..*see* **Mussaf sacrifice**, page 432
Sacrifices of Shabbos and Yom Kippur..Shabbos 114a
Sacrifices of Shavuos..Menachos 45b
Sacrifices of Succos, division between watches...Succah 55b
Sacrifices of Yom Kippur...Yoma 70a-70b
Sacrifices on *Chol HaMoed*...Temurah 14b
Sacrifices on Shabbos, consecrating...............Shabbos 148b; Pesachim 66b; Beitzah 36b
Sacrifices on Shabbos...*see* **Shabbos**, page 605
Sacrifices on Yom Tov.........Beitzah 19a-19b, 20b-21a; Chagigah 7b, 17a; Menachos 100b; Megillah 5a

Laws —
Sacrifice, absorbed taste...Zevachim 97a-97b
Sacrifice, complete year...Arachin 18b-19a; Niddah 47b-48a
Sacrifice, not fit to be offered to king...Succah 50a
Sacrifice, not from tithe money...................Beitzah 19b-20a; Zevachim 50a, 98a; Menachos 82a-83b;
....Pesachim 71a; Chagigah 7b-8a
Sacrifices, consecrating in sacrifice.................Kiddushin 52b-53a; Bava Kama 12b-13a
Sacrifices, deductions..Zevachim 49b-51a
Sacrifices, exempt from shoulder and priestly gifts.................................Chullin 130a

Sacrifices in present times .... Zevachim 60b, 62a, 107b; Megillah 10a-10b; Shevuos 16a; Makos 19a;
.... Eduyos 8:6; Chagigah 3b; Temurah 21a

Sacrifices of moderate holiness, place .... Zevachim 55a-55b, 63a; Menachos 8b-9a

Sacrifices, taste in mixture .... Chullin 98b-99b

Sacrifices, unfit, transferred to graze .... Pesachim 73a; Nazir 25b; Zevachim 5b, 112a, 115b;
.... Menachos 4a; Temurah 18a

Placed on Altar —

Sacrifice became disqualified after offering, taken down Altar .... Zevachim 27b; Niddah 41a

Sacrifices, before throwing, not brought down from Altar .... Zevachim 83b, 85a-85b; Meilah 7b

Sacrifices, disqualified, placed on Altar .... Zevachim 83a-84a, 85a; Sanhedrin 34a-34b;
.... Meilah 2b-3b, 7b

Sacrifices, not taken down inside Altar .... Zevachim 27b

Sacrifices out of place, placed on Altar .... Menachos 79a

Sacrifices placed on Altar .... Zevachim 27b, 84a-84b; Sanhedrin 34a-34b; Niddah 40a-41a

Requirement —

Sacrifice, collateral .... Kiddushin 13b; Menachos 4b; Kinin 2:5

Sacrifice of city led to idolatry .... Yevamos 9a; Horayos 8a

Sacrifices, numerous transgressions .... Krisos 9a-9b, 15b-16a

Sacrifices of one's wife .... Nazir 24a-24b

Sacrifices, several, according to realization .... Shabbos 71b

Various sacrifices —

Sacrifice, burnt offering .... *see* **Burnt offering**, page 81

Sacrifice, communal .... *see* **Communal sacrifice**, page 118

Sacrifice for impurity of Temple .... Nazir 56b; Shevuos 6b-10b

Sacrifice for leper .... Yoma 62b; Krisos 9b; Negaim 14:7-13; Menachos 5a

Sacrifice for leper, guilt offering .... Yoma 61b; Zevachim 47b; Yevamos 7a

Sacrifice for secular use .... Bava Kama 111a; Krisos 22b, 26b-27a; Kiddushin 12a

Sacrifice for voluntary transgression .... Krisos 9a

Sacrifice for *zav* .... Krisos 8a; Zavim 1:3-6

Sacrifice of wood .... Menachos 20b-21a, 106b; Shekalim 6:6

Sacrifice *oleh veyored* .... *see* **Variable guilt offering**, page 720

Sacrifice outside .... *see* **Slaughtering outside Temple, prohibition**, page 636

Sacrifice, peace offering .... *see* **Peace offerings**, page 477

Sacrifice scheduled for too late .... *see* **Piggul**, page 487

Sacrifice, sin offering .... *see* **Sin offering**, page 627

Sacrifice when anointing *Leviim* .... Horayos 5b

Sacrifices of Tabernacle dedication .... Zevachim 101a-101b; Menachos 51b, 78a

Who —

Sacrifice of convert .... Krisos 8b-9a; Rosh Hashanah 31b

Sacrifice, sanctifying for someone else .... Nedarim 35b-36a; Arachin 21a-21b

Sacrifices for heir .... Nazir 27b-28a; Krisos 27b

Sacrifices for women .... Kiddushin 36a-36b

Misc. —

Sacrifice from Temple Treasury .... Temurah 32a-32b; Bechoros 53b

Sacrifice, how much to slaughter .... Chullin 29a-29b

Sacrifice, Treasury of Temple .... Temurah 6b, 13a; Yoma 63b; Zevachim 113b

Sacrifices, causing them to become invalid .... Zevachim 75b-76a; Pesachim 13b; Beitzah 19b;
.... Bechoros 60b-61a; Niddah 70b

Sacrifices *kitz mizbeach*, which ones .... Shevuos 12a-12b; Menachos 90a-90b; Kesubos 106b

Sacrifices of dead, idolatry..Avodah Zarah 29b
Sacrifices offered in Tabernacle...Menachos 45b
Sacrifices to *Kohanim*, source...Zevachim 44b; Menachos 73a

Sacrifice for idolatry
Sacrifice for idolatry, public..Menachos 52a
Sacrifice for idolatry, slave...Horayos 7b
Sacrifice for idolatry, speech...Sanhedrin 63a

Sacrifice for mistake of *beis din*
Sacrifice for mistake of *beis din*, variable guilt offering.............Horayos 8b; Shevuos 17b
Sacrifice for mistake of *beis din*, cloth partition...Zevachim 41b
Sacrifice for mistake of *beis din*, *Kohanim*..Yoma 50a
Sacrifice for mistake of *beis din*, lobe of liver..Zevachim 41b
Sacrifice for mistake of *beis din*, majority..............................Horayos 3a-3b, 4b-5a
Sacrifice for mistake of *beis din*, one of community died...............................Horayos 6a
Sacrifice for mistake of *beis din*, partial mistake.................Horayos 4a-4b, 7b
Sacrifice for mistake of *beis din*, *semichah*...Sanhedrin 13b
Sacrifice for mistake of *beis din*, Temple Treasury.....................................Menachos 52a
Sacrifice for mistake of *beis din*, tribe...........................Horayos 3a, 4b-5a, 5b
Sacrifice for mistake of *beis din*, when................Horayos 2a, 3b, 4b, 5a, 7b

Sacrifice for *nazir*
Sacrifice for fellow *nazir*, expressions of commitment..................................Nazir 12b
Sacrifice for fellow *nazir*, source...Temurah 10a
Sacrifice for impure *nazir*, exempt..Nazir 19a-19b
Sacrifice for impure *nazir* woman, after annulment...........Nazir 19a, 22a; Nedarim 83a
Sacrifice for *nazir*, "I also"..Nazir 11b, 12b
Sacrifice for *nazir* and leper, doubt.............Nazir 55b-56a, 59b-60b; Niddah 70a-70b
Sacrifice for *nazir*, became impure again......................Nazir 18a-18b; Krisos 9b
Sacrifice for *nazir*, cooked shoulder..Chullin 98a-99a
Sacrifice for *nazir*, doubt..Nazir 59b, 57a
Sacrifice for *nazir*, heir.................................Nazir 27b, 30a-30b; Sotah 23a
Sacrifice for *nazir*, intentionally and forced..Krisos 9a
Sacrifice for *nazir*, Shimon Hatzaddik..Nazir 4b
Sacrifice for *nazir*, vow...Temurah 14b
Sacrifice for *nazir*, without precise aim..Krisos 27a
Sacrifice for pure *nazir* woman, after annulment.................Nedarim 83a; Nazir 19a, 22a

Sacrifice for oath
Sacrifice for oath, abjured or voluntary...Shevuos 34b-35a
Sacrifice for oath, about past.................Shevuos 3a-3b, 21a-21b, 25a-26a; Temurah 3b
Sacrifice for oath, *beis din*...Shevuos 49b; Bava Metzia 36a
Sacrifice for oath, did not benefit.....................................Bava Metzia 36a; Shevuos 49b
Sacrifice for oath, for bad and for good..Shevuos 26a
Sacrifice for oath, for denying sacrifice..Bava Metzia 58a-58b
Sacrifice for oath, Rabbinical...Yoma 73b-74a

Sacrifice for oath by custodian
Sacrifice for oath by custodian, cases..Shevuos 49a-49b
Sacrifice for oath by custodian, to exempt...Bava Metzia 35b-36a
Sacrifice for oath by custodian, warning...Shevuos 36b-37a

Sacrifice for woman after birth
Sacrifice for woman after birth, *aggadah*..................Niddah 31b; Shevuos 8a; Krisos 26a

Sacrifice for woman after birth, caesarian birth..Krisos 7b
Sacrifice for woman after birth, doubt.......................Nazir 29a-29b; Krisos 8a-8b, 22b, 26b;
....Bava Basra 166a;Taharos 4:13
Sacrifice for woman after birth, maidservant...Krisos 7b
Sacrifice for woman after birth, miscarriage..............Nazir 64b; Krisos 7b-8a, 9b; Pesachim 3a;
....Eduyos 4:10
Sacrifice for woman after birth, two women..Krisos 7b

Sacrifices, highest degree of holiness
Sacrifices, highest degree of holiness, at south...Zevachim 36a-36b
Sacrifices, highest degree of holiness, chest and leg..Chullin 45a
Sacrifices, highest degree of holiness, Jerusalem...Zevachim 55a
Sacrifices, highest degree of holiness, north............Zevachim 20a, 48a-48b; Menachos 55b-56a
Sacrifices, highest degree of holiness, place for eating...........Zevachim 63a; Menachos 8b-9a
Sacrifices, highest degree of holiness, slaughtered on Altar......................Zevachim 58a

Sacrifice of rejoicing
Sacrifice of rejoicing, in which case must he offer......................................Pesachim 71a
Sacrifice of rejoicing, which sacrifices..Chagigah 8a-8b
Sacrifice of rejoicing, who must offer..............................Pesachim 70b-71a; Chagigah 2b-3a
Sacrifice of rejoicing, Yom Tov..Chagigah 6b
Sacrifices of rejoicing, *Shemini Atzeres*..Succah 48a

Sacrificial
Sacrificial animal, grazes until becomes blemished..............Pesachim 73a; Nazir 25b; Shevuos 12a; T
....emurah 20b
Sacrificial knife, lifting and cleaning..Zevachim 25a

Saddle of animal, Shabbos..Shabbos 53a

Sadducees

Distortions —
Sadducees, date of Shavuos..Menachos 65a-66a
Sadducees, incense of Yom Kippur..Yoma 19b, 53a
Sadducees, sanctifying new month...Rosh Hashanah 22b
Sadducees, water libation..Succah 48b

Episodes —
Sadducee and Rav Sheishess, king..Berachos 58a
Sadducee, impulsive people......................................Shabbos 88a; Kesubos 112a
Sadducee *Kohen Gadol*, incense...Yoma 19b
Sadducees, "rejoice sterile woman"..Berachos 10a
Sadducees, answers..........................Bava Basra 115b-116a; Yadayim 4:8; Menachos 65b

Misc. —
Sadducees, "do not let them rule"..Parah 3:3
Sadducees acknowledge, bull offered for mistake of *beis din*........................Horayos 4a
Sadducees fear Sages...Yoma 19b
Sadducees, impurity..Niddah 33b-34a
Sadducees, questions on verses................................Berachos 7a; Avodah Zarah 4b
Sadducees, renting domain, *eruv*..Eruvin 68b

Safeguards man in his youth, Torah..Kiddushin 82a

Safety fence
Safety fence, apartment building..Chullin 136a
Safety fence, evil comes about by guilty man.................................Shabbos 32a
Safety fence, four by four cubits...Succah 3a-3b

Safety fence, roofs exempt..Bava Kama 51a
Safety fence, synagogue...Chullin 136a
Sage..*see also* **Wise**, page 753; **Rabbinical**, page 533
  Aggadah —
  Sage better than prophet..Bava Basra 12a-12b
  Sage, in front of ignoramus..Sanhedrin 52b
  Sage saying exactly like another Sage..Bava Basra 12a
  Sage who died, no one like him...Horayos 13a
  Sage who forgot his learning..Berachos 8b
  Sage without fear of G-d...Yoma 72b
  Sages, compared to kings..Gittin 62a
  Sages increase peace.................................Berachos 64a; Yevamos 122b; Nazir 66b; Krisos 28b; Tamid 32b
  Sages, mutually tolerant..Megillah 32a
  Sages, virtues..Taanis 4a; Yoma 71a
  Behavior —
  Sage, avenging and bearing grudge...Yoma 23a
  Sage, behavior...Berachos 43b; Bava Basra 57b-58a; Niddah 16b
  Sage, clean place..Berachos 24b
  Sage, does not beg for money..Shabbos 151b
  Sage, examining his bride...Bava Basra 168a
  Sage, first to house of study...Berachos 43b
  Sage, making known his knowledge..Nedarim 62a
  Sage, protection..Berachos 54b; Bava Basra 7b
  Sage, responsibility of his city...Moed Katan 6a
  Sages, be careful with your words...Avos 1:11
  Episodes —
  Sage, "You confirmed words of Sages"...Negaim 9:3, 11:7
  Sage and scribe, Rabbi Meir...Gittin 67a
  Sage died, another was born..Kiddushin 72b
  Sage, does not recognize woman...Bava Basra 167b-168a
  Sage, son of inferior Sage, episode...Taanis 21b
  Sage when he wants, Rabbi Yehudah...Gittin 67a
  Sages, "our saintly Sages in *Eretz Yisrael*"...Pesachim 113b
  Sages make trouble..Eruvin 26a
  Sages of Athens...Bechoros 8b-9a
  Sages of Babylon, angels...Kiddushin 72a
  Sages of Babylon, hate...Pesachim 113b
  Sages of *Eretz Yisrael* and Babylon.......................Taanis 23b; Megillah 28b; Sanhedrin 24a; Chullin 122a
  Sages preceded you, forger..Bava Basra 167a
  Sages speak inexactly..Tamid 29a
  Sages take people's garments..Shevuos 41a
  Sages, very tall...Bava Metzia 84a; Niddah 24b
  Laws —
  Sage permitted, denying..Kesubos 72a
  Sage ruled, piece of meat..Chullin 44b
  Sage, trustworthiness for himself....................Yevamos 77a, 98a; Bechoros 31a, 38b; Kiddushin 70b
  Sage who annulled vow..Nedarim 77b-78a
  Sage who died, laws...Moed Katan 25a; Shabbos 105b

S

Sage who forbade, his colleague cannot permit ...... Avodah Zarah 7a; Chullin 44b; Berachos 63b; .... Niddah 20b
Sage who permitted, suspicion .... Chullin 44b, 141b

Rabbinical Decrees —
Sages, authority to annul law from Torah .... Yevamos 89b-90b
Sages did not make differences .... Shabbos 29b; Chullin 107b-108a
Sages strengthened Rabbinical Decree .... Bava Metzia 55b; Eruvin 77a, 85b; Rosh Hashanah 19a; .... Kesubos 56a-56b
Sages' words, deduction .... Yadayim 3:2
Sages' words are more cherished .... Avodah Zarah 35a

Rights —
Sage and old man, precedence .... Bava Basra 120a
Sage, exempt from tax .... Nedarim 62a-62b; Bava Basra 7b-8a
Sage, exempt from testifying .... Shevuos 30b
Sage, expenses for city .... Bava Metzia 108a; Bava Basra 8a
Sage, judge inferior to him .... Kiddushin 70a
Sage, precedence right .... Horayos 13a
Sage, precedence to *Kohen* .... Megillah 28a
Sage, rights in *beis din* .... Shevuos 30a-30b
Sage, searching defense in *beis din* .... Shabbos 119a
Sages, expenses for well .... Bava Basra 8a

Misc. —
Sage, blessing for sick person .... Bava Basra 116a; Taanis 8a
Sage, dishonest, keeping away from him .... Taanis 7a
Sage, supporting .... *see* **Supporting Torah**, page 665
Sage, young, standing before him .... Kiddushin 32b
Sages, "what benefit do we have from them," heretic .... Sanhedrin 99b-100a
Sages are not pleased with him .... Sheviis 10:9
Sages did not refer to fool .... Bava Basra 7a
Sages, precision in measures .... Rosh Hashanah 13a
Sages, scorn of heretics .... Sanhedrin 100a

Sage who sinned
Sage who sinned at night, repentance .... Berachos 19a
Sage who sinned, his Torah .... Chagigah 15b
Sage who sinned, honor .... Menachos 99b; Moed Katan 17a
Sage who sinned, possibility to correct .... Chagigah 15a

Said
Said during sleep, teaching ...... Yevamos 24b, 91a, 109b; Bava Kama 47b, 65a; Bechoros 23b; Niddah 60a
Said, woman, *kiddushin* .... Kiddushin 5b, 4b
Say little and do much .... Avos 1:15
Say little and do much, righteous .... Bava Metzia 87a; Nedarim 21b
Say to wisdom, your are my sister .... Shabbos 145b; Sanhedrin 7b
Saying "permitted," considered as not liable .... Makos 7b, 9a
Saying "permitted," non-Jew .... Makos 9a
Saying in name of Sage who said it .... Megillah 15a; Chullin 104b; Avos 6:6; Niddah 19b

Sailors
Sailors, decisions .... Bava Kama 116b
Sailors, farmers in the future .... Yevamos 63a
Sailors, looking forward to come to land .... Tamid 32a

S

Sailors, who is considered a sailor..Nedarim 30a-30b

Salamander
Salamander blood, Hezekiah..Sanhedrin 63b
Salamander, greatness of G-d's works..Chullin 127a

Salary
Prohibitions —
Salary, building for idolatrous purpose..Avodah Zarah 19b
Salary for idolatry, destroying..Avodah Zarah 62b
Salary for work on Shabbos, addition to *kesubah*...Kesubos 64a-64b
Salary for work on Shabbos, included...Nedarim 37a-37b; Bava Metzia 58a
Salary of schoolteacher, prohibition...Nedarim 36b-37b; Bechoros 29a
Salary of worker in wine of idolaters...Avodah Zarah 62a-62b, 65a-65b
Salary of worker, Sabbatical year..Avodah Zarah 62a-62b; Sheviis 8:4-5
Salary, sanctifying and sprinkling water..Kiddushin 58b; Bechoros 29a
Salary, thing forbidden to have benefit thereof.......................................Avodah Zarah 63b-64a
Misc. —
Salary for returning lost item...Bava Kama 116a-116b; Bava Metzia 31b
Salary for work, not forgotten...Bava Basra 45b; Shevuos 45b-46a
Salary, like city inhabitants...Bava Metzia 87a
Salary of craftsmen, Temple Treasury..Temurah 31b
Salary of expert, firstborn..Bechoros 28b-29a
Salary of scribe, divorce certificate..Gittin 20a; Bava Basra 168a
Salary of scribe, who must pay..Bava Basra 168a
Salary of worker, from beginning to end.......................Kiddushin 48a-48b, 63a; Bava Kama 99a-99b;
....Bava Metzia 65a, 73a, 110b; Avodah Zarah 19b; Arachin 18a
Salary of worker...*see also* **Worker**, page 761
Salary, paid at end of work...Bava Metzia 65a
Salary for unemployment
Salary for unemployment, business investment...Bava Metzia 68a-68b
Salary for unemployment, judge..Kesubos 105a; Bechoros 29b
Salary for unemployment, lost item...Bava Metzia 31b

Sale..*see also* **Sell**, page 600
Cancelled sale —
Sale on credit, buyer refuses to pay..Bava Metzia 77b
Sale for one day...Bava Metzia 14a
Sale of burial place, family flaw......................................Bava Basra 100b; Kesubos 84a; Bechoros 52b
Sale, reason cancelled...Kesubos 97a
Sale, sick man..Bava Basra 149a
Sale which became cancelled, money in custody..Bava Metzia 49a
Sale with intention to return..Bava Metzia 65b, 67a
Consecrated items Treasury —
Sale of animal tithe.....................................Bechoros 31b, 32a-32b; Bava Kama 13a; Temurah 5b, 8b
Sale of firstborn....Zevachim 75b; Temurah 5b, 7b-9a; Bechoros 31b-32a; Maaser Sheni 1:2; Bava Kama 12b-13a
Sale of redeemed sacrifices....Bechoros 31a-31b, 33b; Beitzah 28a; Chullin 133b; Temurah 8a, 21a, 24a
Sale of sacrifice...Pesachim 89b-90a
Sale to consecrated items Treasury...Shekalim 4:9; Menachos 90a-90b
Prohibitions —
Sale by forbidden act..Bava Kama 70b
Sale, concern for idolatry...Avodah Zarah 12b-14b, 32b-33a

S

Sale, *mi shepara* for one who reneges .... Bava Metzia 63b, 74b
Sale of *chametz*, custodian .... Pesachim 13a
Sale of *chametz* to non-Jew .... Pesachim 13a, 21a-21b; Shabbos 18b
Sales forbidden to non-Jew .... Avodah Zarah 15b; Nedarim 62b

Various items —
Sale by partner .... Gittin 31b
Sale of deposit which decays .... Bava Metzia 38a-38b; Pesachim 13a-13b
Sale of ox which gored .... Bava Kama 33a-33b, 34a, 36a
Sale of promissory note .... Bava Basra 76a, 173a
Sale, priestly gifts .... Chullin 131a, 132a, 138a-138b; Bava Kama 115a

Woman —
Sale by brother of decedent's childless husband .... Kesubos 80b
Sale by married woman .... Kesubos 50a, 78a-78b; Bava Kama 59b, 88a-88b
Sale by widow .... Kesubos 96a-97a, 98a-98b, 100a; Bava Metzia 32a
Sale of dowry by husband .... Kesubos 79b; Yevamos 66b-67a
Sale of *kesubah*, she sold .... Bava Kama 89a
Sale, she accepted to sell to second customer .... Bava Kama 59b
Sale to one's wife .... Bava Basra 51a-51b
Sale, to please my husband .... Kesubos 95a; Bava Basra 49b-50a; Gittin 55b
Sale, wife's property .... Kesubos 79b; Yevamos 66b

Misc. —
Sale at cost price .... Bava Metzia 51b
Sale contradicting loan .... Kesubos 110a
Sale of all rights, including .... Bava Kama 8b; Arachin 31b
Sale of father for mother's *kesubah* .... Yevamos 99a
Sale of field, danger of death .... Gittin 55b, 58a-58b; Bava Basra 47b, 48a
Sale of first acquisition, unfavorable sign .... Kiddushin 59a
Sale of item, easy .... Nedarim 31a-31b
Sale of land, precision of dimensions .... Bava Basra 104b-105a
Sale of Joseph .... Sotah 11a
Sale without knowing quantity, act of acquisition .... Bava Metzia 46b
Sale without knowing quantity, *demai* .... Demai 2:5

Salt
Health —
Salt, coarse, health .... Kiddushin 62a
Salt, cure .... Berachos 40a
Salt during meal, health .... Berachos 44a
Salt, health .... Shabbos 65a; Bava Kama 92b
Salt, how to eat .... Horayos 13b
Salt of Sodom .... Chullin 105b
Salt, too much is harmful .... Berachos 34a

Temple —
Salt for Altar, benefit .... Menachos 21b-22a; Shekalim 7:7
Salt for ramp of Altar .... Eruvin 104a
Salt in Temple, where .... Menachos 21b

Misc. —
Salt, cooking on Shabbos .... Shabbos 42a
Salt for *Hamotzie* slice .... Berachos 40a
Salt for money, giving some away to charity .... Kesubos 66b

S

Salt in lamp..Shabbos 67b
Salt of non-Jews...Avodah Zarah 39b
Salt, requirement to separate tithes...........Maasros 4:3; Bava Metzia 89b; Beitzah 35a

Salted
Salted and bland, absorption...................................Chullin 112b-113a
Salted, like boiling.................Chullin 97b, 111b, 112a-113a; Pesachim 76a
Salted water, Shabbos..........................Shabbos 108a-108b; Eruvin 14b

Salting
Salting meat..Menachos 21a; Chullin 113a
Salting on Shabbos...Shabbos 108a-108b
Salting skin on Shabbos...Shabbos 75b

Salting sacrifice
Salting sacrifice, how...Menachos 21a
Salting sacrifice, indispensable requirement.................Menachos 19b-20a
Salting sacrifice, which parts..................................Menachos 20a-21a

Sam orchosav baolam hazeh........*see* **Self-inspection, reward**, page 599
Sambatyon, Shabbos...Sanhedrin 65b

Same
Same day, paying salary of worker........................Bava Metzia 110b-112a
Same woman, repentance...Yoma 86b

Samson
Samson, his mother's name.......................................Bava Basra 91a
Samson, *nazir*..Nazir 4b
Samson, story..Sotah 9b-10a
Samson was struck in his strength......................................Sotah 10a

Samuch al shulchano...............*see* **Supported at his table**, page 664
Samuch levesta.......................*see* **Close to menstruation**, page 111

Samuel
Samuel and Korah, lineage...Megillah 14a
Samuel, comparable to Moses and Aaron...............................Taanis 5b
Samuel, dread of judgment..Chagigah 4b
Samuel, feared Saul...Nazir 66a
Samuel, gave ruling in front of his teacher.........................Berachos 31, b
Samuel, his sons..Shabbos 55b-56a
Samuel, integrity..Makos 23b
Samuel, premature old age..Taanis 5b
Samuel, princes of mankind...Succah 52b
Samuel, site of Temple..Zevachim 54b
Samuel the prophet, *nazir*...Nazir 66a
Samuel, Torah and greatness...Gittin 59a
Samuel, traveled from town to town..................................Shabbos 56a
Samuel, wealth...Nedarim 38a
Samuel, year of reign..............................Temurah 14b; Zevachim 118b

Sennacherib
Sennacherib, Ammonites permitted..................Berachos 28a; Yadayim 4:4
Sennacherib, death of his army...........Shabbos 113b; Sanhedrin 94a-94b, 95b-96a
Sennacherib, names and episode.................................Sanhedrin 94a-96a
Sennacherib, pride..Chullin 89a
Sennacherib, Ravshakeh's blasphemy.............................Sanhedrin 60a

Sennacherib, Shemayah and Avtalyon .... Gittin 57b
Sennacherib, ten tribes .... Sanhedrin 94a

Sanctification
Sanctification, first, of *Eretz Yisrael* .... Megillah 10a-10b; Shevuos 16a; Zevachim 60b, 107b
Sanctification of G-d's name .... *see* **Self-sacrifice**, page 599
Sanctification, second, Ezra .... Arachin 32b; Megillah 10a-10b; Shevuos 16a

Sanctified
Sanctified, order of precedence .... Zevachim 89a-89b, 90b-91a; Horayos 12b
Sanctify yourself in permitted things .... Yevamos 20a
Sanctifying *Kohanim*, source .... Gittin 59b; Moed Katan 28b; Nedarim 62a; Horayos 12b
Sanctifying oneself, being sanctified .... Yoma 39a

Sanctifying hands
Sanctifying hands, death .... Sanhedrin 83b
Sanctifying hands for burning Red Heifer .... Zevachim 20b
Sanctifying hands of *Kohanim*, how .... Zevachim 19b, 21a; Yoma 37a
Sanctifying hands, when .... Zevachim 19b-21a; Yoma 22a, 28a; Pesachim 2b
Sanctifying hands, Yom Kippur .... Yoma 19a, 30a, 31a-32b, 71a; Zevachim 19b

Sanctifying month
Sanctifying month .... *see also* **Testimony for new moon**, page 684
Sanctifying month, "Sanctified" .... Rosh Hashanah 24a
Sanctifying month, agents .... Rosh Hashanah 19b, 21b
Sanctifying month, at daytime .... Rosh Hashanah 25b; Sanhedrin 11b
Sanctifying month, Baithusim .... Rosh Hashanah 22b
Sanctifying month, episode .... Rosh Hashanah 25a
Sanctifying month, fires .... Rosh Hashanah 22b-23a; Beitzah 4b
Sanctifying month, meal .... Sanhedrin 70b
Sanctifying month, Moses .... Menachos 29a
Sanctifying month, sight .... Arachin 9b
Sanctifying month, when .... Sanhedrin 10b; Rosh Hashanah 24a
Sanctifying month, willful .... Rosh Hashanah 25a

Sand
Sand becomes flour, episode .... Taanis 24b
Sand, deeds of righteous .... Bava Basra 7b
Sand of sea, Israel .... Yoma 22b

Sandal
Sandal .... *see also* **Shoe**, page 619
Sandal, *chalitzah* .... Yevamos 102a
Sandal, nailed, *muktzeh* .... Shabbos 60b
Sandal, nailed, Shabbos .... Shabbos 60a-60b; Beitzah 14b, 15a
Sandals in summer .... Bava Basra 58a

Sanegor ein naaseh kategor .... *see* **Defender, accuser**, page 157

Sanhedrin
Sanhedrin, avoiding death penalty .... Makos 7a
Sanhedrin, exiles .... Shabbos 15a; Rosh Hashanah 31a-31b; Avodah Zarah 8b
Sanhedrin, for which town .... Sanhedrin 17b-18a
Sanhedrin in exile, death penalty .... Sanhedrin 41a; Shabbos 15a; Avodah Zarah 8b
Sanhedrin, king .... Sanhedrin 18b
Sanhedrin, *Lishkas HaGazis* .... Yoma 25a; Sanhedrin 88b
Sanhedrin, Mordechai .... Megillah 16b

Sanhedrin, number of judges .... Sanhedrin 16b-17a
Sanhedrin, order of sitting .... Sanhedrin 36b-37a
Sanhedrin outside Israel .... Makos 7a; Sanhedrin 14a
Sanhedrin, ox to be stoned .... Sanhedrin 15a
Sanhedrin, praise in *Shir Hashirim* .... Sanhedrin 36b-37a
Sanhedrin, *semichah* for judges .... Sanhedrin 37a
Sanhedrin, *sotah* .... Sotah 7a-7b
Sanhedrin, war .... Sanhedrin 16a-16b
Sanhedrin, what do they judge .... Sanhedrin 15b-16a
Sanhedrin, who are the judges .... Sanhedrin 17a-17b; Menachos 65a
Santer, significance .... Bava Basra 68a-68b
Sar chamishim, significance .... Chagigah 14a
Sarah
Sarah, "here, in the tent" .... Yevamos 77a
Sarah, "I am old" .... Yevamos 65b
Sarah, "She is my sister" .... Sanhedrin 58b
Sarah, age of her father at her birth .... Sanhedrin 69b
Sarah, beauty .... Megillah 15a; Bava Basra 58a
Sarah, episode with Abimelech .... Bava Kama 92a; Makos 9a-9b
Sarah, prophecy .... Megillah 14a-14b
Sarah, Sarai .... Berachos 13a
Sarah, spirit's defense .... Sanhedrin 44b
Sarah, sterile .... Yevamos 64a
Sarah, when did she conceive .... Rosh Hashanah 11a
Sarah, Yiskah .... Megillah 14a
Sarai, *yud* letter cried .... Sanhedrin 107a
Saris .... *see* **Sterile man**, page 656
Sarsur .... *see* **Broker**, page 77
Sason and Simchah, episode .... Succah 48b
Sasum min hameforash .... *see* **Undefined from explicit**, page 714
Satan
Episodes —
Satan always wins .... Tamid 32a
Satan, Giving of Torah .... Shabbos 88b-89a
Satan, Job .... Bava Basra 16a
Satan, Pelimo, episode .... Kiddushin 81a-81b
Satan, sin of golden calf .... Shabbos 89a
Misc. —
Satan, does not harm two nations together .... Shabbos 32a
Satan, evil urge .... Bava Basra 16a
Satan, numerical value of Yom Kippur .... Yoma 20a
Satan, to confuse .... Rosh Hashanah 16a-16b
Satiety, G-d proclaims .... Berachos 55a
Satisfied with little
Satisfied with little .... Avos 6:4
Satisfied with little, episodes .... Nedarim 49b-50a; Berachos 17b; Sanhedrin 20a; Taanis 24b; Chullin 86a
Sauce
Sauce of fish, impurity .... Bechoros 22a, 23b; Machshirin 6:3
Sauce of fish, scales .... Avodah Zarah 39b-40a

Sauce of forbidden fish..Chullin 99b; Terumos 10:8

Saul

Saul anointed with oil flask...Horayos 12a; Krisos 6a
Saul, asked for forgiveness...Yoma 22b
Saul, asking for a king...Sanhedrin 20b
Saul, improper request...Taanis 4a
Saul, inheritance of his kingdom...Zevachim 102a
Saul, mistakes..Yoma 22b
Saul, modesty..Berachos 62b; Megillah 13b
Saul, next to Samuel in World to Come..................Berachos 12b; Eruvin 53b
Saul, princes of mankind..Succah 52b
Saul, righteousness...Yoma 22b; Moed Katan 16b
Saul, women's answer..Berachos 48b
Saul, years of reign....................................Temurah 14b; Zevachim 118b

Save

Fellow's money —

Saving, asked for overpayment...Bava Kama 116a
Saving fellow's money, for oneself.................Bava Kama 115a-115b, 116b
Saving fellow's money, losing one's own.............Bava Kama 81b, 114b
Saving fellow's money, source..Bava Metzia 31a
Saving oneself through fellow's belongings.......Bava Kama 60b, 117b
Saving partnership money..Bava Kama 116b

Shabbos —

Saving, died on Shabbos..................................Shabbos 43b-44a; Yoma 85a
Saving from fire, Shabbos..................Shabbos 117b, 120a-120b; Eruvin 95b
Saving holy books..Shabbos 115a-117b
Saving, rare, *muktzeh*...Shabbos 42b-43a
Saving, removing bread from oven............................Shabbos 117b

Misc. —

Save us from impudent men..................................Berachos 16b; Shabbos 30b
Saved from forbidden relations, miracle...................................Kiddushin 40a
Saving community by handing over individual...........................Terumos 8:12
Saving fellow from danger.........Sanhedrin 73a; Bava Kama 81b; Bava Metzia 62a
Saving oneself from non-Jew, non-Jewish court...........................Gittin 44a

Saving a life

Saving a life, adding to permitted quantity.................Menachos 64a-64b
Saving a life, doubt...............Shabbos 129a; Yoma 83a, 84b-85a; Kesubos 15a; Bava Kama 44b, 90a; Bava Basra 50b; Sanhedrin 79a
Saving a life, healing eye on Shabbos.............................Avodah Zarah 28b
Saving a life, healing on Shabbos.....................................Yoma 84a-84b
Saving a life, injury to internal parts.............Avodah Zarah 28a; Shabbos 109a
Saving a life, Jew..Sanhedrin 37a
Saving a life, life for a few hours...Yoma 85a
Saving a life, majority..Yoma 84b-85a
Saving a life, permission......................Shabbos 132a, 151b; Yoma 85a-85b
Saving a life, person in danger...Yoma 82a
Saving a life, prohibitions..................................Yoma 82a; Shabbos 129a
Saving a life, sick..................................Shabbos 29b-30b; Yoma 84b
Saving a life, wanted to catch fish..........................Menachos 64a

Saw .... *see also* **Consider**, page 125; **Looking at**, page 377
Saw act and remembered law, Pinchas .... Sanhedrin 82a
Saw episode and remembered law, Hillel .... Pesachim 66a
See what you raised! .... Kesubos 45a
See your children's children, peace upon Israel .... Kesubos 50a
Seeing from afar, size of item is reduced .... Succah 22b
Seeing from end of world, fetus .... Niddah 30b
Seeing his intended bride, Sage .... Bava Basra 168a
Seeing inside barrel, pillar of cloud .... Shabbos 22b
Seeing king's face, leap year .... Sanhedrin 10b
Seeing teacher's face, learning .... Horayos 12a; Krisos 6a
Seeing the future .... Avos 2:9
Seeing without eating, danger .... Kesubos 61a-61b
Seeing woman before marrying her .... Kiddushin 41a
Seeing leprous marks
Seeing leprous marks, *Kohen* .... Negaim 2:3, 3:1; Niddah 50a; Moed Katan 8a
Seeing leprous marks, one's own .... Negaim 2:5
Seeing leprous marks, standing .... Negaim 2:4
Seeing leprous marks, time .... Moed Katan 7a-8a; Negaim 1:4, 2:2, 3:2
Scalding
Scalding, *kashering* wine press .... Avodah Zarah 75a; Niddah 65b
Scalding, leavening .... Pesachim 39b
Scales of fish .... Avodah Zarah 39a; Chullin 66a-66b; Niddah 51b
Scales
Scales .... *see also* **Weighing**, page 740
Scales, impurity by moving .... Zavim 4, 4-7; Shabbos 83a-83b
Scales, *zav* moving item .... Zavim 4:4-7
Scalps, impurity .... Chullin 123a
Scarecrow .... Shabbos 90a; Menachos 107a; Middos 37a
Scattering
Scattering to wind, *chametz* .... Pesachim 28a
Scattering to wind, idol .... Avodah Zarah 43b-44a
Scholar
Scholar .... *see also* **Sage**, page 583
Scholar, accepting him .... Demai 2:2-3; Bechoros 30b; Avodah Zarah 39a
Scholar, repented .... Bechoros 31a
Scholar, small one sharpens great one .... Taanis 7a
Scholar surely tithed .... Pesachim 4b, 9a; Niddah 15b; Avodah Zarah 41b; Eruvin 32a
Scholar, trustworthiness .... Avodah Zarah 39a
School, children .... Kesubos 50a
Schoolteacher
Aggadah —
Schoolteacher, his righteousness endures forever .... Kesubos 50a
Schoolteacher, punishment .... Bava Basra 21b
Schoolteacher, reward and punishment .... Sanhedrin 91b-92a, 99a, 99b; Temurah 16a
Schoolteacher, reward from G-d .... Bava Basra 8b
Episodes —
Schoolteacher, Ben Shilas .... Bava Basra 8b
Schoolteacher, merit for rain .... Taanis 24a

S

Schoolteacher, Rabbi Chiya..Bava Metzia 85b
Schoolteacher who hit too much...Gittin 36a; Makos 16b
Misc. —
Schoolteacher, blows..Makos 22b
Schoolteacher, complaint about noise...Bava Basra 20b-21a
Schoolteacher, dismissing.....................Gittin 36a; Bava Basra 21a-21b; Makos 16b
Schoolteacher, how...Kesubos 50a
Schoolteacher, salary.....................................Nedarim 36b-37b; Bechoros 29a
Schoolteacher, school..Bava Basra 21a
Schoolteacher, who...Bava Basra 21a-21b

Sciatic nerve
Sciatic nerve, benefit..Pesachim 22a, 23b
Sciatic nerve, extracting...Chullin 92b, 96a-96b
Sciatic nerve, from when is it forbidden...Chullin 101b
Sciatic nerve in bird and animal..Chullin 92b
Sciatic nerve in impure animal...Chullin 100b; Pesachim 22a
Sciatic nerve in sacrifice...Chullin 90a-90b
Sciatic nerve, on the left.....................................Chullin 90b-91a; Pesachim 83b
Sciatic nerve, ramifications...Chullin 92b
Sciatic nerve, spot..Chullin 91a, 93b; Pesachim 83b
Sciatic nerve, taste...Chullin 99b, 100b-101a
Sciatic nerve, *treifah*...Chullin 54a

Scoffer
Scoffer, Bar Kapara's disciple..Berachos 39a
Scoffer, burning excrement...Eruvin 21b
Scoffer, death...Bava Basra 75a; Sanhedrin 100a
Scoffer, Sadducee..Berachos 58a
Scoffers, groups...Sanhedrin 103a; Sotah 42a

Scoffing
Scoffing..*see also* **Laughter**, page 354
Scoffing about idolatry...Sanhedrin 63b
Scoffing, abundance in the future...Shabbos 30b
Scoffing at pauper................................Berachos 3b, 18a; Sotah 43b; Menachos 41a
Scoffing at Sages' words...Bava Basra 75a
Scoffing, resentment...Berachos 39a

Scorn
Scorn of non-Jews for Israel, cherubs..Yoma 54b
Scorn towards Sages, heretic...Sanhedrin 100a
Scorpio, south...Pesachim 94a; Eruvin 56a
Scorpion
Scorpion and frog, episode..Nedarim 41a
Scorpion, comes by distraction..Sanhedrin 97a
Scorpion, cure for baby bitten..Kesubos 50a
Scorpion in Deenor river..Berachos 58b
Scorpion of Adiebe, danger..Shabbos 121b
Scraping
Scraping, cases...Shabbos 75b
Scraping, dressing...Eruvin 102b

Scratching

Scratching during prayer..Nazir 59a
Scratching for dead, women..Kiddushin 35b
Scratching oneself on Shabbos..Shabbos 147b
Scratching sacrifice to slaughter it..Sotah 48a
Scratching skin for dead, mourning...Makos 20b-21a

Scribe

Scribe, divorce certificate..Gittin 22b-23a
Scribe, sign of blessing...Pesachim 50b
Scribes, letters..Kiddushin 30a
Scribes of judges, knowledge.....................................Bava Basra 136a; Sanhedrin 29b
Scribes of Solomon, death..Succah 53a

Script, *ashuris*, **origin**..Sanhedrin 21b-22a; Zevachim 62a

Scroll

Scroll..*see also* **Book**, page 72
Scroll by scroll, Torah given..Gittin 60a-60b
Scroll flying, Zechariah..Eruvin 21a
Scroll, impurity of hands..............................Yadayim 3:4-5; Shabbos 14a-14b, 116a
Scroll, incomplete, Torah reading..Gittin 60a
Scroll of Esther..*see* **Megillas Esther**, page 402
Scroll, writing parts of Torah..Gittin 60a; Yoma 37b-38a
Scrolls, impurity...Keilim 15:6

Scroll of *sotah*

Scroll of *sotah*, personal..Eruvin 13a-13b; Sotah 20b
Scroll of *sotah*, Queen Helen..Yoma 37b
Scroll of *sotah*, writing...Sotah 17a-18a; Berachos 15b

Se'ah bese'ah...*see* **Seah for seah, interest**, page 593

Se'es, leprous marks..........................Negaim 1:1-4; Shevuos 2a, 5b-6b; Shabbos 2b; Zevachim 88b

Se'ir laAzazel...*see* **Goat to Azazel**, page 253

Se'orah...*see* **Barley, quantity**, page 42

Sea

Sea bay flowing into courtyard...Eruvin 12a
Sea, concern that it cancels partition..Eruvin 8a, 99b
Sea creatures similar to land creatures...Chullin 127a
Sea, danger...Pesachim 50b
Sea, Dead Sea, drowning..Shabbos 108b
Sea, boundaries of *Eretz Yisrael*..Gittin 8a
Sea, immersion...Mikvaos 5:4; Shabbos 109a; Parah 8:8
Sea, Mediterranean, blessing...Berachos 59a
Sea, number of drops...Horayos 10a
Sea of Solomon, dimensions.............................Eruvin 14a-14b; Pesachim 109b
Sea of Solomon, Temple..Eruvin 14a-14b
Sea waves, wonders..Bava Basra 73a
Seas of *Eretz Yisrael*..Bava Basra 74b

Seah

Seah for *seah*, interest.................................Shabbos 148b; Bava Metzia 44b, 45a, 74b-75a
Seah, measure...Eruvin 82b

Seal

Seal, G-d's seal is truth...Sanhedrin 64a

S

Seal, hole in barrel..Avodah Zarah 69b
Seal, keeping food *kosher*...Avodah Zarah 31a-31b; Shabbos 122a
Seal, keeping wine...Shabbos 122a; Avodah Zarah 31a
Seal of slave, carrying on Shabbos...Shabbos 58a
Seal, opening on Shabbos...Beitzah 31b-32a
Seal, Exilarch..Shabbos 58a
Seal, vinegar of non-Jew..Avodah Zarah 29b-30a

Search
Searched and did not find, impurities...Niddah 61a; Pesachim 10a
Searching and finding corresponding Beraisa, episode...Gittin 27a
Searching for unclean object...Bechoros 25b; Niddah 61a
Searching for survivors under rubble, Pesach lamb...Pesachim 91a
Searching with sheets...Niddah 61a

Searching for *chametz*
Searching for *chametz*, blessing...Pesachim 7a-7b
Searching for *chametz*, lamp..Pesachim 7b-8a
Searching for *chametz*, maybe one will eat....................................Pesachim 10b-11a; Menachos 67b-68a
Searching for *chametz*, places..Pesachim 8a-8b
Searching for *chametz*, possible times...............................Pesachim 2b, 10b; Menachos 67b
Searching for *chametz*, Rabbinical..Pesachim 4b
Searching for *chametz*, tenant...Pesachim 4a-4b
Searching for *chametz*, time...Pesachim 4a
Searching for *chametz*, trustworthiness...Pesachim 4a-4b

Season
Season of tithes...Maasros 1:1-4
Seasons, adding a month...Rosh Hashanah 21a; Sanhedrin 12b-13b
Seasons and *gematrios*, companion to wisdom...Avos 3:18
Seasons of the year..Bava Metzia 106b

Sechach...*see* **S'chach**, page 576
Sechiro ulekito.......................*see* **Worker for non-Jew, hiring his domain for Shabbos**, page 762
Sechirus..*see* **Renting**, page 558
Sechitah..*see* **Squeezing**, page 653
***Sechvi*, explanation**...Rosh Hashanah 26a

Seclusion
Women —
Seclusion before wedding..Kesubos 9b, 12a
Seclusion, general...............................Kiddushin 80b-81b; Sanhedrin 21a-21b; Avodah Zarah 36b; Sotah 7a
Seclusion, is wife forbidden...Kesubos 13a-13b; Kiddushin 81a
Seclusion with former wife, *kiddushin*...Gittin 73b, 81a-81b; Eduyos 4:7
Seclusion, with *niddah* bride...Kesubos 4a
Seclusion with non-Jewish woman...Avodah Zarah 36b
Seclusion with *sotah* wife..Sotah 7a, 25a; Kiddushin 80b-81a

Misc. —
Seclusion, male..Kiddushin 82a
Seclusion of *Kohen* for Red Heifer, Room of Stone...Yoma 2a
Seclusion with animal..Kiddushin 81b, 82a
Seclusion with non-Jew...Avodah Zarah 25a-25b
Seclusion of *Kohen* for Red Heifer.......................................Parah 3:1-5; Yoma 3b, 8a-8b

S

Second

Second act, levirate marriage ....Yevamos 50a-52a, 53a-53b, 96a-96b
Second agent for divorce ....Gittin 66a-67a, 71b-72a
Second blow, episode about Chanan Bisha ....Bava Kama 37a
Second creditor is preferable to me ....Bava Basra 30b, 43b; Kesubos 109a
Second sanctification, Ezra ....Arachin 32b; Megillah 10a-10b; Shevuos 16a
Second table, impurity ....Berachos 52b
Second Tanna comes to add ....Bava Basra 93b
Second Yom Tov .... *see* **Yom Tov** *Sheni*, page 772

Second Temple

Second Temple, beauty ....Succah 51b
Second Temple, building ....Rosh Hashanah 3a-4a; Megillah 10a, 12a
Second Temple, destruction ....Gittin 55b-56b
Second Temple, differences ....Yoma 9b-10a, 21b; Bava Basra 3a
Second Temple, events ....Avodah Zarah 8b-9a; Shabbos 15a
Second Temple, Herod ....Succah 51b; Bava Basra 3b, 4a
Second Temple, population ....Bava Metzia 28a

Second tithe

Eating —

Second tithe, anointment ....Yevamos 74a
Second tithe, bitter herbs ....Pesachim 39b
Second tithe, *chagigah* ....Chagigah 7b-8b
Second tithe, forbidden to buy ....Maaser Sheni 1:5-7; Kiddushin 55b-56b
Second tithe, *matzah* and *esrog* ....Pesachim 36b, 37b-38a; Succah 35a
Second tithe, Nov ....Zevachim 119a
Second tithe, oil ....Maaser Sheni 2:1-4
Second tithe, redeeming through food to be eaten ....Maaser Sheni 2:10, 4:8
Second tithe, sacrifices ....Beitzah 19b-20a; Zevachim 50a, 98a; Menachos 82a-83b; Chagigah 7b-8a
Second tithe, spice ....Niddah 51b
Second tithe, together with food ....Maaser Sheni 1:3-4, 3:12-13; Eruvin 27a-28a
Second tithe, uses ....Maaser Sheni 1:1, 3:1; Avodah Zarah 62a-62b; Shabbos 22a-22b

Jerusalem —

Second tithe, became impure in Jerusalem ....Maaser Sheni 3:9-11; Makos 19b; Pesachim 38a;
....Bava Metzia 53a-53b; Sanhedrin 112b-113a; Zevachim 49a
Second tithe, close to Jerusalem ....Makos 19b; Temurah 21b
Second tithe, coming in Jerusalem ..Maaser Sheni 3:5-6; Bava Metzia 53a-53b; Makos 20a; Beitzah 5a
Second tithe, house at Jerusalem boundary ....Maaser Sheni 3:7
Second tithe in present times, Jerusalem ....Zevachim 60b; Makos 19a; Temurah 21a
Second tithe, selling in Jerusalem ....Pesachim 75b
Second tithe taken out of Jerusalem ....Chullin 68b
Second tithe, tree branches in Jerusalem ....Makos 12a-12b; Maasros 3:10; Maaser Sheni 3:7

Redeeming —

Second tithe, coin ....Bava Kama 97b; Bava Metzia 52b, 47b; Succah 41a
Second tithe, exemption from fifth ....Maaser Sheni 4:4-5; Gittin 65a
Second tithe, gold ....Bava Metzia 44b-45b; Maaser Sheni 2:7
Second tithe, married woman's fifth ....Kiddushin 24a
Second tithe, *perutah chamurah* ....Bava Metzia 52b-53a
Second tithe, redemption by owner ....Maaser Sheni 4:3; Arachin 27b
Second tithe, redeeming coins through coins ....Bava Metzia 55b-56a; Demai 1:2; Maaser Sheni 2:6

S

Second tithe, value corresponding to money .... Bechoros 51a

Value —
Second tithe, appraisers .... Sanhedrin 14b; Maaser Sheni 4:2
Second tithe, change of value .... Maaser Sheni 4:6; Kiddushin 54b
Second tithe, estimate .... Maaser Sheni 4:1-2; Sanhedrin 14b
Second tithe, less than *perutah* .... Bava Metzia 52b-53b, 55a; Arachin 27a

Misc. —
Second tithe, animal .... Kiddushin 55b-56a; Succah 40b-41a
Second tithe, *challah* .... Pesachim 37b-38a; Succah 35a-35b; Sanhedrin 112b
Second tithe, Divine property ..... Sanhedrin 112b; Pesachim 38a; Succah 35b; Kiddushin 24a, 53a-53b, 54b
Second tithe eaten outside Jerusalem, lashes .... Makos 19b-20a; Krisos 4b-5a
Second tithe, giving .... Maaser Sheni 1:1, 3:1
Second tithe, ignoramus .... Tevul Yom 4:5
Second tithe, immersed that day .... Yevamos 74b, 75a
Second tithe, impurity .... Makos 19b; Yevamos 73b; Zevachim 43b
Second tithe, intermingled coins .... Maaser Sheni 2:5-6; Beitzah 10b; Bava Metzia 55b-56a
Second tithe, keeping purity .... Maaser Sheni 2:3-4
Second tithe, less severe than *terumah* .... Yevamos 73a-74a; Chagigah 18b; Bava Metzia 52b-53a;
.... Bikurim 2:2
Second tithe, lost coins .... Bava Kama 98a
Second tithe, mixture .... Maaser Sheni 2:1; Bava Metzia 53a
Second tithe, money .... Maaser Sheni 2:7-9; Eduyos 1:9-10; Bava Metzia 44b-45b
Second tithe, second level of impurity .... Chullin 33b; Chagigah 18b, 19b; Sotah 30a; Parah 11:5
Second tithe, selling .... Maaser Sheni 1:1, 3:1
Second tithe, *terumah* .... Maaser Sheni 3:2; Zevachim 76a
Second tithe, uncircumcised .... Yevamos 73a-74a
Secondary degree relatives, testimony .... Sanhedrin 28a
Secondary category
Secondary category of damages
Secondary category of damages by man .... Bava Kama 3b
Secondary category of damages, fire, one's stone .... Bava Kama 3b
Secondary category of damages, horn .... Bava Kama 2b
Secondary category of damages, leg .... Bava Kama 2b-3a
Secondary category of damages equivalent to primary .... Bava Kama 2a-2b
Secondary category of damages, ox and pit .... Bava Kama 28a-28b
Secondary category of damages, tooth .... Bava Kama 2b-3a
Secondary category of forbidden relations
Secondary category of forbidden relations, converts .... Yevamos 22a
Secondary category of forbidden relations, definition .... Yevamos 20a, 21a-22a
Secondary category of forbidden relations, source .... Yevamos 21a
Secondary category of forbidden relations, supporting .... Yevamos 84a, 85a-85b; Kesubos 100b
Secondary category of labors
Secondary and primary category of labors, sin offerings .... Krisos 16a-16b;
.... Shabbos 68a, 75b, 96b, 97b; Bava Kama 2a
Secondary and primary category of labors, why .... Bava Kama 2a; Shabbos 96b
Secondary category of labors, cases .... Shabbos 73b, 94b-95a
Secondary category of labors, how many sin offerings .... Krisos 16a-17a
Secondary level of impurity
Secondary level of impurity, how .... Pesachim 20a

Secondary level of impurity, how many subcategories............Pesachim 18b-19a, 20a; Chullin 33b;
....Parah 11:4-6; Taharos 2:3-7
Secondary level of impurity, making secondary degree ....Chullin 34a
Secondary level of impurity, ordinary food..................................Taharos 2:3-7; Chullin 33b-35b
Secondary level of impurity, Rabbinical Decree................................Zavim 5:12; Pesachim 19b
Secondary level of impurity, second tithe.......Chullin 33b; Chagigah 18b, 19b; Sotah 30a; Parah 11:500
Secondary level of impurity, what does it make impure..Bava Kama 2b

Secret
Secret..*see also* **Revealed secret**, page 565
Secret, care to keep.............................Yoma 4b; Sanhedrin 31a, 100b; Yevamos 63b; Bava Basra 4a
Secret, episode about disciple who revealed secret...Sanhedrin 31a
Secret in field..Berachos 8b
Secret of G-d for those who fear Him..Sotah 4b
Secret of lunar cycle..Rosh Hashanah 20b
Secret of lunar cycle, experts..Beitzah 4b
Secrets are revealed to him, Shmuel..Chullin 59a
Secrets of Torah, to whom..Chagigah 13a

Section
Section for righteous in World to Come..................................Shabbos 152a; Bava Metzia 83b
Section of *Hachodesh*..Megillah 30a-30b
Section of *Parah*..Megillah 30a-30b
Section of *Shekalim*..Megillah 29b-30b
Section of *tzitzis*, *Shema*..Berachos 12b
Section of *Zachor*..Megillah 18a, 29b-30b
Section, reading part of..Berachos 12b; Taanis 27b; Megillah 22a
Section repeated, new law.................Sotah 3a-3b; Bava Kama 64b; Shevuos 19a; Menachos 10a
Section, weekly, four sections..Megillah 29b, 30b
Sections in Torah, closed and open..Shabbos 103b
Sections of *tefillin*..Menachos 34b-35a
Sections of Torah, intermingled, oath..Bava Kama 107a

Secular use..*see* **Personal use**, page 483

Security
Security..*see also* **Collateral**, page 114; **Warranty**, page 732
Security, agent..Bava Basra 169b
Security, goods in borrower's hands..Bava Metzia 13a
Security of *kesubah*..Kesubos 82b; Shabbos 16b
Security of *kesubah*, betrothal..Kesubos 43b
Security, scribe's mistake....................Kesubos 51a-51b; Bava Basra 169b; Bava Metzia 13a, 14a, 15b

Seder
Seder hamaarachah, Abbaye..Yoma 14b, 33a-34a
Seder Olam, Beraisa..Yevamos 82b
Seder night
Seder night, dishes..Pesachim 114b
Seder night, harmful creatures..Pesachim 109b
Seder night, Pesach..Pesachim 116a-116b
Seder night, procedure..Pesachim 108b-109a, 115b

Seder..*see* **Order**, page 462

Seduced
Seduced girl, by one's father, forbidden relations................................Yevamos 4a-4b, 97a

S

Seducing husband before intimate relations, reward .... Nedarim 20b; Eruvin 100b
Seducing minor girl, penalty .... Kesubos 29a, 36a, 40b; Chullin 26b; Yevamos 33b
Seducing to forbidden marriages, who .... Yevamos 85b
Seducing wife before intimate relations .... Nedarim 20b

Seducer
Seducer, can divorce .... Kesubos 39b-40a
Seducer, inheritance .... Kesubos 42b
Seducer, she refuses to marry him .... Kesubos 39b
Seducer who admitted, flaw of virgin .... Kesubos 41a

See .... *see* **Saw**, page 591

Seed
Seed and skin of grapes, *nazir* .... Nazir 34a-35a, 38b-39a; Pesachim 41b
Seeds considered as fruit .... Orlah 1:8; Berachos 36b
Seeds of *terumah* .... Terumos 11:4-5
Seeds of vegetables, inedible, tithes .... Maasros 5:8

Seedlings
Seedlings of *terumah* .... Terumos 9:1-3
Seedlings of *terumah* which became impure .... Terumos 9:7
Seedlings of *tevel* and tithe ..... Terumos 9:6; Maasros 5:1-2; Menachos 69b-70a; Nedarim 57b-59b; Pesachim 34a

Seek
Seek G-d when He is present .... Yevamos 49b, 105a; Rosh Hashanah 18a
Seeking G-d, learning .... Berachos 63b

Sefer
Sefer Haftorah, Shabbos .... Gittin 60a
Sefer Hayashar .... Avodah Zarah 25a
Sefer Yetzirah, creation of man .... Sanhedrin 65b, 67b
Sefer Yetzirah, permission .... Sanhedrin 67b
Sefer Yuchasin, Divrei Hayamim .... Pesachim 62b

Sefer Torah .... *see* **Torah scroll**, page 697

Sefichin, Sabbatical year .... Sheviis 9:1; Pesachim 51b

Sefiras Haomer .... Menachos 65b; Chagigah 17b; Rosh Hashanah 5a
Sefiras Haomer .... *see* **Counting Omer**, page 130

Segan Kohen Gadol .... Yoma 12b-13a, 39a; Megillah 9b; Nazir 47b; Sotah 42a; Horayos 12b
Segan Kohen Gadol .... *see* **Assistant to** *Kohen Gadol*, page 34

Segulah
Segulah against evil eye .... Berachos 55b; Bava Basra 118a-118b
Segulah, cure .... Shabbos 61a-61b, 66b; Eruvin 26a
Segulah, investment for minor .... Bava Basra 52a; Bava Kama 87b
Segulah, stone for pregnant woman placement .... Shabbos 66b

Seifa .... *see* **End**, page 196

Seizing
Seizing before collecting from borrower .... Bava Basra 174a
Seizing borrower's property .... Bava Kama 112b
Seizing grindstone, prohibition .... Bava Metzia 115a-116a

Seizure
Seizure, "take money" .... Kesubos 91b
Seizure, *beis din* .... Bava Basra 34b
Seizure, borrower's right to take back .... Bava Metzia 16b, 35a-35b
Seizure, borrower's consent .... Bava Basra 44b-45a

S

Seizure from lender or for another .... Kesubos 90a-90b, 94a; Gittin 11b-12a; Bava Kama 34a; Arachin 7b

Seizure from orphan to collect .... Kesubos 84a-85a, 110a; Bava Kama 14b

Seizure, from when fruit belong to him .... Kesubos 104b; Bava Metzia 35b

Seizure in one's absence .... Kesubos 88a; Bava Kama 112b; Arachin 22b

Seizure, legal documents .... Bava Basra 169a

Seizure, money in doubt as to proper owner .... Bava Metzia 116a; Bava Basra 36a

Seizure of debt from gift .... Gittin 50b

Seizure of firstborn by *Kohen* .... Bava Metzia 6a-6b

Seizure of property, *beis din* .... Bava Kama 112b; Shevuos 41a

Seizure of your houses, mistake in ruling .... Bava Kama 12a

Seizure, property left to borrower .... Bava Metzia 113b-114a; Arachin 23b-24a; Bava Kama 11b

Seizure, property left to borrower for consecration .... Bava Metzia 113b-114a;
.... Arachin 7b-8a, 23b-24a

Seizure, third customer .... Kesubos 92a-92b

Seizure, to adjudicate by expert judges .... Bava Kama 15b, 84a

Seizure to pay *kesubah* .... Nedarim 65b-66a

Seizure, two men holding .... Bava Metzia 2a-2b; Bava Basra 170a

Seizure, unsold property became damaged .... Kesubos 95a-95b

Seizure, vicious circle .... Kesubos 95b

Sela

Sela, coin .... Kiddushin 12a

Sela coin, like fig .... Shabbos 78b

Sela coin, size .... Chullin 50b

Selah, explanation .... Eruvin 54a

Selecting

Selecting and winnowing, labors .... Shabbos 73b

Selecting judges .... Sanhedrin 23a-24b, 31b

Selecting on Shabbos .... Shabbos 95a

Selecting on Shabbos, general .... Shabbos 74a-74b, 142b

Selecting pebble in wheat, damage .... Bava Basra 93b-94a; Beitzah 38b

Self-critic, loud voice .... Sotah 32b

Self-examination .... Eruvin 13b; Moed Katan 5a; Bava Basra 78b; Avos 2:100

Self-help .... Bava Kama 27b-28a

Self-injury .... Bava Kama 91a-91b

Self-inspection, reward .... Moed Katan 5a; Sotah 5b

Self-understood monetary claim .... Bava Basra 35b

Self-sacrifice

Self-sacrifice, "with all your soul" .... Berachos 61b; Pesachim 25a; Yoma 82a; Sanhedrin 74a

Self-sacrifice, circumcision .... Shabbos 130a

Self-sacrifice, forbidden relations ...... Kiddushin 39b-40a; Pesachim 25a-25b; Yoma 82a; Sanhedrin 74a-74b

Self-sacrifice, generations decline .... Berachos 20a

Self-sacrifice, Hillel .... Yoma 35b

Self-sacrifice, idolatry .... Pesachim 25a-25b; Yoma 82a; Sanhedrin 74a

Self-sacrifice, men put to death by government .... Bava Basra 10b

Self-sacrifice, Pappus .... Taanis 18b

Self-sacrifice, sick because of desire .... Sanhedrin 75a

Self-seeded produce of Sabbatical year .... Sheviis 9:1; Pesachim 51b

S

Sell .... *see also* **Sale**, page 585
  Prohibitions —
    Selling synagogue ....Megillah 25b-26b, 27b
    Selling Torah scroll ....Megillah 27a; Bava Basra 151a
    Selling wine to idolater ....Avodah Zarah 65b, 71a-71b, 72b
    Selling wine to idolater who made it forbidden ....Avodah Zarah 59b
  Women —
    Selling her *kesubah*, widow's right to alimony ....Kesubos 53a, 54a, 97b-98a
    Selling maidservant to relatives ....Kiddushin 18b, 19b-20a, 44b
    Selling right to wife's earnings ....Kesubos 80a-80b
    Selling wife's property for income ....Kesubos 79a, 101a
  Misc. —
    Sell, except coat ....Yevamos 63a
    Selling fruit of Sabbatical year ....Succah 39a-39b; Bechoros 31b
    Selling inheritance before death ....Bava Metzia 16a-16b
    Selling one's daughter, sign of blessing ....Megillah 27a
    Selling oneself, Hebrew slave ....Kiddushin 14b-15a
    Selling priestly gifts ....Chullin 138a-138b
    Selling property to emigrate to *Eretz Yisrael* ....Kiddushin 49b
    Selling sewing accessories, parable ....Sotah 40a
Seller sad and buyer joyous ....Berachos 5a
Semen
  Semen .... *see also* **Discharge**, page 165
    Semen and discharge, differentiating ....Niddah 35b
    Semen, impurity ....Shabbos 86b; Niddah 61b
    Semen in vain ....Niddah 13a-13b, 16b, 43a
    Semen in vain, cases ....Niddah 13b-14a; Berachos 13b; Kiddushin 82a
    Semen like arrow or by feeling ....Niddah 43a
    Semen, liquid coming out of body ....Zevachim 79b
    Semen of horses, idolaters' semen ....Yevamos 98a
Semichah
  ***Semichah* on sacrifice —**
    Semichah, did not press his hands ....Menachos 93b
    Semichah, how ....Yoma 36a; Chagigah 16b; Menachos 93b
    Semichah immediately before slaughtering ....Zevachim 33a; Berachos 42a; Beitzah 20a;
      ....Menachos 93a
    Semichah, impure person ....Zevachim 32a-33a
    Semichah, not indispensable requirement ....Zevachim 39b
    Semichah on intermingled sacrifices ....Zevachim 74b-75b
    Semichah, on which sacrifices .....Beitzah 20a; Menachos 55b, 62b, 88a, 92a-93a; Zevachim 11a, 33a, 48b
    Semichah on Yom Tov ....Beitzah 20a-20b
    Semichah on Yom Tov, episode ....Beitzah 20a-20b
    Semichah, partners ....Menachos 93a-94a
    Semichah, who ....Menachos 93a-93b; Temurah 2a; Kiddushin 36a; Chullin 2b; Arachin 2a-2b
    Semichah, women ....Kiddushin 36a; Chagigah 16b; Eruvin 96b; Rosh Hashanah 33a; Chullin 85a
  Which sacrifices —
    Semichah, bull offered for mistake of *beis din* ....Sanhedrin 13b
    Semichah of *Kohen Gadol* on sacrificial parts ....Menachos 94a; Tamid 7:3
    Semichah on bull of Yom Kippur ....Zevachim 40a

S

Semichah on leper's guilt offering..Zevachim 33a
Semichah, remainder of Pesach..Pesachim 89a
Misc. —
Semichah, "rule, he will rule"...Sanhedrin 5a-5b
Semichah, Eli's sons...Sanhedrin 14a
Semichah, Rebbi to Shmuel...Bava Metzia 85b
Semichah, Rabbi Yehudah ben Bava.................................Sanhedrin 13b-14a; Avodah Zarah 8b
Semichah, songs...Kesubos 17a; Sanhedrin 14a
Semichah to judge and to decide law..........................Sanhedrin 5a-5b, 13b-14a, 30b
Semichah, to teach a law..Sanhedrin 30b
Semichah ke'amidah..*see* **Leaning like standing**, page 357
Semichah lekirah.............................*see* **Putting next to stove-top on Shabbos**, page 512
Semichas geulah litefilah.............*see* **Juxtaposing mention of redemption and prayer**, page 330
Semolina (wheat)
Semolina, to whiten skin of young girls...............Shabbos 80b; Moed Katan 9b; Pesachim 42b-43b
Semolina, washing wheat...Pesachim 40a
Semolina for meal offering
Semolina for meal offering, from where...Menachos 85a-85b
Semolina for meal offerings, blemish...Menachos 85b
Semolina for meal offerings, dust..Menachos 85a
Semolina for meal offerings, source...Zevachim 50a
Semuchin, *dayanim*...*see* **Ordained judges**, page 462
Semuchin, *hekesh*...*see* **Analogy**, page 22
Sending
Sending agent for divorce...............................Gittin 29a-30a, 62b-63a; Bava Metzia 76a-76b
Sending away mother bird.....................................Chullin 138b-142a; Bava Metzia 102a
Sending gifts of food on Purim...Megillah 7a-7b
Sent away from house of study...Bava Basra 23b, 165b
Sending out of camps
Sending out of camps, desert and Temples...Zevachim 116b-117a
Sending out of camps, impurity..Pesachim 67a-68a
Sending out of camps, Tabernacle travelled...Menachos 95a-95b
Sensation
Sensation, *niddah*...Niddah 57b
Sensation, seminal discharge..Niddah 43a
Separate
Separate into groups, prohibition..Yevamos 13b-14a
Separated forcefully, impurity..Krisos 15b
Separating *challah* on Shabbos...Beitzah 37a
Separating first fruit..Bikkurim 3:1
Separating from friend, law..Berachos 31a; Eruvin 64a
Separating head of bird, burnt offering.................Zevachim 64b-65a; Chullin 21a-22a
Separating three baskets from Temple Treasury.........Shekalim 3:1-4, 4:1-2; Kesubos 106a-106b;
        Moed Katan 6a
Separating from wife
Separating from wife after days of purity...Pesachim 113b
Separating from wife before Giving of Torah...Shabbos 86a-86b
Separating from wife close to menstruation........Shevuos 18b; Yevamos 62b; Niddah 15a-15b, 63b
Separating from wife close to menstruation, journey..............................Yevamos 62b

S

Separating from wife, to learn .... Kesubos 61b-62a

Separating tithe .... *see also* **Tithe**, page 693

   Disqualified —

Separating impure tithe, intentionally and unintentionally ...... Yevamos 89a-89b; Terumos 2:2;
.... Pesachim 33a; Menachos 25b

Separating tithe, doubt about when became lost .... Gittin 31a

Separating tithe, from food about to be lost .... Bava Kama 115b

Separating tithe, from forbidden food .... Kiddushin 46b

Separating tithe, impure on impure .... Bava Kama 115b

Separating tithe, impure *terumah* .... Terumos 2:1-2; Pesachim 33a; Yevamos 89a; Menachos 25b

Separating tithe, inedible *terumah* .... Kiddushin 46b; Terumos 3:1; Yevamos 89a

Separating tithe, insufficient part of tithes .... Terumos 4:1-2

Separating tithe on ship, episode .... Bava Metzia 11a-11b; Kiddushin 26b-27a; Maaser Sheni 5:9

Separating tithe, wine which turned to vinegar .... Bava Basra 96a; Kiddushin 79a; Niddah 2b

   How —

Separating first tithe from sheaves .... Eruvin 31b; Berachos 47a-47b; Shabbos 127b; Pesachim 35b;
.... Beitzah 13b; Temurah 5b

Separating tithe by estimate, do not do it often .... Avos 1:16

Separating tithe by estimate, how ...... Beitzah 13b; Gittin 31a; Menachos 54b-55a; Bechoros 58b-59a;
.... Terumos 1:7

Separating tithe by estimate, *terumas maaser* .... Beitzah 13b; Bechoros 58b-59a; Gittin 31a

Separating tithe, determining fruit .... Terumos 3:5; Eruvin 37b

Separating tithe, from nearby produce .... Eruvin 30b, 32b; Gittin 30b; Chullin 7a; Niddah 71b

Separating tithe from one basket to another .... Demai 7:6; Temurah 4a

Separating tithe, intent .... Beitzah 13b; Bechoros 58b-59a; Gittin 30b, 31a; Menachos 54b-55a

Separating tithe, precision in amount .... Terumos 4:6

Separating tithe, text .... Demai 5:1-2

Separating tithe, wheat in straw .... Maasros 5:4

   When —

Separating tithe, *chametz* on Pesach .... Pesachim 33a-33b

Separating tithe on Shabbos .... Demai 4:4; Beitzah 37a

Separating tithe on Shabbos, penalty .... Gittin 53b

Separating tithe, Shabbos eve for Shabbos .... Yevamos 93a-93b

   Who —

Separating tithe, guardian of orphans .... Gittin 52a

Separating tithe, from one's produce for fellow's .... Nedarim 36b; Yoma 50b; Zevachim 6a;
.... Temurah 2b-3a, 10a

Separating tithe, last year of childhood .... Niddah 46b; Terumos 1:3

Separating tithe, non-Jew .... Temurah 3a

Separating tithe, non-Jew for himself .... Terumos 3:9; Gittin 23b; Kiddushin 41b; Arachin 6a

Separating tithe, partners .... Terumos 3:3; Temurah 13a

Separating tithe, permission given by married woman .... Yevamos 86a

Separating tithe, who .... Terumos 1:1-3, 1:6; Shabbos 153b; Yevamos 113a

   Misc. —

Separating tithe, on condition .... Succah 23b-24a; Demai 7:4-5; Gittin 25a-25b

Separate waiting-room, blood-letter .... Taanis 21b

Separation between man and wall, prayer .... Berachos 5b

Septuagint .... *see* **Translation of Torah, Talmai**, page 700

Serah bas Asher .... Sotah 13a

S

Sereifah .... *see* **Burning penalty**, page 81
Serenity, wicked .... Avos 4:15
Seriousness, prayer .... Berachos 30b
Serisim, Daniel and his friends .... Sanhedrin 93b
Servant
  Servant during meal, blessings .... Chullin 107b
  Servant during meal, eating .... Kesubos 61a; Eruvin 53b; Chullin 107b
  Servant, Elijah withdrew .... Kesubos 61a
  Servant handing garments .... Berachos 51a
  Servant, ignoramus .... Berachos 52b
  Servant to group, salary .... Pesachim 86b
  Servants of righteous and of wicked .... Chullin 4b
Served
  Served at kings' table .... Yevamos 46a; Avodah Zarah 38a-38b, 59a
  Serving Ishmaelite rather than worst man .... Shabbos 11a
  Serving one's teacher and Sages .... Kesubos 96a; Berachos 7b
  Serving Sages, episodes .... Eruvin 54a
  Serving Sages, ignoramus .... Berachos 47b; Sotah 22a
  Serving, wine of idolaters .... Avodah Zarah 58a-58b
Service
  Temple —
    Service consecrates them .... Sanhedrin 16b; Shevuos 15a; Menachos 50a; Yoma 12b
    Service, invalid, correcting .... Zevachim 15a, 26b, 34b; Menachos 6b-7a, 26b; Meilah 5b
    Service of *Kohen Gadol, mussaf* of Yom Kippur .... Yoma 56b
    Service of *Kohen Gadol* on weekdays .... Yoma 17b; Tamid 7:1, 7:3; Menachos 94a
    Service of Yom Kippur in Temple .... Yoma 30a-71b
    Service, usual manner, sacrifice .... Zevachim 24a
    Services in Temple, most difficult .... Menachos 11a; Yoma 47b, 49b; Zevachim 64b
  Misc. —
    Service, eating *terumah* .... Pesachim 72b-73a
    Service, calf whose neck is broken .... Sotah 45b-46a; Avodah Zarah 23a
    Service of the heart, prayer .... Taanis 2a
Setting
  Setting next to pot, Shabbos .... Shabbos 48a
  Setting next to stove-top on Shabbos .... Shabbos 37a
  Setting aside a place for prayer .... Berachos 6b, 7b
  Setting aside time to learn Torah .... Shabbos 31a
Seudah
  Seudah .... *see* **Meal**, page 395; *see also* **Feast**, page 218
  Seudah mafsekes, Tisha B'Av .... Taanis 29b, 30a-30b; Sanhedrin 70a
  Seudah mafsekes, Yom Kippur .... Yoma 81b; Rosh Hashanah 9a-9b
  Seudas mitzvah .... *see* **Meal (Meals for commandments)** page 395
Sevara .... *see* **Logical deduction, does not need verse**, page 376
Seven
  Seven blessings .... Kesubos 7a-8a
  Seven commandments of non-Jews .... Sanhedrin 56a-57a, 74b-75a
  Seven commandments, punishment .... Bava Kama 38a
  Seven communal leaders .... Megillah 27a
  Seven days of mourning .... Moed Katan 20a

Seven gates in Temple Courtyard .... Middos 1:4-5
Seven heads, snake .... Kiddushin 29b
Seven liquids, susceptibility to become impure and impurity .... Machshirin 6:4
Seven men encompassed history .... Bava Basra 121b
Seven men not touched by worms .... Bava Basra 17a
Seven months of pregnancy .... Sanhedrin 69a
Seven nations, marriage .... Yevamos 76a
Seven of *Adar*, Moses .... Kiddushin 38a; Megillah 13b
Seven parts of Torah scroll .... Shabbos 116a
Seven shepherds .... Succah 52b
Seven sons of Hannah .... Gittin 57b
Seven species, precedence .... Berachos 41a-41b
Seven subjects of *treifos* .... Chullin 42a-43a
Seven things in wise man .... Avos 5:7
Seven things unrevealed to men .... Pesachim 54b
Seven *treifos* laws .... Chullin 42a-43a
Seven ways, checkings of *zav* .... Nazir 65b; Kiddushin 2b; Zavim 2:200
Seven years of conquest, *Eretz Yisrael* .... Arachin 13a; Zevachim 118b
Seven years of famine, craftsman .... Sanhedrin 29a
Seven years, proverbs .... Sanhedrin 29a
Seven years, proverbs .... Sanhedrin 29a

Seven cleaning substances
Seven cleaning substances, blood of sin offering .... Zevachim 95a-95b
Seven cleaning substances, leprous mark .... Zevachim 95a
Seven cleaning substances, stain of *niddah* ...... Niddah 61b-63a; Sanhedrin 49b; Zevachim 95a-95b

Seven days of purity
Seven days of purity, bride .... Niddah 66a
Seven days of purity, examination .... Niddah 7b, 68b-69a
Seven days of purity, episode .... Shabbos 13a-13b
Seven days of purity, *zav* .... Pesachim 81a; Niddah 22a, 33a-33b, 37a; Zavim 1:2
Seven days of purity, *zavah* .... Niddah 37a-37b, 54a-54b

Seventeenth of *Tammuz*
Seventeenth of *Tammuz* .... Rosh Hashanah 18b
Seventeenth of *Tammuz*, episodes .... Taanis 28b

Seventy
Seventy cubits around city .... Eruvin 57a-57b
Seventy one, *Sanhedrin* .... Sanhedrin 16b-17a
Seventy souls, Egypt .... Bava Basra 123a-123b
Seventy years, exile in Babylon .... Megillah 11b-12a
Seventy years, old age .... Moed Katan 28a

Seventy languages
Seventy languages, Giving of Torah .... Shabbos 88b
Seventy languages, *Sanhedrin* .... Sanhedrin 17a-17b; Menachos 65a
Seventy languages, stones of Jordan .... Sotah 35b

Sever panim yafos .... *see* **Pleasing countenance**, page 492

Sewing
Sewing, Alexandrian way .... Moed Katan 26b
Sewing on *Chol HaMoed* .... Moed Katan 10a
Sewing on Shabbos .... Shabbos 74b-75a, 105a

S

Sewing tear, mourner..Moed Katan 22b, 24a, 26a-26b
Sewing, Shabbos work...Shabbos 74b-75a, 105a
Sewing *tefillin*, linen...Makos 11a
Sewing Torah scroll, leaving part of scroll....................................Megillah 19b
Sewing Torah scroll, linen...Makos 11a
Sewing torn Torah scroll...Menachos 31b
Sewn on garment, carrying out on Shabbos..................................Shabbos 57a, 58a

Sexual relations...*see* **Intimate relations**, page 316
Sfek sfeika..*see* **Double doubt**, page 176
Shaar
   Shaar Haashpos, two weavers..Shabbos 15a
   Shaar Nikanor..Middos 2:3; Yoma 38a
Shaas kosher..*see* **Time of validity**, page 692
Shaas hadechak..*see* **Case of necessity, Rabbinical Decree**, page 89
Shaas hashmad................................*see* **Time of religious persecution, self-sacrifice**, page 691
Shabbos
   Aggadah —
      Shabbos, additional soul...Beitzah 16a; Taanis 27b
      Shabbos, borrow on My account..Beitzah 15b
      Shabbos, Divine punishment..Shabbos 33a
      Shabbos, *Gehinnom*...Sanhedrin 65b
      Shabbos, if Israel kept two Shabbosos..................................Shabbos 118b
      Shabbos, ignoramus does not lie...Demai 4:1-2; Chullin 75b
      Shabbos, non-Jews claim Jews do not keep...........................Avodah Zarah 70a
      Shabbos, Ov sorcery...Sanhedrin 65b
      Shabbos, punishment by fire..Shabbos 119b
      Shabbos, reward..Shabbos 10b, 118b; Beitzah 16a
      Shabbos, reward for enjoyment..Shabbos 118a-118b
      Shabbos, Sambatyon...Sanhedrin 65b
      Shabbos, semblance of the World to Come............................Berachos 57b
      Shabbos, two angels...Shabbos 119b
      Shabbos, wealth..Shabbos 119a

   Commandments —
      Shabbos, *Bircas HaMazon*...Berachos 48b
      Shabbos, daytime meal more important................................Pesachim 105a
      Shabbos, enjoyment...Pesachim 68b
      Shabbos, getting up early to prepare....................................Shabbos 117b
      Shabbos, overrides death penalty........................Yevamos 6b-7a; Sanhedrin 35b-36a
      Shabbos overrides *lulav*..Succah 42b-43a, 44a
      Shabbos, prayer starting earlier..Megillah 23a
      Shabbos, quantity of bread eaten..Eruvin 82b
      Shabbos, running to perform a *mitzvah*..............................Berachos 6b
      Shabbos, *tefillin*..Eruvin 95b, 96a; Menachos 36b
      Shabbos, Temple building..Yevamos 6a
      Shabbos, unusual eating habits...Nedarim 37b

   Episodes —
      Shabbos, "Whose Shabbos," Rabban Gamliel........................Berachos 28a; Chagigah 3a
      Shabbos, destruction of Jerusalem......................................Shabbos 119b
      Shabbos, episode about extingushing fire..............................Shabbos 121a

S

Shabbos, episode about fence..Shabbos 150b
Shabbos, like Hillel and Shamai..Beitzah 16a
Shabbos of two pairs..Sotah 13b
Shabbos, pearl in fish...Shabbos 119a
Shabbos, Sages prepared by themselves..................Shabbos 119a; Kiddushin 41a
Shabbos, spice of Shabbos to emperor..Shabbos 119a
Shabbos, wealth for butcher...Shabbos 119a

Kabbalas Shabbos —
Shabbos, "Come bride"..................................Shabbos 119a; Bava Kama 32a-32b
Shabbos prayer on Shabbos eve...Berachos 27a
Shabbos, welcoming early..Shabbos 118b

Prohibitions —
Shabbos, act of acquisition by Shabbos desecration...........................Bava Kama 70b
Shabbos, act of acquisition by sick person....................................Bava Basra 156b-157a
Shabbos, annulling vows..................................Shabbos 46b, 157a; Nedarim 77a-77b
Shabbos, buying house in *Eretz Yisrael*.......................Bava Kama 80b; Gittin 8b
Shabbos, non-Jew who kept Shabbos..Sanhedrin 58b-59a
Shabbos out of his courtyard, *eruv*...............................Eruvin 47a, 62b, 86a
Shabbos, permitting vow..Nedarim 77a
Shabbos, since it was permitted...Eruvin 17a, 93b-94a
Shabbos, testimony about new moon overrides Shabbos......Rosh Hashanah 19b-20a, 21b-22a

Sacrifices —
Shabbos, communal sacrifice.........................Yoma 50a; Menachos 64b; Temurah 14a
Shabbos, leftover burned parts of sacrifices...............................Yoma 46a-46b
Shabbos, limiting labors to offer sacrifice.........................Menachos 63b-64a
Shabbos overridden, daily offering.....................................Pesachim 66a, 66b
Shabbos, overridden for blood sprinkling...............................Beitzah 20b-21a
Shabbos, overridden for burning sacrifices.................Pesachim 68b; Shabbos 20a
Shabbos, Pesach lamb...............Pesachim 65b-66a, 68a-69b; Eruvin 103a
Shabbos, sacrifice with fixed date..............................Yoma 50a; Temurah 14a
Shabbos, several sin offerings...............Shabbos 70b-71a; Sanhedrin 62b; Beitzah 34b-35a
Shabbos, skinning Pesach lamb...........Shabbos 116b-117a, 133b; Menachos 63b-64a

Various Shabbosos —
Shabbos *Chazon*, *Haftorah*...Megillah 31b
Shabbos, four sections..Megillah 30a-30b
Shabbos, Pesach eve...Pesachim 13a, 20b, 49a
Shabbos Rosh Hashanah...Rosh Hashanah 29b-30a

Misc. —
Shabbos, blowing *shofar* or prayer because of calamity................Bava Basra 91a
Shabbos confines...*see* **Techum**, page 675
Shabbos, consecration by *beis din*...................................Nedarim 78a-78b
Shabbos, doubt in desert..Shabbos 69b
Shabbos, mourning...Moed Katan 23a-24a
Shabbos now, we do not request...Shabbos 12a-12b
Shabbos, penalty for doing work...........Gittin 53b-54a; Terumos 2:3; Shabbos 38a; Beitzah 17b;
                                                   Kesubos 34a; Bava Kama 71a; Chullin 15a
Shabbos, requirement to give tithe...........Beitzah 34b-35a; Maasros 4:2; Terumos 8:3; Eduyos 4:10
Shabbos, until Tuesday...Gittin 77a
Shabbos, wording of vow..Nedarim 60a-60b

S

Shabbos labors

Food —

Shabbos labors, coloring by slaughtering .... Shabbos 75a-75b
Shabbos labors, cooking .... *see* **Cooking on Shabbos labors**, page 128
Shabbos labors, extinguishing .... *see* **Extinguishing**, page 211
Shabbos labors, filtering .... Shabbos 138a, 139b-140a, 109a, 134a
Shabbos labors, grinding .... Shabbos 74b, 141a
Shabbos labors, harvesting .... Shabbos 81b, 103a; Chullin 127b
Shabbos labors, hunting .... Shabbos 106a-107a; Beitzah 23b-24a
Shabbos labors, kneading .... Shabbos 18a, 140a, 155b-156a; Zevachim 94b
Shabbos labors, pickling food .... Shabbos 108b
Shabbos labors, scattering to wind .... Shabbos 73b; Bava Kama 60a
Shabbos labors, selecting .... Shabbos 74a-74b, 142b; Beitzah 14b
Shabbos labors, sifting .... Shabbos 73b
Shabbos labors, squeezing .... Shabbos 143b-145a
Shabbos labors, threshing grain .... Shabbos 75a, 128a; Beitzah 13b

Garments —

Shabbos labors, combing wool .... Shabbos 106a
Shabbos labors, cutting off hair .... Makos 20b; Shabbos 94b
Shabbos labors, cutting off skin .... Bechoros 24b
Shabbos labors, rubbing mud .... Shabbos 141a
Shabbos labors, rubbing shirt .... Shabbos 140a
Shabbos labors, sewing .... Shabbos 74b-75a, 105a
Shabbos labors, soaking garment .... Zevachim 94b
Shabbos labors, spinning .... Shabbos 74b, 106a
Shabbos labors, shaking garment .... Shabbos 146b-147a
Shabbos labors, tearing .... Shabbos 105b
Shabbos labors, tearing to sew .... Shabbos 74ba
Shabbos labors, washing .... Shabbos 106a
Shabbos labors, weaving .... Shabbos 75b, 105a, 106a

Building —

Shabbos labors, breaking seals .... Beitzah 31b-32a
Shabbos labors, building by assembling items .... Shabbos 47a-47b
Shabbos labors, building in utensils .... Shabbos 74b
Shabbos labors, destroying bricks building .... Beitzah 31b
Shabbos labors, destroying to build in another place .... Shabbos 31b
Shabbos labors, hole in barrel .... Shabbos 146a-146b
Shabbos labors, smallest building .... Shabbos 102b

Creatures —

Shabbos labors, cutting wart .... Pesachim 68b; Eruvin 103a-103b
Shabbos labors, clipping nails .... Shabbos 94b
Shabbos labors, cut wound .... Shabbos 107a, 107b
Shabbos labors, injury to reptiles .... Shabbos 107a-107b
Shabbos labors, killing harmful creatures .... Shabbos 121b
Shabbos labors, killing lice .... Shabbos 107b
Shabbos labors, skin pieces .... Shabbos 94b

Writing —

Shabbos labors, making two marks .... Shabbos 103b
Shabbos labors, writing .... Shabbos 104b-105a

S

Shabbos labors, writing large letter..Shabbos 75b
Shabbos labors, writing two letters...Shabbos 103a-103b

Leather —
Shabbos labors, catching lice...Shabbos 107b
Shabbos labors, cutting..Shabbos 75b
Shabbos labors, cutting chilazon..Shabbos 75a
Shabbos labors, etching lines...Shabbos 75b
Shabbos labors, hunting, which species...Shabbos 106b
Shabbos labors, instances of tearing..Shabbos 74b
Shabbos labors, mud on shoe...Shabbos 141a-141b
Shabbos labors, pulling fish out of water..Shabbos 107b
Shabbos labors, scraping...Shabbos 75b
Shabbos labors, tanning..Shabbos 75b
Shabbos labors, washing leather.................................Zevachim 94a-94b; Shabbos 142b

Knot —
Shabbos labors, knots..Shabbos 111b-113a
Shabbos labors, noose...Shabbos 111b; Pesachim 11a
Shabbos labors, tying knot in Tabernacle...Shabbos 74b
Shabbos labors, tying harp string...............................Eruvin 102b-103a, 105a
Shabbos labors, untying knot in Tabernacle.....................................Shabbos 74b

Misc. —
Shabbos labors, bandage..Eruvin 102b
Shabbos labors, carrying out.............................*see* **Carrying out**, page 88
Shabbos labors, coloring..Shabbos 106a
Shabbos labors, final touch.......................................Shabbos 75b, 102b-103a
Shabbos labors, virgin, injury...Kesuvos 5b-7a
Shabbos labors, wringing hairs..Shabbos 128b

Shacharis
Shacharis, bircos hashachar...Berachos 60b
Shacharis, blame on who delays...Berachos 28a
Shacharis, close to getting up..Berachos 5b
Shacharis, importance..Berachos 6b

Shachnatziv, city of scoffers...Pesachim 112b

Shadai
Shadai, erasing Name...Shevuos 35a
Shadai, Who said "enough" to His world...Chagigah 12a

Shade
Shade, cool, fourth hour..Berachos 27a
Shade, moon and tree, demons.................................Pesachim 111a-111b
Shade more abundant than sunlight...Succah 7b
Shade of Temple, discourses..Pesachim 26a

Shadi nofo bassar ikaro.............................*see* **Branches, putting down**, page 74

Shadow
Shadow of grave, calculation system...Eruvin 43b
Shadow of wisdom, money..Pesachim 53b

Shaking
Shaking *lulav*...Succah 37b-38a
Shaking of *Eretz Yisrael*......................Sotah 49b; Bava Kama 82b; Menachos 64b
Shaking table, *muktzeh*..Shabbos 143a

S

Shaking tallis, on Shabbos .... Shabbos 147a

Shakud, Shmuel .... Kesubos 43b

Shaliach .... *see* **Agent**, page 14

Shalish .... *see* **Intermediary**, page 315

Shalmei simcha .... *see* **Sacrifice of rejoicing**, page 582

Shalmei tzibur .... *see* **Peace offerings, communal**, page 477

Shalom

   Shalom .... *see also* **Greeting**, page 258

   Shalom, cut *vav* letter .... Kiddushin 66b

   Shalom, Divine name .... Shabbos 10b

   Shalom, erasing G-d's name .... Succah 53a-53b; Makos 11a; Shabbos 116a; Nedarim 66b; Chullin 141a

   Shalom in bathhouse .... Shabbos 10a-10b

   Shalom to demon, prohibition .... Sanhedrin 44a

   Shalom to non-Jew .... Gittin 62a

Shalom bayis .... *see* **Peace, domestic**, page 477

Shalom malchus .... *see* **Peace of government, prayer**, page 477

Shamai

   Shamai and Hillel, planted sword .... Shabbos 17a

   Shamai, Ben Uziel's strong reply .... Bava Basra 133b-134a

   Shamai, honoring Shabbos .... Beitzah 16a

   Shamai, rejected converts .... Shabbos 31a

Shamash .... *see* **Servant**, page 603

Shamayim, fire and water .... Chagigah 12a

Shame

  Damage —

   Shame, different cases .... Bava Kama 86a, 86b, 91a; Kesubos 66a

   Shame, estimate .... Bava Kama 85a-86a

   Shame, indemnity for wife's .... Kesubos 65b-66a

   Shame, intention .... Bava Kama 27a, 35a, 86b; Yevamos 54a

   Shame, man who uncovered woman's hair .... Bava Kama 90b

   Shame, responsibility of food vendor .... Bava Basra 93b

   Shame of slave .... Bava Kama 88a; Sanhedrin 86a

   Shame to oneself .... Bava Kama 91a-91b

  Shame and loss of value

   Shame and loss of value, inheritance .... Kesubos 42b

   Shame and loss of value, source .... Arachin 14b-15a

   Shame and loss of value, to whom and how .... Kesubos 40a-40b

  Misc. —

   Shame because of transgression, atonement .... Berachos 12b

   Shame, burning one's dish in public .... Berachos 17b

   Shame, decrees .... Moed Katan 27a-27b

   Shame, do not shame and do not be *ashamed* .... Moed Katan 9b

   Shame, no greater shame than this .... Bava Kama 86a

   Shame, virtue .... Nedarim 20a; Yevamos 79a

Shamed

   Shamed by his sin, forgiveness .... Berachos 12b

   Shamed I am by your words, Beis Shamai! .... Chagigah 22b

Shamir worm

   Shamir worm, Solomon .... Gittin 68a-68b

S

Shamir worm, stones in Temple .... Sotah 48b

Shamta .... Moed Katan 17a; Yevamos 52a; Nedarim 7b, 8b; Kiddushin 12b

Shanah meuberes .... *see* **Adding a month, when**, page 11

Shanah upiresh .... *see* **Learned and forsook**, page 358

Shape of letters .... Menachos 29b

Shapur Malka .... *see* **Shvor Malka**, page 622

Shared courtyard, damage .... Bava Kama 13b-14a

Sharing

Sharing .... *see also* **Dividing**, page 168

Sharing, act of acquisition .... Bava Basra 3a

Sharing, bidding for division of property .... Bava Basra 13a-13b

Sharing, lots .... Bava Basra 106b

Sharing by orphans, *beis din* .... Kiddushin 42a-42b; Yevamos 67b; Kesubos 100a; Gittin 34a

Sharing, she lost her *kesubah* .... Bava Basra 132a-133a

Sharing by brothers

Sharing by brothers, bathhouse .... Bava Basra 13a-13b, 172a

Sharing by brothers, canceling .... Kesubos 109b; Bava Kama 9a; Bava Basra 106b-107a

Sharing by brothers, renouncing .... Bava Basra 7a-7b, 65a, 71a

Sharir vekayam .... Bava Basra 160b

Sharp

Sharp and level-headed, preference .... Horayos 14a

Sharp substance, absorption of forbidden substance .... Avodah Zarah 39a

Sharp substance, knife .... Avodah Zarah 39a

Sharp-minded men of Pumpeditha .... Sanhedrin 17b

Sharp-minded, too sharp to see details .... Bava Basra 116b; Eruvin 90a; Bava Metzia 96b

Sharpening

Sharpening disciples by a question .... Berachos 33b; Eruvin 13a; Megillah 25a; Nazir 59b;
Zevachim 13a; Chullin 43b; Niddah 4b, 45a

Sharpening knife on Yom Tov .... Beitzah 28a-28b

Sharpness of mind causes mistakes .... Bava Metzia 96b; Eruvin 90a; Niddah 33b

Shasos, righteous are called .... Sanhedrin 26b

Shatnez

Shatnez, connection .... Kilayim 9:8-11; Yevamos 5b; Shabbos 54a; Menachos 39a

Shatnez, definition .... Kilayim 9:8; Yevamos 5b; Niddah 61b

Shatnez, doubt .... Niddah 61b

Shtanez, honor of human beings .... Berachos 19b-20a

Shatnez in *tzitzis* .... Yevamos 4b, 5b; Menachos 40a-40b

Shatnez, in which items .... Kilayim 9:1-4, 9:7-9; Beitzah 14b-15a; Shabbos 54a, 57b

Shatnez, Kohanim .... Yoma 69a

Shatnez, priestly garments .... Yoma 69a; Tamid 27a-27b

Shatnez, shrouds .... Niddah 61b; Pesachim 40b; Avodah Zarah 65b

Shatnez, species .... Kilayim 9:1-2; Shabbos 26b, 27a; Yevamos 4b; Menachos 39b

Shatnez, wearing .... Beitzah 14b

Shatnez, G, Z, crowns over letters .... Menachos 29b

Shattering oven, impurity .... Keilim 5:7-11a; Chullin 123b-124a

Shav miyediaso .... *see* **Sin offering, sin because of ignorance**, page 627

Shaving .... *see also* **Haircut**, page 265

Prohibitions —

Shaving beard and *peyos* .... Makos 20b-21a; Shevuos 2b-3a

S

Shaving beard, limits..Negaim 10:9
Shaving body hair...Nazir 58b-59a
Shaving by non-Jew and non-Jew...Avodah Zarah 29a
Shaving front hair..Bava Kama 83a
Shaving, mourner..Moed Katan 14b, 19b, 24a, 22b
Shaving on *Chol HaMoed*...Moed Katan 13b-14b, 17b
Shaving, Shabbos...Shabbos 94b; Makos 20b; Bechoros 24b
Shaving, successive periods of mourning.................Moed Katan 17b; Taanis 13a

Nazir —
Shaving of *nazir*, cases of disqualification...Nazir 46b
Shaving of *nazir*, entrance of *Heichal*...Nazir 45a
Shaving of *nazir*, fire...Nazir 45b
Shaving of *nazir*, left two hairs..............................Nazir 42a; Bava Kama 105a
Shaving of *nazir*, leper..Nazir 60b-61a
Shaving of *nazir*, *peah*..............................Nazir 41a-41b, 58a-58b; Yevamos 5a
Shaving of *nazir*, place..Nazir 45a-45b
Shaving of *nazir*, profit...Kiddushin 57b
Shaving of *nazir*, prohibition...Nazir 39b-40a
Shaving of *nazir*, razor..Nazir 39b-40a, 61a
Shaving of *nazir*, liquid of sacrifice poured on hair..........................Nazir 45b
Shaving of *nazir*, washing hair..........Nazir 42a; Shabbos 50b, 81b; Beitzah 35b
Shaving of *nazir*, when..Nazir 5b
Shaving of *nazir*, when does he bring sacrifice.....................................Nazir 44b
Shaving of *nazir*, when is it permitted...Nazir 46a-46b

Misc. —
Shave for dead, women..Kiddushin 35b-36a
Shave, head and beard......................Nazir 40b, 57b-58b; Makos 20b, 21a
Shave, *nazir* and *Kohen*...Nazir 58a-58b
Shave, prohibition...Makos 20a-20b
Shave, whole head..Nazir 41a-41b
Shave, women...Kiddushin 35b
Shaving armpit, episode..Nazir 59a
Shaving, harmful for sick...Berachos 57b
Shaving leprous mark...Negaim 10:5
Shaving, *Leviim*...Nazir 40a; Negaim 14:4
Shaving, payment for shame..Bava Kama 86a
Shaving to purify leper............Yevamos 5a; Nazir 40a-41a; Sotah 16a-16b; Negaim 14:2-4
Shaving, washing hands afterwards...Pesachim 112a

Shaveh kesef..*see* **Value corresponding to money**, page 720
Shavik hetera..................................*see* **Rebel, transgresses without benefit**, page 549
Shavkei likra dedachik..............................*see* **Answer, unsatisfactory, on verse**, page 29
Shavuos
Shavuos, bringing sacrifice later.............Rosh Hashanah 4b-5a; Chagigah 17a-18a; Moed Katan 24b
Shavuos, eulogy on day following...Chagigah 18a
Shavuos, new wine...Bava Basra 146a
Shavuos, Rav Yosef...Pesachim 68b
Shavuos, rejoicing...Pesachim 68b; Chullin 83a
Shavuos, Sadducees...Menachos 65a-66a
Shavuos, sign for the year..Bava Basra 147a

S

Shavuos to Succos, rejoicing..Pesachim 36b

Shavuos, Torah reading...Megillah 30b-31a

Shavuos, when..Rosh Hashanah 6b

Shchiv meira...*see* **Sick person on deathbed**, page 623

She'elah, *she'elos*................................*see* **Inquiries**, page 310; *see also* **Question**, page 514

She'elas Rav...*see* **Asking a *Rav*, law**, page 33

She'uvim..*see* **Water, drawn, to *mikveh*, quantity**, page 736

Sheakar avodah zarah meartzenu...Berachos 57b

Shealtiel, miracle of his conception...Sanhedrin 37b

Sheasa li nes, blessing..Berachos 54a-54b

Sheaves left for poor

Sheaves left for poor, abandoned them when they fell...................................Temurah 25a

Sheaves left for poor, ants..Peah 4:11; Chullin 134a

Sheaves left for poor, how much...Peah 4:10, 6:5

Sheaves left for poor, intermingled..............................Peah 5:1-3; Bava Metzia 105b

Sheaves left for poor, unusual way...Chullin 137a

Sheba ben Bichri, Nevat..Sanhedrin 101b

Shechalak

Shechalak michevodo...Berachos 58a

Shechalak michochmaso..Berachos 58a

Sheichar...*see* **Alcoholic beverage**, page 18

Shechem

Shechem, murderers..Makos 10a

Shechem, predestined to punishment...Sanhedrin 102a

Shechinah...*see* **Divine Presence**, page 169

Shechin..*see* **Boils**, page 71

Shechitah...*see* **Slaughtering**, page 633

Shed..*see* **Demon**, page 158

Shed, partition...Eruvin 79a-79b

Shedi nofo bassar ikaro.......................................*see* **Branches, putting down**, page 74

Sheep

Sheep, age..Parah 1:3

Sheep and loaves on Shavuos, indispensable requirement................Menachos 45b-46b

Sheep, care is difficult...Bava Metzia 69a; Bechoros 26b

Sheep, complete year...Arachin 18b-19a; Niddah 47b-48a

Sheep, dead, emits sounds...Kinin 3:6; Zevachim 68a

Sheep for *Omer* offering..Menachos 89b

Sheep for sacrifice, *hiddur*..Menachos 87a; Sotah 34b

Sheep, gestation and dropping young..Rosh Hashanah 8a

Sheep goes after sheep..Kesubos 63a

Sheep of Shavuos, waving...Menachos 46b

Sheep or goat, preference..Krisos 28a; Pesachim 57a-57b

Sheep, redeeming donkey......Chullin 74b; Bechoros 4b, 10b-12b; Yoma 49b; Bava Kama 78a; Bava Metzia 7a

Sheep, to exclude mixed species....................................Bava Kama 77b-78a; Chullin 78b

Sheep, wealth...Chullin 84a-84b

Sheep, young, sacrifice...............................Chullin 23a-23b; Menachos 91b; Parah 1:3

Sheets, excavations, to determine impurity...Niddah 61a

Shefichus damim..*see* **Murder**, page 431

Shefoferes hanod...............................*see* **Opening in *mikveh*, utensil inside another**, page 461

S

Shegagah..*see* **Inadvertent, page 305**

Shegagah milifnei hashalit................................*see* **Mistake before ruler, fatal, page 416**

Shehakol, blessing..*see* **Blessing, *Shehakol*, page 63**

Shehasimchah bimeono, *sheva berachos*................**Blessing, *Shehasimcha Bimeono*, page 65**

Shehecheyanu

  Festivals —

    Shehecheyanu, festivals................................Eruvin 40b, 47a-48a; Succah 46a

    Shehecheyanu, Rosh Hashanah................................Eruvin 40b

    Shehecheyanu, Shemini Atzeres................................Succah 47a-48a

    Shehecheyanu, succah................Succah 46a, 56a; Pesachim 7b; Menachos 42a

    Shehecheyanu, Yom Kippur................................Eruvin 40b

  Misc. —

    Shehecheyanu, binding *lulav*................................Succah 45b; Pesachim 7b

    Shehecheyanu, blessing on seeing friend................................Berachos 58b

    Shehecheyanu, on which occasion................Berachos 37b, 59b-60a; Eruvin 40b

    Shehecheyanu, redeeming son and circumcision................................Pesachim 121b

Shehiyah beShabbos................*see* **Leaving food on fire on Shabbos, page 360**

Shehiyah..*see* **Interruption, page 315**

Sheishak, treasures of Egypt................................Pesachim 87b

Sheivet..*see* **Tribe, page 703**

Sheiyah bishechitah................*see* **Interruption in slaughtering, page 315**

Shekachah Lo Beolamo................*see* **Blessing, *Shekacha Lo Beolamo*, page 64**

Shekachah Lo Beolamo, blessing................................Berachos 58b

Shekel

  Shekel in desert, three donations................................Megillah 29b

  Shekel in the Torah................Bechoros 49b-50a; Kiddushin 11a-11b; Bava Kama 36b

  Shekel, oath................Bava Metzia 57b-58a; Shekalim 2:1; Yoma 65a

  Shekel, payment for virgin................................Kesubos 38a-38b

Shelachem..*see* **Yours, page 774**

Shelamim..*see* **Peace offerings, page 477**

Sheli shelach shelach shelach................*see* **Mine is yours, yours is yours, page 411**

Sheliach tzibur..*see* **Cantor, page 87**

Shelichus yad..*see* **Using deposit, page 717**

Sheloh Asani..*see* **Blessing, *Sheloh Asani*, page 65**

Sheloh Chiser, trees................................Berachos 43b; Rosh Hashanah 11a

Sheloh kedarkah..*see* **Sodomy, page 641**

Shem

  Shem uMalchus, blessing, Name and Kingship................Berachos 12a, 40b, 49a

  Shem olam, book................................Sanhedrin 93b

Shem miShimon................*see* **Writing on Shabbos, part of word, page 765**

Shem ra................*see* **Bad reputation, not to remarry her after divorce, page 40**

Shem tov..*see* **Reputation, good, page 561**

Shem

  Shem, Ham and Japheth................................Sanhedrin 69b

  Shem, priesthood taken from him................................Nedarim 32b

  Shem, seven shepherds................................Succah 52b

  Shem son of Noah, men who encompassed history................Bava Basra 121b

S

Shema..*see also* **Decree because of concern**, page 154
  How —
    Shema and *Shemoneh Esrei*, order ....Berachos 4b
    Shema, covering eyes ....Berachos 13b
    Shema, from the Torah ....Berachos 21a
    Shema, hearing oneself..........................Berachos 13a, 15a-15b; Megillah 17b, 19b-20a; Sotah 32b
    Shema, in any language ....Berachos 13a; Megillah 17a-17b; Sotah 32b-33a
    Shema, order of paragraphs..Berachos 14b
    Shema, order of paragraphs, indispensable requirement...........Berachos 13a; Megillah 17a-17b;
                                                                                        Sotah 32b
    Shema, serving G-d ....Bava Metzia 107b
    Shema, standing..Berachos 10b-11a
    Shema, while lying on back ....Berachos 13b; Niddah 14a
  Reading —
    Shema, *Baruch Shem* ....Pesachim 56a
    Shema, concentration..Berachos 13a-13b, 16a, 33b-34a
    Shema, did not read ....Berachos 63b
    Shema, doubt about where one made a mistake ....Berachos 16a
    Shema, doubt if read ....Berachos 21a
    Shema, interrupting one's learning..Shabbos 11a
    Shema, paragraph of *tzitzis* ....Berachos 12b
    Shema, precision in reading ....Berachos 15b; Pesachim 56a
    Shema, pronunciation of "*Echad*" ....Berachos 13b
    Shema, Torah learning..Nedarim 8a; Menachos 99b
  Reward —
    Shema, exegesic sources for reward..Berachos 16b
    Shema, reward greater than for learning ....Berachos 10b
    Shema, victory during war ....Sotah 42a
  Time —
    Shema before sunrise ....Berachos 8b-9a
    Shema, midnight..Berachos 4a-4b, 8b-9a
    Shema, time to read at night ....Berachos 2b-3a
    Shema, time to read in the morning ....Berachos 10b
  Shema before sleep
    Shema before sleep, and "*beyadecha*"..Berachos 4b-5a
    Shema before sleep, and *hamapil* blessing ....Berachos 60b
    Shema before sleep, forgiveness ....Megillah 28a
    Shema before sleep, Psalms ....Shevuos 15b
  Misc. —
    Shema, burial ....Berachos 19a-19b
    Shema, greeting ....Berachos 13b-14a; Yoma 19b
    Shema, groom ....Berachos 17b
    Shema, prohibition to signal when reading ....Yoma 19b
    Shema, reading by Rebbi..Berachos 13b
    Shema Shema, silencing ....Berachos 33b; Megillah 25a
Shema veshema ....*see* **Doubt and doubt, monetary matters**, page 179
Shemaiah and Avtalyon
  Shemaiah and Avtalyon, Hillel..Yoma 35b
  Shemaiah and Avtalyon, *Kohen Gadol* ....Yoma 71b

S

Shemaiah and Avtalyon, Sennacherib..Gittin 57b

Shemaiah and Avtalyon, pairs..Chagigah 16a

Shemen hamishchah...*see* **Oil for anointing**, page 456

Shemini Atzeres

Shemini Atzeres, sacrifices...Succah 48a

Shemini Atzeres, separate festival ....Succah 47a-48a; Rosh Hashanah 4b; Yoma 2b-3a; Chagigah 17a

Shemini Atzeres, succah..Succah 46b-47a

Shemirah bebaalim...*see* **Custody with owner**, page 138

Shemitas kesafim...*see* **Cancellation of debts**, page 86

Shemittah...*see* **Sabbatical** year, page 576

Shemoneh Esrei..*see* **Prayer**, page 497

Shen ve'ayin..*see* **Tooth and eye**, page 677

Shenayim mikra ve'echad targum.....................*see* **Twice Torah, once** *Targum*, page 706

Shen...*see* **Grazing**, page 257

Shepherd

Shepherd, difficulty to repent...Bava Kama 94b

Shepherd, disqualified for testimony..Sanhedrin 25b

Shepherd of sheep..Bava Kama 79b-80a; Bava Metzia 5b; Sanhedrin 25b

Shepherd, takes lead ram when angry at flock...Bava Kama 52a

Shepherds of Israel..Succah 52b

Sheretz...*see* **Reptile**, page 561

Sheruyah...*see* **Soaked in water**, *matzah*, page 641

Shesamta chelki, *Beis hamidrash*..Berachos 28b

Shesh, significance...Yoma 71b-72a

Shesuah, significance...Chullin 60b; Niddah 24a-24b

Shetair einai bemeor Torasecha...Berachos 28b

Shetatzilenu miazei panim..Berachos 16b; Shabbos 30b

Shetikah kehodaah.........................*see* **Silence is considered as an admission**, page 626

Shetiten lanu chaim arukim..Berachos 16b

Shetuki...*see* **Child of doubtful lineage**, page 104

Shev shmatsa detreifos.......................................*see* **Seven** *treifos* laws, page 604

Shev ve'al taaseh.........................*see* **Transgressing without act, doubt**, page 699

Sheva berachos...Kesubos 7a-8a

Sheva berachos...*see* **Seven blessings**, page 603

Sheva mitzvos...*see* **Seven commandments**, page 603

Sheva, kingdom...Bava Basra 15b

Shevach...*see* **Increase in value**, page 306

Shevach eitzim bapas.............*see* **Wood, is it a component of baked bread**, page 759

Shevarim teruah..Rosh Hashanah 33b-34a

Sheves...*see* **Inhabiting world, procreation**, page 309

Sheves, *nezek*...*see* **Sick leave**, page 623

Shevet...*see* **Tribe**, page 703

Sheviis...*see* **Sabbatical year**, page 576

Shevisas Keilim...*see* **Work of utensils on Shabbos**, page 761

Shevna, Hezekiah's superintendent..Sanhedrin 26a-26b

Shevna, Hillel's brother, wished to partner with him in Torah..............................Sotah 21a

Shevor Malka...*see* **Shvor Malka**, page 622

Shevuah...*see* **Oath**, page 452

Shevuos, order of Mishnah..Shevuos 2b-3a

S

Shevuyah .... *see* **Captive woman**, page 87

Shfir, miscarriage .... Niddah 24b

Shibud .... *see* **Mortgage**, page 423

Shibuda deRav Nassan .... *see* **Collecting debt from debtor's debtor**, page 114

Shidduch on Shabbos .... Shabbos 12a

Shifchah charufah .... *see* **Maidservant, promised**, page 384

Shifrah and Puah .... Sotah 11b

Shikchah .... *see* **Forgetting**, page 235

Shikor .... *see* **Drunk**, page 182

Shila and Rav Asi, excommunication .... Niddah 36b-37a

Shiloh

    Shiloh, destruction .... Yoma 9a-9b

    Shiloh, Tabernacle .... Zevachim 118a-119b

    Shiloh, years of existence .... Zevachim 118b-119a

Shiluach hakein .... *see* **Sending away mother bird**, page 601

Shiluach machanos .... *see* **Sending out of camps**, page 601

Shimei and David, curse .... Shabbos 105a

Shimi, Amora, questions .... Taanis 9b

Shimon ben Shetah

    Shimon ben Shetah, abundance .... Taanis 23a; Chullin 119b

    Shimon ben Shetah, conspiring witness .... Makos 5b; Chagigah 16b

    Shimon ben Shetah, pairs .... Chagigah 16a

    Shimon ben Shetah, sorceresses .... Sanhedrin 45b

    Shimon ben Shetah, Yannai .... Berachos 48a; Sanhedrin 19a-19b

Shimon Hapakuli, *Shemoneh Esrei* .... Megillah 17b-18a; Berachos 28b

Shimon Hateimani, "discussed in front of Sages" .... Sanhedrin 17b

Shimon Hatzaddik

    Shimon Hatzaddik, Alexander .... Yoma 69a

    Shimon Hatzaddik, Divine voice .... Sotah 33a

    Shimon Hatzaddik, forty years .... Yoma 9a

    Shimon Hatzaddik, *nezirus* .... Nazir 4b

    Shimon Hatzaddik, old man accompanied him .... Yoma 39b; Menachos 109b

    Shimon Hatzaddik, since his death .... Yoma 39a-39b

Shimon, Azariah's brother .... Sotah 21a

Shimshon .... *see* **Samson**, page 587

Shimush chachamim .... *see* **Serving Sages**, page 603

Shin in *tefillin* .... Shabbos 28b, 62a; Menachos 35a

Shinar, Flood .... Zevachim 113b; Shabbos 113b

Shinuy .... *see* **Change**, page 95

Ship

  Monetary matters —

    Ship, instances of grievance .... Bava Metzia 79b

    Ship, items included in sale .... Bava Basra 73a, 78b

    Ship, pulling to purchase .... Bava Basra 75b-76a

    Ship, rent and loss of value .... Bava Kama 97a

    Ship, rent and wear and tear .... Bava Metzia 69b

    Ship, sank .... Bava Metzia 79a-79b

    Ship sinking, load .... Bava Kama 116b

    Ship, ways to purchase .... Bava Basra 75b-76b; Kesubos 85a

Ships, narrow passage .... Sanhedrin 32b

Prohibitions —

Ship, before Shabbos .... Shabbos 19a

Ship, impurity .... Shabbos 83b-84a

Ship, large, Shabbos .... Eruvin 90a-90b

Ship on Shabbos, pretending .... Shabbos 139b

Ship, partitions on Shabbos .... Shabbos 101a

Ship sailing, *techum* .... Eruvin 42b-43a

Ship, tent of corpse .... Shabbos 101b; Oholos 8:5

Ships, connecting to *eruv* .... Shabbos 101b

Misc. —

Ship, checking depth .... Shabbos 100b

Ship drowning, thorn .... Niddah 31a

Ship, episodes of drowning .... Yevamos 121a

Ship, *Eretz Yisrael* .... Gittin 7b-8a

Ship for sixty Sages of Athens .... Bechoros 8b-9a

Ship, Rabban Gamliel separated tithe .... Bava Metzia 11a-11b; Kiddushin 26b-27a; Maaser Sheni 5:9

Ship, star of Rabbi Yehoshua .... Horayos 10a

Ship, whisper .... Pesachim 112b

Shipurei and tavra, excommunication .... Moed Katan 17b

Shipuy kova .... *see* **Ring, large, slaughtering,** page 569

Shir

Shir Hamaalos, parallel to .... Succah 53a-53b

Shir Hashirim, holiness .... Yadayim 3:5

Shir Hashirim, impurity to hands .... Megillah 7a; Yadayim 3:5

Shir shel Yom .... Rosh Hashanah 30b-31a; Tamid 7:4

Shir HaShirim .... *see* **Song of Songs,** page 645

Shirt, only one, poverty .... Beitzah 32b

Shittim

Shittim, Moabite women .... Sanhedrin 106a; Bechoros 5b

Shittim wood standing .... Yoma 72a; Succah 45b

Shittin .... *see* **Subterranean holes,** page 660

Shituf .... *see* **Eruv partnership,** page 199

Shiur .... *see* **Quantity,** page 513; *see also* **Size,** page 631; **Volume,** page 725; **Measure,** page 398

Shiur letalmidim .... *see* **Discourse,** page 166

Shiva Asar B'Tammuz .... Rosh Hashanah 18b; Taanis 28b

Shiva Asar B'Tammuz .... *see* **Seventeenth of *Tammuz*,** page 604

Shivah nekiim .... *see* **Seven days of purity,** page 604

Shiviti Hashem lenegdi .... *see* **I have set G-d before me always,** page 291

Shiyarei dam .... *see* **Remainder of sacrificial blood,** page 556

Shiyarei lishkah .... *see* **Remainder of Temple funds,** page 556

Shiyarei mitzvah .... *see* **Accessories for commandment,** page 5

Shlamim .... *see* **Peace offerings,** page 477

Shlemah .... *see* **Whole food, blessing,** page 742

Shlichus yad .... *see* **Using deposit,** page 717

Shlomo .... *see* **Solomon,** page 642

Shlulis, explanation .... Bava Kama 61a

S

Shmuel (Amora)
  His life —
    Shmuel, blows from his schoolteacher .... Chullin 107b
    Shmuel, his daughters' captivity .... Kesubos 23a
    Shmuel, punishment for belittling him .... Berachos 19a
    Shmuel, ruler's mistake .... Moed Katan 18a
    Shmuel, woman humiliated him .... Nedarim 50b
  Praises —
    Shmuel, Arioch .... Shabbos 53a
    Shmuel, *shakud* .... Kesubos 43b
    Shmuel, Shvor Malka .... Bava Basra 115b; Pesachim 54a
    Shmuel, wisdom .... Berachos 58b; Shabbos 113b
  Rav —
    Shmuel and Rav, excommunication .... Yevamos 121a
    Shmuel, curse from Rav .... Shabbos 108a; Bava Kama 80b
    Shmuel honored Sage at the door .... Bava Kama 80a-80b
    Shmuel rent his garment at Rav's death .... Moed Katan 24a
    Shmuel saved Rav from snake bite .... Chullin 59a
  Ruling —
    Shmuel, "our teachers of Babylon" .... Sanhedrin 17b; Shevuos 47a
    Shmuel, examined stillborn .... Niddah 25b
    Shmuel, cure and *semichah* .... Bava Metzia 85b
    Shmuel, Elijah's ruling .... Kiddushin 72b
    Shmuel, reversed opinion .... Pesachim 27a; Kiddushin 44b
    Shmuel, law .... Shabbos 22a, 40a; Eruvin 90b; Pesachim 101a; Menachos 41b; Bechoros 49b
    Shmuel, leg on a wall .... Kiddushin 70b
    Shmuel, Rav of city .... Bava Basra 153a; Eruvin 94a; Chullin 53b
    Shmuel, reproving look .... Niddah 26b
  Misc. —
    Shmuel, Adam's Book .... Bava Metzia 85b-86a
    Shmuel, barley to Rabbi Elazar .... Kesubos 77a
    Shmuel, Bei Avidan .... Shabbos 116a
    Shmuel, curse to Karna .... Bava Basra 89a
    Shmuel, dance .... Succah 53a
    Shmuel, familiarity .... Kesubos 105b
    Shmuel, episode about partition taken away .... Eruvin 74a-74b
    Shmuel gave food to taste to disciple .... Kesubos 61a
    Shmuel, inquiry to his deceased father .... Berachos 18b
    Shmuel, Mar Ukva .... Moed Katan 16b
    Shmuel ordered to uproot disturbing trees .... Bava Kama 92a
    Shmuel, Rabbi Yochanan .... Chullin 95b
Shmuel Hakatan
  Shmuel Hakatan, fit for Divine Presence .... Sanhedrin 11a
  Shmuel Hakatan, heretics .... Berachos 28b-29a
  Shmuel Hakatan, prophecy .... Sanhedrin 11a
Shmuel Hanavi .... *see* **Samuel**, page 587
Shmuel's father
  Shmuel's father, deposit .... Berachos 18b
  Shmuel's father, Divine Presence in synagogue .... Megillah 29a

S

Shnaim Mikra VeEchad Targum .... Berachos 8a-8b
Shnei kesuvim ke'echad .... *see* **Two verses teaching identical law**, page 709
Shnei shevilei .... *see* **Two paths, impurity**, page 707
Shni tolaas .... *see* **Crimson wool**, page 133
Shnios le'arayos .... *see* **Secondary category of forbidden relations**, page 596
Shochet bachutz .... *see* **Slaughtering outside Temple, prohibition**, page 636
Shoe
  Impurity —
    Shoe, from *neveilah* skin .... Chullin 94a
    Shoe, impurity .... Shabbos 112a-112b; Keilim 26:4
    Shoe, like impurity of *zav's* couch .... Shabbos 66a
  Prohibitions —
    Shoe in Temple .... Shabbos 66b; Chagigah 4b
    Shoe, mourner .... Moed Katan 15b, 20b
    Shoe on communal fast days .... Taanis 12b
    Shoe, Yom Kippur .... Yoma 78a-78b
  Shabbos —
    Shoe .... *see also* **Sandal**, page 588
    Shoe, going out on Shabbos .... Shabbos 60b-61a, 66a, 141b
    Shoe in river, Shabbos .... Yoma 78a
    Shoe on mold, *muktzeh* .... Shabbos 141b
    Shoe, scraping off mud .... Shabbos 141a-141b
    Shoe, tanning with oil .... Shabbos 141b
    Shoe, torn, *muktzeh* .... Shabbos 112a
    Shoes he has but clothes he has not .... Kesubos 65b; Sotah 8b
  Misc. —
    Shoe, behavior .... Shabbos 61a, 129a; Pesachim 112a, 113b; Bava Basra 58a
    Shoe for *chalitzah* .... Shabbos 66a, 112a-112b; Yevamos 102a-104a; Kiddushin 14a
    Shoe, priestly blessing .... Sotah 40a; Rosh Hashanah 31b
    Shoe, sleeping with shoes on .... Yoma 78b
    Shoe, too big .... Kiddushin 49a
    Shoes for prostitutes, episode .... Pesachim 113b
    Shoes, mourning for Temple destruction .... Bava Kama 59b
    Shoes of Sages, dog .... Moed Katan 17a
    Shoes, order of putting on .... Shabbos 61a
    Shoes, patched, barefoot .... Yoma 77a
    Shoes, patched, Sage .... Berachos 43b; Shabbos 114a
Shoelace, religious persecution .... Sanhedrin 74b
Shoel .... *see* **Borrower**, page 73
Shofar
  Shofar .... *see also* **Blowing *shofar***, page 68
  Shofar, called trumpets .... Shabbos 36a; Succah 34a
  Shofar, *muktzeh* .... Shabbos 35b-36a
  Shofar of Jubilee .... Rosh Hashanah 9b
  Shofar, gold plated, temple .... Rosh Hashanah 27a
  Shofar, shapes .... Rosh Hashanah 26b
  Shofar, unfit .... Rosh Hashanah 27a-27b
  Shofar, women .... Eruvin 96b

S

Shofaros, consecrated, in Temple .... Menachos 104a, 107b-108a; Yoma 55a-55b; Shekalim 6:5;
.... Temurah 23b

Shofaros for consecrated money of bird sacrifices .... Pesachim 90b

Shofar on Rosh Hashanah
   Shofar on Rosh Hashanah, gold coated .... Rosh Hashanah 27a
   Shofar on Rosh Hashanah, polishing .... Rosh Hashanah 33a
   Shofar on Rosh Hashanah, unfit .... Rosh Hashanah 28a
   Shofar on Rosh Hashanah, vow not to use .... Rosh Hashanah 28a
   Shofar on Rosh Hashanah, which animal .... Rosh Hashanah 26a

Shofaros hekdesh baMikdash .... *see* **Boxes, consecrated, in Temple**, page 74
Shofet, shoftim .... *see* **Judge**, page 327
Shoftim, who wrote .... Bava Basra 14b
Shogeg .... *see* **Inadvertent**, page 305
Shoham stones .... Sotah 36a-36b

Shok
   Shok, definition .... Chullin 45b
   Shok vehealeha, significance .... Avodah Zarah 25a

Sholchin, fields .... Bava Basra 68a-68b
Shomer .... *see* **Custodian**, page 136; *see also* **Guardian**, page 260
Shomer letumah .... *see* **Protection concerning impurity**, page 508
Shomeres yom .... *see* **Zavah of one day**, page 775

Shomron
   Shomron and Babylon, cursed .... Berachos 58a
   Shomron, Omri .... Sanhedrin 102b

Shoneh halachos .... *see* **Learning laws**, page 358
Shor haniskal .... *see* **Ox to be stoned**, page 469
Shor muad .... *see* **Ox goring regularly**, page 469
Shor tam .... *see* **Ox goring occasionally**, page 468

Short
   Short and long way .... Eruvin 53b
   Short *Shemoneh Esrei* .... Berachos 29a
   Short way, teaching .... Pesachim 3b; Chullin 63b

Shortcoming in yourself .... Bava Kama 92b

Shortcut
   Shortcut, synagogue .... Berachos 62b-63a
   Shortcut, Temple .... Berachos 62b; Megillah 29a

Short-tempered man, his life is no life .... Pesachim 113b
Shot like arrow, semen .... Niddah 43a
Shoteh .... *see* **Demented**, page 232

Shoulder
   Shoulder cooked, *Koheness* .... Zevachim 55a
   Shoulder cooked, sacrifice for *nazir* .... Chullin 98a-99a

Shoulder, cheek and stomach
   Shoulder, cheek and stomach, Abbaye .... Chullin 133a
   Shoulder, cheek and stomach, condition to keep priestly gifts .... Chullin 133b-134a
   Shoulder, cheek and stomach, consecrating its value .... Temurah 10b
   Shoulder, cheek and stomach, crossed animal .... Chullin 79b-80a, 132a; Bikurim 2:10
   Shoulder, cheek and stomach, doubt .... Chullin 132a; Bechoros 18a-18b
   Shoulder, cheek and stomach, eating .... Chullin 132b

S

Shoulder, cheek and stomach, firstborn..Chullin 132a-132b
Shoulder, cheek and stomach, for *Koheness*..Chullin 131b-132a
Shoulder, cheek and stomach, *Kohen*..Chullin 132b
Shoulder, cheek and stomach, law concerning butcher.............................Chullin 132b
Shoulder, cheek and stomach, *Levi*..Chullin 131a-131b
Shoulder, cheek and stomach, non-Jewish partner......................................Chullin 133a-133b
Shoulder, cheek and stomach, sacrifices..Chullin 130a
Shoulder, cheek and stomach, what is included...Chullin 134b

Shovach, general of Amon, strength...Sotah 42b

Shover...*see* **Receipt**, page 550

Showbread
Showbread, David..Menachos 95b-96a
Showbread, dimensions and height..Menachos 87b, 96a-96b
Showbread, distribution to *Kohanim*...Pesachim 3b
Showbread, division...Succah 56a-56b; Yoma 17b-18a
Showbread, episode of larceny...Kiddushin 53a
Showbread, Garmu family...Yoma 38a
Showbread, journey of Tabernacle...Menachos 95a
Showbread, molds...Menachos 94a
Showbread, place to prepare...Menachos 63a, 95b-96a
Showbread, positioning...Menachos 97a, 99b
Showbread, preparation...Menachos 94a
Showbread, rendered invalid..Menachos 12b
Showbread, Shabbos...Menachos 95b, 97a
Showbread, shape...Menachos 94a-95a
Showbread, two piles...Menachos 98a
Showbread, warm..Menachos 96b

Showing
Showing coin to money-changer..Bava Kama 99b
Showing place to agent.............................Gittin 65a-65b; Kiddushin 48b-49a; Bava Basra 76b, 165a
Showing the truth, ways to acquire Torah...Avos 6:6

Shrouds
Shrouds of linen..Moed Katan 27b; Kesubos 8b
Shrouds of skin...Sotah 14a
Shrouds, profit..Yevamos 66b
Shrouds, red, Rabbi Yannai....................................Shabbos 114a; Niddah 20a
Shrouds, *shatnez*.....................................Niddah 61b; Pesachim 40b; Avodah Zarah 65b
Shrouds, *tzitzis*..Menachos 41a

Shtar......................................*see* **Legal document**, page 361; *see also* **Promissory note**, page 505

Sh'tei Halechem.......................................*see* **Two loaves of *Shavuos***, page 708

Shuda Dedayna...*see* ***Beis din***, free decision, page 50

Shumah...*see* **Estimate**, page 201

Shunamite woman, Elisha..Berachos 10b

Shushan
Shushan, cubit measures.........................Menachos 98a; Pesachim 86a; Bechoros 39b-40a; Keilim 17:9
Shushan, Temple gate..Menachos 98a; Middos 1:3

Shushan Purim...Megillah 2b, 3b-4a, 5b

Shushbin...*see* **Usher**, page 717

Shutafim..*see* **Partner**, page 473

S

Shutters, opening on Yom Tov .... Beitzah 11b-12a
Shvor Malka
Shvor Malka, destruction of Mezigas Kisri .... Moed Katan 26a
Shvor Malka, dream .... Berachos 56a
Shvor Malka, knife for *esrog* .... Avodah Zarah 76b
Shvor Malka, Persia .... Shevuos 6b
Shvor Malka, rain .... Taanis 24b
Shvor Malka, Shmuel .... Bava Basra 115b; Pesachim 54a
Shvus .... *see* **Rabbinical prohibition for Shabbos**, page 533
Shy
Shy person does not learn .... Avos 2:5
Shy, Israel .... Yevamos 79a
Sichah .... *see* **Anointing**, page 28
Sick
  Aggadah —
    Sick, abjuring suffering .... Avodah Zarah 55a
    Sick, *aggadah* .... Nedarim 41a; Sanhedrin 101a
    Sick, atonement .... Kesubos 111a
    Sick, Divine Judgment .... Shabbos 32a
    Sick, Divine Presence .... Nedarim 40a; Shabbos 12b
    Sick, prayer received .... Rosh Hashanah 16a, 18a
  Episodes —
    Sick, Achadvoi's mother .... Bava Basra 9b
    Sick because of desire for woman .... Sanhedrin 75a
    Sick, Rabbi Chanina .... Berachos 34b
    Sick, soul returning to body .... Bava Basra 10b; Pesachim 50a
  Laws —
    Sick .... *see also* **Visiting the sick**, page 725
    Sick and mourner, not to tell him: sit down! .... Moed Katan 27b
    Sick, *chazakah* for gift .... Kiddushin 79b
    Sick, eating forbidden food .... Yoma 83a-83b, 84b
    Sick, exempt from standing .... Moed Katan 27b
    Sick, forbidden to benefit .... Nedarim 38b-39b
    Sick, sacrifice .... Bechoros 41a; Temurah 28b
    Sick, visiting .... Nedarim 39b-40a, 41a-41b
  Medicine —
    Sick .... *see also* **Medicine**, page 622
    Sick, avoiding too many drugs .... Pesachim 113a
    Sick, blessing from Sage .... Bava Basra 116a; Taanis 8a
    Sick, fever nourishes him .... Sanhedrin 108b
    Sick, harmful things .... Berachos 57b; Nedarim 49a; Avodah Zarah 28b-29a
    Sick, making his sickness known .... Berachos 55b; Nedarim 40a
    Sick, praying for one's fellow .... Berachos 12b
    Sick, text of prayer .... Shabbos 12a-12b
  Times —
    Sick, extinguishing lamp .... Shabbos 29b-30b
    Sick, *muktzeh* permitted .... Chullin 15b
    Sick on Yom Tov .... Beitzah 22a
    Sick, succah .... Succah 25b

S

Sick, *Yom Kippur* .... Yoma 83a
Misc. —
Sick, majority of them survive .... Gittin 28a; Kiddushin 71b; Bava Basra 153b
Sick, news of death .... Moed Katan 26b
Sick, watching .... Berachos 54b
Sick leave
Sick leave, estimate .... Bava Kama 85b, 91a
Sick leave for slave, payment .... Bava Kama 85b-86a
Sick leave, infected wound .... Bava Kama 85a
Sick person on deathbed
Acquisition —
Sick person on deathbed, act of acquisition .... Kesubos 55b-56a;
.... Bava Basra 152a-153a, 156a-156b; Gittin 14b-15a
Sick person on deathbed, bequeathed partial gift .... Bava Basra 146b, 151b
Sick person on deathbed, *chazakah* .... Bava Basra 153a-153b; Kiddushin 79b
Sick person on deathbed ordered: "give" .... Gittin 13a-13b, 65b-66a
Sick person on deathbed, partial gift .... Bava Basra 149b, 150b; Peah 3:7
Sick person on deathbed, Rabbinical Decree .... Bava Basra 147b
Sick person on deathbed who acknowledged debt .... Bava Basra 174b-175a
Divorce certificate —
Sick person on deathbed, divorce certificate .... Gittin 73b-74a, 75b
Sick person on deathbed, divorce certificate on Shabbos .... Gittin 77b
Sick person on deathbed who recovered, divorce certificate .... Gittin 72b-73a
Sick person on deathbed, text of divorce certificate .... Gittin 72a, 74b; Kesubos 2b;
.... Kiddushin 59b, 60a; Bava Basra 136a, 137a
In which matter —
Sick person on deathbed at time of bequest, dividing up his property ...... Bava Basra 148b
Sick person on deathbed, bequest of intangible benefit .... Bava Basra 147b-148a
Sick person on deathbed, bequest of undetermined coin .... Gittin 13a-13b
Sick person on deathbed, consecrated item .... Bava Basra 148b
Retracting —
Sick person on deathbed, freeing slave .... Gittin 8b-9a, 40a; Peah 3:8; Bava Basra 149b-150a
Sick person on deathbed, other sickness .... Gittin 73a
Sick person on deathbed, recovered .... Kesubos 55b
Sick person on deathbed, retracting from bequest .... Bava Basra 148b, 151a-153a
Sick person on deathbed, sale .... Bava Basra 149a
Misc. —
Sick person on deathbed, alimony .... Bava Basra 133a
Sick person on deathbed, doubt .... Bava Basra 153a-153b
Sick person on deathbed, episodes .... Bava Basra 151a-151b
Sick person on deathbed, when his gift is effective .... Bava Basra 137a
Sickness
Sickness because of intimate relations .... Pesachim 112b; Gittin 70a; Kesubos 77b; Niddah 17a
Sickness, causes .... Shabbos 33a-33b; Gittin 70a-70b; Bava Metzia 107b, 113b; Bechoros 44b
Sickness coming from drunkenness .... Gittin 67b
Sickness, duration, sign of dead person .... Moed Katan 28a
Sickness of feet .... Sotah 10a; Sanhedrin 48b
Sickness, since Jacob .... Bava Metzia 87a; Sanhedrin 107b
Sickness, which is the most painful .... Shabbos 11a

S

Sickness, *yerakon* .... Bechoros 44b

Sickness, intestinal

Sickness, intestinal .... Berachos 55a; Shabbos 81a

Sickness, intestinal, cure .... Shabbos 110a

Sickness, intestinal, excrements .... Pesachim 118a; Sotah 42b

Sickness, intestinal, righteous .... Shabbos 118b; Kesubos 103b

Sickness, intestinal, sudden death .... Eruvin 41b

Sickness, intestinal, suffering .... Eruvin 41b

Sickness, intestinal, very painful .... Shabbos 11a

Siddur .... *see* **Seizure**, page 598

Siddur hamizbeach .... *see* **Positioning Altar**, page 495

Side

Side alleys of public domain, act of acquisition .... Bava Metzia 10b

Side alleys of public domain, Shabbos .... Eruvin 94a; Shabbos 6a; Kesubos 31b

Side of utensils, impurity .... Keilim 2:2; Chullin 54b-55a

Sides like front .... Sotah 38b-39a

Sides of animal, *muktzeh* .... Shabbos 154b-155a; Chagigah 16b-17a

Sideburns .... *see* **Corners of head**, page 129

Sidewalk, damages of animal .... Bava Kama 21a-21b

Sifra and Sifri, author .... Sanhedrin 86a; Shabbos 137a; Eruvin 96b; Yoma 41a; Kiddushin 53a;
Shevuos 13a; Bechoros 61a; Krisos 22a

Sifting

Sifting on Yom Tov .... Beitzah 29b

Sifting semolina (wheat) for meal offerings .... Menachos 76b

Sifting, work in itself .... Shabbos 73b

Sigh

Sigh about destruction, episode .... Kesubos 62a

Sigh, body-breaking .... Kesubos 62a; Berachos 58b

Sign

Food —

Signs of animal and wild animal .... Chullin 59a-59b

Signs of birds .... Chullin 61a-63b, 65a

Signs of fish .... Avodah Zarah 39a-40b; Chullin 63b-64a, 66a-66b; Niddah 51b

Signs of fish eggs .... Chullin 63b-64a

Signs of grasshoppers .... Avodah Zarah 37a-37b; Chullin 65a-66a

Signs of twitching, animal in danger .... Avodah Zarah 16b; Chullin 37a, 37b-38b

Gesture —

Sign, divorce by mute person .... Gittin 59a

Sign, purchase by deaf .... Gittin 59a

Sign when reading *Shema* .... Yoma 19b

Signs of hands instead of speech, Rabbi Yehoshua .... Chagigah 5b

Signs of Rachel to Leah .... Bava Basra 123a; Megillah 13b

Lost item —

Sign .... *see also* **Mark**, page 390

Signs, is it from the Torah .... Bava Metzia 18b, 27a-28a; Yevamos 120a-120b; Gittin 27b

Signs of closed utensil .... Bava Metzia 25a

Signs of lost item .... Bava Metzia 22b-23b, 24a

Signs of lost item, on utensil .... Maaser Sheni 4:9-11; Bava Metzia 25a

Signs of lost item, place .... Bava Metzia 22b-23b, 25b-26a

Signs of lost item, two pretender..Bava Metzia 28a
Signs to return contract – promissory note ....Bava Metzia 20a-20b
   Women —
Signs of dead for permitting *agunah* ....Yevamos 120a-120b; Bava Metzia 27b; Bechoros 46b
Signs of puberty, women...Niddah 47a-49a
Signs of virgin's wedding ....Kesubos 16b
   Misc. —
Sign for year, Rosh Hashanah and Shavuos...Bava Basra 147a
Sign, hole near letter ....Gittin 27b-28a
Sign is significant...Horayos 12a; Krisos 6a
Sign of property on wall...Bava Basra 4a-4b
Sign on Jerusalem righteous' forehead..Shabbos 55a
Signs and references to remember Torah.....................................Eruvin 53a, 54b; Shabbos 104a
Signs, Cities of Refuge ....Makos 10a-10b
Signs for valleys etc...Pesachim 53a
Signs of leprous marks ....Negaim 3:3-8, 4:1-7, 4:1-11, 5:2
Signs of puberty, deceased person...Bava Basra 154a
Signs of sterility.......................................Yevamos 79b-80b, 97a; Niddah 47b; Bava Basra 155b
Signs, signatures of Sages ....Gittin 36a, 87b; Bava Basra 161b
  Sign of blessing
Sign of blessing, benefitting Sage..Sanhedrin 92a
Sign of blessing, cases where there is no ....Pesachim 50b
Sign of blessing in one's learning, years...Chullin 24a
Sign of blessing, in which matters..Pesachim 50b
Sign of blessing, no benefit from selling daughter.................................Megillah 27a
Sign of blessing, earnings of wife...Pesachim 50b
Signature
Signature after dash...Bava Basra 163a
Signature, blank space invalidating..Bava Basra 162b-163a
Signature, episodes about forging..Bava Basra 167a
Signature of invalid witnesses with valid ones ....Bava Basra 162b; Gittin 18b, 87b
Signature on blank paper..Bava Basra 167a; Kesubos 21a
Signature on corrections...Bava Basra 161b
Signature on divorce certificate.....................................Gittin 9b-11b, 18b-19a, 36a, 86b-88a
Signature, proof that sale of field was fictitious...................Kesubos 109a-109b; Bava Basra 30b
Signature, who will sign with him...Sanhedrin 23a
Signatures of Sages, sign......................................Gittin 36a, 87b; Bava Basra 161b
Signatures, two, *beis din*..Sanhedrin 30a
Signed
Signed at night ....Gittin 18a-18b
Signed, not signed by Mar berei DeRavina..Yevamos 22a
Sihon, Og's brother...Niddah 61a; Rosh Hashanah 2b-3a
***Sikra* thread**
Sikra thread, Altar.............................Zevachim 53a; Menachos 97b; Bechoros 17b; Middos 3:1
Sikra thread, sprinklings...Zevachim 10b
Silence
Silence, "your silence is preferable to your words" ....Yevamos 65a; Gittin 46b
Silence after receiving *kiddushin* ....Kiddushin 12b-13a
Silence, comforting the bereaved ....Berachos 6b

S

Silence during suffering .... Berachos 61a
Silence, good for Sages .... Pesachim 99a
Silence in front of insults, reward .... Chullin 89a
Silence is considered as an admission, prohibitions .... Kiddushin 65b-66b
Silence is considered as an admission, seizing .... Bava Metzia 6a-6b
Silence, *kosher* lineage .... Kiddushin 71b
Silence of Aaron .... Zevachim 115b
Silence then outcry, seizing objects .... Bava Metzia 6a-6b
Silence to annoy wife, permitting vows .... Nedarim 78b-79a
Silence, virtue .... Avos 1:15, 1:17, 3:13

Silence him .... Berachos 33b; Megillah 25a

Silent
Silent, Aaron's reward .... Zevachim 115b
Silent prayer, source .... Berachos 31a

Siloah, fountain of Temple .... Arachin 10b

Silsul, significance .... Rosh Hashanah 26b; Megillah 18a; Nazir 3a

Silver which turned out to be gold, custodian .... Bava Kama 62a

Siman .... see **Omen**, page 459; see also **Mark**, page 390, **Sign**, page 624

Siman le'acher .... see **Proofs to show that sale is false**, page 626

Simanim shenidaldelu .... see **Windpipe and gullet**, page 749

Simchah and Sason, episode .... Succah 48b

Simchah .... see **Sacrifice of rejoicing**, page 582

Simchas
Simchas beis hashoevah .... Succah 50a-51b, 52b-53a
Simchas Torah, three years .... Megillah 29b

Simfon .... see **Blemish**, page 61

Similar
Similar, *mussaf* sacrifice sheep .... Yoma 62b
Similar words .... see **Gezeirah shavah**, page 249

Similarities
Similarities, deducting money from prohibition .... Kiddushin 3b; Kesubos 40b, 46b
Similarities, deducting prohibition from impurity .... Yevamos 103b
Similarities, primary categories of damage .... Bava Kama 5a-6a
Similarities, refuting .... Chullin 115b-116a; Shevuos 9b
Similarities, secondary categories of damages .... Bava Kama 6a-6b
Similarities, two different stringencies .... Sotah 29b; Makos 4b, 4b; Pesachim 77a; Kesubos 32a

Simmering improves dish .... Shabbos 37b-38a

Simultaneous acts which cannot be done successively .... Eruvin 50a; Kiddushin 50b-51a;
Nedarim 69b

Sin
Sin and G-d will forgive .... Chagigah 16a
Sin, "I shall sin and I shall repent" .... Yoma 87a
Sin of Adam .... Berachos 40a; Sanhedrin 70a-70b
Sin of golden calf .... see **Golden calf**, page 254
Sin, transgression and offense, text .... Yoma 36b, 41b
Sin, unwilling .... Yoma 36b
Sinned, if they had not sinned, Holy Writings .... Nedarim 22b
Sins like scarlet .... Shabbos 89b
Sins, unintentional as intentional .... Chagigah 5a

Sin offering
Disqualified —
Sin offering, after one year..Temurah 22a

Sin offering consecrated in case of loss...Zevachim 112a

Sin offering, disqualifying thought...Zevachim 7b-8b, 10b

Sin offering, in place of lost one...Zevachim 112a; Menachos 80b

Sin offering, offered for another transgression...Zevachim 7a, 9b

Sin offering, owner died...Horayos 6a

Sin offering, owner offered atonement sacrifice.............Meilah 7a-7b; Bechoros 33a; Temurah 24a

Sin offering slaughtered for secular purpose...Zevachim 3a-3b, 46b

Sin offering, stolen, decree...Gittin 55a-55b

Sin offerings, waiting to become blemished........Pesachim 97a-97b; Temurah 22a; Meilah 10b-11a

Sin offerings, waiting to become blemished, source....................Bechoros 16a; Temurah 16a-16b

Numerous —
Sin offerings, according to number of lapses....................Makos 14a; Chullin 82b-83a; Krisos 12b

Sin offerings, numerous acts...Makos 14a-14b

Sin offerings, numerous illicit relations...Krisos 15a

Sin offerings, one eating...Shevuos 24b-25a; Krisos 13b-15a

Sin offerings, separate bodies...Krisos 2b, 15a

Sin offerings, separate names...Krisos 2b-3a

Sin offerings, two *kezayis*...................................Chullin 82b-83a; Shabbos 93b-94a; Nazir 42a; Kiddushin 77b;
....Makos 21a; Krisos 12b

Sin offerings, two prohibitions..Krisos 3a; Makos 14b

Requirement —
Sin offering, because of speech...Krisos 3b-4a; Sanhedrin 65a-65b

Sin offering, community exempt..Horayos 2b

Sin offering, for which sin...Horayos 9a-9b

Sin offering, ruling exempt from sin offering....................Yevamos 87b, 92a; Horayos 2a-4b

Sin offering, sin because of ignorance...............Shevuos 26b; Shabbos 69a; Yoma 80a; Horayos 2a, 11a;
....Chullin 5b

Sin offerings for sins punished by excising of soul, source............Yevamos 8b-9a; Horayos 8a;
....Shabbos 68b-69a

Shabbos —
Sin offerings, forgetting Shabbos and labors............................Sanhedrin 62a; Shabbos 70b-71a;
....Shevuos 19a, 26a; Krisos 3a

Sin offerings, harvesting and planting together.........................Shabbos 73b; Moed Katan 2b

Sin offerings, primary and secondary category of labors...................Krisos 16a-16b;
....Shabbos 68a, 75b, 96b, 97b; Bava Kama 2a

Sin offerings, several works accomplished on Shabbos........Shabbos 6b, 69a, 70b, 73a-73b, 96b;
....Krisos 2b

Sin offerings, Shabbos prohibitions..Sanhedrin 62b; Beitzah 34a

Sin offerings, transgressing several secondary category works.....Krisos 16a-16b; Shabbos 68a, 96b;
....Bava Kama 2a

Sin offerings, transgressions over several Shabbosos...Krisos 16a-17a

Temple service —
Sin offering, libations...Sotah 15a

Sin offering, place of sprinklings...Zevachim 10b, 52b-53a

Sin offering, wording of consecration..Nedarim 6a

Sin offerings, stringencies...Zevachim 94b

S

Various kinds —

Sin offering for *Kohen Gadol* .... *see* **Bull for *Kohen Gadol***, page 79

Sin offering for *Nasi* .... *see* **Nasi**, page 437

Sin offering of *nazir*, money .... Nazir 24b-26a; Menachos 4b; Meilah 11a

Sin offerings for idolatry, how many .... Sanhedrin 62a; Shabbos 72b

Sin offerings of Babylon emigrants, entirely burned .... Horayos 6a; Temurah 15b

Sin offerings, when anointing *Leviim* .... Horayos 5b

Misc. —

Sin offering, money, after owners' atonement .... Temurah 23b-24a

Sin offering of community, transgression by community .... Horayos 3a, 5b

Sin offering, preventing shame .... Sotah 32b

Sin offering, source showing that better to avoid .... Chagigah 7a

Sin offerings which must die

Sin offerings which must die .... Pesachim 97a-97b; Temurah 21b-22a; Meilah 10b-11a

Sin offerings which must die, personal use ..... Temurah 21b-22a; Meilah 3a, 10b-11a; Arachin 5b

Sin offerings which must die, public .... Horayos 6b; Temurah 15a-15b, 16a-16b; Yoma 50a

Sin offerings which must die, source .... Bechoros 16a; Temurah 16a-16b

Sin offerings inside *Heichal*

Sin offerings inside *Heichal*, disqualified .... Zevachim 82a; Pesachim 83a

Sin offerings inside *Heichal*, how were they burned .... Pesachim 75a-75b; Yoma 67b-68a;
.... Zevachim 50a

Sin offerings inside *Heichal*, impurity .... Yoma 68a-68b; Zevachim 104b-106a

Sin offerings inside *Heichal,* impurity of man burning them .... Zevachim 83a

Sin offerings inside *Heichal*, parts of sacrifices .... Zevachim 41a-41b

Sin offerings inside *Heichal*, place .... Zevachim 47a-47b

Sin offerings inside *Heichal*, sprinklings .... Yoma 57a, 58b; Zevachim 40a

Sin offerings inside *Heichal,* taking out and cutting up ..... Yoma 67b-68a; Zevachim 50a-50b

Sin offerings inside *Heichal*, thought .... Zevachim 13b-14a, 44a-45a

Sin offerings inside *Heichal*, where were they burned .... Zevachim 104a-104b, 105b-106a

Sin offering, lost

Sin offering, lost, blood .... Temurah 22b

Sin offering, lost, found .... Temurah 15a, 22b-24a

Sin offering, lost, law .... Pesachim 97a-97b

Sin offering, lost, owner already received atonement .... Temurah 22a

Sin offering of bird

Sin offering and bird burnt offering, substituted by mistake ..... Zevachim 66a-66b, 67b-68a;
.... Kinin 3:3

Sin offering of bird, decapitated .... Zevachim 65b-66a, 66b; Chullin 21b

Sin offering of bird, did not sin .... Temurah 34a

Sin offering of bird, eating .... Zevachim 44b

Sin offerings of bird, doubt ..... Nazir 29a-29b; Krisos 8a-8b, 22b, 26b; Bava Basra 166a; Taharos 4:13

Sinai

"Sinai" and "uproots mountains," preference .... Horayos 14a

Sinai, humility .... Megillah 29a

Sinai, laws taught at .... Chagigah 6a-6b; Sotah 37b; Zevachim 115b

Sinai, names .... Shabbos 89a-89b

Sinai, Rav Yosef .... Berachos 64a; Horayos 14a; Moed Katan 12a

Sinas chinam .... *see* **Baseless hatred**, page 43

Since
Since Sage's death etc., harm..Sotah 49b
Since Yose ben Yoezer's death…..Temurah 15b-16a
Since Temple destruction
Since Temple destruction, counsel was taken away.....................Megillah 12b
Since Temple destruction, curse...Sotah 49a
Since Temple destruction, exemption from prayer......................Eruvin 65a
Since Temple destruction, generations decline........................Sotah 48b-49b
Since Temple destruction, houses of righteous........................Berachos 58b
Since Temple destruction, prophecy.....................................Bava Basra 12b
Since Temple destruction, rain..................Bava Basra 25b; Taanis 19b
Since Temple destruction, roads were ruined......................Rosh Hashanah 23b
Since Temple destruction, *shamir* worm disappeared..................Sotah 48b
Since Temple destruction, sky in its pureness.........................Berachos 59a
Since Temple destruction, taste of fruit...................................Sotah 49a
Since Temple destruction, pleasure of intimate relations............Sanhedrin 75a
Sinews, Pesach lamb........................Pesachim 83b, 84a; Chullin 76b-77a
Singer levite who kept gate, death penalty................................Arachin 11b
Single witness
Forbidden relations —
Single witness, about forbidden relations............Yevamos 87b-88a; Gittin 2b, 90a
Single witness, *agunah*...............Yevamos 87b-88a, 115a, 122a; Bechoros 46b
Single witness, episode about lashes....................................Pesachim 113b
Single witness, *kiddushin*...Kiddushin 65a-65b
Prohibitions —
Single witness, for clearly forbidden thing...............Yevamos 88a; Gittin 2b
Single witness, loses his wages...Gittin 54b-55a
Single witness, oath.................................Kesubos 87b; Shevuos 40a
Single witness, thing he is able to do.............Yevamos 88a; Gittin 54b; Bava Basra 134b
Single witness, owner keeps silent.............Yevamos 87b-88a; Kiddushin 65b-66b
Single witness, second tithe..Sanhedrin 30a
Single witness, trustworthiness if in his power...........................Gittin 54b
Misc. —
Single witness concerning sinner, hating him.......................Pesachim 113b
Single witness, calf whose neck is broken.............................Sotah 47a-47b
Single witness for *kesubah*, oath.......................................Kesubos 87b-88a
Single witness, trustworthy to judge.....Kesubos 85a; Yevamos 101b; Kiddushin 66a; Bava Basra 52a
Sinner
Sinner..*see also* **Wicked**, page 743
Sinner, spirit of folly...Sotah 3a
Sinner, will not gain anything..Yevamos 92b
Sinners, Jewish, by their body..Rosh Hashanah 17a
Sinners, Jewish, fast...Krisos 6b
Sinners will stumble on them..Bava Basra 89b
Sinning (mating)
Sinning animals, thought..Bava Metzia 91a-91b
Sinned with non-Jew, sacrifice.......................................Avodah Zarah 22b-24b
Sinning with animal, cases...Sanhedrin 54b-55a
Sinning with animal, non-Jew..................Avodah Zarah 14b-15a, 22a-23a

S

Sinning with animal, prohibition and sin offerings .... Sanhedrin 54b
Sinning with animal, stoning .... Sanhedrin 54a, 55a-55b
Sinning with bird .... Zevachim 85b; Yevamos 83b; Bechoros 42a
Sinning with male .... Sanhedrin 54a-54b

Sinned with man
Sinned with man, atoning payment .... Bava Kama 40b-41a
Sinned with man or woman, sacrifice .... Bechoros 41a; Temurah 28a-28b; Bava Kama 40b;
.... Zevachim 85b; Niddah 41a
Sinned with man, redeemed sacrifices .... Makos 22a

Sirtut .... *see* **Etching line**, page 202
Sirugin, significance .... Rosh Hashanah 26b
Siruv lebeis din .... *see* **Refusing to obey** *beis din*, page 554
Siryon, Hermon .... Chullin 60b

Sisera
Sisera, episode with Jael .... Yevamos 103a-103b; Nazir 23b; Horayos 10b
Sisera, Red Sea .... Pesachim 118b

Sister
Sister, "we have a little sister," interpretations .... Pesachim 87a; Kiddushin 49b; Sanhedrin 24a
Sister, forbidden relations .... Yevamos 22b-23a; Krisos 15a; Makos 14a-14b
Sister, impurity of *Kohen* .... Yevamos 60a-60b
Sister of Cain .... Sanhedrin 58b
Sister of Lotan, Timna .... Sanhedrin 99b
Sisters, *kiddushin* .... Kiddushin 50b
Sisters, three sisters make a *chazakah* .... Yevamos 64b
Sisters to brothers, levirate marriage .... Yevamos 9b-10a, 20a, 26a-26b, 28a-29a, 30a
Sisters, two, to one brother, levirate marriage .... Yevamos 19a, 28a-29a, 50b-51b
Sister being his sister-in-law, levirate marriage .... Yevamos 9b-10a, 20a, 28a-29a
Sister of *chalutzah*, forbidden by Rabbinical Decree .... Yevamos 40b, 41a, 44a-44b; Kiddushin 45a

Sister of wife
Sister of wife and husband's daughter, hatred .... Yevamos 117a
Sister of wife, forbidden relations .... Yevamos 8b, 96a
Sister of wife, testimony about death .... Yevamos 118b
Sister of wife, wed by mistake, divorce .... Yevamos 94a-94b
Sister of wife, wed by mistake, wife .... Yevamos 54b, 95b-96a

Sister-in-law, hatred .... Yevamos 117a

Sit
"Sit, my son, sit," craftsman .... Chullin 54b
Sit down, is said to mourner and sick person .... Moed Katan 27b
Sits in Abraham's lap .... Kiddushin 72b
Sitting, comforting the bereaved .... Bava Basra 100b; Megillah 23b
Sitting, desecrates service .... Sanhedrin 83b-84a
Sitting, desecrates Temple service .... Sanhedrin 83b-84a
Sitting, disqualified service .... Zevachim 23b-24a; Sanhedrin 84a
Sitting, disqualified service in Temple .... Zevachim 19b, 23b-24a
Sitting, health .... Kesubos 111a-111b
Sitting in Temple Courtyard .... Yoma 69a-69b; Sanhedrin 101b
Sitting next to man praying .... Berachos 31b
Sitting, teacher and disciples .... Megillah 21a
Sitting without sinning, reward .... Makos 23a-23b; Kiddushin 39b

S

Sit kaful .... *see* **Span**, page 648
Site of Temple .... Zevachim 54b
Sitting-place of scoffers
   Sitting-place of scoffers .... Avodah Zarah 18b
   Sitting-place of scoffers, meal .... Avos 3:2
Sivlonos .... *see* **Gifts, concern of *kiddushin***, page 250
Six
   Six disciples in one cubit .... Eruvin 53a
   Six disciples under one *tallis* .... Sanhedrin 20a
   Six forbidden relations, levirate marriage .... Yevamos 3b, 13a
   Six hundred thirteen commandments .... Makos 23b-24a
   Six men were not touched by the Angel of Death .... Bava Basra 17a
   Six thoughts, Temple service .... Zevachim 2b, 46b
   Six thousand years, world existence .... Sanhedrin 97a-97b; Avodah Zarah 9a; Rosh Hashanah 31a
   Six years, Hebrew slave .... Kiddushin 15b
   Six years old, schoolchildren .... Bava Basra 21a
Sixth
   Sixth as profit, Rabbi Yehudah .... Bava Metzia 40a-40b
   Sixth, fraud .... Bava Metzia 50a-50b; Kiddushin 42b; Bava Basra 95a
   Sixth of profit, storekeeper .... Bava Metzia 40b; Bava Basra 90a; Menachos 77a
   Sixth, which things .... Bava Metzia 55a
Sixty
   Sixty children you begot, of what use .... Bava Basra 91a
   Sixty, list about one sixtieth .... Berachos 57b
   Sixty, mixture .... Avodah Zarah 69a; Chullin 98a-99b
   Sixty myriads persons, blessings .... Berachos 58a
   Sixty myriads, population .... Berachos 58a
   Sixty one *issaron*, meal offering .... Menachos 103b
   Sixty years old, Rav Yosef's feast .... Moed Katan 28a
Siyag .... *see* **Fence**, page 219
Siyata dishmaya .... *see* **Divine help**, page 169
Siyum maseches .... *see* **Completion of tractate**, page 119
Siyum maseches, episodes .... Shabbos 118b-119a; Pesachim 68b
Size
  Commandments —
     Size of *eruv* for courtyard .... Eruvin 46b, 80b
     Size of four species .... Succah 32b
     Size of length, succah .... Succah 3a
     Size of leprous marks .... Negaim 6:1-4
     Size of *peah* .... Chullin 137b-138a; Peah 1:2
     Size of slaughtering knife .... Chullin 31a
     Size of stain, *niddah* .... Niddah 58b-59a
     Size of *tallis*, *tzitzis* .... Menachos 40b-41a
  Succah —
     Size of succah, height .... Succah 2a-3a, 7b; Eruvin 2a
     Size to disqualify *s'chach* .... Succah 17a-18a
  Temple —
     Size of Altar .... Menachos 97a-98a; Eruvin 4a; Succah 45a; Zevachim 54a, 59b-60a, 61b-62a;
                                                      Middos 3:1-3

S

Size of Temple Courtyard..Middos 2:6, 5:1-2; Yoma 16a-16b; Menachos 97b
Size of *Heichal*..Middos 4:6-7; Yoma 52a
Misc. —
Size and height of Sages..Bava Metzia 84a; Niddah 24b
Size cannot be different for everyone........................Bava Basra 29a; Shabbos 35b; Megillah 18b;
....Gittin 14a; Chullin 9a, 32a
Size considered as crumbled......................................Succah 31b; Yevamos 103b; Chullin 89b
Size, holes..Bechoros 37b-38a
Size of garments, impurity....................Keilim 27:2-4, 27:6-8, 28:7-8; Shabbos 29a, 63b-64a, 76a, 79a;
....Succah 17b; Meilah 18a; Zevachim 95a
Size of hole in utensils...Keilim 17:5
Size of man, beauty..Berachos 31b; Bechoros 45b
Size of pit..Bava Kama 3a, 51b
Size of Torah scroll...Bava Basra 14a
Size of universe...Tamid 32a
Size of utensils concerning impurity..........................Keilim 27:5-6
Size of world...Pesachim 94a
Skeleton whole
Skeleton whole, comforting.......................................Moed Katan 25a
Skeleton whole, impurity..Niddah 56a
Skewer
Skewer, *muktzeh*...Beitzah 28b
Skewer on Yom Tov..Beitzah 34a
Skewer, roasting Pesach lamb.....................................Pesachim 74a
Skin
Skin a dead animal and do not say: "I am an important person".............Bava Basra 110a
Skinning and cutting up sacrifices, order......Chullin 27a-27b; Shabbos 116b; Yoma 25b; Menachos 77b
Skinning animal, drink before slaughtering................Beitzah 40a
Skinning disqualified burnt offering...........................Zevachim 85a-85b, 104a
Skinning on Yom Tov...Bechoros 33a; Temurah 24a
Skinning Pesach lamb on Shabbos...............Shabbos 116b-117a, 133b; Menachos 63b-64a
Skin
Impurity —
Skin, added impurity...Keilim 27:1
Skin of corpse's head...Chullin 123a
Skin of eight reptiles..Shabbos 107a-107b; Chullin 122a
Skin of man, impurity..................................Chullin 122a; Niddah 55a, 56a; Chullin 122a
Skin of overcooked donkey..Chullin 77a-77b
Prohibitions —
Skin...*see also* **Hide**, page 278
Skin, a part of which became detached on Shabbos.............Shabbos 94b
Skin, prohibition to skin animal on Yom Tov..............Bechoros 33a; Temurah 24a
Skin, skinless animal is *treifah*.................................Chullin 55b-56a
Sacrifices —
Skin of bird, offering..Shabbos 108a
Skin of tail, sacrifice..Zevachim 28a
Skin of tail, thought..Zevachim 27b-28a
Skin of sacrifices
Skin of sacrifices are burned......................................Zevachim 103b-104a; Eduyos 2:2

S

Skin of sacrifices, episode .... Pesachim 57a
Skin of sacrifices, for whom .... Zevachim 103a-103b
Skin of blemished sacrifices .... Bechoros 33a-33b; Temurah 24a

Misc. —
Skin, animal, different layers .... Gittin 22a; Shabbos 79a
Skin, different stages of preparation .... Gittin 22a; Shabbos 79a
Skin of dead cow on her young .... Bechoros 57b

Skin pieces
Skin pieces, circumcision on Shabbos .... Shabbos 133b
Skin pieces, invalidating circumcision .... Shabbos 137a-137b; Yevamos 47b, 71b
Skin pieces, Shabbos .... Shabbos 94b
Skin of firstborn animal .... Bechoros 33a; Temurah 24a; Zevachim 104a

Skinless animal, *treifah* .... Chullin 55b-56a

Skull
Skull of Jehoiakim .... Sanhedrin 82a
Skull, *treifah* .... Chullin 52b, 57b
Skull which does not put on *tefillin* .... Rosh Hashanah 17a

Skullcap, *Kohen Gadol* .... Chullin 138a

Sky
Sky and earth, dimensions .... Tamid 32a
Sky and earth, order of creation .... Tamid 32a; Chagigah 12a
Sky, episode about basket .... Bava Basra 74a
Sky, fire and water .... Chagigah 12a
Sky, firmaments .... Chagigah 12b
Sky in its purity, blessing .... Berachos 59a
Sky in its purity, since Temple destruction .... Berachos 59a

Sky-light, *connects domains* .... Eruvin 76b

Slain
Slain man beneath Temple .... Parah 3:3
Slain men of Lod .... Taanis 18b
Slain people of Beitar and Jerusalem .... Gittin 57a-57b, 58a

Slander
Slander, "your wife is my wife" .... Shabbos 30b
Slander about Rabban Gamliel's sons .... Pesachim 51a
Slander, fool .... Pesachim 3b
Slander gives no benefit .... Arachin 15b
Slander, how many judges .... Sanhedrin 8a-9b
Slander, lashes and penalty .... Kesubos 45b-46a
Slander on previous divorce certificates .... Gittin 5b
Slander, tangible proofs .... Shabbos 56a-56b
Slander, whom .... Kesubos 40b, 44b

Slapping
Slapping in the face, damages done by man .... Bava Kama 27b, 36b, 90a-90b; Kiddushin 11b;
.... Bechoros 50b
Slapping, like slapping Divine Presence .... Sanhedrin 58b

Slaughterer who impaired slaughtering, liability .... Bava Kama 99b; Bava Basra 93b

Slaughtering
Disqualified —
Slaughtering animal and its young .... *see* **Animal and its young,** page 26

S

Slaughtering, animal poisoned by venom .... Chullin 30b
Slaughtering, cases of covered knife .... Chullin 30b
Slaughtering, covered knife in air .... Chullin 30b-31a
Slaughtering, covered nail when cutting off neck of bird .... Chullin 20b
Slaughtering fetus in mother's womb .... Chullin 74a
Slaughtering, first eight days .... Shabbos 136a
Slaughtering, improper .... Chullin 80a-82a, 85a-85b; Bava Kama 71a, 106b; Kesubos 34a; Kiddushin 57a
Slaughtering, improper, penalty .... Kesubos 33b-34a; Bava Kama 72a-72b, 76a-76b, 77b
Slaughtering in partially wrong place .... Chullin 18a-19a
Slaughtering in wrong place .... Chullin 19a-19b, 20a
Slaughtering, interruption .... Chullin 9a, 32a
Slaughtering, neck upon knife .... Chullin 16b
Slaughtering, non deep cut on windpipe .... Chullin 19b, 30a-30b
Slaughtering, relying on examination .... Chullin 3a

How much —
Slaughtering at location of hole .... Chullin 19b
Slaughtering bird, only one pipe .... Chullin 27b-28a
Slaughtering bird, windpipe .... Chullin 28a-28b
Slaughtering, half equal to greater part .... Chullin 28b
Slaughtering, how much .... Chullin 27a, 28b-29b
Slaughtering veins .... Chullin 28b

How —
Slaughtering, blessing .... Pesachim 7b
Slaughtering by arrow .... Chullin 30b-31a
Slaughtering by wheel .... Chullin 16a
Slaughtering chicken, how .... Shabbos 128b
Slaughtering, from beginning to end .... Bava Kama 72a-72b; Chullin 29b-30a, 36a, 128a;
.... Zevachim 30a
Slaughtering immediately after *semichah* .... Beitzah 20a; Zevachim 33a; Berachos 42a; Menachos 93a
Slaughtering in air .... Chullin 30b-31a
Slaughtering in zigzag and slant .... Chullin 19b
Slaughtering, intention .... Chullin 12b, 31a
Slaughtering on neck, source .... Chullin 27a-27b
Slaughtering, place on neck .... Chullin 18a-19a, 43b-45a
Slaughtering, shown to Moses .... Menachos 29a

Impurity —
Slaughtering by disqualified persons, *neveilah* .... Chullin 86a-86b
Slaughtering, impure man .... Chullin 2b-3a
Slaughtering renders pure .... Chullin 32b-33a, 69a, 73a, 74a, 85b, 128b; Zevachim 69b
Slaughtering, susceptible to become impure .... Pesachim 16a-16b, 20a, 22b;
.... Chullin 33a, 35b-36b, 127b-128a; Krisos 22a

Knife —
Slaughtering with forbidden knife .... Chullin 8a-8b
Slaughtering with idolatrous knife .... Chullin 8a-8b
Slaughtering with knife set in earth .... Chullin 15b-16b
Slaughtering with scorching knife .... Chullin 8a, 17b

Prohibitions —
Slaughtering fellow's animal to idol .... Chullin 40a-41a; Avodah Zarah 54a-54b
Slaughtering near water or hole .... Chullin 41a-41b

S

Slaughtering to idol, different cases ....Chullin 13a-13b
Slaughtering to idol, idolater ....Chullin 13a, 38b-39b, 116b; Avodah Zarah 32b
Sacrifices —
Slaughtering, disqualified sacrifices after slaughtering ....Zevachim 25b, 26a; Bechoros 39b
Slaughtering disqualified sacrifices on Shabbos ....Pesachim 73a
Slaughtering on Altar ....Zevachim 58a
Slaughtering Red Heifer ....Yoma 42a, 43b; Chullin 31b-32a; Zevachim 14b, 68b; Menachos 6b
Slaughtering sacrifice, stood outside ....Zevachim 26a, 32b
Slaughtering sacrifice, two men ....Chullin 29b-30a
Slaughtering sacrifice, who ....Zevachim 14b, 31b-32b; Chullin 2b
Slaughtering sacrifices at south, lashes ....Zevachim 36a-36b
Slaughtering sacrifices of Yom Kippur ....Yoma 32b-33a, 42a
Slaughtering signs, sacrifice ....Chullin 29a
Time —
Slaughtered animal, Shabbos ....Chullin 14a-15a; Kesubos 34a; Bava Kama 71a
Slaughtering at night ....Chullin 13b
Slaughtering on Shabbos, coloring ....Shabbos 75a-75b
Slaughtering on Yom Tov ....Beitzah 25a
Who —
Slaughtering, blind ....Chullin 13b
Slaughtering, experts ....Chullin 3b, 9a, 12a-12b
Slaughtering, who ....Chullin 12b
Misc. —
Slaughtering animals causing damage ....Bava Kama 23b
Slaughtering, considered from its beginning ....Chullin 29b-30a, 36a, 128a, Bava Kama 72a-b;
....Zevachim 30a
Slaughtering, demonstrating on one's neck ....Gittin 57b
Slaughtering, exemption for fish ....Chullin 27b
Slaughtering, necessary knowledge for Sage ....Chullin 9a
Slaughtering of bird, from the Torah ....Chullin 4a, 27b-28a, 85b-86a; Nazir 29a; Kiddushin 71a
Slaughtering of Sage on Purim ....Megillah 7b
Slaughtering location, boiling ....Chullin 8b
Slaughtering and selling
Slaughtering and selling consecrated animal ....Bava Kama 68b-69a, 76a, 79a; Gittin 55b
Slaughtering and selling, half ....Bava Kama 71b-72a
Slaughtering and selling, instances ....Bava Kama 65b, 68a-69a, 70b-71b, 78b-79a
Slaughtering and selling, partners ....Shabbos 93b; Bava Kama 78b
Slaughtering and selling, source ....Bava Kama 67b
Slaughtering by pressing
Slaughtering by pressing, instances ....Chullin 30b, 32a
Slaughtering by pressing, *melikah* for bird ....Chullin 20b
Slaughtering by pressing, slaughtering in air ....Chullin 30b-31a
Slaughtering outside
Slaughtering outside, before its time ....Yoma 62b-63a; Zevachim 114a-115b
Slaughtering outside, blemish ....Bechoros 16a
Slaughtering outside, cases ....Zevachim 84b-85a, 108a-108b, 111a-111b
Slaughtering outside, consecrated fetus ....Temurah 12a
Slaughtering outside, goat to Azazel ....Zevachim 113b; Yoma 63a-63b; Temurah 6b, 13a
Slaughtering outside, in present times ....Zevachim 107b

S

Slaughtering outside, invalid..Zevachim 113b-115b
Slaughtering outside, qualified...Zevachim 108a
Slaughtering outside Temple, prohibition...Zevachim 107a-107b
Slaughtering outside, time when private altars are permitted....Zevachim 119b; Meilah 3a-3b
Slaughtering outside, where...Zevachim 107b, 108b

Slav..*see* **Quails**, page 513

Slave

Acquisition —
Slave, acquisition of idolater by idolater...Gittin 37b-38a
Slave, acts of acquisition...Kiddushin 22b-23a, 8a
Slave, bill of sale...Gittin 86a
Slave, fraud.......Kiddushin 11a; Bava Metzia 56a-56b, 57a; Temurah 27a; Bava Basra 92b; Kesubos 57b-58a
Slave, guarantee's act of obligation..Kiddushin 7a
Slave, power to purchase..................Kiddushin 23b; Pesachim 88b; Nedarim 88b
Slave, selling for right to collect penalty..Gittin 42b-43a
Slave tied up, act of acquisition..........................Bava Kama 12a; Gittin 21a, 78a
Slaves, *chazakah*...Bava Basra 36a

Aggadah —
Slave, abandoning him, freedom....................Gittin 39a; Yevamos 48a; Nazir 62b; Kiddushin 72b
Slave, enjoys lack of restraint...Gittin 13a; Kesubos 11a
Slave in front of master, prayer...Shabbos 10a
Slave of king, king...Shevuos 47b
Slave, reason for piercing his ear...Kiddushin 22b
Slave to earth, field...Sanhedrin 58b
Slave to his subjects, king..Horayos 10a
Slaves, love one another..Pesachim 113b
Slaves, reward for who is vigilant in *tzitzis*.......................................Shabbos 32b

Commandments —
Slave, circumcision...Shabbos 135b
Slave, half...*see* **Half slave**, page 266
Slave, participating in Pesach lamb..Pesachim 88a
Slave, quorum of ten..Gittin 38b; Berachos 47b
Slave, searching for *chametz*...Pesachim 4a-4b
Slave, slaughtering sacrifice...........................Zevachim 31b-32a; Chullin 2b
Slave, *zimun*...Berachos 47b

Conversion —
Slave, immersed to convert..Yevamos 45b-46a
Slave refusing to convert...Yevamos 48b
Slave, willingly converting..Yevamos 47b-48a

Disqualified —
Slave, agent for divorce certificate.......................................Gittin 23a-23b; Kiddushin 41b
Slave, disqualified for kingship..Bava Kama 88a
Slave, testimony..Bava Kama 88a, 15a

Episodes —
Slave, arrogant, Rav..Kiddushin 70a-70b
Slave, bad, acts then asks for permission...Bava Basra 4a
Slave before king, Rabbi Chanina ben Dosa.......................................Berachos 34b
Slave colored his beard...Bava Metzia 60b
Slave of *Kohen*, mistake in testimony................................Kesubos 28b; Yevamos 99b

S

Slave of Yannai, death punishment..Sanhedrin 19a-19b
Slaves of Abraham, woman screamed ....Succah 31a
Slaves of exilarch, debt..Shabbos 121b; Yevamos 120a
Slaves of exilarch, episodes................................Gittin 67b-68a; Avodah Zarah 38b

Freedom —
Slave becoming public property, correcting situation................................Gittin 40a
Slave, before certificate of freedom, penalty for atonement................Gittin 42b
Slave before freedom certificate, atoning payment................................Gittin 42b
Slave belonging to wife, tooth and eye................................Bava Kama 89b-90a
Slave, cases of freedom................................Gittin 39b; Kiddushin 23a-23b
Slave, eye after tooth................................Bava Kama 74a-74b
Slave, freed, order of precedence................................Horayos 13a
Slave, freedom and financial independence, together................Kiddushin 23a
Slave, gift when freed................Kiddushin 15a, 16b-17b; Bava Metzia 31b
Slave, how is he freed in Jubilee year................Rosh Hashanah 8b
Slave, limbs................Kiddushin 24b-25a; Bava Kama 26b, 91a, 98a
Slave, made captive................................Gittin 37b-38a
Slave, prohibition to free him................Gittin 38a-38b; Berachos 47b; Sotah 3b
Slave, security for loan, freed................................Gittin 40b-41a
Slave, sold outside *Eretz Yisrael*................................Gittin 44b-45a, 8a
Slave, sold to idolater................................Gittin 43b-44a
Slaves of convert who died................................Kiddushin 22b-23a

Monetary matters —
Slave, "I will not support you"................Gittin 12a-12b; Kesubos 43a, 58b; Bava Kama 87b
Slave, acknowledging part of claim................Bava Metzia 100a-100b
Slave, atonement payment for half slave................Gittin 42a-42b
Slave, atonement payment for ox................Bava Kama 43a-43b
Slave, collecting *kesubah*................................Yevamos 99a
Slave, cure................................Gittin 12b
Slave, custodians not liable................Bava Metzia 57b; Shevuos 43a
Slave, his body is purchased................................Yevamos 46a
Slave, item he found................................Bava Metzia 12b
Slave, like movable goods................Bava Kama 11b-12b, 96b-97a; Bava Basra 68a, 150a; Yevamos 99a; Gittin 39a
Slave, oath................Bava Metzia 57b; Shevuos 42b-43a; Bava Kama 63a
Slave, one benefits without the other losing................Bava Kama 97a; Bava Metzia 64b-65a
Slave, payment of sick leave................Bava Kama 85b-86a
Slave, seizing debt from him................Bava Basra 128a; Bava Kama 11b
Slave, shame................Bava Kama 88a; Sanhedrin 86a
Slave who damaged................Yadayim 4:7; Bava Kama 4a

Prohibitions —
Slave and resident non-Jew, Shabbos................Krisos 9a; Yevamos 48b
Slave and Israel, intermingled................Yevamos 100a
Slave for woman, suspicion................Bava Metzia 71a
Slave, forbidden relations................Sanhedrin 58b
Slave going out with seal, Shabbos................Shabbos 58a
Slave, member torn from living animal................Gittin 67b-68a, 7a
Slave, new, makes wine forbidden................Avodah Zarah 57a-57b
Slave, *nezirus*................Nazir 61a
Slave who made a vow................Nazir 61a, 62b

***Terumah* —**
Slave, before certificate of freedom, *terumah* .... Gittin 42b
Slave, giving him *terumah* for his master .... Kesubos 28b; Yevamos 99b
Slave of forbidden woman, *terumah* .... Yevamos 66a
Slave, *terumah* .... Gittin 42b
Misc. —
Slave, calling one's fellow .... Kiddushin 28a
Slave, enslaving wicked man .... Bava Metzia 73b
Slave, five nations .... Yevamos 99a
Slave, Hebrew .... *see* **Hebrew slave**, page 274
Slave, his son born of a Jewess .... Yevamos 44b-45b, 70a, 99a
Slave, lineage .... Yevamos 62a
Slave, one or two days .... Bava Kama 90a; Bava Basra 50a-50b
Slave, piercing his ear .... Kiddushin 14b-15a, 21b-22b
Slaves who serve for reward .... Avos 1:3; Avodah Zarah 19a

Sleep
Advice —
Sleep for righteous, harmful .... Sanhedrin 72a
Sleep, hand on forehead .... Pesachim 112a
Sleep in morning .... Avos 3:10
Sleep, noise of water .... Eruvin 104a
Sleep, to dissipate wine .... Eruvin 64b, 65a; Taanis 17b; Sanhedrin 22b
Health —
Sleep at dawn .... Berachos 62b
Sleep, cure .... Berachos 57b
Sleep on ground .... Berachos 62b
Sleep, too much is harmful .... Gittin 70a
Sleep with shoes on .... Yoma 78b
Prohibitions —
Sleep by day .... Succah 26b
Sleep when eating Pesach lamb .... Pesachim 120a-120b
Sleep with *tefillin* on .... Succah 26a-26b, 41b; Berachos 23b; Tamid 27a
Scientific facts —
Sleep of horse .... Succah 26b
Sleep, one sixtieth of death .... Berachos 57b
Sleep, purpose of night .... Eruvin 65a
Sleep, stomach and nose .... Berachos 61b
Sleep, three days without sleep .... Nedarim 15a; Succah 53a; Yevamos 121b; Shevuos 25a
Misc. —
Sleep after death, episode .... Eruvin 65a
Sleep, dozing .... Taanis 12a-12b; Niddah 63a; Pesachim 120b; Megillah 18b; Yevamos 54a
Sleep during *Simchas Beis Hashoevah* .... Succah 53a
Sleep of seventy years, episode .... Taanis 23a
Sleep, small amount, in succah .... Succah 26a

Sleeping
Sleeping alone .... Shabbos 151b
Sleeping in bed with canopy .... Eruvin 63b
Sleeping in house of study .... Sanhedrin 71a
Sleeping in Temple Fire Room .... Tamid 26b

S

Sleeping late, easier than getting up early .... Yoma 22a
Sleeping together, girls .... Shabbos 65a-65b
Sleeping with one's daughter .... Kiddushin 81b; Berachos 24a
Sliced *matzah*, *Seder* night .... Berachos 39b; Pesachim 116a
Sling, impurity .... Eduyos 3:5; G
Slope, partition for Shabbos
Slope, partition for Shabbos .... Shabbos 100a
Slope, partition for Shabbos, walking upon .... Eruvin 22b
Slow to anger
Slow to anger, blessing .... Berachos 57b
Slow to anger, reward .... Bava Kama 50a-50b
Slow to anger, ten generations .... Avos 5:2
Slow to anger towards good and wicked .... Bava Kama 50a-50b; Eruvin 22a; Yevamos 121b
Slow to anger towards idolatry .... Avodah Zarah 54b-55a
Slow to anger towards wicked, Moses .... Sanhedrin 111a-111b
Small
Small amount is good .... Berachos 34a; Gittin 70a
Small depends on big .... Taanis 7a; Bava Basra 12a
Small food makes smaller .... Berachos 44b
Small intestine, *treifah* .... Chullin 48b
Small utensil, but does not have one .... Berachos 33b
Smashed limbs, *treifah* .... Bava Kama 50b-51a; Chullin 51a-52a, 56b, 57a
Smell
Smell of Jacob, apple orchard .... Taanis 29b
Smell of young Jewish men in the future .... Berachos 43b
Smell, pleasure for the soul .... Berachos 43b
Smell, revives man's spirit .... Berachos 57b
Prohibitions —
Smell of forbidden substance in food .... Avodah Zarah 66b-67a; Terumos 10:3-4; Pesachim 76b
Smell of intestinal gas, prayer .... Berachos 24b
Smell of wine of idolaters .... Avodah Zarah 66b
Smell of wine, tasting .... Avodah Zarah 66b-67a
Smell, producing on Yom Tov .... Beitzah 23a
Smell, personal use .... Pesachim 26a; Krisos 6a
Misc. —
"Smell of divorce," *Kohen* .... Gittin 24b-25a, 82b; Yevamos 52a, 94a
Smell, blessing .... Berachos 43a-43b
Smell, good for intelligence .... Sanhedrin 70a; Yoma 76b
Smell, last blessing .... Niddah 51b-52a
Smell of earth, knowing way .... Bava Basra 73b
Smell of radish, episode .... Bava Basra 146a-146b
Smell in mouth
Smell in mouth, water and salt .... Berachos 40a
Smell of mouth, blemishes of *Kohen* .... Kesubos 75a
Smell of mouth, pepper .... Shabbos 65a; Kesubos 75a
Smell, pleasant
Smell, pleasant, sacrifice owner's intention .... Zevachim 46b
Smell, unpleasant, distance .... Berachos 25a
Smell, unpleasant, distance from city .... Bava Basra 25a

S

Smell, unpleasant, during prayer..Eruvin 65a
Smell, unpleasant, sneezing..Berachos 24b

Smelling
Smelling myrtle and *esrog*...Succah 37b
Smelling plant connected to earth, Shabbos...............................Succah 37b
Smelling wine of idolaters..Avodah Zarah 66b

Smiling to fellow, importance...Kesubos 111b

***Smoch miuta*...*see* **Minority,** page 413

Smoke
Smoke, *chazakah*..Bava Basra 22b
Smoke of Altar..Yoma 21b; Bava Basra 147a

Snake
Eve's sin —
Snake and Eve, curse...Yoma 75a
Snake and Eve, impurity.................Shabbos 145b-146a; Yevamos 103b; Avodah Zarah 22b
Snake, if it had not been cursed..Sanhedrin 59b
Snake, punishment...Sotah 9b

Episodes —
Snake, Ben Dama..Avodah Zarah 27b
Snake, does it kill...Rosh Hashanah 29a
Snake, giant, killed by embers.................................Nedarim 25a; Shevuos 29b
Snake, merit of charity...Shabbos 156b
Snake of onion, episode..Eruvin 29b
Snake, Rabbi Akiva's daughter..Shabbos 156b
Snake, seven heads..Kiddushin 29b
Snake, to punish murderer.....................................Sanhedrin 37b; Shevuos 34a
Snake, toilets...Berachos 62b
Snake, transgressor of Rabbinical Decree.................Shabbos 110a; Avodah Zarah 27b
Snakes, drank wine..Avodah Zarah 30a

Prohibitions —
Snake, bitten animal...Chullin 58b
Snake, stepping on snake as if by accident on Shabbos...............Shabbos 121b
Snake, whisper on Shabbos..Sanhedrin 101a
Snake-like slander, reproof..Arachin 15b

Scientific facts —
Snake, eating earth...Yoma 75a
Snake, giant...Bava Basra 74b
Snake, healing by running...Shabbos 109b
Snake, hind bringing forth...Bava Basra 16a
Snake like beam of oil press...Shevuos 29b
Snake of *Eretz Yisrael*, danger...Shabbos 121b
Snake, old, strength...Shabbos 77b; Avodah Zarah 30b
Snake, poison...Sanhedrin 78a; Bava Kama 23b
Snake, spine of dead...Bava Kama 16a
Snake, use in remedy..Shabbos 77b

Misc. —
Snake, bite...Shabbos 109b-110a; Pesachim 112b
Snake, Divine supervision...Shabbos 121b
Snake, finding extenuating circumstances for inciter...................Sanhedrin 29a

S

Snake, human, episode about birth ....Niddah 24b
Snake, making snake bite someone ....Sanhedrin 78a
Snake, not to provoke it ....Pesachim 113a
Snake of copper ....Rosh Hashanah 29a
Snake of copper, Hezekiah ....Pesachim 56a

Sneezing
Sneezing, during prayer ....Berachos 24a-24b
Sneezing, healing ....Berachos 57b

Snow
Snow, crushing on Shabbos ....Shabbos 51b
Snow, impurity ....Niddah 17a
Snow of mountains, benefit ....Taanis 3b

"So that my son will live," charity ....Bava Basra 10b; Pesachim 8a-8b; Rosh Hashanah 4a

Soaked
Soaked bread, blessing ....Menachos 75b; Berachos 37b
Soaked in water, *matzah* ....Pesachim 39b
Soaking is laundering ....Zevachim 94b

So-and-so I want to marry ....Kiddushin 41a, 81b

Socher ....*see* **Tenant farmer**, page 680

Sochet beShabbos ....*see* **Squeezing on Shabbos, which fruit**, page 653

Society
Society, not to stay out of ....Berachos 49b-50a
Society's benefit, decree ....Gittin 32a-53a

Sod haibur ....*see* **Secret of lunar cycle**, page 597

Sodom
Sodom attitude, refusing even at no loss ....Bava Kama 20a-21a; Eruvin 49a; Kesubos 103a;
....Bava Basra 12b, 59a, 168a
Sodom, corruption ....Sanhedrin 109a-109b
Sodom, fake judgments ....Sanhedrin 109a-109b; Niddah 69a
Sodom, years of sin ....Shabbos 10b-11a

Sodomy
Sodomy, bestiality ....Sanhedrin 54b-55a
Sodomy, marital relations ....Yevamos 34b; Nedarim 20a-20b
Sodomy, forbidden relations ....Sanhedrin 54a
Sodomy, *Kohen Gadol* ....Yevamos 59a-59b
Sodomy, non-Jew ....Sanhedrin 58b
Sodomy, virgin ....Kiddushin 9b-10a

Sof daato ....*see* **Rabbi Meir, depth of thought**, page 525

Sof tumah latzes ....*see* **Impurity eventually goes out**, page 302

Sofam mishum techilasam ....*see* **Permission of second act, to perform first**, page 481

Sofo letame tumah chamurah ....*see* **Impurity, primary source, susceptible to become impure**, page 304

Sofo mochiach ....*see* **End proves intention**, page 197

Soft like reed, Rabbi Elazar ben Rabbi Shimon ....Taanis 20a-20b

Soldiers
Soldiers of David's wars ....Kiddushin 76b
Soldiers of Nebuchadnezzar, strength ....Sotah 42b

Soles ....*see* **Semolina**, page 601

Solidifying food on Shabbos ....Shabbos 95a

S

Solomon
  Kingdom —
    Solomon, feasts .... Bava Metzia 86b
    Solomon, his throne greater than his father's .... Sanhedrin 105b
    Solomon, pleasures .... Gittin 68a
    Solomon, reign and fall .... Sanhedrin 20b; Megillah 11b; Gittin 68b
    Solomon, superintendents .... Sanhedrin 12a
    Solomon, Torah and greatness .... Gittin 59a
  Mistakes —
    Solomon, Bathsheba's rebuke .... Sanhedrin 70b
    Solomon, horses .... Sanhedrin 21b
    Solomon, mistake because of his wives .... Shabbos 56b; Sanhedrin 21b
    Solomon, Pharaoh's daughter .... Yevamos 76a-76b; Sanhedrin 21b
    Solomon, Jeroboam's rebuke .... Sanhedrin 101b
  Temple —
    Solomon, Ashmedai and *shamir* worm .... Gittin 68a-68b
    Solomon, opening of Temple gates .... Shabbos 30a
    Solomon, sacrifices .... Zevachim 59a-60a
    Solomon, Temple .... Sanhedrin 104b; Niddah 70b
  Wisdom —
    Solomon, impurity of sprinkling water .... Niddah 9a
    Solomon, judgment concerning dead child .... Makos 23b
    Solomon, reasons for commandments .... Sanhedrin 21b
    Solomon, request for wisdom .... Rosh Hashanah 21b
    Solomon, wisdom .... Eruvin 21b; Yevamos 21a
  Misc. —
    Solomon and Hiram .... Shabbos 54a
    Solomon, G-d's name .... Shevuos 35b
    Solomon, his scribes' death .... Succah 53a
    Solomon, no harm .... Sanhedrin 103a-103b; Berachos 55b
    Solomon, quickness .... Sanhedrin 104b
    Solomon, World to Come .... Sanhedrin 104b
Some
  Some people acquire their world in one instant .... Avodah Zarah 10b, 17a, 18a
  Some say, Rabbi Nassan .... Horayos 13b-14a
Something which will be discovered ...... Bechoros 36a-36b; Rosh Hashanah 22b; Yevamos 93b, 115a, 116b
Son .... *see also* **Education**, page 187
  Aggadah —
    Son gives merit to his father .... Sanhedrin 104a
    Son, if your heart is wise .... Eruvin 21b; Shabbos 14b
    Son, like his father's loins .... Eruvin 70b
    Son, male, with his loaf in hand .... Niddah 31b
    Son of ignoramus, Torah .... Bava Metzia 85b
    Son of righteous man, prayer .... Yevamos 64a
    Son of village, sees king .... Chagigah 13b
    Son to inherit him, Divine anger .... Bava Basra 116a, 141a
    Son's strength superior than his father's .... Shevuos 48a; Chullin 49b, 63a
    Sons like plants, commentaries .... Pesachim 87a
    Sons sinned, argument against Patriarchs .... Shabbos 89b

S

Sons to your sons, peace..Kesubos 50a

Commandments —

Son, commandments...Kiddushin 29a, 30b

Son depends on him, what about his daughter...Kesubos 52b

Son, learning...Kiddushin 29b

Son, marriage..Sanhedrin 76b

Son, not to make preferences..Shabbos 10b

Son of ignoramus, reward for who teaches him Torah.....................................Bava Metzia 85a

Son, teaching him a trade.......................................Kiddushin 30b, 82a-82b; Berachos 63a

Son, teaching him trade...Pesachim 113a

Sons, raising for Torah study..Pesachim 113b

Personalities —

Sons of Keturah, disciples..Zevachim 62b

Sons of Keturah, name of impurity...Sanhedrin 91a

Sons of Noah, Shem Ham and Japheth...Sanhedrin 69b

Sons of Saul, hanged..Yevamos 78b

Sons of Samuel, sinned...Shabbos 55b-56a

Sons of Josiah..Horayos 11b; Krisos 5b

Episodes —

Son of Koziba...Sanhedrin 93b

Son of Koziba, years of reign...Sanhedrin 97b

Son of Misha, human sacrifice..Sanhedrin 39b; Taanis 4a

Son of Rabbi Yishmael, captivity..Gittin 58a

Son of Resh Lakish, Rabbi Yochanan...Taanis 9a

Son of Shunamite woman, purity..Niddah 70b

Son of Talmion, episode..Meilah 17b

Sons, "My sons defeated Me," Achnai..Bava Metzia 59b

Sons, lazy, episode...Pesachim 89a

Sons of holy men...Avodah Zarah 50a; Pesachim 104a

Sons of Levi, golden calf...Yoma 66b

Sons of nations, Shemaiah and Avtalyon...Yoma 71b

Filiation —

Son, from forbidden relation...Yevamos 22a-22b

Son from maidservant, lineage..Yevamos 23a; Kiddushin 68b

Son of betrothed girl.......................................Yevamos 69b-70a; Kiddushin 75a; Kesubos 13b

Son of different disqualified to marry persons.......................................Kiddushin 66b-67b

Son of non-Jew from Jewish woman..Yevamos 44b-45b, 70a, 99a

Son of non-Jewess and Jewish man.............................Yevamos 23a; Kiddushin 68b

Israel —

Sons, life and livelihood..Moed Katan 28a

Sons of kings, Israel...Shabbos 128a, 67a, 111a; Bava Metzia 113b

Sons of poor, Torah..Nedarim 81a

Sons of prophets, Israel...Pesachim 66a

Sons of Israel...*see* **Israel**, page 318

Sons of Israel, from when..Chullin 101b

Sons to G-d, Israel..Kiddushin 36a; Bava Basra 10a

Sons, whether sons or slaves..Bava Basra 10a

Laws —

Son, adult, excommunication for father who hits...Moed Katan 17a

Son, *chazakah* of land .... Bava Basra 47a, 52a
Son, damages .... Bava Kama 87b
Son, exemption from levirate marriage .... Yevamos 87b
Son, item he found belongs to his father .... Bava Metzia 12a-12b
Son of king, inherits kingdom .... Kesubos 103b; Horayos 11b
Son of widow, honoring .... Kiddushin 31a
Son, rebellious .... *see* **Rebellious son**, page 550
Son, transgressor, fine .... Moed Katan 12b-13a; Bechoros 34b-35a; Gittin 44a-44b
Son, trustworthiness of father .... Yevamos 47a; Kiddushin 74a, 78b; Bava Basra 127b
Son, widow eating *terumah* .... Niddah 44a

Righteous men —
Sons of Aaron, death .... Sanhedrin 52a; Zevachim 115b; Yoma 53a
Sons of Beseira, Hillel .... Pesachim 66a; Bava Metzia 85a
Sons of Beseira, humility .... Bava Metzia 85a
Sons of Benjamin .... Sotah 36b
Sons of Hannah, self-sacrifice .... Gittin 57b
Sons of Kimchis, *Kohen Gadol* .... Yoma 47a
Sons of Rabban Gamliel .... Pesachim 51a
Sons of Rabbi Eliezer, modesty .... Nedarim 20b
Sons of Rabbi Yose .... Shabbos 118b
Sons of Rehab, wine .... Bava Basra 91b
Sons of Jethro, *Sanhedrin* .... Sanhedrin 104a, 106a; Sotah 11a

Support —
Son, charity to support him .... Kesubos 50a
Son, *mitzvah* to support him .... Kesubos 49a-49b
Son, support from dim-witted father and who ran away .... Kesubos 48a
Son, supporting him until six years old .... Kesubos 65b
Sons and daughters, few .... Kesubos 108b; Bava Basra 139b, 140a-140b

Misc. —
Son, agent in presence of his father .... Gittin 66a
Son, making his father agent .... Kiddushin 45b
Son of slave sells his father .... Yevamos 99a
Sons have made me into a song, Torah .... Sanhedrin 101a
Sons, how to beget sons .... Bava Basra 9b, 10b
Sons, is grandson included .... Bava Basra 143b
Sons like signs .... Yevamos 12b-13a
Sons like their mother's brothers .... Bava Basra 110a
Sons males, how .... Shevuos 18b; Niddah 70b-71a
Sons of hated wife, nine bad character traits .... Nedarim 20b
Sons of Noah .... *see* **Non-Jew**, page 448
Sons of Sages, how .... Makos 10a
Sons will be orphans, explanation .... Bava Metzia 38b
Sons, wisdom .... Bava Basra 9b, 10b

Sons die
Sons die, atonement .... Sotah 48b-49a; Berachos 5b
Sons die, punishment .... Sanhedrin 27b; Makos 24a; Berachos 7a; Shabbos 32b; Kesubos 72a
Sons die, wicked .... Shabbos 32b

Sons of Eli
Sons of Eli, Abbaye and Ravah .... Yevamos 105a; Rosh Hashanah 18a

S

Sons of Eli, curse and atonement .... Yevamos 105a; Rosh Hashanah 18a
Sons of Eli, *semichah* .... Sanhedrin 14a
Sons of Eli, sinned .... Shabbos 55b; Yoma 9a-9b

Sons of Haman
Sons of Haman, episode .... Megillah 15b
Sons of Haman, *megillah* .... Megillah 16b
Sons of Haman, written like a Song .... Megillah 16b

Sons of Rabbi Chiya
Sons of Rabbi Chiya, drunkenness .... Sanhedrin 38a
Sons of Rabbi Chiya, learning .... Berachos 18b
Sons of Rabbi Chiya, prayer .... Bava Metzia 85b

Sons of Sage
Sons of Sage, place of sitting and honor .... Horayos 13b
Sons of Sages, episodes about repentance .... Bava Metzia 85a
Sons of Sages, ignoramus .... Menachos 53a
Sons of Sages, modesty .... Bava Metzia 85b
Sons of Sages, not Sages themselves .... Nedarim 81a

Soneh matanos .... *see* **Hating gifts**, page 271

Song of Songs
Song of Songs, holiness .... Yadayim 3:5
Song of songs, impurity of hands .... Megillah 7a; Yadayim 3:5

Song
***Aggadah* —**
Song, Divine Presence .... Pesachim 117a; Shabbos 30b
Song in future .... Sanhedrin 91b
Song of angels and Israel .... Menachos 87a; Chullin 91b-92a; Chagigah 12b
Song of angels at night .... Avodah Zarah 3b

Commandments —
Song every day .... Sanhedrin 99a
Song of day, *Leviim* .... Rosh Hashanah 30b-31a; Tamid 7:4
Song, Torah learning .... Megillah 32a
Songs at *Simchas Beis Hashoevah* .... Succah 53a
Songs during Shabbos meal .... Megillah 12b
Songs of Tanach, writing .... Menachos 31b-32a; Shabbos 103b; Megillah 16b

Episodes —
Song, five worlds .... Berachos 10a
Song of earth, in Hezekiah's place .... Sanhedrin 94a
Song, Saul's fall .... Moed Katan 16b
Song to Rabbi Avuhu .... Kesubos 17a; Sanhedrin 14a
Song, when Ark started its journey .... Avodah Zarah 24b
Song, when Ark was returned from Philistines .... Avodah Zarah 24b
Songs for Sages' *semichah* .... Kesubos 17a; Sanhedrin 14a

Prohibitions —
Song of women, preference .... Sotah 48a
Song, since Temple destruction .... Sotah 48a-48b; Gittin 7a
Song, verse .... Sanhedrin 101a

Temple —
Song, burnt offering and libations .... Arachin 11a-12a; Berachos 35a
Song, by mouth or instrument .... Succah 50b-51a; Arachin 11a; Taanis 27a; Avodah Zarah 47a

S

Song, how many *Leviim* and instruments .... Arachin 13b
Song of Hogras, mentioned derogatorily .... Yoma 38a-38b
Song of *Leviim*, indispensable requirement .... Arachin 11a
Song of *Leviim*, source .... Arachin 11a-11b
Song of *Rosh Chodesh* .... Rosh Hashanah 30b; Succah 54b-55a; Beitzah 4b-5a
Song of Rosh Hashanah .... Rosh Hashanah 30b
Song, which *Levi* is fit to sing .... Arachin 11a
Song, wine libation .... Berachos 35a; Arachin 11a, 12a

Misc. —
Song, not when My creatures drown in the sea .... Sanhedrin 39b
Song of Sea .... Sotah 30b-31a; Berachos 50a; Kesubos 7b
Songs were Your statutes for me .... Sotah 35a

Son-in-law
Son-in-law, distance from mother-in-law .... Pesachim 113a; Kiddushin 12b; Yevamos 52a; Bava Basra 98b
Son-in-law, first, his mother-in-law .... Pesachim 113a
Son-in-law of Rebbi, haircut .... Nedarim 51a; Sanhedrin 22b
Son-in-law screamed at you, come in .... Eruvin 86a

Sorcerer
Sorcerer, Amgosha .... Shabbos 75a
Sorcerer, *Baal Ov* .... Sotah 12b; Sanhedrin 65a, 65b; Krisos 3b
Sorcerer digs in graves .... Bava Basra 58a
Sorcerers of Egypt .... Menachos 85a
Sorceresses, hanging .... Sanhedrin 45b

Sorcery
Episodes —
Sorcery, donkey and garments .... Sanhedrin 67b
Sorcery, episode about squash .... Sanhedrin 68a
Sorcery, Herod's birds .... Chullin 139b
Sorcery, noble woman .... Shabbos 81b-82a; Chullin 105b
Sorcery, pairs, episode about divorcee .... Pesachim 110b
Sorcery, Rabbi Chanina .... Sanhedrin 67b

Misc. —
Sorcery, *aggadah* .... Chullin 7b; Sotah 12b
Sorcery, cases .... Sanhedrin 65a, 65b, 67b; Eruvin 64b; Krisos 3b; Chullin 105b; Shabbos 81b-82a
Sorcery, *chover chaver* .... Krisos 3b; Sanhedrin 65a
Sorcery, dangers .... Chullin 105b; Niddah 17a; Shabbos 82a
Sorcery, non-Jews .... Sanhedrin 59b-60a
Sorcery, Ov does not understand .... Sotah 12b
Sorcery, Ov, on Shabbos .... Sanhedrin 65b
Sorcery, punishment .... Sanhedrin 67a-67b
Sorcery, which is permitted .... Shabbos 67a-67b, 75a; Sanhedrin 68a; Chullin 77b-78a
Sorcery, women .... Sanhedrin 67a

Soreg of Temple .... Middos 2:3; Yoma 16a
Sotah .... *see also* **Warning**, page 731, **Woman guilty of forbidden relations**, page 758
Examining —
Sotah, blessings for innocent woman .... Sotah 26a; Berachos 31b
Sotah, container .... Sotah 15b
Sotah, curse and blessing .... Sotah 17a
Sotah, death .... Sotah 9b, 28a

S

Sotah, death of her partner .... Sotah 27b-28a
Sotah, drinking in public .... Sotah 8b
Sotah, earth .... Sotah 15b-16a
Sotah, erasing scroll .... Sotah 18a
Sotah, her husband sinned .... Sotah 28a, 47b; Yevamos 58a; Kiddushin 27b; Shevuos 5a
Sotah, humiliating her in Temple .... Sotah 8a-8b
Sotah, impure thoughts because of uncovered parts .... Sanhedrin 45a; Sotah 8a-8b
Sotah, inquiries about drinking .... Sotah 18a
Sotah, *Kohen* adjures her .... Sotah 32b
Sotah, order of drinking .... Sotah 14b, 19a-19b, 20b
Sotah, order of water and dust .... Sotah 16b; Temurah 12b
Sotah, refused to drink .... Sotah 19b-20a
Sotah, *Sanhedrin* .... Sotah 7a-7b
Sotah, saving merit .... Sotah 6a-6b, 20b-21a, 22b
Sotah, scroll .... Sotah 17a-18a
Sotah, so that she confesses .... Sotah 7b-8a, 14a-14b
Sotah, taking her out of Temple Courtyard .... Sotah 20b
Sotah, threat .... Sotah 7a-7b
Sotah, two *sotahs* together .... Sotah 8a, 18a
Sotah, uncovering her hair .... Sotah 8a; Sanhedrin 45a
Sotah, water .... Sotah 15b, 20a

Meal offering —
Sotah, burning meal offering .... Sotah 22b-23a
Sotah, meal offering for several suspected men .... Krisos 9b
Sotah, meal offering of barley .... Sotah 15a-15b
Sotah, waving meal offering .... Sotah 19a

Seclusion —
Sotah, circumstances point out .... Sotah 2b, 3a; Niddah 3a
Sotah, contradiction between witnesses .... Sotah 31b-32a
Sotah, drinks a second time .... Sotah 18b-19a
Sotah, forbidden to her husband .... Yevamos 11b
Sotah, had relations with her husband before her partner .... Sotah 24b; Yevamos 58a
Sotah, testimony .... Sotah 2a-2b, 3b, 31a-32a; Sanhedrin 88a
Sotah, time for seclusion .... Sotah 4a-4b
Sotah, witnesses outside *Eretz Yisrael* .... Sotah 6a-7a

Who —
Sotah, betrothed girl .... Sotah 18a-18b, 23b-26a; Yevamos 58a-58b; Kiddushin 27b
Sotah, levirate marriage .... Yevamos 11a-11b; Sotah 5b-6a
Sotah, who .... Sotah 25b-26a, 27a-27b
Sotah, widow awaiting levirate marriage .... Sotah 23b-24a, 25a, 26a; Yevamos 58a-58b;
.... Kiddushin 27b

Misc. —
Sotah in her defilement, *nazir* .... Sotah 2a; Berachos 63a; Nazir 2a
Sotah, prohibition to eat *terumah* .... Sotah 28a-29a, 6a
Sotah, scroll of Helen .... Yoma 37b
Sotah, seclusion with her husband .... Sotah 7a, 25a; Kiddushin 80b-81a

Soul
Soul, additional, Shabbos .... Beitzah 16a; Taanis 27b
Soul and body, punishment .... Sanhedrin 91a-91b

S

Soul, G-d's likeness .... Berachos 10a
Soul in fetus, from when .... Sanhedrin 91b
Soul of converts, Giving of Torah .... Shabbos 146a
Souls saved, episode about Sages' children .... Bava Metzia 85a
Souls will be used up, Messiah .... Yevamos 62a

Sound
Sound, forbidden to make on Shabbos .... Eruvin 104a
Sound of quill pen, divorce certificate .... Gittin 6a
Sound of water, sleep .... Eruvin 104a
Sound, stronger at night .... Yoma 20b
Sounds, emitted by dead sheep .... Kinin 3:6; Zevachim 68a
Sounds heard in Temple .... Yoma 20b, 39b; Tamid 30b

Soup
Soup during meal, health .... Berachos 44a
Soup kitchen, collecting and distributing .... Bava Basra 8b; Peah 8:7
Soup kitchen, from when one must pay .... Bava Basra 8a

Source
Source about cooking by idolater .... Avodah Zarah 37b-38a
Source about explanation .... Chullin 77a
Source about fellow's money .... Bava Metzia 117b
Source about *halacha* to Moses from Sinai .... Pesachim 81b
Source, amounts .... Succah 5b-6a; Eruvin 4a-4b
Source and logic, preference .... Zevachim 96b
Source from Torah for Rabbinical Decrees .... Berachos 19b; Shabbos 23a; Eruvin 21b-22a;
.... Makos 23b; Yevamos 21a
Source from Torah, for Rabbinical Decrees of forbidden relations .... Yevamos 21a
Source of various proverbs, from Tanach .... Bava Kama 92a-92b
South, Elders .... Zevachim 22b-23a Yevamos 45a Chullin 132b
South, Scorpio constellation .... Pesachim 94a; Eruvin 56a

***Sovev* of Altar**
Sovev of Altar, indispensable requirement .... Zevachim 62a
Sovev of Altar, kindling fire upon .... Zevachim 65a

Sowing
Sowing .... *see* **Planting**, page 492
Sowing, secondary category of labor .... Shabbos 73b; Moed Katan 2b

Space
Space between *Chumashim* .... Bava Basra 13b
Space between ramp and Altar .... Zevachim 87b; Pesachim 34a, 77a
Space of a handbreadth, coffins .... Berachos 19b

Span
Span, G-d's and dimension .... Eruvin 21a
Span, Shabbos works .... Shabbos 106a

Sparks
Sparks, comet .... Berachos 58b
Sparks, extinguishing on Shabbos .... Shabbos 47b
Sparks, Rebbi and Rav .... Chullin 137b
Sparks, urine .... Yoma 29b-30a

Speaker
Speaker, duty-bound to offer sacrifice .... Shevuos 22a

S

Speaker, first, Rabbi Yehudah.. Shabbos 33b; Berachos 63b

Speaking

Speaking... *see also* **Speech**, page 649

Speaking during reading of Torah.. Sotah 39a

Speaking harshly towards G-d... Berachos 31b-32a; Taanis 25a

Speaking in a disparaging way about Sages.. Sanhedrin 99b

Speaking, not to speak while eating... Taanis 5b

Speaking without commitment, condition at one's disadvantage.............. Bava Metzia 65b-66a

Speaking without doing... Shevuos 46a

Spoke like humans, Torah.. Kesubos 67b

Spoke, verse spoke in present tense... Bava Kama 54b

Speaking without intention to testify

Speaking without intention to testify, *agunah*.......................... Gittin 28b-29a; Yevamos 121b-122a;

.... Bava Kama 114b

Speaking without intention to testify, *orlah*... Yevamos 122a

Speaking without intention to testify, priesthood... Kesubos 26a

Speaking without intention to testify, Rabbinical Decree....................................... Bava Kama 114b

Specialist's work, *Chol HaMoed*.. Moed Katan 11a

Species on its species, tithe

Species on its species, tithe.. Bechoros 53b-54b, 2:4-6; Temurah 5a

Species on its species, tithe, source.. Bechoros 53b-54b

Specific and general

Specific and general, apart... Niddah 33a; Pesachim 6b; Sanhedrin 45b-46a;

Specific and general, deduction... Chullin 88b; Bechoros 19a

.... Bava Kama 85a; Menachos 55b

Specific and general, how.. Nazir 35a-35b; Eruvin 28a; Bava Kama 63a, 64a

Specific and general, *kol*, deduction to include .... Bava Kama 54b, 63a; Niddah 33a

Specific and general, positive and negative commandments..... Moed Katan 3a; Sanhedrin 113a

Specific and general, when.. Zevachim 4b

Speech

Speech................................ *see also* **Conversation**, page 127, **Expression**, page 210, **Speaking**, page 649

Speech, act of acquisition.. Kesubos 102b; Kiddushin 9a, 9b; Moed Katan 18b

Speech, act of acquisition for consecrated items Treasury........... Kiddushin 28b; Bava Metzia 6a;

.... Bava Basra 133b; Avodah Zarah 63a; Temurah 29b

Speech annuls speech... Kiddushin 59a; Gittin 32b

Speech, baby, from when... Berachos 40a

Speech by fingers.. Berachos 46b

Speech considered like act, *Vayechulu*... Shabbos 119b

Speech, excessively refined.. Kiddushin 70a

Speech, forbidden, on Shabbos... Shabbos 113a-113b, 150a-151a

Speech, lashes for sins involving speech........................... Bava Metzia 90b-91a; Sanhedrin 65b

Speech like act, prohibitions.. Temurah 3a

Speech necessitating sacrifice.. Shevuos 22a

Speech of child, what he heard from his father or mother................................... Succah 56b

Speech of idolatry, sacrifice.. Sanhedrin 63a

Speech of men, vow............................ Nedarim 30b, 49a, 51b; Rosh Hashanah 12b; Yoma 76b; Bechoros 55a;

.... Arachin 9b, 19b

Speech of palm trees, Hillel's disciples... Succah 28a; Bava Basra 134a

Speech of Sages is a blessing... Kesubos 103a

S

Speech of Sages is different .... Avodah Zarah 58b; Chullin 137b
Speech, prohibitions and behavior .... Bava Kama 38b; Kesubos 5b; Yoma 19b
Speech, requirement to bring sin offering .... Krisos 3b-4a; Sanhedrin 65a-65b
Speech, that which will become heard .... Avos 2:4
Speech, usual, Torah ...... Bava Metzia 31b, 94b; Berachos 31b; Yevamos 71a; Kesubos 67b; Nedarim 3a; Gittin 41b;
.... Kiddushin 17b; Sanhedrin 56a, 64b, 85b, 90b; Makos 12a; Avodah Zarah 27a; Zevachim 108b; Arachin 3a; Krisos 11a
Speech, usual, what is included in sale .... Bava Basra 77b; Bava Metzia 40b
Speech when eating .... Taanis 5b
Speech, wine and spices .... Krisos 6b
Spending money for charity, not more than fifth ...... Kesubos 50a, 67b; Arachin 28a
Spice
Spice, cooking on Shabbos .... Shabbos 42a
Spice from second tithe .... Niddah 51b
Spice, impurity of food .... Uktzin 3:4-5; Eduyos 5:3; Niddah 51b-51a
Spice of life and poison, Torah .... Yoma 72b; Taanis 7a; Shabbos 88b
Spice of life, speech .... Avodah Zarah 19b
Spice of Shabbos, emperor .... Shabbos 119a
Spices, cutting off end on Shabbos .... Shabbos 128a
Spices, forbidden mixture .... Orlah 2:10; Avodah Zarah 66a, 68b
Spices, mixture of several .... Orlah 2:10; Avodah Zarah 66a, 68b
Spices of incense .... Krisos 6a-6b
Spider, remedy for scorpion .... Shabbos 77b
Spies
Spies, cluster of grapes .... Sotah 34a
Spies, dates .... Taanis 29a
Spies, defense by Moses .... Berachos 32a
Spies, episode .... Sotah 34b-35a; Menachos 53b; Arachin 15a
Spies, righteous men's response .... Taanis 14b
Spies, Temple destruction .... Menachos 53b
Spies, Tisha Be'*av* .... Taanis 29a
Spies, Israelites died in desert .... Bava Basra 121b
Spinach
Spinach, cure .... Berachos 44b, 57b; Avodah Zarah 29a
Spinach, health .... Berachos 39a, 44b; Eruvin 29a
Spine
Spine and skull, impurity .... Nazir 50a, 52a-52b
Spine, medicine .... Chullin 121a
Spine of corpse, snake .... Bava Kama 16a
Spine, *treifah* .... Chullin 45b-46a
Spinning
Spinning in the street .... Kesubos 72a-72b
Spinning, Shabbos .... Shabbos 74b
Spirit
Spirit, bad .... *see* **Bad spirit,** page 40
Spirit of death, Giving of Torah .... Shabbos 129b
Spirit of folly, transgression .... Sotah 3a
Spirit of impurity, graves .... Niddah 17a; Sanhedrin 65b
Spirit of Naboth, Ahab .... Sanhedrin 89a
Spirits of dead, episode .... Berachos 18b

S

Spitting

Spitting during prayer .... Berachos 24a-24b

Spitting in synagogue .... Berachos 62b-63a

Spitting mucus in front of teacher .... Eruvin 99a

Spitting on fellow, punishment .... Chagigah 5a

Spitting on fellow, shame .... Bava Kama 91a; Kesubos 66a

Spitting on public domain .... Shabbos 8b, 100b

Spitting on Temple Mount .... Berachos 62b

Spittle

Spittle, capacity to make impure .... Keilim 8:10; Machshirin 1:6; Tevul Yom 3:6; Eruvin 99a

Spittle, carrying out on Shabbos .... Eruvin 99a

Spittle, impurity of body liquids .... Niddah 55b-56a

Spittle in mouth, carrying .... Eruvin 99a

Spittle disqualified widow .... Yevamos 104b-105a

Spittle of firstborn .... Bava Basra 126b

Spittle of widow awaiting levirate marriage .... Yevamos 105a, 106b

Spittle, remedy on Shabbos .... Shabbos 108b

Spittle, stepping on spittle as if by accident on Shabbos .... Shabbos 121b

Spleen

Spleen, blood .... Chullin 111a

Spleen, health .... Berachos 44b; Shabbos 110a

Spleen, removal to run faster .... Sanhedrin 21b; Avodah Zarah 44a

Spleen, *treifah* .... Chullin 42b, 55a-55b

Splint for animal, Shabbos .... Shabbos 54b

Splinter from beam .... Sanhedrin 7b; Horayos 3b

Split

Split in two, utensil, impurity .... Keilim 16:1

Split young found in mother's womb .... Niddah 24a-24b

Splitting of Red Sea, how .... Sotah 36b-37a

Splitting of Red Sea, song .... Sotah 30b-31a

Splitting wood, damage .... Bava Kama 32b

Sponge on Shabbos .... Shabbos 143a

Spoon will burn tinsmith .... Pesachim 28a

Spot for cutting, fetus .... Chullin 68a-68b

Spotted *esrog* .... Succah 35b-36b

Spraying wine .... Bava Kama 115b; Pesachim 20b

Spreading tablecloth, *kiddush* .... Pesachim 100a-100b

Springs

Springs of wisdom, Rabbi Akiva .... Sotah 49b

Springs, temperature and source .... Pesachim 94b

Sprinkling .... *see also* **Blood,** page 66, **Throwing blood on Altar,** page 690

   Disqualified —

Sprinkling, hand cut off .... Zevachim 15a

Sprinkling, intermingled sacrifices .... Zevachim 74b-75b

Sprinkling, invalid, correcting .... Zevachim 34b; Meilah 5b

Sprinkling out of place, laws .... Zevachim 26a-27b, 32a

Sprinkling, wart on finger .... Zevachim 40b

Sprinklings, improper thought .... Zevachim 38b

S

Sacrifices —
Sprinkling blood of part of sacrifice ....Pesachim 62a, 77a-78b, 79a; Meilah 15b;
....Zevachim 25b, 104a, 109a-109b; Menachos 9a, 26a; Bechoros 39b
Sprinkling, immersing finger ....Zevachim 93b; Menachos 7b
Sprinkling, one sprinkling hinders................Zevachim 36b-37b; Sanhedrin 4a-4b; Menachos 44b
Sprinklings, indispensable requirement of sin offerings..................................Zevachim 37b-38a
Sprinklings, sacrifice valid without sprinklings ....Zevachim 38b-39a

Which sacrifices —
Sprinkling blood of bird sacrifices..Zevachim 64b
Sprinkling blood of burnt offering, place..Zevachim 51a-52a
Sprinkling blood of cow..Menachos 27b-28a
Sprinkling blood of daily offering...Yoma 15a-15b
Sprinkling blood of guilt offering for leper..Zevachim 47b; Yevamos 7a
Sprinkling blood of guilt offering, *sikrah* thread..Zevachim 10b
Sprinkling blood of Pesach lamb................Pesachim 64b-65a; Zevachim 34b-35a, 37a, 56b-57a
Sprinkling blood of sin offering, place..Zevachim 52b-53a

Misc. —
Sprinkling blood, *Kohen* son of *Kohen* who sprinkled blood.......................Berachos 28a
Sprinkling blood on Shabbos, overrides Shabbos..Pesachim 69a
Sprinkling in due time, commandment..Yoma 8a
Sprinkling on impure person on Shabbos..Pesachim 69a
Sprinkling on *Kohen* for burning Red Heifer...Yoma 8a-8b
Sprinkling on uncircumcised man..Yevamos 71b; Zevachim 118a
Sprinklings on *Kohen Gadol*, Yom Kippur......................................Yoma 4a, 8a-8b, 14a

Sprinklings in *Heichal*
Sprinklings in *Heichal*, cloth partition..Yoma 57a, 58b
Sprinklings in *Heichal*, indispensable requirement................................Zevachim 39a-40a
Sprinklings in *Heichal*, roof caved in ....Zevachim 40a
Sprinklings in *Heichal*, source..Zevachim 40a

Sprinkling of Yom Kippur
Sprinkling of Yom Kippur, similar to lashes..Yoma 15a
Sprinklings of Yom Kippur, Ark cover..Yoma 54b-55a
Sprinklings of Yom Kippur, cloth partition..........................Yoma 56b-57a; Zevachim 57a
Sprinklings of Yom Kippur, golden Altar..Yoma 58b-59a
Sprinklings of Yom Kippur, how to count...Yoma 55a
Sprinklings of Yom Kippur, indispensable requirement....................Zevachim 40a-41b
Sprinklings of Yom Kippur, place..Menachos 27b
Sprinklings of Yom Kippur, place to stand...Yoma 58b
Sprinklings of Yom Kippur, source..Zevachim 42b

Sprinkling outside
Sprinkling outside, cases..Zevachim 111b-112a
Sprinkling outside, exegesic dead..................................Zevachim 107a-107b; Sanhedrin 34b
Sprinkling outside of Temple, part of blood..Zevachim 110a-111a

Sprinkling Red Heifer water
Sprinkling Red Heifer water ....*see also* **Water for sprinkling**, page 736
Sprinkling Red Heifer water, fee..Kiddushin 58b; Bechoros 29a
Sprinkling Red Heifer water, for whom..................Yevamos 72b-73a; Yoma 43a-43b; Parah 5:4
Sprinkling Red Heifer water, how..Parah 12:1-11
Sprinkling Red Heifer water, indispensable requirement............Kiddushin 62a; Parah 12:1-4

S

Sprinkling Red Heifer water, night..Yoma 42b; Parah 12:11a

Spur

Spur, dimension necessary to conduct impurity.....................Shabbos 16b-17a; Oholos 16:1

Spur, words of Torah...Chagigah 3b

Square

Square form of Altar, requisite...Zevachim 62a, 108b, 120a

Square of city, *techum*...Eruvin 55a-55b

Square of *tefillin*...Megillah 24b; Menachos 35a; Shabbos 28b

Squash

Squash, harmful like swords.............................Berachos 57b; Avodah Zarah 11a, 29a

Squash, health...Berachos 57b; Avodah Zarah 11a, 29a

Squash, learning sorcery..Sanhedrin 68a

Squeezing

Squeezing bird sacrifice on Altar..............Zevachim 52a-52b, 65a, 66a; Meilah 8b-9a

Squeezing hair...Shabbos 128b

Squeezing into food...Shabbos 144b-145a

Squeezing on Shabbos, which fruit...Shabbos 145a

Squeezing, possible, absorption..Chullin 108a-109a

Squeezing, preserved food and boiled vegetables..........................Shabbos 145a

Squill

Squill, rebuke to man moving fence..Beitzah 25b

Squill, Joshua...Bava Basra 56a

Sta'm...*see* **Holy parchments, bought from expert**, page 281

Stack

Stack, damage by dog and fire...Bava Kama 23a

Stack, succah..Succah 12a-12b, 15a, 16a

Stadiums, non-Jews...Avodah Zarah 18b

Staff

Staff, carrying out on Yom Tov...Beitzah 25b

Staff for old age..Yevamos 65b; Kesubos 64a

Staff for preparation of olives, impurity..Shabbos 123b

Staff in which coins were hidden, episode about oath................Nedarim 25a; Shevuos 29a

Staff of Aaron, concealed..........................Horayos 12a; Yoma 52b; Krisos 5b

Staff of Aaron, snake...Shabbos 97a

Stain on garment, Sage...Shabbos 114a

Stain of *niddah*

Stain of *niddah*..Niddah 4b-5a, 57b-58a, 59a

Stain of *niddah*, ascribing to other factors........................Niddah 19b-20a, 58b-59a

Stain of *niddah*, checking..Niddah 61b-63a

Stain of *niddah*, description.....................................Niddah 58a, 59a, 60b, 61b

Stain of *niddah*, dimension..Niddah 58b-59a

Stain of *niddah*, doubt from which woman......................Niddah 60b; Kiddushin 73b

Stain of *niddah*, found in street...Niddah 56b

Stain of *niddah*, from which woman...........................Niddah 58a-58b, 59b-61a

Stain of *niddah*, lost..Niddah 61a-61b

Stain of *niddah*, on her body...Niddah 57b, 58a

Stain of *niddah*, place...Niddah 58a

Stain of *niddah*, retroactive impurity...................................Niddah 15a, 53b, 56b

Stains of *niddah*, appearance......................................Niddah 19a-21a; Sanhedrin 87b

S

Stains of *niddah*, episodes about rulings .... Niddah 20a-20b

Stairs
Stairs in Temple .... Yoma 16a; Middos 3:6; Succah 51b
Stairs of Temple Mount .... Middos 2:3

Stake
Stake, mixed species .... Kilayim 6:3
Stakes on pillar, Shabbos .... Eruvin 78a

Stall, sweeping on Shabbos .... Shabbos 140b-141a

Stam Mishnah Tosefta... .... *see* **Mishnah, Tosefta etc., author, page 415**

Stam umachlokes .... *see* **Dispute and undisputed, page 167**

Stama kelishmah .... *see* **Intention, unspecified like specified, page 313**

Stand

Commandments —
Standing before Torah scroll .... Kiddushin 33b; Makos 22b
Standing during *Shemoneh Esrei* .... Berachos 30a
Standing for *chalitzah* .... Yevamos 103a
Standing for service, *Kohen* .... Zevachim 19b
Standing in direction of Jerusalem, prayer .... Berachos 30a
Standing, litigants .... Shevuos 30a
Standing while learning Torah .... Megillah 21a
Standing, witnesses .... Shevuos 30a

Health —
Standing for five activities, danger .... Shabbos 129b; Gittin 70a
Standing, health .... Kesubos 111a-111b
Standing immediately after eating or sleeping, danger .... Shabbos 129b; Gittin 70a
Standing while leaning .... Zevachim 19b

Misc. —
Stand and we shall do our work .... Niddah 49b; Shabbos 59a; Chagigah 23b
Standing before G-d, Eglon .... Sanhedrin 60a
Standing erect .... Kiddushin 31a; Berachos 43b; Sanhedrin 81a
Standing packed in Temple .... Yoma 21a; Avos 5:5
Standing to rest or to load one's burden .... Shabbos 5b; Kesubos 31a-31b

Standing before Sage
Standing before Sage, episodes .... Berachos 28a; Shabbos 31b; Eruvin 28b
Standing before Sage or old man .... Kiddushin 32b-33b; Horayos 13b; Chullin 54b
Standing before Sage, resentment .... Kiddushin 32b, 33a
Standing before Sage who is one's son, episode .... Kesubos 62b
Standing before Sage's wife .... Shevuos 30b
Standing before *Nasi*, difference of opinion, episode .... Horayos 13b-14a
Standing before one another, Sages of Babylon .... Bava Metzia 33a

Star
Star Ayish, place .... Berachos 58b-59a
Star, comet .... Berachos 58b
Star, Rabbi Yehoshua .... Horayos 10a
Stars, answer to heretic .... Sanhedrin 39a
Stars appearing, night .... Berachos 2b; Megillah 20b
Stars appearing, workers stopping work .... Bava Metzia 83a-83b
Stars, astronomy .... Berachos 58b-59a; Pesachim 94a; Eruvin 56a
Stars, flood .... Berachos 59a; Rosh Hashanah 11b

Stars, Israel..Berachos 32b
Staring...*see* **Looking at**, page 377
Starling went to raven...Bava Kama 92b
Staying
Staying alone, punishment for leper...Arachin 16b
Staying without wife...Yevamos 62b
Stealing
Stealing...*see also* **Theft**, page 685, **Thief**, page 686
Stealing less than a *perutah*, idolater.............Avodah Zarah 71b; Eruvin 62a; Yevamos 47b
Stealing, lost item...Bava Metzia 26b
Stealing, money..Sanhedrin 85b-86a
Stealing surreptitiously.................................Sanhedrin 72a-72b; Pesachim 2a-2b; Yoma 85b
Stealing surreptitiously, exempt from payment.................Sanhedrin 72a; Bava Kama 114a-114b
Stealing Temple cup, put to death..Sanhedrin 81b, 82b
Stealing to tease..Bava Metzia 61b
Stealing with intention to pay..Bava Kama 60b
Stolen goods, decree for commerce...Bava Kama 115a
Stolen land, buying land from thief...Bava Metzia 15b-16a
Stealing from an idolater
Stealing from an idolater and not paying him his wages.....................Bava Metzia 111b
Stealing from an idolater, fraud and keeping one's word......................Bechoros 13b
Stealing from an idolater, from Sinai..Bava Kama 38a
Stealing from an idolater, his loan and his lost item...............Bava Kama 113a-113b
Stealing from an idolater, less than a *perutah*......................................Sanhedrin 57a
Stealing from an idolater, worker..Sanhedrin 57a
Stolen item
Stolen item, claiming from buyer..Bava Kama 111b, 115a
Stolen item, consumed, difficulty to return..Chullin 89a
Stolen item, decree for commerce...Bava Kama 115a
Stolen item, subtracting value of fragments........................Bava Kama 11a, 94a
Stolen and lost item, paid custodian.............Bava Metzia 93a-95a; Shevuos 49a
Stolen item, from convert
Stolen item, from convert, general.......................................Bava Kama 108a-109b
Stolen item, from convert, *Kohanim*....Bava Kama 109b, 110a-111a; Menachos 45b; Arachin 28b
Stolen item, from convert, returning........Bava Kama 109a-111a; Kiddushin 21a; Sanhedrin 68b-69a
Stolen item, from convert, sacrifice.................................Bava Kama 110b-111a
Stolen item, from convert to *Kohen*, source............Zevachim 44b; Menachos 73a
Steam
Steam, connecting impurity...Machshirin 5:9-11
Steam, impurity and making susceptible to become impure...........Machshirin 2:1-3
Step
Step, dimension of one cubit...Eruvin 42a
Steps, according to one's food..Shabbos 152a
Steps, large, journey..Taanis 10b
Steps of Rabbi Chanina ben Teradion's daughter.................Avodah Zarah 18a
Steps, prayer..Yoma 53b
Step-sister, permission to marry...Sotah 43b
Sterile, Rav Huna's lecture..Yevamos 62b, 64b

S

Sterile man

Sterile man, and Rabbi Yehoshua ben Korcha .... Shabbos 152a

Sterile man, divorce .... Yevamos 65a

Sterile man, levirate marriage and *chalitzah* .... Yevamos 24a, 79b-80a, 80b; Bechoros 42b-43a

Sterile man, signs .... Yevamos 79b-80a, 80b, 97a; Niddah 47b; Bava Basra 155b

Sterile woman

Sterile woman, forcing husband to divorce her .... Kesubos 77a-77b

Sterile woman, her rights .... Kesubos 101a-101b; Bava Metzia 67a; Yevamos 113a

Sterile woman, *kesubah* .... Yevamos 65a-65b

Sterile woman, levirate marriage .... Yevamos 12a-12b, 20a, 24a

Sterile woman, penalty .... Kesubos 35b-36a

Sterile woman, procreation .... Yevamos 61a-61b

Sterile woman, prohibition to marry .... Yevamos 65a

Sterile woman, signs .... Yevamos 80a, 80b, 97a; Niddah 47b

Sterile woman to *Kohen* .... Yevamos 61b, 81a

Sterile woman, waited ten years .... Yevamos 34b, 64a-64b

Sterile, woman who waited for her husband .... Kesubos 62b

Stern one, you called me .... Sanhedrin 113a-113b

Stick

Stick, dimension necessary to conduct impurity .... Shabbos 16b-17a; Oholos 16:1-2

Stick inserted, *muktzeh* .... Shabbos 140a-140b

Sticks of table in Temple .... Menachos 97a

Still, miracle of sun staying still .... Avodah Zarah 25a; Taanis 20a

Stillborn

Stillborn, examining gender .... Niddah 25a-25b

Stillborn child, firstborn .... Bechoros 46a-47b; Chullin 68a

Stillborn child, impurity of dead .... Bechoros 22a; Oholos 7:4-5

Stillborn child, mourning .... Niddah 44b; Shabbos 136a; Bechoros 49a

Stillborn child, *muktzeh* .... Shabbos 135a; Yevamos 80a-80b; Bava Basra 20a

Stillborn, doubt .... Shabbos 135b-136b; Yevamos 36b, 80b; Niddah 44b

Stillborn, forty days .... Niddah 25b

Stillborn, from when considered born .... Bechoros 46a-46b; Niddah 28a, 29a

Stillborn, murderer exempt .... Sanhedrin 84b

Stilts, impurity .... Shabbos 66b

Stimah .... see **Plugging up barrel**, page 493, see also **Stopping**, page 657

Stimulating evil urge in oneself .... Niddah 13b

Sting, baby .... Kesubos 50a

Stingy, woman towards guests .... Bava Metzia 87a

Stirah .... see **Contradiction**, page 126

Stirring pot on Shabbos .... Beitzah 34a

Stolen .... see **Stealing**, page 655

Stomach

Stomach, meat with milk .... Chullin 116a-116b

Stomach of non-Jew's animal, cheese .... Avodah Zarah 34b

Stomach, old, nose reawakens .... Brachos 61b:

Stomach sleeping, nose awakened .... Berachos 61b

Stomach, *treifah* .... Chullin 50b, 52b

Stone

Damage —
Stone in public domain, damage...Bava Kama 28a-28b
Stone of row, damage..Bava Metzia 118b
Stone which damaged..Bava Kama 3a-3b, 6a
Stone which fell, similar to fire...Bava Kama 3b

Episodes —
Stone of resurrection, episode...Bava Basra 74a-74b
Stones in Jordan..Sotah 33b-34b
Stones of Jacob...Chullin 91b
Stones thrown on public road, episode..Bava Kama 50b

Prohibitions —
Stone for building, positioning on ground, Shabbos...................................Shabbos 102b
Stone from fence, wiping on Shabbos...Bava Kama 81b
Stone, idolatrous, prostrating upon..Megillah 22b
Stone on barrel, *muktzeh*..Shabbos 125b, 142b
Stones of *Markolis*.......................................Avodah Zarah 49b-50a, 51a; Bava Metzia 25b
Stones of mountain, idolatry...Avodah Zarah 46a, 59a
Stones to wipe oneself, Shabbos...Shabbos 81a-81b; Succah 36b
Stones, work on Sabbatical year...Sheviis 3:5-10

Temple —
Stones of Altar...Middos 3:4
Stones of *shoham*...Sotah 36a-36b
Stones of Temple, *shamir* worm..Gittin 68a; Sotah 48b

Misc. —
"Stone will cry from the wall"...Chagigah 16a
Stone, leprous, impurity..Niddah 54b
Stone, *segulah* for pregnant woman...Shabbos 66b
Stone thrown upon fallen person...Kiddushin 20b; Arachin 30b
Stones, tomb, impurity...Chullin 126b; Oholos 2:4, 15:8-9
Stones, Torah written on..Sotah 35b

Stoning
Stoning, "their blood is in them"...Sanhedrin 53a
Stoning, how...Sanhedrin 43a, 45a-45b
Stoning, naked...Sanhedrin 43a, 44b-45a; Sotah 23b
Stoning, not liable to punishment for one labor..Shabbos 6b
Stoning of animal which sinned with man.........................Sanhedrin 54a, 55a-55b
Stoning of ox..*see* **Ox to be stoned**, page 469
Stoning of woman, impure thoughts.........................Sanhedrin 44b-45a; Sotah 8a-8b
Stoning on basis of *chazakah*...Kiddushin 80a, 63b
Stoning, location..Kesubos 45b; Sanhedrin 42b-43a
Stoning, trustworthiness of *kiddushin*..Kiddushin 63b-64a

Stopping
Stopping hole by fat...Chullin 49b-50a
Stopping one's learning, punishment..Avos 3:7

Store
"Store is open," reward and punishment..Avos 3:16
Store in courtyard, preventing...Bava Basra 20b
Store of Jew and non-Jew, *chametz*...Pesachim 31b
Stores, adorned, idolatry...Avodah Zarah 12b-13a

S

Storehouse
Storehouse, clearing on Shabbos .... Shabbos 126b-127a; Beitzah 35b-36a
Storehouse, distance from neighbors .... Bava Basra 20b
Storehouse for *terumah*, sweeping up .... Terumos 11:6-8
Storehouse, *muktzeh* .... Shabbos 126b-127a
Storehouse, path on Shabbos .... Shabbos 127a
Storehouse, searching for *chametz* .... Pesachim 6a
Storekeeper
Storekeeper, child broke bottle .... Bava Basra 87b-88a
Storekeeper with his account book, oath .... Shevuos 47b; Bava Metzia 3a, 6a
Stork
Stork, kind towards its companions .... Chullin 63a
Stork, "Your judgements are like very deep water" .... Chullin 63a
Stove-top
Stove-top, broken, moving .... Shabbos 138b
Stove-top, impurity .... Keilim 6:1-4, 7:1-6
Stove-top, keeping food warm over Shabbos .... Shabbos 38b
Stove-top, preparation for use on Shabbos .... Shabbos 20a, 36b
Straight standing .... Kiddushin 31a; Berachos 43b; Sanhedrin 81a
Strained answer
Strained answer, not adopted as law .... Yevamos 91b; Bava Basra 135a
Strained answer on verse .... Kiddushin 68a; Pesachim 59b; Niddah 33a
Strangulation, death penalty .... Sanhedrin 52b-53a
Strap
Strap of *tefillin*, fast .... Moed Katan 25a
Straps of *tefillin* .... Menachos 35a-35b; Shabbos 28b
Straps to protect animals, Shabbos .... Shabbos 54b
Straw
Straw between courtyards, eating .... Eruvin 79a
Straw between *techumim* .... Eruvin 79b
Straw, closing crack .... Eruvin 78b-79a
Straw, considered like earth for impurity .... Eruvin 78b-79a; Succah 4a; Oholos 15:6-7
Straw in basket, separating on Shabbos .... Shabbos 140a
Straw to dry courtyard .... Eruvin 104a
Straw you sell in place full of straw! sorcery .... Menachos 85a
Stream
Stream for calf whose neck is broken .... Sotah 46a-46b
Stream, parable for Torah .... Berachos 16a
Stream, signs .... Pesachim 53a
Stream with strong current, danger .... Yoma 77b
Streets, lands of the living .... Yoma 71a
Strength
Strength, Divine behavior .... Avodah Zarah 4a
Strength, Divine, humility .... Megillah 31a
Strength, keeping it in old age .... Kesubos 62a
Strength of *Kohanim* in Temple .... Zevachim 64a; Succah 52b
Strength of man .... *see* **Human intervention**, page 287
Strength, second strength implied, fire .... Bava Kama 3b
Strength, son's superior to father's .... Shevuos 48a; Chullin 49b, 63a

S

Strength to wicked, to bear punishment .... Sanhedrin 100b

Strength, indirect

Strength, indirect, damage .... Bava Kama 3b

Strength, indirect, in *karmelis* .... Shabbos 100b-101a, 141a

Strength, indirect, pushing back water in *karmelis* .... Shabbos 141a

Strength, indirect, slaughtering .... Chullin 16a

Strength, indirect, wine of idolaters .... Avodah Zarah 60a

Strength, direct and indirect, murderer .... Sanhedrin 77b-78a; Makos 8a; Chullin 16a

Strengthening Rabbinical Decree .... Bava Metzia 55b; Eruvin 77a, 85b; Rosh Hashanah 19a;

.... Kesubos 56a-56b

Stretch of Cutheans, impurity .... Chagigah 25a

Strict one cannot teach .... Avos 2:5

Strictness towards disciples .... Kesubos 103b

Striking .... *see* **Hitting,** page 279

String, rooster, damage .... Bava Kama 19b

Stringencies

Stringencies about sin offerings .... Zevachim 94b

Stringencies for purity of sacred things .... Chagigah 20b-21a

Stringencies for Red Heifer .... Parah 5:1, 5:4, 10:1-6, 12:6-8; Chagigah 23b

Stringencies of Ezekiel .... Chullin 37b, 44b

Stringencies, purity of sacrifices .... Chagigah 18b, 20b-21a; Chullin 35a-35b

Stringencies, Rabbi Yochanan's city .... Shabbos 46a; Yevamos 14a

Stringency and leniency, stringency .... Niddah 5a

Stringency causing leniency .... Niddah 24a

Stringency, fool in darkness .... Eruvin 6b-7a; Rosh Hashanah 14b; Chullin 43b-44a

Stringency for others .... Sotah 21b

Stringency, if you can do better .... Berachos 30a; Bava Kama 81b

Stringency, important person .... Shabbos 51a, 142b; Pesachim 110a; Megillah 22b; Moed Katan 11b, 12a;

.... Kesubos 52b, 86a; Bava Metzia 73a; Avodah Zarah 8b, 48b

Stringency like Beis Shamai .... Berachos 11a

Stringency like Beis Shamai, "all the more so" .... Berachos 10b-11a

Stringency like two opinions, episode .... Gittin 35a; Bava Kama 99b

Stringency, meat about which Sage ruled .... Chullin 44b

Stringency, not *Bnei Torah* .... Shabbos 139a-139b; Avodah Zarah 58a, 59a; Yevamos 46a

Stringency or leniency, "all the more so" .... Avodah Zarah 46b

Stringency, proof .... Yadayim 4:3

Stringency, slander on divorce certificate .... Gittin 5b

Strip of Cutheans, impurity .... Chagigah 25a

Strong

Strong animals, fear of weak ones .... Shabbos 77b

Strong as a leopard .... Avos 5:20

Strong like lion, episode .... Yevamos 122b

Strong men of *Eretz Yisrael* and pious ones of Babylon ..... Taanis 23b; Megillah 28b; Chullin 122a

Strong men of *Eretz Yisrael*, Resh Lakish .... Yoma 9b

Strong person, *chazakah* .... Bava Basra 36a

Strong person, testimony .... Bava Metzia 39b; Kesubos 27b

Strong things, superseded by stronger ones .... Bava Basra 10a

Strongest man seizes item whose ownership is in doubt ...... Bava Basra 34b-35b; Gittin 60b

Strong-hearted idolaters, did not convert .... Berachos 17b

S

Student
Student .... *see* **Disciple**, page 165
Student for one day .... Chagigah 5b
Student, practical advice .... Shabbos 140b
Student, severity towards .... Kesubos 103b
Study .... *see* **Learning**, page 357
Study partner, he who suggests to learn must arrive first .... Nedarim 8a
Stuffing, putting back into pillow .... Shabbos 48a
Stumble
Stumbled on ground, damage by stone .... Bava Kama 28b
Stumbling, considered liable .... Bava Kama 27b, 29a-29b, 31a
Stumbling-block
Stumbling-block, accident .... Pesachim 40b; Chullin 64a, 93b-94b; Avodah Zarah 65b
Stumbling-block before stumbling-block .... Avodah Zarah 14a
Stumbling-block because of her, idolatrous tree .... Sanhedrin 55a
Stumbling-block, fruit of fourth year .... Bava Kama 69a-69b
Stumbling-block, giving bread .... Chullin 107b
Stumbling-block, hitting grown-up son .... Moed Katan 17a
Stumbling-block, idolatrous item to idolater .... Avodah Zarah 13b-14b
Stumbling-block, keeping forbidden foods ...... Bava Kama 115b-116a; Pesachim 20b-21a, 33b-34a;
.... Chullin 53b
Stumbling-block, righteous men and their animals ...... Chullin 5b, 6a, 7a; Yevamos 99b; Kesubos 28b;
.... Gittin 7a
Stumbling-block, sale and help .... Sheviis 5:6-10; Avodah Zarah 14a, 15a-15b
Stumbling-block, selling to non-Jew forbidden things .... Pesachim 40b; Chullin 64a, 93b-94b;
.... Avodah Zarah 65b; Niddah 61b
Stumbling-block to others, virgin's prayer .... Sotah 22a
Stumbling-block, wheat as salary for idolatry .... Avodah Zarah 62b
Stumbling-block, when forbidden .... Avodah Zarah 6a-6b; Bava Kama 117a
Style of legal document, too refined .... Bava Basra 69b
Substituted
Substituted divorce certificate and receipt .... Gittin 80b-81a
Substituted Tannaim, like Rebbi .... Pesachim 27a
Substituting between *Kohanim*, meal offerings .... Menachos 72b-73a
Substituting bride, Sage .... Bava Basra 168a
Substituting Sage's name, inquiry .... Bava Kama 11b
Substituting Sage's name, episode .... Kiddushin 44b
Substituting without asking permission .... Bava Kama 60b
Subterranean holes
Subterranean holes, digging .... Succah 53a-53b; Makos 11a
Subterranean holes, libations, wine .... Meilah 11b; Succah 49a-49b
Subterranean holes of Altar .... Succah 49a-49b; Zevachim 61b; Middos 3:2-3
Subterranean waters of Babylon .... Shabbos 145b
Subtracting from commandments .... Zevachim 80a
Succah
　Commandment —
　　Succah, blessing .... Pesachim 7b; Succah 45b, 56a
　　Succah, child .... Succah 28b
　　Succah, commandment to eat in it .... Succah 27a; Eruvin 23a; Yoma 79b

Succah, dwelling ....Succah 28b-29a
Succah, dwelling, how ....Succah 28b-29a
Succah, eating a snack ....Succah 26a-27a; Yoma 79a-79b
Succah, eating on first night of Yom Tov ....Succah 27a
Succah, exemptions ....Succah 25b
Succah, from one to another ....Succah 9a, 27a-27b
Succah, night ....Succah 43a-43b; Shabbos 131b
Succah on eighth day, "do not add" ....Succah 48a
Succah on *Shemini Atzeres* ....Succah 46b-47a
Succah, *Shehecheyanu* ....Succah 46a, 56a; Pesachim 7b; Menachos 42a
Succah, woman ....Succah 28a-28b

Kashrus —
Succah, angular walls ....Succah 4b
Succah beneath succah ....Succah 9b-10a
Succah, borrowed ....Succah 27b
Succah, for those obligated ....Succah 8b
Succah, double *s'chach* ....Succah 22a-22b
Succah, fit for seven days ....Succah 23a, 27b
Succah, GNUCH, RKVSH ....Succah 8a
Succah, old ....Succah 9a
Succah on camel ....Succah 23a
Succah on ship ....Succah 7b, 23a
Succah, ordinary wind ....Succah 23a
Succah, stolen ....Succah 31a
Succah stolen, decree ....Succah 31a
Succah, temporary dwelling ....Succah 7b, 21b
Succah under tree ....Succah 9b

Walls and measures —
Succah, correcting ten handbreadths height ....Succah 4a-4b
Succah, dimension ....Succah 3a
Succah, *migo* to Shabbos ....Succah 7a-7b
Succah, necessary height ....Succah 4b-5b
Succah, repairing twenty handbreadths height ....Succah 3b-4a
Succah, round ....Succah 7b-8b
Succah, twenty handbreadths height ....Succah 2a-3a, 7b; Eruvin 2a, 3a-3b
Succah with pointed top ....Succah 7b, 19b

Misc. —
Succah, *chazakah* ....Bava Basra 6b
Succah, *muktzeh* ....Beitzah 30b; Succah 9a, 10a-10b, 46b; Shabbos 22a, 45a
Succah of non-Jews in the future ....Avodah Zarah 3a
Succos in desert ....Succah 11b

Success in business, for one who learns Torah ....Avodah Zarah 19b

Successive
Successive acts impossible to do, simultaneously also ....Eruvin 50a; Kiddushin 50b-51a;
....Nedarim 69b
Successive periods of mourning ....Moed Katan 17b; Taanis 13a

Succos
Succos, Torah reading and *haftorah* ....Megillah 30b-31a
Succos, verses of *mussaf* sacrifice out of *Eretz Yisrael* ....Succah 55a

S

Sucking, circumcision .... Shabbos 133b
Suckling on Shabbos and Yom Tov .... Kesubos 60a; Yevamos 114a
Sudden death, sick .... Eruvin 41b
Suffering
  Episodes —
    Suffering .... *see also* **Pain**, page 470, **Trouble**, page 704
    Suffering, are beloved to you .... Berachos 5b
    Suffering of Manasseh, repentance .... Sanhedrin 101a-101b
    Suffering of Rebbi .... Bava Metzia 85a
    Suffering of Rabbi Elazar son of Rabbi Shimon .... Bava Metzia 84b
    Suffering of Ezekiel .... Sanhedrin 39a
    Suffering, succah .... Succah 25b
    Suffering, Torah learning .... Berachos 5a; Sotah 21a
    Suffering, what is considered .... Arachin 16b-17a
    Suffering, without sin .... Shabbos 55a-55b
    Sufferings, "not them and not their reward" .... Berachos 5b
    Sufferings, adjuring them .... Avodah Zarah 55a
    Sufferings at death .... Moed Katan 28b-29a
    Sufferings, burden of G-d .... Shabbos 145b; Megillah 31b
    Sufferings of lashes, worse than death .... Kesubos 33a-33b
  Misc. —
    Suffering, atonement .... Berachos 5a-5b; Yoma 86a
    Suffering, beloved .... Sanhedrin 101a-101b
    Suffering for *Eretz Yisrael* .... Berachos 5a
    Suffering for one who refrains from learning .... Berachos 5a
    Suffering from illness, atonement .... Kesubos 111a
    Suffering, G-d suffers together with man .... Sanhedrin 46b; Chagigah 15b
    Suffering, joy .... Taanis 8a
    Suffering, keeping silent .... Berachos 61a, 62a; Kiddushin 80b; Zevachim 115b
    Suffering, life is no life .... Beitzah 32b; Pesachim 113b
    Suffering, nodding head .... Yevamos 121a
    Suffering of animals .... Bava Metzia 32b-33a; Shabbos 128b, 154b
    Suffering of converts .... Yevamos 48b
    Suffering of Messiah .... Sanhedrin 93b, 98a, 98b
    Suffering, prayer for mercy .... Berachos 62a
    Suffering with community .... Taanis 11a
  Suffering of Israel
    Suffering of Israel .... Yevamos 47a
    Suffering of Israel, Divine Presence .... Taanis 16a
    Suffering of Israel, for the good .... Sotah 9a; Avodah Zarah 4a
    Suffering of Israel, olive tree .... Menachos 53b
    Suffering of Israel, used to blows .... Succah 29a
  Suffering of righteous
    Suffering of righteous, "better G-d's anger" .... Shabbos 30b
    Suffering of righteous, *ashrei* .... Yoma 87a
    Suffering of righteous, why .... Kiddushin 39b, 40b; Berachos 7a
Sufficient
  Sufficient for slave to be like his master, charity .... Berachos 58b
  Sufficient, misfortune in its time .... Berachos 9b

S

Sufficient that they raise our children .... Yevamos 63a
Sufficient that they save us from sin, bad wife .... Yevamos 63a
Suicide, prohibition .... Bava Kama 91b
Sulfide and salt, destruction .... Yoma 54a
Summer
Summer, end of summer hotter than summer .... Yoma 28b-29a
Summer, seasons .... Bava Metzia 106b
Summer, wording of vow .... Nedarim 61b, 62b
Summoning to judgment
Summoning to judgment, agents .... Bava Kama 112b-113a
Summoning to judgment, going to judge .... Rosh Hashanah 31b
Summoning to judgment, how .... Sanhedrin 8a; Moed Katan 16a
Summoning to judgment, source .... Moed Katan 16a
Summoning to judgment, times .... Bava Kama 113a
Sun
Benefit —
Sun, cure for dust .... Nedarim 8b
Sun, lying in the sun .... Shabbos 129a
Sun on Shabbos, kindness .... Taanis 8b
Sun, precious stone .... Bava Basra 16b
Episodes —
Sun, Hezekiah and Ahaz .... Sanhedrin 96a
Sun, episode about Korah .... Nedarim 39b; Sanhedrin 110a
Sun, miracle of standing still .... Avodah Zarah 25a; Taanis 20a
Scientific facts —
Sun appears in the morning .... Yoma 28b, 29a
Sun, color .... Bava Basra 84a
Sun, deep reverberation, appearance of leprous marks .... Shevuos 6b; Bava Basra 84a; Chullin 63a; Bechoros 41a
Sun, encircles earth .... Bava Basra 25b; Eruvin 56a
Sun, hot, and shade, cool .... Berachos 27a
Sun in middle of sky, strength .... Tamid 32a
Sun, noise .... Yoma 20b
Sun, orbit .... Eruvin 56a; Pesachim 94b
Sun, rainbow and moon are curved .... Rosh Hashanah 23b-24a
Sun, sets in the west .... Sanhedrin 91b
Misc. —
Sun, harmful for animal .... Sanhedrin 76b-77a
Sun in the future .... Sanhedrin 91b
Sun on Shabbos .... Taanis 8b
Sun, placing one's animal in sun .... Bava Kama 56a
Sun, reward and punishment .... Nedarim 8b; Avodah Zarah 3b-4a
Sunday
Sunday, fast more difficult .... Taanis 27b
Sunday, holiday of non-Jews .... Avodah Zarah 6a, 7b; Taanis 27b
Sunflower .... Shabbos 35b
Sunlight greater than shade .... Succah 7b
Sunrise
Sunrise, commandments .... Megillah 20a

Sunrise, morning prayer .... Berachos 9b, 25b
Sunrise, time for morning prayer .... Berachos 29b
Sunrise, time to read *Shema* .... Berachos 9b, 10b, 25b
Sunset, left over sacrificial blood .... Zevachim 56a-56b; Menachos 20b
Superficial learning before in-depth .... Shabbos 63a
Superfluous
Superfluous expression, gift .... Bava Basra 138a-138b
Superfluous priestly garments .... Eruvin 103b-104a; Zevachim 19a-19b
Superfluous teaching in Mishnah .... Horayos 2a-2b
Superfluous word, similar words .... Yevamos 70b, 74a; Niddah 22b-23a; Shabbos 64a, 131a;
.... Bava Kama 25b

Superintendents of Solomon .... Sanhedrin 12a
Supervisor
Supervisor coming out and in .... Chullin 3a, 3b
Supervisors of Temple .... Shekalim 5:1-2; A
Supplications, prayer .... Berachos 29b; Avos 2:13
Support
  Rights —
  Support, "I do not want to be supported" .... Kesubos 58b, 70b, 83a, 107b; Gittin 77b;
.... Bava Kama 8b; Bava Basra 49b
  Supported, Rav Pappa's wife .... Sanhedrin 14b
  Supporting family, no seizure of sold land .... Gittin 50b-51a
  Supporting girls, increase in value .... Bechoros 52a
  Supporting one's wife's daughter .... Kesubos 102b; Gittin 51a
  Supporting slave .... Gittin 12a-12b; Kesubos 43a, 58b; Bava Kama 87b
  Supporting, small inheritance .... Kesubos 43a, 108b; Bava Basra 139b-140b
  Misc. —
  Support, giving away property to sons .... Kesubos 49b-50a
  Support me like a dog and like a raven .... Bava Basra 8a
  Supported at his table, damage .... Bava Kama 87b
  Supported at his table, finds lost item .... Bava Metzia 12b
  Supporting one's children
  Supporting one's children, charity .... Kesubos 50a
  Supporting one's children, commandment .... Kesubos 49a-49b
  Supporting one's children, of father who went abroad .... Kesubos 48a, 107a
  Supporting one's children, until six years old .... Kesubos 65b
  Supporting betrothed orphan girl
  Supporting betrothed orphan girl, her brothers .... Kesubos 53b
  Supporting orphan girl, who can receive .... Kesubos 53b-54a
  Supporting orphan girl, who must support her .... Bava Basra 122b
  Supporting orphan girl, with which goods .... Kesubos 50b-51a
  Supporting orphan girls, her brothers .... Kesubos 43a-43b
  Supporting one's wife
  Supporting one's wife according to their standing .... Kesubos 48a, 61a
  Supporting one's wife, during nursing period .... Kesubos 65b
  Supporting one's wife, eat from your work! .... Kesubos 70a-70b
  Supporting one's wife, fool and husband who ran away .... Kesubos 48a, 106b-107b
  Supporting one's wife, forbidden wife .... Yevamos 84a, 85a-85b; Kesubos 100b
  Supporting one's wife, forcing to divorce .... Kesubos 63a, 77a

Supporting one's wife, necessary items .... Kesubos 70b
Supporting one's wife, one silver coin per week .... Kesubos 58b-59a, 64b
Supporting one's wife, source .... Kesubos 47b-48a
Supporting one's wife, *terumah* .... Kesubos 58a
Supporting one's wife, time of wedding .... Kesubos 2a-2b, 48b, 57a, 70b; Nedarim 73b
Supporting one's wife, what is included .... Kesubos 64b-65a
Supporting one's wife, doubt if wife is divorced .... Kesubos 97a; Gittin 74a; Bava Metzia 12b;
Bava Basra 47b

Supporting Torah
Supporting Torah, "in shade of wisdom" .... Pesachim 53b
Supporting Torah, attached to Divine Presence .... Kesubos 111b
Supporting Torah, blessing .... Sanhedrin 92a
Supporting Torah, like daily offerings .... Berachos 10b
Supporting Torah, like first fruit .... Kesubos 105b
Supporting Torah, like libations .... Yoma 71a
Supporting Torah, source .... Chullin 134b; Yoma 72b
Support
Support, glass utensils .... Shabbos 15b
Support, impurity .... Shabbos 15b, 59b-60a
Support of *s'chach* .... Succah 21b
Supports for basin in Temple .... Yoma 37a
Supports for basin, Munbaz .... Yoma 37a-37b
Surface of two *seah*, pits concerning Shabbos .... Eruvin 22a
Surgery
Surgery for injured man .... Yevamos 76a
Surgery for removal of fat .... Bava Metzia 83b
Surgery of brain .... Kesubos 77b
Surgery on animals, Alexandria .... Sanhedrin 33a, 93a; Bechoros 28b
Surgery on dead, prohibition .... Chullin 11b
Surpluses, prohibition to throw .... Taanis 20b
Surprising things, do not add .... Kesubos 78a
Surreptitiously coming, death .... Sanhedrin 72a-72b; Pesachim 2a-2b; Yoma 85b
Surrounded
Surrounded by city wall, Purim .... Megillah 2b, 3b-4a, 5b
Surrounded me like roosters .... Yevamos 84a
***Sursis*,** inferior language .... Bava Kama 83a
Surya .... *see* **Syria**, page 668
Susceptible to becoming impure
Wanted —
Susceptible to becoming impure, pleased with the water .... Machshirin 3:5-8
Susceptible to becoming impure, unwanted blood .... Keilim 8:11
Susceptible to becoming impure, water is wanted .... Bava Metzia 22a-22b;
Machshirin 1:1-6, 3:1-8, 4:1-5, 4:9-10, 5:1-8
Misc. —
Susceptible to becoming impure, before thought of eating .... Chullin 128a
Susceptible to becoming impure, blood .... Chullin 35b-36b; Niddah 55b-56a
Susceptible to becoming impure, final touch .... Chullin 118a
Susceptible to becoming impure, food impurity .... Chullin 36a, 129a

Susceptible to becoming impure, harvester for wine press........................Shabbos 15a, 17a;
....Avodah Zarah 39b; Chullin 36b
Susceptible to becoming impure, slaughtering..........Pesachim 20a; Chullin 35b-36b, 127b-128a;
....Krisos 22a
Susceptible to becoming impure, when being taken off..Krisos 15b

Suspected
Suspected butcher...Sanhedrin 25a; Chullin 93b
Suspected man, buying from him...Avodah Zarah 39b; Bechoros 29b-30b
Suspected man, certainly sinned..Moed Katan 18b
Suspected man must clear himself from suspicion..Berachos 31b
Suspected man, stumbling-block...Avodah Zarah 15a-15b
Suspected man, testimony..................Sanhedrin 27a-27b; Bechoros 30a-30b, 35a-36a; Yoma 78a
Suspected of forbidden relations, testimony...Sanhedrin 26b
Suspected of one transgression...Bechoros 30a-30b
Suspected of theft.............................Bava Kama 67b-68a, 113a, 113b, 118b-119a; Bava Basra 51b-52a
Suspected, repentance..Sanhedrin 25a, 25b; Bechoros 31a
Suspected Sage, ruling to marry her...Yevamos 24b-26a
Suspected wrongly..Shabbos 118b
Suspecting and suspected..Moed Katan 18b
Suspecting, appeasing afterwards...Berachos 31b
Suspecting innocent..Shabbos 97a; Yoma 19b

Suspected about oath
Suspected about oath, both are suspected..Shevuos 32b, 47a
Suspected about oath, imposing on other litigant..Shevuos 41a
Suspected about oath, who...Shevuos 46b-47a

Suspicion
Suspicion, "you will be innocent"...Shekalim 3:1-4; Yevamos 24b
Suspicion and slander, widow..Bava Metzia 71a
Suspicion, being careful to escape..Shekalim 3:2
Suspicion, *Chanukah* and *peah*..Shabbos 23a
Suspicion, desecrating Sabbatical year, *orlah*...Rosh Hashanah 9b
Suspicion of immorality, *tefillin*..Berachos 23a
Suspicion, ruling for himself......................................Yevamos 77a, 98a; Bechoros 31a, 38b
Suspicion, Sage must avoid..Chullin 44b, 141b

Swans, fattened, Solomon...Bava Metzia 86b

Swarm of bees
Swarm of bees, sale, how many to leave..Bava Basra 80a
Swarm of bees, saving through fellow's money..Bava Kama 114b

Swearing
Swearing to annul a commandment.............................Nedarim 16b; Shevuos 25a, 27a
Swears and not liable, defendant...Shevuos 45a

Swear and collect
Swear and collect!..Bava Basra 128a
Swears and collects, damage...Bava Kama 62a
Swears and collects, informer...Bava Kama 62a
Swears and collects, injured...Shevuos 46b
Swears and collects, stolen items...Bava Kama 114b-115a
Swears and collects, victim of theft...Shevuos 46a-46b
Swears and collects, who...Shevuos 44b-45a

Sweat

Sweat, beneficial for sick .... Berachos 57b
Sweat, blemishes of *Kohen* .... Kesubos 75a
Sweat, blemishes of women .... Kesubos 75a
Sweat of brow, Adam .... Pesachim 118a
Sweat on Shabbos .... Shabbos 40a-40b
Sweat, removing with wine .... Kesubos 75a

Sweeping

Sweeping floor on Shabbos .... Shabbos 95a
Sweeping floor on Yom Tov .... Beitzah 22b
Sweeping on Yom Tov, Rabban Gamliel's household .... Beitzah 22b
Sweeping up *terumah* storehouse .... Terumos 11:6-8

Swift

Swift one is rewarded .... Pesachim 50b
Swift people perform commandments early .... Rosh Hashanah 32b; Pesachim 4a; Yoma 28b

Swiftness

Swiftness and meticulousness, preference .... Yevamos 39a, 39b, 47b
Swiftness, commandment in its time .... Pesachim 105b; Yevamos 39a
Swiftness of girls .... Pesachim 89a; Nedarim 37a; Gittin 25a
Swiftness of *Kohanim* .... Shabbos 20a, 114b; Eruvin 103a; Pesachim 59b, 65a; Beitzah 18a; Bava Basra 90a;
                                                                            Zevachim 35a; Chullin 123b
Swiftness of *Kohanim*, Pesach .... Pesachim 64a-64b
Swiftness of women, parable .... Chagigah 12b

Swimming

Swimming on Shabbos .... Shabbos 40b-41a; Beitzah 36b
Swimming, teaching one's son .... Kiddushin 30b

Swindler

Swindler .... *see also* **Trickery, agent for oneself**, page 704
Swindler, charity .... Peah 8:9; Kesubos 67b-68a
Swindler, claiming lost item .... Bava Metzia 28b
Swindler, remaining until Elijah comes .... Bava Metzia 3a, 37b-38a

Sword

Sword, "with my sword and my bow" .... Bava Basra 123a
Sword for barrel, *muktzeh* .... Shabbos 146a
Sword, for which sin .... Avos 5:8
Sword impure like slain man .... Nazir 53b
Sword in house of study .... Shabbos 17a
Sword of peace, fast .... Taanis 22a
Sword on neck, not to despair from mercy .... Berachos 10a
Sword, sharp, do not despair of mercy .... Berachos 10a
Sword worse than death .... Bava Basra 8b

Symmachus

Symmachus coming to Rabbi Yehudah's lecture .... Kiddushin 52b; Nazir 49b-50a
Symmachus, legal division of items ..... Bava Kama 35b, 46a-46b; Bava Metzia 2b, 6a, 98b, 100a, 100b;
                                                                            Bava Basra 141a
Symmachus, pebbles .... Bava Kama 17b-18a, 19a

Synagogue

Synagogue .... *see also* **House of study**, page 287

Commandments —

Synagogue, bad neighbor .... Berachos 8a

Synagogue, door threshold .... Pesachim 85b
Synagogue, holiness .... Megillah 27b
Synagogue, honor .... Megillah 28a-29a
Synagogue, learning .... Megillah 29a
Synagogue, praying outside .... Pesachim 85b
Synagogue, reward for walking .... Sotah 22a; Bava Metzia 107a
Synagogue, reward for coming early .... Berachos 8a
Synagogue, used to go .... Berachos 6b

Prohibitions —
Synagogue, demolishing .... Megillah 26b; Bava Basra 3b
Synagogue, destroyed .... Megillah 28a-28b
Synagogue, passing behind it .... Berachos 8b, 61a; Eruvin 18b
Synagogue, punishment for calling it "house of the people" .... Shabbos 32a-32b
Synagogue, renting .... Megillah 26b
Synagogue, sale .... Megillah 25b-26b, 27b
Synagogue, changing to house of study .... Megillah 26b-27a
Synagogue, short cut .... Berachos 62b-63a
Synagogue, walking behind .... Berachos 8b, 61a; Eruvin 18b

Misc. —
Synagogue, Divine Presence .... Berachos 6a; Megillah 29a
Synagogue, empty, Angel of Death .... Bava Kama 60b
Synagogue, episode about building .... Bava Basra 3b
Synagogue, height .... Shabbos 11a
Synagogue in Babylon, *Eretz Yisrael* .... Megillah 29a
Synagogue of Alexandria .... Succah 51b
Synagogue in *Eretz Yisrael*, transplanted to Babylon .... Megillah 29a

Syria
Syria, *challah* .... Challah 4:7
Syria, impurity .... Gittin 8b
Syria, like *Eretz Yisrael* .... Gittin 8a-8b
Syria, mixed species in vineyard .... Orlah 3:9; Kiddushin 38b-39a
Syria, Sabbatical year .... Sheviis 6:2; Challah 4:7
Syria, tithes .... Maasros 5:5; Challah 4:7; Gittin 47a-47b

S

T

Taah b'dvar mitzvah..*see* **Mistake**, page 415

Taam ke'ikar....................................*see* **Taste has same law as forbidden food**, page 672

Taama dikra...*see* **Reason of law in Torah**, page 547

Taamei hamikra................................*see* **Cantillation notes of Holy Writings**, page 87

Taanah...*see* **Claim,** *chazakah*, page 109

Taanas besulim..*see* **Virginity (Claim)**, page 724

Taanios..*see* **Fasts**, page 214

Taanu chitim...*see* **Claimed wheat**, page 110

Taaseh velo min haasuy.......*see* **Make but not from what is already made**, page 385

Tabaas gedolah..........................*see* **Ring, large, slaughtering**, page 569

Tabernacle

Tabernacle, beams and curtains.......................................Shabbos 98a-99a

Tabernacle, Bezalel...Berachos 55a

Tabernacle, called *Mikdash*....................................Shevuos 16b; Eruvin 2a-2b

Tabernacle, erection in desert...Kesubos 62b

Tabernacle, hangings...Eruvin 2b

Tabernacle in Shiloh and Nov..Zevachim 118a

Tabernacle, opening of Courtyard....................................Eruvin 2b, 23b

Tabernacle, sacrifices...Menachos 45b

Tabernacle, *terumah*...Megillah 29b

Tabernacle, tools to build...Shabbos 96b

Tabernacles, years of existence..Zevachim 118b-119a

Tabernacle during journeys

Tabernacle during journeys, disqualified sacrifices......Zevachim 60b-61b, 116b; Menachos 95a

Tabernacle during journeys, sacrificial flesh..................Zevachim 60b-61b, 116b; Menachos 95a

Tabernacle during journeys, showbread.........................Menachos 95a

Table

Table atones for man.......................................Berachos 55a; Chagigah 27a; Menachos 97a

Table, called *peturah*..Shabbos 36a; Succah 34a

Table in Temple..................................Pesachim 109b; Menachos 94b, 96a-97a, 98b-99a

Table in Temple consecrates.............................Menachos 87b, 96a

Table, meat and milk on one table..........Chullin 104a-104b, 107b-108a; Shabbos 13a; Eduyos 5:2

Table of butcher in reward for honoring Shabbos............................Shabbos 119a

Table of G-d, *Kohanim's* rights.............Bava Kama 12b-13a; Beitzah 21a; Chullin 120a; Arachin 24b

Table of Sage, behavior .... Bava Basra 57b-58a
Table of showbread, impurity .... Chagigah 26b-27a; Yoma 21a-21b; Menachos 29a, 96b-97a
Table outside of succah .... Succah 3a, 7b, 28a; Berachos 11a; Eruvin 13b
Table, second, impurity .... Berachos 52b
Tables at north of Altar .... Middos 3:5
Tables, Temple .... Tamid 31b; Shekalim 6:4; Menachos 99b
Tablecloth, sign for guests .... Bava Basra 93b
Tablet of *sotah*, Queen Helen .... Yoma 37b
Tablets
Tablets, dimensions and Ark .... Bava Basra 14a-14b; Nedarim 38a
Tablets, first, "good" .... Bava Kama 54b-55a
Tablets in Ark .... Bava Basra 14a-14b; Menachos 99a; Berachos 8b
Tablets, letters .... Shabbos 104a; Megillah 2b-3a
Tablets, reason for breaking .... Shabbos 87a
Tablets, second, Yom Kippur .... Bava Basra 121a
Tablets, Seventeenth of *Tammuz* .... Taanis 28b
Tablets, since they were broken .... Eruvin 54a
Tabor
Tabor and Carmel, Giving of Torah .... Megillah 29a
Tabor, giant animal .... Bava Basra 73b; Zevachim 113b
Tachanun .... Megillah 22b-23a; Berachos 34b
Tachas, in its place or replacement .... Temurah 26b
Tachash in Tabernacle .... Shabbos 28a, 28b
Tachrichim .... *see* **Shrouds,** page 621
Tafasta merubah tafasta .... *see* **Minimum only can be learned from deduction,** page 411
Tafasta merubeh lo tafasta .... Succah 5b
Tagrei .... *see* **Merchant,** page 405
Taharas hakodesh .... *see* **Purity of Temple,** page 512
Tail
Tail, burned parts of sacrifices .... Zevachim 28a
Tail of lizard, twitching .... Bava Basra 142b
Tail of scorpion, zodiac sign .... Berachos 58b
Tail, offering .... Pesachim 3b
Tail to lions .... Avos 4:15
Tail with a thorn in it .... Rosh Hashanah 17a
Tails of animals .... Shabbos 77b
Tails of sheep, episode .... Bechoros 35a
Tailor, clean and easy craft .... Kiddushin 82a; Berachos 63a
Takana .... *see* **Decree,** page 154
Take
"Take your divorce certificate from the floor" .... Gittin 24a, 78a
Take a rod, leader .... Sanhedrin 8a
Take your favors and throw them on thorns .... Shabbos 63b; Beitzah 29b; Kesubos 53b;
.... Bava Kama 83a; Bava Metzia 63b
Taking by means of other object .... Succah 37a-37b, 42a
Taking convert's property .... Bava Kama 49b; Yevamos 52b; Bava Basra 142a
Taking down and not bringing up .... Avodah Zarah 26a-26b; Chullin 13b; Sanhedrin 57a
Taking down fruit from roof on Yom Tov .... Beitzah 35b-36a
Taking down offering from Altar, non-*Kohen* .... Zevachim 69a

Taking from other, proof..Bava Basra 30a, 153a-153b, 159b
Taking fruit outside *Eretz Yisrael*...Bava Basra 90b-91a
Taking off *mezuzah,* closed house where corpse lies...............Bava Basra 12a; Shabbos 146b
Taking off *tefillin*, blessing...Niddah 51b
Taking out...*see also* **Carry**, page 88
Taking out bread from oven, Shabbos.......................................Shabbos 117b
Taking out incense fire pan...Yoma 47a

Taken out of Courtyard
Taken out of Courtyard, flesh of sacrifice...............................Zevachim 82b
Taken out of Courtyard, inside sin offerings...............................Zevachim 104b
Taken out of Courtyard, sacrificial blood...............................Zevachim 82a-82b
Taken out of Temple Courtyard, impurity...............................Pesachim 85a

Taking ash from Altar
Taking ash from Altar, how much...Yoma 24a
Taking ash from Altar, lots...Yoma 22a
Taking ash from Altar, time...............................Yoma 20a-20b; Zevachim 86b
Taking ash from Altar, who...............................Tamid 28a; Yoma 22a-22b, 23a

Takfo Kohen...............................*see* **Seizure of firstborn by** *Kohen*, page 599

Tal umatar
Tal umatar in summer, hot regions...Taanis 14b
Tal umatar, request.............Berachos 33a; Taanis 2a, 4a-5a, 6a, 10a; Bava Metzia 28a

Tallis
Tallis...*see also* ***Tzitzis***, page 711
Tallis of Rabbi Yehudah Nesia...Bava Basra 111a
Tallis, new, Shabbos...Shabbos 147a
Tallis, one for six disciples...Sanhedrin 20a
Tallis, one, for two Sages...Sotah 49a

Talisman...............................*see* **Amulet**, page 21, *see also*; ***Segulah***, page 598

Talk
Talk...*see also* **Speaking**, page 649
Talking while eating...Taanis 5b
Talks to everyone...Kesubos 72a-72b

Tall
Tall in their generation...Niddah 24b
Tall man should not marry tall woman...Bechoros 45b

Talmai, translation of Torah...Megillah 9a-9b

Talmid chacham...*see* **Sage**, page 583

Talmid chaver...*see* **Disciple-Sage**, page 166

Talmudo be'yado...............................*see* **Learning in one's hand**, page 358

Tam...*see* **Ox goring occasionally**, page 468

Tamar
Tamar, Amnon...Sanhedrin 21a
Tamar, episode with Judah...............................Sotah 10a-10b; Megillah 10b; Makos 23b
Tamar, reward for her modesty...Megillah 10b
Tamar, transgression for Heaven's sake...............................Nazir 23b; Horayos 10b

Tamarisk, Abraham...Sotah 10a-10b

Tamchuy...*see* **Soup kitchen**, page 648

Tameh...*see* **Impure**, page 301

Tamid, who arranged this *mesechta*...Yoma 14b

Tamid..*see* **Daily offering**, page 140

Tammuz

Tammuz, full month, Temple destruction..................................Pesachim 77a; Taanis 29a; Shevuos 10a

Tammuz month, danger from *Ketev*..Pesachim 111b

Tamun..*see* **Hidden item, damage by fire**, page 278

Tangible item, vow and oath..Nedarim 13b, 16b; Shevuos 25a

Tanna

Tanna concealed it, do not teach it...Nedarim 23b

Tanna from Jerusalem, easy language..Bava Kama 6b

Tanna, gives non exhaustive list................................Eruvin 27a; Taanis 13b; Kiddushin 16a-16b

Tanna of Beraisa, not considered as another opinion..................Bechoros 23b-24a

Tanna, second, comes to add...Bava Basra 93b

Tanna and can oppose

Tanna and can oppose, Rabbi Chiya..Bava Metzia 5a

Tanna and can oppose, Rav.........Gittin 38b; Eruvin 50b; Kesubos 8a; Bava Basra 42a; Sanhedrin 83b;
....Chullin 122b

Tanna veshier...*see* **List in *Mishnah*, non exhaustive**, page 373

Tannaim

Tannaim, inverted opinions..Beitzah 9b-10a

Tannaim, several said same thing...Shabbos 26b; Succah 7b

Tanner

Tanner and perfumer, crafts...Kiddushin 82b

Tanner, craft..Kesubos 77a

Tanning on Shabbos

Tanning on Shabbos..Shabbos 75b

Tanning on Shabbos, pickling foods..Shabbos 108b

Tanning on Shabbos, rubbing oil on shoe...................................Shabbos 141b

Tanur..*see* **Oven**, page 465

Tapuach hamizbeach...*see* **Ash pile on Altar**, page 33

Tar, lamp of Shabbos...Shabbos 25b

Tarkav, amount..Bava Basra 89b-90a

Targum..*see* **Translation**, page 700

Taryag mitzvos.................................*see* **Six hundred thirteen commandments**, page 631

Tarmod, lineage...Yevamos 16a-16b, 17a; Niddah 56b

Tarshish, two thousand *parsah*..Chullin 91b

Tarumos...*see* **Grievance**, page 259

Tashlumei kefel..*see* **Double payment**, page 176

Tashlumim..*see* **Replacing sacrifice**, page 560

Tashmishei kedushah...*see* **Ritual articles**, page 569

Taste

Taste, absorbed...*see* **Absorption**, page 5

Taste has same law as forbidden food.................Pesachim 44b-45a; Nazir 37a-37b; Chullin 108a

Taste of fruit, since Temple destruction.....................................Sotah 49a

Taste of intimate relations given to wicked................................Sanhedrin 75a

Taste of tree like taste of fruit..Succah 35a

Taste of wine in dates...Bava Kama 92a

Tasting

Tasting dish, blessing...Berachos 14a

Tasting dish during fast..Berachos 14a

Tasting mixture, non-Jew...Chullin 97a-97b, 111b
Tasty food, there is always room for it ....Megillah 7b; Eruvin 82b
Tataah gavar...*see* **Bottom determines, cooking,** page 74
Tattoo..Makos 21a
Tavi
Tavi, blinded by Rabban Gamliel ....Bava Kama 74b
Tavi, Rabban Gamliel's slave ....Berachos 16b; Succah 20b
Tavo alav berachah..Pesachim 32a; Eruvin 29b
Tavo alav berachah...................................*see* **Blessing it shall come to him!,** page 65
Tax
  Idolater's tax —
    Tax, Babylonian government ....Shabbos 149b-150a
    Tax, *challah*..Pesachim 6a
    Tax, enslaving idolater who did not pay ....Yevamos 46a
    Tax, evading by pretending to be idolater..Nedarim 62b
    Tax, fellow's field ....Gittin 58b
    Tax, firstborn..Pesachim 6a
    Tax for crown of Tiberias..Bava Basra 8a
    Tax for fellow...Bava Kama 113b
    Tax, forbidden to profit..Avodah Zarah 71a
    Tax, forced vows ....Nedarim 27b-28a
    Tax, idolatry..Avodah Zarah 12b-13a
    Tax, Jew's slave...Bava Metzia 73b
    Tax, law of country.................................Bava Kama 113a; Nedarim 28a; Bava Basra 54b
    Tax of idolaters, charity ....Bava Basra 9a
    Tax, troubles ....Sanhedrin 98b
  Misc. —
    Tax, city expenses..Bava Metzia 108a; Bava Basra 8a
    Tax, idolatry..Avodah Zarah 12b-13a
    Tax of king, parable...Succah 30a
    Tax, Sabbatical year...Sanhedrin 26a
    Tax, Sage exempt...Nedarim 62b; Bava Basra 7b-8a
  Tax collector
    Tax collector, difficulty to repent...Bava Kama 94b
    Tax collector, disqualified to testify..Sanhedrin 25b-26a
    Tax collector, his family..Shevuos 39a
    Tax collector, law of country..................Bava Kama 113a; Nedarim 28a; Bava Basra 54b, 55a
    Tax collector married scholar's widow ....Bechoros 30b; Avodah Zarah 39a
    Tax collectors, righteous, episodes.........................Sanhedrin 25b-26a; Bechoros 31a
Teach
Teach your tongue to say: "I do not know" ....Berachos 4a
Teaching..*see also* **Learning,** page 357
Teaching Beraisa without approving it ....Niddah 46b; Eruvin 38b
Teaching craft...Kiddushin 82a-82b; Berachos 63a
Teaching in a concise way...Pesachim 3b; Chullin 63b
Teaching in a pleasant way to disciple ....Taanis 8a
Teaching my son only Torah ....Kiddushin 82b
Teaching one thing, duty to honor...Avos 6:3
Teaching others, memory..Eruvin 54a

T

Teaching, remembering one's learning..Eruvin 53a
Teaching trade to son...Pesachim 113a
Teaching, when there is no one else...Berachos 63a

Teaching children
Teaching children, commandment..Shabbos 119b
Teaching children, G-d...Avodah Zarah 3b
Teaching children, how...Kesubos 50a
Teaching children on Shabbos..Nedarim 37a
Teaching children, punishment...Shabbos 119b

Teaching fellow's son
Teaching fellow's son, greater than all commandments..................Bava Kama 17a
Teaching fellow's son, like he gave birth to him...........................Sanhedrin 19b
Teaching Torah to fellow's son, reward.......................................Bava Metzia 85a

Teaching Torah to one's son
Teaching Torah to one's son, commandment...............Kiddushin 30a, 29a, 29b; Sotah 22a;
                                                                                        Berachos 21b, 47b
Teaching Torah to one's sons, excommunication for neglecting.......Pesachim 113b
Teaching Torah to one's son, Shabbos..Shabbos 12a

Teacher
Teacher..see also **Schoolteacher**, page 591
Teacher and disciple, opinions..Sanhedrin 36a-36b
Teacher and father, precedence...Krisos 28a
Teacher and friend..Sanhedrin 106b
Teacher cuts reeds in swamps....................................Shabbos 95a; Sanhedrin 33a
Teacher, everyone has a teacher suitable for him..........................Avodah Zarah 13a
Teacher, leaving him...Yoma 53a-53b
Teacher needs him..Bava Metzia 33a
Teacher, not decent..Chagigah 15b
Teacher, observing him...Chagigah 5b; Horayos 12a
Teacher, only one, learning from..Avodah Zarah 19a-19b
Teacher, only one, remembering Torah..Eruvin 53a
Teacher, precedence for returning lost item..................................Bava Metzia 33a
Teacher, ruling in his place........................Sanhedrin 5b; Kesubos 60b; Eruvin 62b-63b
Teacher, seeing him during learning.............................Horayos 12a; Krisos 6a
Teacher, walking next to him.....................Yoma 37a; Eruvin 54b; Chullin 91a
Teacher who waived his honor..Kiddushin 32a-32b
Teacher's and disciple's instructions, to which must one listen....Sanhedrin 29a; Kiddushin 42b;
                                                                Bava Kama 56a; Temurah 25a; Niddah 14b
Teachers in the south..Yevamos 62b
Teachers of Babylon..Sanhedrin 17b; Shevuos 47a

Teachings
Teachings, "go out and say your teaching outside"........................Bava Kama 34b
Teachings, clear, forgotten..Shabbos 139a
Teachings from deceased, said in this world...............Bechoros 31b; Yevamos 97a; Sanhedrin 90b
Teachings, in the name of Sage who said it..........Megillah 15a; Chullin 104b; Avos 6:6; Niddah 19b
Teachings, prohibition to praise it...Eruvin 64a
Teachings, Sage who died..Kiddushin 13a

Tearing
Tearing by *beis din*, legal document...Bava Basra 168b

Tearing divorce certificate, *kesubah*..Kesubos 89b
Tearing document, by *beis din*...Bava Basra 168b
Tearing during anger, compared to idolater..Shabbos 105b
Tearing off, flowerpot...Shabbos 81b
Tearing off, Shabbos labors..Shabbos 103a
Tearing on Shabbos, ruining...Shabbos 105b
Tearing out hair on Shabbos..............................Shabbos 94b; Makos 20b; Bechoros 24b
Tearing priestly garment..Yoma 72a
Tearing, Shabbos labor..Shabbos 105a-105b
Tearing to sew, Shabbos..Shabbos 74b-75a
Torn animal unfit for consumption...................................see **Tereifah**, page 702
Torn like fish, impurity...Chullin 21a

Tearing garment
Decedents —
    Tearing garment, adding tear for another decedent...............................Moed Katan 26b
    Tearing garment after delayed news of death..Moed Katan 20b
    Tearing garment for decedents, how..Moed Katan 22b, 24a
    Tearing garment for decedents, *Kohen Gadol*..Horayos 12b
    Tearing garment for decedents, laws...Moed Katan 26b
    Tearing garment for decedents, mistake..Nedarim 87a
    Tearing garment for decedents, place and size.................................Moed Katan 26a-26b
    Tearing garment for decedents, punishment...Moed Katan 24a
    Tearing garment for decedents, source..Moed Katan 15a
    Tearing garment for decedents, standing...Moed Katan 20b-21a
    Tearing garment for death of father and mother.............Moed Katan 22a-22b; Horayos 12b
    Tearing garment for death of Sage...Moed Katan 22b
    Tearing garment for other decedent.................Moed Katan 25a, 26a; Shabbos 105b
    Tearing garment, Sages of Babylon one for another..............................Bava Metzia 33a
Misc. —
    Tearing garment for bad news...Moed Katan 26a
    Tearing garment for Temple and cities of Judea....................................Moed Katan 26a
    Tearing garment, Rav Huna...Kiddushin 32a
    Tearing red garment, episode...Bava Basra 168b

Tears
Tears...*see also* **Crying**, page 134
Tears, health..Shabbos 151b
Tears, liquid..Niddah 55b
Tears of Altar, divorce..Sanhedrin 22a; Gittin 90b
Tears, requests heard..Berachos 32b; Bava Metzia 59a

Techeiles...*see* **Blue dye**, page 69
Techias hameisim...................................*see* **Resurrection of dead**, page 563
Techilaso befshiyah.........................*see* **Beginning with negligence**, page 49
Techum
Measure —
    Techum, city inside *techum*..Eruvin 60b-61a
    Techum, city on river...Eruvin 61a
    Techum, close towns..Eruvin 55a-55b, 57a-57b
    Techum, contradicting measures...Eruvin 58b-59a
    Techum, diagonal...Eruvin 56b

Techum, ends at middle of city .... Eruvin 42b, 60b-61a
Techum, ends at middle of domain .... Eruvin 42a
Techum, houses which combine to .... Eruvin 55b
Techum, how to measure .... Eruvin 58a-58b
Techum, including domains .... Eruvin 44b-45a
Techum, large cave .... Eruvin 44b
Techum, leaves hut .... Eruvin 21a
Techum, measuring with rope .... Eruvin 57b-58a
Techum, seventy cubits around city .... Eruvin 57a-57b
Techum, shape of towns .... Eruvin 55a-55b
Techum, square .... Eruvin 51a
Techum, steps .... Eruvin 42a
Techum, walled city .... Eruvin 26a

Territory —
Techum, animal .... Beitzah 37a-37b, 40a; Eruvin 97b
Techum, barrel .... Eruvin 97b
Techum, butcher who saved meat for customer .... Beitzah 40a
Techum, collateral .... Beitzah 39b-40a
Techum, non-Jew .... Eruvin 47b
Techum of borrowed item .... Beitzah 38a
Techum, ownerless items .... Eruvin 45a-45b
Techum, sleeping man .... Eruvin 45a-45b
Techum, traveler .... Eruvin 45a
Techum, waiting for end of Shabbos .... Shabbos 150b; Eruvin 38b-39a
Techum, water .... Beitzah 39a-39b; Eruvin 45b-46a, 47b-48a, 97b; Shabbos 121b

Went out —
Techum, four cubits for who goes out .... Eruvin 48a
Techum, went out and returned .... Eruvin 41b-42a
Techum, went out on two cubits .... Eruvin 44a, 45a
Techum, went out to enclosed area .... Eruvin 42b-43a
Techum, when to come in .... Eruvin 45a, 52b, 105a

Misc. —
Techum, encircling on Shabbos .... Eruvin 42a-42b
Techum higher than ten handbreadths .... Eruvin 43a-43b
Techum, mixture .... Beitzah 38a-39a
Techum of city like city .... Nedarim 56b
Techum, partition for water .... Eruvin 47b-48a
Techum, place of eating .... Eruvin 73a
Techum, prohibition .... Eruvin 17b, 35b, 59a; Sotah 30b
Techum, sailing ship .... Eruvin 42b-43a
Techum, trustworthiness of slave .... Eruvin 58b-59a
Techum, two thousands cubits, source .... Eruvin 51a

Teeth
Teeth, cure .... Shabbos 110a; Berachos 44b
Teeth, health .... Shabbos 111a; Yoma 84a
Teeth, not to extract .... Pesachim 113a
Teeth of old man, livelihood .... Niddah 65a
Tooth damage .... *see* **Grazing**, page 257
Tooth, false, episode .... Nedarim 66a

T

Tooth, golden, Shabbos .... Shabbos 65a
Tooth and eye
Tooth and eye, Canaanite slave .... Kiddushin 24b-25a; Bava Kama 26b, 91a, 98a
Tooth and eye, Hebrew slave .... Kiddushin 20a
Tooth and eye, conspiring witnesses .... Bava Kama 73b-74b
Tefach .... *see* **Handbreadth**, page 268
Tefilas haderech .... Berachos 29b-30a, 60a
Tefillah .... *see* **Prayer**, page 497
Tefillin
  Aggadah —
  Tefillin, "oil of your head" .... Shabbos 153a
  Tefillin, G-d's *tefillin* .... Berachos 6a-6b
  Tefillin, glory .... Megillah 16b
  Tefillin, longevity .... Menachos 44a-44b
  Tefillin, non-Jews revere you .... Menachos 35b; Berachos 6a, 57a; Megillah 16b; Sotah 17a; Chullin 89a
  Tefillin, protection through their merit .... Menachos 43b
  Tefillin, showed to Moses .... Berachos 7a; Menachos 35b
  Blessing —
  Tefillin, blessing when taking off .... Niddah 51b
  Tefillin, blessing when touching .... Succah 46a
  Tefillin, how many blessings .... Berachos 60b; Menachos 36a
  Tefillin, when to say blessing .... Menachos 35b
  Episodes —
  Tefillin, Abraham .... Sotah 17a
  Tefillin, episode about redeeming .... Gittin 45b
  Tefillin, episode about slander .... Berachos 23a
  Tefillin, fast for strap which turned over .... Moed Katan 25a
  Tefillin, Jews did not sacrifice their life .... Shabbos 130a
  Tefillin, miracle for Elisha .... Shabbos 49a, 130a
  Tefillin, slain inhabitants of Bethar .... Gittin 58a
  Prohibitions —
  Tefillin, carrying burden .... Bava Metzia 105b
  Tefillin in bathhouse .... Shabbos 10a
  Tefillin in cemetery .... Berachos 18a
  Tefillin, intimate relations .... Succah 26b
  Tefillin, meal and bed .... Berachos 23b-24a; Tamid 27a; Yoma 69a
  Tefillin, not to add to commandments .... Sanhedrin 88b-89a
  Tefillin of head, side box .... Sanhedrin 89a
  Tefillin, prohibition to hang .... Berachos 24a
  Tefillin, skull which does not put on .... Rosh Hashanah 17a
  Tefillin, toilet .... Berachos 23a-23b, 25a; Shabbos 62a
  Putting on —
  Tefillin, clean body .... Shabbos 49a, 130a
  Tefillin, eight positive commandments .... Menachos 44a
  Tefillin, having only one box .... Menachos 44a
  Tefillin, night .... Eruvin 96a; Menachos 36a-36b; Zevachim 19a
  Tefillin, place to put on .... Menachos 36b-37b; Berachos 13b; Eruvin 95b; Arachin 19b
  Tefillin, putting on according to order .... Menachos 36a; Yoma 33b
  Tefillin, reading *Shema* .... Berachos 14b

T

Shabbos —

Tefillin, carrying out on Shabbos .... Shabbos 61a; Beitzah 15a
Tefillin, finding on Shabbos .... Eruvin 95a-96a, 96b-97b; Beitzah 15a; Shabbos 62a
Tefillin, Shabbos .... Shabbos 61a, 62a; Eruvin 95b-96a; Menachos 36b
Tefillin, Shabbos eve .... Shabbos 12a

Who —

Tefillin, educating child .... Succah 42a; Arachin 2b
Tefillin, mourner .... Succah 25a, 25b; Berachos 11a, 16b; Moed Katan 15a; Kesubos 6b
Tefillin, women .... Berachos 20b; Eruvin 96a-96b

Misc. —

Tefillin are easily purchased .... Bava Metzia 29b
Tefillin boxes .... Menachos 34b, 35a
Tefillin, coated with gold .... Megillah 24b
Tefillin, impurity of hands .... Yadayim 3:3-5; Shabbos 79b
Tefillin, knot .... Eruvin 97a; Menachos 35b
Tefillin, property .... Arachin 24a
Tefillin, pure animal .... Shabbos 28b, 108a; Makos 11a
Tefilin sewn with linen thread .... Makos 11a
Tefilin, square .... Megillah 24b; Shabbos 28b; Menachos 35a
Tefilin, straps .... Menachos 35a-35b; Shabbos 28b
Tefillin which were found, *kashrus* .... Eruvin 96b-97a

Tefusas habayis .... *see* **Pool resources**, page 493
Tefusas rekev hames .... *see* **Decay of dead**, page 152

Tehillim

Tehillim about Absalom .... Berachos 10a
Tehillim, aggadah .... Pesachim 117a
Tehillim before sleep .... Shevuos 15b
Tehillim, chapters .... Berachos 9b-10a
Tehillim, end like beginning .... Berachos 10a
Tehillim, expressions of praise .... Pesachim 117a
Tehillim or *Mishlei,* lecture .... Avodah Zarah 19a
Tehillim, Shir Hamaalos, parallel to .... Succah 53a-53b
Tehillim, verses .... Kiddushin 30a
Tehillim, who wrote .... Bava Basra 14b-15a

Tekiah .... *see* **Blowing *shofar***, page 68
Tekois, episode about olive oil .... Menachos 85b
Telescope, Rabban Gamliel .... Eruvin 43b
Tell me your verse .... Chullin 95b

Temple

Aggadah —

Temple, "rejoicing of his heart" .... Taanis 26b
Temple, between Divine Names .... Berachos 33a; Sanhedrin 92a
Temple, its names .... Pesachim 88a; Taanis 16a; Zevachim 104b
Temple, *Levanon* .... Yoma 39b
Temple, third, in fire .... Bava Kama 60b

Prohibitions —

Temple and *Heichal,* entering .... Menachos 27b; Keilim 1:8-9
Temple and king, order .... Sanhedrin 20b
Temple, entering with shoes on .... Shabbos 66b; Chagigah 4b

Temple, its place..Zevachim 54b, 118b; Yoma 12a
Temple, prohibition to change...Zevachim 33a
Temple, public domain...Pesachim 19b
Temple, Rabbinical prohibitions concerning Shabbos.............Pesachim 47a, 65a; Eruvin 102a
Temple, Shiloh and Nov...Zevachim 118a
Misc. —
Temple, administrators..Shekalim 5:2
Temple, *amah traiksin*..Bava Basra 3a-3b
Temple, called "*mishkan*"...Shevuos 16b
Temple, commandment to be concerned by........................Succah 41a; Rosh Hashanah 30a
Temple Courtyard, dimensions.......................Middos 2:6, 5:1-2; Yoma 16a-16b; Menachos 97b
Temple dedication...Moed Katan 9a; Shabbos 30a
Temple destruction, roads in *Eretz Yisrael*...................................Rosh Hashanah 23b
Temple, high...Kiddushin 69a-69b; Sanhedrin 87a; Zevachim 54b
Temple, holiness...*see* **Holiness of Temple**, page 281
Temple rooms.....................................*see* **Room**, page 571; *see also* **Beis**, page 49
Temple, ravens on roof of *Heichal*, spiked.............Shabbos 90a; Menachos 107a; Middos 37a
Temple, second..*see* **Second Temple**, page 595
Temple Treasury, sacrifice.........................Temurah 6b, 13a; Yoma 63b; Zevachim 113b
Temple, years of existence...Zevachim 118b-119a
Temple Mount
Temple Mount, covered yard....................................Pesachim 13b; Berachos 33b
Temple Mount, encircling...Middos 2:2
Temple Mount, general...Middos 2:1, 35; a 2:3
Temple Mount, slain person..Parah 3:3
Temple utensils
Temple utensils, accuser cannot become defender.......................Rosh Hashanah 26a
Temple utensils, Chonyo...Avodah Zarah 52b
Temple utensils, cornice...Yoma 72b
Temple utensils, from which material................................Sotah 14b; Menachos 28b
Temple utensils in Rome...Meilah 17b
Temple utensils, purity...Chagigah 26a-26b, 26b-27a
Temple utensils, repairing...Zevachim 88a
Temporary
Temporary ruling, Gideon...Temurah 28b-29a
Temporary tent..*see* **Tent, temporary**, page 681
Temurah..*see* **Replacing sacrifice**, page 560
Ten
***Aggadah* —**
Ten generations, after Creation...Avos 5:2
Ten measures etc..Kiddushin 49b
Ten rulers...Nedarim 32b
Ten sayings..................Rosh Hashanah 32a; Yoma 54b; Megillah 21b; Avos 5:1
Ten strong things, overridden by stronger ones...........................Bava Basra 10a
Ten things are one more resistant than the other....................Bava Basra 10a
Ten trials, Abraham...Avos 5:3
Ten trials in desert..Arachin 15a-15b; Avos 5:4
Men —
Ten city workers...Megillah 3b

Ten Jews, Divine Presence..Sanhedrin 39a
Ten males, public prayer...Berachos 21b; Megillah 23b
Ten martyrs...Sanhedrin 11a, 68a
Ten men who first arrived in synagogue..Berachos 47b
Ten men, proclaiming ruling...Kesubos 7b

Misc. —
Ten cubits, breach..Kilayim 4:4
Ten days of Repentance, G-d is close.......Yevamos 49b, 105a; Rosh Hashanah 18a
Ten days of Repentance, prayer...Berachos 12b
Ten decrees by Ezra..Bava Kama 82a-82b
Ten decrees by Joshua...Bava Kama 80b-81b
Ten fields, act of acquisition...........Kiddushin 27a-27b; Bava Kama 12a; Bava Basra 67a-67b
Ten gold coins, commandment..............................Bava Kama 91b; Chullin 87a
Ten lineages...Kiddushin 69a
Ten *parsaos*, one day...Pesachim 93b; Sanhedrin 94a
Ten years, sterile woman...Yevamos 34b, 64a-64b
Ten years without giving birth.....................................Yevamos 64a-65a

Ten Commandments
Ten Commandments, from G-d's mouth..Makos 24a
Ten Commandments, non-Jews acknowledge.............................Kiddushin 31a
Ten Commandments, public reading..Berachos 12a

Ten handbreadths
Ten handbreadths, carrying...Shabbos 92a, 97a
Ten handbreadths, death...Bava Kama 50b-51a
Ten handbreadths from bottom of sea...Shabbos 100b
Ten handbreadths, pit...Bava Kama 3a, 51b
Ten handbreadths, source...Succah 4b-5b
Ten handbreadths, throwing to garbage.......................................Eruvin 8a, 99b

Ten tribes
Ten tribes, exile.......................Yevamos 16b-17a; Shabbos 147b; Sanhedrin 94a
Ten Tribes, lineage of convert...Yevamos 16b-17a
Ten Tribes, World to Come...Sanhedrin 110b
Ten tribes, Josiah..Arachin 33a

Ten kizchi...*see* **Give, like "make an act of acquisition,"** page 251
Tenai..*see* **Condition**, page 120

Tenant farmer
Monetary matters —
Tenant farmer, amount of cereal mound.....................................Bava Metzia 105a
Tenant farmer, *chazakah*...Bava Basra 46b
Tenant farmer, doubt about his share...Bava Metzia 110a
Tenant farmer, eating fruit...Bava Metzia 22a
Tenant farmer, general custom..Bava Metzia 103a-103b
Tenant farmer, other requirements...Bava Metzia 69a
Tenant farmer, sowing other species...Bava Metzia 104b
Tenant farmer, unsuccessful crop..Bava Metzia 103b-104a
Tenant farmer, vow...Shevuos 48b
Tenant, like paid custodian.........Bava Metzia 36a, 80b, 93a, 95b; Bava Kama 45b, 57b; Shevuos 49b

Tithes —
Tenant farmer, right to tithes..Demai 6:3-5

T

Tenant farmer, tithe..Demai 6:1-2
Tenant farmer to non-Jew, tithe................................Challah 4:7; Bava Metzia 101a; Gittin 43b
  Misc. —
Tenant farmer dismissed, episode..Bava Kama 119a
Tenant farmer, Rav Huna's vinegar...Berachos 5b
Tendrils, eating on Yom Kippur...Yoma 81b
Tent
Tent, cracked roof...Oholos 11:1-2
Tent, impurity of leprosy..Negaim 13:6-12
Tent in motion, dead...Chagigah 25a; Nazir 55a
Tent in succah...Succah 10b-11a, 19b, 20b, 21b
Tent, made by man...Oholos 3:7; Succah 20b-21b
Tent, passage of impurity through utensil and man................Oholos 11:3-6, 15:1-3; Eduyos 4:12
Tent, passageway between houses...Shabbos 157a-157b
Tent, *zav* moving tent...Eruvin 35a; Zavim 4:3
Tents impurity, leaning walls......................................Oholos 7:2; Shabbos 138b; Succah 19b
  Tent of corpse
Tent of corpse, boards and barrels..Oholos 15:2-3
Tent of corpse, cradle...Oholos 12:4
Tent of corpse, examples..Oholos 8:1-5
Tent of corpse, impurity by touch..Chullin 125a-125b, 126b
Tent of corpse, opening on roof...Oholos 10:1-5; Succah 18a
  Tent, temporary
Tent, temporary, adding................Shabbos 125b, 137b-138a; Eruvin 44a, 102a-102b; Succah 27b-28a
Tent, temporary, bed canopy.............................Eruvin 102a-102b; Shabbos 45b-46a, 138a-138b
Tent, temporary, cases...Shabbos 138a-138b
Tent, temporary, change...Beitzah 32b-33a; Eruvin 101a
Tent, temporary, disassembling...Beitzah 30b
Tent, temporary, kerchief...Shabbos 139b
Tent, temporary, Shabbos........................Shabbos 125b, 137b-138a; Eruvin 44a, 86b
Tenth
Tenth for daughter's dowry, during father's life..Kesubos 52b
Tenth for dowry, from married woman..Bava Basra 139a
Tenth of property, for dowry....................Kesubos 68a-68b, 69a; Gittin 51a; Bava Basra 66b-67a
Tenth, tithe of animal................Nazir 31b-32a; Bechoros 59a-59b, 60b-61a; Eruvin 50a; Kiddushin 51a
  Tenth of *ephah*
Tenth of *ephah*, meal offering...Menachos 89a
Tenth of *ephah*, meal offering for *Kohen*.....................................Menachos 50b, 87b
Tenth of *ephah*, quantity..Menachos 77a
Tenth of *ephah*, utensil of measure in Temple................Menachos 87b-88a, 90a
Tenufah...*see* **Waving,** page 737
Teruah, *shofar*..Rosh Hashanah 33b-34a
Terumah
  For whom —
Terumah, bringing to *Kohen*..Chullin 134b; Terumos 11:8
Terumah, forbidden to betrothed girl.......................Kesubos 57b, 58b; Kiddushin 5a
Terumah in granary, minor...Succah 42a
Terumah in granary, who is entitled...................Yevamos 86a, 99b-100a; Kesubos 28b
Terumah, married woman and betrothed girl.............Kesubos 57b, 58a; Kiddushin 5a, 10b-11a

T

Terumah, minor girl who married...Kiddushin 45b-46a
Terumah, onein and uncircumcised...Yevamos 68b, 70b-71a

Impurity —
Terumah, death for impure person...Sanhedrin 83a-83b
Terumah, doubt if impure..Kiddushin 80a-80b; Taharos 4:5-6; Niddah 33b
Terumah from outside of *Eretz Yisrael*, impure *Kohen*.......................Niddah 32a; Bechoros 27a-27b
Terumah, immersed that day...Yevamos 75a
Terumah, improper, impurity.............Pesachim 14b-15b, 20b-21a; Bechoros 33b-34a; Terumos 8:8-11;
....Menachos 48a-48b
Terumah, impure person eating...................Makos 14b; Yevamos 75a; Shevuos 7a; Zevachim 43b-44a
Terumah, impure person touching...Makos 14b; Yevamos 75a; Shevuos 7a
Terumah, legumes for animals, purity...Maaser Sheni 2:4; Eduyos 1:8
Terumah, third level of impurity..Chullin 35a-35b

Terumah, impure
Terumah, impure, burning...Shabbos 25a-25b
Terumah, impure, eating..Yevamos 73b
Terumah, impure, unintentional and intentional..Yevamos 89a-89b
Terumah, impure, oil...Terumos 11:10
Terumah, impure, benefit...Pesachim 32a
Terumah, impure, separating..Terumos 2:1-2; Pesachim 33a
Terumah, impure, taking out of *Eretz Yisrael*...Sheviis 6:5-6
Terumah, separating impure for impure...Bava Kama 115b

Mixture —
Terumah, fell into one of two baskets................Terumos 7:5-7; Pesachim 9b, 44a; Yevamos 82a-82b;
....Nazir 36b-37a
Terumah, sweeping up storehouse...Terumos 11:6-8
Terumah which was sown...Terumos 9:1-3

Terumah intermingled
Terumah intermingled, combining...Terumos 4:7-13
Terumah intermingled, dry...Terumos 5:1, 5:4
Terumah intermingled, separating from mixture...................Terumos 5:2-3; Bechoros 22a-23a
Terumah intermingled, Shabbos...Shabbos 142a-142b
Terumah intermingled, taste...Terumos 10:1-2, 10:5-6

Non-_Kohen_ —
Terumah, death for non-*Kohen*...Sanhedrin 83a-83b
Terumah given to rented animal...............................Terumos 11:9; Yevamos 66b; Avodah Zarah 15a
Terumah unintentional, payment.........Pesachim 31b-32b; Terumos 6:1-6; Eruvin 29b; Yevamos 90a;
....Gittin 54a; Bava Metzia 54b
Terumah, permission to benefit...Pesachim 23a
Terumah to non-*Kohen*, quantity...Pesachim 32b-33a
Terumah to non-*Kohen*, unusual way of eating..Yoma 80b-81a

Other *terumos* —
Terumah, new, communal offerings...............................Rosh Hashanah 7a; Yoma 65b; Megillah 29b
Terumah of loaves of thanksgiving.......Menachos 76a, 77b, 78b; Pesachim 37b; Nedarim 12b; Niddah 6b
Terumah of tithe, eaten as snack...Beitzah 13a
Terumah of tithe, from finished produce...Beitzah 13a

Requirement —
Terumah from second tithe..Maaser Sheni 3:2; Zevachim 76a
Terumah in connected to earth produce...Menachos 70a

Terumah in present times..Kesubos 25a; Niddah 46b-47a

Terumah, leaving part non-holy..Eruvin 37b; Pesachim 33b

Terumah, quantity................................Terumos 4:3-5; Kesubos 99b-100a; Kiddushin 41a-41b; Chullin 137b

Terumah, quantity for agent..Terumos 4:3-5

Terumah, requirement to give tithes..Beitzah 35a-35b; Maasros 2:4

Misc. —

Terumah, fruit wastes..Terumos 11:4-5; Eduyos 3:3

Terumah, importing from outside of *Eretz Yisrael*..Sheviis 6:5-6

Terumah, money for *kiddushin*..Kiddushin 53a, 58a-58b

Terumah, moving on Shabbos..Shabbos 127b

Terumah outside *Eretz Yisrael*, leniencies................................Bechoros 27a-27b; Beitzah 9a

Terumah, owner's money..Kiddushin 53a-53b

Terumah, ways of eating..Terumos 11:1

Terumah, widow..*see* **Widow eating *terumah***, page 745

Terumas hadeshen..*see* **Taking ash from Altar**, page 671

Teshuvah..*see* **Repentance**, page 559

Testicle

Testicle, blood..Chullin 93b; Pesachim 74b

Testicle, eating..Chullin 93a-93b

Testimony..*see also* **Signature**, page 625, **Trustworthiness**, page 704

Disqualified —

Testimony, close to himself and his money................................Yevamos 25b; Sanhedrin 9b-10a, 25a

Testimony, complete................................Bava Kama 70a-70b; Bava Basra 56a-56b; Sanhedrin 30b-31a, 86a-86b

Testimony, disqualified because affected................................Bava Basra 43a-44b, 46b-47a; Kiddushin 43b

Testimony, disqualified by Rabbinical Decree................................Rosh Hashanah 22a; Eruvin 82a;
....Sanhedrin 24b-25a, 26b, 27b

Testimony, disqualified witness who was reinstated................Bava Basra 128a-128b; Arachin 17b-18a

Testimony for *agunah*, women hating one another................Yevamos 117a-118a, 119b-120a

Testimony, lower class people are disqualified..Kiddushin 40b

Testimony, man disqualified because of transgression................................Sanhedrin 25b, 26b-27b

Testimony of friend and of enemy..Sanhedrin 29a

Testimony, old..Kesubos 20b

Testimony partly invalid, divorce certificate..Gittin 33a

Testimony partly invalid, third witness................Makos 5b-6a; Bava Basra 160b, 114a; Sanhedrin 9a-9b, 41b

Testimony, pretending to be wicked................................Yevamos 25b; Sanhedrin 9b, 25a

How —

Testimony, "I also"..Sanhedrin 60a

Testimony by estimate..Sanhedrin 37b; Shevuos 34a

Testimony, can be contradicted................................Bava Kama 75b; Sanhedrin 41b, 78a

Testimony, combining two testimonies................................Bava Kama 70a-70b; Bava Basra 56a-56b;
....Sanhedrin 30b-31a, 86a-86b

Testimony, consecutive witnesses..Sanhedrin 30a-30b

Testimony, how..Sanhedrin 6b, 60a; Shevuos 30a

Testimony, not in presence of defendant..Bava Kama 112a-112b

Testimony, of two people individually..Makos 6b; Sanhedrin 81b

Testimony, reminding..Kesubos 20a-20b

Testimony, translator..Makos 6b

Testimony, written..Gittin 71a; Bava Basra 165a-165b

T

Marriage —

Testimony concerning adulterers, what to testify .... Makos 7a; Bava Metzia 91a
Testimony concerning *kiddushin* .... Kiddushin 65a-65b
Testimony concerning *sotah* .... Sotah 2a-2b, 3b, 31a-32a; Sanhedrin 88a
Testimony, woman committing adultery .... Sotah 3b

Monetary matters —

Testimony concerning act of acquisition .... Kiddushin 65b; Bava Basra 40a
Testimony concerning *chazakah* in land .... Bava Basra 29a-29b
Testimony concerning honesty of lost item's owner .... Bava Metzia 28b
Testimony, ox goring regularly .... Bava Kama 24a-24b

Prohibitions —

Testimony about interest, negative commandment .... Bava Metzia 75b
Testimony, false, prohibition .... Makos 23a; Shevuos 31a; Kesubos 19a
Testimony, prohibitions .... Shevuos 30b, 31a

Who —

Testimony of convert .... Yevamos 22a; Kesubos 28b; Bava Kama 88a
Testimony of ignoramus .... Chagigah 22a
Testimony of minor .... Kesubos 28a-28b; Bava Basra 155b-156a
Testimony of non-Jew and slave .... Bava Kama 15a
Testimony of woman .... Shevuos 30a
Testimony, slave disqualified .... Bava Kama 88a

Testimony of relative

Testimony of relative, attestation .... Bava Basra 57a
Testimony of relatives, disqualified .... Bava Basra 159a
Testimony of relatives, guarantee .... Makos 7a
Testimony of relatives, to acquit one's relative .... Sanhedrin 27b-28a
Testimony of relatives, who .... Bava Basra 128a, 129a; Sanhedrin 28a-29a

Misc. —

Testimony about liability to bring sacrifice .... Krisos 11b-12b; Bava Metzia 3b; Yevamos 87b-88a;
.... Kiddushin 65b
Testimony concerning commandments in the future .... Avodah Zarah 2a, 4b
Testimony concerning forbidden relations, two .... Yevamos 88a; Gittin 2b, 90a
Testimony concerning transgressions .... Taanis 11a; Chagigah 16a
Testimony, duty .... Pesachim 113b; Bava Kama 56a
Testimony mistaken, slave .... Kesubos 28b; Yevamos 99b
Testimony of money given, reason unknown .... Shevuos 34a-34b
Testimony of Sage concerning law, trustworthy .... Berachos 30b; Chullin 7a
Testimony, part of it taken into consideration .... Yevamos 25a-25b; Sanhedrin 9b-10a;
.... Bava Basra 134b
Testimony, provable, trustworthiness .... Yevamos 39b
Testimony, retracting .... Kesubos 18b; Bava Basra 167b-168a; Bava Metzia 28b
Testimony, retracting .... Kesubos 18b; Bava Metzia 28b
Testimony, Sage exempt .... Shevuos 30b
Testimony, who will sign with him .... Sanhedrin 23a

Testimony for new moon

Testimony for new moon, examining .... Rosh Hashanah 23b-24a
Testimony for new moon, episode .... Rosh Hashanah 22b
Testimony for new moon, relatives .... Rosh Hashanah 22a
Testimony for new moon, Shabbos .... Rosh Hashanah 19b-20a, 21b-22a

T

Testimony for new moon, trustworthiness..Rosh Hashanah 22a-22b
Testimony for new moon, until when..Rosh Hashanah 30b; Beitzah 4b-5a
Testimony for new moon, Yaazek..Rosh Hashanah 23b

Testing G-d by tithe..Taanis 9a

Tevel

  Mixture —

    Tevel, cases of mixture..Demai 7:7; Challah 3:9
    Tevel, how to tithe a mixture..Menachos 31a
    Tevel, minimal mixture..Avodah Zarah 73b
    Tevel, mixture of *demai*..Chullin 6a

  Misc. —

    Tevel, death..Yevamos 86a; Sanhedrin 83a; Zevachim 11b
    Tevel, impure, benefit..Shabbos 26a
    Tevel, *muktzeh*..Beitzah 34b, 35a; Shabbos 43a, 128a
    Tevel, planting again..Maasros 5:1-2
    Tevel, sale to ignoramus..Maasros 5:3-4
    Tevel, significance..Nedarim 51a
    Tevel, theft..Nedarim 84b-85a; Kiddushin 58b
    Tevel, tithe for poor..Makos 16b-17a; Nedarim 84b; Yevamos 86a

Teveriah..*see* **Tiberias**, page 690

Tevichah umechirah..*see* **Slaughtering and selling**, page 635

Tevilah..*see* **Immersion**, page 299

Tevius ayin..*see* **Recognizes**, page 551

Tevul yom..*see* **Immersed that day**, page 299

Text

  Text of blessing, changing..Berachos 40b
  Text of blessings..Pesachim 7a-7b
  Text of divorce certificate..Gittin 80a
  Text of tithes separation..Demai 5:1-2

Texture of bread..Menachos 75b; Berachos 37a, 37b

Tfos lashon rishon..*see* **First expression determining**, page 225

Thanks to waiter instead of to host..Bava Kama 92b

Thanksgiving

  Thanksgiving, first, Leah..Berachos 7b
  Thanksgiving, four [people] must give thanks..Berachos 54b

  Thanksgiving sacrifice

    Thanksgiving sacrifice..*see also* **Loaves of thanksgiving**, page 376
    Thanksgiving sacrifice from second tithe..Menachos 81b-82a; Zevachim 50a
    Thanksgiving sacrifice intermingled with *temurah*..Menachos 80b-81a
    Thanksgiving sacrifice, lost..Temurah 18b; Menachos 79b-80a; Pesachim 13b

Theaters, prohibition to frequent go to..Avodah Zarah 18b

There is no guardian against immorality..Kesubos 13a-13b; Chullin 11b; Niddah 30b

Theft..*see also* **Thief**, page 686

  Aggadah —

    Theft..*see also* **Stealing**, page 655
    Theft and forbidden relations, cities..Eruvin 21b
    Theft and forbidden relations, desire for..Makos 23b; Chagigah 11b
    Theft, ant..Eruvin 100b
    Theft, considered as murder..Bava Kama 119a; Bava Metzia 112a

T

Theft, consumed stolen item .... Chullin 89a
Theft, curtain is not closed .... Bava Metzia 59a
Theft in burnt offering .... Succah 30a
Theft, punishment .... Shabbos 32b-33a
Theft, reproof by *chatsav* plant .... Beitzah 25b
Theft, taste of bread .... Sanhedrin 104b

Prohibition —
Theft, causing pain and paying penalty .... Bava Metzia 61b
Theft, interest and fraud .... Bava Metzia 61a
Theft, man and money .... Sanhedrin 85b-86a
Theft, more severe than sacred theft .... Bava Basra 88b

Returning —
Theft, denying .... Bava Metzia 43a-43b; Pesachim 32a; Bava Kama 65a-66a, 94a, 96b
Theft, increase in value .... Bava Kama 65a, 66a, 95a-95b; Bava Metzia 43a-43b
Theft of one of five persons, doubt .... Bava Kama 103b-104a; Bava Metzia 37a-37b; Yevamos 118b

Misc. —
Theft, accusation, possible indication .... Bava Kama 114b-115a
Theft, buying from suspected thief .... Bava Kama 67b-68a, 113a, 113b, 118b-119a; Bava Basra 51b-52a
Theft, concealing in forest .... Bava Kama 79b
Theft, *kiddushin* .... Kiddushin 52a-52b, 13a
Theft, large animal .... Sanhedrin 25b
Theft of father, returning .... Bava Kama 108b-109a
Theft, priestly gifts .... Chullin 134a; Bava Kama 115a
Theft, Rabbinical, before act of acquisition .... Bechoros 18a-18b; Bava Metzia 12b; Gittin 30a

These and those are words of the living G-d .... Gittin 6b; Eruvin 13b
Thickness of food, removing prohibited .... Chullin 97a

Thief
Episodes —
Thief, Kidor .... Yoma 83b
Thief, wiped with fellow's coat .... Bava Metzia 24a
Thieves, in different villages .... Chullin 127a
Thieves, persimmon .... Sanhedrin 109a
Thieves, Rabbi Elazar ben Rabbi Shimon .... Bava Metzia 83b

Misc. —
Thief becomes righteous when nothing to steal .... Sanhedrin 22a
Thief, blessing .... Sanhedrin 6b
Thief, changing from owner's will .... Bava Metzia 78a-78b
Thief, *chazakah* .... Bava Basra 47a
Thief, disqualified for testimony .... Sanhedrin 25b
Thief for commandment, indemnity .... Chullin 87a; Bava Kama 91b
Thief, impurity .... Chagigah 26a
Thief , mouse is not, the hole is .... Gittin 45a
Thief, not suspected of being a thief .... Shevuos 46b
Thief, thought for impurity .... Bava Kama 66b, 114a-114b; Keilim 26:8
Thief, who .... Bava Kama 57a, 79b
Thieves of field .... Bava Kama 116b
Thieves, together without shame .... Kiddushin 80b

Thigh
Thigh, definition .... Chullin 45b

Thigh, upper, *treifah* .... Chullin 42b, 54a-54b

Thing

Thing at its time, how good .... Sanhedrin 101a

Thing, improper thing in one's mouth .... Pesachim 3a

Thing in name of who said it .... Chullin 104b

Thing in name of who said it, episode .... Bechoros 31b; Yevamos 96b-97a

Thing which will finally be heard .... Avos 2:4

Things which are written, orally .... Temurah 14b; Gittin 60b

Things which I said are mistaken ..... Eruvin 16b, 104a; Shabbos 63b; Yevamos 20b, 76a; Bava Basra 127a;

Chullin 56a; Niddah 68a

Third

Third, adding to beautify commandment .... Bava Kama 9a-9b

Third and seventh day for impure person, sprinkling .... Yoma 8a

Third generation for first, testimony .... Bava Basra 128a, 129a

Third, growth of grain .... Sanhedrin 69a

Third in land, investments .... Bava Metzia 42a

Third in Scripture, learning .... Kiddushin 30a; Avodah Zarah 19b

Third of growth, tithe of produce .... Rosh Hashanah 12b-13b; Maasros 1:3

Third of shekel to charity .... Bava Basra 9a

Third person seized, land .... Bava Basra 35b

Third level of impurity

Third level of impurity for non-holy food .... Sotah 30a-30b

Third level of impurity, renders sacrifice impure .... Chagigah 24a; Pesachim 18b

Third level of impurity, sacrifice .... Chullin 35a-35b

Third level of impurity, *terumah* ..... Sotah 29a-30a; Chullin 33b-35b; Pesachim 18b-19a; Taharos 2:4-7

Thirteen Attributes .... Rosh Hashanah 17b

Thirty

Thirty nine lashes .... Makos 22a-22b

Thirty nine works, source .... Shabbos 49b, 70a, 97b

Thirty shekels for a half slave .... Gittin 42a-42b

Thirty shekels for a slave, when .... Bava Kama 43a-43b

Thirty six righteous .... Succah 45b; Sanhedrin 97b

Thirty six slain men at Ai .... Bava Basra 121b

Thirty days

Thirty days if not explicitly expressed, *Nazir* .... Nazir 5a

Thirty days, loan .... Makos 3b

Thirty days, prohibitions concerning mourner .... Moed Katan 22b

Thirty days, redeeming firstborn .... Bava Kama 11b; Bechoros 12b, 49a-49b

Thirty days, sacrifice .... Parah 1:4

This

"This is my brother," inheritance .... Bava Basra 135a-135b

"This is my wife," trustworthiness .... Kiddushin 79b-80a

"This is what is called a great man" .... Zevachim 5a

This I did not hear, but I heard a similar law .... Shabbos 108b, 114a

This is a man .... Shabbos 112b; Eruvin 24a; Avodah Zarah 10b

This is known by children .... Gittin 29a; Berachos 5a; Chullin 81b

This is my G-d and I shall glorify Him .... Shabbos 133b; Succah 11b; Nazir 2b

This is my sin offering .... Nedarim 6a

This one looks like that one, *treifah* .... Chullin 48b

T

This Sage forbids and that permits .... Gittin 83b
Thongs for canopy, wearing them as garment .... Shabbos 139b
Thorn
  Prohibitions —
    Thorn, act needed for itself .... Shabbos 42a
    Thorn, clearing away on Shabbos .... Shabbos 42a; Beitzah 28b
    Thorn in cavity, *treifah* .... Chullin 53b
    Thorn in gullet, *treifah* .... Chullin 43b
    Thorn, pulling out on father's body, prohibition .... Sanhedrin 84b-85a
    Thorn, pulling out on Shabbos .... Shabbos 123b
    Thorns in vineyard, mixed species .... Bava Basra 156b; Kilayim 5:8; Shabbos 144b
  Misc. —
    Thorn, saves person from ship drowning .... Niddah 31a
    Thorns, between my eyes .... Kiddushin 71a
    Thorns on wall, damage .... Bava Kama 30a
Thought .... *see* **Intent**, page 311
Thousand foods, figs .... Nedarim 50b
Thread
  Thread in garment, intermingled .... Orlah 3:2-3; Temurah 34a
  Thread of grace, Torah .... Avodah Zarah 3b; Chagigah 12b
  Thread of substance forbidden to profit, in garment .... Orlah 3:2-3; Temurah 34a
  Thread *sikrah,* Altar .... Zevachim 53a; Menachos 97b; Bechoros 17b; Middos 3:1
  Thread *sikrah,* sprinklings .... Zevachim 10b
  Thread, threefold, Sage's offspring .... Bava Basra 59a
  Thread, threefold, three commandments .... Menachos 43b
  Threads extending when cutting *matzah* .... Pesachim 37a
Threatening and not performing .... Shevuos 46a
Three
  Aggadah —
    Three books, Rosh Hashanah .... Rosh Hashanah 16b
    Three come by distraction .... Sanhedrin 97a
    Three men whom evil urge did not dominate .... Bava Basra 17a
    Three partners in man creation .... Niddah 31a
    Three Patriarchs only .... Berachos 16b
    Three, taste of World to Come .... Bava Basra 16b-17a
    Three things prolong life .... Berachos 54b-55a
    Three things, world stands on .... Avos 1:2, 1:18
  Commandments —
    Three commandments, threefold thread .... Menachos 43b
    Three days without learning .... Bava Kama 82a
    Three *Kohanim,* fat and chest of animal .... Menachos 62a
    Three lies permitted to Sage .... Bava Metzia 23b-24a
    Three meals, Shabbos .... Shabbos 117b-118a, 118b; Kesubos 64b
    Three men, *zimun* .... Berachos 45a-45b; Chullin 106a
    Three prayers, source .... Berachos 31a
    Three species, needing three commandments .... Menachos 62b
  Monetary matters —
    Three appraisers to share partnership .... Bava Metzia 31b-32a
    Three, avoiding lawsuit against three litigants .... Pesachim 112b

T

Three banknotes in a bundle, mark..Bava Metzia 20b
Three men, act of acquisition of debt.............Gittin 13a-14a; Kiddushin 48a; Bava Basra 144a, 148a
Three thirds, investment...Bava Metzia 42a
Three years, uncontested holding of real property..............................Bava Basra 28a-29a

Prohibitions —
Three handbreadths, erecting down...............Shabbos 5a, 80a, 92a, 97a, 100a-100b; Eruvin 98b
Three ordinary men, permitting vow...............Yevamos 25b; Nedarim 78a-78b; Bava Basra 120b
Three ordinary men, who..Bechoros 36b-37a
Three transgressions, forgiveness..Yoma 86b
Three windpipes, *treifah*..Chullin 45a, 45b

Purity —
Three by three fingerbreadths, impurity................Shabbos 28b-29b, 39b, 47a; Keilim 28:1-3
Three by three fingerbreadths, leprosy..Shabbos 26a-27a
Three *log*, *mikveh*..Mikvaos 2:4; Shabbos 15a
Three utensils, impurity..Keilim 24:1-16; Shabbos 84a, 84a

Misc. —
Three, beneficial to body...Berachos 57b
Three, *chazakah*...........Yevamos 26a, 64b-65a; Eruvin 97a; Kesubos 43b; Bava Kama 23b; Bava Metzia 106b;
....Bava Basra 28a-28b; Sanhedrin 81b; Niddah 63-64a
Three days for putting barriers..Shabbos 87a
Three days without sleep.................Nedarim 15a; Succah 53a; Yevamos 121b; Shevuos 25a
Three verses teaching identical law...Kiddushin 35a

Three camps
Three camps, desert and Temples..Zevachim 116b-117a
Three camps, impurity...Pesachim 67a-68a
Three camps, journey of Tabernacle..Menachos 95a-95b

Three hundred
Three hundred and ten worlds..Sanhedrin 100a-100b; Uktzin 3:12
Three hundred barrels of oil...Shabbos 13b
Three hundred, overstatement..Chullin 90b; Tamid 29b

Three months
Three months after death, *chalitzah*...............................Yevamos 41a-41b; Eruvin 47a
Three months before remarrying.............Yevamos 34a-35a, 41b-43b; Kesubos 37a; Gittin 18a
Three months, embryo is recognizable.............Yevamos 37a, 42a; Sanhedrin 69a; Niddah 8b

Three year old girl
Three year old girl, convert..Yevamos 60b; Kiddushin 78a, 78b
Three year old girl, forbidden to *Kohen*..Niddah 45a
Three year old girl, intimate relations.............Kiddushin 10a-10b; Niddah 44b-45a; Yevamos 57b;
....Sanhedrin 55b, 69a
Three year old girl, virginity...Niddah 45a
Three year old girl, canopy..Yevamos 57b

Threefold thread
Threefold thread, Sage's offspring...Bava Basra 59a
Threefold thread, three commandments..Menachos 43b
Threefold thread, Torah and occupation..Kiddushin 40b

Threshing
Threshing floor, distance from neighbors...Bava Basra 24b-25a
Threshing, peeling wheat...Beitzah 13b
Threshing, plants...Shabbos 75a

T

Threw

Threw and remembered, Shabbos...Shabbos 102a

Threw arrow and rent garment...Kesubos 31a; Bava Kama 117a

Threw coin to sea, indirect damage...Bava Kama 98a

Threw her *kiddushin*...Kiddushin 8b

Threw knife and slaughtered that way...Chullin 12b, 31a

Threw, murder...Bava Kama 26b-27a

Threw, roofed house..Shabbos 4b-5a, 97a

Threw stone on group...Bava Kama 44b

Threw through private domain..Shabbos 97b-98a

Threw utensil from roof, damage..Bava Kama 17b, 26b

Throwing *chametz* to sea..Pesachim 28a

Throwing cup at face, succah...Succah 29a

Throwing idol to sea...Pesachim 28a; Avodah Zarah 43b-44a

Throwing, not to throw water of cistern...Yevamos 11b, 12a, 44a, 53a

Throwing on Shabbos, deduced from holding out......................................Shabbos 4b, 97a

Throwing benefit, idol..Avodah Zarah 49b

Throwing roasted grain, wedding...Berachos 50b

Throwing blood on Altar

Throwing blood on Altar, determining disqualified sacrifices......................Meilah 8a-9b

Throwing blood on Altar, determining *piggul*..Meilah 3b-4a

Throwing blood on Altar, eating sacrificial flesh before............Pesachim 77b; Sanhedrin 63a;

....Makos 18b

Throwing blood on Altar, even when meat is out of Temple............Zevachim 26a, 89b-90a;

....Meilah 6b-7a, 8b; Menachos 12a, 25b, 47a-47b

Throwing blood on Altar, facing basis...Zevachim 56b-57a

Throwing blood on Altar, impurity before..Zevachim 34a

Throwing blood on Altar, instead of pouring.......................................Pesachim 121a; Zevachim 37a

Throwing blood on Altar, *piggul*, personal use...................Meilah 3b-4b, 5b-6a; Menachos 47b

Throat

Throat, absorbed impurity...Niddah 42b

Throat, egg..Yoma 80a

Throat, impurity...Zavim 5:9

Throne of Glory...Chagigah 12b-13a; Pesachim 54a; Nedarim 39b

Thunder

Thunder, blessing...Berachos 59a

Thunder, origin..Berachos 59a

Thunder, to rectify crookedness of heart...Berachos 59a

Tiberias

Tiberias, Ben Azzai, marketplace of Tiberias..Kiddushin 20a

Tiberias, episode about crown...Bava Basra 8a

Tiberias, names and praise...Megillah 6a

Tiberias, relocations of *Sanhedrin*...Rosh Hashanah 31b

Tiberias, welcoming Shabbos...Shabbos 118b

Tidal wave...Bava Metzia 24a

Tight lid

Tight lid, clay...Chullin 25a

Tight lid, hole...Keilim 9:7-8; Shabbos 95b-96a

Tight lid, how..Keilim 10:1-6

T

Tight lid, impurity of sacrifices ....Chagigah 25a
Tight lid in oven ....Keilim 8:6
Tight lid, leper ....Negaim 13:12
Tight lid, *niddah* who moved item ....Gittin 61b
Tight lid, saving ....Keilim 9:1-2
Tigris, Chidekel ....Berachos 59b
Tikroves avodah zarah ....*see* **Idolatrous sacrifice**, page 295
Tikun ....*see* **Correct**, page 129; *see also* **Repairing**, page 558, **Prepare**, page 501
Tikun haolam ....*see* **Decrees for society's benefit**, page 154
Tile, depth of wall ....Bava Basra 3a
Tiltul ....*see* ***Muktzeh***, page 429
Time of coming of Messiah ....Kesubos 112b; Sanhedrin 97a, 98a-98b
Time of coming of Messiah ....Kesubos 112b; Sanhedrin 97a, 98a-98b
Time of Divine Favor ....Yevamos 72a; Taanis 24b
Time of Redemption, Divine Presence leaves Jacob ....Pesachim 56a
Commandments —
Time dependant commandments, women ....Kiddushin 33b-35a; Eruvin 27a, 96a-96b
Time for donating wood ....Taanis 28a
Time for eating firstborn ....Zevachim 57a; Bechoros 27b-28a
Time for eating sacrifices ....Zevachim 36a
Time for eliminating *chametz* ....Pesachim 13a-13b
Time for searching for *chametz* ....Pesachim 4a
Time for slaughtering daily offering ....Pesachim 58a-58b
Time of daily offerings and *mussaf* sacrifices ....Berachos 26b
Time of immersion, impure persons ....Shabbos 120b-121a; Yoma 6a-6b; Pesachim 90b
Legal documents —
Time of divorce certificate ....Gittin 3b, 17a-18a, 26b, 79b-80b, 86a; Bava Basra 176a
Time of legal document proves ....Gittin 72a-72b, 76b-77a, 85b; Bava Basra 136a; Avodah Zarah 37a
Time of legal document, signed at night ....Gittin 18a-18b
Time written in knotted up divorce certificate ....Bava Basra 164a-164b
Monetary matters —
Time given by *beis din* to demolish dangerous wall ....Bava Metzia 118a
Time limit of *beis din*, damages ....Bava Kama 91a
Time of *beis din* session ....*see* **Beis din**, page 50
Time of convocation to judgment ....Bava Kama 113a
Time of loan ....Makos 3b
Time of workers, to work ....Bava Metzia 83a-83b
Prayers —
Time of *Mincha* ....Berachos 26b-27a, 29b; Yoma 28b; Shabbos 118b
Time of morning *Shema* ....Berachos 10b
Time of prayer separately ....Shabbos 10a
Time of prayers ....Berachos 26b-27a
Time of prayers, delaying ....Berachos 28a
Time of *Shema* at night ....Berachos 2b-3a, 4a-4b
Prohibitions —
Time for leavening, time necessary to walk one *mil* ....Pesachim 46a
Time necessary to make, Shabbos labor ....Eruvin 40a; Beitzah 24b
Time of religious persecution, self-sacrifice ....Sanhedrin 74a-74b
Times require exceptional punishment ....Sanhedrin 46a; Yevamos 90b

Times, wording of vow .... Nedarim 60a-61a

Women —

Time for annulment of vow .... Nedarim 76b, 87b; Shabbos 157a

Time for female formation .... Niddah 30b

Time for intimate relations, pious men .... Niddah 38a

Time for seclusion of *sotah* .... Sotah 4a-4b

Time from betrothal to wedding .... Kesubos 57a-57b; Nedarim 73b

Time of wedding arrived, supporting wife .... Kesubos 2a-2b, 48b, 57a, 70b; Nedarim 73b

Times for intimate relations .... Yevamos 62b; Kesubos 62a-62b

Times of separation from home to learn .... Kesubos 61b-62a

Misc. —

"Time to act," from beginning .... Berachos 63a; Sanhedrin 70a

Time favorable, choosing partner .... Pesachim 112a, 113a

Time necessary to say three words .... Nedarim 87a-87b; Nazir 20b-21a; Bava Kama 73a-73b;
.... Bava Basra 129b-130a

Time necessary to walk one *mil* .... *see* **Mil**, page 410

Time of growth of fruit .... Bechoros 8a; Rosh Hashanah 11a

Time to Act, Oral Torah .... Temurah 14b; Gittin 60a

Time to eat day meals .... Shabbos 10a; Pesachim 12b; Bava Metzia 107b; Berachos 2b

Time of validity

Time of validity, blood of sin offering .... Zevachim 93a

Time of validity, bone of Pesach .... Pesachim 83a

Time of validity, impurity .... Menachos 101a-101b; Bava Kama 77a; Shevuos 11b; Chullin 81b;
.... Bechoros 9b

Timna, Esau's concubine .... Sanhedrin 99b

Timnas city, ascent and decline .... Sotah 10a

Tinok shenishba .... *see* **Captive child, sacrifice**, page 87

Tiomes, *lulav* .... Succah 32a; Bava Kama 96a-96b

Tipach .... *see* **Twenty years old, age for marriage**, page 706

Tipping balance of world, by commandment .... Kiddushin 40b

Tipuach, significance .... Moed Katan 27b

Tircha detzibura .... *see* **Imposing upon the congregation**, page 300

Tirosh, wine and sweet foods .... Yoma 76b

Tisha B'Av

Tisha B'Av, canceling .... Megillah 5b

Tisha B'Av, differences .... Pesachim 54b

Tisha B'Av, greetings .... Taanis 14b

Tisha B'Av, immersion .... Niddah 68a

Tisha B'Av, prohibitions .... Pesachim 54b, 55a; Taanis 29b-30b; Berachos 17b

Tisha B'Av, Shabbos .... Megillah 5a

Tisha B'Av, Torah reading .... Megillah 31b

Tisha B'Av, tragedies .... Taanis 29a

Tisha B'Av, twilight .... Pesachim 54b

Tisha B'Av, washing .... Yoma 78a

Tisha B'Av, who is permitted to eat .... Pesachim 54b

Tishas hayamim .... *see* **Nine days**, page 445

Tishmeru means Mishnah .... Kiddushin 37a

Tishrei

Tishrei, Creation .... Rosh Hashanah 8a, 10b-11a, 27a; Avodah Zarah 8a

Tishrei, non-Jewish kings .... Rosh Hashanah 3a-3b, 8a
Tishrei, Israel will be redeemed in *Tishrei* .... Rosh Hashanah 11b

Tithe .... *see also* **Separating tithe**, page 602; **Requirement to give tithe**, page 561

First tithe —
Tithe, first, to whom .... Yevamos 86a-86b; Kesubos 26a; Chullin 131b
Tithe, first, Israel is allowed to eat it .... Yevamos 74a, 85b-86a; Kesubos 26a
Tithe, immoral *leviyah* .... Yevamos 91a; Bechoros 47a
Tithe, leaving right .... Bava Basra 63a
Tithe, money for *kiddushin* .... Kiddushin 53a, 53b
Tithe of your father by me .... Gittin 30b

From which produce —
Tithe, accessory to fruit .... Maasros 4:5-6
Tithe, consecrated produce .... Peah 4:8; Challah 3:4; Menachos 66b
Tithe, edible seed .... Eruvin 28a
Tithe from gifts for poor .... Sotah 43b; Berachos 40b
Tithe, non-Jew's field .... Terumos 3:9; Menachos 31a, 66b-67a; Bechoros 11a-11b; Gittin 47a-47b, 23b;
.... Kiddushin 41b; Bava Metzia 101a
Tithe, Sabbatical year produce .... Rosh Hashanah 15a

Requirement —
Tithe, from the Torah and by Rabbinical Decree .... Rosh Hashanah 12a; Bechoros 54a;
.... Berachos 36a; Niddah 50a
Tithe in Beth Shean, Rebbi .... Chullin 6b-7a
Tithe in present times .... Kesubos 25a; Niddah 46b-47a
Tithe of produce, from third of growth .... Rosh Hashanah 12b-13b; Maasros 1:3
Tithe, scholar surely separated ...... Eruvin 32a-32b; Pesachim 4b, 9a; Niddah 15b; Avodah Zarah 41b
Tithe, tenant farmer .... Demai 6:1-2
Tithe, tenant farmer to non-Jew .... Challah 4:7; Bava Metzia 101a; Gittin 43b
Tithes, Ammon and Moab .... Yadayim 4:3; Chagigah 3b; Yevamos 16a
Tithes, produce bought .... Bava Metzia 88a-88b

Separating tithe —
Tithe, exchange .... Bava Metzia 11b
Tithe, first generations .... Berachos 35b
Tithe, first, separating from sheaves ...... Berachos 47a-47b; Shabbos 127b; Eruvin 31b; Pesachim 35b;
.... Beitzah 13b; Temurah 5b
Tithe of one's part, how .... Demai 6:7-9
Tithe of wealthy man, G-d proclaims .... Pesachim 113a
Tithe, punishment .... Shabbos 32b; Taanis 7b
Tithe, testing G-d .... Taanis 9a
Tithe, wealth .... Berachos 63a; Makos 23b; Shabbos 32b, 119a; Taanis 9a
Tithes, figs on dried figs .... Menachos 54b-55a

Misc. —
Tithe, according to majority .... Machshirin 2:11
Tithe, doubtful .... *see* **Demai**, page 158
Tithe, exempt to give, bought fruit from non-Jew .... Bechoros 11a
Tithe, giving a name, redeeming .... Maaser Sheni 4:7
Tithe of money .... Kesubos 50a, 67b; Arachin 28a
Tithe, second .... *see* **Second tithe**, page 595
Tithe, so that you become rich .... Taanis 9a; Shabbos 119a
Tithe, subtracting from repayment of loan .... Gittin 30a-30b

Tithes before separation........ Makos 20a; Nedarim 85a; Kiddushin 58b; Bava Basra 123b; Chullin 130b;
.... Bechoros 11a
Tithes by ignoramus .... *see* **Demai**, page 158

Tithe for poor
Tithe for poor, *demai* .... Demai 4:3; Nedarim 84a-84b; Makos 16b-17a
Tithe for poor, right to grant .... Nedarim 84a-84b
Tithe for poor, *tevel* .... Makos 16b-17a; Nedarim 84b; Yevamos 86a
Tithe for poor, to father .... Kiddushin 32a
Tithe for poor, when .... Rosh Hashanah 12b

Tithe of animal
Tithe of animal, agent who made a mistake .... Bechoros 61a
Tithe of animal, before time .... Bechoros 21a-21b, 56a, 57b; Temurah 19b
Tithe of animal, buying .... Bechoros 11a, 55b-56b; Bava Kama 110b
Tithe of animal, combining flocks .... Bechoros 53b-55a
Tithe of animal, doubts .... Bava Metzia 6b-7a; Bechoros 58b
Tithe of animal, exempt because already counted .... Bechoros 59b-60a; Bava Metzia 6b
Tithe of animal, exemptions .... Bechoros 53b, 57a-57b
Tithe of animal, heirs .... Bechoros 56b
Tithe of animal, how to count .... Bechoros 58b-59a, 60a
Tithe of animal, mistake in count .... Bechoros 59a-59b, 60b-61a; Nazir 31b-32a; Eruvin 50a;
.... Kiddushin 51a
Tithe of animal, in present times .... Bechoros 53a-53b, 61a
Tithe of animal, offering .... Zevachim 37a, 56b; Pesachim 64b-65a
Tithe of animal, out of *Eretz Yisrael* .... Bechoros 53a
Tithe of animal, partners .... Bechoros 56b
Tithe of animal, replacing .... Temurah 13b
Tithe of animal, sale .... Bechoros 31b, 32a-32b; Bava Kama 13a; Temurah 5b, 8b
Tithe of animal, sheep redeeming donkey .... Bechoros 11a; Bava Metzia 7a
Tithe of animal, time .... Bechoros 57b-58b; Shekalim 3:1; Rosh Hashanah 7b-8a
Tithe of animal, year .... Rosh Hashanah 8a
Titi li .... *see* **I merit a reward for my behavior**, page 291
Titus
Titus, *Gehinnom* .... Gittin 57a
Titus, Temple destruction .... Gittin 56b
To
To life! drinking wine .... Shabbos 67b
To use its place, carrying together with permitted item .... Shabbos 142a
To use object and place, *muktzeh* .... Shabbos 122b-123a, 123b-124b, 141b; Beitzah 11a
Toanim leyoresh velalokeach .... *see* **Arguments on behalf of purchaser and of heir**, page 31
Toch kedei dibur .... *see* **Time necessary to say three words**, page 692
Toch tocho .... *see* **Utensil inside another**, page 718
Tochachah .... *see* **Rebuke**, page 550
Tocho kebaro .... *see* **Inside like outside, personality**, page 311
Todah .... *see* **Thanksgiving sacrifice**, page 685
Today
Today to accomplish them, reward .... Avodah Zarah 3a, 4b; Eruvin 22a
Today, you are not my wife .... Gittin 83b-84a, 86a; Nedarim 29a
Today you have become a people .... Berachos 63b
Todos, Jew living in Rome .... Pesachim 53a-53b; Berachos 19a; Beitzah 23a

Toeh .... *see* **Mistake**, page 415

Toes, leper .... Yoma 61b

Toevah, significance .... Nedarim 51a

Tofeach al menas lehatfiach .... *see* **Wet to the point of making wet**, page 740

Tofes, standard text in all *gittin* and contracts .... Gittin 26a

Tohu vavohu .... Chagigah 12a

Toil in Torah .... Sanhedrin 99b

Toilets

Toilets .... *see also* **Bodily needs**, page 70

Toilets, *chazakah* .... Bava Basra 22b, 50b

Toilets, close by, wealth .... Shabbos 25b

Toilets close to one's table .... Bava Metzia 107a

Toilets, learning .... Zevachim 102b

Toilets, locking .... Tamid 27b

Toilets, prayer .... Berachos 26a; Shabbos 10a-10b; Nedarim 7a

Toilets, protection .... Berachos 62a

Toilets, seclusion with women .... Sanhedrin 19a

Toilets, snake .... Berachos 62b

Toilets, *tefillin* .... Berachos 23a-23b; Shabbos 62a

Tolaas shani .... *see* **Crimson wool**, page 133

Toladah, Tolados .... *see* **Secondary category**, page 596

Tolerant, G-d loves him .... Pesachim 113b

Tombstone

Tombstone, grave site .... Moed Katan 5a-6a

Tombstones, impurity .... Chullin 126b; Oholos 2:4, 15:8-9

Tomen, amount .... Bava Basra 89b

Tongue

Tongue .... *see also* **Speaking**, page 649, **Speech**, page 649

Tongue, exposed limb .... Kiddushin 25a

Tongue of Rabbi Chutzpis .... Chullin 142a

Tongue of scarlet, Yom Kippur .... Yoma 41b, 67a; Rosh Hashanah 31b

Tongue, pure .... Pesachim 3a-3b

Tongue, pure, episodes .... Pesachim 3b

Too much is harmful, a little is good .... Berachos 34a; Gittin 70a

Took advice from His angels .... Sanhedrin 38b

Tools to built tabernacle .... Shabbos 96b

Tooth .... *see* **Bone** page 71

Top

Top determines, cooking .... Pesachim 75b-76a

Top of the world, neglected things .... Berachos 6b

Tor Malka, destruction .... Gittin 57a

Torah .... *see also* **Learning**, page 357

Aggadah —

Torah begins with kindness .... Sotah 14a

Torah, betrothed to Israel .... Pesachim 49b; Berachos 57a; Sanhedrin 59a

Torah, by suffering .... Berachos 5a

Torah, Creation .... Avos 3:14

Torah, given to Moses like bride to groom .... Nedarim 38a

Torah, no one knows its value .... Shevuos 5a

T

Torah of kindness, definition...Succah 49b
Torah without kindness...Avodah Zarah 17b

Effects —
Torah and kindness, protection from evil urge...Avodah Zarah 5b
Torah, birth pangs of Messiah...Sanhedrin 98b
Torah heals...Eruvin 54a
Torah labors for man...Sanhedrin 99a
Torah leads to watchfulness...Avodah Zarah 20b
Torah protects...Berachos 5a; Avodah Zarah 17b
Torah protects and saves..Sotah 21a
Torah returns to its dwelling...Bava Metzia 85a

Episodes —
"Torah is outside," Rabbi Meir...Horayos 13b
Torah and greatness..Gittin 59a; Sanhedrin 36a
Torah and kindness, Eli's sons........................Yevamos 105a; Rosh Hashanah 18a
Torah and kindness, Issacher...Bava Kama 17a
Torah in ugly container...Nedarim 50b; Taanis 7a-7b
Torah insincere, Doeg...Sanhedrin 106b
Torah it is and I need to learn it....................................Berachos 62a; Megillah 28a
Torah learning in poverty, episode..Sanhedrin 20a

Learning —
"*Torah tzivah*," teaching child...Succah 42a
Torah burns in him..Taanis 4a
Torah by student's name..Avodah Zarah 19a; Kiddushin 32b
Torah, erring then understanding...............Gittin 43a; Shabbos 119b-120a; Chagigah 14a
Torah exhausts...Sanhedrin 26b
Torah in poverty, reward...Sotah 49a
Torah scholars are G-d's paid workers...Eruvin 65a
Torah, encouragement..Berachos 32b
Torah, what will become of it, making a living..Berachos 35b

Writing and giving —
Torah forgotten, Sages taught it anew..Succah 20a
Torah from Sinai, source...Berachos 5a; Megillah 19b
Torah given in whole or by parts...Gittin 60a-60b
Torah, greater part in writing..Gittin 60b
Torah, its writing and conclusion..Gittin 60a-60b
Torah not given to angels..Kiddushin 54a
Torah, oral, covenant...Gittin 60b
Torah, oral, writing...Temurah 14b; Gittin 60b
Torah, stones in Jordan river...Sotah 35b
Torah, Written and Oral...Gittin 60b; Temurah 14b

Misc. —
Torah cares about Jews' money..........................Rosh Hashanah 27a; Menachos 76b, 86b, 88b, 89a;
                                                        Chullin 49b, 77a; Yoma 39a, 44b; Negaim 12:5
Torah, I have only...Yevamos 109b
Torah, means indispensable requirement...Menachos 19a
Torah, not among those who make merry..Sanhedrin 111a
Torah outlook, submitting to...Rosh Hashanah 25a-25b
Torah speaks inexactly...Tamid 29a

Torah testified, clay utensils .... Avodah Zarah 34a
Torah uses man's speech .... Bava Metzia 31b
Torah, writing together with Prophets scroll .... Bava Basra 13b-14a

Torah as a fixed occupation
Torah as a fixed occupation, diligence .... Yoma 19b
Torah as a fixed occupation, first generations .... Berachos 35b
Torah as a fixed occupation, making a living .... Berachos 35b

Torah for its own sake
Torah for its own sake, honor will come in the end .... Nedarim 62a
Torah for its own sake, influences .... Sanhedrin 99b
Torah for its own sake, kindness .... Succah 49b
Torah for its own sake, many things .... Avos 6:1
Torah for its own sake, redemption .... Sanhedrin 99b

Torah reading
How —
Torah reading, how .... Megillah 21a-21b; Sotah 39b
Torah reading, interruption during curses .... Megillah 31b
Torah reading, no translation .... Megillah 25a-25b
Torah reading, number of men called .... Megillah 21b-23a
Torah reading, number of verses .... Megillah 21b; Taanis 27b
Torah reading, omitting section .... Yoma 69b-70a; Megillah 24a; Sotah 41a
Torah reading, signs to reader for cantillation notes .... Berachos 62a
Torah reading, *Targum* .... Berachos 45a; Megillah 23b-24a; Sotah 39b
Torah reading, where to stop .... Megillah 21b-22a

When —
Torah reading, *Anshei Maamad* .... Taanis 27b-28a
Torah reading by king .... Sotah 41a-41b
Torah reading, fasts .... Megillah 30b, 31b
Torah reading, festivals .... Megillah 30b-31b
Torah reading, *Kohen Gadol* .... Sotah 40b-41a; Yoma 69a-70a
Torah reading, *Mincha* of Shabbos .... Megillah 31b-32a; Bava Kama 82a
Torah reading, Monday and Thursday .... Megillah 31b-32a; Bava Kama 82a
Torah reading, *Rosh Chodesh* .... Megillah 21b-22a, 29b; Yoma 70a; Sotah 41a

Misc. —
Torah reading, blessings .... Megillah 21b, 32a
Torah reading, going out and learning during .... Berachos 8a
Torah reading, incomplete Torah scroll .... Gittin 60a
Torah reading, last eight verses of Torah .... Menachos 30a; Bava Basra 15a
Torah reading, prohibition to speak .... Sotah 39a

Torah scroll
Honoring —
Torah scroll, sizes .... Bava Basra 14a
Torah scroll on bed .... Menachos 32b; Moed Katan 25a
Torah scroll, on Sage's coffin .... Bava Kama 17a
Torah scroll open, going out of synagogue .... Berachos 8a
Torah scroll, prohibition to hang .... Berachos 24a
Torah scroll, rolling up .... Megillah 32a
Torah scroll, rolling up towards middle .... Bava Basra 14a
Torah scroll, saving .... Shabbos 115b, 116a

T

Torah scroll, taking it from one place to another .... Berachos 18a
Torah scroll which rolled open on Shabbos .... Eruvin 97b-98b, 103a; Shabbos 5b
Torah scroll without covering, holding .... Shabbos 14a; Megillah 32a

Misc. —
Torah scroll, beauty .... Shabbos 133b; Yoma 70a; Nazir 2b
Torah scroll, borrower and custodian .... Bava Metzia 29b
Torah scroll buried, Rabbi Eliezer's death .... Sotah 49b
Torah scroll, deposit from minor .... Bava Basra 52a
Torah scroll in pain .... Sanhedrin 101a
Torah scroll in Temple .... Bava Basra 14a-14b
Torah scroll, king .... Sanhedrin 21b, 22a
Torah scroll, returning .... Sotah 39b
Torah scroll, sale .... Megillah 27a; Bava Basra 151a
Torah scroll, size .... Bava Basra 14a; Menachos 30a
Torah scroll, torn, episode .... Yevamos 96b
Torah scroll, torn, sewing .... Menachos 31b
Torah scroll, written by heretic .... Shabbos 116a
Torah scrolls, four hundred .... Bava Basra 14a

Toras *Kohanim*
Toras Kohanim, kings of Israel .... Sanhedrin 103b
Toras Kohanim, learning .... Yevamos 72b

Torch, *havdala* light .... Pesachim 8a, 103b

Toref, specifics in all *gittin* and contracts .... Gittin 26a

Tosefes .... *see* **Addition**, page 11

Tosefta, author .... Sanhedrin 86a

Total gift .... *see* **Administrator**, page 12

Touched
Touched by idolater, wine .... Avodah Zarah 55a-56b
Touching dead, impurity .... Avodah Zarah 37b
Touching one's genital member .... Niddah 13a-13b, 16b, 43a
Touching *tefillin* .... Menachos 36b; Yoma 7b-8a; Shabbos 12a
Touching twice, combining for impurity .... Chullin 124b
Touching under one's navel .... Niddah 13b

Touring one's property
Touring one's property, episodes .... Chullin 105a
Touring one's property every day .... Chullin 105a
Touring one's property on Shabbos .... Gittin 38b

Tov .... *see* **Best**, page 55

Tov in first Tablets .... Bava Kama 54b-55a

Tov lev mishteh tamid .... *see* **Good heart, continuous feast**, page 255

Tovas hanaah .... *see* **Right to grant**, page 567

Tovel vesheretz be'yado ... *see* **Immersing while holding dead reptile**, page 298

Towel
Towel for wiping, impurity .... Berachos 52a-52b
Towel, taking back on Shabbos .... Shabbos 147a-147b
Towel, washing hands .... Chullin 107a-107b; Succah 26b-27a

Tower
Tower, impurity of corpse .... Oholos 4:1-3; Sanhedrin 106b
Tower of Babylon causes forgetfulness .... Sanhedrin 109a

Tower of *Haflagah* generation..Sanhedrin 109a
Tower of Nimrod, idolatry..Avodah Zarah 53b

Town

Town and city, advantages..Kesubos 110b
Town in *Eretz Yisrael*, Omri..Sanhedrin 102b
Town inhabitant seeing king..Chagigah 13b
Town of Sachnya, episodes..Gittin 57a
Towns, Purim..Megillah 2a-2b, 4b-5a; Yevamos 13b

Traces of derogatory speech..Bava Basra 164b-165a; Arachin 15b-16a

Tracing on written letters..Gittin 19a

Trade

Trade..*see also* **Sale**, page 585, **Sell**, page 600
Trade, advice..Yevamos 63a; Pesachim 113a
Trade, episode about care to avoid theft..Beitzah 29a
Trade for one's son, Rav..Pesachim 113a
Trade, Rav Yehudah's profit..Bava Metzia 40a-40b
'Trading, advice..Yevamos 63a
Trading, fruit from outside *Eretz Yisrael*..Bava Basra 90b-91a
Trading honestly, questions..Shabbos 31a
Trading in forbidden items..Sheviis 7:3-4; Pesachim 23a
Trading in Sabbatical year fruit, punishment..Kiddushin 20a-20b
Trading, *muktzeh*..Shabbos 19b
Trading, who benefits..Nedarim 31a-31b
Trading with fellow's cow..Bava Metzia 35b, 36b

Tradition

Tradition from teacher, ruling..Pesachim 51a-51b; Shevuos 13a
Tradition, *kosher* birds..Chullin 63b
Tradition of Torah..Avos 1:1

Tragedy which we hope will not happen..Taanis 19a

Training period in *beis din*..Sanhedrin 42a; Shevuos 30b; Horayos 3b

Traiksin, Temple..Bava Basra 3a-3b

Trample

Trampled animal, examination..Chullin 53b-54a
Trampled animal, *treifah*..Chullin 43b, 52b-53a
Trampling underfoot..Avodah Zarah 18a

Transfer of rights, money-changer..Bava Metzia 112a

Transformed into positive commandment, annulled..Makos 16a-16b; Chullin 141a

Transgress

Transgress in order that your friend will not..Shabbos 4a; Eruvin 32b; Kiddushin 55b;
....Menachos 48a-48b
Transgressed twice, seems permitted..Kiddushin 20a, 40a; Yoma 86b; Moed Katan 27b; Sotah 22a;
....Arachin 30b
Transgressing law, *kesubah*..Kesubos 72a-72b, 101a-101b; Sotah 25a
Transgressing law, wife, divorce..Sotah 25a
Transgressing two prohibitions..Yevamos 4a; Pesachim 24a; Chagigah 10b; Nazir 40a; Sotah 44a;
....Bava Metzia 60b, 61a, 111a, 112a
Transgressing without act, doubt..Eruvin 100a-100b

T

Transgression
Episodes —
Transgressions in desert, ten .... Arachin 15a-15b; Avos 5:4
Transgressions, stumbling blocks on Yom Tov .... Kiddushin 81a
Transgressions, Yom Kippur night .... Yoma 19b-20a
Punishment —
Transgression done with lack of restraint, punishment .... Shabbos 33a
Transgression escorts man .... Avodah Zarah 5a; Sotah 3b
Transgression extinguishes merit of commandment .... Sotah 21a
Transgression, fourth, punishment .... Sanhedrin 7a
Transgression in secret, severity .... Sotah 3a; Bava Kama 79b
Transgression obstructs heart .... Yoma 39a
Transgression which produces fruit .... Kiddushin 40a
Misc. —
Transgression for Heaven's sake .... Nazir 23b; Horayos 10b
Transgression in secret, preference .... Chagigah 16a; Kiddushin 40a
Transgression leads to transgression .... Avos 4:2
Transgression, mistake in performance of commandment ..... Shabbos 137a; Pesachim 71b-72b;
.... Succah 42a; Yevamos 34a
Transgression, something resulting from .... Temurah 20b

Transgressor
Transgressor of Rabbinical Decree, snake .... Shabbos 110a
Transgressor, Rabbinical prohibition .... Shabbos 40a

Trans-Jordan, first fruit .... Bikkurim 1:10

Translating
Translating Rabbi Shila's lecture, Rav .... Yoma 20b
Translating verse word for word .... Kiddushin 49a

Translation
Translation incomprehensible .... Avodah Zarah 14b
Translation of Book of Prophets, Yonassan ben Uziel .... Megillah 3a
Translation of Tanach, permitted .... Megillah 3a
Translation of Tanach, reading .... Shabbos 115a-115b
Translation of Torah, Talmai .... Megillah 9a-9b
Translation, testimony .... Makos 6b
Translation, Torah reading .... Berachos 45a; Megillah 23b-24a; Sotah 39b
Translation, verses not to translate .... Megillah 25a-25b

Translator
Translator, episodes about humility .... Sotah 40a
Translator, Rav to Rabbi Shila .... Yoma 20b

Trap for fish .... Sanhedrin 81b

Traveling, food needed .... Pesachim 113a

Treasure
Treasure of fear of Heaven .... Shabbos 31b
Treasures of the Holy Temple, *tzitz* and *paroches* .... Sukka 5a; Meilah 17b
Treasure, Rabbi Akiva .... Gittin 67a
Treasures, Egypt and Korah .... Pesachim 87b, 119a

Treasurer
Treasurer, counting coins .... Bava Basra 9a
Treasurers of Temple .... Shekalim 5:2

T

Treasury

Treasury of consecrated items, ... *see* **Consecrated items Treasury**, page 123

Treasury of Temple, sacrifice .... Temurah 6b, 13a; Yoma 63b; Zevachim 113b

Treatment

Treatment .... *see also* **Medicine**, page 622

Treatment, assessment .... Bava Kama 91a

Treatment, offers of man who caused damage .... Bava Kama 85a

Treatment, plants .... Bava Kama 85a

Tree

***Aggadah* —**

Tree, "how shall I bless you?" .... Taanis 5b-6a

Tree in pure place, righteous man .... Kiddushin 40b

Tree of knowledge .... Berachos 40a; Sanhedrin 70a-70b

Trees, fruitless, future .... Kesubos 112b

Trees of gold in Temple .... Yoma 21b, 39b

Commandments —

Tree, beautiful, *esrog* .... Succah 35a

Tree, cedar, leper .... Sotah 15b

Tree, consecrating .... Bava Basra 71b-73a

Tree, gifts for poor .... Chullin 131a-131b

Tree, redeeming consecrated .... Bava Basra 72a; Arachin 14a-14b

Trees, blessing .... Berachos 43b; Rosh Hashanah 11a

Monetary matters —

Tree, between fields .... Bava Metzia 107a

Tree, branches belonging to buyer .... Bava Basra 82a

Tree, *chazakah* .... Bava Basra 37a-38a

Tree, damage to public domain .... Bava Basra 27b, 60a-60b

Tree, distance from neighbors .... Bava Basra 18a, 26a-26b, 27b, 83a

Tree, included in land sale .... Bava Basra 69a

Tree, keeping away from city .... Bava Basra 24b

Tree, left over for buyer .... Bava Basra 80b; Taanis 25b

Tree, Rabbi Yannai .... Bava Basra 60a-60b

Tree, rights on land .... Bava Basra 27a, 37a-38a, 72a, 72b, 82a-83b

Tree uprooted, lessee .... Bava Metzia 103b

Trees on river banks, episode .... Bava Metzia 107b

Prohibitions —

Tree consecrated to idolatry .... *see* **Asheirah**, page 33

Tree, idolatry .... Avodah Zarah 45b-46a, 48a

Tree in Temple Courtyard .... Tamid 28b

Tree, wasting .... Bava Kama 91b-92a; Bava Basra 26a

Trees, *orlah* .... Orlah 1:1-2, 1:9; Sotah 43b; Bava Metzia 119a; Pesachim 23a

Trees too close, mixed species .... Bava Basra 37b, 83a, 102b; Kilayim 5:2; Eruvin 3b

Shabbos —

Tree, empty land .... Eruvin 15a, 99b-100a; Succah 24b-25a

Tree, *eruv techumin* .... Eruvin 49b-50b, 50b

Tree, *muktzeh* .... Eruvin 100a-100b; Shabbos 155a

Tree roots, *muktzeh* .... Eruvin 100a

Trees of field, *muktzeh* .... Beitzah 31a

T

Misc. —

Tree, *Adar* .... Beitzah 15b
Tree, advice on arboriculture .... Bava Basra 80b; Bava Kama 81a; Shabbos 67a; Pesachim 56a
Tree, branches .... Shabbos 4b, 8a
Tree cut down, trunk grows again .... Bava Basra 80b
Tree, like taste of fruit .... Succah 35a
Tree of *shekem*, plain .... Pesachim 53a
Tree, what is included .... Berachos 40a-40b

Treifah

Bird —

Treifah, brain membrane of bird .... Chullin 56a-56b
Treifah, crop of bird .... Chullin 56b
Treifah, dislodged leg .... Chullin 57a-57b
Treifah, dislodged wing .... Chullin 57a
Treifah, feathers .... Chullin 58b
Treifah, gizzard .... Chullin 43a
Treifah, intestines of bird .... Chullin 56b
Treifah, leg of bird .... Chullin 57a-57b

Bodily parts —

Treifah, additional limb like missing one .... Chullin 58b
Treifah, animal cheek .... Chullin 55b
Treifah, broken bone .... Chullin 76b-77a
Treifah, junction of sinews .... Chullin 76a-76b
Treifah, knee .... Chullin 42b, 57a-57b, 76a
Treifah, rectum .... Chullin 50a-50b
Treifah, ribs and vertebras .... Chullin 42b, 52a-52b; Eruvin 7a
Treifah, sciatic nerve .... Chullin 54a
Treifah, skinless animal .... Chullin 55b-56a
Treifah, skull .... Chullin 52b, 57b
Treifah, spinal cord .... Chullin 45b-46a; Kesubos 7a
Treifah, upper thigh .... Chullin 42b, 54a-54b

Cases —

Treifah animal fell in fire .... Chullin 56b, 57a
Treifah animal which fell .... Bava Kama 50b-51a; Chullin 51a-52a, 56b, 57a
Treifah, cases of trampled animal .... Chullin 43b, 52b-53a
Treifah, egg .... Chullin 58a
Treifah, flesh to be cut by veterinarian .... Chullin 53b
Treifah, *kosher* blemishes .... Chullin 54a
Treifah, number .... Chullin 42a-43a
Treifah, this one resembles that one .... Chullin 48b
Treifah, trampled animal .... Chullin 43b, 52b-53a
Treifah, trampled animal, examination .... Chullin 53b-54a
Treifah, young .... Chullin 58a

Doubts —

Treifah, cases of mixtures .... Zevachim 74b
Treifah, checking and comparing .... Chullin 50a
Treifah, checking brain .... Chullin 56a-56b
Treifah, checking gullet .... Chullin 28a-28b, 43a-43b
Treifah, doubt if torn alive .... Chullin 9a, 10a, 50b-51a; Beitzah 25a

Treifah, needle..Chullin 48b-49a, 50b-51a; Shabbos 36a; Succah 34a; Kesubos 76b
Treifah, splinter from beam...Sanhedrin 7b; Horayos 3b
Treifah, thorn in body cavity...Chullin 53b

Internal organs —
Treifah, brain..Chullin 45a-45b
Treifah, gall bladder...Chullin 43a, 48a
Treifah, gullet..Chullin 43a-43b
Treifah, gullet stuck to cheek...Chullin 43b-44b
Treifah, heart...Chullin 45b
Treifah, intestine...Chullin 48b
Treifah, liver...Chullin 43a, 46a, 48a
Treifah, omasum..Chullin 50b-51a
Treifah, reticulum...Chullin 50b-51a
Treifah, spleen...Chullin 42b, 55a-55b
Treifah, stomach...Chullin 50b, 52b
Treifah, three tubes..Chullin 45a, 45b
Treifah, womb..Chullin 55b, 56b

Other laws —
Treifah, death penalty..Sanhedrin 78a
Treifah, firstborn..Zevachim 104a
Treifah, impurity of Temple..Chullin 73a, 123b
Treifah, murdered man...Chullin 11b
Treifah, murderer and conspiring witnesses...Sanhedrin 78a
Treifah, ox about to be stoned...Sanhedrin 78a
Treifah, sacrifice............................Menachos 5b-6a; Temurah 29a; Avodah Zarah 5b-6a, 51a; Zevachim 116a

Misc. —
Treifah animal, does it give birth and develop.....................Chullin 42a, 57b-58a; Temurah 11b
Treifah, announcement...Chullin 94b-95a
Treifah, cannot be permitted..Chullin 68b
Treifah, experiments..Chullin 57b
Treifah, is it alive.................Chullin 42a, 57b-58a, 75a, 140a; Temurah 11b; Bechoros 3a; Niddah 24a
Treifah, slaughter makes pure..........................Chullin 69a, 74a, 85b, 128b; Zevachim 69b
Trei Asar...*see* **Twelve Prophets, order**, page 706
Trei Asar, order..Bava Basra 14b
Trepik, equal to three *maos*...Kesubos 64a; Gittin 45b
Trial
Trial..*see* **Judgment**, page 329
Trial, not to get oneself into..Sanhedrin 107a
Trial of forbidden relations, miracle..Kiddushin 40a
Trials of Abraham...Avos 5:3
Trials of Israel in desert..Arachin 15a-15b; Avos 5:4

Triangle
Triangle, separation between mixed species..Kilayim 2:7, 3:3
Triangle, wall of succah..Succah 7a

Tribe
Tribe, another, marriage..Bava Basra 120a; Taanis 30b
Tribe, called *kahal*..Horayos 5b
Tribe does not disappear...Bava Basra 115b
Tribe, judging one's tribe...Sanhedrin 16b

T

Tribe, *Kohanim* and *Leviim* .... Horayos 6a-6b
Tribe led to idolatry .... Sanhedrin 15b
Tribe, sacrifice for mistake of *beis din* .... Horayos 5b
Tribes .... *see also* **Jacob's sons**, page 321
Tribes all gave birth to judge, prophet and king .... Succah 27b
Tribes, number .... Horayos 6b
Tribes, permitted to intermarry .... Bava Basra 120a
Trickery, agent for oneself .... Kiddushin 58b-59a
Trigon, Greek .... Bava Basra 164b
Trouble
Trouble .... *see also* **Suffering**, page 662
Trouble, must make trouble known ...... Shabbos 67a; Chullin 78a; Moed Katan 5a; Sotah 32b; Niddah 66a
Trouble of tomorrow .... Sanhedrin 100b
Trouble, praying before it comes .... Sanhedrin 44b
Trouble to care for animals on Shabbos .... Shabbos 53a-53b
Troubles, last ones make first ones forgotten .... Berachos 13a
Troubles of Israel, Divine Presence .... Taanis 16a
Troubles since Rebbi's death .... Sotah 49b
Trough, raking on Shabbos .... Shabbos 140b-141a
True
True judgment .... Peah 8:9; Bava Basra 8b
True words are recognizable .... Sotah 9b
Truffles and mushrooms, blessing .... Berachos 40b
Truly they said, law .... Bava Metzia 60a; Shabbos 92b
Trumpets
Trumpets of Moses .... Menachos 28a-28b
Trumpets of silver, in Temple .... Rosh Hashanah 27a
Trumpets with *shofar* .... Rosh Hashanah 27a
Trunk
Trunk grows again .... Bava Basra 80b
Trunk, how much to leave .... Bava Basra 80b; Bava Kama 81a; Taanis 25b
Trust in G-d
Trust in G-d, avoiding worry .... Berachos 60a; Sotah 48b
Trust in G-d, everything He does .... Berachos 60b
Trust in G-d, exceeding .... Tamid 28a
Trust in G-d, reward .... Menachos 29b
Trustworthiness .... *see also* **Testimony**, page 683
Marriage and filiation —
Trustworthiness, "I was raped," concerning *Kohen* .... Nedarim 90b, 90b-91b; Yevamos 112a
Trustworthiness, convert about himself .... Yevamos 46b-47a
Trustworthiness for divorce .... Gittin 62b, 64a-64b; Bava Basra 134b-135a
Trustworthiness for levirate marriage ...... Kiddushin 64a-64b; Bava Basra 134a-135a; Yevamos 39b
Trustworthiness of *kiddushin*, disagreement .... Kiddushin 63b
Trustworthiness of *kiddushin*, stoning .... Kiddushin 63b-64a
Trustworthiness of midwife .... Kiddushin 73b-74a
Trustworthiness of *niddah* .... Kesubos 22a-22b
Trustworthiness of pregnant woman .... Kesubos 13a-14a, 16a; Kiddushin 74a
Trustworthiness, son's lineage .... Yevamos 47a; Kiddushin 74a, 78b; Bava Basra 127b
Trustworthiness, wife's lineage .... Kiddushin 79b-80a

T

Monetary matters —

Trustworthiness of borrower to lender..Shevuos 42a
Trustworthiness of father about his firstborn, inheritance............Kiddushin 78b; Yevamos 47a;
....Bava Basra 126b, 127b, 128b
Trustworthiness of judge..Kiddushin 74a
Trustworthiness of broker...Sanhedrin 31a-31b; Gittin 64a
Trustworthiness of owner of lost item..Bava Metzia 28b
Trustworthiness of seller, to whom..............................Kiddushin 73b-74a; Bava Metzia 2b
Trustworthiness to disqualify judge...Sanhedrin 23a-24a
Trustworthiness to invalidate witness..Sanhedrin 23a-24a

Prohibitions —

Trustworthiness, "this money is second tithe"..Sanhedrin 30a
Trustworthiness about blemish of firstborn...............Shabbos 145a-145b; Bechoros 28a, 36a
Trustworthiness about firstborn son..Kiddushin 73b-74a
Trustworthiness, blemishes of tithe...Bechoros 36b
Trustworthiness for oneself, forbidden matters..Kesubos 22a, 23b
Trustworthiness for searching for *chametz*...Pesachim 4a-4b
Trustworthiness of ignoramus, food having sacrificial sanctity.............Chagigah 22a-22b
Trustworthiness of *Kohen*, blemish of firstborn............................Yoma 78a; Bechoros 36a-36b
Trustworthiness of Sage for himself............Yevamos 77a, 98a; Bechoros 31a, 38b; Kiddushin 70b
Trustworthiness of scholar.......................Demai 2:2-3; Bechoros 30b; Avodah Zarah 39a
Trustworthiness of scholar, his family members..............Avodah Zarah 39a; Bechoros 30b
Trustworthiness of women for prohibitions..Pesachim 4a-4b

Misc. —

Trustworthiness about oneself...Krisos 12a-12b
Trustworthiness for provable testimony..Yevamos 39b
Trustworthiness *migo*...*see* **Migo**, page 409
Trustworthiness, non-Jews...Chullin 133b
Trustworthiness of one witness............................*see* **One witness, like two when Torah
....requires only one**, page 460
Trustworthiness, proof...*see* **Migo**, page 409
Trustworthiness, reward and importance...Taanis 8a
Trustworthiness, women's signs of puberty...Niddah 48b-49a

Trustworthy

Trustworthy...*see also* **Keeping one's word**, page 333
Trustworthy immediately..Kiddushin 73b-74a
Trustworthy is your employer...Avos 2:14-15, 6:4
Trustworthy like two people, derogatory speech......................................Pesachim 113b
Trustworthy men..Shabbos 119b; Taanis 8a; Chagigah 14a-14b
Trustworthy to him like two people...........Kesubos 85a; Yevamos 101b; Kiddushin 66a; Bava Basra 52a
Trustworthy to swear, only you............................Bava Metzia 36b; Bava Kama 11b

Truth

Truth, absolute, judge................Peah 8:9; Shabbos 10a; Megillah 15b; Bava Basra 8b; Sanhedrin 7a
Truth, *aggadah*...Shabbos 104a
Truth and peace they loved, Beis Shamai...Yevamos 14b
Try, do not try to see your friend's disgrace...Avos 4:18
Tu B'Av...Bava Basra 121a-121b; Taanis 30b-31a
Tu B'Shevat..Rosh Hashanah 14a-14b
Tube, blood of *niddah*...Niddah 21b

Tumah..*see* **Impurity**, page 301
Tumah beluah...*see* **Impurity, absorbed**, page 303
Tumtum...*see* **Gender doubtful**, page 247
Tune, learning...Megillah 32a
Tunic, Joseph..Shabbos 10b; Megillah 16b
Turban of *Kohen*, atones for arrogance...Zevachim 88b
Turn
   Turn it over because everything is in it..Avos 5:22
   "Turning loaf of bread"...Kiddushin 59a
   Turning, always on the right ....Zevachim 62b; Yoma 15b, 17b, 45a, 58b; Sotah 15b
   Turning around, precedence between creditors ....Kesubos 95b
   Turning head away to disapprove.........................Eruvin 94a; Yoma 73a; Shabbos 122b; Succah 11a;
                                    Bava Kama 102a; Avodah Zarah 7a; Chullin 74a;
   Turning one's body for prayer ....Berachos 30a; Yevamos 105b
   Turning to south, to become wise...Bava Basra 25b
   Turning toward Jerusalem, prayer...Berachos 30a
   Turns over to prevent conception.......................Kesubos 37a; Yevamos 35a
Turnip
   Turnip from earth, Shabbos ....Shabbos 50b-51a
   Turnip, health..Berachos 44b
   Turnip, *kashering* knife ....Chullin 111b-112a
Turnus Rufus, Rabbi Akiva..........................Sanhedrin 65b; Avodah Zarah 20a
Turtledove
   Turtledove, pursued among birds...Bava Kama 93a
   Turtledoves for sacrifice, age of *kashrus*..............................Chullin 22a-22b
   Turtledoves for sacrifice, which ones..................................Chullin 62a-62b
Turyanus, Papus' murder ....Taanis 18b
***Tushiah*,** Torah...Sanhedrin 26b
Tuviah
   Tuviah, name of Moses ....Sotah 12a
   Tuviah sinned and Zigud is punished!...................Pesachim 113b; Makos 11a
Twelve
   Twelve months, judgment of wicked..Eduyos 2:10
   Twelve months, wine of idolaters............Avodah Zarah 34a-34b, 75a-75b; Niddah 65b
   Twelve Prophets, order ....Bava Basra 14b
Twenty
   Twenty four hours, concerning which laws..................................Zavim 2:3
   Twenty four priestly gifts...........................Chullin 133b; Bava Kama 110b
   Twenty two thousand, Divine Presence....................Bava Kama 83a; Yevamos 64a
   Twenty years
      Twenty years old, age for marriage ....Kiddushin 29b-30a
      Twenty years old, punishment ....Shabbos 89b
      Twenty years, sale of land.......................................Bava Basra 155a-156a
Twice Torah, once *Targum*...Berachos 8a-8b
Twin
   Twin sisters of Abel and Cain ....Yevamos 62a
   Twins, birth..Niddah 27a
   Twins, firstborn of donkey..Bechoros 9a-9b
   Twins, firstborn of pure animal..........................Bechoros 9a-9b, 17a-18b

Twitching animal in death throes

Twitching animal in death throes, impurity .... Chullin 30a, 117b, 121b; Oholos 1:6

Twitching animal in death throes, limb torn from .... Chullin 121b

Twitching animal in death throes, prohibition to eat .... Chullin 121b; Sanhedrin 63a

Twitching animal in death throes, signs to permit dying animal .... Avodah Zarah 16b;
.... Chullin 37a-38b

Twitching animal in death throes, swallowed pure item .... Chullin 121b

Two

Aggadah —

Two angels, Shabbos .... Shabbos 119b

Two angels to protect man .... Taanis 11a; Chagigah 16a

Two dry pieces of wood kindle a wet one .... Sanhedrin 93a

Two hearts, eating .... Bava Basra 12b

Two Sages, tolerant one towards the other .... Sotah 49a

Two tables, Torah and wealth .... Berachos 5b

Two thousand years of Torah .... Avodah Zarah 9a

Beis din —

Two groups .... *see* **Witnesses**, page 753

Two judges who sat in judgment .... Gittin 32b-33a; Sanhedrin 3a, 5b-6a, 30a, 87b; Kesubos 22a

Two witnesses like a hundred .... Shevuos 42a

Commandments —

Two acts, levirate marriage .... Yevamos 50a-52a, 53a-53b, 96a-96b

Two doors, prayer .... Berachos 8a

Two Sages, learning during journey .... Sotah 49a; Taanis 10b

Two sisters to one *yavam*, levirate marriage .... Yevamos 19a, 28a-29a, 50b-51b

Doubt —

Two baskets, doubt .... Pesachim 9b

Two paths, impurity .... Taharos 5:3-5; Pesachim 10a; Kesubos 27a; Niddah 60a

Two paths, Temple .... Shevuos 19a-19b; Krisos 18b-19a

Two weaknesses, *chazakah* .... Kiddushin 79a; Niddah 2b-3a

Episodes —

Two crowns, Giving of Torah .... Shabbos 88a

Two kings, moon .... Chullin 60b

Two paths, Rabbi Yochanan .... Berachos 28b

Two Sages under one *tallis* .... Sotah 49a

Two wicks, Temple destruction .... Gittin 58a

Monetary matters —

Two coins, of which .... Bava Metzia 55a

Two in *perutah* .... Kiddushin 7b

Two *kesubos*, claiming .... Kesubos 89b-90a

Two legal documents concerning one matter .... Kesubos 43b-44a

Two legal documents, contradiction .... Shevuos 47b

Two lost, one found .... Beitzah 10b; Pesachim 10a; Gittin 51a

Two oxen which pursued, doubt .... Bava Kama 36a

Two persons who raised item together .... Bava Metzia 8a, 9a

Two signatures, *beis din* .... Sanhedrin 30a

Two years, redeeming property .... Bava Metzia 106a; Arachin 14b, 29b, 30a

Two men holding

Two men holding, cases .... Bava Metzia 2a-2b; Bava Basra 170a

T

Two men holding, oath..Bava Metzia 5b
Two men holding promissory note..Bava Metzia 7a-7b; Bava Basra 170a
Two men holding, sharing..Bava Metzia 7b

Prohibitions —
Two acts in one negative commandment...Makos 21a-21b
Two by two, permitted mixture...Zevachim 74a, 77b, 80a
Two death penalties with one act..Krisos 3b
Two death penalties, severest...Sanhedrin 81a
Two negative commandments, father's widow awaiting levirate marriage..........Yevamos 4a
Two negative commandments with one act..Krisos 14b-15a
Two negative commandments, what do they teach...Pesachim 24a
Two penalties of excising of soul with one act..Krisos 3b
Two persons performed work, Shabbos...Shabbos 3a, 92b-93b
Two sins, idolatry...Taanis 5b
Two vertebral columns, hump...Bechoros 43b

Quantities —
Two hairs, holes..Niddah 52a-52b
Two hairs, puberty...Niddah 45b-46a, 48b
Two halves equivalent to whole..Kesubos 109b

Sacrifices —
Two days, *chagigah*...Pesachim 71a-71b
Two days, firstborn and peace offerings...........................Zevachim 57a; Bechoros 27b-28a
Two men who slaughtered sacrifice..Chullin 29b-30a
Two pieces, offering for questionable guilt..Yevamos 113a
Two shekels, guilt offering...Zevachim 90b; Krisos 22b, 27a
Two shekels of guilt offering, value..Kiddushin 12a
Two sprinklings which are four...Zevachim 10b, 53b, 94b

Two loaves of Shavuos
Two loaves of Shavuos, blessing of abundance...Rosh Hashanah 16a
Two loaves of Shavuos, bringing..Menachos 61a
Two loaves of Shavuos, disqualified...Menachos 46b-47b, 74b
Two loaves of Shavuos, dividing up..Succah 55b-56a
Two loaves of Shavuos, from last year produce.........................Menachos 83b-84a; Parah 2:1
Two loaves of Shavuos, from which wheat...Menachos 69b, 83b-84a
Two loaves of Shavuos, how...Menachos 94a
Two loaves of Shavuos, new grain in Temple...Menachos 84b
Two loaves of Shavuos, prepared inside...Menachos 63a, 95b-96a
Two loaves of Shavuos, redeeming..Menachos 48a
Two loaves of Shavuos, Shabbos..Menachos 95b
Two loaves of Shavuos, waving....................................Succah 37b-38a; Menachos 46b, 61a, 62a

Shabbos and Yom Tov —
Two loaves of bread, Shabbos..Shabbos 117b; Berachos 39b
Two meals, *eruv*...Eruvin 82b-83a; Kesubos 64b; Keilim 17:11
Two sanctities, Yom Tov outside *Eretz Yisrael*.............................Eruvin 39b; Beitzah 4b
Two Shabbososos, Redemption..Shabbos 118b
Two thousand cubits for *techum*..Eruvin 51a
Two utensils, *eruv*..Eruvin 48b, 49a

Misc. —
Two became three, walking stick..Shabbos 152a

Two calamities, fast..Taanis 8b
Two dead, combining..........Oholos 3:1, 2:6, 8:6, 15:10; Nazir 52a-52b; Chullin 125a-125b; Meilah 17a
Two honeycombs..Beitzah 36a
Two identical sections in Torah, new law.....Sotah 3a-3b; Bava Kama 64b; Shevuos 19a; Menachos 10a
Two meals, eighteen figs..Eruvin 80b
Two men, imposing on community...Bava Basra 8b
Two men who slaughtered non-holy animal..Chullin 30a-30b
Two prohibitions, number of lashes.................Yevamos 4a; Pesachim 24a; Chagigah 10b; Nazir 40a;
....Sotah 44a; Bava Metzia 60b, 61a, 111a, 112a
Two prophets using same words...Sanhedrin 89a
Two reasons, answer..Sanhedrin 62b
Two sounds, hearing..Rosh Hashanah 27a
Two which are four...Shevuos 3a-5a

Two forbidden substances acting together
    Two forbidden substances acting together................Pesachim 26b-27a; Sanhedrin 80a-80b;
    ....Avodah Zarah 48b-49a; Chullin 58a; Temurah 31a
    Two forbidden substances acting together, father's seed................Chullin 58a; Bechoros 7a
    Two forbidden substances acting together, leaven.............................Avodah Zarah 68a
    Two forbidden substances acting together, leavening...................Orlah 2:8-12; Temurah 12a;
    ....Pesachim 26b; Avodah Zarah 49a, 73b; Chullin 99a-99b

Two heads
    Two heads, episode about inquiry..Menachos 37a
    Two heads, firstborn..Menachos 37a-37b
    Two heads, found in river...Chullin 95b

Two hundred
    Two hundred, annulment of *orlah*...Pesachim 48a
    Two hundred forty eight limbs...Bechoros 45a; Oholos 1:8
    Two hundred *zuz, kesubah*...Kesubos 51a-51b
    Two hundred *zuz*, poor..Peah 8:8; Sotah 21b

Two Tannaim
    Two Tannaim, how is it possible....Rosh Hashanah 7b; Megillah 9b; Shevuos 4a; Chullin 84a, 104a
    Two Tannaim, Mishnayos.................Bava Kama 36b, 40b, 47b; Yevamos 13a; Shevuos 5a;
    ....Rosh Hashanah 7b; Kiddushin 63b
    Two Tannaim, preference...Kiddushin 63b

Two verses
    Two verses, exactly similar law...Bechoros 49a
    Two verses, *gezeirah shavah*...Zevachim 57a; Arachin 14b
    Two verses teaching identical law...Sanhedrin 67b
    Two verses, three...Kiddushin 35a

Two wives
    Two wives, does one marry...Yevamos 65a
    Two wives, jealousy...Megillah 13a; Avodah Zarah 55a
    Two wives, not to marry...Pesachim 113a
    Two women in two cities, marrying...Yevamos 37b; Yoma 18b

Two Yosef ben Shimon
    Two Yosef ben Shimon, concern..Yevamos 115b-116a
    Two Yosef ben Shimon, divorce certificate.................Gittin 24b, 34b; Bava Basra 167b
    Two Yosef ben Shimon, legal document.............Bava Basra 172b-173a; Gittin 24b; Bechoros 48a
    Two Yosef ben Shimon, lost divorce certificate....Gittin 27a-28a; Bava Metzia 18a-19a, 20a-20b

Tying shoe, strength in old age .... Chullin 24b
Tying on Shabbos
   Tying on Shabbos, bucket .... Pesachim 11a
   Tying on Shabbos, cases .... Shabbos 111b-113a
   Tying on Shabbos, rope of weaver .... Shabbos 113a
   Tying on Shabbos, Temple .... Shabbos 74b; Eruvin 102b-103a, 105a
Tyre to Carthage .... Menachos 110a
Tzad echad beribis .... see **Interest, possibility,** page 314
Tzad hashaveh .... see **Similarities,** page 626
Tzaddik .... see **Righteous,** page 568
Tzaddik Yesod Olam .... Yoma 38b; Gittin 61a; Chagigah 12b
Tzadok, *Kohen Gadol* .... Yoma 73b
Tzamid pasil .... see **Tight lid,** page 690
Tzaraas .... see **Leprosy,** page 364
Tzarah .... see **Rival,** page 569
Tzarei atpesah, mezonos .... see **Payment in advance,** page 476
Tzarich, no possible solution .... Yoma 61b; Berachos 15b; Eruvin 48a; Yevamos 9a; Nazir 46b;
          Gittin 40a; Horayos 8a
Tzarus ayin .... see **Miserliness,** page 414
Tzav, urging .... Kiddushin 29a
Tzedakah .... see **Charity,** page 97
Tzedukim .... see **Sadducees,** page 582
Tzelofchad .... see **Zelophehad, daughters of man gathering wood** page 776
Tzeroros .... see **Pebbles, flung,** page 478
Tzes hakochavim .... see **Stars appearing,** page 654
Tzevaos
   Tzevaos, Hannah .... Berachos 31b
   Tzevaos, erasing Name .... Shevuos 35a-35b
Tzevitah, explanation .... Chagigah 22b
Tzibur .... see **Communal prayer,** page 118
Tzidei reshus harabim .... see **Side alleys of public domain,** page 624
Tzidkiyahu .... see **Zedekiah,** page 776
Tziduk hadin
   Tziduk hadin, blessing in cemetery .... Berachos 58b
   Tziduk hadin, text .... Berachos 19a
Tziklono, interpretation by initials .... Menachos 66b
Tzinim upachim .... see **Catching cold, man's responsibility,** page 89
Tzintzenes hamannah .... see **Flask of manna,** page 229
Tzion
   Tzion, commandment to be concerned .... Succah 41a; Rosh Hashanah 30a
   Tzion, redemption for who was born there .... Kesubos 75a
Tzipor, only pure bird .... Chullin 139b-140a
Tzipor metzora .... see **Birds for leper,** page 58
Tzippori .... see **Zippori,** page 777
Tzipuy avodah zarah .... see **Coating idol,** page 112
Tziruf .... see **Combining,** page 114
Tzitz .... see **Forehead-plate,** page 235

Tzitzis

Commandment and reward —
Tzitzis, "your white garments" .... Shabbos 153a
Tzitzis, four commandments .... Menachos 37b
Tzitzis, numerous slaves .... Shabbos 32b
Tzitzis, protection by their merit .... Menachos 43b
Tzitzis, remembering commandments .... Menachos 43b
Tzitzis, reward .... Shabbos 23b; Menachos 43b, 44a
Tzitzis, sky blue and white .... Menachos 38a-38b

Episodes —
Tzitzis, Abraham .... Sotah 17a; Chullin 88b-89a
Tzitzis, dead men in desert .... Bava Basra 74a
Tzitzis, Rabbah's care .... Shabbos 118b
Tzitzis, reproof by angel .... Menachos 41a
Tzitzis, saving from forbidden relations, story of student and prostitute ..... Menachos 44a

How —
Tzitzis, blessing when putting on .... Menachos 43a
Tzitzis, blessing when tying .... Menachos 42a
Tzitzis, from one garment to another .... Menachos 41b; Shabbos 22a, 40a; Pesachim 101a
Tzitzis, hanging on corner .... Menachos 42a
Tzitzis, introducing in hole .... Menachos 42a
Tzitzis, knots and binding .... Menachos 38b-39b
Tzitzis, separating strings .... Menachos 41b
Tzitzis, tying before completion of garment .... Menachos 40b

Kashrus —
Tzitzis, buying in market .... Menachos 43a
Tzitzis, false blue dye .... Menachos 41b
Tzitzis found, validity .... Eruvin 96b
Tzitzis, length of strings .... Menachos 41b-42a
Tzitzis, made for commandment .... Menachos 42b; Succah 9a
Tzitzis, make but not from what is already made .... Succah 11a-11b
Tzitzis, number of strings .... Menachos 39a-39b, 41b; Yevamos 5b; Bechoros 39b
Tzitzis, sewing tear .... Menachos 41a
Tzitzis, species of strings .... Menachos 39b; Shabbos 27b
Tzitzis, spun by non-Jew .... Menachos 42b
Tzitzis torn, how many must remain .... Menachos 38b, 39a
Tzitzis, wool and linen .... Menachos 39b; Shabbos 27b; Yevamos 4b; Nazir 58a

Prohibitions —
Tzitzis, dignity of creatures .... Menachos 37b-38a
Tzitzis, giving to non-Jew .... Menachos 41b
Tzitzis in cemetery .... Berachos 18a
Tzitzis, invalid, on Shabbos .... Shabbos 139b; Menachos 37b-38a
Tzitzis, not to add commandments .... Sanhedrin 88b-89a; Menachos 40b-41a
Tzitzis on shrouds .... Menachos 41a
Tzitzis, selling to non-Jew .... Menachos 43a

Requirement —
Tzitzis, blind .... Menachos 43a
Tzitzis, educating child .... Succah 42a; Arachin 2b
Tzitzis, night and blind .... Zevachim 18b; Shabbos 27b; Menachos 43a

Tzitzis, punishment of who abstains from *tzitzis* .... Menachos 41a, 43b, 44a; Shabbos 32b
Tzitzis, requirement applies to garment .... Menachos 41a, 42b
Tzitzis, requirement in case of partnership .... Chullin 135a-136a
Tzitzis, women .... Menachos 43a; Succah 11a

Tallis —
Tzitzis, size of corner .... Menachos 42a
Tzitzis, folded *tallis* .... Menachos 41a
Tzitzis, leather *tallis* .... Menachos 40b
Tzitzis, linen *tallis* .... Menachos 40a-40b; Shabbos 25b; Eduyos 4:10
Tzitzis, measuring corner .... Bava Kama 119b
Tzitzis, number of corners .... Zevachim 18b; Menachos 37b, 43b
Tzitzis, size of *tallis* .... Menachos 40b-41a

Misc. —
Tzitzis, cut strings .... Menachos 38b, 39a
Tzitzis, reading of *Shema* .... Berachos 12b
Tzitzis, *shatnez* .... Yevamos 4b, 5b; Menachos 40a-40b
Tzitzis, significance .... Menachos 41b

Tziva and Mephiboshet, David .... Shabbos 56a-56b; Yoma 22b
Tzivon, Ana .... Bava Basra 115b; Pesachim 54a
Tzlaf .... *see* **Caper**, page 87
Tznius .... *see* **Modesty**, page 420
Tzoan in Egypt .... *see* **Zoan in Egypt**, page 777
Tzoar, sins are few .... Shabbos 10b-11a
Tzofnas bas Peniel .... Gittin 58a
Tzom Gedaliah (Fast of Gedaliah) .... Rosh Hashanah 18b
Tzomes hagidin .... **Junction of sinews,** *tereifah*, page 330
Tzon barzel .... *see* **Flock which value is fixed**, page 230
Tzorchei tzibur .... *see* **Communal needs**, page 118
Tzorech gufo umekomo .... *see* **To use object and place,** *muktzeh*, page 694
Tzorech hamoed .... *see* **Chol HaMoed,** act needed for festival, page 105
Tzori
Tzori, coin .... Kiddushin 11a; Bava Kama 36b, 90b; Bechoros 50b
Tzori, danger of fire .... Shabbos 26a
Tzori, sap .... Shabbos 25b-26a
Tzrarei atpasa, mezonos .... *see* **Payment in advance, supporting**, page 476
Tzrichah legufah .... *see* **Necessary for itself, not**, page 439
Tzroros .... *see* **Pebbles, flung**, page 478

T

Uchla, amount..Bava Basra 90a

Udder

Udder cooked in grape seeds, episode..Chullin 110a-110b

Udder, meat with milk...Chullin 109a-110a, 111a

Ugly man

Ugly man, episode about Rabbi Elazar..Taanis 20a-20b

Ugly man, success in learning..Nedarim 50b

***Ulam* in Temple**..Yoma 44b; Middos 3:8

Ulla

Ulla, angry stare...Pesachim 53b

Ulla, Babylon..Pesachim 88a; Taanis 9b

Ulla changed his teaching to evade...Bava Kama 11b

Ulla, learning text of Havdala..Pesachim 104b

Ulterior

Ulterior goal leads to Heaven's sake................................Nazir 23b; Horayos 10b

Ulterior service of G-d................Pesachim 50b; Nazir 23b; Sotah 22b, 47a; Sanhedrin 105b; Horayos 10b;
Arachin 16b

Ulterior service of G-d, better not having been created................Berachos 17a

Umdana..*see* **Estimate**, page 201

Unavoidable circumstances

Unavoidable circumstances, beginning with negligence................Bava Kama 21b, 56a, 58a-58b;
Bava Metzia 36b, 42a, 93a

Unavoidable circumstances, custodians................Bava Metzia 36b, 41a, 93a-94a, 106a-106b

Unavoidable circumstances in condition of divorce................Gittin 30a, 34a-34b; Kesubos 2b-3a;
Nedarim 27a-27b

Unavoidable circumstances, levirate marriage................Yevamos 53b-54a

Unavoidable circumstances, man damaging................Bava Kama 28b-29a

Unavoidable circumstances, not liable................Avodah Zarah 54a; Nedarim 27a; Bava Kama 28b

Unavoidable circumstances, rare................Gittin 73a

Unavoidable circumstances to fulfill conditions................Nedarim 27a-27b

Unavoidable circumstances, would have sinned even if he knew................Shevuos 26b

Unblemished ox, consecrating................Temurah 7b, 19b, 33b; Menachos 101a; Pesachim 42a

Uncircumcised
  Prohibitions —
    Uncircumcised child, *terumah* .... Yevamos 71a
    Uncircumcised, second tithe .... Yevamos 73a-74a
    Uncircumcised, *terumah* .... Yevamos 70a-71a
  Sacrifices —
    Uncircumcised, circumcision on Pesach eve .... Pesachim 92a
    Uncircumcised, desecrates service .... Sanhedrin 83b-84a; Zevachim 22b
    Uncircumcised, Pesach for all generations .... Pesachim 96a
    Uncircumcised, Pesach lamb .... Yevamos 71a
    Uncircumcised, thought invalidating Pesach .... Pesachim 61b-63a
  Misc. —
    Uncircumcised, disgust .... Nedarim 31b, 32a
    Uncircumcised, like impure .... Yevamos 72b
    Uncircumcised, punishment .... Sanhedrin 99a
    Uncircumcised, sprinkling and preparing water .... Yevamos 72b; Shabbos 137a; Arachin 3a
    Uncircumcised, sprinkling on him .... Yevamos 71b; Zevachim 118a
Unclean place
    Unclean place, covering one's mouth .... Berachos 24b
    Unclean place, Sage .... Berachos 24b
    Unclean place, sin to read *Shema* .... Berachos 24b
Uncovered
  Snake —
    Uncovered, cat in house .... Shabbos 128b
    Uncovered, crushed garlic .... Beitzah 7b
    Uncovered, doubt .... Chullin 9a-10a
    Uncovered drink, keeping it at home .... Shabbos 128b
    Uncovered drink, others drank .... Avodah Zarah 30b
    Uncovered, filtering .... Terumos 8:7; Bava Kama 115b; Succah 50a; Bava Basra 97b
    Uncovered, from when .... Chullin 9a-10a; Terumos 8:4
    Uncovered, in which food and drink .... Terumos 8:4-6; Avodah Zarah 10a, 30a-30b;
                                                                                    Chullin 10a, 49b; Taanis 30a; Sanhedrin 70a
    Uncovered, libations .... Succah 50a
    Uncovered liquid, cases .... Avodah Zarah 30a-30b
    Uncovered liquid filtered, *kiddush* .... Bava Basra 97b
    Uncovered, non-Jews .... Avodah Zarah 31b
    Uncovered, reptiles .... Avodah Zarah 31b
    Uncovered, water .... Avodah Zarah 30b; Terumos 8:4-5; Bava Kama 116b; Chullin 10a, 49b
  Misc. —
    Uncovered woman's hair, episode .... Bava Kama 90b
    Uncovering shoulder, death of Sage .... Moed Katan 22b
    Uncovering *sotah's* hair .... Sotah 8a; Sanhedrin 45a
Undefined from explicit .... Zevachim 53a; Horayos 6b; Chullin 132a
Under
    Under beam, carrying .... Eruvin 4b-5a, 8b, 9a
    Under bed, food .... Pesachim 112a
    Under the sun, no profit .... Shabbos 30b
Underground passage
    Underground passage of fish, episode .... Yevamos 121a

U

Underground passages in Temple .... Pesachim 67b, 86a; Tamid 27b
Underground passages, resurrection of dead .... Kesubos 111a
Understanding
Understanding, reward for learning .... Berachos 6b
Understanding, superior, given to women .... Niddah 45b
Unemployed
Unemployed persons are numerous .... Berachos 17b; Pesachim 51b
Unemployed persons, streets are full of them .... Berachos 17b; Pesachim 51b, 55a
Unemployment indemnity
Unemployment indemnity, business investment .... Bava Metzia 68a-68b
Unemployment indemnity, judge .... Kesubos 105a; Bechoros 29b
Unemployment indemnity, lost item .... Bava Metzia 31b
Unfinished wood utensils, impurity .... Chullin 25a-25b
Unforeseeable situation, permitting vows .... Nedarim 64a-64b; Nazir 32a-32b
Unfortunate man, peace between rat and cat .... Sanhedrin 105a
Unintentionally
Shabbos —
Unintentionally, as if by accident .... Shabbos 121b
Unintentionally, brushing hair on Shabbos .... Shabbos 50a-50b
Unintentionally, cases .... Beitzah 23a, 23b; Bechoros 24b-25a; Shabbos 29b, 41b, 50a-50b; Pesachim 25b-26b; Kesubos 5b-6a; Nazir 42a; Krisos 20b
Unintentionally, cutting off .... Krisos 19b
Unintentionally, dragging .... Shabbos 29b
Unintentionally, grass .... Eruvin 100b
Unintentionally, hardening iron .... Shabbos 41a-42a; Yoma 34b
Unintentionally, hole .... Chagigah 10a-10b
Unintentionally, plugging up barrel .... Shabbos 111a-111b; Kesubos 6a; Bechoros 25a
Unintentionally, purposeful work .... Bava Kama 26b
Unintentionally, raking coals .... Krisos 20a-20b
Unintentionally, separating straw for animal .... Shabbos 140a
Unintentionally, *chilazon* .... Shabbos 75a
Unintentionally, sponge .... Shabbos 143a
Unintentionally, virgin on Shabbos .... Kesubos 5b
Unintentionally, wiping with clay utensil .... Shabbos 81b
Misc. —
Unintentionally, benefit .... Krisos 19b; Sanhedrin 62b
Unintentionally, cutting off leprous mark .... Shabbos 72a-73a; Sanhedrin 62b; Krisos 19b
Unintentionally, impossible .... Pesachim 25b-26b; Shabbos 29b
Unintentionally, permitted .... Shabbos 46b, 111a-111b
Unintentionally, possible to avoid .... Shabbos 29b; Pesachim 25b-26b
Unintentionally, *shatnez* .... Kilayim 9:2-6; Shabbos 29b, 46b; Pesachim 26b
United, Israel is cherished when united .... Menachos 27a
Unity of G-d, questions on verses .... Sanhedrin 38b
Unleavened food .... *see **Chametz**, page 94*
Unlimited blessing, tithe .... Makos 23b; Shabbos 32b; Taanis 9a, 22b
Unloading
Unloading and loading .... Bava Metzia 31a-33a
Unloading animal, *muktzeh* .... Shabbos 154b

U

Unmarried
Unmarried pregnant girl......................................Kesubos 13a-14a, 16a; Kiddushin 74a
Unmarried woman guilty of intimate relations, to *Kohen*...........Yevamos 61b
Unmarried woman, prohibition of intimate relations................Sanhedrin 76a
Unnecessary
Unnecessary blessing..Berachos 33a
Unnecessary to study this problem...............................Bava Metzia 16a
Unos hareiyah...*see* **Lobe of lung**, page 376
Unrevealed to men...Pesachim 54b
"Until when, lazy one," sleeping by day.....................Succah 26b
Untying knot, in Temple.....................................Shabbos 74b
Unusual
Unusual behavior, damage, no liability..........Bava Kama 20a, 24b, 32a
Unusual cult, idolatry...........Sanhedrin 60b-61a; Avodah Zarah 51a; Zevachim 106a
Unusual manner
Unusual manner, beating grain..................Kesubos 60a; Yevamos 114a
Unusual manner, damages by animal.........Bava Kama 19b-20a, 24b, 32a
Unusual manner in damages, jumped and ate......Bava Kama 19b-20a
Upheaval in *Eretz Yisrael*............Sotah 49b; Bava Kama 82b; Menachos 64b
Uphill and downhill, health.................................Eruvin 56a
"Upon me and upon my neck"............Pesachim 8b; Avodah Zarah 30a
Upper
Upper blanket of *zav*, impurity...............................Niddah 32b-33a
Upper floor, leaving right to.............Bava Basra 63a-63b, 64a, 148a
Upper part of city, learning...................................Pesachim 112a
Upper thigh, *treifah*.........................Chullin 42b, 54a-54b
Upright, Patriarchs...Avodah Zarah 25a
Uprooted
Uprooted tree, lessee..Bava Metzia 103b
Uprooting matter from its place of growth.....Shabbos 107b-108a; Bechoros 24b-25a
Uproots mountains
Uproots mountains and Sinai....................................Horayos 14a
Uproots mountains, Rabbah..............Berachos 64a; Horayos 14a
Uproots mountains, Rabbi Meir..................................Sanhedrin 24a
Uproots mountains, Resh Lakish.................................Sanhedrin 24a
Urah lamah tishan............*see* **"Wake up, why are you sleeping," not to say**, page 728
Urgent for burial, for whom is it recommended...............Moed Katan 22a
Uriah
Uriah, "*Or Yah*"...Bava Basra 25a
Uriah, David's mistakes......Shabbos 56a; Kesubos 9a-9b; Yoma 22b; Moed Katan 16b; Kiddushin 43a
Urim
Urim, priestly vestments................Yoma 73a-73b; Sotah 48b
Urim, second Temple...Yoma 21b
Urim, war.....................Berachos 3b-4a; Sanhedrin 16a-16b
Urinating
Urinating, behavior.......Berachos 40a; Yoma 29b-30a; Bechoros 44b; Niddah 13a
Urinating, carrying out on Shabbos.............................Eruvin 99a
Urinating during prayer..Berachos 22b-23a
Urinating immediately before or after prayer...................Megillah 27b

Urinating in front of bed, exile .... Shabbos 62b; Kiddushin 71b
Urinating naked, poverty .... Shabbos 62b; Niddah 17a
Urinating on side of wall .... Bava Basra 19b

Urine
Urine, impurity of liquids of *niddah* .... Niddah 43a-43b
Urine, *niddah* blood .... Niddah 14b, 57b, 59b
Urine of donkey .... Bechoros 7a-7b
Urine of *zav* .... Zevachim 79b
Urine, prayer .... Berachos 25a-25b; Nazir 38a

Urn, lots for goats of Yom Kippur .... Yoma 39a

Use
Use difficult, public domain .... Shabbos 8b
Use forbidden, *muktzeh* .... Beitzah 11a

Used
"Used like wood," impurity .... Chullin 129a
Used during the day, utensil .... Avodah Zarah 67b, 75b-76a
Used to blows, Israel .... Succah 29a
Used to come to synagogue, G-d asks about him .... Berachos 6b
Used to noise, not troubled by it .... Gittin 56b

Using
Using crown of Torah .... Nedarim 62a; Avos 1:13, 4:5
Using crystal cup even if it breaks .... Berachos 28a
Using lost item .... Bava Metzia 29b, 30a
Using man learning laws, prohibition .... Megillah 28b
Using one's two hands, blemish .... Bechoros 45b
Using scholars, Abraham .... Nedarim 32a
Using Torah student, prohibition .... Megillah 28b

Used to miracles
Used to miracles .... Taanis 25a
Used to miracles, Nahum .... Sanhedrin 108b-109a; Taanis 21a
Used to miracles, Rabbi Shimon bar Yochai .... Meilah 17b

Using deposit
Using deposit, agent .... Bava Metzia 43b-44a
Using deposit, cases .... Bava Metzia 43b-44a
Using deposit, penalty for custodian .... Bava Kama 107b
Using deposit, reducing .... Bava Metzia 41a-41b, 43b
Using deposit, returned it .... Bava Metzia 40b-41a

Useless words, prohibition .... Yoma 19b, 77a

Usha
Usha, decrees .... Kesubos 50a
Usha, relocations of *Sanhedrin* .... Rosh Hashanah 31b
Usha, sale by married woman .... Kesubos 50a, 78b; Bava Kama 88b; Bava Metzia 35a, 96b;
                                                                                                       Bava Basra 50a, 139b

Usher
Usher for Eve .... Berachos 61a
Usher, virginity .... Kesubos 12a

Ushiya "the small," rain .... Taanis 24a

Ushpiz .... *see* **Host,** page 285

Usually counted .... Beitzah 3b; Yevamos 81a-81b

U

Utensil .... *see also* **Item**, page 319, **Vessel**, page 722

Aggadah —
Utensil, "full utensil contains" .... Berachos 40a; Succah 46a-46b
Utensil, "he broke broken utensil" .... Bava Kama 26b
Utensil to prepare meal offering .... Menachos 96a
Utensil to take away ash from Altar .... Tamid 5:5
Utensil used for holy purpose .... Bava Metzia 84b
Utensils for measuring, Temple .... Menachos 8b, 57b, 87a-88b, 90a
Utensils for replacement, Temple .... Chagigah 26b
Utensils, nice, mind at ease .... Berachos 57b
Utensils of Temple .... *see* **Temple utensils**, page 679

Impurity —
Utensil, coating .... Chagigah 26b; Menachos 96b-97a; Keilim 22:1
Utensil, dismantled, impurity .... Shabbos 58b-59a; Succah 16a; Keilim 18:9, 26:1
Utensil, impurity from first source .... Bava Kama 2b
Utensil inside another, clay utensil .... Zevachim 3a; Chullin 25a; Keilim 8:1
Utensil inside another, immersion .... Chagigah 20b-22a; Mikvaos 6:2
Utensil not destined to be moved .... Keilim 15:1; Shabbos 35a; Megillah 26b
Utensil, not movable when full .... Megillah 26b
Utensil receiving impurity from food .... Pesachim 18a-18b
Utensil, reparable, impurity .... Shabbos 58b; Keilim 26:1
Utensil split in two, impurity .... Keilim 16:1
Utensil to consecrate blood for sprinkling .... Pesachim 34b-35a; Chagigah 23a-23b;
.... Parah 5:2-3, 5:5-6; Yadayim 1:2
Utensil with impure back, use .... Berachos 52b
Utensils in walls of oven .... Keilim 9:1

Utensils receiving impurity of couch
Utensils receiving impurity of couch, baby carriage .... Beitzah 23b; Shabbos 66a
Utensils receiving impurity of couch, bed .... Keilim 18:3-5, 23:4; Zavim 2:4
Utensils receiving impurity of couch, chairs .... Keilim 23:4
Utensils receiving impurity of couch, clay utensils .... Shabbos 84a-84b
Utensils receiving impurity of couch, corpse and reptile .... Bava Kama 25b
Utensils receiving impurity of couch, from when .... Keilim 20:4, 22:9-10
Utensils receiving impurity of couch, garments .... Keilim 28:9-10
Utensils receiving impurity of couch, leaning on .... Shabbos 66a-66b
Utensils receiving impurity of couch, or other impurities .... Keilim 22:10
Utensils receiving impurity of couch, pillow and blanket .... Keilim 23:4
Utensils receiving impurity of couch, possibility of immersion ...... Shabbos 84a-84b
Utensils receiving impurity of couch, shoe .... Shabbos 66a
Utensils receiving impurity of couch, stringency for sacrifices ...... Chagigah 22b-23a
Utensils receiving impurity of couch, which are pure .... Keilim 20:6, 27:9-10, 28:5;
.... Bava Kama 66b

Monetary matters —
Utensil, cases of act of acquisition .... Bava Basra 87a
Utensil, damages by pit .... Bava Kama 5b, 10a, 28b, 53b-54a
Utensil of buyer, act of acquisition, place .... Bava Basra 84b-86a; Gittin 78a, 79b;
.... Kiddushin 25b-26a; Bava Metzia 67b; Avodah Zarah 71b
Utensil taken to be examined, broken .... Nedarim 31a-31b; Bava Basra 87b
Utensils which are usually lent .... Shevuos 46b; Bava Metzia 116a; Bava Basra 52b

Prohibitions —

Utensil, concern about use by non-Jew .... Avodah Zarah 74b

Utensil for cooking sacrifice .... Avodah Zarah 76a; Zevachim 93a, 94b-95b, 96b-97a

Utensil of non-Jew, immersion .... Avodah Zarah 75b

Utensils after Pesach, *chametz* .... Pesachim 30a-30b; Zevachim 95b

Utensils for Pesach, *kashering* .... Pesachim 30b

Shabbos —

Utensil and its contents, Shabbos .... Shabbos 93b-94a

Utensil, heavy, *muktzeh* .... Shabbos 35a, 123b, 128a; Eruvin 102a

Utensil under lamp, Shabbos .... Shabbos 42b-43a, 47b

Utensil whose use is forbidden .... Shabbos 122b-124b, 141b; Beitzah 11a

Utensil whose use is permitted .... Shabbos 123b-124a

Utensils, work on Shabbos .... Shabbos 18a-18b

Various utensils —

Utensil of bone, impurity .... Chullin 25b

Utensil of clay .... *see* **Clay utensil**, page 110

Utensil of iron .... *see* **Iron utensil**, page 317

Utensil of leather, impurity .... Shabbos 28a; Sanhedrin 68a; Keilim 17:15, 23:1, 26:1-6

Utensil, of wood and iron .... Keilim 13:6-7, 14:2-3; Shabbos 15b, 59b-60a

Utensil of wood, impurity .... Chullin 25a-25b; Megillah 26b

Utensils for cheating, impurity .... Bava Basra 89b; Keilim 29:16

Utensils of baker, impurity .... Keilim 15:2-5; Eduyos 7:7

Utensils of saltpeter, impurity .... Keilim 2:1

Utensils, flat

Utensils, flat, immersion .... Shabbos 84b

Utensils, flat, impurity .... Keilim 2:1, 15:1

Utensils, flat, impurity of couch .... Bava Kama 25b

Misc. —

Utensil of gold, erosion .... Meilah 19a

Utensil, small, but does not have one .... Berachos 33b

Utensils of non-Jews, absorbed food .... Pesachim 44b; Nazir 37b; Avodah Zarah 75b-76a

Utensil connected to ground

Utensil connected to ground, impurity .... Keilim 11:2, 12:3, 14:3, 20:4-5; Bava Basra 66a

Utensil connected to ground, is it considered like ground .... Bava Basra 65b-66b;

.... Bava Kama 67a

Utensil connected to ground, *mikveh* .... Bava Basra 65b-66b; Bava Kama 67a; Parah 5:7

Utensil connected to ground, watering place .... Mikvaos 4:5; Yevamos 15a-15b; Parah 5:7

Uterus of woman, impurity .... Niddah 16a, 22a, 41b, 66a, 71a

Utterances for Creation .... Rosh Hashanah 32a; Megillah 21b; Avos 5:1

Uva Letzion, *Kedushah* .... Sotah 49a

Uzzah

Uzzah and Azzael .... Yoma 67b

Uzzah, episode about Ark .... Sotah 35a-35b

Uzziah, premature death .... Pesachim 87b

U

V

Va'ani, accepting *nezirus* .... Nazir 13a-13b
Vaed, explanation .... Eruvin 54a
Valid before being disqualified .... Succah 33a-33b; Avodah Zarah 47a; Chullin 87a; Pesachim 73b;
.... Yoma 64a; Zevachim 12a

Valley
    Valley, *karmelis* .... Shabbos 6b-7a; Bava Basra 153b; Taharos 6:7
    Valley, doubtful impurity .... Pesachim 10a; Bava Basra 55b; Avodah Zarah 70a; Taharos 6:5
    Valley open he found, stringency of meat mixed in milk .... Chullin 110a
    Valley, signs .... Pesachim 53a
Value on me, without explaining .... Arachin 4b
Value corresponding to money
    Value corresponding to money, *reiyah* sacrifice .... Bechoros 51a
    Value corresponding to money, redeeming consecrated item .... Arachin 27a
    Value corresponding to money, second tithe .... Bechoros 51a
Vanachnu mah, humility .... Chullin 89a
Vapor in bathhouse, health .... Shabbos 41a
Variable guilt offering
    Variable guilt offering, became poor .... Arachin 17b; Krisos 9b, 27b-28a; Negaim 14:11; Niddah 70a
    Variable guilt offering, became rich .... Yoma 41a-41b; Krisos 27b-28a
    Variable guilt offering, communal .... Horayos 8b; Shevuos 17b
    Variable guilt offering, impurity .... Shevuos 5a, 6b-7b
    Variable guilt offering, leper .... Arachin 17a-18a; Krisos 9b; Negaim 14:11-13
    Variable guilt offering, offered as if he was a poor man .... Yoma 41b; Krisos 28a; Negaim 14:12
    Variable guilt offering, who must offer .... Horayos 8b-9b; Krisos 10b
Vashti
    Vashti .... Megillah 12a-12b
    Vashti, beauty .... Megillah 15a
Vasikin, morning prayer .... Berachos 9b, 25b
Vatodieinu, *havdala* on Yom Tov .... Berachos 33b
Vav
    Vav, cut .... Kiddushin 66b
    Vav, do we deduce laws from *vav* .... Yoma 45a; Yevamos 68b, 69a, 72b, 87a; Moed Katan 8a;
.... Sotah 28a; Sanhedrin 14a, 21a, 51b; Menachos 51b, 87b
Vay .... *see* **Woe,** page 754

Vaychulu, Shabbos night .... Shabbos 119b

Vayedaber, harsh speech .... Makos 11a

Vayehi

"Vayehi binsoa," nun inversed .... Shabbos 115b-116a

Vayehi, expression of trouble .... Megillah 10b

Vayeishev, pain .... Sanhedrin 106a

Vechen lemar .... *see* **Also to you!**, page 19

Vegetable

Commandments —

Vegetable, blessing .... Berachos 40a

Vegetable of Beth Shean, tithe .... Chullin 6b-7a

Vegetable, *peah* .... Pesachim 56b-57a

Vegetable, tithes .... Rosh Hashanah 12a; Niddah 50a

Vegetables, cooked, blessing .... Berachos 38b-39a

Vegetables, cooked, blessing on the water .... Berachos 39a

Health —

Vegetable, healthful characteristics .... Shabbos 140b; Eruvin 55b-56a; Pesachim 42a

Vegetable, importance .... Eruvin 55b-56a

Vegetable in bundle, sorcery .... Chullin 105b

Vegetable, raw, harmful .... Pesachim 42a; Eruvin 55b-56a

Vegetable, small, harmful .... Berachos 44b

Misc. —

Vegetable from outside *Eretz Yisrael* .... Sanhedrin 12a; Nedarim 53b

Vegetable, gathering .... Rosh Hashanah 14a

Vegetable, preparing during Yom Kippur .... Shabbos 114b-115a

Vegetable which grew on a depression between fields .... Bava Metzia 118b-119a; Gittin 22a

Vegetable, wording of vow .... Nedarim 53a-53b

Vegetables, advice to buy .... Shabbos 140b

Vegetables, time of growth .... Rosh Hashanah 11a

Veins

Veins, receiving blood .... Zevachim 25a-25b

Veins, slaughtering .... Chullin 28b

Velamalshinim, blessing in *Shemoneh Esrei* .... Berachos 28b-29a

Venakeh lo yenakeh, which sins .... Yoma 86a

Vengeance .... *see* **Revenge**, page 565

Venom

Venom, animal .... Chullin 58b

Venom of reptiles .... Avodah Zarah 31b

Venom of snake .... Sanhedrin 78a; Bava Kama 23b

Veod, expression of Mishnayos .... Eruvin 23a

Verbal testimony .... Gittin 71a

Verbal expression

Verbal expression, divorce certificate .... Nedarim 5b-6a; Gittin 85b

Verbal expression, general .... Nedarim 6b-7a; Kiddushin 5b; Gittin 85b

Verbal expression, insufficient, *nezirus* .... Nazir 2b-3a; Kiddushin 5b

Verbal expression, invalid, interpretation .... Arachin 5a-5b, 20a; Kesubos 58b; Nazir 9a; Gittin 39a; Temurah 27b

Verbal expression, *nazir* .... Nedarim 3a; Nazir 2b

Verbal expression of vows, incomplete .... Nedarim 3a-3b

V

Verbal expression, vows .... Nedarim 5b-6a; Nazir 2b; Kiddushin 5b

Verdict

Verdict given, accused man fled .... Makos 7a; Gittin 28b, 29a; Sanhedrin 45b

Verdict, wording .... Sanhedrin 6b

Verse

Commentaries —

Verses, pronunciation or written, which determines .... Sanhedrin 4a-4b; Makos 7b-8a;
.... Succah 6b; Kiddushin 18b; Pesachim 86b; Zevachim 37b-38a; Bechoros 34a; Krisos 17b

Verses, tradition forgotten .... Kiddushin 30a

Prohibitions —

Verse, interrupting in the middle .... Taanis 27b; Megillah 22a; Berachos 12b

Verse, song for cure and protection .... Sanhedrin 101a

Verses on legal documents .... Yevamos 106b

Misc. —

Verse, "A verse I explain" .... Taanis 5b

Verse, "tell me your verse" .... Chullin 95b

Verse at its time, good .... Sanhedrin 101a

Verse cannot apply to doubt .... Yoma 74a-74b; Chullin 22b; Bechoros 41b; Chagigah 4a; Krisos 21a

Verse does not lose its simple meaning .... Shabbos 63a; Yevamos 24a; Kesubos 38b

Verse explained from end to beginning .... Berachos 60a, 63a; Sanhedrin 70a

Verse in his mouth, prophecy .... Berachos 55b, 57b

Verse, source for different laws .... Sanhedrin 34a

Verse was in our hand and we forgot it .... Avodah Zarah 52b; Zevachim 59a

Verse, words in inverse order .... Kiddushin 78b

Verses, answers to heretics .... Avodah Zarah 4a

Verses, doubt about way to read .... Yoma 52a-52b

Verses, not to translate .... Megillah 25a-25b

Verses of Torah reading .... Megillah 21b; Taanis 27b

Vertebras, *treifah* .... Chullin 42b, 52a-52b; Eruvin 7a

Ve'sein

Ve'sein berachah .... Berachos 33a; Taanis 2a, 4a-5a, 10a

Ve'sein berachah, forgot .... Berachos 26b, 29a-29b

Ve'sein tal umatar

Ve'sein tal umatar, blessing for years .... Berachos 33a; Taanis 2a

Ve'sein tal umatar, from when .... Taanis 10a

Ve'sein tal umatar, in summer .... Taanis 14b

Ve'sein tal umatar, request .... Taanis 4a-5a, 6a; Bava Metzia 28a

Veshet .... see **Gullet**, page 262

Vessel

Vessel .... see also **Utensil**, page 718

Vessel for cooking, used within day .... Avodah Zarah 67b, 75b-76a; Pesachim 44b

Vessels, broken, giving to child .... Yoma 78b

Vessess .... see **Menstruation**, page 404

Vestibule

Vestibule in Temple Courtyard .... Tamid 28b

Vestibule of Rav's yeshiva, door .... Bava Basra 11b

Vestibule, partition by *pi tikra* .... Eruvin 25a-25b, 90b, 94b-95a; Succah 18b-19a

Veterinary, flesh cut by, *treifah* .... Chullin 53b

Vetzivanu, blessing for Rabbinical commandments .... Shabbos 23a; Succah 46a

V

Vicious circle
Vicious circle, precedence between creditors, turning around .... Kesubos 95b
Vicious circle, precedence between sacrifices .... Zevachim 90b
Victory, episode about Divine Voice .... Sotah 33a
Vidui .... *see* **Confession, page 121**
Vidui maaser .... *see* **Confession for tithe, page 121**
Vihyisem nekiim .... *see* **Suspicion, being careful to escape, page 666**
Villager seeing king .... Chagigah 13b
Vine
Vine, climbing, mixed species in vineyard .... Kilayim 6:1-9; Eduyos 2:4
Vine, climbing, on fruit tree .... Bava Metzia 116b
Vine plants, surrounding garden .... Eduyos 2:4
Vinegar
Episodes —
Vinegar in lamp, Rabbi Chanina ben Dosa .... Taanis 25a
Vinegar of Rav Huna .... Berachos 5b
Vinegar, Rav Zevid's death .... Avodah Zarah 38b
"Vinegar son of wine" .... Bava Metzia 83b; Chullin 105a
Misc. —
Vinegar and wine, two kinds .... Bava Basra 84a-84b
Vinegar, doubt about tithes separation .... Bava Basra 96a
Vinegar for beans .... Avodah Zarah 67a
Vinegar, hot days .... Shabbos 113b
Vinegar, wine of idolaters .... Avodah Zarah 29b
Vinegar, Yom Kippur fast .... Yoma 81b
Vinegar for teeth
Vinegar for teeth, health .... Shabbos 111a
Vinegar for teeth, Shabbos .... Shabbos 111a; Beitzah 18b; Avodah Zarah 28a
Vinegar for teeth, strained answer .... Kiddushin 45b; Taanis 4b
Vineyard
Mixed species —
Vineyard, cases .... Kilayim 4:5-7, 5:1-2, 7:2-3
Vineyard, distance to permit sowing .... Kilayim 4:1-3, 4:8-9, 5:3-4
Vineyard, forbidden species .... Kilayim 5:8; Bava Basra 156b; Menachos 15a-15b
Vineyard, from when is it forbidden .... Kilayim 5:6-7, 7:7
Vineyard, grew by itself .... Kilayim 5:6-7
Vineyard, how much is forbidden .... Kilayim 5:5, 8:1
Vineyard, mixed species and pips .... Kiddushin 39a; Berachos 22a; Bechoros 54a; Chullin 82b, 136b
Vineyard of fellow, mixed species .... Kilayim 7:4-6; Bava Basra 2a-2b; Yevamos 83a-83b; Menachos 15b; Bava Kama 100a-100b
Vineyard outside *Eretz Yisrael* .... Orlah 3:9; Shabbos 139a; Kiddushin 38a, 39a; Berachos 36a
Vineyard, source for prohibition of profit .... Kiddushin 56b; Chullin 115a
Vineyard, species mixed involuntarily .... Kilayim 7:6-7
Vineyard, what is forbidden .... Pesachim 25a; Chullin 116a
Vineyards too close, mixed species .... Bava Basra 37b, 83a, 102b; Kilayim 5, 1-2; Eruvin 3b
Misc. —
Vineyard, "he sold him a name" .... Bava Metzia 104a; Bava Basra 7a
Vineyard, gifts to poor .... Peah 7:3-7; Chullin 131a-131b
Vineyard of Ben Shemen .... Succah 49a

Vineyards, four hundred...Bava Basra 14a

Violent
Violent men, David's sons.............................Kiddushin 76b; Sanhedrin 21a
Violent persons, Jerusalem...Pesachim 57a

Virgin
Rights —
Virgin, claiming *kesubah*..Kesubos 16a-16b
Virgin, inheritance of indemnity...................................Kesubos 42b
Virgin, proof...Kesubos 15b-16a
Virgin, trustworthiness...Kesubos 28a
Virgin's wedding is known...................Kesubos 16a-16b; Bava Basra 92b
Misc. —
Virgin constantly praying...Sotah 22a
Virgin, different meanings..Niddah 8b
Virgin, pregnant from first relation..................................Yevamos 34a
Virgin, pregnant, permitted to *Kohen Gadol*...............Chagigah 14b-15a
Virgin, pre-menstruation...Niddah 8b
Virgin, time of wedding.......................Kesubos 2a, 3a-3b, 4b-5a, 9b
Virgin, union on Shabbos..Kesubos 5b-7a
Virgin's prayer..Sotah 22a
Virgins of Yavesh Gilead...Yevamos 60b

Virginity
Claim —
Virginity, accusation against which women.....................Kesubos 36a-36b
Virginity, Durkati family..Kesubos 10b
Virginity, episodes...Kesubos 10a-10b
Virginity, *kesubah*..Kesubos 9b-10a
Virginity, lashes for plaintiff......................................Kesubos 10a-10b
Virginity, lashes to husband who denies his wife's..........Kesubos 10a-10b
Virginity, opening..Kesubos 9b-10a
Virginity, trustworthiness.................Kesubos 11b, 12b-13a, 16a, 75b
Virginity, until when..Yevamos 111b
Misc. —
Virginity, chain between legs...Shabbos 63b
Virginity, during first three years..................................Niddah 45a
Virginity, *niddah*.......................Niddah 11b, 45a, 64b-65b; Kesubos 6a-6b
Virginity not found, wife could be forbidden......Kesubos 9a-9b, 12a; Niddah 45a
Virginity, suspicion of immorality...............Kesubos 9a-9b, 12a; Niddah 45a
Virginity, without blood...Kesubos 6b, 10a
Virginity, Judah..Kesubos 9b, 12a

Visible
Visible blood traces, covering blood................................Chullin 87a
Visible from outside, partition................Eruvin 9b-10a, 15a; Succah 19a
Visible from outside, succah..Succah 19a

Vision
Vision, Moses...Yevamos 49b
Vision, prophetic, clear........................Succah 45b; Sanhedrin 97b
Vision, sixteen *mil*...Bechoros 54b
Visions of G-d in prophecy...Chagigah 14a

Visiting early in the morning, *shalom* .... Berachos 14a
Visiting teacher
Visiting teacher on festival .... Succah 27b
Visiting teacher on festival, episode .... Chagigah 3a
Visiting teacher, Rebbi .... Shabbos 152a
Visiting the sick
Visiting the sick, "the way in which they will go" .... Bava Metzia 30b; Bava Kama 100a
Visiting the sick, Abraham .... Sotah 14a
Visiting the sick, general .... Nedarim 39b-40a, 41a-41b; Bava Metzia 30b
Visiting the sick, give your hand, healing .... Berachos 5b
Visiting the sick, man forbidden to benefit .... Nedarim 38b-39b
Visiting the sick on Shabbos .... Shabbos 12a-12b
Visiting the sick, praying .... Shabbos 12a-12b
Visiting the sick, Rabbi Akiva .... Nedarim 40a
Visiting the sick, Rabbi Eliezer .... Sanhedrin 101a
V'lados ishah .... *see* **Fetus, ox goring occasionally,** page 220
V'lados tumah .... *see* **Secondary level of impurity,** page 596
Voice .... *see also* **Noise,** page 447, **Sound,** page 648
    Men —
Voice, deep, women's blemishes .... Kesubos 75a
Voice, loud, during prayer .... Berachos 24b
Voice, recognized, reliable proof .... Gittin 23a
Voice, why do people have different voices .... Sanhedrin 38a
    Misc. —
Voice and appearance, secular use of consecrating thing .... Pesachim 26a; Krisos 6a
Voice of woman, nakedness .... Berachos 24a
Voice of Jacob .... Gittin 57b
Voice, omen .... Megillah 32a
Voice, pleasant, recovers man's spirit .... Berachos 57b
Volume
Volume adds to difficulty to carry .... Bava Metzia 80a
Volume of dead reptiles, eating .... Meilah 16b-17a
Volume of olive .... *see* **Olive volume,** page 459
Voluntary prayer .... Berachos 21a-21b; Pesachim 54b
Vomits
"Vomits milk," Torah .... Berachos 63b
Vomiting after immersion .... Mikvaos 10:8
Vomiting, combining for quantity .... Chullin 103b
Vomiting in front of fellow .... Shabbos 12a
Vomiting on Shabbos .... Shabbos 147b
Vomiting, waste .... Shabbos 147b
Vow
    Cases —
Vow, already existing .... Nedarim 85b
Vow in Torah .... Nedarim 14a-14b
Vow, tangible item .... Nedarim 13b, 15a; Shevuos 25a
Vow with condition, prohibition because of doubt .... Nedarim 14b-15b
    Doubt —
Vow, doubt, is it valid .... Nedarim 18b-19b, 61a-61b; Kiddushin 64b

Vow of *nezirus*, clear-cut ....Nedarim 19b, 21a; Eruvin 82a; Chagigah 10a; Nazir 34a, 62a; Sanhedrin 25a
Vows, doubtful wording ....Nedarim 18b-19b, 61a-61b

Expressions —
Vow, bed, what is included ....Nedarim 56a-56b
Vow, explaining one's intention ....Nedarim 20a
Vow, garments, what is included ....Nedarim 55b
Vow, inaccurate wording ....Nedarim 4b-5a, 7a-7b, 10a-10b; Nazir 3a
Vow, wording, vegetable ....Nedarim 53a-53b

Permitted —
Vow by mistake, explained ....Nedarim 65a-65b, 66a
Vows by mistake ....Nedarim 25b; Shevuos 28b
Vows, forced ....Nedarim 27b-28a
Vows of encouragement ....Nedarim 20b-21b
Vows, overstatement ....Nedarim 24b-25a
Vows permitted, permitting them ....Nedarim 21b; Nazir 11b

Permitting —
Vow according to several persons ....Gittin 36a; Bechoros 46a; Arachin 23a; Makos 16a
Vow in public, permitting ....Gittin 36a; Bechoros 46a; Arachin 23a; Makos 16a
Vow known to numerous people ....Gittin 46a; Kesubos 74b
Vow of ignoramus ....Nedarim 20a
Vow permitted in part ....Nedarim 25b-27a, 66a

Prohibitions —
Vow includes oath ....Nedarim 80b
Vow, keeping away from making vows ....Nedarim 20a, 22a, 59a, 60b, 77b; Eruvin 64b;
....Yevamos 109b; Gittin 46b
Vow, not to violate one's word ....Nedarim 3b
Vow, prohibition of item ....Nedarim 2b
Vow to consecrate item, not recommended ....Menachos 81a
Vow, three days without sleeping ....Nedarim 15a; Succah 53a; Yevamos 121b; Shevuos 25a
Vows, death punishment ....Shabbos 32b; Kesubos 72a; Rosh Hashanah 6a; Sanhedrin 22a; Zevachim 29b

Women —
Vow, episodes concerning women ....Nedarim 66a-66b
Vow forbidding marital relations ....Nedarim 15b, 81b
Vow, forbidding her work product to her husband .....Nedarim 79b, 85a-86b; Kesubos 59a-59b
Vow, forbidding benefit to wife, divorce ....Kesubos 61b, 70a-72a; Eduyos 4:10
Vow, forbidding benefit to wife, rebellious husband ....Kesubos 61b
Vow not to marry divorced woman, *Kohen* ....Bechoros 45b-46a; Gittin 35b-36a
Vow of woman, husband's consent ....Nedarim 73b, 74a; Shabbos 46b; Yevamos 29b; Gittin 83b;
....Niddah 46b
Vow of woman when she will marry or divorce ....Nedarim 88b-89a
Vow, suffering, annulment ....Nedarim 79a-79b, 81b; Kesubos 71a-71b
Vow, to be forbidden to all Jews ....Yevamos 112a
Vows, can annul *kiddushin* ....Kesubos 72b; Kiddushin 50a
Vows, forcing to divorce wife ....Kesubos 52a, 61b, 70a, 71a-72a
Vows of wife, agent ....Nedarim 8b
Vows, wife's death ....Shabbos 32b; Rosh Hashanah 6a; Sanhedrin 22a; Zevachim 29b

Misc. —
Vow and donation, warranty ....Megillah 8a; Arachin 20b; Chullin 139a
Vow, eating earth ....Shevuos 24a-24b

Vow with condition, unintentional..Shevuos 28a-28b
Vows of consecration ....*see also* **Consecrated**, page 122
Vows, personal use...................................Yevamos 88a; Nedarim 35a; Shevuos 22a-22b

Vow by comparison
Vow by comparison ....Shevuos 20a-20b
Vow by comparison, firstborn..Nazir 4b
Vow by comparison, for *nazir*, annulling for wife ....Nazir 22a-22b
Vow by comparison, for *nazir*, like who ....Nazir 21a
Vow by comparison, permitted or forbidden state ....Nedarim 11b-13a; Nazir 22b
Vow by comparison, primary state..Nedarim 11b-13a; Nazir 22b
Vow by comparison to juxtaposed word in verse...................................Nazir 3a-3b
Vow by comparison to prohibition..Nedarim 13a, 14a; Nazir 4b
Vow by comparison, wordings...Nedarim 13a-13b, 15b-16a

Vow of *cherem*
Vow of *cherem*, *Kohanim* on watch ....Arachin 28a-28b
Vows of *cherem* for *Kohanim* ....Arachin 29a; Temurah 32a-32b
Vows of *cherem*, general...Arachin 28b-29a; Sanhedrin 88a

Vow of meal offering
Vow of meal offering, forgot which kind ....Menachos 104b-106b
Vow of meal offering, not specified...Menachos 104b-105a
Vow of meal offering, offering another ....Menachos 3a, 102b-103a

Vowed
Vowed small sacrifice and brought large ....Menachos 107b
Vowing, "before he dies"...Nedarim 3b
Vowing and performing for idolatry ....Sanhedrin 63a
Vowing not to support one's wife ....Kesubos 70a-70b
Vowing, permission to wait..Bava Kama 80a
Vowing that wife will not benefit from him, supporting her....................Kesubos 70b-71a
Vowing to be forbidden to her deceased husband's brother ....Yevamos 112a-112b

Vowing woman
Vowing woman, divorce ....Kesubos 52a, 71a-71b
Vowing woman, *kesubah* and *kiddushin* ....Kiddushin 50a; Kesubos 72b

V

W

Wages .... *see* **Salary**, page 585
Wagging tail .... Bava Kama 19b
Wagon
  Wagon, included in sale .... Bava Basra 77b
  Wagon, *muktzeh* .... Shabbos 122a
  Wagons of Tabernacle
    Wagons of Tabernacle, boards .... Shabbos 49b
    Wagons of Tabernacle, public domain .... Shabbos 98a, 99a
    Wagons of Tabernacle, shape .... Shabbos 98a-98b
Waiting
  Waiting after *Shemoneh Esrei* prayer .... Yoma 53b
  Waiting between two prayers .... Berachos 30b
  Waiting for fellow, prayer .... Berachos 5b-6a
  Waiting for payment, interest .... Kiddushin 6b
  Waiting patiently for one's hour .... Berachos 64a; Eruvin 13b
  Waiting to perform vow .... Bava Kama 80a
  Waited ten years
    Waited ten years, *kesubah* .... Yevamos 65a-65b
    Waited ten years, procreation .... Yevamos 64a-65a
    Waited ten years, sterile woman .... Yevamos 34b
Waiting-room of blood-letter, separated .... Taanis 21b
"Wake up, why are you sleeping," not to say .... Sotah 48a
Walk
  Prohibitions —
    Walking annuls partition, Shabbos .... Eruvin 8a, 10b, 22a-22b
    Walking behind woman .... Berachos 61a; Eruvin 18b
    Walking in front of praying man .... Berachos 27a
    Walking like standing, *karmelis* .... Shabbos 5b-6a
    Walking like standing, putting down .... Shabbos 5b; Kesubos 31a-31b; Eruvin 98a
    Walking next to one's teacher .... Yoma 37a; Eruvin 54b; Chullin 91a
    Walking on Shabbos, for weekday purposes .... Eruvin 38b-39a
    Walking with difficulty, Shabbos .... Shabbos 8b, 100b
  Misc. —
    Walk over people's heads .... Horayos 13b

W

Walking, act of acquisition .... Bava Basra 100a
Walking dissipates wine .... Eruvin 64b; Taanis 17b; Sanhedrin 22b
Walking distance of one day .... Pesachim 93b; Sanhedrin 94a
Walking, health .... Kesubos 111a
Walking in darkness, parable .... Sotah 21a
Walking in fellow's field .... Bava Kama 81b
Walking, inattentive when .... Bava Kama 27b
Walking modestly .... Succah 49b; Makos 24a
Walking over holy people's heads, Avdan .... Yevamos 105b
Walking over holy people's heads, judge .... Sanhedrin 7b

Wall .... *see also* **House in walled city**, page 287
Monetary matters —
Wall around city, contributing to expenses .... Bava Basra 7b
Wall, building in front of wall .... Bava Basra 6a
Wall, *chazakah* by means of usage .... Bava Basra 6a
Wall, dangerous, time given by *beis din* to demolish .... Bava Metzia 118a
Wall, dimensions .... Bava Basra 3a, 98b
Wall, distance .... Bava Basra 2b, 19a-19b, 20b, 22a-22b
Wall, foundation of beams .... Bava Basra 6a
Wall of neighbor, payment by surrounded neighbor .... Bava Basra 4b-5a; Bava Kama 20b
Wall of pit, distance .... Bava Basra 17a-17b
Wall of pit, thickness .... Bava Basra 17b
Wall, old, lost item .... Bava Metzia 25b-26a
Wall, participation of neighbor .... Bava Basra 2b
Wall, sign of property .... Bava Basra 4a-4b
Wall, thickness .... Bava Basra 3a
Wall which fell, division .... Bava Basra 4a

Shabbos —
Wall between courtyard, Shabbos .... Eruvin 76b-77b
Wall between roofs .... Bava Basra 2b, 6b
Wall inclined, putting down .... Shabbos 5a-5b; Eruvin 98a-98b
Wall, like private domain .... Shabbos 99b
Walls, angular, domains for Shabbos .... Eruvin 15a, 17b-18a, 19a-20a, 22b-23a; Shabbos 6b; Succah 24b

Succah —
Wall, inclined, *halacha* .... Succah 6b
Wall, inclined, succah .... Succah 4a-4b, 17a-17b
Walls, angular, succah .... Succah 4b
Walls of succah, four handbreadths .... Succah 16b
Walls of succah, how many .... Succah 7a, 7b; Sanhedrin 4a; Niddah 26a

Temple —
Wall of Temple Courtyard, holiness .... Zevachim 56a
Walls of *Heichal*, gold .... Middos 4:1
Walls of Temple .... Rosh Hashanah 4a; Yoma 16a; Middos 2:4
Walls of Temple, holiness .... Zevachim 56a

Misc. —
Wall, "I am a wall," commentaries .... Pesachim 87a; Bava Basra 7b-8a
Wall around city, secular use .... Kiddushin 54a
Wall between one's property and idol .... Avodah Zarah 47a-47b

W

Wall, impurity of corpse .... Oholos 6:3-7, 7:1, 11:9
Wall inclined, recalls sin .... Berachos 55a; Rosh Hashanah 16b
Wall of Jericho .... Berachos 54b
Walls of tents, impurity .... Oholos 5:6-7

Walled city
Walled city, deceased person .... Keilim 1:7
Walled city, houses and wall .... Arachin 32a-32b; Megillah 3b, 5b, 10b
Walled city, how many houses .... Arachin 33b
Walled city, inhabited and walled .... Arachin 33b-34a
Walled city, Purim .... Megillah 2b, 3b-4a, 5b
Walled city, when was it walled .... Arachin 33b-34a

Want
Want, "I want," by coercion .... Rosh Hashanah 6a; Arachin 21a
Wanted to carry out, change .... Shabbos 92b
Wanted to catch fish and saved child .... Menachos 64a
Wanted to conceal, Koheles and Mishlei .... Shabbos 30b
Wanted to conceal, plunder from idolaters .... Bechoros 50a; Avodah Zarah 52b
Wanted to cut picked produce .... Shabbos 72a-73a; Sanhedrin 62b; Krisos 19b
Wanted to eat pork and ate lamb .... Nazir 23a; Kiddushin 81b
Wanted to kill one and killed another .... Sanhedrin 78b-79b; Kesubos 15a; Bava Kama 44b
Wanted to return world to chaos .... Sanhedrin 103a
Wanted to separate *terumah* and said tithe instead .... Terumos 3:8; Pesachim 63a
Wants and does not have .... Chullin 7b
Wants to become wise, learns monetary matters .... Berachos 63b; Bava Basra 175b
Wants to become wise, turns to south .... Bava Basra 25b
Wants to benefit like Elisha .... Berachos 10b
Wants to live, kills himself .... Tamid 32a
Wants to lose one's money, how .... Bava Metzia 29b

War
Episodes —
War against Amalek, Moses' hands .... Rosh Hashanah 29a
War against Sihon .... Rosh Hashanah 2b-3a
War of Aristobolus .... Sotah 49b; Bava Kama 82b; Menachos 64b
War of Abraham .... Nedarim 32a; Sanhedrin 96a, 108b
War of Abraham, his disciples .... Nedarim 32a
War of Pharaoh, Josiah .... Taanis 22a-22b
Wars of David, how .... Berachos 3b-4a; Sanhedrin 16a-16b
Wars of David, soldiers gave divorce certificate .... Kesubos 9a; Shabbos 56a
Wars of Rome and Greece .... Avodah Zarah 8b

Mandated wars —
War, ark .... Sotah 42b-43a
War before Shabbos .... Shabbos 19a
War, everyone goes to war .... Sotah 44b
War, fast .... Taanis 22a
War, Jewish soldiers returning .... Sotah 44a
War, mentioning *malchuyios* .... Taanis 16b-17a
War, merit of learning .... Makos 10a
War, merit of *Shema* .... Sotah 42a
War, policemen .... Sotah 44b

War, returning from war .... Sotah 43a-44a
War, sanctioned by whom .... Sanhedrin 16a-16b
War, Shabbos .... Eruvin 45a

Misc. —
War, *agunah* .... Yevamos 114b-115b
War, beginning with weak soldiers .... Berachos 53b
War, do not go out first .... Pesachim 113a
War, Esau's hands .... Gittin 57b
War, messianic times .... Shabbos 63a
War of Gog and Magog .... Avodah Zarah 3b
War of Torah .... Kiddushin 30b

Warm
Warm up audience during eulogy .... Shabbos 153a
Warm yourself at Sages' light .... Avos 2:10

Warm water
Warm water, health .... Bava Metzia 29b; Chullin 84b
Warm water, kneading meal offerings .... Pesachim 36a; Menachos 53a, 55a
Warm water, *matzah* .... Pesachim 36a

Warning
Warning, accepting death penalty .... Sanhedrin 40b-41a
Warning before penalty, doubtful .... Makos 15b-16a; Pesachim 63b; Yevamos 101a; Shevuos 3b, 21a;
.... Chullin 81a, 82b-83a, 91a; Temurah 3b
Warning craftsman, unnecessary .... Bava Basra 21b
Warning, conspiring witnesses .... Kesubos 33a
Warning, enemy .... Makos 6b, 9b
Warning for positive commandment .... Sanhedrin 56a
Warning household pleasantly before Shabbos .... Shabbos 34a
Warning in Torah about conspiring witnesses .... Makos 4a-4b; Kesubos 32b-33a
Warning, negative commandment, death penalty .... Makos 13a-14a
Warning of severe punishment instead of lenient .... Kesubos 33a; Sanhedrin 80b
Warning, scholar .... Makos 6b, 9b; Sanhedrin 8b, 41a, 72b
Warning, source .... Sanhedrin 40b-41a
Warning, specifying punishment .... Sanhedrin 8b-9a, 80b
Warning to prevent damage .... Bava Kama 31a
Warning to thief coming surreptitiously .... Sanhedrin 72b; Kesubos 34b
Warning, who warns .... Makos 6b; Sanhedrin 9b
Warnings, several lashes for same transgression ..... Nazir 42a; Makos 20a-20b, 21a; Kiddushin 77b;
.... Chullin 82b-83a

Warning to *sotah*
Warning to *sotah*, before seclusion .... Sotah 3a
Warning to *sotah*, by *beis din* .... Sotah 24a, 27a
Warning to *sotah*, canceling .... Sotah 25a; Sanhedrin 88a
Warning to *sotah*, explanation .... Sotah 2b
Warning to *sotah*, from which sin .... Sotah 26b; Yevamos 55b
Warning to *sotah*, from whom .... Sotah 26a-26b
Warning to *sotah*, refrain from speaking to him! .... Sotah 5b
Warning to *sotah*, right or requirement .... Sotah 2a, 3a

Warp without woof, partition .... Eruvin 16b-17a

W

Warranty .... *see also* **Security**, page 597

   Sacrifices —

     Warranty for lost consecrated item .... Chullin 139a-139b; Rosh Hashanah 6a; Megillah 8a; Arachin 20b; Kinin 1:1

     Warranty, guilt offering .... Krisos 24a

     Warranty of redeeming son .... Bechoros 51b

     Warranty, redeeming donkey .... Bechoros 12b

     Warranty, sacrifices .... Megillah 8a; Arachin 20b; Chullin 139a

   Misc. —

     Warranty, non-Jew took away .... Bava Basra 45a

     Warranty of food vendor, indemnity .... Bava Basra 93b

     Warranty of non-Jew's *chametz* .... Pesachim 5b-6a

Warrior

   Warrior, in Torah .... Chagigah 14a

   Warriors, David's .... Kiddushin 76b

Wart

   Wart, blemish of sacrifice .... Bechoros 40b

   Wart, blemishes of *Kohen* .... Kesubos 75a

   Wart on finger, sprinkling .... Zevachim 40b

   Warts, cutting on Shabbos .... Pesachim 68b; Eruvin 103a-103b

Washing .... *see also* **Laundering**, page 354, **Bathing**, page 44

   Health —

     Washing baby .... Yoma 78b

     Washing baby for circumcision .... Shabbos 86a, 134b

     Washing, cure for eyes .... Shabbos 108b

     Washing face, wiping .... Shabbos 133b-134a

     Washing, harmful for sick person .... Berachos 57b

     Washing, how .... Shabbos 41a, 61a

     Washing on Yom Tov .... Beitzah 21b; Shabbos 39b

     Washing oneself, health .... Nedarim 81a; Chullin 24b

     Washing, too much is harmful .... Gittin 70a

     Washing, with relatives .... Pesachim 51a

   Prohibitions —

     Washing dishes on Shabbos .... Shabbos 118a

     Washing during communal fast day .... Megillah 5b

     Washing floor on Shabbos .... Shabbos 40b, 95a; Pesachim 65a

     Washing, forbidden acts when *niddah* .... Kesubos 4b, 61a

     Washing in bad waters, Shabbos .... Shabbos 109a-109b

     Washing in teacher's presence .... Pesachim 51a

     Washing leather on Shabbos .... Zevachim 94a-94b; Shabbos 142b

     Washing, mourner .... Taanis 13a-13b; Moed Katan 15b

     Washing, mourner being a refined person .... Berachos 16b

     Washing on Shabbos, cases .... Shabbos 40a-40b, 147a-147b

     Washing on Shabbos, prohibition .... Shabbos 39b-40a, 147b

     Washing on Yom Kippur .... Yoma 77b

     Washing, vow of affliction .... Nedarim 79b-81b

   Misc. —

     Washing, "I lost blessing" .... Shabbos 25b

     Washing, *ayef* .... Yoma 77a

W

Washing before immersion .... Bava Kama 82a-82b; Niddah 66b, 67b-68a
Washing, death for *Kohen* who neglected .... Sanhedrin 83b
Washing on Shabbos eve .... Shabbos 25b
Washing on Shabbos eve, episode .... Shabbos 25b
Washing sacrificial blood, place .... Zevachim 94b

Washing wheat
Washing wheat for meal offerings .... Pesachim 36a, 40a
Washing wheat, leavening .... Pesachim 36a, 39b-40a, 42a; Sanhedrin 5b
Washing wheat to make semolina .... Pesachim 40a

Washing hands
How —
Washing hands, container .... Yadayim 1:2
Washing hands, halfway .... Gittin 15b-16a; Yadayim 1:1, 2:1
Washing hands, human intervention .... Yadayim 1:5
Washing hands in a canal .... Chullin 107a
Washing hands in fruit juice .... Zevachim 22a
Washing hands in hot water .... Chullin 105a-105b, 106a
Washing hands in mud and worms .... Zevachim 22a
Washing hands in wine .... Berachos 50b; Zevachim 22a
Washing hands, intention .... Chagigah 18b-19a
Washing hands, intervening substance .... Chullin 106a-106b
Washing hands, quantity of water .... Yadayim 1:1, 2:1; Nazir 38a; Gittin 15b; Chullin 107a
Washing hands, raising hands .... Sotah 4b
Washing hands, saying blessing immediately after .... Berachos 42a
Washing hands, up to where .... Chullin 106a-106b
Washing hands, water .... Yadayim 1:3-5
Washing hands, wiping .... Sotah 4b
Meal —
Washing hands, decree .... Chullin 106a
Washing hands, doubt .... Yadayim 2:4
Washing hands during war .... Eruvin 17a-17b
Washing hands, for whole day .... Chullin 106b-107a
Washing hands, giving to eat .... Yoma 77b; Chullin 107b
Washing hands, inattentive .... Pesachim 115b; Yoma 30a
Washing hands, source .... Berachos 53b
Washing hands, towel .... Chullin 107a-107b; Succah 26b-27a
Washing hands, up to one *parsah* .... Pesachim 46a; Chullin 122b-123a; Berachos 15a
Washing hands, volume of olive of bread .... Succah 27a

Washing hands after meal
Washing hands after meal, episode about deposit .... Chullin 106a; Yoma 83b
Washing hands after meal, how .... Chullin 105a-105b; Sotah 4b
Washing hands after meal, immediately before *Bircas HaMazon* .... Berachos 42a
Washing hands after meal, indispensable requirement for blessing .... Berachos 53b
Washing hands after meal, source .... Berachos 53b
Washing hands after meal, table companions .... Berachos 43a, 46b
Misc. —
Washing hands, bad spirit .... Shabbos 108b-109a; Pesachim 111b-112a
Washing hands before learning .... Bava Kama 17a
Washing hands before prayer .... Berachos 14b-15a, 22a

W

Washing hands, blows from schoolteacher .... Chullin 107b
Washing hands, by one who did not wash .... Berachos 51a
Washing hands, fear .... Pesachim 111b-112a
Washing hands, food dipped in liquid .... Pesachim 115a-115b
Washing hands, fruit .... Chagigah 18b; Chullin 106a
Washing hands in Temple .... *see* **Sanctifying hands**, page 588
Washing hands in the morning .... Berachos 60b
Washing hands, meat after milk .... Chullin 104b, 105b
Washing hands, poverty .... Shabbos 62b
Washing hands, punishment .... Sotah 4b; Shabbos 62b
Washing hands, Rabbi Akiva .... Eruvin 21b
Washing hands, refrained from washing and ate pork .... Chullin 106a; Yoma 83b
Washing hands, reward .... Shabbos 62b
Washing hands, second tithe .... Chagigah 18b

Waste

Waste, cases .... Bava Kama 91b
Waste, crumbs .... Berachos 52b; Shabbos 143a
Waste, leftover food .... Taanis 20b
Waste of food .... Berachos 50b, 52b; Shabbos 50b
Waste, oil for lamp .... Shabbos 67b
Waste, one's own body .... Shabbos 129a, 140b
Waste, tree .... Bava Kama 91b-92a; Bava Basra 26a
Waste, vomiting .... Shabbos 147b

Watch

Watch, blessing .... Berachos 11b-12a
Watch of Bilgah .... Succah 56b
Watch of *Kohanim*, gifts to *Kohanim* .... Arachin 28a-28b
Watches .... *see also* **Anshei Maamad**, page 29
Watches, festival .... Succah 55b-56a; Moed Katan 17b
Watches of *Kohanim* .... Taanis 27a-27b; Arachin 12b-13a
Watches, sharing of sacrifices .... Succah 55b-56b
Watches, Succos sacrifices .... Succah 55b

Water

Aggadah —

Water Above, *aggadah* .... Chagigah 15a
Water is kept in clay vessels .... Taanis 7a
Water, one does see its end .... Yevamos 121a-121b
Water, parable for Torah .... Taanis 7a-7b; Bava Kama 17a, 82a; Avodah Zarah 5b
Water, refers to Torah .... Bava Kama 82a
Water reverberating smiling face, thus is man .... Yevamos 117a
Waters stolen, forbidden relations .... Sanhedrin 75a

Commandments —

Water, blessing .... Berachos 44b-45a
Water in which vegetables cooked, blessing .... Berachos 38b-39a
Water remaining in vessel, washing hands .... Chullin 107a
Water to preserve *lulav* .... Succah 42a
Water, washing hands .... Yadayim 1:3-5
Water which rested overnight, *matzah* .... Pesachim 42a

Episodes —

Water, "we drink their water," Rabbi Meir .... Horayos 14a

Water, "we drink your water," Rabbi Yehoshua .... Chagigah 3a

Water absorbs water, Sages of Athens .... Bechoros 9a

Water, episode about Nakdimen .... Taanis 19b-20a

Water in desert, miracle .... Berachos 54a

Water which rested overnight, episode .... Pesachim 42a

Waters of Dispute, Moses .... Shabbos 55b

Health and danger —

Water and salt during meal .... Berachos 40a

Water, boiling, on stomach .... Shabbos 40b

Water borrowed, danger .... Pesachim 111a

Water, danger from harmful forces .... Chullin 105b-106a

Water, danger of leech and sickness .... Avodah Zarah 12b; Pesachim 112a

Water, danger of river and lake .... Pesachim 112a

Water, danger of stream with strong current .... Yoma 77b

Water, danger on Shabbos and Wednesday .... Pesachim 112a

Water drunk by demons .... Chullin 105b

Water, harmful to wound .... Yevamos 47b, 120b, 121a

Water uncovered .... Avodah Zarah 30b; Chullin 10a, 49b; Terumos 8:4-5; Bava Kama 116b

Water, warm, health .... Bava Metzia 29b; Chullin 84b

Immersion —

Water, colored, *mikveh* .... Makos 3b-4a; Eruvin 29b; Chullin 20a; Mikvaos 7:3-5

Water connected to *mikveh* .... Mikvaos 6:1-2; Zevachim 22a

Water pumped which flowed horizontally, *mikveh* .... Temurah 12a-12b; Mikvaos 4:4

Water, spoiled, *mikveh* .... Mikvaos 1:8

Water touches first, intervening substance .... Mikvaos 7:7

Prohibitions —

Water, clear, in lung .... Chullin 55b

Water connected to earth, idolatry .... Avodah Zarah 58b-59a

Water from olives, to *kosher* utensils .... Avodah Zarah 75a; Niddah 65b

Water or hole, slaughtering .... Chullin 17a, 41a-41b

Purity —

Water, cases of desired water .... Krisos 15b; Machshirin 1:1-6, 3:1-5, 4:1-5, 4:9-10, 5:1-8

Water connected to earth, impurity .... Mikvaos 1:1-6; Machshirin 4:6-8

Water for ash of Red Heifer .... Parah 8:8-11

Water, impure, mixture .... Machshirin 2:3-4

Water of swamp-egg, episode .... Sanhedrin 5b

Water to wash hands, impurity .... Yadayim 2:1-3

Water wanted, susceptible to become impure .... Bava Metzia 22a-22b; Machshirin 1:5

Water which pleased, susceptible to become impure .... Machshirin 3:5-8

Shabbos —

Water, carrying out voluntarily, impurity .... Krisos 15b

Water, cold, placed on pot, Shabbos .... Shabbos 48a

Water from gutter, drinking on Shabbos .... Eruvin 99b

Water in wheel, Shabbos .... Eruvin 104a-104b

Water on body, carrying .... Shabbos 141a

Water, partition for *techum* .... Eruvin 47b-48a

Water, putting down on Shabbos .... Shabbos 5b, 99b-100a

W

Water, salted, Shabbos..Shabbos 108a-108b; Eruvin 14b
Water, *techum*...........................Beitzah 39a-39b; Eruvin 45b-46a, 47b-48a, 97b; Shabbos 121b

Temple —
Water libation..*see* **Libation of water**, page 368
Water, mixing meal offering...Menachos 57b
Water of basin in Temple..Zevachim 19b, 21b-22a
Water of basin in Temple, staying overnight.................................Zevachim 20a, 21a-21b

Misc. —
Water in desert, precedence for drinking..Bava Metzia 62a
Water in public domain, damage..Bava Kama 28a-28b, 30a
Water in which eggs cooked, taste...Chullin 64b
Water, not to throw water of cistern.................................Yevamos 11b, 12a, 44a, 53a
Water of Babylon...Shabbos 145b; Bechoros 44b
Water of well, source..Succah 53b

Water, drawn
Water, drawn, came out from mud..Mikvaos 2:6
Water, drawn, cases.......................................Shabbos 16b; Mikvaos 2:7-9, 4:1-2
Water, drawn, combining................................Mikvaos 2:5-6, 3:1-4, 6:3, 6:11
Water, drawn, impurity..Shabbos 14a; Gittin 16a
Water, drawn, *kashering* for *mikveh*..Mikvaos 3:1-3
Water, drawn, *mikveh*..Bava Basra 66a
Water, drawn, sponge and bucket..Mikvaos 6:4
Water, drawn, three holes..Mikvaos 2:5
Water, drawn, to *mikveh*, quantity........................Mikvaos 2:4; Shabbos 15a
Water, drawn, utensil...Mikvaos 4:3, 6:10, 7:6

Water of sewage
Water of sewage, danger...Pesachim 111a
Water of sewage, episode about forgiveness...Yoma 87a
Water of sewage, Shabbos...Eruvin 88a-89a

Water, warm
Water, warm, health....................................Bava Metzia 29b; Chullin 84b
Water, warm, *matzah*...Pesachim 36a
Water, warm, meal offerings...............................Pesachim 36a; Menachos 53a, 55a

Water for sprinkling
Impurity —
Water for sprinkling, cases of impurity...Parah 11:3, 11:6
Water for sprinkling drunk by cow....................................Pesachim 17b-18a; Parah 9:5
Water for sprinkling, impurity.......................................Parah 9:5, 9:8, 12:4-6
Water for sprinkling, purity..Zevachim 93a
Water for sprinkling which was used, impurity...Eduyos 5:3
Water for sprinkling, who becomes impure?.........................Yoma 14a-14b; Niddah 9a

Misc. —
Water for sprinkling, became impure...........................Parah 11:1-2; Chullin 9b-10a
Water for sprinkling, bird drank..................Gittin 86b; Chullin 62a-62b; Parah 9:3
Water for sprinkling, decrees.................Yevamos 116b; Chagigah 23a; Parah 8:2, 9:6
Water for sprinkling, filling..................................Parah 6:4-5; Zevachim 25b
Water for sprinkling, mixed...................Zevachim 80a, 93a; Parah 9:1-4, 11:1
Water for sprinkling, quantity........Zevachim 75a-75b, 80a, 93a; Yoma 14a-14b; Niddah 9a
Water for sprinkling, supervising...........................Parah 6:1, 7:1-12, 8:1

W

Water for sprinkling, work ...... Parah 6:1, 7:1-12, 8:1, 4:4

Wave
Wave, immersion ...... Mikvaos 5:6; Chagigah 19a; Chullin 31a-31b
Wave, immersion of needle ...... Mikvaos 7:7
Waves of the sea, wonders ...... Bava Basra 73a

Waving
Which item —
Waving first fruit ...... Makos 18b-19a; Menachos 61a-61b; Succah 47b
Waving, ram and meal offering of *nazir* ...... Nazir 46a-46b
Waving, *sotah* meal offering ...... Sotah 19a; Succah 47b; Kiddushin 36b
Waving, two loaves of Shavuos ...... Succah 37b-38a; Menachos 61a, 62a
Waving, what must be waved ...... Menachos 61a-61b, 62b
Waving, breast and hind leg ...... Menachos 62a-62b
Waving, sheep of Shavuos ...... Menachos 46b
Misc. —
Waving, did not wave ...... Menachos 93b
Waving, how ...... Kiddushin 36b; Succah 47b; Menachos 61b-62b
Waving, owners ...... Kiddushin 36b; Succah 47b; Sotah 19a; Makos 18b; Menachos 61a-61b
Waving, partners ...... Menachos 62b, 93b-94a
Waving, reasons of commandment ...... Menachos 62a; Succah 37b
Waving, when ...... Menachos 62b
Waving, who ...... Menachos 61a-62b

Wax
Wax, honey waste ...... Shabbos 20b
Wax in ears, sickness ...... Bava Metzia 107b
Wax on forehead, disguise ...... Yevamos 120a

Waxing floor on Shabbos ...... Shabbos 40b

Way
Way, "in which way," death ...... Berachos 28b
Way of evil urge, "do this" ...... Shabbos 105b; Niddah 13b
Way of Torah ...... Avos 6:4
Way on which one wants to go ...... Makos 10b
Way, other, distance from women ...... Bava Basra 57b
Way, right, *Pirkei Avos* ...... Avos 2:1, 2:9
Way, short and long, Rabbi Yehoshua ...... Eruvin 53b
Way, short, to teach ...... Pesachim 3b; Chullin 63b
Ways, breadth dimensions ...... Bava Basra 100a-100b
Ways of Emorite ...... Shabbos 67a-67b; Chullin 77b-78a
Ways of Emorite, burning ...... Avodah Zarah 11a-11b
Ways of Heaven, why intervene ...... Berachos 10a
Ways, pleasant ...... Succah 32a; Gittin 59b
Ways to acquire Torah ...... Avos 6:5-6
Ways, peaceful
Ways, peaceful, non-Jews ...... Gittin 61a
Ways, peaceful, theft ...... Gittin 60b-61a
Ways, peaceful, Torah ...... Gittin 59b

We
"We are witnesses," what one holds belongs to him ...... Bava Metzia 3a
"We did not see" is not proof ...... Kesubos 23a

W

We shall do and we shall listen..Shabbos 88a

Weak animals, inspire fear in strong ones..Shabbos 77b

Weakness

Weakness after discourse, episode..Beitzah 21a

Weakness of *Kohen Gadol*..Zevachim 20a

Weakness of Sage...Yoma 71a

Wealth

   Episodes —

      Wealth from nothing, oil of Ludkiya..Menachos 85b

      Wealth kept to cause detriment..Pesachim 119a

      Wealth of Prophets...Nedarim 38a

      Wealth of Rabbi Elazar ben Azariah..Beitzah 23a

      Wealth of Rabbi Elazar ben Charsum...Yoma 35b

      Wealth, Rav Huna's blessing...Megillah 27b

      Wealth to cause detriment, Korah.................................Sanhedrin 110a; Pesachim 119a

   How —

      Wealth, honoring one's wife...Bava Metzia 59a

      Wealth, incense..Yoma 26a

      Wealth is not frequent..Gittin 30b

      Wealth of head of community...Yoma 22b

      Wealth, reward for honoring Shabbos..Shabbos 119a

      Wealth, reward for separating tithe.............Berachos 63a; Makos 23b; Shabbos 32b, 119a; Taanis 9a

      Wealth, too much is harmful..Gittin 70a

   Misc. —

      Wealth, forgetting G-d..Berachos 32a

      Wealth, how..........................Niddah 70b; Shabbos 119a; Pesachim 112a, 113a; Bava Kama 93a

      Wealth of Sages, crown..Sotah 49b

      Wealth, two tables...Berachos 5b

Wealthy

   Aggadah —

      Wealthy and poor, Torah and charity..Temurah 16a

      Wealthy by his ox, suffering...Pesachim 118a

      Wealthy denying G-d, mind cannot tolerate...Pesachim 113b

      Wealthy, happy with one's lot..Avos 4:1

      Wealthy man separating tithe, G-d proclaims...Pesachim 113a

      Wealthy, who is considered...Shabbos 25b

   Episodes —

      Wealthy men, Bonias...Eruvin 85b-86a

      Wealthy men of Babylon, curse...Zevachim 113b

      Wealthy people of Jerusalem..Gittin 56a

      Wealthy, Rav Nachman...Gittin 31b

   Wealthy women

      Wealthy women, Marta..Gittin 56a

      Wealthy women, Mechuza...Shabbos 32b-33a; Pesachim 50b

      Wealthy women, Nakdimen...Kesubos 65a, 66b

   Misc. —

      Wealthy, honoring them...Eruvin 86a

      Wealthy, receiving charity...Peah 5:4; Bava Kama 7a-7b; Chullin 130b

      Wealthy spend less..Chullin 46a; Menachos 86a

Weapons

Weapons for house of study .... Sanhedrin 82a
Weapons for hunt, impurity .... Keilim 15:6, 23:5
Weapons, selling to thieves and non-Jew .... Avodah Zarah 15b-16a
Weapons, Shabbos .... Eruvin 45a; Shabbos 62a, 63a
Weapons upon her, woman .... Avodah Zarah 25b

Wearing

Wearing, advice .... Shabbos 146b, 147b
Wearing black garments, transgression .... Chagigah 16a; Kiddushin 40a
Wearing, carrying on Shabbos .... Nedarim 55b
Wearing clothing on Shabbos, coins in garment .... Shabbos 147a
Wearing, folded garment .... Shabbos 58a, 142a, 147a
Wearing, nut in garment .... Shabbos 65b
Wearing priestly garments .... Yoma 5b-6a, 24b; Tamid 5:3
Wearing, ribbons .... Shabbos 139b
Wearing, what is considered .... Shabbos 62a; Nedarim 55b
Wearing woman's dress .... Nazir 59a

Weaver

Weaver, separating strands on Shabbos .... Shabbos 75b
Weavers, witnesses .... Shabbos 15a

Weaving machine, *muktzeh* .... Shabbos 113a

Wedding

How —

Wedding .... *see also* **Marriage**, page 390
Wedding, ash to commemorate Temple destruction .... Bava Basra 60b
Wedding at night .... Kesubos 56a
Wedding ceremony, performed according to Sages ..... Gittin 33a, 73a; Yevamos 90b; Kesubos 3a
Wedding, crown to commemorate Temple destruction .... Gittin 7a; Sotah 49a, 49b
Wedding, customs .... Berachos 50b
Wedding, father accompanied bride .... Kesubos 48b-49a; Nedarim 89a; Sanhedrin 66b
Wedding, feast .... Pesachim 49a; Succah 25b; Chullin 83a
Wedding, glass cup to commemorate Temple destruction .... Berachos 31a
Wedding, joy .... Berachos 6b; Kesubos 16b-17a; Succah 25b

Misc. —

Wedding, annulling condition of *kiddushin* .... Yevamos 107a
Wedding, died before ceremony .... Kesubos 3b-4b
Wedding gifts, mutual .... Bava Basra 144b-145b
Wedding on *Chol HaMoed* .... Moed Katan 8b-9a, 18b; Chagigah 8b
Wedding, time of ceremony .... Kesubos 2a, 3a-3b, 4b-5a, 56a

Wedding canopy

Wedding canopy, "Worth coming for this teaching" .... Berachos 16a
Wedding canopy, act of acquisition like *kiddushin* .... Kiddushin 3a, 5a-5b
Wedding canopy, annulment of condition .... Yevamos 107a
Wedding canopy at night .... Kesubos 56a
Wedding canopy for disqualified women .... Yevamos 57b-58a
Wedding canopy, girl less than three years old .... Yevamos 57b

Weeding on Shabbos .... Moed Katan 2b

Week

Week of *Tisha B'Av* .... Yevamos 43a-43b; Taanis 26b

Week of *Tisha B'Av*, laundering .... Taanis 29b
Week, until Tuesday .... Gittin 77a
Weeks of quarantine for leper .... Negaim 3:3-8
Weekly section, four parshios .... Megillah 29b, 30b
Weighing
Weighing, meat of firstborn animal .... Bechoros 31b
Weighing on Yom Tov .... Beitzah 28a
Weight, adding weight .... Bava Basra 88a-88b
Weight
Weight, missing, prohibition .... Bava Metzia 61a-61b; Bava Basra 89b-90a
Weight, missing, punishment .... Bava Basra 88b, 90b; Yevamos 21a
Weight, precision .... Bava Basra 89a-89b
Weight, sign for lost item .... Bava Metzia 23b
Welcoming Shabbos
Welcoming Shabbos by mistake .... Berachos 27b
Welcoming Shabbos, episodes .... Shabbos 119a; Bava Kama 32a-32b
Well (noun)
Well dried up, lessee .... Bava Metzia 103b
Well, flowing to utensil and pool .... Mikvaos 5:1-2
Well flowing with ever-increasing strength .... Avos 2:8
Well, expenses for digging .... Bava Basra 8a
Well from which you drank .... Bava Kama 92b
Well, immersion .... Mikvaos 1:7
Well, Miriam's merit .... Taanis 9a
Well, mixture .... Mikvaos 5:3, 5:5
Well of Miriam, Carmel .... Shabbos 35a
Well of Siloah .... Arachin 10b
Well, precedence and diverting .... Gittin 60b
Well, private, usage .... Bava Kama 81b
Well, repair expenses .... Bava Metzia 108a
Well, source of its water .... Succah 53b
Well (stream) in Temple, in the future .... Yoma 77b-78a; Menachos 98a; Sanhedrin 100a
Well (adjective)
Well done that you broke .... Shabbos 87a; Yevamos 62a; Bava Basra 14b; Menachos 99b
Well speaks and well applies .... Yevamos 63b
West, Divine Presence .... Bava Basra 25a
Wet nurse
Wet nurse, non-Jewish .... Avodah Zarah 26a
Wet nurse, paid, laws .... Kesubos 60b
Wet nurse, work of married woman .... Kesubos 59b, 61a
Wet to the point of making wet
Wet to the point of making wet, connecting foods .... Taharos 8:8-9
Wet to the point of making wet, *mikveh* .... Gittin 15b-16a; Avodah Zarah 72a
Wet to the point of making wet, urine .... Berachos 25a-25b
What
What a humble man, what a pious man! .... Berachos 6b
What a pious man, what a humble man! .... Sanhedrin 11a; Berachos 6b
What can son do so as not to sin, parable .... Berachos 32a
What can we do, saying to mourner .... Bava Kama 38a

W

What difference between these and those .... Sanhedrin 111b
What do you seek in *aggadah* .... Sanhedrin 38b, 67b; Chagigah 14a
What does *Kohen* do in cemetery .... Sanhedrin 5b
What shall I eat tomorrow .... Sotah 48b
What slave bought .... Kiddushin 23b; Pesachim 88b; Nedarim 88b
What to do to become wealthy .... Niddah 70b
What use is there in Rabbinical Decrees .... Bava Metzia 17b

Wheat
  Blessing —
    Wheat, blessing on bread cake .... Berachos 37a, 37b; Menachos 75b
    Wheat, blessing on drink .... Berachos 38a
    Wheat, blessing on whole grain .... Berachos 37a
    Wheat, mixed, blessing .... Berachos 36b-37b, 39a
  Commandments —
    Wheat among dung, meal offerings .... Menachos 69a
    Wheat, *challah* .... Menachos 70a-70b; Challah 1:1
    Wheat, communal meal offerings .... Menachos 76b
    Wheat, puffed, for children on Pesach night .... Pesachim 108b-109a
  Prohibitions —
    Wheat, absorbing forbidden substance .... Avodah Zarah 65b
    Wheat on Pesach, *kiddushin* .... Pesachim 7a, 21b
    Wheat submerged in river, *chametz* .... Pesachim 40b
    Wheat, wording of vow .... Nedarim 55a; Moed Katan 13b
  Misc. —
    Wheat, baby .... Berachos 40a
    Wheat, *chitah* and *chittim* .... Nedarim 53b
    Wheat, fell from clouds .... Menachos 69b
    Wheat fell in cloud, episode .... Menachos 69b
    Wheat he eats?, help to husband .... Yevamos 63a
    Wheat in earth, fraud .... Menachos 69a; Bava Metzia 56a
    Wheat on wound .... Kesubos 103a; Pesachim 39b
    Wheat sown, like soil .... Bava Metzia 56b-57a
    Wheat, what is included .... Challah 1:1-2; Nedarim 55a; Menachos 70a-70b

Wheel
  Wheel of poverty turns around .... Shabbos 151b
  Wheel or *mazal* revolves .... Pesachim 94b
  Wheel, ritual slaughter .... Chullin 16a
  Wheel to draw water, Shabbos .... Eruvin 104a-104b

When
  "When he comes to you, send him to me" .... Bava Kama 40a
  When, comes to explain .... Eruvin 82a; Sanhedrin 24b-25a
  When I am for myself, who am I .... Avos 1:14
  When it leaves his possession, vow .... Nedarim 42a-42b, 47a
  When it will come into his possession, consecrated item .... Arachin 20b-21a
  When will come drop of semen, righteous .... Niddah 31a
  When will it come and I perform it .... Berachos 61b
  When will you come, Messiah .... Sanhedrin 98a

Whether sons or slaves .... Bava Basra 10a

W

Whey
Whey, milk .... Chullin 113a-114a
Whey, wording of vow .... Nedarim 51b-52b
Whip of schoolteacher, parable .... Succah 29a
Whisper
Whisper for snake, Shabbos .... Sanhedrin 101a
Whisper to annul sorcery .... Pesachim 110a-110b
Whispers, cases .... Shabbos 66b, 67a; Pesachim 112b
Whispers, Emorite ways .... Shabbos 67a-67b; Chullin 77b-78a
Whispering
Whispering on Yom Kippur, episodes .... Yoma 82b-83a
Whispering to pregnant woman, Yom Kippur .... Yoma 82b
White
White geese, impure thoughts .... Berachos 20a
White geese, take people's garments .... Kesubos 85a; Gittin 73a
White hair, prohibition to tear out .... Shabbos 94b
White spot, leprous marks .... Shevuos 2a, 5b-6b; Negaim 1:1, 1:4; Shabbos 2b; Zevachim 88b
White teeth better than milk .... Kesubos 111b
Whitening girls' skin .... Shabbos 80b; Moed Katan 9b; Pesachim 42b-43b
Who
Aggadah —
Who depends on whom, small depends on big .... Taanis 7a; Bava Basra 12a
Who gives livelihood gives life .... Taanis 8b
Who is accustomed to hit .... Succah 29a
Who is rich .... Shabbos 25b
Who is wise, strong etc. .... Avos 4:1; Tamid 32a
Who moves back before whom .... Taanis 16a; Megillah 29a
Blessings —
Who creates different creatures, blessing .... Berachos 58b
Who did not make me etc., blessings .... Menachos 43b
Who did not omit .... Berachos 43b; Rosh Hashanah 11a
Who formed with justice, blessing .... Berachos 58b
Who gave of His wisdom and of His honor .... Berachos 58a
Who has kept us alive .... *see* **Shehecheyanu**, page 613
Who has thus in His world, blessing .... Berachos 58b
Who made miracle for me, blessing .... Berachos 54a-54b
Who revives the dead, meeting friend .... Berachos 58b
Who sanctified us, Rabbinical .... Shabbos 23a; Succah 46a
Misc. —
Who answered to etc., fast day .... Taanis 15a-15b, 16b-17a
Who are kings? Our Sages .... Gittin 62a
Who revealed this secret .... Shabbos 88a
Who wants life .... Avodah Zarah 19b
Whoever worked before Shabbos will eat on Shabbos .... Avodah Zarah 3a
Whole
Whole and sliced, *matzah* .... Berachos 39b
Whole food, blessing .... Berachos 39a-39b
Whole loaf, *eruv* .... Eruvin 80b
Whole, sacrifices .... Menachos 74b

Wholesaler, *demai* .... Demai 2:4-5
Why
  Why did I come, quorum .... Berachos 6b
  Why should a living man complain .... Kiddushin 80b
  Why should I involve myself in this case, judge ... Sanhedrin 6b
Why etc., answers .... Shabbos 145b
Wicked
  Aggadah —
    Wicked during their lives, dead .... Berachos 18b
    Wicked, from wicked comes wickedness .... Makos 10b
    Wicked in your own eyes .... Avos 2:13
    Wicked know they will die .... Shabbos 31b
    Wicked, nodding head .... Yevamos 121a
    Wicked prepares and righteous wears .... Bava Metzia 61b
    Wicked, telling his bad actions .... Yoma 38b
  Behavior —
    Wicked, calling someone "wicked" ... Kiddushin 28a; Bava Metzia 71a
    Wicked, do not associate with them .... Avos 1:7
    Wicked man, avoiding to provoke him ... Berachos 7b; Megillah 6b
    Wicked, one may ill-treat a man who called him "wicked" ... Bava Metziah 71a; Kiddushin 28a
  Laws —
    Wicked, cursing and hitting wicked ... Sanhedrin 85a-85b; Makos 8b
    Wicked, disqualified to testify .... Sanhedrin 25b-27b
    Wicked, looking at .... Megillah 28a
    Wicked, prohibition to praise him .... Sotah 42b
    Wicked, sacrifice accepted .... Chullin 5a; Eruvin 69b
  Reward and punishment —
    Wicked, G-d's pain at his death .... Sanhedrin 39b
    Wicked, G-d's patience .... Eruvin 22a
    Wicked, good for him to die .... Yevamos 63b
    Wicked, opening of *Gehinnom* .... Eruvin 19a
    Wicked, prosperous .... Kiddushin 40a, 40b; Berachos 7a
    Wicked, reward in this world .... Yoma 87a
    Wicked, serenity .... Avos 4:15
    Wicked who was killed, atonement .... Sanhedrin 47a-47b
    Wicked will be destroyed, Moses .... Sanhedrin 111a-111b
  Wicked men —
    Wicked, deceitful .... Sotah 21b
    Wicked good to men .... Kiddushin 40a
    Wicked, his servants .... Chullin 4b
    Wicked, Rabbinical prohibition .... Niddah 12a
    Wicked son of wicked, blame .... Sanhedrin 52a
    Wicked, vows .... Nedarim 9a, 22a, 77b
  Wicked of Jerusalem
    Wicked of Jerusalem, confidence ... Shabbos 139a; Yoma 9b
    Wicked of Jerusalem, immorality .... Shabbos 62b-63a
    Wicked of Jerusalem, prostrated themselves to sun ... Yoma 76b-77a; Kiddushin 72b; Succah 51b

W

Misc. —

Wicked, do we speak about wicked men ....Yevamos 33b
Wicked government, Edom ....Bava Basra 60b
Wicked Jew, worse than corrupted nations ....Sanhedrin 39b
Wicked, no World to Come ....Sanhedrin 104b-105a
Wicked, not called *"amcha"* ....Makos 8b; Yevamos 22b; Bava Kama 94b; Bava Metzia 48b, 62a;
....Bava Basra 4a; Sanhedrin 85a
Wicked, permission to make him work hard ....Bava Metzia 73b
Wicked, see yourself as wicked ....Niddah 30b
Wicked son of wicked, illegitimate child ....Yevamos 97b

Wicks

Wicks, flickering on Shabbos ....Shabbos 28b-29a
Wicks, *menorah* ....Shabbos 21a; Yoma 23a; Succah 51a
Wicks, Shabbos lamp ....Shabbos 20b-21a

Widow

Kohen —

Widow, doubt if permitted to *Kohen* ....Kesubos 14a; Eduyos 8:3; Kiddushin 75a
Widow, eating breast and leg of sacrifice ....Yevamos 87a
Widow to *Kohen Gadol* ....Yevamos 59a-59b, 61a

Rights —

Widow and daughter, insufficient inheritance ....Bava Basra 139b-140b; Kesubos 43a
Widow and lender, precedence ....Kesubos 84a
Widow awaiting levirate marriage, kesubah ....Kesuvos 82b
Widow, buying back her own dowry ....Yevamos 66a-67a
Widow, deducting price of garments from her *kesubah* ....Kesubos 54a
Widow, dwelling ....Kesubos 103a
Widow, exempt from oath ....Kesubos 55a
Widow, exemption from oath ....Kesubos 87a
Widow, healing expenses ....Kesubos 52b
Widow, not liable to pay for her burial ....Kesubos 48a
Widow, oath for *kesubah* ....Gittin 34b-36a
Widow, oath to be able to sell ....Kesubos 98a
Widow, redeeming ....Kesubos 52a
Widow, sale ....Kesubos 96a-97a, 98a-98b; Bava Metzia 32a
Widow who sold, warranty ....Kesubos 97a, 100a

Widow's right to alimony

Widow's right to alimony ....Kesubos 95b-96a
Widow's right to alimony, does she lose her alimony ....Kesubos 53a, 54a, 97b-98a
Widow's right to alimony, reserved field ....Kesubos 54b
Widow's right to alimony, sick man ....Bava Basra 133a
Widow's right to alimony, until when ....Kesubos 54a
Widow's right to alimony, widow awaiting levirate marriage ......Yevamos 41b; Kesubos 107b
Widow's right to alimony, widow who delayed asking for it ....Kesubos 96a

Misc. —

Widow, Abbaye, episode ....Kesubos 65a
Widow, marriage ....Pesachim 112a-112b
Widow, prohibition of seizure ....Bava Metzia 115a; Sanhedrin 21a
Widow, things forbidden because of suspicion ....Bava Metzia 71a; Avodah Zarah 22b
Widow, too friendly ....Sotah 22a

W

Widow awaiting levirate marriage
Widow awaiting levirate marriage, "I did not have relations with *yavam*" ....Yevamos 111b-112a
Widow awaiting levirate marriage, *agunah* ....Yevamos 92a-92b, 93b-94a, 114b, 118b; ....Shevuos 32b; Eduyos 1:12
Widow awaiting levirate marriage, annulling vow ....Nedarim 74a-75a; Yevamos 29b
Widow awaiting levirate marriage, burial ....Kesubos 80b-81a
Widow awaiting levirate marriage, goes to *yavam* ....Sanhedrin 31b
Widow awaiting levirate marriage, grew with brothers ....Yevamos 102b
Widow awaiting levirate marriage, how is she acquired ....Kiddushin 13b-14a; Yevamos 54a
Widow awaiting levirate marriage, married or had forbidden relations ....Gittin 80b; ....Yevamos 81a, 92b, 96a; Sotah 18b
Widow awaiting levirate marriage, of father ....Yevamos 4a
Widow awaiting levirate marriage, *sotah* ....Sotah 23b-24a, 25a, 26a; Yevamos 58a-58b; ....Kiddushin 27b
Widow awaiting levirate marriage, *terumah* ....Yevamos 56a, 58b; Kesubos 58a
Widow eating *terumah*
Widow eating *terumah*, disqualified to *Kohanim* ....Yevamos 57b-58a
Widow eating *terumah*, disqualifying persons ....Yevamos 67b-68a
Widow eating *terumah*, general ....Yevamos 86b-87b
Widow eating *terumah*, grandson ....Yevamos 70a
Widow eating *terumah*, illegitimate child ....Yevamos 70a
Widow eating *terumah*, offspring ....Yevamos 70a
Widow eating *terumah*, who ....Yevamos 86b-87b
Wife ....see also **Married woman**, page 391
Bad wives —
Wife curses him, poverty ....Shabbos 62b
Wife, dominating ....Beitzah 32b
Wife dominating, prayer not answered ....Bava Metzia 75b
Wife forbidden, distinctive sign made by relatives ....Kiddushin 70a, 70b; Kesubos 28b
Wife, husband's demand for modesty ....Gittin 90a-90b
Wife transgressing law, divorce ....Sotah 25a
Wife, bad
Wife, bad, divorce her ....Gittin 90a-90b; Yevamos 63b
Wife, bad, embitters his life ....Bava Basra 145b; Sanhedrin 100b
Wife, bad, his life is no life ....Beitzah 32b
Wife, bad, husband's distress ....Yevamos 63a-63b
Wife, bad, leprosy ....Yevamos 63b; Sanhedrin 100b
Wife, bad, suffering ....Eruvin 41b
Wife, bad, worse than anything ....Shabbos 11a
Closeness —
Wife, accepting her advice ....Bava Metzia 59a
Wife, blessing is found thanks to her ....Bava Metzia 59a
Wife, excessive conversation ....Chagigah 5b
Wife, honoring her greatly ....Bava Metzia 59a; Sanhedrin 76b; Chullin 84b
Wife, importance of loving her ....Sanhedrin 76b
Wife, midget, take her advice ....Bava Metzia 59a
Wife, not to reveal one's secret ....Sanhedrin 100b

W

Commandments —
Wife for one's son, *mitzvah* .... Kiddushin 30b
Wife, her husband cheers her .... Kiddushin 34b; Rosh Hashanah 6b
Wife of father, honor .... Kesubos 103a
Wife of *Kohen Gadol*, Yom Kippur .... Yoma 13a-13b
Wife of Sage, standing before her .... Shevuos 30b

Death —
Wife, cause of death .... Sanhedrin 22a; Rosh Hashanah 6a; Zevachim 29b
Wife deceased, her husband's pain .... Sanhedrin 22a-22b
Wife died, when can husband remarry .... Moed Katan 23a
Wives, widows .... Bava Metzia 38b

Episodes —
Wife, "my home" .... Shabbos 118b; Gittin 52a
Wife, "your wife is my wife," slander .... Shabbos 30b
Wife amputated, episode .... Shabbos 53b
Wife committed adultery, episode .... Kiddushin 66a
Wife of Korah and On ben Peles .... Sanhedrin 109b-110a
Wife of Lot, blessing .... Berachos 54b
Wife of Lot, impurity .... Niddah 70b
Wife of Potiphar .... Sotah 36b; Shabbos 49b; Yoma 35b

Forbidden relations —
Wife of brother, marriage by mistake .... Yevamos 95b
Wife of father, forbidden relations .... Sanhedrin 53a-54a
Wife of father, his children's enemy .... Yevamos 63b; Berachos 56a
Wife of minor, how .... Kiddushin 19a; Sanhedrin 52b
Wife of non-Jew, not liable .... Sanhedrin 52b
Wives exchanged at wedding .... Yevamos 33b

Levirate marriage —
Wife of brother, during his life .... Yevamos 9a-9b, 17a-17b, 18b-19b
Wife of two dead men, levirate marriage .... Yevamos 31b-32a, 96b; Gittin 43b, 82b
Wife of two dead men, maidservant .... Gittin 43a-43b

Marriage —
Wife, first, divorce .... Sanhedrin 22a; Gittin 90b
Wife, husband trustworthy about her lineage .... Kiddushin 79b-80a
Wife, man does not accept her blemishes .... Kesubos 75b-76a
Wives, they give their wives away .... Gittin 84a

Righteous' wives —
Wife of Elazar, lineage .... Sotah 43a
Wife of Rabbi Akiva .... Nedarim 50a; Kesubos 62b-63a
Wife of Rabbi Chanina .... Kesubos 62b
Wife of Rabbi Chanina, chest .... Bava Basra 74a-74b
Wife of Rabbi Chiya, sterility .... Yevamos 65b
Wife of Rabbi Meir, Bruriah .... Eruvin 53b; Pesachim 62b
Wife of Rav Ashi .... Beitzah 29b
Wife of Rav Pappa, "I shall not be supported" .... Sanhedrin 14b
Wife of Turnus Rufus, Rabbi Akiva .... Avodah Zarah 20a
Wives of David .... Sanhedrin 19b, 21a
Wives of Solomon .... Shabbos 56b; Sanhedrin 21b
Wives of tribes .... Pesachim 50a

Wife of scholar
Wife of scholar, standing before .... Shevuos 30b
Wife of scholar, tax collector .... Bechoros 30b
Wife of scholar, trustworthy .... Avodah Zarah 39a

Rights —
Wife, her rights parallel to which husband's rights .... Kesubos 47b
Wife, proxy .... Gittin 48b
Wife, support, vowed she will not benefit from him .... Kesubos 70b-71a
Wife, supporting them according to their standing .... Kesubos 48a, 61a
Wife, vow .... Kesubos 86b

Shabbos —
Wife, first, happiness .... Sanhedrin 22a-22b; Yevamos 63b
Wife, good-looking, advantage .... Berachos 57b
Wife helps her husband .... Yevamos 63a

Misc. —
Wife, act of acquisition for *eruv* .... Nedarim 88b; Eruvin 79b
Wife of *Kohen* .... *see* **Koheness**, page 348
Wife of youth .... Sanhedrin 22a
Wife, pregnant, prayers .... Berachos 60a
Wives of Sages, reward .... Yoma 77a

Wife like oneself
Wife like oneself, reading *Shema* .... Berachos 24a
Wife like oneself, right to compensation for shame .... Kesubos 65b-66a
Wife like oneself, trustworthy .... Bechoros 35b

Wife's property
Wife's property .... *see also* **Profits, wife's property**, page 391
Wife's property, are divorced without receiving kesubah .... Kesubos 101a
Wife's property, as borrower or as lessee .... Bava Metzia 96a-96b
Wife's property, concealing .... Kesubos 78b-79a; Bava Basra 151a a150b
Wife's property, expenses .... Kesubos 79b-80a; Bava Metzia 39a
Wife's property, selling for profits .... Kesubos 80a-80b
Wife's property, waiving his right to .... Bava Basra 49a-49b

Wig
Wig, city led to idolatry .... Sanhedrin 112a; Arachin 7b
Wig, dead woman .... Arachin 7b
Wig, Shabbos .... Shabbos 64b

Wild
Wild animal .... *see* **Beast**, page 46
Wild ox, fat and covering of blood .... Chullin 80a

Wild donkey
Wild donkey, episode about punishment .... Chullin 127a
Wild donkey, greatness of G-d's works .... Chullin 127a
Wild donkey, Rabbi Chanina ben Dosa .... Berachos 33a
Wild donkey, work .... Avodah Zarah 16b

Will
Will, giving more to one son .... Bava Basra 129a-131a; Yevamos 36b
Will of *beis din*, conversion .... Kesubos 11a
Will of Canaan to his sons .... Pesachim 113b
Will of husband, episode .... Nedarim 66b

Will of Rebbi......Kesubos 103a-103b
Will, So and so will inherit him......Bava Basra 128b-131a, 133a
Will to disinherit, not recommended......Bava Basra 133b
Wills, ethical, from Sages......Berachos 28b
Wills, Rabbi Banaah......Bava Basra 58a-58b

Willful transgression
Willful transgression like unintentional, ignoramus......Bava Metzia 33b
Willful transgressions like merits......Yoma 86b
Willful transgressions like unintentional, repentance......Yoma 36b

Willow
Willow and poplar, exchanging names......Shabbos 36a; Succah 34a
Willow, definition......Succah 33b-34a
Willow, dimension......Succah 32b
Willow, *Hoshana Rabba*......Succah 34a, 43b-44b; Taanis 3a; Moed Katan 3b; Zevachim 110b
Willow, how many......Succah 34b
Willow, importance of Israel......Succah 34a
Willows of Motza......Succah 45a

Wind
Scientific facts —
Winds, after rain......Taanis 3b
Winds, do not cease......Taanis 3b; Avodah Zarah 10b
Winds, fierce......Berachos 59a
Winds, harm and benefit......Bava Basra 25a-25b; Gittin 31b-32a
Winds, rain and yield......Bava Basra 147a
Misc. —
Wind blowing, fatal danger......Bava Metzia 107b
Wind, episode about wind blowing......Bava Metzia 86a
Wind hastened death of slaughtered man......Yevamos 120b-121a
Wind helping, damages from fire......Bava Kama 60a H
Wind, mentioning in prayer......Berachos 33a; Taanis 3a-3b
Wind, unusual, damage......Bava Kama 29a
Wind, usual, partition......Succah 24b-25a
Wind, usual, succah......Succah 23a
Winds, blessing......Berachos 59a
Winds, parable for Israel......Taanis 3b; Avodah Zarah 10b
Winds, smoke of Altar......Bava Basra 147a; Yoma 21b
Wind, northern
Wind, northern, at night......Yevamos 72a
Wind, northern, blows with all other winds......Bava Basra 25a-26b
Wind, northern, desert......Yevamos 72a
Wind, northern, learning......Eruvin 65a; Megillah 28b

Window
Window, blocking on Shabbos......Shabbos 125b-126b; Eruvin 44a; Succah 27b
Window, *chazakah*......Bava Basra 59a, 60a
Window, connecting domains......Eruvin 76a, 76b
Window, damage done by sight......Bava Basra 2b, 59b
Window of tent of corpse, boarding up......Bava Basra 19b-20b
Window, tent of corpse......Eruvin 30a; Oholos 3:6-7, 13:1-4a
Windows in Temple, not for light......Menachos 86b

W

Windows, place for prayer..Berachos 31a, 34b

Windpipe
Windpipe and gullet, became loose..Chullin 42b, 44a, 53b
Windpipe and gullet, torn...Chullin 20a-20b
Windpipe, cases of *treifah*..Chullin 44a-45a, 54b
Windpipe, heart, lung, liver, *treifah*...Chullin 45a, 45b
Windpipe, including all internal organs, liver...Chullin 110b
Windpipe, needle...Chullin 48b-49a
Windpipe, *neveilah*...Chullin 32a-32b
Windpipe of bird, slaughter...Chullin 28a-28b
Windpipe, of Rava, oath...Nedarim 25a; Shevuos 29a
Windpipe, place of slaughtering...Chullin 18a-19a, 45a
Windpipe stuck to cheek, *treifah*...Chullin 43b-44b

Wine   *see also* **Drunkenness**, page 182
Aggadah —
Wine goes in, secret comes out..Eruvin 65a; Sanhedrin 38a
Wine for righteous, damage...Sanhedrin 72a
Wine is absorbed, oil floats...Sanhedrin 104b
Wine is offered by host and we thank the waiter..Bava Kama 92b
Wine is strong, sleep drives it away...Bava Basra 10a
Wine, kept for the future...Berachos 34b; Sanhedrin 99a
Wine, non-Jew fearing to touch it...Avodah Zarah 61b
Wine, scream...Yoma 76b
Wine spilled, blessing...Eruvin 65a-65b
Wine, Torah...Taanis 7a-7b

Benefit —
Wine, appetite...Berachos 35b; Pesachim 107b-108a
Wine, cure...Bava Basra 58b
Wine for woman...Kesubos 64b-65a
Wine, joy...Berachos 35b
Wine, quick-wittedness..............................Sanhedrin 70a; Bava Basra 12b; Yoma 76b
Wine, satiates...Berachos 35b; Succah 49b
Wine to produce milk, nursing woman...Kesubos 65b
Wine, too much is harmful...Gittin 70a

Commandments —
Wine, before execution...Sanhedrin 43a
Wine, blessing...Berachos 35b, 42a-42b, 59b; Bava Basra 95b-96a
Wine, discharging another by one's blessing..Berachos 43a
Wine for *havdala*, destined to World to Come..Pesachim 113a
Wine for *kiddush*...Bava Basra 97a-97b
Wine for Pesach night...Pesachim 99b, 108a-108b
Wine on Purim...Megillah 7b
Wine, rejoicing on Yom Tov...Pesachim 109a
Wine to mourner...Sanhedrin 70a; Eruvin 65a
Wine to Sage, libations..Yoma 71a
Wine, washing hands...Zevachim 22a; Berachos 50b

Wine for *Bircas HaMazon*
Wine for *Bircas HaMazon*, drinking..Succah 49b
Wine for *Bircas HaMazon*, forty gold coins..Chullin 87a

Wine for *Bircas HaMazon,* general .... Berachos 51a-51b
Wine for *Bircas HaMazon,* generous man .... Sotah 38b
Wine for *Bircas HaMazon,* how .... Pesachim 105b-106a, 107a; Berachos 50b, 51a-51b
Wine for *Bircas HaMazon,* requirement .... Berachos 52a; Pesachim 105b, 117b

Wine for libations

Wine for libations, congealed in subterranean holes .... Meilah 11b; Succah 49a-49b
Wine for libations, forty days .... Eduyos 6:1
Wine for libations offered to Altar .... Zevachim 91b-92a; Menachos 104a-104b
Wine for libations offered to Altar, how .... Zevachim 91b-92a
Wine for libations offered to Altar, quantity .... Menachos 104a-104b
Wine for libations, preparing and examining .... Menachos 86b-87a
Wine for libations, taste of fig .... Bechoros 17a
Wine for libations, uncovered .... Succah 50a
Wine for libations, which is fit .... Bava Basra 97a-97b; Menachos 86b-87a

Episodes —

Wine, emperor's daughter .... Nedarim 50b; Taanis 7a-7b
Wine for blessing, Yalta .... Berachos 51b
Wine for *kiddush,* episodes .... Megillah 27b
Wine from apples, Rebbi .... Avodah Zarah 40b
Wine, new on Shavuos .... Bava Basra 146a
Wine of Judea and Edom .... Pesachim 42b
Wine of Rav Huna turned sour .... Berachos 5b
Wine of swindler, *kiddushin* .... Bava Metzia 101b
Wine, Jethro's offspring .... Bava Basra 91b

Monetary matters —

Wine, "this wine," commitment to buy .... Bava Metzia 73b-74a
Wine at virgin's wedding .... Kesubos 16b
Wine, fraud .... Bava Metzia 59b-60a
Wine, liability of seller .... Bava Basra 96a-96b, 97b-98a
Wine on market day .... Bava Metzia 99b
Wine, supporting one's wife .... Kesubos 64b-65a
Wine, trade .... Pesachim 113a
Wine, wordings of sale .... Bava Basra 93b-94a, 95a-95b, 97b

Prohibitions —

Wine and oil, remedies on Shabbos .... Shabbos 134b
Wine and vinegar, remedies on Shabbos .... Shabbos 109a
Wine becoming sour, *terumah* .... Bava Basra 96a; Kiddushin 79a; Niddah 2b
Wine, impurity and susceptibility to become impure .... Pesachim 33b, 34b; Shabbos 144b-145a
Wine in non-Jew's cup, *muktzeh* .... Beitzah 21b
Wine, judges for capital cases .... Sanhedrin 42a
Wine of *mitzvah, nazir* .... Nazir 3b-4a, 5a, 44a
Wine of oath, *nazir* .... Nazir 4a
Wine, priestly blessing .... Taanis 26b-27a
Wine, uncovered .... Avodah Zarah 30a-30b, 31b; Chullin 9a-10a; Shabbos 128b; Bava Kama 115b;
.... Succah 50a; Bava Basra 97b
Wine, when ruling .... Eruvin 64b; Krisos 13b; Kesubos 10b

Quality —

Wine congealed .... Succah 12a
Wine, diluted in water .... Berachos 50b; Shabbos 76b-77a; Eruvin 29b; Bava Basra 96b; Niddah 19a

Wine, fate......Bava Basra 98a
Wine for sprg......Bava Kama 115b; Pesachim 20b
Wine, old......Pesachim 42b; Bava Basra 98a-98b
Wine, smell of fig......Bechoros 17a
Wine sold in store......Bava Basra 95b-96a

Misc. —

Wine and alcohol, how to drink......Berachos 51a
Wine and vinegar, two types......Bava Basra 84a-84b
Wine, bones of deceased......Niddah 24b
Wine, drunkenness......Yoma 74b-75a; Sanhedrin 70a; Berachos 29b
Wine from residues, connection to *mikveh*......Chullin 25b-26a Pesachim 42b Maasros 5:6;
......Maaser Sheni 1:3; Bava Basra 96b-97a Maasros 5:6
Wine from residues, tithes......Maasros 5:6; Pesachim 42b; Bava Basra 97a; Chullin 25b
Wine, helps thinking......Eruvin 65a
Wine, numerical value......Eruvin 65a; Sanhedrin 38a
Wine, proper manners in drinking......Pesachim 86b; Beitzah 25b
Wine, song......Berachos 35a; Arachin 11a, 12a

Wine for *nazir*

Wine for *nazir*, prohibitions......Nazir 34a-35a, 38b-39a
Wine of *nazir*, permission of profit......Pesachim 23a
Wine of *nazir*, quantity......Nazir 38b

Wine of idolaters

How —

Wine of idolaters, cases of doubt......Bava Basra 24a
Wine of idolaters, doubts about touch......Avodah Zarah 70a-70b
Wine of idolaters, moved indirectly by non-Jew......Avodah Zarah 60a, 58b
Wine of idolaters, non-Jew left alone, how much time......Avodah Zarah 69b
Wine of idolaters, non-Jew left alone with wine......Avodah Zarah 60b, 61b, 69a-70a
Wine of idolaters, poured as libation not in presence of idol......Avodah Zarah 59b
Wine of idolaters, pouring......Avodah Zarah 60a, 72b
Wine of idolaters, pouring to throw away......Avodah Zarah 33a
Wine of idolaters, pressing......Avodah Zarah 56b
Wine of idolaters, serving......Avodah Zarah 58a-58b
Wine of idolaters, shaking without intention......Avoda Zarah 57b-58a
Wine of idolaters, touched by non-Jew......Avodah Zarah 55a-56b, 71b, 72b
Wine of idolaters, touching......Avodah Zarah 56b-57a, 59b-61a, 72a-73a
Wine of idolaters, touching to preserve......Avodah Zarah 60b
Wine of idolaters, touching unintentionally......Avodah Zarah 56b-58b, 59b

Prohibitions —

Wine of idolaters, concern of mixture......Avodah Zarah 31b-32a
Wine of idolaters, containers......Avodah Zarah 32a, 33a-34a
Wine of idolaters, impurity......Avodah Zarah 30b-31a
Wine of idolaters, mixture......Avodah Zarah 49b, 56b, 73a-74a
Wine of idolaters, sold to who made it forbidden......Avodah Zarah 59b
Wine of idolaters, throwing to Dead Sea......Avodah Zarah 49b
Wine of idolaters to non-Jew, sale......Avodah Zarah 65b, 71a-71b, 72b

Who —

Wine of idolaters, Cutheans......Avodah Zarah 31a-31b
Wine of idolaters, renegade......Chullin 13a

Wine of idolaters, resident non-Jew .... Avodah Zarah 64b
Wine of idolaters, slave and child .... Avodah Zarah 57a-57b
Misc. —
Wine of idolaters, decree .... Avodah Zarah 36b
Wine of idolaters, fearing to touch it .... Avodah Zarah 61b
Wine of idolaters, *kashering* wine press .... Avodah Zarah 60b, 74b-75a; Niddah 65a-65b
Wine of idolaters, seal .... Avodah Zarah 29b-30a
Wine of idolaters, source .... Avodah Zarah 29b
Wine of idolaters, twelve months .... Avodah Zarah 34a-34b
Wine press
Wine press, episode about *kashering* .... Avodah Zarah 74b
Wine press, *kashering* .... Avodah Zarah 60b, 74b-75a; Niddah 65a-65b
Wine press, purity .... Avodah Zarah 75a-75b; Taharos 10:8
Wine press, requirement to give tithe .... Eruvin 99b; Maasros 4:4; Shabbos 11b
Wing
Wing, hole in lung .... Chullin 57a
Wings of dove, *tefillin* .... Shabbos 49a, 130a
Wings of righteous, future .... Sanhedrin 92b
Winning in dispute, punishment for disciple who rejoiced .... Menachos 68b
Winnowing
Winnowing, blowing on cereal peel to separate it from kernel .... Beitzah 12b-14a
Winnowing, work in itself .... Shabbos 73b
Winter, seasons .... Bava Metzia 106b
Wiping
Wiping after bodily needs, how .... Berachos 55a, 62a; Shabbos 81a, 82a
Wiping after bodily needs, Shabbos .... Shabbos 81a-81b; Succah 36b; Bava Kama 81b
Wiping clean, *kashering* wine container .... Avodah Zarah 74b-75a; Niddah 65b
Wiping face, cure .... Shabbos 133b-134a
Wiping in fellow's garment .... Bava Metzia 24a
Wiping out Amalek .... Megillah 7a; Bava Basra 21a-21b
Wiping with clay, sorcery .... Shabbos 82a
Wiping with clay utensil, intentionally .... Shabbos 81b
Wiping with reed .... Chullin 16b
Wisdom
Wisdom, "I am wisdom" .... Sotah 21b
Wisdom, "say to wisdom you are my sister" .... Shabbos 145b; Sanhedrin 7b
Wisdom and not work .... Shabbos 117b, 131b; Rosh Hashanah 29b
Wisdom and understanding, in Creation .... Chagigah 12a; Berachos 55a
Wisdom, cunning .... Sotah 21b
Wisdom gives life to Sage .... Yoma 83b
Wisdom, Greek, episode .... Sotah 49b; Bava Kama 82b; Menachos 64b
Wisdom, Greek, prohibition .... Bava Kama 82b-83a; Menachos 99b
Wisdom illuminates man's face .... Nedarim 49b
Wisdom in *Eretz Yisrael* .... Bava Basra 158b
Wisdom, more powerful than ten rulers .... Nedarim 32b
Wisdom of captives .... Sanhedrin 104a-104b
Wisdom of Jews, non-Jews .... Chagigah 5b
Wisdom of Rebbi, saw Rabbi Meir from behind .... Eruvin 13b
Wisdom of Solomon .... Eruvin 21b

W

Wisdom of women, in their spindle .... Yoma 66b

Wisdom of women, On ben Peles .... Sanhedrin 109b-110a

Wisdom, repentance and good deeds .... Berachos 17a

Wisdom, to wise man .... Berachos 40a, 55a; Succah 46a-46b

Wise

Wise and humble .... Sanhedrin 88b

Wise man better than prophet .... Bava Basra 12a-12b

Wise man understanding by himself .... Chagigah 13a

Wise of heart will take commandments .... Sotah 13a

Wise or foolish, fetus .... Niddah 16b

Wise, seven things .... Avos 5:7

Wise, who is .... Shabbos 114a

With

With all your soul .... Berachos 61b; Pesachim 25a; Yoma 82a; Sanhedrin 74a

With my sword and my bow .... Bava Basra 123a

Withholding worker's salary .... Bava Metzia 61a, 111a

Witness

Disqualified —

Witness from witness, *agunah* .... Yevamos 87b, 122a; Shabbos 145a-145b; Bechoros 46b

Witness from witness, firstborn .... Shabbos 145a-145b; Bechoros 36a

Witness, plotting, from when is he disqualified .... Bava Kama 72b-73a; Sanhedrin 27a

Witness thief, episode .... Sanhedrin 27a-27b

Witness, third witness disqualified .... Makos 5b-6a; Bava Basra 160b, 114a; Sanhedrin 9a-9b, 41b

Witnesses accomplished their mission .... Gittin 63b

How —

Witnesses about monetary matters, examination .... Sanhedrin 2b-3a, 30b-31a, 32a-32b;

.... Yevamos 122b

Witnesses, contradicting during examination .... Sanhedrin 41a

Witnesses, examination .... Sanhedrin 9b, 29a, 30b-31a, 32a-32b, 40a-40b, 41b, 81b; Pesachim 12a

Legal documents —

Witness, disqualified after having signed .... Bava Basra 159a-159b

Witness, disqualified, signed on legal document .... Bava Basra 162b; Gittin 18b, 87b

Witness, in writing and verbal .... Bava Basra 165a-165b

Witnesses, "we were forced to sign" .... Kesubos 18b-19a

Witnesses, appeal on contract .... Kesubos 19b

Witnesses, contract on condition .... Kesubos 19b

Witnesses of legal document, attest invalidity .... Bava Basra 48b-49a; Kesubos 19b

Witnesses of transfer and signature .... Gittin 23a, 26a, 3a-4a, 86b

Witnesses on legal documents, reading .... Gittin 19b

Witnesses, signature on divorce certificate .... Gittin 9b, 10a-10b, 11b, 18b-19a, 36a, 86b-88a

Witnesses signed, as if examined by judges .... Kesubos 18b; Gittin 3a

Witnesses who do not know how to sign .... Gittin 9b, 19a-19b

Witnesses on attestation of legal document

Witnesses on attestation of legal document, minor .... Kesubos 28a

Witnesses on attestation of legal document, relative .... Bava Basra 57a

Witnesses on attestation of legal document, who .... Bava Metzia 20b

False —

Witness, one like two, denying .... Yevamos 88b, 117b; Sotah 31b-32a, 47b; Kesubos 22b

Witnesses, conspiring .... *see* **Conspiring witnesses**, page 125

W

Witnesses, false, despised .... Sanhedrin 29a
Witnesses, two like a hundred .... Shevuos 42a
Witnesses who were refuted, lashes .... Bava Kama 74b

Monetary matters —
Witness becomes judge .... Gittin 5b; Rosh Hashanah 25b-26a; Kesubos 21b; Bava Kama 90b;
.... Bava Basra 114a; Sanhedrin 34b
Witness or judge, bequest .... Bava Basra 113b-114a; Sanhedrin 34b
Witnesses, "do not pay me" .... Shevuos 41a-41b
Witnesses about loan, requirement .... Bava Metzia 75b
Witnesses are present, oath not trusted .... Bava Metzia 83a
Witnesses, armless, death .... Sanhedrin 45b
Witnesses, designated, acknowledgment .... Sanhedrin 29a-29b
Witnesses testifying about part of sum, oath .... Bava Metzia 3a-4a, 5a
Witnesses vs. *migo* .... Bava Basra 31a, 33b

Misc. —
"Witnesses we are," against *migo* .... Bava Metzia 81b; Kesubos 27b; Bechoros 36a
Witness, single .... *see* **Single witness**, page 629
Witnesses about seclusion, intimate relations .... Gittin 73b, 81b; Eduyos 4:7
Witnesses concealed, inciter to idolatry .... Sanhedrin 67a
Witnesses in capital cases, threat .... Sanhedrin 32b, 37a-37b
Witnesses in east .... Kiddushin 12b; Kesubos 23a; Bava Basra 135a
Witnesses, only to prevent a lie .... Kiddushin 65b
Witnesses who made a mistake, requirement to bring sacrifice .... Yevamos 87b

Woe
Episodes —
Woe, Noah's drunkenness .... Sanhedrin 70a
Woe that I gave my bread to an ignoramus .... Bava Basra 8a
Woe that it should happen in my days .... Taanis 24b
Woe to me because of powerful men .... Pesachim 57a
Woe to me that I used the crown of Torah .... Nedarim 62a
Woe to that shame .... Bava Basra 75a
Woe to us who have seen you thus .... Taanis 21a

Eulogies —
Woe about those who were lost .... Sanhedrin 111a
Woe good man!, eulogy .... Berachos 16b
Woe to ship which lost its captain .... Bava Basra 91a-91b
Woe to world whose leader died .... Bava Basra 91a-91b

Misc. —
"Woe to monetary loss" .... Bava Metzia 23a
Woe that I swore, exile .... Bava Basra 74a
Woe to complainer more than to victim of complaint .... Bava Kama 93a
Woe to his father who taught him Torah .... Yoma 86a
Woe to his wife and her sister .... Yevamos 29a, 109a
Woe to idolaters who do not know what they lost .... Succah 55b
Woe to man whose children are girls .... Kiddushin 82b
Woe to me from my Creator .... Berachos 61a
Woe to men for the disgrace of Torah .... Avos 6:2
Woe to sons exiled from their father's table .... Berachos 3a
Woe to wicked, this world .... Yoma 87a

W

Woe to wicked, woe to his neighbor..Succah 56b

Wolf

Wolf and lion etc., killing..Sanhedrin 15b

Wolf, swallowed dead and evacuated him................................Taanis 22b; Menachos 69b

Wolves, paid custodian..Bava Metzia 41a, 93b, 106a

Woman................................*see also* **Looking at women**, page 377, **Thought**, page 311

Aggadah —

Women, causes of death..Shabbos 31b-32a

Women, get up early..Chagigah 12b

Women, how do they gain merit................................Berachos 17a; Sotah 21a

Women, promise..Berachos 17a

Women punished by lashes, parable................................Yoma 86b

Women, righteous, redemption from Egypt................................Sotah 11a

Women, run after them..Shabbos 152a

Women, tranquil, promise..Berachos 17a

Bad women —

Woman, bad, husband's life is bad................................Bava Basra 145b; Sanhedrin 100b

Woman, bad, leprosy..Yevamos 63b; Sanhedrin 100b

Women, haughty..Megillah 14b

Beauty —

Woman, beautiful, Ben Sira..Yevamos 63b

Woman, how to beautify herself................................Shabbos 80b; Kesubos 59b

Woman's purpose is etc...Kesubos 59b; Taanis 31a

Women, beauty and lineage..Taanis 31a; Kesubos 59b

Women, for beauty, children, etc.................................Kesubos 59b; Taanis 31a

Characteristics —

Woman, greater understanding..Niddah 45b

Woman, her ability in her spindle..Yoma 66b

Woman, large like storehouse..Berachos 61a

Woman, reason of certain traits..Niddah 31b

Woman shouts, when no food at home................................Temurah 16a

Woman understands guests' character................................Berachos 10b

Woman, visits her relatives..Yevamos 26a

Woman, wears her weapons on her................................Avodah Zarah 25b; Yevamos 115a

Women are easily swayed, "*daatan kalos*"................................Kiddushin 80b; Shabbos 33b

Women are talkative..Berachos 48b

Women, character traits..Megillah 14b

Women, guests..Berachos 10b; Bava Metzia 87a

Women hating one another..Yevamos 117a

Women, limbs..Bechoros 45a

Women, people apart..Shabbos 62a

Women, zealous, parable..Chagigah 12b

Commandments —

Women, blowing of *shofar*..Rosh Hashanah 33a

Women, commandments of Pesach................................Pesachim 43a-43b; Megillah 91b

Women, exempt from redeeming son................................Kiddushin 29a

Women, exempt from sons' commandments................................Kiddushin 29a-29b

Women, honoring father and mother................................Kiddushin 30b

Women, *kiddush*..Shevuos 20b; Berachos 20b

W

Women, *megillah* reading..Megillah 4a
Women, permission for tithe..Yevamos 86a
Women, Pesach lamb..Pesachim 79b, 91a-91b; Sanhedrin 12b
Women, positive commandments............Berachos 20a-20b; Kiddushin 33b-35a; Eruvin 27a, 96a-96b
Women, *semichah*...................Chagigah 16b; Eruvin 96b; Rosh Hashanah 33a; Kiddushin 36a; Chullin 85a
Women, source for commandments and punishments.............Kiddushin 35a-35b; Bava Kama 15a;
....Pesachim 43a; Succah 28a-28b; Yevamos 84b; Temurah 2b; Niddah 48b
Women, *tefillin*..Eruvin 96a-96b
Women, Torah learning..Sotah 21b
Women, *tzitzis*...Menachos 43a; Succah 11a
Women, waving sacrifice...Menachos 61a-61b

Distance —
Women, contact prohibited..Shabbos 13a; Avodah Zarah 17a
Women, distance...Kiddushin 70a-70b, 81b-82a
Women, forbidden jobs..Kiddushin 82a
Women, her son in front of her...Sanhedrin 19a
Women, partition to separate...Kiddushin 81a; Succah 51b
Women, passing between them..Pesachim 111a
Women, *Simchas Beis Hashoevah*...Succah 51b-52a; Middos 2:5
Women, toilets..Sanhedrin 19a
Women, walking behind women..Berachos 61a; Eruvin 18b

Episodes —
Woman cursed Rava..Bava Basra 153a
Woman, episode about Sage's mistake...Bava Basra 167b-168a
Woman, one-armed, episode...Shabbos 53b
Woman whose two husbands died, episode of Abbaye.........................Yevamos 64b
Women, bad, stories...Yevamos 63b; Sanhedrin 22b
Women, beautiful women in Tanach....................Megillah 15a; Bava Basra 58a; Sanhedrin 39b
Women in tent, Matriarchs...Sanhedrin 105b
Women of Mechuza, theft..Shabbos 32b-33a
Women of Shachnetziv, eulogy..Moed Katan 28b
Women, signs of puberty...Niddah 47a-49a

Forbidden —
Woman, "*katlonis*"...Kesubos 43b; Yevamos 26a, 64b
Woman sinned with to animal, *Kohen Gadol*...Yevamos 59b
Woman forbidden to *Kohen*, her prohibition..Yevamos 85a
Woman, permitted to husband and not to *yavam*.............................Yevamos 84a-84b
Woman whose two husbands died, marriage...............Kesubos 43b; Yevamos 26a, 64b
Women forbidden, negative commandment, *kiddushin*.................Kiddushin 64a, 68a;
................Yevamos 10b, 23a, 52b, 69a, 92a-92b; Kesubos 29b-30a; Sotah 18b; Sanhedrin 53a; Temurah 29b
Women forbidden to *Kohen Gadol*..Yevamos 59b-60a
Women, king...Sanhedrin 21a

Immorality —
Woman, immoral, turns over..Kesubos 37a; Yevamos 35a
Woman sinning with animal, to *Kohen Gadol*..Yevamos 59b
Woman suspected of adultery..*see* **Sotah**, page 646
Woman unmarried, lineage of her fetus...Kiddushin 74a
Woman, unmarried, prohibition of intimate relations................................Sanhedrin 76a
Women whose husbands were exchanged...Yevamos 34a

Impurity —

Woman having blood flow .... *see **Zavah**, page 775*
Woman having no menses .... Niddah 12b, 39a
Woman, sprinkling and sanctification .... Yevamos 72b; Parah 5:4; Yoma 43a; Arachin 3a
Women, differences for leprous woman .... Krisos 8b
Women, leprosy and *nezirus* .... Sotah 23b; Arachin 3a; Krisos 8b
Women, leprous mark, *nesek* .... Kiddushin 35b

Marriage —

Woman .... *see also **Marriage**, page 390; **Wife**, page 745*
Woman does not lie, divorce .... Kesubos 22b, 23a; Yevamos 116a; Nedarim 91a; Gittin 64b, 89b
Woman, one-armed, *chalitzah* .... Yevamos 105a
Woman vowing to be forbidden to her deceased husband's brother ..... Yevamos 112a-112b
Woman whose husband is missing .... *see **Agunah**, page 15*
Women, agent for divorce certificate .... Gittin 62b
Women hating one another, *agunah* .... Yevamos 117a-118a, 119b-120a

Monetary matters —

Woman and property, claims .... Kiddushin 65b
Woman, *beis din* .... Gittin 41a
Woman injured by stick, *kesubah* .... Kesubos 11a-12a, 13a
Woman like her husband, testimony .... Sanhedrin 28a-28b
Woman, order of inheritance .... Bava Basra 113a-113b, 115a
Woman transgressing law, *kesubah* .... Kesubos 72a-72b; Sotah 25a
Women, *chazakah* .... Bava Basra 50b-51a
Women, disqualified for testimony .... Shevuos 30a
Women, sale .... Kesubos 50a, 78a-78b; Bava Kama 88a-88b
Women, source for monetary laws .... Kiddushin 35a-35b; Bava Kama 15a

Praise —

Woman, "I did not find in all these" .... Gittin 45a
Woman, "I lost blessing" .... Shabbos 25b
Woman, assistance to her husband .... Yevamos 63a
Woman, good, advantage .... Yevamos 63b; Bava Basra 145b; Sanhedrin 100b
Woman, good-looking, advantage .... Sanhedrin 100b
Woman, pious, brings wealth .... Shabbos 25b
Women, honoring their husband .... Megillah 12b; Kiddushin 31a; Krisos 28a
Women, joy of their husband .... Shabbos 152a
Women, staying without wife .... Yevamos 62b

Procreation —

Woman and children, procreation .... Yevamos 61b-62b
Woman desires, journey .... Yevamos 62b
Woman inquires before marrying, *agunah* .... Yevamos 115a
Woman makes covenant .... Sanhedrin 22b
Woman, run after her .... Bava Basra 145b
Woman wants to marry more than man .... Yevamos 113a; Kesubos 86a; Gittin 49b
Women, procreation .... Yevamos 65b-66a
Women, using sponge during intimate relations .... Yevamos 12b, 100b; Kesubos 39a;
.... Nedarim 35b; Niddah 45a

Prohibitions —

Woman carrying out intervening item on Shabbos .... Shabbos 57a-57b
Woman's dress, prohibited to a man .... Nazir 59a

W

Women, death by hanging .... Sanhedrin 45b-46a; Sotah 23a
Women go out, pieces of jewelry .... Shabbos 57b, 59a-60a, 62a-62b, 64b
Women, sorcery .... Sanhedrin 67a
Women, trustworthiness about prohibitions .... Pesachim 4a-4b

Woman guilty of forbidden relations
Woman guilty of forbidden relations and her daughter, marriage .... Sotah 26b-27a
Woman guilty of forbidden relations, circumstances showing .... Yevamos 24b-25a
Woman guilty of forbidden relations, delayed birth .... Yevamos 80b
Woman guilty of forbidden relations, destroys her house .... Sotah 3b
Woman guilty of forbidden relations, episode about blind man's wife ..... Kiddushin 66a
Woman guilty of forbidden relations, immodest behavior .... Gittin 89a
Woman guilty of forbidden relations, lineage of her fetus .... Kiddushin 74a
Woman guilty of forbidden relations, misconduct and rumor .... Yevamos 24b-25a
Woman guilty of forbidden relations, one son legitimate .... Bava Basra 58a
Woman guilty of forbidden relations, prohibition of relations out of wedlock ....
.... Sanhedrin 76a; Avodah Zarah 36b
Woman guilty of forbidden relations, right to remainder of her property ....
.... Kesubos 101a-101b
Woman guilty of forbidden relations, single witness .... Sotah 3b
Woman guilty of forbidden relations, testimony .... Kesubos 9a
Woman guilty of forbidden relations, to *Kohen* and for *terumah* .... Yevamos 44b, 61b, 68a-69a;
.... Kiddushin 74b-75a
Woman guilty of forbidden relations turns upside down, months of examination ....
.... Yevamos 34b-35a; Kesubos 37a
Woman guilty of forbidden relations, will in the end use services of immoral man ....
.... Avodah Zarah 17a

Misc. —
Woman, considered circumcised .... Avodah Zarah 27a
Woman giving seed, male .... Niddah 25b, 28a, 31a; Berachos 60a
Woman in street, Sage does not speak to .... Berachos 43b
Woman, married .... *see* **Married woman**, page 391
Woman, married, counting for Pesach lamb .... Pesachim 87a, 88a
Woman, same, repentance .... Yoma 86b
Woman, slaughtering sacrifice .... Zevachim 31b-32a; Chullin 2b
Women coming back from funeral .... Berachos 51a
Women, dead, coffin in the street .... Moed Katan 27b-28a
Women, death and theft .... Sotah 23b
Women, how to participate in funerals .... Sanhedrin 20a
Women, participated in miracle .... Shabbos 23a; Pesachim 108b; Megillah 4a; Arachin 3a
Women, trustworthiness about puberty .... Niddah 48b-49a
Women's gallery, *Simchas Beis Hashoevah* .... Succah 51b-52a; Middos 2:5
Women's gallery, Temple .... Middos 2:5; Yoma 16a

Woman after birth
Woman after birth, catching cold during immersion .... Shabbos 129a
Woman after birth, days of purification .... Krisos 10a-11a; Niddah 11a-11b, 35b-36a, 71b
Woman after birth, impurity and sacrifice .... Niddah 28a, 40a, 42b
Woman after birth, protection .... Berachos 54b

Woman giving birth
Woman giving birth .... *see also* **Miscarriage**, page 414, **Birth**, page 59

W

Woman giving birth, completed months ..... Niddah 27a, 38a; Rosh Hashanah 11a; Yevamos 42a;
.... Bechoros 20a-20b
Woman giving birth, die suddenly .... Eruvin 41b
Woman giving birth, overrides Shabbos .... Shabbos 128b-129a; Arachin 7a-7b
Woman giving birth, saving her life .... Oholos 7:6; Sanhedrin 72b
Woman giving birth swears, sacrifice .... Niddah 31b; Shevuos 8a; Krisos 26a
Women giving birth, causes of death .... Shabbos 31b-32a

Women, precedence
Women, precedence for charity .... Kesubos 67a-67b
Women, precedence in *beis din* .... Yevamos 100a
Women, precedence to men .... Yevamos 100a; Kesubos 67a-67b; Horayos 13a

Womb
Womb, external part, *niddah* .... Niddah 41b
Womb of animal, *treifah* .... Chullin 55b
Womb of woman, impurity .... Niddah 16a, 22a, 41b, 66a, 71a
Womb opening, blood of *niddah* .... Niddah 21b, 22b, 38a, 66a; Krisos 10a

Wonder
Wonder of generation .... Chullin 103b
Wonder performed by prophet .... Sanhedrin 89b
Wonders performed by false prophets .... Sanhedrin 90a

Wonderful character traits, Rabbi Akiva .... Gittin 67a

Wood
  Prohibitions —
Wood, cooking on Shabbos .... Shabbos 74b
Wood for heating, Sabbatical year .... Succah 40a; Bava Kama 101b-102a
Wood, forbidden to profit .... Pesachim 26b-27b, 75a
Wood, gathering on Yom Tov .... Beitzah 33b
Wood, is it a component of baked bread .... Pesachim 26b-27b, 75a
Wood, *muktzeh* .... Beitzah 33a; Shabbos 143a
Wood to fire idolaters .... Nedarim 62b
Wood which fell, *muktzeh* .... Beitzah 4b; Shabbos 29a

  Misc. —
Wood between rows of stones, Temple .... Rosh Hashanah 4a
Wood, episode about loading .... Bava Metzia 30b
Wood of *shittim* standing .... Yoma 72a; Succah 45b
Wood, picking in fellow's field .... Bava Kama 80b-81b
Wood, quantity for cooking .... Gittin 56a
Wood utensils, flat .... Chullin 25a
Wood utensils, unfinished, impurity .... Chullin 25a-25b
Wood which bounced and damaged .... Bava Kama 32b

  Wood for Altar
Wood for Altar, arranging .... Zevachim 62b
Wood for Altar, at night .... Yoma 27b
Wood for Altar, changing name of sacrifice .... Menachos 89b
Wood for Altar, daily offering .... Yoma 26b
Wood for Altar, donation .... Menachos 20b, 106b-107a; Shekalim 6:6; Meilah 19b
Wood for Altar, episode about government decree .... Taanis 28a
Wood for Altar, impurity .... Pesachim 24b; Chagigah 35a; Zevachim 34a, 46b; Chullin 36b
Wood for Altar, public offering .... Menachos 22a

W

Wood for Altar, rare...Menachos 101a
Wood for Altar, size...Zevachim 62b
Wood for Altar, times for endowment...Taanis 28a
Wood for Altar, *Tu B'Av*...Bava Basra 121b; Taanis 31a
Wood for Altar which grew wormy, defect...............Menachos 85b, 101a; Middos 2:5
Wood for Altar, which is fit......................Menachos 22a; Tamid 29b-30a; Zevachim 116b

Woof without warp, partition..Eruvin 16b-17a

Wool
Wool and linen, *shatnez*........................Yevamos 4b; Shabbos 26b, 27a; Menachos 39b
Wool and linen, *tzitzis*..................Menachos 39b; Shabbos 27b; Yevamos 4b; Nazir 58a
Wool, nature of fiber...Yoma 71b; Zevachim 18b
Wool or linen, impurity...Shabbos 26a-27a

Word
Word, doubled, commentaries...Bava Metzia 31a-31b
Word, improper word in one's mouth...Pesachim 3a
Word is worth a coin, silence is worth two..Megillah 18a
Word of G-d, favorable, not revoked...Berachos 7a; Shabbos 55a
Word of G-d, soul cut off for despising.......................................Sanhedrin 99a; Shevuos 13a
Word, superfluous, similar words.......Yevamos 70b, 74a; Niddah 22b-23a; Shabbos 64a, 131a; Bava Kama 25b
Words given to second agent for divorce certificate...................Gittin 66b, 71b-72a
Words in inverse order, in verse...Kiddushin 78b
Words of prophecy....................................Eruvin 60b; Bava Basra 12a; Bechoros 45a
Words of Sages are more cherished...Avodah Zarah 35a
Words of Sages, learning...Yadayim 3:2
Words of sick man...Kesubos 55b
Words of Torah, City of Refuge...Makos 10a
Words of Torah during meal..Avos 3:3
Words of Torah, no impurity..Berachos 21b-22a
Words, similar...*see Gezeirah shavah*, page 249
Words, similar, prophets...Sanhedrin 89a
Words, slave is not disciplined by words...Kesubos 77a
Words, these are words of the living G-d...............................Gittin 6b; Eruvin 13b
Words, true, are recognizable..Sotah 9b
Words which were exchanged..Shabbos 36a; Succah 34a

Work
Festivals —
Work of expert, *Chol HaMoed*..Moed Katan 11a
Work on Pesach eve..Pesachim 2b, 50a-50b, 51b, 55a
Work on Pesach eve, custom..Pesachim 51b, 55a
Work on *Rosh Chodesh*...Rosh Hashanah 23a; Arachin 10b
Work on Yom Tov, numerous lashes.......................Makos 21b-22a; Pesachim 48a
Work permitted on Yom Tov, lighting...Pesachim 5b
Work permitted on Yom Tov, not for food...Beitzah 12a-12b
Prohibitions —
Work by animal for sacrifice..Sotah 46a; Bechoros 14a
Work by items forbidden to benefit thereof.........................Avodah Zarah 63b-64a
Work for work, interest...Bava Metzia 75a-75b
Work, mourner......................................Moed Katan 11b, 15b, 21b, 26b-27a
Work, not for leaders..Kiddushin 70a

Work, redeemed sacrifices .... Bechoros 15a, 25a; Chullin 137a
Works on Sabbatical year .... Moed Katan 4b
Works on Sabbatical year, from the Torah .... Moed Katan 2b-3b

Rights —
Work of one's daughter .... Kesubos 40b, 46b, 47a; Kiddushin 3b-4a; Niddah 47a
Work of orphan girl .... Kesubos 43a-43b
Work of widow .... Kesubos 43a, 81a, 95b-96a
Work of wife .... Kesubos 58b, 70b, 83a, 107b; Gittin 77b; Bava Kama 8b; Bava Basra 49b
Work, penalty higher for ox than for sheep .... Bava Kama 79b

Shabbos —
Work at end of Shabbos .... Pesachim 50b
Work before *havdala* .... Shabbos 150b
Work continuing on Shabbos .... Shabbos 18a
Work of utensils on Shabbos .... Shabbos 18a-18b
Work of weekdays .... Shabbos 143b
Work on Shabbos, distinct prohibitions .... Shabbos 6b, 69a, 70b, 73a-73b, 96b; Krisos 2b
Work on Shabbos eve .... Pesachim 50b
Work on Shabbos, prohibition to use .... Chullin 15a; Bava Kama 71a; Kesubos 34a; Terumos 2:3;
.... Gittin 53b
Work on Shabbos, result forbidden until when .... Eruvin 40a; Beitzah 24b
Work, Yom Tov .... *see* **Yom Tov**, page 771
Works, numerous, on Shabbos, cases .... Shabbos 74b
Works of Shabbos, Tabernacle .... Shabbos 49b
Works, Shabbos .... *see* **Shabbos labors** page 607

Misc. —
Work accessory, livelihood .... Berachos 35b
Work by animals .... Sanhedrin 59b; Bava Metzia 91b
Work does not enrich nor impoverish .... Kiddushin 82b
Work done by others .... Berachos 35b
Work, first, impurity .... Keilim 16:1
Work honors those who perform it .... Nedarim 49b
Work, too much is harmful .... Gittin 70a

Work of married woman
Work of married woman, blessing .... Pesachim 50b
Work of married woman, for whom .... Kesubos 58b, 83a, 107b
Work of married woman, nursing .... Kesubos 59b, 61a
Work of married woman, parallel to which right .... Kesubos 47b
Work of married woman, surplus .... Kesubos 66a
Work of married woman, which .... Kesubos 59b, 61a, 61b
Work of married women, Mechuza .... Shabbos 32b-33a

Worker
Commandments —
Worker, requirement to give tithes .... Maasros 2:7-8, 3:1-3
Worker, separating tithes .... Terumos 3:3-4
Worker, *Shema* and prayer .... Berachos 16a

Damage —
Worker who caused damage, liability .... Bava Kama 99b; Bava Metzia 80a, 80b, 82b-83a
Worker who damaged, dismissed .... Bava Basra 21b
Worker who damaged, retracted .... Bava Metzia 109a-109b

W

Worker who made a mistake, alcoholic beverage................Bava Metzia 42b-43a
Worker who made a mistake, responsibility........................Bava Kama 99b

Prohibitions —
Worker, *Chol HaMoed*...Moed Katan 13a
Worker, delaying his salary...Bava Metzia 110b-112a
Worker, feeding him from food forbidden to benefit........Avodah Zarah 63a-63b
Worker prevented from eating, exemption from lashes......Bava Metzia 88b
Worker, withholding his salary.......................................Bava Metzia 61a, 111a

Rescinding —
Worker, caused damage because of his rescission..............Bava Metzia 78a
Worker, employer changing his mind..............................Bava Metzia 49a
Worker, permitted to quit work..............Bava Metzia 10a, 76b-77b; Bava Kama 116b
Worker, who retracted from work...................Bava Metzia 10a, 76b-77b
Workers in Mechuza, work addicted................................Bava Metzia 77a

Salary —
Worker, "take your work as a fee"....................................Bava Metzia 118a
Worker, agent who changed sum of wage.......................Bava Metzia 76a-76b
Worker asked for overpayment, "I was joking"...............Bava Kama 116a
Worker, garments...Kesubos 54a
Worker, made him work at fellow's job.............Bava Metzia 76a, 111a, 118a
Worker, oath.............................Shevuos 45a-45b; Bava Metzia 103a, 112b-113a
Worker, oath leading to another.....................................Shevuos 49a
Worker, paid like city inhabitants..................................Bava Metzia 87a
Worker, salary from beginning to end.............Kiddushin 48a-48b, 63a
Worker who brought remedy to ill person who died........Bava Kama 116a-116b

Rights —
Worker, eating consecrated produce...............................Meilah 13a
Worker, eating produce............Bava Metzia 87a-87b, 88b-89b, 91b-92a, 93a; Maasros 2:7-8
Worker, found item...........................Bava Kama 116b; Bava Metzia 10a, 12b
Worker, meal..Bava Metzia 86a-87a
Worker, receiving leftovers...Bava Kama 119a-119b

Misc. —
Worker, came in with permission....................................Bava Kama 33a
Worker, changing from customer's order.........Bava Kama 98b-99a, 100b-101a, 102a
Worker, *chazakah* on movable items...............................Bava Basra 45a-46a
Worker for non-Jew, hiring his domain for Shabbos.......Eruvin 64a
Worker, responsibility of custodian................................Bava Metzia 80b-81a
Worker, working hours..Bava Metzia 83a-83b
Workers broke barrel, episode...Bava Metzia 83a
Workers of city, decisions...Bava Basra 8b, 9a
Workers, Torah scholars are G-d's paid workers.............Eruvin 65a
Workers, working with them..Bava Metzia 29b-30a

Worker unemployed
Worker unemployed, *heter iska*......................................Bava Metzia 68a-68b
Worker unemployed, judge..................Kesubos 105a; Bechoros 29b
Worker unemployed, lost item.......................................Bava Metzia 31b

Working
Working on communal fast days......................................Taanis 12b
Working while burning Red Heifer..................................Parah 4:4

Working with permission, partner .... Bava Basra 42b
Working with two species of animals .... Kilayim 8:2-4; Bava Metzia 8b
Working without permission, payment .... Bava Metzia 101a-101b; Kesubos 80a

Working animal

Working animal in unusual manner .... Pesachim 66b
Working animal on Shabbos, decrees .... Avodah Zarah 15a
Working animal on Shabbos, prohibition .... Shabbos 153b-154b; Avodah Zarah 15a
Working animal on Shabbos, sale to non-Jew .... Avodah Zarah 15a

World

World, "may you see your future world in your life" .... Berachos 17a
World, comparable to porch or ball .... Bava Basra 25b
World continues its way, in spite of acts of wicked .... Avodah Zarah 54b
World created for righteous .... Shabbos 30b; Berachos 6b
World destroyers, Mishnah .... Sotah 22a
World exists for righteous man .... Berachos 6b
World is built by kindness .... Sanhedrin 58b
World is dark for him .... Beitzah 32b
World is like wedding .... Eruvin 54a
World sustained by Rabbi Chanina's merit .... Berachos 17b; Taanis 24b; Chullin 86a
World upside down did I see .... Bava Basra 10b; Pesachim 50a
World was created for me .... Sanhedrin 37a
Worlds in the future, righteous' wings .... Sanhedrin 92b
Worlds in the future, three hundred and ten .... Sanhedrin 100a-100b; Uktzin 3:12
Worlds in which G-d drifts .... Avodah Zarah 3b
Worlds, righteous can create .... Sanhedrin 65b

World, this world

World, this world created with "*heh*" letter .... Menachos 29b
World, this world different from next world .... Berachos 17a
World, this world is comparable to night .... Pesachim 2b
World, this world is like a hallway .... Avos 4:16
World, this world was created for wicked .... Berachos 61b

World to come

Episodes —

World to come, Amoraim's yeshivah .... Bava Metzia 85b
World to come, do I merit it .... Avodah Zarah 18a
World to come, Doeg and Ahitophel .... Chagigah 15b
World to come, generation of desert .... Sanhedrin 110b
World to come, jesters .... Taanis 22a
World to come, men destined to .... Taanis 22a
World to come, Solomon .... Sanhedrin 104b
World to come, wicked kings .... Sanhedrin 104b-105a

Semblance —

World to Come, Patriarchs .... Bava Basra 16b-17a
World to Come, Shabbos .... Berachos 57b
World to Come, three things .... Berachos 57b

Misc. —

World to come and messianic period ..... Sanhedrin 91b, 96a-99a; Berachos 34b; Shabbos 63a, 151b
World to come, created with *yud* letter .... Menachos 29b
World to come, non-Jews .... Sanhedrin 105a

W

World to come, righteous enjoy radiance of Divine Presence.............................Berachos 17a
World to come, suffering.............................Berachos 5a

Worm

Worm coming out of lung.............................Chullin 49a
Worm coming out of Tanna's ear, episode.............................Bava Metzia 84b
Worms, after one year.............................Chullin 58a-58b
Worms, dead.............................Berachos 18b; Shabbos 13b, 152a
Worms, did not attack Patriarchs.............................Bava Basra 17a
Worms, health and names.............................Shabbos 90a; Pesachim 116a
Worms in fruit meat and fish.............................Chullin 58a-58b, 67a-67b
Worms in king's garments.............................Berachos 56a-56b; Bava Metzia 78b
Worms in liver, sickness.............................Shabbos 109b
Worms, length of life.............................Chullin 58a-58b
Worms of flax, blood.............................Chullin 85b
Worms, red, washing hands.............................Zevachim 22a
Worms, righteous people.............................Bava Basra 17a
Worms, utensils and pits.............................Chullin 66b-67a

Worn out garments

Worn out garments, divorced women.............................Kesubos 101a-101b
Worn out garments, woman's right.............................Kesubos 65b

Worry

Worry, do not worry about tomorrow's troubles.............................Sanhedrin 100b
Worry for livelihood.............................Menachos 103b-104a; Yevamos 63b
Worry, forgetting Torah.............................Sanhedrin 26b
Worry, mourner.............................Moed Katan 27b
Worry, push aside.............................Berachos 60a; Sanhedrin 100b
Worry, speak of it.............................Sotah 42b; Yoma 75a; Sanhedrin 100b
Worry, whole group must worry.............................Shabbos 105b-106a

Worst quality land.............................*see* **Land of worst quality**, page 353

Worth

Worth like *Sanhedrin's* majority.............................Berachos 62b
Worth *perutah, kiddushin*.............................Kiddushin 12a
Worth *perutah*, which.............................Bava Metzia 55a

Wound

Wound, ascribing blood of *niddah* to wound.............................Niddah 15a-16a
Wound, carrying out dressing.............................Shabbos 50a
Wound to internal parts, Shabbos.............................Avodah Zarah 28a; Shabbos 109a

Wrapping

Wrapping head, how.............................Moed Katan 24a
Wrapping head, mourner.............................Moed Katan 15a
Wrapping like Ishmaelites, mourner.............................Moed Katan 24a

Wrinkle themselves on Torah.............................Chagigah 14a

Write

Write and give, divorce certificate.............................Kesubos 55a; Bava Basra 135b-136a, 152a; Gittin 9b
Write! divorce certificate.............................Gittin 65b
Write! they said to scribe.............................Gittin 29a, 66a-66b, 71b-72a
Writing and giving, selling legal document.............................Bava Basra 76a, 173a
Writing and lending books.............................Kesubos 50a
Writing, ben Kamtzar.............................Yoma 38a-38b

W

Writing between lines, holy parchments .... Menachos 30a-30b
Writing explanation, impossible .... Sanhedrin 35a
Writing four letters together .... Yoma 38b
Writing holy parchments, by copying .... Megillah 18b; Menachos 32b
Writing legal document .... *see* **Legal document**, page 361; **Bill**, page 57
Writing of scribe, divorce certificate .... Gittin 66b-67a, 71b-72a
Writing of the Torah on stones .... Sotah 35b
Writing on words to validate Name .... Gittin 20a, 54b; Shabbos 104b
Writing on written letters .... Gittin 19a
Writing one's property on king's name .... Nedarim 47b-48a
Writing one's property over to sons, support .... Kesubos 49b-50a
Writing or pronunciation, which determines .... Sanhedrin 4a-4b; Makos 7b-8a; Succah 6b; Kiddushin 18b;
.... Pesachim 86b; Zevachim 37b-38a; Bechoros 34a; Krisos 17b
Writing parts of Torah .... Gittin 60a; Yoma 37b-38a
Writing promise of dowry .... Kesubos 102b
Writing, slaughtering and circumcising, Sage .... Chullin 9a
Writing Torah scroll, commandment .... Sanhedrin 21b; Menachos 30a
Writing Torah scroll, earned .... Eruvin 64a-64b
Writing, uniformity, holy parchments .... Menachos 30a
Writing verses in amulets .... Shabbos 61b, 115b
Writing verses on legal documents .... Yevamos 106b
Wrote promissory note to borrow in *Tishrei* .... Bava Metzia 12b-13a, 17a, 19a
Wrote to divorce, *Tishrei* .... Bava Metzia 19a

Writing on Shabbos
Writing on Shabbos, cases .... Shabbos 104b-105a
Writing on Shabbos, how much .... Shabbos 78b, 80a; Krisos 16b-17a, 103a-103b, 97b
Writing on Shabbos, like putting down .... Shabbos 80a
Writing on Shabbos, making mark .... Shabbos 103a-103b
Writing on Shabbos, part of word .... Shabbos 103a-103b
Writing on Shabbos, quantity .... Shabbos 75b, 103a-103b
Writing on Shabbos, tracing on written letters .... Gittin 19a

Written
Written at daytime and signed at night .... Gittin 18a-18b
Written explicitly .... Zevachim 49b
Written testimony .... Gittin 71a

W

Yaal kegam .... *see* **Abbaye and Rava, ruling**, page 2

Yaaleh Veyavo

Yaaleh Veyavo, Bircas HaMazon .... Berachos 49a-49b; Shabbos 24a

Yaaleh Veyavo, doubt about *Rosh Chodesh* .... Eruvin 40a

Yaaleh Veyavo, forgot .... Berachos 29b, 30b

Yaaleh Veyavo on Shabbos .... Eruvin 40b; Beitzah 17a

Yaaleh Veyavo, when .... Shabbos 24a-24b

Yaavetz

Yaavetz, deduction of measures .... Yoma 80a

Yaavetz, Otniel .... Temurah 16a

Yaakov .... *see* **Jacob**, page 321

Yachid .... *see* **Individual**, page 308

Yachid mumcheh .... *see* **Expert judge**, page 210

Yachloku .... *see* **Dividing up**, page 168

Yad

Yad Absalom .... Sotah 10b-11a

Yad, definition .... Arachin 19b

Yad letumah .... *see* **Handle (Impurity)**, page 268

Yadayim mochichos .... *see* **Verbal expression**, page 721

Yados nedarim .... *see* **Verbal expression of vows, incomplete**, page 721

Yael .... *see* **Jael**, page 321

Yagdil Torah veyaadir .... *see* **Fins and scales, why did both need to be written**, page 223

Yagon, explanation .... Berachos 28a

Yah, *Hallelujah* and *kes kah* .... Pesachim 117a

Yahrzeit .... Nedarim 12a

Yair, slain men at Ai .... Bava Basra 121b

Yalta

Yalta, broke wine barrel .... Berachos 51b

Yalta, imitation of forbidden food .... Chullin 109b

Yalta, Rabbi Nachman's wife .... Berachos 51b

Yam shel Solomon .... *see* **Sea of Solomon**, page 593

Yam Suf .... *see* **Red Sea**, page 551

Yamim means a year .... Kesubos 57b

Yannai
Yannai, judgment of his slave...Sanhedrin 19a-19b
Yannai murdered Sages...Kiddushin 66a
Yannai, possibly illegitimate...Kiddushin 66a
Yannai, Shimon ben Shetach...Berachos 48a
Yannai, Yochanan *Kohen Gadol*...Berachos 29a
Yarchei Kallah, reward for listening to lecture...Berachos 6b
Yardein...*see* **Jordan, page 324**
Yatzia, explanation...Bava Basra 61a
Yavam...*see* **Brother of deceased childless husband, page 78**
Yavan...*see* **Greece, page 258**
Yavesh Gilead, virgins...Yevamos 60b
Yavneh
Yavneh, relocation of *Sanhedrin*...Rosh Hashanah 31b
Yavneh, Sages...Berachos 63b
Yawning, prayer...Berachos 24a-24b
Yayin nesech...*see* **Wine of idolaters, page 751**
Ye'ush...*see* **Despairing, page 161**
Year...*see also* **Age, page 13**

Abundance —
Year, good, Divine mercy...Berachos 55a
Year, poor in the beginning...Rosh Hashanah 16b
Years of life turning for good...Yoma 71a
Years, success in learning...Chullin 24a

Long life —
Years of life...Yevamos 49b-50a
Years of righteous, filled...Sotah 13b; Kiddushin 38a; Rosh Hashanah 11a
Years of son, like his father's...Eduyos 2:9

Prohibitions —
Year, complete or not...Arachin 18b-19a; Niddah 47b-48a
Year, remainder of wine of idolaters...Avodah Zarah 34a-34b, 75a-75b; Niddah 65b
Year, wording of vow...Rosh Hashanah 12b; Nedarim 60a-61a

Sacrifice —
Year, new, sacrifice...Yoma 65a-66a; Rosh Hashanah 7a; Megillah 29b
Year of animal tithe...Rosh Hashanah 8a
Year of firstborn...Rosh Hashanah 5b, 6b-7a; Bechoros 27b, 28a; Temurah 21b; Zevachim 29a-29b
Year without three festivals...Rosh Hashanah 6b

Times —
Year, "days"...Kesubos 57b
Year of Sabbatical year, reckoning...Avodah Zarah 9b
Year of sun and moon...Arachin 9b, 31b; Rosh Hashanah 6b; Yoma 65b-66a; Nazir 8b
Year, part like whole...Rosh Hashanah 2b, 10a-10b; Chagigah 5b; Makos 3b; Niddah 44b-45a
Year, wording of rent...Rosh Hashanah 7b
Years, counting months...Megillah 5a; Nazir 7a

Misc. —
Year, heavenly judgment...Eduyos 2:10
Year when they did not blow *shofar*...Rosh Hashanah 16b
Years in which G-d will renew His world...Sanhedrin 92b

Years for tithe
Years for tithe, grain .... Rosh Hashanah 12b-13b
Years for tithe, legumes .... Rosh Hashanah 13b-14a
Years for tithe, tree .... Rosh Hashanah 15b
Years for tithe, vegetables .... Rosh Hashanah 14a
Years for tithe, produce of earth .... Sheviis 2:7-10
Years of kings' reign
Years of kings' reign, how .... Rosh Hashanah 2a-3b, 8a; Avodah Zarah 10a
Years of kings' reign, in divorce certificate .... Yadayim 4:8
Years of kings' reign, incomplete .... Megillah 11b-12a
Years of kings' reign, legal documents .... Rosh Hashanah 2a-2b, 8a; Avodah Zarah 9b-10a
Years of *orlah*
Years of *orlah*, bending branch over .... Orlah 1, 5
Years of *orlah*, how .... Rosh Hashanah 9b-10b; Yevamos 83a
Years of *orlah*, replanted tree .... Orlah 1:3-4
Yechoniah .... *see* **Jechoniah**, page 322
Yechezkel .... *see* **Ezekiel**, page 212
Yedios lechiuv korban .... *see* **Realizing, requirement to offer sacrifice**, page 547
Yefes, in tents of Shem .... Megillah 9b
Yefas toar .... *see* **Beautiful captive**, page 46
Yehalelucha, Pesach .... Pesachim 117b-118a
Yehavecha, significance .... Rosh Hashanah 26b
Yehei Shemei Rabba
Yehei Shemei Rabba, followed by *mevarach* .... Succah 39a
Yehei Shemei Rabba, G-d's pain .... Berachos 3a
Yehei Shemei Rabba, interrupting during *Shemoneh Esrei* .... Berachos 21b
Yehei Shemei Rabba, maintains world .... Sotah 49a
Yehei Shemei Rabba, reward .... Shabbos 119b
Yehi ratzon
Yehi ratzon, prayers .... Berachos 16b-17a; Avos 5:20
Yehi ratzon, with congregation .... Berachos 30a
Yehi ratzon .... *see* **May it be His will**, page 395
Yehoachaz ben Josiah .... *see* **Jehoahaz ben Josiah**, page 322
Yehonasan, *Av Beis Din* .... *see* **Jehonathan,** *Av Beis Din*, page 322
Yehonasan ben Menasheh .... *see* **Jehonathan ben Manasseh**, page 322
Yehoshafat .... *see* **Jehoshaphat**, page 322
Yehoshua .... *see* **Joshua**, page 325
Yehoshua ben Gamla
Yehoshua ben Gamla .... Yevamos 61a; Yoma 18a
Yehoshua ben Gamla, decree .... Bava Basra 21a
Yehoshua ben Perachia, pairs .... Chagigah 16a
Yehoshua *Kohen Gadol*, Nebuchadnezzar .... Sanhedrin 93a
Yehoyachin .... *see* **Jehoiachin**, page 322
Yehoyakim .... *see* **Jehoiakim**, page 322
Yehu .... *see* **Jehu**, page 322
Yehudah .... *see* **Judah**, page 326
Yehudah ben Rabbi Chiya
Yehudah ben Rabbi Chiya .... Kesubos 62b
Yehudah ben Rabbi Chiya came back home late .... Kesubos 62b

Yehudah ben Rabbi Chiya, prayer .... Bava Metzia 85b
Yehudah ben Shamua, demonstration .... Rosh Hashanah 19a; Taanis 18a
Yehudah ben Tabai, pairs .... Chagigah 16a
Yehudi, denies idolatry .... Megillah 13a
Yekuthiel, Moses .... Megillah 13a
Yemei hamiluim .... *see* **Days of Tabernacle dedication,** page 148
Yemei sefiro .... *see* **Days of counting, leper,** page 148
Yemei tohar .... *see* **Days of purification,** page 148
Yemos Hamashiach .... *see* **Messianic times,** page 407
Yerakon fever, cure .... Shabbos 110a-110b
Yerei shamayim .... *see* **G-d-fearing,** page 246
Yeret, interpretation by initials .... Menachos 66b
Yericho .... *see* **Jericho,** page 322
Yeridah .... *see* **Decline** page 154
Yeridah letzorech aliyah .... *see* **Decline needed for ascent,** page 154
Yerovoam .... *see* **Jeroboam,** page 322
Yerushalayim .... *see* **Jerusalem,** page 323
Yes
   "Yes yes," wording of oath .... Shevuos 36a
   "Yes" honest, keeping one's word .... Bava Metzia 49a
Yesh
   Yesh, leniency and stringency .... Arachin 13b-15a
   Yesh omrim, Rabbi Nassan .... Horayos 13b-14a
Yesharim, Patriarchs .... Avodah Zarah 25a
Yeshayah, Yeshayahu .... *see* **Isaiah,** page 318
Yeshivah
   Yeshivah at his door .... Eruvin 26a
   Yeshivah for healing of sick .... Eruvin 26a
   Yeshivah, Heavenly .... Berachos 18b; Bava Metzia 85b
   Yeshivah of Rabbi Afes .... Bechoros 18b
   Yeshivah on grave .... Bava Kama 16b-17a
   Yeshivah, since our Patriarchs' days .... Yoma 28b
Yeshnah lischirus .... *see* **Rent,** page 558
Yeshurun became fat and kicked .... Berachos 32a
Yetzer hara .... *see* **Evil urge,** page 204
Yetzer hatov .... *see* **Good urge, forgotten,** page 255
Yetzias Mitzrayim .... *see* **Exodus, mentioning,** page 209
Yevamah .... *see* **Widow awaiting levirate marriage, kesubah,** page 744
Yibum .... *see* **Levirate marriage,** page 367
Yichud .... *see* **Seclusion,** page 594
Yichus .... *see* **Lineage,** page 371
Yid'oni
   Yid'oni, does not understand .... Sotah 12b
   Yid'oni, general .... Sanhedrin 65a, 65b
Yiftach .... *see* **Jephtah,** page 322
Yihyu leratzon, prayer .... Berachos 4b, 9b
Yiras shamayim .... *see* **Fear of G-d,** page 218
Yirmiyah .... *see* **Jeremiah,** page 322
Yisachar .... *see* **Issacher,** page 319

Y

Yisachar from Barkai .... Krisos 28b

Yishai .... *see* **Jesse**, page 323

Yishmael .... *see* **Ishmael**, page 318

Yishmael ben Nesaniah, wicked son of wicked .... Megillah 15a

Yishmael ben Piabi, second Temple .... Yoma 9a

Yishmael My son, bless Me! .... Berachos 7a

Yishmaelim .... *see* **Ishmaelites**, page 318

Yiskah, Sarah .... Megillah 14a

Yisrael .... *see* **Israel**, page 318

Yisro .... *see* **Jethro**, page 323

Yisurim .... *see* **Suffering**, page 662

Yitzchak .... *see* **Isaac**, page 318

Yiud .... *see* **Marrying Hebrew maidservant**, page 392

Yiush .... *see* **Despairing**, page 161

Yoav .... *see* **Joab**, page 324

Yochanan ben Nerbai .... Pesachim 57a; Krisos 28a-28b

Yochanan *Kohen Gadol*

    Yochanan *Kohen Gadol*, decrees .... Sotah 47b-48a; Maaser Sheni 5:15

    Yochanan *Kohen Gadol*, Divine voice .... Sotah 33a

    Yochanan *Kohen Gadol*, eighty years .... Yoma 9a; Berachos 29a

    Yochanan *Kohen Gadol*, Yannai .... Berachos 29a

Yocheved .... *see* **Jochebed**, page 324

Yochni, episode .... Bechoros 57b

Yoel .... *see* **Joel the prophet, drought**, page 324

Yoke **of Torah,** reward .... Avos 3:5

Yom beshanah keshanah .... *see* **Day in year, counts like a year**, page 148

Yom hashanah .... *see* **Yahrzeit**, page 766

Yom keneged yom .... *see* **Day of impurity,** *zav*, page 148

Yom keneged yom, *zav* .... Niddah 72a-72b; Zavim 1:1

Yom Kippur

   Commandments —

    Yom Kippur, *havdala* .... Pesachim 53b-54a

    Yom Kippur, honoring .... Shabbos 119a

    Yom Kippur, joy .... Bava Basra 121a

    Yom Kippur, *Neilah* .... Yoma 87b-88a

    Yom Kippur, prayer starts later .... Megillah 23a

    Yom Kippur, sacrifices .... Yoma 70a-70b

    Yom Kippur, Torah reading .... Megillah 30b-31a

   Prohibitions —

    Yom Kippur, children .... Yoma 82a

    Yom Kippur, combining for forbidden consumption .... Yoma 80b, 81a

    Yom Kippur, drinking .... Yoma 80a-80b

    Yom Kippur, fast .... Yoma 81a

    Yom Kippur, hardships .... Yoma 74a, 74b, 76a-77b

    Yom Kippur, improper food .... Yoma 81b; Berachos 36b

    Yom Kippur, pregnant woman .... Yoma 82b

    Yom Kippur, quantity of food .... Yoma 78b

    Yom Kippur, rubbing oil on body .... Yoma 77b

    Yom Kippur, service .... *see* **Kohen Gadol**, page 346

Y

Yom Kippur, shoe...Yoma 78a-78b
Yom Kippur, sick...Yoma 83a, 84b
Yom Kippur, sin offerings for several forbidden works...................................Krisos 18b
Yom Kippur, washing..Yoma 77b-78b; Nedarim 80b

Misc. —
Yom Kippur, atonement...................Yoma 85b-86a, 87a; Shevuos 2b, 12b-13b; Krisos 7a, 18b, 25a-26b
Yom Kippur, Babylonians' mistake..Rosh Hashanah 21a
Yom Kippur, episode about transgressions...Yoma 19b-20a
Yom Kippur, episode concerning decree..Chullin 101b
Yom Kippur, final verdict..Rosh Hashanah 8a-8b, 16a
Yom Kippur, garments..Yoma 12b, 35a-35b
Yom Kippur, guilt offering for doubtful culpability.................................Yoma 85b
Yom Kippur, no accusation..Yoma 20a
Yom Kippur, Temple dedication.................................Moed Katan 9a; Shabbos 30a
Yom Kippur, Yom Tov *Sheni*...Rosh Hashanah 21a

Yom o yomayim...*see* **Day or two, slave**, page 148

Yom Tov
Animals —
Yom Tov, caring for animal...Beitzah 23a
Yom Tov, covering blood..Beitzah 7b-8b; Chullin 84b
Yom Tov, driving animal..Beitzah 33a
Yom Tov, feeding animal.............................Beitzah 20b, 21a-21b; Megillah 7b
Yom Tov, firstborn..........................Beitzah 25b-27b; Shabbos 136a; Chullin 51b
Yom Tov, meat...Beitzah 11a-11b, 28a
Yom Tov, nursing..Yevamos 114a
Yom Tov, preparing animal...Beitzah 25a
Yom Tov, skinning...Beitzah 11a-11b; Bechoros 33a
Yom Tov, slaughtering..Beitzah 25a, 28b, 34a

Food for Yom Tov —
Yom Tov, change in work.....................Shabbos 148a-148b; Beitzah 14a-14b, 29b-30a
Yom Tov, food...Beitzah 11a
Yom Tov, food, *muktzeh*...Beitzah 31b
Yom Tov, food which can be prepared on weekdays...........Shabbos 134a; Beitzah 14a-14b
Yom Tov, for weekday..Beitzah 22b
Yom Tov, identical for all..Kesubos 7a
Yom Tov, is it permitted to heat water to wash feet..................Beitzah 34a
Yom Tov, oven...Beitzah 32b
Yom Tov, preparing for second day of Yom Tov........................Beitzah 17a
Yom Tov, preparing for Shabbos......................................Pesachim 46b
Yom Tov, preparing utensils...........Beitzah 28a-28b; Shabbos 137b; Megillah 7b
Yom Tov, work so as to eat after Yom Tov......Pesachim 46b-48a, 62a; Beitzah 21a

Rabbinical prohibitions —
Yom Tov, *challah*...Beitzah 9a
Yom Tov, clay utensils...Beitzah 33b-34a
Yom Tov, decree because of Shabbos.............................Shabbos 124a
Yom Tov, died on Yom Tov....................Beitzah 6a, 22a; Shabbos 139a-139b
Yom Tov, drawing water..Shabbos 148a-148b
Yom Tov, *eruv chatzeiros*......................Eruvin 38a-39a; Beitzah 16b-17a
Yom Tov, *eruv techumim*.......................................Beitzah 16b-17a

Yom Tov, food for non-Jew .... Beitzah 21a-21b
Yom Tov, immersion .... Beitzah 18a-18b
Yom Tov, ladder .... Beitzah 9a-9b
Yom Tov, leniencies .... Beitzah 9b-10a
Yom Tov, loan .... Shabbos 148b
Yom Tov, measuring .... Beitzah 29a-30a
Yom Tov, *muktzeh* .... Beitzah 30a, 31b-32a; Shabbos 124a
Yom Tov, pretending .... Beitzah 37a; Shabbos 117b, 124a, 139b
Yom Tov, producing a smell .... Beitzah 23a
Yom Tov, sale .... Beitzah 27b, 29b
Yom Tov, sending .... Beitzah 14b, 15a; Shabbos 60a
Yom Tov, sick person .... Beitzah 22a
Yom Tov, sweeping house .... Beitzah 22b
Yom Tov, using scale .... Beitzah 28a
Yom Tov, washing .... Beitzah 21b; Shabbos 39b

Works —
Yom Tov, building .... Beitzah 32b
Yom Tov, burning sacrifice .... Shabbos 23b-25a; Menachos 46b
Yom Tov, carrying out .... Beitzah 12a, 25b
Yom Tov, cutting off wood .... Beitzah 33a-33b
Yom Tov, cutting wood .... Beitzah 31b
Yom Tov, destroying .... Beitzah 31b-32a
Yom Tov, differences in works .... Makos 21b-22a; Pesachim 48a
Yom Tov, extinguishing .... Beitzah 22a
Yom Tov, gathering wood .... Beitzah 33b
Yom Tov, kindling .... Beitzah 21b, 33b; Pesachim 5b
Yom Tov, positive and negative commandment .... Beitzah 8b; Shabbos 25a
Yom Tov, selecting .... Beitzah 12b, 14b, 29b
Yom Tov, works .... Beitzah 12b, 14a-14b, 29b, 34a

Misc. —
Yom Tov and Shabbos, differences .... Shabbos 124a, 137b; Beitzah 2b, 28a, 35b-37a
Yom Tov, count for mourning .... Moed Katan 19a-20a, 24b
Yom Tov, days of mourning .... Moed Katan 19a-20a; Nazir 15a-15b
Yom Tov, episode about ruling .... Beitzah 4a
Yom Tov, eulogy .... Moed Katan 8a-8b
Yom Tov, mourning .... Moed Katan 14b
Yom Tov, prayer starts later .... Megillah 23a
Yom Tov, staying at home .... Succah 27b
Yom Tov, stumbling-blocks .... Kiddushin 81a

Yom Tov *Sheni*
Yom Tov *Sheni*, blessings .... Shabbos 23a
Yom Tov *Sheni*, custom .... Pesachim 51b-52a; Beitzah 4b
Yom Tov *Sheni*, *eruv techumin* .... Beitzah 17a
Yom Tov *Sheni*, excommunication .... Pesachim 52a
Yom Tov *Sheni*, *havdala* .... Beitzah 4b
Yom Tov *Sheni*, outside *Eretz Yisrael* .... Rosh Hashanah 20b-21a
Yom Tov *Sheni*, two holy days .... Eruvin 38a, 39b; Beitzah 4b
Yom Tov *Sheni*, Yom Kippur .... Rosh Hashanah 21a

Yoma
Yoma depagra..Shabbos 129b
Yoma tava leRabbanan, recovery..................................Berachos 46a
Yoma, who arranged this tractate................................Yoma 14b
Yoma depagra...............*see* **Day of vacation,** *yoma depagra*, page 148
Yonah...*see* **Jonah**, page 324
Yonassan, bread to David................*see* **Jonathan, bread to David**, page 324
Yonassan, translation of Book of Prophets....................Megillah 3a
Yonassan Aryeh overcame group of robbers....................Yevamos 122b
Yonassan ben Uziel
Yonassan ben Uziel................................Succah 28a; Bava Basra 134a
Yonassan ben Uziel, inheritance..................Bava Basra 133b-134a
Yonassan the demon..........................Yevamos 122a; Gittin 66a
Yored bireshus...............*see* **Working with permission, partner**, page 763
Yosam...*see* **Jotham**, page 326
Yose ben Yoezer
Yose ben Yoezer......................................Temurah 15b-16a
Yose ben Yoezer consecrated his property......Bava Basra 133b
Yose ben Yoezer, pairs................................Chagigah 16a
Yose de'min Yokrat, episode.........................Taanis 24a
Yosef..*see* **Joseph**, page 325
Yosef ben Shimon
Yosef ben Shimon, concern........................Yevamos 115b-116a
Yosef ben Shimon, divorce certificates....Gittin 24b, 34b; Bava Basra 167b
Yosef ben Shimon, two........Bava Basra 172b-173a; Gittin 24b; Bechoros 48a
Yosef ben Simai, fire on Shabbos....................Shabbos 121a
Yosef ben Yochanan, pairs..........................Chagigah 16a
Yosef Habavli
Yosef Habavli, his face shone..........................Menachos 18a
Yosef Habavli, how beloved is Your Torah..........Menachos 18a
Yosef Habavli, Isi ben Yehudah............Pesachim 113b; Yoma 52b
Yosef permitting..........................Avodah Zarah 37a; Eduyos 8:4
Yosef son of Rabbi Yehoshua, "upside down" world......Bava Basra 10b; Pesachim 50a
Yosef the demon, *techum*..........................Eruvin 43a
Yosef who honors the Shabbos....................Shabbos 119a
Yoshiahu..*see* **Josiah**, page 326
Yotam..*see* **Jotham**, page 326
Yotzeh...............*see* **Taken out of Courtyard, flesh of sacrifice**, page 671
Yotzeh dofen...............................*see* **Cesarean birth**, page 91
Yotzeh secharo behefsedo...............*see* **Advantage outweighed by loss**, page 12
Yotzeh venichnas...............*see* **Coming out and in, person guarding**, page 115
Yotzer Or
Yotzer Or, blind reciting..............................Megillah 24b
Yotzer Or, missing *Shema*..............................Berachos 10b
Yotzer Or, text..Berachos 12a
You
You and donkey, act of acquisition........Bava Basra 143a; Kiddushin 51a
You are called Man........Yevamos 61a; Bava Metzia 114b; Krisos 6b

Young

Young, advantage .... Shabbos 152a
Young *Kohanim* .... Tamid 26b-27a
Young *Leviim* .... Arachin 13b
Young man and girl in *Eretz Yisrael* .... Bava Basra 91b
Young men, commentaries .... Pesachim 87a
Young men of Israel, smell in the future .... Berachos 43b
Young men shame sun, beauty .... Sanhedrin 92b

Young animal

Damage —

Young of cow to be stoned .... Sanhedrin 80a-80b; Avodah Zarah 24a; Temurah 30b
Young of goring cow, collecting .... Bava Kama 47a

Sacrifices —

Young animal replacing burnt offering .... Temurah 18b-19b, 20b-21a
Young of animal forbidden on Altar ..... Temurah 30b-31a; Sanhedrin 80a-80b; Avodah Zarah 24a, 46b-47a
Young of consecrated animal, atonement .... Krisos 27a
Young of guilt offering, consecrated as burnt offering .... Temurah 25b; Bava Kama 73b
Young of redeemed sacrifices .... Bechoros 15b-16a
Young of sacrifice, in its mother's womb ...... Zevachim 98a, 114a; Temurah 11a, 19a-19b, 24b-25a;
.... Menachos 83a; Chullin 89b-90a; Krisos 23b; Niddah 41a

Misc. —

Young animal belonging to woman, divorce .... Kesubos 79b
Young animal from wife's property .... Kesubos 79a
Young of *treifah* animal .... Temurah 30b-31a; Chullin 58a; Bechoros 7a

Young girl

Young girl, agent for divorce .... Gittin 64b; Kesubos 47a; Kiddushin 43b-44a
Young girl, divorce .... Gittin 64b; Kesubos 47a
Young girl, father's rights .... Kesubos 43b
Young girl, from city named Neuron .... Chullin 5a
Young girl, *kiddushin* .... Kiddushin 43b-44a
Young girl, *kiddushin* to widow awaiting levirate marriage .... Kiddushin 43b-44a
Young girl, signs .... Niddah 47a-49a
Young girl, six months until adulthood .... Niddah 65a; Kesubos 39a; Kiddushin 79a
Young girl to old man, marriage .... Yevamos 44a

Your daughters, would you have also neglected?

.... Moed Katan 18a

Yours

Yours, *lulav* .... Pesachim 38a; Succah 41b; Bava Basra 137a-137b
Yours, *matzah* .... Pesachim 38a

Yov

.... *see* **Job**, page 324

Yovel

.... *see* **Jubilee**, page 326

Yud

Yud and *heh*, worlds .... Menachos 29b
Yud in *tefillin* .... Shabbos 62a
Yud letter in Sarai's name, crying .... Sanhedrin 107a
Yud of *ein*, deduction .... Kiddushin 4a

Yuvla, ram

.... Rosh Hashanah 26

Z

Z'man hazeh...*see* **Present times**, page 501

Zachor, reading..Megillah 18a, 30a-30b

Zachor veshamor...*see* **Remember and keep**, page 557

Zachur latov, commentaries on Book of Ezekiel.......................................Menachos 45a

Zachur latov.................*see* **Remembered for the good, commentaries on Book of Ezekiel**, page 557

Zaken, he who acquired wisdom...Kiddushin 32b

Zaken mamreh..*see* **Rebellious elder**, page 550

Zar..*see* **Non-Kohen**, page 449

Zav

  Discharges —

    Zav...*see also* **Discharge of zav**, page 165

    Zav, "small," first discharge.......................Niddah 32b, 34b-35a; Arachin 3a

    Zav, discharges and days...Bava Kama 24a

    Zav, first discharge..Niddah 72a-72b; Zavim 1:1

    Zav, pure discharges...........Yoma 18a-18b; Nazir 65b; Niddah 35a-35b, 37a; Zavim 2:2

  Sacrifices —

    Zav, considered before time...Chagigah 9b

    Zav, Pesach lamb..................Pesachim 66b-67a, 95b; Bechoros 33a; Krisos 10a

    Zav, sacrifice...Krisos 8a; Zavim 1:3-6

  Misc. —

    Zav, "small" and "great".........................Megillah 8a-8b; Niddah 43b

    Zav, cure..Shabbos 110a-110b

    Zav, impurity.......................................Oholos 1:5; Niddah 32b-33a

    Zav, impurity of non-Jews.......................Avodah Zarah 36b-37a; Shabbos 17b

    Zav, living water...Parah 9:1-4

    Zav, who...Zavim 2:1

    Zav who had intimate relations......................................Niddah 73a

Zavah

  Zavah and *niddah*, calculations about doubt...........Arachin 8a-8b; Niddah 53b-54b, 69a-69b

  Zavah, continuous flow...Nazir 15b

  Zavah, part of day.....................................Pesachim 81a; Nazir 15b

  Zavah, when.......................................Niddah 72b-73a; Sanhedrin 87a

  Zavah for one day

    Zavah for one day, deductions..........................Niddah 73a; Horayos 4a

Zavah for one day, relations and couch..Niddah 73a
Zavah for one day, retroactive impurity...Pesachim 81a; Nazir 15b-16a
Zavah for one day, time of immersion...Megillah 20a-20b
Zavah for one day, when..Niddah 54a, 71b-72b
Ze Eli vaanvehu................................*see* **This is my G-d and I shall glorify Him, page 687**
Zeal for commandment, Lot's daughter................Bava Kama 38b; Nazir 23b-24a; Horayos 11a
Zealous ones kill
Zealous ones kill, impure person...Sanhedrin 82b-83a
Zealous ones kill, who..Sanhedrin 81b, 82b
Zealots kill man having relation with non-Jewess............Sanhedrin 81b-82a; Avodah Zarah 36b
Zebulun
Zebulun, his share in *Eretz Yisrael*...Megillah 6a
Zebulun, praises coast...Pesachim 4a
Zechariah
Zechariah, avenging his blood..Sanhedrin 96a-96b; Gittin 57b
Zechariah, perfect in deeds...Megillah 23a
Zechariah, wicked men's answer..Sanhedrin 105a
Zecher Lechorban.......................*see* **Commemorating Temple destruction, page 117**
Zecher litzias Mitzraim..*see* **Exodus, date, page 209**
Zecher tzaddik livrachah...............*see* **Memory of righteous for a blessing, page 403**
Zechus avos....................................*see* **Merit of fathers, until when, page 405**
Zedekiah
Zedekiah, "you will die in peace"..Moed Katan 28b
Zedekiah, exile...Arachin 12a
Zedekiah, false prophet..Sanhedrin 89a
Zedekiah, his righteousness..Sanhedrin 103a
Zedekiah, Nebuchadnezzar and hare..Nedarim 65a
Zedekiah, princes of mankind...Succah 52b
Zedekiah, Temple destruction in his days...Sanhedrin 103a
Zedekiah was struck in his eyes..Sotah 10a
Zedekiah, Josiah's son...Horayos 11b; Krisos 5b
Zeh
Zeh Eli veanvehu..Shabbos 133b; Succah 11b; Nazir 2b
Zeh hayom techilas maasecha, Rosh Hashanah..Rosh Hashanah 27a
Zeh mechashev vezeh oved......................*see* **Intent in fellow's sacrificial service, page 312**
Zeh neheneh......................*see* **Benefits without the other losing, consecrated item, page 54**
Zeh vezeh gorem..................*see* **Two forbidden substances acting together, page 709**
Zeh yachol...........................*see* **Two persons performed work, Shabbos, page 708**
Zeirei
Zeirei, death of woman with whom he deposited money...Berachos 18b
Zeirei, Rabbi Yochanan's daughter..Kiddushin 71b
Zephaniah, princes of mankind...Succah 52b
Zelophehad, daughters of man gathering wood...Shabbos 96b-97a
Zeman grama...............................*see* **Dependent on time, women, page 159**
Zera haav..*see* **Offspring of father, page 455**
Zera levatalah....................................*see* **Semen in vain, page 600**
Zeres...*see* **Span, page 648**
Zerikah.............................*see* **Throwing blood on Altar, page 690**
Zeriyah.............*see* **Connection of water to *mikveh*, considered as sowing, page 122**

Z

Zerizus .... *see* **Swiftness, page 667**

Zerubbabel, Nehemiah .... Sanhedrin 37b

Ziboris .... *see* **Land of worst quality, page 353**

Zichrono livrachah .... Kiddushin 31b

Zichrono livrachah .... *see* **May his memory be a blessing, page 395**

Zikah .... *see* **Bond before levirate marriage, page 71**

Zikuy harabim .... *see* **Merit of multitude, page 405**

Zimah, significance .... Nedarim 51a; Yevamos 37b

Zimri and Kozbi .... Sanhedrin 82a-82b

Zimun

   Zimun by ignoramus, episode .... Berachos 47b

   Zimun, combining .... Berachos 45a-45b, 47a-48b, 50a-50b; Arachin 4a

   Zimun, guest .... Berachos 46a

   Zimun, how .... Berachos 45b, 47a, 50a

   Zimun, on fruit .... Chullin 106a

   Zimun requirement .... Berachos 45a-48b, 55a

   Zimun, text .... Berachos 46a, 49b-50a

   Zimun, two men .... Berachos 45a-45b; Chullin 106a

   Zimun, who .... Berachos 47a

Zion .... *see* **Tzion, page 710**

Zipporah, "*kushis*" .... Moed Katan 16b

Zippori

   Zippori, marketplaces .... Bava Basra 75b

   Zippori, end of Shabbos .... Shabbos 118b

   Zippori, praise of *Eretz Yisrael* .... Megillah 6a

Zmiros Shabbos .... *see* **Songs during Shabbos meal, page 645**

Zo ve'ein tzarich zo .... *see* **Superfluous teaching in *Mishnah*, page 664**

Zoan in Egypt .... Kesubos 112a

Zochalin lemikveh .... *see* **Flowing water, *mikveh*, page 231**

Zomeim, zomemim .... *see* **Conspiring witness, page 125**

Zomer .... *see* **Pruning, secondary category of work, page 509**

Zonah .... *see* **Woman guilty of forbidden relations, page 758**

Zore'a .... *see* **Sowing, page 648;** *see also* **Planting, page 492**

Zoreh .... *see* **Winnowing, page 752**

Zorek .... *see* **Throwing on Shabbos, deduced from holding out page 690**

Zos HaTorah, deductions about sacrifices .... Zevachim 97b-98a; Menachos 82b-83a

Zov .... *see* **Discharge, page 165**

Zroa beshelah .... *see* **Shoulder cooked, page 620**

Zroa lechayaim vekeivah .... *see* **Shoulder, cheek, and stomach, page 620**

Zugo .... *see* **Pairs, danger, page 471**

Zutra bar Tuviah, rebuke .... Moed Katan 16b

Zuz

   Zuz, dinar .... Kesubos 64a

   Zuz unusable, tasting in store .... Shabbos 129a

Z

יום ידים עוקצין ברכות פאה דמאי כלאים שביעית תרומות מעשרות מעשר שני
קטן חגיגה יבמות כתובות נדרים נזיר סוטה גיטין קידושין בבא קמא בבא מציעא בב
רכין תמורה כריתות מעילה תמיד מדות קנין כלים אהלות נגעים פרה טהרות מקוא
מעשר שני חלה ערלה בכורים שבת ערובין פסחים שקלים יומא סוכה ביצה ראש הש
בא מציעא בבא בתרא סנהדרין מכות שבועות עדיות עבודה זרה אבות הוריות זבח
ה טהרות מקואות נידה מכשירין זבים טבול יום ידים עוקצין ברכות פאה דמאי כלא
סוכה ביצה ראש השנה תענית מגילה מועד קטן חגיגה יבמות כתובות נדרים נזיר סו
אבות הוריות זבחים מנחות חולין בכורות ערכין תמורה כריתות מעילה תמיד מדות ק
פאה דמאי כלאים שביעית תרומות מעשרות מעשר שני חלה ערלה בכורים שבת ערו
דים נזיר סוטה גיטין קידושין בבא קמא בבא מציעא בבא בתרא סנהדרין מכות שבוע
תמיד מדות קנין כלים אהלות נגעים פרה טהרות מקואות נידה מכשירין זבים טבול
רים שבת ערובין פסחים שקלים יומא סוכה ביצה ראש השנה תענית מגילה מועד ק
הדרין מכות שבועות עדיות עבודה זרה אבות הוריות זבחים מנחות חולין בכורות ערכ
שירין זבים טבול יום ידים עוקצין ברכות פאה דמאי כלאים שביעית תרומות מעשר
ענית מגילה מועד קטן חגיגה יבמות כתובות נדרים נזיר סוטה גיטין קידושין בבא קמ
ת חולין בכורות ערכין תמורה כריתות מעילה תמיד מדות קנין כלים אהלות נגעים פ
תרומות מעשרות מעשר שני חלה ערלה בכורים שבת ערובין פסחים שקלים יומא סו
ושין בבא קמא בבא מציעא בבא בתרא סנהדרין מכות שבועות עדיות עבודה זרה אב
הלות נגעים פרה טהרות מקואות נידה מכשירין זבים טבול יום ידים עוקצין ברכות פ
וקלים יומא סוכה ביצה ראש השנה תענית מגילה מועד קטן חגיגה יבמות כתובות נדר
עבודה זרה אבות הוריות זבחים מנחות חולין בכורות ערכין תמורה כריתות מעילה תמ
צין ברכות פאה דמאי כלאים שביעית תרומות מעשרות מעשר שני חלה ערלה בכור
מות כתובות נדרים נזיר סוטה גיטין קידושין בבא קמא בבא מציעא בבא בתרא סנהד
ריתות מעילה תמיד מדות קנין כלים אהלות נגעים פרה טהרות מקואות נידה מכשי
ערלה בכורים שבת ערובין פסחים שקלים יומא סוכה ביצה ראש השנה תענית מגי
בא בתרא סנהדרין מכות שבועות עדיות עבודה זרה אבות הוריות זבחים מנחות חו
ות נידה מכשירין זבים טבול יום ידים עוקצין ברכות פאה דמאי כלאים שביעית תרומ
שנה תענית מגילה מועד קטן חגיגה יבמות כתובות נדרים נזיר סוטה גיטין קידושין ב
מנחות חולין בכורות ערכין תמורה כריתות מעילה תמיד מדות קנין כלים אהלות נג
ביעית תרומות מעשרות מעשר שני חלה ערלה בכורים שבת ערובין פסחים שקלים יו
א קידושין בבא קמא בבא מציעא בבא בתרא סנהדרין מכות שבועות עדיות עבודה ז
ים אהלות נגעים פרה טהרות מקואות נידה מכשירין זבים טבול יום ידים עוקצין בר
חים שקלים יומא סוכה ביצה ראש השנה תענית מגילה מועד קטן חגיגה יבמות כתוב
דיות עבודה זרה אבות הוריות זבחים מנחות חולין בכורות ערכין תמורה כריתות מע
וקצין ברכות פאה דמאי כלאים שביעית תרומות מעשרות מעשר שני חלה ערלה בכו
מות כתובות נדרים נזיר סוטה גיטין קידושין בבא קמא בבא מציעא בבא בתרא סנהד
ריתות מעילה תמיד מדות קנין כלים אהלות נגעים פרה טהרות מקואות נידה מכש
חלה ערלה בכורים שבת ערובין פסחים שקלים יומא סוכה ביצה ראש השנה תענית מג
בתרא סנהדרין מכות שבועות עדיות עבודה זרה אבות הוריות זבחים מנחות חולין בכו
מכשירין זבים טבול יום ידים עוקצין ברכות פאה דמאי כלאים שביעית תרומות מעש
ענית מגילה מועד קטן חגיגה יבמות כתובות נדרים נזיר סוטה גיטין קידושין בבא ק
ת חולין בכורות ערכין תמורה כריתות מעילה תמיד מדות קנין כלים אהלות נגעים
תרומות מעשרות מעשר שני חלה ערלה בכורים שבת ערובין פסחים שקלים יומא ס
ושין בבא קמא בבא מציעא בבא בתרא סנהדרין מכות שבועות עדיות עבודה זרה אב
לות נגעים פרה טהרות מקואות נידה מכשירין זבים טבול יום ידים עוקצין ברכות
וקלים יומא סוכה ביצה ראש השנה תענית מגילה מועד קטן חגיגה יבמות כתובו
זרה אבות הוריות זבחים מנחות חולין בכורות ערכין תמורה כריתות מעילה
רות פאה דמאי כלאים שביעית תרומות מעשרות מעשר שני חלה ערלה ערל